NEW

WITHDRAWN

W9-BYQ-392

ENCYCLOPEDIA OF WORLD BIOGRAPHY

1

ENCYCLOPEDIA OF
WORLD BIOGRAPHY

SECOND EDITION

A

Barbosa

1

GALE

DETROIT • NEW YORK • TORONTO • LONDON

Staff

Senior Editor: Paula K. Byers
Project Editor: Suzanne M. Bourgoin
Managing Editor: Neil E. Walker

Editorial Staff: Luann Brennan, Frank V. Castronova, Laura S. Hightower, Karen E. Lemerand, Stacy A. McConnell, Jennifer Mossman, Maria L. Munoz, Katherine H. Nemeh, Terrie M. Rooney, Geri Speace

Permissions Manager: Susan M. Tosky
Permissions Specialist: Maria L. Franklin
Permissions Associate: Michele M. Lonoconus
Image Cataloger: Mary K. Grimes

Production Director: Mary Beth Trimper
Production Manager: Evi Seoud
Production Associate: Shanna Heilveil
Product Design Manager: Cynthia Baldwin
Senior Art Director: Mary Claire Krzewinski

Research Manager: Victoria B. Cariappa
Research Specialists: Michele P. LaMeau, Andrew Guy Malonis, Barbara McNeil, Gary J. Oudersluys
Research Associates: Julia C. Daniel, Tamara C. Nott, Norma Sawaya, Cheryl L. Warnock
Research Assistant: Talitha A. Jean

Graphic Services Supervisor: Barbara Yarrow
Image Database Supervisor: Randy Bassett
Imaging Specialist: Mike Lugosz

Manager of Data Entry Services: Eleanor M. Allison
Data Entry Coordinator: Kenneth D. Benson

Manager of Technology Support Services: Theresa A. Rocklin
Programmers/Analysts: Mira Bossowska, Jeffrey Muhr, Christopher Ward

Copyright © 1998
Gale Research
835 Penobscot Bldg.
Detroit, MI 48226-4094

ISBN 0-7876-2221-4 (Set)
ISBN 0-7876-2541-8 (Volume 1)

Library of Congress Cataloging-in-Publication data is available.

Printed in the United States of America
10 9 8 7 6 5 4 3 2

INTRODUCTION

The study of biography has always held an important, if not explicitly stated, place in school curricula. The absence in schools of a class specifically devoted to studying the lives of the giants of human history belies the focus most courses have always had on people. From ancient times to the present, the world has been shaped by the decisions, philosophies, inventions, discoveries, artistic creations, medical breakthroughs, and written works of its myriad personalities. Librarians, teachers, and students alike recognize that our lives are immensely enriched when we learn about those individuals who have made their mark on the world we live in today.

This new edition of the *Encyclopedia of World Biography* (*EWB*) represents a unique, comprehensive source for biographical information on nearly 7,000 of those people who, for their contributions to human culture and society, have reputations that stand the test of time. Bringing together the first edition of *EWB*—published nearly 25 years ago—and the supplemental volumes that appeared over the years, this set features fully updated and revised versions of *EWB*'s original articles, including expanded bibliographic sections, as well as a cumulative index to names and subjects. Also, to round out the first set's already illustrious, carefully selected list of entrants, an additional 500 articles enhance *EWB*'s coverage of women and multicultural figures who, in the past, may not have received adequate attention in general biographical reference works.

Articles. Arranged alphabetically following the letter-by-letter convention (spaces and hyphens have been ignored), the articles begin with the full name of the person profiled in large, bold type. Next is a boldfaced, descriptive paragraph that includes birth and death years in parentheses and provides a capsule identification and a statement of the person's significance. The long essay that follows is an average of 800 words and is a substantial treatment of the person's life. Some of the essays proceed chronologically while others confine biographical data to a paragraph or two and move on to a consideration and evaluation of the subject's work. Where very few biographical facts are known, the article is necessarily devoted to analysis of the subject's contribution.

Following the essay are a Further Reading section and, when applicable, a list of Additional Sources with more recent biographical works that have been published on the person since the original edition of *EWB*. Bibliographic citations contain both books and periodicals; in addition, this publication of *EWB* marks the first inclusion of Internet addresses for World Wide Web pages, where current information can be found.

Portraits accompany many of the articles and provide either an authentic likeness, contemporaneous with the subject, or a later representation of artistic merit. For artists, occasionally self-portraits have been included. Of the ancient figures, there are depictions from coins, engravings, and sculptures; of the moderns, there are many portrait photographs.

Index. The exhaustive *EWB* Index, contained in volume 17, is a useful key to the encyclopedia. Persons, places, battles, treaties, institutions, buildings, inventions, books, works of art, ideas, philosophies, styles, movements—all are indexed for quick reference just as in a general encyclopedia. The Index entry for a person includes a brief identification and birth and death dates. And every Index reference includes the title of the article to which the reader is being directed as well as the volume and page numbers.

Because *EWB* is an encyclopedia of biography, its Index differs in important ways from the indexes to other encyclopedias. Basically, this is an Index about people, and that fact has several interesting consequences. First,

V

the information to which the Index refers the reader on a particular topic is always about people associated with that topic. Thus the entry "Quantum theory (physics)" lists articles on people associated with quantum theory. Each article may discuss a person's contribution to quantum theory, but no single article or group of articles is intended to provide a comprehensive treatment of quantum theory as such. Second, the Index is rich in classified entries. All persons who are subjects of articles in the encyclopedia, for example, are listed in one or more classifications in the index—abolitionists, astronomers, engineers, philosophers, zoologists, etc.

The Index, together with the 16 volumes of articles, make *EWB* an enduring and valuable source for biographical information. As the world moves forward and school course work changes to reflect advances in technology and further revelations about the universe, the life stories of the people who have risen above the ordinary and earned a place in the annals of human history will continue to fascinate students of all ages.

We Welcome Your Suggestions. Mail your comments and suggestions for enhancing and improving the *Encyclopedia of World Biography* to:

The Editors
Encyclopedia of World Biography
Gale Research
835 Penobscot Bldg.
Detroit, MI 48226-4094
Phone: (800) 347-4253
Fax: (313) 961-6599

ENCYCLOPEDIA OF WORLD BIOGRAPHY

1

A

Hugo Alvar Henrik Aalto

Hugo Alvar Henrik Aalto (1898-1976) was a Finnish architect, furniture designer and town planner. More broadly, he was a comprehensive designer with a humanistic concern for man and his total environment.

On Feb. 3, 1898, Alvar Aalto was born in Kuortane. After service during the war of national liberation, he studied architecture at the Helsinki Polytechnic Institute and graduated in 1921.

His first major design was for the Municipal Library, Viipuri (now Vyborg, Russia), which won the competition of 1927, although local conservatism prevented construction until 1934. The building includes an auditorium at ground level with a glazed wall overlooking the parkland. The library accommodation, in contrast, has blank walls and indirect lighting to prevent direct sunlight from annoying the readers. Aalto's building for the newspaper *Turun-Sanomat* in Turku (1928) demonstrates his feeling for structure, especially in the use of tapered columns.

The qualities of the Viipuri library and the Turku newspaper office emerge again in perhaps the most humanitarian design of the 20th century, Aalto's Tuberculosis Sanatorium in Paimio (1929-1933). The building is carefully sited among pine trees. The patients' rooms have full morning sunlight; artificial light is from behind the patient's head. Rooms are painted in soft tones with darker ceilings to create a restful effect. Sound is absorbed by carefully positioned insulation, cupboards are hung for ease of floor cleaning, windows are designed to be draftproof, faucets of washbasins are tilted to prevent splashing, and doorknobs are shaped to fit the hand. Aalto designed the furniture specifically for hospital use. The whole scheme is an essay in consideration by the designer for the user.

In 1932 Aalto designed his first chair with a plywood seat and back in one piece on a tubular metal frame. Soon he made his furniture entirely of wood, achieving in this material what Ludwig Mies van der Rohe and Marcel Breuer had done a few years earlier in tubular steel. Aalto perfected designs which could readily be mass-produced.

Aalto's competition entry for planning the Munkkiniemi district of Helsinki (1934), his Sunila Cellulose Factory and adjacent housing near Kotka (1935), and his plan for the city of Varkaus (1936) led him into the realm of urban development. His Finnish Pavilion (1938-1939) for the New York World's Fair resulted in a teaching appointment at the Massachusetts Institute of Technology, Cambridge, where he designed the Baker House Dormitory (1947-1948).

In 1944, at the conclusion of the Finnish-Russian War, Finland was forced to cede to the Soviet Union the Karelian Isthmus and resettle one-fifth of the nation's population. Aalto's planning schemes provided a lead in this immense task. The first reconstruction plan Aalto made was for the city of Rovaniemi. The garden city of Tapiola, designed by the National Housing Foundation of Finland in 1952, was an outgrowth of Aalto's concepts.

His most famed sculpture is at Suomussalmi, where the Finns successfully halted a Russian attack in 1940. The memorial, a leaning bronze pillar 30 feet high, was designed in 1960. His architectural masterpieces include the municipal building in Säynätsalo (1952) and the Vuoksenniska Church (1959).

1

Aalto's buildings are carefully integrated into the landscape. They also have internal spatial relationships that are enhanced by furniture and sculpture of his own design and by his concern for the workability of each component part within the building. "The very essence of architecture consists of a variety and development reminiscent of natural organic life. This is the only true style in architecture," Aalto said in *Alvar Aalto; The Decisive Years*.

A member of the Academy of Finland since 1955, Aalto died in Helsinki on May 11, 1976.

Further Reading

The complete works of Aalto, with plans and photographs, were edited by him and Karl Fleig in *Alvar Aalto* (1963; 2d ed. 1965). See also Frederick Gutheim, *Alvar Aalto* (1960) and Schildt, Göran, *Alvar Aalto; The Decisive Years*, Rizzali, 1986. Aalto's furniture is discussed in the New York Museum of Modern Art publication, *Architecture and Furniture: Aalto* (1938). □

Henry Louis (Hank) Aaron

Henry Louis (Hank) Aaron (born 1934) was major league baseball's leading homerun hitter with a career total of 755 upon his retirement in 1976. He broke ground for the participation of African Americans in professional sports.

enry (Hank) Aaron was born in Mobile, Alabama, in the midst of the Great Depression on February 5, 1934. He was the son of an African American shipyard worker and had seven brothers and sisters. Although times were economically difficult, Aaron took an early interest in sports and began playing sandlot baseball at a neighborhood park. In his junior year he transferred out of a segregated high school to attend the Allen Institute in Mobile, which had an organized baseball program. He played on amateur and semi-pro teams like the Pritchett Athletics and the Mobile Black Bears, where he began to make a name for himself. At this time Jackie Robinson, the first African American player in the major leagues, was breaking the baseball color barrier. Gaining immediate success as a hard-hitting infielder, the 17-year-old Aaron was playing semi-professional baseball in the summer of 1951 when the owner of the Indianapolis Clowns, part of the professional Negro American League, signed him as the Clown's shortstop for the 1952 season.

Record Breaker

Being almost entirely self-trained, Aaron in his early years batted cross-handed, " . . . because no one had told him not to," according to one of his biographers. Nevertheless, Aaron's sensational hitting with the Clowns prompted a Boston Braves scout to purchase his contract in 1952. Assigned to Eau Claire, Wisconsin, in the minor Northern League (where coaching corrected his batting style), Aaron batted .336 and won the league's rookie-of-the-year award. The following year he was assigned to the Braves' Jackson-

ville, Florida team, in the South Atlantic (Sally) League. Enduring the taunting of fans and racial slurs from fellow players in the segregated south, he went on to bat .362 with 22 homers and 125 runs batted in (RBIs). This achievement won him the title of the League Most Valuable Player in 1953.

During the winter of 1953-1954 Aaron played in Puerto Rico where he began playing positions in the outfield. In the spring of 1954 he trained with the major league Boston Braves (later the Milwaukee Braves) and won a starting position when the regular right-fielder suffered an injury. Although Aaron was sidelined late in the campaign with a broken ankle, he batted .280 as a rookie that year. Over the next 22 seasons, this quiet, six-foot, right-handed batting champion established himself as one of the most durable and versatile hitters in major league history.

In 14 seasons playing for the Braves Hank Aaron batted .300 or more; in 15 seasons he hit 30 or more homers, scored 100 or more runs, and drove in 100 or more runs. In his long career Aaron led all major league players in runs batted in with 2,297. He played in 3,298 games, which ranked him third among players of all time. Aaron twice led the National League in batting and four times led the league in homers. His consistent hitting produced a career total of 3,771 hits, ranking him third behind Pete Rose and Ty Cobb. When Aaron recorded his 3,000th hit on May 7, 1970, he was the youngest player (at 36) since Cobb to join the exclusive 3,000 hit club. Aaron played in 24 All-Star games, a record shared with Willie Mays and Stan Musial. Aaron's lifetime batting average was .305, and in his two World Series encounters he batted .364. Aaron also held the record of hitting homeruns in three consecutive National League playoff games, a feat he accomplished in 1969 against the New York Mets.

A Quiet Superstar

Although Aaron's prodigious batting ranked him among baseball's superstars, he received less publicity than such contemporaries as Willie Mays. In part this was due to Aaron's quiet personality and to lingering prejudice against African American players in the majors. Moreover, playing with the Milwaukee Braves (which became the Atlanta Braves in 1966) denied Aaron the high level of publicity afforded major league players in cities like New York or Los Angeles. During Aaron's long career the Braves won only two National League pennants, although in 1957, the year Aaron's 44 homers helped him win his only Most Valuable Player Award, the Braves won the World Series. The following year Milwaukee repeated as National League champions, but lost the World Series.

Aaron perennially ranked among the National League's leading homerun hitters, but only four times did he win the annual homer title. It wasn't until 1970 that Aaron's challenge to Babe Ruth's record total of 714 homers was seriously considered by sportswriters and fans. By 1972 Aaron's assault on the all-time homer record was big news and his $200,000 annual salary was the highest in the league. The following year Aaron hit 40 homers, falling one short of tying the mark. Early into the 1974 season Aaron hit the tying homer in Cincinnati. Then on the night of April 8, 1974, before a large crowd at Atlanta and with a nationwide television audience looking on, Aaron hit his 715th homer off pitcher Al Downing of the Dodgers to break Ruth's record. It was the peak moment of Aaron's career, although it was tempered by an increasing incidence of death threats and racist hate mail which made Aaron fear for the safety of his family.

A New Career

In the Fall of 1974 Aaron left the Braves and went on to play for the Milwaukee Brewers until his retirement in 1976. At the time of his retirement as a player, the 42-year-old veteran had raised his all-time homer output to 755. When he left the Brewers he became a vice president and Director of Player Development for the Braves, where he scouted new team prospects and oversaw the coaching of minor leaguers. His efforts contributed toward making the Braves, now of Atlanta, one of the strongest teams in the National League, and he has since become a senior vice president for that team. In 1982 Aaron was voted into the Baseball Hall of Fame at Cooperstown, New York, and in 1997 Hank Aaron Stadium in Mobile, Alabama, was dedicated to him.

Further Reading

Begin with Hank Aaron's autobiography, *I Had A Hammer: The Hank Aaron Story* (1992). Available biographies of Hank Aaron include Rick Rennert, Richard Zennert, *Henry Aaron (Black Americans of Achievement)* (1993), and James Tackach, *Hank Aaron (Baseball Legends Series)* (1991). A good book for younger readers is Jacob Margolies, *Home Run King (Full-Color First Books)* (1992). Other books that look at Aaron's place in baseball history are Clare Gault, Frank Gault, *Home Run Kings: Babe Ruth, Henry Aaron* (1994) and James Hahn and Lynn Hahn, *Henry Aaron* (1981). Joseph Reichler, *Baseball's Great Moments* (1985) covers the two highlights of Aaron's career—when he struck his 3,000th hit and when he broke the homer record in 1974. Recent published articles include Hank Aaron, "When Baseball Mattered," *The New York Times* (5/03/97, Vol. 146), "Aaron Still Chasing Ball No. 755," *The New York Times* (8/27/96, Vol. 145), and "Aaron honored With New Stadium," *The New York Times* (8/27/96, Vol. 145). Jules Tygiel, in *Baseball's Great Experiment* (1984), gives an excellent historical account of black players seeking admission into major league baseball. Art Rust, Jr., in *Get That Nigger Off the Field* (1976), furnishes sketches of black players who entered the majors during Aaron's time. David Q. Voigt, in *American Baseball: From Postwar Expansion to the Electronic Age* (1983), treats the black experience within the context of major league history since World War II. □

Abba Arika

The Jewish scholar Abba Arika (ca. 175-ca. 247), also known as Rav, founded a yeshiva, or academy, in Sura, Babylonia. The school remained an important center of Jewish learning until the 11th century.

Abba Arika was born to an aristocratic family in Kafri, Babylonia. As a young man, he went to Palestine to study at the academy of the eminent rabbi Judah I. Rabbi Judah had compiled the Mishna, a work containing the Oral Law, or body of unrecorded Jewish teachings or traditions. After acquiring considerable knowledge, Abba returned to Babylonia, where he became an inspector of markets and a lecturer at the academy at Nehardea. About 219 he moved to Sura on the Euphrates River and opened his own academy. His school gained an excellent reputation and attracted many students; in time its importance as a center of learning surpassed that of the academies in Palestine. Abba became known as Rav (master par excellence).

Rav was deeply concerned not only with the training of scholars but also with the education of all the members of the Jewish community. He therefore taught workers in the hours preceding and following the regular school day. Twice a year, in the spring and the fall, some 12,000 students came from all parts of the country to listen to lectures and discussions on Jewish law.

The Mishna was the basic text taught at Sura, where it was analyzed, discussed, and expounded. The debates on the Mishna in the Babylonian academies over the centuries were incorporated in the Gemara, an encyclopedic work which was completed about 500. The Mishna and the Gemara compose the Talmud. The Palestinian schools produced a Talmud in the 5th century, but it was not well preserved. The Babylonian Talmud thus became authoritative. Rav was a member of the last generation of *Tannaim* (teachers who are mentioned in the Mishna); he also belonged to the first generation of *Amoraim* (scholars whose commentaries are recorded in the Gemara).

In addition to his scholarly work, Rav wrote a number of prayers which were incorporated in the traditional liturgy. Among them is the inspiring *Alenu,* which entreats God to perfect the universe as a kingdom of the Almighty. He also composed the major poetic selections of the *Musaf,* or supplementary service, for the New Year.

Rav was devoted to the study of Judaism and valued this activity above worship and sacrifice in the temple. He extolled the importance of work and earning a livelihood, but he also displayed an affirmative attitude toward life and pleasure. ''A person will be called to account,'' he warned, ''for having deliberately rejected the permissible pleasures he can enjoy.'' Rav indulged in mystical speculation, but he abhorred superstition and discouraged indulgence in astrology. He always stressed that redemption can come only through repentance and good deeds.

Rav guided his school until his death about 247. The academy continued to exist until 1034.

Further Reading

It will be helpful to examine at least one tractate of the Mishna in relation to the Gemara in *The Babylonian Talmud,* edited by Isidore Epstein (trans., 34 vols., 1935-1948). Hermann L. Strack, *Introduction to the Talmud and Midrash* (trans. 1931), discusses the *Tannaim* and *Amoraim* and their contributions. For a list of the *Tannaim* and *Amoraim* by generations consult George F. Moore, *Judaism in the First Centuries of the Chris-*

tian Era, vol. 2 (1927); this work provides an excellent basic orientation in the Talmud. □

Abbas I

Abbas I (1571-1629), called ''the Great,'' was a shah of Persia, the fifth king of the Safavid dynasty. He brought Persia once again to the zenith of power and influence politically, economically, and culturally.

The greatest shah of the Safavids, Abbas I had a precarious beginning. His mild-mannered and ascetic father, Shah Mohammad Khodabandeh, could not cope with the leaders of the seven Turkish Shii tribes known as Qizilbash (Redheads), who helped the Safavids come to power. But they were so greedy for land and power that though they controlled the king they quarreled among themselves. They preferred an oligarchy to a central government with an autocratic shah. To weaken the dynasty and ensure their success, the Qizilbash killed most of the Safavid princes, including the heir apparent and his mother.

Abbas was born on Jan. 27, 1571. When his older brother, the crown prince, was killed, Abbas was rescued and taken to Khorasan, a northeastern province of Persia. A few years later, in 1588, he ascended the throne with the reluctant consent of his father and the help of loyal friends. In addition to internal difficulties, Shah Abbas was faced with impending attack by the colossal Ottoman Empire to the west and the constant menace of the Uzbeks to the northeast.

Early Military Conquests

Shah Abbas made peace with the Ottomans and concentrated on fighting the Uzbeks and on pacifying the country. In nearly 14 years of constant warfare he drove the Uzbeks beyond the Oxus. He took advantage of the weakness of the Russians after the death of Ivan the Terrible in 1584 and secured for Persia the provinces on three sides of the Caspian Sea whose rulers had been depending for protection upon the power of Russia. Abbas also sent his armies south and subdued the provinces on the northern shores of the Persian Gulf.

All of these advances would have come to naught had Abbas not been able to establish a strong central government with himself at the top. The main obstacles in his way were the power-hungry Qizilbash chieftains, with whose military and administrative help the Safavids had been ruling the Persians. Abbas decided to take away their power and influence.

Shah Abbas therefore had to establish direct contact with the Persian population and depend upon their loyalty. This he accomplished with great success. He moved the capital from Qazvin to Esfahan, which was not only more centrally located but was more Persian. He became an enthusiastic patron of Persian civilization and appointed Persians to posts of leadership and authority. Furthermore,

he robbed the Qizilbash of their military power by creating two new regiments: a cavalry regiment made up of Christians from the Caucasus and an infantry regiment recruited from the Persian peasantry. Their use of muskets and artillery not only overshadowed the sword and lance of the Qizilbash but prepared Persia in the struggle against the Ottomans.

War with the Ottoman Empire

Shah Abbas was fortunate in that the height of his power coincided with the decline of the Ottoman Empire. He was the contemporary of no less than five Ottoman sultans. Shah Abbas opened his campaigns against the Ottomans in 1602 and the hostilities lasted some 12 years, mostly with the Persian armies in control. In the peace treaty of 1614 the Ottomans agreed to retreat to the boundaries that existed before the victorious campaign of Sultan Selim I in 1500. With these victories Shah Abbas expanded the territory of Persia to its pre-Islamic limits. Partly for security and partly for commercial and political reasons, he transferred thousands of Armenian families from their homes in Armenia and settled them in the interior of Persia. The bulk of them were settled in New Jolfa, just across the Zayandeh Rud (river) from Esfahan. The thriving community still exists.

The struggle between the Persians and the Ottomans was not only religious, territorial, and military; it was diplomatic and commercial as well. The rising nations of Europe wanted to revenge themselves after centuries of Ottoman domination and at the same time clear the way for commerce between Europe and Asia. Realizing the animosity between the Ottomans and the rulers of Persia, they sent delegates to try to arrange coordinated assaults on Turkey from both east and west.

Relations with Europe

The early Safavids had been fanatic Shii Moslems and did not want to have any dealings with the infidel Christians. Shah Abbas, however, was tolerant. The coordinated assault never materialized, but he saw the diplomatic and commercial advantages of contact with Europe. Consequently, during his reign a long string of ambassadors, merchants, adventurers, and Roman Catholic missionaries made their way to Esfahan. Shah Abbas welcomed them all and used them for the advancement of his own policies. Two adventurers from England, the famous Sherley brothers, Anthony and Robert, were very close to the Shah. They helped him train the new army and took part in the campaign against the Ottomans. Later the Shah sent them in turn as ambassadors to the monarchs of Europe. He was lavish in his entertainment of accredited ambassadors, and sometimes he himself went a few miles out of the city to welcome them.

His religious tolerance was almost exemplary. On official occasions, especially when a foreign ambassador was being entertained, he would invite the religious leaders of Christians, Jews, and Zoroastrians. He was especially tolerant of the Christians, partly because they were the largest minority in Persia and also because he wanted to impress the Christian leaders of Europe. He built churches for the Armenian community in New Jolfa and allowed them to own their houses, ride horses, and wear any kind of clothes they pleased—privileges which non-Moslems did not have before or for long after Shah Abbas until modern times. Furthermore, he permitted the Christian monks from Europe, who had come to Persia for missionary purposes, to build their centers in the Moslem section of Esfahan. He was so friendly to the monks that they thought he was about ready to become a Christian. Shah Abbas did not discourage this illusion.

Opening of the Persian Gulf

Perhaps the main purpose of Shah Abbas in building friendly relations with Europe was commerce. Persian products, especially silk, were in demand in Europe. Knowing that trade with Europe through the vast Ottoman Empire was not practical, he turned his attention to the Persian Gulf. The Portuguese had come to the region about a century earlier and had virtual monopoly of the trade. To Shah Abbas, who wanted to do business with all the countries of Europe, the Portuguese monopoly was too limiting. In a series of maneuvers in which he used the British fleet somewhat against the latter's plans, Shah Abbas defeated the Portuguese in 1622. Having become master of the Persian Gulf, he opened it to Portuguese, Spanish, British, Dutch, and French merchants. He gave Europeans special financial, legal, and social privileges. He gave orders to all provincial governors to facilitate travel and lodging for them. These same privileges, which were granted by a strong government for the purpose of enhancing trade, were later used by the strong

European governments as means of imperialism in all of the Middle East. Usually Armenians acted as agents of the Shah for trade with the European merchants.

Shah Abbas was as cruel and suspicious in his relations with the Qizilbash leaders as he was kind and open in his dealings with the common people. Having been brought up in an atmosphere of intrigue, he, like many monarchs of the time, had his complement of executioners who were kept quite busy. One of the victims was his own son and heir apparent. His power was more absolute than that of the sultan of Turkey. While the sultan was limited by the dictates of the Moslem religious laws as interpreted by the chief religious leader of the realm, the Shii Safavids were not so limited. Theirs was a theocracy in which the shah, as representative of the hidden imam, had absolute temporal and spiritual powers. He was called the Morshed-e Kamel (most perfect leader) and as such could not do wrong. He was the arbiter of religious law. Later, when Persian kings became weak, the interpreters of religious law, Mujtaheds, dominated the religious as well as the temporal scene.

On the other hand, the love of the common people for him was genuine, and the cry of "long live the Shah" whenever he passed among them was spontaneous. From the records it appears that he spent most of his time among the people. He was a frequent visitor of the bazaars and the teahouses of Esfahan. Often he mixed with the people in disguise to see how the common people were faring. These practices produced a wealth of stories about Shah Abbas that Persian mothers still tell their children.

He was an enthusiastic patron of Persian architects and with their help built Esfahan into one of the most beautiful cities of his time. In order to make Shiism, which is more a manifestation of Persian nationalistic mystique than of its Arab Islamic origin, somewhat self-sufficient with a center of its own, Shah Abbas built a beautiful mausoleum over the tomb of the eighth imam in Mashhad. He inaugurated pilgrimages to the shrine of Imam Reza by walking from Esfahan to Mashhad. He built roads, caravansaries, and public works of all sorts. Undoubtedly, the Safavid period was the renaissance of Persian civilization since conquest by the Arabs in the 7th century. That this was done by a dynasty of Turkish origin signifies the assimilating power of Persian culture. Shah Abbas died in the forty-second year of his reign in Mazanderan on Jan. 21, 1629.

Further Reading

The best short account in English of the life of Abbas I is in Percy Sykes, *A History of Persia,* vol. 2 (1915; 3d ed. 1930). Other background studies which discuss Abbas include Donald N. Wilber, *Iran: Past and Present* (1948; 4th ed. 1958); A. J. Arberry, ed., *The Legacy of Persia* (1953); and Richard N. Frye, *Persia* (1953; 3d ed. 1969). □

Ferhat Abbas

Ferhat Abbas (1899-1985) was the first president of the provisional government of the Algerian Repub-

lic. His political career reflected the failure of the middle-class moderate elements to dominate Algerian nationalism.

Ferhat Abbas was born on Oct. 24, 1899, at Taher in the department of Constantine, Algeria, into a pro-French family of provincial administrators and landowners. In 1924, while a student of pharmacy at the University of Algiers, he helped to found the Association of Moslem Students, over which he presided for 5 years. He graduated in 1932, opened a pharmacy in Sétif, and served on municipal and provincial councils in eastern Algeria.

Until World War II Abbas accepted the validity of the colonial system and became a major spokesman for political reforms and the assimilation of Algerians and the French. In 1936 he even wrote, "I will not die for the Algerian fatherland, because this fatherland does not exist," a point of view which he later jettisoned. Although he joined the French army medical corps in 1939, in February 1943 he drew up the Manifesto of the Algerian People, which marked a rupture with the assimilationist dream and called for the internal autonomy of Algeria. After spending time in jail, in March 1944 he founded the Friends of the Manifesto, but following riots and massacres in Sétif on May 8, 1945, he was again interned.

In 1946 Abbas was released and served as a member of the French Constituent Assembly in Paris. The same year he founded a new party, the Democratic Union of the Algerian

Manifesto. In 1947 he became a member of the Algerian Assembly.

By 1954 Abbas, who had married a Frenchwoman and championed dialogue with France, finally realized that the Algerian condition could not be changed through legal means. French colons in Algeria refused to fulfill the promises that Paris had made to Algerian nationalists and attempted to repress the nationalist movement. Nonetheless, the insurrection of November 1954, which ignited the 8-year Algerian revolt, surprised Abbas and other moderates. In May 1955 he secretly joined the National Liberation Front and openly rallied to its ranks on April 22, 1956, by meeting in Cairo with the chiefs of the rebellion. On Aug. 20, 1956, he became a member of the National Council of the Algerian Revolution.

After the French arrested Ahmed Ben Bella, the revolutionary leader, in October 1956, Abbas assumed a more important role in the struggle for independence, and on Sept. 18, 1958, he was named president of the first provisional Algerian government. He lost this post in 1961 and took no part in the negotiations at Évian, which led to Algerian independence in July 1962.

In the subsequent civil war between Ben Bella's forces and the provisional government, Abbas supported Ben Bella and became president of the first Algerian Constituent Assembly. His political experience and profound knowledge of middle-class Algerian personalities made him a convenient ally for the more radical victors. But he criticized the new constitution and the regime for its "fascist structures," and on Aug. 14, 1963, he resigned as president of the Assembly.

In July 1964, when an insurrection broke out, Abbas was put under house arrest. Freed in June 1965, on the eve of the coup which replaced Ben Bella with Col. Houari Boumediene, Abbas retired from public life to Sétif. He died in 1985.

Further Reading

There is no biography of Ferhat Abbas in English. Several general books deal with his activities: Edward Behr, *The Algerian Problem* (1961); Joan Gillespie, *Algeria, Rebellion and Revolution* (1961); and William B. Quandt, *Revolution and Political Leadership: Algeria, 1954-1968* (1969). ☐

Berenice Abbott

Bernice Abbott (1898–1991) was one of the most gifted American photographers of the 20th century.

Berenice Abbott's work spanned more than 50 years of the twentieth century. At a time when "career women" were not only unconventional but controversial, she established herself as one of the nation's most gifted photographers. Her work is often divided into four categories: portraits of celebrated residents of 1920s Paris; a 1930s documentary history of New York City; photographic

explorations of scientific subjects from the 1950s and 1960s; and a lifelong promotion of the work of French photographer Eugène Atget. As a woman and a serious artist, Abbott faced numerous obstacles, not least of which was denial of the recognition she was due. Only recently has the high quality of her work been adequately appreciated. As one writer put it, "She was a consummate professional and artist."

Bernice Abbott was born into a world of rigid social rules, especially for women, who were expected to accept without question certain cultural dictates about clothing, manners, proper education, and other areas of everyday life. Abbott was an independent and somewhat defiant girl who hated such arbitrary constraints. One of her earliest acts of "rebellion" was to change the spelling of her name; Bernice became Berenice. "I put in another letter," she told an interviewer, "made it sound better."

Abbott's childhood was not especially happy. Her parents divorced when she was young, and though Abbott remained with her mother, her brothers were sent to live with their father. She never saw them again. This was a severe blow and may partly explain why Abbott never married or had her own family. She said she never wed because "marriage is the finish for women who want to work," and in her era this was largely true.

"Reinvented" herself in New York

At age 20 Abbott headed for New York City to "reinvent" herself, as one writer put it. She rented an apart-

ment, studied journalism, drawing, and sculpture, and formed a circle of friends, many of whom were ''bohemians'' rebelling against the strict social rules of the day. Friends who remembered her from those days said Abbott was shy and ''looked sort of forbidding.'' After three years Abbott had had her fill of New York and decided to go to Paris, something unmarried young women rarely did by themselves. In fact, that such a move was sure to generate controversy probably contributed to Abbott's decision to pursue it.

Photography became her calling

In Paris Abbott studied sculpture, but she ultimately found it unsatisfying. In 1923 photographer Man Ray, whom she had known in New York, offered her a job as his assistant. Abbott knew nothing about photography but accepted the job. ''I was glad to give up sculpture,'' she said. ''Photography was much more interesting.'' She worked for Man Ray for three years, mastering photographic techniques sufficiently to earn commissions of her own. Indeed, her work became so successful that she decided she had finally found her calling and opened her own studio.

Photographic portraits had become quite fashionable in Paris, and Abbott gained a solid reputation. She photographed some of the most distinguished people of the day, including Irish writer James Joyce; French writer, artist, and filmmaker Jean Cocteau; and Princess Eugénie Murat, granddaughter of French emperor Napoleon III. Her works have been called ''astonishing in their immediacy and insight,'' revealing much of the personality of her sitters, especially women. Abbott herself commented that Man Ray's photographs of women made them ''look like pretty objects''; she instead allowed their character to come through.

Championed work of Eugène Atget

While her star was on the rise, Abbott ''discovered'' some pictures of Paris that she called ''the most beautiful photographs ever made.'' She sought out the photographer, an aged, penniless man named Eugène Atget. For almost 40 years Atget had been making a poor living photographing buildings, monuments, and scenes of the city and selling the prints to artists and publishers. Abbott's keen eye detected the originality of these photos, and she befriended the old man. When Atget died in 1927, Abbott arranged to purchase all of his prints, glass slides, and negatives—more than a thousand items in all. She became obsessed with this massive collection, spending the next 40 years promoting and preserving Atget's work, arranging exhibitions, books, and sales of prints to raise money. She donated the collection to New York's Museum of Modern Art in 1968, by which time she had almost singlehandedly brought Atget from total obscurity to worldwide renown. Some critics have claimed that Abbott's devotion to Atget's works hampered her career. But she denied this, insisting, ''It was my responsibility and I had to do it. I thought he was great and his work should be saved.''

Photographs documented New York City

Abbott's career took a new turn when she returned to New York in 1929. Inspired by Atget's work and by the excitement she felt in the air, she began a new project: photographing the city as no one ever had. She spent most of the 1930s lugging her camera around, shooting pictures of buildings, construction sites, billboards, fire escapes, and stables. Many of these sites disappeared during the 1930s as a huge construction boom in New York swept away the old buildings and mansions to make way for modern sky-scrapers. Several of these photos were published in a 1939 book called *Changing New York.* In it Abbott wrote, ''To make the portrait of a city is a life work and no one portrait suffices, because the city is always changing. Everything in the city is properly part of its story—its physical body of brick, stone, steel, glass, wood, its lifeblood of living, breathing men and women.''

This task of documenting the city was not an easy one, especially for a woman. Abbott was ''menaced by bums, heckled by suspicious crowds, and chased by policemen.'' Her most famous anecdote of the period came from her work in the rundown neighborhood known as the Bowery. A man asked her why a nice girl was visiting such a bad area. Abbott replied, ''I'm not a nice girl. I'm a photographer.'' Finances presented further obstacles, and she spent her own money on the project until 1935, when the Federal Art Project of the Works Progress Administration began to sponsor her work. Until 1939 she was able to earn a salary of $35 a week and enjoyed the participation of an assistant. When funding ran out, however, she had to abandon the project.

Took on scientific community

Abbott continued working during the 1940s and 1950s, though largely outside the spotlight. She became preoccupied during this period with scientific photography, hoping to record evidence of the laws of physics and chemistry, among other phenomena. She took courses in chemistry and electricity to expand her understanding. Again her iron determination served her well.

The scientific community looked on her efforts with suspicion, both because of its skepticism about photography's usefulness and its hostility toward women who ventured into the virtually all-male enclave of science. She spent years trying to convince scientists and publishers that texts and journals could be illustrated with photographs, fighting the conventional belief that drawings were sufficient. In all, as Abbott told an interviewer, the project was a minefield of sexism: ''When I wanted to do a book on electricity, most scientists . . . insisted it couldn't be done. When I finally found a collaborator, his wife objected to his working with a woman. . . . The male lab assistants were treated with more respect than I was. You have no idea what I went through because I was a woman.''

Photographs showed beauty in science

Political events rescued Abbott when the Soviet Union launched the first space satellite in 1957, initiating the ''space race.'' The U.S. government began a new push in the field of science. In 1958 Abbott was invited to join the Massachusetts Institute of Technology's Physical Science Study Committee, which was charged with the task of improving high school science education. At last Abbott was vindicated in her insistence on the value of photography to science. Her biographer, Hank O'Neal, has said that her scientific photos were her best work. This is a subject of some debate, but many agree that she was able to uniquely demonstrate the beauty and grace in the path of a bouncing ball, the pattern of iron filings around a magnet, or the formation of soap bubbles.

In her later years Abbott did some photography around the country, in particular documenting U.S. Route l, a highway along the East Coast from Florida to Maine. During this project she fell in love with Maine and bought a small house in the woods of that state, where she lived for the rest of her life. As the popularity of photography grew in the 1970s and her life's work became recognized, Abbott was visited there by a string of admirers, photography students, and journalists. She became something of a legend in her own time, honored as a pioneer woman artist who conquered a male-dominated field thanks to "the vinegar of her personality and the iron of her character." But perhaps most importantly, students of the medium recognized the talent and artistry behind Abbot's work, among which reside some of the prize gems of twentieth-century photography.

Further Reading

Abbott, Berenice, *Berenice Abbott,* Aperture Foundation, 1988.
Abbott, Berenice, *Berenice Abbott Photographs,* Smithsonian Institution Press, 1990.
O'Neal, Hank, *Berenice Abbott: American Photographer,* McGraw-Hill, 1982. □

Grace Abbott

The social worker and agency administrator Grace Abbott (1878-1939) awakened many Americans to the responsibility of government to help meet the special problems of immigrants and of children.

Grace Abbott was born and raised in Grand Island, Nebraska. Her father was lieutenant-governor, and her mother was an abolitionist and suffragist. Grace received her bachelor's degree from Grand Island College in 1898 and taught for several years at Grand Island High School. She did graduate work in political science and in law at the University of Chicago, receiving a master's degree in 1909. The year before, greatly attracted to the pioneering social work of Jane Addams, she became a resident of Hull House in Chicago and collaborated effectively with Addams for over a decade.

She shared Addams' interest in the cause of world peace, and she worked effectively to advance women's suffrage. But very early she became preoccupied with the problem of immigrants. For over 20 years many Americans

had been worried that the flood of immigrants—as many as a million in a single year—arriving from eastern and southern Europe constituted a severe threat to American life and institutions. These "new immigrants"—as they were called—seemed dangerously "different" in language, dress, religion, and their disposition to cluster in the cities (as most people in this era were also doing). Other Americans—like Addams and Abbott—believed that it was not the immigrants who were "new," but America—increasingly urban, industrial, impersonal; to them, the problem was how to help the newcomers find and maintain their families, get jobs, and learn to play a knowledgeable part in a democracy.

From 1908 to 1917 Abbott directed the Immigrants' Protective League in Chicago. Close personal contact with immigrants made her aware of how difficult it was for new arrivals from Poland, or Italy, or Russia to find the relatives or friends they depended on; how hard it was to get jobs that were not exploitative; and how tricky it was not to be abused by the political machines. A trip in 1911 to eastern Europe deepened her understanding of the needs and hopes of the immigrants. Abbott's point-of-view is eloquently summarized in her *The Immigrant and the Community* (1917). To Abbott, the "new immigrants" were every bit as desirable as additions to America as were the older arrivals. In modern American society, they needed help; and, while the states and local philanthropic organizations such as the Immigrants' Protective League could and should help, the federal government had an important role to play. It was wrong, she argued, to concentrate on restricting or excluding immigration; the government should plan how best to accommodate and integrate the newcomers. She was not successful in redirecting federal policy; the acts of 1921 and 1924 drastically reduced the number of new immigrants. But her writings and her work with the Immigrants' Protective League helped develop a more widespread and a more generous understanding of the difficulties the immigrants encountered.

Work in the Children's Bureau

In 1912 Congress established the Children's Bureau in the recognition that children were entitled to special consideration in schools, in the workplace, in the courts, and even in the home. In 1916 Congress passed a law prohibiting the shipment in interstate commerce of products made by child labor. It remained for the Children's Bureau to make the law effective. Julia Lathrop, the first head of the bureau, in 1917 asked her friend Abbott to head up the child labor division. She proved to be an exceptionally able administrator. However, within a year the Supreme Court invalidated the law as an infringement upon the rights of the states to deal with child labor as they thought best. Abbott resigned and for the rest of her life worked to secure an amendment to the Constitution outlawing child labor. To her regret, this effort, too, was frustrated by states-rights feelings and by the concern that the amendment would jeopardize the rights of parents and churches to supervise the rearing of children.

After a brief period back in Illinois, Abbott returned to Washington in 1921 as the new head of the Children's

Bureau. Probably her most important responsibility was to administer the Sheppard-Towner Act (1921), which extended federal aid to states that developed appropriate programs of maternal care. Abbott had been appalled to find that infant mortality was higher in the United States than in any country where records were kept, and she was convinced that the best way to reduce that mortality was to improve the health of the mother, before and after childbirth. The Supreme Court rejected protests against this dramatic extension of federal government responsibilities for social welfare. Abbott, while seeing to it that the over 3,000 centers across the country met federal standards, showed herself sensitive to the special concerns of localities. Though Congress terminated the program in 1929, the act, as administered by Abbott, was a pioneering federal program of social welfare.

Abbott never lost faith that the American people would, when properly informed and led, support enlightened welfare programs. She was optimistic that the New Deal of Franklin Roosevelt and of her old friend Frances Perkins would realize many of her dreams. She had the satisfaction of helping draft the Social Security Act of 1935 which, among other things, provided federal guarantees of aid to dependent children.

Ill health prompted her to resign in 1934. She became professor of public welfare at the University of Chicago, where her sister, Edith Abbott, was a dean. She lived with Edith until her death in 1939. Quiet and forceful, compassionate and efficient, singularly immune to cant or prejudice, Grace Abbott epitomized the enormous contribution made by her generation of women. She helped make America a more decent place.

Further Reading

There is an excellent summary of Abbott's life in *Notable American Women* (1971). Edith Abbott wrote three helpful articles about her sister in *Social Service Review* (1939 and 1950). Grace Abbott's role is clearly indicated in Clarke A. Chambers, *Seedtime of Reform: American Social Service and Social Action, 1918-1933* (1963). Abbott wrote many reports, articles, and books. Among the most instructive are *The Immigrant and the Community* (1917) and two volumes of documents, with critical introductions, *The Child and the State* (1938).

Additional Sources

Costin, Lela B., *Two sisters for social justice: a biography of Grace and Edith Abbott,* Urbana: University of Illinois Press, 1983. □

Lyman Abbott

Lyman Abbott (1835-1922) was American Protestantism's foremost interpreter of the scientific, theological, and social revolutions challenging the nation after the Civil War.

Lyman Abbott was born on Dec. 18, 1835, in Roxbury, Mass., the son of Jacob Abbott, clergyman and author of the celebrated "Rollo" books for children. Upon graduation from New York University, young Abbott successfully practiced law but soon entered the Congregational ministry. His first pastorate after ordination in 1860 was in Terre Haute, Ind., and although Civil War sympathies in the community were divided, Abbott ardently upheld the Union. With the coming of peace, he joined the American Union Commission in the healing work of reconstruction. When a subsequent New York pastorate left him discouraged, he turned to a new calling, journalism. He wrote for *Harper's Magazine* and edited the new *Illustrated Christian Weekly,* then joined Henry Ward Beecher in the editorship of the *Christian Union* (after 1893 the *Outlook*). With Beecher's withdrawal in 1881, Abbott became editor in chief; until his death in 1922, this influential journal was Abbott's major vehicle of expression.

Abbott also succeeded Beecher in 1888 as pastor of the prestigious Plymouth Congregational Church in Brooklyn. For 10 years his quiet, conversational sermons (quite in contrast to those of the colorful Beecher) and his Sunday evening lectures on current topics brought him widening fame, as did his many speaking engagements and much-admired books. In sum, no Protestant leader had so large a following over such a long period as did Abbott, and no churchleader surpassed him in interpreting the great issues of the day for American Protestants.

It was Abbott's mission to persuade Americans that science and faith were compatible, that the new scientific

theory of evolution was "God's way of doing things," and that the new liberal theology did not mean the death of God. For him the new science and scholarship further proved that God governed the world, man was essentially good and constantly improving, and history was progressing in accordance with a divine plan. He wished to make religion relevant to life, believing that ethics rather than creeds were central to Christianity and that the churches should speak to social problems.

Abbott possessed a rare ability to sense the way the wind was blowing, and he seldom attempted to go against it—not because he was cowardly but because he was by nature a moderate who distrusted radicalism in all forms. He was an evolutionist but not a Darwinian, a religious liberal but not an agnostic, an antislavery man but not an abolitionist, a temperance advocate but not a prohibitionist, and an industrial democrat but not a socialist.

Abbott had a long and full and satisfying life, knowing the love of his wife and six children and the adulation of thousands. When he spoke, an entire generation of Protestants listened.

But Abbott was neither an original nor a profound thinker, and the limitations of his moderate, essentially middle-class position are suggested by the fact that he acquiesced in the increasing segregation of African Americans, lamented the extension of political rights to women, deplored labor violence, rationalized American imperialism, vociferously urged early intervention in World War I (following the lead of his friend Theodore Roosevelt, whom he had backed in 1912 for the presidency on the Progressive party ticket), and approved the suppression of wartime dissent.

Further Reading

Ira V. Brown, *Lyman Abbott* (1953), is a fine biography. Abbott's own *Reminiscences* (1916) is helpful. For Protestantism's response to the challenges of modernism, industrialization, and urbanization see Charles H. Hopkins, *The Rise of the Social Gospel in American Protestantism, 1865-1915* (1940); Aaron I. Abell, *The Urban Impact on American Protestantism, 1865-1900* (1943); Henry F. May, *Protestant Churches and Industrial America* (1949); and Francis P. Weisenburger, *Ordeal of Faith: The Crisis of Church-going America, 1865-1900* (1959). □

El Ferik Ibrahim Abboud

El Ferik Ibrahim Abboud (1900-1983) was a military leader who instituted the first military government of the independent Sudan, but who yielded to civilian rule when he was unable to solve the country's problems.

Ibrahim Abboud was born on Oct. 26, 1900, at Mohammed-Gol, near the old port city of Suakin on the Red Sea. He trained as an engineer at the Gordon Memorial College and at the Military College in Khartoum. He received a

commission in the Egyptian army in 1918 and transferred to the Sudan Defense Force in 1925, after its creation separate from the Egyptian army. During World War II he served in Eritrea, in Ethiopia, with the Sudan Defense Force, and with the British army in North Africa. After the war, Abboud rose rapidly to commander of the Sudan Defense Force in 1949 and assistant commander in chief in 1954. With the declaration of independence for the Sudan in 1956, he was made commander in chief of the Sudanese military forces. After the Sudanese army staged a coup d'etat in November 1958, overthrowing the civilian government of Abdullah Khalil, Gen. Abboud led the new military government.

Between 1956 and 1958 Sudanese nationalist leaders from both major parties sought to find solutions to the seemingly intractable problems of building a nation, developing the economy and creating a permanent constitution. Neither Ismail al-Azhari, leader of the Nationalist Unionist party and the first prime minister of the Sudan, nor his rival, Abdullah Khalil, the Umma party leader and successor to al-Azhari as prime minister, was able to overcome the weaknesses of the political system or to grapple with the country's problems. Parliamentary government was so discredited that Gen. Abboud, who formerly had remained studiously aloof from politics, led a coup d'etat on Nov. 16, 1958, to end, in his words, "the state of degeneration, chaos, and instability of the country."

Chief of the Military Government

At first Abboud and his ruling Supreme Council of Twelve had the tacit support of the Sudanese politicians and

people. The country was tired of the intrigues of the politicians and was prepared to permit the military to inaugurate an efficient and incorruptible administration. There was opposition only within the military in the first few months of the military government. This was the result of disagreements among the senior military leaders. But within a year many younger officers, and even cadets, rose to challenge Abboud's position. All of them were quickly suppressed.

Abboud's Regime

Abboud moved swiftly to deal with the Sudan's problems. The provisional constitution was suspended and all political parties dissolved. The price of Sudanese cotton was lowered, and the surplus from the crop of 1958 and the bumper crop of 1959 was sold, easing the financial crisis. An agreement was reached with Egypt concerning the division of the Nile waters, and although the Sudan did not receive as great an allotment as many Sudanese thought equitable, Egypt recognized the independence of the Sudan, and frontier conflicts ceased. Finally, in 1961, an ambitious 10-year development plan was launched, designed to end the Sudan's dependence on cotton exports and many foreign manufactured imports.

Although Abboud dealt with the important economic problems and improved foreign relations, he made little attempt to capitalize on his successes to forge a political following outside the army. His political independence certainly enabled him to act decisively, but his actions frequently alienated large segments of the population, which his government ultimately needed to remain in power without resort to force. He sought to meet demands of the population for increased participation in government by instituting a system of local representative government and the "erection of a central council . . . in a pyramid with the local councils as a base." The creation of such councils clearly shifted increased power to the rural areas, whose conservatism would counter complaints from the more liberal urban critics who were becoming increasingly frustrated by increasingly arbitrary administration.

"Southern Problem"

In spite of its weaknesses, Abboud's government might have lasted longer if not for the "southern problem." Abboud was personally popular or, at least, respected. He was even invited to the White House in 1961, where President John F. Kennedy praised the Sudan for having set a good example for living in peace with its neighbors.

In the non-Arabic, non-Moslem southern Sudan, however, the arbitrary rule of the military government produced a more negative reaction than in the north. Thus, the government's vigorous program of Arabization and Islamization in the south provoked strikes in the schools and open revolt in the countryside. Opposition to the government was met by force, and many southerners fled as refugees into the neighboring countries. By 1963 the conflict had escalated to a civil war in which the northern troops held the towns while the southern guerrillas roamed the countryside. Finally, in August 1964, in a desperate attempt to find a solution to the enervating campaign in the south,

Abboud established a 25-man commission to study the problem and make recommendations for its solution. When the commission, in turn, asked for public debate on the "southern question," the students of Khartoum University initiated a series of debates that soon turned into a forum for open criticism of all aspects of the administration. The government banned these debates, precipitating student demonstrations in which one student was killed. The situation rapidly deteriorated, and within two days the civil service and the transport workers were on strike. Demonstrations followed in the provinces. Rather than suppress the opposition by armed force and bloodshed, Abboud dissolved his government on Oct. 26, 1964, and called for the formation of a provisional cabinet to replace the Supreme Council. Abboud himself was forced to resign on Nov. 15 in favor of a civilian provisional government, and he retreated into retirement, thus ending the Republic of the Sudan's first period of military rule.

Abboud lived in Britain for several years, but died in Khartoum on Sept. 8, 1983, at the age of 82.

Further Reading

Abboud is discussed in Rolf Italiaander, *The New Leaders of Africa* (1960; trans. 1961); Thomas Patrick Melady, *Faces of Africa* (1964); and Kenneth D.D. Henderson, *Sudan Republic* (1966). □

Abd al-Malik

Abd al-Malik (646-705) was the ninth caliph of the Arab Empire and the fifth caliph of the Umayyad dynasty. He overcame the dissidents in the Second Civil War and reorganized the administration of the Islamic Empire.

The son of Marwan I, Abd al-Malik was born in Medina and lived there until he was forced to leave in 683 at the beginning of the Second Civil War. In this war the rule of the reigning Umayyad family was challenged by Abdullah ibn-az-Zubayr from Mecca. Marwan I was proclaimed caliph in Damascus in 684 and secured his position in Syria and Egypt before his assassination in 685.

Abd al-Malik succeeded to the caliphate in a difficult situation. Shiite rebels occupied much of Iraq, and there were also troubles in Syria. To free his hands, Abd al-Malik made a truce with the Byzantine emperor in 689. He then attacked Iraq, but it was not until 691 that the Zubayrid army there was defeated. A year later Mecca fell after a siege to Abd al-Malik's general al-Hajjaj, and Abdullah ibn-az-Zubayr was killed. The empire remained disturbed, and three separate revolts by men of the Kharijite sect were not quelled until 697. The final pacification was largely effected by al-Hajjaj, governing Iraq and the lands to the east from Al Kufa, but his severity provoked many wellborn Arabs of Iraq to revolt under Ibn-al-Ashath from 701 to 703.

With the restoration of Umayyad rule over the empire it became possible once again to mount campaigns on the frontiers. Abd al-Malik achieved little in Central Asia, Afghanistan, and Anatolia, but in North Africa the Byzantines were defeated, Carthage was occupied in 697, and a base was established at Kairouan; thus the way for the Arab advance to Morocco and into Spain was prepared.

In administrative matters Abd al-Malik took the important step of making Arabic the official language of Islam. He also unified fiscal and postal administration, eliminating the local systems that had been retained in the provinces conquered from the Byzantine and Persian empires. Similarly, he discouraged the use of Byzantine coinage that carried the emperor's likeness, and he struck golden dinars and silver dirhems inscribed with passages from the Koran. These measures made the Arab Empire more definitely Islamic and helped to counteract the divisive influence of tribalism. Abd al-Malik began the building of the magnificent Dome of the Rock at Jerusalem on the site of the Jewish Temple. Through the efforts of al-Hajjaj an improved way of writing the Koran with vowel marks was first developed during Abd al-Malik's reign.

Further Reading

There is no work no Abd al-Malik in English. The sources for the events of his reign are studied in detail in Julius Wellhausen, *The Arab Kingdom and Its Fall* (1902; trans. 1927). There are brief accounts in such works as Carl Brockelmann, *History of the Islamic Peoples* (1939; trans. 1947), and Philip K. Hitti, *History of the Arabs* (1940). □

Abd al-Mumin

The Berber Abd al-Mumin (ca. 1094-1163) was the founder of the Almohad dynasty in North Africa and Spain.

L ittle is known of the background of Abd al-Mumin except that he was born about 1094 in a village close to Tlemcen (in present-day Algeria) and was a member of the Berber Zenata confederation. As a young man, he studied religious science at Tlemcen. About 1117, while on a visit to Bougie seeking to further his knowledge, Abd al-Mumin became a student and disciple of Ibn Tumart, the founder of the Almohad reform movement. For 13 years Abd al-Mumin was one of the principal supporters of Ibn Tumart, accompanying him into banishment in the Atlas Mountains, where he served on the council of advisers to Ibn Tumart and took part in Almohad military expeditions.

Some time before Ibn Tumart died in 1130, he designated Abd al-Mumin to succeed him in leading the Almohad community. But probably because Ibn Tumart had ruled by dint of his personal religious and charismatic qualities, neither his death nor Abd al-Mumin's succession was announced for 3 years. Possibly also of significance was the fact that Abd al-Mumin did not belong to the Masmuda confederation of Berbers, from which the main

body of the Almohads was drawn. In 1033 Abd al-Mumin proclaimed himself caliph (*amir al-muminin*), which signified, over and above his leadership of the Almohads, his independence of the Abbasid caliphate in Baghdad.

Abd al-Mumin's 30-year reign as caliph is noteworthy for the propagation of the Almohad reform movement by conquest and for the establishment of a unified Berber empire in North Africa and Spain. The first target for conquest was the Almoravid state in Morocco, against whose immorality and espousal of the Maliki school of law the Almohad movement had been directed. A long campaign, which consisted first of raids and eventually of siege operations against the Almoravid center, culminated in the conquest of the capital, Marrakesh, in 1147. This, however, did not signal the conquest of Morocco, as two simultaneous Berber uprisings in the south and on the Atlantic coast proved. Abd al-Mumin ruthlessly suppressed these uprisings, and he used them as an occasion to purge those of his followers whose loyalty was suspect. Thousands are said to have been slain.

Having built a strong, reliable base in Morocco and western Algeria, Abd al-Mumin undertook the conquest of Spain and of present-day Algeria and Tunisia. Moslem, that is, southern Spain was captured from the Almoravids in a series of campaigns between 1146 and 1154, when Granada fell; Algeria was taken from its Berber and Arab rulers by 1151; and in 1159 Abd al-Mumin led an expedition against Tunisia, parts of which had been occupied by the Normans of Sicily. Thus, by 1160 Abd al-Mumin had built in North Africa and Spain the largest empire ever ruled by Berbers, united by both religious and political affiliation.

In the opinion of some scholars, Abd al-Mumin ultimately compromised, if not betrayed, the religious principles of the Almohad movement by securing the succession to the caliphate for his son, thus establishing a dynasty based on heredity rather than piety. Nevertheless, it cannot be denied that Abd al-Mumin deserves equal credit with Ibn Tumart as a founder of the movement which dominated political and religious life in the Moslem West until the early 13th century.

Further Reading

There is no detailed study of Abd al-Mumin. Relevant material may be found in Henri Terrasse, *History of Morocco* (2 vols., 1949-1950; trans., 1 vol., 1952). □

Abd al-Rahman I

Abd al-Rahman I (731-788) was emir of Islamic Spain from 756 to 788. Known as "the Immigrant," he established the rule of the Umayyad dynasty in the Iberian Peninsula.

Born near Damascus, Syria, Abd al-Rahman I was the son of the Umayyad prince Muawiya ibn Hisham and a Berber concubine named Rah. In 750 he was one of the few members of his family to escape slaughter by the Abbasids, and thus, as the Umayyad line was extinguished in the East, he made his way to the western Islamic world to establish a base of power. Accompanied by his freedman Badr, he traveled across North Africa, finally gaining refuge among his mother's tribe, the Nafza Berbers of Morocco. Using this base, he sent Badr to Spain to prepare the groundwork for his political aspirations.

On Aug. 14, 755, Abd al-Rahman landed at Almuñécar and was soon acknowledged as chief by various settlements of Syrian immigrants, still loyal to his family. Finally, after defeating the last governor of Islamic Spain, Yusuf al-Fihri, he entered the capital, Cordova, on May 15, 756, and was proclaimed emir in the main mosque there.

News of Abd al-Rahman's triumph spread quickly across the Islamic world, striking terror in the hearts of the rival Abbasids but gladdening thousands of Umayyad supporters, who soon flocked to Spain. Many of the prince's relations and Syrian aristocrats who had been removed from power in the East became the new upper crust of Cordovan society. During his 32-year reign Abd al-Rahman had to deal with numerous uprisings, several of which were supported by the Abbasids. One of the most serious was the revolt of the Yemenite Arab al-Ala ibn Mugith, whom Abd al-Rahman ordered decapitated. From 768 to 776 the emir faced an even more serious revolt led by the Berber chief Shakya. Later, a coalition of disaffected Arab chiefs called on Charlemagne for help against the Umayyad ruler. The Frankish king vainly besieged Saragossa in 778, and part of his army was wiped out in the Pass of Roncesvalles by a Basque ambush as it returned to France, an episode chronicled in the *Song of Roland.*

Through his policy of attracting opposing interest groups and dealing sternly with rebellion, Abd al-Rahman achieved a modicum of stability. He perfected the Syrian administrative bureaus introduced earlier in the century and further centralized government operations in Cordova, which by the end of his reign began to resemble a great capital. Blond, habitually dressed in white, and blind in one eye, he was skilled in oratory and poetry no less than in the military arts. On Sept. 30, 788, Abd al-Rahman I died in Cordova.

Further Reading

A short biography of Abd al-Rahman I is in Philip K. Hitti, *Makers of Arab History* (1968). For general background see W. Montgomery Watt, *A History of Islamic Spain* (1965). □

Abd al-Rahman III

Abd al-Rahman III (891-961) was the greatest of the Umayyad rulers of Spain and the first to take the title of Caliph. During his reign Islamic Spain became wealthy and prosperous.

Abd al-Rahman III, called al-Nasir or the Defender (of the Faith), was born at Cordova on Jan. 7, 891, the son of Prince Muhammad and a Frankish slave. Like most of his family, he was blue-eyed and blond, but he dyed his hair black to avoid looking like a Goth. In 912 he succeeded his grandfather, Abd Allah, as emir. The first period of his half-century reign was marked by campaigns of pacification against various rebellious groups. Between 912 and 928 he steadily wore down the forces of Umar ibn Hafsun, whose coalition of neo-Moslem peasants from southern Spain proved the most serious challenge yet mounted against Cordova's authority.

During the next phase of his reign Abd al-Rahman was able to concentrate his energies on foreign problems. He applied pressure to his Christian enemies to the north and waged a diplomatic campaign against Fatimid influence in North Africa. In 920 he stopped the southward advance of King Ordoño III of León and in 924 sacked Pamplona, the capital of Navarre. Abd al-Rahman was defeated at Simancas in 939 by Ramiro II of León, who was unable, however, to press his advantage further. In 927 Abd al-Rahman captured Melilla on the Mediterranean coast of Morocco as an advanced defense against possible moves by the Tunisia-based Fatimids; this was followed in 931 by the conquest of Ceuta. From these two bases the Spanish ruler extended an Umayyad protectorate over much of western North Africa which lasted until the end of the century.

An astute politician, Abd al-Rahman adopted the supreme titles of Caliph and Prince of the Believers in 929, a significant political decision designed to legitimize his imperial pretensions over the claims of Abbasid and Fatimid rivals. The assumption of the caliphal title reflected the total pacification of Islamic Spain, for the powerful group of orthodox Islamic theologians had always opposed any challenge to the religious unity of Islam, symbolized in the Abbasid caliphate.

After reigning for 25 years, Abd al-Rahman III launched the construction of a luxurious pleasure palace and administrative city, Madinat al-Zahra, just outside Cordova. Begun in 936, the construction took 40 years, and for a while the Caliph spent one-third of his annual income on it. He occupied the palace in 945, moving most of the governmental administrative bureaus there. Cordova itself, as the capital of Islamic Spain, became during his reign the greatest metropolis of western Europe, rivaling Constantinople.

Abd al-Rahman III died at the apex of his power on Oct. 15, 961. He had pacified the realm, dealt ably with his Fatimid rivals, and stabilized the frontier with Christian Spain.

Further Reading

The definitive study of Islamic Spain during the lifetime of Abd al-Rahman III is in French, E. Lévi-Provençal, *L'Espagne musulmane au X siècle* (1932). For a general survey in English see W. Montgomery Watt, *A History of Islamic Spain* (1965). □

Abd el-Kadir

The Algerian political and religious leader Abd el-Kadir (1807-1883) was the first national hero of Algeria. In 15 years of armed struggle against the French occupation of Algeria, he became a symbol of tenacious resistance to colonialism.

I n May 1807 Abd el-Kadir was born in the province of Oran into a famous family of marabouts (holy men). He received a traditional education and mastered the subtleties of Islamic theology. At the end of his adolescence he visited Mecca and several Middle Eastern countries. The trip greatly influenced his development.

In November 1832, 2 years after the French occupation of Algiers had begun, the Algerian tribes designated Abd el-Kadir to conduct a holy war against the invaders. At the age of 24 this pious marabout became transformed into an energetic and highly capable warrior. In the struggle that followed, his vision was always more religious than nationalistic, but his example helped forge the embryo of the Algerian nation.

Abd el-Kadir's first task was to unite under his authority tribes torn by internal rivalries and others content to collaborate with the invaders. French errors facilitated his task: in an 1834 treaty they recognized Abd el-Kadir's sovereignty over the province of Oran and gave him the arms and the money to consolidate his power.

Once Abd el-Kadir felt strong enough, he revolted against the French, who reacted in 1836 by sending to Algeria the 19th-century master of counter insurgency warfare, Marshal Bugeaud de la Piconnerie. Bugeaud defeated his adversary but proved to be a better soldier than a diplomat, since the Treaty of Tafna (1837), which he negotiated with Abd el-Kadir, extended the control of the marabout over a portion of the province of Algiers.

During the following years Abd el-Kadir reorganized the territory under his command and founded a theocratic state. He set up an administration, organized a regular army, levied taxes, and created an arsenal. By 1839 two-thirds of Algeria acknowledged his sovereignty.

Disturbed by his success, the French government again ordered Bugeaud to contain the upstart. Abd el-Kadir was defeated and took refuge in Morocco. The French used his presence there to declare war against the Moroccans and defeated them at the battle of Isly in 1844. Abd el-Kadir returned to Algeria and organized the resistance anew. Abandoned by his followers and declared an outlaw by the Moroccan sultan, Abd el-Kadir surrendered in 1847.

He ended up in a French prison, where he remained until 1852, when the French allowed him to retire to Damascus. In 1865 he refused the offer of Napoleon III to become the viceroy of Algeria. In 1870 he condemned the insurrection of the Algerian Kabyle Berbers. Abd el-Kadir died in Damascus on May 26, 1883.

Further Reading

The most complete biography of Abd el-Kadir in English is Wilfrid Blunt, *Desert Hawk: Abd el Kadir and the French Conquest of Algeria* (1947). An older study is Charles Henry Churchill, *The Life of Abdel Kader* (1867). Background information is contained in G. B. Laurie's military history, *The French Conquest of Algeria* (1909). □

Mohamed ben Abd el-Krim el-Khatabi

The Moroccan Berber leader Mohamed ben Abd el-Krim el-Khatabi (ca. 1882-1963) organized the resistance against European colonialism in northern Morocco from 1920 to 1927. He inspired a generation of militant nationalists, who liberated Morocco in 1956.

S on of an Islamic schoolteacher, Abd el-Krim was born at Ajdir in the Rif mountains into the important Berber tribe of the Beni Ouriaghel. After his Koranic studies his family moved to Tetuán in 1892, where he attended a Spanish school and came into contact with European culture. He completed his studies in Fez at the Moslem university of Qarawiyin.

In 1906 Abd el-Krim edited an Arabic supplement of a Spanish newspaper in Melilla. In the following year he became a secretary in the Spanish Bureau of Native Affairs; his work provided him with a precise knowledge of the mining resources of the Rif and the abusive aspects of colonialism. In 1914 he was named the chief religious judge for the region of Melilla and emerged as an important figure in northern Morocco. He was familiar with the Occident and the ideas which agitated the world on the eve of World War I. He commanded enough influence in his tribe to incite the Beni Ouriaghel to fight against the pretender Bou Amara, who revolted against the Moroccan sultan.

In 1917 Abd el-Krim's father was accused by the Spaniards of collusion with the Germans and he took to the maquis. In August 1917 Abd el-Krim was imprisoned for protesting against the French and Spanish presence in Morocco.

A few months after his release in 1919, Abd el-Krim and his younger brother joined their father in the mountains. Their goal was to established an independent state in the Rif. When his father died in September 1920, Abd el-Krim assumed the leadership of the rebellion. He organized the Rifian tribes, uniting them in the face of opposition from leaders of religious orders. He also delegated emissaries to propagandize his cause overseas and to obtain aid from foreigners. Tactically, he prepared for a long guerrilla war, taking advantage of the region's steep mountainous terrain and the inaccessibility of the Rifian coastline.

During the spring of 1921 his forces defeated 50,000 Spanish troops at Anual. They chased the Spaniards to

Melilla but failed to attack the city, a strategic error which later cost Abd el-Krim dearly.

Following his success at Anual, Abd el-Krim created a permanent political organization for his conquered territories. The tribal chiefs meeting in a national assembly created the Confederated Republic of the Rif Tribes with a central government presided over by the prince, or emir, Abd el-Krim. His financial resources included tax revenues, ransom demanded for captured Spaniards, and outright subsidies paid by German concerns interested in exploiting the mining riches of the Rif. The army, amounting to about 120,000 men, was well equipped but operated along traditional Moroccan military lines.

Nothing in Abd el-Krim's physical appearance revealed princely qualities. He was short and stout with a ruddy complexion and always dressed in rustic mountaineer robes. Married to four women, as permitted by the Moslem religion, and the father of four children, he nevertheless led an austere life. Although a devout Moslem, he was no fanatic: his ideals were nationalistic, not religious. He was a legendary figure in the whole country, but only a few Rifians met him directly. His despotic temperament made him more feared than loved, and on several occasions he became the target of assassins.

In 1925 the French, fearful of the repercussions of Abd el-Krim's victories on their own protectorate in southern Morocco, advanced on the Rif. Initially, the emir obtained brilliant military victories and even menaced the city of Fez, but a successful counterattack by a coalition of Franco-Spanish forces in 1927 led Abd el-Krim to surrender.

The French deported him with his family to Réunion Island, where he remained in exile for 20 years. In 1947 Paris authorized him to move to France, but during the trip through the Suez Canal he jumped ship and demanded asylum from King Farouk. When Col. Nasser came to power in 1952, Cairo was transformed into the center of the Arab nationalist movements, and the old Abd el-Krim became the historical and spiritual reference for all anti-colonial resistance. He died in Cairo on Feb. 6, 1963, without over having returned to independent Morocco.

Further Reading

Two books dealing with Abd el-Krim and his resistance to colonialism are David S. Woolman, *Rebels in the Rif: Abd El Krim and the Rif Rebellion* (1968), and Rupert Furneaux, *Abdel Krim: Emir of the Rif* (1967). □

Muhammad Abduh ibn Hasan Khayr Allah

The Egyptian theologian and nationalist Muhammad Abduh ibn Hasan Khayr Allah (1849-1905) was a founder of modernist reform in Islamic religion, of the Arabic literary renaissance of the last hundred years, and of Egyptian nationalism.

Muhammad Abduh, born to peasant stock, was brought up in the village of Mahallat Nasr in the Nile Delta. His first education consisted of the traditional memorization of the Koran. In 1862 he studied at the Ahmadi mosque-academy in the provincial city of Tanta. In 1866 Abduh left Tanta for Cairo, where he completed the course of study at the Azhar mosque-university. In contrast to many of his fellows, Abduh pursued secular subjects such as history and natural science.

One of the turning points in Abduh's life was the arrival in Cairo in 1872 of the enigmatic political activist Jamal ud-Din al-Afghani, who, over three continents, clamored for the regeneration of the Moslem world. The two men became fast friends, and under Jamal's influence Abduh began to extend the range of his vision from Egypt to the whole Moslem world.

Teacher and Journalist

Having finished his studies in 1877, Abduh became a teacher at both the Azhar and the new Dar al-Ulum (seat of learning). In 1880 he was asked to edit *Al-Waqai al-Misriyah* (Egyptian Events), the official gazette. Under his editorship it became the model for a new standard of modern, straightforward prose as well as a vehicle for liberal opinion.

But Abduh's life was not yet to become tranquil. When the revolt of Col. Urabi took place in 1882, Abduh was implicated and was exiled. He took up residence in Beirut and then went to Paris, where Jamal ud-Din had established himself. Together they edited the short-lived but highly influential journal *Al-Urwa al-Wuthqa* (The Strongest Bond), which called for reform at home and lashed out against colonialism in the Moslem world.

Abduh spent 1884 and 1885 traveling before taking up residence again in Beirut, where he began to teach from his home and to lecture in mosques. He was soon invited to teach in an official school. In 1888 Abduh returned to his native land, where he had become a national figure. He shortly entered the judiciary of the "native courts," serving first in the provinces and then, in 1890, in Cairo.

Official Career

In 1899 the khedive appointed Abduh chief mufti (jurisconsult) of Egypt, and in the same year he was also appointed to the advisory legislative council. His tenure as mufti was marked by his liberalism in interpretation of the law and by reform of the religious courts.

Abduh's career also attained great distinction in his advocacy of educational reforms. In 1895 Khedive Abbas II appointed him to a newly formed commission charged with reforming the venerable Azhar, and Abduh was thus able to implement at least in part many of his liberal ideas.

Abduh tried to mediate between the teachings of Islam and Western culture. To this end he ceaselessly prodded the hidebound traditionalists at home while fending off Western writers who he felt misunderstood Islam. After his return to Egypt, he advocated the efficacy of education over that of revolution in national regeneration.

Literary Output

Abduh's writings were considerable. Among his religious books special mention should be made of *Risalat al-Tawhid* (1897; Epistle on the Unity [of God], a work summarizing his theological views); *Al-Islam wa-al-Nasraniyah maal-Ilm wa-al-Madaniyah* (1902; Islam and Christianity in Relation to Science and Civilization); and *Al-Islam wa-al-Radd ala Muntaqidih* (1909; Islam and a Rebuttal to Its Critics).

In the area of language and literature Abduh wrote extensive commentaries on several classical Arabic literary works and coedited a 17-volume work on Arabic philology; in the mundane field his *Taqrir fi Islah al-Mahakim al-Shariyah* (1900; Report on the Reform of the Shariyah Courts) should be noted.

Most ambitious of all Abduh's works was his *Tafsir al-Quran al-Hakim* (1927-1935; Commentary on the Koran). The huge project was never completed, but the 12 volumes that appeared are the most important expression of modernist views of the scripture of Islam.

Further Reading

The principal studies on Abduh in English are in C. C. Adams, *Islam and Modernism in Egypt* (1933); Uthman Amin, *Muhammad Abduh* (trans. 1953); and Malcolm H. Kerr, *Islamic Reform: The Political and Legal Theories of Muhammad Abduh and Rashid Rida* (1966). Relevant but more general are J. M. Ahmed, *The Intellectual Origins of Egyptian Nationalism* (1960); Nadav Safran, *Egypt in Search of Political Community* (1961); and Albert Hourani, *Arabic Thought in the Liberal Age* (1962). A serious study which includes a discussion of Abduh, is Majid Fakhry, *A History of Islamic Philosophy* (1970). □

Abdul-Hamid II

The Turkish sultan Abdul-Hamid II (1842-1918) was a ruler of the Ottoman Empire. A reactionary autocrat, he delayed for a quarter century the liberal movement in the empire.

Born on Sept. 21, 1842, Abdul-Hamid was the son of Sultan Abdul-Medjid and of Tirimujgan, a Circassian. He obtained the throne in 1876, when his brother Murad V was ousted by a liberal reform group led by the grand vizier Midhat Pasha.

In fulfillment of promises made before his accession, Abdul-Hamid issued the empire's first constitution on Dec. 23, 1876, a document largely inspired by Midhat Pasha. It provided for an elected bicameral parliament and for the customary civil liberties, including equality before the law for all the empire's diverse nationalities. The issuance of the constitution undercut European ambitions and stalled, at least temporarily, pressure for reform.

The Sultan, however, was an autocrat by nature. In February 1877 Midhat Pasha was dismissed and exiled.

Abdul-Hamid's reactionary measures continued when he prorogued the new parliament in May. From this time until 1908, the Sultan ignored the constitution.

The excuse for the Sultan's actions was war with Russia, declared April 24, 1877. Military successes by the Slavic states and losses in the Caucasus caused the Ottomans to bow to the Russian presence at Yesilkoy (San Stefano) only 10 miles from Istanbul. The settlement of San Stefano in March 1878 was harsh for Turkey because it provided for Bosnian-Herzegovinian autonomy, the independence of Serbia, Montenegro, and Romania, establishment of "Greater Bulgaria," and an indemnity and cession of territory to the czar. The terms were ameliorated by a revision announced in Berlin on July 13, 1878.

Economic Reforms

Domestically, German influence was on the rise (British support had helped Midhat Pasha). Germans reorganized the army and the country's tangled finances. Foreign control over finances was confirmed by a decree issued December 1881 consolidating the public debt and creating the Ottoman Public Debt Administration. Its function was to collect assigned revenues, such as those from monopolies on tobacco and salt and assorted excise taxes, and to use these funds to reduce the indebtedness owed European bondholders.

The Ottoman Public Debt Administration proved a spirited agency for economic betterment. Tax collection techniques improved and revenues increased; technologi-

cal innovations were introduced in industries supervised by the agency; Turkish public administration training began here; improvements were made in transportation with railroad mileage increasing notably; and the credit of the empire improved to a point where foreign economic investments resumed.

Abdul-Hamid was anxious to appear as a religious champion against Christian encroachment. He encouraged the building of the Mecca railroad to make Islam's holy places more accessible. He subsidized the pan-Islamic policy of Jamal-ud-Din al-Afghani, whom he invited to Istanbul but virtually imprisoned there, and encouraged widespread support for himself as the head of the caliphate.

Rebellion in the Empire

Neither pan-Islamic nationalism nor efforts at economic development could quiet internal unrest, however. Revolts broke out in various parts of the empire; Yemen, Mesopotamia, and Crete were particularly troubled. In Armenia, whose inhabitants wanted changes promised at Berlin, a series of revolts occurred between 1892 and 1894, culminating in persecutions and massacres of an estimated 100,000 Armenians. Abdul-Hamid became known as "Abdul the Damned" and the "Red Sultan."

The government engaged increasingly in espionage and mass arrests. By 1907 both military and civilian protests were widespread. Leadership in the movement fell to a Salonika-based liberal reform group, the Committee of Union and Progress. In the summer of 1908, dogged by police, the leaders fled to the hills; but when the III Army Corps threatened to march on Istanbul unless the constitution was restored, Abdul-Hamid complied. He also called for elections and appointed a liberal grand vizier.

On April 13, 1909, Abdul-Hamid, unreformed as ever, supported a military-religious counter coup which ousted the liberal Young Turk government. Again the III Army Corps intervened, Istanbul was occupied, and on April 27 the committee deposed the Sultan in favor of his brother, Mehmed (Mohammed V). Abdul-Hamid was confined at Salonika until that city fell to the Greeks in 1912. He died at Magnesia on Feb. 10, 1918.

Further Reading

A good biography is the contemporary account by Sir Edwin Pears, *Life of Abdul Hamid* (1917). More recent is Joan Haslip, *The Sultan: The Life of Abdul Hamid* (1958). Background information is in M. Philips Price, *A History of Turkey from Empire to Republic* (1956; 2d ed. 1961); E. E. Ramsaur, *The Young Turks: Prelude to the Revolution of 1908* (1957); Bernard Lewis, *The Emergence of Modern Turkey* (1962; 2d ed. 1968); and, from a more European viewpoint, W. N. Medlicott, *The Congress of Berlin and After: A Diplomatic History of the Near Eastern Settlement, 1878-1880* (1938; 2d ed. 1963). □

Shaykh 'Abdullah al-Salim al-Sabah

Shaykh 'Abdullah al-Salim al-Sabah (1895-1965) ruled Kuwait for 15 years (1950-1965), a period of spectacular development and change, both human and material. His crowning achievement came when Kuwait attained independence from Great Britain in 1961.

Shaykh 'Abdullah al-Salim al-Sabah succeeded his cousin Shaykh Ahmad al-Jabir al-Sabah as the Amir of Kuwait on February 25, 1950. Long before his accession to the throne, Shaykh 'Abdullah had been supportive of the political reform movement that emerged during the period between world wars; in fact, he was an early favorite of the reformers. Before the advent of the oil boom, leading merchant notables constituted the primary source of the Arab shaykhdom's prosperity, contributing the largest share of the government's revenues. In 1921 these notables had successfully challenged the autocratic rule of the Sabah family, demanding the establishment of a consultative council (*al-Majlis al-Istishari*) and participation on the issue of succession.

As a result, a council was established, but it lasted only two months; rivalry and infighting crippled it and resulted in its voluntary dissolution. The ruler remained sole authority. Propelled by the deteriorating economic situation of the 1930s, the merchants once again rose up, demanding parliamentary government. In 1938 they formed a secret society—*al-Harakah al-Wataniyyah* (The National Bloc)—that demanded the restoration of the 1921 council. The ruler, Shaykh Ahmad al-Jabir, eventually consented in order to avoid confrontation; a second council was established in 1939, headed as before by Shaykh 'Abdullah.

Architect of Modern Kuwait

During the next 11 years, 'Abdullah played a leading role on the domestic political scene, handling administrative and financial responsibilities with facility. After ascending to the throne in 1950, he began presiding over the swiftest and most complete transformation of the country in its history. A spectacular development program made impressive gains in the fields of education, health, and other social services. Hundreds of schools were built to meet the demands of increasing numbers of students; the government recruited large numbers of highly qualified teachers from more advanced Arab countries such as Egypt and Palestine. A full range of health services was provided for Kuwaitis and expatriates alike; Kuwaiti citizens were entitled to free housing and guaranteed employment. Similarly, Shakyh 'Abdullah laid the infrastructural foundations for the tremendous material progress in modern Kuwait.

Once cognizant of the full extent of its tremendous wealth, Kuwait offered help to the less fortunate Arab countries, both for humanitarian reasons and as part of its quest for recognition and Arab solidarity. The Kuwait Fund for Arab Economic Development (KFAED) was established by Shakyh 'Abdullah immediately after independence in 1961. The disbursement of large sums of development aid remained a respected tradition and a major plank in Kuwait's foreign policy, both in Africa and the Arab world.

Independence and Prosperity

During the first decade of 'Abdullah's reign, Kuwait was still a British protectorate; the British political agent was solely responsible for foreign affairs. In the late 1950s and early 1960s, however, in a time of growing Arab nationalism, certain political events took place in the Arab East that left their impact on Kuwaitis as well as on British imperialists. The rise of the Kuwaiti intelligentsia, influenced by Nasserism and by the Iraqi revolution of 1958 and the subsequent overthrow of the pro-British Hashemite dynasty there, induced Shakyh 'Abdullah in 1961 to terminate the 1889 "Exclusive Agreement" with Great Britain. Britain in turn was becoming more and more aware of the need for decolonization, especially after the 1956 Suez War fiasco. Kuwait was declared a sovereign and independent Arab state in June 1961. Within a month the new state joined the Arab League.

Shakyh 'Abdullah promulgated Kuwait's first constitution on November 11, 1961, and the first elections to the new 50-member National Assembly were held on January 23, 1963. Kuwait joined the United Nations that same year. The constitution guaranteed freedom of the individual and the press; discrimination on the grounds of race, social origin, or religion was forbidden by law. Islam was designated the official state religion; however, other religious practices were permitted as long as they did not violate public order or morality. All male citizens 20 years and older could run for public office—not as candidates of political parties but on independent platforms. While political parties were prohibited, trade unions were allowed.

The constitution designated Kuwait a hereditary emirate and limited succession to the descendents of Shaykh Mubarak (ruler of Kuwait, 1896-1915). The ruler, or Amir, was declared immune and his person inviolable. Government was divided into three branches: executive, legislative, and judiciary. However, the Amir, as head of state, and a council of ministers appointed by him held executive power, while legislative power was shared by the Amir and the National Assembly. Technically all legislation had to pass by a two-thirds vote of the assembly; but in actuality its legislative powers were eclipsed by the more powerful Amir, whose cabinet constituted one-third of the assembly. While the cabinet ministers were held accountable to the assembly, the prime minister (always the crown prince, by tradition) was not. In other words, ministers could be subjected to a vote of confidence, but the prime minister could not. Thus, Shakyh 'Abdullah and the Sabah family retained firm control of the government.

The tremendous social and political changes that occurred during Shakyh 'Abdullah's reign led to the transformation of Kuwait from a benevolent, autocratic government to a representative one. It thereby became a model for other Gulf states yet to embark on modernization. Today, Shakyh 'Abdullah is remembered as the wise, prudent, and benevolent *pater familias* who introduced democracy and development to that small city-state.

Further Reading

Although Shakyh 'Abdullah al-Salim al-Sabah is listed in *International Who's Who,* there is no authoritative biography of him in English; his reign is briefly treated, however, in a small number of books, the most important of which is H. R. P. Dickson's *Kuwait and Her Neighbours* (London, 1956). The author was a long-time British political agent in the Gulf. Other sources include: Zahra Freeth and H. V. F. Winstone, *Kuwait: Prospect and Reality* (1972); Ahmad Mustafa Abu Hakima, *The Modern History of Kuwait* (London, 1983); and Jacqueline S. Ismail, *Kuwait: Social Change in Historical Perspective* (1982). For inter-Arab politics in the late 1950s and early 1960s see Malcolm Kerr, *The Arab Cold War: Gamal 'Abd al-Nasir and His Rivals, 1958-1970* (1971). □

Abdullah ibn Husein

Abdullah ibn Husein (1882-1951) was an Arab nationalist and political leader who established and became king of the Hashemite Kingdom of Jordan.

Born in the Islamic holy city of Mecca, Abdullah ibn Husein was the second son of Husein ibn Ali in the city's leading family, which claimed descent from the prophet Mohammed. In 1891 he moved to Constantinople (modern Istanbul) and was raised and educated in the Ottoman capital. Following the Young Turk Revolution in 1908, the new Ottoman government appointed Husein ibn Ali the sharif of Mecca, the protector of the holy places, which was a position his family had often held. Abdullah represented the Hejaz Province of western Arabia in the reorganized Ottoman parliament and participated in Arab political movements concerned with the question of autonomy or independence for Arab areas of the multinational Ottoman Empire.

Even before the outbreak of World War I in 1914, Abdullah had discreetly contacted British officials in Egypt to learn Great Britain's attitude toward Arab political aspirations in the event of Ottoman involvement in war. Consequent negotiations led in part to the Arab Revolt of June 1916, in which Abdullah and Arab troops assisted British efforts to drive the Turks out of Syria.

Following the war, Britain could not harmonize the pledges it had made to the French, the Zionists, and the Arabs—especially the Arab expectation for a separate and fully independent Arab state for the Fertile Crescent and Arabia. The Arab National Congress at Damascus in 1920 elected Abdullah king of Iraq and his brother Faisal king of Syria, but the French seizure of Damascus in July 1920 upset the plans. Abdullah moved north in 1921 with troops to support Faisal's claims, but the pragmatic Abdullah acquiesced in Britain's immediate proposal to accept the newly created emirate of Transjordan, the largely arid territory east of the Jordan River. This land became formally independent in 1946, and the Hashemite Kingdom of Jordan in 1949.

During the first Palestinian War of 1948-1949, Abdullah's British-trained Arab Legion held central Palestine, which Abdullah annexed in 1950 over the objections of Palestinians and the other Arab states. Because of this and the general opinion that he was a moderate and was willing to reach an accommodation with Israel, Abdullah was killed by an embittered Palestinian on July 20, 1951, in Jerusalem—the nationalist of one generation assassinating the nationalist of an earlier one.

Between World Wars I and II Abdullah had ruled as a realistic, capable desert emir, but he was not cognizant of new social and political forces emerging in the Arab world following World War II and the Palestinian conflict. Abdullah failed completely in his ambitious dream of building a greater Syrian union with himself as king, just as his father had failed before him.

Further Reading

Two volumes by Abdullah are *Memoirs of King Abdullah of Transjordan,* edited by Philip P. Graves (trans. 1950), and *My Memoirs Completed* (trans. 1954). James Morris, *The Hashemite Kings* (1959), presents a popular story of Husein ibn Ali and his sons. British views of Abdullah are provided by Alec S. Kirkbride, a personal friend and adviser, in *A Crackle of Thorns: Experiences in the Middle East* (1956), and by John Bagot Glubb, the leader of the Arab Legion, in *The Story of the Arab Legion* (1948) and *A Soldier with the Arabs* (1957). Ann Dearden, *Jordan* (1958), is a good survey of the emirate. P. J. Vatikiotis, *Politics and the Military in Jordan: A Study of the Arab Legion, 1921-1957* (1967), includes material on history and politics during the interwar era.

Additional Sources

Abdullah, King of Jordan, *My memoirs completed "Al Takmilah,"* London; New York: Longman, 1978.
Wilson, Mary C. (Mary Christina), *King Abdullah, Britain, and the making of Jordan,* Cambridge, Cambridgeshire; New York: Cambridge University Press, 1987. □

Abdullah ibn Yasin

The North African religious leader Abdullah ibn Yasin (died 1059) was the founder and spiritual leader of the Moslem Almoravid movement.

Little is known of the life of Abdullah ibn Yasin until he stepped into North African history about 1050 as a missionary to the Sanhaja Berbers of the western Sahara. Himself a Berber, Ibn Yasin had been trained in the Maliki school of jurisprudence. He was living in the town of Nafis in the Moroccan High Atlas when he was invited by two Sanhaja leaders to instruct the Berber tribesmen of the Sahara in the true principles of Islam. Ibn Yasin proved to be a stern disciplinarian in the Maliki tradition, insisting that

the Berbers abide by the letter of Moslem law in such matters as marriage, taxation, and punishment of criminals. Rather than give up their traditional practices, the Berbers denounced Ibn Yasin and his preaching.

Discouraged by this failure, Ibn Yasin withdrew with a small group of loyal followers to a Senegal island. There he established a ribat, or monastery-fortress, whose inhabitants (Arabic, al-Murabi-tun; English, Almoravids) gave their lives to religious instruction and devotion and to holy war against infidels. This combination of religious instruction, military discipline, and communal life directed from the ribat was as noteworthy for its success as his previous preaching was remarkable for its failure. In spite of the fact that the rules which Ibn Yasin imposed on his followers were strict and the corporal punishment which he personally inflicted for infractions, severe, his adherents soon numbered in the thousands, enough to subdue those very Berbers who had rejected his teachings. There is little doubt that the opportunity which Ibn Yasin gave the tribesmen for raiding and the taking of booty lent his doctrines an attraction which they had lacked at first.

About 1055 Ibn Yasin felt his forces were strong enough to undertake the conquest of urban centers in Morocco and Ghana. It is indicative of the increasing importance of warfare in the Almoravid movement that he turned over the leadership of the armies to one of his earliest followers, Yahya ibn Umar, retaining for himself the direction of spiritual and civil affairs. With this division of command, expeditions were sent against Sijilmasa in the north and Aoudaghost in the south.

The motives for attacking Sijilmasa were probably complex. Ostensibly, religion provided the occasion for the attack, inasmuch as a group of religious scholars had complained to Ibn Yasin that they were being persecuted by the ruler of the city. Tribal feelings were probably involved too, since the Berbers ruling the city belonged to the Zenata confederation while the Almoravids were Sanhaja. Finally, the fact that large amounts of booty were taken indicates the possibility that economic factors were involved. Northward expansion was continued in subsequent years into the cities of southern and central Morocco, in all of which Ibn Yasin attempted to impose the Maliki code of Islamic law. Thus, before his death in battle in 1059, he had created a base for the military expansion of the Almoravid empire into North Africa and Spain and laid down the guidelines by which it was to be governed.

Further Reading

In the absence of any detailed biographical study of Ibn Yasin see Henri Terrasse, *History of Morocco* (2 vols., 1949-1950; trans., 1 vol., 1952). □

Kobo Abe

An important figure in contemporary Japanese literature, Kobo Abe (1924-1993) attracted an international audience for novels in which he explored the

nihilism and loss of identity experienced by many in post-World War II Japanese society.

Abe's works were often linked to the writings of Franz Kafka and Samuel Beckett for their surreal settings, shifting perspectives, grotesque images, and themes of alienation. The labyrinthine structures of his novels accommodated both precisely detailed realism and bizarre fantasy, and his use of symbolic and allegorical elements resulted in various metaphysical implications. Scott L. Montgomery stated: "Abe's most powerful books . . . displace reality in order to highlight the fragility of an identity we normally take for granted."

Many critics contended that Abe's recurring themes of social displacement and spiritual rootlessness derived from his childhood in Manchuria, a region in northern China seized by the Japanese Army in the early 1930s, and by his brief association during the late 1940s with a group of avant-garde writers whose works combined elements of existentialism and Marxism. In 1948, the year that he published his first novel, *Owarishi michino shirubeni,* Abe earned a medical degree from Tokyo University. Although Abe never practiced medicine, his background in the sciences figured prominently in his fiction. For example, *Daiyon kampyok* (1959) is a science fiction novel set in a futuristic Japan that is threatened by melting polar ice caps. The protagonist of this novel is a scientist who designs a computer capable of predicting human behavior. After the machine foretells that its creator will condemn government

experiments on human fetuses that would insure Japan's survival in a subaqueous environment, the scientist's wife gives birth to a child with fish-like fins instead of arms. While a reviewer for the *Times Literary Supplement* deemed the novel's plot "too phantasmagorical and implausible," several critics favorably noted Abe's accurate use of scientific terminology.

Abe garnered international acclaim following the publication of *Suna no onn* (1962; *Woman in the Dune*). This novel relates the nightmarish experiences of an alienated male teacher and amateur entomologist who is enslaved by a group of people living beneath a huge sand dune. Condemned to a life of shoveling the sand that constantly endangers this community, the man gradually finds meaning in his new existence and rejects an opportunity to escape. William Currie remarked: "Like Kafka and Beckett . . . , Abe has created an image of alienated man which is disturbing and disquieting. But also like those two writers, Abe has shown a skill and depth in this novel which has made it a universal myth for our time." With Hiroshi Teshigahara, Abe wrote the screenplay for a film adaptation of *Woman in the Dune* which was awarded the Special Jury Prize at the 1964 Cannes Film Festival.

Abe's next three novels further examined human estrangement and loss of identity. *Tanin no ka* (1964; *The Face of Anothe*) details a scientist's attempts to construct a mask that covers his disfiguring scars. *Moetsukita chiz* (1967; *The Ruined Ma*) follows a private detective who gradually assumes the identity of the person he has been hired to locate. *Hakootok* (1973; *The Box Ma*) focuses upon a man who withdraws from his community to live in a cardboard box in which he invents his own idyllic society. Jerome Charyn commented that *The Box Ma* "is a difficult, troubling book that undermines our secret wishes, our fantasies of becoming box men (and box women), our urge to walk away from a permanent address and manufacture landscapes from a vinyl curtain or some other filtering device." In Abe's succeeding novel, *Mikka* (1977; *Secret Rendezvou*), the wife of a shoe salesman is mysteriously admitted to a cavernous hospital even though she is not ill. While searching for her at the facility, the woman's husband discovers that the hospital is run by an assortment of psychopaths, sexual deviants, and grotesque beasts.

Abe's novel *The Ark Sakur* (1988) is a farcical version of the biblical story of Noah and the Flood. Mole, the protagonist, is an eccentric recluse who converts a huge cave into an "ark" equipped with water, food, and elaborate weapons to protect himself from an impending nuclear holocaust. Mole's vision of creating a post-apocalyptic society inside his ark is thwarted by a trio of confidence men whom he enlists as crew members and by the invasion of street gangs and cantankerous elderly people. Edmund White observed: *The Ark Sakura* may be a grim novel, but it is also a large, ambitious work about the lives of outcasts in modern Japan. . . . It is a wildly improbable fable when recalled, but it proceeds with fiendishly detailed verisimilitude when experienced from within."

Further Reading

Chicago Tribune, January 24, 1993, section 2, p. 6.
Los Angeles Times, January 23, 1993, p. A22.
Times (London), January 25, 1993, p. 19.
Washington Post, January 23, 1993, p. C4.
Contemporary Literary Criticism, Gale, Volume 8, 1978, Volume 22, 1982, Volume 53, 1989.
Janiera, Armando Martins, *Japanese and Western Literature,* Tuttle, 1970.
Tsurutu, Kinya, editor, *Approaches to the Modern Japanese Novel,* Sophia University, 1976.
Yamanouchi, Hisaaki, *The Search for Authenticity in Modern Japanese Literature,* Cambridge University Press, 1978.
Atlantic, October, 1979.
Chicago Tribune Book World, October 7, 1979.
Commonweal, December 21, 1979. □

Iorwith Wilber Abel

Labor organizer Iorwith Wilber Abel (1908-1987) helped introduce industrial unionism during the 1930s. He later served 13 years as president of the United Steelworkers of America.

Iorwith Wilber Abel was born on August 11, 1908, in Magnolia, Ohio, a small town fifteen miles south of the industrial city of Canton. Abel was reared in a typical working-class family by parents of mixed ethnic origins. His father, John, a skilled blacksmith, was of German background, and his mother Welsh. Abel attended the local elementary schools and graduated from Magnolia High School. In 1925 he went to work for the American Sheet and Tin Mill Company in Canton, where he became a skilled iron molder. Abel changed jobs frequently, finding employment in the 1920s with the Malleable Iron Company and Timken Roller Bearing, among other Canton firms. He also found time to study for two years at the Canton Business College. Then in 1930 the Great Depression hit and Abel found himself unemployed. Desperate for work (he had married in June 1930), he took a job in a brickyard where he did unskilled labor for twelve hours a day at minimal wages. Abel subsequently claimed that his experience as an "exploited" worker taught him the need for social reform and the virtues of trade unionism.

By the middle of the 1930s Abel again had a job as a skilled foundryman with the Timken Company. There he participated actively in the labor upheaval of the 1930s which gave birth to the Congress of Industrial Organizations (CIO) and industrial unionism for the nation's mass-production workers. In 1936 he helped found Local 1123 of the Steel Workers Organizing Committee (SWOC) at Timken and served successively as the local's financial secretary, vice president, and president. He was known around Canton as a union hell-raiser and in one year alone allegedly led 42 wildcat (unauthorized) strikes. But he also served as a responsible, competent union official, one who caught the eye of SWOC president Philip Murray.

In 1937 Murray appointed Abel to the SWOC staff as a field representative. Five years later, in February 1942, Murray appointed him director of SWOC District 27 in the Canton region and that same year he was elected to the position by the first constitutional convention of the United Steelworkers of America (USA). He held the district director's position for ten years, until the death of Philip Murray in 1952, when Abel moved up to the secretary-treasurer's office. Abel served as secretary-treasurer for twelve years, during which time he traveled around most of the United States and Canada meeting various local union officers and acquainting himself with the grievances of members. He played a major role in three national steel strikes and kept in closer touch with rank-and-file union members than the increasingly distant and debonair union president, David McDonald.

Elected USA President

As McDonald's aloof leadership style precipitated discontent among USA members, Abel in November 1964 announced his candidacy for the union presidency. In a heated campaign Abel charged McDonald with "tuxedo unionism" and with selling out the workers to the bosses through the steel industry's Human Relations Committee, which was supposed to eliminate strikes. He promised to be more militant and to bargain harder with employers. The election proved so bitter and contested that more than a month passed before final results were tabulated. Abel won by a margin of a little more than 10,000, of which over

7,000 came from Canadian locals. In December 1965, Abel was also elected to a vice presidency of the AFL-CIO.

Although he had promised to give rank-and-file members a greater voice in the union and to be more aggressive in bargaining with employers, Abel behaved in a manner similar to McDonald. In practice, he preferred to reach accommodations with employers rather than call workers out on strike. As he watched technological change raise productivity and reduce the need for labor, Abel sought to win union members a shorter work week, earlier retirement, better pensions, and more leisure time. Working cooperatively with members of the steel industry and federal officials, Abel at first won many of his goals. But as foreign competition increasingly threatened the steel industry in the 1970s, the union found itself on the defensive. Thus in 1973 Abel signed an agreement with the steel companies which promised to eliminate strikes for a four-year period. The so-called Experimental Negotiating Agreement (ENA) worked well between 1973 and 1977 and was renewed that year. This arrangement was later abandoned when the steel industry went into recession.

When Abel voluntarily retired from office in 1977, the union had increased its membership by over 40 percent, from under one million members to 1.4 million. Abel had campaigned for laws which improved workplace health and safety and to insure pension guarantees. One of Abel's chief critics was Edward Sadlowski, a Chicago union leader who ran for the presidency when Abel stepped down. But Abel supported Lloyd McBride, who won.

After retiring, Abel moved to Sun City, Arizona. Right before his death in 1987 he returned to his roots, settling in Malvern, Ohio, a few miles from Canton. Abel died of cancer a day before his 79th birthday and was survived by his second wife and two daughters. As reported by Robert D. McFadden in the *New York Times* from an interview with the Associated Press a year prior to his death, Abel thought public opinion in regards to organized labor had turned for the worse. He attributed this decline to people forgetting the struggles of early laborers, current fears as to the state of the economy, and the younger element who "think they get benefits like we have and holidays, vacations, medical insurance and all that because employers want to give them that." Until the end, he remained one of the staunchest advocates for workers, but not against management. Rather, he believed in workers working with management to meet common goals.

Further Reading

There is no full biography of Abel. A brief sketch is available in Gary Fink, ed., *Biographical Dictionary of American Labor Leaders* (1984). For histories of the steelworkers' union and Abel's role see Lloyd Ulman, *The Government of the Steel Workers' Union* (1962); John Herling, *Right to Challenge: People and Power in the Steelworkers' Union* (1972); and the autobiography of David McDonald, *Union Man* (1969). For Abel's own ideas on unionism and collective bargaining, see the published version of his Fairless Lectures at Carnegie-Mellon University, *Collective Bargaining, Labor Relations in Steel: Then and Now* (1976). Obituaries can be found in the August 24, 1987 issues of *Time* and *Newsweek*. □

Peter Abelard

The French philosopher and theologian Peter Abelard (1079-1142) was a leading thinker of the Middle Ages. His reputation outside academic circles is based upon his more human qualities as reflected in his love affair with Heloise.

In comparison with the literary and intellectual activity of the 9th century (the so-called Carolingian Renaissance), the period from 900 to 1050 contained few figures of cultural importance. Toward the end of the 11th century, however, the monastic and cathedral schools of northern France began to produce a series of gifted thinkers. This reawakening was part of the social, economic, and cultural transformation of Europe during the 12th century. The intellectual revival in particular was significant in laying the foundations for the development of scholastic philosophy and theology. The two most important figures in the early stages of this development were Anselm of Canterbury and Peter Abelard.

Although writing before most of the works of Aristotle had been recovered, Abelard made an important contribution to philosophy and logic by his solution to the problem of universals. His theological writings also had great influence, especially his work on Christian ethics and his contribution to the development of the scholastic method.

Abelard was born at Le Pallet in Brittany near Nantes in 1079. His father, Berengar, was lord of Pallet. Since Abelard was the eldest son, it was expected that he would be knighted and succeed his father. He sought, however, an ecclesiastical career as a teacher in one of the cathedral schools that then flourished in northern France. Leaving home at the age of 15, he studied logic or dialectic under Roscelin of Compiègne. Several years later, having been at various schools, he went to Paris to study under William of Champeaux, head of the cathedral school and archdeacon of Notre Dame. Abelard must have seemed a difficult student, for he questioned the method and conclusions of his master and raised points in class that embarrassed William in front of his students. According to Abelard, it was in such public debate that he later forced William to rethink his position on the question of universals.

Early Career

In 1102 Abelard set up his own school at Melun. He quickly attracted students and, on the basis of his growing reputation, shifted his lectures to Corbeil, closer to Paris. About 1106 poor health forced Abelard to visit his home in Brittany. He returned to Paris in 1107 and taught at the cathedral school. But under pressure from William, Abelard moved his lectures to Melun and later to the church of Ste-Geneviève, located on a hill on the southern edge of Paris. There he taught until the entrance of his parents into monastic life about 1111 forced him to return to Brittany to help reorganize family affairs.

Although many of Abelard's works in logic were written later in his life, his thinking on this subject seems to have been formed in the early period of study and teaching. Eventually he was to produce two sets of glosses on the parts of Aristotle's logic that were then known, *Categories* and *De interpretatione*. He also glossed the logical treaties of Porphyry and Boethius. Much of this material was eventually drawn together in an extensive work entitled *Dialectica*.

The problem of universals was the most pressing philosophical question in Abelard's day. This problem concerned the degree of reality possessed by a universal concept, such as "man" or "tree." Some thinkers approached the problem with Platonic presuppositions and tended to give a high degree of reality to the universal concept. According to this ultrarealist position, the universal exists in reality apart from the individuals embraced by that category. This separately existing universal is the archetype and cause of the individual things that reflect it. On the other hand, the ultranominalist position maintained that the universal was only a concept in the mind, a term that conveniently related individual things which, apart from such an arbitrary classification, would have little or nothing in common.

Abelard took a different approach to this problem. Beginning with the question of how men come to know a universal, he maintained that they know such only through their experience with individual things that make up a class. According to Abelard, the quality that individual things in a class have in common is a universal, but such a universal never exists apart from the individual thing.

Affair with Heloise

The decision of his parents to enter the religious life or the development of his own interests led Abelard upon his return to Paris to seek instruction in theology. Journeying to the cathedral school at Laon, northeast of Paris, Abelard studied under the most renowned master of this subject, the elderly Anselm of Laon. As had happened so often in the past, Abelard found the teaching shallow and boring, and in response to the urging of his fellow students he lectured on the scriptural book of Ezekiel. The resulting breach between Abelard and Anselm precipitated Abelard's expulsion from Laon, and in 1113 he returned to the cathedral school in Paris, where he taught theology for a number of years in relative peace.

By mutual agreement of Abelard and Fulbert, a canon at the Cathedral in Paris, Abelard became a resident in Fulbert's house and tutor of his young, cultured, and beautiful niece Heloise. Abelard and Heloise fell in love, and after some months Fulbert discovered their affair and forced Abelard to leave his house. At this time Abelard was about 40 years old and Heloise about 18.

Heloise, however, soon found that she was pregnant, and with Abelard's cooperation she left Paris in order to have the child in the more secluded and secure surroundings of Le Pallet, where Abelard's relatives lived. She gave birth to a son, Astralabe, and soon afterward at the request of Fulbert and over her objections Heloise and Abelard were married in Paris. The marriage initially was to have remained a secret in order to protect Abelard's reputation as a committed philosopher and to leave the way open for his advancement in a Church career. Fulbert, however, was concerned about his own reputation and that of his niece, and he openly acknowledged Abelard as his nephew-in-law.

The denial of the marriage by Abelard and Heloise angered Fulbert, and Abelard in order to protect her sent her to the convent at Argenteuil. Fulbert, thinking that Abelard was seeking to annul the marriage by forcing Heloise into the religious life, hired men to seize Abelard while he slept and emasculate him. This crime resulted in the disgrace of Fulbert and the death of those who had attacked Abelard. More importantly, it brought a temporary end to Abelard's teaching career, and both he and Heloise adopted the monastic life, she at Argenteuil and he at St-Denis, the famous Benedictine monastery north of Paris.

Monastic Years, 1118-1136

Abelard's life at St-Denis was difficult not only because of the public disgrace occasioned by his emasculation and the exposure of his affair with Heloise, but also because separation from the cathedral schools and subjection to the authority of an abbot were new and unpleasant experiences for him. Abelard's reputation attracted students, and his abbot permitted him to set up a school in a daughter priory separate from the monastery.

The resumption of teaching by Abelard brought criticism from his rivals, especially Alberic and Lotulf of Rheims, who maintained that a monk should not teach philosophy and that Abelard's training in theology was insufficient. They specifically attacked a work on the Trinity that Abelard had written for his students at St-Denis. Alberic in particular was instrumental in calling a council at Soissons in 1121 which condemned Abelard's work and placed him under "house arrest," first at St-Médard and then at St-Denis. Additional friction with his fellow monks forced Abelard to flee to a priory of St-Denis in Provins, located in the territory of the Count of Chartres, who was friendly toward him.

In spite of these reversals, Abelard still found time to write for his students. His most famous work, *Sic et non,* seems to have been written in this period. It was intended to provide source materials for students to debate theological questions. Conflicting quotations from earlier Christian authorities were placed side by side, and the introduction indicated the procedures the student should follow in arriving at a solution to the problems. The work did not attack traditional authorities, but it suggested that reliance on authority should be combined with a critical examination of the theological issues involved in each problem as well as an examination of the intention and merits of the authorities quoted.

In 1122 the abbot of St-Denis allowed Abelard to found a primitive hermitage on a piece of land between Provins and Troyes. There he built a school and a church, which he dedicated to the Paraclete, or Holy Spirit. This period of quiet teaching away from the centers of civilization was interrupted in 1125 by opposition from representatives of a new type of piety, probably Norbert of Prémontré and Bernard of Clairvaux. Seeking the safety of his homeland, Abelard returned to Brittany to accept the abbacy of the unruly monastery of St-Gildas, on the coast near Vannes. For 10 years Abelard struggled to bring order to the monastery at the risk of his life, and he was able to befriend Heloise and her fellow nuns, expelled from Argenteuil by the abbot of St-Denis, by deeding to them the hermitage of the Paraclete.

Return to Teaching

In 1136 Abelard returned to Paris to teach at the church of *Ste-Geneviève.* For the next 4 years he continued to attract students as well as opposition from Bernard and others. During this period Abelard wrote a work on ethics which took as its title the Socratic admonition, "Know thyself." In this work Abelard stressed the importance of intention in evaluating the moral or immoral character of an action.

The opposition of Bernard was instrumental in provoking a second trial of Abelard's orthodoxy. A council was convened at Sens in 1140, which resulted in the second condemnation of Abelard. Convinced of his innocence, Abelard decided to take his case before the Pope. He began his journey to Italy, but illness forced him to terminate his journey in Burgundy at the Cluniac priory of St-Marcel near Chalon-sur-Saône under the protection of his former pupil Peter the Venerable, Abbot of Cluny. There he died on April 21, 1142.

Further Reading

Abelard's autobiography is available in an excellent translation by J.T. Muckle, *The Story of Abelard's Adversities* (1964); written in a clever and convincing style, it presents only Abelard's side of events and issues. A scholarly study based on the life of Abelard and his relationship with Heloise is Étienne Gilson, *Heloise and Abelard* (1938; trans. 1951). The delightful historical novel of the English medievalist Helen Waddell, *Peter Abelard* (1933), provides insight into the period. See also Cedric Whitman, *Abelard* (1965). The best introduction to the thought of Abelard remains J.G. Sikes, *Peter Abailard* (1932). The lengthy introduction to the translation of one of Abelard's most important works, *Christian Theology,* edited by J. Ramsay McCallum (1948), is informative. The influence of Abelard's teaching is covered by D.E. Luscombe, *The School of Peter Abelard* (1969).

Additional Sources

Ericson, Donald E., *Abelard and Heloise: their lives, their love, their letters,* New York, N.Y.: Bennett-Edwards, 1990.

Luscombe, D. E. (David Edward), *Peter Abelard,* London: Historical Association, 1979.

Marenbon, John., *The philosophy of Peter Abelard,* New York: Cambridge University Press, 1997. ☐

4th Earl of Aberdeen

The British statesman George Hamilton Gordon, 4th Earl of Aberdeen (1784-1860), was noted for his work in the area of foreign affairs. He was prime minister of Great Britain at the outbreak of the Crimean War in 1853.

George Hamilton Gordon was born on Jan. 28, 1784, in Edinburg, Scotland. His father died when George was 7 and his mother when he was 11; he was brought up by his guardians, William Pitt and Henry Dundas (Lord Melville). George was educated at Harrow and St. John's College, Cambridge. On the death of his grandfather in 1801, he became the 4th Earl of Aberdeen.

Travels on the Continent during 1802-1804, especially in Greece, quickened Aberdeen's interest in classical studies and archeology. In 1805 he married Lady Catherine Elizabeth Hamilton. She died in 1812, and in 1815 he married her sister-in-law, Harriet, the widow of Lord Hamilton.

Aberdeen's diplomatic career began in the Napoleonic era. He was sent by the foreign secretary, Lord Castlereagh, as special ambassador to Austria in 1813 to effect a final coalition against Napoleon. Aberdeen signed the Treaty of Töplitz with Austria and was present at the Battle of Leipzig in October 1813. Somewhat at odds with the more conservative Castlereagh, Aberdeen retired after the Treaty of Paris was signed in 1814; he was created a peer of the United Kingdom.

For the next decade Aberdeen remained in relative seclusion, improving his estates in Scotland. The Greek war of independence returned him to an active role; he joined the Duke of Wellington's Cabinet in 1828, first as chancellor of the duchy of Lancaster and then as foreign secretary. In the short-lived Wellington government (1828-1830), Aberdeen helped design a settlement guaranteeing the territorial integrity of an independent Greece. He was again out of public office until he joined Prime Minister Robert Peel's first Cabinet as secretary for war and the colonies in 1834. This brief ministry ended in 1835, and Aberdeen was out of office until 1841.

The most important part of Aberdeen's public career began in 1841, when he became foreign secretary in Peel's second ministry. Both men were advocates of free trade, and an entente with France was basic to this policy. Aberdeen, who had convinced Wellington in 1830 to recognize the Louis Philippe regime, now worked closely with F. P. G. Guizot, the French foreign minister, and avoided the danger of war in several disputes. Aberdeen also settled two boundary questions with the United States by the Webster-Ashburton Treaty of 1842 and the Oregon Treaty of 1846. The most notable action of this ministry was the repeal of the British Corn Laws in 1846; Aberdeen supported Peel in this and continued to identify with him after his government fell later that year. Aberdeen was especially opposed to the belligerent foreign policy of Lord Palmerston.

On Peel's death in 1850, Aberdeen was recognized as the leader of the Peelites (Tory liberals), and in December 1852 he became prime minister of a coalition government. His Cabinet contained six Whigs, six Peelites, and a Radical. It was a Cabinet of talent but also of strong personalities (William Gladstone, Lord Palmerston, and Lord Russell), and Aberdeen was unable to maintain control. The major differences were in foreign policy. The fear of Russian power by Palmerston and Russell was not shared by Aberdeen and Gladstone, but public opinion through the press forced a reluctant Aberdeen into the Crimean War in March 1854. The war at the outset was popular, but the Aberdeen Cabinet was soon accused of mismanaging it. Stories of inadequate shelters, archaic medical care, and mounting British casualties flooded the press. Aberdeen could not withstand the parliamentary attack and resigned in January 1855 to be replaced by his rival, Palmerston.

The Crimean War marked the end of Aberdeen's public career. The war sickened him, and he never ceased to blame himself for Britain's involvement. He died in London on Dec. 14, 1860.

Aberdeen, as a politician and diplomat, was a compromiser. This characteristic was both his strength and his weakness. It helped to make his career as a foreign secretary, but he was too timid to lead the country in a time of crisis.

Further Reading

Two standard biographies of Aberdeen are Arthur Hamilton Gordon Stanmore, *The Earl of Aberdeen* (2 vols., 1893), and Lady Frances Balfour, *The Life of George, 4th Earl of Aberdeen* (1923); both are sympathetic but not very penetrating. An excellent discussion of the domestic impact of the Crimean War is in Olive Anderson, *A Liberal State at War: English Politics and Economics during the Crimean War* (1967). For Anglo-American relations during this period see Wilbur Devereux Jones, *Lord Aberdeen and the Americas* (1958).

Additional Sources

Chamberlain, Muriel Evelyn, *Lord Aberdeen, a political biography,* London; New York: Longman, 1983.
Iremonger, Lucille, *Lord Aberdeen: a biography of the fourth Earl of Aberdeen, K.G., K.T., Prime Minister 1852-1855,* London: Collins, 1978. □

William Aberhart

As premier of the province of Alberta, Canada, from 1935 to 1943, William Aberhart (1878-1943) was the first political leader who made the theories of social credit a basis for government.

William Aberhart was born on a farm in Huron County, Ontario, on Dec. 30, 1878. He was educated in the local schools, attended business college, and later received a teacher's certificate. After 2 years in a rural school, he moved to the small manufacturing city of Brantford and became a public school principal. In 1910 he received a bachelor of arts degree extramurally from Queen's University, an achievement which gave him great satisfaction. In the same year he moved with his wife and two daughters to Calgary, Alberta.

In 1915 Aberhart was appointed principal of a new high school in a prosperous, middle-class area. Although his enormous energy and organizing abilities brought him wide respect as a principal, he was less admired as a teacher of mathematics and commercial subjects because of his dependence on rote.

Religious revivalism was a strong influence in Aberhart's boyhood. In Brantford he had led a Bible class associated with a Presbyterian church and espoused premillennialist teachings. He established Bible classes successively in one Presbyterian and two Methodist churches in Calgary, leaving each because of disagreements with clergy more theologically liberal than himself and his inability to work with any group he could not dominate. From 1915 he built up a large Bible class in association with a local Baptist church, and this led to the establishment of the nondenominational Prophetic Bible Institute, directed by Aberhart.

As one of the first regular broadcasters on the Canadian prairies, Aberhart had a ready-made audience among his religious followers. He responded to the devastating effects of the Great Depression on the farm economy of Alberta by adding to his evangelical radio message the doctrines of social credit, which had originated with an English engineer, Clifford Hugh Douglas. Always the teacher who reduced complexity to simple formula, Aberhart asserted that the answer to poverty in the midst of plenty was to make purchasing power equal to productive power by issuing paper credit. Promising $25 a month to every Albertan, the new Social Credit party under Aberhart's leadership swept into office in the provincial election of 1935, ousting the United Farmers of Alberta government, in office since 1921. After considerable delay and a threatened revolt within the party, Aberhart's government passed legislation to give the province control over banking and credit, but these measures were either disallowed or declared unconstitutional in the courts.

By Aberhart's death on May 23, 1943, social credit theories were disappearing before wartime prosperity, and they were lost entirely when the province became rich on oil and natural-gas development. Increasingly conservative Social Credit governments continued to hold power in Alberta thereafter.

Further Reading

Much of Aberhart's career may be traced in numerous volumes on social credit; his character is examined in John A. Irving, *The Social Credit Movement in Alberta* (1959). Also useful are C. B. Macpherson, *Democracy in Alberta: The Theory and Practice of a Quasi-Party System* (1953), and J. R. Mallory, *Social Credit and the Federal Power in Canada* (1954).

Additional Sources

Elliott, David Raymond, *Bible Bill: a biography of William Aberhart,* Edmonton, Alta., Canada: Reidmore Books, 1987.
William Aberhart and Social Credit in Alberta, Toronto: Copp Clark Pub., 1977. □

Ralph David Abernathy

Civil rights leader Ralph David Abernathy (born 1926) was the best friend and trusted assistant of Martin Luther King, Jr., whom he succeeded as president of the Southern Christian Leadership Conference, a nonviolent civil rights organization.

Ralph David Abernathy, one of 12 children, was born in Marengo County, Alabama, about 90 miles outside of Montgomery. Originally named David, he was nicknamed Ralph by one of his sisters after a favorite teacher. His father William, the son of a slave, supported his family as a sharecropper until he saved enough money to buy 500 acres of his own, upon which he built a prosperous self-sufficient farm. He eventually emerged as one of the leading African Americans in the county, serving as a deacon in his church and on the board of the local African American high school and becoming the first African American there who voted and served on the grand jury. Ralph aspired early on to become a preacher and was encouraged by his mother to pursue that ambition. Although Abernathy's father died when he was 16 years old, the young man was able to obtain a Bachelor of Science degree in mathematics from Alabama State University and a Master's degree in sociology from Atlanta University in 1951. During this time he worked as the first African American DJ at a

white Montgomery radio station. While attending college he was elected president of the student council and led successful protests for better cafeteria conditions and living quarters. He earned the respect of both students and administrators, and he was later hired as the school's dean of men.

Montgomery Bus Boycott

Before obtaining his first degree, Abernathy was ordained as a Baptist minister and, after completing his education, served as minister at the Eastern star Baptist church in Demopolis, near his home town of Linden. When he was 26 he accepted a position as full time minister at the First Baptist Church in Montgomery, Alabama. Three years later, Martin Luther King accepted a call to another of Montgomery's leading African American churches, Dexter Avenue Baptist. During this time King and Abernathy became close friends.

In 1955 an African American seamstress from Montgomery named Rosa Parks refused to relinquish her bus seat to a white passenger and she was arrested and later fined. This began an important historic phase of the civil rights movement. Through hurried meetings in their churches ministers, along with the National Association for the Advancement of Colored People (NAACP), began a boycott of the city busses until all African Americans were assured better treatment. The ministers formed the Montgomery Improvement Association (MIA)—a name suggested by Abernathy—to coordinate the boycott and voted a young minister named Dr. Martin Luther King, Jr. their president.

The MIA convinced African American taxi-cab drivers to take African American workers to their jobs for a ten cent fare. When the city government declared that practice illegal, those with cars formed carpools so that the boycotters wouldn't have to return to the busses. After 381 days, the boycott was over and the busses were completely desegregated, a decision enforced by a United States district court. During 1956 Abernathy and King had been in and out of jail and court, and toward the end of the boycott on January 10, 1957, Abernathy's home and church were bombed. By the time the boycott was over it had attracted national and international attention, and televised reports of the activities of the MIA encouraged African American protesters all over the South.

Nonviolent Civil Rights Movement

King and Abernathy's work together in the MIA commenced their career as partners in the civil rights struggle and sealed their close friendship, which lasted until King's assassination in 1968. Soon after the boycott they met with other African American clergymen in Atlanta to form the Southern Christian Leadership Conference (SCLC) and press for civil rights in all areas of life. King was elected president and Abernathy the secretary-treasurer. This group began to plan for a coordinated nonviolent civil rights movement throughout the South, the ultimate purpose of which would be to end segregation and to hasten the enactment of effective federal civil rights legislation. In the early 1960s when the civil rights movement began to intensify because of student lunch counter sit-ins, nonviolent demonstrations, and efforts to desegregate interstate busses and bus depots, Abernathy moved to Atlanta, Georgia, to become the pastor of West Hunter Baptist Church. In Atlanta he would be able to work more closely with the SCLC and King, who had returned to the city at an earlier date.

The SCLC attempted to coordinate a desegregation movement in Albany, Georgia, in December 1961, but were not as effective as they hoped to be with their work there. Abernathy was arrested along with King during the Albany demonstrations, but they were quickly released from jail because the city leaders did not want to attract national attention to conditions in the city. In the spring of 1963 the leaders of the SCLC began to coordinate their efforts to desegregate facilities in Birmingham, Alabama. Publicity about the rough treatment of African American demonstrators at the hand of Eugene "Bull" Conner, the city's director of public safety, directed the eyes of the world on that city's civil rights protest. Abernathy found himself in jail with King once again. More than 3,000 other African Americans in the city also endured periods of incarceration in order to dramatize their demands for equal rights. The Birmingham demonstrations were successful and the demands for desegregation of public facilities were agreed upon. In the wake of the demonstrations, desegregation programs commenced in over 250 southern cities. Thousands of schools, parks, pools, restaurants, and hotels were opened to all people regardless race.

March On Washington

The success of the Birmingham demonstration also encouraged President John F. Kennedy to send a civil rights bill to Congress. In order to emphasize the need for the bill, leaders of all the nation's major civil rights organizations, including the SCLC, agreed to participate in a massive demonstration in Washington, D.C. The "March on Washington" on August 28, 1963, attracted over 250,000 African American and white demonstrators from all over the United States. By the next summer the Civil Rights Act had been signed into law, and a year later, in 1965, the Voting Rights Act had passed.

On April 4, 1968, during a strike by city sanitation workers in Memphis, Tennessee, King was assassinated, and Abernathy succeeded him as the leader of the SCLC. Abernathy's first project was the completion of King's plan to hold a Poor People's Campaign in Washington during which white, African American, and Native American poor people would present their problems to President Lyndon B. Johnson and the Congress. Poor people moved into Washington in mule trains and on foot and erected "Resurrection City." Abernathy once again found himself in jail, this time for unlawful assembly. After the Poor People's Campaign, Abernathy continued to lead the SCLC, but the organization did not regain the popularity it held under King's leadership.

Abernathy resigned from the SCLC in 1977 and made an unsuccessful bid for the Georgia fifth district U.S. Congressional seat vacated by prominent African American statesman Andrew Young. Later, he formed an organization called Foundation for Economic Enterprises Development (FEED), designed to help train African Americans for better economic opportunities. He continued to carry out his ministerial duties at the West Hunter Street Baptist Church in Montgomery, and lectured throughout the United States. In 1989 Abernathy published his autobiography, *And The Walls Come Tumbling Down* (Harper, 1989), which garnered criticism from other civil rights leaders for its revelations about the alleged extramarital affairs of Martin Luther King.

Further Reading

Ralph Abernathy's biography is *And the Walls Came Tumbling Down: An Autobiography* (1991). The first published biography of Abernathy is Catherine M. Reef, *Ralph David Abernathy (People in Focus Book)* (1995). There is a substantial amount of biographical material about him in Stephen Oates' biography of Martin Luther King, Jr., *Let the Trumpet Sound* (1982). Some information about Abernathy is also available in Flip Schulke, editor, *Martin Luther King, Jr.; A Documentary . . . Montgomery to Memphis* (1976) and in David J. Garrow, *The FBI and Martin Luther King, Jr.* (1981). There is information about Abernathy in a publication by the Southern Christian Leadership Conference entitled *The Poor People's Campaign, a Photographic Journal* (1968). □

Israel Abrahams

The British Jewish scholar Israel Abrahams (1858-1925) wrote works on Jewish history, literature, and sociology. He aided immensely in the popularization of many areas of Jewish knowledge previously accessible only to scholars.

The son of a scholarly family, Israel Abrahams served both as student and teacher in Jews' College in London. He was reader in rabbinics and Talmudic literature at Cambridge as successor to Solomon Schechter, who came to the United States to head the Jewish Theological Seminary.

Abrahams's endeavors included founding of the Jewish Historical Society of London, editing (1888-1908) with Claude G. Montefiore the *Jewish Quarterly Review,* contributing to many encyclopedias, and lecturing in England and the United States. He enjoyed a felicity of style in the use of the English language, which made his writings very attractive to lay people who desired authoritative Jewish information.

One of Abrahams's major works is *Jewish Life in the Middle Ages* (1896). He presents much new information in this portrayal of medieval Jewish life—including the Jews' daily routine and basic beliefs and practices, as well as their relations with other Jewish and non-Jewish communities. Contrary to the opinion of other scholars who asserted that the Jews sought isolation from the Christian community in order to preserve their autonomy, Abrahams insisted that the Jews did not eschew contacts with the Christians whenever the political climate permitted. The book is not arranged according to countries but into sections that deal with the home, family relations, personal rites, synagogue and school, business dealings, and relations between Jews and non-Jews.

Another major work by Abrahams is *Hebrew Ethical Wills* (2 vols., 1926), in which he presents with English translations a vast array of spiritual wills prepared by Jewish saints and scholars over the ages. His other works include *Chapters in Jewish Literature* (1899), *A Short History of Jewish Literature* (1906), *The Book of Delight* (1912), an annotated edition of the Authorized Daily Prayer Book (1912), and *Studies in Pharisaism* (2 vols., 1917-1924). He was coauthor with David Yellin of a biography of Maimonides (1903).

Abrahams tended toward the Reform interpretation of Judaism. While he did not accept political Zionism, he was greatly devoted to the Hebrew language and worked for the introduction of the natural method in Hebrew language instruction. His departure from the orthodox philosophy of Judaism was undoubtedly responsible for otherwise inexplicable errors in his exposition of some Jewish ritual practices.

Pioneer endeavor like that performed by Abrahams in making English translations and interpretations of basic Jewish scholarly texts available to the large reading public stimulated the publication of Jewish classics for the general reader by organizations such as the Jewish Publication Society of Philadelphia.

Further Reading

Abrahams's own *The Book of Delight* (1912) is a collection of lectures, which reveal his interests and insights. A biography is Herbert Loewe, *Israel Abrahams* (1944). □

Creighton W. Abrams

An outstanding tank commander in the U.S. Army during World War II, General Creighton W. Abrams (1914-1974) continued to serve in the army in various capacities including commander of U.S. forces in Vietnam from 1968 to 1972 and as Army chief of staff from 1972 to 1974.

Creighton W. Abrams was born on September 15, 1914, in Springfield, Massachusetts. He graduated from West Point in 1936 with a mediocre academic record and a reputation as a prankster. After finishing the Cavalry School at Fort Bliss, Texas, he served with the First Cavalry Division and later with the newly created First Armored Division.

During World War II, Abrams emerged as one of the most aggressive and effective tank commanders in the U.S. Army. He was promoted to lieutenant colonel in September 1942 and in September 1943 he was given command of the 37th Tank Regiment. His regiment led the sweep of Gen. George Patton's Third Army across Europe. In December 1944 it broke through German lines to relieve the defenders of Bastogne. Abrams himself is said to have worn out six tanks during the war, and his outfit was credited with having destroyed more than 300 German vehicles, 150 guns, and 15 tanks. No less an authority than Patton designated Abrams the "best tank commander in the Army."

Following World War II, Abrams carried out a variety of tasks. As director of tactics at the Armored School at Fort Knox, he rewrote the field manual on armored tactics. He subsequently commanded the 63rd Tank Battalion in Europe and the Second Armored Cavalry Regiment. In the Korean War he served as chief of staff of three different army corps.

Promoted to the rank of brigadier general in 1956, Abrams served as deputy assistant chief of staff and as a division commander in Europe. During the domestic crisis caused by racial integration of the universities of Mississippi and Alabama in the early 1960s, he assumed command of the federal troops readied for possible intervention. He was subsequently promoted to major general and appointed vice chief of staff.

Top Commander in Vietnam

In April 1968, Abrams succeeded his West Point classmate Gen. William Westmoreland as commander of U.S. forces in Vietnam. In style, at least, the two men were polar opposites. Westmoreland was formal in manner, immaculate in attire, and by-the-book in approach, while Abrams was informal, even casual, studiedly rumpled in appearance, and crusty in manner. Earthy in language and usually found chomping on a cigar, Abrams also loved gourmet food and classical music. Soft-spoken and tactful, he could, however, in Westmoreland's words, "erupt like a volcano, face crimson, fist pounding the table."

His task in Vietnam was among the most complex and challenging ever faced by an American military leader. During what has been called the Vietnamization period, he was responsible for holding the line militarily in South Vietnam while the United States executed a gradual withdrawal and turned over military responsibility to the South Vietnamese. Although the number of U.S. troops available to him was reduced much more rapidly than he would have preferred, Abrams maintained relentless pressure on Vietcong and North Vietnamese positions in South Vietnam. He gradually shifted American strategy from the search and destroy operations Westmoreland had favored to one that concentrated on defending the population of South Vietnam. He also presided over a vast augmentation of the South Vietnamese armed forces, leaving them with one of the largest and best equipped armies in the world. To buy time for Vietnamization, Abrams planned and executed incursions against North Vietnamese supply lines in Cambodia in 1970 and in Laos in 1971.

Succeeds Westmoreland Again

In all, Abrams handled a thankless assignment capably. He won the respect and in some cases the devotion of those under him, and in contrast to Westmoreland his plain and earthy demeanor won accolades from a skeptical U.S. press corps. He went out of his way to win the confidence of his Vietnamese counterparts, and he acquired in Vietnam a kind of "father-savior image." When he left Vietnam in June 1972, the South Vietnamese Army was much stronger than when he had come. (In the fierce battles following the North Vietnamese Easter offensive, South Vietnam, with heavy U.S. air support, turned back the enemy.)

Abrams succeeded Westmoreland as Army chief of staff in October 1972. During the little more than two years he served in that capacity, he struggled to protect the Army against the anti-military backlash that developed in the aftermath of the Vietnam War. He presided over a major reorganization which increased the number of divisions from 13 to the 16 he felt the United States needed to maintain its global commitments. He made possible this expansion by streamlining the army's support services, eliminating seven headquarters around the world at an annual savings of millions of dollars.

Abrams died on September 4, 1974, of complications from surgery for lung cancer.

Further Reading

A good overview of the European campaigns of 1944-1945 is found in Russell Weigley, *Eisenhower's Lieutenants* (1981). Abrams's command in Vietnam is sympathetically appraised in Bruce Palmer, Jr., *The 25-Year War: America's Military Role in Vietnam* (1984), and more critically assessed in Guenter Lewy, *America in Vietnam* (1978).

Additional Sources

Sorley, Lewis, *Thunderbolt: General Creighton Abrams and the army of his times,* New York: Simon & Schuster, 1992. □

Isaac ben Judah Abravanel

The Jewish philosopher and statesman Isaac ben Judah Abravanel (1437-1508), or Abarbanel, is noted for his biblical commentaries and for his attempt to prevent the expulsion of the Jews from Spain in 1492.

Isaac Abravanel, a descendant of an old and distinguished Spanish family, was born in Lisbon, Portugal. In addition to intensive religious training, he received a broad liberal education and acquired a thorough grounding in Greek, Latin, and Christian literature. Like his father, Isaac was highly successful in both his commercial and diplomatic careers. He served as treasurer under the Portuguese kings Alfonso V and John II. Falsely charged with plotting against the monarchy, Abravanel fled in 1483 to Castile, Spain. There he devoted himself to his commentary on several biblical books of the prophets.

In 1490 Abravanel was appointed treasurer to the Spanish monarchs Ferdinand and Isabella. But in 1492 Torquemada, the head of the Spanish Inquisition, persuaded the royal couple to expel the Jews from Spain. Despite Abravanel's important services to the Crown, his attempts to have the decree of expulsion revoked were unsuccessful. He went into exile with his fellow Jews and moved to Naples, where he was soon given a financial post in the government. In 1495 a French invasion forced him to leave Naples. After some years of intermittent wandering, he settled in Venice in 1503. He died there in 1508 and was buried in Padua.

His Writings

Abravanel's most important works are the commentaries which he wrote on almost all the books of the Old Testament. He employed what might be termed a critical or scientific approach in his biblical studies. He examined the historical episodes in the Bible in the light of economic, political, and social factors and often drew analogies to his own times. In dating biblical books, he often deviated from tradition, and he did not hesitate to consult the works of Christian scholars.

Abravanel also wrote a number of philosophical and theological works. His *Rosh Amana* (Pillars of Faith) and

Sefer Mifalot Elohim (Book of God's Works) show the influence of the 12th-century Jewish philosopher Maimonides. In general Abravanel developed a negative view of culture and civilization. He was influenced by the Stoics in his condemnation of luxurious living and by the Cynics in his criticism of the political state. His pessimism was balanced, however, by a firm belief in the miraculous coming of the Messiah, which he expounded in *Maayene Hayeshuah* (Founts of Salvation), *Yeshuath Meshiho* (Salvation of His Messiah), and *Mashmia Yeshua* (Proclaimer of Salvation). These works contributed to the subsequent rise of false messiahs.

Further Reading

The major scholarly work on Abravanel is B. Netanyahu, *Don Isaac Abravanel: Statesman and Philosopher* (1953), which contains an extensive bibliography. Specialized studies are Jacob S. Minkin, *Abarbanel and the Expulsion of the Jews from Spain* (1938), and the chapter on Abravanel in Joseph Sarachek, *The Doctrine of the Messiah in Medieval Jewish Literature* (1932; 2d ed. 1968). A brief general summary of Abravanel's life and thought is in Meyer Waxman, *A History of Jewish Literature* (4 vols., 1930-1931; 5 vols. in 6, 1960). Julius Guttman, *Philosophies of Judaism* (1933; trans. 1964), includes a brief discussion of his thought. □

Abu Bakr

Abu Bakr (ca. 573-634) was the first caliph, or successor of Mohammed as ruler of the Arab state. He held together the political structure created by Mohammed at Medina, defeated separatist revolts, and initiated the expansion of Islam into Syria and Iraq.

Friend of Mohammed and three years younger, Abu Bakr was born in Mecca of the tribe of Quraysh and became a merchant. He was possibly the first mature man to accept Mohammed as the Prophet and to become a Moslem. After conversion he spent much of his wealth in buying and setting free Moslem slaves. However, his clan gave him little protection, and he suffered indignities from Mohammed's opponents. As Mohammed's closest friend and adviser, he alone accompanied him on his Hijra, the migration from Mecca to Medina in 622.

In Medina, Abu Bakr helped Mohammed in many unobtrusive ways, and his knowledge of the genealogies and intrigues of the numerous Arab tribes was a great asset. The two men were further bound together by Mohammed's marriage to Abu Bakr's daughter Aisha in 623 or 624. Abu Bakr did not command any important military expedition for Mohammed, but he was the leader of the pilgrimage to Mecca in 630 and was appointed to lead the public prayers during Mohammed's last illness. By signs as slight as these, he was marked out as caliph.

On Mohammed's death in June 632, the future of the state was uncertain, but the oratory of Omar (later the second caliph) persuaded the men of Medina to accept Abu

Bakr as caliph. Much of his reign was occupied with quelling revolts. One had already broken out in Yemen, and soon there were about five others in different parts of Arabia. The leaders mostly claimed to be prophets, and the revolts are known as "the wars of the apostasy," though the underlying reasons were mainly political. The chief battle was that of Yamama in May 633, when Musaylima, the strongest insurgent leader, was defeated and killed by a Moslem army under Khalid ibn al-Walid.

Mohammed had foreseen the need for expeditions outside Arabia to absorb the energies of his Arab allies and prevent their fighting one another; and Abu Bakr, despite the threatening situation after Mohammed's death, sent an expedition from Medina toward Syria. As Arabia was pacified after the revolts, other expeditions were sent to Iraq, then a part of the Persian Empire, and to Syria. Shortly before Abu Bakr's death in August 634, his general Khalid, following a celebrated desert march from Iraq to Damascus, defeated a large Byzantine army at Ajnadain in Palestine and gave the Arabs a foothold in that country. Thus, in the short reign of Abu Bakr the embryonic Islamic state was not only preserved intact but was launched on the movement of expansion which produced the Arab and the Islamic empires.

Further Reading

There is no work solely on Abu Bakr by any Western scholar. His reign is briefly treated in Carl Brockelmann, *History of the Islamic Peoples* (1939; trans. 1947); Philip K. Hitti, *History of the Arabs* (1937; 8th rev. ed. 1963); and Bernard Lewis, *The Arabs in History* (1950). □

Abu-L-Ala al-Maarri

Abu-l-Ala al-Maarri (973-1058) was a celebrated Arab poet who lived in what is today Syria and Iraq. A writer of poems, commentaries, elegies, and religious tracts, he was a skeptic and cynic.

Abu-l-Ala was born in Maarra, a small town in northern Syria near Aleppo; his family was highly respected. He received a good education for his day, in spite of the fact that he was partially blinded by smallpox at the age of 4. Syria was recognized at that time as a highly intellectual and cultural area, and Abu-l-Ala received his education in Aleppo, Tripoli, and Antioch under the best Syrian scholars. He seems to have studied to be a professional encomiast like his predecessor al-Mutanabbi but soon rejected this calling because of his proud nature.

Soon after the age of 20 Abu-l-Ala returned to Maarra, where he lived off the fees he received from his pupils until 1010. He then moved to Baghdad, the intellectual center of Islam. But he left after 19 months because he refused to write flattering verses for those in power. This period was the turning point in his life. To date, he had won distinction as an erudite savant and as an accomplished poet in the

style of al-Mutanabbi, a poet he admired. But Abu-l-Ala's great works appear only after his visit to Baghdad. His later poetry is filled with many unorthodox ideas that he could have come across only in Baghdad.

He reached his hometown to find his mother had died. This affected him immensely. It is said that afterward he lived in a cave and adopted ascetic habits. He was nicknamed "the double prisoner" because of his blindness and seclusion.

But Abu-l-Ala's fame continued to draw students to him. He eventually amassed great wealth in his retreat. He passed his last 40 years in retirement but not idleness. This is evident by his long list of compositions. He is best known for two collections of poems entitled *Sakt al-Zand* and *Luzumiyat* and for many letters.

The problem of Abu-l-Ala's orthodoxy is often debated. He is usually held to be a heretic because of his chiding works on the Koran. His ideas are unusually skeptical of many accepted doctrines of his day. He was a monotheist, but his God was little more than an impersonal fate. He did not accept the theory of divine revelation. Religion in his view was the product of man's superstitions and the need for society to control these feelings. And he was always against religious leaders' taking advantage of their unsuspecting followers for their own personal benefit. He did not believe in a future life, and it was against his better wisdom to have children because of the miseries of living. He was a vegetarian and an ascetic. He did believe in a religion of active piety and righteousness, and thus his ideas were much like the Indian thought of his time.

Further Reading

There are a few fine works that translate some of Abu-l-Ala's compositions and include biographical and critical commentary: D. S. Margoliouth, *The Letters of Abu-l-Ala* (1898); Ameen F. Rihani, *The Quatrains of Abu-l-Ala* (1904); and Henry Baerlein, *The Diwan of Abu-l-Ala* (1908). One of the best descriptive works on Abu-l-Ala is in German: Carl Brockelmann, *Geschichte der arabischen Litteratur* (2 vols., 1898-1902; rev. ed. 1943-1949). The best work in English is Reynold A. Nicholson, *A Literary History of the Arabs* (1907; 2d ed. 1930). Nicholson also wrote the valuable *Studies in Islamic Poetry* (1921). More general works are Philip K. Hitti, *The History of the Arabs* (1937; 8th rev. ed. 1963), and James Kritzeck, ed., *Anthology of Islamic Literature* (1966). □

Abu Musa

Abu Musa (born about ca. 1930) left the Jordanian army in 1970 to join the Palestine Liberation Army (PLO). In 1983 he emerged as a leader of the hardline PLO opposition to Yasser Arafat.

Abu Musa was born Said Musa Maragha in the West Bank area of what was then Palestine in the early 1930s. During the Arab-Jewish fighting of 1948 the

Jordanian army entered the West Bank, ostensibly to help the Palestinian Arabs defend themselves. After the Palestinian Arabs were defeated, however, the Jordanians stayed on, and later annexed the West bank to their own kingdom.

When he reached adulthood, Abu Musa joined the Jordanian army. His unit participated in the Arab-Israeli War (Six Day War) of 1967, which resulted in the Israeli occupation of the West Bank, along with other Arab territories.

Three years later Abu Musa found himself in the middle of the fighting between the Jordanian army and the guerrillas from the Palestinian Liberation Organization (PLO) who had set up base camps in Jordan to support their fight against Israel. Like many others of the West Bankers in the Jordanian army, Abu Musa found his first allegiance was to his Palestinian roots. He became one of the highest-ranking officers in the PLO's Yarmouk Brigade, which was made up of defectors from the Jordanian army.

Despite these defections, the Jordanian forces soundly defeated the PLO, which then moved most of its military bases to South Lebanon. The Palestinians became deeply entangled in the civil war which wracked Lebanon from 1975 onwards: PLO fighters combined with the Lebanese leftist militias in the "Joint Forces." In 1976 Abu Musa was the commander of the Joint Forces in South Lebanon at a time when the Syrians were trying to suppress them. In the course of one of the many battles against the Syrians, in the Lebanese town of Nabatiyeh, Abu Musa was wounded in the leg and had to leave active duty.

Returning to action, Abu Musa became deputy chief of operations for all the PLO forces. When Israel invaded Lebanon in 1982 he was one of the chief strategists in the PLO's defense of the capital, Beirut. After the PLO was finally evacuated from Beirut, Abu Musa joined a convoy to the Syrian-occupied parts of eastern Lebanon.

A few weeks later Abu Musa was one of the most prominent of a group of Palestinian fighters who publicly accused PLO leader Yasser Arafat of authoritarianism, favoritism, and other shortcomings. Their opposition to Arafat was soon backed by the Syrians who were critical of Arafat's move toward favoring negotiations with Israel. In December 1983 Abu Musa led those Palestinians (this breakaway group was sometimes referred to as the "Fatah Uprising") who, with help from the Syrian army, moved against the remaining positions of Arafat loyalists in northern Lebanon. Soon after, this group became known as the Palestinian National Liberation Organization and remained pro-Syria.

In 1984 Abu Musa was one of the leaders of the National Salvation Alliance, which from its headquarters in the Syrian capital, Damascus, contested Arafat's leadership of the Palestinian movement. The alliance was unable to command a majority of Palestinian support during its first year's existence. Slowly it increased its influence. In 1989 Abu Musa stated that if given the chance, his group would try Arafat for treason. As peace talks flowed and ebbed throughout the Middle East in the late 1980s and early 1990s, Abu Musa and his followers became more and more vocal about their support for King Hussein of Jordan. As reported in the *New York Times* in 1994, Musa summed up

this support by stating, "In essence, the Palestinians of Jordan trust the King. I know we are not getting a good deal. I know that it may be that we are not all going to have the chance to go back to Palestine. But I also know he has done his best and will continue to do so." Impeding peace negotiations, Musa's Palestinian National Liberation Organization sometimes claimed responsibility for terrorist attacks, as when it took responsibility for killing three Israeli soldiers on Israel's frontier with Jordan in 1996.

Little is known about Abu Musa's personal history. Generally admired in Arab circles for his military capability, he retained some affectations from his days as a regular army officer, including his habit of usually carrying a cane.

Further Reading

There are no works in English which say much about Abu Musa in person. However the general political background to his emergence can be understood from a reading of Quandt, Jabber, and Lesch, *The Politics of Palestinian Nationalism* (1973), or from Helena Cobban, *The Palestinian Liberation Organization: People, Power and Politics* (1984). Three worthwhile newspaper articles can be found in the *New York Times*, November 12, 1989; July 24, 1994; and July 3, 1996. □

Abu Nuwas

Abu Nuwas (ca. 756-813) was the most famous Arab poet of the Abbasid era. His style was extravagant, and his compositions reflected well the licentious manners of the upper classes of his day.

Abu Nuwas was born in Ahwaz on the Karun River in western Persia. His father was Arab and his mother was Persian. At a young age he was sold into slavery because of family poverty; a wealthy benefactor later set him free. By the time Abu Nuwas reached manhood, he had settled in Baghdad and was writing poetry. It was at this time that because of his long hair he acquired the name Abu Nuwas (Father of Ringlets).

Gradually he attracted the attention of the caliph Harun al-Rashid and was given quarters with the other poets at court. His ability as a poet no doubt was one reason for Abu Nuwas's success with the Caliph, but after a while he became known as a rake and participated in less reputable pastimes with the ruler. Abu Nuwas spent some time in Egypt but soon returned to Baghdad to live out his remaining years. It is said he lived the last part of his life as an ascetic.

Abu Nuwas wrote about the way he lived. His chief topics were wine and pederasty. The Persian poets of a later era used wine in their poems only as a metaphorical symbol, but for Abu Nuwas the glories of debauchery and dissipation could never fully be expressed. He depicted with humorous realism his experiences in life, admitted his sins with remarkable frankness, and wrote that he would never repent although he recommended that others not follow his example. With ironic tones he composed a dirge for his own body wasting away from bad habits. He closed one poem by stating that he never expected his sins to be found out by God because he was too unimportant for God to take notice of his actions.

When reading Abu Nuwas's poetry, one must recognize that the majority of Arab poets—far more than Western poets—are more interested in clever formulations of their poems than in the actual content of their ideas. Thus exaggeration is to be expected.

Further Reading

The vast body of Abu Nuwas's work remains untranslated from Arabic. In English the only major work about Abu Nuwas, which also contains many of his poems, is W.H. Ingrams, *Abu Nuwas in Life and Legend* (1933). Ingrams divided his biographical discussion into three parts: the actual, the apocryphal, and the mythical. Two other most reliable works are Reynold A. Nicholson, *A Literary History of the Arabs* (1907; 2d ed. 1930), and Philip K. Hitti, *The History of the Arabs* (1937; 8th rev. ed. 1963). In both these works Abu Nuwas is seen in relation to his contemporaries. See also James Kritzeck, ed., *Anthology of Islamic Literature from the Rise of Islam to Modern Times* (1966). □

Bella Stavisky Abzug

Liberal lawyer and unconventional politician, Bella Stavisky Abzug (born 1920) works energetically for civil and women's rights. She served three terms as a New York Congresswoman.

Bella Stavisky Abzug was born on July 24, 1920, in the Bronx, New York. She was the daughter of Emanuel and Esther Savitsky, Russian Jewish immigrants who owned a local meat market. During her youth she worked in her father's store until it failed in the 1920s and he turned to selling insurance. In 1930 her father died, which left her mother to support the family with his insurance money and jobs in local department stores. She attended an all-female high school in the west Bronx and eventually entered Hunter College, where she excelled as a student, earning her degree in 1942.

Student Activist

Abzug was elected as president of her high school class and later as student body president at Hunter College. She taught Hebrew and Jewish history on the weekends and marched in protest against the spread of Nazism in Europe and against British and American neutrality during the Spanish Civil War. In World War II she joined the ranks of thousands of American women entering war production industries and worked in a shipbuilding factory. In 1944 she married Maurice Abzug, a stockbroker and novelist. They had two daughters.

By the time she entered Columbia Law School Bella's career as a litigation lawyer, politician, and activist was well along. At Columbia she was editor of the *Columbia Law*

Review. After her graduation in 1947 she joined a firm that specialized in labor law, one of the most confrontational areas of law practice. In the 1950s she worked as a labor lawyer and represented civil rights workers. She launched a lifelong commitment to helping poor and oppressed people gain justice and a decent life in the days following World War II. During this time such commitments were viewed with suspicion as part of the "red scare." She defended many individuals, such as New York school teachers accused of subversive activities during the anti-communist crusade of Senator Joseph McCarthy.

Civil Rights

In the early 1950s she was deeply involved in the early Civil Rights movement. While carrying her second child in 1962, she undertook a case to defend an African American man accused of raping a white woman with whom he had been having an affair. Although she ultimately lost the case, Abzug was able to delay the man's execution for two years by appealing the conviction twice to the Supreme Court. Her arguments in the case were nearly two decades ahead of their time, and the Warren and Burger Courts would eventually accept similar arguments made for guaranteeing a fair trial and prohibiting cruel and unusual punishment.

During the 1960s Abzug joined in the movement to ban nuclear testing. She helped to found the Woman's Strike for Peace organization, leading the organization in demonstrations that took place in New York and Washington, D.C. After the signing of the Nuclear Test Ban Treaty she helped to refocus the antinuclear movement into an antiwar movement as the U.S. became more deeply involved in the Vietnam War.

In the late 1960s Abzug struggled to forge a broad, progressive coalition across party lines to address the concerns of the poor, ethnic minorities, and women's groups in shaping a new national agenda. During these years she became active in the Democratic party, and after the insider fiasco at the Chicago Democratic Convention in 1968 she joined with other liberal Democrats to found the New Democratic Coalition.

Elected to office

Running for office in 1970, supported by her ties to labor and a strong backing from the Jewish vote, Abzug was elected to the U.S. House of Representatives from New York City's 19th ward. During her first year in Congress she gained national attention by her bold and daring political initiatives on behalf of liberal causes, as well by wearing her wide, trademark hat within the halls of congress. On her first day in office she introduced a bill calling for the withdrawal of troops from Vietnam by July 4, 1971. Although conservative forces in Congress defeated the bill within a week, Abzug established herself immediately as an unconventional politician who would take on her opponents using a brusque and often confrontational style. During her tenure she co-authored the Freedom of Information and Privacy Acts, she was the first to call for President Nixon's impeachment in the 1970s, and she cast one of the first votes for the Equal Rights Amendment.

In 1972 redistricting eliminated Abzug's congressional district, and she decided to run in the 20th district against a popular liberal incumbent, William Fitz Ryan. She lost the primary, but Ryan died before the general election in November, and Abzug became the Democratic nominee. She won in the November election and served in the House until 1976 when she gave up her seat to run for the Senate, a race she lost to Daniel Patrick Moynihan. She then ran in the Democratic mayoral primary in New York, but was defeated by Edward Koch. Never one to give up, she told reporters who assumed she was finished with politics, "I'll thank you not to write my obituary."

Continuing Activism

Abzug continued to make headlines fighting for peace and women's rights long after leaving office. President Jimmy Carter appointed her as co-chair of the National Advisory Committee for Women, but was apparently unprepared for the demands that the committee would make. When the committee met with President Carter, several of the members spoke to him about the cuts in social services and pointed out their negative impact on the nation's women. After that meeting Abzug was dismissed from the committee, an action that sparked the resignation of several members, including the other co-chair, and gave rise to a massive public outcry against Carter for the firing.

Throughout her long and controversial political career, Abzug has retained a place in the limelight with her characteristic sharp tongue and unconventional style. Her hats along with her defiance of codes of dress and demeanor have won her a reputation as a nonconformist. But above and beyond the flair of her personality, it is the issues she supports that are her deepest concern. As she wrote in the introduction to her autobiography, "I am not evoking a wild fantasy when I claim that I'm going to help organize a new political coalition of the women, the minorities and the young people, along with the poor, the elderly, the workers, and the unemployed, which is going to turn this country upside down and inside out."

Abzug continues to devote her energies to women's rights and reproductive freedom. As chair of New York City's Commission on the Status of Women she directs a National Parity Campaign to increase the number of women in elective office. In 1991, she presided over the Women's Congress for a Healthy Planet and her presence at the United Nations 4th Women's Conference in Beijing garnered considerable attention. She is also co-chair of the Women's Environmental Development Organization (WEDO), and as senior advisor to UNCED Secretary General Maurice Strong she successfully campaigned to incorporate key issues of the women's agenda into official statements approved at the Earth Summit.

Further Reading

Bella Abzug has written her own autobiography, *Bella,* edited by Mel Ziegler and published by the Saturday Review Press in 1972. While it chronicles Abzug's political career up to that time, she remained in Congress four more years and was active later. There is a biography of her by Doris Faber, *Bella Abzug* (William Morrow, 1976). She is listed in *Political Profiles: The Nixon/Ford Years,* Facts on File, v. 5 (1979). She has also been written up in the *New York Times Biographical Service* in February and December, 1978. Numerous contemporary articles have appeared about her in publications such as *Time, Newsweek, The New Republic,* and *Life.* □

Chinua Achebe

Chinua Achebe (born 1930) is one of the foremost Nigerian novelists. His novels are primarily directed to an African audience, but their psychological insights have gained them universal acceptance.

Chinua Achebe was born into an Ibo family on Nov. 15, 1930, at Ogidi in Eastern Nigeria. He was educated at a government college in Umuahia, and he graduated from the University College at Ibadan in 1954.

While working for the Nigerian Broadcasting Corporation, he composed his first novel, *Things Fall Apart* (1959), at a time when Nigerian prose fiction was represented solely by the fantastic folklore romances of Amos Tutuola and the popular stories of urban life of Cyprian Ekwensi. Achebe's novel introduced serious social and psychological analysis into Nigerian literature. It is set in the early days of colonization and tells the tragedy of a warrior hero who rigidly identifies with the values of traditional Ibo society. For this reason, he lacks the required flexibility of mind and heart to adapt to changing conditions under incipient European impact. This novel won immediate international recognition.

With his next novel, *No Longer At Ease* (1960), Achebe turned to the last phase of the colonial regime, describing with his usual poise and insight the tragic predicament of the young African idealist. His foreign education has converted him to modern standards of moral judgment without alleviating the inner and outer pressures of traditional mores. The catastrophe derives from the hero's inability to make his choice; it is the drama of a bungled destiny in a bewildering time of rapid cultural change.

Arrow of God (1964) reverted to the past once more. As the high priest of the village deity, the central character is a tribal intellectual who sees the weaknesses of the traditional outlook and senses the need for change. His mental alertness and consequent skepticism lay him open to the charge of betraying his own people. In a desperate outburst of arrogance he attempts to restore his prestige and to reassert the power of his god, but he merely succeeds in alienating the villagers, who begin to turn to the Christian missionaries.

So far, Achebe had been concerned with the clash of cultures, which is an all-pervading theme in the African novel. But by the mid-1960s the exhilaration of independence had died out in Nigeria as the country was faced with the terrific political problems common to the many poly-ethnic states of modern Africa. The Ibo, who had played a dominant role in Nigerian politics, now began to feel they were being reduced to the status of second-class citizens by

the Moslem Hausa people of Northern Nigeria. Achebe turned his creative insight to an imaginative critique of public mores under independence. The result was *A Man of the People* (1966), a bitter portrayal of a corrupt Nigerian politician. The book was published at the very moment a military coup swept away the old political leadership and its abuses. That timing made some Northern military officers suspect Achebe played a role in the coup, but there was never any evidence supporting the theory.

During the Biafran succession from Nigeria (1967-70), however, Achebe served Biafra as a diplomat. He traveled to different countries publicizing the plight of his people, focusing especially on the Ibo children being starved to death and massacred. He wrote articles for newspapers and magazines about the Biafran struggle and living in Enugu, the designated capital of Biafra, and founded the Citadel Press with Nigerian poet Christopher Okigbo.

Writing a novel at this time was out of the question, he said during a 1969 interview: "I can't write a novel now; I wouldn't want to. And even if I wanted to, I couldn't. I can write poetry—something short, intense, more in keeping with my mood." Three volumes of poetry emerged from this mood, as well as a collection of short stories and children's stories.

After the fall of the Republic of Biafra, Achebe continued to work as a senior research fellow at the University of Nigeria at Nsukka, a position he had assumed several years before. He also devoted much time to the Heinemann Educational Books' Writers Series, which was designed to promote the careers of young African writers, became director of Nwamife Publishers, Ltd., and founded *Okike: A Nigerian Journal of New Writing*.

In 1972, he came to the United States to become an English professor at the University of Massachusetts at Amherst (he taught there again in 1987), and in 1975 he joined the faculty of the University of Connecticut. He returned to the University of Nigeria at Nsukka in 1976 and was appointed a professor emeritus there in 1985.

His novel *Anthills of the Savanna* was published in 1987 and appeared on the short-list for the Booker Prize. Set in the imaginary West African nation of Kangan, it tells the story of three boyhood friends and the deadly effects of one's obsession with power and being elected "president for life." Its release coincided with Achebe's return to the United States and teaching positions at Dartmouth College, Stanford University and Bard College, among other universities.

Over the years, Achebe has received dozens of honorary doctorates and several international literary awards. He is an honorary member of the American Academy and Institute of Arts and Letters, and his work has been translated into more than 40 languages. In 1994, he fled to Europe from the repressive Nigerian regime, which threatened to jail him. However, he later returned to Nigeria to serve as president of the town union of his native village of Ogidi, honored as such because of his dedication to his ancestors' myths and legends.

Further Reading

Information on Achebe is in Gerald Moore, *Seven African Writers* (1962); Ulli Beier, ed., *Introduction to African Literature: An Anthology of Critical Writings from 'Black Orpheus'* (1967); Cosmo Pieterse and Donald Munroe, eds., *Protest and Conflict in African Literature* (1969); *Contemporary Literary Criticism* Vol. 51 (1989); Zell, Hans M. et al, *A New Reader's Guide to African Literature* (1983). □

Dean Gooderham Acheson

The American lawyer and statesman Dean Gooderham Acheson (1893-1971) served as secretary of state in President Harry Truman's Cabinet.

Dean Acheson was born in Middletown, Conn., on April 11, 1893, the son of Edward Campion and Eleanor Gooderham Acheson. His father, the Episcopal bishop of Connecticut, provided a genteel upbringing which led to Groton and afterward Yale, where Acheson received his bachelor's degree in 1915. During the succeeding 3 years he served briefly as an ensign in the U.S. Navy and earned his law degree at Harvard. In May 1917 he married Alice Stanley. Three children were born to the Achesons—Jane, David Campion, and Mary Eleanor.

From the beginning Acheson seemed destined for a successful career. Possessed of high intelligence, a deep sense of moral rectitude, and aggressive energy, he had in addition the grace of the patrician and the friendship of such distinguished and influential people as Felix Frankfurter of the Harvard Law School and, later, the Supreme Court of the United States.

Following his graduation from Harvard, Acheson became private secretary to Supreme Court justice Louis D. Brandeis. In 1921 he entered the prominent Washington law firm of Covington, Burling, and Rublee, where he practiced for the next 12 years. President Franklin D. Roosevelt first brought Acheson into public service in May 1933 with an appointment as undersecretary of the Treasury. Acheson resigned 5 months later following a disagreement on the President's gold-purchasing program and returned to his Washington law practice.

In 1941 Acheson again entered the government, this time as assistant secretary of state for economic affairs. He remained in the State Department, except for one brief interlude, until 1953. His long and significant record there reflected a practical rather than a contemplative mentality, which attracted him especially to Harry Truman's forthright leadership. As undersecretary of state from 1945 to 1947, Acheson broke with Truman only on the Palestinian question, convinced that the nation was embarking on a unilateral commitment to Israel's defense against the Arab states which could ultimately prove embarrassing, if not costly.

Acheson's most memorable contributions, as undersecretary and, from 1949 to 1953, as secretary of state, came in his implementation of the containment policy from the Marshall Plan to NATO. Despite his achievements, these years in the State Department were trying ones. The alleged loss of China to Communist leadership in 1949 exposed the Truman administration to charges of treason. Acheson, always loyal to his friends and associates, refused to testify against Alger Hiss, then under trial for spying, or to condemn past American policy toward China. These actions rendered him totally vulnerable and roused a storm of accusations such as few commanding public figures in American history have faced.

Upon his retirement from the State Department in 1953, Acheson returned to Covington and Burling, remaining in public life only as a member of special governmental committees, as a presidential adviser, and as a critical observer of men and events. He served in the late fifties as foreign policy chief of the Democratic Advisory Council of the Democratic National Committee. He died in Sandy Spring, Md., on Oct. 12, 1971.

Further Reading

Acheson's own writings are voluminous. Three of his books which develop his views of external policy, politics, and government are *A Democrat Looks at His Party* (1955), *A Citizen Looks at Congress* (1957), and *Power and Diplomacy* (1958). His autobiography, *Morning and Noon* (1965), terminates with his appointment to the State Department in 1941. Acheson's personal record of his State Department experience is *Present at the Creation: My Years in the State Department* (1969).
No book-length biographies of Acheson have yet appeared. McGeorge Bundy, ed., *The Pattern of Responsibility* (1952),

includes excerpts and paraphrases of Acheson's many speeches during his secretarial years and is a good source of information on his views toward world affairs. The volumes covering the years 1949 to 1952 of *The United States in World Affairs* (1950-1953), prepared by Richard P. Stebbins for the Council on Foreign Relations, are replete with observations on Acheson's leadership. Also useful is the survey of postwar American foreign policy, William Reitzel and others, *United States Foreign Policy, 1945-1955* (1956). Acheson's role as an adviser to Kennedy is discussed in Seyom Brown, *The Faces of Power* (1968). ☐

John Emerich Edward Dalberg Acton

John Emerich Edward Dalberg Acton, 1st Baron Acton (1834-1902), was a major English scientific historian and Catholic philosopher. His work is distinguished by the application of rigorous standards of accuracy and ethical principles to history.

John Acton was born on Jan. 10, 1834, in Naples. He was educated in England at Oscott College and in 1848 went to Munich, then a center for the general revival of Catholic scholarship. Ignaz von Döllinger, a member of the Munich group and follower of Leopold von Ranke, introduced Acton to Ranke's new scientific history and to recent developments in Catholic scholarship.

When Acton returned to England in 1859, he succeeded John Henry Newman as editor of the Catholic monthly *Rambler* (after 1862 the *Home and Foreign Review*). Acton advocated the application of scientific historical methods to Christianity, believing it possible to reconcile Christianity with the findings of history and thus to strengthen the Roman Catholic Church. Acton's *Review* was publicly censored in 1862 by Cardinal Wiseman. In 1864, after Pius IX rejected Döllinger's appeal for a less hostile attitude toward historical criticism of Christianity, Acton abandoned his editorship of the *Review*. During the controversy in 1870 over papal infallibility, Acton attacked papal temporal power and continued to criticize the misuse of history. He further provoked English Roman Catholic circles in 1874 with his letters to the *Times*, citing historical examples of papal inconsistency.

Acton's historical writings consist largely of lectures. However, his importance resulted less from his published works than from his personal influence, his insistence on scientific methods, and his prescient concern with political morality. His essay "Democracy in Europe" (1878) and two lectures delivered at Bridgnorth in 1877 (published in 1907)—"The History of Freedom in Antiquity" and "The History of Freedom in Christianity"—are the only completed portions of his projected *History of Liberty*. Influenced by Edmund Burke and Alexis de Tocqueville, Acton saw liberty threatened by democracy and socialism as well as by the evils of highly concentrated state power. Con-

science, the fount of freedom, had higher claims than those of the state. He was a critic of racism and nationalism, with his liberalism rooted in Christianity.

Acton was one of the founders of the *English Historical Review* and wrote an essay on modern German historians for the first volume (1885). He was appointed professor of modern history at Cambridge University in 1895. His inaugural lecture, "The Study of History," and his courses, "Lectures on the French Revolution" and "Lectures on Modern History," made a great impression on scientific historiography at the time. Acton was to be the editor of the great multivolume *Cambridge Modern History*, but only the first volume appeared before his death in 1902.

Further Reading

The best book on Acton is Gertrude Himmelfarb, *Lord Acton: A Study in Conscience and Politics* (1952). Other works are David Mathew, *Acton: The Formative Years* (1946), and Lionel Kochan, *Acton on History* (1954).

Additional Sources

Chadwick, Owen, *Acton and Gladstone,* London: Athlone Press, 1976.
Himmelfarb, Gertrude, *Lord Acton: a study in conscience and politics,* San Francisco, CA: ICS Press, 1993.
Mathew, David, *Acton, the formative years,* Westport, Conn.: Greenwood Press, 1974.
Schuettinger, Robert Lindsay, *Lord Acton: historian of liberty,* LaSalle, Ill.: Open Court, 1976.
Tulloch, Hugh, *Acton,* New York: St. Martin's Press, 1988. ☐

Robert and James Adam

The British architects Robert (1728-1792) and James (1730-1794) Adam were the leading practitioners of the neoclassic style in the late 18th century. Their graceful, elegant work is based chiefly on ancient Roman and Renaissance motifs.

Robert Adam was born on July 3, 1728, at Kirkcaldy, Fifeshire, Scotland. James Adam was born in Edinburgh on July 21, 1730. They were the second and third sons of William Adam (1689-1748), a prominent Scottish architect. There were two other sons—John, the oldest of the children, and William—and six daughters. Robert was educated at Edinburgh High School and the university and received a sound architectural training from his father.

About 6 months before their father's death, John and Robert took over control of the family business. John practiced little as an architect, confining his attention more to the business side of the firm. One of the daughters, Elizabeth, became an efficient member of the business.

Robert's principal work from 1750 to 1754, in collaboration with James, was the completion of their father's masterpiece, Hopetoun House, West Lothian, Scotland. They reacted against the ponderous moldings and robust decoration of the Palladian school and introduced in the Yellow and Red Drawing Rooms (the latter not finished until 1758) a fresh note of rococo lightness and elegance in the ceiling plasterwork in accordance with the French taste then fashionable in England. Robert also redesigned the outlying pavilions of the house in a manner that anticipates his mature neoclassic style.

His first independent work was the design of Dumfries House, Scotland (1751-1754), again with remarkably fine rococo ceiling decorations. It was probably here that the cabinetmaker Thomas Chippendale commenced his long association with Robert in the furnishing of Adam houses.

In 1754 Robert traveled to Rome; during 4 years' study there under the guidance of the artist C. L. Clérisseau, Robert made thousands of drawings of classical and Renaissance buildings and monuments, of decorations in the ancient tombs, and of the "grotesques" in the Loggias of the Vatican painted by Raphael and his pupil Giovanni da Udine. After an excursion to Dalmatia, Robert published *The Ruins of the Palace of the Emperor Diocletian at Spalatro* (1764).

On his return to Britain in 1758, Robert set up an architectural practice in London with James. Robert executed new interiors at Hatchlands, Surrey (1758-1761), for Admiral Boscawen. Through the same patron's influence, Robert was employed to design the new screen and gateway to the courtyard of Admiralty House, Whitehall, London (1760). In 1759 he revised the plans of John Carr of York for Harewood House, Yorkshire, and designed all the interiors, which were carried out during the following 12 years.

The interior decorations of these houses mark the breakaway from the fashionable Palladian and rococo taste and the rise of the neoclassic style, which was to be popular for the next 30 years. The style was based on the enormous repertoire of classical motifs that Robert had built up in Rome: festoons of husks and bellflowers, swags and garlands, vines, vases, tripods, gryphons, sphinxes, paterae, formal arabesques, and scrolls of foliage. Many of these motifs had been used earlier by Sir Christopher Wren, James Gibbs, William Kent, and other architects, but the freshness of the Adam style lay in the highly personal refinement, delicacy, and elegance that Robert gave them. He attenuated the height of columns beyond the proportions laid down by the Roman architect Vitruvius and by Andrea Palladio (Osterley Park House, Middlesex) and combined both Roman and Greek elements in a single Ionic capital (Syon House, Middlesex), thus giving it the dignity of one and the elegance of the other. Robert scaled down the elements of a design to give it a lightness and grace unknown in the early Georgian age.

In 1773 the brothers published the first volume of *The Works in Architecture of Robert and James Adam*, the second volume followed in 1779, and the third was published posthumously in 1822. In the introduction to this work, they claimed "to have brought about . . . a kind of revolution in architecture and decoration, against the pretensions of numerous imitators" and "by means of a series of delicate ornaments and mouldings" to have recaptured "the beautiful spirit of antiquity."

Robert died in London on March 3, 1792, and was buried in Westminster Abbey. James died in London on Oct. 20, 1794. Some 3000 drawings by Robert and other members of his firm are preserved at Sir John Soane's Museum in London.

Architecture and Furniture

The work of Robert Adam falls roughly into three phases of stylistic development. His early exteriors, as at Bowood, Wiltshire (1761-1767), and Kedleston Hall, Derbyshire (1765-1770), are composed of boldly projecting masses with giant orders of Roman character, heavy architraves, entablatures, and pulvinated friezes. At Kedleston, Robert again took over from another architect, in this case, as at Nostell Priory, Yorkshire, from James Paine. The south front of Kedleston, with the bold convexity of its dome contrasting with the concave curve of the sweeping perron below, illustrates the quality of "movement" which Robert expressed powerfully in his early work: "the rise and fall, the advance and recess, with other diversity of form in the different parts of a building, so as to add greatly to the 'picturesque' of the composition." In this early work Robert displays much influence of Sir John Vanbrugh and Kent, two architects whom he greatly admired. Similar bold characteristics appear in Robert's early interiors, such as the Marble Hall and Saloon at Kedleston (1765); the Anteroom at Syon (1759), where he achieved a sense of Roman magnificence; and the Drawing Rooms at Kedleston and Saltram House, Devonshire. The ornament of his early ceilings is bold and sparse and sometimes of compartment form (Croome Court, Worcestershire, 1760; Syon, 1759). His fireplaces are bold in scale, with fully sculptured caryatid figures (Hatchlands, 1758-1761; Harewood, 1759-1771; Kedleston, 1765-1770).

Robert's later exteriors, as in his London street houses (ca. 1769-1780), lose the three-dimensional quality and become more flat and linear, with shallow relieving arches, flush windows, and recessed porticoes. His interiors likewise at this time lose their bold ornament in favor of fine-scale motifs in shallow relief but still of satisfying quality, as in the Galleries at Harewood and Syon (1759). After 1780 his ornament became more finicky in character and crowded closely into the containing spaces, as in the later rooms at Osterley (1761-1780). His later fireplaces became smaller in scale; they had formal neoclassic ornament in shallow relief or were merely inlaid in colored marbles.

The same development is apparent in Robert's furniture designs, from the bold character of the early Syon side tables with straight, square, tapering legs to the mature form of the Osterley Drawing Room side tables and eventually to the excessively attenuated forms of the late designs, especially for looking glasses (Apsley House, London, ca. 1775). Chippendale is proved by bills to have made furniture to Robert's designs for Sir Laurence Dundas (1765), and Chippendale absorbed the neoclassic spirit so successfully that he continued to supply furniture in the new idiom for most of Adam's important houses (Nostell; Harewood; and Newby Hall, Yorkshire).

The final phase of Robert's career was that of large-scale public works. Examples are the Register House, Edinburgh (1772-1792), and Edinburgh University (1788-1792).

James Adam assisted his brother, especially in his later commissions. James's important independent works were the facades of Portland Place, London (1776), and Glasgow Infirmary (1792-1796).

Influence of the Adam Style

Although the Adam style was much criticized by Sir William Chambers, Horace Walpole, and other architects, it was universally adopted not only throughout Great Britain and Ireland but in the United States (by Charles Bulfinch and Samuel McIntire), Russia, and Sweden. The imitation of Adam ornament of excessively fine scale and finicky character in poor materials such as *papier-mâché* contributed toward the discrediting of the style after 1780 and the consequent reaction in favor of plainness and severity of decoration as expressed in the work of Henry Holland and James Wyatt. But at the height of its vogue, and later in Victorian, Edwardian, and modern times, when Adam revivals took place, the style was recognized as achieving a distinctive beauty, charm, and elegance unsurpassed in the history of architecture and decoration.

Further Reading

The primary work on the Adam brothers is their own *The Works in Architecture of Robert and James Adam* (3 vols., 1773-1822; facsimile reproduction, 1959). The first monograph is John Swarbrick, *Robert Adam and His Brothers* (1915). The most complete study of the brothers, their drawings, and their works is Arthur T. Bolton, *The Architecture of Robert and James Adam, 1758-1794* (2 vols., 1922). Both Swarbrick and Bolton include photographs of Adam buildings and interiors that no longer exist.

A valuable general work is James Lees-Milne, *The Age of Adam* (1947), covering the development of the Adam style, its antecedents, and its influence abroad. An account of the early life and tours abroad of the two brothers, based on letters, drawings, and family papers, is admirably presented in John Fleming, *Robert Adam and His Circle in Edinburgh and Rome* (1962).

The interior style is exhaustively studied in Damie Stillman, *The Decorative Work of Robert Adam* (1966). The first systematic study of the furniture designed by Robert Adam is Eileen Harris, *The Furniture of Robert Adam* (1963). The most comprehensive general work on the furniture, including neoclassic work by Chippendale, is Clifford Musgrave, *Adam and Hepplewhite and Other Neo-Classical Furniture* (1966). For discoveries in connection with the authorship of Adam furniture see the remarkable monograph by Anthony Coleridge, *Chippendale Furniture* (1968).

For the history of the neoclassic movement in architecture see Mario Praz, *On Neoclassicism* (1940; trans. 1969); John Summerson, *Architecture in Britain, 1530 to 1830* (1953; 4th ed. 1963); and Hugh Honour, *Neo-Classicism* (1968). A short biography and lists of works are contained in H. M. Colvin, *A Biographical Dictionary of English Architects, 1660-1840* (1954).

Additional Sources

Rykwert, Joseph, *Robert and James Adam: the men and the style*, Milano: Electa; New York: Rizzoli, 1985. □

Ansel Adams

Ansel Adams (1902-1984) was not only a masterful photographic technician but a lifelong conservationist who pleaded for understanding of, and respect for, the natural environment. Although he spent a large part of his career in commercial photography, he is best known for his majestic landscape photographs.

Ansel Easton Adams was born on February 20, 1902, in San Francisco, California, near the Golden Gate Bridge. His father, a successful businessman, sent his son to private, as well as public, schools; beyond such formal education, however, Adams was largely self-taught.

His earliest aspiration was to become a concert pianist, but he turned to photography in the late teens of the century; a trip to Yosemite National Park in 1916, where he made his first amateurish photos, is said to have determined his direction in life. Subsequently, he worked as photo technician for a commercial firm.

He joined the Sierra Club in 1919 and worked as a caretaker in their headquarters in Yosemite Valley. Later in life, from 1936 to 1970, Adams was president of the Sierra Club, one of the many distinguished positions that he held.

Ansel Adams decided to become a full time professional photographer at about the time that some of his work was published in limited edition portfolios, one entitled *Parmelian Prints of the High Sierras* (1927) and the other, *Taos Pueblo* (1930), with a text written by Mary Austin.

His first important one-man show was held in San Francisco in 1932 at the M. H. de Young Memorial Museum. Subsequently, he opened the Ansel Adams Gallery for the Arts, taught, lectured, and worked on advertising assignments in the San Francisco area; during the 1930s he also began his extensive publications on the craft of photography, insisting throughout his life on the importance of meticulous craftsmanship. In 1936 Alfred Stieglitz gave Adams a one-man show in his New York gallery, only the second of the work of a young photographer (in 1917 Paul Strand was the first) to be exhibited by Stieglitz.

In 1937 Adams moved to Yosemite Valley close to his major subject and began publishing a stream of superbly produced volumes including *Sierra Nevada: The John Muir Trail* (1938); *Illustrated Guide to Yosemite Valley* (1940); *Yosemite and the High Sierra* (1948); and *My Camera in Yosemite Valley* (1949).

In 1930 Adams met the venerable Paul Strand while they were working in Taos, New Mexico, and the man and his work had a lasting effect on Adams' approach to photography by shifting his approach from a soft formulation of subjects to a much clearer, harder treatment, so-called "straight photography." This orientation was further reinforced by his association with the shortlived, but influential, group which included Edward Weston and Imogen Cun-

ningham and called itself f/64, referring to the lens opening which virtually guarantees distinctness of image.

Throughout much of his early career Adams worked both on commercial assignments and in pursuit of his own vision. He saw no inherent conflict between the two approaches since, as he affirmed, "I don't have any idea that commercialism or professionalism is on one side of the fence and the creative side is on the other. They're both interlocked."

In one sense Ansel Adams' work is an extensive documentation of what is still left of the wilderness, the dwindling untouched segment of the natural environment. Yet to see his work only as documentary is to miss the main point that he tried to make: without a guiding vision, photography is a trivial activity. The finished product, as Adams saw it, must be visualized before it is executed; and he shared with 19th century artists and philosophers the belief that this vision must be embedded within the context of life on earth. Photographs, he believed, are not *taken* from the environment but are *made* into something greater than themselves.

During his life, Ansel Adams was criticized for photographing rocks while the world was falling apart; he responded to the criticism by suggesting that "the understanding of the inanimate and animate world of nature will aid in holding the world of man together."

Further Reading

A great deal has been written by and about Ansel Adams; of particular value are two books that are superbly illustrated with his work. Nancy Hewhall's *Ansel Adams: The Eloquent Light* (1963) provides a good analysis of his work and place in the history of photography; and Ansel Adams' book *Examples: The Making of 40 Photographs* (1983) is a firsthand account of his working methods. For a deeper understanding of his thinking see his essays "What is good photography?" (1940), "A personal credo" (1944), and "Introduction to Portfolio One" (1948) all in Nathan Lyons, *Photographers on Photography* (1966). In 1985 *Ansel Adams: An Autobiography,* written with Mary S. Alinder, was published with 277 illustrations. □

Charles Francis Adams

An American diplomat and politician, Charles Francis Adams (1807-1886) was minister to England during the Civil War. By helping to preserve the neutrality of the British, he frustrated Confederate hopes for foreign aid and intervention in the war.

Charles Francis Adams was born in Boston on Aug. 18, 1807. He spent 8 of his first 10 years in Europe, where his father, John Quincy Adams, was a diplomat. After graduating from Harvard in 1825, the young Adams studied law and began to practice 4 years later. His deep interest in public affairs led him into political activity, and he served several terms in the Massachusetts Legislature during the 1840s. Never an abolitionist, although he believed slavery to be wrong, Adams worked with the Conscience Whigs and Free Soil party to prevent slavery's geographical extension. In 1848 he was the vice-presidential candidate of the Free Soilers. He became a Republican in the mid-fifties and was elected to Congress in 1858 and 1860. He advocated compromise with the South during the secession crisis of 1860-1861 to prevent civil war. His appointment by President Abraham Lincoln as minister to England in 1861 was a reward for his long career as an able advocate of Whig-Republican principles and moderate antislaveryism.

Adams's ministry was marked by a series of crises in Anglo-American relations resulting from the exigencies of the Civil War and from Confederate diplomatic maneuvers. He had to contend not only with the British, who disliked the disruption in trade caused by the war, but also with Confederate agents, who, believing that British aid to the South could assure its success, sought diplomatic recognition and material aid. Adams's main preoccupation, therefore, was to prevent British sympathy for the South from being translated into active support. A severe test of his diplomatic skills occurred in November 1861, when an American warship stopped the British ship *Trent* and removed two Confederate diplomats on board. Alarmed by angry British reaction to this event, Adams recommended the immediate release of the Confederates; the Lincoln administration finally agreed.

Adams's efforts met with general success, as the British remained officially neutral throughout the war. Occasion-

Shepherd, Jack, *The Adams chronicles: four generations of great-ness,* Boston: Little, Brown, 1975. □

ally, however, the Confederates were able to circumvent England's official policy, as when they purchased the warships *Nashville, Florida,* and *Alabama* from British ship-builders. The evidence that Adams collected to demonstrate such violations of neutrality later enabled the United States to sue for damages. Furthermore, his persistent protests to the British government led to the detention of other ships being built for the Confederacy.

After a series of Confederate defeats in 1863, the diplomatic situation eased, and for the remainder of Adams's ministry he faced relatively minor problems. Following his resignation in 1868 and his return from England, he became active in politics again as an opponent of Radical Reconstruction. In 1872 the Liberal Republicans considered nominating him for president, and in 1876 the Massachusetts Democrats ran him for governor. Unsuccessful in both, Adams spent the remainder of his time in literary pursuits until his death in Boston in 1886.

Further Reading

The most complete biography is Martin B. Duberman's excellent *Charles Francis Adams, 1807-1886* (1961). The background of Adams's work can be followed in the old but still useful Ephraim D. Adams, *Great Britain and the American Civil War* (2 vols., 1925).

Additional Sources

Adams, Charles Francis, *Charles Francis Adams,* New York: Chelsea House, 1980.

Gerald Adams

Gerry Adams (born 1948) is the elected president of Sinn Fein, the political arm of the Irish Republican Army (IRA) in Northern Ireland. Although his reputation has been somewhat tarnished because of his ties to the admitted terrorist organization, Adams has gained worldwide attention for his part in the historic IRA cease-fire that lasted from August, 1994, until February, 1996, and the peace talks with England. Although the cease-fire broke within 18 months, Adams will no doubt be a major player in any subsequent negotiations.

B efore the Government of Ireland Act was passed by the British Parliament in 1920, the island of Ireland was united and was a colony of Great Britain. In 1921, the country was partitioned into two sections. The independent Republic of Ireland contained 26 of Ireland's original 32 counties, while Northern Ireland consisted of six counties and remained under British rule. Since the country was divided, violent skirmishes have occurred between Northern Ireland's Protestants, some of whom, as unionists, support the retention of ties with Great Britain, and the Catholic minority, a percentage of whom favor the republican cause and seek a union with the Republic of Ireland, refusing to accept the division of Ireland or retention of ties with the British. Northern Ireland's Catholics protest what they see as gerrymandering, or dividing their country in such a way as to give an advantage to one group. Indeed, Protestants are a majority in Northern Ireland; in the late 1990s, the population stood at approximately 900,000 Protestants and 600,000 Catholics. This minority status hinders any republican efforts; treaties stipulate that any change of the status of Northern Ireland can only come about with the consent of a majority of the people in the country.

This was the backdrop in Northern Ireland on October 6, 1948 when Gerry Adams, the eldest of ten children, was born in a working-class area of Belfast. He was educated at the Catholic schools of St. Finain's and St. Mary's. As a teenager, Adams worked as a bartender in a pub that had mostly Protestant patrons. He became active in politics in 1964 when republican demonstrators rioted against the Royal Ulster Constabulary (RUC), Northern Ireland's largely Protestant police force. Adams subsequently joined Sinn Fein, although the organization was illegal at that time. Meaning "we ourselves" or "ourselves alone" in Irish Gaelic, Sinn Fein is a party committed to an independent Ireland free of British intervention; it also considers itself the only lawful government of Ireland.

By the end of the 1960s, Adams was playing a prominent role in Sinn Fein, helping to launch groups to target

discrimination against Catholics in housing, employment, and civil rights. Another aim of the republican crusade was the repeal of the Special Powers Act which gave police the power of search, arrest, detention and imprisonment and included the right of police to deny inquests into their activities. Protests by Sinn Fein and its supporters met with threats by loyalist extremists. Tensions were further ignited because Sinn Fein viewed the RUC as being biased in supporting the loyalist cause and failing to protect republican demonstrators.

As unrest grew, paramilitary organizations increased their activity. The IRA was formed in 1919 as a nationalist organization seeking a united, independent Ireland; it claimed that terrorism was necessary to prompt unification. In 1969, the outlawed IRA split into two branches, the Officials and Provisionals, and the Provos embarked on an intensified terrorist campaign. Illegal Protestant paramilitary groups—such as the Ulster Volunteer Force and the Ulster Defense Association/Ulster Freedom Fighters—responded with their own terrorist operations. As violence burgeoned, British army troops took to the streets of Belfast and Derry in August of 1969. The British subsequently instituted the Emergency Provisions Act (EPA) and the Prevention of Terrorism Act (PTA). The EPA allowed British forces to stop and questioned anyone, while the PTA allowed anyone to be arrested and detained for up to seven days.

In the midst of this civil uprising, Adams married Colette McArdle in 1971. The couple eventually had three children. As a prominent republican leader, however,

Adams was forced to lived apart from his family for safety reasons.

On January 20, 1972, a day henceforth known as "Bloody Sunday," British troops killed 13 unarmed Catholic protestors and injured 150. In March of that same year, the British removed the Ulster government and directly ruled Northern Ireland from England. The partisan violence, which became known as "The Troubles," continued. Between 1971 and 1975, more than 2,000 people in Northern Ireland were jailed without being charged or put on trial. Adams himself was arrested in 1972 and interred on a British prison ship.

In January of 1973, by which time Adams had been released from prison, the New York Times reported the killing of five Catholics, supposedly in response to IRA bombings. The reporter noted, "there is speculation that the renewed violence is connected with the take-over of a new chief of staff, Gerry Adams." Although he has never confirmed it, Adams was allegedly a member of the IRA and a Belfast brigade commander. On July 20, 1973, Adams, along with 16 other suspected IRA members, was arrested by security forces. Adams, who was visiting his wife and new baby, was seized after soldiers burst into his home. In the New York Times, a spokesman for the British Army called the arrests a "major coup" that "dealt a severe blow to the . . . IRA command structure in Belfast."

Adams was imprisoned under the Special Powers Act and was held without trial from 1973 to 1977. During this time, Adams preached the republican cause to other inmates. His writings in Long Kesh prison camp became the basis of his book Cage Eleven. After being released from Long Kesh, Adams traveled to London during an IRA truce to take part in secret negotiations with William Whitelaw, the British administrator of Ulster. Such an assignment spoke of Adams's growing influence in Sinn Fein. Indeed, Adams was elected vice-president of the party in 1978. That same year, he was arrested again when police detained 20 suspects following a bombing in Belfast that killed 12 people.

In 1981 international support for Sinn Fein grew when ten Catholic prisoners died after staging hunger strikes to protest British policy in Northern Ireland. When Britain allowed Northern Ireland to again convene its own Parliament in 1982, Adams won a seat, but he refused to accept it because it required taking an oath to the British crown. Adams advanced even further in Sinn Fein, being elected president in 1983. The high-profile post had its risks; Adams was shot four times in a 1984 daytime attack by a squad of Protestant gunmen. With Adams's ascension into Sinn Fein's top political office, the group gained the presence of an author and speaker who vowed to give voice to the opposition of Britain's presence in Northern Ireland. He would not be seen on television, however; in 1988 legislation was passed that prohibited broadcast media from interviewing republican spokespersons.

In 1993 Adams's stateside publisher, Sheridan Square Press, wanted to bring him over to publicize two books: The Street, a collection of short stories about Belfast, and Cage Eleven, Adams's memoirs about time spent in an Irish prison. The United States denied Adams a visa, something they had done eight times since he had been elected president of Sinn Fein. As Adams's Irish publisher told *Publishers Weekly,* the visa denial was the work of British influence: "They don't want anyone as articulate as Gerry Adams . . . talking about the situation." (Adams was banned from British soil until 1995.) However, American President Bill Clinton ignored British opposition and broke precedent in 1994 when he granted Adams a visa to travel to the United States on three separate occasions. A reporter for *Time* later called the move "an enormous step in giving [Adams] international stature."

Part of the reasoning behind the United States's new stance was the recognition of Adams's work to resolve the conflict in his homeland. In May of 1987, Sinn Fein published *A Scenario for Peace* which offered a political solution to Northern Ireland's continuing troubles. Beginning in 1988, Adams and John Hume had held discussions concerning peace in Northern Ireland. Hume is the centrist left-wing leader of the Social Democratic and Labour Party (SDLP), who, like Adams, is a leading Roman Catholic figure in Belfast. In September of 1993, Hume, Adams, and Albert Reynolds helped revive the Irish Peace Initiative which outlined principles and suggested processes to build peace in Northern Ireland. This spurred further developments such as the Downing Street Declaration and the Joint Framework Document. In the Downing Street Declaration, British Prime Minister John Major stated that his government would engage in peace talks if Sinn Fein's leaders and the IRA would adopt a nonviolent policy.

In August of 1994, the IRA announced a cease-fire; six weeks later, Protestant forces also invoked a cease-fire. Political leaders around the world praised the cease-fire and the notion of all-party talks. Former Irish Prime Minister Albert Reynolds stated, "In the silence offered by the stifling of the guns, none of us should be afraid to talk peace." After 25 years of violence and centuries of discontent, hopes were raised that the various factions in Northern Ireland could negotiate a form of government acceptable to all of its citizens.

The efforts of Adams and Hume were critical in convincing the IRA that a cease-fire would bring political results. Adams became a champion of the peace process, stating in 1994, "I want to take the gun out of Irish politics." However, a reporter for Britain's *Guardian* newspaper commented, "As the Republican movement's most visible leader, all the IRA's worst atrocities inevitably land at his door." Still, during the cease-fire, Adams traveled extensively promoting the republican platform.

Both Sinn Fein leadership and the IRA grew frustrated by the changing demands the British government placed on inclusion to the talks. Britain insisted on unilateral disarmament by the IRA, but the IRA refused, viewing it as a ploy by Britain to promote the view that the IRA had surrendered. Irish representative Reynolds noted that disarming "was not a condition laid down before the cease-fire." Then the British government stipulated that elections in Northern Ireland could replace an arms surrender as a precondition to admitting parties to the talks. Such elections would determine the number of delegates each group could send to all-party talks, another stipulation that Sinn Fein viewed as tacitly unfair.

As the months passed without progress, dissatisfaction with the British government increased. In the fall of 1995, Adams allegedly twice kept the IRA from breaking the cease-fire and resuming bombings. On February 9, 1996, however, a bomb exploded in London, killing two people. The IRA claimed responsibility, ending the cease-fire and halting the peace process. Within 48 hours, 500 soldiers were deployed to republican strongholds in Northern Ireland. Adams claimed that he did not know in advance that the IRA would end the cease-fire. Nonetheless he was quoted in *Time* as saying, the British "broke the commitments they made when the IRA agreed to the cease-fire. They promised all-party talks, but after 18 months we got nothing."

Another IRA bomb exploded in London on February 18, 1996. Yet in Northern Ireland, hope remained that peace could be salvaged. In *Time,* Catholic priest Denis Faulk noted, "three years ago we would have been slagging each other off over a bombing like the one in London. but now everyone is talking about maintaining the peace. The days of the paramilitaries are numbered. No one wants to go back to war."

The renewed terrorist campaign raised questions about the influence Adams actually has with the IRA and if anyone can control the fragmented (by design) organization. In response to the bombings, the British government banned high-level contacts with Sinn Fein. On May 30, 1996, elections took place in Northern Ireland, with Sinn Fein coming in fourth and garnering more than 15 percent of the vote. Despite Britain's earlier statement that these elections would determine the number of delegates each political group could send to the peace talks, British Prime Minister John Major said a resumption of the IRA cease-fire was a prerequisite for Sinn Fein's inclusion. Still, Adams remains an important figure in the peace process. Belfast city councilor Alex Attwood commented in *Time* in 1996 that "Adams and his first-line managers are the best and the brightest. People may not like them, but they need to be sustained if we are going to secure peace." In 1997, Adams won a seat in the British parliamentary elections as a Member of Parliament for West Belfast in Northern Ireland. As in 1982, he refused to accept it because it required taking an oath to the British crown.

Further Reading

Adams, Gerry, *Before the Dawn: An Autobiography,* William Morrow (New York), 1997.
Keena, Colm, *Gerry Adams, a Biography,* Mercier Press (Dublin), 1990.
Economist, May 13, 1995; August 19, 1995.
Monthly Review, May 1989.
New York Times, February 1, 1973; July 20, 1973; February 19, 1978; May 18, 1993; February 3, 1997.
People, December 26, 1994.
Publishers Weekly, June 14, 1993.
Time, November 5, 1990; November 8, 1993; February 26, 1996.
US News & World Report, August 14, 1995.
Vanity Fair, January, 1997. □

Hank Adams

Originally a staunch supporter of the Kennedys, Hank Adams (born 1944) moved into the arena of Native American activism in 1964. Eventually he became the director of the Survival of American Indians Association, a group dedicated to the Indian treaty-fishing rights battle.

Hank Adams

Hank Adams was born in 1944 on the Fort Peck Indian Reservation in Montana at a place known as Wolf Point, but more commonly referred to as Poverty Flats. He graduated in 1961 from Moclips High School, where he was student-body president, editor of the school newspaper and annual, and a starting football and basketball player. Following graduation he developed an interest in politics and moved to California where he was a staunch supporter of President John F. Kennedy and a campaign worker for the president's brother, Robert F. Kennedy, in the 1968 Democratic primary.

In 1964, Adams played a behind-the-scenes role when actor Marlon Brando and a thousand Indians marched on the Washington State capitol in Olympia to protest state policies toward Indian fishing rights. Indians reserved the right to take fish in "the usual and accustomed places" in numerous treaties negotiated in the 1850s. State officials and commercial and sports fisherman tried to restrict the amount, time, and places where Indian people could fish, thus prompting the treaty-fishing rights battles.

Adams began his activist career in April 1964 when he refused induction into the U.S. Army until Indian treaty rights were recognized. His attempt failed and he ultimately served in the U.S. Army. In 1968, Adams became the director of the Survival of American Indians Association, a group of 150 to 200 active members primarily dedicated to the Indian treaty-fishing rights battle. Late in 1968, he actively campaigned against state regulation of Indian net fishing on the Nisqually River near Franks Landing, Washington. For this and his role in the fishing-rights battles, Adams was regularly arrested and jailed from 1968 to 1971. In January 1971, on the banks of the Puyallup River near Tacoma, Washington, Adams was shot in the stomach by an unknown assailant. He and a companion, Michael Hunt, had set a fish trap about midnight and remained to watch it. That section of the Puyallup River had been the scene of recent altercations as Indian people claimed fishing rights guaranteed by treaties, despite state laws to the contrary. Adams recovered from the gunshot wound and continued to fight for Indian fishing rights in the state of Washington into the mid-1970s. □

Henry Brooks Adams

The American historian and author Henry Brooks Adams (1838-1918) lived in an era of remarkable change and recorded the implications of the period with great perception. He is best known for "Mont-Saint-Michel and Chartres" and "The Education of Henry Adams."

Henry Adams was born in Boston on Feb. 16, 1838, the fourth of seven children of Charles Francis and Abigail Brooks Adams. Henry's mother was the daughter of one of Boston's wealthiest men; his father was the son of John Quincy Adams, sixth president of the United States, and the grandson of John Adams, second president. The boy grew up in a household which contained Boston's largest private library and in which politics and history were perpetually present.

Entering Harvard in 1854, Adams proved himself an able student, but the proffered reward of high class standing did not tempt him to become a conformist even in this period of rigid college regulations. He wrote for the *Harvard Magazine,* acted for the Hasty Pudding Club, and at his graduation in 1858 was chosen Class Day Orator. Although he had learned far more than a reader of his autobiography might imagine, he graduated without academic distinction. In the autumn he traveled to Germany, intending to study law at the University of Berlin. When he discovered that his German was inadequate for university study, he entered a gymnasium (secondary school) for one semester. He toured Europe for 2 years, sending reports to a Boston newspaper.

Private Secretary

When Adams returned to America in 1860, he became private secretary to his father, newly elected to Congress, and again arranged to act as correspondent for a newspaper in his native city. The plans of father and son were abruptly altered in March 1861, when President Lincoln appointed the elder Adams minister to Great Britain. By the time the new minister and his private secretary sailed, Southern forces had fired on Fort Sumter and the Civil War had begun. Henry thought of seeking a commission, but his elder brother Charles, himself in the army, urged him to remain in England and advance the Union cause as a writer. Whether or not the reports Henry published in the *New York Times* and elsewhere contributed to the war effort is an open question, but the 7 years he spent with his father in England unquestionably contributed greatly to his education. He met Sir Charles Lyell and John Stuart Mill and at their urging read the works of Auguste Comte and Herbert Spencer; in the course of time these influences would reorient his thinking on politics, economics, and science. During this period Henry Adams published three long and promising articles in the influential *North American Review.*

The Educator

Adams returned to the United States in 1868 and settled in Washington, where he reported on the political scene for the *Nation* and for some newspapers. The Adams family was accustomed to wielding power, and he doubtless dreamed from time to time of holding high office, but the political realities of Washington in the "gilded age" seem to have brought him quickly to the conviction that his role would be that of critic and commentator rather than political leader. His brilliant, acerbic articles were soon making him famous and men in and near the White House infamous. In the autumn of 1870 he reluctantly quit Washington for Boston to become editor of the *North American Review* and assistant professor of history at Harvard.

At Harvard, Adams's teaching assignments were concentrated in the medieval period, but his methods were modern and innovative, emphasizing student participation rather than lectures, and critical understanding rather than the memorization of names and dates. In 1872 Adams married the wealthy and intelligent Marian Hooper and took her to Europe for a year-long wedding trip. This was the beginning of the happiest and most productive period of his life— a period which, ironically enough, he omits entirely from his autobiography. By 1876 he was ready to offer his Harvard students a course on the history of the United States from 1789 to 1840. From that course he developed materials for the books upon which his reputation as a historian rests: *Documents Relating to New England Federalism, 1800-1815* (1877); *The Writing* and *The Life of Albert Gallatin* (1879), a classic political portrait; *John Randolph* (1882); and the monumental *History of the United States during the Administrations of Jefferson and Madison* (9 vols., 1889-1891).

Observer and Critic of Society

Adams resigned as editor of the *North American Review* in 1876 in an election-year dispute with the loyal Republican publishers. The following year he left Harvard and settled with his wife in Washington, where he could more easily pursue his historical research. In 1879 they returned to Europe, spending much of the winter in London, often in the company of their close friend Henry James. Before their return to America in the fall of 1880, an anonymous novel treating the political and social life of Washington appeared under the title *Democracy;* Adams's authorship of this sprightly piece was to remain a well-kept secret until 1909.

Living in Washington again, the Adamses established their own little court—a splendid circle of sentimental cynics which included John Hay and his wife, the brilliant geologist and writer Clarence King, and the aging senator Don Cameron and his wife, Elizabeth. Elizabeth, always a favorite of Adams, served as the model for Catherine in his second novel, the pseudonymous *Esther* (1884). The title character was based on Adams's wife, and it is a tender and touching portrait. In 1885 Marian Adams's father died; she sank rapidly into a manic-depressive condition and on December 7 committed suicide. "For twelve years I had everything I most wanted on earth," Henry Adams wrote to a friend; suddenly he seemed to have nothing.

Six months after his wife's death, Adams and the artist John La Farge set out for Japan. Adams returned in time to stand by his father's deathbed in November 1886. He went to Washington next and completed the *History.* More travels followed, notably a trip to Polynesia, again with La Farge, in 1890. One of the native women Adams admired provided materials for *Memoirs of Marau Taaroa, Last Queen of Tahiti* (1893). From the South Seas the writer-traveler journeyed to France.

In 1904 Adams privately printed *Mont-Saint-Michel and Chartres,* a classic study of the architecture, thought, and spirit of the Middle Ages (a trade edition appeared in 1913). In this book the Virgin of Chartres stands as a symbol of 13th-century unity. For his next major work he also found a dominant symbol in France: the dynamo he observed at the Paris Exposition of 1900 somehow expressed for him the "multiplicity" of the 20th century. This was the subject of the book for which he is best remembered, *The Education of Henry Adams* (private edition 1907; published 1918). Customarily called his autobiography, it is really the history of an era.

Adams spent his last years in Washington, surrounded by nieces and visited by a new generation of America's social and political elite. He approved of President Wilson's decision to enter World War I because he hoped it would lead the country into a permanent Atlantic alliance. Adams died quietly in his home on March 26, 1918. He was buried in Rock Creek Cemetery beside the grave of his wife with no marker save the beautiful statue he had commissioned Augustus Saint-Gaudens to execute for her.

Further Reading

Ernest Samuels's exemplary biography in three volumes is the standard authority: *The Young Henry Adams* (1948), *Henry Adams: The Middle Years* (1958), and *Henry Adams: The Major Phase* (1964). J. C. Levenson, *The Mind and Art of Henry Adams* (1957), is rigorous and thorough. George Hochfield, *Henry Adams: An Introduction and Interpretation* (1962), is also useful. □

Herbert Baxter Adams

As a historian and teacher, Herbert Baxter Adams (1850-1901) was important in establishing the professional study of history in American universities.

Herbert Baxter Adams was born in Shutesburg, Mass., on April 16, 1850. He entered Amherst College in 1868 and initially showed interest in journalism, editing the college newspaper and occasionally reporting for papers in Amherst, Boston, and New York. However, according to Adams himself, hearing one lecture during his senior year changed his mind and made him decide to study history.

After graduation Adams taught for one year, but he knew that the pursuit of his goal required foreign study, and so in 1874 he left for Heidelberg and Berlin. He received his doctorate from Heidelberg in 1876, having already accepted a position at the newly established Johns Hopkins University, where he would remain until his death. It is not coincidental that Adams began his career at the same time that Johns Hopkins opened its doors, for the educational goals of the man and the institution were identical. The university was to be a research institution where graduate-level instruction using the seminar method would be available for advanced students. Adams, with his German training, was determined to inaugurate through the seminar system the scientific study of history based on careful, critical examination of the sources. He hoped to make the study of history an independent professional pursuit rather than a mere branch of literature.

In 1881 Adams was put in charge of the Historical Seminary, the institution for the training of advanced students, in which he supervised several men who were to become famous historians. In 1882 he issued the first number of the *Johns Hopkins University Studies in Historical and Political Science,* which he founded so that scholars at the university could publish the results of their research. He continued as editor for 18 years.

As a historian, Adams specialized in the study of local political institutions of America's colonial period. He tried to show the derivation of these institutions from German and English models—an approach usually called the "germ theory" of American politics. His primary role, however, was as a teacher, editor, and organizer. After 1883 he did not publish any of his own scholarly work in history except for a biography of the American historian Jared Sparks in

1893. After 1884 he was secretary of the American Historical Association, of which he was the leading founder and the effective executive head until declining health forced him to resign in 1900. He died on July 30, 1901.

Further Reading

Adams's career may be traced in W. Stull Holt, ed., *Historical Scholarship in the United States, 1876-1901: As Revealed in the Correspondence of Herbert B. Adams* (1938). John Martin Vincent's essay in Howard W. Odum, ed., *American Masters of Social Science* (1927), is more directly biographical, but it does not reveal as clearly Adams's contributions to the historical profession. John Higham and others, *History* (1965), places Adams in historical context. □

James Luther Adams

James Luther Adams (1901-1994) was the leading 20th century Unitarian theologian and a skillful proponent and defender of religious and political liberalism. A major American social ethicist, he combined a concern for the Christian tradition with openness to the social sciences and active involvement in religious and secular associations.

Adams was born in Ritzville, Washington, on November 12, 1901. His family background prepared him hardly at all for a role as a champion of liberalism. His father, James Carey Adams, was a Baptist country preacher, a premillenarian who later became a Plymouth Brother. Letta Barrett Adams, his mother, was also a devout believer. It was his educational experiences that provided the foundation of his liberal thinking. The "new law" he came to live by at the University of Minnesota was the scientific humanism of John Dietrich and the "new prophecy" he proclaimed was the anti-Rotarianism of H. L. Mencken. But Adams's railing against religion was a turbulent eddy, catching the eye but hiding the deep currents of a profound religious sense. He entered Harvard Divinity School in 1924 and was greatly influenced by Unitarianism, the tradition of social responsibility, and the historical, critical methods of the school. Marxism and Anglo-Catholicism, with their emphasis on community, provided Adams with a necessary complement to humanism's "individual psychology of self-culture."

Adams's journey to Europe in the summer of 1927, following his ordination as a Unitarian minister, had a lasting effect on his approach to ethics and theology. While there, he became familiar with the writings of Paul Tillich and witnessed the Nazi festival in Nuremberg. These experiences deeply influenced his understanding of culture and human nature and his assessment of liberal theology. Upon his return from Europe he married Margaret Anne Young in September of 1927 and became pastor of the Second Church in Salem, Massachusetts.

Given his active involvement in and commitment to the development of the Unitarian Church, it was no surprise in 1935 that he was called to teach at the Unitarian Seminary in Chicago. Before taking up that charge he returned for a year of study in Europe where he placed himself under the spiritual direction of a Roman Catholic priest and researched the liturgical movement at Maria Laach (a Benedictine monastery). In Germany he studied the relation of religion to fascism and democracy. He sought to bring both secular and sacred together in his personal religious journey, a journey which led to his detention by the Gestapo on more than one occasion. Adams supported the Allied cause in the war, a war which he understood as related to a wider issue: the linkage between the totalitarianism of the Axis and the social inequalities in the United States. The strength and vitality of his religious liberalism and the constant interplay between principles and events are evident in his criticism of all parties in the war.

On his return from Europe in 1936, Adams had begun a teaching career at the University of Chicago, a career he continued at Harvard Divinity School and other universities. His influence on ethicists and theologians is legendary. He wrote several books and hundreds of essays and reviews. He continued to teach informally through prolific correspondence, lectures, writing, translating, and, most importantly, personal contact. One consistent way in which he interacted with events and societal problems, thereby fleshing out his teaching and writing, was through memberships in associations. He was president of the Society of Christian Ethics, the Society for the Scientific Study of Religion, and the American Theological Society, as well as an active member of the American Civil Liberties Union along with a host of other religious and political organizations.

Over six decades he strongly influenced American Christian ethics through his translation and introduction of European thinkers to American theologians. Paul Tillich's theology is widely known in America primarily due to Adams's editing and translating. Adams's interpretation of Tillich's thinking in *Paul Tillich's Philosophy of Culture, Science and Religion* is the classic text on the German theologian's early years. Conversely, Adams's influence on Tillich was strong: in the latter's words: "I have learned from him (Adams) the emphasis on the practical, social as well as the political, application of the principle of *agape* to the situation of the society in which we live."

The influence of metaphysicians such as Tillich on Adams is counterbalanced by the strong historical sense evident in his biblical prophetic awareness and his analysis of the left wing of the Protestant Reformation. Concern for the person in society and history consistently led him to the field of sociology. Karl Marx, Ernst Troeltsch, Max Weber, Karl Mannheim, and Ferdinand Toennies profoundly affected Adams's interpretation of social ethics and the historicity of men and women.

One of Adams's most important contributions to 20th century theology was his reformulation of religious liberalism. His method of reformulation was forcefully dialectical, focussing now on community, then on the individual, now on God, then on man. Adams's dialectical sense fos-

tered in others a willingness to engage in the task of translating ethical formulations for a new age, yet cautioned that new understandings were not the final answer. Thus, vital reformulation results only if theory and practice exist dialectically. They do in Adams primarily because no answer is final and because community facilitates discernment of the interaction between theory and practice. Theory may be correct, but the test is application to the present situation and reflection upon the interaction of event and theory.

Adams was a driving force in the United States in social ethics for the second half of the 20th century. His last book, *An Examined Faith: Social Context and Religious Commitment* (1991), was published when he was 89 years old. Through his writings and teachings, Adams developed a version of natural law doctrine based in liberal religion. His aim was to critique contemporary social injustices while simultaneously informing action to reshape these unjust practices. Adams died of heart failure at his home in Cambridge, Massachusetts, in 1992.

Further Reading

The best introduction to James Luther Adams is his volume of essays entitled *On Being Human Religiously,* edited and introduced by Max L. Stackhouse (1976). An analysis of Adams's theological ethics and an extensive bibliography will be found in John R. Wilcox's *Taking Time Seriously: James Luther Adams* (1978). His last book is *An Examined Faith: Social Context and Religious Commitment,* Beacon Press (1991). Adams is profiled in "Remembering James Luther Adams," *The Christian Century,* December 7, 1994; and his version of natural law is discussed in Douglas Sturm, "Natural Law, Liberal Religion, and Freedom of Association: James Luther Adams on the Problem of Jurisprudence," *Journal of Religious Ethics,* Spring 1992. □

John Adams

The second president of the United States, John Adams (1735-1826) played a major role in the colonial movement toward independence. He wrote the Massachusetts Constitution of 1780 and served as a diplomatic representative of Congress in the 1780s.

John Adams was born in Braintree (now Quincy), Mass. His father was a modest but successful farmer and local officeholder. After some initial reluctance, Adams entered Harvard and received his bachelor's degree in 1755. For about a year he taught school in Worcester. Though he gave some thought to entering the ministry, Adams was repelled by the theological acrimony resulting from the period of the Great Awakening and turned to the law. After studying under James Putnam, Adams was admitted to the Boston bar in 1758. While developing his legal practice, he participated in town affairs and contributed his first essays to the Boston newspapers. In 1764 he married Abigail Smith of

Weymouth, who brought him wide social connections and was to share with sensitivity and enthusiasm in the full life that lay ahead.

Early Political Career

By 1765 Adams had achieved considerable distinction at the Boston bar. With the Stamp Act crisis he moved into the center of Massachusetts political life. He contributed an important series of essays, *Dissertation on the Canon and Feudal Law,* to the *Boston Gazette* and prepared a series of anti-Stamp Act resolutions for the Braintree town meeting, which were widely copied throughout the province.

In April 1768 Adams moved to Boston. He defended John Hancock against smuggling charges brought by British customs officials and acted as counsel for Capt. Thomas Preston, the officer in charge of British troops at the Boston Massacre. Adams undertook the Preston defense somewhat reluctantly, fearing its consequences for his own local popularity, but the need to provide Preston with a fair trial persuaded him to act—with no damage, in the end, to his own reputation or practice. Indeed, a few weeks later Adams was elected representative from Boston to the Massachusetts Legislature.

In the spring of 1771, largely for reasons of health, Adams returned to Braintree, where he divided his attention between farming and the law. Within a year, however, professional and political considerations drew him back to Boston. In 1773 he celebrated the Boston Tea Party as a dramatic challenge to British notions of parliamentary su-

premacy. The next year he was one of the representatives from Massachusetts to the First Continental Congress, where he took a leading role in developing the colonists' constitutional defense against the Coercive Acts and other British measures. Although Adams favored the various petitions Congress made to the King, Parliament, and the English people, as well as the scheme of nonimportation agreements, he nonetheless hoped for more vigorous measures. All the while, however, he had to guard against the suspicion held by many other delegates that the New Englanders were plotting independence. Upon his return to Massachusetts, Adams was chosen for the governor's council but was negatived. During the winter of 1774-1775 he carried on, under the pseudonym Novanglus, an extended debate with Daniel Leonard over the proper constitutional relations between the Colonies and Parliament. Adams's recommended solution at this point was a commonwealth system of empire, with a series of coequal parliaments joined by common allegiance to the Crown.

After the battles of Lexington and Concord, Adams returned to Congress, carrying the welcome instructions from the General Court for measures to establish American liberties on a permanent basis, secure from attack by Britain. He now believed that independence would probably be necessary. Congress, however, was not yet willing to agree, and Adams fumed while still more petitions were sent off to England. The best chance of promoting independence, he concluded, was through the device of instructing the various colonies to adopt new forms of government following the breakdown of their provincial regimes. Replying to petitions from several provinces seeking advice on their governments (petitions which Adams and others had solicited), he recommended that they adopt new governments modeled on their colonial regimes and framed by special conventions.

By February 1776 Adams was back in Congress. There he presented, first privately in response to the requests of several delegates and then publicly in a pamphlet entitled "Thoughts on Government," his specific proposals for the reconstruction of the provincial governments. Adams was at last fully committed to American independence. In May, Congress finally passed a resolution that, where no adequate governments existed, measures should be taken to provide for the "happiness and safety" of the people. For this resolution Adams wrote a preamble which in effect asserted the principle of independence. A month later he seconded Richard Henry Lee's resolution for the formal declaration of independence, the contracting of foreign treaties, and the construction of a continental confederation. A member of the committee appointed to bring in the formal statement, Adams contributed little to the content of the Declaration of Independence but served, as Thomas Jefferson later reported, as "the pillar of its support on the floor of the Congress." On another committee Adams drew up a model treaty that encouraged Congress to enter into commercial but not political alliances with European nations. Exhausted by his duties, he temporarily left Philadelphia in mid-October for Massachusetts. For the next year or so he continued to serve in Congress.

Diplomatic Career

On Nov. 28, 1777, Congress elected Adams commissioner to France, replacing Silas Deane, and in February Adams embarked from Boston for what was to prove an extended stay. Upon arrival, Adams found that France had already granted diplomatic recognition to the United States and contracted treaties of commerce and amity. With nothing specific to do, Adams spent the next year and a half trying to keep busy: attempting to secure badly needed loans for Congress, transmitting lengthy letters on European affairs, and learning with mixed fascination and repugnance about the ways of French court and national life.

When he learned that Benjamin Franklin, one of his fellow commissioners, had been appointed sole American plenipotentiary in France, Adams returned to Boston, where in the fall of 1779 he was elected from Braintree to the state constitutional convention. For the next few months he devoted his time to the convention, preparing what became the basic draft of the new Massachusetts constitution.

In the meantime Adams had been tapped by Congress for another diplomatic post, this time as commissioner to contract peace and then a commercial treaty with Great Britain. He embarked in mid-November and arrived in Paris on Feb. 9, 1780. Again he found his situation frustrating, largely because he had been instructed to make no significant moves without the prior approval of the Comte de Vergennes, the French foreign minister. Between Adams and Vergennes there quickly developed a mutual dislike—duplicated in Adams's relations with Franklin, a man more flexible and less demanding in his relations with the French foreign minister. In the face of all this, Adams spent considerable time writing his friends in Congress to complain of his difficult position. Having been further commissioned minister plenipotentiary to the United Provinces, Adams finally secured recognition by The Hague in the spring of 1782, and in October he signed the first of several desperately needed loans with a group of Dutch bankers.

He returned to Paris to negotiate the terms of peace with the British representatives. Adams and the other two American commissioners, Franklin and John Jay, ignored their instructions to make no agreement without first consulting Vergennes; they feared (correctly) that France wished to pressure the United States into peace arrangements inconsistent with national interest (for example, leaving certain coastal areas in British hands). The American commissioners concluded provisional articles of peace and sent the results home to Congress. These were duly signed as the definitive treaty of peace on Sept. 3, 1783.

The Dutch loans and the treaty of peace were the major products of the diplomatic phase of Adams's public career. Before returning permanently to the United States, however, he spent 3 frustrating years as American envoy to the Court of St. James in London, attempting without success to negotiate a commercial treaty and to clear up various diplomatic issues carried over from the Revolution. Rebuffed by British officials and unsupported by a weak Congress, Adams finally asked to resign. Formal letters of recall were sent in February 1788. During the last year and a half of his stay, he composed his three-volume *Defense of the Constitutions of Government of the United States of America,* an extended attempt to defend the American concept of balanced government against the criticisms of the French statesman A.R.J. Turgot.

The Presidency

With his return to Boston, Adams began the final stage of his public career. He was chosen vice president in 1789 under the new Federal constitution, a position he was to fill, again with considerable frustration because of its powerlessness, during both of Washington's administrations.

As the election of 1796 approached, the Jeffersonian Republicans began forming an opposition to the Federalists' financial program and seemingly pro-British foreign policy. The Republicans presented Jefferson as their presidential candidate. The Federalists split into two factions, with Adams as one candidate and Thomas Pinckney (backed by Alexander Hamilton) as the other. In spite of Hamilton's efforts, Adams ran well ahead of Pinckney and became the second president of the United States. Jefferson, a scant three electoral votes behind, became vice president.

Adams took office on March 4, 1797. From the first his presidency was a stormy one. His Cabinet, inherited from Washington and dominated by Hamilton's followers, proved increasingly difficult to control. Foreign policy problems, generated by the outbreak of war between revolutionary France and a counterrevolutionary coalition of European nations, created internal political crises of magnitude. The outbreak of revolution in France had tended to polarize political discussion in the United States as well as in Europe between "aristocratic" and "democratic" positions. More particularly, the war between England and France raised questions of whether the United States would maintain a strict neutrality—in fact impossible because of efforts by both England and France to control American trade—or align itself, at least sympathetically, with one of the countries. While most Americans professed the desire to remain neutral in the contest, the Jeffersonians were sympathetic with France and the Federalists with England. Adams found himself caught in the middle.

In 1797 French diplomats attempted to bribe the three-man commission sent by the United States to negotiate various points in dispute between the two nations. The immediate result was an outburst of anti-French sentiment, which the Hamiltonians worked hard to inflame. Adams became caught up in the furor as well, making numerous statements during the spring and summer of 1798 that fanned emotions even higher. Taking advantage of the situation, the Federalists in Congress, with Adams's tacit approval, developed a war program consisting of substantial increases in the American navy, a large provisional army, the Alien and Sedition Acts (aimed at controlling potential subversives within), and a system of tax measures to finance the entire program. The Federalist goals were two: to prepare for an expected war with France and to attack the Jeffersonian opposition.

For a while it seemed that the Federalist measures would carry the day. But during the late summer and fall of 1798 the prospect of peaceful accommodation with France increased, and public discontent with the Federalist war program (helped along by the cries of the Jeffersonians) broke through the surface. President Adams, at home in Massachusetts during much of this time, became convinced that war with France was not necessary and that the Federalist policies, if continued, were likely to result in serious internal disorder. Early in 1799 he committed himself to a plan of peaceful accommodation with France—a decision that enraged most of the Hamiltonians and left them sitting far out on a political limb, with a military establishment and no foreign invader to fight.

By 1800 the split between Adams and the Hamiltonian wing of the Federalist party was complete. Adams dismissed the main Hamiltonians from his Cabinet, and Hamilton openly opposed Adams for reelection. But the President's peace initiatives were both enlightened statesmanship and good politics. The young nation was unprepared for any major external war, and the possibility of serious internal conflict if the war program was continued seems to have been real. Moreover, as various individuals reported, by late 1799 France was prepared for an honorable accommodation with the United States, so there was no longer reason for conflict. Politically, Adams's peace decision made comparable sense. The Federalist split no doubt weakened his chances in 1800, but the Jeffersonians were already scoring heavily in their attacks on Federalist policies. Continued defense of such policies would almost certainly have led to political disaster. In the end Adams lost the election to Jefferson by a narrow margin.

Adams later described his peace decision as "the most splendid diamond in my crown," more important than his leadership in the revolutionary crisis, his constitutional writings, or his diplomatic service. He left the capital, however, bitterly disappointed over his rejection by the American people, so distressed that he even refused to remain for Jefferson's inaugural in 1801.

Adams spent the remainder of his life in political seclusion, though he retained a lively interest in public affairs, particularly when they involved the rising career of his son, John Quincy Adams. John Adams divided his time between overseeing his farm and carrying on an extended correspondence concerning both his personal experiences and issues of more general political and philosophical significance. He died at the age of 91, just a few hours after Jefferson's death, on July 4, 1826.

Further Reading

The most complete modern biography is Page Smith, *John Adams* (2 vols., 1962), although Smith does not differentiate clearly enough the central themes of Adams's career. Still useful is Gilbert Chinard, *Honest John Adams* (1933). For the early career of John Adams see Catherin Drinker Bowen, *John Adams and the American Revolution* (1950). Adams's election to the presidency is fully detailed in Arthur M. Schlesinger, ed., *History of American Presidential Elections* (4 vols., 1971). Manning J. Dauer, *The Adams Federalists* (1953), and Stephen G. Kurtz, *The Presidency of John Adams: The Collapse of Federalism, 1795-1800* (1957), examine Adams's feud with Hamilton and the split within the Federalist party. For the political thought of Adams three studies are relevant: Correa M. Walsh, *The Political Science of John Adams* (1915); Edward Handler, *America and Europe in the Political Thought of John Adams* (1964); and John Howe, *The Changing Political Thought of John Adams* (1966). □

John Couch Adams

The English mathematical astronomer John Couch Adams (1819-1892) was a principal figure in the discovery of the planet Neptune.

Born at Laneast, Cornwall, on June 5, 1819, to a farm family of modest station, John Couch Adams early demonstrated a remarkable capacity for mathematics. He was admitted to Cambridge University on a scholarship in the fall of 1839, and when he graduated in 1843 he was appointed to the faculty, spending virtually the rest of his life there.

The chain of events in which Adams figured so prominently began long before his birth. In 1781 William Herschel had discovered the planet Uranus. From then on, astronomers had sought to account for the movement of Uranus according to the rules which governed the motions of the other planets. By Adams's day it was apparent that their attempts had failed. Although a new orbit had been computed as late as 1820, the refractory planet was already departing from its predicted path by about 1 minute of arc. Although such a small angle is almost inconceivable by the layperson (it is the angle subtended by a nickel at a distance of 100 yards), it represented an intolerable error for 19th-century astronomy.

Finding the Unknown Planet, Neptune

Adams's initial attack on Uranus, begun upon his graduation in 1843, lasted 2 1/2 years. Like earlier efforts, it was based on the law of universal gravitation, according to which the planet describes an essentially elliptical orbit around the sun with slight deviations caused by the attractions of other planets. Adams premised his work on the assumption that the computations of previous mathematicians had been spoiled by an unknown planet, whose actions on Uranus they necessarily failed to take into account. In September 1845 he presented his result to the director of the Cambridge observatory, indicating the approximate spot in the sky where the unknown planet should be found.

So unprecedented was Adams's prediction that no one knew how to treat it. Not until June 1846, when U.J.J. Leverrier in France published a similar result, did the English decide to drop their observational commitments and undertake the extensive search program to locate the planet. As was to appear later, they actually charted the planet on August 4 and 12 among the thousands of observations made. Before they could analyze all the data, however, the planet was discovered at Berlin on September 23 from the computations of Leverrier. Although Adams officially lost the honor of the discovery, the merit of his work was recognized, and his scientific reputation was established.

During the remaining 45 years of his life, he made important contributions to celestial mechanics and received many honors. He died in Cambridge on Jan. 21, 1892.

Further Reading

Adams's professional work is republished in *The Scientific Papers of John Couch Adams* (2 vols., 1896-1900). There is no biography. Two accounts of Adams's greatest achievement are Sir Harold Spencer Jones, *John Couch Adams and the Discovery of Neptune* (1947), and Morton Grosser's highly readable *The Discovery of Neptune* (1962). □

John Quincy Adams

John Quincy Adams (1767-1848) was the sixth president of the United States. A brilliant statesman and outstanding secretary of state, he played a major role in formulating the basic principles of American foreign policy.

B orn in Braintree (now Quincy), Mass. on July 11, 1767, John Quincy Adams was the eldest son of John and Abigail Smith Adams. In 1779, at the age of 12, he accompanied his father to Europe. Precocious and brilliant—at 14 he accompanied Francis Dana, the American minister, to Russia as a French translator—he served as his father's secretary during the peace negotiations in Paris. Except for brief periods of formal education, he studied under his father's direction. When he entered Harvard in 1785, he was proficient in Greek, Latin, French, Dutch, and German.

After his graduation Adams studied law and began to practice in Boston in 1790. More interested in politics than the law, he made a name for himself with political essays supporting the politics of President George Washington. Those signed "Publicola" (his answer to Thomas Paine's *Rights of Man*) were so competent that they were ascribed to his father, who was then vice president.

The Diplomat

In 1793 Washington appointed young Adams minister to the Netherlands. From this vantage point he supplied the government with a steady flow of information on European affairs. Sent to London in connection with Jay's Treaty, he met Louisa Catherine Johnson, the daughter of the American consul, and married her on July 26, 1797. Although it was not a love match, the marriage was a happy one marked by deep mutual affection. In 1797 Adams became minister to Prussia, concluding a commercial treaty incorporating the neutral-rights provisions of Jay's Treaty.

On his return to the United States in 1801, Adams was elected to the Massachusetts Senate. Two years later he became a U.S. senator. Nominally a Federalist, he pursued an independent course. He was the only Federalist senator from New England to vote for the Louisiana Purchase. The Massachusetts Federalists forced him to resign in 1808 be-

cause they were angered by his support of Jefferson's commercial warfare against Great Britain and his presence at a Republican presidential nominating caucus.

Adams severed his connections with the Federalists and in 1809 accepted an appointment from Republican president James Madison as minister to Russia. He did much to encourage Czar Alexander's friendly disposition toward the United States. It was partly due to Adams's encouragement that Russia made an offer to mediate between Great Britain and the United States, which led to direct peace negotiations to end the War of 1812. As a member of the peace commission at Ghent, Adams and his colleagues (Henry Clay, Albert Gallatin, James A. Bayard, and Jonathan Russell) found the British commissioners so intransigent that they were obliged to conclude a treaty short of American expectations. In 1815, as minister to great Britain, Adams worked to lessen the tension between the two nations by welcoming Lord Castlereagh's friendly overtures.

The Secretary of State

In March 1817 President James Monroe appointed Adams secretary of state. Adams, who was then 50, was not a prepossessing figure. He was short, plump, and bald; his best feature was his penetrating black eyes. Inclined to be irascible, and very much aware of his own intellectual powers, he disciplined himself to conceal his impatience. "I am," he wrote in his diary, "a man of reserved, cold, austere, and forbidding manners. . . . " He was ill at ease in large gatherings, but in intimate circles he could be an entertaining companion. Imposing rigid moral standards on himself, he was inclined to judge others harshly. He had an almost Puritan sense of duty and a passion for work, which kept him at his desk for long hours not only in connection with official duties but in the scholarly researches that gave him so much pleasure. Every day he found time to make lengthy entries in his diary, which constitutes one of the most revealing sources for the political events of his era. His wife, witty and gracious, somewhat compensated for her husband's social shortcomings; Louisa Adams's weekly evening parties were among the most popular in the capital.

Adams and Monroe worked together in the greatest harmony and understanding, for they were in complete agreement on the basic objectives of American foreign policy. They wished to expand the territorial limits of the nation, to give American diplomacy a direction distinct from that pursued by the European states, and to compel the other powers to treat the United States as an equal. Monroe closely controlled foreign affairs, but he relied heavily on Adams, who proved a shrewd adviser, an adroit negotiator, and a talented writer whose state papers formulated administration policy with logic and a tremendous command of the relevant facts.

The most difficult negotiations undertaken by Adams were those culminating in the acquisition of Florida and the definition of the western boundary of Louisiana. In 1819 Adams was able to exploit Andrew Jackson's invasion of Florida to force Spain to settle both issues in the Transcontinental Treaty, which Spain ratified in 1821. Adams's familiarity with the complexities of the history of Louisiana enabled him to obtain a boundary settlement favorable to the United States and to fix the northern boundary so that American interests in the Columbia River region were protected. During the crisis precipitated by Jackson's unauthorized seizure of Spanish posts in Florida, Adams was the only Cabinet member to recommend that the administration completely endorse the general's conduct.

Equally taxing and less successful were the prolonged negotiations with the French minister over indemnities for confiscation of American ships and cargoes during the Napoleonic Wars, France's commercial rights in Louisiana, and trade relations in general. In 1822 Adams concluded a treaty providing only for a gradual reduction of discriminatory duties. His efforts to persuade Great Britain to open West Indian trade to American ships were unsuccessful. In the midst of these demanding negotiations, Adams conducted an extensive correspondence with American diplomats, reorganized the State Department, and drafted a masterly report for Congress on a uniform system of weights and measures. In 1822 Monroe formally recognized the new independent states in Latin America. Adams's instructions to the first American emissaries reflected his misgivings about the future of these states, which were largely dominated by authoritarian regimes.

When France intervened in Spain in 1823 to suppress a revolution, Adams did not share the view that this presaged a move on the European powers, who had banded together in the Holy Alliance, to restore Spanish authority in South America. He was far more concerned about Russian attempts to expand along the Pacific coast. Consequently, he welcomed Monroe's decision in 1823 to make a policy declaration expressing American hostility to European intervention in the affairs of the Americas. To the President's declaration, later known as the Monroe Doctrine, Adams contributed the noncolonization principle, which affirmed that the United States considered the Americas closed to further European colonization. In 1824 the American minister in Russia, acting on instructions from Adams, obtained an agreement in which Russia withdrew north of latitude 54'40'', but Adams was not able to persuade the British to vacate the Columbia River region.

The President

In 1824 Adams was involved in a bitter four-cornered presidential contest in which none of the candidates received a majority of the electoral votes. Adams with 84 votes, largely from New England and New York, ran behind Andrew Jackson with 99 but ahead of William H. Crawford with 41 and Henry Clay with 37. The contest was resolved in Adams's favor in the House of Representatives when Clay decided to support him. Adams's subsequent choice of Clay as secretary of state raised a cry of "corrupt bargain"; there was no overt agreement between them, but the charge was most damaging.

Adams's presidency added little to his fame. In the face of the absolute hostility of the combined Jackson-Crawford forces, he was unable to carry out his nationalist program. His proposals for Federal internal improvements, a uniform bankruptcy law, federally supported educational and scientific institutions, and the creation of a department of the interior were rebuffed. His sole success in dealing with Congress was the appointment in 1826 of two delegates to attend the Panama Congress, arranged by Simón Bolívar. This Adams achieved only after acrimonious debates in which hostile congressmen made much of the fact that American delegates would be participating in a conference attended by black representatives from Haiti.

Committed to a protectionist policy, Adams signed the Tariff of Abominations (engineered by the Jacksonians in 1828), although it was certain to alienate the South and displease New Englanders, whose manufactures were not granted additional protection. He never permitted political expediency to override his rigid sense of justice. Consequently, he alienated much Southern and Western opinion by his efforts to protect the interests of the Cherokees in Georgia. He also declined to use the power of patronage to build up a national following, although Postmaster General John McLean was appointing only Jackson men. Pilloried as an aristocrat hostile to the interests of the "common man," Adams was overwhelmingly defeated by Jackson in the election of 1828.

The Congressman

At the end of his presidency, Adams expected to concentrate on the scholarly interests which had always absorbed so much of his time, but his retirement was brief. In 1831 he was elected to the House of Representatives, where he served for eight successive terms until his death. Although generally associated with the Whigs, he pursued an independent course. For 10 years he was chairman of the Committee on Manufactures, which drafted tariff bills. He approved Jackson's stand on nullification, but he considered the compromise tariff of 1833, which was not the work of his committee, an excessive concession to the nullifiers. After 1835 he was identified with the antislavery cause, although he was not an abolitionist. From 1836 to 1844, when his efforts were finally successful, he worked to revoke the gag rule that required the tabling of all petitions relating to slavery. Session after session "old man eloquent," as he was dubbed, lifted his voice in defense of freedom of speech and the right to petition. True to his nationalist convictions, he continued to advocate internal improvements and battled to save the Bank of the United States.

Adams suffered a stroke on the floor of the House of Representatives on Feb. 21, 1848. He was carried to the Speaker's room, where he died 2 days later without regaining consciousness.

Further Reading

The most important printed sources are Adams's diary, *Memoirs of John Quincy Adams. ..,* edited by Charles Francis Adams (12 vols., 1874-1877), and Worthington Chauncey Ford's edition of *The Writings of John Quincy Adams* (7 vols., 1913-1917), which stops in 1823. The best biography is Samuel Flagg Bemis's two volumes, *John Quincy Adams and the Foundations of American Foreign Policy* (1949) and *John Quincy Adams and the Union* (1956). Adams's election to the presidency is covered fully by Arthur M. Schlesinger, Jr., ed., *History of American Presidential Elections* (4 vols., 1971). Studies of Adams's diplomacy are Dexter Perkins, *The Monroe Doctrine, 1823-1826* (1927; new ed. 1966); Philip C. Brooks, *Diplomacy and the Borderlands: The Adams-Onis Treaty of 1819* (1939); Arthur Preston Whitaker, *The United States and the Independence of Latin America, 1800-1830* (1941); Bradford Perkins, *Castlereagh and Adams: England and the United States, 1812-1823* (1964). See also George A. Lipsky, *John Quincy Adams: His Theory and Ideas* (1950). □

Peter Chardon Brooks Adams

The American historian Peter Chardon Brooks Adams (1848-1927) stimulated studies of his field in the United States by outlining his belief that economic and geographic conditions affect the course of history.

Brooks Adams was born on June 24, 1848, in Quincy, Mass. His father, Charles Francis Adams, was the son of one U.S. president and the grandson of another. His mother, Abigail, was the daughter of Peter Chardon Brooks, a wealthy Massachusetts merchant.

After an unhappy childhood, Adams entered Harvard in 1866. He graduated from Harvard Law School and was admitted to the bar in 1873. But the practice of law never appealed to him, and so, independently wealthy because of a legacy from his maternal grandfather, he decided to pursue his own interests in writing and politics. He achieved prominence in the Massachusetts Democratic party and was widely mentioned in 1898 as a possibility for the governorship, but he broke with his party on the issues of imperialism and expansion, being an unremitting advocate of both. He was poorly suited to politics anyway, and all who knew him agreed that he was shy, gloomy, and eccentric.

He achieved real prominence through his writings. His first important historical work was *The Emancipation of Massachusetts* (1887), in which he attempted to show that Puritan Massachusetts had been a theocracy where freedom of religion, of speech, and of opinion had no place. More importantly, the book contained the first expression of Adams's primary preoccupation as a historian: the search for and demonstration of a law of history establishing the relationship between historical events and economic conditions.

This concept was sharpened by current political events in the United States. The controversy between the advocates of the free and unlimited coinage of silver and those who supported the gold standard imparted immediacy to his ideas, resulting in *The Law of Civilization and Decay* (1895), in which Adams argued that the course of civilization was determined primarily by economic conditions. The book attracted the favorable attention of Theodore Roosevelt, who, when he became president in 1901, gave Adams a considerable role as an adviser. In this position Adams advocated imperial expansion along with stringent regulation of American business.

In 1903 Adams became a lecturer at the Boston University Law School, remaining there until 1909. In 1912 he worked for Roosevelt's nomination by the Republican party. His efforts failing, he left to take a rest in Germany. This became the pattern of his life: frequent trips in search of health and occasional writing and lecturing, in which usually he merely repeated his previously expressed ideas. He died in Quincy, Mass., on Feb. 13, 1927.

Further Reading

The standard biography of Adams is Arthur F. Beringause, *Brooks Adams: A Biography* (1955), but its organization makes it somewhat difficult. Timothy Paul Donovan, *Henry Adams and Brooks Adams: The Education of Two American Historians* (1961), is an illuminating examination of the brothers' ideas. Thornton Anderson, *Brooks Adams: Constructive Conservative* (1951), is probably the clearest exposition of Adams's thought.

Additional Sources

Beringause, Arthur F., *Brooks Adams: a biography*, New York: Octagon Books, 1979. □

Samuel Adams

The colonial leader Samuel Adams (1722-1803) helped prepare the ground for the American Revolution by inflammatory newspaper articles and shrewd organizational activities.

A fundamental change in British policy toward the American colonies occurred after 1763, ending a long period of imperial calm. As Great Britain attempted to tighten control over its colonies, Adams was quick to sense the change, and his invective writings at first irritated and finally outraged the Crown officials. As a prime mover in the nonmilitary phases of colonial resistance, Adams undoubtedly pushed more cautious men, such as John Hancock, into leading Whig roles. However, his service in the Continental Congress and as a state official lacked political finesse. Once the struggle shifted from a war of words to one of ideas and finally of military encounters, Adams's influence declined.

Samuel Adams was born on Sept. 27, 1722, in Boston, Mass., the son of a prosperous brewer and a pious, dogmatic mother. When he graduated from Harvard College in 1740, his ideas about a useful career were vague: he did not want to become a brewer, neither did work in the Church appeal to him. After a turn with the law, this field proved unrewarding too. A brief association in Thomas Cushing's firm led to an independent business venture which cost

Adams's family £1,000. Thus fate (or ill luck) forced Adams into the brewery; he operated his father's malt house for a livelihood but not as a dedicated businessman. In 1749 he married Elizabeth Checkley.

When his father suffered financial reverses, Adams accepted the offices of assessor and tax collector offered by the Boston freeholders; he held these positions from 1753 to 1765. His tax accounts were mismanaged and an £8,000 shortage appeared. There seems to have been no charge that he was corrupt, only grossly negligent. Adams was honest and later paid off the debts.

Adams's wife died in 1757 and in 1764 he married Elizabeth Wells, who was a good manager. His luck had changed, for he was about to move into a political circle that would offer personal opportunity unlike any in his past.

Growth in Politics

Adams became active in politics, and politics offered the breakthrough that transformed him from an inefficient taxgatherer into a leading patriot. As a member of the Caucus Club in 1764, he helped control local elections. When British policy on colonial revenues tightened during a recession in New England, passage of the Sugar Act in 1764 furnished Adams with enough fuel to kindle the first flames of colonial resistance. Thenceforth, he devoted his energies to creating a bonfire that would burn all connections between the Colonies and Great Britain. He also sought to discredit his local enemies—particularly the governor, Thomas Hutchinson.

Enforcement of the Sugar Act was counter to the interests of those Boston merchants who had accepted molasses smuggling as a way of life. They had not paid the old sixpence tax per gallon, and they did not intend to pay the new threepence levy. Urged on by his radical Caucus Club associates, Adams drafted a set of instructions to the colonial assemblymen that attacked the Sugar Act as an unreasonable law, contrary to the natural rights of each and every colonist because it had been levied without assent from a legally elected representative. The alarm "no taxation without representation" had been sounded.

Mature Propagandist

During the next decade Samuel Adams seemed a man destined for the times. His essays gave homespun, expedient political theories a patina of legal respectability. Eager printers hurried them into print under a variety of pseudonyms. Meanwhile Parliament unwittingly obliged men of Adams's bent by proceeding to pass an even more restrictive measure in the Stamp Act of 1765. Unlike the Sugar Act, this was not a measure that would be felt only in New England; Adams's audience widened as moderate merchants in American seaports now found more radical elements eager to force the issue of whether Parliament was still supreme "in all cases whatsoever." In one of many results, Governor Hutchinson's home was nearly destroyed by a frenzied anti-Stamp Act mob.

Adams's hammering essays and unceasing activities helped crystallize American opinion into viewing the Stamp Act as an odious piece of legislation. Through his columns in the *Boston Gazette,* he sent a stream of abuse against the British ministry; effigies of eminent Cabinet members hanged from Boston lampposts testified to the power of his incendiary prose. Adams rode a crest of popularity into the provincial assembly. As calm returned, he knew that the instruments of protest were developed and ready for use when the next opportunity showed itself.

The Townshend Acts of 1767 furnished Adams with a larger and more militant forum, projected his name into the front ranks of the patriot group, and earned him the hatred of the British general Thomas Gage and of King George III. Working with the Caucus Club, the radicals overcame local mercantile interests and demanded an economic boycott of British goods. This nonimportation scheme became a rallying point throughout the 13 colonies. Though its actual success was limited, Adams had proved that an organized, skillful minority could keep a larger but diffused group at bay. Adams worked with John Hancock to make seizure of the colonial ship *Liberty* seem a national calamity, and he welcomed the tension created by the stationing of British troops in Boston. Almost singlehandedly Adams continued his alarms, even after repeal of the Townshend duties.

In the succession of events from the Boston Massacre of 1770 to the Boston Tea Party and the Bill, Adams deftly threw Crown officials off guard, courted the radical elements, wrote dozens of inflammatory newspaper articles, and kept counsel with outspoken leaders in other colonies. In a sense, Adams was burning himself out so that, when the time for sober reflection and constructive political activity came, he had outlived his usefulness. By the time of the battles of Lexington and Concord in 1775, when he and Hancock were singled out as Americans not covered in any future amnesty, Adam's career as a propagandist and agitator had peaked.

Declining Power

Adams served in the Continental Congress between 1774 and 1781, but after the first session he occupied himself with gossip, uncertain as to what America's next steps should be or where he would fit into the scheme. He failed to perceive the forces loosed by the Revolution, and he was mystified by its results. While serving in the 1779 Massachusetts constitutional convention, he allowed his cousin John Adams to do most of the work. Tired of Hancock's vanity, he let their relationship cool; Hancock's repeated reelection as governor from 1780 on was a major disappointment. Against Daniel Shays's insurgents in 1786-1787, Adams shouted "conspiracy," showing little sympathy for the hard-pressed farmers.

As a delegate to the Massachusetts ratifying convention in 1788, Adams made a brief show as an old-time liberal pitted against the conservatives. But the death of his son weakened his spirit, and in the end he was intimidated by powerful Federalists. He was the lieutenant governor of Massachusetts from 1789 to 1793, when he became governor. As the candidate of the rising Jeffersonian Republicans, he was able to exploit the voter magnetism of the Adams name and was reelected for three terms. He did not seek reelection in 1797 but resisted the tide of New England federalism and remained loyal to Jefferson in 1800. He died in Boston on Oct. 2, 1803.

Further Reading

Harry Alonzo Cushing edited *The Writings of Samuel Adams* (1904-1908). Ralph V. Harlow, *Samuel Adams, Promoter of the American Revolution: A Study in Psychology and Politics* (1923), is a brave attempt at interpretive analysis. John C. Miller, *Sam Adams, Pioneer in Propaganda* (1936), is readable and reliable. An older standard work is William V. Wells, *The Life and Public Services of Samuel Adams* (1865). Stewart Beach, *Samuel Adams: The Fateful Years, 1764-1776* (1965), is a useful study. Philip Davidson, *Propaganda and the American Revolution, 1763-1783* (1941), and Arthur M. Schlesinger, Sr., *Prelude to Independence: The Newspaper War on Britain, 1764-1776* (1958), provide background information. □

Jane Addams

As social worker, reformer, and pacifist, Jane Addams (1860-1935) was the "beloved lady" of American reform. She founded the most famous settlement house in American history, Hull House in Chicago.

Jane Addams was born in Cedarville, Ill., on Sept. 6, 1860, the eighth child of a successful miller, banker, and landowner. She did not remember her mother, who died when Jane was 3 years old. She was devoted to and profoundly influenced by her father, an idealist and philanthropist of Quaker tendencies and a state senator of Illinois for 16 years.

Jane Addams attended Rockford Female Seminary in northern Illinois, from which she graduated in 1881. The curriculum was dominated by religion and the classics, but she developed an interest in the sciences and entered the Women's Medical College in Philadelphia. After 6 months, illness forced her to discontinue her studies permanently and undergo a spinal operation; she was never quite free of illness throughout her life.

Finding a Career

During a long convalescence Addams fell into a deep depression, partly because of her affliction but also because of her sensitivity to the lot of women of her station in 19th-century America. Although intelligent middle-class women were frequently well educated, as Jane Addams was, society dictated a life of ornamental uselessness for them as wives and mothers within a masculine-dominated home. During a leisurely tour in Europe between 1883 and 1885 and winters spent in Baltimore in 1886 and 1887, Addams sought solace in religion. Only after a second trip to Europe in 1887-1888, however, when she visited Toynbee Hall, the famous settlement house in London, did she find a satisfactory outlet for her talents and energies.

Toynbee Hall was a social and cultural center in the slums of London's East End; it was designed to introduce

young ministerial candidates to the world of England's urban poor. Jane Addams hit upon the idea of providing a similar opportunity for young middle-class American women, concluding "that it would be a good thing to rent a house in a part of the city where many primitive and actual needs are found, in which young women who had been given over too exclusively to study might restore a balance of activity along traditional lines and learn of life from life itself."

Creation of Hull House

Hull House, in one of Chicago's most poverty-stricken immigrant slums, was originally envisioned as a service to young women desiring more than a homemaker's life. But it soon developed into a great center for the poor of the neighborhood, providing a home for working girls, a theater, a boys' club, a day nursery, and numerous other services. Thousands visited it annually, and Hull House was the source of inspiration for dozens of similar settlement houses in other cities. Its success catapulted Jane Addams into national prominence. She became involved in an attempt to remedy Chicago's corrupt politics, served on a mediation commission in the Pullman railroad strike of 1894, supported the right of labor to organize, and spoke and wrote widely on virtually every reform issue of the day, from woman's suffrage to pacifism.

Jane Addams served as an officer for innumerable reform groups, including the Progressive party and the Women's International League for Peace and Freedom (of which she was president in 1915), and she attended international peace congresses in a dozen European cities. Her books cover wide-ranging subjects: prostitution and woman's rights (*A New Conscience and an Ancient Evil,* 1912, and *The Long Road of Woman's Memory,* 1916), juvenile delinquency (*The Spirit of Youth and the City Streets,* 1909), and militarism in America (*Newer ideals of peace,* 1906). She received honorary degrees from a half dozen American universities and was an informal adviser to several American presidents. She died on May 21, 1935.

Further Reading

Most of the biographies of Jane Addams are satisfactory. Her two autobiographical works are of great interest: *Twenty Years at Hull-House* (1910) and *The Second Twenty Years at Hull-House* (1930). *Jane Addams: A Centennial Reader* (1960) is the best book of selections from her writings and includes valuable introductions by other authors. John C. Farrell, *Beloved Lady: A History of Jane Addams' Ideas on Reform and Peace* (1967), provides a fascinating analysis of her ideas.

Additional Sources

Addams, Jane, *The social thought of Jane Addams,* New York, N.Y.: Irvington, 1982, 1965.
Hovde, Jane, *Jane Addams,* New York: Facts on File, 1989.
Levine, Daniel, *Jane Addams and the liberal tradition,* Westport, Conn.: Greenwood Press, 1980, 1971. □

Joseph Addison

The English essayist and politician Joseph Addison (1672-1719) founded the "Spectator" periodical with Sir Richard Steele.

Joseph Addison was born on May 1, 1672, the son of the rector of Milston, Wiltshire. He was educated at the Charterhouse, an important boarding school, and then at Oxford, where he received a bachelor's degree in 1691.

Addison used poetry to further his political ambitions; his earliest poems include flattering references to influential men. In 1699 Addison was rewarded with a grant of money which allowed him to make the grand tour, a series of visits to the main European capitals, which was a standard part of the education of the 18th-century gentleman. One record of his travels is his long poem *Letter from Italy.*

In 1703 Addison returned to England to find that the Whigs, the party with which he had allied himself, were out of power. But his poem on the Battle of Blenheim won him an appointment as commissioner of appeal in excise. Addison continued to combine literary with political success. He was elected to parliament in 1707, and in 1709 he went to Dublin as secretary to the lord lieutenant of Ireland. In 1710 he founded the *Whig Examiner* to counter the Tory views of the *Examiner,* a periodical managed by Jonathan Swift.

In 1709 Addison had begun to write for the *Tatler,* a magazine edited by his friend Sir Richard Steele; Addison contributed in all 42 essays. The last issue of this periodical was published in January 1711. Two months later, under the

Further Reading

The best biography of Addison is Peter Smithers, *The Life of Joseph Addison* (1954; 2d ed. 1968). Addison was much admired by the Victorians, and there is a long biographical essay in Thomas Babington Macaulay, *Essays: Critical and Miscellaneous* (1843). For a more recent view see Bonamy Dobrée, *Essays in Biography, 1680-1726* (1925). An invaluable guide to Addison's intellectual milieu is Alexandre Beljame, *Men of Letters and the English Public in the Eighteenth Century: 1660-1744* (1881; 2d ed. 1897; trans. 1948).

Additional Sources

Addison and Steele, the critical heritage, London; Boston: Routledge & K. Paul, 1980.

Otten, Robert M., *Joseph Addison,* Boston: Twayne Publishers, 1982. ☐

Thomas Addison

The English physician Thomas Addison (1793-1860), one of a famous group of physicians at Guy's Hospital, London, was the first to describe a disease of the endocrine glands and the type of anemia now known as Addison's disease.

Thomas Addison was born in April 1793 at Long Benton near Newcastle-upon-Tyne. His father, Joseph Addison, was a grocer and flour dealer. Thomas studied medicine at the University of Edinburgh and took his doctorate in medicine in 1815. He then held various posts in London hospitals, and in 1819 he was admitted a licentiate of the Royal College of Physicians of London. Although now a fully qualified physician, he entered as a student at Guy's Hospital about 1820. In 1824 he was appointed assistant physician to that hospital and in 1837 full physician. An acute clinical observer and a brilliant teacher, he did much to create the fame of the medical school at Guy's.

Addison's medical writings were not numerous but very important. In 1829, in collaboration with John Morgan, he published the first work on toxicology in English. Much of his work—including his important observations on pneumonia, pulmonary tuberculosis, and fatty liver—appeared in the *Guy's Hospital Reports.* He gave the first description of appendicitis in his and Richard Bright's *The Elements of the Practice of Medicine* (vol. 1, 1839), most of which was written by Addison.

In 1849 Addison read to a London medical society a paper on anemia with disease of the suprarenal bodies. This type of anemia was unlike the anemias then known (it was always fatal) and at autopsy Addison had sometimes found disease of the suprarenals. The paper passed unnoticed. After further investigation Addison published in 1855 his classic work *On the Constitutional and Local Effects of Disease of the Supra-renal Capsules,* in which he described Addisonian (pernicious) anemia and Addison's disease.

joint editorship of Addison and Steele, the first number of the *Spectator* appeared. Published every day, it ran for 555 numbers (the last issue appeared on Dec. 6, 1712). Although its circulation was small by modern standards, it was read by many important people and exercised a wide influence. Addison and Steele wrote 90 percent of the essays. Their purpose was, in their words, to bring "Philosophy out of Closets and Libraries, Schools and Colleges, to dwell in Clubs and Assemblies, at Tea-Tables, and in Coffee-Houses." Some of the essays are concerned with literary and philosophical questions; others comment on good manners and bad, life in the country and in the town. Addison and Steele invented characters who represent different types, notably the old-fashioned country gentleman, Sir Roger de Coverley.

In 1713 Addison wrote *Cato: A Tragedy,* a play in which he undertook to imitate and to improve upon classical Greek tragedy. The play was a success, probably because some of the audience took it to be a political allegory. Alexander Pope wrote the prologue, and Samuel Johnson later praised the play as Addison's noblest work.

In 1714 Queen Anne died, and Addison shared in the Whigs' rise to power. He was known as a temperate, conciliatory politician. In 1717 he was appointed secretary of state; he retired the next year with a generous pension. Addison died on June 17, 1719.

Addisonian Anemia

This disease is described in the short introduction to the book. He gave a general description of this anemia, on which he had been lecturing since 1843. It occurred in persons past middle age and was almost always fatal. As he did not know its cause, he called it "idiopathic anaemia."

Addison's clinical description of this anemia is, so far as it goes, a classic, and hence it is often called Addisonian anemia. But in his time little was known about the microscopical examination of the blood, and he therefore did not know about the characteristic blood picture. These and some other features were first described in 1872 by Anton Biermer of Zurich, who called the disease "pernicious anaemia." Outside the English-speaking world it is often called Biermer's anemia. The discovery in the period 1925-1930 of the cause of the disease and of satisfactory methods of treatment completely changed the outlook, and the term "pernicious" is now no longer appropriate.

Addison's Disease

The whole of the text of Addison's book is devoted to his description of a new disease characterized by "anaemia, general languor and debility, remarkable feebleness of the heart's action, irritability of the stomach, and a peculiar change of colour in the skin, occurring in connection with a diseased condition of the 'supra-renal capsules.'"The excellence of his clinical description of the disease, and its priority, has never been doubted, and his account of the peculiar bronze color of the skin is outstanding. He described 11 cases, with an autopsy in each. In each he found a lesion in the suprarenal glands, and three-quarters of these lesions were due to tuberculosis.

Before Addison wrote, nothing whatever was known about either the function or the diseases of the suprarenal glands, and his book makes clear that one of its main objects was to stimulate others to investigate their function. But important scientific investigations of these glands, leading to the discovery of adrenaline (epinephrine) and cortisone and other steroids, were not begun until the end of the 19th century. By 1855 no disease of any other endocrine gland had been discovered, and Addison was therefore the founder of clinical endocrinology.

Later Life

Addison's interests all centered in Guy's Hospital, and he paid little attention to private practice. In the late 1850s his health began to decline, and in the hope of effecting an improvement he resigned his hospital posts early in 1860 and moved to Brighton. He died there on June 29, 1860.

Further Reading

There is an excellent biography of Addison by Sir Samuel Wilks, his former pupil and successor at Guy's Hospital, in *A Collection of the Published Writings of the Late Thomas Addison, M.D.*, edited by Wilks and Daldy (1868). Some additional details are in W. Munk, *Roll of the Royal College of Physicians of London*, vol. 3 (1878). For a discussion of later work on the adrenals see C. Singer and E. A. Underwood, *A Short History of Medicine* (1962).

Additional Sources

Pallister, George., *Thomas Addison, M.D., F.R.C.P. (1795-1860)*, Newcastle upon Tyne: The Author, 1975. ☐

Konrad Adenauer

The German statesman Konrad Adenauer (1876-1967) was chancellor of the Federal Republic of Germany (West Germany) from 1949 to 1963.

A conservative, Francophile Rhinelander, Konrad Adenauer successfully presided over the creation of a Western-oriented German state after World War II. By providing an efficient political mechanism for German life, he aided the astonishing recovery of West Germany and its acceptance into the Western bloc during the cold war. As a statesman, he was often compared to the 19th-century German leader Otto von Bismarck. But while Bismarck led a largely Protestant, militarist, and aristocrat-dominated government, Adenauer shaped a heavily Catholic, civilian, business-dominated "half-Germany" firmly tied to the West.

Early Life

Konrad Adenauer was born in 1876 in Cologne, and his career was always closely connected with this city in the Rhineland region of Germany. Although his father was a Prussian soldier and minor civil servant, Adenauer shared the common ambivalence of the Rhinelanders to the Prussian-dominated German Empire.

Even as a young man, Adenauer was reserved, somewhat ascetic, and hardworking rather than brilliant in his studies. Severe thrift and the support of friends enabled him to study law at the universities of Freiburg im Breisgau, Munich, and Bonn. Adenauer then worked for an influential Cologne lawyer, who was the head of the local German Center party organization. (The German Center party had been formed by Catholics to protect their interests against the Protestant-dominated government.) Through hard work, ambition, and party contacts, Adenauer became an assistant to the lord mayor of Cologne in 1906. He soon became the equivalent of deputy mayor and finally lord mayor in 1917. During these years Adenauer had married and had three children.

Tenure as Lord Mayor

Adenauer faced many crises in his 16-year tenure as mayor. He successfully dampened the fires of revolution that swept Cologne at the end of World War I. After flirting with movements for a Rhenish state separate from Prussia (and possibly even Germany), Adenauer became noted as a strong representative of Rhineland interests against the central government in Berlin. As a leading member of the Center party, he was chairman of the upper house of the Prussian state legislature from 1920 to 1933.

drew up the political foundations for a new German republic composed of the British, American, and French occupation zones.

Tenure as Chancellor

When the first federal parliamentary elections in 1949 resulted in a victory for the CDU, Adenauer outmaneuvered his many adversaries to become the first chancellor. The decisive single vote which gave him a majority was his own. He was reelected in 1953, 1957, and 1961.

As chancellor, Adenauer was often criticized for behaving more autocratically than the Basic Law (constitution) of 1949 intended. He generally left economic matters in the hands of private enterprise and of Ludwig Erhard, his capable economics minister. Although Adenauer had never before held a diplomatic post, he developed great stature as a statesman. He served as his own foreign minister from 1951 to 1955. A Franco-German rapprochement and a strong tie to the United States formed the basis of Adenauer's European and world policies. Although opponents scornfully dubbed him the "chancellor of the Allies," Adenauer's negotiations with Germany's former enemies resulted in a plan of West European unity and prosperity which rivaled Charlemagne's empire in scope. From the early 1950s on, Adenauer offered to contribute to the European Defense Community and in 1954 to raise a new German army within NATO. Under his guidance West Germany became an active member of the Council of Europe, the West European Union, and the European Economic Community (European Union).

By the early 1960s Adenauer was an octogenarian and had come to be called *Der Alte* (the Old Man). He was increasingly out of touch with the new generation, liberal opinion, and the thaw in East-West relations. He resigned the chancellorship under heavy political pressure from his own party in 1963. When he died in 1967, his funeral occasioned an almost unprecedented foreign tribute to a German chancellor.

Further Reading

Adenauer's *Memoirs* (4 vols., 1965-1968; trans., vol. 1, 1966) is an important if not objective source. No fully adequate biography of Adenauer exists. Paul Weymar, *Adenauer* (1955; trans. 1957), suffers from being an "authorized" version of the Chancellor's life. Both Charles Wighton, *Adenauer: A Democratic Dictator* (1963), and Rudolf Augstein, *Konrad Adenauer* (1964; trans. 1964), tend to be hostile. For a good broad evaluation of Adenauer's role after 1945 see Richard Hiscocks, *The Adenauer Era* (1966). Arnold J. Heidenheimer, *Adenauer and the CDU: The Rise of the Leader and the Integration of the Party* (1960), treats domestic politics. Edgar Alexander, *Adenauer and the New Germany: The Chancellor of the Vanquished* (1956; trans. 1957), is a study of the man and his personality and an assessment of present-day political Germany. See also Gordon A. Craig, *From Bismarck to Adenauer: Aspects of German Statecraft* (1958; rev. ed. 1965), and Wolfram F. Hanrieder, *West German Foreign Policy, 1949-1963* (1967).

Additional Sources

Gotto, Klaus., *Konrad Adenauer,* Stuttgart: Bonn Aktuell, 1988.

Adenauer's life was not without dark sides. His first wife died during World War I, and he suffered severe facial injuries in an automobile accident which left him a victim of insomnia. In 1933 Adenauer, an opponent of Nazism, was driven from office by the new regime of Hitler. He was persecuted sporadically, and in 1934 and 1944 he was arrested by the Gestapo. On the latter occasion his second wife was mistreated and later died. Adenauer narrowly escaped being sent to the concentration camp at Buchenwald. But for the most part he spent the years from 1933 to the end of World War II quietly in his villa on the Rhine, cultivating his garden and avoiding politics.

West German State

When American troops seized Cologne, Adenauer was offered his old post of lord mayor. Although he was almost 70, his reputation as a good administrator untainted by Nazism gave him a political edge. Conflicts with the British occupation authorities late in 1945, however, led to Adenauer's dismissal. He then threw himself into reviving German Center party activities. He concurred with other former leaders of the party that it must broaden its base to include all faiths that supported democratic institutions. To achieve this end, he was a cofounder of a new political party—the Christian Democratic Union (CDU). With the backing of the Catholic Church and influential Cologne businessmen, Adenauer rapidly advanced from head of the local CDU (1945) to chairman of the party for the British Zone (1946) and finally for all of West Germany (1949). In 1948 he was elected president of the Parliamentary Council, a body that

Schwarz, Hans-Peter, *Konrad Adenauer: a German politician and statesman in a period of war, revolution, and reconstruction*, Providence, RI: Berghahn Books, 1995. ☐

Alfred Adler

The Austrian psychiatrist Alfred Adler (1870-1937) founded the school of individual psychology, a comprehensive "science of living." His system emphasizes the uniqueness of the individual and his relationships with society.

Although the psychiatrists Alfred Adler and Sigmund Freud (1856-1939) lived at the same time and in the same place, their views could hardly have been more opposite. Freud's theory of psychoanalysis was rapidly accepted and overshadowed Adler's individual psychology during their lifetimes. However, Freud's position has since been modified, largely by his own followers, and numerous new schools of psychology have emerged whose tenets are increasingly compatible with Adler's original position.

Alfred Adler was born in a suburb of Vienna, the second of seven children of a Hungarian-born grain merchant. In his childhood he suffered some illnesses and the death of a younger brother; these experiences contributed to his early decision to become a physician.

He attended classical secondary school and received a degree from the University of Vienna Medical School in 1895. He married Raissa Epstein, a Russian student.

Adler's early career was marked by a zeal for social reform, often expressed in articles in socialist newspapers. His first professional publication was a social-medicine monograph on the health of tailors.

In 1902 Freud invited Adler to join a small discussion group, which became the illustrious Vienna Psychoanalytic Society. Adler was an active member but did not consider himself a pupil or disciple of Freud. He could not agree with Freud's basic assumption that sex was the main determinant of personality, and all that this implied: the dominance of biological factors over the psychological; the push of drives, making for identical, predictable patterns; the part commanding the whole; pleasure-seeking as man's prime motivation. Whereas Freud tried to explain man in terms of his similarity to machines and animals, Adler sought to understand and influence man precisely in terms of what makes him different from machines and animals (concepts and values). This humanistic view characterized all the principles of his theory. Adler's views diverged ever more from those of Freud, and in 1911 he resigned from Freud's circle to formulate and found his own school.

Adler spent 3 years of World War I in military-hospital service. In 1919 he organized a child-guidance clinic in Vienna and also became a lecturer at the Pedagogical Institute. He was perhaps the first psychiatrist to apply mental hygiene in the schools. Working with teachers in child-

guidance clinics, he carried out his innovative counseling before a restricted audience and dealt with the family and teacher as well as the child. This was probably the first "family therapy" and "community psychiatry" on record.

Beginning in 1926, Adler spent much time in the United States lecturing and teaching. When he saw the Nazi threat to Austria in 1932, he emigrated with his wife to New York. On May 28, 1937, he died suddenly while on a lecture tour in Aberdeen, Scotland. Two of his four children, Alexandra and Kurt, took up the practice of psychiatry in their father's tradition in New York City.

Adler had piercing eyes, a soft voice, and a friendly manner. He spoke slowly, with occasional silences, in a conciliatory, persuading tone. He was unusually open to people and was very sociable and hospitable. He loved the arts, especially music, and had a fine voice and enjoyed singing. He was a tireless worker, leaving little time for sleep. In therapeutic relationships he had a gift for disarming gentleness, acceptance, and encouragement.

Adler's Theory

Individual psychology, though not easy to master, has the kind of simplicity which comes with concreteness, dealing as much as possible with what can be observed and as little as possible with what must be taken on faith. Thus it can be explained in everyday language and can readily be demonstrated on actual cases. It probably covers more aspects of the personality than any other theory in that it deals with the healthy as well as the abnormal, individual and group relations, and the physical and the psychological. Yet it hangs together with a marked self consistency because all the principles are interrelated. This cohesiveness reflects Adler's view of the person as an organism: a unit in which all the parts function cooperatively, even when differently, in subordination to an overall plan for the whole.

Goal-striving

Adler saw man imbued with a unitary dynamic force, a striving from below to above. Since this striving is an "intrinsic necessity of life itself, like physical growth," there is no need to infer a further source of energy for it. Adler described it as directed toward superiority, overcoming, perfection, success, significance—always as these are variously envisioned by each individual. In the goal is "the root of the personality." To understand the personality or any behavior, one must seek its purpose.

Self-determination

Adler found that an individual might respond to a perceived inferiority with greater or lesser inferiority feelings and with discouragement, compensation, or overcompensation. Thus the individual is not completely determined by objective factors. Within certain limitations, such subjective factors as interpretation and opinion are always decisive. Adler called this degree of self-determination man's creative power. It includes not only the ability to choose between several ways of regarding or reacting but also, more importantly, man's potential for spontaneity. Through it the individual arrives at his style of life.

Life Style

In spite of a certain unpredictability thus lent to all humans, there is a self-consistency in a person's actions which characterizes him uniquely. This "coherence and unity of the individual in all his expressions," as Adler expressed it, is his life style. From the beginning, the young child checks his impressions, successes, and failures against one another. Soon practical requirements of the environment are learned, perceptions become selective, practiced responses become habitual, value guidelines are set up, and "the child arrives at a style of life, in accordance with which we see him thinking, feeling, and acting throughout his whole life."

Social Ties

Adler's psychology has been judged the first in a social-science direction. "In addition to regarding an individual's life as a unity, we must also take it together with its context of social relations . . . [it] is not capable of doing just as it likes but is constantly confronted with tasks . . . inseparably tied up with the logic of man's communal life." Adler specified three main tasks of life: occupation, association with others, and love and marriage. He also referred to them as social ties, for they all require cooperation for their solution. Man's very uniqueness is influenced by his relations to others: "The style of the child's life cannot be understood without reference to the persons who look after him."

Social Interest

Adler also assumed an innate potentiality for coping with society, termed social interest. Unlike an instinct, it must be evoked and developed. Its subjective development is based in man's native empathy; the objective "development of the innate potentiality for cooperation occurs first in the relationship of the child and the mother." Social interest represents a transcendence of the self, an absence of self-centeredness. It is a trait, like intelligence, and as such influences the direction of the striving, but it is the most important trait in the life style.

Adler stated unequivocally that social interest is the criterion of mental health. He based this finding solely on his observations as a psychiatrist that mentally healthy persons "feel at home on this earth with all its advantages and disadvantages, and act as true fellowmen"; that is, they demonstrate a developed social interest.

The "failures in life"—the neurotics, psychotics, and offenders—on the other hand, are characterized by intense inferiority feelings that keep them continuously concerned with themselves, or self-bound. They may become convinced of their inability to cope with life (the much-cited inferiority complex) or may strive for a personal goal of superiority, useful or meaningful to themselves only, in accordance with their private sense rather than common sense. They have most often developed a pampered life style in that they expect to receive without giving. Normality in these terms is tantamount to maturity, which involves growing away from helplessness toward taking responsibility for others, becoming an asset rather than a burden.

Therapist and Patient

The therapist's function, according to Adler, is not to treat "mental disease" but to divine the error in the patient's way of life and lead him to greater maturity. To this end Adler introduced a number of diagnostic approaches. Among these, his theory of dreams, the meaning of early childhood recollections, and the role of birth order in the family have become widely known and adopted. The understanding of the patient achieved in this way is not one of depth but of context in the larger whole of his total transactions. This is the basis for changing the patient's picture of himself and the world. In addition to this reorganization, Adler wished the patient to appreciate his own power of self-determination and have the courage to exercise it. To encourage the patient, the therapist must express a disinterested concern that evokes and fosters feelings of trust and fellowship—fulfilling a function at which the mother had failed.

Further Reading

The comprehensive source book for Adler is *The Individual Psychology of Alfred Adler,* edited by H.L. and Rowena R. Ansbacher (1956), which is a selection of Adler's own writings and is intended as a textbook on individual psychology. *Alfred Adler: Superiority and Social Interest: A Collection of Later Writings,* also edited by the Ansbachers (1964), includes a paper on religion and several case studies. Two standard biographies of Adler are Phyllis Bottome, *Alfred Adler: Apos-*

tle of Freedom (1939; rev. ed. 1957), and Hertha Orgler, Alfred Adler, the Man and His Work: Triumph over the Inferiority Complex (1939; 3d ed. 1963). Ruth L. Munroe, Schools of Psychoanalytic Thought: An Exposition, Critique and Attempt at Integration (1955), is a general consideration of psychoanalytic theory.

Additional Sources

Alfred Adler, as we remember him, Chicago: North American Society of Adlerian Psychology, 1977.

Hoffman, Edward, The drive for self: Alfred Adler and the founding of individual psychology, Reading, Mass.: Addison-Wesley Pub. Co., 1994.

We knew Alfred Adler, London: Adlerian Society of Great Britain, 1977. □

Felix Adler

Felix Adler (1851-1933), American educator and social reformer, was one of the creators of the Society for Ethical Culture, a liberal religious movement in the United States and Europe. The motto of the society was "Deed not creed."

Felix Adler was born on Aug. 13, 1851, at Alzey in the Rhineland, Germany. He was the son of a rabbi. The family emigrated to the United States when Felix was 6. Adler graduated from Columbia College, New York, with highest honors in 1870. He prepared for the rabbinate in Berlin and Heidelberg, receiving a doctorate summa cum laude from the latter university in 1873. His exposure to biblical criticism, however, and growing concern with earthly human problems led him to renounce his rabbinical office upon his return to America. He soon became affiliated with the Free Religious Association, a group whose transcendentalist leanings had attracted the aging Ralph Waldo Emerson, and ultimately Adler succeeded the association's founder, Octavius Frothingham, as president. But in 1876 Adler and his friends formed a new group, the Society for Ethical Culture.

The Ethical Culture movement, which eventually spread abroad to London, Berlin, and Vienna, became Adler's main enthusiasm. His major writings expressed the society's philosophy: Creed and Deed (1877), The Religion of Duty (1905), An Ethical Philosophy of Life Presented in Its Main Outlines (1918), and The Reconstruction of the Spiritual Ideal (1924). Drawing upon Immanuel Kant's moral imperative (which stated that a man must treat his fellowmen as ends in themselves, not means), Adler contended that each man achieves individual excellency only through involvement in experiences which develop the excellencies of other men. Adler believed that a man's deeds, rather than his religious creed, are the essence of the religious life. The philosophy of Ethical Culture drew upon Judaism, Christianity, Emersonian transcendentalism, and socialism.

Adler lived according to his philosophy. Involved in education, he founded the free Workingmen's School in 1880 and other progressive schools and took part in projects leading to the establishment of the Child Study Association in 1907. In social work he participated in innovations in district nursing, cooperative workshops, settlement houses, and political reform clubs. He also served on governmental committees concerned with slum housing, vice, and child labor. From 1902 to 1933 Adler was professor of social and political ethics at Columbia University.

Adler married Helen Goldmark in 1880; they had five children. On April 24, 1933, after a short illness, Felix Adler died. A dedicated reformer who sought to advance ethics as the basis for human and social fulfillment independent of theism, he succeeded in inspiring a movement which has carried on his devotion to ethics in action.

Further Reading

Part 1 of Adler's An Ethical Philosophy of Life Presented in Its Main Outlines (1918) is autobiographical. Material may also be found in The Fiftieth Anniversary of the Ethical Movement, 1876-1926 (1926); Horace J. Bridges, ed., Aspects of Ethical Religion: Essays in Honor of Felix Adler (1926); and Henry Neumann, Spokesmen for Ethical Religion (1951). David Saville Muzzey, the noted historian, includes a brief sketch of Adler in Ethics as a Religion (1951).

Additional Sources

Friess, Horace Leland, Felix Adler and ethical culture: memories and studies, New York: Columbia University Press, 1981.

Guttchen, Robert S., *Felix Adler,* New York: Twayne Publishers 1974.

Kraut, Benny, *From Reform Judaism to ethical culture: the religious evolution of Felix Adler,* Cincinnati: Hebrew Union College Press, 1979. □

Adonis

Adonis, born Ali Ahmad Said in 1930, was a Lebanese poet whose work reflected a radical vision of Arab history and culture, as well as a hunger for change and modernity.

Adonis is the pen name of Ali Ahmad Said, one of the most prominent Arab writers in the post-World War II period. Born in January of 1930 in Qassabin, a small mountain village in western Syria close to the Mediterranean, he studied at Damascus University, receiving his Licence es-Lettres, Philosophy in 1954. After a six-month spell of imprisonment in Syria in 1955 because of his political activities and membership in the Syrian National Socialist Party, he escaped to Lebanon to settle there in 1956, becoming a Lebanese national.

In 1960-1961, at a crucial stage in his intellectual development, he received a scholarship which enabled him to study in Paris. Adonis wrote extensively during this time. His poetry represented an attempt to create a fusion of his early influences, as he tried also to give poetic expression to his political and social beliefs. These urgings included the quest for national identity and the powerful drive to achieve the "great leap forward" of Arab society.

In 1957, at a significant point in the development of what was called the New Poetry, he joined another poet, Yusuf al-Khal, in founding the avant-garde journal *Shi'r* (*Poetry*), which was destined to play a major role in the development of Arabic poetry. In 1968 he established the equally influential, but more culturally and politically oriented journal *Mawaqif* (*Situations*), which became the avant-garde literary magazine in the Arab world.

From 1970 to 1985 Adonis was a professor of Arabic literature at the Lebanese University. He was deeply affected by the 10 years of horror during the Lebanese civil war, as reflected in his writings. In 1973, he obtained his Doctorat d'Etat at St. Joseph University in Beirut. In 1976 he held a visiting professorship at Damascus University, and in 1980-1981 he was a professor of Arabic at the Sorbonne in Paris. In 1985 he taught for a semester at Georgetown University in the United States. He also taught at the prestigious academic institution College de France, where he lectured on Arabic poetics. He later held a professorship at the University of Geneva, where he lectured on Arabic poetry.

Adonis's youthful years coincided with the years of upheaval, revolutionary fever, struggle against colonialism, and search for modernization and revival throughout the Arab world. The achievements of such figures as Kahlil Gibran (author of *The Prophet*) had contributed significantly to the burgeoning of a new sensibility, a fresh poetic language, and new imagery and rhythmic structures. Adonis's formative years had been strongly influenced by this new trend, as well as by his readings in European poetry. Yet he had also been educated in the classical traditions of Arabic poetry by his father, a man well steeped in classical culture and Islamic theology.

In this intense atmosphere of search, lust for change, and political upheavals (particularly after the struggle for Palestine and the foundation of Israel in 1948), the New Poetry began to explode, taking the form first of a rebellion against the prosodic and rhythmic system of organization which had dominated Arabic poetry from its earliest days. What became known as *al-shi'r al-hurr* (roughly, free verse) came into being, and Adonis's role in the evolution of this mode of writing was crucial.

The turning point in Adonis's work came with *The Songs of Mihyar the Damascene,* published in 1961, in which he seemed to discover the secrets of creating a balance between the social-political role assigned to poetry and the demands of a subtle, esthetically appealing, and symbolic language of absence. Adonis's poetry became richer, more dramatic, multi-voiced, more complex, and far more experimental, especially on the level of language and structure. But in the view of many, it never managed to surpass the songs of the magical *Mihyar.*

The most complex of his works, his 400-page *Mufrad bi-Sighat al-Jam'* (*Singular in the Plural Form;* 1977), is a dazzling piece of writing, but one which has remained a closed, esoteric world to the majority of readers.

Adonis is both a poet and a theorist on poetry, as well as a thinker with a radical vision of Arab history and culture. This philosophy is embodied at its most provocative stage in his major work, *al-Thabit wa al-Mutahawwil* (*The Static and the Changing*), a study of conventionalism and innovation in Arabic culture. Adonis has exerted a powerful influence on thinking about poetry, creativity, change, and modernism among both his contemporaries and the younger generations of Arab poets.

His name has become synonymous with rebellion, rejection, radical writing, and modernism (expressed in Arabic by the word *hadatha*), which he, more than any other figure, has labored to define, preach, and provide with a powerful poetic embodiment. Such books as his *Zaman al-Shi'r* (*The Time of Poetry*) and *Sadmat al-Hadatha* (*The Shock of Modernity*) are landmarks in the history of critical contemplation in the Arab world.

Well acquainted with the Western literary traditions, especially in poetry, Adonis produced some fine and influential translations of European, and especially French, poetry. Of particular importance are his translations—or more accurately, perhaps, his Arabic renderings—of the complete poetical works of St. John Perse and the dramatic works of the French poet of Lebanese origin Georges Schehadeh.

Some of Adonis's later poetry lost much of the abstractness and cerebrality of the works he produced in the

1970s. It also lost much of the lyricism and tone of yearning of his poetry in the 1960s. He displayed a new fondness for what may be called *the poetry of place,* in contrast to *the poetry of time* that had dominated his previous work.

In 1985, Adonis wrote a provocative book of literary criticism, *Al Shi riyya Al-Arabiyya* (*Arabic Poetics*), which was published in Beirut. Adonis focused on the "dual siege" of the Arab writer, who is caught between Western thought and Islamic traditions. In 1990, Adonis wrote *Introduction to Arab Poetics,* published by the University of Texas.

In 1994, his book *The Pages of Day and Night* (translated by Samuel Hazo) was released, and it received widespread acclaim. Many of the poems had a distinct aura of mystical timelessness to them. The works included lyrical, fantastical, and revelatory writings.

In Adonis's long writing career, he has twice been nominated for a Nobel Prize, and has published more than 20 books.

Further Reading

Additional information on Adonis can be found in *Adonis, Ali Ahmad Sa'id* (1983), which also includes a small selection of Adonis's poems; Abdulla al-Udhari (editor), *Victims of a Map* (London: 1985); Issa Boullata (editor), *Modern Arab Poets 1950-1975* (1976); Salma al-Khadra al-Jayyusi (editor), *Modern Arabic Poetry: An Anthology* (1988); and Kamal Abu-Deeb, "The Perplexity of the All-Knowing," in *Mundus Artium* (1977).

Adonis' writings in English translation include *The Blood of Adonis,* selected and translated by Samuel Hazo (1971); *Mirrors,* translated by Abdullah al-Udhari (London: 1976); *Transformations of the Lover,* translated by Samuel Hazo (1983); *Orbits of Quest and Desire,* selected and translated by Kamal Abu-Deeb (1992); and *An Introduction to Arab Poetics,* translated by Catherine Cobham (1990). A number of translations into other European languages, especially French, are also available. □

Theodor W. Adorno

Retaining his intellectual roots in Hegel and Marx, the German philosopher Theodor W. Adorno (1903-1969) moved freely across diverse academic disciplines to probe into the nature of contemporary European culture and the predicament of modern man. He was a leading member of the influential intellectual movement known as the Frankfurt School.

Theodor W. Adorno was born in Frankfurt-am-Main, Germany, on September 11, 1903, as the only son of an upper middle class family. His father, Oskar Wiesengrund, was an assimilated Jewish merchant, and his mother, Maria Calvalli-Adorno, was a musically gifted person of Italian-Catholic descent. He adopted his mother's patronomic Adorno in the late 1930s.

An economically secure and artistically rich home environment were conducive to the development of his talents in both music and the humanities. While attending a gymnasium in Frankfurt, he was encouraged by his mother to take piano lessons. His mastery of the skills of piano playing deepened and sustained his interest in the philosophical as well as technical aspects of music.

At 17 Adorno enrolled at the Frankfurt University. Although his chief interest was in philosophy, he took courses in psychology, sociology, and music, and wrote a dissertation on Husserl's phenomenology. Impressed by the power and novelty of *Wozzeck,* Alban Berg's opera, Adorno decided to undertake a serious study of music. The two years that Adorno spent in Vienna among a group of innovative composers including Berg and Arnold Schoenberg provided him with a first-hand professional knowledge of contemporary music and led him even to attempt musical composition. But his gift was manifested in his consideration of the nature and genesis of the modern music, especially the atonal system of Schoenberg. In a number of articles Adorno propounded the view that Schoenberg had discarded the tonality which was bound up with the bourgeois phase of cultural development and therefore was not a universal or perennial form of music.

Upon his return to Frankfurt in 1925 Adorno wrote a *Habilitationsschrift,* the writing which qualifies a person for university appointment, dealing with the philosophical and psychological issues of that time in Germany. It was not approved. He was successful, however, with a writing on Soren Kierkegaard, sponsored by the theologian Paul Tillich. The chief contention of his *Habilitationsschrift* was that Kierkegaard, having rejected Georg Hegel's grandiose sys-

tematization of philosophy, retreated into pure subjectivity of his soul unhinged from the concrete social reality.

Adorno became associated with the Institute for Social Research, which was established in 1923 as an affiliated body of the Frankfurt, but it was personal rather than formal because of his youth and student status. It was Max Horkheimer, eight years Adorno's senior, who introduced Adorno to other senior scholars there who were embarked on a variety of projects aimed at determining the social conditions of Europe. Although Marxist and progressive in outlook, the researchers at the Institute were concerned with intellectual work rather than direct political action. Together they constituted what came to be known as the Frankfurt School credited with the creation of the Critical Theory.

Adorno began teaching philosophy at his alma mater in 1931 but the seizure of political power by Hitler disrupted his academic career and eventually forced him into exile. He took refuge first at Oxford, England, between 1934 and 1937 and thereafter in the United States until his return to Germany in 1949 to resume teaching at the Frankfurt University. The sufferings of the Jews and the crimes of the Third Reich became two of the major concerns in his philosophical reflections to the end of his life.

Early Writing Career

Adorno's association with the Institute was marked by the inclusion of his article entitled "The Social Condition of Music" in the first issue of the Institute's official journal in 1932. His article entitled "Jazz" in the same journal in 1936 revealed his life-long prejudice against that form of music which he argued was devoid of any aesthetic value.

Of more lasting value is his article on "The Fetish Character of Music and the Regression of the Listeners" in the 1936 issue of the Institute's journal. Here Adorno makes the observation that the commercially oriented music industry manipulates the musical tastes of the listeners by seductive psychological methods. He points out how helplessly the listeners are seduced into accepting the arbitrary cuts and interruptions in radio broadcasting. He maintains that such cuts are made for commercial gains and at the expense of the integrity of the original composition and performance and in utter disregard for the intelligence of the listeners. This article is valuable because it contains his lines of arguments against the culture industry to be developed more fully in his later writings.

During his stay in the United States between 1937 and 1949 Adorno was engaged in a number of projects which the members of the Institute for Social Research conducted individually or collectively. Although Adorno was disappointed by the quantitative analysis of cultural phenomena which he undertook at Princeton, he played a leading role in a large collaborative project which resulted in the publication of the influential book *Authoritarian Personality*.

Toward the end of the war Adorno and Horkheimer wrote *Dialectic of Enlightenment* published in Amsterdam in 1947. Defining enlightenment as demythologizing, the authors trace the process of taming of nature in Western civilization. The main thrust of the argument is that in the name of enlightenment a technological civilization which sets humans apart from nature has been developed and that such a civilization has become a cause of dehumanization and regimentation in modern society. They contend that the notion of reason is accepted in that civilization mainly in the sense of instrument for controlling nature, and subsequently people, rather than in the sense of enhancing human dignity and originality. In the new edition of the book published in 1969, shortly before Adorno's death, the authors declare that the enlightenment led to positivism and the identification of intelligence with what is hostile to spirit (Geistfeindschaft).

Return to Germany

After World War II many members of the Frankfort School remained in the United States or in Great Britain, but Horkheimer and Adorno returned to Germany. They were expected to provide intellectual leadership for postwar Germany. Horkheimer accepted the position of the Rector of the Frankfurt University and invited Adorno to join him. Adorno returned to Germany in 1949 although he spent a year in the United States in 1952.

Adorno lived up to what was expected of him by pouring out articles and books and by training a new generation of German scholars. His writings, voluminous as they were, however, did not contain many innovative ideas but rather restatement, in more elaborate forms and in a somewhat extravagant writing style, of the ideas which he had presented in his previous articles and books. But the true extent of his originality cannot be determined until the projected 23 volumes of his complete works are available.

In 1951 he published *Minima Moralia: Reflections from Damaged Life* consisting of articles which he wrote during the war. The most personal of his writings, the short essays in this book were written in an aphoristic style reminiscent of Arthur Schopenhauer and Friedrick Nietzsche. The purpose of the book is to examine how "objective forces" determine even the most intimate and immediate experience of an individual in contemporary society.

The *Negative Dialectics,* published in 1966, is a sustained polemic against the dream of philosophers from Aristotle to Hegel to construct philosophical systems enclosing coherently arranged propositions and proofs. One of the most terse statements in the book is "Bluntly put, closed systems are bound to fail." As this statement indicates, his aim in this book is to vindicate the vitality and intractability of reason.

Prisms, another major work published in 1967, contains essays on a wide range of topics from Thorstein Veblen to Franz Kafka. However, the main theme running throughout the book is the gradual decomposition of culture under the impact of instrumental reason. In this book and in *Aesthetic Theory,* his last major work unfinished at the time of his death in 1969 but edited and published posthumously, Adorno advances the thesis that the integrity of creative works lies in the autonomous acts of the artists who are at once submerged under and yet triumphant over social forces.

A persistent critic of positivism in philosophy and sociology and a bitter foe of commercialism and dehumanization promoted by the culture industry, Adorno championed individual dignity and creativity in an age increasingly menaced by what he regarded as mindless standardization and abject conformity. At a time when many academic philosophers were weary of dealing with large questions for fear of violating the canon of rigorous philosophical reasoning, Adorno boldly asserted that the function of philosophy is to make sense out of the totality of human experience.

Adorno, who was hailed as one of the ideological godfathers of the New Left Movement in the 1960s because of his indictment of both capitalism and communism, was criticized and humiliated by his former followers for his opposition to violent social activism. He was once forced out of his lecture room by female students at the Frankfurt University.

Further Reading

Theodor Adorno has the reputation of being one of the most obscure writers of this century. Virtually all of his translators into English seek the readers' forbearance for the inadequacy of their translations. The Suhrkamp Verlag, a German publisher, has embarked on the publication of his complete works in 23 volumes under the editorship of Rolf Tiedemann. David Held, *Introduction to Critical Theory: Horkheimer to Habermas* (1980) and Martin Jay, *The Dialectical Imagination: A History of the Frankfurt School and the Institute of Social Research, 1923-1950* (1973) are useful guides to the Frankfurt School and contain valuable information on Adorno's role in the movement. Martin Jay, *Adorno* (1984) contains a brief biography of Adorno followed by expositions of his major ideas. Friedemann Grenz, *Adornos Philosophie in Grundbegriffen* (Suhrkamp Verlag, 1974) offers a clear and authoritative interpretation of Adorno's philosophy.

Additional Sources

Hohendahl, Peter Uwe, *Prismatic thought: Theodor W. Adorno,* Lincoln: University of Nebraska Press, 1995.

Jay, Martin, *Adorno,* Cambridge, Mass.: Harvard University Press, 1984.

Reijen, Willem van, *Adorno: an introduction,* Philadelphia: Pennbridge Books, 1992. □

Edgar Douglas Adrian

The English neurophysiologist Edgar Douglas Adrian, 1st Baron Adrian of Cambridge (born 1889), shared the Nobel Prize for Physiology or Medicine with Sir Charles Sherrington for their discoveries regarding the functions of neurons.

Edgar Douglas Adrian, born in London on Nov. 30, 1889, was the second son of A. D. Adrian, legal adviser to the Local Government Board. He entered Trinity College, Cambridge, in 1908 and graduated with honors in the natural sciences in 1911. He then embarked

on research in physiology, and in 1913 he was elected a fellow of Trinity. Thereafter he took his clinical courses at St. Bartholomew's Hospital, London, and he graduated in medicine at Cambridge in 1915. During the remainder of World War I he studied service men suffering from nerve injuries and nervous diseases, and after the war he lectured on the nervous system at Cambridge. There he was Foulerton research professor of the Royal Society from 1929 until 1937, when he became professor of physiology in Cambridge University.

Early Researches on Single Nerve Fibers

Much experimental work during the 19th and early 20th centuries had shown that, when an isolated motor nerve was stimulated electrically, the resulting nerve impulse not only caused contraction of the muscle associated with that nerve but was accompanied by a change of electric potential (the action current) at the active point of the nerve. This current passed along the nerve at great speed. It was sufficiently strong to be measured by a very delicate capillary electrometer, and the oscillations produced in the mercury level could be recorded by photography on a moving strip of paper. At any point on the nerve the activity lasted for only a few thousandths of a second, and that point became temporarily refractory to further stimulation as soon as the impulse had passed it. In 1909 Keith Lucas proved the important "all-or-none" principle in muscle, that is, in a motor nerve. This principle implied that, in a nerve fibril, a stimulus just strong enough to cause a contraction in the muscle fibers which it supplied produced a maximum con-

traction in these fibers. In a motor nerve an increase in the stimulus acted by bringing more nerve fibers into action.

By the early 1920s practically all the work in this field had been done on motor nerves because the instruments then available were not sufficiently sensitive to detect the extremely minute impulses produced by the stimulation of sensory nerves. Adrian had been a pupil of Keith Lucas, and before the war, while he was Lucas's assistant, they had discussed the possibility of amplifying the minute currents in sensory nerves and of sensitive methods for recording them. Lucas died in an airplane accident in 1916, and when Adrian returned to Cambridge after the war he began experiments on the lines previously discussed with Lucas. By 1927, using a three-or four-valve amplifier, he had attained a 5000 amplification. By varying the tension in a frog's muscle Adrian showed that the "all-or-none" principle applies also to sensory nerves. But he soon found that his results were influenced by the fact that even the smallest sensory nerves receive impulses from many end organs. It was therefore necessary to study the reactions in single nerve fibers.

The reactions in a single nerve fiber were first demonstrated in 1926 by Adrian, working at Cambridge with a Swedish collaborator. In a frog muscle they were able to dissect out a strip containing a single muscle spindle attached to a single nerve fiber. When this muscle spindle was stimulated by stretching the muscle strip, they obtained a regular series of responses at intervals of 0.03 second. Adrian also found that in all the sense organs that give a prolonged discharge under a constant stimulus—such as muscle spindles and tactile endings—the record shows a rhythmic series of impulses, their frequency depending on the rate of development of the stimulus and on its intensity. In the case of a muscle spindle the frequency therefore depends on the extent and rapidity of the stretch. The stimulus acts as a trigger to release a nerve impulse. The total activity of a fiber can be increased by increasing the frequency of the impulses produced, but not by increasing the strength of the stimulus. The message in a nerve fiber can therefore be varied only by changing the frequency and duration of the discharge.

These experiments also showed that nerves possess the power of adaptation. A steady current passed through a frog muscle produced only one impulse, owing to the very rapid adaptation of the nerve. But steady tension on a muscle spindle, in which adaptation is very slow, produces a succession of impulses in the nerve fiber.

Adrian then turned to the sequence of events in sensory end organs in general. By 1928 he had shown that, in the case of pressure on the skin, the frequency of the impulses varied with the rate of increase of pressure and declined when the pressure remained constant. But when an object touches the skin, there is at that moment a sudden and rapid outburst of impulses, after which the impulses cease. In the case of pain he was unable to obtain clear-cut results or to confirm that pain is due to impulses in specific pain fibers. It seemed possible that pain might be due to very slow impulses.

Activity of Nerve Cells

In 1931 Adrian began to study impulses arising automatically in the brain, for example, in the cells of the respiratory center. In the isolated brain of a goldfish he found the impulses had a regular frequency of 20 to 60 a minute, corresponding in frequency with the gill movements of an intact fish. In an attempt to reduce the number of nerve cells concerned in the reactions, he next investigated the persistent activity that occurs in excised portions of the central ganglia of the water beetle *Dytiscus,* in which the activity shows the characteristic rhythm of the respiration in that insect. He concluded that the activity of nerve cells is probably due to a slow depolarization of the cell body or its dendrites. The active state in a group of nerve cells implies a surface change like that in the nerve fiber, but, contrary to the momentary change in the nerve fiber, it can persist for long periods and vary in intensity.

It was for the researches described up to this point that Adrian shared the Nobel Prize in 1932.

Rhythm of the Higher Centers

In 1929 Hans Berger discovered that, if electrodes were applied to the head of a conscious subject, a rhythmic disturbance having a frequency of about 10 per second could be recorded. These waves—Berger's alpha rhythm—were often present when the eyes were closed but disappeared when they were opened. The tracing recording the waves was called an electroencephalogram (EEG). About 1934, and later, Adrian studied these waves thoroughly and greatly extended their usefulness in conditions such as epilepsy. He showed that the rhythm occurs essentially in an inattentive subject. If the subject's eyes, when open, gaze at a uniform screen or are covered by glasses that blur the vision, the rhythm decreases only slightly. Adrian found that the waves were produced in a large area of the occipital and parietal regions of the cortex. He also found that, if the subject looked at a screen illuminated by a light flickering at, say, 18 flickers a second, the brain rhythm kept pace with the rate of flicker. In 1934 he also showed that the cerebellum has a spontaneous rhythm of very high frequency waves (150 to 250 per second).

Special Senses and Cortical Representation

A cat, when dropped in any position from a height, always lands on its feet owing to positional impulses received by the vestibular nucleus in the hindbrain. During the war Adrian found that this nucleus reacted to two different kinds of responses, and he studied variations in them induced by changes in the position of the body. In 1943 he studied the impulses received by the cerebellum of a monkey when various parts of its body were moved passively, and he was able to define the different areas in the cerebellum associated respectively with the forelimb, the hindlimb, and the face region.

In 1943 Adrian also studied the relative sizes of the sensory receiving areas of the cerebral cortex connected with different parts of the body in various animals. He found that the size of an area depended on the importance of the information received by it. In humans, the fingers, important in exploring the environment, received generous representation. In the cat the emphasis is on the forelimb, and in the pig the whole of the receiving area appears to be devoted to the snout. In 1946 Adrian found that in the pony and sheep the area devoted to the nostrils is as large as that for the whole of the rest of the body.

Adrian's last writings on neurophysiology (1950-1956) dealt with the olfactory sense. The primary olfactory fibers are so short and thin that it was not possible to record from them, but he obtained records from the olfactory bulb. Deep anesthesia suppressed the spontaneous discharges from the olfactory bulb, and records were then made of the discharges produced by the animal inhaling various odoriferous substances. In the cat he distinguished three different types of discharge, associated respectively with ethereal, oily, and fishy odors. He also obtained important evidence of a process of adaptation in the olfactory nerves.

Later Life

In 1951 Adrian retired from his chair and became Master of Trinity College, Cambridge, an office which he held until 1965. He was vice-chancellor of the University of Cambridge from 1957 to 1959 and chancellor from 1968. He was also the first chancellor of the University of Leicester. In 1942 he was appointed to the Order of Merit, and in 1955 he was created 1st Baron Adrian of Cambridge.

Adrian was the recipient of many honors in addition to his Nobel Prize. In 1923 he was elected a Fellow of the Royal Society. He was its Croonian Lecturer in 1931 and its Ferrier Lecturer in 1938; he received its Royal Medal in 1934 and its Copley Medal—its highest award—in 1946. He served as its Foreign Secretary from 1946 to 1950, and he was president of the society from 1950 to 1955. In 1924 he was elected a Fellow of the Royal College of Physicians of London, and he received several honors in that college. He was president of the Royal Society of Medicine in 1960-1962, and he was awarded that society's Gold Medal in 1950. From 1962 to 1965 he was a trustee of the Rockefeller Institute. He was an honorary fellow of many foreign learned societies, and he received honorary degrees from 33 universities throughout the world.

Throughout his career Adrian wrote numerous scientific articles and published three books, each of which marks a stage in his researches: *The Basis of Sensation* (1928), *The Mechanism of Nervous Action* (1932), and *The Physical Background of Perception* (1947).

On August 4, 1977, Adrian died in London, England. Although he retired from Cambridge in 1965, he continued to live at the college almost until his death. Throughout his life, Adrian was active, enjoying sports such as mountain climbing, fencing, sailing, and bicycle riding. Adrian also took a keen interest in the arts, and particularly enjoyed painting, even meriting an exhibition of 80 of his works at Cambridge.

Further Reading

A short biography of Lord Adrian will be found in *Nobel Lectures, Physiology or Medicine, 1922-1941* (1965). This work also contains his Nobel Lecture, which summarizes his earlier work, mainly on single nerve fibers and the end organs. There is a brief discussion of Adrian's work in general in C. Singer and E. A. Underwood, *A Short History of Medicine* (1962); and a few extracts from his writings are given in E. Clarke and C. D. O'Malley, *The Human Brain and Spinal Cord* (1968). Reference may also be made to J. F. Fulton, *Physiology of the Nervous System* (1949). Later biographical material appears in *Notable Twentieth-Century Scientists,* Volume I (Detroit: Gale, 1995) and *Nobel Laureates in Medicine or Physiology* (1990), edited by Daniel Fox, Marcia Meldrum, and Ira Rezak. □

Aelfric

The Anglo-Saxon monk Aelfric (955-ca. 1012) was a scholar and writer. His works, especially his collections of sermons, are stylistically the most accomplished in Old English. They were designed to explain Christianity to his fellow citizens in an organized fashion.

Aelfric was born near Winchester, England. His youthful studies at Winchester coincided with the revival of Benedictine monasticism in England. To this movement he contributed varied writings which preserved, translated, and disseminated the Christian tradition. Aelfric was undoubtedly influenced in his task by the recent example of King Alfred, who wished to make the learning of the past available to his subjects in the vernacular instead of Latin.

The chronology of Aelfric's works is not absolutely certain, but soon after he became a monk at Cerne Abbas, Dorset, in 987, he began producing texts explaining Christianity's message and history. He wrote his first series of 40 Catholic homilies in 989 and his second series in 992. These two collections explained the Gospel as it was read to the faithful every Sunday and on feast days; they utilized the critical interpretations of Saints Augustine, Ambrose, Jerome, and Bede and were theologically conservative in aim and outlook. Their prose is rhetorically brilliant yet always clear. In the second series Aelfric introduced such refinements as heavy alliteration, balanced clauses, and a rhythmic sentence ending, or cursus. For these innovations he drew on both ornamented Latin prose and traditional Old English poetry.

Between 992 and 1002 Aelfric revised and expanded the *Catholic Homilies*, produced other didactic religious writings and translations, and wrote three Latin works intended to aid students of the language: a grammar, a glossary, and the *Colloquy*, a charming exercise text for use in vocabulary drills, which is full of information about Anglo-Saxon occupations and livelihoods. A series of *Lives of the Saints* and free translations, often including commentary, of the first seven Old Testament books (the Heptateuch) occupied much of his time between 1002 and 1005.

In 1005 Aelfric became abbot of a new monastery at Eynsham, where during his remaining years he continued to revise and expand his cycles of homilies and to write supplementary works of instruction and edification, including letters to Wulfstan, Archbishop of York, himself a noted vernacular homilist. Aelfric died between 1010 and 1012.

Further Reading

The most comprehensive accounts of Aelfric's life, writings, and chronology are the two chapters by Peter Clemoes in Peter Clemoes, ed., *The Anglo-Saxons* (1959), and in Eric G. Stanley, ed., *Continuations and Beginnings: Studies in Old English Literature* (1966). For background on the Anglo-Saxon Church see Margaret Deanesly, *The Pre-Conquest Church in England* (1961). Stanley B. Greenfield, *A Critical History of Old English Literature* (1965), surveys Aelfric's literary context. Peter Hunter Blair, *An Introduction to Anglo-Saxon England* (1956), provides an excellent guide to Anglo-Saxon history, institutions, and culture.

Additional Sources

White, Caroline Louisa, *Aelfric: a new study of his life and writing,* Hamden, Conn.: Archon Books, 1974. □

Aeschylus

The Greek playwright Aeschylus (524-456 B.C.) is the first European dramatist whose plays have been preserved. He is also the earliest of the great Greek tragedians, and more than any other he is concerned with the interrelationship of man and the gods.

Aeschylus was born at the religious center of Eleusis. His father, Euphorion, was of a noble Athenian family. In 499 B.C. Aeschylus produced his first tragedy, and in 490 he is reputed to have taken part in the Battle of Marathon, in which the Athenians defeated the Persian invaders.

In 484 Aeschylus won first prize in tragedy in the annual competitions held in Athens. In 472 he took first prize with a tetralogy, three tragedies with a connecting theme and a comic satyr play. It embraced *Phineus, The Persians, Glaucus of Potniae,* and the satyr play *Prometheus, the Fire Kindler.* Defeated in one dramatic competition by Sophocles in 468, Aeschylus later won first prize with another tetralogy: *Laius, Oedipus, The Seven against Thebes,* and the satyr play *The Sphinx.* In 463 he won first prize with the tetralogy now known as *The Suppliants, The Egyptians, The Danaids,* and the satyr play *The Amymone.* In 458 he gained his last victory with the trilogy *Oresteia.* The date of another trilogy, the *Prometheia,* is unknown, but it was probably produced sometime between *The Seven against Thebes* and the *Oresteia.* Only 7 of the perhaps 90 plays that Aeschylus wrote are preserved.

Aeschylus was acquainted with the Greek poet Ion of Chios, and he may also have known Pindar, Greece's greatest lyric poet. Aeschylus's son and the descendants of Aeschylus's sister also wrote tragedies. The legend that Aeschylus stood trial for divulging the Eleusinian Mysteries but was acquitted on the grounds that he was never initiated may be simply a reflection of his religious environment. He was greatly influenced by the poet Homer, describing his own works as "slices of Homer."

Aeschylus retired to Sicily, and tradition says that he was ignominiously killed by an eagle which, in its desire to split open a turtle it was carrying, mistook his bald head for a boulder. His tomb at Gela in Sicily became a shrine, and his own epitaph recorded his military, not his literary, exploits.

Contributions, Style, and Philosophy

Because Aeschylus was writing for the Greek theater in its formative stages, he is credited with having introduced many features that became associated with the traditional Greek theater. Among these were the rich costumes, decorated cothurni (a kind of footwear), solemn dances, and possibly elaborate stage machinery. Aeschylus also added parts for a second and a third actor; before his time plays were written for only one actor and a chorus. He is said to have acted in his own plays and designed his own choral dances.

Aeschylus is a master of the grand style. His language is ingeniously elaborate. He loves to impress his audience, and he does not hesitate to display his geographic knowledge in long, pompous descriptions. His character drawing is handled chiefly through contrast. The chorus is not always more intelligent than the characters, but its importance is formidable. Some have said that the style of Aeschylus is more lyric than epic.

Corresponding with his grand style are his grand ideas. Mighty themes and mighty men cross his stage. Aeschylus has been described as a great theologian who attempts to present a purified conception of the godhead and who is deeply interested in the problem of theodicy, or vindicating the justice of a god in permitting evil. In a real sense, in the figure of the supreme Greek deity, Zeus, Aeschylus completes the concept of henotheism, concerned with the worship of one god without denying the existence of other gods and developed by Hesiod and Solon.

The Plays

Modern scholarship has shown that the first of Aeschylus's plays was *The Persians* (*The Suppliants* was formerly thought to be the earliest because of its heavily lyric content). *The Persians* is the only play on a historical subject that survived from Greek drama. The play is set at the Persian capital soon after the Battle of Salamis. The queen, Atossa, is disturbed by a dream which portends disaster for her son Xerxes, who is on an expedition against the Greeks. A messenger arrives and announces terrible losses and defeat for the Persians. The ghost of Darius, father of Xerxes, warns against any further invasions of Greece.

This play is seen from a Persian point of view, and not a single Greek is mentioned. Aeschylus does not seek to glorify the Greeks but to show how an entire people can be guilty of national hubris, or pride. The gods are credited with the victory. Overweening hubris and imprudence can lead to destruction.

In *The Suppliants* the chorus is the protagonist. There are 50 sons and 50 daughters and only three characters: Danaus, Pelasgus, and the Egyptian herald. Pursued by the 50 sons of Aegyptus, the 50 daughters of Danaus seek refuge with Pelasgus, King of Argos. The Danaids do not want to marry the sons of Aegyptus, who are their cousins, and Pelasgus, after a democratic consultation, decrees that the State will protect them. The action ends with prayer and supplication to Zeus. Whether the theme of this play is abhorrence of incest is not clear; what is clear is the emphasis placed on Zeus as the upholder of justice.

Aeschylus was probably the first to dramatize the Oedipus story in *The Seven against Thebes*. The play concentrates on Eteocles, son of Oedipus and king of Thebes. The city is attacked by Polynices, Eteocles's brother, and six other warriors, and the brothers die at each other's hands. Eteocles is the first real character in Greek drama. This is the first play with a prologue and the chorus is less important. There is little action but considerable stiff stylization.

Prometheus Bound has often been described as a static play because the main character, Prometheus, is chained to a mountain peak and cannot move. He is being punished for defying the authority of the newly established cosmic ruler, Zeus, by bringing fire to mankind. Prometheus bemoans his

lot and proclaims that he will be freed by a descendant of Io—Heracles—13 generations later. He indicates clearly that he has saved mankind from destruction and is the source of all knowledge. Zeus is depicted as an absolute tyrant and Prometheus as a suffering but defiant rebel. Both are guilty of hubris. Both must learn through suffering: Zeus to exercise power with mercy, understanding, and justice, and Prometheus to respect authority. Absolute power is no more acceptable than absolute defiance. Reason (Prometheus) and power (Zeus) must be balanced to promote a harmonious society.

Aeschylus's masterpiece is the *Oresteia,* the only extant trilogy from Greek drama. The three plays—*Agamemnon, The Choephori,* and *The Eumenides*—though they form separate dramas, are united in their common theme of *dikē,* or justice. King Agamemnon returns to his home in Argos after the Trojan War only to be murdered by his scheming wife, Clytemnestra, in collusion with her paramour, Aegisthus. Orestes, the son of Agamemnon and Clytemnestra, is in exile; he is enjoined by Apollo to wreak vengeance on his mother and Aegisthus. Orestes' sister Electra assists him in carrying out the vengeance. For the killing of his mother Orestes is pursued by the blood deities, the Furies. On his flight he reaches Athens, where he is tried and acquitted by the tribunal, called the Areopagus. The Furies are gradually transformed into the "Kindly Ones," the Eumenides.

The *Oresteia* is concerned with the problem of evil and its compounding. The evil of the Trojan War brings on evil at home, which in turn must be avenged. In the act of vengeance another evil is also committed, for the ancient law says that "unto him that doeth it shall be done." How can this seemingly endless chain of evil be broken? Aeschylus proclaims that Zeus is the answer to this problem of theodicy. Aeschylus believes that suffering is an innate part of the pattern of the universe and that through suffering emerges a positive good.

Albin Lesky has noted (1965) that "Aeschylean tragedy shows faith in a sublime and just world order, and is in fact inconceivable without it. Man follows his difficult, often terrible path through guilt and suffering, but it is the path ordained by god which leads to knowledge of his laws. All comes from his will."

Further Reading

A good study of the plays of Aeschylus is Herbert Weir Smyth, *Aeschylean Tragedy* (1924). Another treatment, which includes other writers' views on Aeschylus, is Leon Golden, *In Praise of Prometheus: Humanism and Rationalism in Aeschylean Thought* (1966). More specialized studies of Aeschylus are Gilbert Murray, *Aeschylus: The Creator of Tragedy* (1940); Friedrich Solmsen, *Hesiod and Aeschylus* (1949); J. H. Finley, Jr., *Pindar and Aeschylus* (1955); and Anthony J. Podlecki, *The Political Background of Aeschylean Tragedy* (1966). Peter D. Arnott, *An Introduction to the Greek Theatre* (1959), includes scholarly background material as well as an in-depth treatment of Aeschylus and the *Agamemnon.*
Chapters discussing various aspects of Aeschylus's works are contained in the following books: Gilbert Norwood, *Greek Tragedy* (1920; 4th ed. 1953); H. D. F. Kitto, *Greek Tragedy: A Literary Study* (1939; 3d ed. 1961), *Form and Meaning in*

Drama: A Study of Six Greek Plays and of Hamlet (1956; 2d ed. 1968), and *Poiesis: Structure and Thought* (1966); William Chase Greene, *Moira: Fate, Good, and Evil in Greek Thought* (1944); and D. W. Lucas, *The Greek Tragic Poets* (1955; 2d ed. 1959). A fine work, which includes discussions of Aeschylus and his times, is Albin Lesky, *Greek Tragedy* (1938; trans. 1965; 2d ed. 1967). □

Affonso I

Affonso I (1460-1545) was a king of Kongo whose reign marked the high point of Portuguese and Christian influence in the kingdom, as well as the failure to establish relations between Europe and Africa on the basis of equality.

After the Portuguese navigator Diogo Cão reached the Kingdom of Kongo in west-central Africa in 1482, contacts between Kongo and Portugal multiplied. The Portuguese dispatched a technical assistance mission to Kongo, and in 1491 the Kongo king Nzinga Nkuwu was baptized under the name João I.

One of João's sons, Nzinga Mvemba, was baptized Affonso and upon his father's death in 1506 he assumed the throne of Kongo. Thereafter, relations between Portugal and Kongo became much more active. Missionaries, teachers, masons, carpenters, and military advisers were dispatched to King Affonso, who paid for their services with slaves, copper, and ivory. Serious problems soon developed, because many of the Portuguese preferred to engage in trade—especially the slave trade—rather than to exercise their crafts. Portuguese commercial establishments on the island of São Tomé also interfered in Kongo-Portuguese exchanges.

In 1512 Affonso requested tighter royal control over the activities of Portuguese nationals. King Manuel I decreed a royal monopoly over trade with Kongo, dispatched an envoy with jurisdiction over all Portuguese nationals, and submitted an extensive plan for the acculturation of Kongo involving the adoption of the Portuguese legal system, feudal titles, and court etiquette. Manuel's instructions were largely ineffective, and the Portuguese colony in Kongo was soon divided between a royal faction and a faction favorable to São Tomé interests, with the latter increasingly gaining the upper hand. The slave trade became the predominant European occupation; although Affonso himself was involved in this activity and did not object to it in principle, he strongly resented the traders' indiscriminate seizure of Africans, even including members of the Kongo nobility.

Portuguese missionary and educational activities declined. The number of missionaries during the reign of Affonso seems never to have exceeded 10, all of them residing at court. One of Affonso's sons, Dom Henrique, studied in Lisbon and Rome and served as bishop of São Salvador, the capital of Kongo, from 1520 until his death in 1526. By that time, however, the disruptive effects of the Portuguese presence had reached such dimensions that Affonso decreed the expulsion of all Europeans except missionaries and teachers. But he was forced to rescind his order and to content himself with setting up a board of inspectors to control all commercial transactions conducted by foreigners. Affonso's efforts in 1529 and 1539 to secure Vatican support through the dispatch of a mission to Rome met with no real success. The increasing disruption of Kongo royal authority culminated with the attempt by eight Portuguese to shoot Affonso in church on Easter Day, 1540. With this incident the reign of King Affonso ended, although the actual date of his death is not known. Portuguese factions supported rival contenders for the throne, and one of Affonso's grandsons, Diogo I, eventually ascended to the throne.

The reign of King Affonso left lasting memories in Europe and Africa. Kongo remained nominally Catholic during the following century, and lineal descent from Affonso became a recognized requirement for succession to the throne. At the same time, whatever illusions might have been entertained on both sides regarding the possibility of peaceful interaction between the cultures of western Europe and Africa were shattered in the reign of King Affonso; and a relationship that had started on a quasi-idyllic note deteriorated in less than one generation into the ruthless exploitation of Africa by Europeans.

Further Reading

There are discussions of Affonso I in Jan Vansina, *Kingdoms of the Savanna* (1966), a political history of Central Africa, and in James Duffy, *Portuguese Africa* (1959), which stresses colonial problems caused by Portuguese occupation. □

Aleksandr Nikolaevich Afinogenov

The Soviet dramatist Aleksandr Nikolaevich Afinogenov (1904-1941) mixed lyricism, melodrama, and comedy in his portrayals of average Russians in everyday pursuits.

On April 4, 1904, near Ryazan, Russia, Aleksandr Afinogenov was born. His father was a railroad worker, an active Communist, and, after the Revolution, a writer. Aleksandr grew up in proletarian surroundings during the consolidation of proletarian ideology. The characters in his plays often come from the proletariat and reflect that point of view. Afinogenov was too young to take part in the Revolution, which began in 1917. He graduated from the Moscow Institute of Journalism in 1924.

His first play, *Robert Tim,* was performed in 1924. During the 1920s Afinogenov's creative writing took second place to his political activity. He joined the Communist party in 1922 and soon became a leader of Proletcult, the organization for the development of proletarian culture.

Afinogenov's task was to train playwrights and actors and disseminate proletarian literary views. He directed the First Moscow Workers' Theater of Proletcult during the late 1920s; it performed plays designed to uplift the workers' spirit and encourage the building of communism. Specifically for this purpose, Afinogenov adapted and staged a story by Jack London, the American author, as well as several of his own plays. One play was *The Eccentric* (1929), which depicts the obstacles that bureaucratism and careerism present to the progress of communism.

The most popular, and sensational, of Afinogenov's plays is *Fear,* first performed in 1930 by the Moscow Art Theater. At the time Afinogenov was deeply dedicated to furthering a new Communist art, based on Marxist principles of dialectical materialism. He was not blind, however, to the corruption and weaknesses in the Soviet bureaucracy, and he did not favor using terror to advance communism. *Fear* portrays a research scientist who is partial to the views of the prerevolutionary intelligentsia. The scientist publishes a study of those sense stimuli that condition the behavior of high Soviet bureaucrats. Fear is found to be the main stimulus. Although one character defends the Soviet bureaucracy as preferable to the czarist bureaucracy, the public saw *Fear* as a direct attack on the regime, and the play was attacked by orthodox Marxist critics. It became popular again in the 1950s, when the Soviet premier, Nikita Khrushchev, attacked the bureaucratic legacy of Joseph Stalin.

During the 1930s Afinogenov continued in his dual capacity as director and playwright. His *Salute to Spain!* (1936) praised the Republican forces in the Spanish Civil War. His dramas of the late 1930s were lyrical, psychological portrayals of everyday Soviet life. *On the Eve* (1941) was an expression of outrage at the Nazi invasion of the Soviet Union. Afinogenov was killed on Nov. 4, 1941, during an aerial bombardment of Moscow.

His diaries and notebooks, published in 1960, are a valuable source of information on Soviet writers of the 1920s and 1930s. His plays are very popular in the Soviet Union.

Further Reading

There is no adequate biography of Afinogenov in English. In Russian see A. Karaganov, *Aleksandr Afinogenov* (1964). Afinogenov's work is discussed in Vera Alexandrova, *A History of Soviet Literature, 1917-1964: From Gorky to Solzhenitsyn* (1963). For a more detailed discussion of Afinogenov's drama in the context of Soviet theater consult Spencer E. Roberts, *Soviet Historical Drama: Its Role in the Development of a National Mythology* (1965). □

Michel 'Aflaq

Michel 'Aflaq (1910-1989) was the founder and spiritual leader of the Arab Socialist Resurrection party, called the Ba'th party, for more than 25 years. He lived in Syria until 1966, and after being forced into exile, he assumed power within the Ba'th party in Iraq.

Michel 'Aflaq was born in 1910 in the Midan Quarter of Damascus, Syria, to a Greek Orthodox family of five children. His father was a local wheat dealer. 'Aflaq was educated in Greek Orthodox schools in Damascus and won a scholarship to study at the Sorbonne in Paris. He graduated from the Sorbonne with honors in history in 1936 and returned to Damascus to teach at the Tahjiz secondary school. 'Aflaq quit teaching in 1944 to concentrate full time on political activities.

While in France 'Aflaq was close to many Communists and wrote articles for several French Communist publications. In the late 1930s he became disenchanted with the Communists and the Syrian Communist party, and in 1940 he founded the Arab Resurrection party, known as the Ba'th party. He also in 1946 founded the party newspaper, *al-Ba'th,* which became a principal vehicle for his prolific writings.

Michel 'Aflaq was a dedicated Arab nationalist and a firm believer in socialism. A philosopher and visionary more than a practical politician, he had a strong personality and was highly intelligent. His long political career ultimately left him with influence in various parts of the Arab world outside his native land. In the 1940s and 1950s 'Aflaq organized political meetings and rallies in Syria and motivated party workers by providing long-range political analysis. He would often rely on his long-time friend, close companion since childhood, and party co-founder Salah al-Din al-Bitar to put these theories into policies.

'Aflaq's long political career took many turns. In 1947, and again in 1949, he ran unsuccessfully for the Syrian Parliament. But in between, in August 1949, he served as minister of education in a Hashim al-Atasi cabinet. In 1954 the party he and al-Bitar founded merged with the Socialist party of Akram al-Hawrani under the new name Arab Socialist Resurrectionist party. Al-Hawrani was a populist from the northern Syrian city of Hama. The new party also made the decision in 1954 to expand operations into neighboring Arab countries, and party leaders were present at several international socialist conferences in the mid-1950s.

Between 1958 and 1963, when the Ba'th party took power in both Syria and Iraq, 'Aflaq was engaged in considerable political maneuvering. He and his party initially supported the 1958 union of Egypt and Syria, but only 18 months later 'Aflaq fled to Beirut, Lebanon, disillusioned. He returned to Syria in September 1961 when the union with Egypt was dissolved and immediately tried to reassert his authority, which al-Hawrani had in the meantime tried to usurp. A May 1962 party national congress expelled al-Hawrani, but factionalism continued to plague the party as some in the party wanted to reestablish links with Egypt.

In February 1963 the Ba'th party took power in Iraq. The party also seized power in Syria the following month. But the party's rise to power only intensified party factionalism in Syria and Iraq, and the process undermined 'Aflaq's leadership of the Ba'th party movement. Over the years 'Aflaq had been unable to develop strong ties with the young military members in the Syrian Ba'th party who paid little attention to the older civilian leaders of the party. In 1965 'Aflaq lost his position as secretary general of the party, a position he had held for 25 years, but was given the honorary title of founder-leader.

Although he was in exile from Syria after February 1966, this was not the first time he had trouble or had to leave his country. During the 1940s and 1950s he was jailed frequently. He went into exile briefly in 1953, in 1959, and in 1964. In November 1966 the young military leaders of the Ba'th party in Syria threw 'Aflaq out of the party. However, he went on to become a leader of an international branch of the party from a base in Baghdad. Branches of the Ba'th party existed in most Arab countries, and 'Aflaq was the visionary for many of their leaders.

From the party's beginning 'Aflaq was the chief author of its ideology. The basic doctrine of the Ba'th party was summarized by its slogan: "Unity, liberation, socialism: One Arab nation having an immortal mission." This Arab nation was a permanent entity in history, and Arabism was defined as the feeling and consciousness of being Arab. For 'Aflaq and his supporters, the Arab nation comprised the entire area between the Sahara desert and the Atlantic and the Persian Gulf. The party proposed to make this Arab nation modern and secular, with full rights of citizenship for women. Islam would be secularized and made part of Arab culture, and all religious, communal, regional, racial, or tribal divisions would be subsumed into one Arab nation.

The overriding priority of the party was given to Arab unity, but the party did not develop a clear strategy for achieving unity. Liberation, the second Ba'th goal, was exceedingly popular with the post-World War II Arab generation, which wanted to be done with all forms of foreign domination. The third part of 'Aflaq's triad, socialism, in the early years of the party played a secondary role to concerns about Arab nationalism and unity and liberation. The form of socialism envisaged then was mild and allowed for private enterprise. Despite 'Aflaq's close ties in the early 1930s to Communism, the party constitution did not show any strong ties to Marxism.

The role of the party in 'Aflaq's conception was to be the vanguard of the people, and this vanguard represented the new Arab generation which would bring the people out of decades of neglect and backwardness into a new nation. Ba'th means resurrection. While the elitist role of the party was evident, in the early, formative years the system of government which the party espoused was not clear. The Ba'th party did use the electoral process to gain access to power in Syria, but abandoned that process in 1957 when the opportunity of unity with Egypt emerged.

'Aflaq clearly captured the imagination of politically aware Arabs in many countries, especially in the period 1946 to 1956. This was a time of incredible expansion of his party in Syria and elsewhere. The stress on nationalism, unity, and liberation won many hearts and minds. In the late 1960s and 1970s, however, when these parties obtained power in Syria and Iraq, practical considerations of policies and running governments divided the Ba'th party elites, and

a new generation with different views emerged, leaving 'Aflaq with vastly diminished status in his movement in his later years.

'Aflaq lived his last years with the title of Pan-Arab General Secretary of the Iraqi Ba'th party, a position which ceremonially placed him above Iraqi President Saddam Hussein, though 'Aflaq's contributions to politics were minimal. He lived in Baghdad in virtual isolation until his deteriorating health necessitated a move to Paris to seek treatment. On June 10, 1989, 'Aflaq underwent heart surgery but never left the hospital, dying two weeks later. At the time of his death, a statement was issued by the Ba'th party leaders, stating 'Aflaq "led Arab masses for decades in their struggle against imperialism and for Arab unity." The statement also claimed that 'Aflaq had converted from Christianity to Islam during his life, but did not want this information to be interpreted politically, so he didn't make this announcement during his lifetime.

Further Reading

Michel 'Aflaq and the Ba'th Party are discussed prominently in several good books written about postindependence Syria. Among the better books are: *Political Leaders of the Contemporary Middle East and North Africa,* edited by Bernard Reich (1990); *The Struggle for Syria: Study of Postwar Arab Politics, 1945-1958,* by Patrick Seale (1965); *The Ba'th Party: A History from Its Origins to 1966,* by John F. Devlin (1976); *Syria,* by Tabitha Petran (1972); *The Arab Ba'th Socialist Party History, Ideology, and Organization,* by Kamel S. Abu Jaber (1966); *The Struggle for Power in Syria,* by Nikolaos van Dam (1979); and *Syria Under the Ba'th, 1963-1966,* by Itamar Rabinovich (1972). □

Aga Khan

Aga Khan (chief commander) is the title of the imam, or spiritual leader, of the sect of Moslems known as Nizari Ismailis. The title was granted in 1818 by the Shah of Persia.

The Ismailis are Shias, one of the two great sects of Islam. Unlike the Sunnis, the major group, the Shias believe that the imam must be a descendant of the prophet Mohammed through Hasan and Husain, the sons of his daughter Fatima. The Ismailis, who trace their origin to the 8th century, were formed around the followers of Ismail, a descendant of Husain. One branch, the Nizari Ismailis, established itself in Persia in a number of strong fortresses in the 11th century.

Aga Khan I

Hasan Ali Shah (1800-1881) had the title Aga Khan bestowed on him for his services to Fath Ali, the Persian ruler, whose daughter he married. The Aga Khans thus have the status of princes of the royal house of Persia. Aga Khan I rebelled against Fath Ali's successor and had to flee to India in 1840. He was welcomed by the British rulers of India as an ally since they were then on bad terms with Persia. In return for his support during the war against Afghanistan (1839-1842) and in the conquest of Sind, he was given a pension and the title of Highness.

The British valued the Aga Khan's support, as they hoped this would show the large Moslem population of India that they were not anti-Moslem, even though they were making war on Moslem countries. The Aga Khan's support was of particular importance in western India, where there were considerable numbers of Ismailis. Most belonged to the group known as Khojas, descendants of converts made in the 14th century by missionaries sent by the Ismailis from Persia. These converts belonged mainly to the trading classes, with businesses centered in Karachi and Bombay but with links to East Africa and other points along the coast of the Indian Ocean. Aga Khan I used these trading links to knit the Khojas into a tightly organized group. Because they regarded him as a semidivine figure, they were willing to pay, as the tenets of the sect demanded, about an eighth of their income to him. This became the Aga Khan's source of immense wealth. His son Aga Khan II, Ali Shah, died in 1885 after only 4 years in office.

Aga Khan III

Aga Khan III, Sultan Sir Muhammad Shah (1877-1957), was born on Nov. 2, 1877, in Karachi. At the age of 8 he succeeded his father, Aga Khan II, as imam. Under him the office reached its greatest influence. The Aga Khan enjoyed

Aga Khan III

international fame, and his personal charm, great wealth, and intelligence made him a popular figure in European society. His friendships with the great and famous in politics, business, and the arts were enhanced by his devotion to horse racing. This was a family tradition, and the Aga Khan's stables were among the finest in the world. His horses won the Derby three times, in addition to many other famous races.

To outsiders the Aga Khan's luxurious style of living and his enthusiasm for horse racing seemed incongruous with his position as the spiritual leader of his people. It must be remembered, however, that he did not hold office by virtue of his own spiritual merit; the office itself was sacred, and his inheritance of it by direct line from the Prophet assured his sanctity. Nor did his followers regard the pleasures that he enjoyed with such gusto as unbecoming an imam. On the contrary, these were precisely the pleasures they believed all men should enjoy. Furthermore, as a public man he worked for causes of importance to Moslems everywhere, and as imam of the Ismailis he was deeply concerned with their welfare.

The Aga Khan's highly placed friends in England, including King Edward VII, were responsible for his first major public appointment—membership in 1902 in the Council of the Viceroy of India. This honor was a continuation of the attention the government of India had paid to his family, and for the next 40 years he was closely involved with Indian politics, especially when Moslem interests were affected. His good standing with the British, as well as his natural dignity and charm, led to his choice by Moslem groups in India as their spokesman and representative.

He presided over the meeting of the All-India Moslem Educational Conference in Delhi in 1904. His value for Moslem interests, even though he belonged to a sect regarded as heretical by the orthodox, was recognized by Mohsin-ul-Mulk, the head of the trust that ran the Moslem college at Aligarh. The Aga Khan became involved in the college's fundraising projects and its transformation into a full-fledged Moslem university. The Aga Khan's real entrance into the political life of Indian Islam came in 1906, however, when he led a delegation to the governor general to argue for special safeguards for Moslems in any constitutional changes that would take place in India. The Indian National Congress was demanding the introduction of representative government, and the Moslems were afraid that this would mean their domination by the Hindu majority. The governor general gave the Aga Khan's delegation an encouraging response, and the Moslem leaders then organized the All-India Moslem League to watch over their political interests. The Aga Khan was elected its first president in 1906 and retained the office until 1913. By then the league was becoming more critical of the British government, and the Aga Khan was anxious to maintain his political neutrality.

In the years immediately after World War I, the Aga Khan sought without much success to get the British government to deal not too harshly with Turkey, which had been an ally of Germany. He was also unable to make any contribution to Indian politics in the early 1920s, when Gandhi was seeking to work for Moslem-Hindu cooperation against the British by supporting the Khilafat movement, which was based on loyalty to the sultan of Turkey as the caliph, or spiritual leader, of Islam.

The Aga Khan's ability to bring together the various factions of Indian Moslems led to his choice as their spokesman at the Round Table Conferences, which were held from 1931 to 1933 in London to discuss India's political future. By this time the Moslems were not the only ones concerned about their fate if India should become free, and other minority groups were demanding protection from the "threat" of Hindu majority rule. Once more the Aga Khan used his diplomatic skills to press for separate representation for the different minority groups under the new constitution. The result was the Communal Award of 1933, which was regarded by the Indian National Congress, the major proponents of nationalism, as a divisive force in Indian politics. During these years the Aga Khan was his country's delegate to the League of Nations, and he was elected president of the League in 1937.

The Aga Khan was also very active as imam of his religious community. He saw the responsibilities of his office not as religious in the sense that they entailed a concern with theology and worship, but as social and economic, to strengthen the Ismaili community. He was particularly interested in the advancement of women, and he forbade those of his group to veil their faces, as did Moslem women in most countries. He used his great wealth to establish banks that lent money at low interest rates to his followers, thus encouraging trade and commerce. He also encouraged the construction of schools and hospitals in India, East Africa, and the Middle East, sometimes in cooperation with local governments. One widely publicized aspect of his career, the ceremony of weighing him on anniversaries against gold, diamonds, or platinum, was directly related to these philanthropic interests. The money raised on such occasions was used for furthering the social concerns of the group.

The Aga Khan spent most of his adult life in France, partly because of his enjoyment of French culture but also for the important political reason that this arrangement kept him from being identified too closely with any one of the geographic areas where he had followers.

He married four times. His first wife was a cousin, whom he divorced after what he called "a sour sham of marriage." In 1908 he married the first of his three European wives, the ballerina Theresa Magliano. They had one son, Aly Khan. After her death in 1926, he married Andrée Carron in 1929 and divorced her in 1943. They had one son, Sadruddin. Yvette La Brousee, whom he married in 1944, survived him. He died on July 12, 1957, in Geneva.

It had been assumed that the Aga Khan would appoint his oldest son, Aly Khan, as his successor to the office of iman, but he named instead Prince Karim, Aly Khan's son. He explained that he believed it was in the interest of the Shia Moslem Ismaili community that he be succeeded by "a young man brought up and developed during recent years and in the midst of the new age and who brings a new outlook on life to his office as imam."

Aga Khan IV, Prince Karim, was born in Geneva on Dec. 13, 1936. In contrast to his father, he was noted for his serious approach to life. He traveled to the different centers of the Ismaili community throughout the world to be acknowledged as "Imam of the Time."

Further Reading

Aga Khan III wrote an autobiography, as Sultan Muhammad Shah, *The Memoirs of Aga Khan: World Enough and Time* (1954). His political views are in his *India in Transition: A Study in Political Evolution* (1918). Another useful source is Naoroji M. Dumasia, *The Aga Khan and His Ancestors* (1939). A relevant religious group is discussed in Syed Mujtaba Ali, *The Origin of the Khojas and Their Religious Life Today* (1936). S. M. Ikram, *Modern Muslim India and the Birth of Pakistan* (1950; 2d ed. 1965), places Aga Khan III in the context of the Indian nationalist movement. □

Jean Louis Rodolphe Agassiz

Jean Louis Rodolphe Agassiz (1807-1873), a Swiss-American naturalist, was an outstanding comparative anatomist. He promulgated the glacial theory and opposed Darwin's theory of evolution by natural selection.

Paleontology was just beginning to emerge as a science during Agassiz's time; speculations about the distribution of species and their relationships to each other were becoming a major preoccupation of naturalists, and science was taking on an increasingly important place in the curricula of educational institutions. Agassiz played an important role in all these developments, both in Europe and in America.

Louis Agassiz was born at Môtier-en-Vuly in French Switzerland on May 28, 1807. His father, the last of a line of seven Protestant clergymen, instilled in Louis the religious qualities that marked his life, and his mother, Rose Mayor Agassiz, encouraged the precocious taste for science that led him to neglect his books in order to collect a huge assortment of pets.

Early Education

Destined for a career in medicine, Agassiz was sent to school at Bienne at the age of 10, and at 15 to the College of Lausanne. In 1824 he began medical training at the University of Zurich, and in 1826 he matriculated at Heidelberg, where his interest in natural history increased under the influence of the distinguished staff, which included Friedrich Tiedemann and Heinrich Bronn. In the following year at the University of Munich, he came under the lasting influence of Ignaz von Döllinger, a pioneer embryologist.

While at Munich, Agassiz, then only 21 years old, published the work that launched him on his long and distinguished scientific career, *The Fishes of Brazil* (1829), prepared from the collections of two eminent naturalists, J.B. von Spix and Karl von Martius. This was the most

important account of a local fish fauna published to that time. During the following winter he began work on his *Recherches sur les poissons fossiles* (1833-1844).

Influence of Cuvier

Agassiz moved to Paris in the fall of 1831. Still pursuing medical studies, he nevertheless spent a part of each day with the fossil fish collection in the Museum of Natural History of the Jardin des Plantes. Georges Cuvier, the brilliant comparative anatomist (who at this time was developing a new system of animal classification), immediately became interested in the young naturalist, gave him a corner in one of his own laboratories, and offered him the material he himself had been collecting for years for his own work on fishes. Agassiz worked under Cuvier and adopted his views of the plan of creation, which put Agassiz bitterly at odds with all "developmental" or evolutionary theories.

Cuvier had noted the succession of types in geological history but saw no genetic connection between any of the four great classes he recognized—Vertebrates, Articulates, Mollusks, and Radiates. Working with Cuvier's delineation of types, Agassiz regarded his own investigations as glimpses into the divine plan, of which the structures of the types were the expression. Divine ideas, he held, were especially embodied in animal life, each species being the "thought unit." Agassiz viewed the marvel of structural affinity in creatures of widely diverse habits and outward appearance as a result of the association of ideas in the divine mind— not, as Charles Darwin thought, as proof of common descent. Agassiz further developed the notion that species

were created in the localities where they were destined to pass their lives, that is, common forms found in widely separated areas were proof not of migration but of separate creation. Throughout his life he used these ideas to combat every form of evolutionism.

Work on Glaciers

While teaching at Neuchâtel in 1836, Agassiz became interested in glacial action. He concluded that it had probably been a major agency in shaping the topography from the North Pole to the Mediterranean and Caspian seas. He studied ongoing glacial action and other parts of Europe, and in 1840 he published his first comprehensive discussion in *Études sur les glaciers* (2 vols.). This was followed by other works in 1846 and 1847, in which he established his expanding theory of general glacial action wherever the earth's surface bears drift material and polished or striated erratic boulders.

Move to America

Agassiz left for America in September 1846. On his arrival in Boston, the following month, he was hailed as an internationally famous scientist and was lionized by the scientific community. He gave lectures at Lowell Institute and embarked on an extremely successful lecture tour, which included most of the major eastern cities. Charmed by the enthusiastic receptions he received, convinced that America offered unprecedented opportunities for a naturalist, and disturbed by political problems in Europe, Agassiz decided to make America his permanent home. In 1848 he accepted the chair of zoology and geology that had been created especially for him by Abbott Lawrence at Harvard University. His first wife had died in Switzerland, and in 1850 he married Elizabeth Cabot Cary of Boston. His son, Alexander, and two daughters joined their father in America.

Although Agassiz remained America's most popular naturalist until his death and gained a reputation as a great teacher, he produced no more works of the caliber of those published in Europe. His *Contributions to the Natural History of the United States* (1857-1862), a projected 10-volume work of which only 4 were published, was his most ambitious undertaking. Its most important portion, the "Essay on Classification," was a statement of the idealistic point of view about to become outmoded because of the Darwinian revolution. Agassiz had no sooner published his first volume than he embarked on a bitter debate with Asa Gray, a fellow Harvard professor and enemy of several years' standing, over the theory of evolution.

Institutional Accomplishments

Agassiz was a fund-raiser without parallel in 19th-century American science. He was instrumental in securing legislative grants and private gifts to establish Harvard's museum of comparative anatomy, where an enormous working collection for the specialist and a series of displays for general instruction were assembled. He became the museum director in 1859. The museum's profound influence during the next few decades as a center of scientific research and study can hardly be exaggerated. With other members of the elite group of American scientists (led by Alexander Dallas Bache) with whom he had become associated, Agassiz helped found the National Academy of Sciences during the Civil War. Only a few months before his death, Agassiz secured an endowment to establish a summer school of science on Penikese Island, which became the first American teacher-training institute. Here teachers learned to see nature and to teach others how to see it by the method of direct experience that Agassiz had used successfully at Harvard.

Agassiz was ill at frequent intervals for several years. He died in Cambridge on Dec. 14, 1873. His last work, another argument against the theory of evolution, appeared in the *Atlantic Monthly* shortly afterward.

Further Reading

The outstanding work on Agassiz is Edward Lurie, *Louis Agassiz: A Life in Science* (1960). Other works are valuable for his correspondence and for assessment by contemporaries: Arnold Guyot, *Memoir of Louis Agassiz, 1807-1873* (1883); Elizabeth Cary Agassiz, ed., *Louis Agassiz: His Life and Correspondence* (2 vols., 1885), especially important for the many letters to and from eminent European and American scientists; Jules Marcou, *Life, Letters, and Works of Louis Agassiz* (2 vols., 1896), which includes a complete bibliography; and Lane Cooper, *Louis Agassiz as a Teacher* (1917; rev. ed. 1945), which offers testimony of students about Agassiz's methods. For general background on Agassiz's mode of thought, John T. Merz, *A History of European Thought in the Nineteenth Century* (4 vols., 1904-1912), is still without a rival. A. Hunter Dupree, *Science in the Federal Government* (1957), gives the institutional background for Agassiz's work in America. □

James Agee

The writer James Agee (1909-1955) was a poet, journalist, novelist, and screenwriter. He also was the author of *Let Us Now Praise Famous Men,* an eloquent and anguished testimony about the essential human dignity of impoverished sharecroppers during the 1930s. The book is regarded as one of the most significant literary documents associated with the Great Depression.

Born November 27, 1909, in Knoxville, Tennessee, James Agee was the son of Hugh James and Laura (Tyler) Agee. His father worked for a small construction company founded by his father-in-law, while his mother had close ties to the Anglo-Catholic church and enjoyed writing poetry. His father's death in a car accident when James was six strongly influenced his life. He later described the incident in his autobiographical novel *A Death in the Family,* which was published posthumously (1957) and won a Pulitzer Prize. For most of his career he was a journalist writing for Henry Luce publications (*TIME,*

Fortune, LIFE) and a screenwriter. As a reporter in 1936, his encounter with three families of sharecroppers in Alabama became the basis for the very personal documentary-style book *Let Us Now Praise Famous Men,* which was an ambitious literary attempt to honor people enduring extreme poverty.

Not long after his father's death Agee moved with his family to the mountains in south-central Tennessee where he attended St. Andrews, a small Episcopalian school, from 1919 to 1924. He established a deep friendship with Father James Harold Flye that developed into a life-long correspondence. While at St. Andrews he experienced the spiritual crisis which he later described in his novel *The Morning Watch* (1951).

He spent one year at high school in Knoxville before attending Philips Exeter Academy in New Hampshire from 1925 to 1928. As a student at Harvard College (1928-1932) he wrote numerous short stories, poems, and essays. His work on a parody of *TIME* magazine helped him get a job after graduation as a reporter for *Fortune* magazine. Through another *Fortune* writer, the poet Archibald MacLeish, Agee submitted a collection of poems that was selected by the Yale Series of Younger Poets and published as *Permit Me Voyage* (1934).

For *Fortune* (1932-1938), Agee wrote long articles on a wide range of business and cultural topics, including the Tennessee Valley Authority and the American highway system. In 1936 he was assigned to do an article on tenant farming in the South. Accompanied by photographer

Walker Evans, who was employed by the Farm Security Administration, Agee spent several weeks with three poor families in Alabama.

A departure from traditional journalism, his impassioned article was rejected by the magazine. He spent several more years writing a book that made use of a number of literary techniques to describe the dignity of these anonymous people. Combining elements of documentary journalism, poetry, autobiography, and philosophy, and including many of Evans' photographs, the work was published as *Let Us Now Praise Famous Men* (1941). It initially sold only 600 copies; however, after it was reissued in 1960 it was recognized by scholars and critics as one of the most significant literary documents produced during the Great Depression

In 1939 Agee took a job reviewing books for *TIME* magazine. From 1941 to 1948 he wrote film reviews for *TIME,* and, after writing a cover piece on the impact of the atom bomb in August 1945, he wrote on political and cultural issues until 1947. From 1942 to 1948 he also wrote film reviews for *The Nation* magazine that established him as one of the nation's best-known and respected writers about films and the movie industry. In 1949 and 1950 he contributed several long film essays (on Charlie Chaplin, D.W. Griffith, and John Huston) to *LIFE* magazine.

To support his work on two novels (*The Morning Watch* and *A Death in the Family*) that were based on experiences from his childhood, Agee shifted his attention in the late 1940s from journalism to screen writing. He was involved with two independent productions: *In the Street,* about children in Harlem, and *The Quiet One,* about a school for delinquent children, which won an award for best film at the Venice Film Festival. For Hollywood, he worked on adaptation of Stephen Crane's *The Bride Comes to Yellow Sky* and *The Blue Hotel,* as well as director John Huston's *The African Queen,* which earned an Oscar nomination for best screenplay (1952).

In the early 1950s he worked for the Twentieth-Century Fox studio, wrote a script about Abraham Lincoln for the television series *Omnibus,* wrote a screenplay based on the life of the French Impressionist painter Paul Gauguin, and worked on scripts about the Tanglewilde Music Festival and colonial Williamsburg.

Agee's lifestyle, included heavy drinking and smoking, vices that interfered with his writing and severely impaired his health. He suffered the first of several heart attacks in 1951 while working on *The African Queen,* and later died of a heart attack on May 16, 1955, at the age of 45.

Although he was employed for almost his entire writing career as a journalist or scriptwriter, and despite his early death, Agee produced a considerable and diverse body of creative work, including poetry, essays, and novels. *Let Us Now Praise Famous Men* challenged the traditional conventions of reporting and literature and helped define a new genre of personal journalism that became more common in the 1960s.

Although Agee never fulfilled his personal ambition as a writer, the critical success of his novel *A Death in the Family,* published after his death, and the delayed recognition of *Let Us Now Praise Famous Men* established his reputation as one of the most talented writers of his generation.

In the 1930s Agee was twice married and divorced (to Via Saunders and to Alma Mailhouse, with whom he had one child) and was later married to Mia Fritsch, with whom he had three children.

Further Reading

To appreciate Agee as a writer one should read *Let Us Now Praise Famous Men* (1941) and the novel *A Death in the Family* (1957). To understand his religious and personal struggles one can read his short novel *The Morning Watch* (1951) and also the *Letters of James Agee to Father Flye* (1962). For perspective on Agee as a film critic and screenwriter, see the two volumes of *Agee on Film* (1958, 1960). Agee's poetry can be found in *The Collected Poems of James Agee* (1968) and examples of his journalism are available in *James Agee: Selected Journalism* (also 1968).

For information on Agee's life the best biography is *James Agee: A Life,* by Laurence Bergreen (1984). Also valuable is *The Restless Journey of James Agee* (1977) by Genevieve Moreau, which includes more analysis of his writing. Views of Agee by those who knew him can be found in *Remembering James Agee* (1974), edited by David Madden, and *Agee: His Life Remembered* (1985), edited by Ross Spears and Jude Cassidy. For a look at the legacy of the people and conditions featured in *Let Us Now Praise Famous Men,* see *And Their Children After Them* by Dale Maharidge and Michael Williamson (1989). □

Agesilaus II

Agesilaus II (ca. 444-360 B.C.), a Spartan king and general, dominated Spartan politics. Through military might he made his state supreme in Greece by about 380 B.C.

Agesilaus was a son of the Spartan king Archidamus II. Agesilaus was not in the direct line of succession after his elder brother King Agis II died, but the powerful military commander Lysander contrived to have Agis's son disqualified as a bastard fathered by Alcibiades and engineered Agesilaus's election as king about 399. Lysander hoped to exploit the lame and inexperienced Agesilaus, but the new king asserted his power and dismissed Lysander from service.

Agesilaus's first command was in Asia Minor against the Persians in 396-394. He failed to gain any permanent advantage but amassed a huge amount of booty. Meanwhile Sparta's supremacy in Greece was broken by the states in central Greece. Lysander was killed in Boeotia, and the other of Sparta's dual kings, Pausanias, was banished for incompetence in the face of the enemy. Agesilaus was recalled from the field and marched his army homeward. He broke through the enemy lines at Coronea, where he was wounded, and reached Sparta well laden with loot.

Agesilaus thus became in effect sole king, and he dominated the politics of Sparta until his death.

From 394 to 388 Agesilaus tried in vain to break a stalemate with the states of central Greece, which held the Isthmus of Corinth. He therefore entered into an alliance with Persia and negotiated a general peace with Persian backing in 386. Thebes alone remained independent; Agesilaus mustered his troops and subdued Thebes.

The King's Peace, as it was called, was a triumph for Persia and restored Sparta's supremacy. Agesilaus, however, failed to reform Sparta's ways and in particular to offset its dwindling population. He enforced Sparta's rule in Greece by ruthless methods, which appealed to the militarist strain in the Spartan character, and between 385 and 379 he subdued Mantinea, Phlius, Thebes, and the Chalcidian League. Sparta now dominated the Greek world, with Persia in the east and Syracuse in the west as allies.

The tide turned in 379-378. Thebes broke away from Spartan dominance. Athens followed Thebes into a coalition when a Spartan officer, Sphodrias, made an unsuccessful treacherous attack on Athens in time of peace and Agesilaus shielded him from the consequences. Saddled with a war against Thebes and Athens, Agesilaus invaded Boeotia in 378 and 377 but achieved nothing. In 376 he became ill, and his coruler at the time, Cleombrotus, failed to invade Boeotia. Thebes resurrected the Boeotian League, and Athens formed a maritime coalition. In 371 a new King's Peace was made, but Agesilaus again broke it. This time Epaminondas, the Theban commander, was not intimidated. A Spartan army under Cleombrotus invaded Boeotia and was decisively defeated by Epaminondas; Sparta's empire collapsed. The old king Agesilaus organized Sparta's defenses in 370 and again in 362. He led a Spartan force fighting the Persians in Egypt in 361 and died at sea while returning.

Further Reading

Ancient sources on Agesilaus II are Xenophon's *Agesilaus* and *Hellenica;* "Life of Agesilaus" in Plutarch's *Lives;* and "Agesilaus" in *The Lives of Cornelius Nepos.* Modern works which discuss Agesilaus II include J. B. Bury, *A History of Greece to the Death of Alexander the Great* (1900; 3d rev. ed. 1951); M.L.W. Laistner, *A History of the Greek World from 479 to 323 B.C.* (1936; 3d rev. ed. 1957); N.G.L. Hammond, *A History of Greece to 322 B.C.* (1959; 2d ed. 1967); and A. H. M. Jones, *Sparta* (1967).

Additional Sources

Cartledge, Paul., *Agesilaos and the crisis of Sparta,* Baltimore: Johns Hopkins University Press, 1987. □

Agha Mohammad Khan

Agha Mohammad Khan (ca. 1742-1797) was the founder of the Qajar dynasty that ruled Persia until 1924. The memory of this vengeful ruler is universally execrated; yet he did keep Persia intact at a time of struggle.

Following the death of Nader Shah in 1747, many tribal chiefs rose in revolt in the hope of taking over the leadership of the country. In the melee Mohammad Hoseyn Khan, the head of the Qajar tribe, was killed, and his son Mohammad, 5 years old, was castrated by order of Adel Shah, the nephew of Nader Shah. Henceforth, the boy's name was prefixed by "Agha," a title used in Persia for eunuchs. This cruel deed was perhaps one of the chief causes of the evil in Agha Mohammad's character and behavior. He became a misanthrope and hostile to everyone.

After years of warfare among the rivals for the throne of Nader Shah, Karim Khan Zand became the undisputed ruler in 1750. He married Agha Mohammad's sister and ordered his young brother-in-law to live in Shiraz, his capital, as a hostage. Agha Mohammad was quite free in Shiraz and was even permitted to venture out of the city for hunting. But his hatred was so strong that whenever he was in Karim Khan's presence he would secretly cut the rug on which he was sitting.

In 1779, when Karim Khan was at the point of death, Agha Mohammad found excuses to remain out of the city. By prearrangement his sister notified him when Karim Khan had died. Agha Mohammad immediately galloped toward the north and reached Esfahan, a distance of 316 miles, in

less than 3 days. From there he hurried to the southern shores of the Caspian Sea and was welcomed by his tribesmen. While he was busy uniting and strengthening the Qajars, the Zands were torn by fratricide and a bitter struggle for succession.

In the end, the two protagonists for the throne of Persia were Lotf-Ali Khan Zand, a grandnephew of Karim Khan, and Agha Mohammad Khan. These two were of opposite character. The cruelty and treachery of Agha Mohammad were matched against the nobility and gallantry of Lotf-Ali. Agha Mohammad won the contest in 1794, aided by the treachery of Haji Ebrahim, a counselor of Lotf-Ali Khan. The young prince was blinded and strangled, and the province of Kerman, which had aided Lotf-Ali, was devastated and its population savaged.

Agha Mohammad Khan chose Tehran as his capital and from there solidified his rule and expanded his domain. His main foreign foe was Catherine the Great of Russia, and their dispute was over Georgia, whose governor, Heraclius, had renounced his allegiance to Persia and had accepted Russia's protection. In the ensuing struggle Catherine, who had her hands full in Europe, did not come to her protégé's aid. As a result, Agha Mohammad captured Tiflis and put the population to the sword. On his return he was crowned shah of Persia in March 1796.

Catherine sent a punitive expedition which reached as far south as Baku, but she died and her son Paul reversed her orders. Agha Mohammad, delighted at the news, decided to go to the Caucasus and capture Shisha, the one city which had resisted him the previous year. The city surrendered without a struggle, but three days later in June 1797 three of his servants killed Agha Mohammad Shah.

Sir John Malcolm, a British representative at the time, in his *History of Persia* describes the eunuch shah's character: "The person of that monarch was so slender that at a distance he appeared like a youth of fourteen or fifteen. His beardless and shrivelled face resembled that of an aged and wrinkled woman; and the expression of his countenance, at no times pleasant, was horrible when clouded, as it very often was, with indignation. . . . The first passion of his mind was power; the second avarice; and the third revenge. In all these he indulged in excess, and they administered to each other. . . . His knowledge of the character and feelings of others was wonderful; and it is to this knowledge, and his talent of concealing from all the secret purpose of his soul, that we must refer his extraordinary success in subduing his enemies."

Further Reading

The best account of Agha Mohammad Khan's life in English is in Sir John Malcolm, *History of Persia* (2 vols., 1815; rev. ed. 1829). Sketches of his life are in E. G. Browne, *A Literary History of Persia* (2 vols., 1902-1906; new ed., 4 vols., 1953-1956), and in Percy Sykes, *History of Persia* (2 vols., 1915; 3d ed. 1930). More modern studies include W. B. Fisher, ed., *The Cambridge History of Iran*, vol. 1 (1968), and Hamid Algar, *Religion and State in Iran: 1785-1906* (1969). □

Agis IV

Agis IV (ca. 262-241 B.C.) was a Spartan king who tried with youthful idealism to return Sparta to the ancient laws of the country and paid for his failure with his life.

Agis, the son of Eudamidas II, was elected one of Sparta's dual kings in 244 B.C. At that time full Spartan citizenship depended on the possession of land and the ability to subscribe to the *syssition,* the daily group meal which constituted a civil and social occasion. The number of citizens had shrunk rapidly as the ownership of land became concentrated in the hands of a few families, and circulation of foreign money widened the gulf between rich and poor. Agis proposed that all land be redistributed to 4,500 men as citizens and to 15,000 noncitizens, or *perioeci,* who served in the military, and that all debts and mortgages be canceled.

To show his good faith, Agis surrendered the royal estates. Though his altruism gained him support among the younger men, vested interests opposed him. Nonetheless, Agis and his friend Lysander, one of the ephors, pushed his proposals through the assembly after deposing the other of Sparta's dual kings, Leonidas. Agis, however, was unable to implement these proposals because the newly elected ephors of 242 B.C. were in opposition (the five ephors were magistrates who exercised control over the kings). He therefore instigated a bloodless revolution, replacing the ephors with men he trusted. One was his uncle, Agesilaus, a very wealthy and astute man, who persuaded Agis to burn all records of debts and mortgages but then obstructed the actual redistribution of land. This delaying tactic began to undermine Agis's position.

At this critical time the Achaean general Aratus asked for a Spartan army to defend the Isthmus against attack by the Aetolian League. As sole king and Sparta's military commander, Agis left for war, and most of his supporters went with him. In his absence Leonidas returned, was reinstated as king, organized all those whose vested interests were in danger, and got his own supporters elected ephors in 241.

Agis returned disheartened by the treachery of Agesilaus, but he did not use the army for a coup d'etat, preferring to take sanctuary in the temple of Athena. Decoyed onto common ground, he was arrested, put in prison, and condemned in a mock trial. Agis, his mother, and his grandmother were executed.

Agis had the merits and the failings of a young king. He was a puritan, a visionary, and a statesman who saw the need for reform; but he was ingenuous, impetuous, and impractical. His mistake was to use unconstitutional methods to reform the constitution and to dethrone Leonidas when he himself relied on Leonidas's royal position. Agis's inexperience caused him to underestimate the strength and the unscrupulousness of the vested interests of financial conservatism, and his bad judgment of individuals caused his own failure. But his short reign was important. The status quo had been revealed as a folly, and his martyrdom in the cause of social justice and Spartan nationalism was both an inspiration and a warning to the next royal reformer, Cleomenes III.

Further Reading

Plutarch's *The Lives of the Noble Grecians and Romans* contains a good biography of Agis IV. Background works which discuss him briefly are Max Cary, *A History of the Greek World, 323-146 B.C.* (1932; 2d rev. ed. 1951), and Humphrey Michell, *Sparta* (1964).

Additional Sources

King Agis of Sparta and his campaign in Arkadia in 418 B.C.: a chapter in the history of the art of war among the Greeks, New York: AMS Press, 1978. □

Giovanni Agnelli

Italian industrialist Giovanni Agnelli (born 1920) was a leading capitalist in Italy, controlling a group of enterprises that employed 360,000 workers and had annual sales of over $15 billion.

Giovanni Agnelli reigned for thirty years as one of the most prominent industrialists in Europe, spending his youth as one of the most notorious playboys in Europe. Born in Turin, Italy, he was known as Gianni Agnelli or "L'Avvocato" (the lawyer) because he once received a law degree. His grandfather, Giovanni Agnelli, Sr. (1866-1945), established FIAT (Fabbrica Italiana Automobili Torino, the Italian Car Factory, Turin) at the beginning of the 20th century. When Giovanni's son, Edoardo Agnelli, died in an airplane accident, Gianni and his younger brother Umberto became heirs of the largest private enterprise in Italy.

At the time of their father's death, neither Gianni nor Umberto were willing or able to take over the management of the FIAT empire. During the years of Fascism their grandfather allowed all management and power to be concentrated in the hands of Vittorio Valletta. Valetta found it profitable for FIAT and himself to collaborate with the Italian Fascists and German Nazis before and during the war and all the way to the 1943 armistice. The Valletta reign continued after the war and after the death of Giovanni Agnelli, Sr. in 1945. Giovanni Jr. was not prepared for the task, even though from childhood his main goal was to become the head of FIAT and manufacture automobiles. Valletta retired in 1966 and died in 1968.

Playboy to Patriarch

Giovanni Agnelli, Jr. was 46 when he took over FIAT, and his 20 years in the "wilderness" had been spent mostly as a millionaire playboy rather than as a financial and industrial genius. He finally arrived at the headquarters of FIAT in Turin during a period of extraordinary economic expansion in Italy ("the economic miracle"). After 1966 he found himself with total power over a company which had major problems. Valletta had reigned in the old heavy-handed paternalistic style and left Giovanni with an ossified organization incapable of adjusting to the new economic realities of the 1960s. The great empire was overwhelmed by confusion, disorganization, and internal power struggles among its executives. Neither executives or engineers were willing to accept major changes in procedure or attitude for fear of losing the power of their particular fiefdoms. The scenario which developed presented Agnelli in public as "Mr. Capitalist" of the Italian business world, while inside his own company he was confronted by colleagues who wanted to stop him from affecting any real changes. The story of Giovanni Agnelli is that of a continual battle for control and renewal of FIAT between 1966 and 1985, from which he emerged eventually as the victor.

Successes and Failures

His record at the helm of the industrial giant is marked with both successes and failures through some very difficult times. Where Valletta had conducted an unrelenting and autocratic witch hunt against leftists and labor organizers, Agnelli pursued pragmatism above everything. He made alliances in a business-like fashion regardless of politics, using persuasion and strategy to subdue even his strongest rivals. At the beginning of his reign, Agnelli invisioned expanding FIAT internationally, much as Volkswagen had done. This turned into disaster, and a grandiose scheme of joining with French car makers dried up sooner than the ink on the agreement.

The 1970s were trying times for Agnelli, as well as for every established industry connected with the automobile. The 1974 OPEC crises made the Western world vulnerable to oil producers' blackmail. Agnelli's main battle was with government controlled or protected enterprises. He believed in strong administrations in the Valetta tradition, but always retained the ultimate controls himself. At the time many believed that FIAT was a lost cause. But Agnelli never lost optimism, although he put up a front of desperation to convince his workers to produce more for less money.

He attempted to forge an alliance with workers and unions in a grand design for a renaissance of capitalism. He played cat-and-mouse with unions but took advantage of their errors so as to make them inconsequential in the decision-making process at FIAT. In the 1980s he eventually succeeded in putting a car on the market whose popularity once more made FIAT a profitable enterprise. Furthermore, in the 1980s he waged a battle against publicly owned enterprises by taking control of some and helping in the privatization of others.

The Agnelli Empire

By the end of his reign in 1996, the $46.5 billion FIAT empire included a major publishing company, a food producer, an insurance company, and accounted for 25 percent of the capitalization of the Milan Stock Exchange. In 1927 the grandfather Giovanni Agnelli, Sr. created IFI, a financial holding company that sold preferred stock to outsiders but retained all the common stock for the Agnelli family. IFI owns 33 percent of FIAT, as well as common stock in large insurance companies, a department store chain, an important Italian newspaper, a soccer team, and numerous other enterprises. Agnelli's empire is one of the largest in Europe. Out of 20 million Italian workers, about 1.5 million are directly or indirectly dependent upon FIAT and the decisions made be Giovanni Agnelli and his heirs.

In 1996 Agnelli, diagnosed with cancer, finally retired from his post as chairman of FIAT, being replaced by a loyal lieutenant, Cesare Romiti. His son Giovanni, also a member of the board, is being groomed as his eventual replacement.

Further Reading

A history of Agnelli's influence on Italian power is Alan Friedman, *Fiat and the network of Italian Power* (1989). Giovanni Agnelli is discussed as part of the "economic miracle" in *Fortune* (May 1968). A journalistic approach to Agnelli between 1966 and 1985 is Guiseppe Turani, *L'AVVOCATO,* Spreling & Kupfer, editors (Milan 1985). An earlier book on the period, Antonio Mosconi, *Il gruppo dell' impressa industriale,* analyzes the dichotomy between public and private capitalism in Italy. Articles about the end of Agnelli's reign include John Tagliabue, "Agnelli says he will retire from Fiat post," *New York Times* (Dec. 12, 1995), and Maureen Kline, "Fiat Chairman Agnelli to End Era By Stepping Down," *Wall Street Journal* (Dec. 12, 1995). An account of the recent history of the Fiat empire is Charles P. Wallace, "The Next Mr. Fiat?," *Fortune* (Oct. 14, 1996). □

Spiro Theodore Agnew

Between the time of his nomination as Richard Nixon's running mate in August 1968 to his resignation in October 1973, Vice President Spiro T. Agnew (1918-1996) was a leading spokesman for those Nixon called "The Silent Majority" of Americans. The charge of bribe-taking, which forced Agnew's resignation from office, preceded by less than one year President Nixon's own resignation.

Spiro Theodore Agnew was born November 9, 1918, in Baltimore, Maryland, to Greek immigrant restaurant owner Theodore S. Anagnostopoulous and a Virginia-born widow named Margaret Akers. The family surname went through two changes after it left Gargaliani, Greece, metamorphosing from Anagnostopoulous to Aganost before arriving at Agnew. The elder Agnew lost his business during the Depression, but had restored his fortunes by the time his son was ready for high school. Agnew attended public schools in Baltimore before enrolling in Johns Hopkins University in 1937, where he studied chemistry. He was, in his own words, a "typical middle class youth" who spoke and wrote very well, gaining experience writing speeches for his father's many appearances before civic, ethnic, and community groups.

After three years of studying chemistry Ted Agnew transferred to law school at the University of Baltimore, where he attended night classes. He supported himself by working for an insurance company, where he met his future wife "Judy," Elinor Isabel Judefind.

Service in Two Wars

In September of 1941 Agnew became one of the early draftees in President Franklin D. Roosevelt's peace time Selective Service System. After the attack on Pearl Harbor, Agnew was sent to Fort Knox to train as a tank officer. He married Judy after graduation in May 1942. Sent to the European theater, Agnew commanded a tank company in the 10th Armored Division, won the Bronze Star, took part in the Battle of the Bulge, and was discharged a captain.

He returned to civilian life with the great wave of hundreds of thousands of veterans seeking to recover their old lives or build new ones. The first of four children was born to Agnew and his wife in 1946, spurring Agnew to complete his interrupted legal studies in 1947. He had a good job with an insurance company and had just purchased a new home in Baltimore County when the Korean War broke out in 1950. Abruptly recalled to active duty for a year, he lost both his income and his home.

Successful Legal Career

Mustered out a second time, Agnew joined the lower management levels of a Baltimore supermarket chain. He was not only a skillful personnel manager, but developed a friendship with Judge Herbert Moser, who served on the

company's board of directors. Moser helped him make connections, and soon Agnew's legal career took off.

Agnew had all the attributes of the successful American attorney. He was articulate, persuasive, flexible, knowledgeable, confident, well-groomed, and energetic. As clients became more numerous, the growing Agnew family prospered.

Entrance into Politics

Despite his growing law practice, or perhaps because of a desire to expand it, Agnew became involved in Baltimore County local politics. His father was a well-connected Democrat, and Agnew registered as a Democrat early in his adult life. A friend and associate, Judge E. Lester Barrett, persuaded him to switch to the Republican party where he began working for local and national campaigns. In 1957 he served his first public office when he was appointed to the Zoning Board of Appeals of Baltimore County. In 1960 he ran his first campaign, for associate circuit judge. Although he lost that election, the next year saw him winning the seat of Baltimore county executive, the first Republican to do so in seventy years.

His run as county executive was generally considered to be very successful, and he gained a popular following which served him well when he ran for governor of Maryland in 1966 and won. He ran against Democratic civil rights hard-liner and millionaire contractor, George Mahoney. Notwithstanding the overwhelming Democratic edge

in registration, Agnew captured half of the votes, defeating Mahoney 453,000 to 371,000.

Turn to the Right

Governor Agnew proved to be a progressive, urban-oriented executive with moderate civil rights leanings and liberal credentials. While in office he passed tax reform, increased funding for anti-poverty programs, passed legislation removing barriers to public housing, repealed a law banning interracial marriage, spoke out against the death penalty, passed a more liberal abortion law, and drafted the nation's toughest clean water legislation. However, around the time of the urban riots and the rise of the anti-war movement in 1968, the tone and tolerance of Agnew's administration began to undergo alteration. He began arresting civil rights demonstrators, speaking harshly against the rising waves of protest, encouraging a sharp increase in police powers and the use of the military in civil disturbances.

At the 1968 Republican Convention in Miami Beach, Agnew was persuaded to place Richard Nixon's name in nomination. When Nixon won the nomination he accepted Agnew as his running mate. A key sentence uttered by Agnew in his vice presidential acceptance speech was, "I fully recognize that I am an unknown quantity to many of you." In truth, as the governor of a small southern state he was relatively unknown within the party. Former Vice President Nixon wanted someone who was a Southerner, an ethnic American, an experienced executive, a civil rights moderate, a proven Republican vote-getter with appeal to Democrats, and a law and order advocate. Agnew fit all these qualifications.

Agnew's strengths generally helped the ticket, although several of his racially offensive gaffs created momentary fears about the wisdom of the choice. The Nixon-Agnew victory over Humphrey-Muskie was close yet clear cut, with a half million popular votes separating victors and losers.

Vice President—and Resignation

As vice president, Agnew was assigned a then-unprecedented office in the White House and was urged to help shape federal-state policies and other domestic matters. He learned his job quickly, making up for a lack of foreign and national experience by attacking administration opponents through attention-getting speeches. Relying on a crack team of writers led by William Safire, Patrick Buchanan, and Cynthia Rosenwald, the vice president became noted for coining phrases, lashing out against college radicals, dissident intellectuals, American permissiveness, and a "liberal" media elite. In New Orleans on October 19, 1969, he lamented that "a spirit of national masochism prevails, encouraged by an effete corps of impudent snobs who characterize themselves as intellectuals." At the Ohio State graduation ceremony of June 1969 he characterized the older generation's leadership as the "sniveling hand-wringing power structure." With these and similar speeches Agnew became widely known and much sought after as a speaker. The media became attracted to him and gave him considerable attention.

Resigning In Disgrace

Agnew won renomination to Nixon's team in 1972 and undoubtedly contributed to the overwhelming victory over McGovern-Shriver in that year. However, early into his second term he was advised that he was under investigation by federal prosecutors looking into allegations that he had regularly solicited and accepted bribes during his tenure as county executive and Maryland governor. As the cloud of Watergate began to envelope Richard Nixon and the presidency, the situation became increasingly untenable.

This intolerable political situation developed into an intricate plea bargaining process. As a result, federal authorities produced Agnew's "nolo contendere" plea of October 1, 1973. He pleaded no contest in Federal court to one misdemeanor charge of income tax evasion and was fined $10,000 and put on probation for three years. He was also forced to resign his office. His legal expenses, fines and other fees, totaling $160,000, were paid by his good friend Frank Sinatra. He was disbarred by the state of Maryland in 1974. The second of America's vice presidents to resign (John C. Calhoun had done so the previous century), Agnew was the only one to quit under a cloud of scandal.

After retreating from politics Agnew rearranged his life with considerable resiliency, becoming an international business consultant and the owner of several lucrative properties in Palm Springs, California, and in Maryland. He also wrote a best selling novel, *The Canfield Decision* (1986), and a book defending his record, *Go Quietly . . . Or Else* (1980), in which he suggests that Richard Nixon and Alexander Haig had planned his assassination if he refused to leave his post. In 1981 he was sued by three citizens of Maryland who sought to have the money he had reportedly received illegally from the state returned. After a few years of legal maneuvers the citizens won their case and Agnew had to reimburse $248,735 to the state coffers.

Agnew died of leukemia on September 17, 1996, at the age of 77.

Further Reading

The key to Spiro Agnew's importance to America lies in his speeches, which take up a good part of John R. Coyne, Jr.'s *The Impudent Snobs* (1972). Other collections are found in Spiro T. Agnew, *Frankly Speaking* (1970). Early biographies by Jim G. Lucas, *Agnew Profile in Conflict* (1970), and Robert Curran, *Spiro Agnew: Spokesman For America* (1970), shed light on Agnew's pre-vice-presidential career. His own book, *Go Quietly . . . Or Else* (1980), alleged his innocence of the charges that drove him from the office of vice-president. ☐

Shmuel Yoseph Agnon

The Israeli author Shmuel Yoseph Agnon (1888-1970) is noted for his folkloric yet sophisticated novels. He received the Nobel Prize for literature in 1966.

On July 17, 1888, S. Y. Agnon was born Shmuel Yoseph Czaczkes in the town of Buszacz, Eastern Galicia (then part of Austro-Hungary). His father was descended from a long line of Talmudic scholars. The young Shmuel's studies encompassed the whole gamut of Jewish writings: the Bible, Talmudic and Midrashic lore, medieval philosophical treatises, rabbinic writings, and Hasidic tales.

As a youth of 15, Shmuel began to publish his stories and poems in Hebrew and Yiddish. In 1908 he arrived in Palestine, where young *halutzim* (pioneers) were establishing the base for a Jewish state. There he assumed the name of Agnon, and his fame as an original and colorful novelist began to spread. Dwelling chiefly on Hasidic folklore and legend, his tales captured the spirit and flavor of a way of life deeply rooted in Jewish tradition.

From 1913 to 1924 Agnon lived in Germany, where he married Esther Marks. They later had a son and a daughter. While in Germany, he collaborated with Martin Buber on a book of Hasidic tales. In 1924 he returned to Palestine and settled in Jerusalem, a city to which he always remained deeply attached.

Agnon's works mirror Jewish life from the 18th century to the present. In *The Bridal Canopy* (1931) he unfolds a picaresque tale of a pious man, Reb Yudel Hasid, who travels throughout town and village to solicit dowries for his three marriageable daughters. This work is set in a world bygone, anchored in faith and governed by a benevolent providence. This seemingly simple, pietistic way of life is

also reflected in a shorter novel, *In the Heart of the Seas* (1935), which tells of the journey of a group of Hasidim to the land of their ancestors in the early 19th century.

In *A Simple Story* (1935) and *A Guest for the Night* (1939) the reader is ushered into the 20th century with its new and threatening forces. *A Guest for the Night is* based on Agnon's journey to his birthplace in the mid-1930s. World War I has shattered the old faith and traditions and on the horizon looms the still greater menace of World War II. *Yesteryear* (1945) is based on Agnon's experiences in Palestine before World War I. The protagonist of the novel, Yitzhak Kumer, is a somewhat weak, naive, and simple pioneer in search of self-fulfillment but overwhelmed by problems. The work tells the deeply moving story of characters struggling to turn an age-old dream into reality.

In the last decades of his life, stirred by the atrocities of World War II, Agnon infused new currents and nuances into his writings. His stories became more symbolic and took on a Kafkaesque quality. In *Betrothed, A Whole Loaf,* and *Edo and Enam,* Agnon appears as a master of enigma. The settings of these later works are often phantasmagoric, and the plots are frequently parables of the vicissitudes of modern life. Through Midrashic and mystic allusions, Agnon provides the key for deciphering the hidden meanings of these later tales.

S. Y. Agnon died on Feb. 17, 1970, and was buried on the Mount of Olives with great honors.

Further Reading

Two major works on Agnon are Arnold J. Band, *Nostalgia and Nightmare: A Study in the Fiction of S. Y. Agnon* (1968), a biographical as well as critical study, and Baruch Hochman, *The Fiction of S. Y. Agnon* (1970), an evaluation of Agnon's works against historical and literary backgrounds.

Additional Sources

Fisch, Harold, *S. Y. Agnon,* New York: F. Ungar Pub. Co., 1975.
Shaked, Gershon, *Shmuel Yosef Agnon: a revolutionary traditionalist,* New York: New York University Press, 1989. □

Agostino di Duccio

The Italian sculptor Agostino di Duccio (1418-1481) evolved a highly personal style in relief sculpture. He executed his major works in Rimini and Perugia.

One of 10 children of a weaver, Agostino di Duccio was born in Florence. He left the city in 1433. This early departure and the style of his first independent work, an altarpiece with scenes from the life of St. Gemignano (Modena, ca. 1442), suggest that he may have studied sculpture under Jacopo della Quercia in nearby Bologna.

Agostino returned to his birthplace in 1442, but by 1446 he was forced to leave Florence for Venice because he was charged with the theft of silver from the Church of SS.

Annunziata. Perhaps by 1450, and certainly by 1454, Agostino was engaged in the most important enterprise of his life: the sculptural program for the Tempio Malatestiano in Rimini. His collaborator was Matteo di Pasti.

Executed with extraordinary precision, assurance, and delicacy, the reliefs of Rimini are carved in a style so dependent on finely incised curvilinear patterns that they evoke such far-ranging analogies as Oriental calligraphy, the ''Neo-Attic'' style of Greco-Roman art, and the ethereal designs of Agostino's younger compatriot Sandro Botticelli.

From 1457 to 1462 Agostino was in Perugia, chiefly engaged on the facade of the small oratory of S. Bernardino. The main emphasis is on the tympanum over the entrance door; the sensitive, frail figure of the saint is framed by angels playing musical instruments, and the angels are surrounded by a ring of gay and charming cherubim heads.

In 1463 Agostino worked briefly in Bologna preparing a model for the facade of S. Petronio. That same year he received commissions for two colossal figures for the Cathedral of Florence. The first, probably executed in stucco, is lost; the second, in marble, was not finished by Agostino, and the marble block was used 40 years later by Michelangelo for his *David.* During the next decade Agostino completed various smaller works, including the attractive tabernacle for the Church of the Ognissanti in Florence. In 1473 he again left Florence and spent his last years in Perugia executing a series of commissions that reveal a somewhat weary repetition of his fresher and more incisive earlier works. Agostino is presumed to have died after 1481.

Further Reading

There is no adequate monograph on Agostino. Useful information and critical insights are presented in John Pope-Hennessy, *The Virgin and Child by Agostino di Duccio* (1952) and *Italian Renaissance Sculpture* (1958), and in Charles Seymour, Jr., *Sculpture in Italy, 1400-1500* (1966). □

Georgius Agricola

The German mineralogist and writer on mining Georgius Agricola (1494-1555) is a major figure in the history of technology. His main contribution was his book on mining and metallurgy, ''De re metallica.''

Georgius Agricola, whose real name was Georg Bauer, was born at Glachau in Saxony on March 24, 1494. Virtually nothing is known of his family, his childhood, or his schooldays. At school his teachers Latinized his name to Georgius Agricola, a customary practice at the time.

Years of Study and Research

Agricola entered the University of Leipzig at the age of 20 and was awarded a degree in 1517. He began teaching Latin and Greek in the town school of Zwickau in 1518, and within a year he was made the principal. From 1522 to 1524 Agricola was a lecturer in the University of Leipzig. Then, in order to further his studies of the natural sciences, philosophy, and medicine, he spent 3 years studying in Italy at the universities of Bologna, Padua, and Venice.

By 1526 Agricola had returned to Germany, and a year later he took the job of physician in the little town of Joachimsthal, Bohemia. At that time Joachimsthal was in the center of one of the most productive metal mining regions in Central Europe, and Agricola was soon deeply involved in studying the closely related techniques of mining and metallurgy. After 3 years' residence in Joachimsthal, he finished his first book on mining, a hand-book on mineralogical and mining terms.

By now Agricola was fully committed to his research into mining and metallurgy. Around 1530 he left his medical post in Joachimsthal and toured German mines for 3 years. However, the lure of his native Saxony brought Agricola to Chemnitz in 1533, and he was appointed city physician. He lived and worked there for his remaining years. In 1543 he married a widow of Chemnitz, and they had at least five children.

Publications and Civic Activities

Five of Agricola's books were published in a one-volume edition in 1546 in Basel, comprising *De ortu et causis subterraneorum*, a pioneer study of physical geology; *De natura eorum quae effluunt ex terra*, dealing with subterranean waters and gases; *De natura fossilium*, the second in

importance of Agricola's works, being the first proper study of mineralogy; *De veteribus et novis metallis*, dealing mostly with the history of metals; and *Rerum metallicorum interpretatio*, a dictionary of Latin and German mineralogical and metallurgical terms. In 1548 a curious little book, *De animantibus subterraneis*, appeared; it is a not very sound study of animals which live underground. He wrote more than two dozen works, many of which have survived, on mining, metallurgy, medicine, and religion.

In 1546 Agricola began to take an active interest in public affairs. He became a burgher of Chemnitz and served four terms as burgomaster. Although he was a staunch Catholic living under a Protestant monarchy, other political duties and civic responsibilities came his way and indicate the high esteem with which he was regarded. He died on Nov. 21, 1555.

"De re metallica"

Agricola's masterpiece, *De re metallica*, was the most important 16th-century book on any aspect of technology. He appears to have begun it about 1530, when he left Joachimsthal, and it took 20 years to complete. The printing was delayed until 1553, because of the time required to prepare the illustrations, and its publication in Basel in 1556 was a year too late for the approval of the author.

De re metallica consists of 12 books and covers every aspect of the industry. Hundreds of mining operations are described, and there are sections dealing with such related problems as surveying, geology, smelting, assaying, and administration. No less important and interesting than the text are the hundreds of delightful wood-cuts, which are technical drawings the like of which had not been printed before. Although they are not the only surviving illustrations of 16th-century engineering, they are the most realistic and reliable because they are based on actual practice rather than on speculation.

For 2 centuries *De re metallica* was the standard work in its field. Agricola had, for the first time in mining history, attempted to place the subject on an organized and scientific footing. More than a dozen editions appeared before 1700 in Latin, German, and Italian.

Further Reading

Agricola's *De re metallica* is his essential work. The fully documented translation by Herbert Clark Hoover and his wife, Lou Henry Hoover (1912), is recommended. There is a biography of Agricola in German but no full-length biography in English. Bern Dibner, *Agricola on Metals* (1958), is primarily an analysis of *De re metalica* but also provides some information on Agricola's life. Background material is in Frank Dawson Adams, *The Birth and Development of the Geological Sciences* (1938), and William B. Parsons, *Engineers and Engineering in the Renaissance* (1939), which contains a description of Agricola's techniques of mining and metallurgy. □

Emilio Aguinaldo

The Philippine revolutionary leader Emilio Aguinaldo (1869-1964) fought for independence of the Philippine Islands, first against Spain and then against the United States.

B orn on March 23, 1869, Emilio Aguinaldo grew up in Kawit in Cavite Province and was educated in Manila. Appointed to a municipal position in his home province, he was also the local leader of a revolutionary society fighting Spanish rule over the Philippines. By an agreement signed with rebel leaders in January 1898, Spain agreed to institute liberal reforms and to pay a large indemnity; the rebels then went into exile.

When war broke out between Spain and the United States in April 1898, Aguinaldo made arrangements with the U.S. consuls in Hong Kong and Singapore and with Commodore George Dewey to return from exile to fight against Spain. On June 12 Aguinaldo proclaimed the independence of the Philippine Islands from Spain, hoisted the national flag, introduced a national anthem, and ordered a public reading of the declaration of independence.

When he realized that the United States would not accept immediate and complete independence for the Philippines, he organized a revolution against American rule that resulted in 3 years of bloody guerrilla warfare. He was captured on March 23, 1901, by Gen. Frederick Funston. Funston and several other officers, bound hand and foot, pretended to be prisoners and were taken to Aguinaldo's camp by Filipinos loyal to the United States. Released and given weapons, they easily captured Aguinaldo, who then took an oath of allegiance to the United States and issued a peace proclamation on April 19. The bitterness caused by the war was soon transformed into friendship as Americans and Filipinos joined to work toward Philippine independence. Aguinaldo retired to private life, and his son entered West Point in the same class as Gen. Funston's son.

In 1935 Aguinaldo ran unsuccessfully for president of the Philippine Commonwealth against Manuel Quezon. After the Japanese invasion of the Philippines in 1941, he cooperated with the new rulers, even making a radio appeal for the surrender of the American and Filipino forces on Bataan. He was arrested as a collaborationist after the Americans returned but was later freed in a general amnesty. He explained his action by saying, "I was just remembering the fight I led. We were outnumbered, too, in constant retreat. I saw my own soldiers die without affecting future events. To me that seemed to be what was happening on Bataan, and it seemed like a good thing to stop."

In 1950 he was named to the Council of State, an advisory body for the president, and in his later years he was chairman of a board which dispensed pensions to the remaining veterans of the revolution. He died in Manila on Feb. 6, 1964.

Further Reading

Aguinaldo tells his own story in *A Second Look at America* (1957). The outstanding early work on Philippine affairs is W. Cameron Forbes, *The Philippine Islands* (2 vols., 1928; rev. ed. 1945). Leon Wolff is more sympathetic to the Philippine rebels in *Little Brown Brother: How the United States Purchased and Pacified the Philippine Islands at the Century's Turn* (1961). A more scholarly account is Garel A. Grunder and William E. Livezey, *The Philippines and the United States* (1951).

Additional Sources

Turot, Henri, *Emilio Aguinaldo, first Filipino president, 1898-1901,* Manila, Philippines: Foreign Service Institute, 1981. □

Ahad Haam

The Russian-born author and philosopher Ahad Haam (1856-1927), whose real name was Asher Tsvi Ginzberg wrote essays on the Jewish nation that caused great debate within the Zionist movement.

A sher Ginzberg was born in Skwera in the Russian district of Kiev. His father, a fervent Hasid, was learned and affluent, and he educated his son in the spirit of Hasidism. Even as a youth, Asher was renowned as an expert in Talmudical and Hasidic literature. At the age of 17 he married, remaining in his father's home while continuing his studies of all aspects of Jewish learning. He later became interested in secular culture, Western languages, and science.

In 1884 Ginzberg settled in Odessa, where he remained for the next 20 years. There he actively joined in the work of the Lovers of Zion. In 1889 he published his first programmatic article, "This Is Not the Way," under the pseudonym Ahad Haam (meaning "one of the people"). In this essay he attempted to demonstrate that, without a revival of the national consciousness which had dwindled over the long years of exile, the program of the Lovers of Zion could not succeed. In the same year he founded in Odessa the Sons of Moses, an organization dedicated to providing the future leadership for a Jewish national revival.

In 1891 Ahad Haam made his first visit to Palestine. He wrote the article "Truth from Palestine," which aroused intense reactions and vehement opposition among Zionists. In 1896 he became head of Achiasaph, an important Hebrew publishing house in Warsaw. In the following year he founded in Berlin the monthly *Hashiloach* and remained its editor until 1902. He then was employed by the Wisotsky Tea Company, first in Odessa and from 1907 in London.

Ahad Haam visited Palestine five times and in 1922 permanently settled there. He undertook the collection of his many articles and letters, took an active part in the community life, and continued in his Zionist speculations. In 1927 he died and was buried in Tel Aviv.

Ahad Haam was an original and penetrating thinker. He was one of the first opponents of Theodor Herzl's political Zionism, and he proposed instead national redemption through a spiritual Zionism. Such a goal, he thought, could be reached only through a center of learning, ethics, philosophy, and science in Palestine. This center would safeguard the Jewish nation against cultural assimilation and would strengthen feelings of national solidarity among Diaspora Jewry. He argued that solutions to the economic and political problems of millions of Jews were unattainable, since "an ingathering of the exiles would be nothing short of miraculous." But he stressed that a spiritual revival of Judaism was well within the realm of the possible. The influence of Ahad Haam upon Jewish literature and Zionist thought was great, and he found many adherents among both political leaders and Jewish authors.

Further Reading

For a collection of Ahad Haam's works in English see *Ahad Haam: Selected Essays,* translated by Sir Leon Simon (1912). Simon also wrote a biography, *Ahad Haam, Asher Ginzberg* (1960). For a general introduction see Shalom Spiegel, *Hebrew Reborn* (1930), and Meyer Waxman, *A History of Jewish Literature* (4 vols., 1930-1936; new ed., 5 vols. in 6, 1960).

Additional Sources

Zipperstein, Steven J., *Elusive prophet: Ahad Ha'am and the origins of Zionism,* Berkeley: University of California Press, 1993. □

Ahmadou Ahidjo

Ahmadou Ahidjo (1924-1989) was the president of the Federal Republic of Cameroon and one of the most influential leaders of the French-speaking African states.

Ahmadou Ahidjo was born in August 1924, in Garoua, an inland river port on the Benue River in northern Cameroon. The son of a Fulani chief, he attended secondary school in Yaoundé, the Cameroon capital, to prepare for a career in the lower echelons of the civil service. Unable to complete his education, he became a radio operator for the post office, a position he held until 1946 when he entered territorial politics. In 1947 he was elected to the trust territory's first Assembly and was reelected in 1952. His growing importance in Cameroon politics was emphasized when, in 1953, in addition to his functions as territorial deputy, he was elected to the Assembly of the French Union. He served that body as one of its secretaries in 1954 and as vice president for the 1956-1957 session.

Cameroon was granted responsible government in 1957, and André Marie Mbida, leader of the Démocrates Camerounais party, became the territory's first prime minister. Ahidjo, who had joined the Démocrates during the previous year and whose influence among the northern

deputies was widely acknowledged, was appointed vice premier and minister of the interior in the Mbida government. When Mbida was forced to resign in February 1958, Ahidjo, who had broken with him earlier, took over as premier.

On January 1, 1960, the former French Cameroon Trust Territory became an independent republic, and in May Ahidjo was elected his country's first president. When, on October 1, 1961, the Cameroon Republic and the former British Trust Territory of the Southern Cameroons merged to become the Federal Republic of Cameroon, he became president of the federation. On March 23, 1970, Ahidjo, as the only candidate of the ruling Cameroon National Union (CNU), was reelected to his second seven-year term as president.

Personality and Political Views

Ahidjo began his career as a deputy from the Benué region in the north, representing northern sectional interests. As his outlook broadened, he helped found a number of northern-based political associations. Then in 1956 he joined the Démocrates, a party that had been founded by Catholic intellectuals in the south. A devout Moslem, he brought to the Démocrates both northern support and a national outlook. In 1958, following his break with Mbida, he organized a new political party, the Union Camerounaise (UC), which became the governing party when Ahidjo succeeded Mbida as prime minister. The UC came to dominate Cameroon's political scene, absorbing other parties and groups until 1966, when it merged with the

remaining East and West Cameroon parties and became the country's only party, under the new name of the Cameroon National Union. Since Ahidjo was president of the UC, he also became president of the CNU.

Ahidjo was by nature retiring and not given to personal ostentation and flamboyant public display. These qualities contributed to a political style marked not only by dignity and an air of quiet command, but also by a capacity for occasional firm, even ruthless, action (as demonstrated in 1962 when, at a single stroke, he jailed all four leaders of opposition parties). His political philosophy included espousal of the single-party state, a commitment to pan-African ideals, and a somewhat vaguely defined brand of African socialism. He was a firm proponent of intra-African cooperation—trying to bring peace between rival factions in Cameroon's north and south—and his government played key roles in various regional organizations, as well as in the broader-based Organization of African Unity.

Voluntary transfer of power

In November 1982, Ahidjo resigned the presidency and handed over power to his prime minister and long-time associate, Paul Biya, but stayed on as head of the country's single political party. A power struggle broke out, however, and Ahidjo was accused of plotting against the government.

He went into exile in France in August 1983 and in early 1984 was sentenced to death in absentia by a Cameroon court. Though the sentence was later commuted to an indefinite term of detention, Ahidjo never returned to Cameroon. He died of a heart attack November 30, 1989, in Dakar, Senegal.

Further Reading

For information on Ahidjo see Victor T. Le Vine, *The Cameroons: From Mandate to Independence* (1964); Claude E. Welch, Jr., *Dream of Unity: Pan Africanism and Political Unification in West Africa* (1966); and Willard R. Johnson, *The Cameroon Federation: Political Integration in a Fragmentary Society* (1970). ☐

Conrad Aiken

Conrad (Potter) Aiken (1889-1973), poet, essayist, novelist, and critic, was one of America's foremost men of letters and a major figure in American literary modernism.

I n Conrad Aiken's "Silent Snow, Secret Snow," a young boy named Paul withdraws from his parents, teacher, and people with authority over his life. He enters a private, autistic world in which it seems as if he were cut off from everyone else by a wilderness of silence and snow. That private world seems mysterious in a delightful way, and by the end of the story, Paul has completely enveloped himself in it. There is no sign that anyone will ever be able to reach him again.

"Silent Snow, Secret Snow" is one of Aiken's most powerful stories. One of its principal achievements lies in making the reader sense the force and pleasure that a private world like Paul's can have.

A world like that might once have been attractive to Aiken himself. He was the son of wealthy, socially prominent New Englanders who had moved to Savannah, Georgia, where his father became a highly respected physician and surgeon. But then something happened for which, as Aiken later said, no one could ever find a reason. Without warning or apparent cause, his father became increasingly irascible, unpredictable, and violent. Then, early in the morning of February 27, 1901, he murdered his wife and shot himself. Aiken (who was eleven years old) heard the gunshots and discovered the bodies.

The violent deaths of his parents overshadowed Aiken's life and writings. Throughout his life, he was afraid that, like his father, he would go insane, and, like Paul in "Silent Snow, Secret Snow," he withdrew from threats in the world around him. He disliked large gatherings and refused to give public readings from his works. He became deeply interested in psychoanalytic thought, and it became a central concern in his works.

After the tragedy, Aiken was taken to Massachusetts to live with relatives. He graduated from the Middlesex School and Harvard, where his classmates included T.S. Eliot, with whom he established a lifelong friendship. He lived in England for several years, but his main home for most of his life was Massachusetts. During his last 12 years, however, his

home was the brickfront rowhouse in Savannah next to the one in which his parents died.

Aiken wrote or edited more than 50 books, the first of which was published in 1914, two years after his graduation from Harvard. His work includes novels, short stories (*The Collected Short Stories* appeared in 1961), criticism, autobiography, and, most important of all, poetry. He was awarded the National Medal for Literature, the Gold Medal for Poetry from the National Institute of Arts and Letters, the Pulitzer Prize, the Bollingen Prize, and the National Book Award. He was awarded a Guggenheim Fellowship, taught briefly at Harvard, and served as Consultant in Poetry for the Library of Congress from 1950 to 1952. He was also largely responsible for establishing Emily Dickinson's reputation as a major American poet.

The best source for information on Aiken's life is his autobiographical novel *Ushant* (1952), one of his major works. In this book he speaks candidly about his various affairs and marriages, his attempted suicide and fear of insanity, and his friendships with Eliot (who appears in the book as The Tsetse), Ezra Pound (Rabbi Ben Ezra), and other accomplished men.

In an interview for the *Paris Review* toward the end of his life, Aiken claimed that Freud's influence could be found throughout his work. In both his poetry and his fiction, Aiken tried to realize motivations buried in the subconscious. He believed that if they were left there, unspoken and unacknowledged, they could have as disastrous an effect as they had on his father's life. For Aiken, literature was a means to awareness, a route by which a man could become aware of the dark motivations hidden within himself.

Psychoanalytic thought is central in Aiken's writings. In his novel *Great Circle* (1933), for example, the central character has to learn to accept his past—with, of course, the help of a psychoanalyst. *Blue Voyage* (1927) is ostensibly about a voyage to England, but in fact the real voyage in this stream-of-consciousness novel is in the mind.

Aiken was principally successful as a poet, but his poetry has also been severely criticized. The central problem with much of the poetry is that it seems to lack great intensity. It conveys feelings of indefiniteness; emotion seems dispersed or passive. But those who criticize the poetry in this way have missed the nature of Aiken's poetic task. He cannot speak with the intensity and precision of other poets because he is, as it were, seeing and showing us things for the first time. He is dealing with aspects of man's psychology that are by their very nature indefinite and, in any precise way, undefinable. In this respect, his poetry reminds us strongly of the work of Mallarmé and other French symbolists.

Like the symbolists, Aiken is also a master of poetic music. Some poets are read less for the sound of their verse than for their ideas. Although Aiken presents grand intellectual schemes rooted in psychoanalytic thought, his greatest achievement is in the sound of his poetry—that is, in the creation of formal patterns of sound. There is great pleasure in simply reading and hearing the sound of his verse.

Aiken trained himself comprehensively in traditional English prosody, but his poetry shows little awareness of the revolutions in prosody that Pound and William Carlos Williams were effecting during his life. But the poetic effects he created are reminiscent of experiments in other arts in the late 19th and early 20th centuries. The sound of his poetry reminds one of the music of Debussy or, to name one of Aiken's American contemporaries, Charles Tomlinson Griffes. In painting, he reminds one of Whistler, particularly the Whistler of the Nocturnes.

Aiken sketches out moods, sensations, feelings, and attitudes with the music of his verse, but it is done as impressionistically as in, for example, Griffes' "The White Peacock" and "Nightfall." Aiken was at his best in poetic evocations of emotional and subconscious states which are better understood through suggestion than through direct statement.

Aiken's experiments with poetic music link him to some of the major poets of the New York School, particularly John Ashbery. The New York poets have generally been somewhat more experimental technically, but in the creation of "pure poetry"—poetry dependent on internal music for its unity and effect—they have clear affinities with him. Aiken should be seen in part as a transitional figure between the fin-de-siècle world of aestheticism and symbolism, on the one hand, and the poetic experiments of Ashbery and the New York School, on the other.

The magic of Aiken's poetry is in its ability to suggest through sound, image, and rhythm the things that would otherwise remain unknown to us. That accomplishment by itself places him among the most significant American poets of his generation.

Further Reading

The critical work on Aiken is vast. Reuel Denney's *Conrad Aiken* (1964), Frederick John Hoffman's *Conrad Aiken* (1962), and Jay Martin's *Conrad Aiken, a Life of His Art* (1962) are essential works. *Selected Letters of Conrad Aiken*, Joseph Killorin, ed., was published in 1978.

Additional Sources

Butscher, Edward, *Conrad Aiken, poet of White Horse Vale*, Athens: University of Georgia Press, 1988.
Conrad Aiken: a priest of consciousness, New York: AMS Press, 1989. □

Alvin Ailey

Alvin Ailey (1931-1989) founded the Alvin Ailey American Dance Theatre and won international fame as both a dancer and choreographer.

During the 1960s and 1970s, Alvin Ailey shaped modern dance into a popular art form. In 1969, he founded the American Dance Center, a dance school that teaches a variety of techniques. Five years later he founded the Alvin Ailey Repertory Ensemble, a junior dance company. But mainly through the auspices of the Alvin Ailey American Dance Theater established in 1959, Ailey greatly impacted the dance world. Known for its "vibrant artistry and repertory, and for Ailey's motivating humanist vision," his company drew enthusiastic responses from audiences, while touring the world.

The 30-member company has executed more than 150 pieces in some 67 countries. Ailey's modern dance company has presented classic pieces by early dance pioneers, including the dancer, choreographer, and anthropologist Katherine Dunham, whose Afro-Caribbean-based works had a lasting impact on Ailey. In addition, his company has performed many works by younger black choreographers such as Bill T. Jones, Ulysses Dove, Judith Jamison, and others.

Ailey also produced his own celebrated dance pieces, dealing with his memories of church services and forbidden dance halls in the all-black neighborhood of the Texas town where he spent his early years. His energetic, diverting dances also used blues, jazz, Latin, and classical music. About Ailey's works John Gruen wrote in *The Private World of Ballet,* "His work is marked by the free use of disparate elements of the dance vocabulary. At its best, the Ailey group generates an uncommon exhilaration, achieved by a tumultuous and almost tactile rhythmic pulse. Ailey's own best works are charged with a dazzling and uninhibited movement and life. The exuberance and poignancy of the black experience are well served in Ailey's splendid [dance pieces] *Revelations, Blues Suite,* and *Cry.*"

In addition, Ailey staged dance productions, operas, ballets, and had works performed on television. He received honorary degrees in fine arts from colleges and universities and prizes for his choreography, including a *Dance* magazine award in 1975; the Springarn Medal, given to him by the National Association for the Advancement of Colored People (NAACP) in 1979; and the Capezio Award that same year. In 1988 he was awarded the Kennedy Center Honors prize.

Inauspicious Beginnings

Alvin Ailey, Jr. was born into a large extended family on January 5, 1931, in Rogers, Texas, a small town not far from Waco. Alvin Sr., a laborer, left his son's mother, Lula Elizabeth, when Alvin Jr. was less than one-year-old. While the United States was in the midst of the economic Great Depression, jobs were particularly scarce for black men and Alvin Sr. struggled to make ends meet. Six years later, Alvin Jr. was sent to his mother. At the age of six, Alvin Jr. moved with his mother to Navasota, Texas, where he recalled in an interview in the *New York Daily News Magazine,* "There was the white school up on the hill, and the black Baptist church, and the segregated theaters and neighborhoods. Like most of my generation, I grew up feeling like an outsider, like someone who didn't matter."

In 1942, when Ailey was 12, he and his mother relocated to Los Angeles, where his mother worked in an aircraft factory. As a teenager Ailey showed an interest in athletics, joining his high school gymnastics team and playing football. An admirer of pioneering dancers Gene Kelly and Fred Astaire, Ailey took tap dancing lessons at the home of a neighbor. But his interest in dance was really stimulated when a high school friend took him to visit the Hollywood modern dance school run by Lester Horton, whose company was the first racially integrated one in America. Unsure of what opportunities would be available for him as a dancer, however, he left Horton's school after one month.

After graduating from high school in 1948, Ailey contemplated becoming a teacher. He entered the University of California in Los Angeles and began studying the romance languages. When Horton offered him a scholarship in 1949, Ailey went back to the dance school but left again after one year, this time to attend San Francisco State College.

Directed Horton's Troupe

For a time Ailey danced in a San Francisco nightclub, then he returned to the Horton school to finish his training. By 1953, when Horton took the company east for a New York City debut performance, Ailey was with him. When Horton died of a heart attack, the young Ailey took charge as the company's artistic director, choreographing two pieces in Horton's style to be presented at the Jacob's Pillow festival. After the works received poor reviews from the festival manager, the troupe broke up.

Despite the setback, Ailey's career stayed on track. A Broadway producer invited him to dance in *House of Flowers,* a musical adaptation of Truman Capote's book. While a member of the cast, Ailey spent the next five months broadening his dance knowledge by taking classes at the

Martha Graham school with Doris Humphrey, and with Charles Weidman and Hanya Holm. He also studied ballet with Karel Shook, cofounder of the Dance Theatre of Harlem, and acting with legendary acting instructor Stella Adler. From the mid-1950s through the early 1960s, Ailey appeared in theatrical and musical productions on and off-Broadway, among them *The Carefree Tree; Sing, Man, Sing; Jamaica;* and *Call Me By My Rightful Name.* He also played a major theatrical part in the play, *Tiger, Tiger, Burning Bright.*

In the spring of 1958, Ailey and another dancer with an interest in choreographing recruited 35 dancers to perform several concerts at the 92nd Street Young Men's and Young Women's Hebrew Association (YM-YWHA) in New York City, a place where modern dances and new choreographers were seen. Ailey's first major piece was inspired by blues music. Viewers saw the debut performance of *Blues Suite,* set in a Southern "bawdyhouse." Observed Julinda Lewis-Ferguson in her book, *Alvin Ailey, Jr.: A Life in Dance,* "The characters interact with anger, tenderness, love, and a whole range of familiar and recognizable emotions." The performance drew praise, with Jack Anderson of the *New York Times* calling *Blues Suite* "one of Mr. Ailey's best pieces." Ailey scheduled a second concert at the Y, to present his own works, and then a third, which featured his most famous piece, *Revelations.* Accompanied by the elegant jazz music of Duke Ellington, *Revelation's* audience is deftly pulled into African-American religious life. Julinda Lewis-Ferguson described the piece in her book: "*Revelations* begins with the dancers clustered together in a group, in the center of the stage, arms stretched over their heads. . . . They appear to be bathed in a golden blessing from heaven. . . . The highly energetic final section of the work starts off with three men running, sometimes on their knees, trying to hide from their sins or from the punishment for their sins. . . . The finale, "Rocka My Soul in the Bosom of Abraham," is both a spiritually powerful conclusion to the suite and a purely physical release of emotion." In the *New York Post* Clive Barnes described *Revelations* as "powerful and eloquent" and a "timeless tribute to humanity, faith, and survival."

Established Own Dance Company

Ailey established the Alvin Ailey American Dance Theater, composed of a troupe of eight black dancers, in 1959. One year after formation, Alvin Ailey's dance theater became the resident dance company at the Clark Center for the Performing Arts at the 51st Street and Eighth Avenue Young Men's Christian Association (YMCA) in New York City. In 1969, they moved to Brooklyn, New York, as the resident dance company of the Brooklyn Academy of Music, an arts center with three theaters. But they were unable to create the Lincoln Center they had hoped for in that borough and moved back to midtown Manhattan in 1971.

By the mid-1960s Ailey, who struggled with his weight, gradually phased out his dancing and replaced it with choreographing. He also oversaw administrative details as the director of his ambitious dance company. By 1968, the company had received funding from private and public or-

ganizations but still had financial problems, even as its reputation spread and it brought modern dance to audiences around the world. Ailey also had the leading African-American soloist of modern dance, Judith Jamison, and having been using Asian and white dancers since the mid-1960s, Ailey had fully integrated the company. He had organized his dance school in 1969, and by 1974, he had a repertory ensemble too.

In the early 1960s the company performed in Southeast Asia and Australia as part of an international cultural program set up by President John F. Kennedy. Later they traveled to Brazil, Europe, and West Africa. Ailey was choreographing dances for other companies too. He created *Feast of Ashes* for the Joffrey Ballet, three pieces for the Harkness ballet, and *Anthony and Cleopatra* for the Metropolitan Opera at Lincoln Center in New York City.

Ailey also worked on projects with other artists, including one with the jazz musician Duke Ellington for the American Ballet Theater. His company also gave a benefit performance for the Southern Christian Leadership Conference (SCLC). For Ailey the decade culminated with the performance of *Masekela Language,* a dance about the need for racial equality in South Africa, based on the music of Hugh Masekela, a black South African trumpeter who lived in exile for speaking out against apartheid. In her book Julinda Lewis-Ferguson described the piece as "raw, rough, almost unfinished, just like the buildings of the South African townships."

Ailey's Solo *Cry* A Smash Hit

By the late 1970s Ailey's company was one of America's most popular dance troupes. They continued touring around the world, with U.S. State Department backing. They were the first modern dancers to visit the former Soviet Union since Isadora Duncan's dancers performed there during the 1920s. In 1971, Ailey's company was asked to return to the City Center Theater in New York City after a performance featuring Ailey's celebrated solo, *Cry;* danced by Judith Jamison, she made it one of the troupe's best known pieces.

Dedicated to "all black women everywhere—especially our mothers," the piece depicts the struggles of different generations of black American women. It begins with the unwrapping of a long white scarf that becomes many things during the course of the dance, including a wash rag, and ends with an expression of unquestioning belief and happiness danced to the late 1960s song, "Right On, Be Free." Of this and of all his works, Ailey told John Gruen in *The Private World of Ballet,* "I am trying to express something that I feel about people, life, the human spirit, the beauty of things. . . . My ballets are all very close to me—they're very personal. . . . I think that people come to the theater to look at themselves, to look at the state of things. I try to hold up the mirror. . . ."

In 1980, Ailey suffered a mental breakdown which put him in the hospital for several weeks. At the time he had lost a close friend, was going through midlife crisis, and was experiencing financial difficulties. Still, he choreographed a number of pieces for the company during the 1980s, and his reputation as a founding father of modern dance grew during the decade.

Ending a legendary career, Ailey died of a blood disorder called dyscrasia, on December 1, 1989. Thousands of people flocked to the memorial service for him held at the Cathedral of St. John the Divine. "Alvin Ailey was a giant among American artists, a towering figure on the international dance scene," Gerald Arpino, the artistic director of the Joffrey Ballet, told the *Washington Post*. "His works have elated and moved audiences throughout the world. His spirit soars in his creations and he has enriched and illuminated our lives." Indeed, African American modern dance has firmly been entrenched in popular culture thanks to the presence of Ailey, creator of 79 dance pieces.

Further Reading

Earl Blackwell's Celebrity Register, Times Publishing Group, 1986, pp. 3-4; Gale Research Inc., 1990, pp. 2-3.
Ferguson, Julinda Lewis, *Alvin Ailey, Jr.: A Life in Dance,* Walker and Company, 1994, pp. 1-74.
Gruen, John, *The Private World of Ballet,* Viking, 1975, pp. 417-23.
Jamison, Judith, with Howard Kaplan, *Dancing Spirit: An Autobiography,* Doubleday, 1993, pp. 66-236.
Newsmakers, Gale Research Inc., 1989, 1990.
Rogosin, Elinor, *The Dance Makers: Conversations With American Choreographers,* Walker and Company, 1980, pp. 102-117.
Ballet News, November, 1983, pp. 13-16.
Chicago Tribune, December 3, 1989, Sec. 2, p. 16.
Dance Magazine, December, 1983, pp. 44, 46, 48; October, 1978, pp. 63-4, 66, 68, 72-4, 76.
Los Angeles Times, December 2, 1989, Sec. A-38.
Newsday, December 4, 1988, Part II, pp. 4-5, 27.
New York Times, December 2, 1989, pp. 1, 14.
Washington Post, December 2, 1989, Sec. A-1, A-12; Sec. C-1, C-9. □

Pierre d'Ailly

The French scholar and cardinal Pierre d'Ailly (1350-1420) is known chiefly for his efforts in healing the Western Schism of the Church. His scientific and philosophical writings are also important.

Pierre d'Ailly was born at Compiègne. He spent most of his life in association with the University of Paris, graduating in theology from the College of Navarre in 1380 and becoming master of the college in 1384 and chancellor of the university in 1389.

One of the university's chief concerns was the Western Schism (1378-1417), in which rival popes claimed legitimacy. At first D'Ailly supported the Avignon pope Benedict XIII, but he soon became a radical leader of the Conciliar movement. The Conciliarists argued that a general council of the Church is superior to the pope and that therefore a general council could end the schism by choosing a new pope satisfactory to all parties. D'Ailly played a prominent part at the Council of Pisa (1409), which elected a new pope, Alexander V. In 1411 Alexander's successor, John XXIII, made D'Ailly a cardinal. When the rival popes refused to resign, however, the Council of Constance (1414-1418) was called. D'Ailly was an acknowledged leader and effected the decision to have the contending popes abdicate. The council then elected a new pope, Martin V, and the schism was ended. D'Ailly himself was a candidate for the papal throne, but he lost the election because of opposition from France's enemies, England and Burgundy. He retired for safety to Avignon, where he served Martin V.

Pierre d'Ailly wrote prolifically. His works on the nature of the Church had the most lasting influence. He developed the theory of conciliarism and the concept that the only infallible body in the Church is the whole of the faithful. These ideas were later shared by the Protestant reformers. He was an advocate of the calendar reform later made by Pope Gregory XII; and, like many important thinkers of his day, he took great interest in astrology, which he felt was consistent with religion. His book on geography, *Imago mundi,* was read carefully by Columbus, who said that it inspired his voyage of 1492 by suggesting the feasibility of sailing from Spain west to India. D'Ailly also wrote on astronomy, meteorology, mathematics, logic, metaphysics, and psychology. He died in Avignon in 1420.

Further Reading

A biography of Pierre d'Ailly in English is John P. MacGowen, *Pierre d'Ailly and the Council of Constance* (1936). There are two good studies for D'Ailly's conciliar theories: E.F. Jacob, *Essays in the Conciliar Epoch* (1943; rev. ed. 1963), and Brian Tierney, *Foundations of the Conciliar Theory: The Contribution of the Medieval Canonists from Gratian to the Great Schism* (1955). For D'Ailly's actions at Constance and some documents of the event see Louise Ropes Loomis, *The Council of Constance: The Unification of the Church* (1961).

Additional Sources

Guenaee, Bernard, *Between church and state: the lives of four French prelates in the late Middle Ages,* Chicago: University of Chicago Press, 1991. □

William Maxwell Aitken

William Maxwell Aitken (Lord Beaverbrook; 1879-1964) was a Canadian businessman and politician who left an indelible mark on politics and journalism on both sides of the Atlantic. Aitken rose to prominence as a merger king in Canada before gravitating into British politics and mass-circulation journalism. In 1916 he was elevated to the peerage as Lord Beaverbrook.

William Maxwell Aitken was born in Maple, Ontario, on May 25, 1879, the fifth of ten children of Jane and William Aitken. His father's itinerant career as a minister of the Church of Scotland left a moral and geographic imprint on young Max, who grew up in New Brunswick on Canada's Atlantic coast. He imbibed Presbyterian values in a region that was seeing its once strong prowess in the wood, wind, and water industries eroded by technological and regional shifts in the Canadian economy. Max's early personality displayed a bumptious opportunism brought on by the limited scope for advancement in Atlantic Canada; Aitken's entire career may be seen as a steady gravitation from the margins of economic, social, and political power to its center—from the Atlantic provinces to Montreal and ultimately to London, the seat of imperial political and financial power. Other New Brunswick "boys" would follow similar patterns: Louis B. Mayer to Hollywood and Richard Bedford Bennett to the Canadian prime ministership.

An apt student with a penchant for math and reading, Max cut his entrepreneurial teeth selling magazines and insurance door-to-door. The study of law briefly beckoned but did not overcome his restlessness, and in 1898 Aitken headed for Canada's "last best west," where in Calgary he joined his boyhood friend R.B. "Dick" Bennett in operating a bowling alley. Sensing that finance capitalism was the lifeblood of Canada's booming economy, Aitken returned east to use his persuasive personality in the possibilities of company promotion. As secretary to Halifax promoter John F. Stairs, Aitken quickly acquired a reputation and growing wealth as the seller of bonds in Canadian industrial and utility ventures, some of which extended south to Cuba and the Caribbean. The limited capital pool of the maritime provinces prompted Aitken to shift his focus in 1906 to Montreal, Canada's financial hub. Aitken's arrival in the Canadian business establishment was reinforced by his marriage that same year to Gladys Drury, daughter of a well-placed Halifax family; three children followed: Janet (1908), Max (1910), and Peter (1912).

In Montreal Aitken capitalized on the opportunities for industrial consolidation in the hothouse of national industrial development. He assembled integrated companies out of hitherto fragmented industries, the creation of Canada Cement in 1909 and the Steel Company of Canada in 1910 being the best examples. These activities had a two-fold outcome. They made Aitken very wealthy; he was by 1910 a millionaire with a reputation as a bold "money spinner" capable of remaking the Canadian industrial landscape. They also drew him deeper into the transatlantic web of financial dependence that underlay the Canadian economy. At the same time, Aitken's business methods—alleged stock watering and questionable promotional tactics—affixed a lifelong stigma to his name.

From his arrival in England in 1910 to his death in 1964, Aitken was principally concerned with British politics and journalism. Few abiding principles pervaded his activities in these years; as in business, he was interested in power and the deal-making that underlay it. Aitken understood the power of modern mass democracy—so evident in the sway of his mass-circulation daily newspapers—and the necessary accommodations that turned broad public sentiment into policy. His ventures into amateur history bespoke this instinct: titles such as *Politicians and the Press* (1925) and *Men and Power, 1917-1918* (1956) were best-sellers.

In 1910 Aitken won election as a Conservative member of Parliament for Ashton-under-Lyne; it would be his only elected office. While he excelled at the rhetoric of politics, he faded in the day-to-day practice of politics. Knighted in 1911, he drifted into back room political intrigue and began investing in the *Daily Express,* a profitable example of mass-circulation "new journalism." World War I gave scope to his charismatic qualities: he sensed the importance of "propaganda" on the home front. He extolled the exploits of Canadian troops in Flanders and later headed the Pictorial Propaganda Committee in England. He drew poets, writers (including Rudyard Kipling and Arnold Bennett) and filmmakers into the war effort. In 1918 he became Britain's minister of information. He played a role in the downfall of Prime Minister Asquith in 1916 and then served his successor, Lloyd George. In 1916 he received a peerage as Lord Beaverbrook, a move some alleged was designed by Lloyd George to forestall the bumptious Canadian from seeking his own job.

In the interwar years Beaverbrook continued to build his journalistic empire; he became a prototype of the modern "press lord." His control of the *Daily Express* was complemented by addition of the *Sunday Express* and the *Evening Standard.* The papers often reflected Beaverbrook's personal enthusiasms: empire free trade in the late 1920s and a fascination with Europe's totalitarian regimes. He visited both Stalin's Russia and Hitler's Germany. When war came again in 1939, Beaverbrook quickly abandoned his inclination to appeasement and rallied to the cause of war, serving his friend Churchill as minister of aircraft production in 1940-1941 and then as an adviser in various guises, including a continued championing of Russia as an ally. Despite his penchant for organization and quick results, the "Beaver" proved a mercurial colleague, prone to egotism and intrigue.

Peace saw Beaverbrook devote his energies to his newspaper empire and to his philanthropic nostalgia for his New Brunswick birthplace. He relished his social eminence in England, in Canada, and at his holiday homes in Jamaica and the south of France. Widowed in 1927, Beaverbrook maintained a wide circle of amorous relationships, including friendships with novelist Rebecca West and actress Tallulah Bankhead. In 1963 he married the widow of his childhood chum Sir James Dunn (1874-1956), a millionaire steel maker. Within a year Beaverbrook died of cancer, on June 9, 1964, and was buried in Newcastle, New Brunswick.

Further Reading

Beaverbrook was author of 11 books. As author, he was by turns amateur historian, political insider, and polemicist. His work is best sampled and not exhaustively read. *Canadians in Flanders* (1916), *Success* (1921), and *Men and Power* (1956) are most characteristic. Anne Chisholm and Michael Davie have written a definitive biography, *Beaverbrook: A Life*

(1992), a book that overshadows A. J. P. Taylor's *Beaverbrook* (1972), a work clearly influenced by Taylor's own friendship with Beaverbrook. □

Jalal-ud-din Mohammed Akbar

Jalal-ud-din Mohammed Akbar (1542-1605) was the third Mogul emperor of India. The administrative system that he built was copied by the British, and it is discernible in contemporary India.

On Nov. 23, 1542, Akbar was born at Umarkot, Sind, while his father, the emperor Humayun, driven from the throne of Delhi, was escaping to Persia. Humayun died in 1556 soon after his return to Delhi, and Akbar was proclaimed emperor on February 14, under the regency of Bairam Khan. The regent wrested control of northern India from the Afghans, who had defeated Humayun, but in 1560 Akbar rid himself of the regent and assumed full imperial powers. By 1605 Akbar had made himself the master of the Indo-Gangetic Basin, Kashmir and Afghanistan in the north, Gujarat and Sind in the west, Bengal in the east, and part of the Deccan to the Godavari River in the south.

The Emperor presided over a Hindu-Moslem cultural synthesis which culminated in a golden age of culture. Though he never learned to read or write, he was a cultivated man, and surrounded himself with the best minds of his generation. He patronized liberal Moslem intellectuals such as Shirazi, Faizi, and Abul Fazl, the author of *Ain-i-Akbari* and *Akbar Nama,* two important Mogul historical works. Akbar welcomed to his court mystics such as Salim Chishti and engaged in dialogues with Jesuit priests. He also invited Abul Fatah Gilana, who had written a commentary on Avicenna, to his court.

Committed to the policy of universal tolerance (*sulahkul*), Akbar considered himself the ruler of all his subjects and the Commander of the Faithful. Through his marriages with Rajput princesses, he brought Hindus to the ruling dynasty and gave three of the highest positions in his cabinet to Hindus. He abolished taxes such as the *jizya,* a poll tax, that discriminated against non-Moslems. Akbar patronized Indian music and arts, and in many buildings, notably at Fatehpur Sikri, near Agra, he adopted Hindu elements in architecture. Every week he appeared in public, and he held an open court.

Akbar participated in the religious festivities of all groups, allowed the Jesuit fathers to establish a church at Agra, and discouraged cow slaughter. In 1575 at Fatehpur Sikri he built a house of worship to which Moslem, Hindu, Jain, Christian, Parsi, and other theologians were invited for dialogue. In 1582 he promulgated a new religious movement, *din-i-ilahi,* which did not attract many converts.

Jalal-ud-din Mohammed Akbar (on chair)

In administration Akbar introduced far-reaching changes in revenue collection. To achieve balance of power, he separated revenue collection in each province from military administration, thereby using the collector to check the power of the commander. He built up a military cadre, preferring to pay cash salaries rather than award land grants. The emperor died on Oct. 17, 1605.

Further Reading

The best biography of Akbar is Vincent A. Smith, *Akbar, the Great Mogul: 1542-1605* (1917; 2d ed. 1958). The fullest information on Akbar's reign is provided by Abul Fazl in *Ain-i-Akbari,* edited by S. L. Goomer (trans., 3 vols., 1871; 2d ed. 1965), and in *Akbar Nama* (trans., 3 vols., 1897-1921); see also Laurence Binyon, *Akbar* (1932). There is a chapter on Akbar in Bamber Gascoigne's *The Great Moghuls* (1971), a scholarly and beautifully illustrated work. Histories of the Moguls include Michael Prawdin (pseudonym for Michael Charol), *The Builders of the Mogul Empire* (1963), and A. B. Pandey, *Later Medieval India: A History of the Mughals* (1963). □

Anna Akhmatova

The Soviet poet Anna Akhmatova (1889-1966) is the best-known member of the Acmeist movement. Her work is characterized by subtle understatement,

careful variations in rhythm, and spontaneous re-cording of everyday emotions.

Anna Akhmatova, the pen name of Anna An-dreyevna Gorenko, was born on June 23, 1889, near the Black Sea port of Odessa. Her father, a retired naval officer, moved the family to St. Petersburg when Anna was a young girl. She attended the Tsarskoe Selo Women's Gymnasium near St. Petersburg, where she met Nikolai Gumilev, whom she married in 1910. He was also a poet of the Acmeist movement, which proclaimed a return to precise, direct expression of poetic emotion.

Anna Akhmatova lived mainly in St. Petersburg and at her nearby country home, Komarovo, but traveled abroad several times: in 1910-1911 to Paris; in 1912 to northern Italy; and in 1965 to Oxford, England, where she was awarded an honorary degree. Throughout her life St. Petersburg played an important thematic role in her poetry. It was the city of such great writers as Fyodor Dostoevsky, Nikolai Gogol, and Aleksandr Pushkin, and it represented Anna Akhmatova's affinity to the 19th-century Russian prose tradition.

Her early life was marked by immediate success in poetry and the anguishing failure of her marriage to Gumilev, whom she divorced in 1918. Her first books, *Evening* (1912), *Rosary* (1914), and *Anno Domini MCMXXI* (1921), testify to the trials of her marriage. Gumilev was executed in 1921 as a counterrevolutionary, and their only

son, a historian, spent most of the years from 1939 to 1956 in a Soviet prison camp. These events compounded Anna Akhmatova's misfortune and led to the book of poems *Requiem* (1963), which is a testament to the suffering not only of the poet but of all Russians during the horrifying days of Stalin's purges. In 1946 Anna Akhmatova was hounded by Stalin's minister of culture, Andrei Zhadanov, called "a mixture of nun and harlot," and expelled from the Union of Soviet Writers. She had been reduced to silence before, from 1925 to 1940; she did not emerge from this final rebuke until after the death of Stalin. During the late 1950s and the 1960s she devoted herself to translations and to her own poetry.

Anna Akhmatova's poetic diction and her predominantly psychological themes were drawn from the humanistic tradition of 19th-century Russian prose. Her poetry imitates the rhythm and structure of conversational speech. Her work, like that of Boris Pasternak, whom she admired, was a sincere response to the inhuman cruelties of the age.

Anna Akhmatova was at work on her book *The Death of Pushkin,* a tribute to the perishing of genius at the hands of an insensitive society, when she died of a heart attack on March 6, 1966. She was accorded a Russian Orthodox funeral and was buried near Komarovo.

Further Reading

There is no adequate biography of Anna Akhmatova. Personal reminiscences about her are in the moving account by Osip Mandelstam's widow, Nadezhda Mandelstam, *Hope against Hope: A Memoir* (trans. 1970). Helen Muchnic, *Russian Writers: Notes and Essays* (1971), has an interesting discussion of Anna Akhmatova and her contemporaries. The definitive critical book on her poetry is in Russian: Boris M. Eikhenbaum, *Anna Akhmatova* (1923). A useful study is Leonid Strakhovsky, *Craftsmen of the Word: Three Poets of Modern Russia* (1949). The broadest selection of her poetry in English is *Forty-seven Love Poems,* translated by Natalie Duddington (1927).

Additional Sources

Anna Akhmatova and her circle, Fayetteville, Ark.: University of Arkansas Press, 1994.

Davies, J. (Jessie), *Anna of all the Russias: the life of Anna Akhmatova (1889-1966),* Liverpool: Lincoln Davies, 1988.

Haight, Amanda., *Anna Akhmatova: a poetic pilgrimage,* New York: Oxford University Press, 1976.

Reeder, Roberta., *Anna Akhmatova: poet and prophet,* New York: St. Martin's Press, 1994. ☐

Akiba ben Joseph

The Palestinian rabbi Akiba ben Joseph (ca. 50-ca. 135) was a founder of rabbinic Judaism. He developed a method of Hebrew scriptural interpretation.

The early life of Akiba ben Joseph is enshrouded in legends, anecdotes, sayings, and numerous references in the Talmud. He was born in the vicinity of Lydda to a humble peasant family. Until well on in years, he was an illiterate shepherd employed by the wealthy Ben Kalba Sabua, whose daughter Rachel married Akiba on condition that he devote himself to learning. Her father opposed the match and banished Rachel from his home.

Akiba labored hard to earn a meager livelihood. When his child started school, Akiba accompanied him, and together they learned to read. Despite many discouragements, Akiba persevered in his studies and at the age of 40 entered the rabbinical academy of Johanan ben Zakkai, a Pharisaic teacher, at Yabneh (Jamnia). In the academy Akiba, himself a commoner, invariably championed the plebeian viewpoint rather than the patrician.

In the year 96 Akiba went with other rabbis on a mission to Rome to persuade the emperor Domitian to revoke an anti-Jewish edict. Shortly after their arrival, Domitian was assassinated, and his successor, Nerva, adopted a more humane policy toward the Jews. From a convert to Judaism in Rome, Akiba received a generous bequest, which enabled him to establish an academy at Bnei Berak near Jaffa. He attracted thousands of students, to whom he lectured under the shady boughs of a palm tree.

Akiba developed a new method of textual interpretation which attached significance and meaning to every word, letter, jot, and tittle of the scriptural text. It was imaginative, but unlike the logical system employed by Hillel, it was rather artificial. With this new approach Akiba was able to adjust the law to the needs of the times. His disciples applied this approach in the Midrashic (biblical expositional) works they compiled.

Another of Akiba's outstanding contributions to scholarship was his arrangement according to subject matter, in divisions and subdivisions, of the earlier collections of the Oral Law, which heretofore had been organized hazardly. His system was further developed by his disciple Rabbi Meir, and it was set up in its present form, the Mishnah, by Judah I (Judah Hanasi, the Prince) about 200.

Akiba played an important role in the Bar Kochba revolt against Rome (132-135) and insisted on continuing to teach the Law, though to do so was a capital offense. He was imprisoned, tortured, and executed by the Romans, dying with the *Shema Yisroel* ("Hear O Israel," Deuteronomy 6:4), Israel's profession of faith, on his lips.

Further Reading

Herbert Danby's translation of the Mishnah (1933) is excellent. A splendid account of Akiba's life, times, and thought is in Louis Finkelstein, *Akiba: Scholar, Saint and Martyr* (1936). Finkelstein's chapter, "Akiba," in Simon Noveck, ed., *Great Jewish Personalities in Ancient and Medieval Times* (1959), is essentially a summary of his book-length study. Morris Adler, *The World of the Talmud* (1959), deals with the background of the Talmud.

Additional Sources

Finkelstein, Louis, *Akiba: scholar, saint, and martyr,* Northvale, N.J.: J. Aronson, 1990.
Rabbi Akiva: sage of all sages, Woodmere, N.Y.: Bet-Shamai Publications, 1989. ☐

Akihito

The 125th emperor of Japan, Akihito (born 1933), succeeded to the throne upon the death of his father, Hirohito, Jan. 7, 1989. He formally took office Nov. 12, 1990.

Crown Prince Akihito was born Dec. 23, 1933, to Emperor Hirohito and Empress Nagako. In keeping with rigid tradition, the boy was separated from his parents (except for once-a-week visits) at the age of three and brought up by court attendants. It was evidently a loveless, lonely existence made worse by World War II, when he was moved out of Tokyo for safety from Allied bombing attacks.

At war's end, the American occupying forces ended the boy's isolation, enabling him to attend high school and college with the sons of the established privileged classes. In addition, a Philadelphia Quaker, Elizabeth Gray Vining, was hired to tutor the royal heir in Western customs and values. It was a happy choice. Vining awakened the young man's interest in many things besides tropical fish and horseback riding.

The postwar constitution of Japan, written by the United States, stripped the emperor of all but ceremonial powers and religious obligations as chief priest of Shinto. Emperor Hirohito never seemed comfortable in the new role of being only the "symbol of the state," and after a long illness he died on Jan. 7, 1989, at the age of 87. Although Akihito became emperor at once, he had to observe a long period of mourning before official enthronement.

During this time, tradition and rituals enabled the new emperor to hold the attention of his nation. He further endeared himself to the people by establishing his goal of serving as a constitutional monarch (not unlike British rulers). And unlike his father, Akihito adopted an informal style in dealing with his subjects, sometimes shaking hands instead of waiting to receive a bow. In general, the emperor won the affection of his people.

Akihito was the first emperor to marry a commoner, Michiko Shoda, in 1959, daughter of a successful industrialist, whom he met on a tennis court. Akihito also became the first emperor to raise his own children. Such innovations made the empress unpopular with her mother-in-law and others at the imperial court. In time, however, Michiko's style and grace prevailed. The couple raised Crown Prince Naruhito, Prince Akishino, and daughter Nori.

On Nov. 12, 1990, at the age of 56, Akihito ascended the Chrysanthemum Throne in an elaborate ritual attended

harp. They make their home in a Western-style house outside of Tokyo.

Further Reading

For background information on Japan see *The Japanese* (1977) by Edwin O. Reischauer, U.S. ambassador to Japan, 1961-1966. A later assessment is Richard J. Samuels, "Japan in 1989," in *Asian Survey* (January 1990). The education of the young Akihito is described by his tutor Elizabeth Gray Vining in *Windows for the Crown Prince* (1952). An insightful look at Akihito's Japan is Steven R. Weisman's "Japan's Imperial Present," in the *New York Times Magazine* (August 24, 1990). The preparation for the enthronement ceremony was reported by Elizabeth Bumiller in the *Washington Post* (November 11, 1990). □

Lucas Alamán

The Mexican statesman Lucas Alamán (1792-1853) was the leading spokesman and theorist for the Conservative party. He is also one of Mexico's major historians, especially of the 19th century, although his works were written to justify the Conservative position.

Lucas Alamán was born in Guanajuato on Oct. 18, 1792, of an aristocratic family, which owed its fortune to the district's silver mines. He attended the Mexico City College of Mining. In 1810 he witnessed the sack of Guanajuato by rebels under Father Miguel Hidalgo y Costilla, and much of his conservative sentiment stemmed from his vivid memory of this event. He studied in Europe from 1814 to 1820, principally in Spain and France.

Alamán was a member of the Mexican delegation to the Spanish Cortes from 1821 to 1823, and upon his return to Mexico he was installed as minister of foreign relations, serving until 1825. The short, stout, spectacled Alamán soon demonstrated that he was a shrewd and subtle politician despite his diffident manner, and he became a prominent figure on the Mexican political scene. He is credited with obtaining British recognition of the Mexican republic and with establishing the National Archives and the Museum of Anthropology. Alamán returned to the Cabinet as minister of foreign relations in 1830, becoming the dominant figure throughout the regime of Gen. Anastasio Bustamante. Alamán's accomplishments included improving Mexican credit in international financial markets, a law closing Texas to further North American settlement, and substantial efforts to stimulate economic development. He advocated a protective tariff to encourage wealthy landowners to invest in industry, and in 1830 he founded the Banco de Avío, a government-sponsored institution which offered loans to private individuals at modest rates to assist modernization and expansion of existing industry. Alamán headed the bank until 1833.

Alamán is remembered principally, however, for his historical works. He wrote them during the 1830s and

by representatives of 158 countries. Empress Michiko ascended her own smaller throne (the Michoda) set up nearby. The ceremony cost an estimated $80 million, and included 3,400 guests, with many world leaders and dignitaries in attendance. Akihito continued a 2,600-year line of successor emperors, but he stated before the coronation that a monarch still should be accessible. "I find it natural that the imperial family should not exist at a distance from the people," Akihito said.

The Emperor and Empress travel the world representing Japan, and wherever they go, it is a major event. In 1992, they toured China in an effort to improve relations and build commerce. In 1994, the royal couple made a whirlwind 16-day tour of the United States, their first since ascending the throne, and their stay included a large white tie dinner with President Bill Clinton and First Lady Hillary Rodham Clinton. In a speech in Washington, D.C., Akihito talked about the 50 years of support between the United States and Japan. "It is my earnest hope that peaceful interchange will continue to flourish for many more years to come and that the Pacific will become a true ocean of peace," the Emperor said. The tour included 10 cities, including Los Angeles, where the royal couple visited the Japanese American National Museum.

The royal couple is described as sincere, respectful, and diplomatic. Wherever they travel, it becomes a large media event, yet they appear to handle the notoriety with grace. Both the couple and their children are accomplished musicians; Akihito plays cello, and the Empress plays the

Pedro Antonio de Alarcón

The Spanish writer and politician Pedro Antonio de Alarcón (1833-1891) is best known for his novels and short stories, which depict in a lively, humorous manner the customs of the Spaniards of his region, Andalusia.

Pedro Antonio de Alarcón was born in Guadix in the province of Granada on March 10, 1833, the fourth of 10 children. He studied law and soon became involved in politics. A radical revolutionary, he led an insurrection in Granada against the clergy and army. In 1853 he went to Madrid to pursue a literary career but returned to Granada the following year. He was a member of the famous Cuerda Granadina (Granada Club), a group of dissident young artists and bohemians.

Alarcón soon returned to Madrid, where he contributed political articles to journals and became widely known as the editor of *El Látigo* (The Whip), an anticlerical, antidynastic newspaper. His first novel, *El final de Norma* (1851; The End of Norma), an extravagant, adolescent work about the love of a violinist for a singer, attests to his romantic temperament. In 1859 he served with the army in Morocco during Spain's war with the Moors; he described his experiences in *Diario de un testigo en la guerra de Africa* (1859-1860; Diary of a Witness of the African War).

Alarcón changed his radical political views as a result of a duel in which his life was spared. He became a conservative and a staunch defender of religion and embarked upon a political career. In 1863 he was elected a deputy to the Cortes, and after the revolution of 1868, which ended the reign of Isabella II, he was appointed minister to Sweden but renounced the post before serving. He became a member of the Council of State in 1875.

Alarcón wrote his masterpiece, *El sombrero de tres picos* (The Three-Cornered Hat), in 1874. This novel, based on a popular ballad, presents a vivid, detailed picture of Andalusia in the days of Charles IV. The colorful setting, fast pace, and wit inspired Manuel de Falla's ballet as well as operas in French, German, and English. Another short novel, *El capitán Veneno* (1881; Captain Venom), and a collection of short stories, *Historietas nacionales* (1881; Native Stories), demonstrate considerable narrative skill. Alarcón also published three popular travel books and a volume of poems.

In 1877 Alarcón became a member of the Spanish Royal Academy. His subsequent preoccupation with morality in art, the subject of his address on admission to the academy, mars his longer novels, such as *El escándalo* (1875; The Scandal) and *La pródiga* (1881; The Prodigal). They are too moralistic and melodramatic. With the failure of *La pródiga*, Alarcón withdrew from public life and ceased to write fiction. In his autobiography (1884) he remarked bitterly on the adverse criticism many of his books had received. He died in Madrid on July 20, 1891, after a prolonged illness.

1840s, when he became the chief Conservative theorist and spokesman and edited the party's newspapers, *El Tiempo* and *El Universal*. History was a political weapon for Alamán, and his books were dedicated to defending the Conservative cause. His principal works were *Disertaciones sobre la historia de la república méjicana* (3 vols., 1844-1849; Dissertations on the Mexican Republic), covering the period from the conquest to independence, and *Historia de Méjico* (5 vols., 1849-1852; History of Mexico), examining the years 1808 to 1848. Employing a biographical approach in the style of William H. Prescott, he glorified Agustín de Iturbide, the Conservative who had won Mexican independence, and condemned Father Hidalgo, characterizing his uprising as a proletarian revolt against civilization. Alamán extolled the virtues of the Spanish colonial heritage, stressing its superiority to the liberal doctrines of the United States. Yet he also criticized colonial governmental abuses and defended Mexican independence.

Alamán returned to the Ministry of Foreign Relations in 1853, heading a Conservative coterie that restored Gen. Antonio López de Santa Ana to the presidency. Alamán's plan to dominate the government collapsed with his death on June 2, 1853.

Further Reading

There are few studies of Alamán in English. The best is Charles A. Hale, *Mexican Liberalism in the Age of Mora, 1821-1853* (1968). □

Further Reading

The definitive book on Alarcón is in Spanish, José Fernández Montesinos, *Pedro Antonio de Alarcón* (1955). Works on Spanish literature in English include James Fitzmaurice-Kelly, *A New History of Spanish Literature* (1898; rev. ed. 1926); Ernest Mérimée, *A History of Spanish Literature* (1908; rev. ed. and trans. 1930); George Tyler Northup, *An Introduction to Spanish Literature* (1925; 3d rev. ed. by Nicholas B. Adams., 1960); and Richard E. Chandler and Kessel Schwartz, *A New History of Spanish Literature* (1961). □

Juan Ruiz de Alarcón y Mendoza

The Spanish playwright Juan Ruiz de Alarcón y Mendoza (1581-1639) was a major figure of Spain's Golden Age, 1580-1680. His work is distinguished by mastery of humorous dialogue and by use of a thesis, or basic premise, to satirize common human failings.

Juan Ruiz de Alarcón was born in Mexico to parents from distinguished Spanish families. He was educated in both Mexico and Spain and obtained two law degrees. He returned to Spain in 1614 and became a playwright, and there he received most of his acclaim.

Perhaps Alarcón's colonial background and certainly his physical defect (he was hunchbacked) inspired the monstrous jibes directed at him, such as "dwarfed camel," "monkey," and "trunk poet." Although Alarcón returned the barbs in kind, bitterness may account for the presence in his plays of characters who lack physical grace but possess impressive moral strength. At the same time, several of his physically attractive characters invite disapproval because of some moral defect. For example, the handsome but scandalmongering Don Mendo in *Las paredes oyen* (*The Walls Have Ears*) loses the lovely Ana to Don Juan de Mendoza, who describes himself as "poor, ugly and with a very undistinguished appearance."

Alarcón wrote less than 30 plays, all in verse. In spite of his output, relatively small in his day, he ranks among the European comic geniuses. His most famous play is *La verdad sospechosa* (*The Suspected Truth*), which the French dramatist Pierre Corneille adapted and in part literally translated as *Le Menteur* (1644; *The Liar*). *The Suspected Truth* tells the story of a personable young university graduate who is, in the 17th century sense, a complete caballero except for one notable moral defect: impulsive lying. From this Alarcón developed multiple situations affording sparkling entertainment while pointing out a moral.

Many of his protagonists have a ruling passion, a convention adopted by the French playwright Molière in, for example, *L'Avare* (1668; *The Miser*). One early play by Alarcón, *No hay mal que por bien no venga* (*From Evil Good Always Springs*), features a protagonist to whom comfort is the motive for every decision or act, whether important or trivial, except in matters of honor. In *Mudarse por mejorarse* (*His Eye on the Main Chance*) the indecisive Don Garcia loses the love of the beautiful, wealthy Clara because of his vacillation between her and her niece.

Occasionally Alarcón departed from writing his customary thesis plays. Then he abandoned his usual moderation for a more exuberant style, as in *El anticristo* (*The Anti-Christ*) and the second part of *El tejedor de Segovia* (*The Segovian Weaver*).

Further Reading

There is no biography of Alarcón in English. He is included in two general studies, George Tyler Northup, *An Introduction to Spanish Literature* (1925; 3d ed., revised by Nicholas B. Adams, 1960), and Richard E. Chandler and Kessel Schwartz, *A New History of Spanish Literature* (1961). His complete works have been published in Spanish, *Obras completas de Juan Ruiz de Alarcón,* edited by Agustin Millares Carlo (3 vols., 1957-1968). □

Alaric

Alaric (ca. 370-410) was a leader of the Visigoths who clashed repeatedly with the Roman Empire and led his troops in the sack of Rome in 410.

The Visigoths had been driven from their homeland in central Europe into Roman territory by the attacks of the neighboring Huns. After the Visigoths inflicted a massive defeat on the Eastern Roman army in 378, they were persuaded by the emperor Theodosius I to settle in the Roman province of Lower Moesia (northern Bulgaria) as Roman mercenaries.

Alaric was born near the mouth of the Danube about 370. The Visigothic troops in Roman service chose him as their leader about 390. In 395, dissatisfied by the commands given him, Alaric attacked Thrace, Macedonia, and Greece. In 397 the strongman of the Western Roman Empire, General Flavius Stilicho, sailed to Greece and convinced Alaric to leave there and settle in Epirus.

In 401 Alaric invaded Italy for the first time. After a battle with Stilicho in April 402, he was persuaded to withdraw. He returned in 403 and was defeated at Verona, but Stilicho allowed him to escape to the Dalmatia-Pannonia area.

Alaric became restless again in 408 and demanded heavy payments for his services from the emperor Honorius. The fall of Stilicho and the massacre of many families of barbarian mercenaries in Roman service provided Alaric with excuses for attacking Italy. He laid siege to Rome but withdrew on the payment of 5,000 pounds of gold. In 409, when the Emperor refused to meet his renewed demands, Alaric returned to Rome. He set up a rival emperor, Priscus Attalus, but removed him when Attalus began to act too independently.

Alaric was still interested in coming to terms with the Roman government. However, when his camp was treacherously attacked in July 410 by Sarus, a Visigoth loyal to the Emperor, Alaric saw this as an act approved by the imperial government and decided to attack Rome. He entered the city on August 14, and for the first time in 800 years barbarians sacked the city. Although Alaric on the whole spared the holy places, perhaps because the Visigoths were Christians, the population suffered heavily. He carried away numerous captives, including Galla Placidia, the sister of the emperor Honorius.

Alaric moved south, seeking food and land for his people. His ultimate destination appears to have been Africa. He sacked Capua and Nola on the way but failed to take Naples. He reached Rhegium (Reggio Calabria) on the coast, but the fleet that was to carry him to Africa was wrecked. Turning north again, he died at nearby Consentia (Cosenza) in 410 and was buried in the Bucentus (Busento) River.

While his sack of Rome gained Alaric the reputation of a terrible barbarian, he was actually a man who passed most of his life within the imperial system, trying only to profit as much as possible from his own power.

Further Reading

Some ancient sources on Alaric are translated in Colin D. Gordon, *The Age of Attila* (1960). Still the best accounts in English are J. B. Bury, *A History of the Later Roman Empire* (1923), and Thomas Hodgkin, *Italy and Her Invaders* (8 vols., 1880-1899). □

Ala-ud-din

Ala-ud-din (died 1316) was the second sultan of the Khalji dynasty of Delhi in India. His totalitarian rule marked the beginning of the imperialistic period of the sultanate and the rise to power of native Indian Moslems.

Not much is known of the early life of Ala-ud-din. He was appointed governor of Kara by his uncle and father-in-law, Sultan Jalal-ud-din Khalji, in 1292. Three years later he invaded Malwa, captured Bhilsa, a wealthy commercial center, and drew up plans to usurp the sultanate. In 1296 he became the first Moslem invader to penetrate the Vindhya Mountains into the Deccan and, after defeating the Hindu raja of Devagiri, obtained a booty that contained 17,250 pounds of gold, 200 pounds of pearls, and 28,250 pounds of silver. Supported by crack troops and armed with these riches, he assassinated his father-in-law and proclaimed himself the sultan of Delhi in 1296.

For the next 15 years Ala-ud-din waged wars relentlessly. By 1303 the western Hindu kingdoms of Gujarat, Ranthambhor, Chitor, and Rajasthan had been subdued. During the next 3 years he checked the advance of the Mongols into India and restored tranquility to India's northwest frontier. In 1305 he overran central India, bringing under his domination Malwa, Ujjain, Chanderi, and Mandawar. Two years later he made a second attempt on Devagiri, and by 1309 his army had reached the southernmost tip of India at Cape Comiron. By 1311 he was the richest sultan in the history of Delhi. He toyed with the idea of starting a new religion and of world conquest, even issuing coins referring to himself as Alexander II. But his advisers dissuaded him from pursuing such self-glorification.

A tyrannical ruler, Ala-ud-din instituted several harsh measures to quell rebellions. A widely pervasive secret service was established, marriage alliances among the nobility were forbidden without his express permission, and private property of the nobles was reduced. He revised the taxation system, reorganized the army, and stamped out corruption in the supplying of horses for the cavalry by requiring that they be branded. The Hindus were treated with special severity, and they bore the heaviest taxation. They were not allowed to possess weapons, ride on horseback, or cultivate luxury habits. The prices of all the necessities of life were controlled.

Such rigid price controls and the wealth that poured into the Sultan's treasury after the conquests in southern India enabled Ala-ud-din to undertake cultural and architectural activities on a lavish scale. Literati, physicians, astronomers, and historians thronged Delhi—many from Baghdad and Central Asia, which had been sacked by the Mongols. Delhi became the metropolis of the Moslem East under Ala-ud-din, and architecture was its greatest cultural achievement. Delhi's Jamaat Khana Mosque is highly ornate, spacious, and crowned by an immense dome.

But the excesses of a luxurious life made Ala-ud-din an invalid, and he became dominated by Malik Kafur, his most successful field commander. Ala-ud-din died in January 1316, and the Khalji dynasty came to an end only 4 years later.

Further Reading

Ala-ud-din's career is superbly traced in K. S. Lal, *History of the Khaljis, A.D. 1290-1320* (1950; rev. ed. 1967). See also R. C. Majumdar, A. D. Pusalker, and A. K. Majumdar, eds., *The Delhi Sultanate* (1960); Vidya Dhar Mahajan and Savitri Mahajan, *The Sultanate of Delhi* (1961; 2d ed. 1963); A. B. Pandey, *Society and Government in Medieval India* (1965); and K. S. Lal, *Studies in Medieval Indian History* (1966).

Additional Sources

Niazi, Ghulam Sarwar Khan., *The life and works of Sultan Alaud-din Khalji*, Lahore, Pakistan: Institute of Islamic Culture, 1990.
Warsi, Sultan Hameed., *History of Ala-ud-Din Khilji*, Lahore: Iqbal Publications, 1987. □

Alaungpaya

The Burmese king Alaungpaya (1715-1760) ruled from 1752 to 1760. Founder of the Konbaung dynasty, he infused new vigor into his people and engaged in conquests that expanded Burma's (now Myanmar) borders to an unparalleled extent.

Alaungpaya was born in the village of Moksobo on the western bank of the Irrawaddy River and given the name of Aung Zeya by his parents. His father was headman of the village, and when he later decided to relinquish the post, Aung Zeya succeeded him.

In 1737, when Aung Zeya was only 22, the belief spread among the superstitious people of the countryside that a new leader of great valor and courage would emerge among them to replace the ruler of the then weak Burman dynasty. After consulting various astrologers, the king arrested Aung Zeya, who denied that he was the would-be leader. He was released, and for the next 16 years he lived quietly among his fellow villagers of Moksobo.

In the intervening years the Mon, who were rivals of the Burmans and had been inhabitants of the country before the Burmans entered, renewed their attacks on the monarchy, toppling it in 1752. Their victory was short-lived, however. Aung Zeya, then 38, rose to lead the Burman resistance to Mon conquest and established a new dynasty that year at Moksobo, which he renamed Shwebo (as it is still known today). For himself Aung Zeya appropriated the title of Alaungpaya (the ruler who will someday become a Buddha).

After freeing upper Burma of Mon control, Alaungpaya moved down the Irrawaddy Valley against the adversary, finally capturing in 1755 the river port of Dagon, which he

renamed Rangoon ("end of the battle;" today Burma's capital).

Completing the conquest of lower Burma in 1757, Alaungpaya returned to upper Burma to end the attacks of raiders from Manipur to the west and to defeat the Shan princes as far east as the Salween River. In his series of conquests he was helped by his sons Hsinbyushin and Bodawpaya. Alaungpaya also played a major role in reestablishing and reforming many other aspects of Burmese life, such as ending a schism among the Buddhist clergy, prohibiting the drinking of liquor, and decreeing an end to cattle slaughter (for economic as well as religious reasons).

Alaungpaya died of wounds suffered in the explosion of one of his own siege guns during an assault on the Thai capital of Ayuthia. He had attacked Thailand to bring back Mon refugees and some Thai to repopulate lower Burma. The Konbaung dynasty, which he established, was the last dynasty to rule over Burma until the country's fall to British colonial rule in 1885.

Further Reading

Alaungpaya and his military victories in particular are the subject of a chapter in D. G. E. Hall, *Burma* (1950; 3d ed. 1960), one of the best histories of the country. A sensitive, accurate appraisal by the Burmese historian Maung Htin Aung is offered in *A History of Burma* (1967). There is also a good treatment of Alaungpaya and his place in Myanmar's history in John F. Cady, *A History of Modern Burma* (1958). □

Duke of Alba

Fernando Álvarez de Toledo, Duke of Alba (1507-1582), or Alva, was a Spanish general and statesman. Known as the Iron Duke because of his ruthlessness, he almost succeeded in putting down the rising in the Low Countries against Spain.

Fernando Álvarez de Toledo was born at Piedrahita on Oct. 29, 1507, into one of the oldest and most distinguished noble families of Spain. His father died when Fernando was young, and he was reared by a stern grandfather to be a strict Roman Catholic, a loyal servant of the king, and a disciplined soldier. By the age of 14 he was serving as an officer in the campaigns of Emperor Charles V against the French.

From 1531 Alba played a leading role in operations against the Turks, was promoted to general in 1533, and distinguished himself during the siege of Tunis in 1535. After defending Perpignan against a French assault in 1542, he was appointed by Charles V to serve Prince Philip as military adviser during the Emperor's absence from Spain. Alba joined Charles V in Germany in 1546 with the outbreak of the Schmalkaldic War and commanded the cavalry, which contributed heavily to the imperial victory at Mühlberg in 1547. In 1552 he took over general command of the Spanish forces in Italy, but when Maurice of Saxony rose unexpectedly and successfully against the Emperor and won the alliance of Henry II of France, Charles recalled Alba to Germany to lead the resistance to the French armies. However, Alba could not prevent the defeat of the imperial forces, which led to the Emperor's abdication in 1556.

Philip II, on becoming king of Spain, named Alba governor of Milan and commander in Italy. There Alba waged a war against the papal army of Paul IV, a French ally. Avoiding a direct attack upon Rome lest there be a repetition of the sack of 1527, Alba compelled the Pope to accept a peace in 1557, which consolidated Spanish domination of Italy for more than a century. Returning to the Low Countries, Alba participated in the negotiations which resulted in the Peace of Cateau-Cambrésis (1559).

Rioting by Calvinist mobs in the Netherlands in 1566 led to Philip II's decision to send Alba to the Low Countries to crush them, root out Protestantism, and replace the ancient institutions of local and provincial government by ruling organs responsible only to Philip. Alba entered Brussels on Aug. 22, 1567, took over as governor general, and set up the Council of Troubles (called the Council of Blood by the people) to put down heresy and rebellion. The council operated with harsh rigor; even two of the most important noblemen in the country, the counts of Egmont and Hoorn, were arrested, tried, and beheaded; and over 1,000 men of all ranks were similarly punished (it was originally believed that the victims numbered about 6,000). Thousands fled abroad for safety.

Alba defeated the rebel armies of William the Silent and his brother, Louis of Nassau, in their forays into the Netherlands. He introduced a system of taxation into the Low Countries based primarily on the Spanish system of a sales tax of 10 percent on each transfer of goods; although the provinces bought their way out for the moment by lump-sum payments, there was profound anxiety that the prosperity of the Low Countries was being undermined. In 1572, the rebellion led by William the Silent shifted to the northern Netherlands. The next year Alba asked Philip II to allow him to return to Spain, and he sailed away from the Netherlands, still torn by rebellion, on Dec. 18, 1573.

On his return to Spain, Alba found himself in the King's disfavor. Nonetheless, in 1580 Philip entrusted the conquest of Portugal to him. Alba died in Lisbon on Dec. 11, 1582.

Further Reading

A brief account of Alba's career was written by the Duke of Berwick and Alba, *The Great Duke of Alba as a Public Servant* (1947). For background see Roger Bigelow Merriman, *The Rise of the Spanish Empire in the Old World and in the New,* vol. 4 (1918); William Thomas Walsh, *Philip II* (1937); Sir Charles Petrie, *Philip II of Spain* (1963); and John Lynch, *Spain under the Hapsburgs,* vol. 1 (1964). Alba's role in the Netherlands is detailed in Pieter Geyl, *The Revolt of the Netherlands, 1555-1609* (1932; rev. ed. 1958); Cecil John Cadoux, *Philip of Spain and the Netherlands* (1969); and Edward Grierson, *The Fatal Inheritance: Philip II and the Spanish Netherlands* (1969). Also useful is C.V. Wedgwood, *William the Silent* (1944).

Additional Sources

Maltby, William S., *Alba: a biography of Fernando Alvarez de Toledo, third duke of Alba, 1507-1582,* Berkeley: University of California Press, 1983. □

Hassan Al-Banna

An Egyptian religious leader, Hassan Al-Banna (1906-1949) was the founder of the Muslim Brotherhood, which is considered the forerunner of contemporary movements of Islamic revivalism.

H assan Al-Banna was born in the village of Mahmoudiyya, located northwest of the city of Cairo, to a traditional lower middle-class family. His father was a watch repairer and a teacher at the local mosque school where Al-Banna received his first lessons in Islam.

His religious inclination, activism, charismatic appeal, and leadership potential were evident from an early age. By the time he was 14 years old he had memorized the Koran, the holy book of Islam, and while still in secondary school he began to organize committees and societies stressing Islamic principles and morals. Later, while attending the Teacher's College in Cairo, Al-Banna attended lectures at the Al-Azhar, the foremost Islamic university, where he was exposed to current religious thought as well as to Sufism—Islamic mysticism—which opened a new inner dimension towards Islam and helped in forming his future beliefs. It was in the city of Isma'illiyya, where Al-Banna was given the job of grammar teacher, that he began to preach his ideas and won his first followers, who encouraged him to form the Society of the Muslim Brethren in 1928.

The association's activities were in fact a reaction to conditions in the Islamic world and in Egypt during the 1920s and 1930s. World War I had brought about the defeat of the Ottoman Empire and an end to the Caliphate, the symbol of Islamic power and unity for the Islamic world. Secularization and Westernization were becoming acceptable to the various governments that ruled Muslim nations. Egypt, which had been occupied by British troops since 1882 and was ruled by a corrupt government and ineffectual king, was undergoing deep structural changes caused by modernization underway since the 19th century reforms of Muhammad Ali Pasha. In turn, modernization was accompanied by the penetration of capitalism and industrialization. These two forces undermined traditional crafts, trade, and village life, resulting in social dislocations as well as a growing economic gap between the rich and poor of the country.

Furthermore, the accompanying process of secularization posed a real threat to Islam, because only where the Shari'a (Islamic law) was the established legal system could there be a true Islamic society and could Muslims live out their lives within the true faith. Traditional elements were also concerned by the threat posed to their society and traditions by Western ideas, press, cinema, theater, and other cultural practices.

Rise of Conservative Ideals

During the second half of the 19th century Egypt had witnessed vigorous reformist efforts directed towards making Western thoughts and institutions more acceptable to Islamic society without undermining Islam itself. Such efforts had been led by important religious leaders such as Jamal Al-Din Al-Afghani, Muhammad Abdu, and Rashid Ridda. However, by the 1920s, with increasing political, social, and economic problems, Egypt witnessed a period of resurgence of conservative Islamic ideals. Al-Banna was the disciple of these earlier reformers; unlike them, however, he did not look for a way of compromise with Western ideas. What he called for was the institution of an Islamic state with a caliph as its leader and the Koran as the basis of its law.

The Ikhwan of the Muslim Brethren was to be the means of achieving these goals; the program reflected the ideas of Al-Banna, its "Supreme Guide," regarding social, religious, and economic matters. Among other things, it called for a moral society in Islamic terms and an end to Westernization. Since the ills of society were blamed on the habits of the Europeanized upper classes who preferred to wear Western clothes, speak European languages, and bring up their children according to Western customs, habits of the rich were to be combatted.

Economically the wrongs enforced upon the urban and rural masses would be corrected by calling attention to poor conditions in villages, enforcing the religious Zakat tax intended to enable all to share in the wealth of the few, preventing usury, and adjusting government salaries by eliminating the huge gaps between upper and lower level jobs, as well as public sharing in the profits of industrial and other monopoly companies. Special attention was to be given to the technical and social needs of workers so as to help raise their standard of living.

As for the social program, one of the main concerns of the Ikhwan was the breakdown in the traditional role of the family and in familial interrelationships. What with the growing poverty, immigration of rural masses to urban centers, and other dislocation in Egyptian society, the family, the basic unit of Islamic society, was breaking down and the young, widows, and older members were often left homeless. The state had not stepped in to fill the gap caused by this dislocation. The Ikhwan's program, therefore, called for safeguarding the family and family traditions through enforcement of morality by a ban on prostitution, alcohol, night-clubs, and theater productions of immoral nature and censorship of radio programs, newspapers, and books. The morality of women was to be guarded carefully, no association of the sexes before marriage would be allowed, and even though women were to be educated, schools would be segregated at all levels.

Activity on the Political Level

On the political side, the program was quite nationalist in orientation. It called for a one-party structure, a party that would have the good of the nation and not that of its membership at heart. The building of a strong national army would be given priority, and ties with the Islamic world strengthened. Government corruption would be put to an end and the bureaucratic structure made more efficient. The ulama class of scholars would find a place within the government by becoming employed by it in both the civil service and the army.

Thus the Ikhwan began as a religious association with the intent of fighting Westernization and re-instituting Muslim laws and morality. They were concerned with the social dislocations of their time and searched for an answer to them. Their program proved to be popular, particularly among the urban masses and the traditional elements of society, as well as with the young professionals and university graduates who were aware of the poor social and economic conditions of Egypt and of the government's inability to deal with them.

Al-Banna himself was one of the chief sources of the popularity of the Ikhwan, whose membership was conservatively estimated at one million in the 1930s. He was described as a charismatic leader, a man of conviction who inspired great faith in his followers. He was not a violent person; however, he brought into existence the *Nizan Al-KhASS,* the secret military arm of the Ikhwan which undertook various acts of terrorism, such as the 1952 burning of foreign and Jewish institutions in Cairo and the murder of Egypt's Prime Minister Al-Nuqrashi in 1948. The latter killing provoked the assassination of Al-Banna himself in 1949 at the hands of King Farouk's secret police. The king, who once was allied with Al-Banna, had now found him too dangerous and eliminated him, even though Al-Banna declared himself innocent of Nuqrashi's death.

After the death of the Supreme Guide, the Ikhwan went underground. There was a brief interval of friendship with the Nasser regime after the 1952 revolution, but in 1956, after a failed assassination attempt on the life of Nasser, the Ikhwan were driven underground once more. Since the ideas of the Ikhwan were more moderate than some other contemporary militant Islamic sects operating in Egypt, the Ikhwan were becoming more acceptable to the Egyptian people and government in the 1980s. The government, however, continued to refuse to recognize the Ikhwan as an official political party with the right to join the political process in the country.

Further Reading

Additional information can be found in J. HeyworthDume, *Religious and Political Trends in Modern Egypt* (1950); Albert Homain, *Arab Thought in the Liberal Age: 1798-1939* (London, 1978); Ishak Musa Husiami, *The Moslem Brethren* (Beirut, 1956); B. Lewis, "The Return of Islam," in *Commentary* (January 1976); Richard P. Mitchell, *The Society of the Muslim Brotherhood* (London, 1969); and Charles Wendel, *Five Tracts of Hasau Al-Banua: 1906-1969* (1978).

Additional Sources

Memoirs of Hasan al Banna Shaheed, Karachi: International Islamic Publishers, 1981. □

Edward Franklin Albee III

American playwright Edward Franklin Albee, III (born 1928), achieved great success in the early 1960s with his early one-act plays and the immensely popular full-length work *Who's Afraid of Virginia Woolf?*

Edward Franklin Albee, III, was born on March 12, 1928, and as an infant was adopted by Reed A. and Frances Albee. His adoptive father was a part owner of the Keith-Albee theater circuit, which controlled many playhouses across the country presenting vaudeville acts, plays, and movies.

Albee attended private schools and spent the year 1946-1947 as an undergraduate at Trinity College in Hartford, Connecticut. Leaving college, he went to New York City, where he worked as a continuity writer for radio station WNYC, an office boy in an advertising agency, a record salesman for a music publisher, a counterman in a luncheonette, and a Western Union messenger. While working at these jobs, he had modest success as a poet.

In 1958 he began to write for the theater, and his first two one-act plays, *The Zoo Story* and *The Death of Bessie*

Smith, debuted in Berlin in German translations in 1959 and the following year were taken to New York.

He also wrote *The Sandbox* in 1959 for the Festival of Two Worlds in Spoleto, Italy, where it was not performed, but it was produced in New York the following year. *The American Dream,* seen by some as an expanded version of *The Sandbox,* was presented in Manhattan in 1961. The brief one-act *Fam and Yam* premiered in Westport, Connecticut, in 1960. Critics called some of these plays "brilliant" and "excellent" and found them "packed with untamed imagination." A few hailed Albee as the first American playwright of the absurd and hence a seminal figure.

The most exciting development in European drama in the post-World War II period was the advent of the so-called Theater of the Absurd, which had it philosophical roots in the existentialist school led by Jean-Paul Sartre and Albert Camus. As old as Aristotle, this school's undergirding was the view that existence precedes essence, or, in overly-simplified terms, that the concrete precedes the abstract. But the French existentialists added these refinements: reason alone is not adequate to explain human existence; anguish is common to all those who try to confront life's problems; and morality demands participation.

As filtered through the Theater of the Absurd, these ideas were altered or expanded to include the notions that the human condition is senseless and devoid of purpose or ideals and that, as psychoanalyst Philip Weiss puts it, "conventional logical communication" must be de-empha-

sized or regarded as well-nigh impossible. In Europe, Eugene Ionesco was considered the most consistent practitioner of Absurdist drama. In the words of Jacques Guicharnaud and June Beckelman, Ionesco's plays can be summarized as "a return to nihilism," offering "the message . . . that there is no message."

In the words of Tom Driver in *History of the Modern Theater,* "it was necessary, to have a popular playwright of the absurd [in America]. It was in this context that Edward Albee became a culture hero . . . after . . . *The Zoo Story,*" because, as John MacNicholas puts it, this play was "an exploration of the farce and agony of human isolation," a common Absurdist theme.

Years of Success and Criticism

After co-authoring the libretto of the opera *Bartleby* with James Hinton, Jr., in 1961, Albee had his greatest hit with *Who's Afraid of Virginia Woolf?* in 1962. Robert Corrigan in *The Theater in Search of a Fix* observed, "Great drama has always shown man at the limits of possibility. . . . In *Virginia Woolf* Albee has stretched them some, and in doing so he has given not only the American theatre but the theatre of the whole world, a sense of new possibility." John Gassner in *Dramatic Soundings* called it "pulsating moment-by-moment drama . . . [which] reaches the same order of harrowing dramatic power as Elizabethan melodrama." Even those whose general reception of the play was cool found something to praise, like Richard Gilman, who commented that "the rhetoric . . . is straight-forward, cocky, brutal, knowing . . . tremendously *au courant* . . . and very funny." The play won the 1963 Antoinette Perry Award (Tony) as the best new drama of the season.

In the next five years Albee divided his talents between adapting the works of others and continuing to compose original plays. In selecting works to adapt, Albee showed an unfortunate predilection for the second-rate: in 1963 he dramatized Carson McCuller's novella *The Ballad of the Sad Café;* in 1966 he produced *Malcolm,* based on a James Purdy novel of no distinction; and in 1967 he rewrote the play *Everything in the Garden* by the then-deceased Giles Cooper.

In 1964 Albee's *Tiny Alice* was staged and, like most of those which followed, was greeted by either raves or boos. Thomas Adler thought it reminiscent of Pirandello in showing "the universal human need to concretize the abstract, to discover or . . . to create a manageable representation of the unknown." Richard Gillman considered it "far and away the most significant play on Broadway this year." At the other end of the spectrum, novelist Philip Roth blasted *Tiny Alice* for "its tediousness, its pretentiousness, its galling sophistication, its gratuitous and easy symbolizing, its ghastly pansy rhetoric and repartee."

In 1966 came *A Delicate Balance,* which won its author his first Pulitzer Prize, although such influential critics as Robert Brustein and John Simon dismissed it, the former declaring that "its empty chatter is passed off as profound observation with the aid of irrelevant portentous subordinate clauses. . . . "

In 1968 came a double-bill of short plays, *Box* and *Quotations from Chairman Mao Tse-Tung,* which, the playwright explained, "both . . . deal with the unconscious primarily" and which represented his closest approach to Absurdist theater. *All Over,* a play about death, came to New York in 1971 and encountered the range of critical reactions that was becoming standard.

Awarded a Second Pulitzer Prize

Albee won his second Pulitzer Prize with *Seascape* in 1975, which Harold Clurman (long an Albee supporter) in the *Nation* found "rather charming" and Brendan Gill in the *New Yorker* judged to be "wryly written and sometimes touching," its plot "a charming toy." But the naysayers were out in force again, with Jack Kroll in *Newsweek* summing it up as "the ultimate in pure nagging."

The year 1977 brought *Counting the Ways: A Vaudeville,* first presented in London, and *Listening: A Chamber Play,* which debuted in Hartford. Martin Esslin in *Plays and Players* found the former "full of beauties," and Thomas Adler in the *Educational Theatre Journal* thought it had "considerable charm and wit."

The Lady from Dubuque in 1980 fared rather badly with the critics. Brustein wrote, "It really is quite an awful piece," and Simon added that it featured "the ultimate in witless nastiness, gratuitous offensiveness and, above all, . . . verbal infelicity." Albee did little better with his adaptation of Nabokov's novel *Lolita* in 1981, although more than one critic raised the question of whether the novel itself was not dated.

The Man Who Had Three Arms in 1982 drew from Dan Sullivan in the *Los Angeles Times* the grudging admission that "[t]here is some juice in this one, even if it is mostly bile," but Frank Rich in the *New York Times* blasted it because "it isn't a play—it's a temper tantrum in two acts."

Finding the Sun (1983) provoked the comment from Linda Ben-Zvi in *Theater Journal,* "There is much that is strong and theatrical about the piece . . . it plays well." *The Marriage Play* (1987) drew from Dana Rufolo-Hörhagen in *Plays and Players* the encomium that it "is a resonant, poetical, and cleanly hewn-work." In 1994 *Three Tall Women* debuted in Manhattan. Essentially a monologue in the first act, it had an ingeniously-wrought second act in which the monologue was continued by three actresses, representing the protagonist at different stages in her life. This play won the Pulitzer Prize in 1994.

Besides writing for the theater, Albee directed some of his own plays and those of others at various off-Broadway houses and in Los Angeles and won an award from the *Village Voice* for directing Len Jenkins' *Five of Us.* Further, he joined with Richard Barr and Clinton Wilder to form the New Playwrights Unit Workshop, which assisted aspirant writers for the theater. Albee also served as chairman of the Theater Department of Fordham University in New York.

Albee wrote four screenplays, including an adaptation of *The Death of Bessie Smith;* composed an introduction to *Three Plays by Noel Coward;* contributed to the *National*

Playwrights Directory; and authored a biography of Louise Nevelson.

Albee's position in the history of American drama is difficult to assess. He had ardent admirers such as Ruby Cohn, who called him "the most skillful composer of dialogue that American has produced" in *Dialogue in American Drama,* and John MacNicholas, who wrote in the *Dictionary of Literary Biography* that his "ideals about man and art and his formidable technical skills . . . place him in the first rank of the dramatists of his century." On the other hand, Driver thinks he "achieved a popular and critical success out of all proportion to his substance and skill." The best and probably the fairest summary of Albee's career thus far is that of C.W.E. Bigsby in *Edward Albee: A Collection of Critical Essays:* "Albee has remained at heart a product of off-Broadway, claiming the same freedom to experiment, and, indeed, fail, which is the special strength of that theater." Another assessment is Albee's receipt of three Pulitzer Prizes. Tennessee Williams and August Wilson won two Pulitzers each, the only other multiple winners among American playwrights. In 1997 Albee was the recipient of the Steinbeck Award for literary and humanitarian contributions by a writer.

Further Reading

There has been no definitive biography of Albee; until one appears, the essay by MacNicholas in the *Dictionary of Literary Biography* (1981) will have to suffice. Three collections of essays about Albee's work are worth attention: the aforementioned anthology edited by Bigsby (1975) with contributions by such critics as Esslin and Clurman; *Edward Albee,* edited by Harold Bloom (1987); and *Critical Essays on Edward Albee,* edited by Philip Kolin and J. Madison Davis (1986). Information regarding the Steinbeck award can be reviewed at http://www.southhampton.liunet.com. □

Issac Albéniz

The Spanish composer and pianist Issac Albéniz (1860-1909) played an important part in the creation of a national Spanish music. His most famous work is the piano suite *Iberia*.

saac Albéniz was born in Camprodón, in the province of Gerona, on May 29, 1860. An extraordinarily precocious child, he made his debut as a pianist in Barcelona at the age of four. When he was six his mother took him to Paris, where he took lessons from Antoine Marmontel, professor of piano at the Conservatoire. She tried to have him admitted as a student there, but, although he did brilliantly on his entrance examinations, the jury felt he was too young. On his return to Spain in 1868 he went on a concert tour of Catalonia with his father and was hailed as a child wonder. In 1869 the family moved to Madrid, where Albéniz enrolled at the Conservatory and studied with Mendizábal. In 1870, at the age of ten, he ran away from home and gave concerts in various cities of northern Spain.

Being robbed on the road on this first adventure did not deter him from running away again in 1872 after a short return to his parents' home. This time he played concerts in Andalusia in the south of Spain and, in Cádiz, embarked as a stowaway on a steamship headed for South America.

In Buenos Aires he led a beggar's life until he received help in arranging some concerts. After a successful tour of South America that earned him good money, he went to Cuba. There he met his father, who, by a strange coincidence, had been transferred to Havana as a customs inspector. Although the father attempted to persuade his son to return to the family, young Albéniz asserted his independence and left for New York. Having spent all his money, he supported himself there as a porter and by playing in dockside bars. One of his money-making tricks was to turn his back to the piano and to play with the backs of his fingers. After a stay in San Francisco, he returned to Europe in 1873, going first to Liverpool and London and then to Leipzig, where he studied with Jadassohn and Reinecke.

In 1877 he returned to Spain and was able to obtain financial aid from Count Guillermo Morphy, private secretary to King Alfonso XII, to continue his studies at the Brussels Conservatory. His teachers there were Gevaert for composition and Brassin for piano. After a leave from the Conservatory for a trip to Cuba and the United States, he returned to Belgium and, in 1879, won first prize for piano at the Conservatory. In 1880 he met and auditioned for Franz Liszt, who accepted him as a student. After following Liszt to Weimar and Rome and travelling once more to South America, he settled in Barcelona in 1883. In the same year he married one of his students, Rosina Jordana, and came under the influence of Felipe Pedrell, a musicologist, composer, and folklorist, who encouraged him to compose in a nationalistic idiom.

Albéniz's adult career as a virtuoso pianist lasted a little more than a decade, and from about 1890 he devoted himself almost exclusively to composition. After studying with Dukas and d'Indy in Paris for a time, he lived in London from 1890 to 1893. There, in 1891, he met Francis Burdett Money-Coutts (Lord Latymer), a London banker whose avocation was writing poetic dramas. He offered to pay Albéniz handsomely if he would agree to set his dramas to music. Enticed by the generous remuneration, Albéniz agreed. Because Money-Coutts' librettos were weak and their subject matter held no particular appeal for Albéniz, the collaboration resulted in several mediocre operas (*Merlin,* part of *Lancelot, Henry Clifford*), the only exception being *Pepita Jiménez,* adapted by Money-Coutts from a novel by Juan Valera.

In 1893 Albéniz moved to Paris. He became part of its active musical life and was appointed an assistant teacher of piano at the Schola Cantorum. Frequent and stimulating contact with musicians such as Vincent d'Indy, Gabrielle Fauré, Claude Debussy, Ernest Chausson, and Charles Bordes forced him to reevaluate his accomplishments as a composer and to strive for greater mastery. The same year saw the first performance of Albéniz's opera *The Magic Opal* (libretto by Arthur Law) in London, followed by the premieres of *Henry Clifford* and *Pepita Jiménez* in 1895 and

1896, respectively, in Barcelona. In 1900 he moved back to Barcelona, returned to Paris in 1902, and settled in Nice in 1903.

During his last years, plagued by mental depression and severe physical illness (he was a victim of Bright's disease), he wrote his most celebrated work, the piano suite *Iberia,* published in four books from 1906 to 1909. Each of the four books was given its first performance by the French pianist Blanche Selva successively in 1906, 1907, 1908, and 1909. On May 18, 1909, Albéniz died in Cambô-les-Bains, in the French Pyrenees. He left two unfinished piano works, *Navarra* (completed by Déodat de Séverac) and *Anzulejos* (completed by Enrique Granados). The French government awarded him the Grand Cross of the Legion d'honneur posthumously.

Although Albéniz composed some interesting orchestral works (*Catalonia, Rapsodia española,* and a piano concerto) and two good works for the stage *Pepita Jiménez* and the operetta *San Antonio de la Flórida*), he is known primarily as a composer for the piano. His contact with Felipe Pedrell influenced him to become a serious and ambitious composer and encouraged him to draw on Spanish folk material as a basis for his works. Albéniz turned to the folk music of Andalusia. He was captivated by its landscape, its people, and its folklore. He believed that he had Moorish blood in him, and he often stated that the one place where he felt most comfortable was the Alhambra in Granada. In his compositions Albéniz distills the essence and flavor of the haunting melodies, the strumming of the guitar, the exuberant rhythms, and the clicking of castanets, and presents them in a stylized, idealized artistic form. This approach is evident in a number of his popular compositions written before 1900: the *Seguidillas, Granada, Sevilla, Córdoba,* and the Tango in D Major.

His masterpiece, the piano suite *Iberia,* is a remarkable musical portrait of Spain. Although based on Andalusian folk material, it manages to capture the sights, sounds, colors—the soul—of all Spain. Fiendishly difficult technically, it challenges even the most gifted pianists. After reading the manuscript of the first book, the pianist Blanche Selva declared the piece unplayable. However, she eventually mastered it and went on to premiere the entire work. Musically the work is characterized by a variety of stylized Spanish dance rhythms, bold and piquant harmonies, unexpected modulations, rich textures, and occasional passages in which the piano imitates the guitar or castanets.

Debussy's reaction to the last piece in the fourth and final book, *Eritaña,* is a worthy summary of the entire work: "Never before has music captured so many varied impressions, all of different colors. Our eyes eventually close, dazzled with having seen so many images."

Further Reading

The following books have sections on Albéniz: Gilbert Chase, *The Music of Spain* (1941, 1959); Ann Livermore, *A Short History of Spanish Music* (1972); Harold C. Schonberg, *The Great Pianists* (1963) and *The Lives of the Great Composers* (1970); and David Ewen, *The World of Twentieth-Century Music* (1968). □

Juan Bautista Alberdi

The Argentine political theorist Juan Bautista Alberdi (1810-1884) wrote extensively on his nation's political problems. His ideas were incorporated in the Constitution of 1853.

Born in Tucumán on Aug. 29, 1810, Juan Bautista Alberdi was orphaned when still a young boy. He was then sent to Buenos Aires to continue his schooling. The new and unsettling environment caused him to leave school, but a strong attachment to his studies drew him again to the classroom. He decided on a legal career and entered law school in Buenos Aires.

Alberdi's intellect was not limited to legal matters. A man of charm and musical ability, he moved in select social circles. He founded and contributed to a journal of music and wrote a piano instruction booklet. In all this activity he did not neglect his law studies and frequently authored legal works.

The most important event in his student life was his introduction into the literary salon of Marcos Sastre. Sastre sponsored a group of young intellectuals renowned in Argentine history as the "Generation of 1837." Led by the poet Esteban Echeverria and the educator Domingo Sarmiento, they devoured the latest philosophical and literary imports from France. No mere imitators, they formulated concepts which would eventually reshape Argentine life. Unfortunately their ideas incited the wrath of the dictator, Juan Manuel de Rosas, and most of them soon fled Argentina.

Alberdi joined the extensive expatriate community in Montevideo, Uruguay, in 1838. This was the beginning of a 40-year exile. He drifted briefly to Europe and basked in the vibrant intellectual atmosphere of Italy and France, then left for Chile, where he expanded his reputation with incisive works on international law, as well as poetry, satire, and polemics.

Immediately upon hearing of the fall of dictator Rosas in 1852, Alberdi wrote *Bases and Points of Departure for the Political Organization of the Argentine Republic.* In this masterwork of political science, Alberdi carefully constructed proposals for building a democratic and federal republic, drawing ideas from Jean Jacques Rousseau, Echeverria, and the Constitution of the United States. The plans he presented were written into the Constitution of 1853.

Still Alberdi remained absent from his homeland. His personality had evidently soured in exile, and his acerbic wit and biting sarcasm did little to endear him to his fellows. Convinced of the rectitude of his own views, he found little ground for compromise or conciliation. Consequently, he gladly accepted an appointment as Argentina's roving European minister. In 1880 Alberdi returned to Argentina to serve an abbreviated legislative term but soon went again to Europe. He died in Paris on June 18, 1884.

An exile most of his adult life, Alberdi wielded his broad influence almost exclusively through his profound writing. He was steeped in philosophy, law, and political science and applied them to the special circumstances and needs of his country. The brilliance of Alberdi's work is seen in the long-lived constitution so largely inspired by him.

Further Reading

The outstanding biography of Alberdi is in Spanish: Jorge M. Mayer, *Alberdi y su tiempo* (1963). This may be supplemented by another work in Spanish, Pablo Rojas Paz, *Alberdi, el ciudadano de la soledad* (1941). José L. Romero, *A History of Argentine Political Thought* (1946; trans. 1963), discusses Alberdi's concepts, especially in relation to the Generation of 1837. Recommended for general background are James R. Scobie, *Argentina: A City and a Nation* (1964), and Henry S. Ferns, *Argentina* (1969). □

Josef Albers

Josef Albers (1888-1976) was one of the leading artists and art and design teachers of the 20th century. His emphasis was on color as a medium in its own right.

Josef Albers was born in 1888 in Bottrop in the Ruhr District of West Germany. After receiving his education at the Teachers' Training School in Langenhorst and then at the Teachers College in Büren, he began his career as a teacher in the primary grades in the public school of Bottrop. His interest in art began with a visit to Munich and its museums and galleries in 1908. By 1913 he had completed his first abstract painting, and soon after he mastered the art of printmaking, especially woodcuts and lithographs.

In 1920 Albers became a student at the Bauhaus in Weimar, founded by Walter Gropius, and remained as a teacher when the Bauhaus was relocated first to Dessau and then to Berlin. During his years at the Bauhaus, both as an artist and as a teacher, Albers was concerned with the interrelationship of the fine and applied arts. Thus he taught furniture design and calligraphy in addition to painting and drawing. Among his designs was the first laminated wood chair intended for mass production. He used commercial methods to produce glass paintings and collages, as well as stained glass windows for architectural use. In his glass paintings of the 1920s Albers explored variations in optics and perception—both concerns that would be of great importance in his art as well as his teaching.

On the recommendation of the Museum of Modern Art, Josef and Anni Albers (also an artist, whom he married in 1925) were invited to teach at the newly-founded Black Mountain College in North Carolina. He became the first of the Bauhaus teachers to leave Germany, in the fall of 1933. Albers was a mature and accomplished artist when he arrived in America, and soon after he began an active lecture and seminar tour. Through these numerous public appearances and academic presentations, his ideas and methods reached a wide audience and ideas developed at the Bauhaus were brought to the United States.

Albers left Black Mountains College in 1949 and became chairman of the Department of Art at Yale University in 1950. Here he began his well-known series of paintings and prints to which he gave the title *Homage to the Square.* Albers' format for these works—a structure of three or four squares superimposed over one another according to precise ratios—allowed him to explore the optical and perceptual qualities of color in a neutral, non-representational manner. The squares represent only squares; they do not refer to objects in the natural world. Within this apparently limited format he demonstrated the endless and changing effects and relationships when different colors are combined. Color was allowed to function as a medium in its own right, rather than as a means to describe or refer to natural objects. The individual and his perceptions became Albers' subject. He rejected scientific and theoretical interpretations of his work, insisting that his interest lay in the magical properties of color, or color as a means of aesthetic revelation.

Until the mid-1960s Albers was known primarily as one of the leading teachers of art and design in the United States. Then in 1965 his work was included in the important and popular exhibition titled "The Responsive Eye," presented by the Museum of Modern Art in New York. As a result of this exhibition the beauty of his paintings and prints was recognized and the historical importance of his experiments with perception was acknowledged. From then until his death in 1976 Albers' work was exhibited throughout the world, and he received numerous honorary degrees and awards.

In 1963 Albers had published *Interaction of Color,* the major statement of his artistic philosophy. The book is dedicated to his students, and the chapters explain problems to the reader and offer a series of visual exercises in the same way that Albers would present his ideas in the classroom. *Interaction of Color* represents Albers' legacy as a teacher and as an artist, the summation of a long and distinguished career.

Further Reading

Albers published his philosophy of art in an important and influential book, *Interaction of Color* (1963). Another major discussion of his art is F. Bucher, *Josef Albers: Despite Straight Lines. An Analysis of His Graphic Constructions* (1961). His paintings and prints are discussed in numerous exhibition catalogues from museums throughout the world. His contributions to the art of the 20th century are also discussed in major texts on modern art, such as H. H. Arnason, *Modern Art* (1977). □

Albert

Albert (1819-1861) was the husband of Queen Victoria and the Prince Consort of Great Britain. His most important achievements were the strengthen-

ing of the constitutional monarchy and the establishment of the royal family as a moral force in the life of the nation.

Albert was the second son of Ernest, Duke of Saxe-Coburg-Gotha, and of Louise, daughter of Augustus, Duke of Saxe-Coburg-Altenburg. He was born on Aug. 26, 1819, at Rosenau, Germany. Educated by a private tutor, he was advised and encouraged by his uncle Leopold, who became king of Belgium in 1831, and by Baron Stockmar, a friend and confidant of the Coburg family. After a short visit to England in 1836, Albert spent 10 months studying in Brussels. He then attended Bonn University and toured Italy with Stockmar.

Marriage to Victoria

His marriage to Victoria had, in effect, been settled in 1836, but they did not announce their betrothal until November 1839, more than 2 years after Victoria ascended the throne. Although the marriage was arranged for political and dynastic reasons, Victoria had fallen deeply in love with Albert, and he returned her devotion. Their marriage in February 1840 was not, however, enthusiastically supported by the English. Albert was never to win the unanimous support either of the populace or of the aristocracy.

During the first period of their marriage, Victoria was unwilling to offer Albert royal tasks commensurate with his real abilities. "I am only the husband, and not the master in

the house," he wrote to a close friend less than 3 months after his wedding. It took time for Albert to influence the Queen in public affairs, and even then he never fulfilled the role assigned to him by Stockmar of acting as her "constitutional genius." However, he was a personality in his own right, keenly interested in music and in the progress of science and technology and deeply concerned about the duties of royalty in a changing social context.

Change of Albert's role came gradually following the birth of the Princess Royal in November 1840 and the replacement of Lord Melbourne as prime minister by Sir Robert Peel in 1841. Above all, the retirement to Germany in September 1842 of Baroness Lehzen, Victoria's devoted Hanoverian attendant, strengthened Albert's position. His increasing involvement in government affairs was also guaranteed by the domestic happiness that he afforded the Queen. A keen gardener and a fine shot, he was always happy in the country with his family. As Albert and Victoria shared the delights and the difficulties of bringing up their nine children, sketched and painted together, and played duets, she came to rely upon him more and more. In 1857 he received the title Prince Consort.

Domestic Policies

Albert respected Peel, with whom he had much in common—a distaste of faction, a strong sense of duty, and a high-minded seriousness; moreover, both recognized that politics had to take into account the economic and social changes that were transforming Britain into an industrially based economy. The events of 1848, a year of European revolutions, confirmed Albert's view that in the course of social change the interests of workingmen had to be safeguarded as well as those of the middle classes. "The unequal division of property . . . is the principal evil," he wrote in 1849. "Means must necessarily be found, not for *diminishing riches* (as the communists wish) but to make facilities for the poor. . . . I believe this question will first be solved here in England."

Albert was one of the main architects of the Great Exhibition of 1851, which was held in London's newly built Crystal Palace. This exhibition was designed to display in international as well as national terms how society was being reshaped by science and technology. On the opening day of the exhibition, Victoria wrote in her diary, "All is owing to Albert—All to Him." Although this was an exaggeration, it was certainly true that Albert's zeal and enthusiasm had inspired everyone connected with the originally hazardous and controversial enterprise.

Foreign Affairs

Deeply suspicious of Lord Palmerston, who had become foreign minister in 1846, Albert had his own network of foreign intelligence sources and his own approach to international relations. He and Victoria did not hide their feelings about the Palmerstonian policies that they honestly believed to be perilous. Their first clash with Palmerston came in 1847 on the issue of Portugal, and there soon were differences on France and Spain. When Palmerston resigned in 1851, there was sharp criticism both of Albert and of the Queen. On the eve of the Crimean War (1853-1856), Albert was strongly attacked in the press for what were condemned unjustifiably as pro-Russian sympathies. Between the end of the Crimean War and his death, Albert remained strongly interested in European, and particularly German, politics. He was sympathetic to German unification under Prussian leadership. His advice was frequently taken on difficult issues, but in 1859 there were renewed differences both with Palmerston and with Lord John Russell on the Italian question. In 1861 Albert used his influence to prevent Britain from becoming embroiled in the American Civil War as a result of an incident involving the mail steamer *Trent.*

Albert died on Dec. 13, 1861, after an attack of typhoid fever. The Queen was desolate and throughout the rest of her long reign tried to model her actions on what she thought her beloved Albert would have done.

Further Reading

The standard biography of Albert is Sir Theodore Martin, *The Life of His Royal Highness the Prince Consort* (5 vols., 1875-1880). Other biographies are Roger Fulford, *The Prince Consort* (1949); Frank Eyck, *The Prince Consort: A Political Biography* (1959); and Hector Bolitho, *Albert, Prince Consort* (1964). Kurt Jagow's edition of *Letters of the Prince Consort, 1831-1861* was translated by E. T. S. Dugdale in 1938.

Additional Sources

Bennett, Daphne, *King without a crown: Albert, Prince Consort of England, 1819-1861,* Philadelphia: Lippincott, 1977.

Hobhouse, Hermione, *Prince Albert, his life and work,* London: H. Hamilton, 1983.

James, Robert Rhodes, *Albert, Prince Consort: a biography,* London: Hamish Hamilton, 1983.

James, Robert Rhodes, *Prince Albert: a biography,* New York: Knopf: Distributed by Random House, 1984, 1983.

Scheele, Godfrey, *The Prince Consort: man of many facets: the world and the age of Prince Albert,* London: Oresko Books, 1977. □

Albert I

Albert I (1875-1934) was king of the Belgians from 1909 to 1934. He was especially concerned with the social welfare of his subjects and the development of commerce and industry in Belgium.

Albert was born in Brussels on April 8, 1875, the son of Philip, Count of Flanders, and Princess Marie of Hohenzollern. His uncle Leopold II was the reigning king of Belgium. The death of the only son of Leopold II in 1869 and the death of Albert's older brother in 1891 made Albert the heir to the Belgian crown. In 1900 he married Elisabeth, a daughter of the Duke of Bavaria. They had three children: Leopold, Duke of Brabant (1901), Charles, Count of Flanders (1903), and Marie José (1906). Albert began his reign on the death of Leopold II in 1909.

Both Albert's granduncle Leopold I and uncle Leopold II accepted the principle that Belgium was a parliamentary monarchy, but they had often taken a very strong executive stance toward Parliament. During Albert's reign the principle would be firmly established that the prime minister and his cabinet must enjoy the confidence of the Chamber of Deputies, the lower house of Parliament, and must be responsible to that body. During the years before World War I, the Catholic party emerged as the majority party within the Chamber of Deputies. The major issue in Belgian public life was universal manhood suffrage. In 1893 the Chamber had enacted it, but the measure was modified to award plural votes on the basis of marital status, education, and occupation. The Belgian Labor party launched a series of demonstrations and strikes to force the repeal of this law and the adoption of the "one man, one vote" principle, but to no avail.

With the onset of World War I on Aug. 1, 1914, Albert refused a German ultimatum demanding free passage of German troops over Belgian soil. He assumed command of the Belgian army and staged a successful retreat onto French soil where he established headquarters at La Panne. During the war the government-in-exile constituted a national union of Liberals, Catholics, and, for the first time, the Belgian Labor party. In 1918 Albert led the Allied offensive which recovered the Belgian coast.

With the end of the war Belgium returned to cabinet regimes and normal parliamentary politics, and the years from 1918 to 1929 were spent in restoration and reconstruction. In 1919 the controversial vote structure was repealed and replaced by a "one man, one vote" statute. Belgium was struck very hard by the global economic crisis after 1929, and the last 5 years of Albert's reign were marked by strong efforts to control rising unemployment and sociopolitical strife.

On Feb. 17, 1934, Albert I was killed while mountain climbing at Marche-les-Dames in southern Belgium. He was succeeded by his older son, Leopold, who reigned as Leopold III.

Further Reading

The War Diaries of Albert of Belgium, edited by R. van Overstraeten, was published in 1954. There is no definitive biography of Albert. Useful biographies include Emile Galet, *Albert, King of the Belgians in the Great War: His Military Activities and Experiences* (trans. 1931); Emile Cammaerts, *Albert of Belgium: Defender of Right* (1935); and Charles d'Ydewalle, *Albert and the Belgians: Portrait of a King* (1935). The Flemish question became increasingly important during Albert's reign, and Shepard B. Clough, *A History of the Flemish Movement in Belgium* (1930), is the best introduction to this subject in English. For general background see Adrien de Meeüs, *History of the Belgians* (trans. 1962). □

Albert II

The sixth king of the Belgians, Albert II (born 1934), succeeded to the throne upon the death of his

brother, Baudoin, July 31, 1993. He was formally sworn in August 9, 1993.

Belgium found itself unexpectedly with a new king when King Baudoin died on July 31, 1993. Baudoin had no children, and nine days later his younger brother, Albert, took the oath as king of the Belgians (the constitutional title of the Belgian monarch). Albert, born in Brussels on June 6, 1934, to King Leopold III and Queen Astrid, was only three years younger than Baudoin. He did not step aside in favor of his son, Philippe, as had been anticipated; at 33 years of age Philippe was rumored to be still unready for the responsibilities of the monarch.

The throne of Belgium was no longer itself in peril, as it had been under Leopold III because of his disputed role in the surrender of Belgium to the Germans in World War II. After Leopold's abdication in 1950, Baudoin had brought stability but not harmony to a country gripped by a struggle between Dutch-speaking Flanders and French-speaking Wallonia. At the time of his death Belgium had begun a far-reaching federalization that made the maintenance of Belgian unity as a country questionable. The wave of mourning over Baudoin's passing brought Flemings and Walloons together in support of the monarchy, and there was no support for an anarchist deputy who shouted in favor of a European republic before Albert took his oath. It was thought by some that the rush to full separation into independent states, anticipated for early in the next century, would be halted by the new king's influence and the resurgent commitment to the dynasty.

The extent to which Albert would be able to play the part of mediator and peacemaker remained uncertain, however. As a constitutional monarch, the king of the Belgians may take no independent political action. (When Baudoin, as a devout Catholic, found himself unwilling to sign a law permitting abortion, he withdrew from his office for a day to permit it to go into effect.) The monarch is compelled to be extremely careful in using his influence as a symbol, especially since the reigns of two previous kings, Leopold II and Leopold III, had been marked by bitter and never fully resolved controversy over their policies.

Subtlety, persuasiveness, patience, and imperturbability, as well as deep knowledge and understanding of issues, are required for a king. This is where there was anxiety about whether the new king could effectively carry through the healing and reconciliation for which he pleaded in his speech to the Parliament on taking the throne. His experience, apart from the largely honorary offices bestowed upon him as heir to the throne, was chiefly as an enthusiastic supporter of Belgian business interests abroad. Honorary chairman of the Belgian Office of Foreign Trade since 1962, he was often called "Belgian's traveling salesman." As such he had been known as an affable head of numerous economic missions, with considerable expertise particularly in transportation issues. While leaving the hard work of negotiating to businessmen and economists, he provided the flattering presence of what the British call a "royal." How effective he would be in the hornet's nest of

Belgian domestic politics remained to be seen. His obvious desire to preserve Belgian national unity was aided by the fact that he had not taken sides in the Flemish-Walloon conflict.

The serene aura of King Albert II's Belgium was marred in 1996 by a series of unsettling scandals in the region. The murders of several children led to the discovery of a pedophile ring. Investigations surrounding these crimes started a chain reaction which ultimately led to the discovery of excess, corruption, and other serious inadequacies in the nation's system of law enforcement. The king, who has no powers of government, spoke out freely and expressed his outrage on more than one occassion. He called for "profound change" in the wake of nationwide demonstrations over the incidents.

On the personal side, King Albert II is an ardent fan of fast motorcycle driving (sometimes halted but not charged by highway police). He is known to enjoy good living, although he was not a member of the international "jet set." Like his predecessors on the throne, he was lucky in his marriage. After a storybook romance, he married an Italian princess, Paola Ruffo di Calabria, in 1959. She became very popular in Belgium, so that Albert was soon dubbed "Paola's husband." They had three children, Philippe, Astrid, and Laurent. In 1984 Princess Astrid married Lorenz, Archduke of Austria-Este. The couple's four children, Amedeo, Maria, Laura, and Luisa Maria, were born in Belgium. Because of uncertainty about Philippe's eventual readiness to follow his father to the throne, there was some speculation that Astrid might become queen, the first in Belgian history.

King Albert II and the members of the royal family take a deep interest in social and humanitarian issues including health care, wildlife, and the environment. These modern royals sponsor a site on the Internet with news and tourist information concerning the Kingdom of Belgium.

Further Reading

At the time of the king's inauguration biographical information was limited to brief press accounts.

Information can be found online at http://belgium.fgov.be. □

Leon Battista Alberti

Leon Battista Alberti (1404-1472) was an Italian writer, humanist, and architect. Through his theoretical writings on painting, sculpture, and architecture, he raised them from the level of the mechanical arts to that of the liberal arts.

Leon Battista Alberti, as a scholar and philosopher who moved in humanist circles in Florence and the papal court in Rome, was involved in all the central concepts of the Renaissance. He was concerned with reforming his society and the arts in the image of ancient Roman culture. Throughout most of his writings the problem of man's relation to society is fundamental.

Leon Battista Alberti was born in Genoa on Feb. 14, 1404. He was the illegitimate son of Lorenzo Alberti, who belonged to one of the most prominent and oldest Florentine families but had been banished in 1401 from his native city. As a young boy, Leon Battista attended the famous school of the humanist Gasparino Barzizza in Padua, probably at the time Lorenzo Alberti was in Venice (1414). By 1421 Leon Battista was at the University of Bologna; while there he wrote a Latin comedy, *Philodoxeus* (ca. 1424). He received a degree in canon law prior to 1428, and it is probable that after earning his degree in Bologna he went to Rome. Sometime before 1431 Alberti was appointed prior of S. Martino in Gangalandi, Tuscany, which benefice he held until his death. In 1431 and early 1432 he accompanied Cardinal Albergati on a tour of northern Europe. On his return to Rome, Alberti became secretary to the patriarch of Grado and in October 1432 abbreviator at the papal court.

Soon after this Alberti wrote *Descriptio urbis Romae* as an index for an archeological map of Rome and in 3 months composed the first three books of *Della famiglia,* which is concerned with domestic life and the education of children. The fourth book of the treatise on the family, dealing with friendship, was written in Florence in 1437, and the entire work was revised in 1443. The sociological approach of this treatise remained central to his later writings.

The Treatises

In June 1434 Alberti accompanied the court of Pope Eugenius IV to Florence when it fled from the unrest in Rome. Florence, under the leadership of artists such as Donatello, Masaccio, and Filippo Brunelleschi, was then the art capital of Europe. Here Alberti composed his theoretical treatises on the visual arts. His treatise in Latin on painting, *De pictura,* was completed in 1435; the following year he prepared in Italian a briefer, more popular version, *Della pittura.* The Latin edition, dedicated to Gianfrancesco Gonzaga of Mantua, was written to persuade patrons that the art of painting was not merely a mechanical craft. The treatise explained for the first time in writing the mathematical foundations of one-point linear perspective as it was developed by the architect Brunelleschi, to whom the Italian version was dedicated; it also discussed antique themes and their appropriate expression. A Latin treatise on sculpture, *De sculptura,* may have originated at this time, although there is much uncertainty about its date.

As a member of the papal court, Alberti accompanied the Pope to Bologna in April 1436, and in January 1438 he was at Ferrara for the convocation of the council of the Latin and Greek churches. During this period Alberti wrote a work on law, *De iure* (1437), and another on the priest, *Pontifex* (1437). In 1442 Leonello d'Este, the ruler of Ferrara, recalled Alberti to advise him on a memorial equestrian statue of his father, Niccolo d'Este. Alberti's treatise on the horse, *De equo animante,* is related to this commission. His philosophical dialogue on peace of mind, *Della tranquillità dell'animo,* probably dates from the same period.

Alberti followed the papal court back to Rome in September 1443 and, probably at the instigation of Leonello d'Este, began to write the first five books of his important Latin treatise on architecture, *De re aedificatoria.* After Nicholas V was elected pope in 1447, Alberti finished the remaining five books, and the complete work was presented to the Pope in 1452 (first printed in 1485). The treatise not only relates architecture to the classical principles enunciated by the ancient Roman writer Vitruvius but, inspired by Alberti's previous concern for the family and society, studies architecture as a sociological phenomenon. For the remainder of his life, however, Alberti was more involved with the design and execution of architecture than with theoretical treatises.

The Architecture

The Rucellai Palace in Florence was begun by Alberti about 1447 and completed in 1451. The facade has three superimposed stories of classical pilasters. His first design for the facade was probably square and had a single entrance portal, but Bernardo Rossellino, who executed the building, lengthened the palace and constructed two portals, which contradicted Alberti's architectural principles.

In 1450 Sigismondo Malatesta commissioned Alberti to refurbish the Gothic church of S. Francesco at Rimini, later known as the Tempio Malatestiano. Alberti enclosed the exterior in a classical envelope of arcades at the sides and a triumphal arch motif on the facade. The great domed sanctuary, depicted in the foundation medal of 1450 and related, according to Alberti in a letter of 1454, to the Pantheon at Rome, was never executed, as the building was left incomplete at the death of Sigismondo in 1466.

In 1450, under the aegis of Pope Nicholas V, a great building program for the city of Rome was formulated, including additions to the Vatican Palace and the rebuilding of St. Peter's and the portion of the city near the Vatican called the Leonine Borgo. Except for some preliminary work at St. Peter's, this project was not carried out, but several features of the urban plan and of the palace additions suggest at least the counsel of Alberti.

Giovanni Rucellai, whose palace Alberti had designed, commissioned him in 1458 to complete the facade of the great Gothic church of S. Maria Novella in Florence. Limited by the medieval work of the lower part of the facade, Alberti created an ingenious compromise design in the classical mode that harmonized with the earlier portion. He also renovated the family chapel in S. Pancrazio for Rucellai and executed the Shrine of the Holy Sepulcher for the chapel in 1467.

In May 1459 Alberti followed Pope Pius II to Mantua. Probably at this time Lodovico Gonzaga of Mantua commissioned Alberti to build the church of S. Sebastiano, since its model was prepared by February 1460 and the foundation begun the following month. Alberti designed a centralized church plan with monumental entrance stairs leading up to a temple front facade; he altered the design of the facade in 1470, but it was never completed.

Late in 1464 Pope Paul II dismissed the papal abbreviators, including Alberti, which gave Alberti more time for his architectural commissions. For the church of S. Andrea in Mantua, he designed in 1470 a great Latin cross plan with transept and domed crossing; he described it as an ''Etruscan temple.'' Construction began in 1472, the year of his death, and was continued until 1493 by Luca Fancelli, who supervised Alberti's Mantuan commissions. Only the nave flanked by chapels was executed in the 15th century; S. Andrea was finally completed in the 18th century.

Lodovico Gonzaga was the patron of the Church of S. Annunziata in Florence, and in 1470 he commissioned Alberti to revise Michelozzo's earlier plan for the rotunda of the church. At the same time Alberti wrote a treatise on morality, *De iciarchia,* lamenting the corruption of the times. In September 1471, he served as a guide to the antiquities of Rome, when Lorenzo de' Medici and the Florentine representatives came to pay homage to the newly elected pope, Sixtus IV. In 1472, probably early in April, Alberti died at Rome.

Widespread Influence

Alberti's treatises on painting and architecture exerted a great influence on 16th- and 17th-century artistic thought. The teachings of the French 17th-century academies of painting and architecture represent a codification of artistic principles first formulated less rigidly by Alberti.

Of his architecture, the plan of S. Andrea, through its impact on Giacomo da Vignola's design for the Jesuit church, the Gesù, at Rome, was important for two centuries of church architecture. In the same way, the facade of S. Maria Novella, with its great scrolls, became the model for classicizing church facades, as seen also in the Gesù. In both his architecture and architectural theory Alberti paved the way for the High Renaissance architecture of Rome, exemplified in Donato Bramante's work of the early 16th century.

Further Reading

Alberti's treatises include *Ten Books on Architecture,* edited by Joseph Rykwert and translated by James Leoni (1955); *On Painting,* translated with an introduction by John R. Spencer (1956; rev. ed. 1966); and *The Family in Renaissance Florence,* translated with an introduction by Renée N. Watkins (1969). The standard biography of Alberti is in Italian: Girolamo Mancini, *Vita di Leon Battista Alberti* (1882; 2d rev. ed. 1911). A study in English is Joan Gadol, *Leon Battista Alberti* (1969). The fundamental study of his architectural style and theory is in Rudolf Wittkower, *Architectural Principles in the Age of Humanism* (1949; 3d rev. ed. 1962).

Additional Sources

Borsi, Franco., *Leon Battista Alberti,* Oxford: Phaidon, 1977. ☐

St. Albertus Magnus

The German philosopher and naturalist St. Albertus Magnus (ca. 1193-1280), also known as Albert the Great, was a dominant figure in the evolution of Christian scholastic thought and a precursor of modern science.

Albert was born in Lauingen, Swabia. His family, the counts of Bollstädt, members of the lesser nobility, sent him to study at the new University of Padua in Italy. After two decades of liberal-arts study Albert was accepted into the Dominican order of mendicant friars in 1223. He studied theology in Germany and was the first German Dominican to become a master of theology at the University of Paris.

The political and social violence of the epoch was accompanied by equally bitter conflicts in the realms of philosophy and theology. In 1256 Pope Alexander IV ordered Albert to his court to defend the Mendicants against the professors of the University of Paris, who were members of the secular clergy. In 1263-1264 he served as the Pope's legate, preaching the crusade in Germany.

Biological and Physical Sciences

The works of Albertus Magnus embrace all the knowledge of the time in natural science and philosophy as well as in theology. His botanical writings, particularly *De vegetabilibus et plantis,* are noted for their accuracy and detailed descriptions of plant anatomy. His clear grasp of the empirical basis of a taxonomic scheme for plant evolution, evident in his explanation of mutable forms, was not to be surpassed until the Renaissance botanists rediscovered na-

ture. He also had qualities of the practical farmer and intuitive conservationist, advocating the proper use of manure, the planting of trees to arrest soil erosion, and the cultivation of vineyards.

Following the lead of Aristotle, he wrote voluminously of the animal world as well. *De animalibus* contains descriptions of many animal forms and sections on reproduction and embryology. Albertus Magnus had little knowledge of internal anatomy, treated anthropology philosophically rather than empirically, and presented an Aristotelian classification scheme for the animal kingdom. Furthermore, he was one of the first western European scholars to take careful note of the adaptation of animal form to the environment.

In the physical sciences he commented extensively on chemistry, geology, petrology, and the complex problem of the stability of mineral forms. Here he followed the Aristotelian conception of the four elements and the four qualities and avoided the fanciful notions of the alchemists by retaining a skeptical attitude toward the possibility of a true transformation of the base metals into gold or silver. He isolated the element arsenic, compiled a list of about 100 minerals and their properties, and made accurate observations of fossils. His "chemical writings" discriminate the basic processes of protochemistry, that is, sublimation, distillation, pulverization, grinding, heating, cementing, dissolving, coagulation, and liquefaction.

Autonomy of Reason

The operational principles underlying the scientific work of Albertus Magnus are evident in the following statements taken from his works:

> In science we do not have to investigate how God the Maker by His free will uses that which He has created for a miracle by means of which He manifests His power, but rather what may happen in natural things on the ground of causes inherent in nature.

> Science does not consist simply in believing what we are told, but in inquiring into the nature of things.

> A conclusion that is inconsistent with our senses cannot be believed; a principle that does not agree with experience gained by sense perception is not a principle, but rather the reverse of it.

> The investigation of nature should be pursued even unto individual things; knowledge of the natures of things in general is only rudimentary knowledge.

These precepts are indeed remarkable for a 13th-century scholar. They provide eloquent support for the claim that it was Albertus Magnus who first clearly established the autonomy of reason in the sphere of science and hence, at a critical moment in European history, prevented the rational studies of nature from being outlawed by the Church as a form of magic or necromancy or from being inundated by the tides of mysticism or dogmatic orthodoxy.

Further Reading

A modern biography of St. Albertus Magnus is S. M. Albert, *Albert the Great* (1948). The best analysis of his role in the evolution of medieval thought appears in the various writings of the great French historian Etienne H. Gilson: *Christianity and Philosophy* (1936; trans. 1939) and *The Spirit of Medieval Philosophy* (1932; trans. 1936). See also E. J. Dijksterhuis, *The Mechanization of the World Picture* (trans. 1961), and Fritz Paneth, *Chemistry and Beyond: A Selection,* edited by Herbert Dingle and G. R. Martin (1964). □

Madeleine Korbel Albright

A professor and foreign policy expert, Madeleine Korbel Albright (born 1937) was appointed by President Bill Clinton in 1992 to be the U.S. permanent representative to the United Nations and head of the U.S. delegation to that body. President Clinton was also responsible for her appointment as the Secretary of State in 1997.

I n filling the sensitive diplomatic post of ambassador to the United Nations (U.N.), President Clinton turned to a prominent Washington insider with an extensive background in academia together with strong political connections. Rewarding Madeleine Albright for her support of

Democratic Party candidates and making her the second woman to serve as chief of mission at the United Nations, he also signaled the weight to be assigned to international frameworks in American foreign policy by making her a member of his cabinet.

Madeleine Korbel Albright was born on May 15, 1937, in Prague, the daughter of a Czech diplomat. At the age of 11 she came to the United States, joining her father, Josef Korbel, who was on an official assignment for his country at the U.N. but who then used the opportunity to seek political asylum in the United States for himself and his family.

Becoming a naturalized citizen, Albright pursued an academic career, starting with a B.A. from Wellesley College (1959). Pursuing graduate work at Columbia University, she received a master's degree in international affairs (1968), specializing in Soviet studies, and her Ph.D. in 1976.

Albright's subsequent career record highlights a combination of scholarly research and political activity. She was a coordinator for the unsuccessful presidential candidacy of Senator Edmund S. Muskie of Maine in 1976, later becoming his chief legislative assistant. In 1978 Albright was asked by one of her former professors at Columbia University, Zbigniew Brzezinski, National Security Adviser under President Carter, to join the National Security Council staff as a legislative liaison, where she remained until 1981. The following year was spent writing a book about the role of the press in bringing about political change in Poland in the period 1980 to 1982, a project conducted under a fellow-

ship from the Woodrow Wilson Center for Scholars at the Smithsonian Institute.

Albright's next important career milestone came in 1982, when she joined the faculty of Georgetown University and expanded both her interests and personal contacts. As a research professor of international affairs and director of women students enrolled in the foreign service program at the university's School of Foreign Service, she taught undergraduate and graduate courses in international studies, U.S. foreign relations, Russian foreign policy, and central and eastern European politics. She was also instrumental in developing programs designed to enhance professional opportunities for women in international affairs. She also became affiliated with the Georgetown University Center for Strategic and International Studies as a senior fellow in Soviet and eastern European affairs. In October of 1989 she took over the presidency of the Center for National Policy, a Washington-based nonprofit research organization formed in 1981 as a Democratic think tank with a mandate to generate discussion and study about domestic and international issues. Having been divorced, she did all this while over the years raising three daughters by herself, and still found the time to be a board member on numerous institutes, national commissions, and civic organizations ranging from the Atlantic Institute, the Boards of Trustees of Wellesley College and of Williams College, and the National Democratic Institute for International Affairs to the Black Student Fund and the Washington Urban League.

Parallel with her research and teaching, Albright deepened her involvement in Democratic Party politics. She acted as an adviser to both Walter Mondale and Geraldine Ferraro during the 1984 presidential election year; and as an adviser to Michael S. Dukakis in 1988 when he failed in his bid to defeat Republican George Bush. She was more successful, however, in 1992, when she endorsed Arkansas Governor Bill Clinton's candidacy. During the campaign she served as his senior foreign policy adviser, and in the transition period as foreign policy liaison in the White House prior to her U.N. posting.

Based clearly on the strength of her personal views and familiarity with world politics, Ambassador Albright immediately became a presence to be reckoned with at the United Nations, especially since she also represented the world's most powerful country and largest contributor to the organization's activities and budget.

Already during the first year it became evident that she saw herself as a spokesperson to three different audiences: first, to the delegations assembled in debate at the New York headquarters, articulating the American position and preferences on global problems dominating the world organization's agenda; second, to President Clinton and his administration, formulating the stand of the U.S. government on U.N.-related topics; and third, to the American public, mobilizing support for policies pursued at, and through, the United Nations. Consequently, Madeleine Albright found herself involved simultaneously in political debate, maneuvering, and consultation in the U.N. arena over such controversial questions as peace-keeping, expanding the Security Council's membership to include possibly both Germany and Japan, and clarifying the precise authority and powers of Secretary-General Boutros-Ghali; in the U.S. policymaking process in Washington; and in the ongoing national debate over the direction of American foreign relations in the 1990s.

Madeleine Albright was nominated by President Clinton in 1996 for the position of Secretary of State. In 1997 the U.S. Senate unanimously confirmed her nomination. This appointment made Albright the first female to hold the position of Secretary of State. This designation also bestows her with the title of highest-ranking female within the United States government.

Shortly after her confirmation, Albright's Czech cousin revealed to reporters at the *Washington Post* that Albright's family were Czech Jews and not Catholics as she believed, and that three of her grandparents had perished in concentration camps. Albright stated that she was not totally surprised by the news and was quoted in *Newsweek* as saying, "I have been proud of the heritage that I have known about and I will be equally proud of the heritage that I have just been given." A few months later, Albright flew to Prague, toured the Old Jewish Cemetery and the Pinkas Synagogue, and was honored by the Czech president.

Meanwhile, in her diplomatic duties, she continued to play hardball. She made efforts to charm North Carolina Senator Jesse Helms, Chair of the Senate Foreign Relations Committee. She interrupted her world travels to tour his home state, speak at his alma mater, and give him a t-shirt inscribed with "Somebody at the State Department Loves Me." Her efforts paid off as Helms was persuaded to work on a measure where the U.S. would repay funds owed to the U.N.

Albright began a peace mission in the Middle East in the fall of 1997, first meeting with Israeli Prime Minister Benjamin Netanyahu in September to discuss Israeli-Palestinian relations. At a joint news conference, there appeared to be a wide gap between the goals of the Clinton administration and the Israeli government. Although Albright condemned terrorist activities, she also urged Netanyahu to make concessions. While in Jerusalem, she also visited the Hall of Remembrance at Yad Vashem, Israel's Holocaust Memorial.

She then conferred with Palestinian leader Yasser Arafat before addressing Jewish and Arab students in Jerusalem, and met with Syrian President Hafez al-Assad, Egyptian President Hosni Mubarek, King Fahd of Saudi Arabia, and King Hussein of Jordan. Albright vowed not to meet with Israeli and Palestinian leaders again until they were "ready to make the hard decisions."

Further Reading

Madeleine Albright's views on foreign policy can be found in her writings, which include *Poland, the Role of the Press in Political Change* (1983); *The Role of the Press in Political Change: Czechoslovakia 1968* (1976); and *The Soviet Diplomatic Service: Profile of an Elite* (1968). Information regarding her appointment as Secretary of State may be viewed at http:// secretary.state.gov. Also see *Time,* July 28, 1997; August 4, 1997; September 15, 1997; *Newsweek,* February 24, 1997; September 15, 1997; *U.S. News & World Report,* September 1, 1997; September 22, 1997. □

Afonso de Albuquerque

The Portuguese nobleman Afonso de Albuquerque (ca. 1460-1515) is best known as governor of India. He is also considered to be the founder of the Portuguese imperial system.

Afonso de Albuquerque was born to a family of minor Portuguese nobility. He fought in Portugal's wars in Spain and Africa. He was sent on a voyage to India in 1503-1504 and went to the East again in 1506 with Tristão da Cunha. In 1507 they captured the island of Socotra in the Arabian Sea, from where Tristão da Cunha sailed for India and Albuquerque for Hormuz. Albuquerque took Hormuz, the principal spice-distributing center for the Persian Gulf, and proceeded to India. He reached Cannanore in December 1508 and revealed his secret instructions to supersede Viceroy Francisco de Almeida, with the title of governor. Almeida, refusing to give up command, imprisoned him until a powerful Portuguese fleet under Fernando Coutinho arrived in October 1509 with a confirmation of Albuquerque's appointment. He then assumed power.

Albuquerque was the major figure in the establishment of the Portuguese sea empire in the East. In 1510 he captured Goa, which he fortified and made the chief trading post and permanent naval base in India. To give it a stable character, he offered lands and subsidies to Portuguese men who would marry native women. In 1511 Albuquerque captured Malacca; from this base he could control the trade from the East Indies and the coast of China. During his governorship Portuguese vessels touched on the coast of China and sailed to some of the islands of the East Indies, gaining naval ascendancy in the Far East.

In Goa again in 1512, Albuquerque strengthened Portuguese administration there and in other coastal cities and prepared a fleet for a campaign along the coasts of Persia and Arabia. His unsuccessful attack on Aden in 1513 failed to close the Red Sea to Moslem shipping. On his return to India, he secured from the King of Cambay the right to construct a fortress in Diu. His success brought friendly overtures from the Shah of Persia, the Samorin of Calicut, and the kings of Siam and Malacca, as well as several other rulers.

Portugal now controlled the principal strategic points from the east coast of Africa to Malacca, with the exception of the Red Sea. A system of licenses (called *cartazas*) required all ships to prove that they had paid customs duties at Malacca, Goa, or Hormuz. An unlicensed ship, particularly if it belonged to Moslems, was subjected to seizure and sinking. Albuquerque's policies thus had made the Portuguese the predominant, although not the only, commercial force in the East until the 17th century.

In 1515 Albuquerque was superseded by enemies he had previously sent back to Portugal as prisoners. He voiced his bitterness: "I am in ill favor with the king for love of men, and with men for love of the king." He died at sea on Dec. 16, 1515.

Further Reading

The best source for material on Albuquerque is by his son, Afonso de Albuquerque, *The Commentaries of the Great Afonso Dalboquerque* (1774; trans. with an introduction by W. de Gray Birch, 4 vols., 1875-1884). Edgar Prestage, *Afonso de Albuquerque, Governor of India* (1929), is a brief account. Elaine Sanceau, *Indies Adventure: The Amazing Career of Afonso de Albuquerque* (1936), is a pro-Portuguese treatment that makes extensive use of the sources. Richard Stephen Whiteway, *The Rise of Portuguese Power in India, 1497-1550* (1899; 2d ed. 1967), and Charles R. Boxer's scholarly *The Portuguese Seaborne Empire, 1415-1825* (1969) are excellent background works that rely on the writings of 16th century Portuguese historians for source material. See also K. G. Jayne, *Vasco da Gama and His Successors* (1910). □

Alcibiades

The Athenian general Alcibiades (ca. 450-404 B.C.) served Athens and its enemies alike and caused damage to every state that employed him.

Alcibiades was the son of Cleinias, a brilliant but unstable Athenian politician. Wealthy, handsome, and aristocratic, Alcibiades was brought up in the house of his guardian, Pericles, and groomed for a political career. He had every possible advantage and in addition possessed exceptional charm and ability as a conversationalist, thinker, and diplomat. Entering politics in the wartime atmosphere of the Peloponnesian War, he represented youth and became an intimate of the teacher of young men, Socrates. (They were portrayed together by Plato in his dialogues *Alcibiades* and *Symposium.*)

Alcibiades chose extreme democracy and an aggressive, imperialistic policy. In 420 B.C., during an uneasy peace with Sparta, by clever tactics he drove Athens into an alliance with Argos and other Greek states against Sparta. This policy, which never gained the full support of the majority in Athens, failed completely in 418, when Sparta defeated the coalition's forces at Mantinea. The debacle caused Athens to conduct an ostracism in order to decide between the conservative Nicias, the advocate of peace with Sparta, and the aggressive Alcibiades. With characteristic ingenuity Alcibiades arrived at a compromise with Nicias, a third party was ostracized, and the fundamental difference of policy was not resolved.

Even in the permissive society of his day, Alcibiades became proverbial for his extravagant and reckless behavior, and the distrust he aroused wrecked his career. In 415 he was the prime mover of the proposal to attack Syracuse and, together with Nicias and Lamachus, commanded the naval expedition to Sicily. Alcibiades was soon recalled on

charges of having profaned the Mysteries and of having mutilated religious statues (hermae) in a drunken spree on the eve of the fleet's departure.

On the way home Alcibiades escaped, reached Sparta, and became a military adviser to the Spartans. He gained for Sparta the alliance of Persia, instigated revolt by some colonies of Athens, and encouraged Sparta to base troops inside Attica against Athens. But he fell into disfavor with the Spartan king Agis, whose wife he seduced. Alcibiades subsequently transferred his services to Persia and then to Athenian antidemocratic extremists, with whom he planned a coup d'etat in Athens. When he failed to obtain Persia's aid, they discontinued to support him and seized power in Athens without him.

Alcibiades's political career now swung full circle. With the help of the Athenian extreme democrats, who still controlled the fleet, he was installed as commander of the navy. Winning brilliant victories against Sparta, which resulted in the restoration of democracy in Athens, he came home in 407 as the favorite of the democrats. But when the Athenian navy under a subordinate officer was defeated at Notium by the Spartan naval commander Lysander, Alcibiades anticipated trouble and withdrew into retirement near the Dardanelles. After the Peloponnesian War, Sparta demanded his head, and he was assassinated while a fugitive in Phrygia.

Further Reading

Ancient sources on Alcibiades include Thucydides's *The History of the Peloponnesian War,* Books V-VIII; Xenophon's *Hellenica I;* Plato's *Symposium* and *Alcibiades I;* and the "Life of Alcibiades" in Plutarch's *Lives.* For modern accounts see the chapter by W.S. Ferguson in J.B. Bury and others, eds., *The Cambridge Ancient History,* vol. 5 (1927), and H. D. Westlake, *Individuals in Thucydides* (1968). Background information is in J.B. Bury, *A History of Greece to the Death of Alexander the Great* (1900; 3d rev. ed. 1951), and N. G. L. Hammond, *A History of Greece to 322 B.C.* (1959; 2d ed. 1967). □

James Lusk Alcorn

James Lusk Alcorn (1816-1894) was a prominent member of the Whig party in Mississippi before the Civil War. After the war he became a leader of the Republican party in his state and served as governor and U.S. senator during the Reconstruction period.

James Lusk Alcorn was born on Nov. 4, 1816, in Golconda, Ill., and raised across the Ohio River in Livingston County, Ky. Here as deputy sheriff under his uncle, he learned how to deal with lawlessness, earned a reputation for physical bravery, and studied law, receiving his license to practice in 1838.

In 1844 he traveled down the Ohio and Mississippi rivers to the newly settled town of Delta in northwestern Mississippi. Aggressive and energetic in his law practice and

in the acquisition of land, he quickly became a leading citizen. He joined the aristocratic Whig party and a year after his arrival was elected to the state legislature, where he served either as a representative or senator until 1857. He also became the foremost advocate of a centralized levee system to protect the rich delta lands of Mississippi from flooding.

During the period before the Civil War, Alcorn was a staunch unionist, but as a delegate at the secession convention he dramatically reversed his stand and voted for secession. After serving briefly as a state general, he retired to his plantation and limited his loyalty to his state, defying both the occupying Union Army and the Confederate government.

Considering the Republican party the successor to the Whig party, Alcorn joined it after the war, and he was elected governor in 1869. He made progress in reconstructing his war-torn state but had trouble handling the increasing violence inspired by the Ku Klux Klan. Although a former slave owner, he accepted the emancipation of the slaves and supported enfranchisement of African Americans, viewing them as a new lower class, like lowerclass whites, for whom he and others of his class would provide leadership. In 1871 he became a U.S. senator, but by this time another faction had formed in the Republican party advocating complete equality for African Americans. This split within the Republican party, plus a program of intimidation and violence by the Klan, enabled the Democrats to regain control of the state government in 1875. Since Alcorn, unlike many other former Whigs, refused to join the

Democrats, his political career ended with the expiration of his term as senator in 1877. In 1890 he emerged from retirement to participate in the state convention which rewrote Mississippi's constitution that disfranchised African Americans. Alcorn died on Dec. 20, 1894, and was buried in the family cemetery on his plantation in the Mississippi Delta.

Further Reading

The only full-length biography of Alcorn is Lillian A. Pereyra, *James Lusk Alcorn: Persistent Whig* (1966), which emphasizes his public career. Material on Alcorn and Reconstruction can be found in James Wilford Garner, *Reconstruction in Mississippi* (1901). □

Amos Bronson Alcott

Amos Bronson Alcott (1799-1888), the most brilliant and visionary American educator of his time, was also the most extreme of the New England transcendentalists.

Bronson Alcott was born near Wolcott, Conn., on Nov. 29, 1799. His was an old New England family which had fallen on hard times, with the result that Alcott received only scanty schooling. However, he educated himself through much of his long life. He early discovered that he wanted to educate others, and he traveled as far away as Virginia to seek a post. Unsuccessful there as elsewhere, he turned to peddling in Virginia and the Carolinas. After his return to New England in 1823, he spent the next decade in a variety of teaching positions and seldom stayed long in any one place.

The school system in the United States at this time was marked by narrowness and rigidity, stressing memorization and discipline. Alcott felt that the basic impulses in the human being were noble ones and that education should consist in freeing the child from restrictions and giving full rein to his imagination. Education should encourage the child mentally, morally, spiritually, esthetically, and physically. For Alcott the body was as important as the mind, so he introduced into his classes such innovations as organized play and gymnastics; he also tried to introduce the study of human physiology. Alcott treated the children as adults through such devices as the honor system, and he led them to discover their personal views through constant use of the Socratic dialogue. But the picture of Alcott gently questioning a 6-year-old about infinity or punishing himself when a child misbehaved was enough to startle any school board, and it is no wonder he became an educational nomad.

If school boards found him shocking, the members of the emerging transcendentalist movement found him admirable though at times exasperating. His philosophy was eclectic. To the Quaker idea of inner vision, he added the idea of intuitive knowledge; he adopted the notion of preexistence; he believed that spirit was the only reality and that man's everyday world was merely an emanation of it; and he permeated this mystic philosophy with a feeling that was close to the ecstatic. He proved to be more Emersonian than even Ralph Waldo Emerson (the leading transcendentalist). The transcendentalists as a group were often accused of being visionary and impractical; Alcott was the personification of those qualities.

His impracticality showed in his family life. Married in 1830, he soon fathered a large family for which he could never provide. Besides schoolteaching, he attempted a bit of farming, a brief stint in communal living at Fruitlands (a cooperative community which he helped found near Harvard, Mass.), itinerant lecturing in the guise of paid "conversations" in the Socratic mode, and some writing. But it was not till he was an elderly man that his family's financial plight was relieved, when his daughter Louisa May Alcott published *Little Women,* a best seller.

Alcott's achievement lay in establishing the first "progressive school" in America, in Boston's Masonic Temple. *The Record of a School, Exemplifying the General Principles of Spiritual Culture* (1835) consists of his observations there as edited by his assistant, Elizabeth Peabody. The school lasted till 1839 despite Alcott's notoriously unorthodox methods. The blow that killed the school was his enrollment of a Negro girl.

In 1859 Alcott's friends got him appointed superintendent of the public schools of Concord, Mass., the native home of transcendentalism. Though he remained as innovative as ever, Concord had become tolerant and allowed him to do a good job. In 1879 he started the Concord Summer School of Philosophy and Literature for adults, which carried on until his death. Besides writing on education, he contributed mystical "Orphic Sayings" to the transcendentalist magazine, the *Dial,* and published poetry and reflective essays.

Thomas Carlyle caught the flavor of Alcott's unique personality: "The good Alcott; with his long, lean face and figure, with his worn gray temples and mild, radiant eyes; all bent on saving the world by a return to acorns and the golden age; he comes before one like a venerable Don Quixote, whom nobody can laugh at without loving."

Further Reading

There is little current work on Alcott, with the notable exception of *The Letters of A. Bronson Alcott,* edited by Richard L. Herrnstadt (1969). The only adequate biography is Odell Shepard, *Pedlar's Progress: The Life of Bronson Alcott* (1937), which corrects and extends the memoir of Alcott by F.B. Sanborn and William T. Harris, *A. Bronson Alcott: His Life and Philosophy* (1893; repr. 1965). The former can be supplemented by Hubert H. Hoeltje, *Sheltering Tree: A Story of the Friendship of Ralph Waldo Emerson and Amos Bronson Alcott* (1943). Alcott as an educator is treated in Dorothy McCuskey, *Bronson Alcott, Teacher* (1940).

Additional Sources

Dahlstrand, Frederick C., *Amos Bronson Alcott, an intellectual biography,* Rutherford N.J.: Fairleigh Dickinson University Press; London: Associated University Presses, 1982. □

Louisa May Alcott

Louisa May Alcott (1832-1888) is one of America's best-known writers of juvenile fiction. She was also a reformer, working in the causes of temperance and woman's suffrage.

L ouisa May Alcott was born in Germantown, Pa., in 1832. She was the daughter of Bronson Alcott, the Concord transcendentalist philosopher and educator. She and her three sisters spent their childhood in poverty. However, they had as friends, and even as tutors, some of the most brilliant and famous men and women of the day, such as Henry David Thoreau, Ralph Waldo Emerson, Margaret Fuller, and Theodore Parker. This combination of intellectual plenty and physical want endowed Alcott with an ironical sense of humor. She soon realized that, if she or her sisters did not find ways to bring money into the home, the family would be doomed to permanent poverty.

In her early years Alcott worked at a variety of menial tasks to help financially. At 16 she wrote a book, *Flower Fables* (not published for 6 years), and she wrote a number of plays that were never produced. By 1860 she was publishing stories and poems in the *Atlantic Monthly*. During the Civil War she served as a nurse until her health failed, and her *Hospital Sketches* (1863) brought the first taste of widespread public attention.

The attention seemed to die out, however, when she published her first novel, *Moods,* in 1865, and she was glad to accept in 1867 the editorship of the juvenile magazine *Merry's Museum.* The next year she produced the first volume of *Little Women,* a cheerful and attractive account of her childhood, portraying herself as Jo and her sisters as Amy, Beth, and Meg. The book was an instant success, so in 1869 she produced the second volume. The resulting sales accomplished the goal she had worked toward for 25 years: the Alcott family was financially secure.

Little Women had set the direction, and Alcott continued a heavy literary production in the same vein. She wrote *An Old-fashioned Girl* (1870), *Little Men* (1871), and *Work* (1873), an account of her early efforts to help support the family. During this time she was active in the causes of temperance and woman's suffrage, and she also toured Europe. In 1876 she produced *Silver Pitchers,* a collection containing "Transcendental Wild Oats," an account of her father's disastrous attempts to found a communal group at Fruitlands, Mass. In later life she produced a book almost every year and never wanted for an audience.

Alcott died on March 6, 1888, in Boston. She seems never to have become bitter about her early years or her dreamy, improvident father, but she did go so far as to say that a philosopher was like a man up in a balloon: he was safe as long as three women held the ropes on the ground.

Further Reading

Ednah Cheney, ed., *Louisa May Alcott: Her Life, Letters, and Journals* (1889), is an early biography. Also of interest are

Katharine S. Anthony, *Louisa May Alcott* (1938), and Marjorie M. Worthington, *Miss Alcott of Concord* (1958). A documented, full-length study of Miss Alcott's works is Madeleine B. Stern, *Louisa May Alcott* (1950). □

Alcuin of York

The English churchman Alcuin of York (c. 730-804) was an educator, statesman, and liturgist. In the total range of his talents he was unequaled by any other man of his time.

B orn in or near York, Alcuin was early entrusted to the cathedral school there under the master teacher, Egbert, who had been a pupil of the great English historian Bede. When Egbert became archbishop of York, Alcuin had the rare good fortune to study under the scholars Aelbert and Eadbert. With the former, Alcuin visited the Continent to secure books and art treasures to enrich the library at York, which until its demolition in the Danish wars was the greatest library in the Western world.

Alcuin's education was firmly classical, since at this time the vast resources of Mediterranean erudition were being poured into England by such men as Paulinus, Theodore, and Hadrian. And under the impact of Bede, such secular studies as literature, science, history, and music, which were uncommon in early monastic schools, were also included in the curriculum. Dedicated to learning, Alcuin was promoted by the time he was 30 from student to teacher, and later to master. In the meantime he was ordained deacon, but he never advanced to the priesthood.

Coming back from a visit to Rome in 781, Alcuin happened to meet the future emperor Charlemagne at Parma. The serious, learned, and sagacious teacher made a deep impression on the Frankish leader. He urged Alcuin to take charge of the palace school, which had been established not only to educate royalty and nobility, but also to prepare missionaries and scholars to instruct the heathen tribes he intended to integrate into his projected Christian empire. The proposal was approved by the Northumbrian bishops, and Alcuin gradually weaned himself from his beloved York. In 782 he joined Charlemagne in Frankland. From then on he visited England only occasionally as an agent and personal representative of Charlemagne.

Alcuin set about developing the school. His was not an original mind, but he brought to his task great persistence and a mind that was an extraordinarily capacious storehouse of knowledge. Gradually Charlemagne drew him into an ever-closer collaboration on matters of state-craft.

Besides establishing his school, which became a center of Western culture, Alcuin wrote important political and liturgical works. He composed a number of significant official documents, which were believed until recently entirely the work of Charlemagne. These included decisions of the thorny problems of iconoclasm and the Spanish heresy of adoptionism. Alcuin's liturgical guide took into account both universally and locally observed rites and served as the basis of the Missal until the Second Vatican Council.

After serving Charlemagne for many years, Alcuin withdrew to the abbey of St. Martin of Tours and died there in 804.

Further Reading

Eleanor Shipley Duckett, *Alcuin, Friend of Charlemagne: His World and His Work* (1951), is a definitive study of Alcuin's life, times, and work. Luitpold Wallach, *Alcuin and Charlemagne: Studies in Carolingian History and Literature* (1959), concentrates on Alcuin's political influence and examines the question of authorship of the state papers prepared for Charlemagne. Gerald Ellard, a renowned liturgist, in *Master Alcuin, Liturgist, a Partner of Our Piety* (1956), shows how capably Deacon Alcuin reorganized the sacramentary at the behest of Charlemagne. The best background studies of the age of Charlemagne are in German and French, but for a study of England in the 8th and 9th centuries Peter Hunter Blair, *An Introduction to Anglo-Saxon England* (1956), is excellent. See also Philippe Wolff, *The Cultural Awakening* (trans. 1968). □

Nelson Wilmarth Aldrich

United States senator Nelson Wilmarth Aldrich (1841-1915) was the ablest of a group of Republican conservatives who fought a rearguard action against progressivism during the administrations of Theodore Roosevelt and William Howard Taft.

A descendant of Roger Williams, Nelson Aldrich was born in Foster, R.I., on Nov. 6, 1841, and educated in the common schools of the area. His marriage to Abby Chapman in 1865 brought him a measure of wealth and gave him entry to society, but he was essentially a self-made man. After service in the Civil War, he rose to partnership in a wholesale grocery business. He invested shrewdly and ultimately became one of Rhode Island's foremost financiers.

A resourceful leader, Aldrich was a man of extraordinary charm, lucidity, and willpower. He served two terms in the Rhode Island Legislature and one in Congress before being elected to the U.S. Senate in 1881. There for 30 years he represented the corporate and financial world's point of view with wit, irony, and intelligence. He shared power with a half dozen other conservatives through the McKinley and first Roosevelt administrations but stood virtually alone as the spokesman of the Old Guard thereafter. More than any other senator, he was able to thwart, retard, or modify Roosevelt's progressive recommendations between 1905 and 1909.

Aldrich's conservatism reflected the arrogance of the self-made man and an almost unqualified belief that what was good for big business was good for the nation. He supported the gold standard and the protective tariff and generally opposed the regulation of business. He was also unsympathetic to social-justice measures and democratic procedural reforms. Yet he was realistic enough to accept the inevitability of change, and he endeavored to shape change along lines congenial to his own views.

In 1906 Aldrich succeeded in having the Hepburn rate bill amended to the railroads' partial satisfaction. The next year he sponsored the Aldrich-Vreeland emergency banking bill. As head of the National Monetary Commission created by that measure, he declared, "I am going to have a central bank in this country." In 1911 his proposals, the so-called Aldrich Plan, were unveiled with strong banking and civic support. Many of these recommendations were incorporated in the Federal Reserve Act of 1913. Significantly, however, Aldrich opposed two of the act's key provisions: public control of the central board and the issuance of government notes.

For all his indomitable qualities, Aldrich was a gracious, pleasure-loving man. A connoisseur and collector of paintings, he maintained a luxurious estate and consorted almost exclusively with the social and economic elite. His daughter Abby was the wife of John D. Rockefeller, Jr. Aldrich died on April 16, 1915.

Further Reading

There is no modern biography of Aldrich. Nathaniel Wright Stephenson, *Nelson W. Aldrich: A Leader in American Politics* (1930), is a brilliant character study which suffers from its uncritical tone. Background studies of the period include Mathew Josephson, *The President Makers: The Culture of*

Politics and Leadership in an Age of Enlightenment, 1896-1919 (1940) and *The Politicos: 1865-1896* (1938); George E. Mowry, *The Era of Theodore Roosevelt and the Birth of Modern America, 1900-1912* (1958); and David J. Rothman, *Politics and Power: The United States Senate, 1869-1901* (1966). □

Sholom Aleichem

Probably the foremost writer of Yiddish literature, Sholom Aleichem (1859-1916) was a catalyst for its revival at the turn of the century. He is also "The Jewish Mark Twain," a folk artist who faithfully recreated the *shtetl*, village life of Russian Jews before modernity, anti-Semitism, and war destroyed that world forever.

Sholom Aleichem was born March 2, 1859. He grew up in Woronko, a Ukranian village which he later recalled with affection. When he was 12, his father failed in business and the family moved to nearby Pereyaslav. A year later his mother died and his father remarried. The stepmother harrassed the children, and her curses, which Sholom recorded, became his first writing. He also composed *The Jewish Robinson Crusoe,* modeled on Daniel Defoe, and *The Daughter of Zion,* an imitation of a Hebrew novel by Abraham Mapu.

Early Writings

Recognizing Sholom Aleichem's intelligence and talent, his father enrolled him in a Russian school where he received a secular education and graduated with honors. But because he was eligible for the draft—eventually he avoided conscription—he was refused admission to a teachers' institute. He found employment as tutor to a young girl, Olga Loyeff, in 1877. When a romance developed he was abruptly dismissed by the girl's father. In 1880 he became the certified rabbi of Louben, the Jewish community's representative to the government. A Hebrew article he wrote during this period came to Loyeff's attention. Tutor and pupil were reunited. They married in 1883, and, after reconciliation with her father, moved to his estate. There, Sholom Aleichem began publishing stories in Yiddish under his pseudonym (Hebrew for "Peace be with you") because Yiddish was considered an inferior dialect for serious writing.

In 1887 he moved to Kiev and produced more stories, mainly about childhood, and novels, including *Sender Blank, Yossele Solovey,* and *Stempanyu.* In 1888 he founded *Die Yiddishe Folksbibliotek,* a magazine containing works by Yiddish authors. He was famous. But writing did not pay, and he supported his family as a trader on the stock exchange. In 1890, after losing his money, he moved to Odessa, then back to Kiev in 1893. Between 1890 and 1903 some of Sholom Aleichem's best known works—the letters of Menachem-Mendel, the Tevye and Kasrilevka stories, subjects to which he later returned—appeared. By 1903 he had left business altogether to write full time.

His life reflected the fortunes of European Jewry. Following the 1905 revolution and pogroms, he fled Russia. Until 1908 he lived in Switzerland, but after a bout of tuberculosis he had residences in the more healthful climates of Italy and Germany. At the outbreak of World War I he was forced, as a Russian alien, to leave Germany for Denmark. In December 1914 he came to America, where he lived until his death on May 13, 1916.

Writings in Exile

During his exile he continued writing stories, novels, and plays. Sholom Aleichem also went on reading tours, including a brief visit to America in 1907. Everywhere he was a celebrity. In Austro-Hungary students carried him from the stage on their shoulders and pulled his carriage home. Crowds greeted him on both arrivals in America. In 1909 admirers held an international jubilee honoring his 50th birthday and 25th anniversary as a writer. But, despite his fame, finances were meager. Books were pirated, publishers owning rights to the works withheld royalties, magazine editors failed to pay. The move to New York in 1914 was financed by its Yiddish cultural community.

In America he disliked the materialism and rivalries among Jewish groups, newspapers, and theaters. Two plays, a dramatization of *Stempanyu* and *Samuel Pasternak,* had disastrous runs in 1907. In 1914 he was ill and depressed over the death of a son, Misha. Though he contributed regularly to the Yiddish press and his stories appeared in translation in *The New York World,* money remained a problem. But his popularity never waned. Huge audiences attended his readings, and over 100,000 people were at his funeral in 1916.

Early Yiddish fiction tended to be sentimental, romances with happy endings. Sholom Aleichem's subjects were real people and their problems. Menachem-Mendel moves from one financial catastrophe to another. Tevye is a milkman with seven daughters to support; Mottel, a cantor's son, an orphan. There are three major fictional settings: Kasrilevka, a *shtetl;* Yehupetz, a city; and Boiberick, a country town. Generally, the characters narrate their stories, capturing the rich vocabulary and cadences of Yiddish.

The works are studies of European Jews in recent times. But the themes are universal: poverty, endurance in adversity, conflict between tradition and progress, and nostalgia for a simpler life. The characters are treated with gentle humor. "Laughter is healthful," Sholom Aleichem said.

Concerned with form, he studied Dickens, Tolstoy, Goethe, and Chekhov, as well as the major Jewish authors—Mendele, Bialik, and Peretz. In his works Yiddish was no longer a "jargon" reserved for commonplace affairs but a literary language, the inspiration for a new generation of Yiddish writers. His works have been translated into many languages, and the musical adapted from his stories, *Fiddler on the Roof* (1964), had productions world-wide.

Further Reading

Sholom Aleichem's works run to 28 volumes. All the major books, *The Adventures of Menachem-Mendel* (1969), *The Adventures of Mottel* (1961), and *The Great Fair* (an autobiography, 1958), are available in English, as are the novels, plays, and many of the stories. Among the story collections are *Inside Kasrilevka* (1948), *The Old Country* (1946), *Old Country Tales* (1966), *Stories and Satires* (1968), and *Tevye's Daughters* (1949). In addition, stories appear in anthologies, notably Melech Grafstein, *Sholom Aleichem Panorama* (1948) and Irving Howe and Eliezer Greenberg, *Treasury of Yiddish Stories* (1965). These also contain critical essays. Marie Waife-Goldberg's *My Father, Sholom Aleichem* (1969), an affectionate memoir, interweaves anecdotes with research. Frances and Joseph Butwin, *Sholom Aleichem* (1977) and Sol Gittelman, *Sholom Aleichem: A Non-Critical Introduction* (1974) analyze the works.

Additional Sources

Samuel, Maurice, *The world of Sholom Aleichem,* New York: Atheneum, 1986, 1970. □

O Aleijadinho

The Brazilian architect and sculptor Antônio Francisco Lisbôa, called O Aleijadinho (1738-1814), an exponent of the rococo style, is acknowledged to be his country's greatest architect and sculptor.

O Aleijadinho (a nickname meaning "the little cripple") was born in Ouro Preto in the state of Minas Gerais. He was the illegitimate son of the architect Manuel Francisco Lisbôa and a Negro slave girl. A lost document, dated 1790, was cited by his first biographer (Rodrigo Brêtas in the newspaper of Ouro Preto, 1858), who quoted from it extensively. The anonymous, contemporary author praised O Aleijadinho fulsomely, calling him "the new Praxiteles, [who] honors architecture and sculpture equally."

O Aleijadinho became physically disabled in his mid-30s and was described as "so sickly that he has to be carried everywhere and has to have his chisels strapped to him to be able to work." Despite the contemporary recognition of his genius, social malice added to his physical agonies. He was not permitted to join the artists' religious fraternity but obliged to join one for mulattoes. Many commissions that he both designed and executed were assigned contractually to others while he was listed as a laborer.

In architecture, classicistic mannerism persisted in Brazil into the 18th century. About 1760, particularly in Minas Gerais, where gold and diamond rushes made the state prosperous, the rococo style began to be employed. Essentially it was a style of elliptical curves and sinuous rhythms enriched with irregular ornament. Ultimately it was derived from the architectural designs of Francesco Borromini through the Portuguese works of Italians: Guarino Guarini in Lisbon in the 17th century and Nicolò Nasoni in Oporto in the 18th century. O Aleijadinho's works are outstanding in the rococo both for inventiveness and harmony.

The undoubted architectural masterpiece of O Aleijadinho is the church of São Francisco de Assis, Third Order, in Ouro Preto (1766-1794). The ground plan is an attenuated rectangle. The central bay of the facade is a flat plane, and the lateral bays, concavely curved, end in round towers. A side view of the exterior offers an interesting rhythm of projections and recessions: the concave lateral bay of the facade, the convex curves of the tower, the flat nave wall, the polygonal forward thrust of the wider sanctuary area, its flat wall, and, finally, a slight, orthogonal saliency of a box-shaped, terminal spatial unit.

O Aleijadinho's designs are characterized by an effective blending of the straight and the curved. The facade of São Francisco, seen in elevation, is an interesting example. The flat, central bay is flanked by Ionic columns in the round; the apertures offer a variety of curves, as does the cresting; and straight pilasters mark the junctures of the curved lateral bays and round towers. O Aleijadinho executed the rococo medallion above the portal depicting St. Francis receiving the stigmata, the sculptural ornament above the portal, and all the interior sculpture.

O Aleijadinho's sculpture includes pulpits, portals, balconies, altars, statues, processional images, and caryatids. His sculpture always enhanced, as well as harmonized with, his architecture. The most dramatic example is his soapstone group of 12 prophets (1800-1805) for the church of Bom Jesus de Matozinhos at Congonhas do Campo. The atrium of the church is enclosed by a low wall which is opened in the front by a multiflight, monumental stairway. The figures of the prophets are so disposed atop the atrium wall and staircase railing that the ensemble has been compared to a tremendous ballet. Ascending and descending the winding staircase, one is offered innumerable compositional arrangements. It is as though one could view Auguste Rodin's *Burghers of Calais,* from diverse angles *within* the group. The prophets' figures are in no way rococo. They loom above one's vision portentously as though hewn by a Romanesque Michelangelo.

Further Reading

The best sources of information on O Aleijadinho and his works are in Portuguese and French. In English important information is provided in Pál Kelemen, *Baroque and Rococo in Latin America* (1951). □

Mateo Alemán

The Spanish novelist Mateo Alemán (1547-c. 1615) wrote the first full-fledged picaresque novel, *Guzmán de Alfarache.* The book was widely read and translated and was imitated in Germany, France, and England.

Mateo Alemán was born in Seville and christened on Sept. 28, 1547. His parents were the physician Hernando Alemán, who practiced at the royal prison, and Juana de Enero, both descendants of converted Jews. By his own admission, Alemán received a very good education. He probably studied with the humanist Juan de Mal Lara. Alemán graduated from University of Seville (then called Colegio de Maese Rodrigo) in 1564. He studied medicine at the universities of Alcalá de Henares and Salamanca and in 1568 was licensed to practice.

Alemaán returned to Seville, where he quickly ran into economic and romantic problems (they followed him all his life). He married Catalina de Espinosa, in a manner not unlike a shotgun wedding. By 1571 he had joined a branch of the Ministry of Finances as an auditor. He was imprisoned for debt in 1580. After serving as a judge in Usagre and another term in jail for debt, he rejoined the Ministry of Finances in 1586. Alemán was a judge again in 1593, this time in the quicksilver mines of Almadén. The work was performed by criminals, whom he got to know well and about whom he wrote an unpublished confidential report. The importance of this experience is evident in the genesis of his picaresque novel.

The prologue to *Proverbios morales* (Moral Proverbs) of Alonso de Barros was Alemán's first published work. The first part of *Guzmán de Alfarache,* which came out in 1599, was an immediate success, and 23 editions were published before 1605. It was probably during these years that he visited Italy. Literary success, however, did not imply financial success. Back in Seville, Alemán was again imprisoned and was released after pawning 500 copies of *Guzmán.* This period coincides with his very close friendship with the writers Lope de Vega and Vicente Espinel. In Valencia in 1602 there appeared a spurious second part of *Guzmán,* signed with the pseudonym Mateo Luján de Sayavedra, almost certainly the Valencian lawyer Juan Martí. Alemán, who had finished in manuscript his second part, decided to rewrite it entirely (he gave Luján a place among his new characters), and it appeared in 1604. That year also saw the publication of his hagiographical work, *San Antonio de Padua,* which by 1623 had four editions.

Not long after, Alemán fulfilled his youthful desire to go to the Indies; he sailed from Cadiz on June 12, 1608, in the same fleet with the playwright Juan Ruiz de Alarcón and the new archbishop of Mexico, Alonso Garcia Guerra. Alemán apparently entered the service of the archbishop, and in Mexico in 1609 he published *Ortografía castellana* (Castilian Spelling), a book in which he propounded an unorthodox spelling, used in his *Sucesos de Don Frai Garcia Gera* (1613; The Life of Don Frai Garcia Gera), a biography of his master but mainly of autobiographical interest. Nothing is known of Alemán after that.

Guzmán de Alfarache was the work that gave final form to the picaresque, which had been developing since *Lazarillo de Tormes* was published in 1554. Alemán's novel profoundly influenced the German *Simplicissimus,* the English *Moll Flanders,* and the French *Gil Blas,* and many other works. *Guzmán* was translated into many languages, and the English version by James Mabbe, entitled *The Rogue* (1622), had five editions in 11 years.

Guzmán de Alfarache, the literary character, is born in Seville and is almost predestined, by family and surroundings, to be a delinquent. He tells the story of his life in the first person and with many digressive moralizations, which have been violently criticized. If the novel is interpreted, however, as a literary product of the Roman Catholic Reformation following the Council of Trent (1545-1563) and as a mirror of the moral and theological preoccupations of the age, then the meaning and structure of *Guzmán* emerge more clearly.

Further Reading

Donald McGrady, *Mateo Alemán* (1968), is the standard biography. An excellent study of *Guzmán de Alfarache* in its literary and historical perspectives is in Alexander A. Parker, *Literature and the Delinquent: The Picaresque Novel in Spain and Europe, 1599-1753* (1967). □

Miguel Alemán Valdés

Miguel Alemán Valdés (1902-1983), the president of Mexico from 1946 to 1952, represented a new generation in Mexican political life, one that had not fought in the revolution. He pushed the industrialization of Mexico.

iguel Alemán was born on Sept. 27, 1902, in Sayula, Veracruz, the son of a local revolutionary hero. After studying law at the National University, he entered political life and served as a judge and a senator for the state of Veracruz. From 1936 to 1940 he was governor of that state.

In 1940, Alemán directed the successful presidential campaign of Manuel Ávila Camacho and was rewarded with the key Cabinet portfolio of secretary of the interior. He was in charge of enemy aliens during the war and of the relations of the central government with the states. He followed a hard-line policy, crushing strikes and disorders attributed to pro-Axis and rightist elements.

The election of the handsome Alemán to the presidency in 1946 swung the political pendulum to the right. He filled his Cabinet with businessmen and technocrats and emphasized industrialization rather than agrarian reform as the solution of Mexico's problems. Loans were negotiated for highway construction and the transformation of the national petroleum industry. National finance was given broad new powers as a development corporation.

Labor no longer held a favored position. The forced industrialization with its curb on wages and decline in real wages produced labor unrest. Workers and farmers were paying a high price to build an industrial society. Agricultural improvements including irrigation, fertilizers, mechanization, diversification, and colonization of new zones displaced land reform. In fact, larger individual holdings were permitted.

Alemán constructed grandiose public works, such as river valley projects in Michoacán and Veracruz, highways, and a magnificent university city in the Federal District. Social reform was not forgotten during Alemán's term. Social security coverage was extended, and the construction of schools and housing was pushed. The results of his efforts could be counted in multiplying industrial units, increased agricultural production and rising per capita income and gross national product.

In 1952, Alemán backed as his successor the minister of the interior Adolfo Ruiz Cortines, who pledged a more balanced national development. But Alemán remained a political force, the focal point for more conservative elements in the party and for the new middle-class banking, industrial, and commercial interests which had risen to power in Mexico. As president of the National Tourism Council, he played a major role in the development of the resort town of Acapulco and the promotion of the 1968 Olympics.

He died of a heart attack May 14, 1983, at his home in Mexico City.

Further Reading

There have been campaign biographies and some journalistic publications on Alemán but no scholarly study. The best work is George S. Wise, *El México de Alemán* (1952). Useful material is contained in Oscar Lewis's chapter "Mexico since Cárdenas" in Richard N. Adams and others, *Social Change in Latin America Today* (1960); in Howard F. Cline, *Mexico: Revolution to Evolution, 1940-1960* (1962); and in Frank Brandenburg, *The Making of Modern Mexico* (1964). General discussions of the Alemán administration may be found in Harry Bernstein, *Modern and Contemporary Latin America* (1952); in Hubert Herring, *A History of Latin America* (1955; 3d ed. 1968); and in Helen Miller Bailey and Abraham P. Nasatir, *Latin America: The Development of Its Civilization* (1960; 2d ed. 1968). ☐

Jean le Rond d'Alembert

The chief contribution by the French mathematician and physicist Jean le Rond d'Alembert (1717-1783) is D'Alembert's principle, in mechanics. He was also a pioneer in the study of partial differential equations.

ean le Rond d'Alembert was born on Nov. 16, 1717, and abandoned on the steps of the church of St-Jean-le-Rond in Paris. He was christened Jean Baptiste le Rond. The infant was given into the care of foster parents named Rousseau. Jean was the illegitimate son of Madame de Tencin, a famous salon hostess, and Chevalier Destouches, an artillery officer, who provided for his education. At the age of 12, Jean entered the Collège Mazarin and shortly afterward adopted the name D'Alembert. He became a barrister but was drawn irresistibly toward mathematics.

Two memoirs, one on the motion of solid bodies in a fluid and the other on integral calculus, secured D'Alembert's election in 1742 as a member of the Paris Academy of Sciences. A prize essay on the theory of winds in 1746 led to membership in the Berlin Academy of Sciences. D'Alembert wrote the introduction and a large number of the articles on mathematics and philosophy for Denis Diderot's *Encyclopédie*. He entered the Académie Française as secretary in 1755.

D'Alembert had a generous nature and performed many acts of charity. Two people especially claimed his affection; his foster mother, with whom he lived until he was 50, and the writer Julie de Lespinasse, whose friendship was terminated only by her death. D'Alembert died in Paris on Oct. 29, 1783.

Rigid Body and Fluid Motion

D'Alembert's principle appeared in his *Traité de dynamique* (1743). It concerns the problem of the motion of a rigid body. Treating the body as a system of particles, D'Alembert resolved the impressed forces into a set of effective forces, which would produce the actual motion if the particles were not connected, and a second set. The principle states that, owing to the connections, this second set is in equilibrium. An outstanding result achieved by D'Alembert with the aid of his principle was the solution of the problem of the precession of the equinoxes, which he presented to the Berlin Academy in 1749. Another form of D'Alembert's principle states that the effective forces and the impressed forces are equivalent. In this form the principle had been applied earlier to the problem of the compound pendulum, but these anticipations in no way approach the clarity and generality achieved by D'Alembert.

In his *Traité de l'équilibre et du mouvement des fluides* (1744), D'Alembert applied his principle to the problems of fluid motion, some of which had already been solved by Daniel Bernoulli. D'Alembert recognized that the principles of fluid motion were not well established, for although he regarded mechanics as purely rational, he supposed that the theory of fluid motion required an experimental basis. A good example of a theoretical result which did not seem to correspond with reality was that known as D'Alembert's paradox. Applying his principle, D'Alembert deduced that a fluid flowing past a solid obstacle exerted no resultant force on it. The paradox disappears when it is remembered that the inviscid fluid envisaged by D'Alembert was a pure fiction.

Partial Differential Equations

Applying calculus to the problem of vibrating strings in a memoir presented to the Berlin Academy in 1747, he showed that the condition that the ends of the string were fixed reduced the solution to a single arbitrary function. D'Alembert also deserves credit for the derivation of what are now known as the Cauchy-Riemann equations, satisfied by any holomorphic function of a complex variable.

Research on vibrating strings reflected only one aspect of D'Alembert's interest in music. He wrote a few of the musical articles for the *Encyclopédie*.

He favored the views of the composer Jean Philippe Rameau and expounded them in his popular *Élemens de musique théorique et pratique* (1752).

Further Reading

D'Alembert's more important mathematical works are available in English, as are his many contributions to the *Encyclopédie,* the most significant of which is his *Preliminary Discourse*. His contributions are discussed in Thomas L. Hankins, *Jean d'Alembert: Science and the Enlightenment* (1970; reprinted, 1990). Excellent studies on D'Alembert as a *philosophe* are Ronald Grimsley, *Jean D'Alembert* (1963), and John Nicholas Pappas, *Voltaire and D'Alembert* (1962). The standard biography, in French, is Joseph Bertrand, *D'Alembert* (1889). A full account of D'Alembert's work in dynamics appears in René Dugas, *A History of Mechanics* (1950; trans. 1955). □

Arturo Alessandri Palma

Arturo Alessandri Palma (1868-1950) was twice president of Chile. He substantially altered Chilean society and paved the way for sweeping social and economic changes of later years.

The grandson of an Italian immigrant, Arturo Alessandri was born near Linares on Dec. 20, 1868. He graduated from the University of Chile with a degree in law in 1893. His political career began with his election as deputy to Congress in 1897, in which capacity he served until 1915, when he was elected senator. While in Congress he also held several Cabinet posts.

Alessandri, popularly known as "The Lion of Tarapacá" because of his oratorical abilities, felt that Chile desperately needed social reformation, and he quickly became a leader of the Liberal Alliance, a coalition of parties organized to support this effort. For the presidential election of 1920, Alessandri was selected as the alliance's candidate. He won by a slim margin. His efforts to secure reform legislation were hampered by conservative control of the Senate, however, and not until March 1924 did the alliance secure majorities in both houses. But when the alliance broke up into bickering factions, the military intervened to force Congress to pass the reform bills in September 1924. Alessandri then resigned, seeing that the military demanded the dissolution of Congress and further political reforms, and left for Europe. The military group controlling the government increasingly was managed by conservatives, and a second military coup in January 1925 overturned the junta and recalled Alessandri.

Alessandri returned in March and immediately called a constitutional convention. The resultant Constitution of 1925 was designed to overhaul the political structure of the country and fortify executive power. However, Alessandri resigned again in October, when Carlos Ibáñez, his minister of war, refused to obey presidential orders. During the subsequent dictatorship of Ibáñez, Alessandri was forced to leave Chile and return to Europe.

After a short but intense period of chaos following the downfall of Ibáñez in July 1931, Alessandri was reelected president in October 1932. He inherited a country with an economy in shambles and on the brink of social revolution. He ruled sternly and, with the assistance of able but unpopular subordinates, managed to restore order and bring back a semblance of prosperity. He served out his full term and in December 1938 turned over the government to Pedro Aguirre Cerda. Alessandri returned to public service in 1944, when he was elected to the Senate, and remained there until his death on Aug. 24, 1950.

Further Reading

A short and well-balanced summary of Alessandri's career appears in Robert J. Alexander, *Prophets of the Revolution: Profiles of Latin American Leaders* (1962). One of the best studies of the Alessandri era is in John R. Stevenson, *The Chilean Popular Front* (1942).

Additional Sources

Alexander, Robert Jackson, *Arturo Alessandri: a biography,* Ann Arbor: Published for Latin American Institute, Rutgers University, by University Microfilms International, 1977. □

Jorge Alessandri Rodriguez

Jorge Alessandri Rodriguez (1896-1986/1987) was a president of Chile who attempted to restore national prosperity while dealing with problems of reconstruction following the catastrophic earthquake of 1960.

Jorge Alessandri, son of the Chilean president Arturo Alessandri, was born on May 19, 1896. More reserved than his father and less drawn to politics, he graduated in 1919 with a degree in civil engineering and at first taught engineering. Also a successful businessman, he held the directorship of the major paper factory in Chile and was vice president of the Bank of South America.

Alessandri's introduction to politics, aside from a brief career as a congressman in 1925, came when he was named minister of finance (1948-1950) during the presidency of Gabriel González Videla. Alessandri balanced the nation's budget and actually secured a surplus, an unusual achievement in inflation-ridden Chile. In 1956 he was elected senator from Santiago.

Alessandri earned a reputation for being aloof and austere but able. A bachelor, he was said to be a father figure for the Chileans. Alessandri possessed a well-known name, was not closely connected officially with the traditional political parties, and was an outspoken critic of the increasingly unpopular Ibáñez administration (1952-1958). Thus, he was nominated for the presidency in 1958 by a

Further Reading

There is no adequate study of Alessandri in English. Two works which deal with Chile during his administration are Federico G. Gil, *The Political System of Chile* (1966), and Frederick B. Pike, *Chile and the United States, 1880-1962* (1963; 2d ed. 1965). Both provide valuable insights into the character of the Alessandri government. ☐

Alexander I

Alexander I (1777-1825) was emperor of Russia from 1801 to 1825. His leadership in the defeat of Napoleon and his statesmanship at the Congress of Vienna contributed to a rare attempt at massive political reconstruction of Europe.

The eldest son of Czar Paul I, Alexander was born on Dec. 12, 1777. He was removed from the care of his parents and brought up under the careful guidance of his grandmother, Empress Catherine II. His principal tutor was César La Harpe, a Swiss revolutionary who, however, was willing to compromise with czarist absolutism as a means to achieve his end. La Harpe was an ardent disciple of the Enlightenment and instilled in his student a sincere attachment for its philosophy. Alexander did not master the Russian language, but he spoke fluent English and excellent French. He ended his formal education after his marriage to Elizabeth (Princess Louise of Baden) in September 1793.

The Succession

At the court of Catherine II, Alexander was groomed to become her successor. But at his father's residence in Gatchina, where Alexander was a frequent visitor in the later years of Catherine's reign, he learned the art of warfare according to Prussian style. The exact military drill demanded of the soldiers by Paul I appealed to Alexander. At Gatchina, Alexander befriended Aleksei Arakcheev, who later became a close adviser.

Since the relationship between Catherine and her son Paul was hostile, she attempted to change the succession to Alexander. A letter from Alexander to Catherine in 1796, the year of her death, reveals that he was fully aware of the plan and had approved it. Paul reigned for 5 years. On March 11, 1801, a palace uprising led to Paul's murder, with the collaboration of Alexander. None of the participants in the conspiracy was tried or officially punished, but there is evidence that Alexander never entirely freed himself from the memories of that night.

Foreign Policy

The succession of Alexander I to the throne brought closer relations between Russia and England. Alexander ordered the recall of the Cossacks that Paul had sent to conquer India, and diplomatic relations were improved. This disturbed Napoleon because in 1801 France was at war with England, and he had made plans to dispatch a French

coalition of independent and conservative groups. Alessandri promised to give the nation an efficient administration manned not with politicians but with technical experts. His program appealed to the wealthy and middle classes, and in one of the closest elections in Chilean history, Alessandri won over Salvador Allende, the Socialist-Communist nominee.

Alessandri kept his campaign promises and attempted to deal with Chile's runaway inflation by instituting a strict austerity program. Between 1958 and 1960 he had some success in stemming the rise in the cost of living and in stabilizing the currency. However, his efforts at economy were halted when devastating earthquakes rocked southern Chile in May 1960. Huge outlays of money to rebuild the territory were required. Alessandri's essentially rightist orientation and his reluctance to attack the pressing problems of agrarian reform, unemployment, and housing resulted in a loss of popularity for the conservative parties. In the presidential election of 1964, Eduardo Frei, a Christian Democrat, was victorious, and conservative domination of Chile was shattered.

Alessandri's political fortunes subsequently took a turn for the better, and in 1970 he was supported by a revitalized conservative coalition for the presidency. Beaten in the election by Socialist Salvador Allende, Alessandri endorsed the winner in the subsequent run-off election in Congress which had become necessary because of Allende's narrow margin of victory in the general elections. Alessandri then retired but maintained his independent political stance. He died around 1986.

Domestic Policy

When Alexander became czar, he was expected to initiate far-reaching constitutional and social reforms because of his liberalism. These hopes were nurtured by the early enlightened measures of his regime: the annulment of vexatious prohibitions enacted by Paul, provision for a broad amnesty, liberation of trade, permission to import foreign publications, removal of restriction on traveling abroad, and partial reform of the harsh penal procedure.

At Alexander's request Speranski drew up plans for constitutional reform. He recommended reforms of the government based on the doctrine of separation of powers—legislative, executive, and judicial—all of them, however, emanating from the czar. The right to vote was to be granted to all property owners. Although Speranski favored the eventual abolition of serfdom, he saw the difficulties in achieving emancipation.

Alexander rejected the doctrine of separation of powers, but Speranski did persuade Alexander to create a state council, a body to review laws passed by the emperor, although its decisions were not binding on the Crown. Alexander also approved Speranski's legislation of 1810-1811 for the reconstruction of the executive departments.

Speranski raised the civil service standards and instituted financial reforms. These measures infringed on the privileges of the landowning and bureaucratic classes, and to placate the nobility Alexander dismissed Speranski in 1812.

Alexander created the Holy Alliance in 1815, an agreement between the rulers of Russia, Austria, and Prussia that they would conduct themselves according to Christian principles. The Alliance became a symbol of repression and reaction, and Alexander's policies became more and more conservative.

The fact that Speranski's constitutional reforms were not carried out and that Alexander failed to fulfill his promise resulted in the emergence of organized political opposition in the form of secret societies. This opposition came from members of the upper classes and led to an abortive coup d'etat on Dec. 14, 1825. Alexander I had died on November 19.

Further Reading

The historian Nikolai M. Karamzin, a contemporary of Alexander I, described the achievements of Alexander I in *Karamzin's Memoir on Ancient and Modern Russia,* translated with an analysis by Richard Pipes (1959). Marc Raeff, *Michael Speransky: Statesman of Imperial Russia, 1772-1839* (1957), is a biographical study with extensive analyses of the political activities and projects of Count Speranski. Evgenii V. Tarle, *Napoleon's Invasion of Russia, 1812* (1938; trans. 1942), is imbued with patriotism and often alludes to parallels between the Napoleonic invasion and threatened attack by Nazi Germany.

A good biography of Alexander I is Alan McConnell, *Tsar Alexander I: Paternalistic Reformer* (1970). Recommended for general historical background is vol. 2 of Michael T. Florinsky, *Russia: A History and an Interpretation* (1953), the most thorough narrative of prerevolutionary Russian history available in English, which is particularly strong on the 19th and early

expedition to join the Russian force undertaking the conquest of India. Alexander distrusted Napoleon and resented the unceremonious way in which he dealt with the crowned heads of the German and Italian states. In spite of their differences, a Franco-Russian treaty of amity was signed on Oct. 11, 1801, which called for close cooperation in all matters of common interest and for joint endeavors to keep peace.

In June 1802 Alexander, without consulting the minister of foreign affairs, Count Kochubey, established a personal friendship with Frederick William III of Prussia that lasted through peace and war.

On April 11, 1805, an Anglo-Russian treaty was signed for the liberation of Holland, northern Germany, Italy, and Switzerland from Napoleonic rule. In the ensuing war an Austro-Russian army of 90,000 men commanded by Gen. Mikhail Kutuzov was routed at the Battle of Austerlitz (Dec. 2, 1805). Alexander wept like a child during the retreat.

The war continued until July 1807, when the Franco-Russian treaty was signed at Tilsit. The alliance with France was not popular in Russia, and Mikhail Speranski, Alexander's secretary of state, felt that the Treaty of Tilsit contained practically all the ingredients of a future war between Russia and France. His fears were realized when Napoleon's army invaded Russia in June 1812. The severe Russian winter, however, proved insurmountable and led to disaster for Napoleon. By the Final Act of the Congress of Vienna on June 9, 1815, part of Poland was set up as a constitutional kingdom, and Alexander became its king.

20th centuries. Alexander A. Kornilov, *Modern Russian History from the Age of Catherine the Great to the End of the Nineteenth Century* (1917; trans. 1943), gives an excellent picture of internal policies. The setting of Leo Tolstoy's novel, *War and Peace* (1868), is the Napoleonic invasion of Russia during the reign of Alexander I.

Additional Sources

Evreinov, Ludmila, *Alexander I, Emperor of Russia: a post-Communism reappraisal,* New York: Riverrun Press, Calder Publications, 1995.

Hartley, Janet M., *Alexander I,* London; New York: Longman, 1994.

Troyat, Henri, *Alexander of Russia, Napoleon's conqueror,* New York: Dutton, 1982. □

Alexander II

Alexander II (1818-1881) was emperor of Russia from 1855 to 1881. He is called the "czar liberator" because he emancipated the serfs in 1861. His reign is famous in Russian history as the "era of great reforms."

Eldest son of Nicholas I, Alexander was born in Moscow on April 17, 1818. Vasili Zhukovski, the poet and courtier, was his principal tutor. Alexander spoke Russian, German, French, English, and Polish. He acquired a knowledge of military arts, finance, and diplomacy. From an early age he traveled extensively in Russia and abroad; in 1837, for example, he visited 30 Russian provinces, including Siberia, where no member of the royal family had ever been. Unlike his father, Alexander had experience in government before he acceded to the throne. He held various military commands and was a member of the state council (from 1840) and of the committee of the ministers (from 1842); during Nicholas's absence Alexander acted as his deputy.

Alexander's political philosophy eludes precise definition. However, there is ample evidence to indicate that he was an admirer of Nicholas's autocracy and bureaucratic methods.

Emancipation of the Serfs

Before he became czar, Alexander was not sympathetic to emancipation. He changed his mind because of Russia's technological and military backwardness in the Crimean War and because he believed that the liberation of the serfs was the only way to prevent a peasant uprising. Through a burdensome arrangement in which local commissions made studies and reported their findings to the government, an emancipation law was eventually formulated and proclaimed in 1861.

The new law stated that serfs were free to marry, acquire property, engage in trades, and bring suits in courts. Each estate proprietor had to prepare within a year an inventory determining the area of land actually in the possession of the peasants and defining the annual payment or services due from the liberated serfs. Each peasant household received its homestead and a certain amount of land (generally the same amount the family had cultivated for its own use in the past). The land usually became the property of the village commune, which had the power to redistribute it periodically among the households. The government bought the land from the owners, but the peasants had to redeem it by payments extending over 49 years. The proprietor kept only the portion of his estate that had been farmed for his own purposes.

The emancipation law of 1861, which liberated more than 40 million serfs, has been called the greatest single legislative act in history. It was a moral stimulus to peasant self-dignity. Yet there were many problems. The peasants had to accept the allotments, and generally they did not receive enough land and were overcharged for it. Since they became obligated for the payment of taxes and redemption reimbursements, their mobility was greatly limited. The commune replaced the proprietor as master over the peasants. The settlement, however, was on the whole liberal, despite some unsolved problems and the agrarian crises that emerged in part from its inadequacies.

Domestic Reforms

Because the emancipation of the serfs ended the landlords' rights of justice and police on their estates, it was necessary to reform the entire local administrations. The statute of 1864 created provincial and district assemblies, which handled local finances, education, scientific agriculture, medical care, and maintenance of the roads. The elaborate electoral system dividing voters into categories by class provided substantial representation to the peasants in the assemblies. Peasant and proprietor were brought together in order to work out local problems.

During Alexander's reign other reforms were initiated. The cities were granted municipal assemblies with functions similar to those of the provincial assemblies. The Russian judicial system and legal procedures, which were riddled with inequities, were reformed. For the first time in Russian history, juries were permitted, cases were debated publicly and orally, all classes were made equal before the law, and the court system was completely overhauled. Censorship was relaxed, and the universities were freed from the restrictions imposed on them by Nicholas I. The army, too, was reformed by Gen. Dimitri Miliutin, military schools were reorganized along liberal lines, and conscription was borne equally by all social groups.

Despite all these reforms, Alexander II became the target of revolutionaries in 1866. Terrorist activity continued throughout the 1870s. The underlying reasons were the lack of far-reaching social and constitutional reforms; the bloody suppression of the peasant uprisings, especially the slaughter of Bezna; the Polish insurrection of 1863 and its bloody defeat; and the general ultrareactionary trend of official policies. Conservatives and nationalists were welcomed by the Czar, but the liberals were alienated. The radicals went underground and espoused the cause of political and social revolution. A member of a terrorist group murdered Alexander II on March 1, 1881.

Foreign Policy

Encroachments begun under Nicholas I against Chinese territory in the Amur River valley were regularized by treaty in 1860. The Russians successfully repressed the Polish uprising of 1863. In 1877 Alexander went to war against Turkey on behalf of the rebellious Balkan Christians of Bosnia, Herzegovina, and Bulgaria.

Further Reading

Two full-length biographies of Alexander II are E. M. Almedingen, *The Emperor Alexander II* (1962), and Walter M. Mosse, *Alexander II and the Modernization of Russia* (1958; rev. ed. 1962). Jerome Blum, *Lord and Peasant in Russia, from the Ninth to the Nineteenth Century* (1961), is a comprehensive study of the social and economic conditions of rural Russia from earliest times to the emancipation of the serfs in 1861. Geroid T. Robinson, *Rural Russia under the Old Régime* (1932), begins where Blum's book stops, and it discusses the peasant question from the emancipation act to the Revolution. George Fischer, *Russian Liberalism, from Gentry to Intelligentsia* (1958), traces the evolution of liberal forces from 1855 to 1905 as a transition from domination by the gentry to domination by professional groups. Hugh Seton-Watson, *The Decline of Imperial Russia, 1855-1914* (1952), is a thorough and well-balanced survey of both internal and foreign policies.

The most thorough narrative of prerevolutionary Russian history available in English, particularly good for the 19th and 20th centuries, is Michael T. Florinsky, *Russia: A History and Interpretation* (1953). Alexander A. Kornilov, *Modern Russian History from the Age of Catherine the Great to the End of the Nineteenth Century* (1917; trans. 1943), gives an excellent picture of internal policies in the 19th century. □

Alexander III

Alexander III (1845-1894) was emperor of Russia from 1881 to 1894. During his autocratic reign Russian absolutism asserted itself for the last time.

Alexander was born on Feb. 26, 1845. His father, Alexander II, appointed the historian K. P. Pobedonostsev to tutor the heir apparent in Russian history and law in 1861. Alexander's mind and character were largely molded by Pobedonostsev, who instilled ardently nationalistic views in his young pupil. As heir apparent, Alexander took part in the administration of the state. During the war with Turkey in 1877-1878 he held a military command.

Alexander married Princess Sophie Frederica Dagmar of Denmark (known in Russia as Maria Fedorovna) and was a devoted husband and the father of five children. He preferred country life at Gatchina to the pomp of the St. Petersburg court.

Alexander's autocratic opinions were profoundly influenced by Pobedonostsev, who became director general of the Holy Synod of the Russian Orthodox Church in 1880, and by the journalist M. N. Katkov. Alexander followed Pobedonostsev's advice in making political decisions and in appointing personnel to higher offices. Katkov's influence was exercised through his articles in the reactionary *Moscow News*, which Alexander read regularly.

Counterreforms and Policies

Alexander issued an imperial manifesto on April 29, 1881, which ended the constitutional reforms of his father and proclaimed the absolute power of the emperor. The law of Aug. 14, 1881, empowered the government to declare a state of emergency in any part of the realm; administrative officials in the areas under the emergency regime were vested with broad extrajudicial and executive powers: arrest, imposition of fines, and confiscation of property without trial; transfer of cases from criminal court jurisdiction to that of military tribunals; the closing of schools; the suspension of periodicals; and the removal of officials. Enacted as a provisional measure for 3 years, the law was renewed and operated until the Revolution of 1917. The law of July 12, 1889, retained the township as a peasant institution but subjected it to the control of a new official, the land captain, who was empowered to suspend or remove elective peasant officials, arrest and fine peasant officials without a trial, and veto decisions of township and village assemblies.

The act of 1890 introduced significant restrictions in the organization of the provincial assemblies. The electors who chose the members of the assemblies were segregated in three electoral colleges on a class basis: nobles, all other

Further Reading

Hugh Seton-Watson, *The Decline of Imperial Russia 1855-1914* (1952), thorough and well balanced, surveys both internal and foreign policies. Michael T. Florinsky, *Russia: A History and an Interpretation,* vol. 2 (1953), is the most complete narrative of prerevolutionary Russian history in English and is particularly strong on the 19th and early 20th centuries. □

Alexander VI

Alexander VI (1431-1503) was pope from 1492 to 1503. Because of his worldly life, he is often considered the most notorious of the Renaissance popes.

On Jan. 1, 1431, Alexander VI was born Rodrigo Borja at Játiva, Spain. He studied law at the University of Bologna and first rose to prominence in 1455, when his uncle was elected pope as Calixtus III. Like his uncle, Rodrigo changed his name to Borgia, the Italian form of Borja. When Borgia was 25, his uncle made him a cardinal, and at 26 he became vice chancellor of the papal court, a position he filled competently for 35 years. Borgia lived a secular life in Rome and did not become a priest until 1468, when he was 37 years old. Priesthood, however, did not change the character of his life. He had children by several mistresses, but there is certainty only about the mother of four of his children—Cesare (1475), Giovanni (1476), Lucrezia (1480), and Goffredo (1481); she was Vanozza de' Catanei. Handsome and attractive to women, Borgia was also intelligent, a good public speaker, and popular with the citizens of Rome.

The Pope

At the conclave of Aug. 6-10/11, 1492, the cardinals elected the 61-year-old Borgia as pope, and he took the name of Alexander VI in honor of the ancient empire builder Alexander the Great. His pontificate began well. The populace was pleased by his election, and he began extensive building projects and worked industriously at papal business. But trouble began in 1494, when King Ferrante of Naples died. The Kingdom of Naples had once been a possession of the French throne, and King Charles VIII of France decided to reclaim it. He invaded Italy and reached Rome in December 1494. Alexander feared deposition but managed to negotiate his freedom. He then joined forces with Venice, Germany, Spain, and Milan and expelled Charles from Italy.

Meanwhile, Alexander faced the monumental task of regaining control of the Papal States, which had fallen into the hands of local nobles during the pontificate of his predecessor, Innocent VIII. Alexander delegated this task to his son Cesare Borgia, who accomplished it with brutal determination. But Cesare's marriage to the French princess Charlotte d'Albret in 1499 forced his father into a very unwise course of action. The marriage committed Alexander to friendship with the new French king, Louis XII. In exchange for French help in reconquering the Papal States,

electors except peasants, and peasants. Women were denied direct vote but could exercise their electoral rights through male representatives. Jews were totally disfranchised. The act of 1892 limited the right to vote in municipal elections to owners of real estate of a specified value and to proprietors of important commercial and industrial enterprises.

The law of Dec. 28, 1881, made it compulsory for serfs to redeem their land allotments, although the payments were lowered. Measures were taken to promote the expansion of peasant landholding areas, and a bank was founded to assist peasants in buying land. But under the passport law of June 1894, peasant were still denied a passport—that is, the right to seek employment outside the village—without the consent of the village assembly.

The government strove to prevent depreciation of the paper ruble and to link it eventually to precious metal by building up the gold reserve. Beginning in 1880, the government took an active part in building and administering the railways, and by 1894 it had taken over 24 lines.

Alexander III is known as the "czar peacemaker" because under his rule the empire remained at peace except for minor, although costly, military expeditions in central Asia. Relations with England were greatly improved, and France replaced Germany as Russia's ally. He died on Oct. 20, 1894.

Alexander did not hinder Louis's conquest of Milan. Thus Alexander betrayed his countrymen and reversed his anti-French policy. Alexander VI died on Aug. 18, 1503, perhaps of malaria.

An Evaluation

Alexander VI has been widely condemned for his conduct. He disregarded priestly celibacy and preferred political machinations to spiritual leadership. He practiced simony (selling Church offices) and was notorious for his nepotism. He used his position to enrich his children, supported a mob of Spanish relatives in Rome, and created 19 Spanish cardinals. He shocked his contemporaries by openly acknowledging his children.

In Alexander's favor it must be said that his morals were no worse than those of his contemporaries and that he had the real virtue of sincere love for his family. He was devastated with grief when his son Giovanni was mysteriously murdered; and although he used his daughter Lucrezia as a political pawn in her three marriages, he could hardly bear to be separated from her. Alexander was frequently maligned and satirized in his own day, but the more vicious rumors (that he poisoned his enemies, for example) are unfounded. Alexander VI was a genial, intelligent, and able man who reflected the morality of his times; if he is to be condemned as a pope, he should nevertheless not be judged too harshly as a man.

Further Reading

The classic account of Alexander VI's career is Ludwig Pastor, *The History of the Popes from the Close of the Middle Ages,* vol. 6 (trans. 1923). Good discussions may be found in M. Creighton, *A History of the Papacy during the Period of the Reformation* (5 vols., 1882-1894; rev. ed., entitled *A History of the Papacy from the Great Schism to the Sack of Rome,* 6 vols., 1897), and in Philip Hughes, *A History of the Church,* vol.3 (1947). A shorter account, absorbing and vivid, is by Will Durant in *The Story of Civilization* vol. 5: *The Renaissance: A History of Civilization in Italy from 1304-1576* (1953). □

1st Earl Alexander of Tunis

The British field marshal Harold Rupert Leofric George Alexander, 1st Earl Alexander of Tunis (1891-1969), was the supreme Allied commander of the Mediterranean theater in World War II. He was governor general of Canada from 1946 to 1952 and British minister of defense from 1952 to 1954.

Harold Alexander was born in Northern Ireland on December 10, 1891, the third son of the 4th Earl of Caledon and of Lady Elizabeth Graham Toler, daughter of the 3d Earl of Norbury. Educated at Harrow and Sandhurst, Alexander served in the British army with distinction in France during World War I. Wounded three times and mentioned in dispatches five times for gallantry in action, he received the Distinguished Service Order and the Military Cross.

Following graduation from the Staff College and the Imperial Defence College, he saw combat in India in 1935 and was again mentioned in dispatches. He served in various staff and command positions, and as a major general he commanded the 1st Division at the outbreak of World War II. The division went to France in 1939 as part of the British Expeditionary Force. When the German blitzkrieg of May 1940 forced France to surrender, Alexander, then a lieutenant general and commander of the I Corps, directed the evacuation of British and French troops from Dunkirk.

Alexander became a full general and took command of the British army forces in Burma in March 1942. He successfully carried out a difficult withdrawal to India, where the British, soon reinforced by American troops, prepared for offensive operations in Southeast Asia.

In August 1942 Alexander was assigned to take command of the British Middle East forces. He defeated Field Marshal Rommel's Italo-German army at Alam Halfa in late August and early September. On October 23 in the Battle of El Alamein, Alexander launched an offensive that precipitated a German and Italian retreat of 1,500 miles across Libya to southern Tunisia with the British in pursuit.

Meanwhile, Anglo-American forces under the supreme Allied commander Dwight D. Eisenhower had landed in French Northwest Africa on November 8, 1942, and to-

Alexander of Tunis (far right)

gether with French forces moved into Tunisia. On February 19, 1943, at the height of an American disaster inflicted by Rommel at Kasserine Pass, Alexander became Eisenhower's deputy and commander of the 18th Army Group. Alexander took command of all the Allied ground forces. They expelled the Germans and Italians from Tunisia in May 1943 and cleared the entire North African shore of Axis troops.

As commander of the 15th Army Group, Alexander directed the Allied invasion of Sicily in July 1943 and the subsequent ground operations, which included General Bernard Montgomery's British 8th Army and General George Patton's U.S. 7th Army. Alexander's leadership was largely responsible for the conquest of the island in 38 days.

Alexander then played an important role in the secret negotiations leading to the surrender of Italy. He headed the ground forces that invaded southern Italy in September 1943 and directed Montgomery's 8th Army in the eastern part of the country and General Mark Clark's U.S. 5th Army west of the Apennines. Alexander coordinated the capture of Naples and the Foggia airfields by October 1, 1943.

Then he began what turned out to be a grueling advance toward Rome. Through tangled, easily defended terrain, in the face of incredible difficulties, and against tenacious German opposition, Alexander engineered the Allied progress to the Gustav Line in the Cassino area. Attempting to go around the resistance, he executed the Anzio amphibious landing on January 22, 1944. It failed to dis-

lodge the Germans from the Gustav Line or from Rome. As a consequence, battles at Cassino and Monte Cassino were fought during January, February and March, but they resulted in a stalemate. Alexander then shifted the bulk of the 8th Army west of the Apennine Mountains in April. On May 11 he launched the massive Operation Diadem. This broke the Gustav Line, brought relief to the beleaguered Anzio beachhead, and liberated Rome on June 4. Later in 1944, promoted to field marshal, Alexander became supreme Allied commander of the Mediterranean theater. He engineered the air, sea and ground movements that broke the German Gothic Line, seized all of Italy and compelled the Germans to capitulate in April 1945.

In 1946, Alexander was made a viscount and named governor-general of Canada. He served there until 1952, when he was named both an earl and minister of defense in Sir Winston Churchill's cabinet. He retired in 1954 and was involved in business until he died on June 16, 1969, in Slough, England.

A man of great personal charm, Alexander was handsome, self-possessed, modest and distinguished in appearance. Field Marshal Alan Brooke, Chief of the Imperial General Staff, said Alexander was always "completely composed and appeared never to have the slightest doubt that all would come out right in the end." Eisenhower called him "broad-gauged," meaning that he worked on an Allied rather than a narrowly nationalistic basis. His most important qualities were his ability to impart and instill confidence among superiors, colleagues and subordinates and his capacity to persuade a multitude of Allied contingents to work together toward common goals. He was known for his charm and imperturbability.

Further Reading

The Alexander Memoirs, 1940-45 (1962) is disappointing but cannot be disregarded. The best portraits of Alexander and the best assessments of his contributions are found in the histories of World War II and in the memoirs of other high-ranking participants. Among the latter are Dwight D. Eisenhower, *Crusade in Europe* (1948); Mark W. Clark, *Calculated Risk* (1950); Winston S. Churchill, *Closing the Ring* (1951); Lucian K. Truscott, *Command Missions: A Personal Story* (1954); and Sir Arthur Bryant, *The Turn of the Tide* (1957). □

Alexander of Yugoslavia

Alexander (1888-1934) was king of the Kingdom of the Serbs, Croats, and Slovenes from 1921 to 1929 and, after changing the name of his country in 1929, king of Yugoslavia until 1934.

Alexander Karageorgevich was born on Dec. 16 (N.S.; Dec. 4, O.S.), 1888, at Cetinje, Montenegro, the second son of Peter I, King of Serbia, and Princess Zorka of Montenegro. Alexander shared his father's exile in Geneva, Switzerland, until 1899, when he was sent to the imperial Russian court in St. Petersburg to be educated. He returned to Serbia in 1909, succeeding his brother George as heir to the throne held by Peter I since 1903.

Having led the first Serbian army to victory over the Turks at Kumanovo on Oct. 24, 1912, in the First Balkan War, Alexander was also in command during the Second Balkan War against Bulgaria in 1913. Advanced age and declining health led Peter I to appoint Alexander regent of Serbia on June 24, 1914. As commander in chief of the Serbian armed forces, Alexander shared the privations of the Serbian retreat across Albania before the advancing Austro-German armies in 1915. He led his victorious forces into Belgrade on Oct. 31, 1918. On December 1 the Kingdom of the Serbs, Croats, and Slovenes was proclaimed with Alexander as prince regent.

The kingdom's adoption of the centralist "Vidovdan" constitution on June 28, 1921, angered the Croats, who favored a federal state organization guaranteeing autonomy to the historical regions. At the death of Peter I on August 16, Alexander became king. On June 8, 1922, he married Marie (1900-1961), a daughter of King Ferdinand of Romania. They had three sons: Peter (born Sept. 6, 1923), Tomislav (1928), and Andrea (1929).

The murder of the Croatian leader Stefan Radić and a follower in the Skupština (Diet) on June 20, 1928, by a Montenegrin Serb deputy resulted in the withdrawal of the Croatian deputies from the Skupština. Convinced of the failure of the parliamentary system, Alexander abrogated the Vidovdan constitution on Jan. 6, 1929, changed the country's name to Yugoslavia on October 3, and began a

period of authoritarian, personal rule. On Sept. 3, 1931, he proclaimed a new constitution, allowing only a "government's" party to exist, which was to receive two-thirds of the Skupština seats upon gaining a plurality in the national elections. This constitution increased Croatian disaffection.

In foreign affairs Alexander, a consistent friend of France, supported the French-backed Little Entente, which opposed Hungarian and Bulgarian revisionism, and hoped for French support against Italy. On a state visit to France, King Alexander and French Foreign Minister Louis Barthou were assassinated at Marseilles on Oct. 9, 1934, by a Macedonian terrorist subsidized by the Croatian fascist organization called Ustaše, which was in the service of Italy and Hungary. The young Peter II succeeded his father under a regency headed by Alexander's first cousin, Prince Paul.

Alexander's death deprived Yugoslavia of strong leadership at a time when, because of internal disorder and the hostility of Germany and Italy, it was most needed. As a founder of the great South Slav state, Alexander was opposed by those favoring the weakening or dismemberment of Yugoslavia, as well as those who resented his authoritarian rule.

Further Reading

Few works have been written dealing primarily with the career of King Alexander. Stephen Graham, *Alexander of Yugoslavia: The Story of the King Who Was Murdered at Marseilles* (1938), provides a sympathetic picture of the King. The relevant sections of Robert J. Kerner, ed., *Yugoslavia* (1949), are useful. See also Alan Roberts, *The Turning Point: The Assassination of Louis Barthou and King Alexander I of Yugoslavia* (1970). A contemporary account of Alexander's Yugoslavia is Charles A. Beard and George Radin, *The Balkan Pivot: Yugoslavia, a Study in Government and Administration* (1929). For the political background of the Balkans during Alexander's reign see Hugh Seton-Watson, *Eastern Europe between the Wars: 1918-1941* (1945; 3d ed. 1962). □

Alexander the Great

Alexander the Great (356-323 B.C.) was the king of Macedon, the leader of the Corinthian League, and the conqueror of Persia. He succeeded in forging the largest Western empire of the ancient world.

With his Macedonian forces Alexander subdued and united the Greeks and reestablished the Corinthian League after almost a century of warfare between the Greek city-states following the Peloponnesian War. Thus Alexander set the stage for his conquest of the Persian Empire, motivated both by personal ambition and by the Greeks' centuries-old hatred for their perennial Asian foes since the Persian Wars. His campaigns were not only wars of liberation of Greek colonies in Asia Minor but also revenge for Persian depredations in Greece in years past. Within 11 years Alexander's empire stretched from the Balkans to the Himalayas, and it included most of the eastern Mediterranean countries, Mesopotamia, and Persia. He died in Babylon contemplating the conquest of Carthage and perhaps Rome. His legacy was a fragmented empire, but he had inspired a new Hellenistic age of cosmopolitan culture.

Alexander was born in 356 B.C. to King Philip II of Macedon and Queen Olympias, the daughter of Neoptolemus, King of the Molossians. Alexander's sister was born the following year, and the two children grew up at the royal court in Pella. Since his paternal grandmother, Eurydice, was an Illyrian, Alexander was barely Macedonian in blood but clearly so in temperament. Of average height, he had deep-set dark eyes which shone out beneath a heavy brow, and a mass of dark, curly hair. As a youth, Alexander rarely saw his father, who was embroiled in long military campaigns and numerous love affairs. Olympias, a fierce and overly possessive mother, consequently dominated her son's early years and filled him with a deep resentment of his father and a strong dislike for women and wine, in which his father heavily indulged.

Education by Tutors

One of Alexander's first teachers was Leonidas, a relative of Olympias, who struggled to curtail the uncontrollable and defiant boy. Philip had hired Leonidas to train the youth in arithmetic, horsemanship, and archery. Alexander's favorite tutor was the Acarnian Lysimachus, who devised a game whereby Alexander impersonated the hero Achilles. This delighted Olympias, for her family claimed

J. Chapman sc.

the hero as an ancestor. In Alexander's youthful mind, Achilles became the epitome of the aristocratic warrior, and Alexander modeled himself after this hero of Homer's *Iliad.*

In 343 Philip summoned the philosopher and scientist Aristotle from Lesbos to tutor Alexander. For 3 years in the rural Macedonian village of Mieza, Aristotle instructed Alexander and a small group of friends in philosophy, government, politics, poetry and drama, and the sciences. Aristotle prepared a shortened edition of the *Iliad,* which Alexander always kept with him. Aristotle believed in despotic control of the Persians, but Alexander agreed with the ideas expressed in Isocrates's *Philip* that Macedon should free the barbarians from despotism and offer them Greek protection and care.

Beginnings of the Soldier

The education at Mieza ended in 340. While Philip campaigned against Byzantium, he left the 16-year-old prince as regent in Pella. Philip's general Antipater cautiously but strongly advised Alexander, but other generals looked on Alexander as a pawn, more easily managed than Philip. Within a year Alexander undertook his first expedition against the Thracian tribes, and in 338 he led the Companion Cavalry and helped his father smash the Athenian and Theban forces at Chaeronea.

The brief relationship and military cooperation with his father ended soon after Philip had united all the Greek states except Sparta into the Corinthian League, over which Philip then governed as military leader. When Philip married Cleopatra, the daughter of his general Attalus, and expelled Olympias, Alexander with his mother and his closest friends fled Macedon and lived in Epirus with Olympias's family until Demaratus of Corinth brought about a reconciliation between father and son.

Alexander as King

In the summer of 336 at the ancient Macedonian capital of Aegai, Alexander's sister married her uncle Alexander, the Molossian king. In the festival procession Philip was assassinated by a young Macedonian noble, Pausanias. The reason for the act was never discovered.

Alexander sought the acclamation of the Macedonian army for his bid for kingship, and the generals, Antipater, and Alexander's own troops which had fought at Chaeronea proclaimed him king. Alexander then systematically killed all possible royal claimants to the throne, and Olympias murdered the daughter of Philip and Cleopatra and forced Cleopatra to commit suicide.

Although elected feudal king of Macedon, Alexander did not thus automatically gain command of the Corinthian League. The southern Greek states rejoiced at Philip's assassination, and Athens, under the staunch democrat Demosthenes, sought to lead the League. Throughout Greece independence movements arose. Immediately Alexander led his armies southward, and Thessaly quickly recognized him as leader. Alexander summoned members of the League to Thermopylae and received their recognition of his command. At Corinth in the autumn of 336 Alexander renewed the treaties with the member states. Sparta refused to join. The League entrusted Alexander with unlimited military powers to campaign against Persia.

A Panhellenic Leader

A spirit of Panhellenism ruled the first stages of Alexander's career. A united Greece free of petty wars would bring to the barbarian worlds the Hellenic culture. As the descendant of Achilles, Alexander would correct the ills Persia had created for Greece and remove Persian intervention in Greek affairs. Although he became a Panhellenic leader, he nevertheless remained a Macedonian king bent upon conquering new territories.

Alexander did not prepare for war with Persia immediately. In the spring of 335 he conquered the Thracian Triballians south of the Danube. He secured Macedon and its northern borders without the help of the general Parmenion, who was already in Asia Minor, and Antipater, who governed as Alexander's regent in Macedon.

Destruction of Thebes

In Asia, Darius III, King of Persia, had become aware of Parmenion's presence in Asia and of Alexander's future plans. Darius attempted to bribe the Greek states to revolt, but only Sparta accepted the gold. However, when a rumor spread that Alexander was dead, Demosthenes prodded the Athenian assembly to unilaterally consider the Corinthian League defunct and Athens independent. Thebes at once rejoiced and slew its Macedonian garrison. Alexander, very much alive, raced southward and besieged Thebes. In the name of the League, Alexander waged war against the rebellious members but still attempted to negotiate peace. When Thebes rejected Alexander's demands, he leveled the city, killed the soldiers, and sold the women and children into slavery, sparing only the temples and the house of the poet Pindar. Alexander destroyed the city to warn others of the price of rebellion. Athens revoked its declaration of withdrawal from the League, honored Alexander, and offered to surrender Demosthenes.

Asiatic Campaign

In October 335 Alexander returned to Macedon and prepared his Asiatic expedition. In numbers of troops, in ships, and in wealth, Alexander's resources were markedly inferior to those of Darius. Parmenion was recalled to Pella to be Alexander's chief aide. The army was not Panhellenic but essentially Macedonian, led by a Macedonian king, and the expedition quickly became the royal Macedonian's personal campaign for aggrandizement and empire.

In the early spring of 334 the army crossed the Hellespont (modern Dardanelles) to Abydos, and Alexander visited ancient Troy. There he sacrificed and prayed, dedicated his armor to Athena, and took an antique sacred shield for his campaign. Not far away at the Granicus River, Alexander met Darius's army in May, employed for the first time his oblique battle formation, and defeated the Persians. To commemorate the victory, Alexander sent 300 sets of Persian armor to the Parthenon in Athens with the dedicatory inscription: "Alexander the son of Philip, and the Greeks, all but the Spartans [dedicated these] from the barbarians who

inhabit Asia." Alexander thus maintained the official propaganda that he was not only a king but the Panhellenic leader.

Western Asia Minor and Darius's capital at Sardis fell easily, followed by Miletus and Halicarnassus. The territories Alexander conquered retained their satrapal administrations, continued to pay the same taxes as before, and formed the foundations of his Asian empire.

By autumn Alexander had crossed the southern coast of Asia Minor, and Parmenion had entered Phrygia. Both armies spent the winter at the Phrygian capital of Gordium. Divine portents and miracles were ascribed to Alexander by the local peoples, Greeks, and barbarians. When Alexander cut the famous Gordian Knot to fulfill a prophecy, he himself started to believe the myths circulated about him.

When news reached Alexander of Greek naval victories in the Aegean, he sped eastward to the passes of the Taurus and Syria. By the late summer of 333 Alexander was in Cilicia, south of Darius and his armies. At Issus the two kings met in battle. Alexander was outnumbered, but utilizing the oblique formations he rushed the Persian center line and Darius turned his chariot and fled. The Persian line crumbled. In November, Alexander attacked the Persian royal camp, gained hoards of booty, and captured the royal family. He treated Darius's wife, mother, and three children with respect. Darius's army was beaten, and the King became a fugitive. Alexander publicly announced his personal claim to the throne of Persia and proclaimed himself king of Asia.

But before he could pursue his enemy into Persia, he needed to control the seas and the coastal territories of Phoenicia, Palestine, and Egypt to secure his chain of supply. Aradus, Byblos, and Sidon welcomed Alexander but Tyre resisted. In January 332 Alexander began his long and arduous siege of Tyre. He built moles to the island city, employed siege machines, fought off the Tyrian navy and army, and 8 months later seized the fortress.

Darius now sought to come to terms with Alexander and offered a large ransom for his family, a marriage alliance, a treaty of friendship, and the part of his empire west of the Euphrates. Alexander ignored Darius's offer, planning to conquer all.

Campaign in Egypt

From Tyre, Alexander marched south through Jerusalem to Gaza, besieged that city, and pushed on into Egypt. Egypt fell to Alexander without resistance, and the Egyptians hailed him as their deliverer from Persian hegemony. In every country Alexander had respected the local customs, religions, and peoples. In Jerusalem he had retained the priestly rule of the Temple, and in Egypt he sacrificed to the local gods. At Memphis the Egyptian priesthood recognized him as pharaoh, offered him the royal sacrifices, and invested him as king on the throne of Ptah. They hailed Alexander as a god. When Alexander visited the oracle of the Phoenician god Ammon at Siwa, the priest greeted him as the son of Ammon. From this time he seems to have accepted the idea of his own divinity. All across his Asian empire, oracles confirmed Alexander's divinity, and the people paid him divine honors.

Alexander promoted Greek culture in Egypt. In 331 he founded the city of Alexandria, which became the center of Hellenistic culture and commerce. Devoted to science, Alexander dispatched an expedition up the Nile to investigate the sources of the river and the true explanation for its inundations.

Arbela, Babylonia, and Persia

In September 331 Alexander defeated the Persians at Arbela (modern Erbil); the event is also called the Battle of Gaugamela. The Persian army collapsed, and Alexander pursued Darius into the Kurdish mountains.

Abandoning the chase, Alexander systematically explored Babylonia, the rich farmlands, palaces, and treasuries which Darius had abandoned. In Babylon, Alexander celebrated the New Year's Festival in honor of the god Marduk, whereby the god extended his divine pleasure and confirmed the lawful monarchy. Alexander became "King of Babylon, King of Asia, King of the Four Quarters of the World."

The royal palace of Susa and its treasuries fell to Alexander in the summer of 331, and he set out for Persepolis, the capital of the Persian Empire. To prevent a royal uprising and to exact punishment for the Persian destruction of Athens in 480, Alexander burned Persepolis, a rash but symbolic act. In the spring of 330 he marched to Darius's last capital, Ecbatana (modern Hamadan). There Alexander left Parmenion in charge of the vast confiscated treasuries and all communications and set off in pursuit of Darius.

Darius had fled beyond the Caspian Gates with his eastern satraps. When Alexander caught up with them in July 330, the satraps had assassinated Darius. Alexander ordered a royal funeral with honors for his foe. As Darius's successor and avenger, Alexander captured the assassins and punished them according to Persian law. Now Persian king, Alexander began to wear Persian royal clothing and adopted the Persian court ceremonials. As elsewhere, Alexander employed local officials in his administration. He did, however, maintain his position of leader of the Corinthian League toward the Greek ambassadors.

Iran and India

At the Caspian Sea, Alexander became occupied with geography, the location of the Eastern Ocean, and its relation to the Caspian Sea. Consequently, he pushed eastward and for 3 years campaigned in eastern Iran. He secured the region, founded cities, and established colonies of Macedonians. In the spring of 327 he seized the almost impregnable high rock fortress of Ariamazes and captured the Bactrian prince Oxyartes. Alexander married Oxyartes's daughter Rhoxana to bind his Eastern empire more closely to him in a political alliance.

The Macedonians began to resent Alexander's Oriental customs and dress and his demand that they prostrate themselves before him. Parmenion's son Philotas conspired against Alexander, who executed the traitor according to

Macedonian law and also ordered the death of Parmenion on false charges.

In the summer of 327 Alexander marched to the Punjab and the Indus Valley. The following year his first son died in India. In northern India, Alexander defeated the armies of King Porus. Impressed with his bravery and nobility, Alexander reestablished Porus as king and gained his loyalty. Continuing his progress eastward, Alexander reached the Ganges, where his armies refused to go farther, and after 2 days of struggle Alexander turned back. The army returned westward along the Indus, but when Alexander was seriously wounded while fighting the fierce Malli warriors, his army was overwhelmed with grief. They cheered his recovery, and all animosities were forgiven.

By July 325 the army and its fleet had reached the Indus Delta. The fleet continued north in the Persian Gulf, while the army began to march along the barren and inhospitable coast. Hardship and death brought havoc to the army, which joined up with the fleet weeks later. In January 324 Alexander reached Persepolis, which he had left 5 years earlier, and in February he was in Susa. But disorder had spread throughout the empire during Alexander's campaigns in the East.

Festival at Susa

Greatly concerned with the rule of his empire and the need for soldiers, officers, and administrators, Alexander attempted to bind the Persian nobility to the Macedonians to forge a ruling class. At Susa he ordered 80 of his Macedonian companions to marry Persian princesses. Alexander, although married to Rhoxana, married Stateira, a daughter of Darius, to legitimize his sovereignty.

When Alexander incorporated 30,000 Persians into the army, his soldiers grumbled. At Opis that summer, when he decided to dismiss his aged and wounded Macedonian soldiers, the angry soldiers condemned his Persian troops and his Persian manners. Alexander arrested 13 of their leaders and executed them. He then addressed the army and movingly reminded them of their glories and honors. After 3 days the Macedonians repented, and in a thanksgiving feast the Persians joined the Macedonians as forces of Alexander—but not as brothers.

Alexander's Death

In the spring of 323 Alexander moved to Babylon and made plans to explore the Caspian Sea and Arabia and then to conquer northern Africa. On June 2 he fell ill with malaria, and 11 days later, at the age of 32, he was dead. A few months later his wife Rhoxana bore him a son, who was assassinated in 309.

Alexander's empire was little more than a vast territory improperly ruled by the king and his bureaucrats. Nations and peoples did not blend harmoniously together but were governed by Macedonians for their King. The empire collapsed at his death, and nations and generals vied for power. The Greek culture that Alexander introduced in the East had barely developed. But in time, and under the "successor" kingdoms, the Oriental and Greek cultures blended and flourished as a by-product of the empire.

Further Reading

The most thorough study of Alexander, and perhaps the most accurate interpretation, is Ulrich Wilcken, *Alexander the Great* (1931; trans. 1932). Andrew R. Burn, *Alexander the Great and the Hellenistic Empire* (1947; 2d ed. 1962), is a delightful brief sketch and a fine interpretation of Alexander. W. W. Tarn, *Alexander the Great* (2 vols., 1948-1950), misrepresents Alexander's goals. Charles A. Robinson, Jr., has compiled a good general study of Alexander, *The History of Alexander the Great* (2 vols., 1953-1963). See also Kurt Emmrich, *Alexander the Great: Power as Destiny* (1965; trans. 1968). John W. Snyder discusses Alexander's military campaigns in *Alexander the Great* (1966). Margarete Bieber, *Alexander the Great in Greek and Roman Art* (1964), considers his portraits. A well-illustrated biography is Peter Bamm, *Alexander the Great* (1968). See also F. A. Wright, *Alexander the Great* (1934); Lewis V. Cummings, *Alexander the Great* (1940); and J. F.C. Fuller, *The Generalship of Alexander the Great* (1958). □

Samuel Alexander

The British philosopher Samuel Alexander (1859-1938) was a forceful exponent of metaphysics at a time when that subject had largely fallen into disrepute. His work shows a fine capacity for synthesis and system.

Samuel Alexander was born in Sydney, New South Wales, Australia, on Jan. 6, 1859. His early education was at Wesley College in Melbourne. He went to England in 1877 with a scholarship to Balliol College, Oxford, where he took the *literae humaniores* (humanities) degree, reading mathematics and philosophy. After graduation he stayed on at Oxford as a fellow of Lincoln College, where he taught philosophy. He was the first Jew to be a fellow at Oxford.

While at Oxford, Alexander was awarded the Green Moral Philosophy Prize for a dissertation in ethics, which formed the basis for his first publication, *Moral Order and Progress* (1889). This book secured Alexander a wide reputation and, in 1893, a chair of philosophy at the University of Manchester, which he held until his retirement in 1924. After retirement he continued to live in Manchester, where he was well known and well loved, a nearly legendary figure. The city and the university honored him in 1925 by erecting an impressive bust by the sculptor Jacob Epstein.

Alexander's major work came late in life with his Gifford Lectures, later published as a book, *Space, Time and Deity* (1920). The book is a complex metaphysics in the grand manner, portraying the world as an evolving hierarchy of emerging qualities: space-time, matter, life, mind, and finally deity. Each new quality depends on the lower ones but at the same time presents something genuinely novel.

In 1933 Alexander collected some of his papers on ethics and esthetics and issued them under the title *Beauty and the Other Forms of Value*. More of his papers were issued in book form after his death. Many of these pieces show a geniality and sense of fun quite different from his systematic works. Reading them, one comes to understand why a friend characterized him as "deep but gay."

In appearance Alexander was forceful and impressive. He looked every inch the philosopher, with a flowing beard, high forehead, and penetrating glance. A bachelor, he had a genius for friendship with persons of all ages and situations.

Further Reading

Alexander's *Philosophical and Literary Pieces* (1939), edited by his literary executor, John Laird, is prefaced by a long memoir which is a synthesis of information and anecdotes obtained from friends of Alexander. The volume also contains a complete bibliography. John W. McCarthy, *The Naturalism of Samuel Alexander* (1948), is a good critical work. For a contrary view see Milton R. Konvitz, *On the Nature of Value: The Philosophy of Samuel Alexander* (1946). Bernard Bosanquet, *The Meeting of Extremes in Contemporary Philosophy* (1921), contains valuable background material. □

Sherman Alexie

Winner of Washington State Arts Commission poetry and National Endowment for the Arts poetry fellowships, Sherman Alexie (born 1966) has published poems, stories, translations, and several books.

Sherman Alexie was born in 1966 and grew up in Wellpinit, Washington, on the Spokane Indian Reservation. Winner of a 1991 Washington State Arts Commission poetry fellowship and a 1992 National Endowment for the Arts poetry fellowship, Alexie has published more than two hundred poems, stories, and translations in publications such as *Another Chicago Magazine, Beloit Poetry Journal, Black Bear Review, Caliban, Journal of Ethnic Studies, Hanging Loose Press, New York Quarterly, Red Dirt, Slipstream, ZYZZYVA,* and others. His first book of poetry and short stories, *The Business of Fancydancing* was published by Hanging Loose Press in January 1992 and quickly earned a favorable front-page review from *The New York Times Book Review.* This first poetry book was the result of poems and stories written in Alexie's first creative writing workshop at Washington State University in Pullman. Alexie soon published a second collection, *I Would Steal Horses,* which was the winner of *Slipstream's* fifth annual Chapbook Contest in March 1992. In January 1993, he published a third poetry book, *Old Shirts and New Skins* (UCLA American Indian Studies Center). By early 1993, Alexie had written three books. Atlantic Monthly Press contracted to publish a collection of Alexie's short stories, *The Lone Ranger and Tonto Fistfight in Heaven.*

The Lone Ranger and Tonto Fistfight in Heaven was published to much critical acclaim. The short stories in this collection, like many of Alexie's other works, reveal his

about the identity and the plight of the American Indian'' through his characters.

Although Alexie's writing is often emotionally cathartic, he writes for his people as well as for himself. In a 1995 interview he told the *Milwaukee Journal Sentinel* that he cherishes the difference his stories and poems have made in the lives of reservation Indians and he continues to write for this audience. Alexie feels that many Native American writers focus on the angst of Native Americans living in urban settings and the reservation Indians, who play prominent roles in his stories and poetry, are unfortunately ignored. Alexie told an audience of writers at the Native American Journalists Association that only American Indian writers can write of their people as only they, regardless of the sincerity of non-Indian writers, have the empathy and the intrinsic awareness of their people's emotions, lives, and humor. □

Alexis Mikhailovich Romanov

Alexis Mikhailovich Romanov (1629-1676), czar of Russia from 1645 to 1676, was an extreme conservative, a devoted churchman, and a firm believer in the divine origin of his power.

B orn on March 10 (O.S.), 1629, in Moscow, Alexis was the son of Michael Romanov, the first of the dynasty which was to rule Russia until 1917. When Michael died in 1645, Alexis, only 16 years of age, succeeded to the throne. Although his formal education had been rudimentary and had stopped when he was 10 years old, Alexis was actually well educated by Moscow standards and had literary pretensions, even trying his hand at writing poetry.

Alexis's reign was beset by many popular revolts, the most serious one in southeastern Russia under the Cossack leader Stenka Razin. Other outbreaks included an insurrection by monks of the Solovetskii Monastery and civil revolts in the cities of Pskov, Novgorod, and Moscow. Although Alexis suppressed the uprisings, he also took steps to improve administration and justice in order to quiet the general discontent. Of major importance was his introduction of a new legal code in 1649. Although a great improvement over its predecessors, the reform had the unfortunate result of tying the peasants even more closely to the land and their landlords.

Alexis presided over renewed Russian expansion in the tradition of earlier Muscovite monarchs, but he was by no means a fighting ruler. Significantly his chief territorial acquisition, a large Polish territory centered on the Dnieper River and part of the later Ukraine, was gained by invitation from the Ukrainian Cossack inhabitants. After a prolonged conflict with Poland, the boundaries of the annexed territory

awareness of the despair, poverty, and alcoholism that is an unescapable part of the daily life of many Native Americans. Alexie poignantly stated: ''[Indians] have a way of surviving. But it's almost like Indians can easily survive the big stuff. Mass murder, loss of language and land rights. It's the small things that hurt the most. The white waitress who wouldn't take an order, Tonto, the Washington Redskins.''

While growing up in Wellpinit, Alexie read everything he could get his hands on, including auto repair manuals in the public library. He had aspirations of becoming a doctor until fainting three times in a high school anatomy class and deciding that an early career change was in order. He attended college for a while, but before dropping out, over 200 of his poems had been published. Alexie often refers to his writing as ''fancydancing,'' a name given the changes Native American veterans of World War II made to their traditional dances. Through the early 1990s many of Alexie's characters were wrought with hopelessness fueled by alcohol. By 1995 however the thrust of his writing was beginning to change and *People* called his then just-published *Reservation Blues* '' . . . a high-flying, humor spiked tale of culture and assimilation.'' Alexie told *People* that although many regard Native Americans as overly stoic, humor in fact is an essential part of their culture. In 1996 Alexie's next novel, *Indian Killer,* was released to favorable reviews. A thriller stocked with a cast of Indian characters representing facets of Native American culture, the novel presents a gripping mystery as well as historical facts and Indian myths. Judith Bolton-Fasman in the Christian Science Monitor commented, ''Alexie has profound things to say

were confirmed by the Armistice of Andrusovo with Poland in 1667.

A conflict with Nikon, the patriarch of the Russian Orthodox Church, also figured prominently in Alexis's reign. Despite the dispute and Nikon's eventual exile to a northern monastery, the patriarch did enact, with Alexis's approval, the ecclesiastical reforms which led to the great schism within the Russian Church.

Unofficially titled "the Quietest One," Alexis also displayed rougher characteristics. He often lost his temper and once slapped his father-in-law in the face, pulled his beard, kicked him out of the room, and slammed the door on him.

Alexis was married twice, first to Maria Ilinishna Miloslavskii and after her death to Natalya Kirillovna Naryshkina. Alexis died suddenly on Jan. 29 (O.S.), 1676, in Moscow at the age of 47. Three sons and six daughters survived him, the two elder sons, Feodor and Ivan, by his first wife, and Peter, the future emperor, by the second.

Further Reading

The best sketches of the Czar are in Ronald Hingley, *The Tsars: 1533-1917* (1968), and in Robert N. Bain, *The First Romanovs (1613-1725): A History of Moscovite Civilisation and the Rise of Modern Russia under Peter the Great and His Forerunners* (1905; repr. 1967). The classic study of the Nikon episode is William Palmer, *The Patriarch and the Tsar* (6 vols., 1871-1876). See also John Bergamini, *The Tragic Dynasty: The History of the Romanovs* (1969).

Additional Sources

Fuhrmann, Joseph T., *Tsar Alexis, his reign and his Russia,* Gulf Breeze, FL: Academic International Press, 1981.
Longworth, Philip, *Alexis, tsar of all the Russias,* New York: F. Watts, 1984. □

Alexius I

Alexius I (ca. 1048-1118) was Byzantine emperor from 1081 to 1118. He saved the empire from almost certain disaster and led it through the first encounter with the Crusades.

Nephew of the emperor Isaac I Comnenus (reigned 1057-1059), Alexius was raised by his strong willed mother, Anna Dalassena. Even as a youth, he was noted for his great military successes. Surviving shifts in regime, Alexius became the strong right arm of successive emperors and put down a number of rebellions. Driven to revolt himself, he secured the support of other aristocratic leaders and was proclaimed emperor on April 4, 1081.

Saving the Empire

When Alexius assumed power, the empire seemed about to collapse. Internal affairs were in chaos, and external enemies closed on all sides for the kill. Asia Minor, the empire's former heartland and chief source of manpower and revenue, was all but lost since the disastrous Battle of Manzikert (1071) had exposed it to devastation and occupation by the Seljuk Turks. To the north, the Asiatic Patzinaks (Petchenegs) menaced the Balkan frontiers. And Robert Guiscard, the Norman bandit chieftain who had forged a powerful state in southern Italy, was preparing to attack the empire in quest of a great Eastern realm of his own.

Alexius had little with which to work. He accepted humiliating terms with the Turks, scraped together hasty forces, and purchased naval aid from Venice to face the urgent Norman threat. The Normans were repulsed, and Alexius devoted the next years to freeing the Balkan provinces from combined menaces of a Bulgarian revolt and of invasions by the Patzinaks and another Asiatic tribe, the Cumans. Despite defeats, Alexius played them off against each other, and with Cuman help he defeated the Patzinaks crushingly at Levurnion in 1091. This victory, a turning point in Alexius's struggles, enabled him to consolidate his grasp on the throne.

First Crusade

Alexius turned next to the grim situation in Asia Minor. He realized his need for greater military strength, and at the same time he was anxious to cooperate with the papacy in ending the schism of 1054 between the Eastern and Western Churches. He therefore sent appeals to the Pope and others, urging Westerners to help him fight in the East. Prompted also by other, specifically Western motivations, the Latin response was the First Crusade. Desiring mercenary auxilia-

ries, the Byzantines were faced instead by a massive outpouring of uncontrolled and irresponsible military adventurers. The initial rabble, under Peter the Hermit, arrived in early 1096 and crossed precipitously to Asia to be massacred by the Turks. The main Crusader army arrived during the following winter.

In June 1097 the Crusaders and Byzantines jointly took Nicaea from the Turks. But ill feelings grew between them, and the Crusaders plunged on their own across Asia Minor toward Syria. The Emperor's failure to aid them in their siege of Antioch in 1097-1098 completed their estrangement. Alexius, however, remained determined to assert his rights of suzerainty over the principalities which the Crusaders established in the Holy Land after their conquest of Jerusalem in 1099. Meanwhile, Bohemund, Guiscard's ambitious son, seized Antioch for himself and returned to Italy to organize a new invasion of the Balkans. In the fighting that ensued from 1104 to 1108, Alexius beat Bohemund to a standstill and brought him to terms. But Bohemund's death in 1111 left the question of Alexius's claims to Antioch and to other Crusader territories unsettled, a problem which would be unraveled by later Byzantine emperors. In the closing decade of his life, Alexius renewed campaigns against the Seljuks, and a victory in 1117 won back for the empire at least some areas of Asia Minor.

The keynotes of Alexius's internal policies were the careful husbanding of limited resources and the astute conversion of liabilities into strengths. The realm he left behind was no longer the greatest power in Christendom, as it had been a century earlier, but it was on its way to a genuine recovery. Before Alexius died on Aug. 16, 1118, he was able to make a clear transfer of power to his son, John II Comnenus, who was to prove perhaps the most noble and admirable sovereign of the entire dynasty.

Further Reading

Alexius is the idealized subject of a biographical history by his daughter, Anna Comnena, *The Alexiad of the Princess Anna Comnena* (trans. 1928). The chief scholarly study of Alexius is in French: F. Chalandon, *Essai sur le règne d'Alexis I Commène* (1900). Chalandon's views are abridged and translated in his account in *The Cambridge Medieval History*, vol. 4, edited by H. M. Gwatkin (1923). For background information see G. Ostrogorsky, *History of the Byzantine State* (1940; trans. 1956; rev. ed. 1969), and *The Cambridge Medieval History*, vol. 4 (2d ed. 1966), part 1, edited by J. M. Hussey.

Additional Sources

Comnena, Anna, *The Alexiad of the Princess Anna Comnena: being the history of the reign of her father, Alexius I, Emperor of the Romans, 1081-1118 A.D.*, New York: AMS Press, 1978.
☐

José Eloy Alfaro

José Eloy Alfaro (1842-1912) was an Ecuadorian revolutionary leader and president. He is the great hero of Ecuadorian radicals.

José Eloy Alfaro was born on June 25, 1842, in Montecristi in the coastal province of Manabi. His father, Manuel Alfaro, was a Spaniard who came to the town as a buyer of straw hats and settled down to live with Natividad Delgado, a girl with mixed white, Indian, and African ancestry. They had eight children, and their common-law marriage was legalized through a church wedding in 1863.

Eloy Alfaro was 22 years old when he started his revolutionary career by taking prisoner the governor of the province. From then till 1889, he was constantly engaged in efforts to subvert the successive governments of Ecuador, either as an independent guerrilla leader, as an officer in a bigger revolutionary movement, or as the backer of other revolutionaries. His originally successful business ventures in Panama and his marriage there to Doña Ana Paredes y Arosemena gave him the financial means to pursue these activities. Even though he invariably failed, his constant activity led to his recognition by liberals as a general, and his prestige further increased as a result of contacts with outstanding liberal revolutionaries from other countries.

In 1895 the coalition of moderates and extreme conservatives in power in Ecuador split, with the conservatives revolting. The liberals seized the opportunity and rose in the coastal city of Guayaquil. Lacking a military leader with sufficient prestige, they remembered Alfaro and called him back. The Old Fighter, as he was known, marched with his army on Quito and soon had his authority established over the country.

Alfaro occupied the presidency from September 1895 until January 1901. His successor, Gen. Leónidas Plaza, had been his first choice for the post, but at the last moment he pressed for Plaza's withdrawal. Alfaro was unsuccessful, and relations between the two men remained cool. When, in 1905, Plaza handed over the presidency to his own candidate, Lizardo García, Alfaro overthrew the new president within 4 months and on Jan. 17, 1906, assumed that office himself.

Alfaro remained president until Aug. 11, 1911, when he was ousted for refusing to hand over the presidency to his legally elected successor—again originally handpicked by himself—Emilio Estrada. Alfaro and his followers were sent into exile. But within 4 months President Estrada died, and Alfaro immediately returned to Guayaquil to launch a revolt against the provisional government, which was favorable to Gen. Plaza. His attempt failed, and Alfaro was captured with his most important followers and sent to Quito. On the day of their arrival, Jan. 28, 1912, they were lynched by a mob that broke into the prison.

Alfaro did not deserve the way he died, but he certainly had been courting a violent death. With the exception of his years in the presidency, he had been a threat to his country's political stability for 50 years. As president, he condoned and occasionally even ordered political murders. Under him rapacious militarism became the curse of the country, and electoral fraud and nepotism were institutionalized. He pursued a bungling foreign policy. The essential aspect of his reforms was the separation of Church and State, by no means an unmixed blessing in the case of Ecuador. He was able to reduce the political influence of the great landowners of the central highlands, though at the cost of strengthening the power of the coastal oligarchy. Perhaps the greatest achievement of his 11 years as president was the completion of the railroad linking Guayaquil to Quito, through the efforts of Archer Harman, an entrepreneur from the United States.

Further Reading

There are several good biographies of Alfaro in Spanish. In English, Emeterio S. Santovenia, *Eloy Alfaro* (trans. 1935), is a biased, uncritical work. Background studies which discuss Alfaro include John Edwin Fagg, *Latin America: A General History* (1963; 2d ed. 1969), and Edwin E. Erickson and others, *Area Handbook for Ecuador* (1966). □

Conte Vittoria Alfieri

The Italian playwright and poet Conte Vittorio Alfieri (1749-1803) was a fervent adversary of political tyranny. His vigorous defense of freedom, the keystone of all his works, made him the idol of Italian patriots during the Risorgimento.

orn into a noble Piedmontese family on Jan. 16, 1749, Vittorio Alfieri received his early education at the Military Academy of Turin. Later, in characterizing his squandered adolescence, he especially criticized this school, where he was "a donkey amongst asses, a fool being taught by the foolish."

Travels in Europe

Alfieri spent most of the decade following 1766 in travel throughout Europe. He frequently had the opportunity to meet European sovereigns, but he generally declined because of his deep aversion to autocratic power. He was particularly repelled by the despotic and militaristic regimes of Prussia and Russia. Only in England was Alfieri pleased with the form of government and the freedom of the citizens.

During his travels Alfieri began a process of self-education. He discovered the works of the great Italian writers Dante, Petrarch, Boccaccio, and Machiavelli, as well as foreign classics. These 10 years also exposed Alfieri to the temptations of love to which he frequently yielded both at home and abroad. But in 1776 he met Louise de Stolberg, Countess of Albany, who was the wife of Charles Edward Stuart, the "Young Pretender" to the British throne. Alfieri rescued her from her much older, irascible, and alcoholic husband. They began living together in 1784 and spent most of the years until 1792 in Paris and in Colmer in Alsace. Then, opposed to the excesses of the French Revolution, Alfieri and the countess escaped with difficulty to Florence, where they remained until his death.

Dramatic Works

Alfieri is considered the greatest Italian tragic dramatist. His career as a tragedian began in 1775 with *Cleopatra,* a work he later renounced. Next there appeared two plays, *Filippo* and *Polinice,* which were first written in French and later cast into Italian verse. His subsequent tragedies are tightly written dramas in harmony with prevailing tradition and polished in their technique. While generally respecting the classical unities of time, place, and action, Alfieri sought greater plot advancement through action rather than narration. He gave a larger role to soliloquies and minimized the use of lengthy speeches to confidantes. Building upon the theatrical examples of Voltaire and Scipione Maffei, Alfieri wrote five-act verse tragedies dealing with illustrious figures and great problems. His protagonists often embody political stances—heroism, tyranny, treachery, or freedom.

Three major sources offered Alfieri material for his tragedies. Classical literature inspired *Antigone, Virginia, Orestes,* and two plays on Brutus (*Bruto I* was dedicated "To George Washington, Liberator of America"). Modern history was the genesis for *Mary Stuart, Don Garcia,* and *The Pazzi Conspiracy.* The Bible inspired *Abel* and *Saul.* The latter is considered Alfieri's masterpiece. While his other tragedies generally display clear conflict between oppressor and oppressed, in *Saul* the tension exists solely within the mind of the protagonist, whose envy, hate, and suspicion give rise to self–torment. The collected tragedies were published in 1789.

Political Writings

Alfieri's first treatise on statecraft, *Of Tyranny* (1777), reflected both his personal views and his reading of the *Discourses* of Machiavelli and the *Spirit of the Law* of the French philosopher Montesquieu. Alfieri, although aware that his essay was neither original nor polished, nevertheless took pride in the youthful defiance and righteous anger which emanated from every page. In this book, dedicated "To Liberty," Alfieri's fundamental premise—like Machiavelli's—is that the most perfect form of government was the Roman republic, where all citizens were protected by impartial laws. Like Machiavelli too, Alfieri believed that a tyrant's usurpation of power should be stopped by popular uprising. Alfieri also considered organized religion and the military unalterable enemies of free men. He alleged that anyone who accepted papal authority would be equally acquiescent to a political despot. In his concluding chapter—"What Government Would Be the Best Substitute for a Tyranny?"—Alfieri resists facile and general solutions. Instead, he cautiously urges all enlightened men to cherish freedom and to be aware that "it is at the cost of many tears and much blood (never otherwise) that people pass from slavery to freedom."

Among his other political works, *The Prince and Literature* (completed in 1786) is also important. In this treatise Alfieri states that literature is based on truth and morality and will flourish only in an atmosphere of freedom.

Later Works

After settling in Florence, Alfieri initiated a series of new literary activities. While polishing *The French-Hater* (an anti-French work in prose and verse), Alfieri taught himself Greek and translated numerous plays from that language. In six satirical comedies (published in 1803), he criticizes the faults of monarchy, oligarchy, and popular government. During these Florentine years Alfieri also wrote his autobiography, an important but sometimes imperfect source of personal history, which he completed only months before his death.

Alfieri died on Oct. 8, 1803. The sculptor Antonio Canova executed a marble monument which marks his tomb in the Church of Sta Croce in Florence, the burial place of innumerable illustrious Italians.

Further Reading

The Life of Vittorio Alfieri Written by Himself was translated by Sir Henry McNally in 1953. An 1810 anonymous translation of this work, entitled *Memoirs,* was revised by E. R. Vincent in 1961. An excellent translation of Alfieri's *Of Tyranny,* with notes and introduction, is by Julius A. Molinare and Beatrice Corrigan (1961). Gaudence Megaro, *Vittorio Alfieri: Forerunner of Italian Nationalism* (1930; reprinted, 1975), affords a wide view of Alfieri's role. See also Charles R. D. Miller, *Alfieri* (1936). There is an essay on Alfieri in William Dean Howells, *Modern Italian Poets* (1887). □

Raúl Ricardo Alfonsín

Raúl Ricardo Alfonsín (born 1927) was an Argentine politician who opposed the ruling military junta from 1976 to 1982. In 1983 Alfonsín was elected president of Argentina.

Raúl Ricardo Alfonsín was born in Chascomús, Buenos Aires province, Argentina, on March 13, 1927. After completing primary school, he entered the General San Martín Military Academy, graduating five years later as a second lieutenant (reserve). He joined the Unión Cívica Radical (Radical Civic Union, UCR, also known as Radical party) in 1945 and soon became active in the Movimiento de Intransigencia y Renovación (Movement for Intransigence and Renovation). This was a reform movement that attempted to give new life to the Radical party after its defeat in the February 1946 presidential elections which brought Gen. Juan Domingo Perón to power.

The same year he joined the Radical party, Alfonsín entered law school. Upon graduation in 1950 he returned to his hometown, where he began to practice law, published a newspaper (*El Imparcial*), and was elected a member of the Chascomús city council.

After the September 1955 military coup put an end to nine years of Peronist rule and banned all political activity by Gen. Perón's followers, the Radical party emerged as the best organized and strongest political force. However, before the 1958 presidential elections took place the party split. It went to the polls divided into the Unión Cívica Radical Intransigente (Radical Intransigent Union, UCRI), which eventually changed its name to MID, Movimiento de Integración y Desarrollo (Movement for Integration and Development), led by Arturo Frondizi and the Unión Cívica Radical del Pueblo (The People's Radical Civic Union, UCRP) under the leadership of Ricardo Balbín. Alfonsín joined Balbín's party and was elected provincial deputy, although Frondizi won the presidency.

In 1960 Alfonsín was reelected for a four year term, but his mandate was terminated in 1962 when President Frondizi was deposed by another military coup. The following year the military held elections. Since the Peronist party was still banned, Arturo Illia, the UCRP candidate, won the contest. Alfonsín was elected national deputy for a four year term and became vice-president of the Radical caucus, but once again a military coup put an abrupt end to his mandate when Gen. Juan Carlos Onganía deposed President Illia in 1966.

Return of Perón

The new military regime sought to transform Argentina and announced widescale reforms. Six years and two military coups later the armed forces decided to return the government to civilians, allow the Peronists to run for office, and put an end to Perón's long exile, permitting his return to Argentina. The call for elections brought about a heated debate within the Radical party. Balbín's longstanding leadership was challenged by a new reform movement, the Movimiento de Renovación y Cambio (Movement for Renewal and Change), created in 1972. Alfonsín was one of its founders and became its presidential candidate. Balbín and the party old guard successfully contained Alfonsín's challenge.

Defeated, Alfonsín supported Balbín, who received the endorsement of the Radical party. The March 1973 elections, however, returned the Peronists to power and eventually led to Perón's third term in office.

The Peronists stayed in power until 1976 when another military coup deposed President María Estela Martínez de Perón (Isabel), who had succeeded her husband in 1974. The coup put an end to a period marked by significant right-wing and left-wing violence, government corruption and inefficiency, and economic chaos.

The "Dirty War"

Headed by a junta composed of the commanders-in-chief of the three armed forces, the new government announced the beginning of the "Proceso de Reorganización National" (Process of National Reorganization). While enacting unprecedented liberal policies intended to bring about economic development, it proceeded to establish a rigid authoritarian regime which became the most repressive government in the history of modern Argentina. Responding to guerrilla violence with state terrorism, the junta launched a brutal campaign that led to large scale human rights violations and killed thousands of innocent persons, including children.

Despite the ban on political activity, Alfonsín was an early critic of the junta's human rights violations. He was a co-founder and active member of the Asamblea Permanente por los Derechos Humanos (Permanent Assembly for Human Rights) which included prominent jurists, politicians, and churchmen. He also became its president, together with Monsignor Jaime de Nevares, Bishop of Neuguén.

By 1980 the armed forces faced serious economic difficulties and found themselves increasingly unable to solve the problems created by their anti-guerrilla campaign, especially the question of the *desaparecidos* (disappeared), persons who had been kidnapped by security forces and had literally disappeared. The defeat of the Argentine armed forces in the April-June 1982 war with the United Kingdom over the Falkland/Malvinas Islands hastened the deterioration of the military regime. A transition government headed by Gen. Reynaldo Bignone was given the task of holding elections and negotiating assurances that the armed forces would not be held accountable for their acts during the "dirty war," as the military itself called the anti-guerrilla campaign. General Bignone failed to reach an agreement with political parties, and elections were set for October 30, 1983.

Alfonsín Takes Command

Taking the initiative, Alfonsín successfully altered the minority status of Renovación y Cambio within UCR and won his party nomination. Then, while the Peronists were still seeking a nominee, Alfonsín launched his campaign. He defined the elections as a contest in which the Radical party's democratic credentials were far superior to those of the Peronist party. He emphasized the need to restore the rule of law to Argentina, extolled democratic values, and projected an image of honesty and hope in the future that found a response not only among the middle class, but also made inroads in the traditionally Peronist working class. When the returns came in, Alfonsín had won the elections with 52 percent of the vote.

When Alfonsín took office on December 10, 1983, he faced a difficult task. He had to strengthen democratic institutions, weakened by successive military coups since 1930; curb the armed forces; dismantle the security forces that had carried out the repressive campaign of the 1970s; satisfy the demands of human rights groups and relatives of *desparecidos;* and bring about the economic recovery of a country burdened by a $45 billion foreign debt. Taking an exceptional step, he brought the members of the three military juntas that ruled Argentina between 1976 and 1982 to trial. Although he failed in his attempt to democratize the labor movement, he tackled inflation with a bold economic plan and, despite his austerity measures, managed to increase his support in the 1985 congressional elections.

Carlos Saul Menem, from the (Peronist) Justicialist Party, was elected President of Argentina in 1989 and reelected in 1995. Alfonsín remains the leader of the Radical Civic Union Party.

Further Reading

There is no full-length biography of Alfonsín in either English or Spanish. For more information on modern Argentine history, James R. Scobie, *Argentina: A City and A Nation* (1964, 2nd ed. 1971) provides an excellent background. For radicalism, see Peter G. Snow, *Argentine Radicalism: The History and Doctrine of the Radical Civic Union* (1965); David Rock, *Politics in Argentina, 1890-1920: The Rise and Fall of Radicalism* (1975); and David Rock (editor), *Argentina in the Twentieth Century* (*1975*). For current information on the World Wide Web, see: http://www.yendor.com/vanished/conadep.html (information on the disappeared); and http://www.buenosairesherald.com/thisweek/onth1.htm (Buenos Aires news weekly). □

Alfonso I

Alfonso I (1109?-1185) was the first king of Portugal. An accomplished warrior, he won independence from Castile and enlarged his realm at the expense of the Moslems.

Alfonso Henriques was born at Guimarães in the castle of his father, Henry of Burgundy, Count of Portugal. His ambitious mother, Teresa, daughter of Alfonso VI of León and Castile, ruled the county as regent after Henry died in 1112. When Alfonso rebelled against his mother in 1127 and took control of the county, he immediately faced an invasion by his cousin, the new king of León, Alfonso VII. The Leónese king refused to recognize the independence of Portugal until 1143, when Alfonso Henriques became a vassal of the pope; the two cousins then signed a treaty in Zamora under the auspices of the Church.

Alfonso was now free to enlarge his domain by conquering lands from the Moslems. His first great victory had been against the Almoravids at Ourique on July 25, 1139. This battle established Alfonso's reputation as a warrior, and it was about this time that he abandoned the title of count for that of king. On March 15, 1147, he captured Santarém, setting the stage for the major campaign of his career. In May a company of English, German, and Flemish Crusaders en route to the Holy Land arrived in Portugal and entered into a lucrative agreement with Alfonso. They joined the royal forces in the 17-week siege of Lisbon, which ended with the Moslems' capitulation on October 25.

Alfonso now addressed himself to the task of settling the Tagus Valley in order to assure its security against Moslem attack. Several of the Crusaders had accepted his offer of land grants, but the population was still not dense enough to resist Moslem incursions. The defense of this region was therefore entrusted to the Knights Templar, and the task of populating the empty lands between Lisbon and Leiria was assigned to the Cistercian monastic order.

Between 1150 and 1169 Alfonso campaigned constantly in the south. He succeeded in containing the Moslems and in making some territorial conquests. To secure peace with the new king of León, Ferdinand II, Alfonso offered him his daughter Urraca, whom Ferdinand married in 1165. Two years later, however, the kings quarreled and Alfonso invaded Galicia, the southern part of which was in dispute. In 1169 Alfonso aided in the siege of Badajoz but was in turn besieged by Ferdinand's troops, who had come to help the surrounded Moslems. Seeking to escape, Alfonso was caught in the gate of the city and broke his leg. He was captured by Ferdinand, and as part of the ransom arrangements he was forced to abandon all claims upon Galicia. As a result of his accident, the King never fought again, and the burden of military leadership passed to his son Sancho.

The year 1171 brought a heightening of the Almohad threat, but in 1172 Alfonso negotiated a 5-year truce with the caliph. As the decade drew to a close, Pope Alexander III officially recognized Alfonso's conquests and bestowed full royal dignity on him and on his successors. The last years of Alfonso's reign were marked by a continuation of the struggle with the Almohads. He died at Coimbra on Dec. 6, 1185, having reigned for 57 years.

The significance of Alfonso's reign as the beginning of a Portuguese national state is clear. But how and why Portugal was able to emerge as an independent power at this time are complex questions. Explanations based on a hypothetical Lusitanian spirit must be rejected in favor of answers founded on the political and geographic realities of the epoch. Although northern Portugal is well protected from Spanish incursions by the rugged Douro Gorge, the most significant roots of Portuguese independence lie in the political weakness of 12th-century Castile, which was unable to prevent the independence of either León or Portugal. Alfonso must thus be seen as a consummate politician who took full advantage of the moment to declare his country's independence.

Further Reading

A summary of Alfonso I's achievements, as well as a discussion of the political and geographic factors in the emergence of the Portuguese state, may be found in H.V. Livermore, *A New History of Portugal* (1966). □

Alfonso III

The Portuguese king Alfonso III (1210-1279) reigned from 1248 to 1279. He completed the conquest of Portugal from the Moslems and presided over the country's first parliaments.

On May 5, 1210, Alfonso was born in Coimbra, the second son of Alfonso II and Urraca. In 1227 he went to France, where he fought as a vassal of Louis IX against Henry III of England and in 1238 married Matilda, Countess of Boulogne.

While Alfonso was in France, a struggle developed in Portugal between his older brother King Sancho II and the Church hierarchy. When Pope Innocent IV directed the

Portuguese in 1245 to select a worthier king, the ambitious Alfonso was summoned, and he arrived in Lisbon in early 1246. Alfonso controlled only southern Portugal, and the civil war which broke out soon after his arrival was more hard-fought than his forces had anticipated. But the strong Castilian support desired by Sancho failed to materialize, and he abandoned hope of retaining his crown. Retiring to Toledo, Sancho died there in 1248.

To consolidate his rule over the divided kingdom, the usurper, who was declared king Alfonso III, launched a campaign to free southern Portugal from the Moslems. Faro fell in 1249, and the rest of the Algarve was secured for Portugal according to the terms of a 1253 pact with Alfonso X of Castile. Despite the fact that Alfonso III was already wed to Countess Matilda, he agreed to marry Beatrice, an illegitimate daughter of the Castilian monarch. Although this marriage brought Alfonso III into disfavor with the Church, Beatrice was received by the Portuguese with all the honors of a queen.

The hostility shown to him by supporters of his brother accentuated Alfonso's less noble characteristics—his overweening ambition, his lack of scruples, and his taste for vengeance. He confiscated the lands of Sancho's partisans and favored his own supporters with grants of land and money.

In 1254 Alfonso called the Cortes of Leiria, the first Portuguese parliament to include the third estate (commoners). The Cortes approved a number of fiscal reforms which the King had proposed. Throughout his reign Alfonso cultivated the support of the townsmen by protecting them against abuse of power by nobles and clergy.

Even though he owed his throne to the Pope, Alfonso was by no means a loyal servant of the Church. He opposed the Church's attempts to broaden the authority of the ecclesiastical courts, and he strove to preserve his traditional right to select bishops. Finally, in September 1275, the Pope ordered Alfonso to abide by the promise to obey Church authority that he had made in order to secure papal recognition of his status as Portuguese monarch. The King did not comply and was excommunicated; he maintained his political strength, however, until the end of his reign. After being reconciled on his deathbed to the Church, Alfonso III died in Lisbon on Feb. 16, 1279.

Further Reading

The life of Alfonso III is adequately covered in H.V. Livermore, *A History of Portugal* (1947). Also useful for general background is Bailey W. Diffie, *Prelude to Empire: Portugal Overseas before Henry the Navigator* (1960). □

Alfonso VI

Alfonso VI (1040-1109) became king of León in 1065 and of Castile in 1072. A fighting king of the Spanish Reconquest, he later feuded with the Cid and could not cope with the invading Almoravids.

Alfonso was the second and favorite son of Ferdinand I, Count of Castile and King of León. By the terms of his father's division of the realm, Alfonso became king of León in 1065. (The eldest son, Sancho, became king of Castile, and Galicia was allotted to the youngest son, Garcia.) Relations between Alfonso and Sancho were hostile from the start, and Sancho defeated him at Llantada in 1068. In 1071 the brothers joined temporarily to deprive Garcia of Galicia, but the following year Sancho again worsted Alfonso in battle, taking him prisoner but then allowing him to leave for exile in the Islamic kingdom of Toledo.

Alfonso spent 9 months in Toledo as the guest of the king al-Mamun, departing in October 1072 after his sister Urraca had engineered the assassination of Sancho. Alfonso was now king of Castile, but he was forced by Sancho's chief military aide, Rodrigo Diaz (the Cid), to disavow publicly his complicity in the murder of his brother.

From 1072 to 1086 Alfonso adopted an aggressive policy toward the Moslems. He extorted monetary tributes and in 1085 captured the ancient Visigoth capital of Toledo—his most glorious achievement. During this period he also strove to bring Spain out of isolation and into the orbit of European Christianity; he encouraged foreign pilgrimages to Santiago de Compostela, supported the Pope in supplanting the Spanish Mozarab liturgy with that of the Roman rite, and encouraged the activities of French monks.

The final stage of Alfonso's reign, from 1086 to 1109, was marked by a series of frustrating defeats at the hands of the Almoravid Berbers, who invaded Spain at the behest of Spanish Moslem leaders worried about growing Christian power. On Oct. 23, 1086, Alfonso suffered a humiliating defeat at Sagrajas, after which no Christian troops except those of the Cid were to have any success against the invader. The Cid's success in Valencia served only to deepen the hostility between the King and the former champion of his hated brother. The famous line from *Poem of the Cid*—"Were his lord but worthy, God how fine a vassal!"—alludes to Alfonso's pettiness and stubborn jealousy in dealing with the Cid, who remained loyal in spite of the King's rebuffs.

After the Cid's death in 1099, Alfonso finally heeded the call of the hero's widow, Jimena, and joined the Cid's troops at Valencia. But that city had to be abandoned to the Almoravids in 1102. The defeats continued unabated until the bitter battle of Uclés in 1108, in which Alfonso suffered the loss of his only son, Sancho. The King died in Toledo on June 30, 1109, leaving his realm in the hands of his daughter, Urraca, and in a state of insecurity and vulnerability from which it was not to recover fully for another century.

Further Reading

A fairly complete narrative of Alfonso's career, particularly episodes involving the Cid, is in Ramón Menéndez Pidal, *The Cid and His Spain* (trans. 1934). William M. Watt, *A History of Islamic Spain* (1967), is recommended for general background material. □

Alfonso X

Alfonso X (1221-1284) was king of Castile and León from 1252 to 1284. Also known as Alfonso the Wise, he was one of the greatest royal patrons of learning of the Middle Ages.

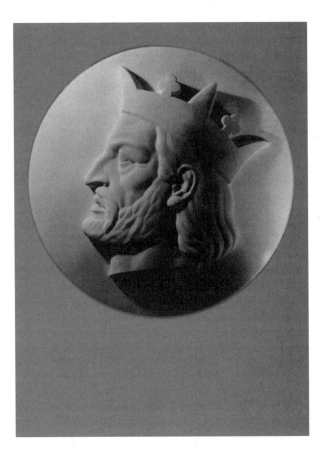

The eldest son of Ferdinand III and Beatrice of Swabia, Alfonso was born in Toledo on Nov. 23, 1221. As a youth, he was tutored in the arts of war and governance. In 1247 he drove the Arabs from Murcia, and in 1248 he played an important role in his father's capture of Seville. The following year he married Violante, daughter of James I of Aragon, who bore him 10 children.

Alfonso became king in 1252 and immediately embarked upon bellicose adventures. He fought Alfonso III of Portugal over some frontier posts in the Algarve. In 1254 he invaded Gascony and soon after laid claim to the throne of Navarre, a move which earned him the hostility of his father-in-law, the King of Aragon, with whom he finally made peace in the Treaty of Soria (1256). Alfonso spent much of the next 20 years in a vain attempt to gain the crown of the Holy Roman Empire, which he claimed by right of his German mother. Opposed in this strategy by three successive popes, he was at last obliged to back down under the threat of excommunication.

Alfonso's frequent absences from the country, moreover, proved an encouragement to rebellion. His Moslem subjects in Andalusia and Murcia revolted in 1262 with the help of Alfonso's tributary, the King of Granada, and the Merinid ruler of Morocco. A series of fresh disturbances followed during which Alfonso's eldest son, Ferdinand de la Cerda, carried the prime burden of military leadership. Ferdinand's death in 1275 precipitated a lengthy struggle over the succession to the throne.

The King's last years were clouded by the contest between the backers of his second son, Sancho, and those of his grandson Alfonso, the son of Ferdinand de la Cerda. In 1282 Sancho declared his father deposed. Alfonso the Wise, deserted even by the Queen, fled to Seville, disinherited Sancho, and called on Abu Yusuf of Morocco for help. Sancho, however, was able to meet this threat and contain the old king within Seville. There Alfonso X died, a tragic figure, cursing his son on his deathbed, on April 4, 1284.

Patron of Learning

Alfonso's greatest legacy was the *Siete partidas* (Seven Divisions of the Law). This work is not so much a legal codex as a learned essay on various kinds of law, covering all aspects of social life. As such, it is a repository of medieval Spanish custom. It had enormous influence on the future course of Spanish law and on the law of Spain's overseas possessions.

The scientific treatises compiled under Alfonso's patronage were the work of the "School of Translators" of Toledo, an informal grouping of Christian, Moslem, and Jewish scholars who made available the findings of Arab

science to Europeans in Latin and Spanish translations. The King's main scientific interests were astronomy and astrology, as indicated by the *Tablas Alfonsíes* (Alfonsine Tables), containing diagrams and figures on planetary movements, and the *Libros del saber de astronomia* (Books of Astronomical Lore), describing astronomical instruments.

Alfonso also patronized two ambitious historical compilations, the *Primera crónica general* (First General Chronicle) and the *General estoria* (General History), designed to present a complete history of the world. These writings mixed fact and fiction, especially when describing the ancient world, but they constitute a faithful representation of medieval man's attitudes toward his past.

Of Alfonso's poems, the most significant are the *Cantigas de Santa Maria* (Canticles of Holy Mary), written in Galician-Portuguese between 1257 and 1279. The canticles are written in troubadour style (the King called himself "the Virgin's troubadour") and contain a wealth of descriptive detail about medieval life. Alfonso also wrote satirical and love poems.

Further Reading

The definitive biography of Alfonso X is in Spanish. A concise historical study in English stressing Alfonso's humanistic pursuits is Evelyn S. Procter, *Alfonso X of Castile, Patron of Literature and Learning* (1951). A useful study of the Alfonsine literary corpus is John Esten Keller, *Alfonso X, el Sabio* (1967). Américo Castro, *The Structure of Spanish History* (trans. 1954), contains numerous insights into the interethnic background of the King's cultural pursuits; the scientific background is treated in Charles Homer Haskins, *Studies in the History of Medieval Science* (1924; 2d ed. 1927).

Additional Sources

Emperor of culture: Alfonso X the Learned of Castile and his thirteenth-century Renaissance, Philadelphia: University of Pennsylvania Press, 1990.

O'Callaghan, Joseph F., *The learned king: the reign of Alfonso X of Castile*, Philadelphia: University of Pennsylvania Press, 1993.

Procter, Evelyn Stefanos, *Alfonso X of Castile, patron of literature and learning*, Westport, Conn.: Greenwood Press, 1980, 1961. □

Alfonso XIII

Alfonso XIII (1886-1941) was king of Spain from 1886 to 1931. His troubled reign was characterized by violent class conflict, political instability, and dictatorship.

Alfonso was born in Madrid on May 17, 1886, 6 months after the death of his father, King Alfonso XII. His mother, Maria Cristina of Hapsburg, served as regent during Alfonso's minority. She was very anxious to build up his physical strength, and he was encouraged to spend much time swimming, sailing, and riding. This Spartan open-air regime gradually changed the delicate child into a strong and energetic young man. His education was carefully supervised, and not for generations had a Spanish sovereign received as thorough an education. He was very fond of history and became an excellent linguist, but his chief joy was military instruction. The love of soldiering evident in his early boyhood was something he never outgrew.

On May 17, 1902, at the age of 16, Alfonso was crowned king of Spain. These were troubled times for his country. In 1898 Spain had suffered a humiliating defeat in the Spanish-American War and had lost Puerto Rico, Cuba, and the Philippines to the United States. The Catalan and Basque peoples in Spain were demanding autonomy, and in the cities socialist and anarchist labor groups were becoming increasingly violent. Political life was very unstable, and between 1902 and 1906 the young Alfonso had to deal with 14 ministerial crises and 8 different prime ministers.

In May 1921 Alfonso delivered a speech denouncing the parliamentary system in Spain, and in July a Spanish force of 10,000 men was annihilated by rebellious tribes in Spanish Morocco. The army and the monarchy came under increasing criticism. The situation became so critical that in September 1923 Gen. Miguel Primo de Rivera took over the government and set up a military dictatorship. Alfonso supported the dictator, and during a visit to Italy he introduced Primo as "my Mussolini."

In early 1930 the dictatorship came to an end; it had become so unpopular that even the army refused to support it. Alfonso's association with the dictatorship had disgraced him and the monarchy, and in the municipal elections of April 1931 the republicans won in Spain's main urban centers. Rather than risk civil war, Alfonso left the country. After traveling to Austria, Switzerland, England, and Egypt, he finally settled in Rome.

In 1931 Spain became a republic. The republicans, however, proved unable to bring political stability and social order to the country. In July 1936 the army rebelled, and the Spanish Civil War began. The war lasted until 1939 and was followed by the long dictatorship of Gen. Francisco Franco.

Alfonso remained abroad during the civil war, since Gen. Franco would not allow him to return. Early in 1941 Alfonso abdicated in favor of his son Don Juan, and on February 28 he died and was buried in Rome.

Further Reading

Good biographies of Alfonso XIII in English are Robert Sencourt, *King Alfonso* (1942); Sir Charles Petrie, *King Alfonso XIII and His Age* (1963); and Vincente R. Pilapil, *Alfonso XIII* (1969). For the social, political, and economic situation in Spain during Alfonso's reign, Raymond Carr, *Spain: 1808-1939* (1966), is highly recommended. □

Alfred

The Anglo-Saxon Alfred (849-899), sometimes called Alfred the Great, was king of Wessex from 871 to

899. He successfully halted the advance of Danish armies seeking to conquer the English, and he stimulated a revival of learning among his war-ravaged people.

The Anglo-Saxons were a group of Germanic tribes who had migrated to the island of Britain in the 5th and 6th centuries and had wrested control of what is now England from the native Britons. After their conversion to Christianity in the 7th century, they absorbed much Latin culture, which blended with their Germanic traditions to form a distinctive civilization and increasingly stable political and social institutions. The process of reducing the many Anglo-Saxon kingdoms to a unified nation under a centralized monarchy was still in its early stages when the Danes, another Germanic nation far more warlike than the Anglo-Saxons had become, began raiding the English coast in the last years of the 8th century. The raids became full-scale invasions. Alfred's courage and military skill, however, prevented the Danes from conquering England, although they were later successful, early in the 11th century.

Alfred was born in 849, the youngest of six children of Ethelwulf, King of Wessex. Alfred's youth was highlighted by two trips to Rome in 853 and 855, where he was honored by the Pope; it was also plagued by sickness and the insecurity of his position as youngest son. Although Alfred could neither read nor write, he loved the traditional poetry of the Anglo-Saxons, which he memorized as it was read to

him. Asser, his biographer, says that on one occasion he was stimulated to learn these heroic songs by a desire to outdo his older brother and win the praise of his mother.

Military Leader

All of Alfred's brothers were dead by 871, and he became king at age 22. Wessex was the only Anglo-Saxon kingdom that had not been conquered by the Danes during the invasion of 866, and by 871 the Danes had established permanent settlements in the North Midlands and in East Anglia. Early in 878, while Alfred's armies were scattered for the winter, an army under Guthrum left Gloucester in Danish-controlled Mercia and made a surprise attack on the West Saxons, capturing much of the kingdom. Alfred, facing disaster, withdrew to the marshlands of Dorset with a small troop. The famous story of his taking refuge in the house of an old lady and, in his distracted state, letting her cakes burn through inattention, is unfortunately a later legend. But Alfred's situation was indeed desperate.

At Easter 878 he fortified the Isle of Athelney in Somerset, and his battles with Danish raiding parties encouraged more and more West Saxons to join him secretly. Seven weeks after Easter, Alfred left Athelney for a rendezvous of the militias of Somerset, Wiltshire, and Hampshire. Ten days later at Edington, near Chippenham, Wiltshire, Alfred's army decisively defeated the Danes. The invaders swore to leave Wessex, and Guthrum was baptized a Christian. The English were saved, and the King began at once to reorganize the land and sea defenses of the West Saxons in order to prevent further Danish inroads. These strategic innovations and Alfred's ability to use his forces well allowed him to turn back another major Danish attack during his reign. Launched from Scandinavia in 892, this invasion ended in 896 without appreciable success despite aid from the Danes already settled in England.

Cultural Influence

Having gained a respite from military crises, Alfred gathered around himself a dedicated group of English and foreign clerics. In 887, when he was 38, he began to learn to read English and Latin. Between 893 and 899 he and his scholars translated several major Latin works to make them accessible to his subjects and thus restore the preeminence in religion and culture England enjoyed before the Danish invasions. Alfred explained his aims in a moving preface to the translation (893) of St. Gregory's *Pastoral Care*. The later translations which he probably initiated or undertook himself included Bede's *Ecclesiastical History*, Orosius's *Universal History*, Boethius's *Consolation of Philosophy*, and St. Augustine's *Solioquies*. In his first attempts at translation, Alfred seems to have had the Latin text read and explained to him and then to have dictated a translation or paraphrase to scribes. In later works the quality of his prose improved, and he interpolated his own views on man's nature, trials, and destiny along with interesting comments on the world as the Anglo-Saxons knew it.

Alfred codified a set of laws for his kingdom and probably aided in the wide dissemination of the *Anglo-Saxon Chronicle*, a quasi-official record of the experiences of his people. His intellect, imagination, and energy seemed to grow in his last years. On his death in 899, he left a record of achievement which earned him his reputation as the greatest Anglo-Saxon king, as well as a legacy of military preparedness and strategy on which were based the victorious campaigns of his immediate successors against the Danes.

Further Reading

The main source of information about Alfred is *Asser's Life of King Alfred*, edited by William Henry Stevenson (trans. 1904), written by Alfred's chaplain, Asser. A modern biography is Eleanor Shipley Duckett, *Alfred the Great* (1956; published in England as *Alfred the Great and His England*, 1957). Also useful is the chapter on Alfred in Christopher Brooke, *The Saxon and Norman Kings* (1963). Alfred's reign and achievements are recorded in G. N. Garmonsway, ed., *The Anglo-Saxon Chronicle* (1953). His career is thoroughly considered and placed in the context of Anglo-Saxon history in R. H. Hodgkin, *A History of the Anglo-Saxons* (2 vols., 1935; 3d ed. 1952), and F. M. Stenton, *Anglo-Saxon England* (1943; 2d ed. 1947). For an assessment of Alfred's contribution to Anglo-Saxon culture see Stanley B. Greenfield, *A Critical History of Old English Literature* (1965). □

Horatio Alger

Horatio Alger (1832-1899) was the American author of prodigiously popular and influential juvenile novels and biographies.

Horatio Alger was born in Revere, Mass., the son of a Unitarian minister. The fervent father so rigorously supervised his son's early training that at 9 the boy was known as "Holy Horatio." Soon he was doing superior work at Gates Academy and, later, at Harvard, from which he graduated at 19. After a few years as a tutor and journalist, he acceded to his father's wishes and enrolled in the Harvard Divinity School; he received his diploma in 1860. But instead of entering the ministry, thanks to an unexpected inheritance he was enabled to go abroad, and free from parental supervision he enjoyed 7 months of bohemian travel. Returning home, he served as a Unitarian minister until 1866, when he moved to New York to make it his home until his very last years.

Having already published four moderately successful books for children, Alger decided to continue writing. With *Ragged Dick, or Street Life in New York* (1868) he scored his first formidable success. Attracted by the book, Charles O'Connor, a social worker, invited Alger to visit the Newsboys' Lodging House. The author served actively in the operation of this home for foundlings and runaways for 30 years. Much of the material for his subsequent books came from interviews with its young male residents: *Fame and Fortune* (1868), *Mark the Match Boy* (1869), *Rough and Ready* (1869), *Sink or Swim* (1870), *Ben the Luggage Boy* (1870), *Paul the Peddler* (1871), *Bound to Rise* (1872). After a trip to the Far West made at the urging of his publisher, Alger wrote *The Young Miner* (1879), *The Young Explorer*

(1880), *Ben's Nugget* (1882), and *Joe's Luck* (1887). His instructive biographies about self-made political leaders sold widely: *From Canal Boy to President* (1881), concerning James A. Garfield; *From Farm Boy to Senator* (1882), about Daniel Webster; and *Lincoln, the Backwoods Boy* (1883). Altogether Alger wrote 109 books averaging 50,000 words each, plus some 100,000 words of shorter material, thus producing about 150,000 words a year during his literary career.

The typical Alger hero was a boy who, born poor, overcame odds by living virtuously and working hard and rose to fame and fortune. The preachment in the books that honesty, perseverance, and industry were certain to be rewarded was taken seriously and followed faithfully by many boys in the late 19th and early 20th centuries who read some of the estimated 20,000,000 copies sold in the United States alone. The author himself lived according to his favorite formula: he rose from poverty to the affluence possible on annual earnings of $20,000 during a period when money had at least three times its present value. Ironically, and unhappily for his credibility, Alger's own life story ended in poverty in his sister's home in Natick, Mass., where he died in 1899.

Further Reading

Frank Gruber, himself a prolific author of popular fiction, is chiefly interested in Alger's bibliography in *Horatio Alger, Jr.: A Biography and a Bibliography* (1961). More valuable for information about the author's life, his influence, and the quality of his writings are John W. Tebbel, *From Rags to*

Riches (1963), and Ralph D. Gardner, *Horatio Alger, or the American Hero Era* (1964).

Additional Sources

Gardner, Ralph D., *Horatio Alger: or, The American hero era*, New York: Arco Pub. Co., 1978, 1971.

Hoyt, Edwin Palmer, *Horatio's boys: the life and works of Horatio Alger, Jr.*, New York: Stein and Day, 1983, 1974.

Scharnhorst, Gary, *Horatio Alger, Jr.*, Boston: Twayne Publishers, 1980.

Scharnhorst, Gary, *The lost life of Horatio Alger, Jr.*, Bloomington: Indiana University Press, 1985. □

Nelson Algren

The American author Nelson Algren (1909-1981) wrote novels and short stories about underworld characters, often set in the slums of Chicago.

Nelson Algren has been called the poet of the under-world. His characters are the pimps and pushers, clowns and con-men, hustlers and hookers, lushes and junkies, grotesqueries and freaks—in short, the born losers of the world who live in what he called "the neon wilderness." For more than half of his works the seamy streets of Chicago are his setting. His social realism has been compared to two other authors who wrote of the Chicago slums, Richard Wright (*Native Son*) and James T. Farrell (the Studs Lonigan series). Algren's work represents a continuation of the American realism begun with Stephen Crane's *Maggie: A Girl of the Streets*, Frank Norris' *McTeague*, and Theodore Dreiser's *Sister Carrie*.

So downbeat is his fiction that one of his most remembered lines is the closing of his frequently anthologized short story "A Bottle of Milk for Mother" in which a young murderer confesses his crime. "I knew I'd never get to be twenty-one anyhow," he tells himself. That short story became part of his second novel, *Never Come Morning* (1942), about a Chicago South Side prizefighter-hoodlum. It was only a little more commercially successful than his scarcely noticed first novel, *Somebody in Boots* (1935), about the end of a Texas family of misfits.

Algren is best known for his novel *The Man with the Golden Arm* (1949), which won the National Book Award and was made into a successful motion picture by Otto Preminger starring Frank Sinatra. It is the story of a professional gambler with a "lucky" arm and a morphine addiction, "a monkey on his back," a phrase Algren heard in the streets and made popular by using it in his novel.

A Walk on the Wild Side (1956), also made into a film, is a sequel to *The Man with the Golden Arm* and, like *Somebody in Boots,* is about a rustic from a Texas town. Critics felt that it was more than a re-writing of his first novel in that here Algren tightened his prose and laced it with comic interludes of Rabelaisian hilarity. But still there is the loser's mentality and Algren's gloomy humor. "Sometimes I almost think it'd be money in my pocket if I'd never been born," one of his characters remarks in A *Walk on the Wild Side.*

Born Nelson Algren Abraham of Jewish, Swedish, and German ancestry in Detroit on March 28, 1909, he grew up in Chicago after his father, a machinist, moved his family there when Nelson was three years old. He lived in ethnic blue-collar neighborhoods of the city and worked his way through the University of Illinois, majoring in journalism and graduating in 1931.

Unable to find work during the Great Depression, he traveled south to New Orleans and Texas, visiting areas that served as the background of his first novel. During his days as a drifter he hustled at a carnival, worked in a service station, and peddled goods as a door-to-door salesman.

It was while he was in Texas that he decided to be a writer. His first step was to steal a typewriter and head back to Chicago. Like the characters in his subsequent stories, he was caught and arrested. He spent four months in jail in Alpine, Texas. The experience gave him material for future stories. When he returned to Chicago he sold one set in a Texas filling station to *Story* magazine.

During World War II he served in the European theater and, again in the fashion of his characters, he emerged as he had entered, a private. He was married twice and divorced each time.

At one point in his life he began a romance with Simone de Beauvoir, the French feminist writer, whom he came to know through a friend who was a French translator. The night Algren met de Beauvoir, he took her to a seedy bar in the Chicago Bowery where they watched drunken old men and women dance to a small band. Later they visited a homeless shelter. The following day Algren took his enthusiastic new friend to see the electric chair, psychiatric wards, cheap burlesque shows, police line-ups, and the city zoo. Subsequently she went to Mexico with him and he visited her in Paris. De Beauvoir wrote about their relationship in several of her books and dedicated *The Mandarins* (1956) to him. He dedicated a book of essays to her. Although she returned to her long-time companion, Jean-Paul Sartre, she was buried wearing Algren's ring.

Algren had one other famous supporter, Ernest Hemingway, who selected him as second only to Faulkner among leading American authors of his day. Curiously, Faulkner and Algren were counterparts in another way. In 1986 the Modern Language Association reported hundreds of articles written on the southern writer with but two on Algren. Yet the Federal Bureau of Investigation's files on Algren outnumber those on Faulkner by 546 pages to 18, indicating a greater interest in the Chicago writer by J. Edgar Hoover and his staff than by literary scholars, many of whom objected to Algren's subject matter. The critic Leslie Fiedler called him "the bard of the stumblebum," and Norman Podhoretz complained that he romanticized hustlers and prostitutes. One of his works, however, *The Neon Wilderness* (1947), a collection of 20 short stories, received generally high critical acclaim.

Algren's last novel, *The Devil's Stocking* (1983), about a black boxer accused of a triple homicide and based on the life of boxer Rubin "Hurricane" Carter, was published posthumously. It had been written after Algren moved east in 1974, living first in New Jersey and later in Sag Harbor, New York.

On May 8, 1981, he complained of pains in his chest and his doctor recommended that he go into nearby Southampton Hospital, but Algren refused, saying that on the following day he was having a party to celebrate his entry into the American Academy of Arts and Letters, an honor which had come to him belatedly. On the morning of his party a friend discovered him dead, lying face-up on his bathroom floor.

Like Chekhov, whose dead body was mistakenly placed in a freight car marked "Fresh Oysters" on route to the cemetery, Algren suffered further indignities after he died. When his tombstone arrived, his name was spelled wrong and had to be re-cut. Then the City of Chicago named a street after him, but residents complained that the new name caused them too much bother, so West Algren Street, like its namesake, vanished from the scene.

Further Reading

Additional information on Nelson Algren and his works can be found in Bettina Drew, *Nelson Algren: A Life on the Wild Side* (1989, 1991); Maxwell Geismar, "Nelson Algren: The Iron Sanctuary" in his *American Moderns: From Rebellion to Conformity* (1958); John Seelye, "The Night Watchmen," with illustrations by Cathie Black, Chicago (February 1988); Nelson Algren, *Conversations with Nelson Algren* (1964); "Nelson Algren, 72, Novelist Who Wrote of Slums, Dies," *New York Times* (May 10, 1981); Saul Maloff, "Maverick in American Letters," *New Republic* (January 1974); George Bluestone, "Nelson Algren," *The Western Review* (Autumn 1957); and Ross MacDonald, "Nelson Algren," *New York Times* (December 4, 1977).

Additional Sources

Cox, Martha Heasley, *Nelson Algren,* Boston: Twayne Publishers 1975. □

Ali

Ali (ca. 600-661), the fourth caliph of the Arab and Islamic Empire, was the cousin and son-in-law of Mohammed. The Shiite branch of Islam regards him and certain of his descendants as inspired rulers and the only true heirs of Mohammed.

Ali was the son of Abu Talib, Mohammed's uncle and for a time his guardian. Abu Talib also was chief of the clan of Hashim of the tribe of Quraysh in Mecca. When Abu Talib was in financial straits, Mohammed took Ali into his household. Ali was there when, about 610, Mohammed received the first revelation and the call to be a prophet. Ali is said by some to have been the first male Moslem, but he could only have been about 10 years old at the time. He joined in the Hijra, the migration to Medina in 622, and shortly afterward married Mohammed's daughter, Fatima, who bore him two sons, Hasan and Husein. After Fatima's death in 632, Ali took other wives. The best known of his other sons was Mohammed ibn-al-Hanafiyya (son of the woman of the tribe of Hanifa). Ali took part in most of the military expeditions sent out by Mohammed from Medina and is reputed to have shown great courage.

After a dispute with Abu Bakr over some lands which Fatima had claimed to have inherited from her father, Ali recognized the caliphs Abu Bakr, Omar, and Othman and lived quietly in Medina. On one occasion he was left in charge of Medina when Omar was absent, and Omar also appointed him to the Council of Six to elect a successor. During the final insurrection against Othman in June 656, Ali remained openly neutral, though he is known to have been friendly with some of the insurgents.

On Othman's assassination Ali was elected caliph by the Moslems in Medina, but he was not recognized either by Muawiya, then governor of Syria, or by a Meccan group led by Aisha, Talha, and Zubayr. This latter group went to Iraq and raised a small army, which was defeated by Ali's troops at the Battle of the Camel near Basra in December 656.

Muawiya was more difficult to deal with. He and Ali with their armies confronted one another at Siffin in July 657, but after some skirmishes they agreed to an arbitration on the question of the caliphate. What happened next is obscure, but Ali refused to accept the decision of the two arbiters. He and Muawiya remained in a state of war, but there were no further hostilities, though Ali had to fight against dissidents among his own supporters known as the

Ali (center, on horse)

Further Reading

The main events of Ali's reign are discussed in Julius Wellhausen, *The Arab Kingdom and Its Fall* (1902; trans. 1927). Erling Ladewig Petersen, *Ali and Muawiya in Early Arabic Tradition* (1964), is a study of the sources. The Shiite account of Ali is summarized by Dwight M. Donaldson in the opening chapters of *The Shiite Religion: A History of Islam in Persia and Irak* (1933).

Additional Sources

Jurdaaq, Jaurj, *The voice of human justice,* Accra: Islamic Seminary, 1982.

Mohy-ud-Din, Atta, *Ali, the superman,* Lahore: Sh. Muhammad Ashraf, 1980.

Nadvai, Abulohasan Alai, *The life of Caliph Ali,* Lucknow, India: Academy of Islamic Research & Publications, 1991. □

Muhammad Ali

Muhammad Ali (born Cassius Clay, 1942) was the only professional boxer to win the heavyweight championship three times. With his outspoken political and religious views he has provided leadership and an example for African American men and women around the world.

Born Cassius Marcellus Clay on January 17, 1942, at Louisville, Kentucky, Muhammad Ali began boxing at the age of 12. A white policeman named Joe Martin featured Ali on his early television show, "Tomorrow's Champions," and started him working out at Louisville's Columbia Gym. An African American trainer named Fred Stoner taught Ali the science of boxing, instructing him to move with the grace and subtlety of a dancer.

"Float Like a Butterfly, Sting Like a Bee"

Ali built an impressive amateur record which led him to both the national Amateur Athletic Union (AAU) and Golden Gloves championships. At the age of 18 he competed in the 1960 Olympic games held at Rome, Italy, and won the gold medal in the light-heavyweight division. This led to a contract with a twelve member group of millionaires called the Louisville Sponsors Group, the most lucrative contract negotiated by a professional in the history of boxing. He worked his way through a string of professional victories, employing a style that combined speed with devastating punching power, described by one of his handlers as the ability to "float like a butterfly, and sting like a bee."

Ali's flamboyant style of boasting and rhyming and outspoken self-promotion garnered considerable media attention as he moved toward a chance to contend for the world heavyweight boxing championship. When he began to write poems predicting the outcome of his many bouts he became known by the another name: "The Louisville Lip." Both the attention and his skill as a fighter paid off, and on

Harurites. While Muawiya brought Egypt and Syria under his control, Ali continued to rule Iraq, most of Arabia, and, at least nominally, the eastern provinces. On Jan. 24, 661, a man called Ibn-Muljam stabbed Ali with a poisoned sword to avenge some of the Harurites. Ali's son Hasan made a feeble effort to claim the caliphate, but he was easily defeated by Muawiya, who was then universally acknowledged as caliph.

Because of the mass of pious legends which have grown up around Ali, it is difficult to know what the real man was like. He seems to have been a devout Moslem but to have had no special gift for politics. Even moderate Shiites, however, claim that he was the most excellent of men after Mohammed and so was designated to succeed him. After his death and still more after the death of his son Husein, Ali's figure caught the popular imagination and a political party was formed around him and his descendants. This is the Shiite or Shia (that is, "the party") sect, which has several subdivisions. For the more moderate Shiites Ali is an inspired or charismatic leader, divinely preserved from sin and error, and his tomb at Nejef, Iraq, is a place of pilgrimage.

Although Shiite Moslems claim that Mohammed designated Ali as his successor, this is denied by Sunnite Moslems. Modern scholars have found no evidence that supports the Shiite claim.

February 15, 1964, at Miami, Florida, when he was only 22 years old, he fought and defeated Sonny Liston for the heavyweight championship of the world.

"Beloved of Allah"

Meanwhile Ali, inspired by human rights activist Malcolm X, embraced the Black Muslim faith and announced that he had changed his name to Cassius X. This was at a time when the struggle for civil rights was at a peak and the Muslims had emerged as a controversial but major force in the African American community. Later he was given the name Muhammad Ali, meaning "beloved of Allah," by the Muslim patriarch Elijah Muhammad.

In his first title defense, held at Lewiston, Maine, on May 25, 1965, he defeated the now challenger Sonny Liston with a first round knockout that many called a phantom punch because it was so fast and powerful that few in attendance saw it. Ali successfully defended his title eight more times.

On April 28, 1967, Ali was drafted into military service during the Vietnam War. As a Muslim and a conscientious objector he refused to serve, claiming an exemption as a minister of the Black Muslim religion. The press turned against him, calling him "unpatriotic, loudmouthed, bombastic." Although he had not been charged or convicted for violating the Selective Service Act, the New York State Athletic Commission and World Boxing Association suspended his boxing license and stripped him of his heavyweight title in May of 1967. Ali's comment to *Sports*

Illustrated at the time was, "I'm giving up my title, my wealth, maybe my future. Many great men have been tested for their religious beliefs. If I pass this test, I'll come out stronger than ever." Eventually Ali was sentenced to five years in prison, released on appeal, and his conviction overturned three years later by the U.S. Supreme Court.

Vindication and Victory

The vindicated Ali returned to the ring in a victorious bout with Jerry Quary in Atlanta in 1971. Four months later he was defeated by Joe Frazier in Manila, who had replaced him as heavyweight champion when the title had been vacated. He regained the championship for the first time when he defeated George Forman (who had beaten Frazier for the title) in a bout held in Zaire in 1974. Ali fought Frazier again in the same year, and in 1975 won both matches and secured his title as the world heavyweight champion. In that year, to welcome Ali back, *Sports Illustrated* magazine named him their "Sportsman of the Year."

Ali began to employ a new style of boxing, one that he called his "rope-a-dope." He would let his opponents wear themselves down while he rested, often against the ropes; then he would lash out in the later rounds. During his ensuing reign Ali successfully defended his title ten more times. Ali held the championship until he was defeated by Leon Spinks on February 16, 1978, in a bout held in Las Vegas, Nevada. Seven months later, on September 15, 1978, Ali regained the heavyweight title by defeating Spinks in a bout held at New Orleans. Ali thus became the first boxer in history to win the heavyweight championship three times. At the end of his boxing career he was slowed by a neurological condition related to Parkinson's disease. His last fight, the 61st, took place in 1981.

Role as Statesman

As his career wound to a close, Ali became increasingly involved in social causes, diplomacy and politics. He has campaigned for Jimmy Carter and other Democratic political candidates and taken part in the promotion of a variety of political causes addressing poverty and children. He even played the role of diplomat, attempting to secure the release of four kidnapped Americans in Lebanon in 1985. As a result, his image changed from gadfly to highly respected statesman.

At the 1996 Summer Games in Atlanta, the world and his country honored Ali by choosing him to light the Olympic torch during the opening ceremonies.

Further Reading

There are numerous books about Muhammad Ali. Some of the best include Thomas Conklin, *Muhammad Ali: The Fight for Respect* (1992), Thomas Hauser's three books, *Muhammad Ali: His Life and Times* (1992), *Muhammad Ali in Perspective* (1996), and *Muhammad Ali: Memories,* with photographer Neil Leifer. Other supplementary texts include Barry Denenberg, *The Story of Muhammad Ali: Heavyweight Champion of the World (Famous Lives)* (1996), *The People's Champ (Sport and Society),* edited by Elliott J. Gorn (1995), Arlene Schulman, *Muhammad Ali: Champion (Newsmakers)* (1996), Jack Rummel, *Muhammad Ali (Black Americans of*

Achievement) (1989), William R. Sanford, Carl R. Green, *Muhammad Ali (Sports Immortals)* (1993), John Stravinsky, *Muhammad Ali: Biography (Biographies from A&E)* (1997). Outstanding accounts of particular events in Ali's life and career are Norman Mailer's book about the return bout with Forman in Zaire, *The Fight* (1997), and Suzanne Freedman, *Clay v. United States: Muhammad Ali Objects to War* (1997). Recent articles on Ali have appeared in *The Boston Globe* (Oct. 1, 1984, Jan. 17, 1992), *Newsweek* (June 22, 1987), *New York Daily News* (Feb. 2, 1989), *New York Post* (July 14, 1987), *New York Times Magazine* (July 17, 1988), *Philadelphia Inquirer* (Aug. 12, 1990), *Spin* (Oct. 1991), *USA Today* (Feb. 25, 1994), and *Washington Post* (June 9, 1991). □

Sunni Ali

Sunni Ali (died 1492) founded the Songhay empire of West Africa. Best known as a great military leader, he was called Ali Ber, or "Ali the Great." There is much controversy about his attitudes toward Islam.

Almost nothing is known about the early life of Ali (who received the title of *sunni,* or *si,* when he became king of Gao) except that he was raised among his mother's people, the Faru of Sokoto, from whom he learned the use of magical powers. When he grew older, he lived with his father, Madogo, the tenth *si* of Gao. Madogo was a strong military leader, and he too taught Ali the techniques of magic. Thus by the time Ali became *si,* he was adept in the arts of both war and magic.

In 1464, when Ali succeeded the fourteenth *si,* Sulaiman Dama, Gao was still a tributary province under the Mali empire, which was then weakening. Trade in the western Sudan was becoming less secure as the Tuareg and the Mossi raided more freely from the north and the south. Thus Ali came to power in a centrally located and relatively strong state at a time when a power vacuum was developing in the Niger Basin, and he immediately advanced against the Mossi and then moved to throw off Mali rule. He succeeded in permanently freeing Gao from the once great Mali empire and laying the basis for the Songhay empire, which was even greater. He could defeat the Mossi only in battles, however, and never even attempted to conquer these formidable non-Moslem foes.

Wars of Conquest

Much of Ali's military career was spent subduing the great cities of the Niger River. During the first year of his reign he began a 7-year siege of the city of Djenné, which according to traditions had resisted 99 assaults by Mali. Meanwhile he expanded further to the west, defeating the Dogon, and the Fulani of Bandiagara. By about 1467 he had added the Hombori to the south.

Timbuktu had been held by the Tuareg since 1433, when they had taken it from Mali. In 1467 the local governor, Umar, petitioned Ali to come and liberate his city from its invaders. In January 1468 Ali advanced with such a

formidable force that both the Tuareg and Umar himself fled. Then the Songhay entered and sacked the city. Ali's ruthless slaughter of most of the Moslem *ulema* there earned him the unanimous disdain and vituperation of the Moslem chroniclers who wrote the *Tarikhs,* which contain the main written sources of his deeds. In the following years Ali mounted additional attacks on the Mossi, Fulani, Tuareg, and other peoples. By 1471 the city of Djenné fell. In contrast to the harsh treatment Ali had accorded the Moslems of Timbuktu, whom he felt to have collaborated with a foreign enemy, here he was generous and accommodated the *ulema.*

During the next decade Ali extended his conquests in all directions, but he continued to nurse a powerful grudge against the Tuareg leader, Akil, who had escaped during the fall of Timbuktu. Akil had fled to Walata, where he still remained in 1480. Since a major part of Ali's military strength lay in his river navy, the isolated plains town of Walata presented special difficulties. Ali conceived a bold scheme to build a canal between Lake Faguibine and Walata in order to deploy his navy in an assault. This was a distance twice that of the modern Suez Canal. Soon, however, work was abandoned when the Songhay had to repel an attack of their nemesis, the Mossi. Ali never resumed construction of this canal, but traces of it are still to be found in Mali.

In the remaining years of his reign Ali led more attacks on the Dogon (1484) and the Gurme, Tuareg, and Fulani (1488-1492). He also again purged Timbuktu Moslems in 1486.

Ali and Islam

A major problem of Sudanic emperors was that of balancing urban, or Moslem, interests against those of the much larger rural, or non-Moslem, population. Rulers were generally Moslems themselves, but they always had to remain tolerant of established, local religions. Ali was a Moslem, and he performed all the routine Islamic rites; but he regarded Islam as a potential threat to his political power. He sought to retain his support in the rural masses, and he feared that he would be cut off from their support if the urban Moslems were granted too many privileges.

Ali's achievements were mainly military. During the early years of his reign he was constantly on the move, and he is remembered as having been undefeated. The task of administrative consolidation was, however, left to his successor, Askia Muhammad. Ali seems to have innovated a system of provincial governors, but it was not developed and Gao's control of its new territories was very tenuous. Songhay agriculture was frequently upset by his military levies, but he eventually alleviated this problem by incorporating more and more war prisoners into his own forces.

Ali depended more upon the fear and respect which he commanded as a strong magician-king than upon the love and admiration of his subjects, as he was a cruel and short-tempered man. He occasionally ordered the execution of even a trusted member of his retinue, only to later regret his loss. His general Askia Muhammad several times escaped such hasty sentences.

On his return from an expedition against the Gurma in late 1492 Ali died, possibly drowning while crossing a river. He was succeeded by his son, Baru, who tried to reject all Islamic influence, and was therefore felled by a Moslem-sanctioned coup led by Askia Muhammad within 4 months.

Further Reading

There is no full-length biography of Ali. A chapter on him, translated from a French source, appears in P. J. M. McEwan, ed., *Africa from Early Times to 1800* (1968). Other sketches of Ali's life can be found in Lavinia Dobler and William A. Brown, *Great Rulers of the African Past* (1965), and Adu Boahen, *Topics in West African History* (1966). Important general sources are E. W. Bovill, *The Golden Trade of the Moors* (1958; 2d ed. 1968); J. Spencer Trimingham, *A History of Islam in West Africa* (1962); and J. O. Hunwick, "Religion and State in the Songhay Empire, 1464-1591," in the International African Seminar, *Islam in Tropical Africa,* edited by I. M. Lewis (1966). □

Ramiz Alia

Following the death of Enver Hoxha, Albania's long-time (1945-1985) dictator in April 1985, Ramiz Alia (born 1925) became the dominant political personality in the country.

Ramiz Alia was born on October 18, 1925, into a poor working-class family from the northern Albanian city of Shkoder. His parents subsequently moved to Tirana, the capital of Albania, where Alia was a student at the city's Gymnasium (academic high school) at the time of the Italian occupation of the country in April 1939.

Like many of his contemporaries, Alia joined the Fascist Lictor Youth Organization. By 1941 he had severed his ties with this group and had become a member of the Albanian Communist Youth Organization. Two years later he abandoned his studies and was admitted to the Albanian Communist Party. The following year he was appointed political commissar with the rank of lieutenant colonel in the Fifth Combat Division of the Albanian Army of National Liberation. His competent performance in this capacity brought him to the attention of Enver Hoxha and marked the beginning of what was to become a close relationship between the two Albanian leaders.

After the end of World War II in 1945, Alia resumed his duties as a member of the Central Committee and Secretariat of the Communist Youth Organization. In November 1948 at the First Congress of the Albanian Party of Labor (APL), the former Communist Party, Alia was elected to its Central Committee and assigned to the party's agitation and propaganda department. The following year he became president of the Communist Youth Organization, a post he held until 1955. In 1950 Alia was sent to the Soviet Union to study Marxist-Leninist theory, and he continued his studies there with several interruptions until 1954.

At this point he began his rapid ascent within the Albanian ruling elite under the patronage of Hoxha. By 1955 Alia was minister of education and the following year he joined the APL Politburo as a candidate (nonvoting) member. In 1958 Alia relinquished his post as minister of education to become the Central Committee's director of agitation and propaganda, a position he held until his appointment in September 1960 as Central Committee secretary for ideology and culture. At the Fourth APL Congress in February 1961, Alia was promoted to full membership in the Politburo.

Alia's rise to the inner circle of the leadership during the mid-1950s and early 1960s occurred at the time when Albania's relations with Russia had soured after Tirana had resisted Soviet pressures to de-Stalinize, improve relations with Yugoslavia, and abandon its industrialization program. Hoxha had rejected these demands on the grounds that they represented a "betrayal" of the doctrines of Marxism-Leninism and posed a threat to Albania's sovereignty. Alia was staunchly loyal to Hoxha during this critical period that culminated in the rupture of Soviet-Albanian ideological and diplomatic ties.

Similarly, Alia supported Hoxha's alignment with China during the 1960s. When tensions developed in the Sino-Albanian relationship following Beijing's rapprochement with the United States and Yugoslavia in the early 1970s, Alia again supported Hoxha's determined opposition to the new Chinese line. Relations between China and Albania reached the crisis stage following the death of Mao Tse-tung in 1976, and two years later economic ties between Tirana and Beijing were suspended. The Sino-Albanian break resulted in the loss of a significant source of foreign assistance for Albania's economic development plans and underscored Albania's diplomatic isolation.

It was against this background that the events leading to Alia's ascent to power unfolded. As Hoxha's health deteriorated following the heart attack he suffered in 1973, the Albanian leader began to give increasing thought to the selection of a successor. It was generally assumed that Prime Minister Mehmet Shehu, the second-ranking member of the leadership, would succeed Hoxha. It appears, however, that differences over both domestic and foreign policy issues had arisen between Hoxha and Shehu and that Hoxha had misgivings about Shehu's temperament and competence to govern effectively. In December 1981 the Albanian press reported that Shehu had committed suicide in "a moment of nervous crisis." Given the massive purge of Shehu's supporters and the arrest of members of his family following his death, it is not improbable that Hoxha had engineered Shehu's demise to pave the way for the succession of Ramiz Alia.

In November 1982 Alia was appointed president of Albania while he continued to hold his important party positions. Upon Hoxha's death in April 1985, Alia was elected APL first secretary without opposition.

After assuming the leadership of Albania, Alia displayed considerable realism and sensitivity toward the problems confronting the country and the discontent these had fostered among the masses. By 1988 he had introduced a modicum of decentralization in economic planning and management, eased restrictions on Albanian intellectuals, and attempted to end Albania's isolation by improving ties with Western Europe and the Balkan states.

These measures, however, did not succeed in solving the nation's economic problems or curbing domestic unrest. The overthrow of the Eastern European communist regimes in 1989 intensified the demands for more radical changes. In response to these pressures, Alia in January 1990 announced a 25-point reform program that provided for the further liberalization of the structure and management of the economy, the legalization of private enterprise and foreign economic investment, significant expansion of civil liberties, and the strengthening of diplomatic and economic ties with other nations. This initiative elicited a mixed reaction from the people. While many Albanians welcomed the promised changes, others expressed their skepticism by fleeing the country or participating in demonstrations against the regime.

To underscore his determination to transform Albania into a "democratic state," Alia purged conservatives and incompetents from leadership positions, disavowed Stalinism, and drafted a new constitution. Bowing to popular pressure, he ended the political monopoly of the Party of Labor by sanctioning opposition parties and calling for free elections in 1991. Irrespective of the outcome of these elections, it appears that Alia's reforms ushered in a new era in the country's history. He set a personal example by resigning all his positions in the Communist Party on May 5, 1991.

Alia resigned as president of Albania on April 3, 1992, after his loss in the March election to Sali Berisha. Berisha subsequently became Albania's first non-Communist president since World War II. Alia may have been ousted from the government regardless of the outcome of the elections, because, even though some Albanians believed that Alia had steered them through a basically nonviolent transition, he had become very unpopular.

Alia was charged with political corruption and placed under house arrest in September 1992. The charges against him included misappropriating government property and funds, misusing power, and abusing the rights of citizens during his five-year term. His detention was converted to imprisonment in August 1993. He and nine other personages were put on trial in April 1994. Although Alia pleaded innocent and expressed the belief that his arrest was politically motivated, he was found guilty on July 2, 1994, and sentenced to nine years in prison. This term was later reduced to five years. Alia had served only about one year of his time when he was released on July 7, 1995. His release was granted by the Court of Appeals because of a new Criminal Code that exempted him from serving his term; however, many believe his release was part of an effort to strengthen European relations, which were strained by the accusations that his imprisonment had been politically motivated. Albania had been admitted to the Council of Europe directly before Alia's release.

Alia's freedom was short-lived. In 1996, he was charged with committing crimes against humanity during his term and imprisoned in March. His trial began on Februrary 18, 1997. However, during a riot on March 1997, during which guards deserted the prison where Alia and other former communists were being held, Alia escaped. On June 9, 1997, the trial of Ramiz Alia was adjourned when he failed to appear before the court. Alia's whereabouts remain unknown.

Further Reading

There is currently no full-length biography of Alia available in English. An excellent recent account of Albanian politics and diplomacy since 1945 is found in Elez Biberaj, *Albania: A Socialist Maverick* (1990). This work includes a useful discussion and interpretation of the policies of the Alia regime between 1985 and 1989. Information on Alia's political career up to 1961 appears in *Who's Who in Eastern Europe: Albania, Bulgaria, Rumania, and Yugoslavia* (1961). Ramiz Alia, *Our Enver* (1988), provides some interesting insights into the relationship between Enver Hoxha and Alia along with details of Alia's rise within the ranks of the Albanian political leadership. Another book that includes discussions of Alia's activities is *The Cold War: 1945-1991* by Benjamin Frankel (1992). Many of Alia's speeches have been published in English translation in pamphlet form, e.g., "Democratization of Socio-Economic Life Strengthens the Thinking of People" (1990) and "The Continuation of the Process of Democratization Is Vital for the Progress of the Country" (1990). The magazines *New Albania* and *Albania Today* are also useful sources of information about Alia's policies and activities. Also see *Business Europa Briefing* (Winter 1995), *Chicago Tribune* (March 14, 1997), *CSCEE/EECR* (Summer 1995), *Current History* (November 1993), *New York Times* (March 16, 1992; April 4,

1992; May 22, 1994; July 8, 1995), and *RFE-RL Research Report* (July 22, 1994).

Saul David Alinsky

Saul David Alinsky (1909-1972) was a leading organizer of neighborhood citizen reform groups in the United States between 1936 and 1972. He also provided philosophical direction for this type of organizing movement.

Saul David Alinsky was born in Chicago, January 30, 1909, the child of Russian-Jewish immigrant parents, Benjamin and Sarah (Tannenbaum). Saul's parents were divorced when he was 13 years old, and he went to live with his father who had moved to Los Angeles. He later returned to Chicago to study at the University of Chicago from which he earned a doctorate in archeology in 1930. Upon graduation he won a fellowship from the university's sociology department which enabled him to study criminology. In 1931 he went to work as a sociologist for the Illinois Division of Juvenile Research while also serving at the Institute for Criminal Research and the Illinois Prison Board. At this time he married Helene Simon, with whom he had two children, a son and a daughter. His wife died in a drowning accident in 1947.

In 1936 Alinsky left his positions with the state agencies to cofound the Back-of-the-Yards Neighborhood Council. This was his first effort to build a neighborhood citizen reform group, a form of activity which would earn Alinsky a reputation as a radical reformer.

Back-of-the-Yards was a largely Irish-Catholic community on Chicago's southwest side near the famous Union Stockyards, which had been deteriorating for many years. Alinsky organized his neighborhood council among local residents willing to unite to protest their community's decline and to pressure city hall for assistance. The council had great success in stabilizing the Back-of-the-Yards neighborhood and restoring the morale of local residents.

With this success behind him, Alinsky in 1939 (with funds from the Marshall Field Foundation) established the Industrial Areas Foundation with himself as executive director to bring his method of reform to other declining urban neighborhoods. His approach depended on uniting ordinary citizens around immediate grievances in their neighborhoods and stirring them to protest vigorously and even disruptively. In Alinsky's first book, *Reveille for Radicals* (1946), he explained how neighborhood residents could be effectively organized as activists for reform.

For many years Alinsky's neighborhood reform work disappeared from public attention, and he became best known instead for his 1949 biography of the famous labor leader John L. Lewis. Alinsky admired Lewis because he had proved especially adept at organization building and using mass pressure to win reforms for his followers. When a wave of reform swept the American nation in the 1960s Alinsky again commanded public attention. A critic of many of the decade's young radicals who spoke the language of violence, Alinsky instead called on reformers to be more practical and to use the self-interest of ordinary citizens as the primary force for increased political participation. "A guy has to be a political idiot," he told radicals, "to say all power comes out of the barrel of a gun when the other side has the guns." For Alinsky, power came from stable local organizations and political participation by aroused citizens fighting for their rights.

President Lyndon B. Johnson's "war on poverty" offered Alinsky a grand opportunity to put his ideas about neighborhood reform into practice. In the mid-1960s he founded a neighborhood (TWO), which the journalist Charles Silberman called "the most significant social experiment going on among blacks in America today." Soon thereafter Alinsky moved to Rochester, New York, where his Industrial Areas Foundation organized local African American residents to pressure the city's largest employer, the Eastman Kodak Company, to hire more African Americans and also give them a role in picking the company's employees. Simultaneously he participated in a federally-funded leadership training institute at Syracuse University which had been created as part of the "war on poverty."

But Alinsky's technique of rubbing a community's sores raw alienated some leaders, and in 1967 Alinsky found himself without a contract. He promptly labeled President Johnson's policies "a huge political pork barrel." At the same time he found it increasingly difficult to work with local African American groups which were then being swept up in the concept of "Black power" and who found it irksome to function under white leadership. Thus at the end of the 1960s Alinsky turned to training white middle-class citizens to organize and protest against the deterioration of their marginal urban and suburban neighborhoods. Always on the move, he organized white worker councils in Chicago, steelworkers in Pittsburgh, Indians in Canada, and Chicanos in the Southwest, where he influenced Cesar Chavez, who was later to found the first successful labor organization among California farm workers.

In 1971 Alinsky published his third book, *Rules for Radicals: A Political Primer for Practical Radicals,* in which he distilled his basic ideas concerning neighborhood reform. A year later, on June 12, 1972, he died of a heart attack near his home in Carmel, California, leaving his third wife Irene (his second marriage in 1947 to the former Ruth Graham had ended in divorce in 1970).

Further Reading

Two brief sketches of Alinsky can be found in *Who's Who in America 1970* and the obituary notice in the *New York Times* June 13, 1972. For Alinsky's ideas about protest and reform one might consult Marion K. Saunders, *The Professional Radical: Conversations with Saul Alinsky* (1956). For a study of one of his neighborhood groups in action in Chicago see Robert Bailey, Jr., *Radicals in Urban Politics, the Alinsky Approach* (1972).

Additional Sources

Finks, P. David, *The radical vision of Saul Alinsky,* New York: Paulist Press, 1984.

Horwitt, Sanford D., *Let them call me rebel: Saul Alinsky, his life and legacy,* New York: Vintage Books, 1992. □

Mohamed Allal al-Fassi

The Moroccan nationalist leader Mohamed Allal al-Fassi (1910-1974) was one of the founders and later the president of the Istiqlal party, an erudite Islamic scholar, and an author.

Mohamed Allal al-Fassi was born in Fez on January 10, 1910, into a family which descended from a companion of the prophet Mohammed and included hundreds of famous Islamic scholars, as well as the first governor general of Moslem North Africa. Allal al-Fassi's father was a doctor of divinity and curator of the famous library of Qarawiyin University in Fez. His mother also belonged to a famous family with considerable influence in northern Morocco.

As a youth, Allal al-Fassi was one of the most fervent, gifted, and revolutionary theologians and nationalists in Morocco. Beginning as a lean boy with piercing blue eyes and blond hair, he developed into a stout spokesman for Morocco's traditional middle class. His personal evolution accurately reflected the transformations of Moroccan nationalism. His eloquence stirred small businessmen, arti-

sans, and traders, who helped support him and the movement. His profound knowledge of Islamic traditions and his writings made him one of the most respected scholars in the Arab world. But his early puritanical drive and his desire to reform and revitalize Islam alienated him from many Moroccan political leaders.

In 1930, five years after he had published his first book of poems, Allal al-Fassi completed his examinations for a divinity diploma at the University of Fez. In the same year he led the attack against France's Berber policy, which appeared designed to intensify divisions in Morocco's population; arrested, he spent 13 months in prison. After he was freed, he became the president of the Movement of Moroccan Action, then of the Nationalist party. By 1937, as a result of his political activities, he was exiled to Gabon and the Congo, where he remained until 1946. During these years he learned French. After nine years of exile he returned to Morocco only to clash with Istiqlal leaders and Sultan Mohammed V. Forced into exile again, he moved to Cairo. In addition, he traveled to Europe, Asia, sub-Saharan Africa, and America, attempting to solidify his position as a Moroccan nationalist spokesman. For several years until 1953, Allal al-Fassi lived in the international city of Tangier, then moved back to Cairo. There, he championed the cause of armed resistance against the French in Morocco.

In 1953 when other politicians turned against the armed Moroccan terrorists who attempted to wrench their country free from France by employing urban guerrilla tactics, Allal al-Fassi became the only important Istiqlal leader to ally himself with them. When France granted Morocco its independence in March 1956, the Istiqlal needed Allal al-Fassi to negotiate with terrorist leaders and win them over to the party. After independence, therefore, he was reintegrated into the Istiqlal. By 1959 he became president, after more radical elements led by the trade unions split off. On June 2, 1962, he became minister of Islamic affairs, a post he resigned on January 5, 1963. In May 1963 he was elected to the parliament, which was disbanded in 1965.

As titular head of the Istiqlal, he then commanded the loyal opposition to King Hassan II. He and his followers campaigned for seven years against Hassan and constitutional reforms that ended parliamentary government, and he remained an outspoken proponent of Morocco's territorial claims to Spanish Sahara and Tindouf. Before Allal al-Fassi could see any real results of these years of work, however, he died of a heart attack May 19, 1974, during a visit to Romania to meet with President Nicolai Ceaucescu.

Further Reading

For Allal al-Fassi's early nationalist activities see John P. Halstead, *Rebirth of a Nation: The Origins and Rise of Moroccan Nationalism, 1912-1944* (1968), and, for his later years, Douglas E. Ashford, *Political Change in Morocco* (1961). One of Allal al-Fassi's books, first published in Arabic in 1948, was translated as *The Independence Movements in Arab North Africa* (1954). □

Ethan Allen

An American Revolutionary War soldier and Vermont leader, Ethan Allen (1738-1789) achieved a place in history by capturing Fort Ticonderoga in 1775. He championed Vermont's drive for statehood.

Ethan Allen was a distinct type of frontier soldier. His influence on the settlers of Vermont was comparable to that of John Sevier on the inhabitants of Watauga, East Tennessee, and of Thomas Sumter on the up-country men of South Carolina. Frontier people possessed clanlike loyalties, and they looked to strong men to lead them. Allen had all the credentials. Tall and broad-shouldered, he had great physical strength, along with "rough and ready humor, boundless self-confidence and a shrewdness in thought and action equal to almost any emergency." When Vermonters were threatened by New York authorities who claimed the area and denied the validity of their land titles, they formed in 1770 a military association, an unauthorized militia which Allen commanded. The members were mostly rough, roistering young men, and they called themselves the Green Mountain Boys.

Allen was born in 1738, the eldest son of a substantial farmer in Litchfield, Conn. His father's early death left him with the responsibility of caring for his mother and seven other children, and it brought his schooling—he was preparing to enter Yale College—to a permanent end. Allen, however, had a genuine intellectual bent, and he was to write a number of pamphlets on such diverse subjects as the taking of Ticonderoga, Vermont's controversies with New York, and religion.

Revolutionary Career

From 1770 to 1775 Allen and his Green Mountain Boys harassed the New York surveyors, sheriffs, and settlers who had invaded Vermont, which was then commonly known as the Hampshire Grants. Allen himself speculated in lands, forming a company to sell tracts along the Onion River. As "chieftain of the Grants," his authority uncontested, Allen sympathized with the colonists elsewhere in their opposition to British imperial policy, although the position of the Vermonters was complicated by the fact that they were currently petitioning the King to be reannexed to New Hampshire.

Even so, Allen felt the need to take British Fort Ticonderoga in case Anglo-American hostilities should erupt. The once-mighty fortress at the juncture of Lake Champlain and Lake George was now a crumbling and lightly garrisoned structure, but New York governor William Tryon had suggested that it be used as a base for bringing Vermont to heel. Moreover, Allen recognized that any large-scale effort by Britain to win an American war would undoubtedly include a southward invasion from Canada along the Lake Champlain-Lake George route.

According to Allen, word of the battles of Lexington and Concord "electrified my mind, and fully determined me to take part with my country." When Allen, with the financial support of Connecticut, proceeded with his plan to grab Ticonderoga, he discovered that Massachusetts had commissioned Benedict Arnold to do the same thing. Allen and his men agreed to let Arnold join them, though it is doubtful that they recognized Arnold as joint commander, as Arnold subsequently claimed. The fracas over authority and the boat trip across the dark, squall-ruffled waters of Lake Champlain to the western shore were more troublesome to the Americans than the Redcoat garrison: 45 officers and men who were "old, wore out, and unserviceable." Just before daylight on May 9, 1775, Allen easily overwhelmed the sleepy garrison "in the name of the great Jehovah and the Continental Congress," or so he later said in describing his ultimatum to the British senior officer. The capture of Ticonderoga's heavy guns, sledged eastward the next winter to Washington's camp, hastened the British evacuation of Boston in 1776.

Soon afterward Allen appeared in Philadelphia and persuaded the Continental Congress to authorize the organization of a regiment of Green Mountain Boys under such officers as the citizens of Vermont should elect. Allen's further advice on the advantages of an invasion of Canada seems to have added some impetus to Congress's order to Gen. Philip Schuyler to advance northward from Ticonderoga against Montreal and other parts of the province. At a public meeting in Vermont, however, Allen's former subordinate Seth Warner was chosen instead of Allen to raise the regiment of Green Mountain Boys—because, according to Allen, the older settlers constituted a majority of the voters at the meeting, and they considered him to be headstrong and radical.

Allen then joined Schuyler's army as a volunteer and was sent to operate behind the British lines with a body of Canadian recruits. He and John Brown, who was leading a similar group, decided to surprise and capture Montreal on their own. Unfortunately for Allen, word got to the town that "Ethan Allen the Notorious New Hampshire Incendiary" was at hand. When Brown's men failed to show up, Allen was easily overwhelmed. "Mr. Allen's imprudence," as Schuyler noted, had brought about his defeat and capture.

Vermont Leader

Following a nearly 3-year captivity spent mainly in England and New York City, Allen was exchanged, but he never again had an active role in the Revolution. During his absence Vermont had declared itself free and independent and had unsuccessfully petitioned Congress for recognition as a state. Allen also failed to bring results, largely because of the opposition of New York and also New Hampshire, which disputed the claims of some Vermonters to lands on the east side of the Connecticut River. Between 1780 and 1788 Allen and his brothers Ira and Levi flirted with British agents in an effort to compel Congress to recognize Vermont's aspirations to statehood. If that body would not, they held up the possibility of conducting a separate peace or, after the war, uniting with Canada. Nothing came of these threats, though Vermont did not become the fourteenth state until 1791, 2 years after Allen's death. Allen is also remembered for authoring the only extended statement of deistic religious principles ever written in America, *Reason the Only Oracle of Man* (1784). Although vigorously condemned by orthodox Christian clergymen, the work probably had little influence at the time since all but a few copies were destroyed in a fire.

Further Reading

Two scholarly biographies of Allen are John Pell, *Ethan Allen* (1929), and Charles A. Jellison, *Ethan Allen: Frontier Rebel* (1969). Stewart H. Holbrook's popularly written *Ethan Allen* (1940) also has merit. Allen's own story of Ticonderoga is available, *The Narrative of Colonel Ethan Allen,* introduction by Brooke Hindle (1961). Recommended for general historical background are Allen French, *The Taking of Ticonderoga* (1928) and *The First Year of the American Revolution* (1934), and Matt B. Jones, *Vermont in the Making* (1939).

Additional Sources

Bellesiles, Michael A., *Revolutionary outlaws: Ethan Allen and the struggle for independence on the early American frontier,* Charlottesville: University Press of Virginia, 1993. ☐

Florence Ellinwood Allen

Florence Ellinwood Allen (1884-1966) was a pioneering woman in the U.S. justice system, serving in a variety of roles in the legal profession previously filled only by men.

F lorence Ellinwood Allen was possibly the premiere pioneer female judge in United States history. In fact, any question that begins, "Who was the first woman judge to . . . " regardless as to how the question ends, the chances are good the answer is "Florence Ellinwood Allen." She was Ohio's first female assistant county prosecutor, the first woman ever to preside over a first-degree murder trial, the first woman to pronounce a death sentence, the first woman to be elected to a Court of Appeals, and the first woman ever appointed to the U.S. Court of Appeals.

Early Life and Education

Allen was born in Salt Lake City, the daughter of Clarence Emir Allen, a professor of classical languages at Western Reserve University in Cleveland. With her father coaching her, she became proficient in Greek and Latin by age seven and was preparing for college by age 13. As a teenager she attended a lecture by suffragist leader Susan B. Anthony. Subsequently, she became Anthony's protégé and a lifelong feminist activist.

She earned a bachelor of arts degree from Western Reserve in 1904, then studied music for two years in Europe with hopes of becoming a concert pianist. That career was derailed by a nerve injury, but upon returning to Cleveland

in 1906 she became music critic for the Cleveland Plain Dealer, a job she held for three years.

Allen became interested in law early in the next decade, but would not be admitted to Western Reserve's law school because she was a woman. She attended the University of Chicago for one year before earning a law degree from New York University in 1913. She worked her way through N.Y.U. by serving as investigator for the New York League for the Protection of Immigrants and lecturing on music for the Board of Education.

Legal Career

Allen overcame discrimination to be admitted to the Ohio bar in 1914 and established a law practice in Cleveland that specialized in women's legal problems. She worked as a volunteer counselor for the Legal Aid Society, worked for the Woman's Suffrage Party of Cleveland and became a leader in Ohio's state campaign for women's voting rights. She was appointed assistant prosecutor for Cuyahoga County in 1919.

In 1921 Allen was the first woman in American history to become judge of a Common Pleas Court when she was elected to the bench in Cuyahoga County. She tried 892 cases from that bench, including eight murder trials. There she developed a reputation as a "no-nonsense" jurist. She did not hesitate to sentence fellow judges to prison when they were caught in wrongdoing. In 1925 she presided over one of her most famous cases, the trial of Frank Motto, who had been accused of murdering two manufacturers in a payroll robbery. Motto was convicted and Allen returned a sentence of death. In 1926 Allen was the first woman to be appointed associate justice on the Ohio State Supreme Court. During the 1920s Allen cultivated a friendship with Eleanor Roosevelt, and in 1934 Mrs. Roosevelt convinced her husband, President Franklin D. Roosevelt, to appoint Allen as the first female judge on the U.S. Court of Appeals, making her the country's foremost female jurist. During her 25 years on the Court of Appeals she handled cases dealing with taxation, patents, personal injuries, forgeries, contracts, interstate commerce, labor laws, and conflicts between federal and state authority. One noted trial in 1937-38 concerned a suit filed by 18 private utility companies against the Tennessee Valley Authority. Judge Allen ruled that the statute creating the T.V.A. was constitutional, and the U.S. Supreme Court upheld the decision.

When Associate Justice George Sunderland retired from the U.S. Supreme Court in late 1937, Allen was widely regarded as a potential successor, but Roosevelt nominated Sen. Hugo Black of Alabama. In 1958, however, Allen became the first woman to serve as the chief judge of a federal appellate court, a position she held briefly until her retirement in 1959. Upon her retirement from active duty she was named a senior judge of the Sixth Circuit Court of Appeals, and worked on her memoirs, titled "To Do Justly." She broke a hip at the age of 81, and suffered ill health until her death one year later.

Further Reading

Florence Ellinwood Allen, *To Do Justly* (Cleveland: Western Reserve University Press, 1965).

Beverly Blair Cook, Entry on Allen, in *Notable American Women: The Modern Period,* edited by Barbara Sicherman and Carol Hurd Green, with the assistance of Ilene Kantrov and Harriette Walker (Cambridge, Mass. & London: Harvard University Press, 1980), pp. 11-13. □

Paula Gunn Allen

As a scholar and literary critic, Paula Gunn Allen (born 1939) has worked to encourage the publication of Native American literature and to educate others about its themes, contexts, and structures. Having stated that her convictions can be traced back to the woman-centered structures of traditional Pueblo society, she is active in American feminist movements and in antiwar and antinuclear organizations.

Paula Gunn Allen is one of the foremost scholars of Native American literature as well as a talented poet and novelist. She also collects and interprets Native American mythology. She describes herself as a "multicultural event," citing her Pueblo/Sioux/Lebanese/Scottish-American ancestry. Her father, E. Lee Francis, born of Lebanese parents at Seboyeta, a Spanish-Mexican land grant village north of Laguna Pueblo, spoke only Spanish and Arabic until he was ten. Due to the lack of a Marionite rite in the area, he was raised Roman Catholic. He owned the Cubero Trading Company and was Lieutenant Governor of New Mexico from 1967 through 1970. Her mother, Ethel, is Laguna Pueblo, Sioux, and Scots. She converted to Catholicism from Presbyterianism to marry Francis.

Allen's great-grandfather, the Scottish-born Kenneth Gunn, immigrated into the area in the 1800s and married her great-grandmother, Meta Atseye, whose Indian name was Corn Tassel. Meta had been educated at the Carlisle Indian School to be, as Allen says in her introduction to *Spider Woman's Granddaughters,* "a literate, modest, excruciatingly exacting maid for well-to-do white farmers' and ranchers' wives," but "became the farmer-rancher's wife instead." Her grandmother, half Laguna, half Scottish-American, Presbyterian, first married a Sioux (Ethel's father) and then remarried a German Jewish immigrant, Sidney Solomon Gottlieb. Her mother grew up speaking and writing both English and Mexican Spanish.

Allen was born in Albuquerque, New Mexico, and grew up in Cubero, New Mexico, a Spanish-Mexican land grant village abutting the Laguna and Acoma reservations and the Cibola National Forest. She attended mission schools in Cubero and San Fidel, but she did most of her schooling at a Sisters of Charity boarding school in Albuquerque, from which she graduated in 1957. Her 1983 novel *The Woman Who Owned the Shadows* and some of

her poetry draws from this experience of being raised Catholic. However, Allen is well aware of the conflicting influences in her background: Catholic, Native American, Protestant, Jewish, and Marionite. In an interview with Joseph Bruchac for *Survival This Way,* Allen says: "Sometimes I get in a dialogue between what the Church taught me, the nuns taught me, and what my mother taught me, what my experience growing up where I grew up taught me. Often you can't reconcile them." Her novel speaks to this confusion as the main character attempts to sort through the varying influences to reclaim a Native American women's spiritual tradition. On her journey, her protagonist uses traditional Laguna Pueblo healing ceremonies as well as psychotherapy, the Iroquois story of Sky Woman, and the aid of a psychic Euro-American woman.

Allen received both her bachelor's degree in English (1966) and her Master of Fine Arts degree in creative writing (1968) from the University of Oregon after beginning her studies at Colorado Women's College. She had three children and is divorced. She received her doctorate in American studies with an emphasis on Native American literature (1975) from the University of New Mexico. Two other writers from Laguna Pueblo are related to Allen—a sister, Carol Lee Sanchez, and a cousin, Leslie Marmon Silko.

Contributions to Native American Literary Scholarship

Allen is recognized as a major scholar, literary critic, and teacher of Native American literature. Her teaching positions include San Francisco State University, the University of New Mexico, Fort Lewis College in Durango, California, the University of California at Berkeley, and the University of California at Los Angeles, where she was a professor of English. Allen's 1983 *Studies in American Indian Literature: Critical Essays and Course Designs,* an important text in the field, has an extensive bibliography in addition to information on teaching Native American literatures. *The Sacred Hoop: Recovering the Feminine in American Indian Traditions,* published in 1986, contains her 1975 germinal essay "The Sacred Hoop: A Contemporary Perspective," which was one of the first to detail the ritual function of Native American literatures as opposed to Euro-American literatures. Allen's belief in the power of the oral tradition embodied in contemporary Native American literature to effect healing, survival, and continuance underlies all of her work.

Allen writes from the perspective of a Laguna Pueblo woman from a culture in which the women are held in high respect. The descent is matrilineal—women owned the houses, and the major deities are female. A major theme of Allen's work is delineation and restoration of this woman-centered culture. Her work abounds with the mythic dimensions of women's relationship to the sacred, as well as the plight of contemporary Native American women, many of whom have lost the respect formerly accorded to them.

Elaborating on the roles and power of Native American women, Allen's "Who Is Your Mother: Red Roots of White Feminism" was published in *Sinister Wisdom* in 1984. In this startling article, Allen articulated Native American contributions to democracy and feminism, countering a popular idea that societies in which women's power was equal to men's never existed. She also has been a major champion to restore the place of gay and lesbian Native Americans in the community. These ideas were first published in 1981 in a groundbreaking essay in *Conditions,* "Beloved Women: Lesbians in American Indian Cultures," and then reworked for the *Sacred Hoop.*

Allen says that her focus on women is intended to affect the consciousness of Euro-American women rather than men because, until the last ten years or so, the women in her culture were never considered weak, and she wants others to know that women were not held down in all cultures. Allen feels some ambivalence about the feminist movement because of this misunderstanding and the cultural chauvinism of Euro-American women, which has been personally hurtful to her and other Native women, but she admits that feminists provide the best audience for her work and have given her much support. In her family, the woman-centered tradition was so strong that her grandfather wanted to name her mother Susan B. Anthony.

Allen was awarded a National Endowment for the Arts Fellowship for Writing in 1978, and she received a postdoctoral fellowship grant from the Ford Foundation-National Research Council in 1984. Also at this time, she served as associate fellow at the Stanford Humanities Institute, coordinating the Gynosophic Gathering, A Woman Identified Worship Service, in Berkeley. She is active in the anti-nuclear and anti-war movements as well as the feminist movement. She won an American Book Award in 1990 for *Spider Woman's Granddaughters: Traditional Tales and Contemporary Writings by Native American Women,* which is an attempt to correct the lack of stories by and/or about Native Women in literature collections. In her 1991 *Grandmother of the Light: A Medicine Woman's Sourcebook,* Allen expands her interest in the ritual experience of women as exhibited in the traditional stories. She traces the stages in a woman's spiritual path using Native American stories as models for walking in the sacred way.

Contributions to Native American Poetry

Besides her extensive work as a scholar, Allen is the author of numerous volumes of poetry. Because of her multicultural background, Allen can draw on varying poetic rhythms and structures, which emanate from such sources as country-western music, Pueblo corn dances, Catholic masses, Mozart, Italian opera, and Arabic chanting. In her work, a finely detailed sense of place resonates with landscapes from the city, the reservation, and the interior. She has been recognized by critics such as A. Lavonne Ruoff for her purity of language and emotional intensity.

Allen became interested in writing in high school when she discovered the work of Gertrude Stein, whom she read extensively and tried to copy. Other influences have been the Romantic poets, Shelley and Keats. Allen took up writing more seriously in college when she read Robert Creeley's *For Love* and discovered that he was teaching at the University of New Mexico, where she was a student. She took his poetry class, although she considered herself a prose writer at the time. Creeley introduced her to the work of the poets Charles Olson, Allen Ginsberg, and Denise Levertov—all of whom have been major influences on Allen. She left New Mexico to finish her bachelor's degree at the University of Oregon and studied with Ralph Salisbury, who was Cherokee, though she did not know it at the time. Feeling isolated and suicidal, Allen says that the presence of a Santee Sioux friend, Dick Wilson, and the discovery of N. Scott Momaday's *House Made of Dawn* made all the difference to her. Recent influences upon her work have been Adrienne Rich, Patricia Clark Smith, and E.A. Mares.

Allen's 1982 *Shadow Country* received an honorable mention from the National Book Award Before Columbus Foundation. Allen uses the theme of shadows—the not dark and not light—to bridge her experience of mixed heritage as she attempts to respond to the world in its variety. Allen's poetry has an infusion of spirits common to Native American literature, but represents not only her Native American heritage, but her multicultural heritage. She also uses her poetry to respond to personal events in her life, such as her mother's suffering with lupus ("Dear World" in *Shadow Country*) and the death of one of her twin sons ("On the Street: Monument" in *Shadow Country*). In the interview with Bruchac, Allen says, "My poetry has a haunted sense to it . . . a sorrow and grievness in it that comes directly from being split, not in two but in twenty, and never being able to reconcile all the places that I am." Allen's multicultural vision allows her to mediate between her different

worlds to make a rich contribution to Native American literature as a scholar, writer, and educator.

Allen continued to receive attention in the 1990s, having her work examined and critiqued in such publications as *The Journal of Homosexuality, The Explicator* and *Ariel.* Also, in 1996 she cowrote an anthology of nine stories about Native Americans for young readers titled *As Long As the Rivers Flow.*

Further Reading

Aal, Katharyn Machan, "Writing as an Indian Woman: An Interview with Paula Gunn Allen," *North Dakota Quarterly,* spring 1989; 149-61.

Allen, Paula Gunn, "Beloved Woman: The Lesbians in American Indian Cultures," *Conditions,* 1981; 65-67.

Allen, Paula Gunn, "Who Is Your Mother? Red Roots of White Feminism," *Sinister Wisdom,* winter 1984; 34-46.

Ballinger, Franchot, and Brian Swann, "A *MELUS* Interview: Paula Gunn Allen," *MELUS,* summer 1983; 3-25.

Bataille, Gretchen M., and Kathleen Mullen Sands, *American Indian Women: Telling Their Lives,* Lincoln, Nebraska, University of Nebraska Press, 1984.

Bruchac, Joseph, "I Climb the Mesas in My Dreams: An Interview with Paula Gunn Allen," *Survival This Way: Interviews with American Indian Poets,* Tucson, Arizona, Sun Tracks and University of Arizona Press, 1987; 1-24.

Caputi, Jane, "Interview with Paula Gunn Allen," *Trivia, a Journal of Ideas,* fall 1990; 50-67.

Coltelli, Laura, *Winged Words: American Writers Speak,* Lincoln, Nebraska, University of Nebraska Press, 1990; 11-39.

Crawford, C.F., John F. William Balassi, and Annie O. Ersturox, "Paula Gunn Allen," in *This About Vision: Interviews with Southwestern Writers,* Albuquerque, University of New Mexico Press, 1990; 95-107.

Hanson, Elizabeth J., *Paula Gunn Allen,* Western Writers Series, Boise, Idaho, Boise State University, 1990.

Milton, John R., "Paula Gunn Allen (Laguna-Sioux-Lebanese)," *Four Indian Poets,* Vermillion, South Dakota, 1974.

Ruoff, A. LaVonne Brown, *American Indian Literatures: An Introduction, Bibliographic Review and Selected Bibliography,* New York, Modern Language Association, 1990; 92-4.

Ruoff, *Literatures of the American Indian,* New York, Chelsea House Publishers, 1991; 95-6.

Swann, Brian, and Arnold Krupat, editors, "Paula Gunn Allen, 'The Autobiography of a Confluence,'" *I Tell You Now: Autobiographical Essays by Native American Writers,* Lincoln, Nebraska, University of Nebraska Press, 1987; 141-54.

Van Dyke, Annette, "The Journey Back to Female Roots: A Laguna Pueblo Model," *Lesbian Texts and Contexts,* Karla Jay and Joanne Glasgow, editors, New York, New York University Press, 1990; 339-54.

Van Dyke, "Curing Ceremonies: The Novels of Leslie Marmon Silko and Paula Gunn Allen," *The Search for a Woman-Centered Spirituality,* New York, New York University Press, 1992.

Van Dyke, "Paula Gunn Allen," *Contemporary Lesbian Writers of the United States: A Bio-Bibliographical Critical Sourcebook,* Sandra Pollack and Denise Knight, editors, Westport, Connecticut, Greenwood Press, 1993. □

Richard Allen

Richard Allen (1760-1831), American Methodist bishop, rose from slavery to freedom to become the first African American ordained in the Methodist Episcopal Church. He was the founder of the African Methodist Episcopal Church.

Richard Allen was born on Feb. 14, 1760, the slave of a Quaker lawyer in Philadelphia who sold him to a planter near Dover, Del. While laboring on his new master's farm, he showed an interest in religion, was converted, and joined a Methodist society. His master, who encouraged his religious work, was in turn converted and allowed Richard and his brother to earn their freedom. Allen educated himself. As a free African American, he traveled through Delaware, Maryland, New Jersey, and Pennsylvania, preaching to both whites and blacks and maintaining himself by cutting wood, laboring in a brickyard, and driving a wagon.

The warm, informal style of early Methodism won Allen's loyalty. He was one of two African Americans who attended the organizing conference of the Methodist Episcopal Church in 1784 at Baltimore. He traveled and preached effectively with white Methodist ministers but declined to accompany Bishop Francis Asbury into the slaveholding South.

In 1786 Allen was invited to preach occasionally at St. George's Church in Philadelphia. Preaching in the early morning or evening, he had particular success among African Americans. By the end of the year his prayer meetings included 42 African American members, and he thought of establishing a separate place of worship. At first he was dissuaded by persons of both races. But when the African Americans discovered that their increasing membership was to be forcefully segregated in the new gallery of St. George's, they refused to submit to this insult and withdrew in 1787. They formed the Free African Society for economic and social reasons. The new organization solicited funds and secured a place to meet, only to find that they had divided loyalties. A minority established the African Protestant Episcopal Church and kept the building, while the majority organized an independent Methodist Church with Allen's leadership and financial undergirding.

Bishop Asbury dedicated the new building, Bethel Church, when it was completed in 1794, and 5 years later he ordained Allen as the first African American deacon in Methodist history. Despite these ties, friction continued between the new congregation and Methodist leaders over supplying ministers and ownership of the Bethel property. When a legal decision supported the congregation's independence in 1816, all official connections with the Methodist Episcopal Church were severed.

African American congregations in other cities had encountered similar problems, and in April 1816 the representatives of 16 churches met at Philadelphia to organize the African Methodist Episcopal Church. Richard Allen was chosen its first bishop. In 1817 he denounced the American Colonization Society's plan to return the free African Americans in the United States to a colony in Africa. In 1830 Allen started the first national movement to resettle free African Americans in Canada. By the time of his death on March 26, 1831, his leadership had solidified the growing denomination and given it national standing. The African Methodist Episcopal Church continued to grow, becoming part of the antislavery movement and the Underground Railroad prior to the Civil War.

Further Reading

Allen's short but essential autobiography is *The Life Experience and Gospel Labors of the Rt. Rev. Richard Allen: To Which Is Annexed the Rise and Progress of the African Methodist Episcopal Church in the United States* (1800; repr. 1960). Charles H. Wesley, *Richard Allen: Apostle of Freedom* (1935), is a well-documented biography. Also useful are William J. Simmons, *Men of Mark: Eminent, Progressive and Rising* (1887; repr. 1968); Carter G. Woodson, *The History of the Negro Church* (rev. ed. 1921); Langston Hughes, *Famous American Negroes* (1954); Emory Stevens Bucke, *The History of American Methodism* vol. 1 (1963); and Richard R. Wright, *The Bishops of the African Methodist Episcopal Church* (1963).

Additional Sources

Mwadilifu, Mwalimu I. (Mwalimu Imara), *Richard Allen: the first exemplar of African American education,* New York: ECA Associates, 1985. □

Woody Allen

Woody Allen (born 1935) has been one of America's most prominent filmmakers, with a series of very personal films about the subjects that have always obsessed him: sex, death and the meaning of life.

"If I sat down to do something popular, I don't think I could," Woody Allen told interviewer Stephen Farber in 1985. "I'm not making films because I want to be in the movie business. I'm making them because I want to say something." When Allen was one of America's most popular stand-up comedians, his fans might have mocked those words, coming from a man whose first role models were Bob Hope and Groucho Marx.

Allen's own films have been made on modest budgets in New York City, where he lives, with no concessions to studio taste or control. Despite the growing seriousness of his work, audiences have never lost sight of Allen the performer and the character he created for himself in his days as a comedian: a nerdy neurotic whose only defense against a hostile universe is his sense of the absurd, which he fearlessly directs at any and all targets, beginning with himself. A very private man, Allen has reluctantly become a public figure, but through all the changes and controversies, "The Woodman" has remained a symbol of uncompromising integrity to his loyal fans. On that subject, he told Farber, "I never hold them cheaply . . . I never write down to them . . . I always assume that they're at least as smart as I am, if not smarter, and . . . I try to do films that they will respect."

Woody Allen was born Allen Konigsberg on December 1, 1935, in the Bronx and grew up in Brooklyn. He changed his name to Woody Allen when at age 17 he began submitting jokes to a newspaper column, eventually attracting the attention of a publicist who hired him to write gags for his clients. After graduation, Allen enrolled in New York University as a motion picture major and then in night school at City College, but dropped out of both to pursue his career as a comedy writer. Years later he told his biographer Eric Lax that when a dean recommended he "seek psychiatric help" if he ever wanted to get a job, he replied that he was already working in show business. "Well, if you're around other crazy people," the dean conceded, "maybe you won't stand out."

Fortunately, Allen had a remarkable gift for his chosen profession. In a recent *New Yorker* article, Adam Gopnik recalled, "Woody was famous among his contemporaries for possessing a pure and almost abstract gift for one-liners . . . that could be applied to any situation, or passed on to any comic, almost impersonally." Before he turned 20 Allen had sold 20,000 gags to the New York tabloids, married his childhood sweetheart Harlene Rosen and landed a job in the writer's development program at NBC. By the time he turned 23 he was writing for the network's biggest comedy star, Sid Caesar, and had signed with talent managers Jack Rollins and Charles Joffe, who would later produce his films. He had also hired a tutor from Columbia University to teach him literature and philosophy at home.

At the urging of his new managers, Allen began performing his own material in a small New York nightclub in 1960. Honing his craft in painful encounters with the audience night after night, six nights a week, he struck a gold mine of comedy material when he and Rosen divorced in 1962. (His jokes about his ex-wife eventually led to a lawsuit from Rosen that was settled out of court.) By this time Allen was beginning to appear on network television and was a hit at Greenwich Village's legendary coffee house, The Bitter End.

Unlike other comics of the time, who favored political humor, Allen made jokes about his own comic persona, the little guy tormented by big philosophical issues and his unfailing hard luck with women. This fact was appreciated by a *New York Times* reviewer, who called him "the freshest comic to emerge in many months."

National recognition was not long in coming. Success in clubs and on television led to a Grammy-nominated comedy album, *Woody Allen,* in 1964, followed by *Woody Allen, Volume Two* in 1965 and *The Third Woody Allen Album* in 1968. Allen's humor found a more up-scale outlet when he began writing humorous essays in the style of S. J. Perelman for the *New Yorker* in 1966. Three collections of these essays have been published: *Getting Even, Without Feathers,* and *Side Effects.*

Allen had long been a lover of movies, American and foreign, but the first one he wrote and acted in, *What's New, Pussycat?* (1965), was a bad experience. Recruited to write a comedy for hip young audiences, he found the experience of sixties-style, big-budget improvisational filmmaking appalling. "I fought with everybody all the time," he told *Cinema* magazine. "I hated everyone, and everyone hated me. When that picture was over, I decided I would never do another film unless I had complete control of it." But the film made a fortune and established Woody Allen as a "bankable" movie talent.

True to his word, he made his directorial debut with a film so modest that no one ever thought to tamper with it. Released by AIP, a company specializing in low-budget action and horror films, *What's Up, Tiger Lily?* (1966) was a Japanese James Bond movie with new dialogue composed of dream-like one-liners put into the characters' mouths by Allen and some friends. "All we did was put five people in a room and keep them there improvising as the film ran," Allen told *Rolling Stone.* Truly for the young and hip, *Tiger Lily* didn't make as much money as *Pussycat,* but it acquired an enduring cult following.

Besides the release of *Tiger Lily,* 1966 was also the year of Allen's marriage to actress Louise Lasser, who supplied one of the voices for *Tiger Lily,* and the Broadway opening of his first play, *Don't Drink the Water,* a comedy about an Jewish American family on vacation who get in hot water behind the Iron Curtain. *Don't Drink the Water* ran for over a year and spawned a movie directed by Howard Morris; Allen directed a television remake of *Don't Drink the Water* in December 1994. The marriage to Lasser ended in divorce after three years, but they remained friends, and she acted in Allen's first three hit comedies: *Take the Money and Run* (1969), *Bananas* (1971), and *Everything You Always Wanted to Know About Sex but Were Afraid to Ask* (1972).

Allen's early comedies, made for United Artists—a company that gave him complete control of his work as writer-director—recall the messy, anything-goes style of classic American comedies built around such free-wheeling talents as the Marx Brothers and W. C. Fields. Like the Marx Brothers, a reviewer for *Time* magazine wrote, Allen was ready "to subordinate everything—plot, plausibility, people—to the imperative of a good joke."

Perhaps because it demanded a more controlled style, he entrusted the film version of his second Broadway hit, *Play It Again, Sam* (1972), to veteran director Herbert Ross. But he played the lead himself, as he had done in the stage version of this romantic comedy about a man who fulfills his dream: to play the last scene of his favorite movie, *Casablanca,* in real life, with himself in the Bogart role. His co-star on stage and in the film was his new off-screen friend and romantic partner, Diane Keaton.

Keaton and Allen also co-starred in the two films written and directed by Allen which mark the end of his "early, funny" period. In *Sleeper* (1973), Allen's character wakes up from a cryogenic sleep to find himself trapped in a future society that looks suspiciously like Los Angeles. And in *Love and Death* (1975), which Allen considers his best comedy, he takes on his favorite themes in an epic satire of all of Russian literature.

It was Keaton's talents as an actress that inspired Allen to make his first serious film, a bittersweet comedy about a failed romance between two neurotics, and it was undoubt-

edly her personality that inspired him to create the title character, *Annie Hall* (1977). (She won an Oscar for her performance; the film won a total of four of the prized gold statuettes.) "What is Woody Allen doing starring in, writing and directing a ruefully romantic comedy that is at least as poignant [distressing] as it is funny and may be the most autobiographical film ever made by a major comic?" asked *Time* magazine. "What he is doing is growing, right before our eyes, and it is a fine sight to behold."

Keaton went on to star for Allen in *Interiors* (1978), and *Manhattan* (1979), a somber black-and-white film about cheating New Yorkers which ends with a salute to the last scene of Charlie Chaplin's *City Lights.* His career as a serious filmmaker had definitely begun.

Annie Hall also marked the beginning of a nine-picture collaboration with cinematographer Gordon Willis in which Allen's growing mastery of film-making techniques enabled him to create a new style for each new film. He imitated the style of Italian director Federico Fellini in his next, most controversial film, *Stardust Memories* (1980), in which he plays a filmmaker who seems to hate his fans. Despite the ensuing hue and cry, Allen told an *Esquire* interviewer in 1987, "The best film I ever did, really, was *Stardust Memories.*"

When the executives who had given him artistic control of his work left United Artists and founded Orion Pictures, Allen worked off his contract with UA and joined them. Coincidentally, the move to Orion also marked the beginning of his collaboration with his new off-screen partner, actress Mia Farrow. Their first four films together all have a fairy-tale quality: *A Midsummer Night's Sex Comedy* (1982) mixes fairies and moonstruck lovers on a country estate; *Zelig* (1983) uses special-effects wizardry to tell the story of a human chameleon who achieved a peculiar kind of fame in the 1920s; *Broadway Danny Rose* (1984) transforms present-day New York into a never-neverland of show-business losers for a poignant romance between a brassy beauty and a hapless agent, and *The Purple Rose of Cairo* (1985) darkens the fairy-tale mood when a hero of the silver screen steps down into real life, with tragic consequences for a Depression-era housewife, touchingly played by Farrow.

Hollywood bestowed three Oscars on their next collaboration, *Hannah and Her Sisters,* in which Hannah (Farrow) is divorced from a hypochondriac, played by Allen, and married to a philanderer, played by Michael Caine. "Tracking the career of Woody Allen is exhausting but exhilarating," began the *New York Times* review of *Hannah.* "Just when we reach the top, another peak appears." But Allen, who told Eric Lax that "the whole concept of awards is silly," was worried by the film's success. "When I put out a film that enjoys any acceptance that isn't mild or grudging," he explained to Lax, "I immediately become suspicious of it."

After *Radio Days* (1987), a light-hearted look at Allen's childhood and the Golden Age of radio, the mood of his films darkened again. *September* (1987) replays the grim psychological dramas of *Interiors,* and *Another Woman* (1988) pairs Farrow with one of America's greatest actresses, Gena Rowlands, in a story of mid-life crisis. Allen briefly returned to comedy in the short *Oedipus Wrecks* (1989), about a man whose problems with his mother take a supernatural turn. He then made his most pessimistic film to date, *Crimes and Misdemeanors* (1989), in which a respectable married man (Martin Landau) murders his mistress (Anjelica Huston) and gets away with it, while Allen's character loses the woman he loves (Farrow) to a shallow fool (Alan Alda).

Before their off-screen relationship ended in a bitter child-custody suit, Allen and Farrow made three more films together: *Alice* (1990), a fairy tale recalling their early collaborations, in which a neglected housewife discovers love and life with the help of a Chinese herbalist who dispenses magic potions; *Shadows and Fog* (1992), a comic salute to the novels of Franz Kafka set in a Middle European country out of some German silent film, and *Husbands and Wives* (1992).

Released in a firestorm of publicity over the custody battle, Allen's last film with Farrow had the press looking for parallels to Allen's real-life romance with Farrow's 21-year-old adopted-daughter, Soon-Yi Farrow Previn. It also marked another new beginning for Woody Allen the filmmaker. Orion's impending bankruptcy obliged him to make the film for Tri-Star, while a less controlled style of filming, with a hand-held camera scampering to keep up with the actors, brought a new sense of life to this savagely funny contemporary look at marriage and infidelity. "It's a good movie," observed the reviewer for *New York* magazine, "yet a decade or so may have to pass before anyone can see it in itself."

The hand-held camera still wobbles noticeably in *Manhattan Murder Mystery*, which reunites him with Diane Keaton, playing a married couple who suspect their next-door neighbor of murder. A pure comedy, Allen's first in many years, *Manhattan Murder Mystery* was a pit-stop for the filmmaker and his loyal fans before his 1994 film *Bullets Over Broadway*, the critically acclaimed melodrama set in the 1920s that focuses on a group of old Broadway stereotypes. He continued with comedy in 1995, releasing *Mighty Aphrodite*, a contemporary tale of a man obsessed with his adopted son's mother interspersed with scenes parodying Greek tragedy. The next release, *Everyone Says I Love You*, surprised his cast and fans alike, marking the director's first foray into musicals. Reports noted that he waited until two weeks after the film's stars signed their contracts to mention that he was making a musical, and that he chose actors who were not necessarily musically trained on purpose in order to evoke more honest emotion in the songs. Reviews were mixed.

Allen's interest in music extended to his off-screen life as well— starting in 1997, he regularly began playing clarinet for the Eddy Davis New Orleans Jazz Band every Monday at a club in New York City. Despite his diverse talents, however, Allen in real life can demonstrate his neurotic tendencies that are trademarks in his films. He told Jane Wollman Rusoff on the "Mr. Showbiz" web site, "I've never made a movie where scholars sat around and said, 'This

ranks with the greatest.' . . . It's a goal, but the trick is to have a great vision. That's not so easy."

Further Reading

Lax, Eric, *On Being Funny: Woody Allen and Comedy*, New York, 1975.

Yacowar, Maurice, *Loser Take All: The Comic Art of Woody Allen*, New York, 1979; rev. ed., 1991.

Palmer, M., *Woody Allen*, New York, 1980.

Jacobs, Diane, . . . *But We Need the Eggs: The Magic of Woody Allen*, New York, 1982.

Brode, Douglas, *Woody Allen: His Films and Career*, New York, 1985.

Pogel, Nancy, *Woody Allen*, Boston, 1987.

Sinyard, Neil, *The Films of Woody Allen*, London, 1987.

McCann, Graham, *Woody Allen: New Yorker*, New York, 1990.

Lax, Eric, *Woody Allen*, New York, 1992.

Groteke, Kristi, *Mia & Woody*, New York, 1994.

Björkman, Stig, *Woody Allen on Woody Allen*, New York, 1995.

Blake, Richard Aloysius, *Woody Allen: Profane and Sacred*, Metuchen, New Jersey, 1995.

Perspectives on Woody Allen, edited by Renee R. Curry, New York, 1996.

Christian Science Monitor, January 24, 1997.

Life (New York), 21 March 1969.

Esquire (New York), 19 July 1975.

Rolling Stone (New York), 16 September 1993.

Esquire (New York), October 1994. □

Edmund Henry Hynman Allenby

The English field marshal Edmund Henry Hynman Allenby, 1st Viscount Allenby (1861-1936), was a commander during World War I. His fame rests largely on his leadership in the Allied victory over the Turkish armies in 1917-1918.

Edmund Allenby was born on April 23, 1861, in Southwell, Nottinghamshire, England. He attended the school of a local clergyman and then went to public school. After twice failing to pass the Indian civil service examination, he succeeded in passing the examination for the Royal Military College at Sandhurst.

Allenby was commissioned in the army in 1882 and sent with his unit to South Africa, too late for the battle of Majuba Hill, won by Boer force. He returned to England in 1886 and continued to advance in the army. He accompanied his regiment to South Africa again after the Boer War started in 1899, and there he made his reputation as an officer in action. The forces under his command were invariably successful in that long war.

At the end of the Boer War, Allenby was promoted from colonel to brigadier general and then to major general by the time World War I began. He was sent to France in command of a cavalry division. He later commanded the V Corps and the 3d Army. He was not an outstanding commander in Europe; his forte was cavalry, and traditional cavalry units were not useful where the front was bogged down in trench warfare. With the need for a new commander in chief in the Middle East, Allenby, because of his unequaled cavalry experience, was chosen. Allenby and Douglas Haig, the British commander in chief in Europe, never had great confidence in each other, and the new assignment for Allenby removed a source of friction on the Western front in Europe. He had unlimited success in his new command. His armies captured Jerusalem and Damascus, defeating the Turkish armies in a brilliant campaign—the last time that cavalry was to be decisive in modern warfare. Allenby and the soldier-scholar T. E. Lawrence of Arabia emerged from that phase of the war as the greatest names.

After the war ended, Allenby was promoted to field marshal, made a viscount, and treated as a hero at home. He was also given the post of high commissioner for Egypt, which he retained until his retirement from public life in 1925.

Lord Allenby was married and had one son. He died on May 14, 1936. Known to his troops as ''the Bull,'' he had exhibited that animal's positive traits of strength and determination but also its weaknesses of bad temper and rash action.

Further Reading

The standard biography is Gen. Sir Archibald Wavell, *Allenby: A Study in Greatness* (2 vols., 1940-1943), a balanced account

by a World War II commander. Brian Gardner, *Allenby of Arabia: Lawrence's General* (1966; British ed. entitled *Allenby,* 1965), is valuable because the author was the first to make use of the Allenby family correspondence. Other sources are Raymond Savage, *Allenby of Armageddon: A Record of the Career and Campaigns of Field-Marshal Viscount Allenby* (1925), and the pertinent chapter in B. H. Liddell Hart, *Reputations, Ten Years After* (1928; repr. in Barrett Parker, ed., *Famous British Generals,* 1951).

Additional Sources

James, Lawrence, *Imperial warrior: the life and times of Field-Marshal Viscount Allenby, 1861-1936,* London: Weidenfeld and Nicolson, 1993. □

Isabel Allende

The author of several novels and a short fiction collection, as well as plays and stories for children, Isabel Allende (born 1942) has received international acclaim for her writing.

Allende earned the Quality Paperback Book Club New Voice Award nomination for her debut novel, *La casa de los espíritus* (1982; *The House of the Spirits*) —which became a best seller in Spain and West Germany in the 1980s and a 1994 movie—and the *Los Angeles Times* Book Prize nomination for *De amor y de sombra* (1984; *Of Love and Shadows*). In 1988 Allende's third novel, *Eva Luna,* was voted One of the Year's Best Books by *Library Journal.*

Many of Allende's books are noted for their feminine perspective, dramatic qualities of romance and struggle, and the magic realism genre often found in Latin American literature. Her female characters survive hardships— imprisonment, starvation, the loss of loved ones—but never lose their spirit or ability to love others. Of Allende's *House of Spirits,* which has been compared to that of the Nobel prize-winning author Gabriel García Márquez's *One Hundred Years of Solitude,* Lori Carlson observed in *Review:* ''There is a lot of love in *The House of the Spirits.* The lovemaking of powerful men and naive women, worn-out married couples and anxious rebels might even conjure up the reader's personal experience. But there is another kind of love in this book with which the reader cannot identify. It is a kind that requires forgiving the person whose torturous hand has shoved your face into a bucket of excrement. A spiritual force that can overcome a world sutured with evil, to beget art. Isabel Allende . . . tells in this, her first novel, a vibrant story of struggle and survival dedicated to her mother, grandmother, and 'other extraordinary' women in a country unnamed. Given the descriptions of events and people in the book . . . Chile quickly comes to mind.''

Allende was born on August 2, 1942, in Lima, Peru. Her parents, Tomás, a Chilean diplomat, and Francisca (Llona Barros) Allende divorced when she was three, and she traveled with her mother to Santiago, Chile, where she

was raised in her grandparents' home. Allende graduated from a private high school at the age of 16; three years later in 1962, she married her first husband, Miguel Frías, an engineer. Allende also went to work for the United Nations Food and Agricultural Organization in Santiago, where she was a secretary for several years. Later, she became a journalist, editor, and advice columnist for *Paula* magazine. In addition, she worked as a television interviewer and on movie newsreels.

Fled Chile

When her uncle, Chilean president Salvador Allende, was assassinated in 1973 as part of a right-wing military coup against his socialist government, Allende's life changed profoundly. Initially, she did not think that the new regime would endure, but later she came to realize that it was too dangerous to stay in Chile. As a result, Allende, her husband, and their two children fled to Venezuela. Although she had established a successful career as a journalist in Chile, Allende nevertheless had a difficult time finding work in journalism in Venezuela.

During her life in exile, Allende was inspired to write *The House of the Spirits.* The novel was adapted for the screen by the Danish writer and director Bille August and released in the United States in 1994. Based on Allende's memories of her family and the political upheaval in her native country, the book chronicles the personal and political conflicts in the lives of successive generations of a family in an anonymous Latin American country. These events are principally communicated through the memories of the

novel's three central characters: Esteban and Clara, the patriarch and matriarch of the Trueba family, and Alba, their leftist granddaughter who falls into the hands of torturers during a military coup.

The House of Spirits was followed by *Of Love and Shadows,* which concerns the switching at birth of two infant girls. One of the babies grows up to become the focus of a journalist's investigation, and the revelation of her assassination compels the reporter and photographer to go into exile. The *Detroit Free Press* described *Of Love and Shadows* as "a frightening, powerful work," in which Allende "proves her continued capacity for generating excellent fiction," while the Toronto *Globe and Mail* commented that "Allende has some difficulty in getting her novel started because she has to weave two stories separately, and seems to be relying initially too much on her skills as a journalist."

On a lecture tour to San Jose, California, to promote the publication of *Of Love and Shadows* in the United States, Allende met William Gordon, a lawyer, who was an admirer of her work and with whom she fell in love. Having been divorced from her first husband for about a year, she married Gordon in 1988, and has lived with him in their suburban home in Marin, California, ever since.

Became Powerful Storyteller

Allende's next book, *Eva Luna,* focuses on the relationship between Eva—an illegitimate scriptwriter and storyteller—and Rolfe Carlé—an Austrian émigré filmmaker haunted by his father's Nazi past. The novel received positive reviews; for example, Abigail E. Lee in the *Times Literary Supplement* wrote, "Fears that Isabel Allende might be a 'one-book' writer . . . ought to be quashed by *Eva Luna.. ..* Allende moves between the personal and the political, between realism and fantasy, weaving two exotic coming-of-age stories—Eva Luna's and Rolfe Carlé's—into the turbulent coming of age of her unnamed South American country." Further, Alan Ryan of the *Washington Post Book World* asserted that *Eva Luna* is "a remarkable novel, one in which a cascade of stories tumbles out before the reader, stories vivid and passionate and human enough to engage, in their own right, all the reader's attention and sympathy."

Allende followed up this novel with *Cuentos de Eva Luna* (1991; *The Stories of Eva Luna*), in which the heroine of *Eva Luna* relates several stories to her lover Carlé. According to Alan Ryan in *USA Today,* "These stories transport us to a complex world of sensual pleasures, vivid dreams and breathless longings. It is a world in which passions are fierce, motives are profound and deeds have inexorable consequences." Anne Whitehouse of *The Baltimore Sun* noted that "Ms. Allende possesses the ability to penetrate the hearts of Eva's characters in a few brief sentences. . . . These are profound, transcendent stories, which hold the mirror up to nature and in their strangeness reveal us to ourselves."

The Eva Luna stories were followed by *El plan infinito* (1993; *The Infinite Plan*) which, in a stylistic departure for Allende, features a male hero in a North American setting. Gregory Reeves is the son of a traveling preacher and prophet who settles in the Hispanic barrio of Los Angeles after becoming ill. As the only Anglo boy in the district, Reeves is tormented by local gang members. Eventually, he finds his way out of the barrio, does a tour of duty in Vietnam, and goes on to study law at Berkeley. *The Infinite Plan* received less praise than Allende's previous books; Michiko Kakutani of The *New York Times* described the novel as a "Bildungsroman-cum-family saga that owes more to Judith Krantz than to Gabriel García Márquez," concluding that it is "disappointing and mechanical." Still, as novelist Jane Smiley pointed out in her *Boston Globe* review, "Not many [émigré authors] have even attempted writing a novel from the point of view of a native of the new country."

Allende's latest work, *Paula* (1995), is a heartrending account of the circumstances surrounding the lengthy illness and death of her daughter in 1991. Commenting on the deeply emotive effect of *Paula,* the reviewer for *Publishers Weekly* declared that "[only] a writer of Allende's passion and skill could share her tragedy with her readers and leave them exhilarated and grateful." In September of 1996, Allende was honored at the Hispanic Heritage Awards for her contributions to the Hispanic American community.

Further Reading

Contemporary Literary Criticism, Yearbook 1985, Vol. 39, Detroit, Gale, 1986, pp. 27-36.
Hart, Patricia, *Narrative Magic in the Fiction of Isabel Allende,* Rutherford, NJ, Fairleigh Dickinson University Press, 1989.
Hispanic Writers: A Selection of Sketches from Contemporary Authors, edited by Bryan Ryan, Detroit, Gale, 1991, pp. 15-18.
Baltimore Sun, March 3, 1991.
Boston Globe, May 16, 1993, pp. B39, B42.
Chicago Tribune Bookworld, May 19, 1985, pp. 37-38.
Christian Science Monitor, June 7, 1985; May 27, 1987.
Cosmopolitan, January 1991.
Dallas Morning News, February 1991, pp. 6J, 8J.
Detroit Free Press, June 7, 1987.
Detroit News, June 14, 1987.
Globe and Mail (Toronto), June 24, 1985; June 27, 1987.
London Review of Books, August 1, 1985, pp. 26-27.
Los Angeles Times, February 10, 1988; December 28, 1990, p. E5.
Los Angeles Times Book Review, June 16, 1985; May 31, 1987.
Mother Jones, December 1988, pp. 42-46.
Nation, July 20/27, 1985, pp. 52-54; March 11, 1991, pp. 314-16.
New Statesman, July 5, 1985, p. 29.
Newsweek, May 13, 1985, p. 82.
New York, April 11, 1994, p. 56+.
New York Newsday, July 23, 1993.
New York Review of Books, July 18, 1985, pp. 20-23.
New York Times, May 2, 1985; May 9, 1985, p. 23; May 20, 1987; February 4, 1988; June 25, 1993.
New York Times Book Review, May 12, 1985, pp. 1, 22-23; July 12, 1987; October 23, 1988; January 20, 1991.
Observer, June 7, 1985, p. 21.
People, June 10, 1985, p. 145; June 1, 1987.
Philadelphia Inquirer, March 3, 1991.
Publishers Weekly, March 1, 1985, p. 70; May 17, 1985; March 20, 1995.
Review, January-June, 1985, pp. 77-78.
Spectator, August 3, 1985.
Time, May 20, 1985, p. 79.
Times (London), July 4, 1985; July 9, 1987; March 22, 1989; March 23, 1989.
Times Literary Supplement, July 5, 1985; July 10, 1987; April 7-13, 1989.
Tribune Books (Chicago), October 9, 1988.
U.S. News and World Report, November 21, 1988.
USA Today, June 7, 1985, p. 4D; March 1, 1991.
Village Voice. June 4, 1985, p. 51; June 7, 1985.
Voice Literary Supplement, December, 1988.
Washington Post Book World, May 12, 1985, pp. 3-4; May 24, 1987; October 9, 1988. □

Salvador Allende Gossens

Salvador Allende Gossens (1908-1973) was President of Chile from 1970 to 1973. He died in the Presidential Palace during the brutal military coup which installed a military dictatorship in Chile in 1973. Allende dedicated his life to the cause of socialism in Chile, serving as a congressman, senator, and government minister during his long public career.

Salvador Allende Gossens was born in Valparaíso, Chile, on July 26, 1908. Allende's family had a long tradition of political involvement in progressive and liberal causes. His father and uncles participated in the reformist efforts of the Radical Party in the 19th and early 20th centuries. His grandfather founded one of the first lay schools in Chile when the Catholic Church claimed hegemony over education. The family also had roots in Chilean freemasonry, with Allende's grandfather serving as a Most Serene Grand Master of the Masonic Order.

In an interview with French Marxist Régis Debray in 1971, Allende also credited an anarchist shoemaker, Juan Demarchi, for contributing to his early political education during his teenage years. In the shoemaker's shop, after school, Allende was introduced to revolutionary theory and the reality of artisan radicalism in early 20th-century Chile.

Following in the footsteps of his uncle Ramon Allende, who was the organizer of Chile's medical services during the country's war with Bolivia and Peru (1879-1883), Salvador Allende began his medical studies at the age of 18 and received his medical degree in 1932. His involvement in university politics as a leader of the Chilean Student Federation found him active in student protests against dictator Carlos Ibáñez (1927-1931), and Allende was arrested on more than one occasion. Allende's brother-in-law was the brother of Marmaduque Grove, leader of Chile's short-lived "Socialist Republic" of 1932. Shortly after Grove's government fell, Allende's father died and at the funeral Allende declared, "I would dedicate my life to the social struggle, and I believe that I have fulfilled that promise."

Allende married Hortensia Bussi, and the couple had three daughters—Paz, Isabel, and Beatriz. His family remained committed to his personal struggles and to his political commitments throughout his life, with Beatriz actually

Cuba in the first month of Fidel Castro's new government and enjoyed close contacts with Fidel, Raul Castro, and Che Guevara. Allende cherished a copy of Che Guevara's *Guerrilla Warfare* inscribed "To Salvador Allende, who is trying to obtain the same result by other means, Affectionately, Che."

In the Chilean Senate Allende consistently defended the interests of the working classes, attacked capitalism and imperialism, defended the Cuban Revolution, and vocally supported the guerrilla movements in Latin America in the 1960s and 1970s. Allende strongly supported OLAS, the Cuban-based solidarity movement for Latin American revolutionaries, and glorified the memory of Che Guevara after his death in Bolivia in 1967. Though rejecting violent revolution for Chile, Allende proclaimed the necessity for revolutionary change, for socialist transformation, "through democracy, pluralism and freedom."

The Allende Presidency

In 1970 Allende was elected president of Chile as the candidate of a leftist coalition called *Unidad Popular,* or Popular Unity. A coalition of Socialists, Communists, Radicals, Catholic leftists, and other minor parties, this coalition represented less than 40 percent of the electorate but was victorious in a three-way election by a narrow plurality. Seeking to carry out dramatic social, economic, and political reforms, including nationalization of Chile's major natural resources, large industries, banking, and trade, the Popular Unity coalition faced stiff internal opposition and the animosity of the Nixon administration in the United States. President Allende attempted to hold together his coalition and to deal with ever more intense internal opposition along with economic sanctions, both overt and covert, applied by the United States. Allende's commitment to socialism, though more moderate than many of his allies, nevertheless generated significant polarization of Chilean society. Economic difficulties, caused both by poor economic planning and by internal and external adversaries, exacerbated political conflict within the country.

By mid-1973 the Chilean economy was experiencing high levels of inflation and serious declines in productivity as the internal opposition to the government became more militant. Finally, on September 11, 1973, the armed forces mounted a nationally coordinated coup d'etat in which large numbers of civilians were killed, wounded, and or imprisoned. President Allende refused to surrender and leave the country as the coup leaders demanded, instead fighting against the military from the presidential palace with an automatic weapon given to him by Fidel Castro. Allende died during the coup, with conflicting reports claiming he committed suicide or was murdered by the soldiers who stormed the presidential palace after it was attacked by air force planes.

In his last broadcast from the palace to the people of Chile, Allende gave inspiration to his followers for the years of military dictatorship that were to follow: "I have faith in Chile and in its destiny. Other men will overcome this dark and bitter moment, when treason stands to conquer. May you go forward in the knowledge that, sooner rather than

shouldering arms alongside her father in the presidential palace during the 1973 military coup. His wife and other family members continued active resistance to the military government both within Chile and from exile after Allende's death in 1973.

Allende and Chilean Socialism

In 1933 Allende joined more well-known political leaders in founding the Chilean Socialist Party. As leader of the Socialists in Valparaíso, where he worked in public health, Allende was elected to the Chilean Congress as a deputy in 1937 and served as minister of health in a "Popular Front" government in 1939 and again in 1941, when he also assumed a major leadership post in the Socialist Party.

In 1943 Allende led a majority faction of the Socialists out of the Popular Front coalition, breaking with the old Socialist *caudillo,* Grove. Allende emerged as secretary general of the splintered party. As he was to do for the rest of his life, Allende declared his commitment to Marxism, socialism, democracy, and nationalism—to promote an independent and unique Chilean road to socialism.

From 1945 until his election as president of Chile, Salvador Allende served in the Chilean senate as a leading member of the Socialist Party. He served five years as vice-president of the Senate and two years as its president. In 1952, 1958, and 1964 Allende was the presidential candidate of leftist coalitions; in 1958 Allende barely lost the presidency to Jorge Alessandri. Shortly thereafter he visited later, the great avenues will open once again along which free citizens will march in order to build a better society."

Further Reading

Much has been written about the presidency of Salvador Allende in Chile, but there is no detailed study of his life and career in English. Allende's own writing and speeches provide a clear idea of his early commitment to improving the life of the majority of Chile's people and of his political values. Examples of Allende's speeches and interview material can be found in Salvador Allende, *Chile's Road to Socialism* (1973); Régis Debray, *The Chilean Revolution* (1971); and "An Interview with Allende" in *New Chile* (1973). A number of books dealing with Allende in the Chilean political system include Stefan de Vylder, *Allende's Chile* (1976); Paul Sigmund, *The Overthrow of Allende and the Politics of Chile, 1964-1976* (1977); Paul Drake, *Socialism and Populism in Chile, 1932-52* (1978); Arturo Valenzuela, *The Breakdown of Democratic Regimes: Chile* (1978); and Brian Loveman, *Chile* (1979). □

Washington Allston

America's first important painter of the romantic movement, Washington Allston (1779-1843) created landscapes, historical scenes, and literary pieces that exude dramatic terror as well as quiet mystery.

Washington Allston was born in South Carolina in 1779. After graduating from Harvard College in 1800, he returned to Charleston and sold his share of the family property to finance his career as an artist. In May 1801 Allston and the miniaturist painter Edward G. Malbone left for England.

Years in Europe

Allston studied at the School of the Royal Academy in London. He learned the use of underpainting and glazes to produce the rich atmospheric effect necessary to the realization of his later romantic paintings. Allston was in Paris in 1803-1804 and in Rome from 1804 to 1808, where he knew the English poet Samuel Taylor Coleridge and the American author Washington Irving. In Italy he especially admired the work of the great Venetian painters Titian, Tintoretto, and Paolo Veronese. He appreciated the bravura of their technique and the resonance of their tone (which, he later wrote, moved not only his senses but his imagination). He tried to emulate these qualities in his own grandiose historical and literary paintings and his landscapes and seascapes, such as the *Rising of a Thunderstorm at Sea* (1804).

Allston returned to America in 1808 and stayed in Boston, occupying the very room that the painters John Copley and John Trumbull had used. During this period he married and did many portraits of his family and friends, such as the soft, languorous portrait of William Ellery Channing (1809-1811), as well as humorous genre scenes. In 1811 he sailed with his wife and Samuel F. B. Morse for

England, where his wife died in 1815. Among the paintings of this second English period were the *Angel Releasing St. Peter from Prison* (1812) and the *Dead Man Revived by Touching the Bones of the Prophet Elisha* (1811-1813), both developed into scenes of Gothic suspense.

American Period

Allston returned to America in 1818 (where he would remain for the rest of his life), residing in Boston but spending much time in Cambridge. His friends at this time included the portrait painter Thomas Sully and the sculptor Horatio Greenough. In 1830 Allston married Martha R. Dana, the sister of the novelist Richard H. Dana; Dana was a cousin of Allston's first wife. The couple settled in Cambridgeport, Mass. Allston continued to lead a rather rarefied existence: his friends were exclusively artists and writers. Allston's lack of sympathy for the widely popular president Andrew Jackson and all that he represented in terms of mass culture was behind his refusal of a commission to decorate the rotunda of the Capitol in Washington.

Times had changed in the United States, and Allston felt out of place. His old confidence was gone. The literati—people like Ralph Waldo Emerson and Dana—admired his work, but to the public he meant nothing. In America, portraiture and, to some extent, landscape were all that most people cared for. In Europe, Allston had painted scenes of either a dramatically bizarre or a sweetly joyous nature. In Europe he had pandered more openly to the emotions, liking especially themes of supernatural salvation; his American paintings are usually more intimate and smaller in scale than those done in Europe.

Allston painted from memory several Italian landscapes, the most memorable being *Moonlight Landscape* (1819); with four mysterious figures in the foreground, it casts a quietly eerie spell. The heroic *Belshazzar's Feast* (1817-1843) was out of keeping with the more subdued mood of the American period. This huge canvas, begun in Europe, was taken up, put down, and taken up again at the end of Allston's life but never finished. Allston was preparing to work on the figure of the King on the day of his death. The painting was commissioned by 10 friends for $10,000; the image of the prophet Daniel interpreting the handwriting on the wall haunted Allston to the point that he found himself unable to undertake other commissions. Dana spoke of it as "that terrible vision . . . the tormentor of his life. . . . " In a sense, Allston's failure to complete this work demonstrates the isolation and frustration of the American artist who wished to do something more than portraiture and landscape in the first half of the 19th century.

Literary Inspiration

Few American painters of Allston's time drew from literature, and certainly none as deeply and broadly as he. He made frequent use of his literary background and interests in his painting: *Uriel in the Sun* (1817) was drawn from Book III of Milton's *Paradise Lost,* and *Flight of Florimell* (1819) from Spenser's *Faerie Queen.* Allston knew the Old and New Testaments well and sometimes chose to depict obscure passages, such as the *Dead Man Revived* from the account of 2 Kings, chapter 13. He produced a volume of poems in 1810 called *The Sylphs of the Seasons, with Other Poems.* "The Sylphs of the Seasons" dealt with the influence of each of the seasons upon the creative imagination. The most important of his writings, *Lectures on Art,* published posthumously in 1850 but neglected until the early 20th century, set forth a theory of art as creation and imagination and dealt systematically with such abstruse topics as invention and originality.

Allston's Importance

Allston probably influenced the course of 19th-century American painting more profoundly than any other artist. He did this not only in a general way by extending the scope of painting beyond the bounds of portraiture but also by originating certain fashions and propounding ideas that were continued. For example, the scene of the tiny figure dwarfed pictorially by the grandeur and vastness of nature (*Elijah Being Fed by the Ravens,* 1818) was taken up by many painters of the later Hudson River school. His tendency to think cyclically in terms of the beginnings and endings of periods of nature and empires (*Belshazzar's Feast*) led to the "catastrophic" paintings of Thomas Cole's "Course of Empire" series and others. Allston's insistence that colors and forms could produce psychological reactions in the spectator, regardless of the subject of the painting, anticipated the work of James McNeill Whistler and the thinking of early-20th-century theoreticians of nonobjective painting. Most specifically, Allston was the first American

painter to draw more from the workings of his personal inner vision than from external reality. In the 19th century alone, he was the forebear of such painters as John Quidor and Albert P. Ryder.

Further Reading

Edgar P. Richardson and Henry W. L. Dana, *Washington Allston: A Study of the Romantic Artist in America* (1948), is a catalogue of the existing and recorded paintings by Allston. See also Oliver W. Larkin, *Art and Life in America* (1949; rev. ed. 1960). Virgil Barker, *American Painting: History and Interpretation* (1950), and James T. Flexner, *The Light of Distant Skies, 1760-1835* (1954; new ed. 1969), offer contrasting interpretations of Allston's work. □

Diego de Almagro

The Spanish conqueror and explorer Diego de Almagro (ca. 1474-1538) had an important share in the Inca conquest and was the first European to visit Chile by land.

Diego de Almagro was a foundling, born probably in the town of Almagro, near Ciudad Real. His first 40 years are obscure, though he appears to have had a military career. He reached America in 1514 with the fleet that brought the Spanish conqueror Pedrarias (Pedro Arias de Avila) to govern the Isthmus of Darien.

In 1524 Almagro formed a partnership with Francisco Pizarro and the priest Hernando de Luque, Vicar of Panama, to investigate reports of Inca wealth to the south. The two lay partners had no financial means, but Luque was able to borrow the money. Pedrarias was uninterested in the enterprise and made no objection, and Pizarro sailed late in 1524. Almagro was delayed several months but then followed the present Colombian coast to a point near modern Buenaventura. Unable to locate Pizarro, he returned to the Isthmus to find him already there.

Gaspar de Espinosa then advanced 20,000 pesos de oro, which enabled the partners to sail again, each in his own ship. Again they divided company: Pizarro after many adventures reached the Inca city of Tumbes, while Almagro returned to Panama ahead of him. Pizarro then went to Spain to secure a royal commission for the Peruvian conquest. Almagro trusted him, as Luque obviously did not, to deal fairly with his associates and was angry upon learning that Pizarro had obtained the major concession for himself. Pizarro somewhat appeased him with explanations, but the two were never friendly thereafter, though Almagro continued to cooperate.

Pizarro invaded Peru first, and Almagro joined him at Cajamarca early in 1533 shortly before the Spaniards executed Sapa Inca Atahualpa. Almagro helped preside over the tribunal that condemned Atahualpa to death.

The four Pizarro brothers now had a firm grip on Peru, so Almagro for a time accepted Francisco's orders. He occu-

pied Riobamba in present-day Ecuador and then met Pedro de Alvarado, who had come from Guatemala to share the Peruvian wealth. Almagro prepared the way for a bargain whereby Pizarro paid Alvarado 100,000 pesos de oro to leave Peru.

Almagro next went to Tchili (Chile), where he hoped to win a rich realm for himself. Suffering great hardships, the party reached Coquimbo and there received an unfavorable report of the country ahead. Almagro turned back to Peru, where the Pizarros meanwhile had nearly crushed the rebellion of Inca Manco. Almagro scattered the remnants of Manco's army and then seized Cuzco, inviting war with the Pizarros. He defeated one Pizarrist army at the Abancay River but was then defeated and captured by Hernando Pizarro at the battle of Las Salinas near Cuzco. Had Francisco Pizarro been present, he might have spared his old partner's life. Hernando, however, had always hated Almagro and had him beheaded in July 1538 after a mock trial in which the major charge was rebellion against the Crown.

Almagro sired a mestizo son in Panama, known to the Spaniards as Almagro the Lad. The Lad headed the conspirators who murdered Francisco Pizarro in Lima on June 26, 1541. Young Almagro was executed by the Pizarrists the following year.

Further Reading

The classic narrative is William Hickling Prescott, *History of the Conquest of Peru* (2 vols., 1847; many later editions). Philip A.

Means, *Fall of the Inca Empire and Spanish Rule in Peru: 1530-1780* (1932), covers Almagro's career in less detail. Frederick A. Kirkpatrick, *The Spanish Conquistadores* (1934; 2d ed. 1946), also deals with Almagro. Hoffman Birney, *Brothers of Doom: The Story of the Pizarros of Peru* (1942), gives the highlights of Almagro's career. Pedro Cieza de Léon's 16th-century work, *Civil Wars in Peru: The War of Las Salinas* (trans. 1923), describes Almagro's fight against the Pizarros and his death. □

Alp Arslan

Alp Arslan (1026-1072) was the second Seljuk sultan of Persia and Iraq and a member of the Turkish dynasty which revitalized Moslem rule in the declining days of the Abbasid caliphate.

Alp Arslan was born Muhammad ibn Daud in the Arab Empire's Persian province of Khurasan in 1026 (or 1029 or 1032). He was the great-grandson of Seljuk, chieftain of the Ghuzz Turkomans, who had invaded southwestern Asia in the 11th century.

Famed as a military leader, Alp Arslan—his name means "Lion Hero"—began his career campaigning extensively for his father, Daud Chaghri Beg, commander of the Turkoman forces in Khurasan. Upon his father's death in 1059/1060, Alp Arslan succeeded. Meanwhile, Seljuk forces under Chaghri's brother, Tughril Beg, had ended a century of Shiite Buyid dominance in Baghdad, whereupon Caliph al-Kaim made him sultan. With Tughril's death in 1063, Alp Arslan succeeded, despite an attempt to enthrone Tughril's brother Suleiman.

The new sultan was immediately faced with internal opposition. His father's cousin, Kutulmish, carried Khurasan into revolt in 1064, and his own brother, Kawurd (founder of the Kirman dynasty), rebelled twice, in 1064 and 1067.

Between the suppression of recalcitrant subordinates, Alp Arslan campaigned against his neighbors. His first major move was a raid in 1064 into Georgia and Armenia, during which the Georgian king acknowledged Seljuk suzerainty. The following year the Sultan led his forces into Transoxiana. In 1070 he took Aleppo during a campaign into Syria. His holdings then reached from central Asia to the Mediterranean.

Alp Arslan was a courageous man, generous in his treatment of opponents. His strength lay in the military realm, domestic affairs being handled by his Persian vizier, Nizam al-Mulk, founder of the administrative organization which characterized and strengthened the sultanate during the reigns of Alp Arslan and his son. Military fiefs, governed by Seljuk princes, were established to provide support for the soldiery and to accommodate the nomadic Turks to the established Persian agricultural scene.

Meanwhile, not only the Seljuks but independent Turkish bands had been harassing the Byzantine frontier. When the Byzantine emperor, Romanus IV Diogenes, led his forces into the sultanate in 1071 in retaliation, Alp Arslan left Syria and on August 26 met the invaders at Manzikert near Lake Van. This battle, which turned largely on the superior Turkish cavalry, was a crucial one since it opened Anatolia to Turkoman appropriation, although Seljuk authority was not consolidated there until the Rum sultanate was founded in 1155. An indication of Alp Arslan's character appears in his generous treatment of Romanus, who was sent home after the peace settlement with presents and a military escort.

In 1072, campaigning in Turkestan, Alp Arslan was stabbed by the captive commander of a recently conquered fortress. He died soon after, on November 24, and was succeeded by his son Malik Shah.

Further Reading

One of the few works on the Seljuks is Tamara Talbot Rice, *The Seljuks in Asia Minor* (1961). General coverage is provided in W. Barthold, *Turkestan down to the Mongol Invasion* (2 vols., 1898-1900; trans. 1928); Sir Percy Sykes, *A History of Persia* (2 vols., 1915; 3d ed. 1930); and Philip K. Hitti, *History of the Arabs: From the Earliest Times to the Present* (1937; 8th rev. ed. 1963). □

Rafael Altamira Y Crevea

The Spanish literary critic, historian, and jurist Rafael Altamira y Crevea (1866-1951) was, in his generation, the foremost Spanish proponent of the scientific method in history. He devoted his life as a jurist to international peace.

Rafael Altamira was born in Alicante on Feb. 10, 1866. He formed a lifelong attachment to his native city and was once described by a disciple as a man with "a southern character, always enthusiastic and optimistic." He received his doctorate at the University of Madrid in 1887. His first major work, *History of Communal Property* (1888), established a European-wide reputation and was soon translated into Russian and German. His next work, *The Teaching of History* (1891), marked him as the major advocate of scientific historical writing in Spain. It gave a new direction to historical scholarship on the Peninsula.

Altamira had already published critical literary articles as a student. He maintained this interest through his early years as a professor, writing novellas and stories as well as literary criticism. In 1895 he founded the *Revista critica de historia y literatura Españolas, Portuguesas y Hispanoamericanas,* the first review of its kind in Spain.

In 1897 Altamira won a professorship at the University of Oviedo. He now set out to promote popular education through the creation of a university extension and to renew Spanish historical scholarship. During the next 15 years he published a monumental *History of Spain* (4 vols., 1900-1911), a *History of Spanish Law* (1903-1904), history text-

books for secondary schools, and numerous articles on Spanish history for the *Grande encyclopédie,* the *Cambridge Modern History,* and the *Revue historique.* In 1909-1910 he made an extended tour of Latin America to establish contacts between Spanish universities and the universities of that area. From 1911 to 1913 he was director of primary education in Spain.

Throughout his work Altamira maintained that true history was cultural history "which the history of kings and battles obeys passively, like the skin obeys the muscles." In the intellectual world of Spain these views were considered revolutionary and made him one of the leaders of the generation immediately preceding World War I.

In 1919 Altamira was named to the committee to create an international court of justice, and in 1921 he was elected to the Permanent International Court at The Hague. Although he continued to teach and write on Latin American history as a professor at Madrid, he now devoted most of his energies to the cause of international peace, lecturing and writing on the subject in addition to his work on the Court.

The Spanish Civil War drove him into exile, first to The Hague, then in 1940 to Bayonne, France, and finally in 1945 to Mexico City. He maintained his interest in historical scholarship to the end. In 1951 he was nominated for the Nobel Peace Prize, but he died on June 1 before the vote was taken.

Further Reading

John E. Fagg's chapter, "Rafael Altamira," in Bernadotte E. Schmitt, ed., *Some Historians of Modern Europe: Essays in Historiography by Former Students of the University of Chicago* (1942), discusses Altamira's historical writing and his reforms in Spanish education. □

Albrecht Altdorfer

The German painter, draftsman, printmaker, and architect Albrecht Altdorfer (ca. 1480-1538) contributed to the evolution of landscape painting. He was a major figure of the so-called Danube school, whose artists created a fantastic, picturesque style of landscape painting.

The son of the engraver Ulrich Altdorfer, Albrecht Altdorfer was probably born at Regensburg. In 1505 Albrecht was listed as a painter from Amberg when he became a citizen of Regensburg. By 1513 he was married and purchased a house at Regensburg.

Throughout his life Altdorfer was active in the affairs of his city. In 1519 he is mentioned as a member of the City Council for External Affairs, and in 1526 he was elected to the City Council for Internal Affairs. That year he was appointed city architect, in which capacity he supervised the building of the city wine cellars and slaughterhouse (1527). In 1528 he declined to allow the city to elect him mayor. His wife died in 1532, leaving him a childless widower. Altdorfer was a member of the council which, in 1533, decided to adopt Lutheranism at Regensburg. In 1535 he traveled to the imperial court in Vienna on an official visit for the city of Regensburg. He died on Feb. 14, 1538, and was buried in the church of the Augustine Cloister, of which he had been named overseer in 1534. A prosperous citizen, at his death he owned several houses and had numerous other possessions.

The Paintings

Altdorfer's earliest preserved works are chiefly engravings and drawings, which show a marked interest in Italian prints, noticeable also in his first signed painting, the *Satyr Family* (1507). This panel, a *St. George in a Wood* (1510), and a *Holy Night* (1510-1515) are small and reveal a characteristically poetic feeling for the minutiae and light of landscape. In *St. George in a Wood* the landscape elements are so fused in color and detail with the figures as to render the latter almost indistinct, and in the *Holy Night* the mysterious moonlight shining on the bricks and wood relegates the figures to a secondary role.

After 1510 Altdorfer's paintings became larger, and he employed a more monumental and heroic language with vivid coloring. Particularly indicative is the altar (ca. 1518) for the monastery of Sankt Florian, near Linz, Austria. Consisting of scenes from the Passion and from the legend of St. Sebastian, the work is striking for its dynamic movements, bold spatial effects with strong foreshortenings and emphatic perspective schemes influenced by the painting of Michael Pacher, and dramatic lighting effects. These characteristics are also present, though more subdued, in the panels of the *Finding of the Body of St. Florian* (ca. 1520) and the *Birth of the Virgin* (ca. 1521). During this period, which lasted until about 1526, Altdorfer produced his first pure landscape paintings, of which the *Danube Landscape near Regensburg* (ca. 1521) is an outstanding example.

In the work of his last period, from about 1526, Altdorfer became increasingly interested in color and in architectural constructions of Renaissance inspiration. This may be observed especially in *Susanna at the Bath* (1526) and the *Allegory of Riches and Poverty* (1531). In *Lot and His Daughters* (1537) and the 22 surviving fragments of fresco decoration that he executed for the Emperor's Bath in the Bishop's Palace, Regensburg, about 1530, Altdorfer adopted Italian Renaissance figure forms but with a flavor that was distinctly German. His most important painting of the period, the *Battle of Alexander* (1529), commissioned by Duke Wilhelm IV of Bavaria, illustrates Altdorfer's ability to organize a multitude of detail of miniaturistic scale in a cosmological vision that embraces both sky and terrain. The personal fate of the protagonists, Alexander and Darius, is subordinated to the agitated action of the armies in the vast panorama.

Drawings and Graphic Work

Among Altdorfer's many drawings, the marginal illustrations he did for the Prayer Book of Emperor Maximilian I in 1515 hold an important place. Altdorfer's engravings share the general characteristics of the Nuremberg school, whose direction was determined by the graphic art of Albrecht Dürer. The earliest ones date between 1506 and 1511, and a larger group belongs to the later years of Altdorfer's life. His graphic work also includes several etchings of landscapes, about 1520, and woodcuts executed mostly between 1511 and 1522 by skilled woodcut artists after his designs.

Further Reading

There is an extensive literature on Altdorfer in German. In English see Emil Waldmann, ed., *Albrecht Altdorfer: Catalogue of Engravings and Etchings* (1923), and F. W. H. Hollstein, *German Engravings, Etchings, and Woodcuts ca. 1400-1700* (1954). For background information see Otto Benesch, *The Art of the Renaissance in Northern Europe* (1945; rev. ed. 1965).

Additional Sources

Wood, Christopher S., *Albrecht Altdorfer and the origins of landscape,* Chicago: University of Chicago Press, 1993. □

John Peter Altgeld

American reformer and jurist and a governor of Illinois, John Peter Altgeld (1847-1902) became nationally prominent when, in 1893, he pardoned three anarchists convicted of the Haymarket bom-

bing and, in 1894, was critical of the Federal government's intervention in the Pullman strike.

John Peter Altgeld was born at Nieder-Selters, Germany, on Dec. 30, 1847, and was brought to the United States by his parents when he was 3 months old. He grew up in Mansfield, Ohio, quitting school at the age of 12 when his father insisted that he work full time on the family farm.

In 1864 Altgeld volunteered for military service in the Civil War. After brief duty on the eastern front, he returned to Mansfield and entered high school against his father's wishes. He did so well in his studies that at 19 he was teaching school himself. At 21 Altgeld went west, working on a railroad-building crew in Arkansas until illness forced him to stop. Virtually penniless and still sick, he wandered eastward to Savannah, Mo., where he settled.

Beginning Politician

Altgeld's fortunes improved rapidly from this point as his talents and immense energy began to assert themselves. While teaching school, he studied law and was admitted to the bar in 1871. The next year he was appointed city attorney. In 1874 he won his first election as the Democratic and Granger candidate for county attorney. He resigned a year later to move to Chicago.

There Altgeld established himself in two areas, real estate and politics. He began to invest in property, and in the early 1880s he started constructing buildings as well.

Soon his transactions in real estate and office buildings involved hundreds of thousands of dollars. At the same time he built up political connections, which led to his nomination in 1884 as Democratic candidate for Congress. Although he failed to carry the normally Republican district, he ran well. In the same year he published *Our Penal Machinery and Its Victims,* in which he criticized the tendency of the penal system to discriminate against poor persons. In 1886 he was elected to the superior court of Cook County as the Democratic and United Labor party candidate.

Altgeld was an impartial and forceful jurist, but he was dissatisfied with the judgeship and worked for higher political office. His public-speaking appearances featured endorsements of antisweatshop legislation, 8-hour laws, and union rights—views published in his book *Live Questions* (1890). Failing in a bid for the U.S. Senate in 1891 and worn out by his varied commitments, he resigned his judgeship to devote himself to his most ambitious construction project, a 16-story skyscraper which he called the Unity Block.

Governor of Illinois

In 1892 Altgeld returned to politics as the Democratic gubernatorial nominee, winning the election by carrying Chicago decisively. As the first Democratic governor of Illinois since the Civil War, Altgeld rewarded loyal Democratic party members with patronage plums, being fairly ruthless in the dismissal of Republican appointees. However, his appointment of Florence Kelley, a leading settlement-house reformer, indicated his commitment to progressive ideas. Though the reform legislation passed during his gubernatorial years was not extensive, it did include a factory inspection law, a women's 8-hour law, and an act prohibiting discrimination against union members.

A National Figure

Altgeld achieved national notoriety in 1893, when he pardoned three anarchists who had been convicted of complicity in the infamous 1886 bomb-throwing incident that had killed several policemen at Haymarket Square, Chicago. (Four of the others convicted had been hanged and one had committed suicide.) Altgeld refused to take the politically expedient course of granting clemency on grounds of mercy; instead he attacked the conviction on legal grounds. His case against the presiding judge was worded very severely. Public reaction was largely negative, branding Altgeld as an anarchist and demagogue who sought to undermine the court system.

Altgeld's conduct during the Pullman strike in 1894 was widely censured, especially by conservatives. In May the men at George M. Pullman's works near Chicago had gone on strike, supported by the American Railway Union's national boycott of Pullman cars. President Cleveland's attorney general, Richard Olney (formerly a railroad lawyer), struck back early in July and got an injunction against the union leadership. Knowing that some minor violence had occurred, Altgeld stood ready to send state troops to maintain order, as he had in earlier strikes. But Olney and Cleveland ignored Altgeld and sent Federal troops to Chicago. In spite of Altgeld's strenuous protest that Federal intervention without the request of state officials was unconstitutional, the strike was broken by the Cleveland administration's decision.

From 1894 to 1896 Altgeld was a leader of the growing anti-Cleveland element within the Democratic party. At the party's Chicago convention in 1896, Altgeld's views triumphed. Although he was not especially impressed with William Jennings Bryan, he was pleased that Bryan's nomination and the free-silver platform decisively repudiated Cleveland's leadership.

The remainder of Altgeld's career was less happy. He had overextended himself financially to build the Unity Block, and debts plagued him. His political power remained great, but his influence brought him little success. He was defeated for reelection in 1896, although he ran ahead of the rest of the Democratic ticket in Illinois. Though he successfully promoted Carter Harrison II for mayor of Chicago, Harrison proved to be very conservative. In 1899 Altgeld ran against Harrison as an independent and finished third in a three-way race. He figured prominently in Bryan's renomination in 1900, only to see Bryan defeated again. At the time of Altgeld's death on March 12, 1902, it seemed that public opinion had rejected his views. However, despite the widespread criticism of his major public acts, he had won the loyalty of many progressives, and his reputation—based on his sympathy for the disadvantaged—has grown rather than diminished in recent years.

Further Reading

Some of Altgeld's major speeches are collected in Henry M. Christman, ed., *The Mind and Spirit of John Peter Altgeld: Selected Writings and Addresses* (1960). There are two excellent books on Altgeld: Harry Barnard, *Eagle Forgotten: The Life of John Peter Altgeld* (1938), and Ray Ginger, *Altgeld's America: The Lincoln Ideal versus Changing Realities* (1958), which discusses some of Altgeld's contemporaries. These studies largely supersede the biography by Waldo R. Browne, *Altgeld of Illinois: A Record of His Life and Work* (1924). See also Arthur and Lila Weinberg, *Some Dissenting Voices* (1970). □

Louis Althusser

Aligned with the French Communist Party, philosopher Louis Althusser (1918-1990) strove to explain contemporary developments by reinterpreting the doctrines of Karl Marx and Friedrich Engels.

Louis Althusser was born at Birmandreis, Algeria (then a colony of France), October 16, 1918. He was briefly imprisoned in concentration camps in World War II. In 1948 he took his degree in philosophy from the Ecole Normale Supérieure in Paris and taught there for the next 32 years. In 1980 he strangled his wife and lived most of the next ten years, until his death in 1990, confined to mental asylums.

Intellectual Revolutionary

Prior to and through World War II, 1939-1945, Althusser was involved in the Roman Catholic youth movement and advocated some of the church's more conservative teachings. During the Nazi occupation of France his thinking underwent a radical transformation, as he along with many others embraced Marxist ideologies. During this time he found himself involved with the French Resistance and attracted to one of its more prominent activists, Helene Legotier, eight years his senior and a member of the French Communist Party (PCF). In 1948 Althusser also joined the party. After the war Legotier continued her activism, while Althusser spent most of his time in academia. His lectures and writings became very influential and he was seen by many to be the party's most outstanding intellectual.

Althusser attempted to reconcile the views of French *structuralism* with those of Marxism by denying the primary role of the individual subject in the face of historically unfolding social structures. His most important works are *For Marx* (1965), *Lenin and Philosophy* (1969), and his contributions to a book of essays called *Reading Capital,* all of which were popular with student revolutionaries during the decade of social upheaval in the 1960s.

While many Marxists were looking for a more "humane" alternative to the totalitarianism unfolding in the Soviet Union and a way to resolve the split caused by the Chinese revolution, Althusser, taking the opposite tack, proposed a purely scientific approach, one he ascribed to the maturing Marx himself in *For Marx,* (1970). In *Reading Capital* and in *Lenin and Philosophy and Other Essays* (1971) he aimed at an objective account of how the total society works from its technological top down, generating the classes that run and do the work of a society. In the latter collection he described how such a structure operates through the languages we speak in common. These, he said, tend to instill in people their sense of reality and of themselves and their social roles, all in the interest of perpetuating the order of the given society: this is the thought-controlling use of language called "ideology."

Structuralist Analysis

Althusser sketched the underlying fabric of a society with the help of French "structuralist" theory. This led to the development of a comprehensive and intricate Marxist model for society as a whole, although access to the model is made difficult by Althusser's style and terminology.

In the structuralist view society cannot be understood through the subjective experience of individuals seen as in some way differentiated from the unfolding processes in which they are enmeshed. A society functions as a single organism in a manner determined by its technology and its modes of production. Every individual action is solely determined by its role in relation to that technology. Althusser's critique was partly in reaction to prevailing individualistic philosophies, as well as the increasingly embarrassing historical degenerations of the Marxist system under Stalin. Critics of Altusser's thinking largely objected to the extreme austerity of a system which denies the primacy of the subjective experience, insisting that a system which so entirely subordinates the individual to the "total" structure can never hope to sustain itself in any realm other than the theoretical.

The Chinese experience reminded Marxists that "contradictions" were the essence of their world view; unity is achieved only through the play of opposites, and all "wholes" contain and even consist of the struggles internal to them. As an organism breaks down food to build up nourishment, the state takes life to protect itself. Later disciples of Althusser would point out that both language and personality reveal inherent tensions in the makeup of the self. These as oppositions can be counted on to result in change and progress as they are products of the internalization of "idealistic" structures in the society as a whole. Marxists who preferred to see change as brought on from "the bottom up" (the oppressed, the working class) criticized Althusser for this scheme of resistance from "the inside out" (the repressed inside any group, body, or system: in the economic system, workers). Others found this to be one of his most fruitful new turns of thought.

Madness and Obscurity

Althusser long suffered as a manic depressive, Legotier acting as his nurse. In 1976 they were married, but in November of 1980 the philosopher strangled his wife to death and was committed to a Paris hospital for the insane. He spent the last ten years of his life in and out of various institutions. During this time he continued to write essays, attempting to explain his homicidal action in the light of a wider social analysis. A posthumous autobiography of collected memoirs, *The Future Lasts Forever,* was published in 1992.

Further Reading

A great deal has been written on Louis Althusser and his theories. The best source of information on Althusser's philosophy is his own published works, including *Essays in Self-Criticism* (London, 1976), *For Marx* (1970), *Lenin and Philosophy and Other Essays* (1971), *Politics and History* (London, 1972), *Reading Capital* (with Etienne Balibar) (London, 1970), and his posthumous *Politics and History* (New York, 1993). Books discussing Althusser and his theories include the first volume of a biography by his friend Yann Moulier Boutang, *Louis Althusser: une biographie, Volume 1: La formation du mythe 1918-1956, Althusser: A Critical Reader* (Cambridge, Mass., 1994); Gregory Eliot, ed., *The Althusserian Legacy* (New York, 1993); E. Ann Kaplan and Michael Sprinker, eds., and Robert Paul Resch, *Althusser and the Renewal of Marxist Social Theory* (Berkeley, 1992). In addition, the following works include discussions of Althusser and his contributions: Perry Anderson, *Considerations on Western Marxism* (London, 1976); Richard and Fernande de George, eds., *The Structuralists from Marx to Levi-Strauss* (1972); Margaret A. Majumdar, *Althusser and the End of Leninism* (1995); Steven Smith, *Reading Althusser: An Essay on Structural Marxism* (Cornell, 1984); Gregory Elliott, *Althusser: A Critical Reader* (1994); Michael Payne, *Reading Knowledge: An Introduction to Barthes, Foucault, and Althusser* (1997); and Ted Benton, *The Rise and Fall of Structural Marxism: Althusser and His Influence (Theoretical Traditions in the Social Sciences)* (1984). Essays on Althusser include John B. Davis, "Althusser's View of the Place of Ethics in Marx's Thought" in *Social Science Journal* (1990, Vol. 27), and Ned Jackson, "The First Death of Louis Althusser or Totality's Revenge," in *History & Theory* (Feb. 1996). □

Thomas J. J. Altizer

The American thinker Thomas J. J. Altizer (born 1927) had a major impact on theology in the last half of the 20th century. Best known as the exponent and developer of "the death of God," his work was little understood in his own time.

A descendant and namesake of Stonewall Jackson, Thomas J. J. Altizer was born September 28, 1927, in Cambridge, Massachusetts; his father was a distinguished attorney. He grew up in Charleston, West Virginia, and graduated there in 1944 from Stonewall Jackson High School. After one year at St. John's College he enlisted in the U.S. Army. Following Army service he enrolled in the College of the University of Chicago from which he graduated with honors in 1948. In 1951 he received the M.A. in theology at the divinity school and in 1955 the Ph.D. in history of religions at the Graduate School of the University of Chicago. His principal mentors during his graduate course were Joachim Wach, Mircea Eliade, and Paul Tillich.

From 1954 to 1956 he taught at Wabash College, and in 1956 he went to Emory University where he taught in the Graduate Institute of Liberal Arts and in the Graduate Division of Religion. In 1968 he became professor of English at the State University of New York at Stony Brook. Retaining his position in English, in 1970 he became chairman of a new interdisciplinary unit in religious studies at Stony Brook. He had already launched a rigorous program of thinking and writing about theology.

No American thinker in the last half of the 20th century worked more productively or with greater singleness of purpose toward the realization of his theological vision than Thomas Altizer. From the beginning that vision encompassed the restoration and realization of the biblical Christian apocalypse and the extension of the claims of that apocalypse to a dialogue with other world religions, notably Buddhism. Seeing Christendom as the historical negation of what had been announced in and by Jesus as the end of history (viz., the Kingdom of God), he saw in the modern "death of God" the historically actual realization of the primal apocalypse, the conscious realization that God had emptied himself of all absolute, transcent otherness and entered fully into the identity and difference of the human cosmos. This *kenosis* (self-emptying), enacted in the Incarnation, had, after centuries of Christian misreading, been realized through the dialectic of history, over which a wholly immanent God prevailed despite the Satanic interventions of Christendom and its orthodox theologians.

The dialectic of the biblical apocalypse—that of the identity of God, of the difference of God from himself and the world, of the world from itself and God—had been

one of its major chapters will be devoted to the work of Thomas J. J. Altizer.''

Further Reading

As of 1997 Altizer had written eleven major books. *Oriental Mysticism and Biblical Eschatology* (1961); *Mircea Eliade and the Dialectic of the Sacred* (1963); *The Gospel of Christian Atheism* (1966); *The New Apocalypse: The Radical Christian Vision of William Blake* (1967); *The Descent Into Hell* (1970); *The Self-Embodiment of God* (1977); *Total Presence* (1980); and *History as Apocalypse* (1985); and *The Theology of Altizer: Critique and Response* , edited by John B. Cobb, Jr. (1970), in which ten contributors evaluated Altizer's theology and he responded. In Thomas W. Ogletree's *The Death of God Controversy* (1966) Altizer's theology is evaluated and compared with that of two other ''radical'' theologians in the 1960s—William Hamilton and Paul van Buren. William Robert Miller in *The New Christianity* (1967) sets Altizer in the context of modern religious thought. In *America and the Future of Theology,* edited by William A. Beardslee (1967), Altizer both commented on the future of theology and had his own contributions to that future commented on by others. The subtlest and most penetrating evaluations of Altizer's last three books are to be found in two major review articles: Charles E. Winquist, ''Thomas J. J. Altizer: In Retrospect,'' *Religious Studies Review* (October 1982) and Mark C. Taylor, ''Altizer's Originality,'' *Journal of the American Academy of Religion* (September 1984). □

preserved and renewed in the epic traditions of the Western world, in Homer and Virgil and above all in Dante, Milton, Blake, and Joyce. Without eschewing—indeed emphasizing—its biblical basis, Altizer's theology thus saw in the conditions of modern consciousness the ultimate fruition of original Christianity, the perfection of Jesus's re-presentation of God. That fruition marked the end of history as known to Western consciousness and, in religious terms, the beginning of the universal (but not absolute) religion.

The power and subtlety of Altizer's work were as little understood by professional theologians as by those in the popular media. That resulted largely from his having distanced himself critically from the two major options of 19th and 20th century Protestant Christian theology. While considered a ''radical'' by everyone, Altizer steadfastly rejected the liberalism of the 19th and 20th centuries (Schleiermacher, Harnack) and its claim to ground Christian faith in the religio-ethical personality of Jesus to which we have access by historical research. Just as steadfastly he rejected the 20th century rejection of liberalism by neoorthodox or neo-reformation theology (Barth, Brunner): in Jesus we have the Word of God thrown into the human condition as an alien word about and of the Wholly, Absolute Other. In high transcendence of these options, Altizer fashioned his theology by utilizing the linguistic forms of Hegel, Kierkegaard, and Nietzsche and the substance of the Bible, mediated by the arts: epic literature, music, painting, and sculpture. The professor Mark Taylor rightly wrote, ''When the history of twentieth century theology is written,

Juan Álvarez

Juan Álvarez (1780-1867) was a Mexican soldier and statesman. A hero of the independence movement and the Mexican Liberal party, he is considered to be the most important liberal military leader before the 1850s.

Juan Álvarez was born in a small town in Guerrero on Jan. 27, 1780. His family, a prosperous one with Indian and Negro blood, moved to Mexico City but returned to Guerrero in 1807. In 1810 Álvarez became a soldier in the guerrilla army of the priest José Maria Morelos y Pavón in the fight for Mexican independence from Spain. Álvarez rose rapidly to commander of the Regiment of Guadalupe. During the long and unsuccessful rebel struggle he lost much of his inherited wealth.

After Morelos's death Álvarez raised troops from his own ranches; he kept fighting in the mountains around Acapulco at a time when most rebels had surrendered. In 1821 the former royalist officer Agustin de Iturbide defected and declared for independence. Álvarez accepted Iturbide's Plan of Iguala and seized the port of Acapulco in October 1821. He held that city until August 1822, when he retired from the military.

After independence Álvarez entered politics as a leader of the Liberal party and as a strong adherent of federalism. He was soon absolute master of the area which later became the state of Guerrero. There he lived modestly on a small ranch, proud of the fact that he personally worked his lands. In 1823 he joined Antonio López de Santa Ana and Vicente Guerrero, a hero of the wars of independence, in a revolt against Iturbide, who had established a monarchy in Mexico. From 1830 to 1832 Álvarez again served with Guerrero, now the Liberal president. After Guerrero's death in 1831, Álvarez continued to fight the Conservatives. In the late 1830s he offered his services against the French invaders, and he extended his political influence over many of Mexico's southern states, Guerrero, Michoacán, Morelos, and Oaxaca.

In the 1840s Álvarez fought against Santa Ana and the Conservatives' attempts to establish a strong centralized government throughout Mexico. He also led a southern Mexican contingent against the North American invaders in 1847. In 1848-1850 he helped found the federal state of Guerrero (then comprising much of southern Mexico) and served as its first governor. In 1853 Santa Ana and the Conservatives again seized power, and Álvarez once more took up arms, keeping much of Guerrero virtually independent of the national government.

In 1855 Álvarez joined Ignacio Comonfort in launching the Plan of Ayutla, resulting in Santa Ana's overthrow and a return to a federal government with a new constitution. The dictator fled in August, and a junta proclaimed Álvarez provisional president, with Benito Juárez as minister of justice. Álvarez's presidency aroused dissension among the Liberals, and he had difficulty maintaining order. In December 1855 he gave the presidency to Comonfort and returned home.

Again during the Three-Year War (1857-1860), Álvarez commanded the Liberal southern division against the Conservatives. In 1864, although 84 years of age, Álvarez took arms against the French and Maximilian. Álvarez died on Aug. 21, 1867.

Further Reading

There are no major works on Álvarez in any language. For information on him and his times see such general histories of Mexico as Hubert Howe Bancroft, *History of Mexico* (6 vols., 1883-1888), and Justo Sierra, *The Political Evolution of the Mexican People* (1940; 2d ed. 1957; trans. 1969). □

Julia Alvarez

In her poetry and prose, Julia Alvarez (born 1950) has expressed her feelings about her immigration to the United States. She was born in New York City of Dominican parents, who returned to their native land with their newborn daughter. After her family's reimmigration to the United States when Alvarez was ten, she and her sisters struggled to find a place for themselves in their new world. Alvarez has used her dual experience as a starting point for the exploration of culture through writing.

lvarez's most notable work, *How the Garcia Girls Lost Their Accents,* fictionally discusses her life in the Dominican Republic and the United States and the hardships her family faced as immigrants. Apparently the culmination of many years of effort, the 15 stories which make up the novel offer entertaining insights for a wide variety of potential readers that includes both Hispanics and non-Hispanics.

Background in the Dominican Republic

Reminiscing about her youth in an article in *American Scholar,* Alvarez wrote, "Although I was raised in the Dominican Republic by Dominican parents in an extended Dominican family, mine was an American childhood." Her family lived close to her mother's family. Life was somewhat communal; Alvarez and her sisters were brought up along with their cousins and supervised by her mother, maids, and many aunts. Although her own family was not as well off as some of their relatives, Alvarez did not feel inferior. Her father, a doctor who ran the nearby hospital, had met her mother while she was attending school in the United States. While such extravagances as shopping trips to America were beyond their financial means, Alvarez's family was highly influenced by American attitudes and goods. Alvarez and her sisters attended the American school, and for a special treat, ate ice cream from the American ice cream parlor. The entire extended family was obsessed with America; to the children, it was a fantasy land.

As Alvarez acknowledges in her article in *American Scholar,* her family's association with the United States may

have saved her father's life. The members of her mother's family were respected because of their ties with America. Alvarez's uncles had attended Ivy League colleges, and her grandfather was a cultural attaché to the United Nations. The dictator of the Dominican Republic, Rafael Leonidas Trujillo Molina, could not victimize a family with such strong American ties. However, when Alvarez's father secretly joined the forces attempting to oust Trujillo, the police set up surveillance of his home. It was rumored that, respected family or not, her father was soon to be apprehended. An American agent and the offer of a fellowship at a New York hospital helped the family escape the country. Describing the scene as their plane landed in the United States in *American Scholar,* Alvarez wrote, "All my childhood I had dressed like an American, eaten American foods, and befriended American children. I had gone to an American school and spent most of the day speaking and reading English. At night, my prayers were full of blond hair and blue eyes and snow. . . . All my childhood I had longed for this moment of arrival. And here I was, an American girl, coming home at last."

American Experiences

Alvarez's homecoming was not what she had expected it to be. Although she was thrilled to be back in America, she would soon face homesickness, alienation, and prejudice. She missed her cousins, her family's large home, and the respect her family name demanded. Alvarez, her parents, and her sisters squeezed themselves and their possessions into a tiny apartment. As she related to *Brújula Compass,* the experience was like a crash: "The feeling of loss caused a radical change in me. It made me an introverted little girl." Alvarez became an avid reader, immersing herself in books and, eventually, writing.

Alvarez went on to college. She earned undergraduate and graduate degrees in literature and writing and became an English professor at Middlebury College in Vermont. She received grants from the National Endowment for the Arts and The Ingram Merrill Foundation in addition to a PEN Oakland/Josephine Miles Award for excellence in multicultural literature. She published several collections of poetry including *Homecoming,* which appeared in 1984, and by 1987 she was working on a collection of stories. When Alvarez published *How the Garcia Girls Lost Their Accents* in 1991, the novel received considerable attention. The past decade had seen a surge of ethnic novels, and *Garcia Girls* came to be known as an exemplary example of the genre.

How the Garcia Girls Lost Their Accents

Rather than a straight narrative, *How the Garcia Girls Lost Their Accents* is a reverse-chronological order series of 15 interwoven stories chronicling four sisters and their parents. A comparison with Alvarez's article in *American Scholar* suggests that these stories are based on her own experience; like her family, the Garcia family is Dominican and displaced in America. Like Alvarez and her sisters, the Garcia girls struggle to adapt to their new environment and assimilate themselves into the American culture.

The first group of stories is dated "1989-1972." Thus, the novel's first story seems to be its ending. Entitled, "Antojos," which is Spanish for "cravings," this story is a memory of one of the sisters, Yolanda, and her return to the Dominican Republic as an adult. Yolanda—whose story ends the novel and who acts as Alvarez's alter ego—has secretly decided to make her home there, having found life in the United States unfulfilling. When she ignores the warnings of her wealthy relatives and drives into the country for the guava fruit she has been craving, she faces disappointment. She is regarded as an American despite her native roots, and although she finds her guavas, her romantic journey is marred by her feelings as an outsider. Alvarez ends this story ambiguously—similar to the rest of the stories. The attempts of Yolanda and her sisters to lead successful lives in the United States are presented more as memory fragments than stories with definite beginnings and endings.

The next story focuses on Sofia, the youngest of the girls. At this point, however, the four girls are women, with husbands and careers. The details of Sofia's break with her father over her decision to take a lover before marriage are presented, and the events at a birthday party she prepared for her father are recounted. Sofia cannot be totally forgiven, nor can she ever return to the Dominican Republic; in the process of becoming an American girl of the 1960s, she has gone beyond the moral limits imposed by her father, who personifies life in the old world.

The third story relates some background information as it reveals a mother's perceptions of her four girls. During a family gathering, Mami tells her favorite story about each of the girls, and the reader learns that Sandi spent time in a mental institution after almost starving herself to death. The fourth story about Yolanda reveals that she too had a mental breakdown of her own after a failed relationship, and in the next story she becomes the narrator. In "The Rudy Elmenhurst Story," Yolanda's tale of her reluctance to sleep with the dashing young man she loved because of his casual approach to the matter explains her ensuing trouble with men as well as her problems assimilating into American youth culture: "Catholic or not, I still thought it a sin for a guy to just barge in five years later with a bottle of expensive wine and assume you'd drink out of his hand. A guy who had ditched me, who had haunted my sexual awakening with a nightmare of self-doubt. For a moment as I watched him get in his car and drive away, I felt a flash of that old self-doubt."

The memories in the second section of the novel recall the years from 1960 to 1970. The girls are younger, and they are experiencing their first years as immigrants. Attempts they made to reconcile themselves to their new culture are challenged by their parents, who want their children to "mix with the 'right kind' of Americans," and the girls are threatened with having to spend time on the island, which they have come to dread. In this section, the girls save their sister from a macho cousin's imposition, a pervert exposes himself to Carla, and Yolanda sees snow for the first time and thinks it is fall-out from a nuclear bomb.

The final story in this section, "Floor Show," focuses on Sandi's perception of events as the family spends a scandalous evening with an American doctor and his drunkenly indiscreet wife in a Spanish restaurant. Sandi is shocked and upset when this woman kisses her father and later dances with the flamenco dancers that the young girl had so admired. Cautioned by her mother to behave at the important dinner, Sandi does as she is told and stays quiet until she is offered a flamenco doll by the American woman, who seems to understand her desire for it. "Sandi was not going to miss her chance. This woman had kissed her father. This woman had ruined the act of the beautiful dancers. The way Sandi saw it, this woman owed her something." The woman gave Sandi something more than the doll; her smile "intimated the things Sandi was just beginning to learn, things that the dancers knew all about, which was why they danced with such vehemence, such passion."

In third and final section, "1960-1956," America is still a dream—the family is still on the island. The first story is divided into two parts and recalls the family's traumatic encounter with the *guardia,* or secret police, and their subsequent flight from their home. From that moment on, the tales regress to the girls' early memories of life in the huge family compound. Yolanda tells of the presents her grandmother brought the children from America and an ensuing encounter with her cousin, Sandi recalls her art lessons and the fright she had at the instructor's home, Carla remembers the mechanical bank her father brought her from F.A.O. Schwartz in New York and the maid who desperately wanted it.

Finally, Yolanda concludes the novel with one of her earliest memories—she stole a kitten from its mother and then abandoned it, even though she had been warned by a strange hunter: "To take it away would be a violation of its natural right to live." The mother cat haunted the girl until she left the island, and, as Yolanda confides in her narration, "There are still times I wake up at three o'clock in the morning and peer into the darkness. At that hour and in that loneliness, I hear her, a black furred thing lurking in the corners of my life, her magenta mouth opening, wailing over some violation that lies at the center of my art."

The praise Alvarez received for her first novel outweighed the criticism that a new novelist often encounters. The *New York Times Book Review* found that Alvarez "beautifully captured the threshold experience of the new immigrant, where the past is not yet a memory and the future remains an anxious dream." *Hispanic* 's critic wrote, "Well-crafted, although at times overly sentimental, these stories provide a glimpse into the making of another American family with a Hispanic surname." And the *Library Journal* reported, "Alvarez is a gifted, evocative storyteller of promise."

Alvarez's second novel, *In the Time of Butterflies,* was published in 1994. This work recounts the lives and tragic end of the Mirabel sisters—Patria, Minerva, and Maria Terese (Mate)—who were assassinated after visiting their imprisoned husbands during the last days of the Trujillo regime in the Dominican Republic. Each sister in turn relates her own aspect of the narrative, beginning with their childhood and gradually defining how they came to be involved in the liberation movement. Their story is framed

by that of the surviving sister, Dedé, who adds her own tale of suffering to the memory of her martyred sisters. *In the Time of Butterflies* received a favorable reaction from reviewers, some of whom admired Alvarez's ability to express the wide range of emotions brought on by the revolution. For example, the reviewer for *Publishers Weekly* observed that "Alvarez captures the terrorized atmosphere of a police state, in which people live under the sword of terrible fear and atrocities cannot be acknowledged. As the sisters' energetic fervor turns to anguish, Alvarez conveys their courage and their desperation, and the full import of the tragedy." The novel was a finalist for the National Book Critics Award in 1994.

A collection of poems entitled *The Other Side/El Otro Lado,* was published in 1995. It deals with similar themes of biculturalism and the power of language. In the book's title poem a spirit conjuror commands Alvarez to serve her own people in the Dominican Republic. But in the end she returns "to the shore I've made up on the other side, to a life of choice, a life of words." Her next work, *Yo!,* published in 1997, is based on Yolanda, one of her characters from her first novel, *How the Garcia Girls Lost Their Accents.* Each section of the novel is told from different characters' perspectives, all of whom depict Yolanda as they see her in order to provide a complex portrait.

Further Reading

American Scholar, Winter 1987, pp. 71-85.
Atlanta Journal, August 11, 1991, p. A13.
Boston Globe, May 26, 1991, p. A13.
Brújula Compass (Spanish-language; translation by Ronie-Richele Garcia- Johnson), January-February 1992, p. 16.
Hispanic, June 1991, p. 55.
Los Angeles Times, June 7, 1991, p. E4.
Library Journal, May 1, 1991, p. 102; August 1994, 123.
Más, (Spanish-language; translation by Ronie-Richele Garcia-Johnson), November-December 1991, p. 100.
New York Times Book Review, October 6, 1991, p. 14; July 16, 1995, p. 20.
Nuestro, November 1984, pp. 34+; March 1985, pp. 52+; January-February 1986, pp. 32+.
Publishers Weekly, April 5, 1991, p. 133; July 11, 1994, p. 62.
School Library Journal, September 1991, p. 292.
Washington Post, June 20, 1991, p. D11. □

Luis W. Alvarez

The importance and variety of the discoveries and contributions of Luis W. Alvarez (1911-1988) are perhaps unmatched by any other 20th-century physicist. He received many awards for his work over the years, including the 1968 Nobel Prize in Physics for his work on a large liquid hydrogen bubble chamber.

Alvarez will probably be best remembered by the public for ingenious experiments that applied physics to other sciences. He x-rayed Chephren's pyramid in Egypt using cosmic radiation, only to find that there were no undiscovered chambers inside. His application of elementary physics to the evidence on the John F. Kennedy assassination verified the Warren Commission finding that only a single assassin was involved. But perhaps his most dramatic discovery was made after his "retirement" by jumping into a totally new field, paleontology and geology. With collaborators that included his son, Walter, he analyzed a 65 million year old clay layer and showed that the great ecological catastrophe that killed the dinosaurs was caused by the impact of an asteroid or comet.

Alvarez was born June 13, 1911, in San Francisco. He began his career at the University of Chicago. His first published paper (as an undergraduate) described a measurement of the wavelength of light using a phonograph record, a parlor lamp, and a yard stick. While reading the original physics literature, he found a paper by Hans Geiger that described a new type of detector for charged particles. He proceeded to construct one of the first Geiger counters in America. Alvarez was the first Chicago undergraduate to present results of his research at the weekly departmental colloquium, sharing the time with a professor who reported on James Chadwick's discovery of the neutron. After hearing the talk, Arthur Compton invited Alvarez to collaborate with him on a study to determine the electric charge of the primary cosmic radiation.

Alvarez's first summer as a graduate student was spent on the roof of the Geneva Hotel in Mexico City, his Geiger telescope resting in a wheelbarrow that allowed him to periodically reverse the east-west orientation of his apparatus. He and Compton determined that the cosmic rays were

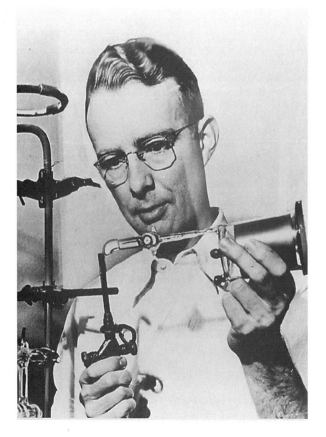

mostly positively charged, and therefore presumably protons. After receiving his Ph.D. in 1936 Alvarez began work with Ernest O. Lawrence at the University of California, in part through family connections. Alvarez's father, a physician on the staff of the Mayo Clinic, had helped Lawrence get money for one of his cyclotrons, and his sister was Lawrence's part-time secretary. Arriving at the Old Radiation Laboratory, Alvarez made the first of his dramatic career changes as he prepared himself to become a practicing nuclear physicist. First, he became thoroughly familiar with all instruments in the laboratory, their use, and the physics that was being done with them. He did this by helping everyone with their experiments while becoming a skilled machine operator and repairman.

Emerging from the laboratory at each day's end, Alvarez would pick up a couple of volumes of physics journals from the university library; he eventually read every published nuclear physics article held there. Years later he would astonish his colleagues by reproducing a curve or a little known fact gleaned in these early efforts. He could usually cite the authors, journal, year, and often the location of the volume in the library and whether the item was on a right-or a left-hand page. By 1937 Hans Bethe had published his three-part compendium of all that was known about nuclear physics. Alvarez chose first to make a measurement that Bethe said couldn't be done and then to disprove one of Bethe's assertions. In just four years Alvarez discovered the radioactivity of tritium and the stability of helium-3, the magnetic moment of the neutron, and that nuclei cannibalize their own atomic electrons. He also demonstrated the spin dependence of the nuclear force, established a new standard of length using mercury-198, and made the first experimental demonstrations in a field now called heavy-ion physics.

World War II ended Alvarez's nuclear physics career. He soon found himself in Boston, figuring how to apply high-frequency radio waves to achieve military goals. Using optics ideas learned in his thesis work, Luie invented the linear phased array, which formed the basis of EAGLE, the first radar bombing system. He also invented VIXEN, a system to outfox German submarines by diminishing an airborne acquisition radar's power as a surfaced sub was approached, so that the listening skipper would believe the attack plane was going away. Alvarez solved the problem of landing planes in bad weather by inventing the radar-based Ground Control Approach (GCA), for which he won the 1946 Collier Air Trophy.

Upon his return to the Berkeley laboratory after the war, Alvarez made another career change, to that of a particle accelerator physicist. He realized the importance of team research and looked to the methods of Lawrence and Ernest Rutherford. Like them, he displayed an ability to select good people to work with him.

His first postwar machine was the proton linear accelerator, which has become the standard injector for many subsequent higher energy circular machines and is still referred to as an "Alvarez accelerator." While preparing for his nuclear physics class one morning, he invented the Tandem van de Graaff, which was commercialized by High

Voltage Engineering. Alvarez was a superb teacher. His course in physical optics was thorough. The students were introduced to the full spectrum of electromagnetic radiation from gamma rays to radio waves with spellbinding tales of how radar was used during the Battle of Britain.

In the mid 1950s Donald Glaser invented a new detector called a bubble chamber. Alvarez immediately saw the potential this had for the study of the newly available high-energy particles, if it could be made to work with liquified hydrogen. He established a group to develop the liquid-hydrogen bubble chamber from the first small steady-state chambers to large pulsed chambers. Characteristically, he grew impatient with the small chambers and proposed a large one 72 inches in length. This was nearly eight times the size of the one then in action at Berkeley, and some people thought this would be too big a step. Alvarez was confident that the chamber could be made to operate and he convinced the money sources to help. The 72-inch chamber aided in the identification of many new particles. It was for this work that he received the Nobel Prize in Physics in 1968.

In 1977 he was presented a piece of rock that had been cut from a hillside in Italy by his geologist son, Walter. The rock had a thin clay layer in it. He was shown how the microscopic fossils ("forams") in the rock became extinct right at the clay layer. These tiny forams had been destroyed at the clay layer. These tiny forams had been destroyed at the same time the dinosaurs had disappeared. Alvarez later described his experience in examining this rock as one of the most exciting moments in his life. The scientific consequences, which include the nuclear winter theory, are still being uncovered by geologists, paleontologists, physicists, chemists, and astronomers.

Alvarez was always solving practical problems that influenced his life. By his early fifties he needed bifocal lenses to correct his eyesight, and this convinced him that there must be a better way to solve this problem. The result was his invention of the variable focus lens and the formation of Humphrey Instruments.

While visiting Kenya, he was frustrated by how the image of the distant animals jumped around in the viewing port of his hand-held camera. He just couldn't hold the camera firmly enough to steady the image. He then invented a series of stabilized optical devices; and eventually he formed Schwem Technologies to develop and market them.

In addition to the 1946 Collier Air Trophy and the 1968 Nobel Prize in Physics, Alvarez also received the Einstein Medal in 1961, the 1964 National Medal of Science, a 1978 membership in the Inventors' Hall of Fame, and the 1981 Wright Prize.

Further Reading

Alvarez produced an extensive autobiography. A single volume version, *Alvarez: Adventures of a Physicist* was published in 1987, a paperback edition in 1989. He was honored by his colleagues with *Discovering Alvarez; Selected Works of Luis W. Alvarez with Commentary by His Students and Colleagues,* edited by W. Peter Trower (1987). □

Jorge Amado

The Brazilian novelist Jorge Amado (born 1912) was best known in the 1930s for his novels of social protest. By the 1950s he had evolved into a compelling storyteller more apt to poke fun at the establishment than to denounce it. His lyricism, imagination, and humor have given him a worldwide reputation and following.

Jorge Amado was born on his father's cacao plantation along the eastern seaboard of Brazil, an area just then emerging from a period of violent struggles for land among the intrepid frontiersmen who opened it up. His novels are almost all set either in this region or in the city of Salvador (Bahia), where he was sent to secondary school. As a 16-year-old contributor to short-lived reviews, he began rebelling against the stuffiness of literary canons, an urge to which he gave further expression in his first halting novel, *O pals do carnaval* (1931; Carnival Country).

In law school in Rio de Janeiro, Amado became increasingly radicalized. *Cacau* (1933; Cocoa) was a proletarian novel set in the region of his childhood, and *Suor* (1934; Sweat) indicated both its aim and its earthy style by its title. In 1935 Amado was jailed; two years later he was exiled and many of his works were banned. He alienated the authorities still further by publishing in 1942 a biography of Luis Carlos Prestes, the charismatic leader of the Brazilian Communist party. After World War II, under a new political regime, Amado served as a Communist member of the Brazilian Chamber of Deputies until the party was outlawed in 1948. He won the Stalin International Peace Prize in 1951.

Subsequently, however, he ceased to take much active interest in political affairs. His later novels lost their preachy quality and became steadily less concerned with social protest. This new aspect can be seen in his first big literary success, *The Violent Land* (1943). It depicts the rough-and-tumble of frontier life but is neither just a "western" nor a radical pamphlet. This novel reveals careful attention to characterization, plot and style. A sequel was published 15 years later, *Gabriela, Clove and Cinnamon.* It offers an especially sharp contrast to his earlier work by its heightened sense of humor and by its concern with the individual caught up in the process of social change, rather than with the broad issues of social justice. Instead of caricatures there are now characters. In its details, the novel is a loving portrayal of the Brazilian lifestyle. It received wide acclaim, was translated into several languages and became a best seller in the United States.

From *Dona Flor and Her Two Husbands* (1966), Amado's best-known novel, through such late works as *The War of the Saints* (1988), his characters gained greater individuality in an often magic, realist, contemporary Bahia. The international success of these works (they've been translated into more than 30 languages) flows from Amado's keen sensitivity for human foibles and his ironic depiction of

inspired Ambedkar and reinforced his commitment to social reform.

Two avenues existed for altering the conditions of Hindu untouchables in the early 20th century. Ambedkar rejected the more traditional approach of changing a caste's habits and image so that they resembled the norms associated with high castes. Instead, he tried to supplant such norms with the Western-based notion that all men, including Mahars, have rights of liberty and equality. Ambedkar made it his mission to create circumstances in which those rights could become fact. Sophisticated, articulate, with a political sense and an independent spirit bordering on egotism, Ambedkar set out to modernize untouchable castes.

Prior to 1935 Ambedkar sought to unify the Mahars through caste conferences, campaigns to enter temples hitherto closed to untouchables, and creation of newspapers for propaganda and communication. In 1924 Ambedkar organized the Depressed Classes Institute of Bombay, which carried on economic and educational uplift. Ambedkar also moved into the political arena because he believed that untouchables must take advantage of opportunities afforded by British constitutional reforms. As a member of the Bombay Legislative Council, he helped the Mahars and other depressed castes receive reserved legislative seats and employment. In the London Round Table Conferences, Ambedkar championed constitutional safeguards for untouchables.

self-serving moralism, especially among those who seek to belittle others in order to give themselves false stature. His simple, almost poetic style, modeled on the ballad rhythms of the folk singer, helps give his novels an emotional intensity checked by his sardonic wit.

In addition to the Stalin International Peace Prize, Amado's honors include the Juca Pato Prize for "Intellectual of the Year" in 1970 from the Union of Brazilian writers. He was elected to the Brazilian Academy of Letters in 1961.

Further Reading

There is no biography of Amado in English. Fred P. Ellison, *Brazil's New Novel* (1954), describes the literary setting and evaluates Amado's work. □

Bhimrao Ramji Ambedkar

Bhimrao Ramji Ambedkar (1891-1956) was an Indian social reformer and politician who devoted himself to improving the life of untouchables, particularly of his own caste, the Mahars.

Bhimrao Ambedkar was born at Mhow, Madhya Pradesh. He attended Columbia University during 1914-1916 and received a doctorate in 1926. While at Columbia, John Dewey and other prominent teachers

These activities brought Ambedkar in collision with Mahatma Gandhi. Although Gandhi paternally sought to improve the condition of untouchables, he rejected Ambedkar's militant demand that untouchables mobilize politically and be given a status separate from that of other Hindus. Conflict between the leaders continued, punctuated by threats of fasts to the death and shaky compromises.

Ambedkar moved in new directions after the 1935 Government of India Act. He established a series of political parties which became foci for untouchable demands. In 1942 he served as legal member on the Governor General's Executive Council and contributed to the drafting of the Indian constitution.

Although political maneuvering brought limited benefits to untouchables, Ambedkar became convinced that he and his caste could not attain self-respect and economic well-being within Hinduism. Following 2 decades of exploring affiliation with other Indian religions, Ambedkar converted to Buddhism just prior to his death on Dec. 6, 1956. This dramatic rejection of Hindu restrictions and a concomitant effort to affirm a new way of life validated Ambedkar's claim to represent the interests and will of his people. Half a million Mahars followed him into Buddhism.

Further Reading

Dhananjay Keer, *Dr. Ambedkar: Life and Mission* (1954; 2d ed. 1962), provides a useful survey of Ambedkar's life.

Additional Sources

Bhandari, C. S., *Dr. Bhim Rao Ambedkar, an outstanding patriot,* New Delhi: Suruchi Prakashan, 1991.

Chandra Mowli, V., *B.R. Ambedkar: man and his vision,* New Delhi: Sterling Publishers; New York: Distributed by Apt Books, 1990.

Dr. Ambedkar: pioneer of human rights, New Delhi: Bodhisattva Publication, Ambedkar Institute of Buddhist Studies, 1977.

Kuber, W. N., *B.R. Ambedkar,* New Delhi: Publications Division, Ministry of Information and Broadcasting, Govt. of India, 1978.

Lobo, C. H. Jacob., *Dr. B.R. Ambedkar: the champion of social democracy in India,* Bangalore, India: Hilerina Publications, 1984. □

Eric Ambler

Eric Ambler (born 1909) is considered one of the masters of the thriller novel involving international intrigue and espionage. Of the six novels he wrote before World War II, four have been adjudged outstanding examples of the genre.

Eric Ambler was born in London on June 28, 1909. In 1927 and 1928 he served as an engineering apprentice, providing background material for the engineer-protagonists who appear in many of his novels. He left engineering to become an actor and then an advertising copywriter, a position he held until 1937, when he became a full-time writer.

Ambler's first novel, *The Dark Frontier,* was published in 1936, and the second, *Background to Danger,* the following year. In his third novel, *Cause for Alarm,* published in 1938, he utilized many of the themes that were to recur in his later works. It is the story of Nicholas Marlow, a British production engineer who is sent to Italy as his firm's representative. His work is especially important to the Italian government, then allied with Germany, because his firm has been supplying high-speed automatic machines for artillery shell production. Marlow's predecessor in the job has allegedly died at the hands of a hit-and-run driver, but actually was murdered.

In Milan Marlow meets a general who claims to be an agent of Yugoslavia, but is actually a spy for Germany, and a Russian agent. Marlow deliberately allows himself to be lured into a scheme to furnish the details of his company's transactions, but the Italian secret police find out about his reports to the general and he becomes a wanted man. He then escapes to Yugoslavia.

In his book of criticism, *Bloody Murder,* Julian Symons notes, "After World War I began, spy stories became unequivocally nationalist in tone and Right-wing in political sympathy." Ambler, however, changed all that when he "infused warmth and political colour into the spy story by using it to express a left-wing point of view." Symons further observes, "Almost all of the best thrillers are concerned, in

one form or another, with the theme of the hunted man." The last third of *Cause for Alarm* is about the attempts to arrest Marlow before he can escape over the border. This portion of the novel also involves a third feature of Ambler's fiction, his interest in "the difficulty of moving from place to place."

Also in 1938 Ambler published *Epitaph for a Spy,* about a foreign language teacher in a Paris school who inadvertently becomes involved in an international intrigue.

In 1939 Ambler published his finest novel, *A Coffin for Dimitrios.* It tells of the attempt by Charles Latimer, a British lecturer in political economy who writes detective stories as an avocation, to trace the history of Dimitrios Talat, who has led a career of murder, theft, and betrayal throughout Europe. Latimer comments on Dimitrios, "It was useless to explain him in terms of Good and Evil . . . Dimitrios was not evil. He was logical and consistent; as logical and consistent in the European jungle as the poison gas called Lewisite and the shattered bodies of children killed in the bombardment of an open town." Symons judges this "[h]is finest book of this period, . . . in which flashback follows flashback."

The following year Ambler published *Journey into Fear,* another demonstration of his expert technique. Most of the novel takes place in the static environment of a small ship bound from Turkey to Greece to Italy. The triggerman in this novel exemplifies what Symons wrote about Ambler's killers in *Critical Occasions.* He states, "The agents and spies involved on both sides are menacing and unpleasant, but not very important men. They murder casually, without any particular passion."

Ambler served in the British Army from 1940 to 1946; he enlisted in the artillery, saw action in North Africa and Italy, and then was named assistant director of army kinematography for the War Office. He achieved the rank of lieutenant colonel and was awarded the Bronze Star.

While in the army he joined with Peter Ustinov to write the screenplay for *The Way Ahead* in 1944 and then wrote *United States* in 1945. On his release from military service he collaborated with David Lean and Stanley Haynes on the screenplay for *One Woman's Story* in 1949. *Highly Dangerous* and *Encore* were written for film in 1951, the same year he published his first novel in 11 years, *Judgment on Deltchev.*

In the 1950s he was more active as a screenwriter than as a novelist. He wrote the screenplays for *The Magic Box* (1952), *The Promoter* (1952), *Shoot First* (1953), *The Cruel Sea* (1953), nominated for an Academy Award, *Lease of Life* (1955), *The Purple Plain* (1955), *Battle Hell* (1957), and *A Night to Remember* (1958). In fiction he produced *The Schirmer Inheritance* (1953) and *State of Siege* (1956), generally considered his best postwar novel. The novel follows the story of an engineer in Sunda, an emerging nation between the Dutch East Indies and Malaysia, who is caught up in a coup d'état that fails (as it is supposed to fail).

The decade of the 1960s saw Ambler active in the novel again, as he wrote *A Passage of Arms* (1960), *The Light of Day* (1963), awarded an Edgar by the Mystery Writers of America, *A Kind of Anger* (1964), *Dirty Story*

(1967), and *The Intercom Conspiracy* (1969). He also published the essay collection *The Ability to Kill* in 1963. Furthermore, he wrote screenplays for *The Wreck of the Mary Deare* (1960) and *Topkapi,* based on *The Light of Day* (1964); he ended his screenwriting with *Love, Hate, Love* (1970).

Besides his other work, Ambler joined with Charles Rodda under the joint pen name of Eliot Reed to produce three novels. Their works include *Skytip* (1950), *Tender to Danger* (1951), and the *The Maras Affair* (1953). In addition to *The Light of Day,* four of his novels have been made into movies: *Journey into Fear* (1942), *Background to Danger* (1943), *The Mask of Dimitrios* (1944), and *Epitaph for a Spy,* filmed as *Hotel Reserve* (1944).

Ambler produced four novels after 1970: *The Levanter* (1972), *Doctor Frigo* (1974), *The Siege of the Villa Lipp* (1977), and *The Care of Time* (1981).

He received many honors, including the Grand Master Award from the Mystery Writers of America, and was given the Order of the British Empire in 1981. Critical opinion of Ambler is best summarized in the words of author Graham Greene, who calls him "our greatest thriller writer."

Further Reading

Here Lies: An Autobiography was published in 1986. Comments on his work can be found in *Critical Occasions* (1966) and *Bloody Murder* (1972), both by Julian Symons, and in *Murder for Pleasure* by Howard Haycraft (1968). □

St. Ambrose

St. Ambrose (339-397) was the bishop of the Italian city of Milan. He was the outstanding leader, preacher, and author in the Western part of the Christian Church during the 4th century.

B orn in the city of Trier (now in Germany), Ambrose was the son of one of the highest-ranking administrative officials of the Roman Empire, the praetorian prefect of Gaul. After the early death of his father, the family returned to Rome, where Ambrose received the liberal education appropriate to a high-ranking Roman who was to practice law and advance to high office in government service. In his late 20s he was employed in legal work at the imperial court, and at about 30 he was named governor of two provinces of northern Italy, in which capacity he resided at Milan. On the death of the bishop of Milan in 374, the people of the city demanded that Ambrose be made bishop, and he reluctantly yielded.

Ambrose's career as bishop had three important aspects: the quality of his thought as a Christian intellectual, his role in the final phase of the Arian controversy, and his impact upon the relations between Church and Empire.

The Western Church of the 4th century was notably lacking in men of high intellectual capacity, especially compared to such Eastern figures as Athanasius and Gregory of

Nyssa. Ambrose went far in the task of integrating the Christian faith with a total world view acceptable to the sophisticated Latin minds of his age. This task was soon to be brought to brilliant fulfillment at the hands of Augustine, who as a young man was much influenced by hearing sermons of Ambrose and who was baptized by him at Easter, 387. Deeply imbued with Neoplatonic currents of thought and widely read in religious authors whose language was Greek, Ambrose succeeded in communicating elevated conceptions of God and of the Christian pursuit of virtue. In particular, he effectively employed allegorical interpretations of the Old Testament and thus freed his hearers from the necessity of entertaining conceptions of God and of God's relations with men which appeared unworthy when understood at a literal level. A number of Ambrose's most important writings, for example, the commentary on Luke's Gospel, were the product of revising and combining the notes taken by enthusiastic listeners to his sermons preached on scriptural texts. His work *On the Duties of the Clergy* is one of the first comprehensive treatments of Christian ethics.

The Arian controversy had raged in the Eastern Church since the early 320s. The central issue was whether belief in Christ as being fully God could be reconciled with strict monotheism. The orthodox answer to this question was affirmative, an answer that was finally ratified in the East at the Council of Constantinople in 381. In the same year a Western council met at the Italian city of Aquileia with Ambrose as president. His commanding leadership and vigilant political maneuvering assured the victory of the orthodox party,

and nonorthodox bishops were removed from their sees by government action. In a series of dramatic incidents in 385-386, Ambrose, defying even an imperial threat on his life, successfully stood his ground in refusing to turn over a church in Milan for use by the nonorthodox party, one of whose powerful supporters was the Emperor's mother.

Ambrose held tenaciously to the central conviction that the Emperor, as a Christian, must execute his responsibilities as ruler in accord with the requirements of Christian faith. Threatening to excommunicate the Emperor, the bishop blocked a powerful movement in 384 toward erecting again the old pagan altar and statue of the goddess Victory in the Senate house at Rome. When, in 390, the emperor Theodosius, in a fit of rage over a bloody riot in the city of Thessalonica, had his soldiers massacre several thousand inhabitants, Ambrose brought the ruler to do public penance for his act of vengeance, again under threat of excommunication. The great bishop of Milan is therefore an important figure in the history of the relations between Church and State in the Western world. Ambrose served as bishop of Milan for 23 years until his death in 397.

Further Reading

The standard comprehensive work on Ambrose is F. Homes Dudden, *The Life and Times of St. Ambrose* (2 vols., 1935). A treatment of smaller scope but of great sensitivity is in Hans von Campenhausen, *Men Who Shaped the Western Church* (trans. 1964). □

Amenemhet I

The pharaoh Amenemhet I (reigned 1991-1962 B.C.), though not of royal blood, was the founder of the Twelfth Dynasty of Egypt.

The mother of Amenemhet was apparently named Nefert and was a native of the nome, or province, of Elephantine, and he himself seems to have been born in southern Upper Egypt. His father was a commoner called Sesostris. Amenemhet is almost certainly identical with the vizier of the same name who was in charge of an expedition to the quarries of Wadi Hammamat in the second year of the reign of Nebtowere Mentuhotep III of the Eleventh Dynasty. Amenemhet was probably middle-aged when he became king after usurping his master's throne. He openly acknowledged his lack of royal ancestry, adopting as the first of three names in his new titulary the epithet Wehem-Meswet (Repeater of Births), thereby identifying himself as the inaugurator of a new era in the history of Egypt.

Amenemhet was a strong supporter of the god Amon of Thebes, whom he raised to the first rank among the deities of Egypt. Mindful of the difficulties his predecessors of the Eleventh Dynasty had experienced in controlling Lower Egypt from Thebes, Amenemhet transferred his seat of government to a site 18 miles south of Memphis, on the boundary between Upper and Lower Egypt, where he built the fortified city of It-towy (Seizer of the Two Lands). He erected his pyramid nearby, west of the modern villages of Lisht and Maharraqa.

The first 2 decades of Amenemhet's reign were mainly spent in an organized effort to consolidate his position. In his bid for the throne, he had evidently received much support from the local nomarchs, or governors, of Egypt, and he made no attempt to abolish their hereditary privileges. However, to prevent rivalry between the nomes and dangerous territorial expansion by any one governor, the boundaries of each nome were strictly established. Early in his reign Amenemhet, accompanied by the nomarch of Beni Hasan, sailed up the Nile with a fleet of 20 ships as far as Elephantine, destroying any remaining pockets of resistance to his government. He may also have conducted an expedition against the inhabitants of Lower Nubia. In the north he carried out a tour of inspection of the Nile Delta, on the eastern frontier of which he repulsed raiding parties of Asiatic nomads. He constructed toward the eastern end of Wadi Tumilat a fortified station called "Walls of the Ruler."

In the twentieth year of his reign, Amenemhet made his eldest son, Sesostris I, coregent. Father and son ruled together for 10 years and dated events to the years of their respective reigns. During this coregency Sesostris seems to have begun the military occupation of Lower Nubia. By the year 29 the area as far as Korosko, halfway between the First and Second cataracts, had been conquered. Amenemhet's name is found in the diorite quarries in the Nubian Desert northwest of Toshka and near the turquoise mines in Sinai. Amenemhet apparently met his death as a result of a palace

conspiracy while Sesostris was on an expedition against the Libyans.

Further Reading

The sources for the rise of the Twelfth Dynasty are discussed in William C. Hayes's chapter "The Middle Kingdom in Egypt" in J. B. Bury and others, eds., *The Cambridge Ancient History*, vol. 1 (2d ed. 1961). Also useful are H. E. Winlock, *The Rise and Fall of the Middle Kingdom in Thebes* (1947), and Alan H. Gardiner, *Egypt of the Pharaohs* (1961). □

Amenhotep III

Amenhotep III (reigned 1417-1379 B.C.) was the ninth ruler of the Eighteenth Dynasty of Egypt. The Pharaoh was a patron of the arts, and during his reign magnificent buildings and sculptures were created.

Amenhotep III came to the throne at a time when his country was at the height of its political power, economic prosperity, and cultural development. As a result of the conquests of his predecessors, particularly Thutmose I and III, Egypt was a dominant power in the Near East, and its sphere of influence stretched from the Fourth Cataract of the Nile to the banks of the Euphrates. Throughout his long and peaceful reign, Amenhotep combined the pursuit of worldly pleasures with a program of self-glorification on a scale grander than any undertaken before.

Amenhotep's reign may be divided into two phases. During his first 10 years he exhibited his skill and prowess as a sportsman in a series of big-game hunts, which were accorded wide publicity. His military career appears to have consisted of a single, relatively unimportant expedition into Upper Nubia in the fifth year of his reign. There is no mention of hunting expeditions after the tenth year or indeed of any activity involving the Pharaoh in physical exertion. In the tenth year Amenhotep arranged a marriage between himself and Gilukhipa, daughter of Shuttarna, King of Mitanni.

The second phase of Amenhotep's reign consisted of nearly 3 decades of luxurious ease, which witnessed an unparalleled output of splendid architectural works, sculpture, and fine craftsmanship. From the middle of his reign onward, Amenhotep probably spent much time amid the luxury of his great palace in western Thebes. Throughout this period the dominant influence in his life was his queen, Tiy, the daughter of a commoner. She occupied this unprecedented position not only in Amenhotep's reign but also in that of their son Ikhnaton.

Amenhotep's mortuary temple on the western plain at Thebes, which was demolished during the Nineteenth Dynasty, was apparently the largest of its class ever built. The two gigantic statues of the Pharaoh, the so-called Colossi of Memnon, which stood in front of the temple, still tower over the plain. Although the Aten (sun disk) probably emerged as

American Horse

American Horse (1840-1876) was a Sioux leader in Red Cloud's War in the 1860s and 1870s which was fought for control of the Bozeman Trail. His capture and death was one in a series of defeats for the Sioux after the Battle of the Little Bighorn and foreshadowed the Sioux surrender in 1877.

American Horse was one of the Lakota leaders during the Indian wars of the 1860s and 1870s. He is perhaps best remembered for his death at Slim Buttes, in revenge for the defeat of George Armstrong Custer and the U.S. Seventh Cavalry at Little Big Horn. He was known among his people as Iron Shield, but also was thought to be called Iron Plume according to newspapermen who reported on the Indian wars. He was often confused with the younger American Horse ["Wasechun-tashunka"], the son of Sitting Bear. The younger American Horse was active in the Ghost Dance Movement of 1889, well after the elder American Horse died, and was a member of the True Oglala, also called the Bear People. Although some writers speculated that the younger American Horse was either a son or nephew to the elder man, George Hyde in *Red Cloud's Folk: A History of the Oglala Sioux Indians,* documented from interviews with He-Dog that the younger man was no relation to the elder American Horse.

a recognized member of the Egyptian pantheon during the reigns of Thutmose III and Amenhotep II, it was not until the reign of Amenhotep III that the new god was officially honored, when the Pharaoh named his flagship and a royal palace after the deity.

During the last decade of his reign Amenhotep was ill and prematurely senile, but there was no reduction in his building activities or the scale of luxury in which he lived. He died at the age of about 55 and was buried in a huge, rock-cut tomb prepared for him in the western branch of the Valley of the Kings.

Further Reading

A well-illustrated account of the reign of Amenhotep III is given in Cyril Aldred, *Akhenaten, Pharaoh of Egypt: A New Study* (1968). This should be read in conjunction with William C. Hayes's chapter "Egypt: Internal Affairs from Tuthmosis I to the Death of Amenophis III" in I.E.S. Edwards, C.J. Gadd, and N.G.L. Hammond, eds., *The Cambridge Ancient History,* vol. 2 (2d ed. 1962).

Additional Sources

Goedicke, Hans., *Problems concerning Amenophis III.,* Baltimore, Md.: Halgo, 1992. □

It is not known when the elder American Horse was born. Historians have speculated that he was born as early as 1801 or as late as 1840. He was the son of Old Smoke, the leader of the Smoke People, who also were referred to as the Bad Faces ["Iteschicha"]. Chief Old Smoke's sister was Walks-As-She-Thinks, who was the mother of the famous Chief Red Cloud. Although not much is known about American Horse's early life, sources indicate his cousin Red Cloud and fellow Lakota Crazy Horse were life-long friends. During the 1830s and 1840s, the Oglala people split into two factions, the Smoke People and the Bear People, over a dispute about the leadership of the tribe. The latter group followed Chief Bull Bear, while the Smoke People were led by Chief Smoke. After the dispute, the Smoke People moved north of Fort Laramie, toward the Black Hills of the Dakotas. They used the Powder River country for buffalo hunting and fought frequently with the Crow Indians over that territory. Some of the Smoke people remained at Fort Laramie. Chief Smoke, who was described as fat and jovial, reportedly took up farming there just before he died in 1864.

American Horse Becomes a Leader

American Horse was one of a select group of "shirt-wearers," who assisted the Oglala chiefs with their duties. Billy Garnett, a white trader, watched the ceremony at which American Horse, Crazy Horse, Young-Man-Afraid and Sword were made "shirt-wearers" in 1865. Steven Ambrose in *Crazy Horse and Custer* described the ceremony. After a feast, one of the wise and knowledgeable elders would describe the duties of a "shirt-wearer." Such warriors were duty-bound to lead warriors in peace and in war, keeping the peace and respecting the rights of the weak. "They must be wise and kind and firm in all things, counseling, advising, and then commanding. If their words were not heard, they could use blows to enforce their orders; in extreme cases, they even had the right to kill. But they must never take up arms against their own people without thought and counsel and must always act with caution and justice."

Following the speeches, each of the warriors was presented with a shirt made from the hides of two bighorn sheep and decorated with scalps they had won in battle, feathers and quill work. After receiving the shirts more speeches were made where the warriors were told to care for the poor, widows, orphans and those who had little power. The four men were chosen, Ambrose said, "because they were greathearted, generous, strong, and brave, and . . . would do their duty gladly and with good heart." Although they were not considered chiefs by their people, the shirt-wearers were looked upon as leaders.

With the California Gold Rush in 1849, settlers began moving west of the Mississippi in greater numbers. In 1862, Congress passed the Homestead Act, which provided western emigrants one-hundred and sixty acres of public land in the plains territory for ten dollars, if they promised to live there and farm the land for at least five years. During the next three years, some three hundred thousand settlers crossed the plains. While Indians periodically attacked settlers, stole livestock and raided newly-built towns, there was no organized warfare because the army was needed for the Civil War.

At about the same time, gold was discovered in Montana. Government treaties with the Indians in the 1850s had set aside the northern Wyoming area for Lakota hunting grounds. Ignoring those treaties, John M. Bozeman blazed a shorter trail to the Montana gold fields through the Lakota territory near the Powder River and Big Horn Mountains in 1862. In 1863 and 1864, he led settlers and miners across the same trail despite attacks from Indians who were protecting their land. In 1865, the Civil War ended and many projects to expand westward settlement began, including a transcontinental railroad, and forts built along the trails travelled by the settlers. Two of those forts were planned for the Bozeman Trail.

The government, well aware that its plans for westward expansion could be thwarted by an Indian war, directed that a peace treaty be signed with the Lakota. In October 1865, Major General S. R. Curtis and Newton Edmunds managed to get the some of the southern Lakotas to sign a treaty that listed all the Lakota bands, including those northern bands hostile to the invading whites. When attacks along the Bozeman Trail continued, the military realized that many of the Indians under such leaders as American Horse, Red Cloud and Crazy Horse had not agreed to the peace.

In January 1866, Colonel Henry E. Maynadier, commander at Fort Laramie, was ordered to do everything possible to get hostile groups to sign the treaty. When only a few of the bands came in to sign, E. B. Taylor of the Indian Office joined Maynadier in June 1866. He sent word to the Oglalas that they would receive guns and ammunition if they signed the treaty. It was enough to entice Red Cloud and some of his followers to Fort Laramie. However, Taylor attempted to deceive the group and did not tell them about the planned army forts. At the same time the talks were proceeding at Fort Laramie, Colonel Henry B. Carrington and seven hundred soldiers were making their way to the Powder River to build the first of the forts. When word reached the chiefs at Fort Laramie, they walked out of the negotiations in a rage.

The Fetterman Fight

In August, 1866, Carrington reached Piney Creek, which was about half way between the Powder and Bighorn Rivers, where he began building Fort Phil Kearny. Two infantry companies were sent further north on the Bozeman Trail to begin work on Fort C. F. Smith leaving Carrington three hundred and fifty soldiers. Fort Phil Kearny was one of the strongest forts ever built during the war for the Plains and provided a clear view all around to prevent any sneak attacks. However, not knowing anything about Indian warfare, Carrington built the fort about five miles away from his supply of wood.

Red Cloud set up his camp with some one thousand followers along the Powder River, close enough to the fort to harass the soldiers daily. As one of Red Cloud's chief lieutenants and a shirt-wearer, American Horse certainly was part of that group, although most historians do not mention him specifically. Charles King, in "Custer's Last Battle," noted that in the 1870s, one of the reservations established in the Black Hills "was the bailiwick of the hero of the Phil Kearny massacre, old Red Cloud, and here were gathered most of his tribe . . . and many of his chiefs; some "good," like Old-Man-Afraid-of-His-Horses and his worthy son, but most of them crafty, cunning, treacherous, and savage, like Red Dog, Little-Big-Man, American Horse, and a swarm of various kinds of Bulls and Bears and Wolves."

The Lakota coordinated their efforts to harass the soldiers at the fort, particularly when they ventured out to get wood for fuel and construction. Throughout the summer, the Indians attacked vulnerable soldiers, killing one or two during each attack. By September, the number of attacks increased. Martin F. Schmitt and Dee Brown in *Fighting Indians of the West* said that when the Indians were not attacking the soldiers they "raided wagon trains, stampeding or capturing horses and mules. They heaped hay on Carrington's beloved mowing machines and set them afire, stole most of his beef herd, shot up the herders, sent pursuing soldiers limping and crawling back to the fort with arrows driven into their bodies."

By December 1866, the number of Indians in Red Cloud's camp had increased to about two thousand. Following Red Cloud's orders, the shirt-wearers planned to use decoys to lure as many of the soldiers into the open as possible for an ambush. In late December after two failed ambushes, the decoys again attacked a group going for wood. Carrington sent Captain William J. Fetterman and eighty soldiers to the rescue, but ordered him not to pursue the Indians past Lodge Trail Ridge. Convinced that he could destroy the entire Lakota nation with only a few men, Fetterman disobeyed orders. The shirt-wearers led by Crazy Horse took charge of the decoys on December 21 and led Fetterman's troops past Lodge Trail Ridge and into Peno Valley where the rest of Red Cloud's forces waited. After about twenty minutes of fighting, Fetterman's entire detachment was killed. A relief column was able to retrieve about half of the bodies while a messenger was sent to Fort Laramie for reinforcements. The next day, Carrington himself led a detachment to retrieve the rest of the bodies. When the reinforcements arrived, Carrington was recalled and Captain H. W. Wessells took over command.

For the next two years, Red Cloud, American Horse and other Lakotas harassed the soldiers at both Fort Phil Kearny and Fort C. F. Smith. In April, 1868, a new peace treaty was drawn up that required Fort Phil Kearny to be burned to the ground. The Lakota returned to the Powder River after the treaty was signed to hunt. In the summer of 1870, American Horse joined Red Cloud and a group of other Lakota leaders on a trip to Washington, where the 1868 treaty was explained in more detail. On the way, the Lakota leaders saw the number of white people inhabiting the country and, although they spoke in anger to the government officials they met, many of the leaders agreed to move to a reservation on the Missouri River. While Red Cloud moved to a reservation, American Horse, Sitting Bull, Crazy Horse, Black Moon, Gall and Man-Afraid-of-His-Horse, chose to remain free to follow the buffalo. There are some references to American Horse at the Spotted Tail Agency and the Red Cloud Agency during the early 1870s, but he apparently only was visiting and did not live at either Agency for any length of time.

Custer's Last Stand

In 1874, George Custer made a discovery during a reconnaissance mission in the Black Hills that eventually led to his death. Gold was discovered in the Black Hills and drew a new wave of miners and speculators to Indian lands. Although the government broke its treaty with the Indians by allowing whites into the Black Hills, it was decided to send a new delegation to the Lakota to negotiate the purchase of the sacred land. Some seven thousand Lakota came to the council with the government in September 1875. Because the Black Hills were (and are today) important to the Lakota religion, the Indians were in no mood to sell. Red Cloud said he would not take less than seventy million dollars as well as beef herds to last seven generations. Others just called for war. No agreement was reached and the miners continued to swarm into the Black Hills. By the New Year, "there were eleven thousand whites in Custer City alone," according to Schmitt and Brown.

In December, 1875, the Lakota were told to move to one of the agencies immediately. Because it was winter, when no one moved about on the northern plains, the Indians remained where they were. Unfamiliar with the area and the tribal customs, the Interior Department ordered the military to force the Indians to the reservations. General George Crook, known to the Indians as Three Stars, was transferred to the region. On March 17, 1865, a detachment of his soldiers surprised a small Lakota camp under the leader He-Dog and destroyed all the tepees and winter stores of food. He-Dog moved his people to Crazy Horse's village. The following month Sitting Bull held a council to talk of war. At the same time General Crook attempted to recruit scouts at the Red Cloud Agency. Several of the older chiefs prevented the young warriors from going with Crook, who finally hired Crow scouts to lead him through the Black Hills. Crook led his troops east in search of more Indians while General Terry made his way to the Big Horn. Terry ordered Custer and the Seventh Calvary to find the Indians' trail and follow it until he found them or Terry himself. As the Indians under Sitting Bull prepared for war and hunted meat, many of the reservation Indians joined them. There were several minor skirmishes between soldiers and Lakotas before summer that year. By June, the Indians made camp at the Little Horn in the Big Horn Mountains.

Depending upon who tells the story, either Custer surprised Sitting Bull's camp or Sitting Bull cleverly ambushed the Seventh Calvary. Whichever version actually occurred, one-hundred and eighty-nine enlisted soldiers, thirteen officers and four civilians died on June 25, 1876 at the Little Big Horn, according to official military records. Others have indicated two hundred sixty-six soldiers were killed with another fifty-four wounded. Historians do not specifically mention American Horse at the battle with Custer, but evidence discovered a few months later indicates he and his band of Lakota probably were participants in the massacre.

After the celebration of their victory, the Lakota broke up into smaller bands and began their usual summer hunting for buffalo. In the fall, many started moving toward the Agencies. American Horse and his band travelled with the Miniconjous leader Roman Nose. In all, there were some two hundred warriors in their camp along with many women and children. They had good conduct certificates identifying them as part of the Spotted Tail Agency and planned to go there for the winter.

The Death of American Horse

The military wanted vengeance for those who had died at the Little Big Horn. When military reinforcements arrived, General Crook began moving down the Rosebud while Terry moved toward Yellowstone in hopes of finding some of the escaping Indians. Crook travelled light with as few provisions as possible so that he could move faster. By September, his supplies were depleted and his troops were slaughtering horses for food. On September 7, he sent Captain Anson Mills, known to the Indians as Bear Coat, and a detachment of one hundred and fifty men to Deadwood to replenish supplies. Late in the afternoon, scout Frank Grouard found fresh signs of Indians at a stream near Slim Buttes and reported it to Mills. The general had accidently come across American Horse's camp of some thirty-five to thirty-seven lodges. He decided to attack it. On the morning of September 9, Mills surprised the sleeping Indians by stampeding the tribe's horses through the camp. Many of the Indians escaped into the surrounding bluffs and started firing back. Believing that Crazy Horse had heard the first shots and come to the rescue, Mills sent a message back to Crook asking for help.

Mills was able to hold the camp until Crook arrived. While herding the horses through the Indian camp that morning, Private W. J. McClinton spotted Custer's Seventh Cavalry guidon hanging on American Horse's tepee. He turned it over to Mills, who later was given American Horses' tepee as a reward. The soldiers also found articles of soldiers' clothing, gloves labeled with the name of Colonel Keogh of the Seventh Cavalry who was with Custer, a large number of guns and ammunition, about one hundred and seventy-five ponies many of which were branded with "U.S." or "7 C," cavalry saddles, a letter addressed to a private in the Seventh Cavalry as well as several tons of meat and other supplies. It was considered more than sufficient proof that American Horse had taken part in the massacre in June. But, according to news reporters at the scene, some of the Indians later said American Horse had not taken part in that battle and that other Indians had brought these things to their camp.

When Crook arrived about eleven o'clock that morning with his two thousand troops, there was still a small group of Indians in a gulch a few yards away from the lodges. They had managed to kill some of Mills' pack mules and harassed the soldiers taking over their camp. When talking failed to get the Indians to come out, Crook ordered Lieutenant William P. Clarke to assault the gulch, but reporters traveling with the army hampered the operation. After some two hours of exchanging shots, Crook heard the squaws' death-chants and ordered the shooting stopped. John G. Bourke in *On the Border with Crook* described the scene around him.

"The women and papooses [sic], covered with dirt and blood, were screaming in an agony of terror; behind and above us were the oaths and yells of the surging soldiers; back of the women lay what seemed, as near as we could make out, to be four dead bodies still weltering in their gore." During the afternoon, Sitting Bull, who was camped nearby, came to rescue the Lakota at Slim Buttes. After exchanging fire with the soldiers he withdrew, realizing he was badly outnumbered.

Further discussions with the hidden Indians resulted in thirteen women and children surrendering. Cyrus Townsend Brady in *The Sioux Indian Wars from the Powder River to the Little Big Horn* said that later it was learned that "even the women had used guns, and had displayed all the bravery and courage of the Sioux." Crook asked the women to return to the gulch to tell the remaining holdouts that they would be treated well if they surrendered. A young warrior came out and received the same assurances, so he went back and helped American Horse out of the gulch along with about nine more women and children. The dead left behind in the gulch included two warriors, one woman and a child. American Horse had been shot in his gut and he was trying to hold his intestines in while he moved toward Crook. He also was biting down on a piece of wood to keep from crying out. He handed Crook his gun and sat down by one of the fires. He refused help from Crook's surgeon, but his wife apparently tried to stem the flow of blood with her shawl.

American Horse died that night. Mari Sandoz in *Crazy Horse: The Strange Man of the Oglalas,* reported American Horse said, "It is always the friendly ones who are struck," before he died. Other writers indicate American Horse said nothing before he died. Some sources reported soldiers scalped him after he died. A total of ten Indians, at least half of them women or children, died in the battle at Slim Buttes, while three soldiers were killed and another twenty were wounded. It was the first of many defeats for the Lakota.

Further Reading

Edwards, Ruthe M., *American Indians of Yesteryear*, Naylor, 1948. □

Adelbert Ames

The American political leader Adelbert Ames (1835-1933) was active in Reconstruction politics, serving as U.S. senator, governor, and leader of the Radical wing of the Mississippi Republican party.

On Oct. 31, 1835, Adelbert Ames was born at Rockland, Maine. He served as a cabin boy aboard a trading schooner, was an outstanding student at school, and developed a strong sense of duty. He received an appointment to West Point Military Academy and graduated fifth in his class just as the Civil War was beginning in 1861. He received the Congressional Medal of Honor for bravery at the First Battle of Bull Run, won promotion to the rank of brigadier general of volunteers, and by the end of the war had become lieutenant colonel in the regular army.

In 1868 he was appointed provisional military governor of Mississippi, where he worked hard to protect the newly freed slaves from harassment by whites and came to regard himself as their protector. As governor, he supervised elections in 1869, in which both black and white citizens participated to ratify a new state constitution and select officials for the civilian government. The newly elected legislature then chose Ames to represent the state in the U.S. Senate. In Washington he helped pass an extension of the Ku Klux Klan Act and emerged as the leader of the Radical wing of the Mississippi Republican party.

He was elected governor in 1873 but was unable to implement his program because of increasing terrorism aimed at intimidating voters, particularly African Americans, in order to reestablish white supremacy. His attempts to suppress this violence were unsuccessful, and Ames saw his party lose the next election to the Democrats. Disillusioned by his failure to aid the African Americans and isolated in the governor's mansion by a hostile Democratic legislature, Ames resigned his office in 1876.

He moved to New Jersey and then to Massachusetts, where he engaged in various business activities. In 1898, when the Spanish-American War began, he was appointed brigadier general of volunteers again and took part in the

siege of Santiago, Cuba. After the war he retired but remained alert and active for the remainder of his long life. He spent his summers in Massachusetts and his winters in Florida, where on April 12, 1933, he died at the age of 98.

Further Reading

Richard N. Current, *Three Carpetbag Governors* (1967), contains a good, short sketch of Ames. Blanche (Ames) Ames, *Adelbert Ames: 1835-1933* (1964), is a long, detailed account of his life by his daughter. A more personal view of Ames can be gained from the book compiled by his wife, Blanche (Butler) Ames, *Chronicles from the Nineteenth Century: Family Letters of Blanche Butler and Adelbert Ames* (2 vols., 1957).

Fisher Ames

The American statesman and political essayist Fisher Ames (1758-1808) was a superb congressional orator, noted for his active support of Alexander Hamilton's policies and for his leadership in the Federalist party.

Fisher Ames was born in Dedham, Mass., on April 9, 1758, the youngest child of Nathaniel and Deborah Fisher Ames, and brother of Nathaniel Ames. The father, a versatile physician, tavern owner, and compiler of a famous almanac, died when Fisher was 6 years old. Ames entered Harvard at 12, studied the classics, was trained in elocution, and in 1774 graduated as an outstanding scholar. During the Revolution he served briefly in the militia, but primarily studied law. As a rising Boston lawyer in the 1780s, he won acclaim with essays condemning Shays' Rebellion and advocating the centralization of governmental power. At the state convention of 1788, Ames's persuasive oratory was influential in obtaining ratification of the Federal Constitution. After one term in the state legislature, he defeated the popular Samuel Adams and became Boston's representative in the first Federal Congress; he was reelected for three terms.

Brilliant, intensely emotional, and urbane, he quickly achieved recognition in the House of Representatives, where his initial objective was to strengthen the new Federal government against encroachment by the states. Gravitating to the emerging Federalist party, Ames vehemently defended Hamilton's financial system against the attacks of James Madison. An advocate of elitist government, he predicted calamity if French Revolutionary ideas spread in America. His opposition both to Madison's resolutions for anti-British commercial policies in 1794 and to the spreading pro-French Democratic societies was a New Englander's response to deteriorating relations with Great Britain. He sought to arouse Federalists against the "French mania," convinced that unless the "Jacobinism" of the Jeffersonian Republicans was uprooted the nation's liberty would be lost.

Ames's greatest political triumph was his memorable speech on April 28, 1796, in defense of Jay's Treaty with

Great Britain. Though weakened by a recent illness, he dramatically persuaded the House to join the Senate in support of the treaty. At 38, discouraged by recurring ill health and by congressional friction, Ames reluctantly retired from Congress.

In 1797 he returned permanently to his Dedham estate, where he enjoyed a congenial family life with his wife, the former Frances Worthington, and their children. He resumed his law practice, experimented with scientific farming, and wrote vivid, opinionated political essays in his role as a spokesman of the Federalist party. Though Ames avoided public life, he served a term on the Governor's Council and in 1800 gave a moving eulogy on Washington. In 1806 he declined the presidency of Harvard. Persistently disagreeing with Nathaniel, his Republican neighbor and brother, Fisher Ames despaired at the triumph of Jefferson. The orator's death on July 4, 1808, gave Federalists an opportunity to rally party members for an impressive funeral, while Nathaniel Ames condemned their "mummery."

Further Reading

Fisher Ames's colorful letters and his essays are contained in Seth Ames, ed., *Works of Fisher Ames* (2 vols., 1854). The only full-length biography of Ames is Winfred E.A. Bernhard, *Fisher Ames: Federalist and Statesman* (1965). Background reading on the Federalist period includes Stephen G. Kurtz, *The Presidency of John Adams: The Collapse of Federalism, 1795-1800* (1957); Broadus Mitchell, *Alexander Hamilton* (2 vols., 1957-1962); John C. Miller, *The Federalist Era, 1789-*

1801 (1960) and *Toward a More Perfect Union* (1970); and Dumas Malone, *Jefferson and His Time,* vol. 3: *Jefferson and the Ordeal of Liberty* (1962).

Additional Sources

Ames, Fisher, *Works of Fisher Ames,* Indianapolis: Liberty Classics, 1983. □

Jeffery Amherst

Jeffery Amherst, Baron Amherst (1717-1797), was commanding general of the British forces in North America and then governor general of British North America.

B orn on Jan. 29, 1717, at Riverhead, Kent County, England, Jeffery, or Jeffrey, Amherst became a page to the 1st Duke of Dorset. Entering the army in 1731, he served as an aide to Gen. John Ligonier in the War of the Austrian Succession and participated in the battles of Dettingen, Roucoux, and Fontenoy. On Dec. 25, 1745, he became lieutenant colonel of the 1st Regiment of Foot Guards, and as an aide to the Duke of Cumberland he was present at the Battle of Laffeldt in 1747. Promoted to the colonelcy of the 15th Regiment of Foot, he accompanied Cumberland as commissary at the Battle of Hastenbeck.

Amherst was recalled to England in January 1758 and was given the rank of major general and command of an army of 14,000 men. His mission was to take the French fort of Louisbourg in Canada, which had been besieged since June 1, 1758; the garrison surrendered on July 26, giving the British their first important victory in the Seven Years War. After securing the Gulf of St. Lawrence, Amherst moved to Albany as commanding general in North America. His task was to drive the French from Lake George and Lake Champlain prior to joining forces with James Wolfe to besiege Quebec.

Ticonderoga fell to Amherst on July 27, 1759, and Crown Point on August 4. After he reached the northern limits of Lake Champlain, he learned of the fall of Quebec and closed his campaign. In recognition of his services, George III appointed him to the sinecure governorship of Virginia. In 1760 Amherst drove down the St. Lawrence from Oswego, meeting British forces from Quebec and from Lake Champlain, to take Montreal, which fell September 8. His conduct of operations during the Indian uprising led by Pontiac in 1763 has usually been criticized as inept. Amherst returned to England during the winter of 1763-1764.

In 1768, when George III decided that all governors should reside in the Colonies, Amherst resigned as governor of Virginia, giving up his military commissions as well. Several months later he was given additional military commissions and 20,000 acres in New York and was appointed to the sinecure governorship of the island of Guernsey. He declined to command the British forces in New England during the American Revolution. In 1776 Amherst served as

military adviser to the Cabinet and was made Baron Amherst. After France entered the war in 1778, he was appointed commander of the military forces in England and was active in the suppression of the Gordon riots. After the war he retired; in view of the approaching war with France in 1792, he was recalled to active duty. He left the army in 1795. A year later he was made a field marshal, the highest rank in the British army. He died on Aug. 31, 1797.

Further Reading

The best biography of Amherst is John Cuthbert Long, *Lord Jeffery Amherst: A Soldier of the King* (1933). An earlier study is Lawrence Shaw Mayo, *Jeffery Amherst: A Biography* (1916). Important background studies include Jack M. Sosin, *Whitehall and the Wilderness: The Middle West in British Colonial Policy, 1760-1775* (1961); Edward P. Hamilton, *The French and Indian Wars: The Story of Battles and Forts in the Wilderness* (1962); and David Hawke, *The Colonial Experience* (1966). □

Cuno Amiet

In addition to his strong personal qualities as a painter, the importance of Cuno Amiet (1868-1961) rests upon his having introduced French Postimpressionism into Switzerland. With Ferdinand Hodler he ranks as the first and most influential modernist Swiss artist.

Cuno Amiet was born in Solothurn, Switzerland, the son of the historian and local archivist J. J. Amiet in 1868. At the age of 15 he was apprenticed to the Swiss realist painter Frank Buchser, a powerful personality whose interest during the 1860s in the transcription of the effects of light prefigured that of the Impressionists. In 1887 and 1888 Amiet was enrolled at the Munich Academy, where he met his life-long friend Giovanni Giacometti (the father of the sculptor, Alberto), and in 1889 he and Giacometti transferred to the Académie Julian in Paris. During the summers he continued to work with Buchser until the latter's death in 1890.

Amiet found his academic training in Paris unsatisfying and, upon the advice of a friend, departed for Pont-Aven in 1892 and remained in that now-famous Breton village for 13 months. There he immediately came into contact with the painters and the work of the Gauguin circle (Paul Gauguin, himself, had left for Tahiti in 1891). It was this experience that made the deepest and most lasting impression on the artist and that made possible his full development as a colorist. While at Pont-Aven Amiet was also introduced to the art of etching by Armand Séguin.

Upon his return to Switzerland in June 1893 Amiet's new paintings were met with ridicule. It was only natural that he should therefore have been drawn to Ferdinand Hodler, an artist 15 years his senior and accustomed to doing battle with critics and the public. From 1898—the year in which he painted Hodler's portrait—through 1903, Amiet fell under Hodler's influence and sought a compromise between the color-rich, painterly manner of Pont-Aven and the strict draughtsmanship that Hodler had distilled from the German tradition. In 1904, when Hodler and Amiet were given major exhibitions at the Vienna Secession, Amiet was viewed as a young follower of Hodler, and he recognized the truth in this judgment. It was at this time that Amiet, returning to the path opened by the modern French art of Pont-Aven, developed into an independent artistic personality, and between 1904 and 1914 he produced some of the finest paintings of his career.

In February 1905 the Künstlerhaus in Zurich gave Amiet a one-man exhibition that, once again, proved to be controversial. This exhibition then travelled to Dresden, where, as the gallery director recognized, it was too far ahead of the public's ability to understand. Nevertheless, it was here that Amiet's work was seen by the future members of the first German expressionist group, called Bridge, or Brücke: E. L. Kirchner, E. Heckel, and K. Schmidt-Rottluff. Several weeks after Amiet's exhibition closed, Brücke was formally organized, and in 1906 Amiet was invited to join this important confraternity that he himself had inspired. He accepted the invitation, and his work was included in the first Brücke exhibition in December 1906. Amiet remained a member of Brücke until its dissolution in 1913, although his participation in its exhibitions and activities diminished in intensity after 1908. In 1907 Amiet had arranged for Brücke to show as a group in his native Solothurn, and was thereby instrumental in introducing yet another modernist current into Switzerland.

Amiet slowly forged his career over the years while working in the idyllic Bernese village of Oschwand. He was aware of the dangers of isolation but apparently needed the beauty of the landscape and the continuing attachment to his homeland for his personal and artistic growth. He settled in Oschwand in 1898, the year of his marriage to Anna Luder, a tavern keeper's daughter, and continued to live there until his death in 1961 at the age of 93.

Amiet had many students, and a stream of distinguished personalities including painters, musicians, writers, and scholars visited his studio. From 1910 onwards he received numerous official and private commissions, notably for the loggia of the new art museum in Zurich, the gymnasium (high school) frescos in Bern, and the exterior wall decoration of the new wing of the art museum in Bern. In 1919 he was awarded an honorary doctorate by the University of Bern.

The artist's physical isolation was largely overcome by a continuing participation in international exhibitions, an activity that reached its peak in 1912 with showings at Dresden, Munich, Cologne, Jena (with August Macke), Berlin, Frankfort, Hamburg, and Amsterdam. Although Amiet had not been in France since his return to Switzerland in 1893, he had by 1904 arrived at a style that remarkably paralleled the achievement of the Fauve painters at the same time. Both the Fauves (Matisse, Derain, Dufy, Vlaminck, Braque) and Amiet, working independently, had developed the possibilities inherent in the Postimpressionist works of Gauguin, Vincent van Gogh, and Georges Seurat. Amiet then exhibited his new paintings at the Salon des artistes independents in Paris during the years 1907-1909.

Although oil painting was Amiet's principal activity, he was a highly gifted watercolorist and printmaker. During the early 1920s he also turned his hand to sculpture and produced a group of expressive portrait busts in bronze and marble.

Amiet's career was singular by virtue of both its length (over three quarters of a century) and an astonishing variety of work that incorporated both French and German modernist elements. In 1934 and 1954 he was honored by major exhibitions at the Venice Biennale. In 1931 over 50 of his paintings, including some early masterpieces, were destroyed in the fire that consumed the Glaspalast (crystal palace) in Munich. Amiet surmounted this blow with an intense activity that ended only with his death 30 years later.

Further Reading

There is no full-length biography of Amiet and only one catalogue of his work in English—*Three Swiss Painters, Cuno Amiet, Giovanni Giacometti, Augusto Giacometti* (Penn State Museum of Art, Harvard University, Guggenheim Museum, 1973). The other sources are in either French or German: George Charensol, *Cuno Amiet* (Paris, 1932); Adele Tatarinoff, *Cuno Amiet* (Solothurn, 1958); Max Huggler, *Cuno Amiet* (Lausanne and Zurich, 1971); and George Mauner, *Cuno Amiet* (Zurich, 1984). □

Idi Amin Dada

As president of Uganda (1971-1979) Idi Amin Dada (born c. 1925) became notorious for massive violations of human rights, economic decline, and social disintegration.

Born between 1925 and 1927 in Koboko, West Nile Province, Idi Amin's father was a Kakwa. The Kakwa tribe exists in Uganda, Zaire (now Congo), and Sudan; some members of the tribe are associated with the Nubi, an uprooted population which emerged as a result of 19th century political upheavals. The Nubi (Nubians) are urbanized and individualistic, have a reputation for homicide and military careers, and are Muslims. Amin embraced Islam and attained a fourth grade education.

Amin was brought up by his mother, who abandoned his father to move to Lugazi. The death of his stepfather soon after separation from his mother led to speculation that he must have been either poisoned or "bewitched" by her.

Amin accompanied his mother and apparently acquired the militaristic qualifications prized by the British at that time: he was tall and strong, spoke the Kiswahili language, and lacked a good education, ensuring subservience. Enlisting in the army as a private in 1946, Amin impressed his superiors by being a good swimmer, rugby player, and boxer. He won the Uganda heavyweight boxing championship in 1951, a title he held for nine years. He was promoted to corporal in 1949.

Friendship with Obote

During the 1950s Amin fought against the Mau Mau African freedom fighters, who were opposed to British colonialism in Kenya. Despite his ruthless record during the uprisings, he was promoted to sergeant in 1951, lance corporal in 1953, and sergeant-major and platoon commander in 1958. In 1959 he attended a course in Nakuru (Kenya) where he performed so well that he was awarded the sword of honor and promoted to *effendi*, a rank invented for outstanding African non-commissioned officers (NCOs). By 1961 Amin and Shaban Opolot became the first two Ugandan commissioned officers with the rank of lieutenant.

In 1962 Amin participated in stopping cattle rustling between neighboring ethnic groups in Karamoja (Uganda) and Turkana (Kenya). Because of atrocities he committed during these operations, British officials recommended to Apolo Milton Obote (Uganda's prime minister) that he be prosecuted. Obote instead reprimanded him, since it would have been unpolitical to prosecute one of the two African commissioned officers just before Uganda was to gain her independence from Britain on October 9, 1962. Thereafter Amin was promoted to captain in 1962 and major in 1963 and was selected to participate in the commanding officers' course at Wiltshire school of infantry in Britain in 1963.

The need for pay increases and the removal of British officers led to an army mutiny in 1964. Amin was called upon to calm the soldiers. The resulting settlement from this

crisis led to Amin's promotion to colonel and commanding officer of the First Battalion Uganda Rifles. The 1964 events catapulted the army into political prominence, something Amin fully understood, and he used the political process to gain favors from his superiors.

Amin's close association with Obote apparently began in 1965 when, in sympathy for the followers of Patrice Lumumba (the murdered prime minister of Congo), Obote asked Amin for help in establishing military training camps. Amin also brought coffee, ivory, and gold into Uganda from the Congo so that the rebels there could have money to pay for arms. The opponents of Obote, such as the *Kabaka* (king) of Buganda (one of Uganda's ancient precolonial kingdoms), wanted an investigation of the illegal entry of gold and ivory into Uganda. Obote appointed a face-saving commission of inquiry and promoted Amin to chief of staff in 1966 and to brigadier and major-general in 1967. An attack on the *Kabaka*'s palace forced the king to flee to Britain, where he died in exile in 1969.

Amin Seizes Control

By 1968 the relationship between Obote and Amin went sour as the latter showed an interest in the young educated army officers and in creating paramilitary units. An attempted assassination on Obote in 1969 and Amin's suspicious behavior thereafter further widened the gap between the two men. These divisions became even more evident when Amin gave unauthorized assistance to the rebels fighting against the Sudanese government. It is unclear in light of these conflicts why Obote promoted Amin

in 1970 to become chief of general staff, a position which gave him access to every aspect of the armed forces. Amin overthrew Obote's government on January 25, 1971.

Ugandans joyfully welcomed Amin. He was a towering charismatic figure and yet simple enough to shake hands with common people and participate in their traditional dances; he was charming, informal, and flexible: and because he married women from different ethnic groups, he was perceived as a nationalist. His popularity increased when he allowed the return of *Kabaka*'s body for a royal burial, appointed a cabinet of technocrats, disbanded Obote's secret police, granted amnesty to political prisoners, and assured Ugandans that he would hand power back to the civilians.

During this euphoric period, Amin's other personality began to emerge: ruthless, capricious, cunning, shrewd, and a consummate liar. His "killer squads" systematically eliminated Obote's supporters and murdered two Americans (Nicholas Stroh and Robert Siedle) who were investigating massacres that had occurred at Mbarara barracks in Western Uganda. It was becoming clear that Amin's apparent friendliness, buffoonery, and clowning were but a mask to hide a terrible brutality.

In 1972 he savagely attacked the Israelis and the British who previously had been his close foreign allies. The bone of contention was his inability to procure arms from these countries. Once Muammar Qaddafi of Libya agreed to help, Amin immediately expelled the Israelis and 50,000 Asians holding British passports. The sudden expulsion of Asian traders not only wrecked Uganda's once prosperous economy, it also earned Amin a negative international image.

Between 1972 and 1979 Amin's overriding policy was to stay in power at any cost. Though outwardly looking brave, Amin was a coward. He was, for example, terrified in 1978 when a story circulated that a "talking tortoise" had predicted his downfall. He constantly changed body guards, travelling schedules and vehicles, and sleeping places. His promiscuous life style enabled him to have several possible sleeping places. At one time he was married to four wives and had over 30 mistresses. He controlled the army through frequent reorganization. The powerful position of chief of defense staff was abolished and replaced by army, air, and paratroop commanders. Similarly, when he was out of the country he entrusted power to a defense council made up of several people, making it hard for opponents to plot against him. He also appeased his forces by lavishing on them free whisky, tape recorders, expensive cars, rapid promotions, and lucrative businesses previously owned by Asian traders.

Trying to Stay in Power

Amin used institutionalized violence or terror to eliminate his real and imaginary enemies. His success in using terror was partly due to divisions among Ugandans who on different occasions became his willing spies. The human cost of Amin's rule was devastating not only in terms of the loss of thousands of Ugandans, but also because of its dehumanizing effects. Human life became less important than wealth. The ritualistic and sadistic methods used in the various murders led to conclusions by reputable doctors that Amin's "mental ill-health" must account for what transpired.

With most national funds devoted to the armed forces and to Amin's personal security, education, health, transport, food and cash-crop production, industrial and manufacturing sectors, and foreign investments were neglected. Despite his growing infamy, Amin was elected chairman of the prestigious Organization of African Unity (OAU) on July 28, 1975. Indeed, 1975 must have been a rewarding year for Amin, as his senior officers promoted him to field marshal. African countries also blocked in 1977 a United Nations resolution which would have condemned Amin for his gross violation of human rights. Through individuals and private companies in the West, Amin received torture equipment for his "killer squads," had his planes serviced and pilots trained, procured hard liquor for the army, and had his coffee sold.

By the late 1970s Amin's luck was running out. Coffee prices had plummeted from a high of $3.18 a pound to $1.28; the United States' stoppage of the purchase of Ugandan coffee in 1978 exacerbated the situation, and Arabs, who had generously donated funds, were concerned about Amin's failure to show how Uganda was being Islamized and why he was killing fellow Muslims. The deteriorating state of the economy made it difficult to import luxury consumer goods for the army. To divert attention from this internal crisis, Amin ordered an invasion of Tanzania in October 1978, allegedly because the latter planned to overthrow his government. The invaders were repelled. Tanzanians and exiled Ugandan soldiers then invaded Uganda and continued their pursuit of Amin until his government was overthrown on April 11, 1979. Amin fled to Libya, which had assisted throughout the years and during the war, but he later moved to Jidda, Saudi Arabia. Amin remained in Saudia Arabia until he was expelled in the early 1990s, when he relocated to Bahrain.

A continuing instability in Uganda attested to the enormous drain which Amin's policies had upon the political, economic, social, and cultural life of that country. Amin has been remembered best as the tyrant of Uganda who was responsible for a reign which was overwrought with mass killings and disarray.

Further Reading

Amin's fortune may be followed in: Iain Grahame, *Amin and Uganda: A Personal Memoir* (London, 1980); David Gwyn, *Idi Amin: Deathlight of Africa* (1977); Henry Kyemba, *State of Blood: The Inside Story of Idi Amin* (1977); Judith Listowel, *Amin* (1973); David Martin, *General Amin* (London, 1974); Ali A. Mazrui, *Soldiers and Kinsmen in Uganda* (1975); and Thomas Medlady and Margaret Medlady, *Idi Amin Dada: Hitler in Africa* (1977). □

Fernando Amorsolo

The Philippine artist Fernando Amorsolo (1892-1972) was a portraitist and painter of rural land-scapes. He is best known for his craftsmanship and mastery in the use of light.

Fernando Amorsolo was born May 30, 1892, in the Paco district of Manila. At 13 he was apprenticed to the noted Philippine artist Fabian de la Rosa, his mother's first cousin. In 1909 Amorsolo enrolled at the Liceo de Manila and then attended the fine-arts school at the University of the Philippines, graduating in 1914. After working three years as a commercial artist and part-time instructor at the university, he studied at the Escuela de San Fernando in Madrid. For seven months he sketched at the museums and on the streets of Madrid, experimenting with the use of light and color. That winter he went to New York and discovered the works of the postwar impressionists and cubists, who became the major influence on his works. On his return to Manila, he set up his own studio.

During this period, Amorsolo developed the use of light—actually, backlight—which is his greatest contribution to Philippine painting. Characteristically, an Amorsolo painting contains a glow against which the figures are outlined, and at one point of the canvas there is generally a burst of light that highlights the smallest detail.

During the 1920s and 1930s Amorsolo's output of paintings was prodigious. In 1939 his oil *Afternoon Meal of the Workers* won first prize at the New York World's Fair. During World War II Amorsolo continued to paint. The Philippine collector Don Alfonso Ongpin commissioned him to execute a portrait in absentia of Gen. Douglas MacArthur, which he did at great personal risk. He also painted Japanese occupation soldiers and self-portraits. His wartime paintings were exhibited at the Malacanang presidential palace in 1948. After the war Amorsolo served as director of the college of fine arts of the University of the Philippines, retiring in 1950. Married twice, he had 13 children, five of whom became painters.

Amorsolo was noted for his portraits. He made oils of all the Philippine presidents, including the revolutionary leader Gen. Emilio Aguinaldo, and other noted Philippine figures. He also painted many wartime scenes, including *Bataan, Corner of Hell*, and *One Casualty*.

Amorsolo, who died in 1972, is said to have painted more than 10,000 pieces. He continued to paint even in his late 70s, despite arthritis in his hands. Even his late works feature the classic Amorsolo tropical sunlight. He said he hated "sad and gloomy" paintings, and he executed only one painting in which rain appears.

Further Reading

Amorsolo is mentioned in Galo B. Ocampo, *The Religious Element in Philippine Art* (1965), and in National Museum, Philippines, *Aspects of Philippine Culture* (1967). □

Amos

Amos (active 8th century B.C.), the first of the literary prophets of ancient Israel, was the author of the biblical book bearing his name.

Amos was born in the Judean town of Tekoa, near modern Bethlehem, Israel. His activities probably took place during the reign of Uzziah, also called Azariah, King of Judah (reigned 783-742 B.C.), and Jeroboam II, King of Israel (reigned 786-745).

In his youth Amos was a shepherd. As a young man he tells of having received a divine commandment to go to the Israelite shrine at Bethel. Once there, he proceeded to fulminate against the popular errors of his day and was ousted by the head priest, Amaziah. Apparently, Amos was a prophet for only a short time, and he did not write down his prophetic messages and utterances. At that time, oracles such as those of Amos were preserved in an oral tradition; that is, they were transmitted by spoken word among Temple circles at Jerusalem. Amos's prophecies were probably written down before the kingdom of Israel was conquered by the Assyrians in 721 B.C.

His oracles are preserved in the biblical book of Amos, which is traditionally placed at the beginning of the Twelve Minor Prophets. Chronologically Amos is the earliest of these prophets, and his book offered a pattern for later prophetic books. The nine chapters are written in a poetic style with a prose introduction. They contain three kinds of composition: oracles telling of impending doom against Judah, Israel, and the neighboring peoples; a brief description of the life of the prophet; and a few verses that scholars generally agree are later additions.

Amos was particularly preoccupied with the moral corruption of his generation and their theological misconceptions. He denounced the corrupt aristocracy and its total neglect of the poor. He criticized those who made sacrifices to God but hypocritically neglected the moral law. He inveighed against those who presumed that they need give no accounting to God for their actions because they were His Chosen People. Above all, Amos shocked his contemporaries by dissociating his message and work from the prophets of his day and by foretelling doom and destruction for Israel. As a counterbalance to this apocalyptic message, Amos also predicted the restoration of the Davidic kingdom and the return of the Exiles. It is at this point that one can find a universalism in Amos which appears again for the first time in vivid form in the writings of Deutero-Isaiah. The God of Amos was not limited to one nation.

Amos has always been important in both Jewish and Christian theology and beliefs. The Talmud (Makkot 24a) states that all 613 commandments of Judaism are contained in one admonition of Amos: "Seek Me and live." Amos is quoted in the New Testament and by the early Christian Church Fathers, who interpreted him as prophesying the doom of Judaism and the rise of Christianity.

Further Reading

Discussions of Amos include R. S. Cripps, *A Critical and Exegetical Commentary on the Book of Amos* (1929; 2d ed. 1955); Julian Morgenstern, *Amos Studies,* vol. 1 (1941); Arvid S. Kapelrud, *Central Ideas in Amos* (1956); Norman H. Snaith, *Amos, Hosea, and Micah* (1956); John D. W. Watts, *Vision and Prophecy in Amos* (1958); and James M. Ward, *Amos and Isaiah: Prophets of the Word of God* (1969). Abraham J. Heschel, *The Prophets* (1962), devotes a chapter to Amos. Background information is in Bernhard W. Anderson, *Understanding the Old Testament* (1957; 2d ed. 1966). ☐

André Marie Ampère

The French physicist André Marie Ampère (1775-1836), with his original and penetrating analysis of the magnetic effects of current-carrying wires, was the founder of electrodynamics.

Born on Jan. 20, 1775, in Lyons, André Marie Ampère was the second child of Jean Jacques Ampère, a prosperous businessman, and Jeanne Antoinette Desutières-Sarcey Ampère. Once the boy had mastered the art of reading under his father's guidance, he showed a voracious appetite for everything in printed form. His principal love was mathematics and geometry. In these subjects his father's library soon failed to provide suitable material, so his father took him to the Lyons library, only to find that some of the best works in mathematics, such as most treatises by Leonhard Euler and Daniel Bernoulli, were in Latin. Young Ampère mastered Latin in a few weeks, as he had not only an uncommon talent for languages but also a consuming interest in the possibility of a universal language.

Intellectual Journey

Ampère married Julie Carron in 1799, and the responsibilities of married life helped him to start systematic work in mathematical physics. The years of his first public teaching position at the Collège de Bourg saw the publication of his essay on probability calculus. As a result, he was called to Paris to take the position of instructor at the Polytechnique. There he developed an absorbing interest in psychology and metaphysics, to the point that he wrote in 1805, "I delve more than ever into metaphysics . . . how admirable is the science of psychology . . . the only thing that still has interest for me."

The phrase is equally indicative of the impulsiveness of Ampère's intellectual journey. Shortly afterward, his brilliant but restless mind turned avidly toward the study of chemistry with the hope of elucidating the fundamental constitution of matter, as shown in his memoirs on molecular and atomic theories. But he kept returning to questions of physics and mathematics. During the first 15 years following his appointment at the Polytechnique, Ampère published memoirs on problems relating to geometry, calculus, mechanics, theory of gases, and optics. At the same time he

was also at work on a book which he wanted to publish under the title "Introduction à la philosophie."

Ampère's admission in 1814 to the Academy of Sciences followed a steady rise in the academic world. In 1808 he became inspector general of the University of Paris, in 1809 professor of analytical mathematics and mechanics at the Polytechnique. As inspector general he had to travel frequently, and it became his custom to name some of his scientific findings after the places where they occurred to him. Thus, he had his Theory of Avignon, his Demonstration of Grenoble, his Theorem of Montpellier, and his Proposition of Marseilles.

Achievements in Electrodynamics

In 1820, at the regular weekly meeting of the Academy of Sciences, Ampère heard a startling report: Hans Oersted, a few months earlier in Copenhagen, had discovered that a current-carrying wire had an influence on a magnetic needle. Two weeks later Ampère began his series of six weekly reports to the academy, much of which was published in the *Annales de chimie et de physique* (1820) and is now known as his first memoir on electrodynamics. In it he disclosed his historic discovery that in Oersted's experiment the magnet can be replaced by another current-carrying wire. Ampère also established that two parallel wires attract one another when the direction of current is the same in both and repel one another when the directions are opposite.

To this crucial experimental discovery Ampère added a wealth of experimental and theoretical details, many of which proved of lasting value. To provide for measurements independent of the earth's magnetic field, he devised a new instrument which he aptly called the "astatic magnetic needle." He showed that current-carrying wire wound as a helix acts in every respect as a bar magnet. He theorized that terrestrial magnetism in part is due to the circulation from east to west of electrically charged material inside the earth. He also anticipated the findings of 20th-century physics as he described ordinary magnets as an assemblage of closed electric circuits. Last but not least, he made the first suggestion about the use of his discovery as a telegraph.

Ampère read his second memoir before the academy in 1822. In it he gave his now-famous formula for the force acting between two current-carrying wires: the force is proportional to the product of the currents in the two wires and to the length of the wires, and inversely proportional to the square of the distance between the two. The memoir was also a classic example of the clarification of a physical problem through the thorough analysis of the geometrical situations involved.

Enormous as was Ampère's achievement in electrodynamics, it was clearly not to be the "last word" in the field of physics. His search for a definitive comprehension of all available information led him to the ambitious project of drawing up a final coordination of all sciences. The first part of his *Essai sur la philosophie des sciences,* or analytical exposition of the natural classification of all human knowledge, was published in 1834. The second part was published posthumously in 1843 by Ampère's son, Jean Jacques, who earned a reputation as a literary critic and author.

Ampère lived his last years in a state of mental exhaustion. Apart from his preoccupation with the classification of sciences, he had no taste or energy for anything. Many of his books remained unopened and uncut. He did not even care to provide the publisher with title and preface for his widely used text on differential and integral calculus. But to the end, he attended faithfully to his official duties. As he left Paris in May, 1836, on one of his tours of inspection, he fell sick and arrived in Marseilles in grave physical condition. There a sudden seizure of fever proved fatal on June 10, 1836.

Further Reading

There are several good biographies of Ampère in French. In English there is an informative, scholarly account of his life in Rollo Appleyard, *Pioneers of Electrical Communication* (1930). M. Arago, "Eulogy on Ampère," is available in English translation in the *Smithsonian Institution, Annual Report for the Year 1872* (1872). Good background sources include Philipp E. A. Lenard, *Great Men of Science: A History of Scientific Progress* (trans. 1933), and Harold I. Sharlin, *The Convergent Century* (1967). □

Roald Amundsen

The Norwegian Roald Amundsen (1872-1928) was the first explorer to reach the South Pole. One of the

greatest figures in the history of polar exploration, he was also the first to sail through the Northwest Passage.

Roald Amundsen was born in Borge. By age 15 he had determined on a career of exploration. He studied sailing techniques, steam navigation, scientific navigation, and terrestrial magnetism, and he trained himself to endure bitter cold and long travel.

After being a mate on an Antarctic expedition, he began at 25 to plan his own expedition. His aims were to attain the Northwest Passage and make magnetic observations near the North Magnetic Pole. His ship, the *Gjöa*, left Christiania harbor on June 16, 1903. Amundsen completed this voyage in 1906 by reaching the Pacific Ocean. He was the first to sail through the Northwest Passage, via Peel Sound, Roe Strait, Queen Maud Gulf, Coronation Gulf, Amundsen Gulf, Beaufort Sea, and Bering Strait. He had completed the first portion of his Arctic polar cap circumnavigation.

Robert E. Peary's attainment of the North Pole on April 6, 1909, convinced Amundsen that he should try to reach the South Pole. He resolved to reach the pole before the British expedition led by Robert F. Scott. After the establishment of three supply depots, on Oct. 29, 1911, Amundsen began the final dash to the pole with four companions and four sleds. On December 14 the Norwegian flag was flying at the South Pole. (Scott and his party did not arrive until Jan.

17, 1912.) On December 17 Amundsen began the return journey, completing 1,860 miles in 99 days.

In 1918 Amundsen left Norway in his ship *Maud;* his objective was to drift across the north polar sea from Asia to North America, but the polar ice pack made this an impossibility. He did reach Alaska, however, via the Siberian coast in 1920 and thus completed the Northeast Passage. This was the second portion of his circumnavigation of the world within the Arctic Circle.

The last phase of Amundsen's life was spent in new feats of polar exploration involving air travel. These were novel projects, more sensational than scientific in nature. In the spring of 1925 he flew in an airplane from Spitsbergen to within 150 miles of the North Pole. The next spring Amundsen, the American aviator Lincoln Ellsworth, and the Italian colonel Umberto Nobile used the dirigible *Norge* on the trans-Arctic flight from Spitsbergen to Teller in Alaska. The *Norge* passed over the North Pole on May 12, 1926. In 1928 Amundsen died in the Arctic during an air relief expedition in search of Nobile and the airship *Italia*.

Further Reading

Amundsen still awaits a definitive biography, but readers will find much in his own works: *The Northwest Passage* (2 vols., trans. 1908); *The South Pole* (trans. 1912); and *My Life as an Explorer* (trans. 1927). Two studies of Amundsen are Bellamy Partridge, *Amundsen: The Splendid Norseman* (1929), and Charles Turley, *Roald Amundsen, Explorer* (1935). There are numerous writings on polar history, but the best is L. P. Kirwan, *The White Road: A Survey of Polar Exploration* (1959; 1960 ed. entitled *A History of Polar Exploration*). □

Anan ben David

Anan ben David (active 8th century) was a Jewish religious leader in Babylonia who is believed to have founded the Karaite, or Scripturalist, sect about 760. The members of the sect were originally known as Ananites.

The account of the role of Anan in launching the Karaite sect must be viewed critically because it was written by a Rabanite opponent several centuries after Anan's death. The factual core contained in the available sources indicates that Anan was next in line of succession for the important hereditary office of exilarch, or head of the autonomous Jewish community in Babylon (now Iraq), because the reigning exilarch had died childless. However, Anan was passed over in favor of his younger brother Hananiah, who was less learned than Anan but more modest and pious. Anan was evidently rejected because he was apparently associated with a pseudo-messianic movement that displayed anti-Talmudic tendencies.

The Moslem chief of the region confirmed Hananiah for the post. Anan then proceeded to launch a secret organization of his followers, who were anti-Talmudists, and they appointed him as their own exilarch. When this was discovered by the authorities, Anan was arrested, imprisoned, and condemned to the gallows. In prison he met a Moslem legal scholar, identified as Abu Hanifa, who advised him to defend his conduct on the ground that Anan's religion was a different and separate one from that of Hananiah and therefore Anan could not be charged with rebellion against legally constituted authority. Abu Hanifa also advised Anan to stress the fact that his group did not follow the fixed calendar introduced by Hillel II about A.D. 350 but determined its calendar, in the Moslem manner, by actual observation of the moon. This defense, bolstered by substantial bribes, helped Anan gain his freedom.

The current of opposition to the Oral Law and rabbinic interpretation of Hebrew Scripture was an outgrowth or continuation of the Saducean tendency that survived the destruction of the Temple. In Babylonian Jewry it took the form of a rebellion against the exilarchate, which was identified with authority and the upper strata of the Jewish community. Of the numerous rebel movements, only the Karaites have survived to this day.

Though Anan opposed the authority assumed by the rabbis in expounding the Law, he did not hesitate to expound the Law himself. He composed his own *Sefer Hamitzvot* (Manual of Precepts) in Aramaic, which reflected his rigorous and ascetic inclinations.

Strict Karaite Doctrines

Anan ben David maintained that in exile no meat should be eaten except that of reindeer and pigeons. He extended the prohibition against kindling a fire on the Sabbath (Exodus 35:3) to apply to the burning of lights on Sabbath eve, though the lights were kindled earlier. His followers could do nothing on the Sabbath, except attend prayer services. Fast days were multiplied in Anan's calendar, and feast days were turned into mourning in accordance with Hosea (8:10), "And I will turn your feasts into mourning and all your songs into lamentation. . . ." The 70 days believed to be the period of Haman's preparation for the massacre of Persian Jewry (Esther 3:12) he designated as a period of mourning along the lines of the Moslem Ramadan. On the theory that a man and his wife shall be one flesh (Genesis 2:24), the relatives of a spouse were not permitted to marry the kin of the other spouse to the fourth degree. Thus permissible marriages were restricted to a ludicrous degree and caused a problem in the Karaite community. The Karaites could not receive medical aid because of the Scriptural verse, "I the Lord am thy Healer." These and similar prohibitions made life a gloomy affair for Anan's followers and impelled subsequent Karaite leaders to modify his rigorous code.

Further Reading

The best treatment of Anan ben David, which includes translated excerpts of his and other Karaite works, is in Leon Nemoy, ed., *Karaite Anthology* (1952). Volume 2 of Jacob Mann, *Texts and Studies in Jewish History and Literature* (1935; rev. ed. 1969), contains an interesting and valuable collection of documents. Good background material on the Karaites is available in Zvi Ankori, *Karaites in Byzantium: The Formative Years, 970-1100* (1959). □

Anaxagoras

The Greek philosopher Anaxagoras (ca. 500-ca. 428 B.C.) was the first to formulate a molecular theory of matter and to regard the physical universe as subject to the rule of rationality or reason.

Anaxagoras was born on the Ionian coast of Asia Minor in the town of Clazomenae, near Smyrna (now Izmir, Turkey). Nothing is known about his life before the age of 20, when he began to study philosophy. About 462 he moved to Athens, which was rapidly becoming an attractive cultural center. Anaxagoras was the first philosopher to take up residence in Athens. His teachings influenced the playwright Euripides, but his most famous pupil was Pericles, who dominated the political life of Athens during the 30 years Anaxagoras lived there.

Anaxagoras did not believe that the sun and moon were divinities, as the Greeks did, and he was prosecuted for his teachings. He returned to Asia Minor to a town allied with Athens, Lampsacus (now Lapseki, Turkey). Here he was treated with respect, and his memory was still honored a century after his death.

"About Nature"

Anaxagoras's views are preserved only in excerpts and summaries, more or less authentic. His book, written in prose, was entitled *About Nature*. It started with this assertion: "All things were together, infinite in number." This abrupt beginning was intended as a blunt contradiction of an earlier contention that the universe was "one continuous whole, which was not in the past," there being only an everlasting unchanging present. In direct opposition to this perpetually static monism, Anaxagoras propounded a constantly changing pluralism. He was the first philosopher to declare the number of separate things to be infinite (the universe as a whole having already been described as infinite).

Each of Anaxagoras's infinitely numerous separate things could be divided and further subdivided endlessly. All the things that were together were infinite not only in number but also in smallness: "Of what is small, there is no smallest part, but always a smaller." By contrast with the thinkers who maintained that matter consisted of those smallest units which were the atoms or indivisible particles, Anaxagoras believed in the infinite divisibility of matter. Nevertheless, as often as this process of subdivision was repeated, the resulting product always emerged as a unit of matter, however infinitesimally small it might be. In this sense Anaxagoras may be regarded as the author of the first molecular theory of matter.

Concept of Mind

His infinitely divisible things, infinite in number, were originally all together. How they had come together and where they had come from were questions not propounded by Anaxagoras. Thus, his universe began with a vast indiscriminate jumble or species of magma, which in the course of time was set whirling by Mind: "The whole rotation was controlled by Mind in such a way that in the beginning there was a vortical motion. At first the turning began on a small scale, but it spins more widely and it will spin even more widely."

What is more, Anaxagoras's Mind itself was not an insubstantial, incorporeal, exclusively mental, spiritual, or divine entity. Unlike a theist, Anaxagoras described his cosmic Mind as being the "most delicate and purest of all things." Nor was Anaxagoras a dualist in the conventional sense of one who counterposes mind against matter, for he declared that "Mind even now is where all other things are too, in the surrounding plenitude as well as in the things that have been assembled and those that have been disassembled."

Anaxagoras rebuked "the Greeks for not thinking correctly about birth and death, since nothing is born or dies; on the contrary, everything is assembled out of existing things and then dissolved. Accordingly, the Greeks would properly call birth 'combination' and death 'dissociation.'" In other words, any individual thing comes into being by combining preexisting components and is dissolved into its constituent parts when its existence is terminated. While individuals come and go, the building blocks or molecular particles persist. They move about freely and enter into new combinations without undergoing any change in their essential nature.

This unceasing flux of migration, combination, dissolution, and recombination is not senseless or chaotic. For Anaxagoras, cosmic Mind "is infinite and absolute; it possesses perfect knowledge of everything, exerts the greatest power, and dominates all living things, the biggest and the smallest." Since all life in Anaxagoras's universe is under the control of Mind, each molecular interchange occurs according to rule. His universe therefore is thoroughly rational, and what he called "Mind" is analogous to what was afterward termed the "laws of nature."

Split-Level Universe

To this overall vision of an orderly cosmos, Anaxagoras contributed some valuable details. Of these, unquestionably the most spectacular was his discovery that the moon does not shine by its own light. By contrast, in the Hebrew Bible the moon was the lesser of the two great lights; like the sun, which was the biblical greater light, the Hebrew moon was self-luminous. Presumably it is because the earth too receives light from the sun that Anaxagoras declared the moon to be earth. His earth and moon resembled each other also in having "flat areas and depressions." Anaxagoras's amazingly prescient description of the moon's ups and downs and his implicit denial that the lunar surface was perfectly spherical waited more than 2,000 years for visual confirmation by Galileo's telescope, and then more than 3

additional centuries for the direct physical proof provided by the American astronauts on the moon.

Anaxagoras believed (mistakenly) that the sun was a red-hot stone. Apparently generalizing from the instances of the sun and moon, he asserted that all the heavenly bodies were stone. His opinion that rock was the material of those bodies may have been inspired by the fall of a huge meteorite, said to have been as big as a wagon, near the Dardanelles when he was a young man. Since Anaxagoras correctly classified the meteorite as an object fallen from the sky to the earth, his universe was all alike. Later the cosmos was divided into an ethereal heaven, reserved for divinities, and the coarse earth, to which mere mortals were consigned. The painful process of reunifying this post-Anaxagorean split-level universe amounted to a return to the one world of Anaxagoras.

Further Reading

Daniel E. Gershenson and Daniel A. Greenberg, *Anaxagoras and the Birth of Physics* (1964), is a collection of the ancient references to Anaxagoras, arranged in chronological order and analyzed as to content; the bibliography is annotated. Also useful is Felix M. Cleve, *The Philosophy of Anaxagoras* (1949). Among the general books on early Greek philosophy that discuss Anaxagoras are John Burnet, *Early Greek Philosophy* (1892; 4th ed. 1930); Theodor Gomperz, *Greek Thinkers: A History of Ancient Philosophy* (3 vols., 1896-1909; trans., 4 vols., 1901-1912); and G. S. Kirk and J. E. Raven, *The Presocratic Philosophers: A Critical History with a Selection of Texts* (1962).

Additional Sources

Schofield, Malcolm., *An essay on Anaxagoras,* Cambridge Eng.; New York: Cambridge University Press, 1980.
Anaxagoras., *The fragments of Anaxagoras,* Meisenheim am Glan: Hain, 1981. □

Anaximander

The Greek natural philosopher and astronomer Anaximander (ca. 610-ca. 546 B.C.) attempted to explain the origins of the universe through his theory of the apeiron.

B orn in Miletus, Anaximander was the son of Praxiades. According to tradition, he was a pupil of the Greek philosopher Thales. Anaximander is said to have taken part in the founding of Apollonia on the Black Sea and to have traveled to Sparta. His book, *On Nature,* a title given by Alexandrian scholars to many works of its type, was still in use some 2 centuries after his death.

Anaximander was concerned with the origin of things. He found an explanation, having abandoned with Thales the old mythological cosmogonies, in his theory of the apeiron (the infinite)—that is, the universe is boundless and formless but is constituted of a single primary substance out of which all individual phenomena arise. This concept is similar in some respects to the "abyss" found in Eastern cosmogonies. Connected with the process of genesis and dissolution is *dikē,* or justice, which works inexorably through the ages. Individual existences commit injustice against each other simply by coming into being and thereby lessening each other's viability, but atonement is made when dissolution comes to the transgressor in its turn.

The earth, in Anaximander's scheme, is shaped like a cylinder and floats at the center of the universe. There would therefore be no reason for it to fall in one direction or another. He believed that the earth was originally covered with water, it dried in part, and man sprang from aquatic forms which had moved onto the drier parts and adapted themselves to the new conditions. The stars, in his bold theory, were really parts of a great outer fire surrounding the compressed air that encircled the earth and they could be glimpsed through holes or vents in that atmosphere.

Anaximander was credited in antiquity with having introduced the gnomon (a sundial with a vertical needle) into Greece, with which he was able to determine the equinoxes. He is also reputed to have been the first Greek to draw a map of the inhabited earth and to teach a doctrine of organic evolution. Although it is difficult to assess his contribution properly because of the defective information about Greek philosophy before Plato, he appears as a boldly imaginative thinker who broke with the mythological explanations of the universe found in the Greek poetic and religious tradition in favor of explanations based on logical premises.

Further Reading

Selected passages from the fragments of Anaximander, with English translation and commentary, are in G.S. Kirk and J.E. Raven, *The Presocratic Philosophers: A Critical History with a Selection of Texts* (1962). Among the specialized studies of Anaximander, Charles H. Kahn, *Anaximander and the Origins of Greek Cosmology* (1960), is noteworthy. There are excellent discussions of Anaximander in John Burnet, *Early Greek Philosophy* (1892; 4th ed. 1930), and Kathleen Freeman, *The Pre-Socratic Philosophers* (1946; 2d ed. 1959). Albin Lesky, *A History of Greek Literature* (1958; new ed. 1963; trans. 1966), is also useful.

Additional Sources

Gnagy, Allan S., *Thalaes, Anaximandros, Anaximenaes,* Athaena: Exantas, 1991. ☐

Anaximenes

The Greek philosopher Anaximenes (active 546 B.C.), last of the important philosophers of Miletus, was perhaps the first philosopher to insist on an underlying physical law governing the universe.

The details of the life of Anaximenes are almost totally unknown, but he is said to have flourished in the year of the fall of Sardis. He wrote at least one work expounding his philosophical views, and although now lost

it probably survived into Hellenistic times. What is known of Anaximenes's views emerges largely from discussion and criticism of his work by Aristotle and others. There is no question that Anaximenes was familiar with Anaximander's writings, since their views are very close.

Anaximenes postulated *aer,* meaning "vapor" or "air," as the basic substance out of which all other things arise. He described it as being invisible when evenly distributed, but by the process of condensation it becomes visible as cloud, water, and finally earth and stone. Rarefaction, on the other hand, causes air to expand and become hot and then turn to fire. Thus, Anaximenes could explain the creation of all forms of matter through the mechanism of condensation and rarefaction of this substance, air, that is obviously composed of discrete particles.

Anaximenes also assumed the air to be in a state of perpetual motion. This provided an explanation for the changes of density which produced the infinite number of worlds that came into being and then disappeared, being reabsorbed into the infinite air. He equated the air that supports the universe with human breath, which is identified with the soul. This implication that air possessed life was compatible with the contemporary belief in the identification of air or breath with life.

In his cosmology Anaximenes describes the earth, the first heavenly body to take shape, as having come into being through condensation; it is flat and floats, as do all heavenly bodies, on the primal and indefinitely extended air. The other heavenly bodies are fire in substance and arose by rarefaction of the water given off by earth. Anaximenes went on to describe the universe not as a complete sphere like Anaximander's but as hemispherical, with the stars passing around, not under, the earth.

In his attempt to present a rational, scientific view, in the form of describing a natural process as responsible for making a world, and by reducing qualitative differences to quantitative differences, Anaximenes was only partially free from mythological beliefs. However, he provided a pattern to be followed by the natural philosophers in the development of science.

Further Reading

There is no full-length biography of Anaximenes, but G.S. Kirk and J.E. Raven, *The Presocratic Philosophers* (1962), gives a good account of his life and work, although it is somewhat difficult to read. Cyril Bailey, *The Greek Atomists and Epicures* (1964), is a very readable exposition in which the ideas of Anaximenes are clarified and placed in historical perspective. See also W.K.C. Guthrie, *A History of Greek Philosophy* (2 vols., 1962), and Felix M. Cleve, *The Giants of Pre-Socratic Greek Philosophy* (2 vols., 1965). ☐

José de Anchieta

José de Anchieta (1534-1597) was an influential Jesuit missionary in Brazil who was especially con-

cerned with the welfare of the Indians under
Portuguese control.

José de Anchieta was born on March 19, 1534, in São
Cristóvão de la Laguna on Tenerife in the Canary Islands.
His well-to-do Spanish family sent him to the Jesuit College at Coimbra University, Portugal, in 1547. He entered
the Society of Jesus in 1551. His biographers credit him with
being an exceptionally intelligent student whose intellectual prowess compensated for physical infirmity.

In 1553 Anchieta accompanied Duarte da Costa, the
second governor general of Brazil, to the New World. In
1549 the Portuguese King had established a central government for the huge but underpopulated American colony.
One of his principal concerns was to introduce to Christianity the various Indian tribes, but this Christianization also
served as an effective means of incorporating the diverse
indigenous inhabitants within the pale of the Portuguese
Empire. The Jesuits, first sent out in 1549, bore the primary
responsibility of concentrating the seminomadic Indians
into *aldeias,* or villages, where they could hear the word of
God and learn the ways of the Portuguese. The Jesuits also
looked after the spiritual welfare of the Portuguese officials
and colonists in their new environment. Anchieta, then, was
one of 128 Jesuits who arrived in Brazil in the 16th century
with the task of transplanting Portuguese Church-centered
civilization to that colony. Though few in number, the Jesuits left a lasting imprint on the new land because of their
exceptional missionary zeal.

Anchieta began to teach in the south in São Vicente,
Portugal's first permanent settlement in Brazil, founded in
1532. He helped to establish several Jesuit schools and in
time taught at most of the important ones. His primary
concern, however, was with the Indians, and wherever
possible he helped to settle them into villages where, in
addition to being instructed in Christian and European
ways, they were protected from the labor demands of the
Portuguese colonists.

Anchieta campaigned vigorously throughout his life to
prevent the colonists from enslaving or exploiting the Indians. On more than one occasion he risked his life to
prevent or to end warfare between the Indians and the
Portuguese, or among the Indians themselves. Frequently he
worked at the side of Father Manuel de Nóbrega, who was
the Jesuit provincial of Brazil, and during one period was his
secretary. Anchieta was instrumental in helping to found
two of Brazil's most important cities, Sao Paulo and Rio de
Janeiro.

The master of several Indian languages, Anchieta
helped to make the Tupi tongue, the language of the principal Indian group along the coast, the lingua franca of the
otherwise heterogeneous Indians. He wrote a grammar of
the Tupi language which was later published in Lisbon and
widely used by missionaries, compiled a Tupi-Portuguese
dictionary, and translated prayers, hymns, and the cate-
chism into the Indian language.

Anchieta's many letters and reports provided later historians with invaluable primary sources for the study of
Brazil's development in the 16th century. They span the
period 1554-1594 and discuss a wide variety of subjects,
such as the civil authorities in Brazil, the bishops and prelates, the French incursions, the Society of Jesus and its
activities, education, and the customs of the Indians.
Anchieta also wrote poetry, composing his verses with
equal ease in Portuguese, Spanish, Latin, and Tupi, as well
as theatrical pieces, principally for didactic purposes.

In 1578 the father general of the Jesuit order in Rome
appointed Anchieta to the office of provincial of Brazil, a
position he held for 8 years. As before, he traveled extensively along the Brazilian coast to visit the principal settlements and missions from Pernambuco in the north to São
Vicente in the south. Retiring from the office of provincial in
1585, he went to Espirito Santo to continue his teaching and
missionary work. He died in Reritiba (today Anchieta) in the
state of Espirito Santo on June 9, 1597.

Further Reading

The only biography of Anchieta in English is Helen G. Dominian,
*The Apostle of Brazil: The Biography of Padre José De
Anchieta, S.J., 1534-1597* (1958). A background study is Bailey W. Diffie, *Latin American Civilization: Colonial Period*
(1945). □

Dorothy Andersen

Dorothy Andersen (1901-1963) was the first medical researcher to recognize the disorder known as cystic fibrosis.

Dorothy Andersen was the first medical researcher to recognize the disorder known as cystic fibrosis. She devoted much of her life to the further study of this disease, as well as to study of congenital defects of the heart. During World War II, Anderson was asked to develop a training program in cardiac embryology and anatomy for surgeons learning techniques of open-heart surgery.

Dorothy Hansine Andersen was born on May 15, 1901, in Asheville, North Carolina. She was the only child of Hans Peter Andersen and the former Mary Louise Mason. Hans Peter Andersen was a native of Denmark and was employed by the Young Men's Christian Association (YMCA) in Asheville. Andersen's mother was a descendent of Benning Wentworth, for whom the town of Bennington, Vermont, was named.

Andersen was forced to take responsibility for her own upbringing early in life. Her father died when she was thirteen years old, leaving behind an invalid wife dependent on her daughter's care. They moved to Saint Johnsbury, Vermont, where Mary Andersen died in 1920. Her death left young Dorothy "with not a single close relative," according to biographer Libby Machol in *Notable American Women.*

Andersen put herself through Saint Johnsbury Academy and Mount Holyoke College before enrolling in the Johns Hopkins School of Medicine, from which she received her M.D. in 1926. While still a medical student, Andersen published in the journal *Contributions to Embryology* two scientific papers dealing with the reproductive system of the female pig. After graduating from Johns Hopkins, Andersen accepted a one-year position teaching anatomy at the Rochester School of Medicine. She then did her internship in surgery at the Strong Memorial Hospital in Rochester, New York. For medical students an internship is normally followed by a residency, which ultimately leads to certification as a physician. Andersen found, however, that she was unable to find a hospital that would allow her to do a residency in surgery or to work as a pathologist, her other major interest. The reason for this slight, according to Machol, was that Andersen was a woman.

Denied the opportunity to have a medical practice, Andersen turned instead to medical research. She took a job as research assistant in pathology at Columbia University's College of Physicians and Surgeons that allowed her to begin a doctoral program in endocrinology, the study of glands. She completed the course in 1935 and was granted the degree of doctor of medical science by Columbia University. From 1930 to 1935 Andersen also served as an instructor in pathology at the Columbia Medical School. Andersen later accepted an appointment as a pathologist at Babies Hospital of the Columbia-Presbyterian Medical Center in New York City, where she stayed for more than twenty years, eventually becoming chief of pathology in 1952. By 1958 she had become a full professor at the College of Physicians and Surgeons.

Andersen's research interests fell into two major categories. The first of these involved a long and careful study of congenital (existing from birth) heart problems based on the examination of infants who had died of cardiac conditions. She began that study during her first year at Babies Hospital and was still publishing her findings on the subject in the late 1950s. Andersen's experience with cardiac problems was put to use during World War II when she was asked to teach courses for physicians who wanted to learn how to conduct open-heart surgery.

The second area of research, for which Andersen is probably best known, evolved out of her discovery in 1935 of cystic fibrosis. That discovery came about during the postmortem examination of a child who had supposedly died of celiac disease, a nutritional disorder. According to Machol, "her researcher's sixth sense alerted, Dr. Andersen searched for similar cases in the autopsy files and in the literature." Eventually she realized that she had found a disease that had never been described in the medical literature, to which she gave the name cystic fibrosis. Cystic fibrosis is a congenital disease of the mucous glands and pancreatic enzymes that results in abnormal digestion and difficulty in breathing; it is believed to affect approximately one in fifteen hundred people. Over the next twenty-six years, Andersen was successful in developing diagnostic tests for cystic fibrosis but less successful in her efforts to treat and cure the disease.

Andersen died of lung cancer in New York City on March 3, 1963. A contributing factor may well have been her smoking habits. As Machol has written: "Ashes from the cigarette that usually dangled from the corner of her mouth were virtually a part of her costume." Among the honors Andersen received were the Mead Johnson Award for Pediatric Research in 1938, the Borden Award for Research in Nutrition from the American Academy of Pediatrics in 1948, the Elizabeth Blackwell Citation for Women in Medicine from the New York Infirmary in 1954, a citation for outstanding performance from Mount Holyoke College in 1952, and, posthumously, the distinguished service medal of the Columbia-Presbyterian Medical Center.

Further Reading

Sicherman, Barbara, and Carol Hurd Green, editors, *Notable American Women, the Modern Period: A Biographical Dictionary,* Belknap Press, 1980, pp. 18-20.
Journal of the American Medical Association, "Andersen, Dorothy Hansine," May 25, 1963, p. 150.
Damrosch, Douglas S., "Dorothy Hansine Andersen," *Journal of Pediatrics,* October, 1964, pp. 477-479. □

Hans Christian Andersen

The Danish author Hans Christian Andersen (1805-1875) enjoyed fame in his own lifetime as a novelist,

dramatist, and poet, but his fairy tales are his great contribution to world literature.

Hans Christian Andersen was born on April 2, 1805, in Odense, Denmark. His father was a shoemaker and his mother a washerwoman, and he was the first Danish author to emerge from the lowest class. At the age of 14, Andersen convinced his mother to let him try his luck in Copenhagen rather than be apprenticed to a tailor. When she asked what he intended to do there, he replied, "I'll become famous! First you suffer cruelly, and then you become famous."

For 3 years he lived in one of Copenhagen's disreputable districts. He tried to become a singer, dancer, and actor but failed. When he was 17, a prominent government official arranged a scholarship for Andersen in order to repair his spotty education. But he was an indifferent student and was unable to study systematically. He never learned to spell or to write the elegant Danish of the period. Thus his literary style remained close to the spoken language and is still fresh and living today, unlike that of most of his contemporaries.

After spending 7 years at school, mostly under the supervision of a neurotic rector who seems to have hated him, Andersen celebrated the passing of his university examinations in 1828 by writing his first prose narrative, an unrestrained satirical fantasy. This, his first success, was quickly followed by a vaudeville and a collection of poems.

Andersen's career as an author was begun, and his years of suffering were at an end.

A lifelong bachelor, he was frequently in love (with, among others, the singer Jenny Lind). He lived most of his life as a guest on the country estates of wealthy Danes. He made numerous journeys abroad, where he met and in many cases became friends with prominent Europeans, among them the English novelist Charles Dickens. Andersen died on Aug. 4, 1875.

Literary Career

In 1835 Andersen completed his first novel, *The Improvisatore,* and published his first small volume of fairy tales, an event that went virtually unnoticed. *The Improvisatore* has a finely done Italian setting and, like most of Andersen's novels, was based on his own life. It was a success not only in Denmark but also in England and Germany. He wrote five more novels, all of them combining highly artificial plots with remarkably vivid descriptions of landscape and local customs.

As a dramatist, Andersen failed almost absolutely. But many of his poems are still a part of living Danish literature, and his most enduring contributions, after the fairy tales, are his travel books and his autobiography. In vividness, spontaneity, and impressionistic insight into character and scene, the travel books (of which *A Poet's Bazaar* is the masterpiece) rival the tales, and the kernels of many of the tales are found there.

World fame came to Andersen early. In 1846 the publication of his collected works in German gave him the opportunity to write an autobiography (published in both German and English in 1847). This book formed the basis of the Danish version, *The Fairy Tale of My Life* (1855).

Fairy Tales

Andersen began his fairy-tale writing by retelling folk tales he had heard as a child. Very soon, however, he began to create original stories, and the vast majority of his tales are original. The first volumes in 1835-1837 contained 19 tales and were called *Fairy Tales Told for Children.* In 1845 the title changed to *New Fairy Tales.* The four volumes appearing with this title contained 22 original tales and mark the great flowering of Andersen's genius. In 1852 the title was changed to *Stories,* and from then on the volumes were called *New Fairy Tales and Stories.* During the next years Andersen published a number of volumes of fairy tales, and his last works of this type appeared in 1872. Among his most popular tales are "The Ugly Duckling," "The Princess and the Pea," and "The Little Mermaid."

At first Andersen dismissed his fairy-tale writing as a "bagatelle" and, encouraged by friends and prominent Danish critics, considered abandoning the genre. But he later came to believe that the fairy tale would be the "universal poetry" of which so many romantic writers dreamed, the poetic form of the future, which would synthesize folk art and literature and encompass the tragic and the comic, the naive and the ironic.

While the majority of Andersen's tales can be enjoyed by children, the best of them are written for adults as well and lend themselves to varying interpretations according to the sophistication of the reader. To the Danes this is the most important aspect of the tales, but it is unfortunately not often conveyed by Andersen's translators. Indeed, some of the finest and richest tales, such as "She Was No Good," "The Old Oak Tree's Last Dream," "The Shadow," "The Wind Tells of Valdemar Daae and His Daughter," and "The Bell," do not often find their way into English-language collections. More insidious, though, are the existing translations that omit entirely Andersen's wit and neglect those stylistic devices that carry his multiplicity of meanings. Andersen's collected tales form a rich fictive world, remarkably coherent and capable of many interpretations, as only the work of a great poet can be.

Further Reading

The only complete collection of Andersen's tales in English is the translation by Jean Hersholt, *The Complete Andersen: All of the 168 Stories* (6 vols., 1949). His novels and travel books have all been translated but not in this century. Still one of the best sources of information about Andersen's life is his autobiography, *The Fairy Tale of My Life,* in a translation by W. Glyn Jones (1954). Excellent biographies are Fredrik Böök, *Hans Christian Andersen* (1938; trans. 1962), and Monica Stirling, *The Wild Swan: The Life and Times of Hans Christian Andersen* (1965). A good introduction to Andersen's method is Paul V. Rubow's essay, "Idea and Form in Hans Christian Andersen's Fairy Tales," in Svend Dahl and H.G. Topsöe-Jensen, eds., *A Book on the Danish Writer Hans Christian Andersen: His Life and Work* (trans. 1955). □

Carl David Anderson

The American physicist Carl David Anderson (1905-1991) opened up the whole field of particle physics for research by his discoveries of the first known antiparticle, the positron, and of the meson.

On September 3, 1905, Carl Daveid Anderson was born in New York City of Swedish ancestry. He attended Los Angeles Polytechnic High School and in 1924 entered the California Institute of Technology, with which he would be associated throughout his life. In 1927 Anderson received his bachelor's degree, and then continuing in graduate school as a Coffin research fellow and next as a teaching fellow, he obtained a doctorate *magna cum laude* in 1930 under the physicist and Nobel laureate R. A. Millikan. After working with Millikan at Cal Tech as a research fellow for 3 years, Anderson was promoted to assistant professor in 1933, to associate professor in 1937, to full professor in 1939, and to chairman of the Division of Physics, Mathematics, and Astronomy in 1962.

In 1946 he married Lorraine Elvira Bergman. The Andersons had two sons, Marshall and David.

Discovery of the Positron

In the years immediately after receiving his doctorate Anderson discovered the positron, or positive electron—a revolutionary discovery because the positron became the first known antiparticle and the first known positively charged particle other than the ordinary proton. Anderson made his discovery during his and Millikan's quest to determine the nature of cosmic rays by allowing them to pass through a Wilson cloud chamber immersed in a strong magnetic field. By 1931 he had found evidence indicating that the rays produced charged particles whose tracks are very similar to those produced by ordinary electrons, except that they are bent by the magnetic field in the opposite direction.

Several explanations of these oppositely bent tracks were possible: that they were due to low-energy protons; that they were due to ordinary electrons moving backward; or that they were due to positive electrons. Although the last hypothesis was the most logical, it was also the most radical, and only after Anderson (with the help of S. Neddermeyer) was able to eliminate definitely the first two did he feel compelled to accept the third. His famous photograph taken on August 2, 1932 unambiguously displayed a positron traversing a lead plate placed in the cloud chamber.

By the following spring, P. M. S. Blackett and G. P. S. Occhialini, working independently at the Cavendish Laboratory in England, produced a number of cloud chamber photographs indicating that a positron-electron pair—that is, matter—can be created by a gamma-ray photon (electro-

magnetic energy) interacting with the intense electromagnetic field surrounding a nucleus. They also recognized, as Anderson at the time had not, that Anderson's positron was the same particle that had been predicted by P. A. M. Dirac's 1928 relativistic quantum-mechanical theory of the electron. (Many physicists had believed Dirac's theory to be imperfect *because* it entailed the yet unobserved positron!) Subsequent work by Anderson and others established beyond doubt the proper experimental conditions for the materialization and annihilation of positrons.

In 1936 Anderson, again aided by Neddermeyer, made a second important experimental discovery: the existence in cosmic radiation of a very penetrating charged particle with a mass of about 200 electron masses, or of about one-tenth the mass of a proton. Anderson named these intermediate-mass particles mesotrons (later shortened to mesons) and believed them to be identical to the nuclear particle H. Yukawa had theoretically predicted less than 2 years earlier. It was later realized, however, that Anderson's meson is actually the mu meson (or muon), and Yukawa's meson is actually the pi meson (or pion). After World War II Anderson continued to cultivate the field of particle physics, which his momentous 1932 discovery had opened up for research.

Anderson received many honors, beginning, at just 31 years of age, with the Nobel Prize for Physics in 1936, which he shared with V. F. Hess. Anderson's contributions to the war effort earned him the Presidential Certificate of Merit in 1945. He received several honorary doctoral degrees and became a member of the National Academy of Sciences.

Anderson maintained his research and teaching activities until his retirement in 1976 with the title professor emeritus.He died in San Marino, California on January 11, 1991, at the age of 85.

Further Reading

There is a brief biography of Anderson as well as his own description of his prize-winning work in a Nobel Foundation publication, *Nobel Lectures Including Presentation Speeches and Laureates' Biographies: Physics, 1922-1941* (1965). Niels H. de V. Heathcote, *Nobel Prize Winners in Physics, 1901-1950* (1953), contains a short biography of Anderson. A historical-philosophical treatment of Anderson's discovery is in Norwood R. Hanson, *The Concept of the Positron* (1963).

☐

Judith Anderson

Judith Anderson (1898-1992) rose to prominence on stage and in films in America in the 1930s and 1940s, playing classical tragic heroines and dark character roles. She was probably most widely known for her film portrayals of the soap opera matriarch Minx Lockridge on NBC's *Santa Barbara* (1984-1987) and as a Vulcan High Priestess in *Star Trek III: The Search for Spock*.

Judith Anderson was born Frances Margaret Anderson in Adelaide, Australia, on February 10, 1898, to an English mother and Irish father. The latter had made (then quickly lost) his fortune in silver mines while his four children were still young. At an early age Judith was given lessons in singing and piano, but displayed a talent for elocution. After winning top honors in an elocution contest for recitation, she signed on as an actress with a touring Australian stock theater company, making her professional debut in 1915 in Sydney in *A Royal Divorce* at the age of 17. Three years later she and her mother traveled to America to explore the possibilities of success in the fledgling American film industry. But a letter of introduction from her Australian theatrical managers to movie director Cecil B. DeMille did little to impress. Anderson's features (not "cute" or "beautiful" by Hollywood standards) and her diminutive size (5 feet 4 inches) made her a liability, rather than an asset, to film acting at that time.

The mother and daughter pair then made their way across country to New York City to attempt to break into the legitimate theater. Judith would travel from one producer's office to the next looking for work, while her mother eked out a living for them as a seamstress in their one-room apartment. As luck would have it, Anderson was "discovered" by the director of the Emma Bunting Stock Company when, tired and ill from the flu, she collapsed in a producer's waiting room. Passing by, he offered her a place in the acting company at $40 a week (although she had to

Judith Anderson (far left)

supply her own costume). Within a year's time she was making $50 a week and playing leading roles. In 1920 she performed in a tour of the play *Dear Brutus* with one of the major stars of the day, William Gillette. Anderson had her first success on Broadway as Elsie Van Zile in a melodrama called *Cobra* (1924).

In the late 1920s and early 1930s she established herself as an actress of great emotional depth in serious dramas such as Eugene O'Neill's *Strange Interlude* and *Mourning Becomes Electra,* Luigi Pirandello's *As You Desire Me,* and Zoë Adkin's *The Old Maid.* She played Gertrude in Guthrie McClintic's production of *Hamlet* with John Gielgud in the leading role and Lillian Gish as Ophelia in 1937 as well as Lady Macbeth to Maurice Evans' Macbeth on Broadway in 1941 (a role she was to repeat several times both on stage and on television).

Perhaps Anderson's greatest stage triumph was the mythic, evil seductress Medea, which she first performed in 1947 in an adaptation especially written for her by her lifelong friend poet Robinson Jeffers (and for which she won a Tony award in 1948). One critic called her Medea "pure evil, dark, dangerous, cruel, raging, ruthless. From beginning to end she maintains an almost incredible intensity . . . she moves with such skill through explored regions of pain and despair that she can hold her audience in suspense throughout the evening."

Anderson's film career initially began in 1933, when she played a gangster's moll in *Blood Money.* She did not adjust well at first to the demands of film acting, but received an Oscar nomination in 1940 for her portrayal of the menacing housekeeper Mrs. Danvers in Alfred Hitchcock's mystery *Rebecca.* Her major films include *Kings Row* (1942), *Stage Door Canteen* (1943), *Laura* (1944), *And Then There Were None* (1945), *The Furies* (1950), *Salome* (1953), *The Ten Commandments* (1956), and *Cat on a Hot Tin Roof* (1958).

Her favorite actress was Sarah Bernhardt, who, like Anderson, excelled in dramatic roles and continued to act well into her seventies. In 1970 Anderson toured in a production of Shakespeare's *Hamlet,* playing the title role of the young, brooding prince at the age of 72. She was much maligned by critics in this endeavor, who, in this day and age of realism, could not overcome the anachronism of having someone of Anderson's age and gender play the role. Responding to questions about accepting roles in soap operas and popular films, she noted in an interview that "Bernhardt . . . would have accepted a daytime drama if they offered her one."

Anderson's acting can be described as very intense, focused, and controlled. She belonged to a generation of American actresses that included Ethel Barrymore, Helen Hayes, Laurette Taylor, and Katherine Cornell, women who represent the "classic" school of American acting, between the histrionic melodramas of the 19th century and the realistic "kitchen sink" dramas of the 20th. Her early training and success in elocution produced a mellifluous speaking voice, rich in tone and depth, which one critic referred to as "heavy" and "haunted," belonging "in the National Archives as a permanent treasure."

She was named Dame Commander of the British Empire in 1960 by Queen Elizabeth II for her outstanding contributions to acting. She also won two Emmys for the two performances as Lady Macbeth she gave on television (1954, 1960) and another Tony award in 1982 playing the nurse to Zoë Caldwell's Medea. Anderson was married and divorced twice. She died of pneumonia at her beloved California home on January 3, 1992 at the age of 94.

Further Reading

Synopses and insights into Anderson's career can be found in the following works: "Theatre Arts Monthly" (1936, 1939), *Great Stars of the American Stage* (1952), and *Actors on Acting* (1970). □

June Anderson

An American opera singer, June Anderson (born 1953) specialized in roles from operas by Donizetti, Rossini, and Bellini that require *bel canto* singing, although she sang operas by many other composers.

June Anderson was born in 1953 in Boston and raised in Connecticut. When she was 11 she began taking voice lessons at her mother's urging. At the age of 14 she performed in her first opera, *The Princess and the Pea* by Ernst Toch. At the age of 17 she sang the part of Gilda in *Rigoletto* and, in the same year, was a finalist in the Metropolitan Opera National Council Auditions. Although she was the youngest singer to be named a finalist at these auditions, she decided not to continue training for a professional career and instead went to Yale University where she majored in French and graduated *cum laude.* She then challenged herself to become a well-known singer in two years, and if she failed to do so, to enter law school.

It was at this point that she began working with the vocal coach Robert Leonard, with whom she studied for many years. He was able to depend on her hard work and high standards to develop excellent breath control, which allowed the natural quality of her voice to project itself unhampered by lack of support. His approach was to build a great voice over time and not to rush the process of growth. Anderson agreed with this approach and frequently declined offers to sing roles that she felt were not suited to her vocal development even though they posed no technical difficulties for her. She worked hard to develop her voice, even though there were many discouraging moments, and as she said, " . . . without a touch of luck, hard work doesn't necessarily pay off." It did, however, and she became a member of the New York City Opera Company, with which she made her debut in 1978 as Queen of the Night in Mozart's *Magic Flute.*

There were many operas in which she sang while at the New York City Opera Company, including *Le coq d'or* by Rimsky-Korsakov, *Rigoletto* by Verdi, the role of Donna Elvira in Mozart's *Don Giovanni,* three different roles in *Les*

Contes d'Hoffmann by Offenbach, *Il barbiere di Siviglia* by Rossini, *Giulio Cesare* by Handel, *La traviata* by Verdi, and a concert version of *I puritani* by Bellini. Although she received good reviews from New York critics, she felt that she was not being given the roles she felt ready for. As she put it, "I sang very few performances and covered just about everything for other singers!"

It was through the recommendation of Sherrill Milnes that Anderson was brought to the attention of Giovanni Lupetin, an agent for European opera houses. He arranged for her to sing in several provincial houses, where she was heard by Italo Gomez, the manager of La Fenice in Venice. He was so impressed by her voice that he offered to mount a production of her choice. Without hesitation she chose *La sonnambula* by Bellini, which she felt "was written for me." Anderson also signed a contract with La Scala, the opera house in Milan, to perform *La sonnambula* and with the opera house in Rome to perform *Semiramide* by Rossini.

European Debuts

It was at this point that June Anderson decided to move to Italy as she perceived her career to be developing more rapidly abroad than at home. Once she had made her debut in the major houses of Italy (she was the first non-Italian to win the prestigious Bellini d'Oro prize), offers to record and to perform came from all over the world. She sang *Die Feen* by Wagner in Munich in 1983. Her strong lyric vocal quality meant that repertoire outside the difficult *bel canto* style was possible for her, but she selected her roles with care. She sang in Canada and on the West Coast in the same year, performing *I puritani* in Edmonton and *Il barbiere di Siviglia* in Seattle.

In 1984 she again sang *Il barbiere di Siviglia,* this time in New Orleans; then *La sonnambula* in Venice; *La fille du regiment* by Donizetti in Parma; *Lucia di Lammermore,* also by Donizetti, in Geneva. In 1985 she began to sing operas that were not in the standard repertoire. In Pittsburgh she sang Verdi's *La battaglia di Legnano;* in Paris, Meyerbeer's *Robert le diable;* she also sang two Handel operas, *Samson* in Chicago and *Giulio Cesare* in Washington, D.C.

Although her life was centered in Italy, Anderson was acclaimed internationally both for the quality of her singing and the intelligence and willingness to work for the sake of the music rather than for herself. As she put it, "I attack the music from the inside out."

The following year Anderson made her debut at Covent Garden where she sang *Semiramide* to critical praise. She returned in 1987 to sing Lucia in *Lucia di Lammermore.* Her desire to explore further the lesser known works of the *bel canto* composers led her to accept roles in *Beatrice di Tenda* by Bellini in Venice, *Maometto II* by Rossini for San Francisco, and *Armida* by Rossini at Aix-en-Provence. She did not confine herself totally to unusual operas, however. During the same period she sang two standard works by Verdi— *La traviata* in Santiago and *Rigoletto* for both Covent Garden and for her Metropolitan Opera debut in 1989.

Recordings and Concerts

Throughout her career Anderson recorded and gave concert performances of several operas. By her own admission, the difficulties she encountered in finding adequately staged productions of *bel canto* operas caused her to consider whether she should increase the number of her recordings and concerts, avoiding the frustrations of the stage and permitting her to exert more control over the final result. In 1983 she presented Albinoni's *Il nasciemento dell' Aurora* in Vicenza and in Venice in concert form. In the same year she filled in for Monserrat Caballe in a concert performance of *Semiramide* at Carnegie Hall. That performance was very widely acclaimed, but resulted in no significant new offers for roles in the United States and was a contributing factor in her decision to move abroad to further her career. She returned to Carnegie Hall many times singing Handel's *Ariodante* and *Beatrice di Tenda* and Berlioz' *Nuits d'Ete.* She sang Bernstein's *Candide* in concert in London and planned to record the work.

Her recordings followed the thrust of her career, including some of the lesser known operas of the early Romantic period. She also recorded some of the French repertoire, which endeared her to the French, so much so that she was asked to perform in July of 1989 at the opening concert of Paris' new Opera Bastille. The French operas she recorded include Bizet's *La jolie fille de Perthe,* Adam's *Le postilion de longjumeau,* Auber's *La muette de portici,* and Halevy's *La juive.* In addition, she recorded Rossini's *Mose in Egito, Maometto II, Les soirees musicales, Il naciemento dell' Aurora,* and, for variety, Carl Orff's *Carmina burana* (a 20th-century work based on medieval Latin texts) and Bernstein's *Candide.*

Anderson's vocal qualities were admired by many critics on both sides of the Atlantic, even when her dramatic skills were not. She was compared to Joan Sutherland, Jennie Tourel, and Nellie Melba. Peter G. Davis in *New York* magazine wrote that her singing "shows off the clarity, evenness and facility of an agile voice with an easy upper extension." Words such as "creamy," "lush," "brilliant," and "assured" have been used to describe her voice. In her own words, she was "a big lyric (soprano) with high notes and agility."

After establishing herself as a prima donna in the United States and in Europe, June Anderson finally reached a level of achievement that placed her among the top international opera singers. Her special affinity for and ability to perform *bel canto* roles gave her career a direction and focus that served her well. The operas that require *bel canto* singing are written in a highly ornamented style that emphasizes the agility of the singer. The style flourished in the early Romantic period in Europe, particularly in Italy from about 1811 to 1843. Many singers find the unusual technical demands of the repertoire, particularly the high range and the rapid runs and ornaments, to exceed their ability to perform it well.

Throughout the 1990s, Anderson performed many roles for the first time, including Elena of *La Donna del Lago* in Milan (1992), Maria in *Mazeppa* at Carnegie Hall (1993), Desdemona in *Otello* in Los Angeles (1995), Rosalinde in

Die Fledermaus at the Metropolitan Opera (1995), Giovanna in *Giovanna d'Arco* in Barcelona and New York (1996), and Tatiana in Tokyo (1996). In 1997 Anderson assumed the role of Norma the Druid priestess for the first time at Chicago's Lyric Opera and received many good reviews. John von Rhein of the *Chicago Tribune* gave Anderson credit for "not only taking on such a tough role at this stage of a comfortably settled career but—amazingly—pulling it off so well" and asserted that her first playing of Norma "had to be reckoned a qualified success."

Anderson's talent was not narrowly confined, however. She appeared in many operas outside of the *bel canto* repertoire. Whatever period of music she sang, her performances were of exceptional quality.

Although some of her critics characterized her as tempermental and moody, her reaction to the impression that people are terrified of her is laughter. She described herself to Kathy Petrere of the *New York Times* in a 1995 interview as "Jell-O with chilies. A really distinct flavor, but in the end it's Jell-O." She admitted to being a perfectionist who "can't stand it" when she made mistakes. Anderson also defined what she deemed most important in life as "friendships," and noted, "If I never sang another note in my life [my friends] would still be there."As she commented in the same interview, "Singing is my job, it's not who I am."

Further Reading

Anderson has been reviewed frequently in magazines and articles. In the August 1986 issue of *Opera News* she appeared on the cover. In the *New York Times* on October 29, 1989, Walter Price wrote an article discussing her career and her debut at the Metropolitan Opera House. See also *Chicago Tribune* (February 7, 1997), *New York Times* (November 6, 1995; April 8, 1997), and *Opera News* (June 1997). Also see the June Anderson page online by Laurent Lacoquelle at http://pages.infinit.net/balza/junea.hmt. □

Marian Anderson

Marian Anderson (1902-1993) is remembered as one of the best American contraltos of all time. She was the first African American singer to perform at the White House and also the first African American to sing with New York's Metropolitan Opera.

Marian Anderson was born in Philadelphia on Feb. 17, 1902, and was educated in the public schools. She displayed a remarkable flair for singing when very young. Local supporters provided funds for study with Agnes Reifsneider and, later, Giuseppe Boghetti. When Anderson was 23, she entered a competition and won first place over 300 other singers, gaining her an engagement with the New York Philharmonic at Lewisohn Stadium. Further sponsorships enabled her to continue her studies in the United States and, after winning the Rosenwald Fellowship, in Europe.

Following debuts in Berlin in 1930 and London in 1932, Anderson concertized in Scandinavia, Germany, South America, and the Soviet Union. In Salzburg, Austria, she gave a sensational performance at the Mozarteum with famous conductor Arturo Toscanini in the audience. Upon hearing her sing, Toscanini reportedly told her she had "a voice heard but once in a century."

Return to the United States

At the end of her European tour, Anderson was an acclaimed sensation in the capitals of Europe, and American impresario Sol Hurok signed her to 15 concerts in the United States. On December 30, 1935, she opened her American tour at New York's Town Hall. The program was typical for Marian Anderson, consisting of songs by Handel, Schubert, Giuseppe Verdi, and Sibelius as well as several black spirituals. The performance was a resounding success, with critics welcoming her as a "new high priestess of song." In the words of a *New York Times* contributor, the concert established her as "one of the great singers of our time."

Over the next several years Anderson sang for U.S. President Franklin Delano Roosevelt at the White House, and she returned to perform for King George VI and Queen Elizabeth of England during their 1939 visit to the United States. She made several cross country tours and soon was booking engagements two years in advance. In one year she covered 26,000 miles in the longest tour in concert history, giving 70 concerts in five months. After World War II ended, she again performed in major European cities. By 1950, it

was estimated that she had performed before nearly 4 million listeners.

Marian Anderson's contralto voice was notable for its power and exceptionally dark texture, particularly in the lowest register. The high voice changed quality—not unusual in a contralto of prodigious range—but idiosyncracies never obliterated the fine musicality and sincere emotion that marked her performances.

Victory Over Racial Discrimination

With Roland Hayes and Paul Robeson, Marian Anderson pioneered in winning recognition at home and abroad for black artists. In 1939, an incident involving the Daughters of the American Revolution did much to focus public attention on racism. The DAR denied Anderson use of their Constitution Hall in Washington, D.C. for an April concert. First Lady Eleanor Roosevelt resigned from the DAR in protest, and the U.S. government placed Lincoln Memorial at Anderson's disposal. Her concert there, on Easter morning, drew a live audience of 75,000, and millions more heard it over the radio.

In 1942 she established the Marian Anderson Award for talented young singers; among the recipients were Camilla Williams, Mattiwilda Dobbs, and Grace Bumbry. Anderson married Orpheus H. Fisher, a New York architect, in 1943.

In 1948 Anderson underwent a dangerous operation for the removal from her esophagus of a cyst that threatened to damage her voice. For two months she was not permitted to use her voice and was unsure if she would ever be able to sing again. When she was finally allowed to rehearse, her voice returned free of impairment. Following her recovery, Anderson made her first post-World War II tour of Europe, including stops in Scandinavia, Paris, London, Antwerp, Zurich, and Geneva.

Her Operatic Debut

On Jan. 7, 1955, Anderson sang Ulrica in Verdi's *Un ballo in maschera* (*The Masked Ball*) at New York's Metropolitan Opera House, and she returned the following season in the same role. This was the first time an African American person had sung with the Metropolitan since it opened in 1883.

Over the years, Anderson continued to add to her accomplishments. She sang at the presidential inaugurations of Dwight D. Eisenhower and John F. Kennedy. In 1957, as an emissary of the State Department, Anderson made a concert tour of India and the Far East that was filmed by CBS-TV. In 1958 President Eisenhower appointed her a delegate to the 13th General Assembly of the United Nations. Anderson gave her farewell concert at Carnegie Hall on Easter Sunday in 1965.

Describing the range and quality of her voice, *New York Times* music critic Harold C. Schoenberg wrote: "Those who remember her at her height . . . can never forget that big resonant voice, with those low notes almost visceral in nature, and with that easy, unforced ascent to the top

register. A natural voice, a hauntingly colorful one, it was one of the vocal phenomena of its time."

Marian Anderson's honors included a doctorate of music from Howard University (1938) and honorary degrees from more than 20 other American educational institutions. She received the Springarn Medal from the National Association for the Advancement of Colored People in 1939 and the Bok Award of $10,000 from her hometown of Philadelphia in 1941. In addition to decorations from many foreign governments, she was awarded the Presidential Medal of Freedom in 1963. At age 89, in 1991, Anderson was honored as the subject of a 60-minute documentary broadcast over public television. She died on April 8, 1993.

Renewed accolades abounded in 1997, the centenary year of Anderson's birth. The Marian Anderson Study Center at the University of Pennsylvania was erected to hold her archives. On February 27, the day that would have been her 100th birthday, Robert Shaw conducted a tribute concert at New York's Carnegie Hall, joined by signers including Jessye Norman, William Warfield, and Roberta Peters. At noon the following Saturday, a gala of spirituals and art songs took place at Union Baptist Church, at 19th and Fitzwater Streets in Philadelphia—the church where Anderson prayed and sang as a little girl.

Further Reading

Information on Anderson can be found in the *Philadelphia Inquirer* (February 26, 1997); Hitchcock, H. Wiley, and Stanley Sadie, *The New Grove Dictionary of American Music* (Macmillan, 1986); Sims, Janet L., *Marian Anderson: An Annotated Bibliography and Discography* (Greenwood, 1981); and Tedards, Anne, *Marian Anderson* (1988). □

Maxwell Anderson

Maxwell Anderson (1888-1959), an American playwright noted for his verse dramas, tried to show men living by their beliefs even in a world where evil tends to dominate.

Maxwell Anderson was born in Atlantic, Pa., on Dec. 15, 1888. Since his father, William, was a Baptist clergyman who changed parsonages frequently, Anderson attended 13 schools in states from Pennsylvania to North Dakota. In 1911 he graduated from the University of North Dakota and married Margaret Haskett. He taught at Stanford University while earning his master's degree and held positions with the *Call-Bulletin* and the *Chronicle* in San Francisco. In New York from 1918 on, he contributed to the *New Republic,* worked on the *Evening Globe* and the *World,* and helped found a poetry magazine, *The Measure.*

The production of *White Desert* (1923) started Anderson's writing career on the New York stage. Of his eight plays produced prior to 1930, four were written in collaboration and one was an adaptation of a novel. His collaboration with Laurence Stallings on *What Price Glory?* (1924) was successful. A realistic portrait of men in war, it proved a welcome contrast to earlier romantic treatments of the subject. *Saturday's Children* (1927), a compassionate though conventional domestic drama, was received favorably. Anderson collaborated on an interesting failure concerned with the Sacco-Vanzetti case, *Gods of the Lightning* (1928), in which propaganda overcame dramatic skill.

Anderson's reputation soared in the 1930s. *Elizabeth the Queen* (1930) is a moving story of love confronted by the realities of politics and ambition. *Mary of Scotland* (1933) has a memorable picture of a woman overcome in a political battle to the death. *Both Your Houses* (1933), with its political intrigue in Congress, received the Pulitzer Prize. Anderson's wife had died in 1931, and he married Gertrude Maynard in 1933. Two years later he won his first Drama Critics' Circle Award with *Winterset,* a mature treatment of the Sacco-Vanzetti materials with a daring use of verse; he won this prize again with *High Tor* (1936), an effective blend of fantasy and reality. *The Star Wagon* (1937) and *Knicker-bocker Holiday* (1938) were popular successes. In 1938 he helped organize the Playwrights Company.

With the exception of *Journey to Jerusalem* (1940), the influence of the war appears in all his plays from *Key Largo* (1939) through *Truckline Café* (1946); the most esteemed is *The Eve of St. Mark* (1942). Columbia University recognized his accomplishments with an honorary doctor's degree in 1946. In the following year his *Off Broadway: Essays about the Theatre* was published.

After World War II Anderson's reputation faded. Of his last eight plays, *Joan of Lorraine* (1946) and *Anne of a Thousand Days* (1948) are notable, but only *Lost in the Stars* (1949), a musical adaptation of a novel on South Africa, was a critical success.

Following the death of his second wife in 1953, Anderson married Gilda Oakleaf. He continued to enjoy relative seclusion and a rural atmosphere while avoiding personal publicity and Broadway habitats. His thirty-second and last full-length play, *The Golden Six* (1958), was a failure. Anderson died in Stamford, Conn., on Feb. 28, 1959.

Further Reading

Barrett H. Clark, *Maxwell Anderson: The Man and His Plays* (1933), and Mabel Driscoll Bailey, *Maxwell Anderson: The Playwright as Prophet* (1957), discuss the plays. The fullest bibliographical treatment is Martha Cox, *Maxwell Anderson Bibliography* (1958). Suggested background reading with critical assessments are Arthur Hobson Quinn, *A History of the American Drama from the Civil War to the Present Day* (1927; rev. ed. 1936); Eleanor Flexner, *American Playwrights, 1918-1938,* (1938); and Walter Meserve, *An Outline History of American Drama* (1965).

Additional Sources

Shivers, Alfred S., *The life of Maxwell Anderson,* New York: Stein and Day, 1983. □

Sherwood Anderson

The works of the American writer Sherwood Anderson (1876-1941) are graced by a psychological complexity absent from earlier American fiction. His stories stress character and mood, and his style is laconic and colloquial.

Sherwood Anderson was born on Sept. 13, 1876, in Camden, Ohio, the third of seven children. His father was an easygoing, improvident man whose itinerant habits resulted in spotty educations for his children. Sherwood had no formal education after the age of 14, although he did attend Wittenberg College for a short time.

Anderson had a belated writing career. He served in Cuba during the Spanish-American War, then began a successful business career in advertising. But it was while owning and managing a paint factory in Elyria, Ohio, that he began, about 1908, to write stories and novels.

The turning point in Anderson's life came in 1912, when, suffering from nervous exhaustion and amnesia, he suddenly deserted his factory. The next year, with his brother Karl, a well-known painter, he went to Chicago and fell in with the "Chicago group"—Theodore Dreiser, Carl Sandburg, and others—through whose efforts his earliest work was published. *Windy McPherson's Son* (1916), his first novel, uses his father as the prototype for Windy, a drifter and teller of tall tales.

A second novel, *Marching Men* (1917), and a collection of prose poems, *American Chants* (1918), followed. Then Anderson published his masterpiece, *Winesburg, Ohio* (1919), a series of fictionalized sketches of "grotesques," his term for people defeated by false dreams, people whose illusions have left them vulnerable to profound hurts from which they never recover. Perhaps the best sketch is "Hands," the story of Wing Biddlebaum, a mournful eccentric who recounts his traumatic experience: he was once a loving small-town schoolteacher, but narrow-minded townspeople, acting on nothing more than a child's agitated and false report, branded Wing as a sexual deviant, drove him from the town, and almost lynched him.

The unity of *Winesburg, Ohio,* established by the presence of a perceptive observer (George Willard, a young reporter) and by the pervasive theme of human frustration, has led some critics to regard the book as a novel, a view taken by Anderson himself. Regardless of its genre, it is a significant expression of a theme associated with D.H. Lawrence—the psychological damage wrought by an industrial civilization—rendered with extraordinary compassion.

Despite his late start, Anderson was a prolific writer. *Poor White* (1920), a novel, was followed by *The Triumph of the Egg* (1921), a collection of stories, the most notable of which is "The Egg," a haunting symbolist tale of a man who has violated his nature by accommodating himself to his wife's ambitions. *Many Marriages* (1923), a novel, was followed by *Horses and Men* (1923), a collection of stories which includes "I'm a Fool," a superb, sympathetic treatment of the theme of American bravado.

Anderson's biggest money-maker, however, was the relatively weak novel *Dark Laughter* (1925), which attempts to measure the white man's crippling anxiety against the black man's tuneful laughter but succeeds only in contributing albeit unwittingly, to racial stereotypes.

Anderson was a heavyset Midwesterner with a leonine head and masses of wavy hair. He was comfortable only in casual clothes. An eccentric man, he once, in the 1920s, bought and edited two rival weekly newspapers in Marion, Va., one Democratic and one Republican. He was married four times; he had two sons and one daughter by his first wife.

Having deserted Ohio for Chicago, he traveled extensively in Europe. Although he continued to write until his death, his later work received scant attention. He died of peritonitis at Colon, Panama, on March 8, 1941.

Further Reading

For a long while the chief obstacle to an understanding of Anderson's life was his own notoriously unreliable autobiographical writings: *A Story-Teller's Story* (1924), *Notebook* (1926), and *Tar: A Midwest Childhood* (1926); the posthumously published *Sherwood Anderson's Memoirs* (1942) was reedited by Ray Lewis White in 1969. Probably the best studies of Anderson and his work are Irving Howe, *Sherwood Anderson* (1951), and James Schevill, *Sherwood Anderson: His Life and Work* (1951). More recent are Ray Lewis White, ed., *The Achievement of Sherwood Anderson: Essays in Criticism* (1966), and David D. Anderson, *Sherwood Anderson* (1967). □

José Bonifácio de Andrada e Silva

José Bonifácio de Andrada e Silva (1763-1838) was a Brazilian-born statesman and natural scientist. He was prominent in scientific and governmental affairs in Portugal and later played an important part in Brazil's struggle for independence.

José Bonifácio de Andrada was born on June 13, 1763, in the Brazilian seaport of Santos. He attended secondary school in nearby São Paulo. At the age of 20 he entered the University of Coimbra in Portugal, where he obtained a degree in philosophy in 1787 and in law in 1788.

In 1790 the Portuguese government commissioned Andrada to make a scientific survey of several countries of Europe. This led him to study mining, mineralogy, and chemistry in Paris and mining in Saxony. The survey took 10 years and gained him a reputation as a natural scientist of note.

After his return to Portugal in 1800, Andrada was appointed general intendant of mines. He also began a teaching career at Coimbra and held technical, scientific, and administrative positions. From 1808 to 1810 he fought against the Napoleonic invasion, rising to the rank of lieutenant colonel and a command position. In 1819, after 36 years' absence from his native land, he returned to Brazil.

Brazil was in a state of political unrest. In 1807 the Portuguese monarch, Dom João VI, had fled before Napoleon's troops from Portugal to Brazil and had brought large numbers of Portuguese to govern the colony. In 1815 he elevated Brazil to the status of a kingdom, but dissension between native Brazilians and the Portuguese continued. Andrada arrived in Brazil at a time when Dom João was being pressured to return to Portugal, and Brazilians feared that the country's status as a kingdom would be lost. Dom João did return in 1821, and Andrada became an adviser and counselor to the prince regent, left behind. Andrada was instrumental in persuading the prince to declare the independence of Brazil and to assume the title of emperor as Dom Pedro I.

Andrada continued as an adviser to Dom Pedro, but his brothers, Martin Francisco and Antônio Carlos Andrada, who were deeply involved in politics, became too outspoken. In July 1823 the Emperor dismissed José Bonifácio from his position as counselor, and the three brothers joined the opposition in the constituent assembly. Pedro dissolved the assembly in November, and the Andrada brothers were exiled to France. In 1824 the Emperor decreed a constitution which was based on a document José Bonifácio and his brothers had formulated.

Andrada returned from exile in 1829 to find once more political unrest in Brazil, with native Brazilians opposing Portuguese-born Brazilians. The latter supported Dom Pedro I, but the strength of the opposition forced the abdication of the Emperor in 1831. He appointed Andrada as tutor to his son, the 5-year old emperor Dom Pedro II.

The Andrada brothers continued to be active in politics, although José Bonifácio, as tutor, was forced into the role of observer rather than participant. Opposition to him as tutor developed, and in 1833 he was suspended from his position and accused of conspiring and disturbing the public order; he was later acquitted. He died at Paquetá, an island near Rio de Janeiro, on April 6, 1838.

Further Reading

Although there are several biographies of Andrada in Portuguese, there is none in English. Histories of Brazil dealing with the period in which he lived are scarce. José Maria Bello, *A History of Modern Brazil, 1889-1964* (1966), contains many references to Andrada's influence on Brazilian history. An older history, Mary Wilhelmine Williams, *The People and Politics of Latin America* (1930; rev. ed. by Ruhl J. Bartlett, 1945), refers to Andrada in brief sketches of Brazilian history. □

Count Julius Andrássy

The Hungarian statesman Count Julius Andrássy (1823-1890) served as prime minister of Hungary and later as foreign minister of Austria-Hungary. He negotiated the Austro-German Dual Alliance of 1879.

Julius Andrássy was born into a distinguished Hungarian aristocratic family at Kassa (now Košice in Slovakia) on Mar.3, 1823. As a young man, he supported the policies of the moderate reformer Count Stephen Széchenyi. Later, however, he switched to the more radical Louis Kossuth, who opposed Austrian control of Hungary and advocated Hungarian nationalism. In 1848 Andrássy took part in the Hungarian revolution against Austria. After Hungary's defeat he lived in exile in Paris and London. By the mid-1850s Andrássy had become an advocate of a Hungarian compromise with Austria. Receiving amnesty in 1857, he returned to Hungary and joined forces with the middle-of-the-road liberals. Together with Francis Deák and Count Beust, he participated in the preparation and execution of the Austro-Hungarian Compromise of 1867. This agreement established the Austro-Hungarian Monarchy, or Dual Monarchy.

Andrássy was appointed prime minister and minister of defense of the new Hungarian government. He was convinced that Hungary's territorial integrity was gravely endangered by Russian-supported nationalistic stirrings among the empire's Slavic minorities and by Russia's own designs on the Balkans. He sought to neutralize this danger by strengthening and perpetuating the German-Hungarian leadership in the monarchy and by increasingly relying on Germany's support. In 1871 Andrássy became foreign minister of the Dual Monarchy, and he worked with much success to strengthen the empire's international position. In

the interest of this policy, he agreed to a partial rapprochement with Russia in the form of the Three Emperors' League (1872), but he made certain that Austria-Hungary's interests would be protected in the Balkan entanglement that followed the crisis of 1875.

At the Congress of Berlin (1878) Andrássy secured the right to occupy Bosnia-Herzegovina. From his viewpoint this action was aimed at counterbalancing Russia's increased role in the Balkans, while also taking account of his compatriots' wish to limit the number of Slavs in the empire. Although this "occupation" (turned into "annexation" in 1908) satisfied Austria-Hungary's immediate political interests, in the long run it proved to be a serious mistake, which contributed much to the eventual dissolution of the empire. For Andrássy personally, its ill effects were more immediate. Domestic dissatisfaction with the policy of expansion, coupled with the difficulties of the occupation itself, led to his resignation in 1879. But before he left office, he capped his career with the conclusion of the Dual Alliance (1879), which united Germany and Austria-Hungary and thus was the ultimate fulfillment of his foreign policy. (It remained the cornerstone of the foreign policies of both empires until 1918.)

Following his resignation, Andrássy withdrew from most political activity and died on Feb. 18, 1890, at Volosca in Istria. He was a man of culture, refinement, aristocratic charm, and broad European outlook. His younger son of the same name (with whom he is often confused) was a distinguished statesman in his own right.

Further Reading

There is no acceptable biography of Andrássy in English. The only major work that includes him is by his son, Count Julius Andrássy, Jr., *Bismarck, Andrássy, and Their Successors* (1927). Among the excellent books in English that deal extensively with Andrássy's foreign policy are Alfred F. Pribram, *The Secret Treaties of Austria-Hungary, 1879-1914* (1920; trans., 2 vols., 1920-1921); William L. Langer, *European Alliances and Alignments, 1871-1890* (1931; 2d ed. 1950); and George H. Rupp, *A Wavering Friendship: Russia and Austria, 1876-1878* (1941). ☐

Andrea del Castagno

The Italian painter Andrea del Castagno (1421-1457) was a leading artist in the early Florentine Renaissance.

Andrea del Castagno was born in a village in the hills east of Florence. He is first recorded in Florence in 1440, when he was commissioned to paint frescoes (now destroyed) showing condemned traitors hanged, a traditional job given to little-regarded artists. Like nearly all the major Florentine artists of the age, he visited Venice (1442), where in collaboration with the otherwise unknown Francesco da Faenza he executed a modest set of saints with God the Father on the vault of a chapel in S. Zaccaria. Back in Florence, Andrea designed a window and executed minor works for the Cathedral (1444-1445). His frescoes for the lawyers' guild in Florence (1444-1445, 1447) are no longer extant, nor are his frescoes completing the life of the Virgin (1450-1452) begun by Domenico Veneziano in S. Egidio, Florence.

No records exist for the great frescoes Andrea painted for the Carducci country house and for the convent of S. Apollonia in Florence (these are now assembled in the Castagno Museum, S. Apollonia). For the hall of the Carducci house he painted a Virgin and Child, Adam and Eve, and nine famous persons—a local version of the "Nine Worthies" common on medieval tapestries. In Andrea's version three Florentine poets, three Florentine soldiers, and three famous women are depicted standing in simulated marble niches, both niche and figure hard and bright. From earlier Renaissance artists like Donatello and Masaccio, Andrea learned to paint massive three-dimensional figures, but unlike his predecessors he was not interested in integrating these figures harmoniously with the environment. Rather, he used his knowledge of perspective to make the figures dominate the space.

Andrea began the frescoes for the refectory of S. Apollonia about 1447. On the upper part of the end wall are the *Crucifixion, Entombment,* and *Resurrection;* the muscular men in twisting robes are presented on a single plane. On the lower part of the wall is Andrea's famous *Last Supper.* Thirteen stony figures sit around a long table in front of a paneled marble wall. There is no emphasis on the figure of Christ but some on Judas, isolated on the other side of the table. The room is actually drawn in rather deep perspective, the side walls half as long as the back one, but a shallow space suggested by the table and figures is what spectators register in this single case of elaborate perspective in Andrea's work. The frescoed monument to the general Niccolò da Tolentino (1456) in the Cathedral of Florence, like Paolo Uccello's earlier one to Sir John Hawkwood next to it, is a simulated sculpture; typically, Andrea eliminates Uccello's perspective brackets and flanks the base with muscular shield bearers. Andrea's other late frescoes, a *Trinity* and a *St. Julian* in SS. Annunziata, are more relaxed, letting light and air tone down the hard ascetic figures.

Andrea del Castagno died of the plague in Florence on Aug. 19, 1457.

Further Reading

The standard work on Andrea del Castagno is in Italian: Mario Salmi, *Paolo Uccello, Andrea del Castagno, Domenico Veneziano* (1936; rev. ed. 1938). There is no satisfactory monograph in English. □

Andrea del Sarto

The Italian painter Andrea del Sarto (1486-1530) was one of the most important painters of the High Renaissance. His highly expressive use of color is unsurpassed in Florentine painting.

With Michelangelo and Raphael working in Rome, Andrea del Sarto became the leading painter in Florence following the death of Fra Bartolommeo in 1517, and through his pupils, Il Rosso and Pontormo, he was a vital formative influence on the development of mannerism.

Andrea was born in Florence on July 16, 1486. He was the son of Agnolo di Francesco, a tailor (Italian, *sarto*), hence the name Andrea del Sarto. According to Vasari, who was a pupil of Andrea, he was trained with a goldsmith from the age of 7. An earlier source identifies Andrea's master, quite convincingly, as Rafaellino del Garbo, a highly competent and successful painter of the late 15th century. About the age of 20 Andrea set up an independent shop with Franciabigio, although he did not matriculate in the painters' guild until Dec. 11, 1508.

Early Period

In 1509 Andrea received his first important public commission for five frescoes in the entrance cloister of the Church of SS. Annunziata, Florence, depicting scenes from the life of St. Filippo Benizzi. Two further frescoes, the *Journey of the Magi* and the *Nativity of the Virgin,* added in 1511 and 1514, illustrate the very rapid development of his style. Of the panel paintings, the beautiful *Mystic Marriage of St. Catherine* (ca. 1512; Dresden) shows his deep understanding of Leonardo's art, particularly in the expressive and compositional use of chiaroscuro (light and shade). Andrea was very selective in the ideas and motifs that he derived from his great contemporaries Fra Bartolommeo, Michelangelo, and Raphael. His figures are not idealized but warmly human and even humorous. He showed a notably early interest in Northern woodcuts by such artists as Albrecht Dürer, Martin Schongauer, and Lucas van Leyden; and his interest in sculpture was not confined to the antique but extended to the use of actual models by his friend Jacopo Sansovino, with whom he shared a workshop from 1511 to 1517.

Middle Period

Between 1511 and 1526 Andrea painted the famous monochrome fresco cycle in the cloister of the Scalzo, Florence, which is one of the masterpieces of High Renaissance art. The elaborate, painted architectural setting and the sculptural clarity of the narrative established new standards in monumental fresco painting.

Outstanding among the panel paintings of this period are the *Madonna of the Harpies* (1517; Florence) and the *Wallace Madonna* (1517-1518; London). In these mature works the outward gaze of the saints and the compelling vibrancy of the color demand the devotional involvement of the spectator.

It was probably in 1517 that Andrea married Lucrezia del Fede, a widow, whose portrait he had included in the *Nativity of the Virgin.* Despite Vasari's condemnation, which was so readily accepted and elaborated in the 19th century, there seems to be no real evidence that Andrea suffered either moral or financial ruin as a result of this marriage.

Summoned by the French king, Francis I, he traveled to France in 1518, but his stay at Fontainebleau was very short for he was back in Florence by the autumn of 1519. The *Charity* (Paris) and the *Portrait of a French Lady* (Cleveland) are the only surviving paintings that he executed in France.

Andrea may have visited Rome in 1519-1520 in connection with the important commission from Pope Leo X for the decoration of the Medici villa at Poggio a Caiano, near Florence, since Andrea's fresco *Tribute to Caesar* (dated 1521) at the villa strongly suggests a direct experience of Raphael's work in Rome.

Late Period

Comparatively little is known of the later part of Andrea's life, although his presence is frequently documented in Florence and his paintings offer no real evidence of any extensive travels. In 1520 he purchased a site on the Via della Crocetta and built a house. In 1524 Andrea took his family to the Mugello to avoid the plague. There he painted the *Pietà* (Florence), which, though more restrained in its color and emotion than the earlier *Pietà* (ca. 1520; Vienna), forms the point of departure for the deliberately appealing beauty of the late works. The increasing idealization and the sometimes arbitrary but acutely expressive color of paintings such as the Quattro Santi (1528; Florence) and *St. Agnes* (1527-1528; Pisa Cathedral) provided a rich source of inspiration for the young generation of mannerist painters. Yet the powerful devotional feeling in these works is evident from the exaggerated praise that Andrea received from writers of the Counter Reformation.

He died of the plague on Sept. 29, 1530, and was buried by the religious confraternity of the Scalzo in the Church of SS. Annunziata.

His Character

Andrea seems to have been a kindly, unassuming man with high professional standards and a profound understanding of humanity. He was genuinely pious, sometimes working for a nominal fee or, as in the case of the *Madonna del Sacco* (SS. Annunziata, 1525), waiving his fee altogether. Vasari interprets this as timidity and weakness, but it is more likely that Andrea, who was patronized by the Pope and the King of France, was sufficiently prosperous to afford such generosity. His popularity in the 16th century is demonstrated by the survival of an exceptional number of copies of his works.

Commonly referred to as Andreino, he was short of stature, as noticeable in the self-portrait in the *Journey of the Magi* (SS. Annunziata). The most reliable record of his features is the self-portrait painted on a tile (1527-1528; Florence).

Further Reading

A complete reappraisal of Andrea del Sarto's role in the High Renaissance and the development of mannerism has been necessitated by two recent monographs that provide a thorough critical study of his life and works: Sydney J. Freedberg, *Andrea del Sarto* (2 vols., 1963), and John Shearman, *Andrea del Sarto* (2 vols., 1965), with a brilliant analysis of Andrea's use of color. An extensive discussion of the artistic developments in the early 16th century may be found in Sydney J. Freedberg, *Painting of the High Renaissance in Rome and Florence* (2 vols., 1961). □

Andrea Pisano

Andrea Pisano (ca. 1290-1348) was the most important 14th-century sculptor in Florence, as well as an architect.

Andrea Pisano, also called Andrea da Pontedera, was born in Pontedera near Pisa. He may have been trained in the shop of Tino di Camaino, a follower of Giovanni Pisano. Andrea's work before 1330 is unknown. According to Lorenzo Ghiberti, Andrea did many things for S. Maria della Spina, Pisa, though nothing extant can be assigned to him with certainty.

In a document of Jan. 22, 1330, Andrea's name appeared for the first time as *maestro delle porte* (artist of the doors) in connection with the first set of bronze doors for the Baptistery in Florence. He was *capomastro* of the Cathedral in Florence (1337-1340) and of the Cathedral in Orvieto (1347). He died sometime before July 19, 1348, when his son's name, Nino Pisano, appeared as *capomastro* in Orvieto.

His Works

The bronze doors of the Baptistery, which now adorn the south portal, are Andrea's masterpiece. In 1329 a member of the cloth merchants' guild, which was responsible for the decoration of the Baptistery, was sent to Pisa to study the doors of the Cathedral and later to Venice to secure a bronze founder for the project in Florence. According to a document of April 2, 1330, Andrea's wax model for the doors was finished. The doors, which were hung by March 15, 1336, are inscribed with Andrea's name. They consist of two large bronze wings decorated with 28 gilded reliefs set in quatrefoils. The lower 8 frames, 4 on each leaf of the doors, show the Seven Virtues plus Humility. The upper 20 frames tell the story of John the Baptist. In the narrative reliefs he relied on the mosaic cycle in the dome of the Baptistery and on Giotto's murals in the Peruzzi Chapel, Sta Croce, both of which tell the story of the Baptist. Andrea's style in these reliefs is Gothic and much closer to Giotto than to the Byzantine style of the mosaics.

The reliefs are medium high with, usually, a few figures moving across a shallow platform before architectural or landscape elements. The movements, dignified and restrained, spring from the rhythms Andrea established across the surface by deeply folded drapery and graceful, swaying postures. The figure sculpture is, in general, subordinate to the overall architectural framework of the portal.

Andrea was also responsible for a number of marble reliefs (1337-1340) on the two lowest registers of the Campanile of the Florentine Cathedral (now in the Cathedral Museum); in style they are similar to the bronze doors. A group of life-size kings, prophets, and sibyls (also in the Cathedral Museum) were intended to decorate niches in the Campanile. Though done more or less in Andrea's style, they are probably not autograph works. Two statues of Christ and St. Reparata (in the same museum), of remarkable quality, are commonly attributed to Andrea.

Further Reading

For the most up-to-date information on Andrea Pisano see John Pope-Hennessey, *An Introduction to Italian Sculpture,* vol. 1: *Italian Gothic Sculpture* (1955). □

Salomon August Andrée

The Swedish engineer and Arctic balloonist Salomon August Andrée (1854-1897) attempted the first balloon flight to the North Pole in 1897, but the three-man team perished.

Salomon August Andrée was born in Grenna, Sweden, on Oct. 18, 1854, the son of an apothecary. He obtained an engineering degree from the Royal Institute of Technology in 1873. After working in industry, he visited the United States in 1876, supporting himself as a janitor at the Swedish exhibit of the Centennial Exhibition in Philadelphia. During his short stay he became interested in ballooning and talked with the American balloonist John Wise of Philadelphia. In 1882-1883, after 2 years as assistant professor at a technical school, he wintered with the International Polar Scientific Program as aeroelectrical observer at the Swedish Spitsbergen Station. He then became first engineer in the Swedish Patent Office.

Andrée's ballooning began in 1893; after a grant to purchase a French balloon, he made a total of nine ascents. In 1895 the Swedish Academy of Sciences accepted Andrée's proposal to use a balloon to reach the North Pole. The balloon, called the *Ornen* (Eagle), was one of the largest ever produced. Made by Lachambre of Paris, it had a volume of 170,000 cubic feet, to be filled with hydrogen, and was constructed of varnished silk with rubberized seams. A cylindrical wicker car hung on suspension ropes. Danes Island (80°N, 11°E) in the Spitsbergen archipelago was selected as the launch location, but the winds proved unfavorable in the summer of 1896. On July 11, 1897, Andrée and two companions began the ascent, heading northeastward. Except for a few inconsequential carrier pigeon messages and marker buoys, no further word or sign was ever received form the party.

In the summer of 1930 a Norwegian scientific expedition accidentally discovered the Andrée campsite on White Island (81°N, 33°E). The bodies were returned to Sweden for heroes' funerals, together with diaries, photographic film, and camp remains. Mystery continued to surround the causes of the men's death, because ample food and fuel were found. However, in 1952 a Danish doctor proved that the deaths were caused by trichinosis contracted from polar bear meat. Although the team did not reach the North Pole, or even get near it, the expedition of the *Ornen* was a pioneering use of aviation in polar exploration.

Further Reading

The best English-language biography of Andrée appears in the Swedish Society for Anthropology and Geography, eds., *Andrée's Story: The Complete Record of his Polar Flight,* 1897 (1930). A popular fictionalized account of the flight is Per Olof Sundman, *The Flight of the Eagle* (trans. 1970). The importance of the Andrée expedition to polar aviation is best reported in John Grierson, *Challenge to the Poles: Highlights of Arctic and Antarctic Aviation* (1964). □

Giulio Andreotti

A long-time leader of Italy's Christian Democratic Party, Giulio Andreotti (born 1919) served his country in many important government positions.

Giulio Andreotti was born in Rome on January 14, 1919. He obtained a law degree with honors during Benito Mussolini's Fascist rule while beginning to participate in Catholic youth movements, especially as a journalist. He was the editor of the Catholic *Azione Fucina,* a weekly university magazine. He also collaborated with the Christian Democratic paper *Il Popolo* during its clandestine period.

When Italy was liberated in 1944 the young Andreotti became a member of the national council of Democrazia Cristiana (DC), the Catholic political party. In 1946 he was elected to the constituent assembly that was charged to draft the constitution of the new Italian Republic. In those same years Andreotti solidified his already prominent position by becoming one of the closest collaborators of Alcide De Gasperi, the Italian premier and indisputable leader of the DC in the post-World War II period. In this manner Andreotti reached the highest ranks within the DC and within the governmental apparatus at the same time, early in his political career.

Conservative Leader of His Party

At De Gasperi's death in 1954 Andreotti remained close to the centrist DC "old guard" leaders: he did not associate with younger Christian Democrats, such as Giuseppe Dossetti, who wanted to move the DC toward more liberal social and economic policies. In the 1960s Andreotti also resisted pressures within his party to form governmental coalitions with the Socialists. However, despite his opposition to the ideas of Christian Democratic

left-wing leaders such as Aldo Moro, Andreotti always managed to maintain good relations with political adversaries within his party. In fact, he was a cabinet minister (Interior, Finance, Treasury, Defense, Industry) throughout the 1950s and 1960s under liberal DC premiers. This continued presence at the highest levels of Christian Democratic and governmental power can be attributed to Andreotti's noted skills in striking compromises with every group while never losing his political autonomy.

Throughout his long political career Andreotti built up a solid basis of personal support among voters within his electoral district in Rome. He was elected to Parliament continuously beginning with the first legislature. He was also noted as one of the Italian political personalities who received the highest number of personal preference votes written manually on the ballots.

In the 1970s Andreotti held the post of president of the Council of Ministers (premier) several times. Of particular note are the cabinets which he headed between July 1976 and early 1979. This was a most difficult time in Italian political life. In addition to a deep economic crisis, there were problems about left-and right-wing terrorism and about the continued growth of the DC's principal rival, the Italian Communist Party (PCI). In 1976 the PCI made consistent gains at the polls, following an extremely tense campaign where it was feared the DC would lose its position as the largest Italian party in favor of the PCI. While this *sorpasso* (overtaking) did not take place at that time, the strength of the Italian left made it extremely difficult for the DC to rule. It was then that Italy's moderate leaders turned to Andreotti and his political pragmatism.

Andreotti Takes Charge

From the point of view of Italian anti-Communist forces it could be said that Andreotti accomplished a political masterpiece with the cabinet he headed, in particular between March 1978 and January 1979. Andreotti managed to form a minority cabinet comprised of Christian Democrats only, but with the external support—in Parliament—of the PCI. In this manner the Communists stayed out of the government, but lent it their support, because they considered this as a first step toward a *compromesso storico* (historical compromise) which they advocated; that is, a nearly unprecedented alliance between the PCI and the DC to form a government together. Andreotti's government, however, simply reaped the benefits of Communist cooperation while avoiding a true *compromesso storico.*

At the end of this experience the losers were the Communists. The PCI lost the support of voters who disliked a cooperation with the Christian Democratic arch-enemy that did not result in a clear PCI influence on governmental programs and policies. The PCI then abandoned its attempts at *compromesso storico* and returned to the more traditional efforts of forming a left-wing government with the Socialists. One of Andreotti's many quips describes well the Communist situation at the time: asked whether power wears one down, Andreotti promptly replied that power wears down "those who do not have it." Prophetic words, as the PCI steadily lost ground in the 1980s. Andreotti's great achievement, in the eyes of Italian anti-Communists then, was to have helped keep the PCI at bay at the time of its greatest strength between 1976 and 1979. Andreotti's ability in striking an unlikely political compromise—the external support by the PCI—was at the core of this success.

In the 1980s Andreotti often held the post of minister of foreign affairs. In that post he was noted for his pro-Arab policies, generally in agreement with other leaders of the European Economic Community but in contrast with American diplomacy. In the summer of 1989 Andreotti became once again premier by pacifying bitter disputes between Socialist and Christian Democratic coalition leaders such as Bettino Craxi and Ciriaco De Mita. Andreotti was considered a leading candidate to become president of the Italian Republic after Francesco Cossiga.

Andreotti began a rapid descent from power in 1992. Two important events occurred during this time that led to his decline: the collapse of communism in Eastern Europe and the occurrence of the most important Mafia trial in history, in which many Mafia bosses were convicted and sentenced to life in prison. The United States had been particularly interested in protecting Andreotti during the cold war, since Italy was on the borderline between East and West, but after the collapse of communism in Eastern Europe, his role was no longer as crucial.

In 1994, the Christian Democratic party collapsed under the weight of corruption investigations. Andreotti was accused of affiliation with the Sicilian Mafia, Cosa Nostra, and went on trial in September 1995. The complex trial was expected to last several years. He was also accused of the 1979 murder of a journalist, Mino Pecorelli, who supposedly had unflattering information about Andreotti that he planned to publish. Andreotti maintained his innocence and claimed the accusations were politically motivated. In reaction to his trial, Andreotti said, "Everything considered, I have been very fortunate in life. . . . I think that in order to merit the next life one must undergo a severe trial. I would rather have had a trial of a different nature. But I believe in the justice of the afterlife and not just on earth, and that gives me a lot of serenity" (*NetNews,* June 16, 1996).

Andreotti is the author of numerous books. Among them (all in Italian) are a biography of Alcide De Gasperi, *De Gasperi e il suo tempo* (1965), and three volumes of recollections and observations about world leaders whom Andreotti met in the course of his long political career: *Visit da Vicino* (1982); *Visti da Vicino-Seconda Serie* (1983); and *Visit da Vicino-Terza Serie* (1985).

Further Reading

Little has been written concerning Giulio Andreotti in English. One may find occasional references in newspapers, such as the *New York Times* and *Washington Post*. See also *Who's Who in Italy* (1986) and *Who's Who in the World* (1996). In the Italian language see Paolo Possenti, *Storia della DC della origini al centrosinistra* (Rome: 1978) and Giulio Andreotti, *Diari, 1976-79: gli anni della solidarieta* (Milan: 1981). See also Alexander Stille, *Excellent Cadavers: The Mafia and the Death of the First Italian Republic* (1995), *The Independent* (September 24, 1995), and the *New Republic* (April 15, 1996). Web sites that contain information on Andreotti include *NetNews,* http://www.liber.se/aw/newnews and Committee for a Safe Society, http://www.alternatives.com./crime. □

Mario Andretti

Mario Andretti's name is virtually synonymous with the sport of race car driving. A versatile driver with a charasmatic personality, he has won numerous races and seen two sons and a nephew become successful in the sport.

For many people all over the world, the name Mario Andretti is synonymous with automobile racing. From humble beginnings in a small Italian village, Andretti went on to become one of the most successful drivers in the history of the sport. Andretti's most amazing accomplishment was his versatility. He excelled in virtually every type of car and on every type of track there is, from 24-hour marathons to the Indianapolis 500. According to a 1989 poll, Andretti's name was better known to the American public than were the names of the next two most famous race car drivers—A. J. Foyt and Richard Petty—combined. During the peak years of his racing career in the 1960s and 1970s, Andretti earned a reputation as one of the sport's most daring drivers, as well as one of its most colorful personalities.

Though an avid racing fan from an early age, the circumstances of Andretti's youth were hardly conducive to a career as a top driver. He was born on February 28, 1940, in Montona, a northern Italian village near Trieste on the Istrian Peninsula. His father, Alvise, was a respected and influential farm administrator. The family lost all of its property during the Second World War, however, and after the war, the region became part of Yugoslavia. The Andrettis spent their first few years after the war in a camp for displaced persons. In 1948, Alvise moved the family to Lucca, a town near Florence, in order to maintain Italian citizenship. There he found a job working in a toy factory.

Bitten by Racing Bug Early

As young children, Mario and his twin brother, Aldo, became fascinated with cars and racing. The course of the Mille Miglia, Italy's famous 1,000-mile road race, went through Florence, and the boys were mesmerized by the noise and excitement of the event. Since the Andrettis lived across the street from a garage, the twins spent a great deal of their time hanging around mechanics and learning as much as they could about cars. Their hero was Alberto Ascari, one of the most famous drivers in Italy at the time. At the age of 13, Mario and Aldo entered a program for young race car driving hopefuls, against the wishes of their disapproving father. The only person Andretti told about his racing was an uncle, who also happened to be his priest. The youth racing program was eventually canceled because so many boys were getting injured, but the Andretti twins continued to pursue their hobby in secret.

In 1955 the entire Andretti family moved to the United States, settling in Nazareth, Pennsylvania, where an uncle already lived. By 1958, the twins had saved enough money to buy their first car, a 1948 Hudson Hornet. They rebuilt the car themselves, and began racing it at the half-mile Nazareth Speedway. One brother would drive the Hudson, while the other would borrow a car. Still keeping their racing a secret from their father, the Andretti boys quickly began to dominate the local racing scene, winning one stock car race after another. Papa Andretti finally learned the truth when Aldo, by most accounts the more aggressive driver of the pair, was seriously injured in racing accident at Hatfield, Pennsylvania. The crash put Aldo into a coma for two weeks, and although he recovered from his injuries, he was never able to successfully resume his driving career.

Meanwhile, Mario's career was getting ready to shift into high gear. Working weekdays as a mechanic, he drove on evenings and weekends, gradually making his way through the ranks of three-quarter midget cars, midget cars, and modified racers. In 1961 he married his high school sweetheart, Dee Ann Hoch. Around the same time, he quit his garage job, and decided to devote his attention to full-time racing. In 1962 Andretti raced sprint cars on the United Racing Club's Eastern circuit. The following year, he won 11 American Race Drivers Club midget car races, including three races in two different states on Labor Day, 1963.

Took USAC Crown as Rookie

By 1964 Andretti had caught the attention of Clint Brawner, chief mechanic for prominent race car sponsor Al

Dean of Dean Van Lines. When Dean's main driver, Chuck Hulse, was injured, he chose Andretti as his replacement. Now in the big leagues of auto racing, Andretti quickly began to make a name for himself on the United States Auto Club (USAC) circuit, finishing in the top ten in a number of races. In 1965, his first full year in top-level racing, Andretti emerged as a star of the speedways, exciting racing fans with his bold driving style. He was signed to a multi-year contract by the powerful Firestone racing team, and although he won only one race that year—the Hoosier Grand Prix at Indianapolis—he was constantly among the leaders, including an impressive third-place finish at the Indianapolis 500. That consistency earned him the USAC national championship for the 1965 season.

Andretti, now an American citizen, repeated as USAC champion in 1966. That season, he won eight of the 15 championship races he entered. During one three-race stretch—the Milwaukee 100, the Langhorne 100, and the Atlanta 300—Andretti led from start to finish, for a total of 500 miles. That phenomenal season established Andretti as the hottest driver on the Indy-car circuit, as well as an international celebrity.

Andretti won eight races again in 1967, but fell just short of the USAC championship, which was taken by A. J. Foyt. As the 1960s continued, he felt the urge to seek out new challenges. For Andretti, that meant trying to duplicate his Indy-car success in other forms of racing. In 1967 he stunned the world of stock car racing by winning the prestigious Daytona 500. The following year, Andretti became involved in the Formula One road racing circuit. He also began to race occasionally on dirt tracks. Although he enhanced his reputation as one of the world's most versatile drivers, Andretti won only four USAC races in 1968, finishing second in the standings to Bobby Unser.

Closed 1960s with Indy Win

After a string of disappointments at the Indianapolis 500, the most important of all races, Andretti finally broke through with a victory in 1969. The win at Indy helped lift Andretti to his third USAC championship in five years. He also won a 12-hour road race at Sebring that season. In 1970 Andretti suffered a series of crashes and mechanical problems, and he failed to win any major races. With an Indy trophy finally in his collection, Andretti decided to focus more energy on Formula One racing during the 1970s. He won the South African Grand Prix in 1971, but struggled through the next several seasons without a Grand Prix victory. He did, however, manage to win the USAC dirt track championship in 1974, a further show of his versatility.

In 1977 Andretti finally began to achieve the kind of success in Formula One racing that he had in Indy cars. He came in third in the standings among Formula One drivers that year, winning the U.S., Spanish, French, and Italian Grand Prix events. The following year, only his second racing Formula One full time, Andretti realized a life-long dream by becoming the Formula One World Champion. By the early 1980s, however, Andretti had pretty much retired from the Grand Prix circuit, and was once more ready to concentrate on Indy cars. In 1984, at an age (46) generally considered over-the-hill for a race car driver, Andretti took his fourth Indy Car championship.

Drove Fast During Career Twilight

Although the victories started to come less frequently, Andretti continued to race competitively through the rest of the 1980s and into the first half of the 1990s, both in Indy Cars and in the occasional Formula One event. He won an Indy Car race in 1988 before encountering an extended dry spell. His last Indy Car win—the 52nd of his career—came in a 1993 race in Phoenix. That year, at the age of 53, Andretti set the all-time qualifying speed record of 234.275 miles-per-hour at the Michigan International Speedway. Andretti retired from racing following the Grand Prix of Monterey at the end of the 1994 season.

Meanwhile, the most famous race car driver in the world had spawned the most successful racing dynasty in history. Son Michael has become one of racing's top drivers in his own right. Andretti's other son, Jeff, and nephew John (Aldo's son) have also shown the Andretti magic behind the wheel. During the early 1990s, several Indy Car fields included four drivers named Andretti.

Mario considered making a one-race comeback in 1996, when a schism developed between Championship Auto Racing Teams (CART) and the upstart Indy Racing League (IRL) over control of the Indianapolis 500 field. As a protest against IRL's attempt to stock the Indy field with its members, CART created the U.S. 500, to be run on the same day as the Indy 500 at the same Michigan track on which Andretti had set his qualifying record a few years earlier. After weeks of contemplation, Andretti eventually decided against entering the U.S. 500. Even in retirement, however, Andretti remains a giant figure among racing fans. He is much in demand for appearances and endorsements. Although he has now left the driving to the next generation of Andrettis, his charisma and diverse skills will be difficult for his successors to match.

Further Reading

Andretti, Mario, *Andretti: Mario on Mario,* Collins, 1994.
Roebuck, Nigel, *Grand Prix Greats,* Patrick Stephens, 1986.
People, August 28, 1978, pp. 37-43.
Libby, Bill, *Great American Race Drivers,* Cowles, 1970, pp. 180-184.
Prentzas, G. S., *Mario Andretti,* Chelsea House, 1996.
Sports Illustrated, May 11, 1992, pp. 78-93.
Road and Track, January, 1995, pp. 117-119.
Sports Illustrated, October 17, 1994, p. 88.
Indianapolis Star, January 18, 1996, p. D1. □

John Albion Andrew

As governor of Massachusetts during the Civil War, John Albion Andrew (1818-1867) energetically organized the state's resources in support of the Union and pressed for vigorous prosecution of the war.

John Andrew was born on May 31, 1818, in Windham, Maine, where his father was the manager of a general store. After graduating from Bowdoin College in 1837, he moved to Boston to study law. A man of deep religious convictions, he became involved in public affairs as a supporter of humanitarian reform movements and then of antislavery. He entered politics as a Whig but helped organize the antislavery Free Soil party in Massachusetts in 1848; its failure left him politically stranded until the emergence of the Republican party in the mid-fifties. He was elected to a single term in the Massachusetts Legislature in 1857; 2 years later he helped organize legal aid for John Brown, an activity which brought him favorable public notice in his home state.

In 1860 Andrew was elected to the first of his five terms as governor of Massachusetts. From the beginning the problem of fighting the Civil War dominated his administration. The Federal government was generally ill equipped at the beginning to organize and carry on the war. The states, therefore, carried a major share of the burden, especially in the war's early years. Andrew readily accepted the challenge. Massachusetts-raised troops were the first to reach Washington after the firing on Fort Sumter, and in the following years Andrew created a state organization that raised emergency funds and enlisted, equipped, and supplied thousands of troops to the Federal cause. His energy and efficiency clearly marked him as one of the leaders of an unusually gifted group of men, the Northern war governors.

Deeply committed to the war, Andrew bombarded President Lincoln with both military and political advice. He was a supporter of Radical Republicanism and favored the speedy emancipation of the slaves and the extensive use of African American troops in the Union Army. Angered by Lincoln's slow response to such ideas, Andrew joined other Radicals in seeking another presidential candidate in 1864. But when it became clear that such a change would only benefit the Democrats, he supported the President. A superb politician, Andrew always retained a sense of the possible, once remarking, "in respect to principles I am always radical. In respect to measures I am always conservative."

After the war Andrew changed course to favor a relatively moderate Reconstruction policy. For example, he wanted the government to deal directly with former Confederate leaders and not, as the Radicals desired, politically proscribe them. He believed that Reconstruction necessitated the support of the South's normal leaders who alone could persuade other Southerners to accept the minimum demands of the North: emancipation, guarantees of civil rights for African Americans, disavowal of secession, and repudiation of the Confederate debt. In 1866 Andrew retired as governor, intending to remain active in politics. He died suddenly of a stroke in 1867 at the age of 49.

Further Reading

The only full-length biography of Andrew is Henry G. Pearson, *The Life of John A. Andrew, Governor of Massachusetts* (2 vols., 1904), which is useful for its detail. Eric L. McKitrick, *Andrew Johnson and Reconstruction* (1960), contains a sketch of Andrew stressing his political pragmatism and analyzing his attitudes on Reconstruction. A useful book on the

Radicals is Hans L. Trefousse, *The Radical Republicans* (1969). □

Charles McLean Andrews

The American historian Charles McLean Andrews (1863-1943) originated the version of colonial history that places the English settlements in America within the larger context of the British Empire.

Charles McLean Andrews was born in Wethersfield, Conn., on Feb. 22, 1863. He graduated from Trinity College in 1884 and began teaching at West Hartford High School. Dissatisfied, Andrews left in 1886 to enter graduate school at Johns Hopkins. There he worked under Herbert B. Adams, a leading figure in the movement to professionalize history and an exponent of the "germ" theory of history, which traced American political institutions from German origins. In keeping with his mentor's interest, Andrews studied towns in Connecticut. However, his dissertation, The River *Towns in Connecticut* (1899), questioned some of Adams's assumptions.

Andrews took his first teaching position at Bryn Mawr in 1889. His continued research to test the germ theory resulted in *The Old English Manor* (1892). The following year Andrews's interest shifted back to American colonial history, although he continued to teach and to write textbooks in European and world history.

Andrews married Evangeline Walker in 1895 and continued to teach at Bryn Mawr, taking a leave sponsored by the Carnegie Institution in 1903-1904 to work on a guide to manuscripts in the British Museum. In 1904 he saw publication of his *Colonial Self-Government, 1652-1689*. By 1907 Andrews's reputation was such that he was asked by Johns Hopkins to fill Adams's chair, which had been vacant 6 years. He moved to Johns Hopkins and published with Francis G. Davenport the *Guide to the Manuscript Materials for the History of the United States to 1783 in the British Museum and Other Depositories* (1908), a work Andrews believed would make him famous.

Unhappy at Johns Hopkins, Andrews moved to Yale to become professor of American history, edit the Yale Historical Series, and teach graduate courses in American colonial history. In 1912 another of his works, *The Colonial Period*, appeared. This book anticipated many of Andrews's later ones, emphasizing the interaction between England and the Colonies and the progressive antiquation of British colonial policy as compared with the innovative nature of colonial institutions. Seven years later Andrews combined his insights in social history and popular culture in two volumes, *The Fathers of New England and Colonial Folkways*.

In 1924 Andrews became acting president of the American Historical Association. His *Colonial Background of the American Revolution* (1924), regarded as one of his best books, maintains that an understanding of British colonial policy is essential to understanding the American Revolu-

tion. The next year Andrews became president of the association.

After his retirement from Yale in 1931, Andrews continued to labor on his final major work, *The Colonial Period of American History* (4 vols., 1934-1938), the first volume of which won a Pulitzer Prize. He failed to complete three additional volumes planned. He died on Sept. 9, 1943.

Further Reading

The standard biography of Andrews is Abraham Seldin Eisenstadt, *Charles McLean Andrews: A Study in American Historical Writing* (1955), which is sympathetic to Andrews and his work. Good evaluations of Andrews's place as a historian may be found in Michael Kraus, *The Writing of American History* (1953); in Harvey Wish, *The American Historian: A Social-Intellectual History of the Writing of the American Past* (1960); and in Lawrence Henry Gipson's "The Imperial Approach to Early American History," an essay by a famous student of Andrews, in Ray Allen Billington, ed., *The Reinterpretation of Early American History: Essays in Honor of John Edwin Pomfret* (1966). □

Fannie Fern Phillips Andrews

Fannie Fern Phillips Andrews (1867–1950) was an educator who fought endlessly for the promotion of peace studies through an international bureau of education.

Fannie Fern Phillips Andrews was an educator who campaigned tirelessly for an international bureau of education to promote peace studies. Born in Lynn, Massachusetts, she was the daughter of a shoemaker father and a mother who was president of the Woman's Christian Temperance Union. Deciding at age three that she wanted to be a teacher, Andrews later attended Salem Normal School in Massachusetts and then taught for six years before receiving her degree in psychology and education from Radcliffe College in 1902. Her work in the public schools of Boston convinced her that students from different ethnic and economic backgrounds had to be taught to communicate and negotiate with each other. Her core belief that men who make war are spurred to conflict by their inability to understand one another's perspectives fueled her interest in "teaching peace".

The American Peace League

In 1908 she founded the American Peace League, an organization which sought to promote peace by teaching the principles of "international justice" in American schools. She extended her influence by organizing the Boston School-Parent group and serving as president of the Boston Home and School Association from 1914-1918. Andrews campaigned nationally for her ideals, and by 1915 League branches had been established in forty states. She envisioned an international bureau of education which would promote understanding among nations. But the era just before the United States entered the World War was an inauspicious time to promote peace. Andrews, who eventually supported American involvement in the war, changed the name of the American Peace League to the American School Citizenship League in 1918, believing that the old title was too provocative during wartime.

International Attention

Andrews and the League received serious consideration from the highest branches of government for her plan to create an international bureau of education. She was engaged in the final planning stages of a multi-national conference to consider the logistics of such an institution when World War I erupted. She had already caught the attention of President Woodrow Wilson , however, and in 1918 he picked Andrews to attend the Paris Peace Conference . There she lobbied for the emerging League of Nations to include in its covenant a provision for her dream of an international bureau of education, but she was unsuccessful. During the war she received a post-graduate degree in international affairs, never losing sight of her goal of an international school curriculum which would promote justice and understanding. Andrews maintained her dedication to promoting peace studies until her death, serving in the International Law Association, the World Peace Foundation, and the International Guild.

Further Reading

J. McKeen Cattell, ed., *Leaders in Education: A Biographical Directory* (New York: The Science Press, 1932).

Alden Whitman, ed., *American Reformers* (New York: H. W. Wilson Co., 1985), pp. l22-123. □

Roy Chapman Andrews

Roy Chapman Andrews (1884-1960) was an American naturalist, explorer, and author whose popular image was that of a romantic explorer in Asia.

Roy Chapman Andrews was born in Beloit, Wis., on Jan. 26, 1884. Fascinated by the natural wonders of southern Wisconsin, he chose his life's work at an early age. Immediately upon his graduation from Beloit College in 1906, he went to New York to seek employment at the American Museum of Natural History, volunteering to scrub floors when no other positions were available.

He assisted in the taxidermy department of the museum and soon received a field assignment to bring in the skeleton of a whale beached on Long Island. This initiated his scientific investigations of whales, and he was soon established as the world's leading whale authority. In his pursuit of these and other studies, Andrews traveled to Alaska, the East Indies, Japan, and Korea. He identified large "devilfish" off the Korean coast as the California gray whale, then considered an extinct species.

After 1915 Andrews concentrated on land explorations; his initial foray had been into the dense northern forests of Korea, but his dream was to test the theory of Henry Fairfield Osborn that central Asia was the home of primitive man and the source of much of the animal life of Europe and America. This work began in 1916 with a small zoological expedition to the periphery of the central Asian plateau in southwestern China and Burma. After a delay caused by World War I, during which Andrews served in Peking for the naval intelligence service, the youthful explorer returned to the United States to plan and finance his ambitious decade-long project. Andrews presented his project as a new type of exploration, a mammoth cooperative venture of various sciences, utilizing innovative techniques, including automobiles for desert exploration. He got the necessary financial support and set out in 1921.

He repeatedly led teams into the less-known portions of China, Borneo, and central Asia. He gained world fame because of his dramatic expeditions into the Gobi Desert, which led to the discovery of rich fossil fields, new geological strata, the first dinosaur eggs known to science, and skeleton parts of some of the largest and oldest known mammals, including the huge *Baluchitherium* and the tiny *Protoceratops andrewsi*. Political turmoil and another war stopped Andrews's Asian exploration in 1930. Two years later, after writing a full report of these expeditions, *The New Conquest of Central Asia,* he entered museum administration.

Andrews had taken a master's degree from Columbia University in 1913; he received honorary doctorates from

Brown University in 1926 and Beloit College in 1928. He served as director of the American Museum of Natural History from 1935 to 1942, then devoted the rest of his life to writing and lecturing. A spellbinding lecturer and story-teller, he relished his popular image as a romantic explorer, but claimed that life was really more dangerous in American cities than in the Gobi Desert. He died in Carmel, Calif., on March 11, 1960.

Further Reading

The best sources on Andrews are his own voluminous writings, particularly his autobiographical works: *This Business of Exploring* (1935); *Under a Lucky Star: A Lifetime of Adventure* (1943); *An Explorer Comes Home: Further Adventures of Roy Chapman Andrews* (1947); and *Beyond Adventure: The Lives of Three Explorers* (1954). The secondary sources are meager. Fitzhugh Green, *Roy Chapman Andrews, Dragon Hunter* (1930), is the only biography. Henry Chester Tracy, *American Naturists* (1930), repeats Andrews's own writings. Geoffrey Hellman, *Bankers, Bones and Beetles: The First Century of the American Museum of Natural History* (1969), recounts Andrews's association with the museum. □

Iury Vladimirovich Andropov

The Soviet leader Iury Vladimirovich Andropov (1914-1984) was the head for 15 years of the Soviet secret police. After Leonid Brezhnev's death in 1982 he became for 16 months the ruler of the Soviet Union.

Iury Andropov was born on June 15, 1914, in the southeastern Russian province of Stavropol, where his father was a railroad worker. He attended a secondary vocational school to learn river navigation, graduating in 1936. By then he was already active in the Young Communist (Komsomol) League, organizing Soviet youth to assist the Communist Party.

For several years he worked as a technician along the waterways in the Volga River basin. In 1940 he began a new career in the Komsomol organization, working to organize youth in the territory just taken from Finland in the Soviet-Finnish war of 1939-1940. He continued this work during the World War II, helping to coordinate guerrilla activities in areas controlled by the Finnish army. Following the war he was promoted to a post of Soviet administrator in the region.

He remained a minor official during the Stalin years. Though he served his Stalinist superiors loyally, he was not implicated in the secret police terror of that period.

His training combined with his lack of involvement in Stalin's crimes made him a good recruit for promotion in the years following Stalin's death in 1953. His advancement began when he entered the Soviet Diplomatic Service. After a short period of training in Moscow, he received in 1953 an appointment to the Soviet embassy in Hungary, a Soviet satellite country. The following year he was named ambassador to Hungary, a position he occupied until 1957. During that time he helped to remove from power the Hungarian Stalinist leader.

In late 1956 the Hungarians attempted to free themselves from Soviet control in a violent uprising, quickly repressed by Soviet troops. Andropov's activity in the repression is not known. He probably assisted in the restoration to power of those Hungarian Communists, led by Janos Kadar, loyal to the Soviet Union. Andropov performed his work well. In 1957 he returned to Moscow to take charge of relations between the Soviet Communist Party and other Communist countries, including the European satellites, the East Asian Communist states, and later Cuba. He held this post for 10 years, acquiring considerable experience in international relations during that time.

In 1967, his political responsibilities increased greatly. That year he was appointed chairman of the Soviet secret police (KGB, acronym for the Committee for State Security). He was chosen by the Soviet leaders in the Politburo for two major reasons. First, he was not a Stalinist; they could rely on him to maintain party control over the secret police. Second, he was not a close supporter of Brezhnev and could be counted on not to let the KGB fall under the control of the new party leader. One of the principal tasks which confronted Andropov was the restoration of the prestige of the secret police, whose reputation had suffered severely in previous years when public denunciation of Stalin's crimes had revealed its terrible abuses of power in carrying out

Stalin's terror. At the same time, he had to silence such Soviet "dissenters" as the physicist Andrei Sakharov and the novelist Alexander Solzhenitsyn, who were demanding further destalinization and publicly protesting violations of human rights in the Soviet Union. Their activities were reported and their writings published in the West.

Andropov remained chairman of the KGB for 15 years, longer than any other secret police chief since Stalin's death. He owed his lengthy term of service to his success at the job. During those years the KGB became one of the most efficient secret police organizations in the world. He organized a public campaign to raise the prestige of the KGB among the Soviet population. He appears to have prevented KGB officers from abusing their power for the sake of personal profit, as other party and police officials were doing. By the early 1980s Andropov had accumulated material from KGB investigations to prove widespread bribery and corruption within the Soviet bureaucracy. He appointed loyal party officials to high positions within the KGB and established his own reputation for efficiency and incorruptibility. His years of secret police leadership made him a major contender to become the next leader of the Soviet Union.

Meanwhile he was able to eliminate public dissent within the Soviet Union. He used several methods of repression. The KGB arrested dissenters for violating laws banning "anti-Soviet propaganda." They were sentenced to years of hard labor in prison camps. Other were sent without trial to psychiatric hospitals for the criminally insane, where they were treated with mind-altering drugs. The most prominent dissenters, protected from harsh punishment by their international fame, had to accept permanent exile abroad. By the end of the 1970s the KGB had virtually wiped out all groups defending human rights and individual liberties in the Soviet Union and had enforced public silence on Stalin's crimes.

Andropov was rewarded for his success. In 1973 he became a member of the ruling party committee, the Politburo. He was its youngest member at that time. In mid-1982, his colleagues on the committee designated him Brezhnev's successor, making him a member of the Secretariat and permitting him to resign his post as chairman of the secret police. Within two days of Brezhnev's death on November 10, 1982, he received the formal party appointment of general secretary.

Andropov had only a brief time to be leader of the Soviet Union. He began in those months to rejuvenate the party leadership and to implement new policies. He appointed to the Politburo younger Communist officials, including a young expert on agriculture named Mikhail Gorbachev. He launched a campaign against corruption, making use of the secret police to hunt out and punish culprits within the state and party apparatus. He tried to improve industrial production by introducing measures punishing absenteeism and rewarding productivity. Finally, he launched a "peace offensive" intended to limit the introduction of new U.S. nuclear missiles in Europe. When in early September 1983 a Soviet fighter plane shot down a South Korean airliner flying over Soviet air space, he defended the hasty action of his frontier forces. The international protest over that incident seriously worsened Soviet relations with Western countries.

In late 1983 Andropov fell seriously ill. Suffering from an incurable kidney disease, he sought the agreement of his colleagues in the Politburo to the appointment of Mikhail Gorbachev as his successor. However, an older Politburo member, Konstantin Chernenko (whom Brezhnev had originally favored), was able to prevent this move and claimed the succession for himself. Andropov died in February 1984.

Further Reading

Biographical information on Andropov is scarce. The best study is Zhores Medvedev, *Andropov: An Insider's Account of Power and Politics within the Kremlin* (1984). References to his work as head of the secret police are found in John Barron, *KGB* (1974). See also Jerry Hough, "The Soviet Succession: Issues and Personalities," in *Problems of Communism,* September-October 1982.

Additional Sources

Beichman, Arnold., *Andropov, new challenge to the West,* New York: Stein and Day, 1983.
Ebon, Martin., *The Andropov file: the life and ideas of Yuri V. Andropov, general secretary of the Communist Party of the Soviet Union,* New York: McGraw-Hill, 1983.
Medvedev, Zhores A., *Andropov,* Harmondsworth, Middlesex, England; New York, N.Y., U.S.A.: Penguin Books, 1984.
Steele, Jonathan., *Andropov in power: from Komsomol to Kremlin,* Garden City, N.Y.: Anchor Press/Doubleday, 1984, 1983.
Yuri Andropov, a secret passage into the Kremlin, New York: Macmillan; London: Collier Macmillan, 1983. □

Sir Edmund Andros

Sir Edmund Andros (1637-1714), an English colonial governor in America, was an able though arbitrary administrator. Because his regime conflicted with the interests of colonial Puritan leaders, he became a symbol of oppression.

Edmund Andros was born in London on Dec. 6, 1637. He was descended from the feudal aristocracy of Guernsey, and his father was master of ceremonies in Charles I's court. The family was royalist during England's civil war, and Andros served in the army following the Restoration. In 1666 he went as a major with an infantry regiment to protect the British West Indies against the Dutch. Six years later he became a landgrave in Carolina colony but showed little interest in the venture, possibly because, on his father's death in 1674, he became both bailiff of Guernsey and governor of the Duke of York's American possessions.

Though plagued by controversy with proprietors in New Jersey, Dutch settlers resenting British regulations, and boundary problems with Connecticut, Andros governed

New York with reasonably success, particularly in defending its Indian frontier and in gaining Iroquois friendship. Yet friction with the colonists increased, and, though an investigation later cleared Andros of charges of financial irregularities and favoritism in trading licenses, he was recalled to England. His knighting in 1681 and other honors show that he was still esteemed by the royal family. After the Duke of York became James II, Andros was named head of the Dominion of New England on June 3, 1686.

The attempt to merge England's separate northern colonies into a single dominion was extremely unpopular in America, and Andros's reputation has suffered accordingly. New England colonists never appreciated the need for consolidating defenses against the French and Indians, and they especially begrudged replacing their own representative assemblies with a single, appointive, advisory council. (Their resistance to this council's reimposition of existing taxes was quickly suppressed.) At first the merchants and large landholders supported Andros, but his vigorous enforcement of the Navigation Acts, his efforts to eliminate piracy, refusal to promote land speculation, and insistence on confirmation of land titles alienated them. Puritan clergymen, outraged when he permitted Episcopal services in Boston, plotted a rebellion. When the news came that William of Orange had landed in England, the Bostonians arose and captured Andros and several Dominion officials. After lengthy delays the prisoners were sent to England, where the charges against them were never pressed.

William and Mary needed competent subordinates and so named Andros governor of Virginia in 1692; thus he

eventually served as executive for every royal province on the American mainland. To Virginia he brought the charter establishing William and Mary College. Though Commissary James Blair believed him unconcerned about the college and established church, Andros was an industrious and respected administrator; Edward Randolph called his the only good government in America. Resigning over differences with Blair, Andros returned to England in 1698, served for a time as governor of Jersey island, and died in London on Feb. 27, 1714. Although he was impatient, skeptical of democracy, and unable to understand Puritans, he had been a conscientious and generally capable official.

Further Reading

Nearly every history of the colonial period deals with Andros and the Dominion, but Viola F. Barnes, *The Dominion of New England* (1923), is most satisfactory. *The Andros Tracts,* edited by W. H. Whitmore (3 vols., 1868-1874), and Charles M. Andrews, *Narratives of the Insurrections, 1675-1690* (1915), provide additional insight. See also Gerard B. Warden, *Boston, 1689-1776* (1970). □

Fra Angelico

The Italian painter Fra Angelico (ca. 1400-1455) achieved a unique synthesis of the mystical, visionary realms of medieval devotional painting with the Renaissance concern for representing the visually perceived world of mass, space, and light.

The monastic life of Fra Angelico began about 1418 in the Order of Dominican Preachers in Fiesole, near Florence. His secular name had been Guido di Pietro, and his monastic name was Fra Giovanni da Fiesole. The appellatives Fra Angelico and Beato Angelico came into use only after his death to recall his spirituality as a man and an artist.

The painter's earliest known works were created at the monastery of S. Domenico at Fiesole in the late 1420s and early 1430s. The *Annunciation* of about 1430 (Museo del Gesù, Cortona) and the *Linaiuoli Altarpiece* (*Madonna of the Linen Guild,* Museo di S. Marco, Florence) reveal the essential directions of Fra Angelico's art. Reminiscences of the style of Lorenzo Monaco, the Camaldolese monk-painter who may have been Fra Angelico's first master in passages of rhythmic line and in the intimate narration of predella panels, are overshadowed by the impact of the more progressive styles of Masaccio and Masolino. The draperies of Fra Angelico's gentle people are modeled in chiaroscuro, and these Virgins, saints, and angels exist in a world constructed on the principles of linear and atmospheric perspective. Numerous large altarpieces and small tabernacles (Madonnas and Saints, Last Judgments, Coronations of the Virgin) were commissioned from the painter and his flourishing shop in the 1430s.

From 1438 to 1445 Fra Angelico was principally occupied with the fresco program and altarpiece for the Domini-

can monastery of S. Marco in Florence. The church and monastic quarters were newly rebuilt at this time under the patronage of Cosimo de' Medici, with Michelozzo as architect for the project. The frescoes by the master and his assistants are situated throughout the cloister, corridors, chapter house, and cells. In the midst of the traditional subjects form the life of Christ, figures of Dominican saints contemplate and meditate upon the sacred events, so that the scenes convey a sense of mystical, devotional transport. At the same time the dramatic immediacy is heightened by the inclusion of architectural details of S. Marco itself in some of the narrative scenes, most notably the *Annunciation* with its view of a corner of the cloister.

A masterpiece of panel painting created at the same time as the S. Marco project is the *Deposition* altarpiece, commissioned by the Strozzi family for the Church of Sta Trinita (Museo di S. Marco, Florence; the pinnacles, as well as the predella now in the Uffizi, were painted earlier by Lorenzo Monaco). The richly colored and luminous figures, the panoramic views of the Tuscan landscape serving as a backdrop to Calvary, and the forthright division into sacred and secular personages reveal Fra Angelico as an artist in tune with the concepts and methods of the Renaissance. And yet, all of the accomplishments in representation do not diminish the air of religious rapture.

The final decade of Fra Angelico's life was spent mainly in Rome (ca. 1445-1449 and ca. 1453-1455), with 3 years in Florence (ca. 1450-1452) as prior of S. Domenico at Fiesole. His principal surviving work of these final years is the frescoes of scenes from the lives of Saints Lawrence and

Stephen in the Chapel of Pope Nicholas V in the Vatican, Rome. The dramatic figure groupings serve to summarize the long tradition of 14th-and early 15th-century Florentine fresco painting. In the rigorous construction and abundant classical detail of the architectural backgrounds, the dignity and luxury of a Roman setting are appropriately conveyed.

In spite of the fact that his life unfolded in a monastic environment, Fra Angelico's art stands as an important link between the first and later generations in the mainstream of Florentine Renaissance painting.

Further Reading

John Pope-Hennessy, *Fra Angelico* (1952), is the standard monograph, but the biography is made obsolete by subsequent documentary findings. Frederick Hartt, *History of Italian Renaissance Art* (1969), is the best comprehensive survey. □

James Rowland Angell

James Rowland Angell (1869-1949) was a pioneer in the development of psychology in America and a leader in higher education.

James Rowland Angell was born May 8, 1869, in Burlington, Vermont, to James Burrill and Sara (Caswell) Angell. His father was president of the universities of Vermont and Michigan and his grandfather was president of Brown University. The Angell home was an academic environment visited by distinguished faculty and guests including Grover Cleveland, Andrew White, and Matthew Arnold. Angell's life was further enriched by travel. His family spent a year and a half in China, where his father served in a diplomatic post, and later traveled around the world.

Academic studies were not taken seriously by the young Angell until he read John Dewey's text on psychology during his sophomore year at the University of Michigan. That experience began an intellectual life which would lead him into the profession of psychology. After graduation (1890) he spent three years in graduate study. The first year he remained at the University of Michigan, receiving a master's degree in philosophy under the direction of John Dewey, a renowned philosopher. The second year he studied at Harvard with William James, a prominent psychologist, and graduated with a master's degree in psychology. The third year he traveled to Germany to further his psychology studies. At the end of that year his doctoral thesis was accepted at the University of Halle, contingent on a revision to improve its German. But instead he accepted a teaching position in psychology at the University of Minnesota. Soon after his arrival in Minnesota, he married his fiance of many years, Marion Watras. They had two children.

Teaching and Research (1893-1914)

One of Angell's chief delights was working with students. Beginning with his first teaching assignment at the University of Minnesota (1893), he worked long into the

nights, seeking to perfect his teaching talents. Using the Socratic method, he developed questions that provoked thinking and continued interesting the students. The next year, as an assistant professor of philosophy and psychology at the University of Chicago, he developed a psychology laboratory where he and graduate students collaborated on experimental research. During his years at Chicago he assisted over 40 doctoral students in psychology, a number of whom later became leaders in psychology (e.g., John B. Watson, an originator of behavioral psychology in America). Angell encouraged his students to study with other professors, particularly recommending minors in philosophy, biology, and education.

In the field of psychology, Angell is viewed as an early originator of functionalism, one of two major competing schools of thought during this period. Seeking to develop psychological principles and to advance the discipline, Angell applied the philosophies of James and Dewey in his laboratory. While his scholarly contributions to psychology have been eclipsed by later works of others, he was a pioneer in standardizing experimental procedures, developing apparatus and laboratory courses, and systematizing the principles of a new science. In addition to scholarly articles, he published two popular texts: *Psychology* (1904) and *Chapters from Modern Psychology* (1912). He was elected president of the American Psychological Association in 1908, the youngest person to have received that honor. During these years at Chicago he developed one of the more prestigious psychology programs in America.

Educational Administration (1912-1937)

As a professor Angell had to supplement his salary by teaching evenings and summers. So he welcomed the opportunity to enter college administration. In 1911 he became dean of faculties. Although he continued editing a psychology monograph series (1912-1922), his work in psychology virtually ended.

Functionalism, losing its chief spokesman, quickly faded in prominence. A leave of absence (1919) allowed him to assume chairmanship of the National Research Council and to oversee the fundraising for and construction of a new building for the National Academy of Sciences. The following year he returned as acting-president at Chicago, to be followed by the presidency of the Carnegie Foundation. Then in 1921 he accepted the presidency at Yale University, the first non-Yale graduate since 1766 to receive that honor.

In his autobiography, Angell raises some doubts as to his success at Yale; however, his alumni, students, and faculty often felt otherwise. During his tenure there the social life of students changed with the division of the university into smaller resident colleges; the curriculum and faculty were expanded with the addition of new programs of nursing and drama and the founding of the Institute of Human Relations; the campus was completely rebuilt with 35 new buildings; and the general financial situation improved—in particular, the endowment quadrupled. In sum, under Angell's leadership, Yale was transformed from a small liberal arts college to a "true" university.

After retiring from Yale in 1937, Angell accepted an appointment as educational counselor to the National Broadcasting Company. He was director of the New York Life Insurance Company, a trustee of the American Museum of Natural History, and a member of the Rockefeller Foundation. He died in Hamden, Connecticut, on March 4, 1949.

Further Reading

A brief autobiography by Angell is in Carl Murchison, ed., *A History of Psychology in Autobiography,* III (1936). A biographical essay by Walter S. Hunter, emphasizing his psychological research, is in *National Academy of Science, Biographical Memoirs,* XXVI. A student's perspective of Angell is found in Maynard Mack's "Portraits from a Family Album," *Yale Literary Magazine* (Nov. 1931). A brief biographical sketch and several republished, complete obituaries are in *Yale Alumni Magazine* (April 1949). His *Chapters from Modern Psychology* (1912) is written for the general audience. A collection of his speeches and essays on education may be found in *Higher Education* (1938). Two critical books which comprehensively describe his tenure at Chicago and Yale are: *The Chicago Pragmatist* by Darnell Rucker (1969) and *Yale: The University College, 1929-1937,* vol. II, by George W. Pierson (1955). □

Maya Angelou

Maya Angelou (born 1928)—author, poet, play-wright, stage and screen performer, and director—is best known for her autobiography, *I Know Why the Caged Bird Sings* (1970), which recalls a young African American woman's discovery of her self-confidence.

Maya Angelou was born Marguerite Johnson on April 4, 1928, in St. Louis, Missouri. Growing up in rural Stamps, Arkansas, with her brother, Bailey, she lived with her pious grandmother, who owned a general store. She attended public schools in Arkansas and California, and became San Francisco's first female streetcar conductor. Later she studied dance with Martha Graham and drama with Frank Silvera, and went on to a career in theater. She appeared in *Porgy and Bess,* which toured 22 countries; on Broadway in *Look Away;* and in several off-Broadway plays, including *Cabaret for Freedom,* which she wrote in collaboration with Godfrey Cambridge.

During the early 1960s, Angelou lived in Egypt, where she was the associate editor of *The Arab Observer* in Cairo. During this time, she also contributed articles to *The Ghanaian Times* and was featured on the Ghanaian Broadcasting Corporation programming in Accra. During the mid-1960s, she became assistant administrator of the School of Music and Drama at the University of Ghana. She was the feature

editor of the *African Review* in Accra from 1964 to 1966. During this time she served as northern coordinator for the Southern Christian Leadership Conference at the request of Dr. Martin Luther King, Jr.

When she returned to the United States, Angelou worked as writer-producer for 20th Century-Fox Television, from which her full-length feature film *Sisters, Sisters* received critical acclaim. In addition, she wrote the screenplays *Georgia, Georgia* and *All Day Long* along with the television scripts for *Sister, Sister* and the series premiere of *Brewster Place.* She wrote, produced, and hosted the NET public broadcasting series *Blacks! Blues! Black!* Angelou also costarred in the motion picture *How to Make an American Quilt* in 1995.

Angelou has taught at several American colleges and universities, including the University of California at Los Angeles, the University of Kansas, Wichita State University, and California State University at Sacramento. Since the early 1980s, she has been Reynolds Professor and writer-in-residence at Wake Forest University.

Angelou has been a prolific poet for decades. Her collections include *Just Give Me A Cool Drink of Water 'Fore I Die* (1971); *Oh Pray My Wings Are Going to Fit Me Well* (1975); *And Still I Rise* (1976), which was produced as a choreo-poem on Off-Broadway in 1979; and *Shaker, Why Don't You Sing* (1983) *Poems: Maya Angelou* (1986); *Life Doesn't Frighten Me,* illustrated by celebrated New York artist Jean Michel Basquiat (1993); *On the Pulse of the Morning* (1993), recited at Bill Clinton's first Presidential Inauguration; *Soul Looks Back in Wonder* (1994); and *I Shall Not Be Moved* (1997), her first book of poetry in over 10 years.

Angelou's poetry is fashioned almost entirely of short lyrics and jazzy rhythms. Although her poetry has contributed to her reputation and is especially popular among young people, most commentators reserve their highest praise for her prose. Angelou's dependence on alliteration, her heavy use of short lines, and her conventional vocabulary has led several critics to declare her poetry superficial and devoid of her celebrated humor. Other reviewers, however, praise her poetic style as refreshing and graceful. They also laud Angelou for addressing social and political issues relevant to African Americans and for challenging the validity of traditional American values and myths. For example, Angelou directed national attention to humanitarian concerns with her poem "On the Pulse of the Morning," which she recited at the 1993 inauguration of President Bill Clinton. In this poem, Angelou calls for recognition of the human failings pervading American history and an renewed national commitment to unity and social improvement.

Although Angelou began her literary career as a poet, she is well known for her five autobiographical works, which depict sequential periods of her life. *I Know Why the Caged Bird Sings* (1970) is about Marguerite Johnson and her brother Bailey growing up in Arkansas. It chronicles Angelou's life up to age sixteen, providing a child's perspective of the perplexing world of adults. Although her grandmother instilled pride and confidence in her, her self-image was shattered when she was raped at the age of eight by her mother's boyfriend. Angelou was so devastated by the attack that she refused to speak for approximately five years. *I Know Why the Caged Bird Sings* concludes with Angelou having regained self-esteem and caring for her newborn son, Guy. In addition to being a trenchant account of an African American girl's coming-of-age, this work affords insights into the social and political tensions of the 1930s. Sidonie Ann Smith echoed many critics when she wrote: "Angelou's genius as a writer is her ability to recapture the texture of the way of life in the texture of its idioms, its idiosyncratic vocabulary and especially in its process of image-making."

Her next autobiographical work, *Gather Together in My Name*, (1974) covers the period immediately after the birth of her son Guy and depicts her valiant struggle to care for him as a single parent. *Singin' and Swingin' and Gettin' Merry Like Christmas* (1976) describes Angelou's stage debut and concludes with her return from the international tour of *Porgy and Bess*. *The Heart of A Woman* (1981) portrays the mature Angelou becoming more comfortable with her creativity and her success. *All God's Children Need Traveling Shoes* (1986) recalls her four-year stay in Ghana.

Widely celebrated by popular audiences and critics, Angelou has a long roster of recognitions, including: a nomination for National Book Award, 1970, for *I Know Why the Caged Bird Sings*; a Yale University fellowship, 1970; a Pulitzer Prize nomination, 1972, for *Just Give Me a Cool Drink of Water 'fore I Diiie*; an Antoinette Perry ("Tony") Award nomination from League of New York Theatres and Producers, 1973, for performance in *Look Away*; Rockefeller Foundation scholar in Italy, 1975; honorary degrees from Smith College, 1975, Mills College, 1975, Lawrence University, 1976, and Wake Forest University, 1977; a Tony Award nomination for best supporting actress, 1977, for *Roots*; and the North Carolina Award in Literature, 1987. In the 1970s she was appointed to the Bicentennial Commission by President Gerald Ford, and the National Commission on the Observance of International Women's Year by Jimmy Carter. She was also named Woman of the Year in Communications by *Ladies' Home Journal,* 1976; and named one of the top one hundred most influential women by *Ladies' Home Journal,* 1983.

Angelou's autobiographical works have an important place in the African American tradition of personal narrative, and they continue to garner praise for their honesty and moving sense of dignity. Although an accomplished poet and dramatist, Angelou is dedicated to the art of autobiography. Angelou explained that she is "not afraid of the ties [between past and present]. I cherish them, rather. It's the vulnerability ... it's allowing oneself to be hypnotized. That's frightening because we have no defenses, nothing. We've slipped down the well and every side is slippery. And how on earth are you going to come out? That's scary. But I've chosen it, and I've chosen this mode as my mode."

Further Reading

For biographical information, see the following periodical pieces: "*The African-American Scholar Interviews:* Maya Angelou," in the *African-American Scholar* (January/February 1977); "I Know Why the Caged Bird Sings," in *Ebony* (April 1970); and Mary Helen Washington, "Their Fiction Becomes Our Reality," in *African-American World* (August 1974). For critical information see: Estelle C. Jelinek, "In Search of the African-American Female Self: African-American Women's Autobiographies and Ethnicity," in *Women's Autobiography* (1980); Claudia Tate, *African-American Women Writers at Work* (1983); Carol E. Neubauer, "Displacement and Autobiographical Style in Maya Angelou's *The Heart of a Woman*," in *African-American Literature Forum* (1983); and Mari Evans, "Maya Angelou" in *African-American Women Writers, 1950-1980* (1983).

Additional information can be found in "Maya-ness is Next to Godliness," in *GQ* (July 1995) and "Maya Angelou: A Celebrated Poet Issues a Call to Arms to the Nation's Artists," in *Mother Jones* (May/June 1995). □

An Lu-shan

The Chinese rebel leader An Lu-shan (703-757) led a great rebellion that nearly overthrew the reigning T'ang dynasty.

An Lu-shan was probably born in Ying-chou on the northwest border of China. His father, a Sogdian, was an officer in the army of the Northern Turks; his mother was probably from a noble Turkish family. Very little is known about his childhood and early life. He eventually became a soldier and by the early 730s was a lieutenant in one of the Chinese garrisons protecting the northeastern border of China against invasion.

This was the beginning of An Lu-shan's career as a rising young officer in the regional army. He appears to have distinguished himself by personally leading raiding parties against threatening Khitan armies. Not all of his exploits were successful. Perhaps overconfident, he was severely defeated in one expedition in 737. He was disgraced, and barely avoided execution. For a short time he lost his rank and titles, but within a year these were restored. By 740 An Lu-shan was second in command in one of the important border armies. After another promotion to deputy military governor, he became governor of the military province of P'ing-lu on the northeast frontier in 742.

Now holding high rank, An Lu-shan had several opportunities to visit the capital of Ch'ang-an. His appearance was that of a rough and simple frontier soldier, though it was later said that this rude exterior hid an already ambitious and scheming man.

During the 740s An Lu-shan enjoyed even greater rank and title as as a frontier commander. He was probably favored by the chief minister because he seemed simple. He was, moreover, illiterate and therefore no threat to any scholar-official in high civil office. In fact, when he came to the court, he played the part of a clown and was said to be immensely amusing to the emperor and his ladies.

There was, however, little burlesque in the career of An Lu-shan during the next decade. In 751 he led a disastrously unsuccessful expedition against the Khitan. Fortunately for him, he still enjoyed imperial favor, and his life and career were saved. In 752 Li Lin-fu, the powerful chief minister who had been his patron, died. For the next 3 years a power struggle took place in which the participants tried to establish political power in the court and military power on the frontier. The aging emperor Hsüan-tsung (reigned 713-756) was unable to control the factions, and in the winter of 755-756 An Lu-shan, now the most powerful of the regional warlords, rose in rebellion against the dynasty. The rebels enjoyed great initial successes, capturing both T'ang capitals and forcing the Emperor to flee to the southwest. An Lu-shan was murdered by his own son in 757.

In 763, after much brutal fighting which devastated China, the rebellion An Lu-shan had begun was finally put down. The dynasty survived for another century and a half, but this rebellion dealt it a blow from which it never fully recovered.

Further Reading

For information on the career of An Lu-shan consult the *Biography of An Lu-shan* (1960), a translation by Howard S. Levy from the *Old T'ang History* (*Chiu T'ang-shu*), the standard, official history of the T'ang, compiled by Liu Hsün and others, A.D. 945. E. G. Pulleyblank, *The Background of the Rebellion of An Lu-shan* (1955), is useful on the period preceding the rebellion. □

Anna Ivanovna

Anna Ivanovna (1693-1740) was empress of Russia from 1730 to 1740. She continued the policy of westernizing Russia initiated by Czar Peter I.

Born in Moscow on Jan. 29, 1693, Anna was the daughter of Ivan V, co-czar of Russia with his half-brother Peter I. After her father's death in 1696, she and her mother and sisters became dependent on Czar Peter I.

In 1710, acquiescing to Peter's wish, Anna married Frederick William, Duke of Courland. Although her husband died shortly after the wedding, the Czar ordered her, as the duke's widow, to take up residence in Mitau, the capital of Courland, counting on her to strengthen Russian influence in the duchy. That arrangement was quickly disrupted by a hostile political faction in Courland, which forced Anna out of Mitau; she was obliged to make her home in Danzig. In 1717 she was permitted to return to Mitau, where she remained as de facto ruler of Courland for 13 years. During that period she received slight attention from her homeland and no special consideration when, after the death of her uncle Peter I, the Russian throne was occupied first by his wife, as Catherine I, then by his grandson, as Peter II.

Anna's Courland experiences had important consequences for her later career: her regard for the German–speaking ruling class made her appear more partial to Ger-

mans than she actually was; her years of existence on a paltry allowance deepened her desire for luxuries; the pervasive political intrigues she encountered reinforced her distrustful nature; and lonely life led her to form an attachment for her secretary, ambitious Johann Ernst Biron, upon whom she became excessively dependent.

When Peter II, the last Romanov male in line of succession, died without having made provision for a successor, the Supreme Privy Council, a small body exercising dominant power in the Russian government, saw Anna as the Romanov most likely to be amenable to their suggestions. Accordingly, they informed her that the throne would be hers if she agreed to certain conditions that would, in effect, transfer power from the ruler to the Council. She agreed to the conditions and returned to Russia in February 1730. Once established as empress, however, she promptly disavowed the conditions.

During her reign Anna was held in generally low esteem. She persisted in her infatuation for Biron, whom she installed in her palace, showered with honors, and treated with unbecoming deference. Some of her official appointments led to the charge that she favored Germans over Russians. Moreover, even by the cruel standards of the time, she was immoderately severe in her treatment of any who aroused her disfavor; she was responsible for the arrest, torture, or exile to Siberia of thousands.

Despite her shortcomings, Anna did not work against Russian interests as they were then interpreted. Rather, she

entrusted major responsibilities to men who had served Peter I and would continue his policies.

As a result, in foreign affairs Russia was strengthened in three strategic areas: the War of the Polish Succession (1733-1735) brought the pro-Russian Augustus III of Saxony to the throne of Poland; the war with Turkey (1735-1739) confirmed Russian possession of Azov; and the selection of Biron as Duke of Courland in 1737 increased that duchy's dependence on Russia and thus improved Russia's position on the Baltic.

In domestic affairs, also, Anna followed in the steps of Peter I, continuing his policy of westernization. She declared St. Petersburg the capital and brought back the offices of government that Peter II had moved to Moscow. She created the Cadet Corps for training officers. She encouraged the sciences, promoted the arts in general, and approved the development of the ballet in Russia.

Having no direct heir, Anna was determined to ensure that her successor would come from her side of the Romanov family—that is, from the descendants of Ivan V rather than those of Peter I. To that end, she chose her niece Anna Leopoldovna to provide the heir and selected her husband. A son was born to them in August 1740 and christened Ivan. Two months later the Empress became gravely ill and, fearing the approach of death, formally named the infant as her heir. Shortly thereafter she appointed Biron to serve as regent during the minority of the child, who would succeed her as Ivan VI. The empress Anna died on Oct. 17, 1740.

Further Reading

R. Nisbet Bain, *The Pupils of Peter the Great: A History of the Russian Court and Empire from 1697 to 1740* (1897), contains a detailed treatment of Anna's reign. See also George Vernadsky, *A History of Russia* (1929; 5th ed. 1961); Nicholas V. Riasonovsky, *A History of Russia* (1963; rev. ed. 1969); and Marc Raeff, *Origins of the Russian Intelligentsia: The Eighteenth Century Nobility* (1966). □

Anne

Anne (1665-1714) was queen of England from 1702 to 1714 and, after 1707, of Great Britain. During her reign England won a long war with France and persuaded Scotland to join in a new united kingdom of Great Britain. She was the last Stuart ruler.

On Feb. 6, 1665, Anne was born in London, the second daughter of James, Duke of York. Her father was a Roman Catholic, but her mother, Anne Hyde, was a Protestant, and Anne was brought up and remained a staunch Church of England Protestant. In 1677 her sister, Mary, to whom she was devoted, married William of Orange and moved to his country, Holland. Six years later Anne married Prince George of Denmark and estab-

lished her own court in London. There the leading figure was Sarah Churchill, to whom Anne was greatly attached. Sarah was the wife of John Churchill, later 1st Duke of Marlborough, and she and her husband's family and friends dominated Anne's court.

Anne's father became king as James II in 1685. His reign was a difficult period for Anne, the more so when her Italian Catholic stepmother produced a male child who blocked the two Protestant princesses from the throne. Public dissatisfaction with James for his Catholicism and his excessive emphasis on royal power was already widespread. The birth of a Catholic heir crystallized discontent into revolution, and James was deposed in 1688. Anne's sister and her husband took the English throne as King William III and Queen Mary II.

With her sister back in England and Sarah Churchill and her friends close by, Anne was happier for a while. Then came Mary's death in 1694 and 4 years later a worse loss. Brought to childbed 15 times, Anne lost every child but one, the Duke of Gloucester, and in 1698 he died at the age of 9. This left no Protestant English heir to the throne and forced Parliament to provide for a German successor should both William and Anne die without surviving children, and this situation did, in fact, occur.

On March 8, 1702, Anne succeeded to the English throne. She was a semi-invalid, content—aside from concern for the Church of England and the appointment of individuals whom she favored—to leave major policy to the Duke of Marlborough and his friend Sidney Godolphin.

They in turn entrusted the management of Parliament to Robert Harley, leader of the Tories. The War of the Spanish Succession against Louis XIV of France was the great issue, and on this Anne loyally backed Marlborough and Godolphin. She rejoiced with them in the victory of Blenheim (1704) and, to a lesser degree, in the union with Scotland (1707).

When the Tories proved less enthusiastic about the war than the Whigs, the government was forced to rely on the Whig party, with its support among Nonconformists and commercial interests. Relations became strained between the Queen and Lady Marlborough, and into the widening gap moved Harley and Abigail Hill, one of the Queen's dressers. Harley strengthened Anne's resolution "not to become the prisoner of a party" (meaning the Whigs). He suggested a moderate government headed by himself. In 1708, despite the Queen's support, he was unable to effect such a change and was forced out of the government.

Two years later Anne recalled Harley to power, and he and his rival, Viscount Bolingbroke, presided over the last 4 years of Anne's reign and concluded the Peace of Utrecht (1713) with France. Meanwhile Anne's health had deteriorated. Her ideal of "moderation above party" vanished in the rivalry between Harley, who was growing lazy and sodden, and the brilliant Bolingbroke, who appealed to the Tory extremists. Perhaps Anne toyed with the idea of having her half-brother succeed her as "James III." Certainly Bolingbroke did, with the hope of becoming the power behind another Stuart. Bolingbroke even got Anne to dismiss Harley, but she could not be persuaded to make Bolingbroke lord treasurer. A few days later, on Aug. 1, 1714, after a lingering illness, the last of the Stuarts died—to be succeeded by the first of the Hanoverian line, George I.

Further Reading

A recent satisfactory biography of Anne is David Green, *Queen Anne* (1970). Many of Anne's letters to Sarah Churchill are printed in the latter's *An Account of the Conduct of the Dowager Duchess of Marlborough* (1742 and later editions). From his reading of this work, Thomas B. Macaulay derived the prejudice against the Marlboroughs and the lack of sympathy for Anne that mark his *History of England from the Accession of James II* (2d ed., 5 vols., 1849-1861). His account is nonetheless worth reading. His grandnephew George M. Trevelyan is kinder to Anne in *England under Queen Anne* (3 vols., 1930-1934), while Geoffrey S. Holmes credits her with still more influence and character in *British Politics in the Age of Anne* (1967). See also G.N. Clark, *The Later Stuarts, 1660-1714* (1934; 2d ed. 1955).

Additional Sources

Gregg, Edward., *Queen Anne*, London; Boston: Routledge & Kegan Paul, 1980. □

Okomfo Anokye

Okomfo Anokye (active late 17th century) was an Ashanti fetish priest, statesman, and lawgiver. A co-

founder of the Ashanti Kingdom in West Africa, he helped establish its constitution, laws, and customs.

The original name of Okomfo Anokye was Kwame Frimpon Anokye (Okomfo means "priest"). Some traditions say that he came from Akwapim in the Akwamu Kingdom southeast of Ashanti, but his descendants claim he was born of an Ashanti mother and Adansi father and was related to the military leader Osei Tutu (the other cofounder of the Ashanti Kingdom) through a maternal uncle. When Osei Tutu succeeded about 1690 to the leadership of the small group of Akan forest states around the city of Kumasi which were already grouped in loose military alliance, Anokye was his adviser and chief priest. Tutu and Anokye, who must be considered together, carried out the expansionist policy of their predecessors, defeating two powerful enemies, the Akan Doma to the northwest and the Denkyera empire to the south. To throw off the Denkyera yoke required a powerful unity that transcended the particularism of the Ashanti segments, and Anokye employed not only the political influence of his priesthood but also added the spiritual ties that transformed the loose Ashanti alliance into a "national" union in 1695.

Anokye and Tutu established rituals and customs of the Ashanti state to diminish the influence of local traditions. They designated Kumasi the Ashanti capital. They established a state council of the chiefs of the preexisting states admitted to the union and suppressed all competing traditions of origin. Finally, they reorganized the Ashanti army.

The war with Denkyera from 1699 to 1701 went badly at first, but when the Denkyera army reached the gates of Kumasi, Anokye's "incantations" supposedly produced defections among their generals. The Ashanti broke the Denkyera hegemony and captured the Dutch deed of rent for Elmina Castle. This gave the Ashanti access to the African coast and involved them henceforth in the commerce and politics of the coastal slave trade. After Tutu's death in 1717, Anokye is said to have returned to Akwapim and died there.

The greatness of Anokye the lawgiver and of Tutu the warrior is measured by the permanency of the nation they created, its symbolism and ritual alive today in the greater state of Ghana. A historical judgment on Anokye is that he enabled the Ashanti "to succeed where Hellas had failed," that is, to retain their national unity after their war of liberation.

Further Reading

The best general work that includes information on Anokye is W.E.F. Ward, *A History of Ghana* (1948; 4th ed. 1967), which treats the rise of the Ashanti in the context of Gold Coast history and gives a historical interpretation of the Okomfo Anokye-Osei Tutu tradition. The Anokye tradition is recorded in R.S. Rattray, *Ashanti Law and Constitution* (1929). Also useful for an understanding of Anokye and the Ashanti is A. Adu Boahen's account, "Asante and Fante, A.D. 1000-1800," in J.F. Ade Ajayi and Ian Espie, eds., *A Thousand Years of West African History* (1965; rev. ed. 1969).

Basil Davidson, *Black Mother: The Years of the African Slave Trade* (1961) and *The Growth of African Civilization: A History of West Africa, 1000-1800* (1965; rev. ed. 1967), treat Anokye enthusiastically and vividly. John E. Flint, *Nigeria and Ghana* (1966), is more scholarly and tries to distinguish between the contributions of Tutu and Anokye. Anthropologist Ivor Wilks appears to doubt the authenticity of the Anokye tradition, or at least to question his contemporaneousness with Tutu; in his "Ashanti Government" in Daryll Forde and P.M. Kaberry, eds., *West African Kingdoms in the Nineteenth Century* (1967), he accounts for the rise of the Ashanti Union without reference to Anokye. □

Jean Anouilh

The French playwright Jean Anouilh (1910-1987) was an accomplished craftsman. His plays, from the frivolous and fanciful to the serious, exploit the artificiality of the theater to elucidate his views of the human predicament.

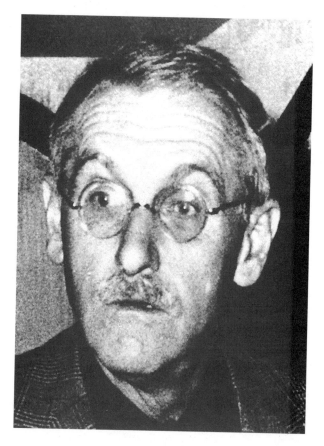

Jean Anouilh was born in Cérisole, near Bordeaux, on June 23, 1910. His father, a tailor, and his mother, a violinist in an orchestra, undoubtedly imparted to their son respect for craftsmanship and a love of art. Anouilh received his primary and secondary education in Paris, where he later studied law for a year and a half. In 1929 he went to work in an advertising agency, for which he wrote publicity and comic film scripts for 2 years. After a period in military service, he was briefly (1931-1932) secretary to the great actor and director Louis Jouvet and married Monelle Valentin, an actress who later created the roles of many of Anouilh's heroines.

From early childhood Anouilh had been fascinated by the stage. He haunted theaters and was writing plays at the age of 12. Like many a stagestruck youth, he tended to confuse real life with the theater, a view which led him to sacrifice in his early plays substance for theatricality. Undaunted by Jouvet's lack of encouragement and by the near or total failure of his first plays, Anouilh stubbornly resolved to devote his life to the theater. Success came in 1937 with *Le Voyageur sans bagages* (*Traveler without Luggage*). Anouilh's popularity steadily increased in the next two decades both in France and abroad.

Profoundly impressed by the plays of Jean Giraudoux and Luigi Pirandello, which broke with the tradition of the realistic theater, Anouilh recognized the value of poetry, of illusion and fantasy, and of irony as a means of portraying basic truths about human life. He held the growing conviction that the essence of the theater, that is, its quality of make-believe, mirrors the pretense and self-delusion of life; this led him to exploit the artificiality of the theater as a way of exposing the falsity of men's motives and even of their allegedly noblest principles and sentiments.

Anouilh's constant preoccupation with the technical production of his plays gradually led him to the role of director. In this capacity he produced, in line with his own views, plays by others, including Molière, as well as his own.

Completely absorbed in his work, Anouilh avoided other involvements and chose a secluded private life. His first marriage ended in divorce, and he married another actress, Charlotte Chardon, in 1953. One of his children, Catherine, also an actress, starred in her father's plays.

Although Anouilh grouped his plays in several categories according to their predominant tone—*pièces* (plays) *roses* (pink), *noires* (black), *brillantes* (brilliant), *grinçantes* (jarring), *costumées* (costumed), and *baroques* (baroque)—they all offer a unified and ever-deepening view of the human condition. His characteristic heroes are essentially rebels, revolting in the name of an inner ideal of purity against compromise with the immoral demands of family, social position, or their past. The fanciful or uncompromising efforts of the early heroes to escape from reality give way in most of the later plays to a profound bitterness caused by the recognition that no escape is possible. Among Anouilh's most admired plays are *Le Bal des voleurs* (1932; *Thieves' Carnival*), *Antigone* (1942), *L'Invitation au château* (1947; adapted as *Ring Round the Moon*), *La Valse des toréadors* (1951; *The Waltz of the Toreadors*), *L'Alouette* (1952; adapted as *The Lark*), *Becket* (1959), and *Ne réveillez pas madameDon't Wake the Lady*).

Anouilh died on October 3, 1987, in Lausanne, Switzerland.

Further Reading

The most exhaustive general study of Anouilh in English is Edward Owen Marsh, *Jean Anouilh, Poet of Pierrot and Pantaloon* (1953). John E. Harvey makes an excellent study of his dramaturgy in *Anouilh: A Study in Theatrics* (1964), and Leonard Cabell Pronko concentrates on the themes and dramatic values in *The World of Jean Anouilh* (1961).
Falb, Lewis W., *Jean Anouilh* (Frederick Ungar, 1977).
New York Times (October 5, 1987). □

St. Anselm of Canterbury

The Italian prelate St. Anselm of Canterbury (1033-1109) was a theologian, Doctor of the Church, and archbishop of Canterbury. He was one of the great thinkers of the Middle Ages.

The 11th century witnessed a dramatic change in European history, the impact of which has been compared to that of the Protestant Reformation or the industrial revolution. Extraordinary economic expansion was accompanied by growth in political institutions and cultural life, especially in Italy and northern France. Anselm spent most of his life in these two countries, and he was involved in many of the cultural changes that took place.

Anselm was born at Aosta in the Italian Alps. His family was noble and seems to have been related to the house of Savoy, the leading territorial magnates of the region. But Anselm's parents no longer possessed political or social prominence, and the family's economic resources were declining.

After the death of his mother about 1056, Anselm argued with his father and left Aosta forever. He traveled across the Alps and contacted his mother's relatives in the kingdom of Burgundy. After a period of study in Burgundy and northern France, he went to the monastery of Bec in Normandy to study under its prior, Lanfranc, a leading teacher in northern Europe.

In 1060 Anselm entered the monastic life at Bec. His proficiency in learning was such that 3 years later, on the occasion of Lanfranc's departure from Bec in order to become abbot of St. Stephen's in Caen, Anselm was appointed prior of Bec and head of the monastic school.

Prior and Abbot of Bec

The office of prior did not initially alter Anselm's love for solitude and meditation. In spite of his teaching activity, little is known of Anselm during his first 10 years at Bec. After 1070, however, he became more active, and the demand from his students to write down some of his teachings resulted in the writing of several works of major import.

The first of these works was the *Monologion* (ca. 1077), a treatise which examines the existence and nature of God. In particular, two arguments are used. In order to make a comparative judgment (that one thing is *better* than another), it is necessary to have a superlative (the best against which everything else can be judged). For Anselm, God is that highest good. Anselm also used the argument of contingency—that is, everything must come into existence through the agency of something prior. It is thus necessary to posit a first cause or being on which everything else depends, for if there were nothing on which it depended, it could not exist. That first cause, for Anselm, is God.

The arguments used in the *Monologion* can be found in previous writers, especially in St. Augustine, on whose work Anselm based most of his thought. The structure and method, however, are new, and Anselm seemed motivated to construct an argument that was rational and could convince the non-Christian.

More revolutionary in nature was the work which Anselm entitled *Proslogion* (ca. 1078). It was the result of a "discovery" of a definition of God, and the ontological argument based upon the definition seemed to Anselm (and to many later philosophers) to be convincing by its very logical simplicity. Anselm's biographer, Eadmer, later described the discovery: "Behold, one night during Matins, the grace of God shone in his heart and the matter became clear to his understanding, filling his whole being with immense joy and jubilation."

The discovery of Anselm was a definition of God that was anticipated in part by Augustine and Seneca; namely, God was that being a greater than which could not be conceived. Using that definition as the basic content of anyone's idea of God, Anselm went on to argue that such a being necessarily existed not only as an idea in the mind but also in external reality. The *Proslogion* was widely circulated and brought Anselm immediate fame among his contemporaries and succeeding generations. Although attacked in his own time and in later centuries, Anselm's ontological argument greatly influenced the course of philosophical and theological thought.

In 1078 Anselm was elected abbot of Bec, a position he held until 1093. In spite of the demands of the office, Anselm found time to complete several works on philosophy and theology. Among them were his philosophical works on grammar and truth and his theological treatises on free will and the devil. While these works are significant in the thought and development of Anselm, they did not make as great an impression on his contemporaries or later generations as did his earlier works.

From 1090 to 1093 Anselm was drawn into two controversies that changed his career. One was over the understanding of the Incarnation of Christ and the doctrine of the Atonement. Beginning in 1092, Anselm wrote two letters on this subject, and the ideas contained therein eventually bore fruit in a lengthy study entitled *Cur Deus Homo*. Although anticipated in part by earlier theologians, such as Tertullian, Anselm wrote the first work to deal so extensively with the Incarnation, and his method of presentation, as well as the precision of his ideas, makes this work one of the most influential in the history of theology.

The other conflict that influenced Anselm in this period was the political and ecclesiastical situation in England. Lanfranc had become archbishop of Canterbury in 1070. After his death in 1089, King William Rufus allowed the position to remain vacant to avoid creating a strong ecclesiastical opponent and to appropriate Church revenues. The King wished to avoid accepting an archbishop who would oppose royal control of the English Church. Illness and fear of eternal retribution, however, finally caused him to appoint a successor to Lanfranc, and to that post he called Anselm. In spite of Anselm's initial reluctance, he was consecrated archbishop of Canterbury on Dec. 4, 1093.

The Archbishop

Anselm's advocacy of Church reform and the recognition of Urban II as the rightful pope precipitated a conflict with the King. To gain support, Anselm convened a council of bishops and noblemen at Rockingham in 1095, but the indecisive results of that council and the growing animosity of the King forced Anselm to flee England in 1097.

Anselm went to central and southern Italy, where he remained for several years as a close associate of the papacy. After the death of William Rufus in 1100, his brother and successor, Henry I, summoned Anselm back to England. The problem of lay investiture and Henry's demand that Anselm renew his oath of feudal homage to the English king brought the two men into conflict. The opposition of the King soon forced Anselm to journey once more to Rome, and Anselm remained away from England until 1106. A compromise was finally worked out whereby the King gave up the right of investiture in return for a guarantee that Anselm would consecrate all candidates for episcopal

and monastic office who had already been appointed by the King and had taken the oath of homage.

On the basis of this agreement, Anselm returned to England as archbishop and remained there for the last 3 years of his life. He found time to return to his writing, and completed works on the Sacraments and on the foreknowledge of God. His work was carried on after his death in 1109 by his students at Bec and Canterbury.

Further Reading

The best study of the life and works of Anselm is R.W. Southern, *Saint Anselm and His Biographer: A Study of Monastic Life and Thought, 1059-c. 1130* (1963), which includes an excellent study of the background and implications of *Cur Deus Homo*. Older but still useful works are R.W. Church, *Saint Anselm* (1870); Martin Rule, *The Life and Times of St. Anselm* (2 vols., 1883); and J. Clayton, *Saint Anselm: A Critical Biography* (1933).

A general survey of the various interpretations of *Cur Deus Homo* is John McIntyre, *St. Anselm and His Critics: A Reinterpretation of the Cur Deus Homo* (1954). Among the many studies of the meaning and importance of the ontological argument for God's existence as expressed in the *Proslogion*, the most significant are Karl Barth, *Anselm: Fides Quaerens Intellectum: Anselm's Proof of the Existence of God in the Context of His Theological Scheme*, translated by I.W. Robertson (1960); Charles Hartshorne, *Anselm's Discovery: A ReExamination of the Ontological Proof for God's Existence* (1965); and John Hick, ed., *The Many-Faced Argument: Recent Studies on the Ontological Argument for the Existence of God* (1967).

Additional Sources

Evans, G. R. (Gillian Rosemary), *Anselm*, London: Geoffrey Chapman; Wilton, CT.: Morehouse-Barlow, 1989.

Evans, G. R. (Gillian Rosemary), *Anselm and a new generation*, Oxford: Clarendon Press; New York: Oxford University Press, 1980.

Jaspers, Karl, *Anselm and Nicholas of Cus*, New York, Harcourt Brace Jovanovich 1974, 1966.

Southern R. W. (Richard William), *Saint Anselm: a portrait in a landscape*, Cambridge; New York: Cambridge University Press, 1990.

Vaughn, Sally N., *Anselm of Bec and Robert of Meulan: the innocence of the dove and the wisdom of the serpent*, Berkeley: University of California Press, 1987.

Ward, Benedicta, *Anselm of Canterbury, a monastic scholar: an expanded version of a paper given to the Anselm Society, St. Augustine's College, Canterbury, in May 1973*, Oxford: S.L.G. Press, 1977. □

St. Anthony

The Egyptian hermit St. Anthony (ca. 250-356) played a large role in the development of Christian monastic life through the influence of his widely recognized sanctity and of his biography, written by St. Athanasius of Alexandria.

Anthony (also called St. Anthony of Egypt and St. Anthony Abbot) was born and raised in a Christian family at Como in Upper Egypt. He and his sister were orphaned when Anthony was between 18 and 20 years old. Six months later, influenced by Christ's words—"If thou wouldst be perfect, go and sell that thou hast and give it to the poor; and come follow me and thou shalt have treasure in heaven" (Matthew 19:21)—Anthony gave his inheritance to the poor. He placed his sister with a group of virgins to be brought up in the holy life, and he went to live as a hermit near his native village. He sought instruction from other men who were also living in solitude.

Anthony's development as a hermit was marked by many temptations by the devil and demons. The terrible and fantastic forms that these took were represented later in literature and art about him. Anthony prevailed against demons in the shapes of wild beasts, evil thoughts, and human persons; his biographer attributes these victories to his constant faith and the use of the sign of the cross and the name of Jesus.

Later Anthony moved from the vicinity of Como to a remote tomb. Here, sustained by bread brought by friends, he continued his inner warfare. When he was about 35, he moved still farther out into the wilderness to an abandoned fort at Pispir across the Nile River. Anthony's reputation grew during the years he spent at the fort, and many hermits came to him for instruction in the discipline of the ascetic life. Finally, in 305, the first religious community of hermits was founded at Pispir.

During the persecution of Christians by the Roman emperor Maximus about 311, Anthony went to Alexandria, where he visited and encouraged the captive Christians and himself sought martyrdom. When the persecution ended, Anthony moved again into the wilderness. He left his mountain on only one more occasion when, about 335, he visited Alexandria to join Athanasius in fighting the Arian heresy. In debates with heretics and philosophers Anthony demonstrated considerable learning and rhetorical skill.

But it was as a holy man that Anthony's fame spread. People came great distances to his wilderness retreat not only for instruction but also to benefit from the miracles reputed to occur at his bidding. He advised the great, such as the Roman emperor Constantine and his sons, and the imperial government.

Anthony died in 356, when he was more than 100 years old. Two disciples buried his body, not embalming it above ground in the Egyptian manner. His grave was unmarked, but his garments were sent to the Egyptian bishops Athanasius and Serapion.

Further Reading

There are various translations and discussions of the *Life of Antony* (*Vita Antonii*), written by St. Athanasius in 357. H. Ellershaw's translation is available in Henry Wace and Philip Schaff, eds., *A Select Library of the Nicene and Post-Nicene Fathers of the Christian Church,* 2d series, vol. 4 (1907). Walter Nigg, *Warriors of God* (1953; trans. 1959), provides a hagiographic account. Herbert B. Workman, *The Evolution of the Monastic Ideal* (1913; rev. ed. 1927), puts Anthony's achievement in historical context. See also Jacques Lacarriere, *Men Possessed by God: The Story of the Desert Monks of Ancient Christendom* (trans. 1964).

Additional Sources

Anthony, of Egypt, Saint, ca. 250-355 or 6., *Lettres,* Begrolles en Mauges: Abbaye de Bellefontaine, 1976.

Athanasius, Saint, Patriarch of Alexandria, d. 373., *The Coptic Life of Antony,* San Francisco: International Scholars Publications, 1995.

Athanasius, Saint, Patriarch of Alexandria, d. 373., *The life of Antony and the letter to Marcellinus,* New York: Paulist Press, 1980.

Cornet, Chantal., *Antoine,* Le Puy: C. Bonneton, 1985. □

St. Anthony (with white beard)

Susan Brownell Anthony

Susan Brownell Anthony (1820-1906) was an early leader of the American woman's suffrage movement and pioneered in seeking other equalities for women. An active abolitionist, she campaigned for emancipation of the slaves.

Susan B. Anthony was born on Feb. 15, 1820, in Adams, Mass., one of seven children. Her family had settled in Rhode Island in 1634. She attended Quaker schools and began teaching at the age of 15 for $1.50 a week plus board. When the family moved to Rochester, N.Y., in 1845, her brilliant father, Daniel Anthony, the dominant influence in her life, worked with important abolitionists. Frederick Douglass, William Lloyd Garrison, Wendell Phillips, and other guests at the Anthony farm helped form her strong views on abolition of slavery.

Woman's Rights

Though her family attended the first Woman's Rights Convention held in Seneca Falls and Rochester, N.Y., in 1848, Anthony did not take up the cause of woman's rights until 1851, when male hostility to her temperance efforts convinced her that women must win the right to speak in public and to vote before anything else could be accomplished. Her lifelong friendship and partnership with Elizabeth Cady Stanton also began in 1851, as did her temporary doffing of corsets in favor of the revolutionary "bloomer" costume—which was women's first major dress reform in the movement. Anthony attended her first woman's-rights convention in 1852; from then until the end of the Civil War she campaigned from door to door, in legislatures, and in meetings for the two causes of abolition of slavery and of woman's rights. The New York State Married Woman's Property and Guardianship Law in 1860 was her first major legislative victory.

Formation of Suffrage Movement

With the outbreak of the Civil War in 1861, woman's rights took second place. Susan Anthony organized the Women's National Loyal League, which mobilized the crucial petitions to force passage of the 13th Amendment to the Constitution to abolish slavery. In 1865 she began her battle in the content of the 14th and 15th Amendments, hoping to gain the franchise for women as well as for African American males. But her former male allies in the abolitionist struggle brushed her aside, saying the time was not yet ripe for woman's suffrage. Saddened but not deterred by this defeat, Anthony worked solely for woman's suffrage from this time to the end of her life, organizing the National Woman Suffrage Association with Stanton. The association's New York weekly, *The Revolution,* was created in 1868 to promote women's causes. After its bankruptcy in 1870, Anthony lectured throughout the nation for 6 years to pay its $10,000 debt.

In the 1872 presidential race Susan Anthony and 15 Rochester comrades became the first women ever to vote in a national election. That they were promptly arrested for their boldness did not dismay her, as she sought to test women's legal right to vote under the 14th Amendment by carrying the case to the U.S. Supreme Court. Her case was singled out for prosecution, and trial was set for 1873 in Rochester. Free on bail of $1,000, Anthony stumped the country with a carefully prepared legal argument, "Is It a Crime for a U.S. Citizen to Vote?" She lost her case, following some dubious legal maneuvering by the judge, but was unfortunately barred from appealing to the Supreme Court when her sentence was not made binding.

Later Years

Susan Anthony spent the rest of her life working for the Federal suffrage amendment—a strenuous effort that took her not only to Congress but to political conventions, labor meetings, and lyceums in every section of the country. Mindful of the nearly total omission of women from historical literature, in 1877 she forced herself to sit down with her colleagues to begin the monumental and invaluable *History of Woman Suffrage* in five volumes. She later worked with her biographer, Ida Husted Harper, on two of the three volumes of *The Life and Work of Susan B. Anthony,* which were drawn largely from her continuous scrapbooks (1838-1900), now in the Library of Congress, and her diaries and letters.

Up to just one month before her death in 1906, Anthony was still active: she attended her last suffrage convention and her eighty-sixth birthday celebration in Washington. She closed her last public speech with the words, "Failure is impossible." When she died in her Rochester home on March 13, only four states had granted the vote to women. Fourteen years later the suffrage amendment, the 19th, was added to the Constitution.

Further Reading

The most complete work on Anthony is Ida Husted Harper, *The Life and Work of Susan B. Anthony* (3 vols., 1898-1908). Katharine Anthony, a distant relative and noted biographer, had access to Miss Anthony's diaries and wrote the best recent biography, *Susan B. Anthony: Her Personal History and Her Era* (1954). Alma Lutz, *Susan B. Anthony: Rebel, Crusader, Humanitarian* (1959) and *Created Equal: A Biography of Elizabeth Cady Stanton* (1940), which also contains considerable material on Anthony, are more solid accounts than Rheta Childe Dorr, *Susan B. Anthony: The Woman Who Changed the Mind of a Nation* (1928). □

Antigonus I

The Macedonian Antigonus I (382-301 B.C.), having served as a general under Alexander the Great, became the most powerful of his immediate successors.

Antigonus was born in Macedon, the son of the minor noble Philip. Nothing is known of his youth; he was 26 years older than Alexander and probably did not associate with him until Alexander became king. In 334 Antigonus campaigned with Alexander in Asia Minor; and after the conquest of its upland regions in the following year, Alexander appointed him satrap of Phrygia for his good service and military ability.

While Alexander marched on through Syria, Egypt, and Persia and into India, Antigonus remained in Asia Minor consolidating his satrapy. Consequently, when Alexander died 10 years later, Antigonus held his territory with greater power and authority than the other "successors," who scrambled for positions elsewhere.

Antigonus governed his kingdom well. In defending Phrygia against Persian partisans, Antigonus suffered the loss of an eye, which gave this tall Macedonian a rather ferocious appearance and gained him the nickname "Monophthalmos" (The One-Eyed). Antigonus ruled his domain with diplomacy and the constant awareness of the greatness of Greek culture and the freedom of the Greek cities in Asia Minor. This won for him the gratitude of the Greeks.

The years which followed Alexander's death were fraught with wars and political intrigues among the most powerful of Alexander's generals, including Antigonus. Alexander's counselor Perdikkas assumed the regency for Alexander's heirs, the half-witted epileptic Philip III Arrhedaeios, who was Alexander's half brother, and the posthumous son Alexander IV. Ptolemy gained control of Egypt and, in a fetishlike manner, of Alexander's body; Lysimachus became satrap of Greek Thrace but never obtained the political power Antigonus had developed in Phrygia; and Antipater continued to rule Macedon and Greece for the royal heirs as he had done earlier for Alexander.

Perdikkas had held the position closest to Alexander since Alexander's beloved Hephaestion had died; he also knew Alexander's last wishes. Perdikkas had persuaded the Macedonian troops in Babylon to await the birth of Alexander's child by the Persian Rhoxana and, if a boy, to elect by their feudal aristocratic methods the child as king. Perdikkas would assume the regency for the boy as grand vizier. Consequently, Perdikkas, as regent over Asia, sharply clashed with Antigonus in Asia Minor. Within a year Alexander's empire appeared to be divided between Antipater in Europe and Perdikkas in Asia. Although though Antigonus's satrapy was extended to include Pisidia, Pamphylia, and Lycia, Antigonus felt hemmed in.

Perdikkas sought to pacify the Asian borders, and he aided Eumenes, Alexander's secretary, in the conquest of the rebelling province of Cappadocia. Perdikkas also ordered Antigonus to send soldiers to help Eumenes, but Antigonus ignored the directive. Antigonus gathered in Europe the support of Antipater and Craterus against Perdikkas, whose ambitions to become king he suspected. Ptolemy also joined Antigonus's new coalition. Since Ptolemy had obtained Alexander's body against Perdikkas's wishes and now had joined Antigonus, Perdikkas in the spring of 321 struck out against Ptolemy's Egypt. Three attempts to cross the Nile Delta failed, and Perdikkas soon after was assassinated.

At the coalition's meeting at Triparadeisus, Antigonus was awarded the command of the royal army in Asia. In 320 Antigonus began several successful campaigns against the rebels Alcestas, who was Perdikkas's brother, and Eumenes.

Antigonus did not adhere to the agreements of the coalition very long, for he intended to obtain sole rule in Asia Minor and to expand his influence into Asia. In 319, when Antipater died, Antigonus alone of all the successor generals had the prospect of reuniting all of Alexander's empire.

Again in 318 Antigonus pursued Eumenes, who had built up a sizable force in Syria. Seleucus, whose power in Babylonia was weak, allied with Antigonus, but as Antigonus entered Syria and Babylonia, Seleucus found himself in a subordinate role and in 316 fled to Ptolemy's protection. Alexander's empire was now divided among Cassander in Macedon and Greece, Ptolemy in Egypt and Cyrene, Lysimachus in Thrace, and Antigonus in Asia from the Aegean Sea to the Indus Valley.

In 315 Ptolemy, Seleucus, and Lysimachus entered a coalition against Antigonus and began a 4-year war against him. Antigonus retained his power but lost Babylonia and the eastern satrapies in 311 to Seleucus. The short-lived treaty of 311 ended the hostilities. Although Antigonus did not emerge as victor, his prestige was enhanced. In 310 he invaded Babylonia unsuccessfully and retreated in 309. Ptolemy, meanwhile, secured Cyprus, invaded Cilicia, and agitated Greece and Athens against Antigonus, who finally struck back in 306. He gained Cyprus in June, when his son Demetrius I Poliorcetes defeated Ptolemy's fleet at Salamis. Though Antigonus and Demetrius now proclaimed themselves kings, they failed to subdue Ptolemy. By 302 Antigonus was master of Alexander's empire with the exception of Egypt.

In the spring of 301 Ptolemy and Lysimachus again challenged Antigonus, and in the ensuing war Antigonus died at the battle of Ipsus that same year. The victors divided his domain.

Further Reading

The formation of the Hellenistic kingdoms and the problems of Antigonus are discussed in Edwyn Robert Bevan, *The House of Seleucus* (2 vols., 1902); W. W. Tarn, *Hellenistic Civilisation* (1927; 3d rev. ed., with G.T. Griffith, 1952); and Pierre Grimal and others, *Hellenism and the Rise of Rome* (1965; trans. 1968). □

Antiochus III

Antiochus III (241-187 B.C.) was a Syrian king of the Seleucid dynasty, Alexander the Great's successors in Asia. Antiochus attempted to restore Alexander's empire to its former greatness, and the magnitude of this undertaking earned Antiochus the name Megas, "the Great."

The second son of Seleucus II and his wife Laodice, Antiochus was born in Babylonia. When his older brother, Seleucus III, was assassinated in Phrygia in 223, Antiochus succeeded him as king at the age of 18. His cousin Achaeus assumed military command and punished Seleucus's assassins. There was strong public support for Achaeus to ascend the throne, but he declined and remained loyal to his cousin. Achaeus governed in Asia Minor.

In 222 Molon and Alexander, the satraps of Media and Persia, revolted. Molon proclaimed himself independent and king, but by 220 his forces had abandoned him, and he and Alexander committed suicide. Then Achaeus sought power and occupied Antioch, but the populace deserted him. Antiochus foolishly overlooked the brief insurrection and instead prepared to attack Egypt. His forces easily gained coastal Phoenicia, Tyre, and Ptolemais, but Antiochus faltered at the fortress of Dora in northern Palestine. This gave Egypt a chance to reorganize its army, and on June 22, 217, Antiochus was defeated in Gaza by Ptolemy IV Philopater. Achaeus grew more and more independent, and the Parthian Arsacids in the northeast gained power. But in Jerusalem the Jews welcomed Antiochus and hailed his confirmation of their religious privileges.

In the winter of 217/216, Antiochus prepared to face the now-powerful Achaeus, and after 2 years of war Antiochus cornered him in Sardis. Through Cretan intrigue Achaeus was captured, mutilated, and then beheaded. Antiochus thus regained his western capital, but the powerful city of Pergamon still remained hostile.

Antiochus then set out to restore the former boundaries of the Seleucid empire. Between 212 and 204 he campaigned in Armenia, regained Parthia and Bactria as vassal kingdoms, and led expeditions into the Kabul Valley in India and across the Persian Gulf into Arabia. About 210 Antiochus made his 10-year-old son Antiochus coruler, as he feared his own death in these campaigns. In 204 Antiochus regained Phoenicia and southern Palestine from Egypt, for in that year Ptolemy IV had died and left his throne to his 4-year-old son Ptolemy V Epiphanes. Antiochus and Philip V of Macedon then decided to divide the Ptolemaic empire.

Fearing the growing strength of Antiochus, Rome dispatched its envoy in 200 to protect Egypt and halt Antiochus, but he disregarded the weak ultimatum. In 197 Antiochus again campaigned in Asia Minor to gain Ptolemaic territories. With Philip's defeat in Greece showing his weakness and with the Ptolemaic empire in distress, Antiochus began to dream of reuniting Alexander's empire. Rome, however, now proclaimed itself champion of Greece's liberty, and Rhodes sought to block Antiochus. After campaigning in Europe, rumors of intrigue regarding Egypt brought Antiochus back to Antioch in 196, where he met and welcomed the defeated Hannibal.

When Antiochus's son died suddenly in 193, rumors of assassination flourished, the anti-Roman faction gained strength, and in 192 war erupted in Greece. Antiochus landed in Greece and surprised the Roman occupation forces. Macedon deserted him and joined Rome, and many of the Greek states vacillated in their loyalties. Roman countercampaigns in 191 forced Antiochus to seek refuge in Chalkis and later in southern Thessaly, where he was defeated. After sea battles in the Aegean, Antiochus feared a Roman invasion of Asia Minor, which finally occurred in 190. Antiochus again met defeat at Magnesia, and the Peace of Apemea in 188 ended a century of Seleucid dominance in Asia Minor. Leaving his son Seleucus in Syria as coruler, Antiochus departed for Luristan, and in the following year he was killed by hostile tribesmen.

Further Reading

Edwyn Robert Bevan, *The House of Seleucus* (2 vols., 1902; repr. 1966), still provides the most thorough discussion of Antiochus III and the Seleucid empire. Pierre Grimal and others, *Hellenism and the Rise of Rome* (1965; trans. 1968), is disappointing in its discussion of Antiochus, as is W. W. Tarn, *Hellenistic Civilization* (1927; 3d rev. ed., with G. T. Griffith, 1952). For background material see W. W. Tarn, *The Greeks in Bactria and India* (1938; 2d ed. 1951), and M. Rostovtzeff, *The Social and Economic History of the Hellenistic World* (3 vols., 1941). ☐

Antiochus IV

Antiochus IV (ca. 215-163 B.C.), called Epiphanes, or "God on Earth," was a king of Syria. He attempted to impose Hellenic culture on the Jews and thus precipitated the rebellion of the Maccabees.

T he third son of Antiochus III, Antiochus IV succeeded his brother Seleucus IV as ruler of the Seleucid empire in 175 B.C. Nicknamed Epimanes, or "Goon on Earth," for his eccentric behavior, Antiochus proved an energetic and capable ruler.

He maintained a vigorous foreign policy. In 169, in response to a planned invasion of Israel and Lebanon by the Egyptian king Ptolemy VI, Antiochus moved first, defeated the Egyptians in the Negeb, and advanced to the Nile at Memphis. He accepted Ptolemy's submission, and when a separatist movement crowned the Egyptian king's brother as Ptolemy VII in Alexandria, he left Ptolemy VI to deal with the usurper. Antiochus withdrew, keeping only Pelusium, the frontier fortress east of the Nile Delta, as pawn. The Ptolemaic brothers united in 168, and Antiochus again invaded Egypt while another of his armies took the Egyptian island of Cyprus. Antiochus was about to besiege Alexandria when an ultimatum from the Roman Senate ordered him to evacuate both Egypt and Cyprus. No match for Rome, Antiochus accepted and had to be satisfied with a "victory over Egypt" festival at Daphne.

Early in his reign Antiochus strengthened his control of Cilicia (modern district of Mersin and Adana), and he reduced Artaxias, the independent ruler of Armenia (modern eastern Turkey), to the status of a client king. In the later years of his reign, Antiochus campaigned in the eastern provinces. He strengthened Media in central Iran against the rising power of Parthia, farther to the northeast. He also attempted an unsuccessful invasion of Susiana in southern Iran, allegedly in order to loot the temple of Anaitis, and an exploration of the Persian Gulf fell short of an invasion of Arabia.

Antiochus relied on Macedonians and Greeks to man his kingdom's administrative services and the armed forces. He tried to increase the reservoir of talent by drawing native peoples into Hellenized cities and by reorganizing native cities along Greek lines, often renaming them Epiphania or Antiochea. These cities included Babylon, Uruk, Ecbatana,

and Jerusalem. Asserting his divinity, Antiochus claimed temple treasures and imposed Greek cults. The policy proved disastrous in Judaea, where confiscation of some temple funds and enforced worship of Zeus Olympius in place of Jehovah caused an uprising and guerrilla warfare by the Maccabees from 167 to 164. Antiochus abandoned the policy before his death in Media in 163, but the tide of Asian reaction to Hellenism was rising, and the circle of Syria's enemies was closing in.

Further Reading

Antiochus IV is discussed in S. K. Eddy, *The King Is Dead* (1961). J.D.C. Pavry, ed., *Oriental Studies in Honor of Cursetji Erachji Pavry* (1933), contains a biography of Antiochus by C. A. Kincaid. There is an extensive treatment of Antiochus in W. W. Tarn, *The Greeks in Bactria and India* (1938; 2d ed. 1951), and a shorter account of his reign in M. Rostovtzeff, *The Social and Economic History of the Hellenistic World* (3 vols., 1941).

Additional Sources

Price, Walter K., *The coming antichris,* Chicago, Moody Press 1974. ☐

Antisthenes

The Greek philosopher Antisthenes (ca. 450-360 B.C.) was a devoted student and follower of Socrates and is credited with founding the Cynic Sect, which exerted great influence on the course of popular philosophy throughout antiquity.

B orn in Athens of an Athenian father and a Thracian mother who may have been a slave, Antisthenes was denied citizenship because of his mother's social status. However, that proved no deterrent to his education, for he studied with the famous Sophist, Gorgias. Antisthenes also became a member of Socrates's circle and on his master's death turned to teaching, meeting with his students in the Gymnasium Kynosarges. It was perhaps from this meeting place that his group became known as Cynics (doglike), although popular etymology links the name with the style of life his followers chose.

Antisthenes wrote 10 volumes, which included a denunciation of Plato (to which Plato's *Euthydemus* is a reply); *Heracles,* which glorified the ancient hero for his benefactions to mankind; *Cyrus,* which praised Cyrus the Elder as a model ruler; *Alcibiades,* which denounced self-centered passion; *Archelaus,* which denounced tyranny; and *Politicus,* in which democracy is accorded the same treatment.

Antisthenes's teachings laid the groundwork for Cynic theory. Happiness may be acquired through virtue which is based on knowledge. This knowledge is not the carefully developed scientific knowledge which the Stoics favored later but simply the concrete knowledge of what words mean. Contrary to Plato, his contemporary and rival, Antisthenes taught that only physical things are real and that a predicate different from the subject to which it refers is impossible to apply. This simplicity of physical theory affected the Cynics' ethics as well. Man must live with the understanding that all except his own individual freedom of spirit is to be held in contempt. Wealth, social position, and, above all, bodily pleasures are to be cast aside in favor of a life of hardship, toil, and concern for others. Heracles is the Cynics' model, and his life was often held up as an example of a human life lived according to the best principles.

As roving mendicants and preachers, the Cynics roundly criticized men for the folly of their conventions and for the delusions under which they lived. Particular targets of their attacks were religious celebrations with their sacrifices and elaborate rituals. In putting into practice their ideal of *anaideia* (shamelessness), they consciously outraged their fellowmen by carrying out acts in public which revealed their utter contempt for the opinions of men.

Antisthenes was important as the founder of a sect which offered a simpler and more natural way of life at a time when the values of the city-state were in serious decline and men had to seek for spiritual guidance elsewhere. If his and his followers' strictures were sometimes coarse, biting, and vulgar, they were nonetheless motivated by a deep concern for their fellowmen and a desire to share with them the freedom which could be found in independence of mind and spirit.

Further Reading

An excellent account of Antisthenes is in Donald R. Dudley, *A History of Cynicism: From Diogenes to the 6th Century A.D.* (1937), and in Farrand Sayre, *Diogenes of Sinope: A Study of Greek Cynicism* (1938). Also useful is Eduard Zeller, *Outlines of the History of Greek Philosophy* (1883; 13th rev. ed. by Wilhelm Nestle, 1928; trans., from Nestle's edition, by L. R. Palmer, 1931). Briefer but good introductory accounts of cynicism in the context of the intellectual history of Greece are in standard histories of Greek literature, such as Albin Lesky, *A History of Greek Literature* (1958; trans. 1966). □

Antonello da Messina

Antonello da Messina (ca. 1430-1479) was one of the first Italian painters to master the oil-paint technique. His further significance stems from his relationship to Flemish painting and his influence on Venetian painters of the late 15th century.

Giorgio Vasari, the 16th-century biographer, said that Antonello da Messina learned oil painting from Jan van Eyck, whom he had visited in Flanders. This is improbable as Jan van Eyck died when Antonello was 11 years old. Nevertheless, critics have continued to postulate a visit to Flanders to explain the Flemish qualities in Antonello's art as well as his mastery of oil painting. A different viewpoint, which has evolved recently, sees his

apprenticeship to the painter Colantonio in Naples and his contact with Petrus Christus, a Flemish follower of Jan van Eyck, as the crucial factors in Antonello's early development.

Antonello was born in Messina, Sicily. Nothing is known of his early years. He was apprenticed to Colantonio probably about 1450. The court in Naples at that time was cosmopolitan, with French, Provençal, Spanish, Burgundian, and Flemish elements present. The youthful Antonello would have had opportunities to study Flemish painting there. By 1456 he was established as an independent master in Messina. In the same year his name appeared on the payroll of Duke Galeazzo Maria Sforza in Milan along with the name of Christus. Whatever Antonello had learned of Flemish art while in Naples would have been reinforced by the presence in Milan of Christus. In 1460 Antonello traveled abroad, though where is not known. From 1460 to 1465 he was in Messina. His whereabouts between 1465 and 1473 is unknown, though he was probably in Messina part of the time. In 1473-1474 he was again in Messina. In 1475-1476 he was in Venice, where, according to Vasari, he had gone to enjoy the licentious pleasures of the city. By September 1476 he was in Messina again. He dictated his will on Feb. 14, 1479, and died in Messina sometime before Feb. 25, the date of a document that speaks of him as dead.

The Works

Antonello's early works reflect a knowledge of Flemish painting. Among them the small *Crucifixion* in Sibiu, Roma-

nia, the *Three Angels* and the small panel *Penitent St. Jerome,* both in Reggio Calabria, and the *Portrait of a Man* in Cefalù are noteworthy. The *Portrait of a Man* is characteristic of Antonello's portrait art. The subject is posed at an angle rather than parallel to the picture plane, as was common among Italian profile portraits. This three-quarter view, characteristic of Flemish portraits, was Antonello's most conspicuous borrowing from the North.

Two panels of the *Virgin Annunciate* in Munich and Palermo are among Antonello's most ingratiating works. The closeup, bust-length pose gives the panels an appealing sense of intimacy. The picture in Palermo is especially fine with its strong geometric pattern and sense of crystalline space.

The altarpiece of St. Gregory in Messina is signed and dated 1473. In it Antonello shows an awareness of the art of Piero della Francesca in the emphatic fullness of the figures, their positions in space, and their rather dour and impassive expressions. There is, however, a certain softness resulting from Antonello's use of light which is his own.

The dismembered altarpiece for the church of S. Cassiano in Venice was Antonello's most influential painting in that city. The central panel, much cut down, is now in Vienna. The altarpiece is a *sacra conversazione* (a type of Madonna and Child painting) set beneath a soaring dome, which forecasts similar compositions by Giovanni Bellini and other Venetian masters of the 16th century. It has the same luminosity and sense of atmosphere so common in Venetian painting.

Further Reading

Two sound monographs on Antonello in English are Giorgio Vigni, *All the Paintings of Antonello da Messina* (1952); trans. 1963), and Stefano Bottari, *Antonello da Messina* (1955). For general background see Cecil Gould, *An Introduction to Italian Renaissance Painting* (1957), and Frederick Hartt, *History of Italian Renaissance Art* (1970). □

Michelangelo Antonioni

The Italian film director Michelangelo Antonioni (born 1912) demonstrated in such compelling and original films as *L'avventura* and *Blow-Up* his belief that the failure of human feelings is the cause of modern tragedy.

Born into an upper-middle-class family in Ferrara, Michelangelo Antonioni took a degree in political economics at the University of Bologna. Having decided on a film career, he worked with the directors Roberto Rossellini and Marcel Carné, among others. The first films Antonioni directed were three notable documentary shorts: *Gente del Po* (1947), *La funivia del Faloria* (1950), and *La villa dei mostri* (1950).

Antonioni's first full-length dramatic effort, *Cronaca di un amore* (1950), was distinguished by its disavowal of the fundamental precepts of Italian neorealism as practiced by the directors Vittorio de Sica and Rossellini and later modified by Federico Fellini. Antonioni's next work, *I vinti* (1952), proved an unsuccessful attempt to lend thematic unity to an episodic and discursive narrative. Considerably more interesting as indicators of the consistent subjects and themes of his film career were *Le amiche* (1955) and *Il grido* (1957). Both these narratives present the spiritual complexities that trouble Antonioni; they show human beings in quest of meaningful life in a hostile world.

With *L'avventura* (1960) Antonioni, after 10 years of virtual obscurity, suddenly set fire to complacent sensibilities of international film audiences and critics. A penetrating voyage into the tortured recesses of the mind, this film explores the difficulty of sustaining love in a cauterized and fraudulent society. This theme also provided the basis for the two subsequent works: *La notte* (1961) and *Eclipse* (1962). In both these films Antonioni stresses the impermanence of love and difficulties of communication.

Red Desert (1964) was Antonioni's first film in color. He used color to create psychological nuances and conceptual patterns not possible in chiaroscuro. The images of *Red Desert* explore the theme of human uneasiness in a world full of the splendors and miseries of technology. *Blow-Up* (1966) is a metaphysical mystery drama set in London. This film is an evocative mixture of asceticism and lyricism, which eludes patterns of interpretation and frustrates conventional expectations of plot and theme. *Zabriskie Point* (1970) suffers from the director's unfamiliarity with his American milieu. A portrait of troubled youth in a wealthy, neofascistic society, the work is nevertheless far superior to its American counterparts. In *The Passenger* (1975), Antonioni again explores the ills of modern society as the hero, a TV reporter, exchanges identities with a dead gun-runner in a futile effort to evade his own fate. *The Oberwald Mystery* (1980) is an adaptation of Jean Cocteau's play *The Eagle Has Two Heads;* shot on video, it is interesting mainly for its experimentation with color. *Identification of a Woman* (1982) follows a movie director's search for a new leading lady; here Antonioni returns to the theme of finding one's identity in contemporary society. The film was awarded a Grand Prix at the 1982 Cannes Film Festival.

Antonioni suffered a paralyzing stroke in 1985 and was unable to complete any film project until 1995, when he released *Beyond the Clouds*. Codirected by German director Wim Wenders, the film presents four stories that each explore the failure of a couple to establish true communication. When the film was shown at the Venice Festival the *Economist* noted that its "main fascination is to watch how Mr. Antonioni looks back on his entire career and yet comes up with something different and modern."

Perhaps no other body of cinematic work depicts the frustrations, delusions, and possibilities of life and love as profoundly and truthfully as that of Antonioni. His characters move in a real world but never make meaningful contact with their environment or with each other in their search for a truth that eludes them.

Further Reading

Analyses of Antonioni's artistry are contained in Jonathan Baumbach's "From A to Antonioni: Hallucinations of a Movie Addict" in W.R. Robinson, ed., *Man and the Movies* (1967); in Stanley Kauffmann's "Some Notes on a Year with *Blow-Up*" in Richard Schickel and John Simon, eds., *Film: Sixty Seven to Sixty Eight* (1968); in Sam Rohdie's *Antonioni* (Indiana University Press, 1990), and in William Arrowsmith's *Antonioni: The Poet of Images,* ed. by Ted Perry (Oxford, 1995). See also the relevant sections in Stanley Kauffmann, *A World on Film: Criticism and Comment* (1966), Dwight Mac-Donald, *Dwight MacDonald on Movies* (1969), *Economist* (September 16, 1995), *New Republic* (October 28, 1996). □

Mark Antony

The Roman politician and general Mark Antony (ca. 82-30 B.C.) was the chief rival of Octavian for the succession to the power of Julius Caesar.

Mark Antony (in Latin, Marcus Antonius) came from a distinguished Roman family. His grandfather had been one of the leading orators in Rome, and his father, Marcus Antonius Creticus, had died in an expedition against pirates. As a young man, Antony became involved in tribunate politics and the Roman East, two areas that were to play a major role in his later life. Among his closest friends was a young man, Curio, who as tribune was a key figure in the conflict between Caesar and the Senate and Pompey. In 58 Antony appears to have been among the supporters of the powerful and violent tribune Clodius.

Career with Caesar

Antony received his first overseas experience in the East when, during 57-55, he served with the Roman governor of Syria, Aulus Gabinius, and distinguished himself as a cavalry officer during campaigns in Palestine and Egypt. From there he went to Caesar in Gaul. In 52 he was elected quaestor in Rome and returned to Gaul to take part in the suppression of the revolt of Vercingetorix. In 50 he was elected tribune, an office that represented the people's interests.

Antony came into the office at a critical time. Caesar's command in Gaul was coming to an end, and a group in the Senate was set on bringing Caesar to trial for alleged misdeeds while consul and proconsul. Caesar depended upon the tribunes to look after his interests in Rome. Curio had played this role masterfully, and Antony tried to emulate him. He vetoed a decree that required Caesar to lay down his arms. When the Senate gave its magistrates special powers to "preserve the state," Antony felt that the measure would be used against him and fled to Caesar. By doing so, he gave Caesar the opportunity to assert his power under the pretext of claiming that he was defending the people's representatives, the tribunes, against the arrogant power of the Senate.

In the course of the civil wars against Pompey, the leader of the Senate faction, Antony was given several important military assignments and distinguished himself. After the victory of Caesar over Pompey at Pharsalus, Antony returned to Italy as Caesar's second in command. In 45 Caesar designated him as consul for 44.

Once again Antony found himself in a key position at an important time. Caesar was rapidly moving in the direction of monarchial government, in fact if not in name, and as a result a conspiracy formed to eliminate him. On March 15, 44, while one of the conspirators detained Antony outside the Senate, Caesar was assassinated. Antony was spared on the grounds that the aim of the conspiracy was to remove an illegal ruler but that slaying the consul, the chief legitimate officer of the Roman state, would besmirch the cause's image.

Second Triumvirate

With the death of Caesar, Antony was forced to fight politically a two-front war. One was against the conspirators. The other was with Caesar's supporters, who were undecided on how to avenge Caesar and also as to who would lead them. Antony initially adopted an attitude that was on the surface conciliatory toward the assassins of Caesar while he strengthened his power position. He might have ensured his supremacy without difficulty if the young Octavian, nephew of Caesar, had not appeared, claiming not only to be Caesar's adopted son and heir but also demanding Caesar's political legacy. Octavian was a man who not only could assume the mantle of Caesar as legitimately as Antony but could also be used by the opponents of Antony as a pawn. Antony tried to strengthen his position by attempting to gain a new 5-year command in Gaul, thus using Caesar's old power base. However, Octavian, stressing his own position as the heir of Caesar, skillfully enticed some of Antony's legions to his side, and Decimus Brutus refused to yield the governorship of Gaul. When Antony attempted to attack Brutus at Mutina (modern Modena), he was in turn attacked by the armies of Octavian and the consuls. He was defeated and forced to retreat north.

In the following months Antony strengthened himself with the armies of the western provinces; while Octavian, realizing that the Senate was trying to use him, began to make political overtures to Antony. The result was the formation of the second triumvirate of Antony, Octavian, and Lepidus. Unlike the first triumvirate of Caesar, Pompey, and Crassus, which was a mere political alliance, this became a constitutionally established organ for ruling the state.

One of the first tasks undertaken by the group was the proscription of leading enemies. The most important of those killed was M. Tullius Cicero, hated by Antony because of his vitriolic oratorical assaults. Antony has often been blamed for these executions. However, this may reflect the propaganda of Octavian, who after the fact wanted to play down his role in the bloody events of these years.

Antony and Octavian now moved eastward to face the army of the conspirators led by Brutus and Cassius. The two forces met at Philippi in 42, and Antony's military skill carried the day.

Antony and Cleopatra

After this battle Antony's career entered its most famous period. While Octavian returned to settle veterans in Italy, Antony went east to order affairs in these provinces. He also prepared a war against Parthia, and needing Egyptian support he summoned Cleopatra, the Ptolemaic queen of Egypt, to Tarsus in 41. An immediate romance followed. This was interrupted when the news arrived that Antony's brother and wife were openly defying Octavian in Italy. Antony moved west and it looked as though fighting would erupt. However, a peace was patched up at Brindisi in 40 and sealed by the wedding of Antony with Octavian's sister, Octavia, after the death of Antony's first wife.

Antony went east again and, except for a return in 37 to aid Octavian against the pirate Sextus Pompey, remained there. In 36 Antony again took up his affair with Cleopatra. He found a complex situation in the East. The area had been seriously disturbed by the wars of Caesar and Pompey and the exactions of Brutus and Cassius. Furthermore, the Parthians were attacking Roman territory. Antony seems to have established good relations with the local dynasts and created for himself a certain amount of popularity, even though his financial exaction must have lain heavily on the provincials. His generals were successful in beating back the Parthians, although an expedition which Antony undertook to Parthia itself turned into a disaster.

In the meantime he was becoming increasingly involved with Cleopatra, politically as well as romantically. Cleopatra saw him as a wonderful opportunity to revive the past glories of the Ptolemies. What the ideas of Antony were is not clear. The picture of Antony enslaved to the Egyptian queen was in part the result of the propaganda efforts of Octavian. However, he certainly was dependent on Cleopatra for money, and he did make territorial concessions and grants of titles to Cleopatra's family.

At the close of 33 the second triumvirate legally came to an end. At the same time the crisis between Octavian and Antony was coming to a head. Antony still had support in Rome. However, Octavian played his cards well, raising public indignation by announcing Antony's divorce of Octavia for Cleopatra, reading Antony's will in which his strong ties to Cleopatra were stressed, and circulating such rumors as Antony's plans to move the capital to Alexandria.

Octavian systematically rallied the support of Italy, while Antony's Roman friends had mixed emotions about waging war on the side of the Egyptian queen. The two men and their armies met off Greece at Actium on Sept. 2, 31. In a confused battle the fleet of Antony was routed. With Cleopatra he fled back to Egypt, where he committed suicide upon the arrival of Octavian.

Further Reading

Ancient sources on Mark Antony are Cicero's *Philippics,* which presents a hostile view, and Plutarch's *Lives.* Arthur Weigall, *The Life and Times of Marc Antony* (1931), is a lively biography. R. Syme, *The Roman Revolution* (1939; corrected repr. 1952), is still the best work for placing Antony in his period. See also Frank Burr Marsh, *A History of the Roman World from 146 to 30 B.C.* (1935; 2d ed. rev. 1953), and Hans Volkmann, *Cleopatra: A Study in Politics and Propaganda* (1953; trans. 1958). □

Juan Bautista de Anza

The Spanish explorer Juan Bautista de Anza (1735-1788) opened the overland route from Mexico to California and established the first settlement at San Francisco.

Juan Bautista de Anza was born in Fronteras, Sonora, Mexico, where his grandfather and father had served as commanders. In 1738 Anza's father submitted a plan for opening a route from Sonora to California, but in 1739 the elder Anza lost his life in a campaign against the Apaches and the plan was dropped.

When Anza was 18 he volunteered for military service and rapidly rose to the rank of captain. In 1759 he became commander of the presidio of Tubac (south of modern Tucson). He led numerous campaigns against the Apaches and achieved a notable reputation as a soldier and leader.

By 1770 the Spanish settlements in California were in desperate condition. Routes by sea and over the peninsula of Baja California could not supply their needs, and there was great fear that California would have to be abandoned. Remembering his father's ambitions, Anza volunteered to open a route from Sonora, and in 1773 Viceroy Antonio Maria de Bucareli granted him permission to attempt the journey. Setting out in January 1774 with 34 men, including the Franciscan Fray Francisco Garcés, Anza traveled to the Colorado River, where he established friendly relations with the Yuma Indians. Turning westward, he broke a trail across the southern desert to San Gabriel in Alta (upper) California.

Bucareli promoted Anza to lieutenant colonel and placed him in charge of recruiting colonists for a new California settlement. In 1775 he left Mexico with 240 colonists, including women and children. In March 1776 the group reached California with the loss of only one life, an almost unheard-of feat in those times.

Anza selected the site for the pueblo of San Francisco and then returned to Mexico, where Bucareli named him governor of New Mexico. Anza proved an excellent governor. His campaigns against the Apaches and Comanches brought peace to the northern frontier, and his reorganization of the defenses of the province strengthened Spanish domination in the area.

In 1781 the Yuma rose against the Spaniards, and Anza, who was unfairly blamed for the revolt, lost his post. However, he soon returned to office and served until 1786, when he requested transfer to a more healthful climate. He went to Tucson as commander and served there until his death in Arizpe in 1788.

Further Reading

An excellent account of Anza's California expeditions is Herbert E. Bolton, *An Outpost of Empire* (1930), the first volume in *Anza's California Expeditions* (5 vols., 1930), which includes the diaries and documents pertaining to Anza's journeys. Anza's career in New Mexico is presented in Alfred Barnaby Thomas, ed. and trans., *Forgotten Frontiers: A Study of the Spanish Indian Policy of Don Juan Bautista de Anza* (1932).

Additional Sources

Brumgardt, John R., *From Sonora to San Francisco Bay: the expeditions of Juan Bautista de Anza, 1774-1776,* Riverside, Calif.: Historical Commission Press, 1976. □

Michel Aoun

Christian Lebanese military leader Michel Aoun (born 1935) served as interim prime minister of Lebanon for two years before being driven out of power by Syrian forces in October 1990.

Michel Aoun was born in 1935 in Harat Hurayk in the southern suburb of Beirut, Lebanon. He obtained his bachelor's degree from the Freres school in Jumayza in Beirut. In 1955 he entered the Military Academy in Beirut and graduated in 1959. He specialized in artillery in his military career. He studied at Challonssur-

Marne in France and at Fort Sill in Oklahoma. From 1978 to 1980 he had training at the prestigious Ecole de Guerre in Paris.

In 1982 he became commander of the newly established 8th Brigade of the Lebanese Army and in August 1983 he was in charge of the Suk al-Gharb region, which witnessed fierce battles in defense of the Lebanese legitimate authorities against the incursions of Syrian-armed proxy militias. On June 23, 1984, Aoun, who became a brigadier general, was appointed commander of the Lebanese Army. He was still in that post when he was chosen, on September 22, 1988, as the prime minister of the six-member Interim Cabinet.

The decision by outgoing President Amine Gemayel, just before his term expired, to appoint an interim cabinet was due to the inability of the Lebanese Parliament to elect a new president. This failure was caused by Syrian President Hafiz Assad's insistence that only his candidate should be elected by the Lebanese Parliament and that the meeting for the election must be held in Syrian-occupied West Beirut.

When President Gemayel appointed Brigadier-General Michel Aoun he was following the precedent set by President Bishara al Khuri in 1952. Before he resigned he appointed as prime minister a Maronite Christian who happened also to be the commander of the Lebanese Army, Brigadier-General Fu'ad Shihab. Although the newly appointed Aoun Cabinet was the legitimate government in accordance with article 53 of the Lebanese constitution, pressure was exerted by Syria on the three Moslem mem-

bers not to accept their cabinet posts. The Syrian authorities went further by claiming that the legitimate cabinet was that of outgoing Prime Minister Al-Huss. Thus from the outset the interim prime minister, Aoun, was faced with Syrian non-recognition and outright opposition. The more he was rebuffed by Syria the more he became adamant in his stand.

In an attempt to avert the resumption of fighting in Lebanon, the foreign ministers of the League of Arab States formed a committee on Lebanon, headed by the Kuwaiti foreign minister, in January 1989. This committee eventually met both Aoun and Al-Huss in Tunis on January 30, 1989. The Arab League Committee on Lebanon also met during the period February to April 1989 in Kuwait with the most prominent Lebanese leaders (both political and religious), but to no avail. These meetings were overshadowed by fighting which erupted between Aoun's Lebanese Army and the Christian Lebanese Forces on the one side and the Syrian Army in Lebanon and the Druze and Shi'a militias on the other side. The fighting was triggered by Aoun's decision, in February 1989, to close all illegal ports, which had adversely affected, among other things, the ports used by Druze and Shi'a militias, which prompted, in turn, the latter to bombard the Lebanese Ministry of Defence and Aoun's headquarters in Baabda in northeast Beirut. Aoun had realized that the conflict was inevitable because of the Syrian attitude toward his cabinet, so he defiantly declared on March 14, 1989, the war of liberation against Syria, hoping to get international support for his cause.

Aoun's appeal was met with the indifference of the West except for France, which supported him diplomatically and provided him with humanitarian assistance. The United States refused to get involved in the conflict between Aoun and Syria, especially as American hostages in Lebanon were being threatened by their pro-Syrian captors. Instead, the United States maintained that the League of Arab States ought to resolve the conflict. The Arab summit held in Casablanca in May 1989, in which Lebanon was not represented, failed to convince Syrian President Assad to withdraw his troops from Lebanon. The Casablanca Summit formed a tripartite committee of the foreign ministers of Saudi Arabia, Morocco, and Algeria to mediate the conflict between Aoun and Syria. Although the first statement issued by this committee was critical of Syria, the latter did not budge, knowing that the tripartite committee would eventually accept the Syrian stand as its military power on the ground was superior to that of Aoun.

In the meantime Syria increased military pressure on Aoun by continued bombardment and by imposing a naval blockade on the areas that were under Aoun's rule. Eventually, in September 1989, the tripartite committee called for a cease-fire, which was accepted by both Aoun and Syria. It also called for the convening of the members of the Lebanese Parliament in Ta'if, Saudi Arabia. In fact, 62 deputies (31 Christians and 31 Muslims) of the total 73 surviving members of Parliament met and agreed upon a blueprint of reforms, known as the Ta'if Accord, which transformed the Lebanese polity from a presidential to a cabinet political system.

While Aoun was not enthusiastic about these internal reforms, he was adamantly opposed to the part of the Ta'if Accord that legitimized the presence of Syrian troops in Lebanon. The accord stipulated that the Syrian troops would be redeployed after two years in the eastern regions of Lebanon but there was no mention of Syrian withdrawal from Lebanon. The accord paved the way for the election of a new president, and Aoun tried to pre-empt the election by issuing a decree dissolving Parliament, but with no success.

Syria's aim in supporting the accord was to delegitimize Aoun, which was not difficult because the latter entangled himself in a violent and destructive conflict with the Christian militia, the Lebanese Forces, during the period January through May 1990. Aoun's popularity, which had been based on his anti-Syrian stand and his call for free elections, a return to the rule of law, and the end of the rule of corrupt politicians and militia leaders, began to erode. Syria, which joined the anti-Saddam (Iraqi) forces by sending troops to Saudi Arabia alongside the U.S. troops, exploited the Gulf crisis to launch a major attack against Aoun on October 13, 1990, and occupied the region which was under Aoun's rule. Aoun sought political asylum in the French Embassy, and the Syrian-dominated cabinet that was installed in December 1990 refused to allow him to leave for France. In August 1991 the Lebanese government granted him a special pardon and, on August 29, Aoun was whisked off to France by French officials, where he continues to live in exile. In a 1995 interview with Daniel Pipes of the *Middle East Quarterly*, Aoun expressed his views on the state of affairs in Lebanon and his hopes for its future: "My conception is a new Lebanon, a modern state, a state of law, all the while respecting public liberty; an honesty in the administration of the state, and very good relations with neighbors."

Although Aoun's five-year suspension of citizenship decreed by the Lebanese government ended in August 1996, Aoun stated that he did not plan to return to Lebanon. According to an interview given to Gary Gambill and Marie Michel El-Zir of *Arab Studies Journal*, Aoun was certain his life would be in danger if he did return because the government fears "that with my return the Lebanese will rally around the idea of independence. . . . They know how unpopular they are and how my popularity remains untouched."

It is true that although Aoun lost his bid for power, he remained popular among the Lebanese communities. Many of his Christian supporters refused to vote in the 1992 election and stayed loyal to Aoun and his ideas. In the United States, the Aounist movement has become a powerful opposition group in the Lebanese emigrant community. Due in part to the lobbying of the Council of Lebanese American Organizations, the U.S. Senate passed Resolution 24 in July 1994 that condemned the Syrian occupation of Lebanon.

Further Reading

For additional information on the rise and fall of Aoun together with background information on the tragedy of war-torn Lebanon, see Augustus Norton, *Amal and the Shi'a Struggle for* the Soul of Lebanon (1987), and Marius Deeb, "The External Dimensions of the Conflict in Lebanon: The Role of Syria," Journal of South Asian and Middle Eastern Studies (Spring 1989), and "Lebanon in the Aftermath of the Abrogation of the Israeli-Lebanese accord," R.C. Freedman (editor), The Middle East from Iran-Contra to the Intifada (1991). See also Economist (August 31, 1991; June 17, 1995; September 7, 1996), Middle East Quarterly (December 1995), New York Times (August 18, 1991; August 30, 1991), Wall Street Journal (August 28, 1991), and Christianity Today (November 19, 1990). Also see the Web site for Americans for a Free Lebanon at http://www.aflnet.com. □

Apelles

Apelles (active after 350 B.C.) was one of the most prominent ancient Greek painters. None of his works has survived, but they are described by ancient writers.

Sources disagree as to whether Apelles was a native of Cos (Pliny), Colophon (Suidas), or Ephesus (Strabo and Lucian). In the early stages of his career he was a pupil of Pamphilus, the guiding spirit of the Sicyonian school of painting, and Apelles seems to have remained associated with that school. During his mature years he executed portraits for Philip of Macedon, according to Pliny in Naturalis historia (XXV, 93). After Philip's death Apelles became court painter to Alexander the Great. Alexander is said to have so admired Apelles' work that he ordered the execution of painted royal portraits to be made Apelles' exclusive prerogative.

After Alexander's death Apelles found employment in Alexandria at the court of Ptolemy I. He was implicated in a conspiracy to overthrow Ptolemy but managed to clear himself and regain the King's favor. The famous allegorical painting Calumny, described in detail by Lucian and recreated in the 15th-century painting by Sandro Botticelli, was perhaps created in an effort to convince Ptolemy of the painter's innocence.

The many anecdotes told about Apelles by ancient writers suggest a spirited, confident, at times even impudent personality, who was always ready to spar with his critics, including Alexander. On one occasion, when Alexander was discoursing on the art of painting, Apelles advised him to be silent because the boys who served as color grinders were laughing at his remarks (Pliny, Naturalis historia, XXV, 85). Apelles is also said to have told Alexander that his judgment in art was inferior to that of a horse (Aelian, Variae historiae, II, 3). Alexander seems to have taken the remarks in his stride.

As is the case with other Greek painters, no work by Apelles has survived, and what the ancient sources tell about his style is in some ways contradictory. On the one hand, he is described as a meticulous technician who never let a day pass without practicing his art, who outdid his contemporary Protogenes in subtlety of line, who was sensi-

tive to criticism of the detail of his works, who painstakingly calculated the effect of his colors, and whose portraits were so precise that diviners claimed to be able to read their sitters' futures from their facial details.

On the other hand, Apelles seems to have written a treatise or memoir in which he conceded his inferiority to some of his contemporaries in composition and proportion (Pliny, Naturalis historia, XXV, 85) but maintained that they lacked his "charm" or "grace" (Greek, charis), an instinctive quality which seems to have involved, among other things, knowing when to stop working on a painting.

Many works by Apelles—portraits, mythological subjects, and allegorical scenes—are mentioned by ancient writers. The two most admired seem to have been Aphrodite Anadyomene (Aphrodite rising from the sea), originally in the Asklepieion in Cos and later placed by Augustus in the Temple of the Divine Caesar in Rome; and Alexander Keraunophoros (Alexander represented as Zeus holding a thunderbolt) in Ephesus. Some echoes of Apelles' works may be preserved in Pompeiian paintings, notably what seems to be a copy of Alexander Keraunophoros in the House of the Vettii.

Further Reading

There is no biography of Apelles. The principal sources on Apelles are translated in J.J. Pollitt, The Art of Greece, 1400-31 B.C.: Sources and Documents (1965). Background works on ancient Greek art include Ernst Pfuhl, Masterpieces of Greek Drawing and Painting (1924; trans. 1926; new ed. 1955); Gisela M.A. Richter, A Handbook of Greek Art (1959; 5th rev. ed. 1967); and Martin Robertson, Greek Painting (1959). □

Virginia Apgar

Medical instructor and researcher Virginia Apgar (1909-1974) revolutionized the field of perinatology—the care of infants around the time of birth—with her development of the Apgar Newborn Scoring System. Her method of rating a newborn's health in five major categories allows doctors to quickly establish if a child requires medical attention. Implementation of this basic practice throughout the United States and around the world resulted in a significant increase in infant survival rates.

Virginia Apgar contributed to many areas of medicine during her career, including anesthesiology, infant care, and the study and prevention of birth defects. It was her work with new babies and mothers, however, that has left the greatest mark in the health sciences. She was the creator of the Apgar Newborn Scoring System, a method of evaluating the health of infants minutes after birth in order to ensure the delivery of proper care. Apgar also contributed to infant health through her discovery that some anesthetics given to women during childbirth had a negative effect on babies. Her findings led doctors across the country to revise their use of painkillers during labor. Later in her career, Apgar was a vital force in the March of Dimes organization, where she directed research efforts, raised money, and educated the public about birth defects. Her lifetime of energetic work resulted in standard medical procedures for mothers and babies that have prevented thousands of infant deaths.

Specialized in New Medical Field

Apgar was born on June 7, 1909, in Westfield, New Jersey. Her childhood home contained a basement laboratory, where her father pursued scientific experiments with electricity and radio waves and built a telescope. Perhaps due to this atmosphere of curiosity and inquiry, Apgar set her sights on a scientific career in the field of medicine. After graduating from high school, she entered Mount Holyoke College with the intention of becoming a doctor. Although she received scholarships that helped to pay for her tuition, she still had to take a number of jobs to support herself through college. Despite the extra work, she graduated with a bachelor's degree in 1929.

Apgar's financial situation did not improve when she enrolled at the College of Physicians and Surgeons at Columbia University in New York City the following September. A month later, the stock market crashed, signaling the beginning of the decade of economic turmoil known as the Great Depression. Determined to stay in school, Apgar borrowed money in order to complete her course work. She emerged in 1933 with a medical degree and a fourth-place rank in her graduating class, but also with the burden of a large financial debt. Her high marks earned her a much sought-after internship in surgery at Columbia, but during this period of training Apgar began to consider how she could best support herself in the medical profession. She saw that even male surgeons had trouble finding work in New York City, and as a woman in what was then a male-dominated profession, she realized that her chances of success were even slimmer. She felt that she was more likely to be successful in the field of anesthesia.

Traditionally, nurses had been responsible for administering anesthesia, but at that time greater emphasis was being to be placed on the importance of anesthetics; doctors had begun entering the field in the hopes of making breakthroughs that would allow for improved surgery techniques. Women physicians, in particular, were encouraged to pursue medical anesthesiology, perhaps because it was still considered a female realm. So after finishing her internship at Columbia in 1935, Apgar began a two-year residency program in anesthesiology, during which time she studied not only at Columbia, but also at the University of Wisconsin in Madison and Bellevue Hospital in New York.

Apgar's choice of career did allow her to realize her goal of securing a job. She was hired as director of the anesthesia division at Columbia University in 1938. Her new position, however, proved to be a challenging one. She was the only person in the anesthesia area, leaving her with a heavy workload. In addition, she struggled to get surgeons to recognize the anesthesiologist as a fellow doctor, not a subordinate, and she fought against the policy that pre-

vented anesthesiologists from being allowed to charge standard doctor's fees. Eventually, Apgar and her department began to receive more support and respect—she gradually increased the number of physicians in the division and won sufficient funding for the area and its employees in 1941, after threatening to quit her post if the school refused her requests. After World War II, anesthesiology began gaining more attention across the nation as an area of specialty and research, and Columbia University created a separate department of anesthesia for training physicians and conducting research. When the chair of the new department was selected in 1949, however, Apgar was passed over in favor of a male anesthesiologist. Instead, she was named a full professor in the department, making her the first woman to reach such a level at Columbia.

Apgar Newborn Scoring System Developed

It was in this position as a teacher and researcher that Apgar would make her greatest contributions to medicine over the next decade. She began to focus her work in the area of anesthesia used during childbirth. Apgar realized that the period immediately following birth was a critical time for many infants; however, babies were usually not evaluated carefully by doctors, who were often more concerned with the welfare of the mother. Because of this lack of an organized examination, many life-threatening conditions were not identified in infants. To provide a quick and efficient means of determining which babies required special care, she devised a five-part test that scored a child's heart rate, respiration, muscle tone, color, and reflexes. The test, known as the Apgar Newborn Scoring System, was to be scored one minute after birth; the recommended timing of the test was later expanded to five and ten minutes as well. Although developed in 1949, a description of the system was not published until 1953. It eventually became a world-wide standard among physicians. A study by Apgar involving a dozen hospitals and more than 17,000 infants evaluated by the Apgar score proved that the testing method was a predictable indicator of a child's survival and rate of development.

Another victory for infant health was won with Apgar's research into the effects of anesthesia given to mothers during childbirth. Collaborating with pediatrician L. Stanley James and anesthesiologist Duncan Holaday, Apgar monitored the blood levels, blood gases, and pH levels of newborns whose mother received anesthesia during labor. These measurements, combined with the application of the Apgar score system, were designed to indicate to doctors what kinds of problems—such as a low oxygen level or a pH imbalance in the blood—needed to be addressed if a baby was doing poorly. To take such measurements and facilitate treatments, Apgar became the first person to place a catheter in the umbilical artery, now a standard practice in neonatal care. In the course of her research, Apgar found that the anesthesia cyclopropane had a noticeable negative effect on a baby's overall condition. Immediately ceasing her use of the gas for mothers in labor, other doctors across the country quickly followed suit after Apgar published her findings.

Conducted Birth Defect Research

After a more than twenty-year career at Columbia, Apgar left her post as professor to earn a master of public health degree at Johns Hopkins University. Her new career took her to the March of Dimes organization in 1959, where she was hired as the head of the division on congenital birth defects. In 1969, she became the head of the March of Dimes research program; during her three-year stint in this role she changed the foundation's emphasis from the prevention of the crippling disease polio to a concentrated effort to prevent birth defects. In an effort to educate the public about the topic, she gave many lectures and cowrote a book titled *Is My Baby All Right?* in 1972. Apgar left her research position in 1973 to become vice president for medical affairs and a fund-raiser. She was a great success in both roles, increasing donations to the charity and channeling the new money into research on birth defects, resulting in better prevention and treatment of many conditions. At the same time, she held a research fellowship at Johns Hopkins University and a position as clinical professor at Cornell University, where she became the first U.S. medical professor to specialize in birth defects.

During her lifetime, Apgar made significant contributions to science not only in the laboratory, but also in the classroom. She instructed hundreds of doctors and left a lasting mark on the field of neonatal care. Apgar received a number of awards recognizing her role in medicine. She was honored with the Ralph Waters Medal from the American Society of Anesthesiologists and the Gold Medal of Columbia University, was named Woman of the Year for 1973 by *Ladies' Home Journal,* and was the recipient of four honorary degrees. In addition, a prize in her name was founded by the American Academy of Pediatrics and an academic chair was created in her honor at Mount Holyoke College.

Apgar, who never married, was unrelenting in her pursuit of knowledge. In her sixties, she began a course of study in genetics at Johns Hopkins University. She also found time, however, for a number of personal interests, including music, gardening, photography, and stamp collecting. On August 7, 1974, Apgar died in New York City at the age of 65. She was remembered as an honest and encouraging teacher who inspired numerous doctors in their medical practice and research. The modern fields of anesthesiology and neonatal care are greatly indebted to her pioneering work.

Further Reading

For more information see Apgar, Virginia, and Joan Beck, *Is My Baby All Right?: A Guide to Birth Defects,* Trident Press, 1972; Calmes, Selma, "Virginia Apgar: A Woman Physician's Career in a Developing Specialty," *Journal of the American Medical Women's Association,* November/December, 1984, pp. 184-188; Diamonstein, Barbaralee, *Open Secrets: Ninety-four Women in Touch with Our Time,* Viking Press, 1972; Vare, Ehlie Ann, and Greg Ptacek, *Mothers of Invention: From the Bra to the Bomb—Forgotten Women and Their Unforgettable Ideas,* William Morrow, 1988. □

Sourou Migan Apithy

Sourou Migan Apithy (1913-1989) was a political leader in Dahomey (now Benin). He led one of the three power blocs which contributed to Dahomean instability.

Sourou Apithy was born in Porto Novo on April 8, 1913 and attended local mission schools. He studied in France, where he received a university degree in political science. He immediately found employment in France as an accountant and later operated his own accounting firm. In 1946 he was chosen to represent Dahomey in the Constituent Assembly and later was elected deputy to the French Assembly. He attended the founding meeting of the Rassemblement Démocratique Africain (RDA) at Bamako, Mali, and was elected one of its vice presidents. Two years later he broke with the RDA and associated himself and his party, the Parti Républicain Dahoméen (PRD), with the socialist aims of Senegal's Léopold Senghor. He was reelected a deputy in 1951 and again in 1956 and became mayor of Porto Novo in 1956.

In the 1957 elections for the legislature Apithy's party was opposed by the Union Démocratique Dahoméene (UDD), which was based in Abomey and was led by Justin Ahomadegbe, and by the northern Mouvement Démocratique Dahoméen (MDD) of Hubert Maga. Apithy's party won 35 of the 60 seats, and he became vice president of the Council. All parties campaigned for the De Gaulle plebiscite in 1958, but Apithy's plan to join Dahomey to the Mali Federation was blocked by Ivory Coast pressure and opposition from UDD.

In the Territorial Assembly elections of 1959, Apithy's party won 37 seats, the MDD 22, and the UDD 11 despite the fact that UDD candidates had received 30,000 more votes than the PRD. Violent protests caused Apithy to concede 9 of the PRD seats to the UDD and to agree to serve under Maga's leadership. Later that year Apithy was forced out of the government by a coalition of Maga and Ahomadegbe.

Troubled Presidency

Dahomey achieved independence in 1960, and Maga became its first president. However, he could not check inflation and unemployment, and he was deposed by a military coup in 1963. The coup leader, Col. Christophe Soglo, reorganized the government and then resigned, and in January 1964 Apithy became president of a civilian coalition government. Economic problems continued, the Bariba in the north revolted, there were strikes, and Apithy and his vice president, Ahomadegbe, differed on policies such as the recognition of Red China. The regional factions inherent in Dahomean politics during this time contributed to the government's instability. In November 1965 Soglo once more intervened and attempted to force the three major parties to cooperate. After fruitless discussions Soglo reestablished a military regime, and Apithy fled the country.

From his exile in France, Apithy played no significant role in the later overthrow of Soglo in 1967, the military regime of Col. Alley, the restoration of civilian government under Emile Derlin Zinsou, and its overthrow in December 1969. After the last coup Apithy joined his old opponents Maga and Ahomadegbe in Dahomey and offered his services to the new regime.

Part of Presidential Council

In an alliance known as the triumverate, the three leaders formed the Presidential Council in May 1970 with the plan to rule Dahomey successively in two-year terms. Maga was the first chairman of the Council. However, the Council's power struggles made them vulnerable to a coup by Major Mathieu Kérékou in 1972, before Apithy's term had begun. He was placed under house arrest, as were Maga and Ahomadegbe.

The 1972 coup marked a distinct break from the previous systems of government, symbolized in the changing of the country's name in November 1975 to the People's Republic of Benin. Kérékou continued to rule and in 1981 released the three former presidents. In poor health on his release, Apithy died on November 12, 1989.

Further Reading

More information may be found in Ronald Segal, *Political Africa* (1961); the section on Dahomey in Gwendolen Margaret Carter, ed., *Five African States* (1963); Ruth Schachter Morgenthau, *Political Parties in French-Speaking West Africa* (1964); and John Hatch, *A History of Postwar Africa* (1965). Also see Allen, Chris, "Benin" in *Benin, The Congo, and Burkina Faso* (Pinter Publishers, 1989), and Decalo, Samuel, *Historical Dictionary of Benin,* 3rd edition (Scarecrow Press, 1995). □

Guillaume Apollinaire

Guillaume Apollinaire (1880-1918) was a great French lyric poet. A leading figure in the avant-garde before World War I, he produced criticism and theortical writings that have significantly influenced esthetic movements from cubism to those of the present day.

Guillaume Apollinaire was the pseudonym of Wilhelm Apollinaris de Kostrowitsky, the illegitimate son of an Italian army officer and a young Polish noblewoman. He was born in Rome on Aug. 26, 1880, and brought up in various towns in southern France where his mother happened to be sojourning. In 1899 Apollinaire went to Paris to live and, without money or diplomas, had difficulty. However, between odd jobs as a literary hack, tutor, bank clerk, and journalist, he managed to travel on the Continent and make two trips to London. Also he had a few love affairs that later figured in his poetry.

The most important aspect of Apollinaire's first years in Paris was his encounter with writers and artists. Jovial and full of enthusiasm, he became the welcome companion of the young modernists in the Bohemia of the day. He helped found little reviews and wrote articles defending what later was dubbed cubism. He wrote fiction, too, and poems that appeared in magazines, ultimately published in 1913 in a volume entitled *Alcools* (Alcohols). The originality of these poems lies more in the subtle handling of image and rhythm to express emotion than in technical innovation. Yet in correcting the proofs, Apollinaire rubbed out all punctuation and placed at the head of the collection a quite recent poem called "Zone," which is a sort of manifesto of modernism and, in form, less orthodox than the others.

When war broke out in 1914, Apollinaire enlisted and found in combat new themes of poetic inspiration. Wounded in 1916, he was sent back to Paris, where the generation of future Dadaists and surrealists greeted him as a chief. In the following year the presentation of *The Breasts of Tiresias,* a burlesque play very much in the modern mood, and a lecture on the "new spirit" gave him considerable notoriety.

His second volume of verse, *Calligrammes,* appeared in 1918. Here Apollinaire demonstrates in metrical innovations the modernism which he preached for poetry in "Zone." There are poems made of snatches of conversation, of enumeration, and of simple notation which infuse daily banalities with lyrical magic. There are the "ideograms," which give the volume its title—"visual" poems which imitate, in typography and in placement on the page, the subject matter.

The year 1918 was one of fulfillment for Apollinaire as an artist and a person. Hitherto unfortunate in love, particularly with the painter Marie Laurencin, he found happiness with Jacqueline Kolb, the "beautiful redhead" of the last poem in *Calligrammes.* They married in May. Six months later, at the age of 38, Apollinaire died of influenza in Paris.

Further Reading

A bilingual edition of *Alcools* was published in 1965 by the University of California Press. Francis Steegmuller provided the fullest biography, *Apollinaire, Poet among the Painters* (1963). Scott Bates, *Guillaume Apollinaire* (1967), enhanced by a bibliography and appendixes, is primarily devoted to an analysis of the poetry but is hampered by exclusive use of English translation. See also Marcel Raymond, *From Baudelaire to Surrealism* (1933, trans. 1950).

Additional Sources

Adlard, John., *One evening of light mist in London: the story of Annie Playden and Guillaume Apollinaire,* Edinburgh: Tragara Press, 1980.
Couffignal, Robert., *Apollinaire,* University: University of Alabama Press, 1975.
Steegmuller, Francis, *Apollinaire: poet among the painters,* Boston, MA: Nonpareil Books, 1980, 1963; New York: Penguin Books, 1986. □

Apollodorus

The Greek painter Apollodorus (active ca. 408 B.C.) was recognized in antiquity as the inventor of a systematic technique for shading to simulate the appearance of mass and space. He achieved this through the modulation of light and shade, a technique which in Greek was called "skiagraphia."

As with all the famous Greek mural and panel painters, no work by Apollodorus survives, but information about him is preserved in ancient literary sources. His invention of shading is most clearly recorded by Plutarch, *De gloria Atheniensium* (*Moralia*, 346A): "Apollodorus, the painter who first invented the fading out (*phthora*) and building up (*apochrosis*) of shadow, was an Athenian . . . ." His surname, *Skiagraphos* (the Shader), is preserved by a scholiast on the *Iliad* and by Hesychius. Pliny the Elder also seems to be referring to the invention of shading when he remarks that Apollodorus "*primus species exprimere instituit*" (*Naturalis historia*, XXXV, 60), a phrase probably to be translated as "he first established a method for representing outward appearance."

The subjects of a few of Apollodorus's paintings are known. Pliny mentions a *Praying Priest* and an *Ajax Burned by Lightning,* both in Pergamon. There are also references to a painting of Odysseus wearing a cap, a *Herakleidai,* and an *Alcmena and the Daughters of Herakles Supplicating the Athenians.* Little progress has been made in identifying echoes of these pictures in the minor arts or in Romano-Campanian painting. Some traces are preserved, however, on Attic white-ground lecythi dating from the late 5th and early 4th centuries B.C.

It seems likely, based on what little monumental evidence there is to document the beginning of shading in Greek painting, that the first steps taken by Apollodorus in developing this technique involved the use of crosshatching and the thickening of inner contour lines as well as the admixture of light and dark tones. The technique seems at first to have been most commonly used for rendering the folds and mass of drapery, less often for rendering anatomy, and scarcely at all for depicting the spatial setting of figures.

The epigram "You could criticize this more easily than you could imitate it" is said by Plutarch to have been connected with the works of Apollodorus, and if the epigram was composed by the painter himself, it suggests an aggressive, confident personality. Pliny ascribes a Latin version of the same epigram, however, to Zeuxis, a younger contemporary of Apollodorus who also played a role in the development of shading.

Further Reading

Most of the ancient sources on Apollodorus are collected and translated in J. J. Pollitt, *The Art of Greece, 1400-31 B.C.: Sources and Documents* (1965). A modern account of Apollodorus is given in Mary Hamilton Swindler, *Ancient Painting* (1929). □

Apollonius of Perga

The Greek mathematician Apollonius of Perga (active 210 B.C.) was known as the "Great Geometer." He influenced the development of analytic geometry and substantially advanced mechanics, navigation, and astronomy.

Very little is known about the life of Apollonius, the last great mathematician of antiquity. He was born at Perga in Pamphylia, southern Asia Minor, during the reign (247-222 B.C.) of Ptolemy Euergetes, King of Egypt. When he was quite young, Apollonius went to study at the school in Alexandria established by Euclid.

Apollonius's fame in antiquity was based on his work on conics. His treatise on this subject consisted of eight books, of which seven have survived. Like most of the well-known Greek mathematicians, Apollonius was also a talented astronomer.

Apollonius had Euclid's great collection, the *Elements,* available and was thus able to draw upon the work of all previous major mathematicians. Also, Euclid's own work on conics, now lost, was a basis for Apollonius's further work.

Conics of Apollonius

The *Conics* was written book by book over a long period of time. The general preface to the work is given in Book I. Apollonius next outlines the contents of the eight books. The first four books are an "elementary introduction," that is, elementary in that they include those properties that are necessary to any further specialization. These books are thus an extension of the earlier conics by other mathematicians such as Euclid. Since most of these results were already well known, one might expect Apollonius's presentation to be more concise and to attempt a greater logic and generality. Beginning with Book V, more advanced topics are taken up. Book V is perhaps the best of the latter four.

Other Works

A number of other works by Apollonius are mentioned by ancient writers, but only one exists in its entirety today. The work, *Cutting-off of a Ratio,* was found in an Arabic version, and a Latin translation was published in 1706. It is concerned with the general problem: given two lines and a point on each of them, draw a line through a given point cutting off segments on the lines (measured from the fixed points on the lines) which have a given ratio to each other.

Another treatise, *Cutting-off of an Area,* was concerned with the same problem as the previous treatise except that the segments cut off were to contain a given rectangle or, in modern terms, have a given product.

Of a similar nature was the treatise *On Determinate Sections.* Here the general problem was: given a line with four points A, B, C, and D on it, determine a fifth point P on the line such that the product of lengths AP and CP is a given constant times the product BP and DP. The determination of point *P* is equivalent to solving a quadratic equation and is no great challenge. But the treatise apparently included more elaborate considerations.

The treatise *On Contacts* (or *Tangencies*) was devoted to the general problem: given three things (points, straight lines, or circles) in position, draw a circle which passes through the points (if any) and is tangent to the lines and circles (if any). For example, if two points and a line are given, then the problem would be to draw a circle through the two points and tangent to the given line. There are ten possibilities; two of them were already in Euclid's *Elements.* Six cases were treated in Book I of *On Contacts,* and Book II dealt with the remaining two, including the most difficult case of three circles. To draw a circle tangent to three given circles became known as the Apollonian problem.

Another treatise was *On Plane Loci.* Restorations of this have been attempted by many geometers. It was presumably concerned with straight lines and circles only and with the problem of showing, given certain conditions on a point, that the point must lie on a straight line or a circle.

A work in applied geometry, *On the Burning-mirror,* was probably about the properties of a mirror in the shape of a paraboloid of revolution. Even though the property is not mentioned by Apollonius in his treatise, he probably knew that light entering such a mirror parallel to its axis is reflected to a single point, its focal point.

Apollonius was also known as a great astronomer. In the *Almagest,* the great astronomical work by Ptolemy (2d century A.D.), Apollonius is mentioned as having proved two important theorems. These theorems, dealing with epicycles and eccentric circles, enabled the points on the planetary orbits to be determined where the planets, as seen from the earth, appeared stationary.

Further Reading

The standard English translation of Apollonius's principal work, with modern mathematical notation, is Thomas L. Heath, ed., *Apollonius of Perga: Treatise on Conic Sections* (1896). Apollonius's work is described and analyzed by Heath in *A Manual of Greek Mathematics* (1931) and by Bartel L. van der Waerden in *Science Awakening* (1950; trans. 1954). For Apollonius's place in the development of analytic geometry see Carl B. Boyer, *History of Analytic Geometry* (1956). □

Aharon Appelfeld

One of the most important writers in the state of Israel, Aharon Appelfeld (born 1932), wrote feelingly of anti-Semitism and the Holocaust. He was a recipient of the Israel Prize for literature.

Aharon Appelfeld was born in 1932 into an assimilated Jewish family in Bukovnia, then part of Poland but later annexed to the U.S.S.R. (now Russia). His mother was killed during the Nazi occupation of Poland, and he was deported to a concentration camp. He managed

to escape and joined the bands of children wandering in the forests of Poland. After three years he was picked up by the Soviet army in 1944 and worked in the kitchens in the Ukraine until the end of the war.

After 1945 Appelfeld traveled to Italy and finally went to settle in what is now Israel in 1946. Until then his main education had been in the concentration camp at Transniestra, and he did not go back to school, even in Israel. However, he studied Hebrew and Yiddish at the Hebrew University in Jerusalem as well as serving in the Israeli army. He also taught at the Haim Greenberg College in Jerusalem.

Appelfeld studiously avoided any realistic depiction of the Holocaust in his writings, preferring allegory to the fictional representation of historical events. He did not consider it easy for a survivor such as himself to play the role of intermediary between contemporary readers and the actual events themselves. There is a danger of the writer hiding the appalling events from himself, though this in turn can lead to what Appelfeld saw as a "covenant of silence."

One way out of this dilemma taken by a number of Jewish writers has been to retell biblical tales which have experiences that parallel those of the Holocaust. Appelfeld, on the other hand, chose a more personal style based upon a concern for small details. He avoided grand themes, and even many Israeli readers found some of his writing frustrating for its apparent placelessness and unwillingness to engage directly with historical events. Appelfeld's main concerns were individual alienation and the struggle by

survivors of the Holocaust to discover meaning in a world where it appeared to be impossible to banish guilt for having survived while so many fellow Jews perished.

The Jews depicted in Appelfeld's stories frequently appear oblivious or reluctant to confront the true reality of their situation. *Badenheim 1939* (first published in English in 1980), for example, portrays a Jewish community in a town in Austria becoming the victims of an escalating anti-Semitism that finally leads to their deportation to Poland by the all-powerful Sanitation Department. Though outwardly life appears to continue as normally as possible, this is really a nightmare world that closely parallels that of Franz Kafka, whom Appelfeld saw as a close model for much of his writing. Even at the final denouement when the community is taken away in cattle trucks, one of the key figures in the story, Dr. Pappenheim, is left speculating that the dirty state of the coaches must mean that they were not going far.

Appelfeld tried to engage less the experience of the Holocaust itself than the social and moral climate among the European Jewish community accompanying its rise. While these Jews are seen as victims of this anti-Semitism, they are not entirely excused from moral guilt in failing to resist it. In *The Age of Wonders* (first English edition 1981) Appelfeld showed the refusal of a cultured literary Jewish family in Austria to face up to the true nature of their situation, with the recent arrival of the *Ostjuden* from Eastern Europe used as the explanation for their predicament. The novel presents a direct encounter between the past, narrated in the third person, and the present, in the first person, through the eyes of Bruno, the son who manages to survive. Within this framework, though, there occurs a vital literature of memory as the family life of assimilated European Jewry is recreated. The bright colors and happy laughter at the start of the novel give way to greyer tones as human relationships become progressively stretched.

Appelfeld's characters have difficulty with social relations. There is a strong suggestion of misogyny in his depiction of women, who are frequently seen as lacking moral depth and easily seduced by men. In a number of his stories the mother-son relationship is shown as the only one with any true meaning, whether it be Bruno and his mother in *The Age of Wonders* or Bartfuss and his mother in *The Age of Bartfuss* (first English edition 1988). Women are often shown as fighting unsuccessfully with their animal natures, such as the servant girl Louise in *The Age of Wonders,* or else remain rather placid and shadowy figures, such as Arna in *The Land of Cattails* (first English edition 1986).

Behind this mother-son relationship lies an unresolved quest for moral purity and social cohesion. *The Land of Cattails* can be read as usurping one of the major genres of European literature, that of the quest for adventure in the form of the romantic hero and his faithful lieutenant, whether this be Don Quixote and Sancho Panza, Kipling's Kim and the llama, or even Batman and Robin. In *The Land of Cattails* the central figure is Rudi, whose mother, Toni, embarks on a quest from Austria back to the homeland of her parents in Eastern Europe. The absurdity of the quest is revealed by the fact that most Jews are trying to flee from the home that Toni has imagined as a rural idyll free from the conflict of Vienna. When she does finally reach her destination ahead of Rudi the Jews are about to be deported, and she disappears. Rudi is left at the end trying to make what meaning he can of his life in the context of the progressive round-up of the Eastern European Jewish population.

Appelfeld's writing ultimately fits into the literary tradition of the outsider trying to establish and defend his or her own area of moral freedom. The sad story of Bartfuss in *The Age of Bartfuss* is set in contemporary Israel. Bartfuss is the quintessential outsider, as in the fiction of Camus or Sartre. He has come to doubt the integrity of his wife, Rosa, whom he avoids as far as possible, and is estranged from his disabled daughter, Bridget, who, after first fearing her father, tries desperately to forge some form of relationship with him. Bartfuss has a few friends from the time he was in Italy before going to Israel, though some refuse to recognize him, finding the past too painful. The one woman, Sylvia, who does recognize him from the past, tragically dies.

Appelfeld continued to be a major literary figure into the 1990s with *The Healer* (1990) and *The Railway* (1991). His books about the Holocaust continued to have a worldwide audience. He made frequent trips abroad, with public appearances to promote his books and to share with others the Holocaust experience. *The Immortal Bartfuss* and *The Healer* were translated into Japanese in 1996. During the 1997 Prague Writers Festival he participated in public conversations with Robert Menasse on "The Disappearance of Central Europe".

Appelfeld felt himself to be a writer still searching for roots in modern Israel. He continued to experiment with a language, Hebrew, that he had to learn as an adult. His relationship with religion was only a tenuous one, since the world of the concentration camps seemed to be one of blind fate. None of the characters in his stories find any solace in religion, and the ultimate hope, Appelfeld has suggested, lies more in the building of tribal and communal bonds than in turning unquestioningly to a religious faith.

Further Reading

For more information on Aharon Appelfeld, see Esther Fuchs, *Encounters with Israeli Authors* (1982); Lawrence L. Langer, *The Holocaust and the Literary Imagination* (1982); Alan Mintz, *Hurban: Responses to Catastrophe in Hebrew Literature* (1984); and David C. Jacobson, *Modern Midrash: The Retelling of Traditional Jewish Narratives by Twentieth Century Hebrew Writers* (1987). More information on Appelfeld and other literary artists can be obtained from the Israel Ministry of Foreign Affairs. □

Adolphe Appia

Adolphe Appia (1862-1928) developed theories of staging, use of space, and lighting which have had a lasting influence on modern stagecraft.

Adolphe Appia was born in 1862 in Geneva, Switzerland. His father, Doctor Louis Paul Amedee Appia, was a highly respected physician. Little is known about Adolphe's mother, Anna, who died when he was 24 years old. Appia's father was a stern Calvinist who was aloof and forbidding to his children, factors that contributed to the young Appia's shyness and introverted nature. The fact that the young Appia suffered from a stutter also must have made him more withdrawn. From an early age Appia had an inclination for the theater, but he grew up in an atmosphere that discouraged such interests. Appia, however, gained his father's permission to study music and in that way was able to pursue his love of the theater.

Appia was especially drawn to Wagner's operas and his theories of staging them. Although he admired the operas, Appia had no love for the use of the proscenium stage, elaborate costumes, or painted sets. Instead, he favored powerful, suggestive stagings that would create an artistic unity, a blending of actor, stage, lighting, and music. After a long study of the operas, Appia concluded that there was disunity because of certain jarring visual elements. The moving actor, the perpendicular settings, and the horizontal floor were in conflict with one another. He theorized that the scenery should be replaced with steps, ramps, platforms, and drapes that blended with the actor's movements and the horizontal floor. In this way the human presence and its beauty would be accented and enhanced. For Appia, space was a dynamic area that attracted both actor and spectator and brought about their interaction. Complementing his concept of space was his belief that lighting should be used to bring together the visual elements of the drama.

Appia, to gain his effect, studied every scene of the opera and worked out how the relationship of actor, scene, dialogue, music, and lighting combined to create a unified harmony. In 1906 he met and was influenced by Emile Jacques-Dalcroze (1865-1960). Dalcroze was the inventor of Eurythmics, a system in which his students responded rhythmically to musical scores. Working with Dalcroze, Appia evolved his own theory that the rhythm inherent in a text is the key to every gesture and movement an actor uses during a performance. He concluded that the mastery of rhythm could unify the spatial and other elements of an opera into a harmonious synthesis.

For most of his life Appia worked alone sketching and writing books and essays regarding his theories. Other innovators such as Gordan Craig (1872-1966) and Jacques Copeau (1879-1949) recognized his genius. Among Appia's important publications were *The Staging of Wagner's Musical Dramas* (1895), *Music and Stage Setting* (1899), and *The Work of Living Art* (1921).

Late in his life, in the 1920s, Appia began to receive the recognition he merited. In 1923 he staged *Tristan and Isolde* for Arturo Toscanini, then artistic director of La Scala. In 1924 he designed the staging for two parts of the *Ring* cycle in Basel. In 1925 he designed the settings and costumes for a production of *Prometheus,* also staged in Basel. The productions were not praised universally. Indeed, the conservative critics who chose to see Wagner as he had always been performed with traditional staging found Appia too

"Calvinistic" for their tastes. Nevertheless, Appia's genius was finally recognized and his theories prevailed in spite of the critics. His theories of staging, use of space, and lighting have had a lasting influence on modern stagecraft.

When Appia died on February 29, 1928, his friend and follower Jacques Copeau wrote a tribute in which he accurately summed up the "Master's" radical reform of the stage: "For him, the art of stage production in its pure sense was nothing other than the embodiment of a text or a musical composition, made sensible by the living action of the human body and its reaction to spaces and masses set against it."

Further Reading

Appia set forth his theories in *The Work of Living Art: A Theory of the Theatre* (1921). Oscar G. Brockett discussed Appia's ideas in *History of the Theatre* (1968). An excellent critical biography is Walther R. Volbach, *Adolphe Appia Prophet of the Modern Theatre: A Profile* (1968).

Additional Sources

Beacham, Richard C., *Adolphe Appia, theatre artist,* Cambridge Cambridgeshire; New York: Cambridge University Press, 1987.
Beacham, Richard C., *Adolphe Appia: artist and visionary of the modern theatre,* Chur, Switzerland; Philadelphia: Harwood Academic Publishers, 1994. □

Jesse Applegate

Jesse Applegate (1811-1888) was an American surveyor, pioneer, and rancher. He is best known for his efforts in the settlement of Oregon, which he helped create as a U.S. territory.

Jesse Applegate was born in Kentucky on July 5, 1811, the son of a Revolutionary War soldier. In 1821 the family moved to Missouri, where Applegate grew to thin, wiry manhood. He attended Rock Spring Seminary (later Shurtleff College) at Shiloh, Ill., and studied mathematics and surveying under John Messenger. Later he taught school and continued private study with Justus Post to perfect his skills as a surveyor.

His education completed, Applegate became a clerk in the surveyor general's office in St. Louis, then worked in western Missouri as deputy surveyor general and farmed in the Osage Valley. In 1832 he married.

In 1843, because of economic hard times and the growing slavery controversy, Applegate joined a wagon train bound for Oregon. He took with him a large herd of cattle and was placed in charge of all the cattle. In Oregon he settled in the Willamette Valley, where he farmed and operated a mill, as well as did survey work. In 1845 he led a pioneer party that opened a southern road into Oregon by way of the Rogue and Humboldt rivers.

A Whig (and later a Republican), he was instrumental in organizing local territorial government in Oregon as a member of the legislative committee. Also, it was he who persuaded the British employees of the Hudson's Bay Company to support this provisional government, thereby bringing political unity to Oregon. He served on the committee that drafted Oregon's appeal for territorial status in 1847 and was principal author of the final draft.

In 1849 Applegate moved to southern Oregon to establish a ranch in the Umpqua Valley. He built a large home, which he called the Yoncalla, raised beef for sale to miners, and dispensed liberal hospitality to visitors. He was known to neighbors as a man who could walk 60 miles in a day.

Using his large library, Applegate wrote extensively for the newspapers, corresponded with prominent public men, and served his political party. He was a member of the Oregon constitutional convention of 1857, but left before it completed its work. Applegate had a hot temper and a dictatorial nature, working best when he was in sole command.

In later years he was called the Sage of Yoncalla, and to his home came such prominent visitors as Schuyler Colfax and Samuel Bowles. He helped throw Oregon's vote to Lincoln in the Republican convention in 1860 and promoted unionist sentiment during the Civil War. He also promoted the Oregon and California Railroad but refused to be subservient to railroad interests. He died on April 22, 1888.

Further Reading

Applegate's *A Day with the Cow-column in 1843* (1934), written during his trek to Oregon, helped popularize that state. See also his autobiographical *Recollections of My Boyhood* (1914). There is background on the history of Oregon and on Applegate's later career in Joseph Schafer, *A History of the Pacific Northwest* (1905; rev. ed. 1918); Charles H. Carey, *A General History of Oregon: Prior to 1861* (2 vols., 1935-1936); and Melvin Clay Jacobs, *Winning Oregon: A Study of an Expansionist Movement* (1938). □

Sir Edward Victor Appleton

The British scientist Sir Edward Victor Appleton (1892-1965) was a pioneer in radio physics who gained fame through his study of the ionosphere— the upper reaches of the atmosphere.

Edward Victor Appleton was born on September 6, 1892, in Bradford, Yorkshire, England. He was a brilliant student who excelled in the study of literature and language as well as science and mathematics. At age 16 he entered the University of London and two years later was awarded a scholarship for study at Cambridge University. Appleton left Cambridge in 1913, graduating with first-class honors in physics. He immediately began postgraduate work in crystallography with the distinguished physicist Sir Lawrence Bragg.

The advent of World War I interrupted this research effort. Appleton enlisted in the Royal Engineers and was assigned to signal duty as a commissioned officer. It was here that he was first introduced to radio, a means of communication then in its infancy in the military. The study of the theory and practice of radio wave propagation and reception, begun during the war, stimulated a life-long interest in the subject and brought Appleton renown as a scientist.

At the end of the war Appleton returned to the Cavendish Laboratory at Cambridge where, in collaboration with Balthazar van der Pol, he began an investigation of the operation of radio vacuum tubes. His original research in this area eventually led to the publication *Thermionic Vacuum Tubes* (1932), a scholarly monograph that long served as an introduction to the physical principles underlying these important electronic components.

In 1924 Appleton, at age 32, was made Wheatstone Professor of Physics at King's College, University of London. While at London (1924-1936) he made his most significant contributions to physics by studying radio transmission and the upper atmosphere. He was aided in this research by Miles Barnett, a young graduate student from New Zealand.

Gugielmo Marconi had succeeded in transmitting radio waves across the Atlantic Ocean for the first time in 1901. English physicist Oliver Heaviside and American physicist Arthur E. Kennelly postulated that this transmission was made possible by the presence of a layer of ionized gases in the upper atmosphere. These gases were believed

to reflect radio waves back toward the earth. The Heaviside-Kennelly layer, which later came to be called the ionoshpere, remained an hypothetical entity until its existence was experimentally verified by Appleton.

Appleton's critical experiments were made using the British Broadcasting Corporation's transmitter at Bournemouth and recording the strength of its signal when received at Cambridge. By varying the frequency of the transmitted signal and noting the interference between the direct (ground) waves and the reflected (sky) waves Appleton was able to prove that the Heaviside-Kennelly layer was located at a height of 60 miles above the surface of the earth. In subsequent experiments Appleton and his co-workers discovered the so-called "Appleton layers," one of which was situated at a height twice that of the Heaviside-Kennelly layer and the other somewhat lower than the Heaviside-Kennelly layer. The electron densities of these layers were calculated, and the daily and seasonal variations of the Appleton layers were determined. The experimental techniques that led to these discoveries were later used by Sir Robert Watson-Watt in the development of radar.

Appleton's scientific achievements were recognized through the bestowal of a number of distinctions. In 1927 he was voted a fellow of the prestigious Royal Society of London; in 1941 he was knighted; and in 1947 he was awarded the Nobel Prize in Physics.

Appleton returned to Cambridge University as Jacksonian Professor of Natural Philosophy in 1936. He continued his ionospheric researches there in a field laboratory built for him by the university. With the coming of World War II Appleton left academic life in order to become a government scientist (1939). In his new role he served as secretary of the Department of Scientific and Industrial Research, a position which ultimately involved him with the organization and management of Britain's nuclear and radar programs.

In 1949 Appleton left government service to accept the post of chancellor at the University of Edinburgh. In addition to his administrative duties he maintained his interest in ionospheric physics and founded the influential *Journal of Atmospheric and Terrestrial Physics,* serving as its editor until his death. During his later years Appleton's international reputation led to his participation in a number of world-wide scientific activities including the International Geophysical Year of 1957. By the time of his death in 1965 Appleton had published 140 scientific papers, the majority dealing with the physics of the upper atmosphere.

Further Reading

For a full-length biographical study of Appleton see Ronald Clark, *Sir Edward Appleton* (1971). His scientific work had been evaluated in two excellent shorter pieces: Charles Süsskind, "Appleton, Edward Victor" in the *Dictionary of Scientific Biography,* edited by C. C. Gillispie (1970) and J. A. Ratliffe, *Biographical Memoirs of the Fellows of the Royal Society,* volume 12 (1966). On the ionosphere, see H. S. W. Massey and R. L. F. Boyd, *The Upper Atmosphere* (1958). □

Nathan Appleton

As a leading member of the New England mercantile-manufacturing community, Nathan Appleton (1779-1861) was instrumental in shaping sound institutions for trade, production, and banking in the early economy of the United States.

Nathan Appleton was born on Oct. 6, 1779, in New Ipswich, N.H. He attended the common schools and the local academy in preparation for college study. At the age of 15 he was admitted to Dartmouth College but decided instead to enter business. He accompanied his elder brother Samuel to Boston and learned bookkeeping in order to work as a clerk in Samuel's mercantile house. When he reached 21 in 1800, he became a full partner in the business, which continued until 1809. In the following year he joined his brother Eben and another merchant, Daniel P. Parker, in a similar venture, which prospered until it was dissolved in 1813.

That year marked Appleton's first move into manufacturing; he invested a portion of his mercantile earnings in a textile manufacturing concern in Waltham, Mass. His copartners were Francis C. Lowell and Patrick T. Jackson. Appleton soon put more capital into the textile business, including the formation in 1821 of the Merrimack Manufacturing Company, which grew into the early industrial town of Lowell, Mass. He and his partners pioneered in developing the production processes, labor system, and distribution methods of the American textile industry. The success of that industry propelled families such as the Appletons, the Lowells, and the Jacksons to positions of great prominence in the New England economic and social world.

Appleton's strong sense of public service led him into a political career during the years in which his business efforts prospered. He was one of two lobbyists chosen by the merchants of Boston to present their views to Congress during the War of 1812, and he served in the Massachusetts House of Representatives for 6 years between 1815 and 1827. He was elected in 1832 as a Whig to the U.S. House of Representatives, serving one full term and a portion of another term 10 years later. In his political life he fought strongly for the principles of high protective tariffs and hard currency.

Throughout his lifetime Appleton actively supported the efforts of the new American nation to establish its economic health and independence. He was a frequent contributor to the public debate on economic issues, writing newspaper articles, making speeches, and publishing pamphlets on money and banking, tariffs, and the need for the development of America's manufacturing sector. As a director of the Boston Bank, he worked toward a conservative, stable banking system, always opposing the inflationary and speculative operations of banks in the backcountry. He was a strong nationalist and a firm believer in Hamiltonian policies for the young nation. Appleton was among the influen-

tial men who did so much to shape the basic institutions of the United States prior to the Civil War.

Further Reading

The best source on Appleton is Robert C. Winthrop, *Memoir of the Hon. Nathan Appleton, LL. D.* (1861; repr. 1969), which contains long sections of Appleton's "Sketches of Autobiography." Also helpful is Kenneth Wiggins Porter, *The Jacksons and the Lees: Two Generations of Massachusetts Merchants, 1765-1844* (2 vols., 1937).

Additional Sources

Gregory, Frances W., *Nathan Appleton, merchant and entrepreneur, 1779-1861,* Charlottesville: University Press of Virginia, 1975. □

Benigno Aquino

Benigno Aquino (1933-1983) of the Philippines was a leading opponent of the rule of President Ferdinand Marcos. His opposition ended in August 1983 when, after living in exile in the United States for three years, he returned to Manila and was gunned down at the airport. His death precipitated massive demonstrations against President Marcos.

"Nino" Aquino was born in 1933 in Tarlac Province, Luzon, to a prominent family. At age 22 he became the nation's youngest mayor in his hometown of Concepcion. Just six years later he became governor of Tarlac province. In 1967 Aquino once again made history when he became the youngest senator elected in the country's history. Meanwhile he married Corazon Cojoangco; they raised five children.

Aquino became famous for his oratorical gifts and his brilliant mind, as well as his immense ambition. He emerged as the leading candidate for the presidency in 1973 when President Marcos was scheduled to leave office after completing the maximum two terms as president. The Marcos government had already begun its campaign against Aquino, labeling him as a Communist sympathizer because of the contacts he had established with insurgency leaders in central Luzon.

Aquino's ambition to be president was dashed when President Marcos declared martial law and dissolved the constitution. Marcos took all power unto himself and jailed his political opponents, including Aquino. Aquino spent over seven years in prison and was found guilty of murder, subversion, and illegal possession of firearms. Aquino denied these charges as well as the legitimacy of his trial and conviction by a military tribunal. In 1980 he was allowed to go to the United States for a heart bypass operation, and he remained in exile as a research fellow at Harvard University until his ill-fated return in 1983.

Following the assassination, and after appointing his own investigative commission of cronies, President Marcos was pressured to appoint a five-person non-partisan investigative board led by Judge Corazon Agrava. Marcos and the military stated that the assassination was carried out by a lone gunman in the pay of the Communist Party. The alleged gunman, Rolando Galman, was shot at the airport immediately following the shooting of Aquino, so he could not be cross-examined. The military carried out its own investigation and reported, not surprisingly, that no military personnel were involved in the death.

The official commission's majority report found that Aquino was not slain by the alleged Communist hireling as claimed by Marcos and the military but was the victim of a "criminal conspiracy" led by the military and including Gen. Fabian Ver, the armed forces chief of staff, the highest ranking general of the country, and a close friend and cousin of President Marcos. Ver's indictment included complicity in attempting to cover up the crime.

The commission's findings were astonishing, although from the beginning most Filipinos doubted the official version of the assassination. Almost no one believed that military generals would order the execution of Aquino on their own initiative, although no proof was ever presented that directly implicated the president. It is true that Aquino posed a threat as a possible unifier of the dispersed opposition. He had been the president's principal adversary for decades.

Ironically, the democratic opposition to Marcos was strongest after it lost its most famous leader. In death Aquino became more powerful than ever. The assassin of Aquino could never have known how seriously the authority of President Marcos would be undermined by his act. As Marcos lost credibility, the economy of the Philippines deteriorated so that by 1985 the nation was in political and economic chaos. At the same time, the opposition used the assassination to its own advantage so that Marcos was forced to relent on many of his most onerous policies. The press began publishing critical commentary and the elections for the National Assembly resulted in a dramatic increase in the number of oppositionists elected.

In December 1985 the court exonerated General Ver and the others charged with Aquino's murder. Marcos promptly reinstated Ver to his former position. But popular unrest with Marcos' rule was growing steadily and within weeks would coalese around Aquino's widow, Corazon.

Further Reading

A biography of the Aquino family written by Nick Joaquin is *The Aquinos of Tarlac: An Essay on History as Three Generations* (Manila, 1983). Other sources include Gerald N. Hill and Kathleen Thompson Hill, *Aquino Assassinated: The Story and Analysis of the Assassination of Philippine Senator Benigno S. Aquino* (1983) and National Library of Australia, *Benigno Aquino: A Select Bibliography of Articles in Periodical Publications Held in the National Library of Australia* (Canberra, 1983). For detailed analysis of the assassination, see the weekly issues of *Asia Week* and *Far Eastern Economic Review* beginning August 21, 1983.

Additional Sources

Aquino, Benigno S., *Testament from a prison cell,* Makati, Metro Manila, Philippines: Benigno S. Aquino, Jr. Foundation, 1984.

Benigno, Teodoro C., *Ninoy, the heart and the soul,* Manila: Office of the Press Secretary, Bureau of Communications Services, 1988.

Hill, Gerald N., *Aquino assassination: the true story and analysis of the assassination of Philippine Senator Benigno S. Aquino, Jr.,* Sonoma, Calif.: Hilltop Pub. Co., 1983.

Joaquin, Nick, *Ninoy Aquino in the Senate: final chapters of The Aquinos of Tarlac: an essay on history as three generation,* Mandaluyong, Metro Manila: Solar Pub. Corp., 1986.

Ninoy Aquino: the man, the legend, Metro Manila, Philippines: Cacho Hermanos, 1984.

Policarpio, Alfonso P., *Ninoy: the willing martyr,* Philippines: Isaiah Books, 1986.

White, Mel, *Aquino,* Dallas: Word Pub., 1989. □

Corazon Cojoangco Aquino

Corazon Cojoangco Aquino (born 1933) was the first woman to run for the office of the president of the Republic of the Philippines. The results of the 1986 election were so fraudulent that both Aquino and her opponent, the incumbent, Ferdinand Marcos declared victory. As a result of the election, the Filipino people rose in protest and Marcos was forced to flee the country and Aquino assumed the office of president.

Corazon Cojoangco Aquino was born on January 25, 1933, the sixth of eight children born to Jose Cojoangco of Tarlac, a prosperous province 65 miles northwest of Manila, the Philippines capital . The Cojoangcos were members of a wealthy landowning family prominent in politics.

Aquino attended an exclusive Catholic school for girls in Manila before travelling to America to attend Philadelphia's Raven Hill Academy. After earning a degree in French and mathematics from New York's Mount Saint Vincent College in 1953, she returned to the Philippines and enrolled in a Manila law school. While at law school she met her future husband, Benigno Aquino and married him in 1954. The marriage united two of Tarlac's most prominent families.

The Politician's Wife

Aquino's husband belonged to a family whose involvement in politics went as far back as the last century. One year after they were married, Aquino's husband was elected mayor of the city of Concepcion at the age of 22. Her husband was considered one of the Philippines' brightest political hopes.

Moving up in politics, Aquino's husband became the youngest territorial governor and later the youngest senator in the Philippines. Through out all her husband's political successes, Aquino stayed in the background, preferring to concentrate her energies on raising their four daughters and a son.

As her husband rose in prominence, he became an outspoken critic of the regime of President Ferdinand Marcos. When Marcos declared martial law on September 21, 1972, Aquino's husband was one of the first persons arrested and put in jail. During the long years of her husband's incarceration from 1972 to 1980, Aquino's role as a quiet wife slowly changed. Becoming her husband's main link to the outside world, she was instrumental in having his statements passed along to the press and to activists outside the prison walls. From inside his cell, Aquino's husband even ran for a seat in Parliament, with his wife conducting a large portion of the campaign.

In 1980, Aquino's husband was released from jail in order to undergo heart surgery in the United States. Aquino's husband worked as a research fellow at Harvard University for the next three years. His family lived with him in the Boston area and his wife described the time as the best years of her life.

In 1983 supporters of the anti-Marcos factions persuaded Aquino's husband to return to the Philippines and to lead their cause. When his plane landed on the tarmac of the Manila International Airport on August 21, 1983, Aquino's husband was assassinated. A commission formed to investigate the murder indicted the military men assigned to escort him as well as their military superiors. However, the court which eventually tried them for the murder acquitted all 26 defendants.

Homemaker Turns Politician

Her husband's assassination served as the turning point of Aquino's life. As her dead husband became the rallying focus of anti-Marcos groups she, as his widow, became the unifying figure for the different factions of the opposition. Aquino was catapulted into the role of keeping the unity alive. On October 15, 1985, the Aquino presidential campaign was launched at the National Press Club in Manila by 250 founding members, many of whom were businesspeople and professionals.

Aquino agreed to run if one million supporters signed an endorsement of her candidacy and if President Marcos called for a snap election. The supporters collected more than one million signatures, and her candidacy was endorsed by six opposition political parties as the common candidate for president in the election called for February 7, 1986. The political support she amassed, and the exoneration of the military men tried for her husband's murder, made Aquino accept the mandate to run for the presidency, "not in vengeance but in search of justice."

She picked Salvador Laurel, leader of the opposition's largest faction, as her running mate. Initial negotiations fell through in a disagreement about which party's name to carry—her husband's LABAN (Fight) Party or Laurel's UNIDO (United Nationalist Democratic Organization). Before the deadline for filing candidacy she and Laurel agreed to run under the UNIDO banner.

Countering Marcos's charges of her political inexperience, Aquino counted as her main asset her diametrical opposition to the president. Her supporters considered her a fresh new face with a reputation for moral integrity. Her main assets in the campaign were her reputation for moral integrity along with her avowal of her slain husband's ideals. To these were added the quiet support of the influential Roman Catholic Church in the Philippines, whose prelate Jamie Cardinal Sin was instrumental in the Aquino-Laurel reconciliation.

The homemaker-turned-politician responded to the challenge with enthusiasm and a singular commitment to the cause of justice. Her opponent, Marcos, had extended his term of office for more than 20 years through a declaration of martial law and constitutional changes that increased his powers. The true results of the election may never be known as the incumbent forces used intimidation, scattered violence, and overt fraud to declare Marcos the winner. The people took to the streets in protest; some army leaders revolted; the United States expressed its indignation. Less than three weeks after his alleged election victory in February 1986, Marcos fled the Philippines. Aquino became the acknowledged president of the republic.

The Presidency and Beyond

Aquino admitted that she faced numerous challenges as the new Filipino president. The release of 441 political prisoners and the forced retirement of 22 pro-Marcos generals were among her first actions as president. She also reinstated the writ of habeas corpus, the right of a prisoner to appear before a judge, and abolished the government's ability to imprison people at will, which had been in effect since 1981. Aquino promised to promote the right to assemble peaceably, and free speech along with prosecuting corruption and abusers of human rights.

Protecting the countryside was another of Aquino's goals. She planned to accomplish this by disarming the private armies that roamed the rural areas and establish industries there. Aquino said she would revitalize the sugar industry by breaking the monopoly. She acknowledged the special relationship with the United States but emphasized that her concern was with the Filipinos, not the Americans.

Aquino knew her popularity would wane and that her leadership would be harshly criticized. At least seven coups were directed at her government during her tenure as president, many times by former allies who had helped her come to power. Besides dealing with factious parties both within her cabinet and in the nation, Aquino had to contend with natural disasters and frequent power failures.

In 1991, a constitutional amendment was passed by referendum which enabled Aquino to remain president until June 30, 1992. Her successor was Fidel Ramos, her former secretary of defense and Marcos' former deputy chief of staff of the armed forces. Ramos, who assisted Aquino in fending off the coup attempts, has continued to support Aquino's democratic ideals. Aquino has still retained her popularity with the Filipino people and works for reform by participating in cooperatives and non-governmental organizations in the Philippines.

Further Reading

Materials on Corazon Aquino include a historical biography of the Aquino family by Nick Joaquin, *The Aquinos of Tarlac; an*

Essay on History as Three Generations (Manila, 1983). Other sources include Gerald N. Hill and Kathleen Thompson Hill, *Aquino Assassination: the Story and Analysis of the Assassination of Philippine Senator Benigno S. Aquino* (1983) and National Library of Australia, *Benigno Aquino: A Select Bibliography of Articles in Periodical Publications Held in the National Library of Australia* (Canberra, 1983). Cover stories in *Time* magazine appeared February 3 and 24 and March 10, 1986. See also "Making Up is Hard to Do," *Time* (March 11, 1996) and "Mac Arthur Park: Manila Postcard," *New Republic* (January 23, 1995). □

Yasser Arafat

Yasser Arafat (born 1929) was elected chairman of the Palestinian Liberation Organization (PLO) in 1969. Though originally an advocate of all-out guerrilla war, from 1974 on he and the PLO sometimes seemed to be seeking a negotiated resolution of the Palestinian problem. He was awarded the Joliot-Curie Gold Medal by the World Peace Council in 1975.

Yasser Arafat was born Abdel-Rahman Abdel-Raouf Arafat al-Qudwa al-Husseini on October 24, 1929 to a Palestinian family living in Cairo, Egypt. He was related, through his mother, to the Husseini family, who were prominent members of the Sunni Muslim community in Jerusalem. His youth was spent in Cairo and Jerusalem. At that time, the area of historic Palestine was ruled by the British, under a mandate (license) from the League of Nations. Palestine was also a magnet for Jewish immigrants from Europe, who sought to build a Jewish homeland there. Jewish immigration was opposed by most of the country's existing population, who for the most part were ethnic Arabs of both the Muslim and Christian faiths.

Youthful Politics

While still in his teens Arafat became involved with a Palestinian Arab nationalist group led by cousins from the Husseini family. When the British moved out of Palestine in 1948, fierce fighting broke out between the Jewish and Arab communities. The Jews were easily able to beat the Palestinians. As a result, around a million Palestinians were forced to flee their ancestral homeland and sought refuge in neighboring Arab nations. Two-thirds of prewar Palestine then became the Jewish state of Israel. The rest came under the control of two Arab neighbors, Egypt and Jordan.

After the Palestinians' 1948 defeat, Arafat went to Cairo, where he studied engineering. He founded a Palestinian student union, which expanded rapidly over the following years. At the end of the 1950s it was one of the main constituent groups in the new Palestinian nationalist movement "Fateh". (The name is a reverse acronym for *Harakat al-Tahrir al-Filastinivva*—the Palestinian Liberation Movement.)

Arafat was one of Fateh's most prominent founders and sat on the movement's central committee. Fateh rejected the many complex ideologies which were fought over in the Arab world in the late 1950s and rejected reliance on any of the existing Arab regimes. Its members argued that Palestinians should seek to regain their own country by their own efforts, which should include guerrilla warfare against Israel. This armed struggle was launched in 1965. The attacks did not seriously scar the Jewish military, but did increase Palestinian morale and Arafat's credibility.

Birth of the PLO

Meanwhile, in 1964, the Arab countries had created their own Palestinian confederation, which they called the Palestinian Liberation Organization (PLO). At that stage the PLO did not take on the Israelis directly.

In 1967, the Israelis defeated the Arabs in the full scale Six-Day War. Israel managed to occupy the rest of historic Palestine, along with chunks of Egyptian and Syrian territory. The Arab states were discredited by their defeat in the Six-Day War and the Fateh guerrillas who had long criticized them seemed vindicated. In 1969, Fateh and its allies were able to take over the PLO apparatus, and Arafat was elected chairman of the executive committee.

Many guerrilla camps were set up in Jordan along the border with Israel. In September 1970 Jordan's King Hussein sent his army against these growing camps, killing many Palestinians in what was known as Black September. Lebanon then became the guerrillas' main base of military operations. After this, the PLO engaged in terrorist acts, including the murder of 11 Israeli athletes at the Munich Olympics.

The Peace Process

In October 1973 Egypt and Syria attacked Israel in the Yom Kippur War, trying to regain the lands Israel had occupied six years earlier. They did not succeed in regaining the lands by force, but their action stimulated American efforts to seek a negotiated settlement in the region. In 1974 the PLO's ruling body, the Palestinian National Council (PNC), voted to seek inclusion in such a settlement, calling for the creation of a Palestinian national authority in those two areas of historic Palestine which the Israelis had occupied in 1967. (These were the West Bank—known by the Israelis as Judea and Samaria—and the Gaza Strip.)

In November 1974 the support of the Arab states enabled Arafat to participate in a debate on the Middle East at the United Nations General Assembly. His famous words there were: "I have come bearing an olive branch and a freedom fighter's gun. Do not let the olive branch fall from my hand." But he failed to use his appearance to spell out the PLO's call for the creation of a Palestinian state *alongside* Israel, so the Israelis still refused to have any dealings with the PLO. In 1975, the United States government vowed to do likewise, at least until the PLO should openly recognize U.N. Security Council resolution 242 of 1967 and Israel's right to exist. Under pressure from Palestinian hardliners, Arafat and the PLO refused to satisfy this condition.

When Egypt's President Anwar Sadat launched his peace process with Israel in 1977-1979, the PLO opposed it. The Camp David accords signed by Egypt, Israel, and the United States in 1978 called for the institution of a Palestinian autonomy plan in the West Bank and Gaza, but this plan never went into effect. Most Palestinian residents of these occupied areas feared that 'autonomy' meant the continuation of Israeli rule, and they supported the PLO's call for an independent Palestinian state there.

In 1982 the Israeli government decided to try to smash the PLO's military capability in Lebanon. The Israeli army knocked out PLO positions in south Lebanon and encircled Arafat and his remaining forces in the Lebanese capital, Beirut. American diplomacy finally resulted in the evacuation of the PLO from Beirut.

In February 1983 the PNC voted to pursue a reconciliation with Jordan and Egypt, with a view to suing for peace with Israel. This angered the Syrians, who set about forming an internal PLO rebellion against Arafat's leadership. Then, in November 1984, Arafat convened a meeting of the PNC in the Jordanian capital. This provoked a final break with his pro-Syrian critics, and afterwards he felt freer to pursue his moves toward the Jordanians.

In February 1985, Arafat and King Hussein healed the rift which had divided them since 1970 and agreed on a joint strategy toward Israel. Their announced aim was the creation of a confederation between Jordan and a Palestinian entity which would be established in the West Bank and Gaza. They sought the help of the United States in pressing the Israelis to agree to this. One obstacle to be overcome was the Americans' ten-year-old ban on talking to the PLO. In midsummer 1985, plans were made for a series of diplomatic moves which would include Arafat's open acceptance of resolution 242. But by early 1986 King Hussein broke off negotiations with Arafat, citing PLO refusal to compromise.

The Oslo Accord was signed by Arafat and Israeli Prime Minister Yitzhak Rabin in the fall of 1993. The accord placed the city of Jericho, the Israeli occupied Gaza Strip, and eventually the remainder of the West Bank under Palestinian self-rule. Arafat was elected president in January 1996.

Late in 1996, Rabin's successor, Benjamin Netanyahu, signed the Hebron agreement with Arafat which removed Israeli occupiers from the last occupied city in the West Bank. In return, Arafat promised to amend the portion of the Palestinian National Charter which calls for the destruction of Israel.

Return to the Status Quo

The decision by Israel to build homes in Jerusalem started up the terrorism campaign in the Middle East. The resulting hostility between the Israelis and the Palestinians placed the peace process on very shaky ground. Jewish settlement in Jerusalem remains a controversial issue.

Further Reading

The major biography of Arafat is Alan Hart, *Arafat: Terrorist or Peacemaker* (1984). An earlier and more critical biography, which contains many errors, is Thomas Kiernan, *Arafat: The Man and the Myth* (1976). The politics of the PLO are detailed in Quandt, Jabber, and Lesch, *The Politics of Palestinian Nationalism* (1973), and Helena Cobban, *The Palestinian Liberation Organization: People, Power and Politics* (1984). One interesting biographical account by a close Arafat colleague is Abu Iyad with Eric Rouleau, *My Home, My Land: A Narrative of the Palestinian Struggle* (1981). Additional Arafat articles include "Don't Insult Me With an Offer Like That," *Time* (June 23, 1997), and "Hope and Fear," *Scholastic Update* (September 20, 1996). □

Louis Aragon

Louis Aragon (1897-1982) was a surrealist author, poet of the French Resistance during World War II, and the leading Communist writer in France.

Louis Aragon was born in Neuilly on Oct. 3, 1897. He was educated to be a physician. In 1917, while in the army medical corps, he met André Breton, who enlisted his support in the "surrealist revolution," a literary and art movement that emphasized the irrational and the unconscious. Aragon's poems and prose pieces of the 1920s are all strongly surrealist. The collections *Feu de joie* (Bonfire) and *Mouvement perpétuel* (Perpetual Motion) show not only the verbal gratuity that surrealism advocated but the lyrical transformation of humdrum reality as well. In prose, too, Aragon demonstrated the "daily marvelous" by drawing a veil of enchantment over a modern city, as in *Le*

Paysan de Paris (1926; Parisian Peasant). In his essays he lambasted everything and everybody representing established values.

When Aragon became a Communist in 1927, the boisterous and brawling surrealist broke with his companions to dedicate himself to a revolution that he considered more viable than Breton's. He married Elsa Triolet, the sister-in-law of the Russian poet V. V. Mayakovsky and an author in her own right.

Aragon radically shifted the basis of his art and wrote a series of four novels during 1933-1944 in a style that harkened back to 19th-century realism. The novels paint a panorama of French life before World War I. Although intended to be an indictment of the bourgeoisie, they do not show Aragon's political views so obviously as the next series, *Les Communistes* (1949-1951; *The Communists*), which deals with France of 1939-1940. For his next novel he went back a century; *La Semaine sainte* (1958; *Holy Week*) is about the painter Théodore Géricault and his times. With *La Mise à mort* (1965; *Death Blow*) Aragon returned to his own times and his own story. His interest in the work of painter Henri Matisse, whose work Aragon collected, led him to write the novel *Henri Matisse* (1971).

Aragon's personal story has been the subject of his poetry for, other than his surrealist "exercises," it is essentially a poetry of self-expression. Its first great theme is patriotism, the sentiment which promoted a remarkable flowering of poetry in France during the Occupation. Among Resistance poetry, Aragon's volumes entitled *Le Crévecoeur* (1941; The Broken Heart), *Le Musée Grévin* (1943; The Grévin Museum), and *La Diane française* (1944; The French Diana) stand with the finest. The second great theme of Aragon's poetry is love, which surrealism exalted in particular. In volume after volume Aragon sang of his love for his wife, Elsa. Just as he rejoined, in the novel, the older tradition of didactic realism, in poetry he pushed back to romanticism for theme and form. With verses as regular as Victor Hugo's, his poetry is eminently accessible and direct in its appeal.

Aragon published numerous essays on art and literature and particularly in support of the political cause to which he devoted all his mature years. In 1937 he became editor of the newspaper *Le Soir*. During the war he helped found the Communist weekly *Les Lettres françaises*. Speaking at Communist meetings and serving in organizations of writers, Aragon gave unstintingly of his time to causes he thought worthy, defending and attacking with the same spirit that had made him the fire-brand of the twenties.

In 1981, French president François Mitterand made Aragon a member of the Legion of Honor. He died in Paris on December 24, 1982.

Further Reading

Hannah Josephson and Malcolm Cowley, eds., *Aragon: Poet of the French Resistance* (1945), contains useful introductions to both the poetry and prose. Catharine Savage, *Malraux, Sartre, and Aragon as Political Novelists* (1964), illuminates the conflict between art and politics for these Marxist writers. Maxwell Adereth, *Commitment in Modern French Literature* (1967), places Aragon in the context of *littérature engagée* Background material is provided by Henri Peyre, *The Contemporary French Novel* (1955), and Germaine Brée and Margaret Guiton, *An Age of Fiction: The French Novel from Gide to Camus* (1957; rev. ed. published as *The French Novel from Gide to Camus* , 1962). See also Adareth, Max. *Elsa Triolet and Louis Aragon: An Introduction to Their Interwoven Lives and Works* (Edwin Mellen Press, 1994); Aragon, Louis, translated by Alyson Waters, *Treatise on Style (Traite du Style)* (University of Nebraska Press, 1991); Becker, Lucille F., *Louis Aragon* (Irvington Publishers, 1971); and the *New York Times* (December 25, 1982). □

Osvaldo Aranha

Osvaldo Aranha (1894-1960) was a leading figure in the group of Brazilian politicians from Rio Grande do Sul who came to power with President Vargas in 1930. During the following 30 years, Aranha remained a major figure in Brazilian political life.

O svaldo Aranha was born in Alegrete in the state of Rio Grande do Sul on Feb. 15, 1894. He graduated from the Porto Alegre Law School in 1916 and for some years practiced his profession.

During the 1920s Aranha served his apprenticeship in politics as mayor of the town of Alegrete, and he was wounded fighting in defense of the state regime during a revolt in 1926. In 1927 he was elected a member of the state legislature, and in 1928 he became a member of the Federal Chamber of Deputies.

When Getulio Vargas became governor of Rio Grande do Sul in 1929, he chose Aranha to head his Cabinet as secretary of justice. In this capacity Aranha became the intermediary of Vargas's government with the rebel group of young military men known as the *Tenentes,* who had organized two revolts against the government during the 1920s.

Vargas ran as opposition candidate for president of Brazil in 1930, and when he took a leave of absence from the governorship during the campaign, Aranha served as acting governor. After Vargas lost to the government of Washington Luiz, Aranha joined with the *Tenentes* in urging Vargas to go along with efforts to organize a revolt. Once Vargas had agreed, the rebels succeeded within 3 weeks in overrunning Brazil's northeast and Amazonian areas, as well as the three southernmost states. Thereupon army leaders in Rio de Janeiro overthrew President Luiz. Aranha was then sent to Rio by the rebel high command to negotiate with the military leaders the transfer of power to Vargas.

Minister and Diplomat

With the installation of President Vargas, Aranha became minister of justice, a post he held until his transfer to the Ministry of Finance in December 1931. In 1934 President Vargas named Aranha ambassador to Washington, D.C. There he worked out a program for resumption of

payment on Brazil's foreign debt, which had been in default for 4 years. When President Vargas led a coup d'etat to establish a semifascist regime in November 1937, Aranha resigned his Washington post in protest. However, in March 1938 Vargas convinced him to enter the government once again, this time as minister of foreign affairs. He continued in this post until 1944.

Aranha was a major force working for alignment of Brazil with the Allies in World War II. Once Brazil had entered the war on the Allied side in 1942, Aranha sought to stimulate popular support for Brazilian participation. To this end, he became vice president of the Society of the Friends of America. When the police refused to allow the society to function, Aranha resigned from the government in August 1944.

At this point Aranha broke with Vargas and became one of the organizers of the antigovernment party, the Uniao Democratica Nacional (UDN). The pressure of the UDN helped force Vargas to call elections for December 1945, but Vargas was overthrown before that date.

During the administration of Vargas's successor, President Eurico Dutra, Aranha returned to diplomacy. He served as ambassador to the United Nations, and in 1947-1948 was president of the UN General Assembly.

With the return of Vargas to the presidency at the end of 1950, peace was made between Vargas and Aranha. Aranha was named minister of finance in 1953, and it was reported that he though this a step toward his candidacy for president. However, President Vargas committed suicide in August 1954, and Aranha immediately resigned from the Cabinet. Aranha did not return to public office but held the status of an "elder statesman" until his death on Jan. 27, 1960.

Further Reading

There is no biography of Aranha in English. Background works that contain information on him include José Maria Bello, *A History of Modern Brazil, 1889-1964* (1940; trans. 1959); Austin F. MacDonald, *Latin American Politics and Government* (1949); and Bryce Wood, *The United States and Latin American Wars, 1932-1942* (1966).

Additional Sources

Cohen, Esther., *Oswaldo Aranha,* Porto Alegre, RS: Tchae!, 1985.
Flores, Moacyr., *Osvaldo Aranha,* Porto Alegre: IEL, 1991. □

Aratus

Aratus (271-213 B.C.) was a Greek statesman and general of distinction whose main goal in life was the destruction of tyrants in the Peloponnesus.

Orphaned at the age of 7 when his family was massacred by a dictator, Aratus alone escaped to Argos. In 251 B.C., as leader of an exile assault force, he scaled the walls of Sicyon unobserved one night, captured the guardroom, and at dawn harangued the Sicyonians into overthrowing their dictator. At the age of 20 he became the idol of the Sicyonian democrats.

Aratus was a shrewd diplomat. He recalled all Sicyonian exiles but averted civil war within Sicyon. He brought Sicyon into the Achaean League, one of the two Greek federations of city-states of the time. From 245 on, the Achaean League elected him general every alternate year. The general, not allowed to succeed himself, implemented federal policy and executed the league's strategy. Aratus now operated in a wider field. In 243 he made a brilliant night attack on Corinth, freeing its fortress, Acrocorinth, from the Macedonian garrison and making Corinth a member of the Achaean League.

Threatened now by the hostility of Aetolia, the other federation, and of Macedon, Aratus found an ally in Agis IV of Sparta, attacked Athens and Argos which were proMacedonian, and by a sudden strike defeated the Aetolians when they invaded Achaea. On the death of Antigonus of Macedon in 240, Achaea and Aetolia formed a coalition against his successor, Demetrius. Their armies attacked Macedon's allies in 237 and 235, Aratus being general in each of these years. Argos survived numerous attacks, but Megalopolis joined the Achaean League, and Achaea and Aetolia divided the other Arcadian cities between them. The alliance broke down in 229, when Aetolia made a separate pact with Antigonus Doson, the successor of Demetrius. However, Aratus won over Argos, bringing the Achaean League to its zenith in the Peloponnesus.

Between 227 and 224 the Spartan king Cleomenes III shattered the Achaean League. Aratus, holding out in Sicyon, called upon Macedon for help and became Antigonus Doson's adjutant in his conquest of the Peloponnesus. Achaea and its army helped Antigonus defeat Sparta at Sellasia in 222. The elimination of Sparta left Achaea and Aetolia again as rivals in the Peloponnesus, and fighting broke out in 220. Aratus mishandled the campaign and persuaded Philip V of Macedon and the Hellenic League to declare war on Aetolia. In 219 an alliance of Aetolia, Elis, and Sparta pounded Achaea until Philip came south and relieved Achaea. As adjutant to Philip, Aratus fostered Achaean interests, but the Achaean army declined and the league was on the verge of collapse when Aratus, again general, reorganized it in 217. Aratus died in 213 as general, being accorded heroic honors at Sicyon.

Further Reading

Ancient sources on Aratus include Plutarch's *Lives of the Noble Grecians and Romans* and Polybius's *Histories*. A good modern account is F.W. Walbank, *Aratos of Sicyon* (1933).

Additional Sources

Plutarch., *Plutarch's Life of Aratus,* New York: Arno Press, 1979. ☐

Jacobo Arbenz Guzmán

Jacobo Arbenz Guzmán (1913-1971) was president of Guatemala from 1951 to 1954, during which time Communists were alleged to have acquired decisive influence. His overthrow by an invasion sponsored by the U.S. Central Intelligence Agency represents a watershed in that country's violent history.

Jacobo Arbenz Guzmán was born in Quezaltenango on September 14, 1913, the son of a Swiss pharmacist and a Latina mother. His father had emigrated to Guatemala in 1901 but, following the failure of his business, committed suicide. A family friend arranged for Arbenz's appointment to the Escuela Politécnica, the national military academy. A brilliant student and superb athlete, he graduated in 1935. Two years later he returned to the academy to teach science and history.

Arbenz soon learned that Guatemala's military structure discriminated against officers from lowly backgrounds. His 1939 marriage to the beautiful María Cristina Vilanova Castro provided his frustration with political content. Born to one of El Salvador's wealthiest coffee-growing families, her sense of noblesse oblige and horror over her father's association with the 1932 "*matanza*" combined to produce within her an intense concern for social justice. Her influence on Arbenz's political consciousness was great.

With his wife by his side, Arbenz played a critical role in the overthrow of long-time Guatemalan *caudillo* Jorge Ubico Castañeda in July 1944 and of his successor Federico Ponce Vaides in October. Arbenz was selected to the three-man junta which governed Guatemala until Juan José Arévalo Bermej's election as president. When Arévalo took office in March 1945, he appointed Arbenz minister of defense.

The 1944 Revolution

Arévalo established the tone for the Guatemalan revolution. His idiosyncratic "spiritual socialism" led to strong government support for social and economic reform. His program held great appeal for Arbenz, who gave to it his wholehearted allegiance. However, it alienated the powerful Guatemalan elite who longed for its halycon days before 1944. Arévalo survived some 25 attempted coups.

With Arévalo statutorily prohibited from serving consecutive terms in office, the two revolutionary parties turned to Arbenz as their candidate. His major opponent was expected to be Francisco Javier Araña, Arévalo's chief of the armed forces. Araña considered the revolutionary program already too extreme. Encouraged by Guatemala's elite, he organized his own party and announced his candidacy for president. Credible rumors circulated, nonetheless, that Araña planned a pre-emptive coup. The National Assembly impeached him for treason. Then, on July 18, 1949, Araña was machine-gunned to death.

Although allegations of Arbenz's complicity in Araña's assassination were never proven, he undeniably benefitted. In November 1950 he garnered over 60 percent of the vote, but he was unable to reconcile the profoundly polarized nation. Counterrevolutionary movements organized beyond Guatemala's borders, sheltered by the neighboring dictators. Arbenz continued to pursue his revolutionary objectives. His most controversial measure was Decree 900, an agrarian reform bill enacted in June 1952. It stipulated that the government would expropriate and redistribute uncultivated acreage from Guatemala's largest landholders. The largest of the large, and therefore the concern that stood to lose the most, was the United Fruit Company, which was a U.S. company.

United Fruit launched a massive public relations and lobbying campaign to convince the U.S. government that Arbenz had fallen prey to Communists. Officials did not need much convincing. Historically wary of Central American instability, Washington's suspicion of the Guatemalan revolution grew apace with the escalating cold war. By the time of Arbenz's election, the Truman administration had instituted an arms boycott. Still, some early State Department assessments predicted Arbenz would guide the revolution toward a more centrist position. Such sanguine forecasts evaporated with the agrarian reform bill. A consensus was reached that Arbenz had allowed the Soviets to establish a beachhead in Guatemala.

In truth, Arbenz was not a Communist and had no intention of turning Guatemala into a Soviet satellite. He realized that Communists were active in Guatemala, that they had their own party, and that they exerted some influence within the government and important societal institutions, particularly labor unions. Yet he understood that their number was small and that so long as they operated out in the open, promoted his program, and were excluded from the army and the police, they posed no substantive danger.

The U.S. Aids Overthrow

The Cold War ethos of the United States precluded drawing such fine distinctions. Either one opposed Communism or one was a Communist. The Eisenhower administration began to plot Arbenz's overthrow within months of taking office. By spring 1954 the Central Intelligence Agency had completed its planning and selected Col. Carlos Enrique Castillo Armas to lead an "Army of Liberation." Desperate and isolated, Arbenz purchased arms from behind the Iron Curtain. Eisenhower initiated "Operation PBSUCCESS."

Castillo Armas' invasion on June 18, 1954, demonstrated that because Arbenz's power base never extended to Guatemala's Maya majority, he remained at the mercy of his armed forces, whose leadership was interested in preserving its own privileged status, not defending the revolution. Hence it was extremely vulnerable to a strategy of deception and psychological warfare. The Army of Liberation was never sufficiently strong to defeat the national army, but through an ingeniously orchestrated combination of clandestine radio broadcasts, bombing sorties, and minor skirmishes, it presented the appearance of such strength. Arbenz's officer corps panicked. So did Arbenz. Distrusting his army's loyalty, he ordered the distribution of arms to peasants and workers. His officers refused, demanding Arbenz's resignation instead. He no longer had the will to resist. Publicly denouncing the United States and United Fruit Company, on June 27 Arbenz, not yet 41, sought asylum in the Mexican embassy.

Guatemala experienced little other than bloodshed and oppression after its revolution ended so abruptly. Time was equally unkind to Arbenz. He and his family wandered from Mexico to Switzerland to Czechoslovakia and then to Uruguay. Increasingly depressed, Arbenz began to drink heavily. He found life no better in Cuba, where he migrated in 1960. He resented Castro's portrayal of him as an object lesson in how not to forge a revolution. He was also devastated by the suicide of his eldest daughter. In 1970 he moved to Mexico City. On January 27, 1971, he was found drowned in his bathtub from uncertain causes. Arbenz's death, like his life, remains an enigma.

Further Reading

There is no biography of Arbenz, but studies of the CIA operation in Guatemala contain valuable information concerning his life and presidency. These include Blanche Wiesen Cook, *The Declassified Eisenhower: A Divided Legacy of Peace and Political Warfare* (1981); Stephen Schlesinger and Stephen Kinzer, *Bitter Fruit: The Untold Story of the American Coup in Guatemala* (1982); Richard Immerman, *The CIA in Guatemala: The Foreign Policy of Intervention* (1982); and Jose Aybar de Soto, *Dependency and Intervention: The Case Study of Guatemala* (1982).

Earlier works tend to be more critical of Arbenz, and they too should be consulted: Ronald Schneider, *Communism in Guatemala, 1944-1954* (1958); Nathan Whetten, *Guatemala: The Land and the People* (1961); Mario Rosenthal, *Guatemala* (1962); Chester Lloyd Jones, *Guatemala Past and Present* (1966); and Richard Newbold Adams, *Crucifixion by Power: Essays on Guatemalan Social Structure, 1944-1966* (1970). □

Diane Nemerov Arbus

The American photographer Diane Nemerov Arbus (1923-1971) specialized in photographs of nontraditional subjects, including gays, the physically challenged, circus performers, and nudists.

Diane Arbus was born Diane Nemerov on March 14, 1923. The daughter of a wealthy New York businessman (the family owned Russeks department store on Fifth Avenue), Arbus led a pampered childhood. Being a member of a prominent New York family, she grew up with a strong sense of what was "acceptable" and what was "prohibited" in polite society. Her world was a protected one in which she never felt adversity, yet it seemed to her to be an unreal world. Ludicrous as it may seem, the sense of being "immune" from hardship was painful for her. An extremely shy child, Arbus was often fearful but told no one of her fantasies. Her closest relationship was with her older brother, Howard.

From the seventh through the twelfth grade Arbus attended Fieldstone School in the Riverdale section of the Bronx, a part of the Ethical Culture educational system. Here she became interested in myths, ritual, and public spectacle, ideas which would later inform her photography. At Fieldstone she also devoted much time and energy to art class—painting, sketching, and working in clay. During this period of her life Arbus and several of her friends began exploring New York on their own, getting off the subway in unfamiliar areas of Brooklyn or the Bronx, observing and following interesting or unusual passersby.

At the age of 14 Diane met Allan Arbus, a 19-year-old City College student who was employed in the art department at Russeks. It was love at first sight. Her parents disapproved, but this only served to heighten Diane's resolve to marry him as soon as she came of age. In many ways, Allan represented an escape from all that was restricting and oppressive in her family life. They were married in a rabbi's chambers on April 10, 1941, with only their immediate families present.

Early Career as Fashion Photographer

To ease financial pressures, Allan supplemented his job at Russeks by working as a salesman and also by doing some fashion photography. Arbus became his assistant. During World War II when Allan was sent to a photography school near Fort Monmouth, New Jersey, Arbus moved to nearby Red Bank and set up a darkroom in their bathroom. Allan taught her everything he was learning at the school. In May

of 1944 Allan was transferred to another photography school, this time in Astoria, Queens. Then, late in 1944, he was sent to Burma. By this time Diane was pregnant with their first child, Doon, who was born April 3, 1945.

During the 1940s Arbus studied briefly under photographer Berenice Abbott. After Allan's discharge from the army, husband and wife teamed up as fashion photographers, working for Russeks and Bonwit Teller. Their first magazine assignment appeared in the May 1947 issue of *Glamour* and marked the beginning of a long association with Condé Nast publishing firm. Their trademark was to shoot models in action. Yet the Arbuses despised the shallowness of the fashion industry. Her real joy during this period was photographing friends and relatives; often she wore her camera around her neck at family meals.

On April 16, 1954, Arbus gave birth to her second daughter, Army. In addition to her fashion work with Allan, she photographed children—strangers in Spanish Harlem, the offspring of close friends, and, of course, Doon and Amy. Throughout the 1950s she also found herself increasingly attracted to nontraditional subjects, people on the fringes of normal society. This provided a release from the oppression she felt in the fashion world. During these years she also suffered from recurring bouts of depression.

In 1957 the couple decided to make a change. He continued to run their fashion studio, freeing her to photograph subjects of her own choice. She briefly attended Alexey Brodovitch's workshop at the New School and, on her own, made a detailed study of the history of photography. But Arbus found herself most drawn to the photographs of her contemporaries Louis Faurer and Robert Frank and, especially, to the unusual images of Lisette Model. In 1958 Arbus enrolled in a class Model was offering at the New School.

It was during this period of work with Model that Arbus decided what she really wanted to photograph was "the forbidden." She saw her camera as a sort of license that allowed her to be curious and to explore the lives of others. Gradually overcoming her shyness, she enjoyed going where she never had, entering the lives and homes of others and confronting that which had been off-limits in her own protected childhood.

Career with a "Candid Camera"

Model taught her to be specific, that close scrutiny of reality produces something fantastic. An early project Arbus undertook involved photographing what she referred to as "freaks." She responded to them with a mixture of shame and awe. She always identified with her subjects in a personal way. Model once referred to Arbus' "specific subject matter" as "freaks, homosexuals, lesbians, cripples, sick people, dying people, dead people." Instead of looking away from such people, as does most of the public, Arbus looked directly at these individuals, treating them seriously and humanely. As a result, her work was always original and unique.

When Arbus and her husband separated in 1960, her work became increasingly independent. During that period she began her series of circus images, photographing midget clowns, tattooed men, and sideshow subjects. She fre-quented Hubert's Freak Museum at Broadway and 42nd Street, fascinated by what she saw. She returned again and again until her subjects knew and trusted her. She also frequented the Times Square area, getting to know the bag ladies and derelicts.

Arbus posed her subjects looking directly into the cam-era, just as she looked directly at them. She said, "I don't like to arrange things; I arrange myself." For her, the subject was always more important than the picture. She firmly believed that there were things which nobody would see unless she photographed them. Arbus created photo essays of these subjects which she sold to magazines such as *Esquire, Harper's Bazaar,* and *Infinity.*

In the early 1960s Arbus began to photograph another group, nudists. She frequented nudist camps in New Jersey and Pennsylvania, agreeing to go naked herself in order to gain her subjects' trust. This period, 1962 to 1964, was a particularly productive one for her. Among Arbus' many accomplishments during this time was winning her first Guggenheim fellowship, which allowed her to photograph "American rites and customs, contests, festivals. . . . "

Three of Arbus' pictures were included in John Szarkowski's 1965 show at the Museum of Modern Art (MOMA), "Recent Acquisitions"—one of two female im-personators back stage and two from her series on nudists. Viewers were shocked and often repelled by these frank images. A few years later her work was included, along with that of Garry Winogrand and Lee Friedlander, in Szarkowski's "New Documents" exhibition at the MOMA. The show, which opened March 6, 1967, marked the pinna-cle of Arbus' career and included some 30 examples of her work. One critic called her "the wizard of odds." Another asserted that she catered "to the peeping Tom in all of us."

From 1966 on Arbus struggled with bouts of hepatitis which often left her weak and depressed. Then, in 1969, Allan Arbus formally divorced her, marrying Mariclare Costello; soon after, they moved to California. During this difficult period Arbus photographed many of the leading figures of the 1960s: F. Lee Bailey, Jacqueline Susann, Coretta Scott King. She also did some lecturing at Cooper Union, Parsons, and Rhode Island School of Design in addition to giving a master class at Westbeth, the artists' community in which she lived.

Arbus committed suicide in her New York apartment on July 26, 1971. Perhaps the words of her longtime friend, photographer Richard Avedon, provide the most fitting epi-thet: "Nothing about her life, her photographs, or her death was accidental or ordinary." Her unique vision, her per-sonal style, and the range of her subject matter provided a seminal influence in 20th-century photography.

Further Reading

The standard work on Arbus' photography is the Aperture mono-graph *Diane Arbus* (1972). Patricia Bosworth's *Diane Arbus, a Biography* (1984) provides a good overview of the photogra-pher's life. In addition, *Magazine Work* (1984), edited by Doon Arbus and Marvin Israel, includes both Arbus' own words and essays by those closest to her. Arbus is also in-cluded in Anne Tucker's *The Woman's Eye* (1973) and is the subject of numerous magazine and newspaper critiques. ☐

Archimedes

The work done by Archimedes (ca. 287-212 B.C.), a Greek mathematician, was wide ranging, some of it leading to what has become integral calculus. He is considered one of the greatest mathematicians of all time.

Archimedes probably was born in the seaport city of Syracuse, a Greek colony on the island of Sicily. He was the son of an astronomer, Phidias, and may have been related to Hieron, King of Syracuse, and his son Gelon. Archimedes studied in Alexandria at the school established by Euclid and then settled in his native city.

To the Greeks of this time, mathematics was consid-ered one of the fine arts—something without practical ap-plication but pleasing to the intellect and to be enjoyed by those with the requisite talent and leisure. Archimedes did not record the many mechanical inventions he made at the request of King Hieron or simply for his own amusement, presumably because he considered them of little impor-tance compared with his purely mathematical work. These inventions did, however, make him famous during his life.

Fact and Fancy

The many stories that are told of Archimedes are the prototype of the absentminded-professor stories. A famous one tells how Archimedes uncovered a fraud attempted on Hieron. The King ordered a golden crown and gave the goldsmith the exact amount of gold needed. The goldsmith delivered a crown of the required weight, but Hieron sus-pected that some silver had been used instead of gold. He asked Archimedes to consider the matter. Once Archimedes was pondering it while he was getting into a bathtub full of water. He noticed that the amount of water overflowing the tub was proportional to the amount of his body that was being immersed. This gave him an idea for solving the problem of the crown, and he was so elated he ran naked through the streets repeatedly shouting "*Heurēka, heurēka!*" (I have discovered it!)

There are several ways Archimedes may have deter-mined the proportion of silver in the crown. One likely method relies on a proposition which Archimedes later wrote in a treatise, *On Floating Bodies,* and which is equiva-lent to what is now called Archimedes' principle: a body immersed in a fluid is buoyed up by a force equal to the weight of fluid displaced by the body. Using this method, he would have first taken two equal weights of gold and silver and compared their weights when immersed in water. Next he would have compared the weight of the crown and an equal weight of pure silver in water in the same way. The difference between these two comparisons would indicate that the crown was not pure gold.

On another occasion Archimedes told Hieron that with a given force he could move any given weight. Archimedes had investigated properties of the lever and pulley, and it is on the basis of these that he is said to have asserted, "Give me a place to stand and I can move the earth." Hieron, amazed at this, asked for some physical demonstration. In the harbor was a new ship which the combined strength of all the Syracusans could not launch. Archimedes used a mechanical device that enabled him, standing some distance away, to move the ship. The device may have been a simple compound pulley or a machine in which a cogwheel with oblique teeth moves on a cylindrical helix turned by a handle.

Hieron saw that Archimedes had a most inventive mind in such practical matters as constructing mechanical aids. At this time one use for such inventions was in the military field. Hieron persuaded Archimedes to construct machines for possible use in warfare, both defensive and offensive.

A Time of War

Plutarch in his biography of the Roman general Marcellus describes the following incident. After the death of Hieron, Marcellus attacked Syracuse by land and sea. Now the instruments of warfare made at Hieron's request were put to use. "The Syracusans were struck dumb with fear, thinking that nothing would avail against such violence and power. But Archimedes began to work his engines and hurled against the land forces all sorts of missiles and huge masses of stones, which came down with incredible noise and speed; nothing at all could ward off their weight, but

they knocked down in heaps those who stood in the way and threw the ranks into disorder. Furthermore, beams were suddenly thrown over the ships from the walls, and some of the ships were sent to the bottom by means of weights fixed to the beams and plunging down from above; others were drawn up by iron claws, or crane-like beaks, attached to the prow and were plunged down on their sterns, or were twisted round and turned about by means of ropes within the city, and dashed against the cliffs. . . . Often there was the fearful sight of a ship lifted out of the sea into mid-air and whirled about as it hung there, until the men had been thrown out and shot in all directions, when it would fall empty upon the walls or slip from the grip that had held it."

Later writers tell how Archimedes set the Roman ships on fire by focusing an arrangement of concave mirrors on them he basic idea is that the mirror reflects to one point all the sun's light entering parallel to the mirror axis.

Marcellus, according to Plutarch, gave up trying to take the city by force and relied on a siege. The city surrendered after 8 months. Marcellus gave orders that the Syracusan citizens were not to be killed, taken as slaves, or mistreated. But some Roman soldier did kill Archimedes. There are different accounts of his death. One version is that Archimedes, now 75 years old, was alone and so absorbed in examining a diagram that he was unaware of the capture of the city. A soldier ordered him to go to Marcellus, but Archimedes would not leave until he had worked out his problem to the end. The soldier was so enraged, he killed Archimedes. Another version is that Archimedes was bringing Marcellus a box of his mathematical instruments, such as sundials, spheres, and angles adjusted to the apparent size of the sun, when he was killed by soldiers who thought he was carrying valuables in the box. "What is, however, agreed," Plutarch says, "is that Marcellus was distressed, and turned away from the slayer as from a polluted person, and sought out the relatives of Archimedes to do them honor."

Archimedes had requested his relatives to place upon his tomb a drawing of a sphere inscribed within a cylinder with a notation giving the ratio of the volume of the cylinder to that of the sphere—an indication of what Archimedes considered to be his greatest achievement. The Roman statesman and writer Cicero tells of finding this tomb much later in a state of neglect.

Other Inventions

Perhaps while in Egypt, Archimedes invented the water screw, a machine for raising water to irrigate fields. Another invention was a miniature planetarium, a sphere whose motion imitated that of the earth, sun, moon, and the five other planets then known (Saturn, Jupiter, Mars, Venus, and Mercury); the model may have been kept in motion by a flow of water. Cicero tells of seeing it over a century later and claimed that it actually represented the periods of the moon and the apparent motion of the sun with such accuracy that it would, over a short period, show the eclipses of the sun and moon. Since astronomy was a branch of mathematics in Archimedes' time, he undoubtedly considered this and his other astronomical inventions much more important than those which could be put to practical use.

Archimedes is said to have made observations of the solstices to determine the length of the year and to have discovered the distances of the planets. In *The sand Reckoner* he describes a simple device for measuring the angle subtended by the sun at an observer's eye.

Contributions to Mathematics

Euclid's *Elements* had catalogued practically all the results of Greek geometry up to Archimedes' time. Archimedes adopted Euclid's uniform and rigorously logical form: axioms followed by theorems and their proofs. But the problems Archimedes set himself and his solutions were on another level from any that preceded him.

In geometry Archimedes continued the work in Book XII of Euclid's *Elements*. In Book XII the method of exhaustion, discovered by Eudoxus, is used to prove theorems on areas of circles and volumes of spheres, pyramids, and cones. Two of the theorems are mentioned by Archimedes in the preface to *On the Sphere and Cylinder*. After stating the result concerning the ratio of the volumes of a cylinder and an inscribed sphere, he says that this result can be put side by side with his previous investigations and with those theorems of Eudoxus on solids, namely: the volume of a pyramid is one-third the volume of a prism with the same base and height; and the volume of a cone is one-third the volume of a cylinder with the same base and height.

There was no direct computation of areas and volumes enclosed by various curved lines and surfaces, but rather a comparison of these with each other or with the areas and volumes enclosed by rectilinear figures such as rectangles and prisms. The reason for this is that the area, for a simple example, of a circle with radius of length one cannot be expressed exactly by any fraction or integer. It is possible, however, to say as is done in Proposition 2 of Book XII of the *Elements* that the ratio of the area of one circle to another is exactly equal to the ratio of the squares of their diameters, or, in a more concise form closer to the Greek, circles are to one another as the squares of the diameters. The proof of this theorem relies on (theoretically) being able to "exhaust" the circle by inscribing in it successively polygons whose sides increase in number and hence which fit closer to the circle. Thus the curved line, the circle, can be closely approximated by a rectilinear figure, a polygon.

Recognizing this, it would be easy to conclude that the circle itself is a polygon with "infinitely" many "infinitesimal" sides. Even by Euclid's time this concept had a long history of philosophic controversy beginning with the well-known Zeno's paradoxes discussed by Aristotle. Archimedes, aware of the logical problems involved in making such a facile statement, avoids it and proceeds in his proofs in an invulnerable manner. However, a student with a knowledge of integral calculus today would find Archimedes' method very cumbersome. It should nevertheless be remembered that the theorems which make the work almost trivial to any modern mathematician were obtained only in the 17th, 18th, and 19th centuries, about 2000 years after Archimedes.

In modern terminology, the area of a circle with radius of length one is the irrational number denoted by π, and although Archimedes knew it could not be calculated exactly, he knew how to approximate it as closely as desired. In his treatise *Measurement of a Circle,* using the method of exhaustion, Archimedes proves that π is between 3 1/7 and 3 10/71 (it is actually 3.14159).

Large numbers seem to have some fascination of their own. A common Greek proverb was to the effect that the quantity of sand eludes number, that is, is infinite. To the Greeks this might seem especially true since their numeral system did not include a zero. Numbers were represented by letters of the alphabet, and for large numbers this notation becomes clumsy. In *The Sand Reckoner* Archimedes refutes the idea expressed by the proverb by inventing a notation which enables him to calculate in a reasonably concise way the number of grains of sand required to fill the "universe." He takes the universe to be the size of a sphere centered at the earth and having as radius the distance from the earth to the sun. After saying this he also points out an alternative view of the universe that had been expressed by a contemporary astronomer, Aristarchus of Samos, namely, that the sun is fixed, the earth revolves about the sun, and the stars are fixed a long distance beyond the earth. Astronomical data, together with the assumption that there are no more than 10,000 grains of sand in a volume the size of a poppyseed, are the basis of calculations leading up to the conclusion that the number of grains of sand which could be contained in a sphere the size of the universe is less than 10^{51}, in modern notation.

Other known works by Archimedes that are purely geometrical are *On Conoids and Spheroids, On Spirals,* and *Quadrature of the Parabola.* The first is concerned with volumes of segments of such figures as the hyperboloid of revolution. The second describes what is now known as Archimedes' spiral and contains area computations. The third is on finding areas of segments of the parabola.

Another of Archimedes' works in mechanics, besides *On Floating Bodies* mentioned previously, is *On the Equilibrium of Planes.* From such simple postulates as "Equal weights at equal distances balance," positions of centers of gravity are determined for parabolic segments.

As is true of all other mathematicians of antiquity, Archimedes usually wrote in a way which left no indication of how he arrived at the theorems; all the reader sees is a theorem followed by a proof. But in 1906 a hitherto-lost treatise by Archimedes, *The Method,* was found. In it Archimedes explains a certain method by which it is possible to get a start in investigating some of the problems in mathematics by means of mechanics. "For," Archimedes writes, "certain things first became clear to me by a mechanical method, although they had to be demonstrated by geometry afterwards because their investigation by the said method did not furnish an actual demonstration." Thus Archimedes is careful to distinguish between a heuristic approach to verifying a theorem and the proof of the theorem. *The Method* utilizes theorems from his mechanical treatise *On the Equilibrium of Planes* and provides an excellent example of the interplay between pure and applied mathematics.

Further Reading

The standard English translation of Archimedes is Thomas L. Health, ed., *The Works of Archimedes* (1897), which includes a supplement, *The Method of Archimedes* (1912). For biographical information see E. J. Dijksterhuis, *Archimedes* (1938; trans. 1956). Archimedes' place in the development of integral calculus is described in Carl B. Boyer, *The History of the Calculus and Its Conceptual Development* (1949). Works on mathematics for the general reader are Thomas L. Heath, *A Manual of Greek Mathematics* (1931); Bartel L. van der Waerden, *Science Awakening* (1950; trans. 1954); and James R. Newman, ed., *The World of Mathematics* (4 vols., 1956). See also Robert S. Brumbaugh, *Ancient Greek Gadgets and Machines* (1966). □

Alexander Archipenko

The Russian-American sculptor and teacher Alexander Archipenko (1887-1964) was an innovator in translating the elements of cubist painting into sculptural form.

Alexander Archipenko was born in the Ukrainian city of Kiev. His father was professor of engineering at the University of Kiev, and his grandfather painted murals for churches. From 1902 to 1905 young Archipenko studied at the art school in his hometown. He was expelled for his rebellious nature: he had criticized his instructors for being too conservative. After working and exhibiting in Moscow for 2 years, he left for Paris at the age of 20 and entered the École des Beaux-Arts. Archipenko stayed there for only 2 weeks, as he found it more profitable to work on his own and to learn from other artists. He set up a studio near Fernand Léger's and through him came to know Pablo Picasso and Georges Braque. Archipenko shared with them an enthusiasm for primitive art, and from them he learned about cubism.

By 1909 Archipenko began to realize his cubist style. This first phase of his development displays no indecision or immaturity. His *Black Seated Torso* (1909) is a fine example of this period. During the next 3 years his style became fully developed, so much so that all his later sculpture tended to be variations of the forms of this period.

Archipenko favored the human female figure, but only as a convention. He interpreted it freely in abstract forms that featured convex and concave characteristics. From the beginning he liked to fuse mass and space in lyrical, rhythmic interplay so as to suggest movement. It has been said that he was influenced by the Italian futurists, notably Umberto Boccioni, whom he knew, but this seems unlikely because Archipenko never adopted the aggressively strident rhythms of the Italians.

In 1912 Archipenko made a number of figures inspired by the circus, his *Médrano* series. These assemblages of various materials such as wood, wire, glass, and mirror are in a quasi-cubist manner. They led to his "sculpto-paintings," in which he combined relief and polychromy. In these and other works he continued to open up voids within the solid mass of the figure, and he also juxtaposed arabesques against a static, frontal plane.

Archipenko received recognition early in his career, especially in Germany. He had his first one-man show at the Hagen Museum in Berlin in 1912. By 1953 he had been given exactly 100 one-man shows.

Archipenko's career as a teacher also began early. In 1912 he established an art school in Paris and soon opened a branch in Berlin. In 1923 he moved to the United States and became an American citizen. He founded the École d'Art in New York City and opened a summer art school in Woodstock, N.Y. He also taught at the Institute of Design in Chicago and numerous American universities. In 1962 he was elected to the National Institute of Arts and Letters.

It is generally agreed that Archipenko did his best work between 1910 and 1920. He was so dexterous that much of his sculpture appears facile. This is particularly true of his later work, in which he often appears to be straining for novelty and effect. For instance, in 1924 he started using motors to cause parts of the sculpture to move; he called this genre "Archipentura." His later sculpture is more complicated and decorative, and he seems to have been distracted by superficialities such as color. Archipenko revealed the extent of his virtuosity when, in the mid-1920s, he executed busts of Fritz Wickerts and Wilhelm Furtwängler in a somewhat naturalistic manner in order to capture a likeness. Archipenko continued work up to the time of his death in New York City on Feb. 2, 1964.

Further Reading

The only recent work on Archipenko is *Archipenko: Fifty Creative Years, 1908-1958* (1960). It contains an autobiographical sketch and essays and statements by 50 art historians. For background, plates, and commentary see C. Giedion-Welcker, *Contemporary Sculpture: An Evolution in Volume and Space* (1955; rev. ed. 1961), and Michel Seuphor, *The Sculpture of This Century* (trans. 1960).

Additional Sources

Nagy, Ildiako., *Archipenko,* Budapest: Corvina, 1980. ☐

Elizabeth Arden

Elizabeth Arden (ca.1878-1966) was instrumental in the development of the modern cosmetics and beauty salon industry. She was also an astute businesswoman.

The 30 years of prosperity that followed the bitter depression of 1893 to 1897 set Americans on the road to the "affluent society" and swept away the old ideas of behavior that had ruled the Victorian age. Particularly notable was the greater freedom achieved by women, who entered the world of daily affairs and began to pay increasing attention to their personal appearance. No one capitalized more effectively on these fundamental trends than Elizabeth Arden, whose dictum to American women—"hold fast to youth and beauty"—helped to create the modern cosmetics and beauty salon industry and made her the sole owner of a $60 million business.

Arden was born Florence Nightingale Graham in 1878 (?) in Woodbridge, a suburb of Toronto, Ontario, Canada, to immigrant parents, her father Scottish and her mother English. Growing up in poverty, she was not able to finish high school but instead drifted from one job to another. In 1908 she moved to New York, where her brother lived. Her entree into the beauty salon business was fortuitous: she took a clerical job in a shop that specialized in "facials," facial massage aided by simple oils and creams and embodying virtually no cosmetic applications. Although Graham was 30 by then, she looked 20 for she was blessed with a smooth, cream complexion. This was her only qualification for taking up the "art of the healing hands," but it was all she needed.

Within a year she and a friend had opened their own shop on Fifth Avenue, a boulevard that was already exchanging its staid mansions in favor of upperclass shops and department stores. Soon she was the sole proprietress, doing business under the name of Elizabeth Arden: Elizabeth, because that was her former partner's name and she saw no reason to scrap its gold leaf lettering on the plate glass window, and Arden from the Tennyson poem, *Enoch Arden.* The new Elizabeth Arden added what became her trademark—a huge red door with a brass name-plate—and a new industry was born.

Cosmetics were still not accepted for "nice" girls in America as the Edwardian era came to a close, but in Paris "*la belle époque*" was ending in a burst of social permissiveness. Ignoring World War I, which had just broken out, and braving the submarine menace to cross the Atlantic, Arden went to France in 1914 and was entranced by what she saw: rouge, lipstick, and mascara which, when applied with skill, produced remarkable effects and were being widely adopted. She came back from Europe with many new ideas for her growing chain of salons and hired chemists to compound smooth, fluffy facial creams and a high-style line of cosmetics that were snapped up at premium prices through her shops.

A course of treatments at Elizabeth Arden's was not cheap, but it did not produce much net profit for the stores, either; some consistently operated at a loss as salons. But as outlets for her constantly expanding line of cosmetics, Arden's shops were very profitable. Innovation, in the classic entrepreneurial style, was her secret of success. Lipsticks came in wider and wider ranges of colors and shades to match a woman's coloring, hair, or costume. Face creams, usually based on petroleum ingredients, had been oily and unpleasant, but Arden's Amoretta was fluffy and luxurious; anything that felt that good had to be good for your skin. Inevitable, the cosmetics line demanded wider distribution, and eventually leading department stores everywhere could not afford to be without it.

Arden's first husband, like most of her other interests, was connected with the business. In 1915 she married her banker, Thomas Jenkins Lewis, who took over management of the cosmetics lines. The partnership flourished but the marriage did not, and they were divorced in 1934. Prince Michael Evlanoff, a Russian émigré, brought little but glamour to her second marriage, and that soon wore thin; they were divorced in 1944, and Arden never married again. Yearning to be accepted by New York society, she achieved it through friendship with Elizabeth Marbury, of an old New York family, and Marbury's ally in the world of high culture, Elsie De Wolfe. The lavish charity balls that they helped with were highly successful, but it is likely that her prominence as a sportswoman was even more important.

Horse racing became Arden's passion, and, true to form, she made money at it at least some of the time. She established Maine Chance Stables (named for her former country home, which she had turned into a health resort), and in 1945 her horses' winnings totaled $589,000. The best was yet to come: in 1946 she appeared on the cover of *TIME* magazine—looking 40 but actually closer to 70—and the next year her horse, Jet Pilot, won the Kentucky Derby.

In business or at play, Arden was all business. Like the true entrepreneur she was, she knew just what she wanted and usually got it. Never losing the outward appearance of the woman who lived for beauty and refinement, she held her own in a violently competitive industry where her closest competitor, Helena Rubinstein ("that woman," she called her), possessed many of the same traits and racked up much the same success. But when it came to letting go, Arden could not, even as she neared 90. At her death on October 18, 1966, she had made no provisions for the disposition of the business in a manner that would minimize the inheritance taxes, and she was still the sole owner. A $4 million bonus to longtime employees; another $4 million to her sister, Gladys, who had managed the Paris branch; and a large bequest to the niece who had been her companion produced taxes that could be paid only by selling the company. It disappeared into the corporate maw of Eli Lilly and Company, but whatever it was that Florence Graham had brought to Elizabeth Arden, the new owners could not supply it and the name declined markedly in the hurly burly world of beauty care products.

Further Reading

Women in business are now getting more attention, along with women's history generally. Arden is included in *Notable American Women—the Modern Period* (1980) and is scheduled for inclusion in the *Dictionary of American Biography,* Supplement Eight. The book *Miss Elizabeth Arden* (1972), by Alfred Allan Lewis and Constance Woodworth, is readable, if not definitive. The best study of Arden is an article in the *New Yorker* magazine, April 6, 1935, "I Am a Famous Woman in This Industry." See also the *TIME* cover story, May 6, 1946. □

Hannah Arendt

A Jewish refugee from Hitler, Hannah Arendt (1906-1975) analyzed major issues of the 20th century and produced a brilliant and original political philosophy.

Hannah Arendt was born in 1906 in Hanover, Germany, the only child of middle-class Jewish parents of Russian descent. A precocious child whose father died in 1913, she was encouraged by her mother in intellectual and academic pursuits. As a university student in Germany (1924-1929) she studied with the finest and most original scholars of that time: with Rudolf Bultmann in New Testament and Martin Heidegger in philosophy at Marburg, with the phenomenologist Edmund Husserl at Freiburg, and with the existentialist Karl Jaspers at Heidelberg. She remained close friends with Heidegger and Jaspers throughout her life.

After receiving her Ph.D. and marrying Gunther Stern, both in 1929, she worked on a biography of Rahel Varnhagen, a noted 19th-century hostess, which analyzed Varnhagen's relationship to her Jewish heritage. In 1933 Arendt was arrested and briefly imprisoned by the Gestapo for gathering evidence of Nazi anti-Semitism. She fled to France where she worked for Jewish refugee organizations until 1940 when she and her second husband, Heinrich Blücher, were interned in southern France. They escaped and made their way to New York in 1941.

Throughout the war years Arendt wrote a political column for the Jewish weekly *Aufbau* and began publishing articles in leading Jewish journals. As her circle of friends expanded to include leading American intellectuals, her writings found a wider audience. Her first major book, *The Origins of Totalitarianism* (1951), argued that modern totalitarianism was a new and distinct form of government which used ideology and terror to control the mass society that

emerged as European nation-states were undermined by anti-Semitism, racism, and imperialism. As the first major effort to analyze the historical conditions that had given rise to Hitler and Stalin, *Origins* was highly acclaimed and widely studied in the 1950s.

Labor, Work, and Action

A second major work, *The Human Condition* (1958), followed. Here and in a companion volume of essays, *Between Past and Future* (1961), Arendt gave explicit and systematic treatment to themes which had been present in her earlier work and which were to characterize all her mature writings. First was the radical character of the modern situation. In the face of unprecedented problems such as totalitarianism, mass society, automation, the possibility of travels through space, and the eclipse of public life, humans were no longer able to find solutions in established traditions of political authority, philosophy, religion, or even common sense. Her solution was as radical as the problem: "to think what we are doing."

In *The Human Condition* Arendt rethinks the *vita activa,* the three fundamental human activities of labor, work, and action, and their relationships. These activities were properly arranged, she argued, only when they were seen in relationship to the distinction between the public and the private. In her view the public provided the space of appearances among humans which speech and action required, and the private protected labor, the interaction of humans with nature and their bodies, from public view. When this distinction breaks down, as it has in modern times, mass society results in which neither true individuality nor true common action is possible.

The Human Condition also developed two other major themes of her work, freedom and worldliness. She was fond of quoting St. Augustine (on whose doctrine of love she wrote her doctoral dissertation): "That there be a beginning, man was created before whom there was nobody." Freedom, or this human capacity for new beginnings, was the "lost treasure" bequeathed by no testament or tradition, rediscovered in every revolution, and radically threatened by mass society and totalitarianism.

The world, comprised of all fabricated things from houses to works of art, Arendt saw as providing a specifically human habitation which protected us and our creations from the ravaging processes of nature. Since this world existed before and continued after the appearance of each individual in it, it offered the possibility of a worldly immortality such that the character and achievements of humans could be remembered after they pass from the world. Here her thought had its most radically secular character. Action, the highest and most worldly human capacity, found worldly rather than divine solutions for its predicaments. Thus she quoted with approval Machiavelli's maxim to "love our country more than the safety of our soul."

The Human Condition established Arendt's academic reputation and led to a visiting appointment at Princeton— the first woman full professor there. Her Princeton lectures became *On Revolution* (1963), a volume which expressed her enthusiasm at becoming an American citizen by exploring the historical background and institutional requirements of political freedom.

The Banality of Evil

In 1961 she attended the trial in Jerusalem of Adolf Eichmann, a Nazi functionary who had been involved in the murder of large numbers of Jews during the Holocaust. Her reports, which appeared first in *The New Yorker* and then as *Eichmann in Jerusalem* (1964), were frequently misunderstood and rejected, especially her claim that Eichmann was more bureaucratic and banal rather than radically evil. Her public reputation among even some former friends never recovered from this controversy.

At the University of Chicago (1963-1967) and the New School for Social Research in New York City (1967-1975) her brilliant lectures and affectionate concern inspired countless students in social thought, philosophy, religious studies, and history. Frequently ill-at-ease in public, she was an energetic conversationalist in smaller gatherings. Even among friends, though, she might sometimes excuse herself and become totally absorbed in some new line of thought that had occurred to her. Playful in the company of men, after the death of her husband in 1970 she attracted marriage proposals from W. H. Auden and Hans Morgenthau.

During the later 1960s she devoted herself to a variety of projects: essays on current political issues (the Pentagon Papers, violence, civil disobedience) published as *Crises of the Republic* (1972); portraits of men and women who offered some illumination even in the dark times of the 20th century, which became *Men in Dark Times* (1968); and a two-volume English edition of Karl Jaspers' *The Great Philosophers* (1962 and 1966).

In 1973 and 1974 she delivered the prestigious Gifford Lectures in Scotland, which were subsequently published as *The Life of the Mind* (1979). Conceived as a volume on the contemplative life parallel to *The Human Condition* on the active life, it too was intended to focus on three human capacities: thinking, willing, and judging. While all three were independent of the active life, the political role of each was also examined, from the role of thinking in opposing evil to the ability of judging to measure the achievements and failures of our public life. Only the first two topics were actually addressed in the lectures she delivered; she died of a heart attack in New York City on December 4, 1975, as she was beginning work on the third. Fortunately, earlier lectures on Kant's *Critique of Judgment* suggested what her approach to judging would have been, and these were published posthumously as *Lectures in Kant's Political Philosophy* (1982).

Honored throughout her later life by a series of academic prizes, frequently attacked for controversial and eccentric judgments, Hannah Arendt died as she lived—a brilliant and original interpreter of human capacities and prospects in the face of modern political disasters.

Further Reading

The definitive biography of Arendt is Elizabeth Young–Bruehl, *For Love of the World* (1982). It includes a comprehensive bibliography. Arendt's political thinking is summarized in

Margaret Canovan, *The Political Thought of Hannah Arendt* (1974). Essays by Arendt on Jewish questions, Zionism, and the Eichmann controversy can be found in Ron H. Feldman, editor, *Hannah Arendt: The Jew as Pariah* (1978).

Several volumes of essays on Arendt have appeared. Melvyn A. Hill, editor, *The Recovery of the Public World* (1979) includes a a response by Arendt, and both *Social Research* (Spring 1977) and *Salmagundi* (Spring-Summer 1983) devoted issues to her. Her teaching style and its effect on students is described by Peter Stern and Jean Yarbrough in *American Scholar* (Summer 1978) and Melvyn A. Hill in *The University of Chicago Magazine* (Spring 1976). Of the many obituaries which appeared following Arendt's death, those in the *New York Review of Books* (January 22 and May 13, 1976) by Mary McCarthy and Robert Lowell are especially revealing.

Additional Sources

Barnouw, Dagmar., *Visible spaces: Hannah Arendt and the German-Jewish experience,* Baltimore: Johns Hopkins University Press, 1990.

May, Derwent, *Hannah Arendt,* Harmondsworth, Middlesex, England; New York, N.Y., U.S.A.: Penguin Books, 1986. □

Moshe Arens

Moshe Arens (born 1925) was an aeronautical engineer who became a leading Israeli statesman, serving as ambassador, minister without portfolio, and defense minister.

Moshe Arens was born in December 1925 in Kovno (Kaunas), Lithuania. His mother was a dentist and his father a businessman. In 1939 he immigrated with his family to the United States where he graduated from high school in New York City and served in the United States Army Corps of Engineers during World War II. He secured a B.S. degree from the Massachusetts Institute of Technology but went to Israel at the outbreak of its 1948 war of independence and served in the Irgun Zvai Leumi under the overall leadership led by Menachem Begin. After the war he settled in Mevo Betar but returned to the United States in 1951 to study at the California Institute of Technology where he received an M.A. degree in aeronautical engineering in 1953. He then worked for a number of years on jet engine development in the aviation industry in the United States.

In 1957 Arens returned to Israel and took a position as an associate professor of aeronautical engineering at the Technion (Israel Institute of Technology) in Haifa. He joined Israel Aircraft Industries in 1962, where he became vice president for engineering, while continuing his relationship with the Technion. He was involved in the design of airplanes and the development of missiles and won the Israel Defense Prize in 1971. He was active in Herut Party politics from the outset and was elected to the Knesset (parliament) in 1974. After the Likud election victory of 1977 he became chairman of the Knesset Foreign Affairs and Defense Committee. He voted against the Camp David Accords in 1978, but subsequently supported the Egypt-Israel Peace Treaty of 1979 as an established fact.

Arens was appointed ambassador to Washington in February where he was well regarded and gained substantial respect. He was seen as cool and articulate and was known for his reliance on detail and logic; he thought and calculated as an engineer. He listened to positions, contemplated them carefully, and provided thoughtful responses. He had close links and a long association with the United States and was among Israel's senior politicians who knew and understood the United States well. He spoke both Hebrew and English with an American accent and tended to speak English in a rapid-fire, somewhat professorial tone.

He regarded the West Bank (Judea and Samaria) as an integral part of Israel in keeping with the views of Vladimir Jabotinsky and Menachem Begin: these territories are historically part of Israel, and they serve a security purpose.

In many respects Arens was an ideological hawk and sought the maximum for Israel, but he often proposed and sought to implement practical/pragmatic policies as a means of achieving his objectives. In 1983 he became defense minister after Ariel Sharon resigned the post following the Kahan Commission's investigation into the massacres at the Sabra and Shatilla refugee camps outside Beirut. As minister of defense Arens established a series of operating principles. Reflecting a lack of experience in the Israeli Defense Forces (IDF), he permitted the generals to do the fighting while he concentrated his efforts on support and policy. His experience was in defense-related industry, and he supported the military during his political career.

Arens' early opposition to the peace treaty with Egypt in 1979 was based on the extent of Israel's concessions. He thought Israel should have tried to retain its two sophisticated air bases in Sinai so new ones would not have to be built. He remarked in February 1982 that Israel "should have tried for a better deal. It almost seems like madness to spend a billion dollars to build a mirror image of the two air bases, six or seven miles to the east of where they are at the present time." He also thought that the settlers in the Yamit area should have been allowed to stay. Furthermore, Egypt should have agreed to sell Israel oil from the Alma oilfields, which Israel discovered, at below market prices instead of the high spot market price.

Although sometimes seen as a potential successor to Prime Minister Yitzhak Shamir, Arens did not always see himself in that role. He expressed preference for airplane design rather than politics. In 1982, just prior to becoming ambassador to Washington, he was quoted as saying: "I'm not crazy about it i.e., politics!. It's difficult, frustrating, much of it quite boring, though it has interesting aspects to it. I don't have driving political ambition to become Prime Minister of Israel."

During the 1980s and early 1990s Arens served in government positions as Minister without Portfolio (1983-1984 and 1988), Minister of Foreign Affairs (1988-1990) and again as Minister of Defense (1990-1992). In 1992 he quit politics after Likud's defeat at the ballot box. With 18 years of government service Arens claimed that he had no plans to return in any official capacity. "We let younger people take charge," he said.

After his retirement from active political life Arens wrote *Broken Covenant: American Foreign Policy and the Crisis between the U.S. and Israel* (1994). He also served on the Board of Governors of the Technion in Haifa, where he was once a professor, and was a deputy director for the investment firm, Israel Corporation Ltd. In an interview with Michael Kapel (*The Australia/Israel Review*, March-April 1997) Arens demonstrated sharp political savvy and insight. Describing Arens lifelong contributions to the Israel government Kapel said, "Arens has indelibly left his mark on the nation and many within Israel's cabinet still seek his influence and guidance even today."

Further Reading

Merrill Simon's *Moshe Arens: Statesman and Scientist Speaks Out* (1988) provides a lengthy collection of statements by Arens and serves as an invaluable guide to his views. The interested reader should also consult more general works on Israeli society and politics. These include: Bernard Reich, *Israel: Land of Tradition and Conflict* (1985); Asher Arian, *Politics in Israel: The Second Generation* (Revised edition, 1989); and Bernard Reich and Gershon R. Kieval, *Israeli National Security Policy: Political Actors and Perspectives* (1988). A major problem at home that had international implications was discussed in Ze'ev Schiff and Ehud Ya'an, *Intifada: The Palestine Uprising—Israel's Third Front* (1990). Interviews with the Israel statesman can be found in publications such as *The Australia/Israel Reviw* and the *Jewish Bulletin of Northern California*. □

Juan José Arévalo

The administration of the Guatemalan president Juan José Arévalo (1904-1990) was marked by significant social welfare legislation, Communist infiltration of labor unions, and friction with the United States.

Juan José Arévalo was born Sept. 10, 1904, in Taxisco to Mariano Arévalo, a farmer and cattle rancher, and Elena Bermejo, a schoolteacher. His early schooling was in Guatemala City; later he won an Argentine government scholarship to study at the University of La Plata, where he earned a doctorate in philosophy in 1934. While in Argentina he married Elisa Martinez, a teacher. After obtaining his degree he became a minor official in the Guatemalan ministry of education, traveled in Europe, and eventually returned to Argentina, where he taught in several universities and wrote books on pedagogy.

When a revolution in 1944 toppled President Jorge Ubico, Arévalo returned to Guatemala and became a presidential candidate for the revolutionary parties. Although Arévalo had gained an international reputation through his writings, he was relatively unknown in Guatemala; thus there were few personal objections. This, together with his civilian, middle-class rural background, professional reputation, youthfulness, and imposing appearance, made his candidacy more acceptable. He overwhelmingly won the election of December 1944.

Beginnings of Reform

A new constitution went into effect on March 13, 1945, and Arévalo's six-year term began two days later. The new president's policy was what he called "spiritual socialism," an ill-defined doctrine of psychological and moral liberation. He was not a "materialistic socialist"; he did not think that man was "primarily stomach." His socialism did not involve redistribution of material goods to equalize men who were economically different. He wanted to give every citizen not only the superficial right to vote but "the fundamental right of living in peace with his own conscience, with his family, with his goods, with his destiny."

During the first years of Arévalo's administration, legislation included a social security law, a labor code, and the Institute for the Development of Production as well as statutes regulating banking and monetary practices and the national airlines. During the latter half of the term, political difficulties caused by disunity within ranks of Arévalo supporters and the presidential ambitions of Col. Francisco Javier Arana, chief of the armed forces, plagued the government. Throughout his presidency Arévalo's attitude toward communism was ambiguous. Some leading Guatemalan Communists were kept out of the country and the party was

background and presidency appear in K.H. Silvert, *A Study in Government: Guatemala* (1954); Robert J. Alexander, *Communism in Latin America* (1957); and Ronald M. Schneider, *Communism in Guatemala: 1944-1954* (1958). See also Gleijeses, Piero, *Shattered Hope: The Guatemalan Revolution and the United States, 1944-54* (Princeton University Press, 1991); Handy, Jim, *Revolution in the Countryside: Rural Conflict and Agrarian Reform in Guatemala, 1944-54* (North Carolina, 1994); *Journal of Latin American Studies: Juan Jose Arévalo and the Caribbean Legion* by Piero Gleijeses (February 1989); and Nyrop, Richard F., ed., *Guatemala: A Country Study* (Federal Research Division, 1983). □

Arnulfo Arias

Arnulfo Arias (1901-1988), thrice elected president of Panama and thrice removed before the end of his term, was an outspoken and popular political figure in his country from the 1930s through the mid-1980s.

Arnulfo Arias was born in Penonomé, Coclé Province, Colombia, August 15, 1901, more than two years before the American-backed revolt made Panama an independent country in November 1903. He went to high school in Binghamton, New York, and then attended the University of Chicago and Harvard University which awarded him a medical degree. After interning at Boston City Hospital, he returned to Panama in 1925.

The Arias family is one of several Panamanian middle-class families prominent in isthmian politics. In the 1930s Arnulfo entered into politics. He criticized the old Panamanian political establishment for being too agreeable to the United States, especially on matters related to the Panama Canal. In 1936, when Arnulfo was representing Panama in various diplomatic posts in Europe, his brother, Harmodio, president of Panama since 1932, negotiated a new canal treaty with the United States. This treaty did not replace the hated 1903 canal arrangement, but at least Panama obtained greater benefits in the Canal Zone. In 1940, after the new treaty was approved, Arnulfo became president of Panama.

Arnulfo took power just as the American military began pressing for greater territorial concessions from Panama to build defense installations to protect the Panama Canal. As a price for these concessions, Arnulfo demanded greater economic concessions from the United States. He championed the Spanish language and excited a generation of *panameños* with his nationalistic rhetoric. Irritated by this outburst of criticism, the U.S. government resisted Arias' demands. In Washington, American officials accused him of being pro-German, but in truth Arias (like Omar Torrijos several decades later) was really expressing the longstanding resistance by Panamanians against American domination of their country. After Arias was tossed out by a palace revolt in October 1941 the United States quickly obtained the defense sites agreement it wanted.

not allowed to register as an official political organization, but Communist infiltration of labor unions and of other political parties was significant. Arévalo's relations with the United States were strained, both because he refused to persecute Communist sympathizers and because his attempts at labor reform interfered with huge American fruit-growing interests in Guatemala. His support for exiled leaders from Caribbean dictatorships was also viewed with suspicion by the State Department.

Diplomat and Author

Leaving office in 1951, Arévalo became an ambassador at large, traveling in Latin America and Europe. After the revolution of 1954, which ousted President Jacobo Arbenz Guzmán, Arévalo went into exile and wrote books extremely critical of United States policy in Latin America. Prior to the scheduled 1963 presidential election, Arévalo announced his intention to run and clandestinely returned to Guatemala, but after the army revolution removing President Miguel Ydigoras Fuentes, he quietly left the country; the election was postponed. While still in exile Arévalo was appointed ambassador to Chile in January 1969. From 1970 to 1972 he served as ambassador to France.

Arévalo died in Guatemala City on October 6, 1990.

Further Reading

Two of Arévalo's books criticizing United States policy in Latin America have been translated into English: *Antikommunism* (sic) *in Latin America* (1959; trans. 1963) and *The Shark and the Sardines* (1961; trans. 1961). Brief accounts of Arévalo's

In 1948 Arias ran again, was elected, but had to wait 18 months before taking power. But once more he so frightened the old families and the national guard with his prolabor policies and anti-American rhetoric that the military kicked him out.

In 1964 Arias ran for a third time, in the months after a bloody confrontation between Americans and Panamanians in January 1964. But once again he was deprived of power by an apparent electoral fraud that gave the executive power in Panama to Marco Robles. Four years later Arnulfo, now aged noticeable but still a vigorous campaigner, ran again. He won a disproportionate victory, but less than two weeks after his inaugural on October 1, 1968, the national guard, under Omar Torrijos, kicked him out.

Arias went to Miami and waited until 1977 to return to Panama. Torrijos was still in power but the Panamanian economy was in trouble. Arias came back to Panama City to a tumultuous welcome from 100,000 enthusiastic followers. Though an old man, he had lost none of his hold on the Panamanian people. "It's the fourth coming," said one of his supporters. True to form, Arias criticized the economic situation, Torrijos and the "cult of personality," and especially the new canal treaties Torrijos signed with the Jimmy Carter administration in Washington.

Torrijos held on to power until his death in a helicopter crash in 1981, but Arias showed that he still had a powerful appeal to the ordinary Panamanians. Age had not mellowed him. He still criticized his followers. "The Panamanian people are like oxen," he once said, "you have to keep

prodding them with a stick to keep them moving." On another occasion he said, "Panama is like a village, what it needs is a mayor, not a president."

In 1984, at 82 and nearly blind, Arias ran yet another time for Panamanian president and narrowly lost to Nicolas Ardito Barleta. Many *panameños* still remembered that Arias made Spanish the official language of Panama and gave women the vote in his first term in 1940-1941. Yet he remained a vigorous anti-communist. It probably did not matter that he lost, some of his supporters said, because the national guard would probably have kicked him out had he won. Arias died in 1988.

Further Reading

For more on Arnulfo Arias consult John and Mavis Biesanz, *The People of Panama* (1955); Walter LeFeber, *The Panama Canal* (1978); and David Farnsworth and James W. McKenney, *U.S.-Panama Relations 1903-1978* (1983). ☐

Oscar Arias Sanchez

Oscar Arias Sanchez (born 1941) was a Costa Rican politician, social activist, his nation's youngest president, and Nobel Peace Laureate (1987). A man of even temperament, Arias worked tirelessly to maintain peace both in Costa Rica and in the wider arena of Central America.

Oscar Arias Sanchez, president of Costa Rica 1986-1990, was born in the rural town of Heredia, not far from the national capital of San José, on September 13, 1941. For several generations his family had been heavily involved in politics and had often served in the national legislature and on several presidential cabinets. The Arias clan were also prominent coffee producers.

Arias was educated in private schools in Heredia and traveled extensively before studying law and economics at the University of Costa Rica. While attending classes there, he became dedicated to national politics, early becoming an active member of the PLN (*Partido de Liberación Nacional,* or National Liberation Party), whose "Grand Old Man" was charismatic ex-President José ("Pepe") Figueres. Through his association with the PLN Arias became devoted to the twin goals of social equity and antimilitarism (Costa Rica had abolished its armed forces under Figueres in the 1940s).

Arias worked feverishly in the unsuccessful presidential campaign of the PLN's Daniel Oduber, gaining insight into political realities, and when he graduated with his bachelor's degree in 1966, he determined to continue his studies abroad. For the next three years he studied in England at the University of Essex and the London School of Economics, where his graduate thesis (published in 1971) had the provocative title *¿Quien gobierna en Costa Rica?* (*Who Governs Costa Rica?*). This work was virtually a sequel to a book published in 1970, after his return to his native country;

Grupos de presión en Costa Rica (*Pressure Groups in Costa Rica*). Hence, by the age of 30, Arias had an unusual set of credentials: he was a highly-educated, extremely well-traveled, published political thinker and activist. He was on the fast-track within the PLN.

Teaching political science at the University of Costa Rica, Arias was offered—and accepted—the crucial post of minister of national planning and political economy on the cabinet of Pepe Figueres, again president. He distinguished himself in his new position and became known for fair-mindedness and for attempting to de-ideologize social tensions in his nation. He held that cabinet post from 1972 to 1976, and also rose to a position of major power within the PLN itself, being named its international secretary in 1975, and later, in 1979, its head of party, or general secretary. He was also a family man, having married (in 1973) Vassar-trained biochemist Margarita Peñón Góngora and fathering a son (Oscar Felipe) and a daughter (Silvia Eugenia).

From 1978 to 1981 he served in the national legislature, where he became known for legislation making the government more accessible and responsive to the common people, leaving that position to help lead the successful campaign of PLN standard-bearer Luis A. Monge, elected president in 1982. Two years later Arias relinquished his duties as PLN general secretary to devote all of his energies to his own presidential campaign. His slogan was "Roofs, jobs, and peace," at a time when the national economy was in stark recession and Central America was badly torn by the insurgencies in Nicaragua and El Salvador. He gained his party's nomination easily, but the election was a close one,

and when he took the oath of office on May 8, 1986, he did so on the strength of 52.3 percent plurality; hardly a landslide or overwhelming mandate.

As president, Arias did his best to realize goals outlined in his earlier books, most notably in *Costa Rica in the Year 2000* (1977), in which he foresaw a more equitable distribution of wealth, more justice and better earnings for farmers and urban workers, a more open "accessible" government, and a true rule of law for all. He acted as he had written, as a non-radical, non-ideological populist.

It was in the realm of foreign affairs, however, that President Arias made his greatest impact. He successfully kept Costa Rica neutral in the threatening Central American upheaval. While he had little sympathy for the undemocratic Marxist Sandinistas in Nicaragua, he successfully resisted pressures from the Costa Rican right wing and Washington to aid and abet the anti-Communist Contra guerrillas. He also refused steadfastly to re-arm his nation, believing that diplomacy was the best answer. To that end he collaborated fruitfully with the governments of the region, met with their leaders, and was a major force in the Contadora Peace Plan first broached in 1986. The following year he produced his own ten-point peace plan, a plan that was applauded (in a nonbinding resolution) in the United States Senate (March 1987) with but one dissenting vote. It was agreed to and signed by all five Central American chief executives on August 7, 1987. The plan stressed withdrawal of all foreign elements from the insurgencies, total amnesty, cessation of hostilities, and democratization (free elections) as well as absolute recognition of national sovereignty.

Although the plan agreed to and signed did not result in immediate peace, it showed President Arias as a genuine international statesman, and the nobility of its ten points convinced the Nobel Prize Committee to award the 1987 Peace Prize to the Costa Rican.

Constitutionally unable to succeed himself, Arias relinquished power in April 1990 to opposition candidate Rafael A. Calderón, announcing that he planned to accept a visiting professorship at Harvard and to write on international affairs and crisis resolution. Following his presidency, Arias pursued these goals through a wide range of initiatives.

The Arias Foundation maintained three programs. The Center for Human Progress was created in 1990, with the objective of eliminating gender discrimination within the Central American Population. The Center for Peace and Reconciliation, also founded in 1990, was founded with the objective of promoting pluralistic participation in building peace in Central America. The Center promoted development in three program areas: demilitarization, conflict prevention and democratization. The Center for Organized Participation was founded in 1993, in collaboration with the Mott Foundation, the Kellogg Foundation and other international donors. Its mission was to strengthen citizen participation in Central America.

Arias was also active in the Carter Center in Atlanta, Georgia. This nonprofit, nonpartisan public policy institute was founded by former U.S. President Jimmy Carter and his wife, Rosalynn, in 1982, and Arias was active in two of the center's 13 programs. The International Negotiation Network (INN) of the Carter Center was an international eminent person's group that included former heads of state and other prominent people who individually or collectively were capable of bringing parties to a conflict together, could serve as mediators in peace negotiations, monitor elections or conduct behind-the-scenes diplomacy. The INN included many distinguished members in addition to Carter and Arias, including: former president Olusegun Obasanjo of Nigeria, Lisbet Palme, Swedish Committee for UNICEF; Shridath Ramphal, former secretary-general of the Commonwealth of Nations; Marie-Angelique Savane, Office of the U.N. High Commissioner for Refugees; Eduard Shevardnadze, former Soviet foreign minister; Archbishop Desmond Tutu of South Africa; former Secretary of State Cyrus Vance; Nobel Peace Prize winner Elie Wiesel, and Andrew Young, former U.S. ambassador to the United Nations.

Arias was also a member of the Carter Center's Council of Freely Elected Heads of Government, a group of 26 current and former heads of government in the Western Hemisphere. The Council mediated and monitored voting, including elections in Panama, Nicaragua, Haiti, Suriname, The Dominican Republic, Guyana, Paraguay and Mexico.

Arias was a member of the Gorbachev Foundation, a think tank founded in 1992 by former Soviet leader Mikhail Gorbachev and located in San Francisco's Presidio National Park. In 1995, the first major forum of the Foundation included not only world leaders, but also scientist Carl Sagan, singer John Denver, and economist Milton Friedman.

The Inter-American Dialogue was an independent organization that sought to foster inter-American relations and which was closely tied to the administration of U.S. President Bill Clinton. The Dialogue's 1994 report, *The Americas in 1994: A Time for Leadership,* was endorsed by six former presidents, including Arias.

Arias also served on the Advisory Council of Transparency International, an independent nonprofit organization based in Berlin, seeking to counter corruption in international commercial transactions and, through its more than 60 national chapters, at national levels.

PeaceJam, an international outreach program, worked with youth in developing the skills of peacemakers. The program offered resources for teachers to guide students in structuring service projects in their communities or in participating in existing global peace projects that exemplified the values of the Nobel Peace Laureates. In 1997, in Amherst, Massachusetts, Arias spoke to high school students in the PeaceJam program. He told the students that at that moment PeaceJam member Aung San Suu Kyi of Burma was being held prisoner by the military for the crime of speaking out for democracy, free speech, and nonviolent protest. Arias said, "My friends, we must not forget that education and free speech are rare-known privileges in many parts of the world." In a 1995 interview with PeaceJam correspondents Dawn Engle and Ivan Suvanjieff at his residence in Costa Rica, Arias was asked what one thing he would say to all the young people of the world. His reply was, "I think the most important thing for the future generations is to understand that it is necessary to have ideals, to dream, to live a

life of principles. It is necessary to understand that the brotherhood is more important than the self. It is necessary to comprehend that the problems of a neighbor in some way affect us too. It is necessary to live in a transparent, crystal-like world where everyone practices what they preach, to end hyprocrisy and to have the courage to fight for what you believe in. I would say don't give in to the naysayers, not to give up one's dreams of bettering the world. Understand that by fighting for the impossible, one begins to make it possible. In that way, no matter how difficult the task is, one will never give up. And it doesn't matter if they call us dreamers, idealists. I always said I would rather be Don Quixote than to be Pancho. Understand that the idealists of today will be the leaders of tomorrow. And we can't stop dreaming."

Further Reading

A work by Oscar Arias published by the Woodrow Wilson International Center for Scholars is *The Quest for World Leadership* (1992). Published material about Arias in English includes Seth Rolbein, *Nobel Costa Rica: A Timely Report on Our Peaceful Pro-Yankee, Central American Neighbor* (1988); Kelli Peduzzi, *Oscar Arias: Peacemaker and Leader Among Nations (People Who Have Helped the World)* (1991); and Kelli Peduzzi, *Oscar Arias, Peacemaker (People Who Made a Difference)* (1993). Publications are available through the Carter Center in Atlanta, Georgia, describing the programs in which Arias was active. See indexes of the *New York Times, Miami Herald,* and *Latin America Regional Reports.* See also the Nobel Prize press release (1987). □

Ludovico Ariosto

The Italian Ludovico Ariosto (1474-1533) was the greatest narrative poet of the Italian Renaissance. His richly human masterpiece, "Orlando furioso," adds a native bent for narration to an exquisitely polished octave stanza.

L udovico Ariosto was born at Reggio Emilia: when he was 14, the family moved to Ferrara, where his father, Niccolò, was in service at the ducal court of the Este family. Five years later his father consented to Ludovico's abandonment of law studies in favor of literature. Ariosto was first employed at court in 1498; 2 years later his father died, leaving him to provide for nine younger brothers and sisters. In 1503 he entered the service of Cardinal Ippolito d'Este, who sponsored performances of Ariosto's neoclassical comedies, *Cassaria* in 1508 and *I suppositi* in 1509. His later comedies are the unfinished *I studenti* (1518-1519), *Il negromante* (1521), and the most successful of them, *La Lena,* performed under his direction in 1529.

In 1513 Ariosto met the beautiful Alessandra Benucci, whom he married secretly in 1527 to avoid the loss of Church benefices. In 1518 he entered the service of the cardinal's brother, Duke Alfonso d'Este. Except for a 3-year period when he governed the bandit-ridden Garfagnana region for the duke, Ariosto was allowed more time for writing than he had been by Cardinal Ippolito. His *Satire* (*Satires*) treat ironically his problems in Ferrara, where the Este brothers failed to recognize his worth, in the Garfagnana, and on missions to the papal court.

Ariosto's *Orlando furioso,* a continuation of Boiardo's *Orlando innamorato,* went through three redactions, or versions (1516, 1521, and 1532). It is a romantic, comicepic retelling of the story of Roland (Orlando), the medieval French hero. Among a myriad of episodes about dauntless knights and enchanting women, the three main narrative threads are the Saracens' siege of Paris and their final rout; the insanity of Orlando, who was driven mad by unrequited love for Angelica, Princess of Cathay; and the love of the warrior woman Bradamante for Ruggiero. The progressive loss of reason by Orlando as he drifts from foreboding dream to hallucination to total madness is finely drawn. Ariosto's wise and realistic portrayal of human nature in all its intricacies in so fantastic a world—which includes even a moon journey—is a remarkable feat of poetry. By no means an outright parody, his poem exalts many values of the world of chivalry, such as love and fidelity. It influenced Cervantes, Spenser, and Shakespeare. Ariosto died in 1533 after completing the last version of his great narrative poem.

Further Reading

An excellent, free-ranging verse translation of Ariosto's masterpiece, *Orlando furioso,* was published in 1591 by the Elizabethan author Sir John Harington (repr. 1963). Later translations include those of Temple Henry Croker in 1755 and William

Stewart Rose in 1825. The recent prose translation by Allan Gilbert (2 vols., 1954) includes his informative appreciation of the poem. The work's unique place in Italian Renaissance narrative poetry is ably discussed by Francesco de Sanctis in *History of Italian Literature* (2 vols., 1870; new ed. 1914; trans. 1931) and by Ernest Hatch Wilkins in *A History of Italian Literature* (1954). See also Edmund G. Gardner, *The King of Court Poets: A Study of the Work, Life and Times of Ludovico Ariosto* (1906; repr. 1968), and Benedetto Croce, *Ariosto, Shakespeare and Corneille* (1920; trans. 1920).

Additional Sources

Ascoli, Albert Russell, *Ariosto's bitter harmony: crisis and evasion in the Italian Renaissance,* Princeton, N.J.: Princeton University Press, 1987.

Griffin, Robert, *Ludovico Ariost,* New York, Twayne Publishers 1974.

Marinelli, Peter V., *Ariosto and Boiardo: the origins of Orlando furioso,* Columbia: University of Missouri Press, 1987. □

Aristarchus of Samos

The Greek astronomer Aristarchus of Samos (ca. 310-230 B.C.) hypothesized that the earth revolves yearly about the sun and daily rotates about its own axis. He attempted to determine the relative sizes and distances of the sun, moon, and earth.

Born on the island of Samos, Aristarchus studied at Athens in the Lyceum under Straton of Lampsacus, who was the head of the Peripatetic school from 288/287 to 270/269 B.C.

Heliocentric System

Though Aristarchus is known to have written on problems of vision, light, and color, his primary work was in astronomy, specifically on the interrelations of the sun, moon, and earth. With respect to their relative positions he pointed out that, mathematically, one can imagine the earth rotating about the sun as easily as the sun about the earth; all that is required is a vastly increased radius of the sphere of the fixed stars and the daily rotation of the earth about its own axis rather than the rotation of the sphere of the fixed stars. Though all serious astronomers in antiquity and the Middle Ages would have realized the mathematical equivalence of the geocentric and heliocentric hypotheses (and many do refer to it), arguments from physics compelled them to accept geocentricity, as Aristarchus himself does in his sole surviving book. Only with the abandonment of Aristotelian physics could the heliocentric hypothesis attain credibility.

Following many predecessors in the 6th to 4th century (Cleostratus, Meton, Eudoxus, and Callippus), Aristarchus tried to fix a "Great Year"—a period in which integer numbers of days, solar years, and the various kinds of months would occur exactly. His Great Year of 2,434 solar years contains 45 exeligmi, and each exeligmus contains three periods in which the period-relation holds: 223

synodic months = 239 anomalistic months = 242 draconic months. Neither the exeligmus nor its third (both Babylonian period-relations) contains an integer number of years, though the exeligmus has an integer number of days. The 45 exeligmi of Aristarchus's Great Year are based on the following period-relations: 30,105 synodic months = 32,265 anomalistic months = 32,670 draconic months = 32,539 sidereal months = 889,020 days = 2,434 solar years.

Relative Sizes of the Sun and Moon

In his treatise *On the Sizes and Distances of the Sun and Moon,* using Euclid's laws of proportions, Aristarchus seeks to define the limits of the ratios of the sizes and distances of the sun, moon, and earth to each other. He uses the situation of a lunar eclipse, assuming that the diameters of the sun and moon are each 2° and the diameter of the disk of the cone of the earth's shadow at the distance of the moon is 4°; thus he uses a diameter of both sun and moon that is about four times what it should be (in another lost work he gave a more correct value of 0:30°) and ignores the variation in the distance and apparent diameter of the moon.

He arrives at the conclusions that the distance of the sun from the earth is between 18 and 20 times that of the moon from the earth, that the diameter of the sun is between 19/3 and 43/6 times the diameter of the earth and the diameter of the earth between 108/43 and 60/19 times the diameter of the moon, and that the diameter of the moon is between 1/30 and 2/45 of the distance of the moon from the earth. Though these results are not correct, their limitations are largely imposed by the state of the mathematics available to Aristarchus, though the erroneous estimate of the moon's diameter contributes. The method was more fully developed and fruitfully applied by Hipparchus a century later.

Influence of Aristarchus

Aristarchus is often called the "Copernicus of antiquity." In a sense this is true, though the identification need not be taken as being in praise of either man. Both realized, as did many others, that a heliocentric system is equivalent to a geocentric system as far as the observed celestial phenomena are concerned; and both were willing, as others were not, to propound this mathematical hypothesis without reference to current theories of physics, and in particular to the laws of motion. Aristarchus wrote when Aristotelian physics and Platonic cosmology were both gaining acceptance and there was no one willing, or perhaps able, to construct an adequate alternative theory embodying his cosmology.

Copernicus was followed by many who questioned and eventually, with the help of new instruments and improved observational methods, disproved Aristotelian physics. The failure of Aristarchus and the success of Copernicus had less to do with their individual merits than with the intellectual milieu in which their views were expounded. In any case, Aristarchus's attempt to measure solar and lunar distance had a far greater influence on his successors than did his heliocentric theory.

Further Reading

The standard work on Aristarchus is Sir Thomas L. Heath, *Aristarchus of Samos, the Ancient Copernicus* (1913; reprinted, 1981). A chapter on Aristarchus appears in J.L.E. Dreyer, *A History of Astronomy: From Thales to Kepler* (1905; rev. ed. 1953). Discussions of his life and work appear in George Sarton's scholarly *A History of Science: Hellenistic Science and Culture in the Last Three Centuries B.C.* (1959) and in Benjamin Farrington's popularly written *Greek Science: Its Meaning for Us* (1949; rev. ed. 1961). See also Marshall Claggett, *Greek Science in Antiquity* (1955), and Giorgio de Santillana, *The Origins of Scientific Thought: From Anaximander to Proclus, 600 B.C. to 300 A.D.* (1961). □

Jean-Bertrand Aristide

The Reverend Jean-Bertrand Aristide (born 1953) was elected president of Haiti by a landslide in 1990 but then was deposed by a military coup in 1991. A radical populist, acclaimed by the masses and feared by Haiti's power elite, he remained in exile until 1994 when a U.S. military occupation of Haiti restored him to power.

Jean-Bertrand Aristide was born on July 15, 1953, in Douyon, a small town along Haiti's southern arm. Orphaned as an infant, he was raised by priests of the Society of St. Francis de Sales of the Roman Catholic Church. The Salesian Order, with European and American houses and members, focused in Haiti on the spiritual instruction of poor and orphaned children. As a dependent of the Salesians, Aristide received his early education in their parochial schools and later attended their seminary in Haiti and the University of Haiti. He was sent to Israel, Egypt, Britain, and Canada for biblical and other learning.

Aristide was ordained a priest in 1982. He also earned a graduate degree in psychology at the University of Montreal. He learned to read and speak French, Spanish, English, Hebrew, Italian, German, and Portuguese in addition to his native Creole. Aristide wrote poetry and composed hymns on his guitar.

In 1988 Aristide was expelled from the Salesian order for preaching too politically and for what Aristide called his "fidelity to the poor." He had been warned by the Vatican and by his local bishop to preach less radically and to cease inflaming his parishioners against the Haitian state. From his ordination, Aristide had condemned Haiti's absence of democracy, arguing from his pulpit in the Church of St. Jean Bosco in the poorest part of Port-au-Prince that only a spiritual and political cleansing could save the country.

For all but the first five years of Aristide's life, Haiti had been ruled by the harsh family dictatorship of Francois (Papa Doc) Duvalier and by Jean-Paul (Baby Doc) Duvalier, his son. Human rights violations were legion. Ordinary Haitians were ceaselessly intimidated by paramilitary thugs known as the tonton macoutes. The ruling family and the

state were synonymous and preyed viciously on the people. Corruption was rife.

Aristide's antagonism to the dictatorship grew out of his religious convictions and his empathy with the sufferings of the Haitian people. He may have foreseen that the Duvalier dictatorship was crumbling; after months of popular protest, some of which was stimulated by Aristide's preachings, in early 1986 Baby Doc and his entourage fled Haiti for France.

The military juntas that succeeded Baby Doc also oppressed the poor. The regimes of both General Prosper Avril and Lieutenant General Henri Namphy were criticized from Aristide's pulpit. In retaliation, the tonton macoutes attacked the Church of St. Jean Bosco, killing 13 members of Aristide's congregation in 1988, two weeks before he was expelled from the Salesian order. The Roman Catholic Church ordered Aristide to Rome. But that "transfer" resulted in one of the largest street demonstrations in Haitian history, with tens of thousands of Haitians angrily blocking Aristide's departure by air.

Aristide had not been defrocked, despite his expulsion from the order. After 1988 he continued to work with the desperately poor of Port-au-Prince by running a halfway house for street children and by opening a medical clinic.

When the United Nations, the United States, and the Organization of American States finally persuaded the military men of Haiti to hold elections, Aristide was neither an early nor an expected candidate. The front runner was Marc Bazin, an experienced international civil servant, but there

were many other well-known men of substance, as well as a leader of the macoutes, who also tendered their candidacies.

The character of the race for the presidency changed dramatically, however, when Aristide decided to run, only a few months before the poll in December 1990. His act was widely regarded as quixotic and sacrificial. But his messianic pledges of redemptive justice for victims of dictatorship and violence struck a responsive chord among the poor, nearly all of whom would be voting for the first time in the nation's only full and free election. He also spoke harshly against the United States, both as a supporter of the Duvaliers and as an exploitative force in the world.

A slight, wispy person, Aristide overwhelmingly vanquished his electoral foes. He won 67 percent of the popular vote, but his Lavalas (Avalanche) Party, which had had little time to organize, took only a comparatively small percentage of the seats in the Haitian parliament. Before Aristide was ousted by military men led by General Raoul Cedras on September 30, 1991, the new president had alarmed the commercial and old-line ruling classes of Haiti by preaching violence against macoutes and leading purges of persons suspected of being secret Duvalierists. His constructive accomplishments in office had been few, particularly since his hold on parliament had been ineffectual.

In the immediate aftermath of the coup the United States, the Organization of American States, and the United Nations embargoed Haitian exports and attempted to bar petroleum and other imports. But those efforts were only partially successful, and the masses suffered from economic sanctions much more than the military junta.

All three groups attempted to broker a settlement between Aristide, living first in Venezuela and later in the United States, and Cedras and his accomplices. Several agreements unraveled when Aristide changed his mind; others fell apart because the military leaders were endlessly suspicious of Aristide's real intentions.

In mid-1993 the Clinton administration and the United Nations persuaded Aristide and Cedras to meet near New York and to conclude an agreement that would return Aristide to the Haitian presidency for the final 27 months of his single, non-renewable term and provide an amnesty for the military. But Haiti's power elite refused to implement the agreement. President Clinton had over 23,000 U.S. troops sent to Haiti in what was termed "Restore Democracy." The task of this military mission was to ensure the safe and successful transition to reinstate Aristide to power. On December 17, 1995, the Haitian presidential election took place and Rene Preval was elected to succeed Aristide.

Further Reading

For a sense of what Haiti was like during Aristide's formative years, read Amy Wilentz, *The Rainy Season: Haiti Since Duvalier* (1989). Amy Wilentz also translated and edited Aristide's writings as *In the Parish of the Poor* (1990). Aristide's own *Autobiography* was translated from the French by Linda M. Maloney (1990). Aristide in exile is described by Catherine Manegold in "Innocent Abroad: Jean-Bertrand Aristide" in the *New York Times Magazine* (May 1, 1994). For

Papa Doc and before, see Robert I. Rotberg, *Haiti: The Politics of Squalor* (1971). Only sketchy journalism describes the brief period of Aristide's ascendancy. □

Aristophanes

Aristophanes (c. 450-after 385 B.C.) was the greatest of the writers of the Old Comedy, which flourished in Athens in the 5th century B.C., and the only one with any complete plays surviving. He wrote at least 36 comedies, of which 11 are extant.

The Old Comedy was a form of drama which has no parallel in subsequent European literature. It was a mixture of fantasy, political and personal satire, knockabout farce, obscenity (probably of ritual origin), and, in the case of Aristophanes at least, delightful lyric poetry. It paid little attention to consistency of time or place or character and was not very interested in the logical development of a dramatic plot. This art Aristophanes practiced with superb skill. He brought to it a command of every kind of comedy, from slapstick to intellectual farce. In dialogue passages he wrote colloquial Attic Greek with splendid clarity and vigor, but he could also write beautiful lyric poetry as well, and he was a parodist of the highest class. He had a devastating way of deflating pomposity in politics, social life, and literature, but above all he had an inexhaustible fund of comic invention and sheer high spirits.

His Life

Knowledge of Aristophanes is confined almost entirely to his career as a dramatist. He was born in Athens between 450 and 445 B.C. into a family of which little is known except that they were not poor. He had an excellent education and was well versed in literature, especially poetry, and above all Homer and the great Athenian tragic dramatists. In addition, he was well acquainted with the latest philosophical theories. He has often been regarded as conservative in his outlook, especially in politics, and he was certainly well aware of the absurdities of some of the new developments of his day. But in many ways he was just as much a product of the new intellectual movement of the second half of the 5th century B.C. as was the tragic poet Euripides; this truth was not missed by his older contemporary and rival in comic drama, Cratinus, who coined the verb "to Euripidaristophanize."

All of Aristophanes's boyhood was spent in the Periclean Age, that interlude of peace between 445 and 431, when Athens was one of the two leading political powers in Greece and also the most important center of artistic and intellectual activity. When the Peloponnesian War broke out in 431, Aristophanes was still a youth. What part he played in the war is not known, but he probably saw some active service before it finally ended in 404. He lived for nearly 20 years after the war and died after 388. One of his three sons, Araros, was a minor comic dramatist.

His Plays

Aristophanes's career as a dramatist started in 427, when he put on a play, now lost, called *The Banqueters*. A year later he brought out another play which has not survived, *The Babylonians*, which had a political theme and expressed some outspoken criticism of Athens's imperial policies. As a result, Cleon, the most influential politician of the day, hauled the author before the Council, apparently on a charge of treason, but no action was taken against Aristophanes. In 425 he produced the earliest of the extant plays, *The Acharnians;* the hero, tired of the war, makes a private peace with the enemy, which brings him into conflict first with the chorus of patriotic Acharnian charcoal burners and later with a swashbuckling soldier.

The following year came *The Knights,* a violent and abusive but often very funny attack on Cleon, who is represented as the greedy and dishonest slave of a dimwitted old gentleman, Demos (the Athenian people personified); the slave is his master's favorite until displaced by an even more vulgar and unscrupulous character, a sausage seller. At the time Cleon was at the height of his influence and popularity, and it says much for the tolerance of the Athenians that even in wartime the play could be produced and, moreover, awarded first prize in the competition for comedies.

In 423 Aristophanes turned from politics to education with *The Clouds,* in which a dishonest old farmer tries to obtain from Socrates an education of the new sophistic type in an attempt to avoid paying his debts. Aristophanes himself thought highly of the play, but it was a failure. A few years later, after 420, he revised it, but the text that has survived is an incomplete revision that could not be performed as it stands. For this reason the play is not entirely satisfactory, but the comic inventiveness of several scenes and the interest of the portrayal of Socrates have always made it very popular. It has sometimes been described as an attack on Socrates, but the sympathetic picture of Aristophanes in Plato's *Symposium* suggests that the dramatist continued to be on quite good terms thereafter with Socrates and his associates.

In 422 Aristophanes produced *The Wasps,* an amusing and good-natured satire on the fondness of the Athenians for litigation. A year later he greeted the prospect of peace between Athens and its enemies with *Peace,* a rapturous and sometimes very bawdy celebration of the delights of peacetime existence in the Attic countryside.

During the 6 years of uneasy truce which followed the conclusion of peace in 421, Aristophanes presumably continued to write plays, but none of them has survived. The next extant play was *The Birds,* produced in 414, soon after the war had begun again with the great Athenian expedition to Sicily. This splendid drama, one of Aristophanes's most poetic and exuberant creations, deals with the adventures of two Athenians who migrate to Birdland; they persuade the birds to found a new city in the skies, Cloudcuckoobury, and then to blockade Olympus till the gods are forced to hand over their power to the birds.

Political unrest in Athens and intrigues in the winter of 412-411 resulted in an oligarchic revolution in May 411. Shortly before this Aristophanes had produced a conspiracy of his own: in *Lysistrata* he depicted the women of Greece banding together to stop the war by refusing to sleep with their husbands until they have made peace. With such a plot the play is inevitably bawdy, and much of the humor is forced, as if Aristophanes did not find it easy to jest in such depressing times. However, Lysistrata herself is one of his most attractive characters, and his sympathy for the plight of women in wartime makes the play a moving comment on the folly of war.

Another of the extant plays, *The Thesmophoriazousai* (Women Celebrating the Thesmophoria, which was a women's festival in honor of Demeter), is also usually dated to 411, but it may equally belong to the following year when the war situation was temporarily brighter for Athens. This lighthearted comedy deals with Euripides, who, faced with a supposed threat by the Athenian women to destroy him, sends an elderly relative in female disguise to speak on his behalf. When his champion is detected, Euripides attempts to rescue him from the police in a series of clever and hilarious parodies of scenes in the plays of the actual Euripides.

After 410 the Peloponnesian War situation gradually worsened, and in the winter of 407-406 Euripides died in Macedonia, to be followed in less than a year by his great rival Sophocles. Aristophanes clearly felt that the great days of tragedy were over, and in *The Frogs,* produced in 405, he showed Dionysus, the patron god of Attic drama, going down to Hades to bring Euripides back. When after many ludicrous adventures the god finally arrives in the

Underworld, he acts as referee in a long poetic dispute between Euripides and Aeschylus, which contains much delightful comedy but also some serious criticism. The play was given the unprecedented honor of a second performance.

Just over a year later the long war finally ended, when the Athenians were starved into surrender in the spring of 404. This calamitous defeat broke something in the spirit of the Athenians, and though they soon regained considerable importance both in politics and in intellectual matters, they were never quite the same again. In the sphere of comedy the uninhibited boisterousness of the Old Comedy disappeared, and it was replaced by a more cautious and reasonable form which points toward the more refined but less fantastic and spirited comedy of manners practiced by Menander and the other writers of the New Comedy.

Aristophanes continued to write plays after the end of the war, and two of the surviving plays date from this period: *The Ecclesiazousai* (Women in Parliament) of 392, a skit on the ideas of communism in marriage and in ownership of property—ideas later put forward by Plato in the *Republic*—and *Plutus* (Wealth) of 388. The two plays are not without interest, but in them Aristophanes is little more than a shadow of the tumultuous comic genius who wrote *The Birds* and *The Frogs.*

Further Reading

There are many translations of Aristophanes's works in prose and verse. The best complete verse translation is probably by B. B. Rogers, *Aristophanes* (3 vols., 1924-1927), but the indelicacies of the original are often smoothed out, and the style of the rhymed verse is no longer fashionable. This is also true of the otherwise excellent versions by Gilbert Murray of *The Frogs* (1908) and *The Birds* (1950). Good modern verse versions of individual plays include: *The Birds,* translated by William Arrowsmith (1961); *The Clouds,* translated by William Arrowsmith (1962); *The Frogs,* translated by Richmond Lattimore (1962); *Ladies' Day (Thesmophoriazousai),* translated by Dudley Fitts (1959); *Lysistrata,* translated by Dudley Fitts (1954); and *Aristophanes against War: The Acharnians, The Peace, Lysistrata,* translated by Patric Dickinson (1957). Gilbert Murray, *Aristophanes: A Study* (1933), is the best book on Aristophanes. Cedric Hubbell Whitman, *Aristophanes and the Comic Hero* (1964), contains a full and interesting discussion of his dramatic technique. There is a detailed treatment of Old Comedy, and of Aristophanes and the other important writers of the group, in Gilbert Norwood, *Greek Comedy* (1931). Katherine Lever, *The Art of Greek Comedy* (1956), includes a short account of Aristophanes and a quite good and not-too-technical account of the development of Old Comedy. A more detailed account of the origins of Old Comedy is in A. W. Pickard-Cambridge, *Dithyramb, Tragedy and Comedy,* edited by T. B. L. Webster (2d ed. 1962). There is an excellent short account of Athens in the second half of the 5th century B.C. in A. R. Burn, *Pericles and Athens* (1948). The social background of the period is examined in Victor Ehrenberg, *The People of Aristophanes: A Sociology of Old Attic Comedy* (1943; 3d ed. rev. 1962). □

Aristotle

The Greek philosopher and scientist Aristotle (384-322 B.C.) organized all knowledge of his time into a coherent whole which served as the basis for much of the science and philosophy of Hellenistic and Roman times and even affected medieval science and philosophy.

Aristotle was born in the small Greek town of Stagiros (later Stagira) in the northern Greek district of Chalcidice. His father, Nicomachus, was a physician who had important social connections, and Aristotle's interest in science was surely spurred by his father's work, although Aristotle does not display a particularly keen interest in medicine as such. The events of his early life are not clear, but it is possible that his father served at the Macedonian court as physician to Amyntas II and that Aristotle spent part of his youth there.

At the age of 17 Aristotle joined Plato's circle at the Academy in Athens. There he remained for 20 years, and although his respect and admiration for Plato was always great, differences developed which ultimately caused a breach. On Plato's death in 348/347 B.C. Aristotle left for Assos in Mysia (in Asia Minor), where he and Xenocrates joined a small circle of Platonists who had already settled there under Hermias, the ruler of Atarneus. Aristotle married Pythias, the niece of Hermias, and in a fine hymn expressed

his shock and dismay over Hermias's death at the hands of the Persians some time thereafter.

After 3 years in Assos with Theophrastus and Xenocrates, Aristotle went to Mytilene for 2 years. Later, Theophrastus and Aristotle made their way to the court of Philip of Macedon, where Aristotle became tutor to Alexander, who later gained immortality by becoming master of the whole Persian Empire. Scant information remains regarding the specific contents of Alexander's education at the hands of Aristotle, but it would be interesting to know what political advice Aristotle imparted to the young Alexander. The only indication of such advice is found in the fragment of a letter in which the philosopher tells Alexander that he ought to be the *leader* of the Greeks but the *master* of the barbarians (foreigners).

Peripatetic School

Aristotle returned to Athens in 335/334. Under the protection of Antipater, Alexander's representative in Athens, he established a philosophical school of his own in the gymnasium Lyceum, located near a shrine of Apollo Lyceus. The school derived its name, Peripatetic, from the colonnaded walk (*peripatos*). Members took meals in common, and certain formalities were established which members had to observe. The lectures were divided into morning and afternoon sessions, the more difficult ones given in the morning and the easier and more popular ones in the afternoon. Aristotle himself led the school until the death of Alexander in 323, at which time he felt it expedient to leave Athens, fearing for his safety because of his close association with the Macedonians. He went to Chalcis, where he died the following year of a gastric ailment. His will, preserved in the writings of Diogenes Laertius, provided for his daughter, Pythias, and his son, Nicomachus, as well as for his slaves.

His Writings

Aristotle produced a large number of writings, but relatively few have survived. Because of the great weight of his authority it was inevitable that several spurious treatises should find their way into the corpus of his work. His earliest writings, consisting for the most part of dialogues, were produced under the influence of Plato and the Academy. Most of these are lost, although the titles are known from the writings of Diogenes Laertius and from one of several *Lives* to come down from antiquity. They include his *Rhetoric, Eudemus (On the Soul), Protrepticus, On Philosophy, Alexander, On Monarchy, Politicus, Sophistes, Menexenus, Symposium, On Justice, On the Poets, Nerinthus, Eroticus, On Wealth, On Prayer, On Good Birth, On Pleasure, and On Education.* These were exoteric works written for the public, and they deal with popular philosophical themes. The dialogues of Plato were undoubtedly the inspiration for some of them, although the divergence in thought between Plato and his pupil—which was to become apparent later—reveals itself to a certain extent in these works too.

A second group of writings is made up of collections of scientific and historical material, among the most important of which is the surviving fragment of the *Constitution of the Athenians*. This formed part of the large collection of *Constitutions*, which Aristotle and his students collected and studied for the purpose of analyzing various political theories. The discovery of the *Constitution of the Athenians* in Egypt in 1890 shed new light not only on the nature of the Athenian democracy of the 5th century B.C., but also on the difference in quality between the historical and scientific works of Aristotle and his successors. The prejudices and errors shown in the *Constitution* reveal a mind influenced by Plato and aristocratic social prejudices, while the factual discrepancies reveal the unreliable historical sources which Aristotle used for this type of treatise. Other works in this category are the *Pythian Victors, Barbarian Customs, Didascaliai* (lists of dramatic performances at Athens), *Homeric Questions, Problems,* and *Olympian Victors*.

The last group of writings is made up of those that have actually survived, and they consist of both philosophical and scientific works. Among them are *Prior Analytics, Posterior Analytics, Topics, Sophistic Arguments, Physics, On Heaven, On Generation and Corruption, Meteorology, On the Soul, History of Animals, On the Origin of Animals, Metaphysics, Nicomachean Ethics, Eudemian Ethics, Politics, Poetics, On Interpretation, On the Movement of Animals, On Feeling and the Senses, On Memory and Recollection, On Dreams, On a Dream, On Divination through Dreams, On the Long and Short Life, On Life and Death,* and *On Breathing.*

Upon the death of Theophrastus, who had kept Aristotle's manuscripts after the master's death in 322, these works were hidden away in a cellar in the Troad and not brought to light again until the beginning of the 1st century B.C., when they were taken to Rome and edited by Andronicus. Our texts derive from Andronicus's recension and probably do not represent works which Aristotle himself prepared for publication. The peculiarly clipped language in which they are written indicates that they are lecture notes of some sort organized from oral discussions of the material by Aristotle. From the time of his death until the rediscovery of these writings, Aristotle was best known for the works which today are the lost writings. Ironically, modern scholars find themselves in possession of works which their ancient counterparts lacked for several centuries, while the works extant in antiquity are lost today.

Philosophical and Scientific Systems

The extant writings, however, are sufficient to show the quality of Aristotle's achievement. The *Topics* and the *Analytics* deal with logic and dialectic and reveal Aristotle's contributions to the development of the syllogism and inductive inference. His view of nature is set forth in the *Physics* and the *Metaphysics,* and we see the premise established in these works which marks the most serious difference between Aristotelianism and Platonism: that all investigation must begin with what the senses record and must move only from that point to abstract thought. As a result of this process of intellectualizing, God, who for Plato is eternal Beauty and Goodness, is for Aristotle the Unmoved Mover, Thought contemplating Itself, the highest form of being which is completely lacking in materiality. Aristotle's God neither created nor consciously controls the universe, although the universe is affected by Him (it). Man is the only creature capable of thought even remotely resembling that of the Unmoved Mover, so man's highest goal is to reason abstractly, and he is more truly human to the extent that he achieves that goal.

But such a conclusion does not lead Aristotle to the moralist position taken by Plato, or by the Stoics or Epicureans in later times. Aristotle views men and their affairs from a cooler and more pragmatic point of view, and in the *Nicomachean Ethics* he analyzes the human situation from the point of view of reality as his researches reveal it to him. Man cannot be happy without the usual necessities of physical life, but those necessities do not suffice for true happiness. Since only the philosopher achieves a level of intellectual activity which might be taken seriously, it is the philosopher who achieves true human happiness through the use of his acutely developed ability to think abstractly.

Aristotle's work was often misunderstood in later times. The cardinal sin which later generations committed against this most dynamic of thinkers was to ascribe to his views a rigidity and certainty which they never had. The scientific and philosophical systems set forth in his writings are not conclusions which must be taken as absolute truth, but rather tentative positions arrived at through careful observation and analysis. Modern scholarship has helped to show the vitality of Aristotle's mind, but in the stagnant intellectual climate of imperial Rome and the totally unscientific Christian Middle Ages Aristotle's views on nature and science were taken as a complete system. As a result, his prestige was enormous but not for any reason that would have pleased him.

Aristotle shares with his master, Plato, the role of synthesizer and catalyst. Each of these two giants showed how the probings of the Pre-Socratics fell short of their goals, and each constructed philosophical systems on premises which they considered sound. Plato had a more direct influence on the development of that great mystical movement in late antiquity, Neoplatonism, and Aristotle had a more profound effect on science. Antiquity produced no greater minds than those of Plato and Aristotle, and the intellectual history of the West would be radically different without them.

Further Reading

Translations of the individual works of Aristotle are too numerous to mention, but a useful starting point is *Works,* translated under the editorship of W.D. Ross (12 vols., 1908-1952). A one-volume *Basic Works* was edited by Richard McKeon (1941). One of the best short introductions to Aristotle's writings is Geoffrey R.G. Mure, *Aristotle* (1964), highly readable but more limited in depth than the useful works of W.D. Ross, *Aristotle* (1923; 5th ed. rev. 1953) and *The Development of Aristotle's Thought* (1957). Other useful general works include D.J. Allan, *The Philosophy of Aristotle* (1952), and John Herman Randall, *Aristotle* (1960). For historical background see M.L.W. Laistner, *A History of the Greek World, from 479 to 323 B.C.* (1957). □

Arius

The Libyan theologian Arius (died ca. 336) was presbyter of the Christian Church in Alexandria and the first of the great heresiarchs.

Nothing is known of the early life of Arius except that he may have been born in Libya and may have studied under Lucian, the revered teacher and martyr of Antioch. It is certain that he was pastor of the Baucalis church on the Alexandrian waterfront, where he won many supporters by his preaching. He may have aspired to the episcopacy in Alexandria, which went instead to his fellow presbyter, Alexander.

Not until 318, however, did Arius become prominent and then only as a heretic. He began by criticizing the Trinitarian views of Bishop Alexander, accusing him of Sabellianism (an early heresy which did not distinguish clearly between the "Persons" of the Trinity). But when Arius explained his position, he caused greater alarm with his own views, and soon he was condemned and exiled from his diocese.

Arius sought refuge in the East, soliciting the support of his friend Eusebius of Nicomedia. Arius contended that the doctrinal error of which he was accused was his belief that the "Son had a beginning but God [alone] is without beginning." And this view, Arius felt, deserved commendation, not persecution. Arius's doctrine of the Son was radically subordinationist; that is, he claimed the Son to be a "creature" of the Father and that "there was [a time when] he was not." Prior to Arius, some religious thinkers had denied the humanity of Christ and some His divinity, but Arius was the first to deny both.

The Arian controversy grew to surprising proportions, soon involving most of the Church in the East and, later, the Church in the West as well. The recently converted Roman emperor Constantine was anxious to utilize the Church in the interests of political unity within the empire. He sent Bishop Ossius of Cordova, his ecclesiastical adviser, to Alexandria to determine the "facts" of the case and try to resolve the dispute. Constantine was not aware of the true nature of the controversy, as is shown by a letter he sent with Ossius, in which he referred to the Arian affair as an "unprofitable question" resulting from a "contentious spirit." But Ossius soon discovered that settling the dispute would be no simple matter. After his investigation he went to Antioch and presided over a council that provisionally condemned Arius and his followers.

The real debate, however, took place a few months later at the first great ecumenical council of the Church at Nicaea in 325. There, with the Emperor presiding and some 220 bishops attending, Arius was condemned—an action that Constantine equated with "the judgment of God." The council also promulgated a credal statement which declared the Son to be "consubstantial" with the Father. This belief could never be accepted by anyone holding Arian views.

After the council the Arian controversy did not die out but intensified. Arius, in exile in Illyricum, was no longer an active participant. In fact, he sought restoration and even wrote a "confession" which he believed to be acceptable to the terms of Nicaea. Not only was he refused admittance to Alexandria, where the great Nicene champion Anthanasius was now bishop, but in addition Constantine ordered Arius's books burned. Apparently, if Athanasius's account is trustworthy, Arius failed to obtain rehabilitation during his life. Technically it had been granted, but on the eve of the day Arius was to receive communion he died suddenly (ca. 336). It was several decades before Arianism itself was defeated and orthodoxy defined.

Further Reading

As with most heretics, Arius is known primarily through the eyes of his opponents; only a few letters of Arius himself survive. Modern studies of Arius and Arianism are scarce: Henry Melvill Gwatkin, *Studies of Arianism: Chiefly Referring to the Character and Chronology of the Reaction Which Followed the Council of Nicaea* (1882; 2d ed. 1900), and John Henry Newman, *The Arians of the Fourth Century* (1833; 4th rev. ed. 1876), are helpful but prejudiced and outdated. Of general surveys, G.L. Prestige, *Fathers and Heretics* (1940); Jean Daniélou and Henri Marrou, *The Christian Centuries*, vol. 1: *The First Six Hundred Years* (1963; trans. 1964); and Henry Chadwick, *The Early Church* (trans. 1967), can be consulted with profit.

Additional Sources

Williams, Rowan, *Arius: heresy and tradition,* London: Darton, Longman, and Todd, 1987.

Kannengiesser, Charles., *Arius and Athanasius: two Alexandrian theologians,* Aldershot, Hampshire, Great Britain: Variorum; Brookfield, Vermont, USA: Gower Pub. Co., 1991. □

Sir Richard Arkwright

The English inventor and industrialist Sir Richard Arkwright (1732-1792) developed several inventions which mechanized the making of yarn and thread for the textile industry. He also helped to create the factory system of manufacture.

Richard Arkwright was born on Dec. 23, 1732, in Preston, Lancashire, England. Little is known of his early life except that he was from a large family of humble origin and obtained only the rudiments of an education. He was apprenticed to a barber in Preston, and when about 18 he set up on his own in Bolton, a textile town in Lancashire.

Sometime in the 1760s Arkwright began working on a mechanical device for spinning cotton thread, the spinning frame, which he patented in 1769. Problems still remained: the raw cotton had to be prepared for the invention by a hand process, and the invention had to be made practical and commercially successful. For this he needed funds and a mill where he could install the frame.

Probably for this reason in 1771 he moved to Nottingham, where a highly specialized kind of weaving, that of stockings, had already been fairly well mechanized. There Arkwright, whose inventions had reduced him to poverty, found a partner who supported his work and backed the construction of a mill run by waterpower (hence the later name of water frame).

Arkwright found that he could successfully use his thread for stockings and also as the warp, or longitudinal threads, in an ordinary loom onto which the weft, or cross threads, were woven. Heretofore, cotton thread had been used for the weft, but only linen threads had been strong enough for the warp. Now a textile made solely of cotton could be produced in England, and it eventually became one of the country's chief exports.

The production of thread was further improved in 1775 by Arkwright's patenting a practically continuous method which prepared the raw cotton for spinning. Apart from a completely mechanical loom, Arkwright had thus eliminated all the major obstacles to producing cotton cloth by machine.

Because thread production was now completely mechanized, all the hitherto separate operations could be coordinated and carried out under one roof, in a mill, or, as it was increasingly called, a factory. Arkwright paid as careful attention to the mill's operation as he did to his inventions. It

was typical of his aggressive entrepreneurship that he was one of the first to apply the steam engine to his mills. While such a concentration of machines, driven by a prime mover, was not a new invention, Arkwright's rationalization of the factory system was nevertheless to become one of the most characteristic features of the industrial revolution.

Wealth and honors, including the bestowal of knighthood, came to him in the 1780s. He died in Nottingham on Aug. 3, 1792.

Further Reading

Two works have been written on Arkwright's relations with associates: George Unwin, *Samuel Oldknow and the Arkwrights* (1924), and R. S. Fitton and A. P. Wadsworth, *The Strutts and the Arkwrights, 1758-1830* (1958). Supplementary accounts of Arkwright's work may be found in T. S. Ashton, *The Industrial Revolution: 1760-1830* (1948; rev. ed. 1964), and in Abbott Payson Usher's "The Textile Industry, 1750-1830," in Melvin Kranzberg and Carroll W. Pursell, Jr., eds., *Technology in Western Civilization,* vol. 1 (1967).

Additional Sources

Fitton, R. S., *The Arkwrights: spinners of fortune,* Manchester, UK; New York: Manchester University Press; New York, NY, USA: Distributed exclusively in the USA and Canada by St. Martin's Press, 1989. □

Giorgio Armani

Characteristically clad in jeans, a white shirt opened at the neck, and a navy cotton pullover, Giorgio Armani (born 1935) designs new fashions in his 16th-century palazzo in Milan. He is a recipient of the coveted Neiman Marcus Award, and has built an international reputation—as well as a fortune—on his revolutionary, unstructured jacket for men.

In April of 1982 *Time* magazine featured Giorgio Armani on its cover. Armani's first radically different blazer appeared in the fashion world under his own label between 1974 and 1975. His sartorial style exhibited a decidedly relaxed, even rumpled look. The designer softened these new jackets by pulling out the padding and lining and leaving out stiffeners of any kind. He combined thinner lapels with baggier pockets and longer jackets. "Armani's unstructured look makes even his English wool suits feel as comfortable as silk pajamas," observed a writer for *People* magazine. And in *Esquire,* Rita Hamilton credited Armani's suit jackets with "the kind of shape that defied the proper Italian establishmentarian look and mirrored the defiant, angry mood of political and social unrest." But, as American designer Donna Karan put it in the *New York Times Magazine,* "fashion evolves." And Armani's designs did change by the end of the 1970s. Creating what would eventually be known as the "wedge-shaped

power suit," Armani extended the shoulders and even added padding to them. The lapels were widened, and the broadest point of the lapel, called the gorge, was lowered. The effect was similar to a style once worn by Hollywood sex symbols like Clark Gable. Still casual and comfortable, the new style was what the *New York Times* called a "second sartorial innovation" that endowed men with a "broad-shouldered, slim-hipped glamour."

In 1980, Giorgio Armani USA offered the American market a hybrid of the two styles. His more fluid sport coats of the first half of the decade could be compared to cardigan sweaters, with comfortable, sloping shoulders. These jackets were teamed up with T-shirts for a studied, informal look. The unmistakable Armani style evolved into an even more simplified version of the original groundbreaking blazer. In his spring 1990 women's collection, Armani "called attention to the generous flow of jackets by stripping them of superfluous detail," wrote Dan Lecca in the *New York Times Magazine.*

Armani's feminine version of the menswear jacket looked like it was borrowed from Greta Garbo's closet, or so imply some fashion critics. "My first jackets for women were in fact men's jackets in women's sizes," he told *Time* magazine. But it's Armani's use of strategically modified menswear fabrics and tailoring in women's suit jackets that is his "special contribution," stated Geraldine Stutz, president of Henri Bendel department store in New York City, in the same publication. "No one had ever done that before." While the jacket forms the foundation of the Armani empire, the Italian designer does create a variety of other garments as well. In 1982, for example, his fall collection featured felt hats, gaucho pants, and light suede hooded sweatshirts in what were described as "jelly bean" colors. Jackets were gold lamé for evening and longer for daytime wear. Fabrics included silk-lined cotton and mixtures of velvet, silk, wool, and linen, in a plethora of patterns and stripes. Whatever Armani chooses to offer in a collection, he is praised for that sense of relaxed comfort. "It's the fit of the armhole," pinpointed Dawn Mello in *Vogue.* And "somehow his clothes never seem to wrinkle." The man with the steel-blue eyes is not only a brilliant designer, he is also an astute business man. A writer for *Forbes* magazine noted that, in general, Armani "sets prices to maximize profits rather than minimize output." The company Giorgio Armani SpA made $350 million in the international market in 1988, $90 million of which came from the United States. The designer has targeted several different markets while maintaining high profit margins. In Italy, Vestimenta sells the priciest line for Giorgio Armani Via. In 1988 it was possible to spend $1,800 for one of Armani's best American suits for men. Blouses ran for between $30 and $400, and blazers ranged from $650 to $800, made by Gruppo GFT. Designed for the 20-years-old-and-up crowd, the Armani label appeared on less pricey suits and sport coats: $700 and $360 respectively.

To capture the younger market, Armani opened a line of stores called Emporio (or Emporium, in English), first in Italy, then in the United States. These boutiques debuted in 1981 to offer quality designs for slimmer pocketbooks. Local merchandise produced in quantity kept the prices low. For example, in 1982 a leather jacket could be purchased for between $250 to $300, skirts went for from $40 to $60, and blouses were priced at around $35. Jay Cocks wrote in *Time* magazine that "One would be hard put to tell the difference, in fact, between a leather jacket from the Emporium and one from the couture line, without resort to the price tag; an X ray would come in handy too." Armani first stocked the Emporio with jeans, T-shirts, and brightly colored cotton bomber jackets. Many of these items were made of extra fabrics from the design studio. And despite the Armani eagle logo (i.e., his initials form an eagle), this clothing had a decided American flair to it: It was even referred to as "Rafaelo Laureno" after Ralph Lauren in the United States. But this style evolved, too, and became more truly Armani. He added dressier and more classic selections, borrowed from his couture line—but at a fraction of the cost. And the jackets alone became available in 250 fabrics and 25 styles by 1989. In that year, Armani opened an Emporio on New York City's Fifth Avenue offering many more items than just clothes. He added a wide selection of accessories, underwear, products for the home, and leather goods. Well-organized and hard-working, Armani has also been described by some of his employees as a "maniac," noted the *New York Times Magazine.* He puts in 12-hour days at the design studio, devoting meticulous care to each phase of his work. In *New York* magazine, he explained, "The more you expose yourself, the more attentive you must be to details." Just before the showing of a new collection, for example, Armani can be found revamping a model's makeup and making other finishing touches. In Milan, he is known as "the Maestro." "A seemingly stoic man who is often silent with strangers," observed Charles Gandee in *House & Garden,* "he is compulsive about using time constructively."

A writer for *Vogue* magazine described Armani as "business class to the tips of his fingers," qualifying this by adding that that's the "class where all the action is." The designer had originally set out to become a doctor, but only studied for three years toward that goal. His mother has been credited with saying he couldn't take the sight of blood. But apparently Armani claims he simply couldn't sit still long enough to do all the reading required of him. If he could start his career all over again, Armani has said he would become a director of plays and films.

After leaving college, Armani fulfilled his requirements in the Italian army by serving as a medical assistant. Three years later he took a job at the Rinascente department store (which has been described as the Sears of Italy) in Milan. There he gained experience as a window dresser and in the style office. And he got to know fashion buyers. From there he moved on to an experimental in-store boutique, where he tested new clothes for the store. Eventually he became acquainted with Nino Cerruti, who was looking for assistance in creating new menswear. Armani designed men's clothes for Cerruti for eight years. Then Sergio Galeotti, an architectural draftsman at a prestigious firm in Milan, convinced Armani to go into business with him. The two became equal partners in various ventures. By the mid-1970s, the team was ready to offer menswear under the now-famous black label of Giorgio Armani. Armani has also done free-lance work on two menswear collections for Emanual Ungaro. This experience taught him the importance of fine tailoring. And he has designed fashions for Zegna, Sicons, Mario Valentino, and Erreuno. By 1984 Armani was designing 29 collections for himself annually. And supplemental to his lines of clothing, he has garnered licensees for a wide scope of accessories, jeans, and perfume.

The private life of Giorgio Armani is "absolutely banal," he told an interviewer in *Vogue.* Perhaps he was referring to the fact that he is a vegetarian who eschews smoking and alcoholic beverages. (He was once a bodybuilder, too.) It is still somewhat difficult to believe that Armani's life could have any commonplace aspect to it, considering that he lives and works in a 400-year-old palazzo (or palace) and owns two other Italian getaway homes (one in Forte dei Marmi and the other on an island near Sicily, called Pantelleria). The palazzo not only encompasses the design studio and Armani's bi-level apartment; it also has its own indoor pool, an apartment for Armani's widowed mother, and an apartment for his partner, Galeotti. And there is a columned amphitheater where Armani can show his latest collections. Now modernized, it was a ballroom in another era.

Twice a year Armani has his studio redecorated, "to suit the style, spirit, and coloring of the season's collection," Gloria Noda reported in *Vogue.* And after having his apartment redesigned by American architect Peter Marino, Armani still wanted to make some refinements. Describing his rooms, he shared these thoughts with *House & Garden* writer Charles Gandee: "I would like to have the time to fill them with personal objects, pictures, which can remove that aesthetically 'too perfect' look. And I would like as well to have the possibility of making some mistakes, thus bringing it closer to human nature." This philosophy is inherent in Armani's clothing designs as well. He fosters a sense of individuality and human sensuousness in his collections. Talking about style, Armani told an interviewer in *Self* magazine that "Each face, each hair texture requires a personalized look." He went on to describe individual style as the "correct balance of knowing who you are, what works for you and how to develop your own character."

The 1991 spring collection of women's clothes by Armani seemed to be designed to enhance the wearer's sense of well-being. The collection included a softly tailored white silk and linen jacket with matching pants. There was also an off-the-shoulder dress paired with shorts, again in a combination of linen and silk, in a muted multiprint fabric design. For evening wear, Armani offered "molten dinner suits and dresses paved in sequins, small crystals and pearls," as described in the *New York Times Magazine.* Cap-sleeved dresses with A-line skirts were also part of the new collection. In another article for the same magazine, Armani told Carrie Donovan that his goal in 1991 was to offer a look that's "just a bit more modern and young."

The 90s have been a busy time for Armani. He has been convicted of bribery (of tax officials in Italy), opened his chain of Armani Cafes, and developed a new fragrance. Giorgio Armani Neve is Armani's men's and women's skiwear and ski casualwear line, developed in 1995. His

1991 project, A/X: Armani Exchange, has been thus far disappointing in terms of sales. The chain of stores represented Armani's attempt to break into the American mass market, offering lower prices for the relaxed chic clothes.

Celebrities still count on Armani to make them look good for Hollywood's major events. Whoopi Goldberg told *People,* Armani "just makes me look elegant." Other star fans of Armani include Jodie Foster and Jack Nicholson.

Further Reading

Economist, May 21, 1994.
Elle, December 1995.
Esquire, May 22, 1979.
Forbes, July 11, 1988.
Harper's Bazaar, May 1984.
House & Garden, January 1990.
New York, March 20, 1989.
New York Times Magazine, January 20, 1980; October 21, 1990;
    February 3, 1991; September 9, 1991; February 7, 1993.
People, July 30, 1979; September 19, 1994.
Self, February 1991.
Time, April 5, 1982.
Vogue, January 1984; August 1984; January 1985; August 1986.
Women's Wear Daily, February 17, 1995; November 7, 1995. □

Jacobus Arminius

The Dutch theologian Jacobus Arminius (1560-1609) criticized the orthodox Calvinist position on the doctrine of predestination. The result was a split in the Dutch Reformed Church, and followers of his position came to be known as Arminians.

Jacobus Arminius was born on Oct. 10, 1560, in Oudewater, Holland. After his early education in Utrecht, he studied at the universities of Leiden, Basel, and Geneva. At Geneva he trained under the French theologian Theodore Beza and won distinction in his studies. In 1588 Arminius was ordained in Amsterdam and eventually achieved the reputation of being a devoted pastor. In 1603 he became professor of theology at the University of Leiden and remained there until his death.

While at Leiden, Arminius became involved in a heated struggle over the teachings of the Dutch Reformed Church. The most important source of controversy was the doctrine of predestination. Dutch Calvinists had divided into two schools of thought: the supralapsarians, who held the orthodox position and taught that God had decreed who would be saved and damned before man's fall in the sin of Adam, and the infralapsarians, who maintained that God did not decree who should be saved and damned until after the fall of man. In either case, human decision was irrelevant to the process of salvation. The supralapsarian position was held by the Reformed Church, and Arminius was asked to refute a man who was preaching infralapsarianism. But Arminius eventually rejected both positions on predestination. Although he did not deny predestination, he held that God did not decree particular individuals to be either saved or damned. He stated that salvation was by faith alone and Christ died for all men. Thus, those who believe will be saved and those who reject God's grace will be damned.

Francis Gomarus, a colleague of Arminius at Leiden, was a strong supralapsarian and vehemently opposed his teachings. At Arminius's death on Oct. 19, 1609, the dispute had not been settled, and his followers, known as Arminians or Remonstrants, continued the strife, although they did not always adhere strictly to his ideas. The position of Arminius against the Calvinist doctrine of predestination was condemned by the national synod of the Dutch Reformed Church in 1618-1619. This step did not, however, end the Arminian movement, and it continued to play a role not only in the Netherlands but also in England.

In addition to his ideas on predestination, Arminius demonstrated a great interest in the reconciliation of all Christian Churches. He believed that conferences, and specifically a general church council, might help to bring Christians together.

Further Reading

James and William Nichols selected and translated *The Works of James Arminius* (3 vols., 1825-1875). The standard biography is still Caspar Brandt, *The Life of James Arminius* (1724; trans. 1857). See also A. W. Harrison, *The Beginnings of Arminianism, to the Synod of Dort* (1926), and Gerald O. McCulloh, ed., *Man's Faith and Freedom: The Theological*

Influence of Jacobus Arminius (1962), which contains an extensive bibliography.

Additional Sources

Bangs, Carl, *Arminius: a study in the Dutch Reformation*, Grand Rapids, Mich.: F. Asbury Press, 1985.

Slaatte, Howard Alexander., *The Arminian arm of theology: the theologies of John Fletcher, first Methodist theologian, and his precursor, James Arminius*, Washington: University Press of America, 1977. ☐

Philip Danforth Armour

Philip Danforth Armour (1832-1901) was a typical American industrial capitalist of the period following the Civil War. He helped build meat-packing into a great industry by using new technology and working out distribution methods for domestic and foreign markets.

Philip Armour was born on May 16, 1832, at Stockbridge, N.Y. His father was a farmer of Scotch-Irish and Puritan origins. Young Armour went to a district school, then to the nearby Cazenovia Academy, from which he was dropped. In 1852 he left for California and worked as a miner and, more successfully, as a contractor selling water and digging water ditches for miners. After 4 years—during which he accumulated some $6,000—he returned to the family farm but soon left it permanently. He became a provisions and grain dealer in Cincinnati and then in Milwaukee, two early hog-packing centers.

Meat-packing (largely of hogs) was a wintertime farm industry: slaughtering took place after the first frost; then the hog products were moved to local markets by commission men or dealers. Armour joined forces with Frederick B. Miles and later, in 1863, with John Plankton. As the Northern armies of the Civil War demanded more and more salt pork, the firm of Plankton, Armour and Company became one of the important suppliers. After 1875 Armour made Chicago his base; by this time his brothers were in partnership with him and were located in Kansas City and New York.

Armour was a leader in modernizing the meat-packing industry. Among new technological devices he introduced were the conveyor-belt system and the use of natural ice, which made continuous operations possible; live animals could be brought to city plants for slaughter and dressing. The early 1880s saw the installation of ice-making and cooling machines and the adaptation of these devices to refrigerate railroad cars and ships. Thus, transportation was revolutionized, making it possible to move dressed meats (and also fruits and vegetables) to branch offices, eastern markets, and Europe.

Armour blazed trails in two ways: his companies owned and operated their own freight cars, forcing special, lower carload rates from the carrier railroads; and he aggressively entered English, German, and French markets, breaking down local resistance to American hog and beef products. Other innovations in which Armour led were the imaginative use of animal by-products (in making soap, glue, fertilizer, neat's-foot oil, and pharmaceuticals) and the use of tin cans for vacuum-packing beef.

At its peak in the 1890s Armour and Company controlled 6,000 refrigerator cars moving over 150,000 miles of railway. This, curiously, was the chief reason for reformer Charles Edward Russell's hostility to the industry; his influential book, *The Greatest Trust in the World* (1905), accused the packers of terrorizing the railroads as well as defying Wall Street. Armour was attacked because he operated family-owned companies rather than publicly owned ones and because he got his working capital from local (Chicago and Kansas City) banks and his investment capital from the plowing back of profits.

Armour also figured prominently in the activities of the Chicago Board of Trade as a trader in grain and pork products, helping establish orderly futures markets. Thus, he broke a bear raid on pork in 1879 and prevented a corner in wheat in 1897-1898. In this connection his system of grain elevators was considered the largest and best in the world.

During the 1890s Armour gave large sums of money for the construction of low-cost housing for his workers and for the establishment of the Armour Institute of Technology and of a preparatory scientific academy. He died on Jan. 6, 1901. Reputed to be worth $50,000,000, he left an estate of $15,000,000.

Further Reading

There is a good biography of Armour by Harper Leech and John Charles Carroll, *Armour and His Times* (1938). See also Rudolf A. Clemen, *The American Livestock and Meat Industry* (1923; abr. 1966) and *By-Products in the Packing Industry* (1927); and Louis F. Swift and Arthur Van Vlissingen, Jr., *The Yankee of the Yards: The Biography of Gustavus Franklin Swift* (1927). ☐

Edwin Howard Armstrong

The American electrical engineer and radio inventor Edwin Howard Armstrong (1890-1954) was one of a small group who made fundamental contributions to the development of radio.

Edwin Armstrong was born in New York City, where his father was the American representative of the Oxford University Press. Armstrong rode his motorcycle to classes at Columbia University, and he took a degree in electrical engineering in 1913. He remained at Columbia for the rest of his life, serving as research assistant to Michael Pupin and, on the latter's death in 1934, as professor of electrical engineering.

Armstrong had one of those turbulent careers typical of so many inventors, especially those working in new and rapidly developing industries. Driven by a thirst for historical vindication and a love of legal combat, perhaps more than by the desire for money, inventors have plagued each other's lives to a remarkable degree. Armstrong took out his first patent before he finished college in 1913, and patents and disputes over them always seem to have occupied an inordinate amount of his time and effort.

His early and long association with Prof. Pupin gave Armstrong direct access to one of the best and most fertile minds in the electrical field. Armstrong's academic base also kept him free of connection with any of the many companies then vying for dominance in the radio field; he was one of the few men to successfully maintain such independence.

The radio was not one invention but a combination of inventions, many of them of disputed origin. Armstrong's first important contribution was his realization of the value of Lee De Forest's audion vacuum tube as a means of amplifying current. To Armstrong this realization appeared to rank alongside the invention of the audion itself. Armstrong's second contribution was the feedback circuit, another means of amplifying current, which he (and others independently) worked out in 1912. The following year he discovered that the audion could be used to generate high-frequency oscillations; again, there were several contemporary claims to this discovery.

While serving as a signal officer in World War I, Armstrong developed in 1918 the superheterodyne circuit, in which incoming high-frequency signals were beaten against low-frequency signals from a local oscillator so that they could be detected. After the war he sold his feedback and superheterodyne patents to the Westinghouse Company for $350,000 and received even more from the Radio Corporation of America (RCA) for a superregenerative invention. His last great contribution was frequency modulation (FM), a method of overcoming static in broadcasting, on which he worked from 1924 to 1933 in the face of indifference and even hostility from large manufacturers and broadcasters.

During his last years perhaps 90 percent of Armstrong's time was taken up by court battles with the National Broadcasting Company, and others; this poisoned his life. He died, an apparent suicide, in 1954.

Further Reading

There is no biography of Armstrong. A brief discussion of his work is in John Jewkes, David Sawers, and Richard Stillerman, *The Sources of Invention* (1958). The standard history of the radio is William R. Maclaurin, *Invention and Innovation in the Radio Industry* (1949). Two other useful books are Donald M. McNicol, *Radio's Conquest of Space* (1946), and Carl F.J. Overhage, ed., *The Age of Electronics* (1962).

Additional Sources

Lewis, Thomas S. W., *The Legacies of Edwin Howard Armstrong: the regenerative circuit, the superheterodyne circuit, the superregenerative circuit, frequency modulatio,* Radio Club of America, 1990. □

Louis Daniel Armstrong

Louis Daniel Armstrong (1900-1971) was an early jazz trumpet virtuoso, and he remained an important influence for several decades.

L ouis Armstrong was born into a poor African American family in New Orleans on July 4, 1900. As a youngster, he sang on the streets with friends. In 1913 he was arrested for a prank and committed to the Waif's Home, where he learned the cornet and played in the band. On his release he began performing with local groups. Joe "King" Oliver, leader of the first great African American band to make records, befriended him, and Armstrong joined Oliver in Chicago in 1922, remaining until 1924, when he went to New York to play with Fletcher Henderson's band.

When he returned to Chicago in the fall of 1925, Armstrong began to cut one of the greatest series in the history of recorded jazz. These Hot Five and Hot Seven recordings find him breaking free from the conventions of New Orleans ensemble playing, his trumpet work notable for its inventiveness, rhythmic daring, improvisatory freedom, and technical assurance. In 1928 he started recording with drummer Zutty Singleton and pianist Earl Hines, the latter a musician able to match Armstrong in virtuosity. Many of the resulting records are masterpieces, the performances highlighted by complex ensembles, unpredictable harmonic twists, and rhythmic adventurousness. During these years Armstrong was working with big bands in Chicago clubs and theaters. His vocals, featured on most post-1925 records, are an extension of his trumpet playing in their phrasing and rhythmic liveliness, and are delivered in a unique guttural style.

By 1929 Armstrong was in New York leading a night-club band. Appearing in the theatrical revue *Hot Choco-lates,* he sang ''Fats'' Waller's ''Ain't Misbehavin','' Armstrong's first popular song hit. From this period his repertoire switched mainly to popular song material, which presented a new challenge because of the relative harmonic sophistication. Some notable performances resulted. His virtuosity reached a peak around 1933; then his style underwent a process of simplification, replacing virtuoso display by a mature craftsmanship that used every note to maximum advantage. He re-recorded some of his earlier successes to considerable effect.

Armstrong continued to front big bands, often of inferior quality, until 1947, by which time the big-band era was over. He returned to leading a small group which, though it initially included first-class musicians, became over the years a mere background for his vaudevillian talents. During the 1930s Armstrong had achieved international fame, first touring Europe as a soloist and singer in 1932. After World War II and his 1948 trip to France, he became an inveterate world traveler, journeying through Europe, Africa, Japan, Australia, and South America. He appeared in numerous films, the best a documentary titled *Satchmo the Great* (1957).

In his later years the public thought of Armstrong as a vaudeville entertainer—a fact reflected in the bulk of his record output. But there were still occasions when he produced music of astonishing eloquence and brilliance. He died in New York City on July 6, 1971.

Further Reading

Armstrong's autobiographical *Satchmo: My Life in New Orleans* (1954) is informative and entertaining on his early years. *Swing That Music* (1936), though ostensibly by Armstrong, was almost certainly ghosted and is of limited interest. Max Jones and John Chilton, *Louis: The Louis Armstrong Story, 1900-1971* (1971), is a superb study and is particularly informative about his life during the 1930s. An outstanding critical study of Armstrong's records of the 1924-1931 period is in Richard Hadlock, *Jazz Masters of the Twenties* (1965). See also Louis Terkel, *Giants of Jazz* (1957). □

Neil Alden Armstrong

The American astronaut Neil Alden Armstrong (born 1930) was the first person to walk on the moon.

Neil Armstrong was born on August 5, 1930, near Wapakoneta, Ohio, the eldest of three children of Stephen and Viola Engel Armstrong. Airplanes drew his interest from the age of six, when he took his first flight, and on his 16th birthday he was issued a pilot's license. A serious pilot even at this age, Armstrong built a small wind tunnel in the basement of his home and performed experiments on the model planes he had made.

Years of Training

Armstrong entered Purdue University in 1947 with a U.S. Navy scholarship. After two years of study he was called to active duty with the Navy and won his jet wings at Pensacola Naval Air Station in Florida. At 20 he was the youngest pilot in his squadron. He flew 78 combat missions during the Korean War and won three Air Medals.

Armstrong returned to Purdue and completed a degree in aeronautical engineering in 1955. He immediately accepted a job with the Lewis Flight Propulsion Laboratory of the National Advisory Committee for Aeronautics (NACA) in Cleveland, Ohio. A year later he married Janet Shearon.

An Aeronautical Career

Shortly afterward, Armstrong transferred to the NACA High Speed Flight Station at Edwards Air Force Base, California. Here he became a skilled test pilot and flew the early models of such jet aircraft as the F-100, F-101, F-102, F-104, F-5D, and B-47. He also flew a B-29 ''drop plane,'' from which various types of rocket-propelled planes were launched. More important for his later role, he became a pilot of the X-1B rocket plane, an earlier version of which had been the first plane to break the sound barrier.

Armstrong was selected as one of the first three pilots of NACA for the X-15 rocket plane, and he made seven flights

in this prototype spacecraft. Once he set a record altitude of 207,500 feet and a speed of 3,989 miles per hour. Armstrong received an invitation from the American space-flight program, but he demonstrated little enthusiasm for becoming an astronaut. His real love was piloting. Largely because of his experience with the X-15, he was selected as a pilot of the Dynasoar, an experimental craft that could leave the atmosphere, orbit earth, reenter the atmosphere, and land like a conventional airplane.

Astronautics: A Step into Space

In 1962, however, sensing that the days of the projected Dynasoar were numbered (it was canceled in 1963), Armstrong decided to become an astronaut and applied for selection and training. In September 1962 he became America's first civilian astronaut and moved to Houston, Texas, to begin training. Armstrong's attitude toward his job, at least prior to his first space mission, was summed up in a statement to a reporter in 1965: "I rule out the possibility of agreeing to go up if I thought I might not come back, unless it were technically indispensable. Dying in space or on the moon is not technically indispensable and consequently if I had to choose between death while testing a jet and death on the moon, I'd choose death while testing a jet."

Armstrong's first flight assignment as an astronaut was as backup, or alternate, command pilot for Gordon Cooper of the *Gemini 5* mission. Armstrong continued his specialized training on the Gemini spacecraft and was selected as the command pilot for the *Gemini 8* mission. With copilot David Scott he was launched from Cape Kennedy (now

Cape Canaveral), Florida, on March 16, 1966. The *Gemini 8* achieved orbit and docked as planned with the Agena vehicle, but shortly afterward the vehicle went out of control. Armstrong detached his craft from the Agena, corrected the malfunction, and brought the Gemini down in the Pacific Ocean only 1.1 nautical miles from the planned landing point. His cool and professional conduct made a strong impression on the officials of the Manned Spacecraft Center in Houston. Armstrong continued his intensive training on the Gemini spacecraft and was selected as the backup command pilot for the *Gemini 11* mission, which was flown, however, by astronauts Charles Conrad, Jr., and Richard Gordon.

As the training for the Apollo program got under way, it was obvious that Armstrong rated high among those being considered for the important role of being the first American on the moon. He undertook his training program with the same cool, analytical, and almost detached approach that had always marked his attitude to flying.

During a routine training flight on the lunar landing research vehicle, a training device that permits astronauts to maneuver a craft in a flight environment similar to that in landing on the moon, Armstrong's craft went out of control. He ejected himself and landed by parachute only yards away from the training vehicle, which had crashed in flames. With his usual imperturbability he walked away and calmly made his report. Again, his behavior and attitude were noted by those who were evaluating candidates for the first crew to the moon.

Selection for the Moon Mission

In January 1969 Armstrong was selected as commander for *Apollo 11,* the first lunar landing mission. On July 16 at 9:32 A.M. Eastern Daylight Time (EDT), Armstrong, together with astronauts Michael Collins and Edwin Aldrin, lifted off from the Kennedy Space Center, Florida, aboard the Saturn 5 space booster.

Apollo 11 passed into the gravitational influence of the moon on July 18 and circled the moon twice. Armstrong and Aldrin entered the lunar module, named the *Eagle,* which then disconnected from the command and service module. As they descended toward the lunar surface, their computer became overloaded, but under continuous instructions from the mission control center at Houston, Armstrong continued the gradual touchdown. Suddenly a boulder field loomed in front of him. He quickly switched to manual control and guided the *Eagle* over it to a smooth landing with only 10 seconds of fuel left. At 4:17:40 P.M. EDT on July 20, a major portion of the earth population was listening to Armstrong's transmission, "Houston, Tranquility Base here. The *Eagle* has landed." At 10:56 P.M. he set foot on the moon, saying, "That's one small step for man, one giant leap for mankind." (Later, he stated that he had intended to say, "That's one small step for a man, one giant leap for mankind.")

Armstrong and Aldrin spent nearly two and a half hours walking on the moon. Armstrong reported: "The surface is fine and powdery. I can pick it up loosely with my toe. It does adhere in fine layers like powdered charcoal to the soles and sides of my boots. I only go in a fraction of an inch, maybe an eighth of an inch, but I can see the footprints of my boots." The astronauts deployed various scientific instruments on the moon's surface, including a seismograph and solar-wind particle collector, and collected rock and soil samples. They also left a mission patch and medals commemorating American and Russian space explorers who had died in the line of duty, along with a plaque reading, "Here men from the planet Earth first set foot upon the Moon. We came in peace for all mankind."

Armstrong and Aldrin returned to the *Eagle* and launched themselves to rendezvous with Collins, who had been orbiting in the *Columbia* spacecraft. On July 24 *Columbia* returned to earth. It splashed down at 12:50 P.M. EDT some 950 miles southwest of Hawaii and only 2.7 miles from its aiming point. After 18 days of quarantine to control any lunar microorganisms, Armstrong and the others traveled around the world for parades and speeches. The mission brought honors including the Presidential Medal of Freedom, the Harmon International Aviation Trophy, the Royal Geographic Society's Hubbard Gold Medal, and accolades from many nations. Armstrong became a Fellow of the Society of Experimental Test Pilots, the American Astronautical Society, and the American Institute of Aeronautics and Astronautics.

Career after NASA

Apollo 11 was Armstrong's final space mission. He joined Nasa's Office of Advanced Research and Technology, where he served as deputy associate administrator for aeronautics. One of his main priorities in this position was to further research into controlling high-performance aircraft by computer. In 1970 he earned a master's degree in aerospace engineering from the University of Southern California.

A private man, Armstrong rejected most opportunities to profit from his fame. He left NASA in 1971 and moved his family back to Ohio to accept a position at the University of Cincinnati. There he spent seven years engaged in teaching and research as a professor of aerospace engineering. He took special interest in the application of space technology to such challenges as improving medical devices and providing data on the environment. In 1978 Armstrong was one of the first six recipients of the congressional Space Medal of Honor, created to recognize astronauts whose "exceptionally meritorious efforts" had contributed to "the welfare of the Nation and mankind."

A member of the board of directors of Gates Learjet Corporation, in 1979 he piloted that company's new business jet to five world-altitude and time-to-climb records for that class of aircraft. Other boards Armstrong served on included those of USCX Corporation and United Airlines. In between his business ventures and such hobbies as fishing and sail-planing, he also chaired the board of trustees of the Cincinnati Museum of Natural History.

Armstrong did accept two further government appointments. In 1984 he was named to the National Commission on Space, which two years later completed a report outlining an ambitious future for American space programs. Also in 1986, Armstrong was named deputy chair of the Rogers Commission to investigate the explosion of the space shuttle *Challenger*. The commission's work resulted in major changes in NASA's management structure and safety practices.

From 1980 to 1982, Armstrong was chair of the board of Cardwell International. He accepted a similar post with Computing Technologies for Aviation (CTA) in 1982. CTA, which was based in Charlottesville, Virginia, provided software for flight scheduling and support activities, allowing corporate jet operators to maximize the efficient use of their aircraft. Armstrong stepped down as head of CTA in 1993. He later presided over the board of AIL Systems, Inc., an electronic systems company headquartered in Deer Park, New York.

In May 1997 Armstrong was named a director at Ohio National Financial Services Inc., a Cincinnati-based provider of diversified financial services. At that time, he also served on the boards of Cinergy Corp. and Cincinnati Milacron Inc. He maintained his residence at a farm near Lebanon, Ohio, and made occasional public appearances in nearby Wapakoneta, his boyhood home and the site of the Neil Armstrong Air & Space Museum.

Further Reading

Information on Armstrong's historic participation in the space program is contained in Chris Crocker, *Great American Astronauts* (1988), Buzz Aldrin and Malcolm McConnell, *Men from Earth* (1989), and Alan B. Shepard, *Moon Shot: The Inside Story of America's Race to the Moon* (1994). Armstrong, together with Michael Collins and Buzz Aldrin, wrote a memoir of the Apollo 11 moon voyage in *First on the Moon* (1970). □

Samuel Chapman Armstrong

As an American educator, Samuel Chapman Armstrong (1839-1893) did much to advance the education of the African American. He was the founder of Hampton Institute in Virginia.

Samuel Chapman Armstrong was born on Jan. 30, 1839, on Maui in the Hawaiian Islands, the child of American missionaries. He spent his early years there, attending the Royal School at Punahou and, when that became Oahu College, continuing for 2 years. In 1860, carrying out the wishes of his father, who had recently died, he sailed for the United States and entered Williams College, in Massachusetts.

Although at first he was not particularly exercised over the issues of the Civil War, Armstrong found the excitement of his classmates infectious, and he volunteered for the Union Army in 1862. Given a captain's commission, he recruited a company near Troy, N.Y., which he led with distinction at the Battle of Gettysburg, earning a promotion to major. Shortly afterward, before his twenty-fifth birthday, he was appointed colonel of the 9th Regiment, United

States Colored Troops. His experiences aroused his interest in the future of the emancipated African American. At the close of the war he received the brevet rank of brigadier general and was referred to as General Armstrong the rest of his life.

Armstrong joined the Freedmen's Bureau, the Federal agency dealing with the problems of former slaves, and in March 1866 took charge of a large camp of African Americans near Hampton, Va. He soon began to consider means of educating his charges and in 1867 interested the American Missionary Association in supporting a school at Hampton.

In setting up the Hampton Normal and Industrial Institution in 1868, Armstrong drew upon his Hawaiian experience. There he had seen the Hilo Manual Labor School, in which the students paid their expenses and tuition by gardening, housework, and carpentry. He was convinced that the best way to train African American youths to be leaders and teachers of their own people was in a school that combined manual with academic instruction. Teaching them to work with their hands as well as their heads would carry out the motto of his institution: "Education for Life." Discipline in the school was rigorous as Armstrong set out to eradicate habits learned in slavery and to equip his students to serve as examples in their personal lives.

Armstrong spent much time raising money from Northern philanthropists, and soon his school exerted a major influence on African American education. He also tried to extend the same principles to training Native Americans.

Although his ideas were later criticized by young African Americans as underestimating the students' capacities, his school met an immediate need, flourished then, and still survives. He died at Hampton on May 11, 1893.

Further Reading

Edith Armstrong Talbot, *Samuel Chapman Armstrong* (1904), is an admiring biography by Armstrong's daughter; it contains extensive selections from his letters and speeches. Francis Greenwood Peabody, *Education for Life* (1913), is an account of the first 50 years of Hampton Institute. Frances B. Johnston, *The Hampton Album* (1966), contains 44 photographs, which, although not taken until 1899-1900, provide a vivid visual image of the school under Armstrong's direction. A favorable evaluation of Hampton, along with moving descriptions of what the school meant to its pupils, is contained in Booker T. Washington, *Up from Slavery* (1901; abr. ed. 1929). Criticisms of the Hampton approach may be found in W. E. B. DuBois, *The Souls of Black Folks* (1903). See Henry Allen Bullock, *A History of Negro Education in the South* (1967), for background.

Additional Sources

Talbot, Edith (Armstrong), *Samuel Chapman Armstrong; a biographical study*, New York, Negro Universities Press, 1969. □

Thomas Augustine Arne

At a time when musical life of England was dominated by foreign music and musicians, Thomas Augustine Arne (1710-1778) was the most successful and popular native composer, keeping alive and advancing the traditions of the English baroque school.

Thomas Arne was born in London on March 12, 1710, the son of an upholsterer and coffin-maker. Educated at Eton, he spent 3 years apprenticed to an attorney before his obvious talents in music persuaded his father to allow him to pursue a career in this field. Arne's first major composition was a setting of Joseph Addison's *Rosamond* (1733). Arne's sister Susannah Maria, 4 years his junior, sang a leading role; later, as Mrs. Cibber, she was a famous dramatic actress and singer. In 1736 Arne married Cecelia Young, a soprano who later gave remarkable performances of music by her husband and by George Frederick Handel.

Arne quickly established himself as a major talent with music to three masques done at the Drury Lane Theatre: *Comus* (1738), adapted from John Milton by John Dalton; *The Judgment of Paris* (1740), by William Congreve; and *The Masque of Alfred* (1740), to a libretto by James Thomson and David Mallet, which concludes with an "Ode in Honour of Great Britain," known now as "Rule, Britannia," Arne's most persistently popular invention. Drury Lane launched a series of revivals of some Shakespearean plays, commissioning Arne to write music to some of the lyrics. *As You Like It* (1740) was followed by *Twelfth Night* (1741), *The Merchant of Venice* (1742), *The Tempest* (1746), and *Love's Labour's Lost* (1747). Many of Arne's most enduring

songs, such as "Under the Greenwood Tree," "When Daisies Pied," and "Where the Bee Sucks," were written for these productions.

Arne spent the years 1742-1744 in Dublin, where he composed his first oratorio, *The Death of Abel*. On his return to London, he became the leader of the orchestra at Drury Lane, and in 1745 he was also appointed official composer for Vauxahll Garden. The music he wrote here, and later for Mary-le-bone and Ranelagh gardens, became extremely popular and was printed in such collections as *Lyric Harmony* and *The Vocal Grove,* then reprinted and rearranged in other publications for many decades in England and the American colonies.

In 1759 Oxford University awarded Arne the degree of doctor of music. Soon he left Drury Lane for Covent Garden, where he wrote operas in a wide range of styles. *Love in a Village* (1762) was a ballad opera, with spoken dialogue alternating with songs, some his own and some arrangements of popular airs of the day. *Thomas and Sally, or the Sailor's Return* (1780) is a true comic opera, with all original music and dialogue set as recitative. His most ambitious work was *Artaxerxes* (1762), an *opera seria* with a libretto adapted and translated by Arne himself from a play by the Italian dramatist Metastasio. It is the only example of a full-length opera in English for a period of many decades. Despite some contradictions in style, it had immediate success and held the stage for many years. A less successful piece was *Olimpiade* (1764), also from Metastasio, in Italian and completely in the Italian style.

Arne's catches and glees, written for the Madrigal Club, have proved to be durable works for social and school singing groups. His second oratorio, *Judith* (1761), is considered by some to be one of his finest works, and his setting of *Libera me* for solo voices and five-part chorus is an interesting and rare example of a setting of a Latin text from this period in England.

Arne also wrote concertos for keyboard, overtures for orchestra, lessons (or sonatas) for harpsichord, and trio sonatas, but this instrumental music has received little attention. He died in London on March 5, 1778.

Arne's dramatic and vocal works are his best; his greatest talent was for graceful, expressive, and memorable melodic lines. His contemporary Charles Burney offers this opinion in *A General History of Music:* "From the death of Purcell to that of Arne, a period of more than fourscore years, no candidate for musical fame among our countrymen had appeared, who was equally admired by the nation at large. . . . In secular music, he must be allowed to have surpassed him [Purcell] in ease, grace, and variety."

Further Reading

Brief biographies of Arne are Burnham W. Horner, *Life and Works of Dr. Arne, 1710-1778* (1893), and Hubert Langley, *Doctor Arne* (1938), neither of which is scholarly. Arne's place in the history of music in England is noted in Frank Howes, *The English Musical Renaissance* (1966). There is a discussion of some aspects of Arne's life and works in Charles Burney, *A General History of Music: From the Earliest Ages to the Present Period* (4 vols., 1786-1789; new ed., with notes by Frank Mercer, 1957).

Additional Sources

Burden, Michael, *Garrick, Arne, and the masque of Alfred: a case study in national, theatrical, and musical politics,* Lewiston: Edwin Mellen Press, 1994. □

Achim von Arnim

The German writer Achim von Arnim (1781-1831) is known chiefly for his novels and his edition of German folk songs. He was an influential member of the German romantic movement.

On Jan. 26, 1781, Achim von Arnim was born in Berlin of an aristocratic Prussian family. He studied science and law at the universities of Halle and Göttingen but soon turned his attention to literature. After becoming acquainted with the poets Johann Wolfgang von Goethe and Clemens Brentano, Arnim traveled extensively through western Europe and England. He then settled in Heidelberg, where he, Brentano, and the poet Johann Josef von Görres formed the Heidelberg group of the German romantic school and founded a literary journal, *Zeitung für Einsiedler* (Newspaper for Hermits). Between 1805 and 1808 Arnim and Brentano compiled *Des Knaben*

Wunderhorn (*The Boy's Magic Horn*), the best-known collection of German folk songs. It consisted chiefly of actual folk poetry, although many of the verses were revised or even composed by the editors. The naive "folk" tone, however, was maintained throughout.

Arnim's personal lyric output was augmented in 1806 by his volume of war songs for use by the Prussian army. In 1808 he moved to Berlin, where he rejoined Brentano and began a series of stories and dramas on historical subjects. In 1809 Arnim published his novel *Gräfin Dolores* "for the instruction and amusement of impoverished young ladies."

In 1811 Arnim married Bettina Brentano, a writer of the romantic school and the sister of Clemens Brentano. At an early age she had become a close friend of Goethe, and her lively exchange of letters with him was published in 1835 as *Goethes Briefwechsel mit einem Kinde* (*Goethe's Correspondence with a Child*).

In 1813 Arnim became a captain in the Prussian army and fought in the war against Napoleon. He was also an editor of the patriotic newspaper *Der Rheinische Merkur.* His unfinished novel, *Die Kronenwächter* (1817; *The Crown Guardians*), concerns the mystical influence of undiscovered royal blood and a secret society on the life of a young adventurer. Arnim later became a gentleman farmer in Wiepersdorf, Brandenburg, where he died on Jan. 21, 1831.

Bettina von Arnim continued her literary work after her husband's death. She wrote polemical treatises for such liberal causes as the rights of workers and women. Her most famous political work was her declaration of principles, *Dies Buch gehört dem König* (1843; *This Book Belongs to the King*). She died on Jan. 20, 1859.

Further Reading

The most significant book in English on Arnim is Herbert R. Liedke, *Literary Criticism and Romantic Theory in the Work of Achim von Arnim* (1937), which emphasizes his theoretical position. An excellent general introduction to his life and writings may be found in Ralph Tymms, *German Romantic Literature* (1955). August Closs, *The Genius of the German Lyric* (1938; rev. ed. 1962), contains a brief discussion of his lyric poetry. L. A. Willoughby, *The Romantic Movement in Germany* (1930), offers a concise appraisal of the role of Bettina von Arnim in German literature.

Additional Sources

Hoermann, Roland., *Achim von Arnim,* Boston: Twayne, 1984.
Hoermann, Roland., *Achim von Arnim's 1854 Kronenwèachter Text: Bettina's forgery or Berthold's forerunner: start of a sequel or end of an Ur-Kronenwèachter?,* Stuttgart: H.-D. Heinz, 1990.
Ziegler, Vickie L., *Bending the frame in the German cyclical narrative: Achim von Arnim's Der Wintergarten & E.T.A. Hoffmann's Die Serapionsbrèuder,* Washington, D.C.: Catholic University of America Press, 1991. □

Benedict Arnold

Although he fought with skill and courage in many campaigns during the American Revolution, Gen. Benedict Arnold (1741-1801) is best known as the man who betrayed his country.

B enedict Arnold was born on Jan. 14, 1741, in Norwich, Conn., of a prominent family. As a young man, he worked for a druggist, fought in the French and Indian War, and engaged in trade with the West Indies. In 1767 he married Margaret Mansfield.

Career as a Soldier

When news of the battles of Lexington and Concord reached Arnold in April 1775, he set out at the head of a company of Connecticut militia for Cambridge, Mass., where George Washington was gathering an army to fight the British forces. His first engagement was the attack the next month on Fort Ticonderoga, where the British had a concentration of artillery. The operation was successful but Arnold got little of the credit, which went mostly to Ethan Allen and his Green Mountain Boys. His second assignment was with an expedition against Canada. Leaving Cambridge on Sept. 19, 1775, Arnold led his troops the length of Maine, by land and water and in snow and storms, reaching Quebec in early November. There he was joined by another column under Gen. Richard Montgomery, which had come by way of Lake Champlain and Montreal. Together the two forces assaulted Quebec on December 31, but the attack failed, costing Montgomery his life and Arnold a severe leg wound. Arnold next went to Lake Champlain to prevent the British from using it as a highway from Canada to New York. He lost two naval battles on the lake in October 1776, but he had effectively delayed the British in their southward advance. In the same month Congress made Arnold brigadier general.

The winter of 1776-1777 was an unhappy one for Arnold. His hot temper, impulsiveness, and impatience had earned him many enemies, who now made all sorts of accusations against him—of misconduct on the march through Maine, of incompetence on Lake Champlain, and more. Worse yet, Congress in February 1777 promoted five brigadier generals, all Arnold's juniors, to major general. Only Washington's pleas kept Arnold from resigning from the army. Fortunately, the coming of spring gave him the chance for a successful operation. While visiting his home in New Haven, Arnold heard of a British attack on American supply depots in Danbury, Conn. He rounded up the local militia and raced to stop the enemy. Although he got there too late to prevent the destruction of the supplies, he did rout the British. A grateful Congress advanced him to major general on May 2, but he was still below the other five in seniority. Meanwhile, he faced a formal charge of stealing goods and property from Montreal merchants during the Canadian campaign. He was exonerated, but his anger at the charges moved him to resign his commission in July 1777.

Once again Washington pleaded with him, and Arnold reconsidered. Washington needed him for service in northern New York to block a bold British plan to split New England from the other colonies by sending Gen. John Burgoyne from Ticonderoga down the Hudson River to New York City. Burgoyne not only failed in his mission; he lost his whole army, which he surrendered at Saratoga, N.Y., in October 1777. Arnold played a major role in the two battles that culminated in the British defeat. Burgoyne himself said of Arnold that "it was his doing." Congress rewarded Arnold by restoring his seniority among the major generals.

Arnold's next assignment was command of the garrison at Philadelphia, which the British had evacuated in June 1778. He married Margaret Shippen, daughter of a wealthy Philadelphian, in April 1779. (His first wife had died some years earlier.) Moving in aristocratic circles, Arnold lived lavishly and beyond his means, and he soon found himself heavily in debt. At the same time he was being charged with a number of offenses connected with using his military office for private gain. He demanded a court-martial, which Congress convened in May. The verdict handed down in December found him not guilty of most charges but ordered Washington to reprimand him. The general did this, but mildly, in April 1780.

End as a Traitor

By this time, however, Arnold had already started on the road to treason. Personally hurt by Congress's treatment and sorely in need of money, he had begun to funnel information on troop movements and strength of units to the British in exchange for money as early as May or June 1779. Early in the summer of 1780, he conceived the idea of turning over the strategic post at West Point, N.Y., to the English for £10,000. He persuaded Washington to place him in command there, but Arnold's plan fell through when his contact, Maj. John André, was captured on September 21 with incriminating documents. André was executed and Arnold fled to the British lines.

Arnold spent the rest of the war in a British uniform fighting his own countrymen. In 1781 he went to London, where he died 20 years later on June 14, despised in America and forgotten in England.

Further Reading

The best biography of Arnold is Willard M. Wallace, *Traitorous Hero* (1954). Arnold's Canadian campaign is well presented by Justin H. Smith, *Our Struggle for the Fourteenth Colony: Canada, and the American Revolution* (2 vols., 1907). For his role in Burgoyne's defeat at Saratoga see Hoffman Nickerson, *The Turning Point of the Revolution* (1928; rev. ed. 1967). Carl Van Doren, *Secret History of the American Revolution* (1941), discusses Arnold's treason. □

Henry Harley Arnold

Henry Harley Arnold (1886-1950) was one of America's first military aviators. He became chief of staff of the Army Air Forces in World War II and was instrumental in the creation of the U.S. Air Force.

Henry Arnold was born on June 25, 1886, in Gladwyne, Pa. He graduated from the U.S. Military Academy in 1907 and joined the infantry. Early in 1911 he went to Dayton, Ohio, to take flying lessons from Orville and Wilbur Wright and later that year earned the twenty-ninth pilot's license issued in the United States. In 1916 he joined the Aviation Section of the Army Signal Corps and during World War I served as commander of the 7th Aero Squadron in Panama. Between the wars he was a vigorous advocate of air power and an active supporter of Billy Mitchell's attempt to create an independent air force.

The Army, however, retained control of the Army Air Corps, as its air arm was then called, and in 1938 Arnold became chief of the corps. He believed that air power would be the decisive weapon in the next war and thought that the airplane, especially the heavy bomber, should not be shackled to the Army. He encouraged development of the "flying fortress," a bomber able to defend itself from enemy fighters and to drop bombs with pinpoint accuracy on industrial targets. Arnold maintained that strategic bombing—the selective destruction of key industries—would force an enemy to an early surrender, even without physical occupation of the country.

Arnold did not get all that he wanted, but in March 1942 the corps became the Army Air Forces and he became the chief of staff. Although technically his organization remained subordinate to the Army, it was actually independent, a fact underscored by Arnold's place as an equal on the Combined Chiefs of Staff (the agency composed of the American and British heads of service) and his promotion to five-star general. Arnold also saw to the development of the type of air force he wanted. His favorite maxim, "A second-best air force is like a second-best hand in poker—it's no good at all," had led to the creation of the world's most powerful air force.

Arnold retired in 1946; a year later, owing largely to his efforts, the U.S. Air Force became an independent service. In his final report he warned that within 30 years the United States would need 3,000-mile-an-hour robot atom bombs, launched from space ships "operating outside the earth's atmosphere." He believed that air power had made mass armies and navies obsolete. He died of a heart attack on Jan. 15, 1950.

Further Reading

Arnold wrote two books, both with Ira C. Eaker, giving his view on air power: *This Flying Game* (1936) and *Winged Warfare* (1941). The best source on Arnold is his memoir, *Global Mission* (1949). There is no satisfactory biography, although a complete account of Arnold's activities as chief of staff of the Army Air Forces is in the official *The Army Air Forces in World War II,* edited by Wesley Frank Craven and James L. Cate (7 vols., 1948-1958). For the military history of the war see J.F.C. Fuller, *The Second World War, 1939-1945* (1948; rev. ed. 1954); Kent Roberts Greenfield, *American Strategy in World War II: A Reconsideration* (1963); and Basil Collier, *The Second World War: A Military History* (1967).

Additional Sources

Coffey, Thomas M., *HAP: the story of the U.S. Air Force and the man who built it, General Henry H. "Hap" Arnold,* New York: Viking Press, 1982.
Copp, DeWitt S., *A few great captains: the men and events that shaped the development of U.S. air power,* Garden City, N.Y.: Doubleday, 1980; McLean, Va.: EPM Publications, 1989. □

Matthew Arnold

The most characteristic work of the English poet and critic Matthew Arnold (1822-1888) deals with the difficulty of preserving personal values in a world drastically transformed by industrialism, science, and democracy.

Matthew Arnold was born at Laleham on the Thames on Dec. 24, 1822. His father, Dr. Thomas Arnold, one of the worthies whom Lytton Strachey was to portray somewhat critically in *Eminent Victorians,* became the celebrated master of Rugby School, and his ideals of Christian education were influential. As a young man, Matthew Arnold saw something of William Wordsworth, Robert Southey, and other veterans of English romanticism. Educated at Rugby and then at Balliol College, Oxford, he early began to write poetry. The closest friend of his youth was Arthur Hugh Clough, a poet and sometime disciple of Dr. Arnold, whose death Matthew Arnold would later mourn in his elegy "Thyrsis."

In 1844 Arnold took a second-class honors degree at Oxford, and the following year he was elected to a fellowship at Oriel College. After some teaching he became private secretary to Lord Lansdowne, who eventually had him appointed to an inspectorship of schools, a difficult, demanding job which required Arnold to do a good deal of traveling and which he held for most of his life.

Several of Arnold's early poems express his hopeless love for a girl he calls Marguerite. Scholars have been unable to identify an original for this girl, and whether she existed at all is a question. In 1851 Arnold married Frances Lucy Wightman, the daughter of a judge. The marriage was a happy one, and some of Arnold's most attractive poems are addressed to his children.

Career as a Poet

In 1849 Arnold, under the pseudonym "A," published a collection of short lyric poems called *The Strayed Reveller;* the sale was poor and the book was withdrawn. In 1852 he published another collection, *Empedocles on Etna and Other Poems,* but this too, after a sale of 50 copies, was withdrawn. Two poems in this collection, however, require special notice. The first, "Empedocles on Etna," is in dra-

matic form, though it consists mostly of a series of monologues in which the hero, a Sicilian philosopher, meditates on the transient glories and satisfactions of human life and then throws himself into the volcano. The second is Arnold's long poem on Tristram and Iseult, which again uses the monologue form. Tristram, watched over by Iseult of Brittany, is dying; he remembers his past happiness with Iseult of Ireland, who arrives just before he dies for a brief, passionate reunion.

In 1853 Arnold published a collection called simply *Poems*; it included poems from the two earlier collections as well as others never before published, notably "Sohrab and Rustum" and "The Scholar Gypsy." The former is a short epic; in style it is frequently reminiscent of John Milton but very beautiful in its own right. The Persian hero Rustum has never seen his son Sohrab, who is raised by the Tatars and becomes one of the bravest of their warriors. The two men meet in single combat, and just as the son recognizes his father, the former falls dead. "The Scholar Gypsy" is based on an old story of an Oxford student who left his university and joined a gypsy band; his spirit is supposed still to haunt the Oxford countryside. The poem contrasts the life of the legendary gypsy with Arnold's own times, which he finds sick, divided, and distracting.

Poems: Second Series (1855) includes another small blank-verse epic, "Balder Dead." Arnold takes his subject from Norse mythology. Balder, god of the sun, has been killed by a trick of the evil Loki, god of mischief. The gods mourn his death, and Hermod goes to the land of the shades to persuade Hela to return Balder to the land of the living. Hela agrees on condition that all living things mourn for Balder; and so they do, with the fatal exception of Loki. Balder is resigned to his death, and at the conclusion of the poem there is a promise of better things when this generation of gods has passed away.

In 1857 Arnold was elected to the professorship of poetry at Oxford, and he held this post for the next decade. He was the first professor of poetry to give his lectures in English rather than in Latin.

In 1858 Arnold published *Merope,* a classical tragedy, which concerns the revenge of a young man on a tyrant who has killed the young man's father and married his mother. *New Poems* (1867) includes "Thyrsis: A Monody," the pastoral elegy in which Arnold again celebrates the Oxford countryside and mourns the death of his friend Clough. The poem invites comparison with other great classical elegies in English—for example, Milton's "Lycidas" and Percy Bysshe Shelley's "Adonais." In 1869 Arnold collected his poems in two volumes. An important new poem is "Rugby Chapel," in which he pays tribute to his father. Although Arnold wrote both epic and dramatic poetry, his best poems are probably his lyrics, such poems as "Dover Beach," "To Marguerite—Continued," and "The Buried Life."

Literary and Social Criticism

In 1861 Arnold published his lectures *On Translating Homer* and in the next year *On Translating Homer: Last Words.* He first isolates the main characteristics of the Homeric style and then consides a number of translations of

Homer and the degree of their success in duplicating these characteristics in English. The books are lively introductions to classical poetry and urge English writers to imitate Homer's "grand style."

Arnold's two-volume *Essays in Criticism* (1865 and 1888) includes essays on a variety of writers—Marcus Aurelius, Heinrich Heine, Leo Tolstoy, and Wordsworth among them. His critical essays are concerned with the discipline and preservation of taste at a time when literary standards were threatened by commercialism and mass education. With schoolmasterly repetitiousness Arnold attacks English provincialism, or "Philistinism" as he calls it. He particularly values the quality of "high seriousness," an author's power to concentrate on the perpetually important issues in human life. Arnold suggests that his readers keep always in mind certain sublime moments in literature which will serve as "touchstones" in the judgment of contemporary work.

Of the several books which Arnold wrote on politics and sociology the most important is *Culture and Anarchy* (1869). He criticizes 19th-century English politicians for their lack of purpose and their excessive concern with the machinery of society. The English people—and the narrow-minded middle class in particular—lack "sweetness and light," a phrase which Arnold borrowed from Jonathan Swift. England can only be saved by the development of "culture," which for Arnold means the free play of critical intelligence, a willingness to question all authority and to make judgments in a leisurely and disinterested way.

Of the four books in which Arnold dealt with the threat to religion posed by science and historical scholarship, the most important is *Literature* and *Dogma* (1873). He argues that the Bible has the importance of a supremely great literary work, and as such it cannot be discredited by charges of historical inaccuracy. And the Church, like any other time-honored social institution, must be reformed with care and with a sense of its historical importance to English culture.

Arnold was one of the great Victorian controversialists, and his books are contributions to a national discussion of literature, religion, and education. His style is witty, ironic, and varied; he exhorts his readers, chides them, even teases them. His books were widely read, and in the magazines in which he regularly published he defended his views against all comers. In 1883 and 1886 he toured the United States and gave lectures, in which he tried to win Americans to the cause of culture.

On April 15, 1888, Arnold went to Liverpool to meet his beloved daughter, and he died there of a sudden heart attack.

Further Reading

Two important collections of Arnold's letters are *Letters of Matthew Arnold, 1848-1888,* edited by George W.E. Russell (2 vols., 1895-1896), and *The Letters of Matthew Arnold to Arthur Hugh Clough,* edited by Howard Foster Lowry (1932). The standard introduction to Arnold is Lionel Trilling, *Matthew Arnold* (1939; 2d ed. 1949). A more recent critical study, synthesizing earlier views, is William A. Madden,

Matthew Arnold: A Study of the Aesthetic Temperament in Victorian England (1967). Two excellent works devoted to Arnold's poetry are Wendell Stacy Johnson, *The Voices of Matthew Arnold: An Essay in Criticism* (1961), and A. Dwight Culler, *Imaginative Reason: The Poetry of Matthew Arnold* (1966). A contrasting approach to the poems is G. Robert Stange, *Matthew Arnold: The Poet as Humanist* (1967).

More specialized works include William Robbins, *The Ethical Idealism of Matthew Arnold* (1959); Patrick McCarthy, *Matthew Arnold and the Three Classes* (1964); and Warren D. Anderson, *Matthew Arnold and the Classical Tradition* (1965). "Matthew Arnold" in T.S. Eliot, *The Use of Poetry and the Use of Criticism* (1932; 2d ed. 1964), is an examination of Arnold by an influential 20th-century critic. ☐

Thomas Arnold

The English educator Thomas Arnold (1795-1842) was a headmaster of Rugby School, and through his efforts it became the model for other English public schools and for boarding schools throughout the Western world.

Thomas Arnold was born in West Cowes, Isle of Wight, England, on June 13, 1795, the seventh child of William and Martha Arnold. His father was the postmaster and customs agent for the Isle of Wight. Arnold received his early education from his mother and an aunt. He attended the preparatory schools Warminster and Winchester from 1803 to 1811, prior to his admittance to Corpus Christi College of Oxford University. He graduated first class in classics in 1814. Through the influence of a friend he became a fellow of Oriel College, Oxford University, in 1814—a position he held until 1819. While there, he was ordained a deacon in the Church of England in 1818.

Arnold married Mary Penrose in 1820. He taught in several preparatory schools until 1827, when he became headmaster of Rugby School. He retained this post until his sudden death on June 12, 1842. Arnold also held a position in the senate of the University of London during 1836-1838 and was appointed a lecturer in history at Oxford in 1841.

Arnold was very much interested in Church reform. A radical in terms of religious thought of the day, he sought a simplified base on which to build a reunited Christian Church. He entered into a well-publicized dialogue with John Henry (later Cardinal) Newman over the nature of the Christian Church and what it ought to be. Arnold's religious ideas influenced the way in which he approached his job as headmaster of Rugby. He assumed the duties of the chaplain when the post became vacant, and he was noted for his sermons to the student body, later published. He emphasized the "Christian scholar" and "good character."

Social reform also interested Arnold. Although he maintained that the class structure of England was essentially natural and unchangeable, he actively sought to improve the lot of the lower and emerging middle classes. His convictions regarding the aristocracy centered on its re-

sponsibility and duty to do what was "right." In short, he wanted a useful aristocracy and a polished middle class. During the height of Parliament's debate over the reform bills of the early 1830s, Arnold published the *Englishman's Register,* a weekly journal supporting reform; it lasted only 3 months.

It is as headmaster of Rugby that Arnold is primarily remembered, however. The whole tone of the school was improved during his tenure. He is credited with broadening its curriculum, improving living conditions, raising the status of the masters, and inaugurating administrative reforms (for example, masters' conferences and student involvement in school affairs). What was once regarded as one of England's worst schools was, by the time of his death, famous for its successful graduates.

Further Reading

T.W. Bamford, *Thomas Arnold* (1960), provides new insight into Arnold's life and work. More traditional views of the headmaster's influence are in Joshua G. Fitch, *Thomas and Matthew Arnold and Their Influence on English Education* (1897), and Norman Wymer, *Dr. Arnold of Rugby* (1953). For a work written by one of Arnold's own students see Arthur P. Stanley, *The Life and Correspondence of Thomas Arnold* (1844).

Additional Sources

McCrum, Michael., *Thomas Arnold, headmaster: a reassessment,* Oxford England; New York: Oxford University Press, 1989.

Stanley, Arthur Penrhyn, *The life and correspondence of Thomas Arnold*, New York: AMS Press, 1978. □

Thurman Wesley Arnold

As assistant attorney general heading the Antitrust Division of the U.S. Department of Justice, Thurman Wesley Arnold (1891-1969) spearheaded the campaign against corporate monopoly carried on by the Roosevelt administration.

Born on June 2, 1891, the son of a prosperous lawyer and rancher, Thurman Arnold grew up in and around Laramie, Wyo., which still retained much of its raw frontier character. At the age of 16, having graduated from the University of Wyoming Preparatory School, Arnold went east to enter Princeton University. Although his years at Princeton were, by his own account, ordinary, he was elected to Phi Beta Kappa, and he determined on a legal career. He received his law degree from Harvard in 1914 and established his practice in Chicago.

In the spring of 1916 Arnold's field artillery unit of the Illinois National Guard was ordered to Texas to assist the United States expedition into Mexico to search for the guerrilla bandit leader Pancho Villa. Arnold was scarcely back in Chicago when the United States declared war against Germany and his unit was again mobilized. Just before going overseas, he married Frances Longan of Chicago. In later years the Arnolds had two sons.

Lawyer, Teacher, and Author

After the war Arnold returned with his wife to Laramie and established a fairly prosperous law practice. He became active in local Democratic party politics, serving one term as mayor of Laramie and several years in the Wyoming Legislature. In 1927, however, with an agricultural depression affecting business in Laramie, Arnold became dean of the University of West Virginia Law School. Three years later he accepted appointment to the law faculty at Yale University.

Arnold soon became known as a leading articulator of legal realism, the new theoretical movement that aimed to create a pragmatic science of the law. In two brilliant books, *The Symbols of Government* (1935) and *The Folklore of Capitalism* (1937), he cut through the abstractions and myths surrounding American political and economic institutions to explain the hard realities of matured industrial capitalism. Meanwhile he gave more of his time to government work under the New Deal, serving as special counsel for the Agricultural Adjustment Administration and as trial examiner for the Securities and Exchange Commission. In March 1938 he accepted an appointment from President Franklin Roosevelt as assistant attorney general in charge of the Antitrust Division of the Justice Department.

Antitrust Campaign

With the economy still badly depressed in 1938 despite persistent efforts to promote recovery, the Roosevelt administration launched an attack on price-fixing and other anti-competitive business practices as part of its effort to reverse the slump. Arnold and his staff, charged with leading the attack, went to work vigorously. Within 3 years the Justice Department had instituted more antitrust prosecutions than it had in the half century since the passage of the Sherman Act (1890). Arnold's staff quickly grew from about two dozen to 190 lawyers. The antitrust campaign had mixed results. Some notable suits were won, particularly that against the aluminum monopoly, and for the first time the government moved against the monopolistic practices of labor unions. But in the year or so before Pearl Harbor (1941), solidification of government-business partnership to maximize war production cut short the antitrust program and left Arnold with little official support within the Roosevelt administration. He finally resigned in 1943 to become associate justice of the U.S. Court of Appeals for the District of Columbia.

Arnold left after 2 years on the Federal bench to form a law partnership with Abraham Fortas and Paul A. Porter, and their firm became one of the busiest and most lucrative in Washington. Arnold generally remained out of the public eye, although he attracted considerable notoriety in the 1950s during several civil-liberties cases which the firm handled for former government officials investigated under the Truman administration's loyalty program. In the following decade Arnold remained reasonably active in his firm despite advancing age. He lived with his wife in Alexandria, Va., until his death on Nov. 7, 1969.

Further Reading

Arnold wrote an autobiography, *Fair Fights and Foul: A Dissenting Lawyer's Life* (1965). An excellent treatment of the realist movement in American legal theory, in which Arnold was a leading figure, is Wilfrid E. Rumble, Jr., *American Legal Realism: Skepticism, Reform, and the Judicial Tradition* (1968). Ellis W. Hawley, *The New Deal and the Problem of Monopoly* (1966), is equally good on the antitrust campaign carried out under Arnold's leadership in the late thirties. Broadus Mitchell, *Depression Decade: From New Era through New Deal, 1929-1941* (1947), and William E. Leuchtenburg, *Franklin D. Roosevelt and the New Deal, 1932-1940* (1963) may also be consulted on Arnold's career in the New Deal.

Additional Sources

Arnold, Thurman Wesley, *Voltaire and the cowboy: the letters of Thurman Arnold*, Boulder: Colorado Associated University Press, 1977. □

Arnold of Brescia

The Italian religious reformer Arnold of Brescia (ca. 1100-1155) preached a doctrine of absolute poverty

and called for the Church to abandon economic and political power.

Arnold was born at Brescia, and little is known of his youth. He became an Augustinian canon regular and later prior of the monastery in Brescia. He first established himself as a severe critic of the Church in the rebellion against Bishop Manfred, the political ruler of Brescia. On this occasion Arnold outspokenly attacked all forms of ecclesiastical worldliness and corruption. Denounced as a schismatic by the bishop to Pope Innocent II, Arnold soon after heard his proposals for reform condemned by the Second Lateran Council (1139), which banished him from Italy.

Arnold went to France, where he became involved in the conflict between Bernard of Clairvaux and Peter Abelard, taking the side of the latter and possibly becoming his student. In 1140 the Council of Sens condemned Abelard and Arnold for doctrinal error, but whereas Abelard submitted to its decision, Arnold did not. He went to Paris, where he opened a school in which he continued his attacks on clerical corruption. He also continued his polemics against Bernard, who retaliated by arranging for Arnold's expulsion from France.

After a brief period in Switzerland and Bohemia, Arnold arrived in Rome in 1145, intending to reconcile himself to the Church and promise obedience to the pope, Eugenius III. But Rome was seething with political instability. Innocent II had died in 1143 in the midst of the crisis surrounding the establishment of a republican government, and a successor, Lucius II, was killed while leading a force against the republicans. Eugenius III had established a truce with the new republican regime, but it proved to be short-lived, and he was forced to flee in 1146. Amid this antipapal turmoil, Arnold's intention to submit to Church authority evaporated, and he began preaching to the populace, calling for an end to clerical corruption and papal politics and for a total reform of the Church. Himself an ascetic, Arnold preached a doctrine of absolute poverty. For Arnold, the gospel taught that all worldly goods belonged to laymen and princes but never to Christians. He thus implied that clergy owning property had no power to perform the Sacraments—a heretical implication which brought down upon him the implacable hostility of the Church. He was excommunicated on July 15, 1148.

Yet Arnold's preaching proved to be very effective among students, the lower clergy, and the poorer classes. A strong-willed and charismatic figure, he acquired such a large following that his movement took on political significance. Arnold's fortunes were tied to those of the republic; from it he received political protection, and to it he gave his learning, eloquence, and following. To control this evangelical and republican movement, Pope Adrian IV, who succeeded Eugenius III in 1154, became allied with the German king Frederick I (Barbarossa). When Frederick took Rome by force in 1155, the republican party was destroyed, and Arnold was seized as a political rebel. He was executed by secular authorities, and his ashes were thrown into the Tiber to prevent their being venerated as relics.

Arnold's career, however, was more that of a religious reformer than of a political agitator or revolutionary. His influence on republicanism was negligible, but his moral and religious teachings spread throughout Italy and abroad and were taken up by various lay and evangelical movements in the 13th and 14th centuries.

Further Reading

The best biography of Arnold is George William Greenaway, *Arnold of Brescia* (1931), which has a good bibliography. Contemporary sources bearing witness to Arnold's career include *The Deeds of Frederick Barbarossa* by Otto of Freising, edited and translated by Charles Christopher Mierow and Richard Emery (1953); and *Memoirs of the Papal Court* by John of Salisbury, edited and translated by Marjorie Chibnall (1956). Extended treatments of Arnold's career are presented in Pasquale Villari, *Mediaeval Italy from Charlemagne to Henry VII* (1910), and in Ferdinand A. Gregorovius, *History of the City of Rome in the Middle Ages* (6th ed., 3 vols., 1953-1957). □

Arnolfo di Cambio

Arnolfo di Cambio (1245-1302) was the most important Florentine sculptor and architect of the last half of the 13th century.

Arnolfo di Cambio was trained in the sculptural workshop of Nicola Pisano, where he assisted in carving the marble pulpit in the Cathedral, Siena (1265-1268). Shortly thereafter he left Nicola's shop to establish himself as an independent artist. Little is known of his activities until 1277, when he was working in Rome under the patronage of Charles of Anjou. Arnolfo's three earliest works date from the period 1265-1277: the monument to Adrian V in S. Francesco, Viterbo, made in collaboration with a Cosmati master; the monument to Cardinal Riccardo Annibaldi, of which remnants are in the cloister of St. John Lateran, Rome; and the seated portrait of Charles of Anjou in the Capitoline Museum, Rome. Arnolfo's early style was characterized by simple, geometric forms that gave the figures a certain blockiness and immobility. Drapery folds were deeply cut and arranged in regular patterns, often falling in V-shaped folds.

Arnolfo's services were requested in Perugia in 1277 for work on a fountain. Charles of Anjou gave him leave to go, though Arnolfo's presence in Perugia is not documented until early 1281. Presumably the fountain he worked on is the one known through three fragments representing *assetati* (thirsty ones) in the National Gallery of Umbria, Perugia, rather than the famous Fontana Maggiore in Perugia by Nicola and Giovanni Pisano, which was completed in 1278. Arnolfo signed his monument to Cardinal Guglielmo DeBraye (died 1282) in S. Domenico, Orvieto. This work, which has lost its canopy, revealed for the first time Arnolfo's assimilation of the style of classical antiquity to which he had been exposed in Rome. This is especially noticeable in the Enthroned Virgin, who has a Junoesque quality. The monument to Cardinal DeBraye established a pattern for 14th-century funerary monuments that was repeated many times, especially in the work of Tino di Camaino.

In Rome, Arnolfo was responsible for erecting two ciboria, or altar canopies, one in S. Paolo fuori le Mura (1285) and the other in S. Cecilia in Trastevere (1293), where he combined his talents as sculptor and architect. Both are Gothic structures with give arches, triangular pediments ornamented with crockets, finials, and figure sculpture at the corners and in the spandrels. The muchadored bronze statue of the seated St. Peter located near the crossing of St. Peter's has been attributed to Arnolfo. This work was derived from an Early Christian marble prototype still preserved in the Vatican Grottoes. Other sculptural works done by Arnolfo in Rome during the 1290s include the statue of Pope Boniface VIII blessing and the funerary monument of Boniface VIII, both in the Vatican Grottoes, and the monument to Honorius IV in S. Maria in Aracoeli.

All of Arnolfo's purely architectural works are in Florence. The major one, the design for the Cathedral, was begun in 1296. This was an enormous undertaking that certainly justified the description of Arnolfo as "the most famous and able church builder in the land." The same document, dated April 1, 1300, reveals that he was *capomastro,* or artistic director and chief builder, for the Cathedral. The Cathedral project included numerous statues for the facade. Those that have survived include the *Virgin Enthroned, Pope Boniface VIII Enthroned,* and the *Nativity* in the Cathedral Museum, Florence, and the *Dormition of the Virgin* in Berlin. A statue of St. Reparata, also in the Cathedral Museum, is usually attributed to Arnolfo. Two other churches in Florence, the Badia and Sta Croce, are associated with Arnolfo's name, as is the massive town hall, the Palazzo Vecchio, in Florence. Arnolfo died on March 8, 1302, in Florence.

Further Reading

The best English-language source on Arnolfo's sculpture is John Pope-Hennessy, *An Introduction to Italian Sculpture,* vol. 1: *Italian Gothic Sculpture* (1955). A standard monograph, in Italian, with numerous black-and-white photographs is V. Mariani, *Arnolfo di Cambio* (1943). Also recommended is G. H. and E. R. Crichton, *Nicola Pisano and the Revival of Sculpture in Italy* (1938).

Additional Sources

Carli, Enzo, *Arnolfo,* Firenze: Casa editrice EDAM, 1993. □

Raymond Aron

Raymond Aron (1905-1983) excelled as an academic scholar, teacher, and journalist. He applied the methods of sociology to the study of economics, international relations, ideology, and war.

Raymond Aron was born in Paris, France, on March 14, 1905, the year that brought the separation of church and state in that country. His father, Gustave, was a professor of law who had married Suzanne Levy. After the world depression struck France, Raymond married Suzanne Gauchon on September 5, 1933. Their union produced two girls, Dominique (Mrs. Antoine Schnapper) and Laurence.

Aron had already graduated from the prestigious Ecole Normale Supérieure, the intellectual center of some of France's greatest thinkers, and in 1928, when only 23 years old, he won his *agrégation* in philosophy. Over the next 10 years he expanded into sociology and economics and received a State Doctorat in 1933. He had already started his career with a lectureship at the University of Cologne in Germany (1930-1931) and as a staff member at the Maison Académique of Berlin (1931-1933).

Having departed just as Hitler assumed power, Aron returned to his native land to become a philosophy professor at the Lycée of Le Havre (1933-1934), and from there he became the secretary of the Center for Social Documentation of the Ecole Normale/Supérieure (1934-1939). Just before World War II began in 1939 he joined the humanities faculty of the University of Toulouse as associate professor of social philosophy. He was active in the military defense

against Germany in 1939-1940, and when France fell he joined Gen. Charles De Gaulle in London. Here he began his career as a journalist, serving as editor-in-chief of *La France Libre* and, after the liberation of France, as an editorial writer of *Combat* (1946-1947) and *Le Figaro*, a right of center newspaper within the old liberal tradition of France. Aron referred to himself as a "Keynesian with a certain nostalgia for economic liberalism." For over 20 years he was one of the leading French columnists and thrived in the liberty allowed him by the paper. Later, when the newspaper was taken over by right-wing financiers led by Robert Hersant, he resigned in 1977 to preserve the editorial liberty that he had devoted his adult life to defending.

Aron remained a man of many talents, combining journalism, university teaching, and voluminous writing. He served as professor at the Ecole Nationale d'Administration and at the Institut d'Etudes Politiques (1945-1955). He then moved to the Sorbonne, where he joined the Faculty of Letters (1955-1968), and finally, in 1970, to that pinnacle of France's educational system, the Collège de France, where he served as professor of sociology until his death in 1983.

Aron's long career as teacher and writer brought him many honors. He was elected to almost all the major academies: Académie des Sciences Morales et Politiques, American Philosophical Society, American Academy of Arts and Sciences (honorary foreign member), British Academy, and Deutsche Akademie für Sprache und Dichtung. His prizes include Prix des Ambassadeurs (1962) for his book *Paix et guerre entre nations;* Prix Montaigne (1968) for the body of his work; Prix des Critiques (1973) for his *République impériale;* and Prix Goethe. He was elected as a chevalier, later officer of the Legion of Honor, and was awarded several honorary doctorates.

Aron's publications may be summarized by a book review by Stanley Hoffman published in the *New York Times Book Review* of June 17, 1979:

> The range of Raymond Aron's interests is immense. He is a philosopher, a sociologist, a political scientist, an economist; he is a scholar and a journalist. His 40-odd books and innumerable articles fall into two broad categories. Some are profound, often erudite reflections on the meaning of history, on the nature and forms of modern industrial society, on international conflict through the ages, on the evolution of political and social thought. . . . The second category consists of books and articles suggested by current events and debates, and especially by the political and intellectual tides in France. . . . What is common to both is Raymond Aron's relentlessly analytical and critical mind and his passionate defense of political liberalism. He is a descendant of the Philosophies of Enlightenment, and his intellectual godfathers are Montesquieu and Tocqueville.

Aron had for many years an intellectual mission: to defend the liberal order of the western world and to expose the left-wing myths that undermine the liberal tradition of freedom and private property. His views tended to range him with conservatively oriented groups; however, he insisted that, as a Keynesian liberal, he was neither rightwing nor left on all issues. His position depended on the issue: economic policy, North African policies, or relations between East and West.

His opposition to Marxism was based on several beliefs. In one of his most popular books, *The Opium of the Intellectuals* (1955, 1957), he contended that Marxism is mental opium and that many learned people create and believe false myths. These myths include the belief that history is progressive and liberating (whereas the victory of Marxism in Russia led to totalitarian controls), and that the proletariat is the collective savior of humanity, while in fact most workers, rather than becoming bearers of Marxism, just want a middle class standard of living.

Another highly influential publication, *The Century of Total War* (1954), presents a study of the inability of men to shape their destiny. "Since . . . bourgeois Europe entered into the century of total war, men have lost control of their history and have been dragged along by the contradictory promptings of technique and passions." What was most decisive about World War I was the "technical surprise," the vast use of deadly weapons. Industry discovered the means to provide the "mass production of destruction." This happened with the replacement of old-time professional armies with armies of people, the masses. Popular passions hardened ideologies, especially nationalism, with the result that the war created a "Europe of nationalities." The folly of men led to World War II, a conflict that became global but failed to bring the peace and liberty that west Europeans sought. "European democracy and freedom and civilization are the victims, even more than Germany, of a victory won in their name." Raymond Aron died in 1983.

Further Reading

Reviews of Aron's work can be found in *New York Times Book Review* (June 17, 1979); *TIME* (July 9, 1979); *Commentary* (September 1979); *Best Sellers* (September 1979); and *National Review* (November 9, 1979).

Additional Sources

Aron, Raymond, *Memoirs: fifty years of political reflection,* New York: Holmes & Meier, 1990.
Colquhoun, Robert, *Raymond Aron,* London; Beverly Hills, Calif.: Sage Publications, 1986. ☐

Jean Arp

The French sculptor and painter Jean Arp (1887-1966) was a pioneer of abstract art. His wooden reliefs and sculpture in the round are biomorphic in form and poetically allusive.

Jean Arp was born in Strasbourg. He studied at the Academy in Weimar in 1905-1907 and at the Académie Julian in Paris in 1908. He came to disapprove of formal instruction and moved to Weggis, Switzerland, where he lived and worked in isolation. In 1912, after meeting Wassily Kandinsky in Munich, Arp exhibited with the Blue Rider group, and in 1913 he exhibited in the first Autumn Salon in Berlin. The following year he met Pablo Picasso, Robert Delaunay, under whose influence he began to work in a cubist vein, Amedeo Modigliani, and Max Ernst. In 1915 Arp settled in Zurich, where he met the painter Sophie Taeuber, whom he married in 1921.

Arp was one of the founders of the Dada group in 1916, which held its tumultuous meetings at the Cabaret Voltaire in Zurich. The Dadaists, reacting to the general disillusionment brought on by World War I, held up non-sense as the chief esthetic value to be realized in art and literature. Arp, now a committed Dadaist, abandoned the cubist rigors of the previous 2 years for an art that was whimsical in spirit and biomorphic in form. At this time he constructed painted wooden reliefs, whose curved shapes vaguely call to mind navels, clouds, and lakes. Arp's Dadaist art represented the fanciful and poetic, rather than the nihilistic and morbid, side of the movement, and he gave his works humorous titles. Among his Dadaist collages was a series in which bits of colored paper were pasted on cardboard; these he titled *Collage with Squares Arranged According to the Laws of Chance* (ca. 1917). But the bits of paper seem to have been placed with a concern for the effectiveness of the design. In 1919 Arp collaborated with Ernst and others to found the Cologne Dada group.

Arp settled in Paris in 1922, where he joined the surrealist movement. He participated in the first surrealist group exhibition held in Paris in 1925 and was officially a surrealist until 1930. In 1931-1932, as a member of the Abstraction-Création group, he made pictures out of bits of twine and torn paper and executed his first sculpture in the round of stone and wood.

His sculpture in the round, like the wooden reliefs, is curving and vaguely suggests the world of nature, such as hills, clouds, or part of a torso, rather than the world of machines. Arp always brought his material, the stone or bronze, to a high degree of finish. He described his sculpture as "concretions." "Concretion," he wrote, "designates solidification, the mass of the stone, the plant, the animal, the man. Concretion is something that has grown." Unlike Constantin Brancusi's sculpture, to which it is superficially similar, Arp's sculpture seems to be expansive rather than distilled or concentrated. Works such as the bronze *Shell and Head* (1933) and marble *Star* (1939-1960) seem to turn out to the world rather than turn in upon themselves.

Arp visited the United States in 1949 and 1950. He died in Basel, Switzerland.

Further Reading

Probably the best overall treatment of Arp in English is James Thrall Soby, ed., *Jean Arp* (1958), with equal attention given to the Dadaist wooden reliefs and the sculpture in the round. It contains essays by the Dadaist Richard Hülsenbeck, Robert Melville, and Carola Giedion-Welcker, as well as an essay by Arp. Two recent book-length treatments of Arp are Sir Herbert E. Read, *The Art of Jean Arp* (1968), and Edward Trier, *Jean Arp, Sculpture: His Last Ten Years* (1968). Hans Arp, *On My Way: Poetry and Essays, 1912-1947* (1948), is a collection of remarkably sensitive poems. Good background material is in A. H. Barr, Jr., ed., *Fantastic Art, Dada, Surrealism* (1936; 3d ed. 1947).

Additional Sources

Andreotti, Margherita., *The early sculpture of Jean Arp*, Ann Arbor, Mich.: UMI Research Press, 1989. □

Svante August Arrhenius

The Swedish chemist and physicist Svante August Arrhenius (1859-1927) is known for his theory of electrolytic dissociation.

Svante Arrhenius was born on Feb. 19, 1859, at Vik near Uppsala, the son of Svante Gustav and Carolina Thunberg Arrhenius. His father was a land surveyor and later a supervisor at the University of Uppsala.

Arrhenius's intellectual abilities became obvious early. Against his parents' wishes, the blond, blue-eyed, rubicund child taught himself to read at the age of 3. He acquired a fantastic arithmetical skill and a pictorial memory by observing his father adding columns in his account books. In his future scientific work, he was especially fond of discovering relationships and laws from masses of data. At the age of 8, he entered the fifth grade of the cathedral school, where he distinguished himself particularly in physics and mathematics and from which he graduated, the youngest and ablest student, in 1876.

Theory of Electrolytes

Arrhenius entered the University of Uppsala, where he studied chemistry, physics, and mathematics. As he was not satisfied with his chief instructor in physics, he left Uppsala in 1881 to work on the conductivities of electrolytes at Stockholm under the physicist E. Edlund. In 1884 Arrhenius presented his results *(Recherches sur la conductibilité galvanique des électrolytes)* together with a new theory of electrolytes *(Théorie chimique des électrolytes)* in a 150-page dissertation for the doctorate at Uppsala. Although he compromised and moderated his radical ideas, his professors were not impressed and only grudgingly passed the dissertation.

Arrhenius's theory of electrolytes encountered widespread resistance from the scientific world, but it eventually found confirmation in the modern theory of atomic structure. Of the 56 theses advanced in his 1884 dissertation, only a few have not withstood the test of time or have had to be greatly modified. In order to explain the nonconductance of solid salt and pure water when tested separately and the conductance of an aqueous salt solution, Arrhenius postulated that when a solid salt is dissolved in water its molecules dissociate or ionize into charged particles, which Michael Faraday had called ions years before. Whereas Faraday assumed that such ions are produced only during electrolysis, Arrhenius proposed that they are already present in solution even without the application of an electric current. Chemical reactions in solutions are thus reactions between ions. Arrhenius's views were essentially correct for weak electrolytes (weak acids, bases, and other covalent substances), but for strong electrolytes his ideas were modified in 1923 by the Debye-Hückel theory of inter-ionic attraction.

Professional Recognition

With the aid of a travel grant from the Swedish Academy of Sciences, Arrhenius devoted his next few years to travel and study. He worked with Wilhelm Ostwald in Riga and Leipzig, with Friedrich Kohlrausch in Würzburg, with Ludwig Boltzmann in Graz, and with J. H. van't Hoff in Amsterdam.

In 1891 Arrhenius was appointed lecturer and in 1895, over strong objections, professor of physics at the Technical University of Stockholm, of which he became rector in 1896. During this time he courted and married Sofia Rudback. The couple had a son, Olav Vilhelm, who became a worker in soil science and agricultural botany. Three children were born of his second marriage, to Maria Johansson.

In 1901 Arrhenius was elected, with strong opposition, to the Swedish Academy of Sciences. The following year he received the Davy Medal of the Royal Society, and in 1903 he became the first Swede to receive the Nobel Prize in chemistry for his theory of electrolytic dissociation. He was appointed rector of the newly founded Nobel Institute for Physical Research at Stockholm in 1905, a position he held until his retirement in the spring of 1927.

Spectrum of Scientific Achievement

After his theory was accepted by the entire scientific world, Arrhenius turned his attention to other topics. He became interested in the widest application of the fundamental theory of chemical reactions. In 1902 he began to apply the laws of theoretical chemistry to physiological problems, especially those of serum therapy (immunochemistry). He found that organismic changes follow the same laws as ordinary chemical reactions and that no essential difference exists between reactions in the test tube and those in the human body.

Arrhenius became active in the fields of astronomy and cosmic physics, and he proposed a new theory of the birth of the solar system by the collision of stars. He used the ability of radiation pressure to transport cosmic material to explain comets, the corona, the aurora borealis, and zodiacal light. He also hypothesized that spores of living matter are transported by radiation pressure from planet to planet with the resultant spread of life throughout interstellar space. He developed a theory to explain the ice ages and other profound climatic changes undergone by the earth's surface. He reflected upon the world's supply of energy and the conservation of natural resources. He dreamed of a universal language and proposed a modified form of English. There was hardly a field of science to which he did not make original, if not universally accepted, contributions. During his last years he wrote several textbooks and many books of a popular nature, in which he made it a point to indicate what was still to be done in the fields under discussion. Arrhenius had a healthy constitution, but he made great demands upon himself in order to maintain his extraordinary productivity. After a brief attack of acute intestinal catarrh in September 1927, he died on October 2 and was buried in Uppsala.

Further Reading

The biography by Wilhelm Palmaer, "Svante Arrhenius, 1859-1927," originally in German, appears in an abridged translation in Eduard Farber, ed., *Great Chemists* (1961). A thumbnail sketch of Arrhenius and a brief evaluation of the electrolytic dissociation theory are contained in Eduard Farber, *Nobel Prize Winners in Chemistry, 1901-1961* (1963). Benjamin Harrow, *Eminent Chemists of Our Time* (1920), explains how Arrhenius formulated his theory of electrolytic dissociation. A popularized summary of his life and work may be found in Bernard Jaffe, *Crucibles: The Story of Chemistry, from Ancient Alchemy to Nuclear Fission* (1930; rev. ed. 1948).

Additional Sources

Svante Arrhenius, 1859-1927, Moskva: "Nauka," 1990.
Crawford, Elisabeth T., *Arrhenius: from ionic theory to the greenhouse effect,* Canton, Mass.: Science History Publications/ USA, 1996. □

Antonin Artaud

Antonin Artaud (1896-1948) was one of the 20th century's most important theoreticians of the drama. He developed the theory of the Theater of Cruelty, which has influenced playwrights from Beckett to Genet, from Albee to Gelber.

Antonin-Marie-Joseph Artaud was born in Marseilles on September 4, 1896, the son of a wealthy shipfitter and a mother from a Greek background. At age five he suffered a near-fatal attack of meningitis, the results of which remained with him for the rest of his life.

He was educated at the Collège du Sacré Coeur in Marseilles and at 14 founded a literary magazine, which he kept going for almost four years. Still in his teens, he began to have sharp head pains, which continued throughout his life. In 1914 he was the victim of an attack of neurasthenia and was treated in a rest home; the following year he was given opium to alleviate his pain, and he became addicted within a few months.

He was inducted into the army in 1916, but was released in less than a year on grounds of both mental instability and drug addiction. In 1918 he committed himself to a clinic in Switzerland, where he remained until 1920.

On his release, he went immediately to Paris, still under medical supervision, and began to study with Charles Dullin, an actor and director. He soon began to find jobs as a stage and screen actor and as a set and costume designer. Within the next decade, he appeared on film in *Fait Divers*

and *Surcourt—le roi des corsairs* (1924); Abel Gance's *Napoléon Boneparte* (1925); *La Passion de Jeanne d'Arc* (1928); *Tarakanowa* (1929); G. W. Pabst's *Dreigroschenoper,* made in Berlin (1930); and *Les Croix des Bois, Faubourg Montmartre,* and *Femme d'une nuit* (all 1930). On stage he had roles in *He Who Gets Slapped* (1923), *Six Characters in Search of an Author* (1924), and *R.U.R.* (1924).

At the same time, Artaud became seriously interested in the surrealist movement headed by André Breton and in 1923 published a volume of symbolist verse strongly influenced by Mallarmé, Verlaine, and Rimbaud, *Tric trac du ciel* (*Backgammon of the Sky*). Two years later, at the height of his involvement with the surrealists, he published *L'Ombilic des limbes* (*Umbilical Limbo*), a collection of letters, poems in prose, and bits of dialogue; it contained one complete work, the five-minute playlet *Le Jet de sang* (*The Jet of Blood*), which was finally produced in 1964.

Artaud broke with the organized surrealist movement in 1926, when Breton became a Communist and attempted to take his fellow-members with him into the party. Yet Artaud continued to view himself as a surrealist and in 1927 wrote the filmscript for *La Coquille et le clergyman,* perhaps the most famous surrealist film, and *Les Pèse-nerfs* (*Nerve Scales*), another collection containing various literary forms.

As A Producer

It was also in 1927 that he joined with Roger Vitrac and Robert Aron to found the Théâtre Alfred Jarry, named for the author of the 1896 play *Ubu roi,* which had so shocked the theatrical establishment of its time. Their theater had no permanent home, so they leased space in established theaters. In their first year they presented two programs, the first an evening of three one-act plays, one contributed by each of the founders, and Léon Poirier's *Verdun, visions d'histoire.* The following year they produced one evening which combined the film of Maxim Gorky's *The Mother* and the last act of Paul Claudel's *Partage de midi,* another of Strindberg's *Dream Play,* and their final effort, Vitrac's *Victor ou les enfants du pouvoir.*

Working as a theatrical producer gave Artaud an insight into the exigencies of the practical aspects of theater, with which he was not happy. Then, in 1931, he saw a Balinese drama at the French Colonial Exposition in Paris and found in this work, which stressed spectacle and dance, the ideal for which he had been searching.

As A Theoretician

In 1932-1933 he published his first work of dramatic theory, *Manifestes du théâtre de la cruauté* (*Manifestos of the Theater of Cruelty*), and in 1935 staged the first work based on his theories, an adaptation of *Les Cenci,* heavily dependent on the earlier works on that theme by the British poet Shelley and the French novelist Stendhal. Since one of Artaud's theories involved the breaking of the barrier between actors and audience, *Les Cenci* may be have been the first play ever staged in the round. In any event, it was a total failure.

Shattered, Artaud went to Mexico in 1930 and stayed there for the better part of a year, spending some time with the sun-worshipping Tarahumara Indians. On his return to France, he became engaged to a Belgian girl and tried to end his drug dependence. In May of 1937, giving a lecture in Brussels, he went completely out of control and began screaming at the audience. In the fall of that same year, on a visit to Ireland, he was declared mentally unfit, put in a straitjacket, and sent back to France. Ironically, it was shortly thereafter that his most important and influential work, *Le Théâtre et son double* (*The Theater and Its Double*), was published.

Diagnosed as schizophrenic, Artaud spent the next nine years in mental institutions, returning to Paris in triumph, acclaimed as a genius after his three-hour lecture-reading to an audience which included Nobel laureate Andre Gide, future Nobel laureate Albert Camus, and André Breton. Artaud died of cancer on March 4, 1948, in a rest home near Paris. Unlike his fellow theoretician of the drama, Bertolt Brecht, whose plays have been widely honored and frequently performed, Artaud had no success at all with his endeavors in drama, poetry, or fiction. His reputation rests entirely on his critical work.

In a word, Artaud called for a theater that is anti-intellectual. He believed that the drama of the past 400 years had become sterile and had no future. In the essay "No More Masterpieces" he laid the blame for the psychologically oriented drama on Shakespeare and elsewhere blamed Racine, but, wherever the responsibility lies, he asserted that the attempts "to reduce the unknown to the known, to the quotidian and ordinary" had brought the theater to the sorry state in which he found it.

Besides the psychological concerns, he also objected to the emphasis on the written word, the primacy of spoken poetry. In "The Theater of Cruelty (First Manifesto)" he said that "it is essential to put an end to the subjugation of the theater to the text and to recover the notion of a kind of unique language half-way between gesture and thought."

What Artaud offered as a substitute was the Theater of Cruelty. In the essays "Letters on Cruelty," Artaud said, "This cruelty is a matter of neither sadism nor blood-shed. . . . " He went on, "I do not systematically cultivate horror . . . cruelty signifies rigor, implacable intention and decision, irreversible and absolute determination." He added, "It is a mistake to give the word 'cruelty' a meaning of merciless bloodshed and disinterested gratuitous pursuit of physical suffering. . . . Cruelty is above all lucid, a kind of rigid control and submission to necessity. There is no cruelty without consciousness. . . . "

Yet, at the same time, it must be remembered that in one of his staged works Artaud picked as the theme the Cencis, a tale of rape, incest, and murder; that another of his works concerned the warped and dissolute Roman emperor Heliogabalus, and that one of his favorite British plays was *'Tis Pity She's a Whore*, also about incest and murder.

What Artaud's Theater of Cruelty had to offer instead of the conventional was a theater in which spectacle played the main role. Instead of poetic language, there would be a series of sounds and " . . . these intonations will constitute a kind of harmonic balance, a secondary deformation of speech. . . . "

There will be musical instruments, he said, which will be "treated as objects and as part of the set." The lighting will be calculated to produce "an element of thinness, density, and opaqueness, with a view to producing the sensations of heat, cold, anger, fear, etc." The dress should be "age-old costumes of ritualistic intent," while the stage should be "a single site, without partition or barrier of any kind." He adds: "Manikins, enormous masks, objects of strange proportions will appear." As to the set, "There will not be any set." Finally, there will be no script: "We shall not act a written play, but we shall make attempts at direct staging, around themes, facts, or known works."

While Artaud's theory was not successful in eradicating a theater based on texts, it made play-producers more conscious of elaborate sets, of movement (particularly the dance), and of an attention to myth, another of his concerns. Hence, his influence continued to be strong decades after his death in 1948.

Further Reading

No understanding of Artaud would be possible without a reading of the *The Theater and Its Double,* translated by Mary C. Richards (1958). The best biography in English is *Artaud and After* by Ronald Hayman (1977). Another excellent appreciation is *Artaud* by Martin Esslin, and important contributions appear in *The Theater of Revolt* by Robert Brustein (1964) and *Against Interpretation* by Susan Sontag (1966). Any good history of 20th-century theater will contain a good analysis, e.g., *History of the Modern Theater* by Tom Driver (1970).

Additional Sources

Esslin, Martin., *Antonin Artaud,* New York: Penguin Books, 1977, 1976.

Esslin, Martin., *Artaud,* London: J. Calder, 1976; Glasgow: Fontana/Collins, 1976.

Hayman, Ronald, *Artaud and After,* Oxford Eng.; New York: Oxford University Press, 1977. □

Chester Alan Arthur

The twenty-first president of the United States, Chester Alan Arthur (1830-1886) was reputed to be one of the leading spoilsmen in American politics when he took office, but he proved to be a dignified and an able administrator.

Political enemies claimed that Chester A. Arthur was Canadian-born and therefore ineligible to be president of the United States. Arthur himself never replied to the charges and said that he was born on Oct. 5, 1830, in Fairfield, Vt., the eldest of seven children of a Scotch-Irish Baptist minister. He was educated at Union College in Schenectady, N.Y., taught school, and studied law. Moving to New York City, he built up a successful law practice and became interested in Republican party politics.

Arthur rose steadily, if undramatically, in the Republican party by virtue of his willingness to perform the less exciting labors necessary to building a new political movement. New York City was slipping into the clutches of the Democratic party machine of William Marcy Tweed during the Civil War, but Arthur moved up steadily as the protégé of the state's governor. He served as engineer in chief, inspector general, and quartermaster general of New York, raising, equipping, and dispatching state troops for the Federal government. In 1863, when the Republicans were turned out of office, he stepped aside for a Democratic successor. By unanimous agreement he had been an excellent administrator.

Arthur as a Spoilsman

As a reward for his work for the party, in November 1871 President U.S. Grant named Arthur to be collector of customs for the Port of New York. In an age when political parties functioned almost primarily for patronage—the jobs and other "spoils" which accrued to the party in power—Arthur possessed one of the most powerful and lucrative positions in the patronage apparatus by the time he was 41. As collector, he supervised more than 1000 employees, and many of these were troops in the New York State Republican machine. Arthur helped oversee the distribution of the jobs and, at election time, supervised the collection of "assessments"—contributions to Republican campaign funds which were virtually a requirement for holding a Federal job. The Customs House was no stranger to graft but Arthur himself was honest. He once said that "if I had

misappropriated five cents, and on walking down-town saw two men talking on the street together, I would imagine they were talking of my dishonesty and the very thought would drive me mad."

In a sense, corruption would have been superfluous. Arthur was paid by a fee of one-half of all monies he recovered for the government from importers misrepresenting what they owed. In one famous case Arthur and two other officials divided $135,000. His pay generally ran to $40,000 a year until 1874, when his salary was set at $12,000.

Not all of this money stayed in Arthur's bank account. Like all political appointees, he was expected to make large donations to the party. These expenditures earned Arthur a prominent place in New York State's patronage-oriented Republican party. With Alonzo Cornell and Levi Morton, he stood second only to Roscoe Conkling in the control of New York's powerful political organization. His reputation among reformers was disgraceful but, until 1880, he could afford to ignore any pressures but Conkling's.

Arthur's nicknames—"the Gentleman Boss," "the Elegant Arthur,"—indicate the figure he cut. Over 6 feet tall, stoutly built according to the specifications of the times, with a wavy moustache and bushy sidewhiskers, he dressed in fine, fashionable clothing. He was exquisitely urbane, dining well, drinking the best wines and brandies, and entertaining on a grand scale. None of this was extraordinary in middle-class New York City, but it made for a stunning contrast to the conservatively clothed and morally straitlaced Midwestern Republican politicians among whom he moved in Washington.

Accidental President

In 1880 Republicans divided sharply and bitterly over the nomination of a presidential candidate. The two principal hopefuls were former president U.S. Grant (Conkling and Arthur were among his chief advocates) and James G. Blaine. The deadlocked convention resolved the issue only by turning to a dark-horse candidate, James A. Garfield of Ohio. Conkling, the leader of the pro-Grant faction, was furious—for Garfield was friendlier to Blaine than himself—and he insisted that Levi Morton decline the offered vice-presidential nomination. Arthur was the Garfield group's second vice-presidential choice and, though Conkling remained adamant, Arthur accepted. Arthur continued to pay court to Conkling, however, even after the election had made him vice president of the United States. In fact, Arthur was in Albany, lobbying for Conkling's reelection, when news arrived that President Garfield had been shot in Washington by a deranged man who claimed he did it in order to make Arthur president. Garfield died on Sept. 19, 1881, and Arthur became president.

Historians tend to agree that Arthur was a much better president than anyone expected. He seemed sensitive to the dignity of his office, and, while he continued to send most patronage to his old allies, he generally extricated himself from their society. Though he offered Conkling a seat on the Supreme Court, he left one of Conkling's old enemies in the Customs House. Republicans on the side of reform were chagrined at this new president, but Arthur could be surprising. He even supported and signed a landmark civil service bill (providing, among other things, for examinations as a prerequisite to holding some government jobs), and he permitted an investigation of post office frauds, which implicated several cronies.

Arthur remained what he had always been, a good administrator. But, as H. Wayne Morgan (1969) points out, "Arthur liked the appearance of power more than its substance." He designed a flag for himself, relished military ceremonies, refurbished the shabby White House, and presented a perfect presidential appearance. He took little initiative in the significant events of his term, such as the Pendleton Civil Service Act and the construction of a modern navy.

Unfortunately for Arthur's political future (he would have liked to be reelected in 1884), he had alienated old supporters without winning over old enemies. In 1884 he had no real strength at the Republican Convention and was quietly shelved. He died in 1886. He had not inspired his contemporaries, and, though his biographers have been friendly, he has not inspired them either.

Further Reading

There are several biographies of Arthur, none of particular distinction. A standard account is George F. Howe, *Chester A. Arthur: A Quarter-century of Machine Politics* (1934). Matthew Josephson, *The Politicos: 1865-1896* (1938), is a highly readable, if sometimes inaccurate, history of 19th-century politics. H. Wayne Morgan, *From Hayes to McKinley: National Party Politics* (1969), updates Josephson's work and includes brief, incisive portraits of Arthur and other leading personalities of the era. □

José Gervasio Artigas

The patriot José Gervasio Artigas (1764-1850) is often referred to as the father of Uruguayan independence. While such a title is somewhat misleading, certainly Artigas is unchallenged as the greatest hero of Uruguay.

José Gervasio Artigas was born in Montevideo on June 19, 1764. He was a gaucho, or cowboy, until 1810, when he was attracted to a patriotic cause. A revolutionary junta in Buenos Aires desired to take the region of the viceroyalty of the Rio de la Plata out of the jurisdiction of Spanish control. From 1810 to 1811 Artigas commanded Uruguayan patriots in this war of independence against the Spanish. He conquered almost all of Uruguay except for the city of Montevideo. Then Artigas became the spokesman for those who were disenchanted with the leadership of Buenos Aires and wanted more autonomy for the provinces.

In 1813 Artigas-supporting delegates to a constitutional assembly in Argentina were rejected by the Buenos Aires government, and a civil war between the Artigas faction and Buenos Aires began. The differences between the two were fundamental and thus difficult to resolve. Artigas favored a limited federalist government that would leave a great deal of power to the local government. Buenos Aires essentially favored little provincial autonomy and a strong central government located in Buenos Aires.

Militarily, Artigas and Buenos Aires were well matched. He had the support of the region that would become Uruguay and, after 1815, the support of four river provinces that made up the Liga Federal, a confederation of provinces. Buenos Aires, in addition to the population of the province and city, had the revenue of the port facilities and the allegiance of some interior provinces.

Artigas participated in the successful siege of Montevideo, which the Spanish still held, and in 1815 entered Buenos Aires in triumph. But in 1816 he faced ultimate defeat when the Portuguese, hoping to add the provinces around the Rio de la Plata to Brazil, invaded Uruguay. Buenos Aires refused to support him, and after a 4-year struggle Artigas's forces were defeated. From then on Artigas lived in exile in Paraguay, no longer participating in Uruguay's struggle for independence. With the proclamation of Uruguayan independence in 1828, he was invited to return by his victorious followers, but he declined. He died in Asunción on Sept. 23, 1850.

Artigas's significance crossed national boundaries. In Uruguay he is most accurately remembered as the architect of a feeling of uniqueness and regional pride that eventually led to independence. He never favored independence for Uruguay, preferring always the concept of a confederation of all provinces making up the former viceroyalty of the Rio de la Plata. For Argentina he first articulated the principles of federalism in the "Instructions of 13," which were incorporated in the Constitution of 1852. Under this constitution Argentina finally achieved a measure of stability, enabling it to grow into a position of real power in South America.

Further Reading

The most complete work on the life of Artigas is in Spanish. John Street, *Artigas and the Emancipation of Uruguay* (1959), is an excellent treatment in English. See also Simon G. Hanson, *Utopia in Uruguay: Chapters in the Economic History of Uruguay* (1938), and Clarence H. Haring, *The Spanish Empire in America* (1947). □

Cosmas Damian and Egid Quirin Asam

The brothers Cosmas Damian (1686-1739) and Egid Quirin (1692-1750) Asam, German artists who worked in architecture, painting, and sculpture, often as a team, achieved in their works a unity of the arts unequaled in Bavaria during the late baroque period.

The Asam brothers were sons of the painter Hans Georg Asam. Cosmas Damian was born on Sept. 28, 1686, and Egid Quirin on Sept. 1, 1692. They received their early training from their father. The brothers went to Rome in 1711, where they absorbed the style of the Roman high baroque, particularly from the work of the architect and sculptor Gian Lorenzo Bernini and his followers. Upon their return to Bavaria, Cosmas Damian worked as a painter, and his brother continued his studies under the sculptor Andreas Faistenberger in Munich.

The brothers collaborated in 1718 in the construction and decoration of the church of the Benedictine Abbey of Weltenburg on the Danube, near Regensburg, their most famous creation. Cosmas Damian was the architect and painter, and Egid Quirin produced all the sculpture for this most dramatic achievement of the period in Bavaria. The illusionistic ceiling fresco and the sculpture of the high altar, *St. George Slaying the Dragon,* were finished in 1721. The church interior exploits all the illusionistic devices of the Roman baroque—a dynamic oval ground plan, hidden light sources, agitated sculptural forms, and brilliant color and gilding—to give the on-looker a feeling that he is witnessing a heavenly vision in surroundings suggestive of the wonders of Paradise.

The most spectacular of Egid Quirin's works is the lifesize polychromed *Assumption of the Virgin* in the monastery church at Rohr (1718-1722). The group of the Virgin carried by angels floats, seemingly unsupported, in the air, above an altar conceived as a stage. Cosmas Damian executed numerous ceiling frescoes, including those for the church of St. Jakob, Innsbruck (1720-1723), the pilgrimage church at Einsiedeln in Switzerland (1723-1726), Brovnov Abbey near Prague (1731), and the abbey church at Osterhofen in Bavaria (1730-1735). All are noteworthy for complex and daring effects of perspective, rich color, and dramatic massing of figures, clearly revealing the influence of Roman ceiling painting, yet with a certain naive gaiety and heartiness that is distinctively Bavarian.

The last work on which the brothers collaborated was the house and attached church that Egid Quirin began to build in Munich in 1733 as his home and as a private chapel and votive offering. The small church of St. John Nepomuk (popularly called the Asam Church) is, after Weltenburg, the richest display of their respective talents. The ceiling fresco by Cosmas Damian was badly damaged in World War II. The sculpture and stucco decoration of the church are unsurpassed in their complexity, richness of color and forms, and unity of the whole. The group of the Holy Trinity, hanging above the altar, and the sculptures on the confessionals are among Egid Quirin's most startling and moving works.

Cosmas Damian died on May 11, 1739, before the church was finished, and Egid Quirin completed it. He died on April 29, 1750, in his house attached to the church.

Further Reading

The only works in English that discuss the Asam brothers at length are John Bourke, *Baroque Churches of Central Europe* (1958; 2d ed. 1962); Nicolas Powell, *From Baroque to Rococo* (1959); Eberhard Hempel, *Baroque Art and Architecture in Central Europe* (1965); and Henry-Russell Hitchcock, *Rococo Architecture in Southern Germany* (1968). The best monograph, in German, is Erika Hanfstaengl, *Die Brüder Cosmas Damian und Egid Quirin Asam* (1955), which also has the best photographs. □

Francis Asbury

Francis Asbury (1745-1816), English-born American clergyman, broke with the English Methodists in 1787 and established the Methodist Episcopal Church in America.

Francis Asbury was born on Aug. 20 or 21, 1745, in Staffordshire, England. His mother exerted great influence over Francis. She taught him to read the Bible before he was 6 years old and instilled in him a strong fear of sin. A shy, introspective boy who was intimidated by bullying classmates and a harsh schoolmaster, he had only 6 years of formal education.

Asbury had a religious awakening at the age of 14, after which he began to attend meetings of the Methodist Society. He soon became an exhorter and later a preacher. At the Bristol Conference of the Methodists in 1771, he volunteered to go to America as a missionary. He arrived in Philadelphia on Oct. 27, 1771, and went to New York to work under Richard Boardman, one of the first missionaries sent to America by the Methodist Society.

Asbury found church discipline lax and the city sinful. Without asking Boardman's permission, he borrowed a horse and rode into the countryside, thus making his first circuit in America by going to several New York communities.

A morose and solemn man, Asbury constantly subjected himself to spiritual and physical flagellation. A variety of physical problems plagued him during the 45 years in which he traveled the American continent; nevertheless, he rode at least 5,000 miles a year, preaching and exhorting at every opportunity.

Asbury's prestige grew as his circuit widened. He preached first in Pennsylvania, Maryland, Delaware, and Virginia and later in the South and the West. In October 1772 he received a letter from John Wesley informing the preacher that he was to replace Boardman as Wesley's assistant. The following year he was in turn succeeded by Thomas Rankin. There was constant tension between Asbury and Rankin, a result, in part, of Rankin's jealousy of Asbury and, in part, of Asbury's inability to work under anyone. Wesley ordered both to leave America during the Revolutionary War. Rankin returned to England but Asbury chose to remain in America, despite the fact that Methodists were suspected of Tory sympathies. He spent 6 months in seclusion at the Delaware home of Judge Thomas White, but his urge to preach overcame his caution and he returned to circuit riding. By 1780 his influence at the Baltimore

Additional Sources

Asbury, Francis, *Francis Asbury's America: an album of early American Methodism,* Grand Rapids, MI: F. Asbury Press, 1984.

Ludwig, Charles, *Francis Asbury: God's circuit rider,* Milford, Mich.: Mott Media, 1984.

Smeltzer, Wallace Guy, *Bishop Francis Asbury, Field Marshal of the Lord,* Pittsburgh?: Commission on Archives and History of the Western Pennsylvania Conference of the United Methodist Church in cooperation with the author; Denver, Colo.: Available from W.G. Smeltzer, 1982. ☐

Conference was forceful enough to defeat a group of Methodists from the Southern states in a dispute over the Sacraments. He became the acknowledged head of the Methodist Church in America, and when, on Dec. 27, 1784, he was ordained superintendent, he became the titular head.

Asbury ruled his ever-increasing flock imperially, calling himself "bishop." The Methodist Episcopal Church was formally established in America in 1787, when he broke with the English Methodists. His dominance was seriously threatened only once: in 1792 a group of dissidents led by James O'Kelly refused to submit to Asbury's rule and left the Methodist Church to form the Republican Methodist Church.

Eventually Asbury became so ill that he was compelled to accept the appointment of an associate, Richard Whatcoat. In a very real sense, Asbury was the founder of American Methodism. When he became superintendent in 1784, there were 83 traveling preachers and less than 15,000 Methodists. When he died on March 31, 1816, there were 212,000 Methodists, 2,000 local preachers, and 700 circuit riders.

Further Reading

Francis Asbury's own *Journal and Letters,* edited by Elmer T. Clark and others (3 vols., 1958), is an invaluable primary source. Herbert Asbury, *A Methodist Saint: The Life of Bishop Asbury* (1927), is a solid biography, and L. C. Rudolph, *Francis Asbury* (1966), provides additional detail. An excellent reference is Emory S. Bucke, ed., *The History of American Methodism,* 3 vols. (1964).

Shalom Asch

The major works of the Polish-born writer Shalom Asch (1880-1957) are built on an epic scale, show profound insight into human character, and reveal prophetic vision. They depict patriarchal Jewish life with its devotional joys and fateful martyrdom.

Shalom Asch was born in Kutno, Poland, where he studied at a Hebrew religious school. At the age of 18 he left for Wocawek to become a Hebrew teacher. His reading was extensive in Hebrew, Yiddish, Russian, Polish, and German literatures, and he started writing in Hebrew. In 1899 he showed his work to the noted Yiddish writer H. L. Peretz, who advised him to turn to Yiddish as a medium of expression. From that time on, most of Asch's writing was done in Yiddish.

In 1900 he published his first short story, "Moishele." Subsequently his sketches, short stories, and plays appeared in Jewish weeklies and periodicals. Like his childhood, they were steeped in sadness.

When Asch met the Polish writer M. M. Shapira, whose daughter Matilda he later married, his literary horizons broadened. The short story "The Little Town" (1905) opened a new chapter in Yiddish literature. The emphasis on poverty shifted now to the idyllic and romantic atmosphere of the small town, despondency gave way to faith, and satire turned to humor. A year earlier Asch had written his first play, *He Left and Returned.* His two following plays, *The Days of Messiah* and *God of Vengeance,* were performed in several European languages. Asch's reputation grew in the literary centers of the world.

At the outset of World War I Asch emigrated to the United States; several years after the war he returned to Poland. Later he took up residence in France, then moved again to the United States, where he became a citizen in 1938. For many years Asch was a member of the Jewish Agency for Palestine. He later resided in England, then moved to Israel in 1954 with the intention of settling there for the rest of his life. During a visit to his daughter in London he died in 1957.

Scope of the Work

Asch was extremely versatile in his literary forms, and the subjects that absorbed him covered a wide range. He wrote about life in little towns in Poland and in metropolitan New York, about social and religious problems, and about Zionism and the Nazi holocaust. His outstanding works— *Motke the Thief, God of Vengeance, Kiddush Hashem* (The Sanctification of God's Name), *Sabbetai Zvi, The Mother, and Three Cities* —depict the exaltations and degradations of environmental influences. The survival under adversity and the idealism and indestructible spirit of his people are transformed by his pen into sublime drama, comedy, and tragedy. In his Christian trilogy—*The Nazarene, The Apostle,* and *Mary* —he tried to bring out the common elements in Judaism and Christianity.

Asch started by depicting the provincial Jewish town and ended by opening international, intercultural, and interfaith vistas to Jewish literature. He was a writer of the highest order, both an idealist and a realist. His works have been translated into all major languages.

Further Reading

There is little material on Asch in English. Solomon Liptzin, *The Flowering of Yiddish Literature* (1963), includes a chapter on his life and works. Meyer Waxman, *A History of Jewish Literature* (4 vols., 1930-1936; rev. ed., 5 vols., 1960), discusses his work until 1935. For general background see Charles A. Madison, *Yiddish Literature: Its Scope and Major Writers* (1968).

Additional Sources

Siegel, Ben, *The Controversial Sholem Asch: an introduction to his fiction,* Bowling Green, Ohio: Bowling Green University Popular Press, 1976. □

Mary Kay Wagner Ash

Texas make-up tycoon Mary Kay (Wagner) Ash (born ca. 1916) parlayed her early training in direct sales into a multi-million-dollar, Dallas-based cosmetics firm.

Although her choice of a cosmetics career was not unique, Mary Kay Ash proved incomparable at combining the skills she had acquired selling books door-to-door with her understanding of marketing to women. Successful beauty product entrepreneurs before her had proved this a lucrative field for women. A few, such as Madame C.J. Walker, Elizabeth Arden, and Helena Rubenstein, had "invented" a specialized product line and established highly effective sales networks. It was Mary Kay's reliance on women as in-home salespersons, her use of a signature color—pink—as part of the corporate identity, and her shrewd incorporation of premiums and incentives (such as pink Cadillacs and diamond jewelry) into company sales plans that brought her such astonishing financial success.

Clinging to the rather time-worn convention that "a lady never reveals her age," Ash withheld the exact year in which her May 12th birth occurred; it is estimated by those who have known her to be 1916. She was born to Edward and Lula Wagner in rural Hotwells, Texas, and proved to be an eager and dependable student throughout her school years. She was, as well, a mainstay of her family; after her mother left each day for work, Ash prepared her physically challenged father's meals. Her capabilities and intellect were not sufficient, however, to lift her out of the domestic sphere. Due to her family's limited resources Ash was unable to go to college, and at age 17 she married and would go on to have three children.

During an era when it was uncommon for married women with a family to work outside the home, Ash became an employee of Stanley Home Products, often conducting several demonstration "parties" each day at which she sold company products, mostly to homemakers much like herself. As did many parents, Ash sought to provide the best for her children, and she believed that the quickest way to do so was for her to excel at a job. Energetic and a quick learner, Ash found that direct sales suited her well. She rose at Stanley to unit manager, a post that she held from 1938 to 1952. Although she spent a year studying at the University of Houston, she gave up on academics to return to the stimulation of sales challenges.

Following a divorce from her husband soon after the close of World War II, Ash moved in 1952 from her job at Stanley Home Products to a similar sales slot at World Gift

Company, where she remained for another 11 years. Throughout this time she was refining her theory of marketing and sales: provide a quality product, target that product at a specified market, and offer sales incentives not only to the sales force but to the customer as well. During her years at Stanley, Ash had developed effective techniques and strategies, and it was her belief that other women were able to do the same in selling. However, she had hit glass ceilings at both companies, and eventually quit, hoping to write a book about her techniques.

Instead, in 1963 she founded her own company, originally named "Beauty by Mary Kay," a venture based primarily on a special skin care cream to which she had purchased the manufacturing rights. Since Ash had endured several decades of gender discrimination in the predominately male world of commerce and industry, she was determined in her own firm to offer career opportunities to any woman who was willing to devote the energy and creativity required to sell Mary Kay cosmetics. Before long she had built an effective force of female sales representatives who—like their doggedly positive chief executive officer—were eager to prove they were capable of *any* job.

Ash's second husband had died in 1963, only weeks after her company was established. She relied heavily on her oldest son to guide and advise her throughout the start-up phase of her cosmetics company; three years later she married Melville J. Ash and assumed the name that is so well-known today.

A relentless optimist with evangelical leanings, Ash published a carefully laundered autobiography in 1981; in 1984 she wrote *Mary Kay on People Management,* a volume that expanded on the now-familiar God-and-family theory of business success for women; and in 1995, she released another text on working women, *Mary Kay— You Can Have It All.* Among the tenets that she held as basic to her success was her idea that women needed to place "God first, family second, and career third."

Despite her conservative views, conventional approach to combining family and job responsibilities, and ultrafeminine appearance, Mary Kay Ash was a tough business person with a veteran's knowledge of marketing and sales. After her "semi-retirement" she served for a time at the Hastings Center, a think tank in Briarcliff Manor, New York.

Her predilection for flashy pink Cadillacs, gold-plated dinnerware, and layers of make-up aside, Ash helped innumerable women to careers and to the financial security that derives from earning one's own money. Though her personal views may not be typical of other women who have strived for their civil rights, Mary Kay nevertheless encouraged and empowered legions of women. Through her belief in women's abilities and her willingness to give them a chance, she made the dream of self-sufficiency a reality for hundreds of thousands of women worldwide.

Mary Kay Cosmetics now employs over 475,000 beauty consultants in over 25 countries throughout the world. Mary Kay Ash became involved in cancer research through fund raising after her husband, Mel, died of cancer in 1980. In 1993, she was honored with the dedication of the Mary Kay Ash Center for Cancer Immunotherapy Research at St. Paul Medical Center in Dallas. In 1996 a new foundation was started to research cancers which have historically affected women, the foundation was named the Mary Kay Ash Charitable Foundation.

To date, her autobiography *Mary Kay* has sold over one million copies. In 1987 Ash became the chairman emeritus of Mary Kay Inc.

Further Reading

Mary Kay Ash published an autobiography, *Mary Kay* (1981), providing an overview of her personal life and career as a cosmetics entrepreneur. She followed this in 1984 with *Mary Kay on People Management* and in 1995 with *Mary Kay— You Can Have It All* . See also *Contemporary Authors,* Volume 112 (Detroit: Gale, 1985). She also has been profiled in magazines, including portraits, in *People* (July 29, 1985) and *Fortune* (September 20, 1993).Additional information can be obtained from the Mary Kay Inc. web site at http://www.marykay.com. □

Abu al-Hasan Ali al-Ashari

The Moslem theologian Abu al-Hasan Ali al-Ashari (873/883-935) defended the basic Islamic belief that the Koran is the revealed book of God and that upon it and the Traditions of the Prophet the religion of Islam must be based.

Al-Ashari seems to have been born in Basra, in present-day Iraq. As was the custom, his education commenced with long exposure to the Koran and the collected Traditions of the Prophet and his Companions. Having mastered these, al-Ashari became a student of the head of the Mutazilite, or rationalist, school in Basra; eventually he would have succeeded his master had he not experienced a reconversion to the traditionalist position of Islam. This crisis in his life is said to have occurred in 912-913, and al-Ashari gave public notice of his intention to attack the Mutazilites from the pulpit. He spent the remainder of his life composing theological polemics against the enemies of the orthodox position. Al-Ashari died in Baghdad.

The rationalist movement in Islamic theology, whose adherents were known as the Mutazilites, had developed in the early 9th century, some 200 years after the death of the Prophet. The movement was influenced by the Neoplatonic and Aristotelian ideas which became known to Moslems through polemical discussions with Eastern Christians and Arabic translations of Greek philosophy. The rationalists, however, were deemed to have gone too far in attempting to harmonize revelation with reason. They were execrated by the traditionalist thinkers, who dubbed them Mutazilites, or "withdrawers" (from the community). The Mutazilites argued, for example, that God is just; if this is so, His creatures must have free will, or else sinners would be punished not for their own acts but for God's. The traditionalists balked at this type of argument as placing a limit upon God's omnipotence—a limit, moreover, merely devised in the mind of one of His creatures.

This Greek-influenced rationalism in religion, though highly distasteful to the bulk of believers, caught the fancy of three of the early Abbasid caliphs in Baghdad, who persecuted prominent traditionalists with the usual result of producing martyrs for that party. The tide turned in 850, however, after the accession of the traditionalist caliph al-Mutawakkil, who in turn persecuted the Mutazilites. Theological rationalism had thus fallen from official grace by the time al-Ashari was born, but it fought a successful rearguard action for many years and was only finally discredited among the orthodox by al-Ashari and his followers.

In joining battle with the Mutazilites, al-Ashari declared for predestination. Both good and evil are the products of God's will, and the seeming freedom of choice which man has is merely the creation by God in man of the ability to perform an act. Perhaps the most crucial theological arguments of the time revolved around the problem of whether the Koran, which is held by Moslems to have been dictated to the Prophet by God through the angel Gabriel, is eternal with God or merely one of His creations. The Mutazilites argued that the Koran is not eternal, since only God can be eternal; it therefore is created. Al-Ashari held that it is the literal speech of God, therefore one of His eternal attributes, and hence uncreated.

The general tenor of al-Ashari's thought was to rely upon the Koran and the Traditions, as of course the bulk of believers had been doing. His greatest contribution, however, was to make respectable in the eyes of the traditionalists the rationalist apparatus as long as it was employed to support an Islam firmly based upon those two foundations.

Further Reading

The work which best places al-Ashari within his historical and intellectual context is Walter C. Klein's translation of al-Ashari's *Al-Ibanah An Usul ad-Diyanah* (1940). Two other books by al-Ashari were translated, with valuable notes, by Richard J. McCarthy, *The Theology of al-Ashari* (1953). A few other works by al-Ashari exist in Arabic, but they have not been translated into Western languages; the bulk of his writings have been lost. In English the most accessible sampling of al-Ashari's ideas, as well as those of other Moslem theologians, may be found in John Alden Williams, ed., *Islam* (1961). Al-Ashari's importance to early Islamic theology is discussed in W. Montgomery Watt, *Free Will and Predestination in Early Islam* (1948). See also his *Islamic Philosophy and Theology* (1962). □

Arthur Robert Ashe Jr.

World champion athlete, social activist, teacher, and charity worker, Arthur Robert Ashe Jr. (1943-1993) was the first African American player to break the color barrier in the international sport of tennis at the highest level of the game. After early retirement from sports due to heart surgery in 1979, Ashe used his unique sportsman profile and legendary poise to promote human rights, education, and public health.

Arthur Robert Ashe Jr. was born on July 10, 1943, in Richmond, Virginia. He was a member of the eleventh identifiable generation of the Ashe family and a direct descendant of a West African slave. The family line reached back to ownership by Samuel Ashe, an early governor of North Carolina. When Ashe was six years old his mother, Mattie Cordell Cunningham Ashe, died of heart disease at the age of 27.

Ashe's father nurtured both Arthur and his younger brother, Johnnie, with love as a strict disciplinarian. He worked as a caretaker and special policeman for a park named Brook Field in suburban North Richmond. Young Arthur lived on the grounds with four tennis courts, a pool, and three baseball diamonds. This was the passkey to his development as a future star athlete. His early nickname was "Skinny" or "Bones," and he grew to six feet one inch with a lean physique. He was right-handed.

Ashe as Amateur Tennis Player

R. Walter ("Whirlwind") Johnson, an African American general physician and tennis patron from Lynchburg, Virginia, opened his home in the summers to tennis prospects, including the great Althea Gibson several years earlier. Johnson used military-style discipline to teach tennis skills

and also stressed his special code of sportsmanship: deference, sharp appearance, and "no cheating at any time."

Ashe attended Richmond City Public Schools. He received an honorary diploma from Maggie L. Walker High School in 1961. After success as a junior player in the American Tennis Association (ATA, for African American players), he was the first African American junior to receive a United States Lawn Tennis Association (USLTA) national ranking. When he won the National Interscholastics in 1960, it was the first USLTA national title to be won by an African American in the South. The University of California at Los Angeles (UCLA) awarded him a full scholarship.

In 1963 Ashe became the first African American player to win the U.S. Men's Hardcourt championships. He also became the first African American to be named to a U.S. Junior Davis Cup team and played for ten years (1963-1970, 1975, 1976, 1978). (Earlier he could not make the U.S. Junior Davis Cup team because he was denied entry in two of five major events, in Kentucky and Virginia.) He became the National College Athletic Association (NCAA) singles and doubles champion, leading the UCLA Bruins to the NCAA title in 1965. He was All-American from 1963 to 1965.

A year later Ashe graduated from UCLA in the ROTC program with a bachelor's degree in business administration. After serving in the Army for two years, during which he was assigned time for tennis competitions, Ashe introduced a grassroots tennis program into U.S. innercities in 1968. This effort was the forerunner of today's national U.S. Tennis Association/National Junior Tennis League (USTA/NJTL) program, with 500 chapters running programs for 150,000 kids.

Ashe as Professional Tennis Player

Two events changed Ashe's life direction in the late 1960s. The first, in 1968, was a proposed boycott by African American athletes at the Olympic Games in Mexico City. The boycott issue partly involved a protest against racial segregation, or "apartheid," in the Republic of South Africa. Ashe identified closely with such discrimination. The second event was in tennis. He was the first African American USLTA amateur champion and won the first U.S. Open Tennis Championships at Forest Hills, a new prize-money national event. The USLTA ranked him Co-Number One (with Rod Laver). His support changed from $28 per diem as a U.S. Davis Cup player to becoming a top money-winner when he turned professional in 1969. He took the Australian Open title in Melbourne in 1970. In 1971 he won the French Open doubles title with Marty Riessen. The next year he helped found the Association of Tennis Professionals (ATP).

In 1973 Ashe became the first African American to reach the South African Open finals held in Johannesburg and was the doubles winner with Tom Okker of The Netherlands. Black South Africa gave Ashe a name that day: They called him "Sipho," meaning "a gift from God" in Zulu.

The year 1975 was Ashe's best and most consistent season. He was the first and only African American male player to win the "Gentleman's Singles" title in an historic victory on center court at the All-England Lawn Tennis Club at Wimbledon. Ashe dethroned the defending champion, Jimmy Connors. President Lyndon Johnson's comment was "Brooke is the only Senator we got; and Marshall the only justice; and Ashe the only tennis player." In 1975 Ashe was ranked Number One in the world, won a singles title in Dallas, and was named ATP Player of the Year. He played as a member of the U.S. Aetna World Cup team, 1970 to 1976 and 1979.

Due to injuries, he sat out most of 1977. Wearing a footcast, Ashe (33) married Jeanne Moutoussamy (25), a professional photographer and television graphic artist. A decade later the couple had a daughter, Camera Elizabeth.

With Tony Roche, Ashe won the Australian Open doubles title in 1977. He almost defeated John McEnroe in the Masters final at Madison Square Garden in January 1979 and was a semi-finalist at Wimbledon in the summer, before a heart attack soon after the tournament ended his legendary career. After his quadruple bypass heart surgery, Ashe had to announce his retirement from competitive tennis.

Ashe as International Role Model

As his first post-retirement venture Ashe served as Davis Cup captain from 1981 to 1985. He was only the second captain in over 30 years to lead the U.S. team to consecutive victories, 1981 and 1982.

His new life was a rebirth with many directions. Ashe's Davis Cup campaigns, his protests against apartheid in South Africa, and his controversial support of higher academic standards for all athletes received much media attention. But he actually spent most of his time quietly dealing with the challenges of the "real world" through public speaking, teaching, writing, business, and voluntary public service.

In 1983 he had double bypass surgery. Ashe became national campaign chairman for the American Heart Association and the only nonmedical member of the National Heart, Lung and Blood Advisory Council. In the late 1970s he had become a consultant to Aetna Life & Casualty Company. He was made a board member in 1982. He represented minority concerns and, later, the causes of the sick.

Ashe developed social programs such as the ABC Cities program, combining tennis and academics; Safe Passage Foundation for poor children, which includes tennis training; Athletes Career Connection; the Black Tennis & Sports Foundation to assist minority athletes; and 15-Love, a substance abuse program conducted through the Eastern Tennis Association.

Kappa Alpha Psi Fraternity gave him their Laurel Wreath Award in 1986. He was inducted into the UCLA Sports Hall of Fame, the Virginia Sports Hall of Fame, and the Eastern Tennis Association Hall of Fame. He became the first inductee into the U.S. Professional Tennis Association Hall of Fame. He was the first athlete without a link to the Olympic Games to be awarded the coveted Olympic Order.

Ashe spent six years and $300,000 of his own funds to write *A Hard Road to Glory: A History of the African-American Athlete,* a three-volume work published in 1988. Ashe won an Emmy Award for writing a television docudrama based upon his work. The research effort also earned him honorary doctorates from such universities as Virginia Union, Princeton, Dartmouth, Virginia Common-wealth, and South Carolina.

After brain surgery in 1988 came the shocking discovery that he had been infected with HIV, the virus which causes AIDS. Doctors traced this infection back to an unscreened blood transfusion after his second cardiac operation in 1983. To protect his family and his own privacy, he informed only a few friends and associates of his illness. But to avoid possible news reports he publicly disclosed that he was suffering from AIDS at a news conference in April 1992.

Ashe established the Arthur Ashe Foundation for the Defeat of AIDS as a new international organization, with half of the funds generated going to AIDS causes outside the United States. He rallied professional tennis to help raise funds and to increase public awareness of the AIDS epidemic. This foundation coordinated efforts with other groups to provide treatment to AIDS patients and to promote vital AIDS research. He addressed the General Assembly of the United Nations on World AIDS Day, December 1, 1992.

Arthur Ashe died of pneumonia related to AIDS on February 6, 1993, in New York City. Mourners paid their respects as Ashe's body lay in state at the Virginia governor's mansion, at a memorial service held in St. John's Cathedral in New York City, and at the funeral at the Ashe Athletic Center in Richmond. In 1996 Ashe's hometown of Richmond, Virginia announced plans to erect a statue in his honor on Richmond's Monument Avenue. The following year, a new tennis stadium at the National Tennis Center in Flushing Meadows, New York, was named for him. Up until his death, Ashe remained involved in tennis and sports. He served as a television commentator at tennis matches, sports consultant at tennis clinics and a columnist for the *Washington Post*.

Further Reading

Arthur Ashe: Portrait in Motion (written with Frank Deford, 1975, 1993) is a "tennis diary" written between Wimbledon 1973 and Wimbledon 1975. In 1981 he also wrote an autobiography (with Neil Amdur) dedicated to his slave ancestors, entitled *Off the Court*. The last autobiography, *Days of Grace: A Memoir*, co-authored with Arnold Rampersad, was completed by Ashe 48 hours before he died. Ashe's definitive work, *A Hard Road to Glory: A History of the African-American Athlete*, with Kip Branch, Ocania Chalk, and Francis Harris (1988) covered African-American athletic history from ancestral homelands to the present. For an intimate view of Ashe from a family perspective, see the touching book *Daddy and Me: A Photo Essay of Arthur Ashe and His Daughter Camera* (1993), with photographs and words by Jeanne Moutoussamy-Ashe. A balanced commentary by Kenny Moore, "He Did All He Could," appeared in *Sports Illustrated* (February 15, 1993). An article by Terry Pluto, "Statue Right of Way to Honor Ashe," appeared in the *Beacon Journal* (July 13, 1996). □

Ashikaga Takauji

The Japanese warrior chieftain Ashikaga Takauji (1305-1358) rose to a position of military hegemony during the civil wars of the 14th century and founded the second shogunate, or warrior government, of medieval Japan.

The Ashikaga shogunate (known also as the Muromachi shogunate because of the location of its central offices in the Muromachi section of Kyoto), although it underwent many vicissitudes, retained at least titular military overlordship of Japan from 1336 until 1573.

The first shogunate of the medieval age had been founded at Kamakura in the eastern provinces in 1185 by Minamoto Yoritomo. Yoritomo, as shogun or "generalissimo" appointed by the imperial court of Kyoto, had exercised strong personal rule over his vassal followers. When he died in 1199, his two young sons who succeeded him as the second and third shoguns were unable to maintain Minamoto control over the shogunate, and during the early 13th century, leaders of the Hojo family (who were related to Yoritomo by marriage) became the real rulers at Kamakura as shogunate regents.

The Ashikaga were one of the main branch families of the Minamoto clan. During the Kamakura period (1185-1333) they faithfully served the Hojo regents; but, as later events were to prove, they cherished the hope of one day reasserting the primacy of Minamoto authority among the military of the land.

Downfall of the Kamakura Shogunate

Although the Hojo regents were viewed by some as usurpers of the rights of the Minamoto, they administered the government of the Kamakura shogunate on a basis of feudal justice and with marked efficiency during much of the 13th century. The effort and expense required to repulse two attempts by the Mongols in 1274 and 1281 to invade Japan and the need to maintain defenses against a possible third attempt placed a great strain on the Hojo administration and contributed to the family's decline.

By the early years of the 14th century the quality of Hojo rule had deteriorated to the point where voices of discontent were being raised throughout the country. From early in their rise to power in Kamakura the Hojo regents had managed to keep the imperial court at Kyoto, the former seat of central government in Japan, in a state of almost total political impotence. As Hojo control weakened, however, an increasing number of people among both Kyoto courtiers and provincial warriors came to look to the Emperor for new leadership.

In 1324 and again in 1331 the Hojo uncovered plots against them in Kyoto and even went so far as to exile Emperor Daigo II from the imperial capital for his role in the second one. The anti-Hojo movement continued to grow in intensity, and in 1333 the Hojo were obliged to send armies from Kamakura in an attempt to control the fighting that had erupted in the region of Kyoto. One of the commanding generals of the Hojo forces was Takauji, already the head of the Ashikaga family at 28. As he approached the imperial capital, Takauji suddenly announced his support of the exiled Daigo II and attacked and destroyed the branch offices of the shogunate in Kyoto. Almost simultaneously, another military force in the east entered Kamakura and decisively defeated the Hojo leaders and their immediate followers, thus bringing about the collapse of the Kamakura shogunate. The general who led this attack was Nitta Yoshisada, who, like Takauji, was the head of an important branch family (the Nitta) of the Minamoto clan.

Period of Imperial Restoration, 1333-1336

Upon his return to Kyoto from exile, Daigo II attempted to take advantage of the destruction of the Kamakura shogunate to reassert or "restore" the long-dormant authority of the throne. Although there had been powerful sovereigns earlier in Japanese history, the tendency since at least the 9th century had been for other families and groups to arrogate central ruling powers. The courtier family of Fujiwara, by installing themselves as regents to the throne, had, for example, been almost all-powerful at Kyoto during most of the 10th and 11th centuries. And in the 12th century the military of the eastern provinces became the new rulers of Japan through the establishment of the Kamakura shogunate.

Daigo II, an extraordinarily determined and headstrong person, attempted to exercise imperial rule directly and personally from his court in Kyoto. But he and his advisers were markedly unsuccessful in dealing with the needs of the most critical sector of Japanese society of the medieval age, the provincial warrior class. Before long, much of the discontent that had previously been directed at the Hojo regime in Kamakura was turned against Daigo II's court.

Probably the most important determinant of the fate of the brief Restoration government of 1333-1336, however, was the fierce rivalry for leadership of the warrior class that arose between Takauji and Nitta Yoshisada. Yoshisada managed to ingratiate himself with the court and to turn Daigo II and his chief advisers against Takauji. In the eighth month of 1335 Takauji went to the eastern provinces to quell a rising of remnants of the Hojo and their former followers. Three months later the Emperor, charging that Takauji intended to establish an independent territorial base in the east, commissioned Yoshisada to lead a punitive force against him. Thus began a protracted period of battling between the Ashikaga and Yoshisada, who was allied with other supporters of Daigo II. In an attempt to avoid being branded as a rebel, Takauji secured the backing of a rival branch of the imperial family that also aspired to the throne. In name at least, the struggle was thereby elevated to a dynastic dispute over imperial succession.

War between the Courts, 1336-1392

After several shifts in the tide of battle, the Ashikaga succeeded in occupying Kyoto in 1336 and in forcing Daigo II to abdicate in favor of their candidate. A few months later Daigo II escaped from the capital and fled south to Yoshino, where some of his leading supporters awaited him. Daigo II insisted that his "abdication" had been invalid and that he was still the legitimate sovereign of Japan.

From 1336 until 1392 there were two courts in Japan: the Southern court of Daigo II and his successors at Yoshino and the Northern court of Kyoto maintained by the Ashikaga. There was considerable fighting during the first few decades of the war between the courts, and the forces of the Southern court even recaptured Kyoto several times. However, the Ashikaga gradually reduced the opposition, and in 1392 they succeeded in reuniting the courts by persuading the Southern emperor to return to Kyoto and relinquish his claim to sovereignty to the Northern emperor.

Founding of the Ashikaga Shogunate

At the beginning of the war between the courts, Takauji had instituted a new shogunate in Kyoto. As a chieftain from the eastern provinces, Takauji would have preferred to locate his shogunate in Kamakura. But the need to do battle with the Southern court chiefly in the central region of Honshu dictated the advisability of choosing Kyoto as the site for the shogunate's headquarters. Nevertheless, Takauji and his advisers plainly conceived of themselves as the successors to the Kamakura shogunate, which they had helped destroy, and attempted to structure their government along the same lines as the latter.

In comparison with the Kamakura shogunate and the later Edo or Tokugawa shogunate (1603-1867), the Ashikaga shogunate was a weak ruling institution. Although it thoroughly dominated the Northern court and steadily reduced the fighting strength of the rival Southern court, the Ashikaga shogunate was hampered from the outset by a strong tendency toward regional separatism. Takauji and his immediate successors as shogun were obliged to give away much land and relinquish extensive governing rights to their leading generals in order to secure even a loose military hegemony over the land. Yet the Ashikaga hegemony was virtually nonexistent in areas distant from Kyoto, and by the end of the 15th century it had fallen apart completely. During the last hundred years or so of its existence, the shogunate founded by Takauji survived as a national governing body in name only.

Discord within the Shogunate

Nitta Yoshisada was killed in battle in 1338, and Emperor Daigo II died in 1339. Within a few years of the deaths of these great adversaries, Takauji nearly eliminated the offensive fighting power of the Southern court and was in a good position to seek a settlement with it. But in the early 1350s discord arose within the shogunate—involving several prominent vassal chieftains of the Ashikaga as well as Takauji and his brother, Tadayoshi—that precluded such a move.

Tadayoshi had performed important services in the rise of the Ashikaga family to national prominence in the early 14th century and had shared some of the ruling powers of the shogunate with his brother. Yet in the course of reestablishing order within the shogunate, Takauji was driven to kill Tadayoshi, an act that darkened the final years of his life.

When Takauji died in 1358 at the age of 53, he was succeeded as shogun by his son, Yoshiakira. Takauji's life had been devoted almost entirely to fighting, and it remained for Yoshiakira and the third Ashikaga shogun, Yoshimitsu, to stabilize the Ashikaga hegemony and bring to an end the war between the courts.

Takauji's Image in History

The 14th century witnessed the only major dynastic schism in Japanese history, and many later nationalists have felt impelled to deal with what they regard as the major interpretational problem it presents: which of the two courts, the Northern or the Southern, should be regarded as "legitimate"? By the late 19th century the most widely held contention was that, since Daigo II had never freely abdicated, the Southern court was legitimate during its existence from 1336 until 1392. A corollary to this was that those who had fought for the losing cause of the Southern court were loyalist heroes, and the Ashikaga and their allies were viewed as veritable "traitors."

In the period of ultranationalism and military aggression that led to World War II, Takauji in particular came to be vilified as the most heinous person in Japanese history. In 1934 a Cabinet minister, who was also a history buff and who had published an article that showed Takauji in a favorable light, was forced to resign his position. And during the war a noted scholar who many years earlier had tried sympathetically to analyze Takauji's "faith" was severely criticized.

Since the end of World War II Japanese scholars have been able to deal with the dynastic issue and the civil strife of the 14th century without fear of official censure. Their recent studies have evaluated Takauji more dispassionately and appropriately within the context of his times.

Further Reading

The best general treatment of Takauji and the period of the founding of the Ashikaga shogunate is in the early chapters of Sir George B. Sansom, *A History of Japan, 1334-1615,* vol. 2 (1961). A more detailed analysis of the dynastic issue in which Takauji became involved is presented by H. Paul Varley in *Imperial Restoration in Medieval Japan* (1971). This book also traces the course of the historical debate over which of the courts was "legitimate" and the process by which the opprobrium of the Japanese people came to be heaped on the memory of Takauji during the period before World War II.

Additional Sources

Ashikaga Takauji, Taokyao: Fukutake Shoten, Shaowa 59, 1984.
□

Laura Ashley

The British designer Laura Ashley (1925-1985) achieved renown for her genteel, Victorian inspired fashions in women's clothes and for her English Country manor style of furnishings for homes. Through her designs, books, and stores, she may be said to have served as an arbiter of fashion and life style.

Laura (Mountney) Ashley was born September 7, 1925, in Merthyr Tydfil, Wales, and died September 17, 1985, in Coventry, England. She was buried in Wales, where she was educated and grew up and where she established her world famous business of designing, manufacturing, and merchandising women's clothes and household items.

Her name had in her lifetime become synonymous with small, repetitive overall patterns; the use of natural fabrics; and a graceful simplicity in women's styles. Her dresses and blouses were noted for their Victorian-like high necks and full sleeves, the severity relieved by lace and ruffles. Particularly characteristic was her soft, floppy, wool felt hat with a broad flexible brim that could be worn down over the eyes and ears or pushed back so as to reveal the forehead. It became common to speak of a "Laura Ashley look," a term applied to her garments, fabrics, and interior designs and even to the appearance of the young, expressionless, fresh-faced women who modeled her clothes.

She married Bernard Ashley in 1949. On a kitchen table in their flat in the Pimlico section of London they designed placemats, scarves, tablecloths, aprons, and dresses by the silkscreen method. They soon moved to a country home in Surrey and in the late 1950s to Carno, Wales, now the headquarters of the firm's international operations. She concentrated on creating the designs and her husband on printing and merchandising them.

Her life in the Welsh and English countryside, amidst farms and villages, clearly influenced the combination of Puritan function and Victorian nostalgia of her designs. "Living quite remotely as I have done," she once said, "I have not been caught up with city influences and we just developed in our own way." She declared about her success: "It's not really a question of inspiration. What you make as a designer is an expression of yourself. I love music and painting and I prefer life in the country." Another time she said: "The idea of four babies, cooking, sewing, and looking after the home suited me perfectly." Of fashion she remarked: "I don't like ephemeral things; I like things that last forever. . . ."

A major influence on her dress designing was her uniform as a Wren in World War II. She said about it: "The uniform was a very good quality navy gabardine and you could press it and wear it with a clean white cotton shirt and collar and tie. There was a nice, cheeky little hat and comfortable black leather shoes."

At another time, she said: "I reckon that women looked their best at the turn of the century." She studied 18th and 19th century prints in museum collections for her miniature floral patterns. "No one wants to live with a design that jumps out at them," she explained. Her colors, too, were subdued.

Her success was quick and extraordinary. Her fabrics were first sold in two of the smaller but highly fashionable London department stores, Heal's and Liberty's, both of which had a tradition of featuring thoughtfully designed and esthetically pleasing objects. Liberty's, for example, continued to offer fabric and wall paper in patterns originally created by William Morris, the 19th century English poet and book and furniture designer.

Toward the end of the 1960s Ashley opened her first retail store in London. It was marked by natural wood floors, cabinets, and counters; trim painted in a deep blue-green; old-fashioned lounge chairs; and a general air of elegant informality. The first American shop opened in 1974 in San Francisco. By the time of her death there were over 200 Laura Ashley stores throughout the world, each looking much like the original one. The firm had 4,000 employees. In 1984 the stores alone grossed $130,000,000.

The Laura Ashley look, evoking a sense of permanence with its links to the past and its dependence on the natural, proved so popular perhaps because it contrasted dramatically during its emergence with the more transient and extravagant styles of French and Italian designers who appealed to mass clienteles with bolder expectations. "I like the idea of a uniform," she once said. "I think people should hang on to the things they like. They don't need closets full of clothes." One of her admirers, paradoxically, was the late trend-setting Princess Diana, the former wife of the Prince of Wales, heir to the British throne.

Laura Ashley preceded a generation of American designers working in a similar, restrained, classic style: Ralph Lauren, Calvin Klein, Ann Klein, and Perry Ellis. Although the volume of her retail business may have been less than that of other well-known clothes stylists, no other had quite her special influence or lent his or her name so definitively to an immediately recognizable look.

The Laura Ashley firm published three major books during her lifetime: *Fabric of Society: A Century of People and Their Clothes 1770-1870* by Jane Tozer and Sarah Levitt and *A House in the Cotswolds* and *The Laura Ashley Book of Home Decorating* by Elizabeth Dickson and Margaret Calvin, with a foreword by Laura Ashley. Through photographs of entire rooms, these volumes provided vivid glimpses of the environment of such novelists as Austen, Trollope, and Eliot. Perhaps even more, they serve as guides to many young persons today on how to furnish and decorate their homes.

Although early Laura Ashley products appealed mainly to women, the later ones, including upholstered chairs and sofas, furniture and drapery fabrics, wallpapers, and ceramic tiles, proved attractive to men as well. One particularly successful innovation of the Laura Ashley decorating style was to relate objects in a single setting to each other. Thus a Laura Ashley bedroom might have similarly patterned fabrics on bedspread, sheets, pillows, draperies, chaise lounge, and even the tiles in an adjoining bathroom. This organic integration of patterns made the typically small English chamber, however crowded, seem larger and quieter. The Laura Ashley look in home design, with its concentration on miniature and mid-sized floral patterns and its understated use of ornamental touches, provided a comfortable relief to the unrelieved starkness of modernism.

Further Reading

Up to the time of her death, no book had appeared which was devoted to her life and work. The titles mentioned in the text provide a good survey of the range of her interests and achievements in design. Many articles and interviews, indexed in the usual reference sources, may be found in leading American and British periodicals and newspapers, especially in the years immediately preceding her death. General books about fashion, providing a context for placing Laura Ashley, are *Fashion in the Sixties* by Barbara Bernard (1978); *The Fashion Makers* by Barbra Walz (1978); *Fashion from Ancient Egypt to the Present Day*, edited by James Laver (1965); and *Fashion and Reality*, by Alison Gernsheim (1963). □

William Henry Ashley

William Henry Ashley (ca. 1778-1838), American businessman, fur trader and explorer, and politician, was a leading figure in the organization and operation of the Rocky Mountain fur trade during the 1820s.

Willliam Ashley was born in Chesterfield County, Va. His date of birth has been given variously as 1778, 1782, and 1785; modern scholarship tends to accept the earliest date. From Virginia young Ashley migrated to Missouri. By 1805 he had settled in the St. Genevieve area, where he became a supplier for local merchants and businessmen. He married Mary Able, then turned to land speculation, operating a plantation near Cape Girardeau. By 1811 he and Andrew Henry had moved to Washington County, Mo., where Henry worked a lead mine and Ashley processed saltpeter and manufactured gunpowder.

During this time Ashley served as justice of the peace for the St. Genevieve district and as an officer in the territorial militia. During the War of 1812 he received several promotions, becoming a lieutenant colonel in 1814. Five years later he advanced to the rank of colonel and in 1822 became a brigadier general.

He arrived in St. Louis in 1819 and became active in real estate speculation, banking, and politics. In 1820 he was elected the first lieutenant governor of Missouri, and 4 years later he lost a close election for the governorship.

His political activity remained secondary; Ashley's major interest was the fur trade. In 1822, with his former associate Andrew Henry, he advertised for "enterprizing young men" to enter the trade—and from that time on, the American fur business depended upon hired trappers (rather than Native Americans) to obtain the bulk of the furs. Ashley's advertisement encouraged a number of the most famous of the trappers and mountain men to enter the trade.

While working for Ashley, Jedediah Smith brought back news of South Pass; Ashley took wagons over it and later explored parts of the Colorado River Valley. In 1826 Ashley sold his interest in the trade and turned to the less risky business of supplying the trading companies.

In 1825 he married a second time, but Eliza Christy, his bride, lived only 5 years. In 1832 he married Elizabeth M. Wilcox. A slender, energetic man of medium height, Ashley had a narrow face with a prominent nose and jutting chin. His leadership abilities helped him remain in public life, and in 1831 he was elected to Congress to complete the term of Spencer Pettis, who had been killed in a duel.

Ashley claimed to support Andrew Jackson, but at the same time he favored the Second Bank of the United States. He was reelected to Congress in 1832 and 1834. At the close of his third term he ran a second time for the Missouri governorship but lost to Lilburn Boggs. Two years later, in 1838, he died of pneumonia.

Further Reading

There is no biography of Ashley, but Dale L. Morgan, ed., *The West of William H. Ashley* (1964), gives the most complete account of his life. See also Harrison C. Dale, ed., *The Ashley-Smith Explorations and the Discovery of a Central Route to the Pacific, 1822-1829* (1918). Dale L. Morgan, *Jedediah Smith and the Opening of the West* (1953), gives much collateral material. For a general account of the fur trade see Hiram M. Chittenden, *The American Fur Trade of the Far West* (3 vols., 1902; 2d ed., 2 vols., 1935).

Additional Sources

Dale, Harrison Clifford, *The explorations of William H. Ashley and Jedediah Smith, 1822-1829,* Lincoln: University of Nebraska Press, 1991. □

Harry Scott Ashmore

The American journalist Harry Scott Ashmore (born 1916) was the 1958 Pulitzer Prize winner for his reports and commentary on the Little Rock, Arkansas, school integration crisis.

Harry Ashmore was born July 28, 1916, in Greenville, South Carolina, in the northwest part of the state. His father, William Green Ashmore, was a merchant, and the Ashmore traced their lineage in Greenville County to the colonial period of American history. Harry's mother, Elizabeth Scott Ashmore, came from Scotch-Irish roots that began in America with her father's migration from County Antrim, Ireland. The Scotts were strong Presbyterians, but Elizabeth relented to the Baptist loyalties of the Ashmores.

Harry recalled in his boyhood a region marked by numerous textile mills that made it emblematic of the "New South" and its industrial character. Nonetheless, the people of the area were highly partisan in their Old South prejudices. Ashmore remembered that his relatives considered white supremacy a "fact of life" and the social dominance of whites over Blacks as the "natural order" of society. Both of Ashmore's grandmothers related with pride their husbands' military service in the armies of the Confederacy.

Early Newspaper Career

Ashmore graduated from Clemson College in 1937 and began a career in journalism. His work on the *Greenville Piedmont* included an assignment to study living conditions of the poor in northern cities, a report that his editor hoped would retaliate against northern journalists' exposés of wretched conditions in the Greenville area textile mills. Ashmore's investigation of New York City drew a notice in *TIME* magazine and won a measure of vindication for the South, but Ashmore later regretted that the effect was to make the South indifferent to the social evils in its midst.

In 1940 Ashmore married Barbara Edith Laier, a New Englander who was teaching at Furman University. The couple had one child, a daughter Anne. The next year Ashmore attended Harvard University as a Nieman Fellow and focused his studies on American history, primarily with Professors Paul H. Buck, Frederick Merk, and Arthur Schlesinger, Sr. Ashmore then saw extensive military service in World War II, fighting with George S. Patton's Third Army and winning decorations for his achievements.

After his return home, Ashmore became editor of the editorial page of the *Charlotte (N.C.) News,* a job that he accepted in part because his work on the Greenville paper had alienated the reigning Bourbon politicians in the state.

At Charlotte, Ashmore succeeded Wilbur J. Cash, a brilliant writer whose deflation of the South's sentimental mythology in his classic *The Mind of the South* greatly influenced Ashmore.

In 1947 Ashmore joined the *Arkansas Gazette,* a venerable Little Rock newspaper of longstanding Democratic party loyalties. He had by this time become a familiar name as part of a small group of Southern liberal journalists that included his good friends Harry Golden and Ralph McGill. As editor of the editorial page, Ashmore turned the *Gazette* against the segregationist movement in the Democratic Party led by Strom Thurmond of South Carolina and known as the "Dixiecrat" schism of 1948. Ashmore, always a voice of restraint, had initiated reforms in the *Gazette* that called for consistent courtesy titles ("Mr., "Mrs.," and "Miss") for both African-American and white people. Ashmore also headed a team of scholars, organized by the Ford Foundation's Fund for the Advancement of Education, to study race and the public schools in the South. *The Negro and the Public Schools* was published one day before the United States Supreme Court issued its historic desegregation decision in *Brown vs. Board of Education* in 1954.

Work for Civil Rights

That decision raised a defiant South, with campaigns for massive resistance to court-ordered school integration. Ashmore at the *Gazette* won national attention for his calls for moderation and responsibility among Little Rock area citizens. Ashmore repeatedly criticized the defiant position of Arkansas Governor Orville Faubus and answered conservative journalists who spoke for white supremacy and racial segregation, James Jackson Kilpatrick of the *Richmond News-Leader* in particular. In Little Rock and around the state, white Citizens Councils led a boycott against the *Gazette* and had the encouragement of Faubus in their efforts. Ashmore received threats of violence to himself and his family, as Little Rock became the center of the nation's attention in the fall of 1958. Ashmore's coverage of these events was carried by *Life* magazine, and his editorials for the *Gazette* won Pulitzer Prizes in journalism for him and the newspaper.

In 1960 Ashmore accepted the invitation of Robert Maynard Hutchins to join the Fund for the Republic and to become the chairman of the executive committee of its Center for the Study of Democratic Institutions in Santa Barbara, California. The fund had been created by the Ford Foundation to advance the cause of civil rights and civil liberties and had been providing grant support for interracial organizations in the South. Ashmore maintained his interest in race relations in America and took on special assignments for major newspapers. He also served as editor-in-chief of the *Encyclopedia Britannica.*

Ashmore remained throughout his career a Democratic Party stalwart. He worked with the Adlai Stevenson campaigns of 1952 and 1956 as strategist and speechwriter. He is best characterized as a committed but pragmatic liberal. He spoke out against the militant and violent elements that became vocal in the civil rights movement after the death of Martin Luther King, Jr. and warned against the radical ideo-logies of the New Left movement of the 1960s. Ashmore opposed President Lyndon Johnson's conduct of the war in Vietnam, and in 1967 and 1968, with journalist Bill Baggs of the *Miami News,* he undertook an unsuccessful peace mission to Hanoi with the cooperation of the State Department. He also maintained his liberal commitments through his work with the American Civil Liberties Union and his service to that organization as its vice-president.

Harry Ashmore once said that he wanted to make journalism a bridge between the world of ideas and the world of men. His lively writings on history and contemporary affairs reflected that objective.

Further Reading

Ashmore wrote two books in the 1980s: *Hearts and Minds: The Anatomy of Racism from Roosevelt to Reagan* (1982); and *Hearts and Minds: A Personal Chronicle of Race in America* (1988); the former is heavily autobiographical and contains many useful observations of the half-century course of the civil rights movement. Ashmore wrote *Arkansas: A Bicentennial History* (1978) for the Norton series on the American states. *Mission to Hanoi* (1968), with William C. Baggs, recounts the secret diplomatic journey undertaken by the two journalists. Ashmore's *An Epitaph for Dixie* (1957) is a trenchant analysis of the South and its class and racial attitudes, and his article "The Untold Story Behind Little Rock," written for *Harper's Magazine* (June 1958), provides a first-hand account of the integration crisis. A *TIME* magazine article, "Damned Good Pro" (October 14, 1957), is an appreciative tribute to Ashmore's editorial campaigns against the segregationists. □

Jehudi Ashmun

Jehudi Ashmun (1794-1828) was the white American governor of Liberia Colony, West Africa, whose leadership enabled the early settlement at Monrovia to survive armed attacks from local Africans.

Jehudi Ashmun was born on a farm near Champlain, N.Y., on April 21, 1794. He studied at Middlebury College and graduated from the University of Vermont in 1816. In 1818 after 2 years as principal of a theological academy in Maine he resigned following a misunderstanding over his marriage of that year. He failed as editor of the *Constellation,* a Baltimore religious weekly, and as editor of the *Theological Repository,* a Washington monthly magazine of the Episcopal Church.

While in Washington in 1820 Ashmun learned of the work of the American Colonization Society (ACS) and wrote several articles supporting it. Intrigued, he started a newspaper, the *African Intelligencer,* to publicize the ACS program of sending free African Americans from America to found a colony in West Africa. The newspaper did not last, but Ashmun was still enthralled by the first settlement established at Monrovia. In 1822 he published *Memoir of the Life . . . of Samuel Bacon,* concerning the ACS official who had helped settle the first contingent of African American emigrants before himself succumbing to malaria. In 1822

Ashmun was put in charge of 37 African Americans who were emigrating to Africa; his wife made the trip with him, for they expected to return to the United States.

When he arrived in Monrovia in August, Ashmun found the colony of about 120 people demoralized, without supplies or leadership from the ACS, and under military threat from hostile Africans. Assuming control without authorization from the ACS, he skillfully directed the fortification and successful defense of the settlement.

Despite the recurring malaria that weakened him and killed his wife and despite the early antagonisms of some ACS officials, Ashmun remained in Africa. Later, in executing the authoritarian orders of the ACS, he made enemies of the settlers, who, under Lott Cary, rebelled and forced him to retreat to the Cape Verde Islands temporarily in 1824. The most enlightened of the white colonial agents, still Ashmun did not believe in the equality of blacks and whites. With the help of Ralph R. Gurley, new secretary of the ACS, Ashmun liberalized the government of the colony and once more won the support of the Liberians. (Gurley later wrote a biography of Ashmun.) Between 1824 and 1828 he governed the settlement, built up and fortified Monrovia, and consolidated Liberian commercial and political control over the coastal areas north and south of the town.

Trade with the Africans was lucrative and most Liberians wanted to be merchants. Although he himself was a trader, Ashmun published a booklet, *The Liberian Farmer* (1826), to encourage agriculture. Ashmun's reports to the

ACS provide the basic history of early Liberia, and he also published *History of the American Colony in Liberia, 1821-1823* (1826).

During his 6 years in Africa, Ashmun was in poor health. Early in 1828 he left Africa for the West Indies and then for the United States, hoping to regain his health. He died on August 25, shortly after his arrival in New Haven, at the age of 34. The survival of Liberia is his principal monument.

Further Reading

The authoritative account of Ashmun's life was written by his close friend, Ralph Randolph Gurley, *Life of Jehudi Ashmun: Late Colonial Agent in Liberia* (1835). It includes a number of letters and other documents written by Ashmun. For a detailed account of his career in Liberia see Charles Henry Huberich, *The Political and Legislative History of Liberia* (2 vols., 1947). A recent evaluation of Ashmun's work in the American Colonization Society is in P. J. Staudenraus, *The African Colonization Movement, 1816-1865* (1961). There is a brief biographical sketch of Ashmun in Stewart H. Holbrook, *Lost Men of American History* (1946). □

Hanan Mikhail Ashrawi

Spokesperson for the Palestinian delegation in the Arab-Israeli peace talks and later chair of a human rights group in the West Bank and Gaza, Hanan Mikhail Ashrawi (born 1946), a professor of English literature and a political activist, won international recognition for her articulate defense of Palestinian national rights. Her innate eloquence is further manifested by her literary accomplishments.

Hanan Mikhail Ashrawi was born October 8, 1946, in Nablus, one of the big cities of what was then central Palestine. The youngest of five children—all female—Hanan and the rest of the Mikhails moved around quite a bit during her childhood, mainly due to the 1948 war of Israeli independence and to demands placed on her father, a physician. From Nablus, her family moved to the warm city of Tiberias in the north where they remained until Israel became a state in 1948. With most Palestinian Arabs of that part of Palestine—now Israel—fleeing the war and ending in refugee camps in southern Lebanon and Syria, Mikhail's family moved to Amman, Jordan. Initially, her father, Daoud Mikhail, remained behind in the war-torn country, but he rejoined his family a bit later. While in Jordan, Hanan's father worked as a health inspector with that government.

Finally, in 1950 the Mikhails returned to the West Bank, settling in Ramallah, a city located six miles north of Jerusalem. The West Bank, which had been annexed by the Amman government in August 1950, came under Israeli occupation during the Six-Day War of 1967.

As a physician, Daoud Mikhail, along with his wife Wadi'a Mikhail, a nurse, provided his family with a comfortable standard of living. Daoud Mikhail was a liberal thinker and quite progressive in his philosophy. Brought up by his sisters when his mother died, he had learned to respect and admire the position of women and favored a greater role for them in society. Contrary to acceptable norms for most girls and women at the time, Hanan grew up believing that there was nothing she could not or should not do only because she was a woman. Her father's status and his social and political views undoubtedly influenced Hanan's personality and character and set her on a path which ultimately led to her activist and leadership roles.

Daoud Mikhail's activities with the Arab National Socialist Party had led to his imprisonment by the Jordanian authorities for a time. Later on he was involved in the establishment of the Palestine Liberation Organization (PLO). He died in 1988.

Hanan Mikhail received her B.A. and M.A. degrees from the American University of Beirut. While there she joined the General Union of Palestinian Students (GUPS) and became its spokesperson. She also taught political awareness classes to Palestinians in that city's surrounding refugee camps. ABC's World News Tonight anchor Peter Jennings met Hanan while in Beirut and described her as "incredibly smart." In 1970, unable to rejoin her family in the West Bank, Hanan left Beirut to go to the United States to complete her graduate studies at the University of Virginia, where she received her Ph.D. in English and Comparative Literature.

Hanan met Yasser Arafat for the first time in 1969 while attending a GUPS convention in Amman; she joined Fateh, the largest of the PLO components, but then she left. She was able to return to the West Bank in 1973 under the Family Reunification Act. There she became involved in the women's rights movement and began to speak about coexistence with Israel and about a two-state solution for the Arab-Israeli conflict.

In 1975 Hanan Mikhail married Emile Ashrawi, an artist, filmmaker, and later a photographer in Jerusalem for the United Nations refugee relief group. They had two daughters.

Hanan Ashrawi came to world attention during her highly praised performance on ABC's Nightline "town meeting" from Jerusalem in April 1988, five months after the breakout of the Palestinian *intifada* (uprising against Israeli rule). That event catapulted her into the world of high politics and placed her under a substantial level of responsibility. Ashrawi, a professor of English literature and the former dean of arts at Beir Zeit University in the West Bank, became very involved in the talks with then Secretary of State James Baker that eventually lead to the 1992 Madrid peace conference. As a resident of East Jerusalem, she was denied a role as a negotiator by Israel, becoming instead the chief spokesperson for the Palestinian delegation. As such, and with the world as her audience, Hanan's articulate conferences on behalf of the Palestinian people, and her information duels with her Israeli counterpart, made her face one of the most recognizable in the world. Along with Faisal Husseini, the chair of the group and another West Bank personality, Hanan sat at the core of an influential team of advisers for the Palestinian delegation.

Ashrawi published many articles, conferred with heads of state, and addressed numerous international conventions. When arrested by the Israeli authorities along with Husseini, former President George Bush said, "Hanan is on my mind." These Palestinians were soon released.

Ashrawi received her share of criticism, and not only from the Israelis. From the Palestinian corner, Ashrawi was criticized as too moderate and too accommodating to both the Americans and the Israelis.

After the signing of the September 13, 1993, agreement between Israel and the PLO, Ashrawi resigned her position on the Palestinian team. She then founded a human rights group that focused on women's issues in the West Bank and Gaza.

Her convictions and determination to bring freedom and democracy to the war-torn country of Palestine are described in her critically acclaimed memoir, *This Side of Peace*. The book draws from the imagery of her native Arabic, but Ashrawi wrote the book in English in order that it might be more widely read. Reviewer William B. Quandt of *Foreign Affairs Magazine* described the book as "an appealing and powerful personal statement from a person of integrity and insight." Ashrawi plans to publish a novel dealing with the realities of the Palestinian-Israeli conflict.

Further Reading

The best source of additional information is *The New Palestinians: The Emerging Generation of Leaders* (1992) by John Wallach and Janet Wallach. See also Mikhail-Ashrawi, Hanan, *This Side of Peace* (Simon & Schuster, 1995); Victor, Barbara, *A Voice of Reason: Hanan Ashrawi and Peace in the Middle East* (Harcourt, Brace & Company, 1994). Periodical articles include *Commonweal,* June 16, 1995; *Foreign Affairs,* July-August 1995; *Interview,* July 1995; *Mother Jones,* March-April 1993; and *Publishers Weekly,* December 5, 1994. ☐

Ashurbanipal

Ashurbanipal (died ca. 630 B.C.) was the last great king of the Assyrian Empire. He was an able soldier and administrator, a scholar, and a patron of art and learning.

The events of the reign of Ashurbanipal are imperfectly known, and the course of his campaigns cannot be chronologically described. Designated crown prince in 672 B.C. by his father, Esarhaddon, Ashurbanipal succeeded to the throne 3 years later; his elder brother Shamash-shum-ukin was proclaimed king of Babylonia in the same year. Ashurbanipal's first task was the settlement of Egypt, recently conquered by Esarhaddon. Native princes were appointed as vassal rulers, but after repeated revolts by Egyptians the country was put under military occupation in 663 and Memphis and Thebes destroyed. Ashurbanipal then defeated Tyre, which had aided Egypt, and made an alliance with Lydia against the threat of Cimmerian hordes to the northeast. In 654 the Egyptians expelled the last Assyrian garrison and regained their independence.

Ashurbanipal spent the middle years of his reign in a bitter struggle with his brother. In 652 Shamash-shumukin rebelled with Elamite aid against Assyrian hegemony, and the revolt was joined by the Chaldeans of South Babylonia, the Arameans and Arabs, and the princes of Palestine. Ashurbanipal attacked Elam, starved the Babylonian cities into submission, and in 648 captured Babylon; Shamash-shum-ukin perished in the flames of his burning city. Ashurbanipal installed a puppet king, Kandalanu, in Babylon and subdued the Arabs. The Elamites after several years of warfare were forced to capitulate, and their capital, Susa, was destroyed. Among those who subsequently paid homage to Ashurbanipal was Cyrus, the first king of Persia.

Little is known of Ashurbanipal's last years, though private documents hint at shrinking frontiers and the dislocation of trade. Assyria's end was not far off, but few at the time of his death, about 630, would have dared to predict it.

The splendid reliefs from Ashurbanipal's palace at Nineveh (near Mosul, Iraq) depict him as a warrior and an intrepid hunter of lions. Thousands of cuneiform tablets found in the ruins of this palace show Ashurbanipal's wide range of interests. The dockets on some tablets show they had been copied, or borrowed, from the ancient temple libraries of Babylonia, and they comprise religious literature, scientific treatises, and historical records. The king's interest sprang from a degree of education unusual among monarchs of the ancient world, for he could read the ancient Sumerian texts and was an expert mathematician. His love of learning and his desire to uncover and preserve the past have earned him the title of the "archeologist king."

Further Reading

For a general account of the reign of Ashurbanipal consult A. T. Olmstead, *History of Assyria* (1923), and J. B. Bury, S. A. Cook, and F. W. Adcock, eds., *The Cambridge Ancient History,* vol. 3 (1925). The principal cuneiform texts are translated in Daniel D. Luckenbill, *Ancient Records of Assyria and Babylonia* (2 vols., 1926-1927), and in the Oriental Institute of the University of Chicago Assyriological Studies, no. 5, Arthur Carl Piepkorn, ed., *Historical Prism Inscriptions of Ashurbanipal I* (1933). Seton Lloyd, *Foundations in the Dust: A Story of Mesopotamian Exploration* (1947), gives an interesting account of the excavation of the palace at Nineveh and the discovery of Ashurbanipal's library. The relief sculptures from this palace are illustrated in E. A. Wallis Budge, ed., *Assyrian Sculptures in the British Museum* (1914); see also C. J. Gadd, *The Stones of Assyria* (1936). ☐

Isaac Asimov

The author of nearly five hundred books, Isaac Asimov (1920-1992) is esteemed as one of the finest writers of science fiction and scientific fact in the twentieth century.

Asimov was born on January 2, 1920, to middle-class Jewish parents in Petrovichi, Russia, then part of the Smolensk district in the Soviet Union. His family immigrated to the United States in 1923, settling in Brooklyn, New York, where they owned and operated a candy store. In 1934, while attending Boys High School of Brooklyn, Asimov published his first story, "Little Brothers," in the school newspaper. A year later he entered Seth Low Junior College, an undergraduate college of Columbia University. He transferred to the main campus in 1936, where he switched his major from biology to chemistry. During the next two years Asimov's interest in history grew and he read numerous books on the subject. He also read science fiction magazines and wrote stories. His first professionally published story, "Marooned off Vesta," appeared in *Amazing Stories* in 1939. Asimov graduated from Columbia University with a B.S. in chemistry in 1939. He later earned an M.A. and Ph.D. After serving in World War II, Asimov became an instructor at Boston University School of medicine. Asimov died in 1992.

Asimov received his greatest popular and critical acclaim for *The Foundation Trilogy: Three Classics of Science Fiction* and his robot series. Comprised of *Foundation, Foundation and Empire,* and *Second Foundation, The Foundation Trilogy* describes the "future history" of a vast galactic empire. His books about robots—most notably *I, Robot;*

The Caves of Steel; and The Naked Sun—did much to legitimize science fiction by augmenting the genre's traditional material with the narrative structures of such established genres as mystery and detective stories, while displaying a thematic concern for technological progress and its implications for humanity. Many critics, scientists, and educators, however, believe Asimov's greatest talent was for popularizing or, as he called it, "translating" science for the lay reader. His many books on atomic theory, chemistry, astronomy, and physics have been recognized for their extraordinary clarity, and Asimov has been praised for his ability to synthesize complex data into readable, unthreatening prose. When asked about his prodigious output in such a wide range of fields, Asimov responded self-deprecatingly by saying he never had a thought that he didn't put down on paper. An editorial in The Washington Post concluded that he redefined the rule "as to how many things a person is allowed to be an expert on" and that his "extraordinary capabilities aside, [his] breadth of interest deserves more admiration than it gets."

Isaac Asimov is "the world's most prolific science writer," according to David N. Samuelson in Twentieth Century Science-Fiction Writers, who "has written some of the best-known science fiction ever published." Considered one of the three greatest writers of science fiction in the 1940s (along with Robert Heinlein and A. E. Van Vogt), Asimov has remained a potent force in the genre. Stories such as "Nightfall" and "The Bicentennial Man," and novels such as The Gods Themselves and Foundation's Edge have received numerous honors and are recognized as among the best science fiction ever written. As one of the world's leading writers on science, explaining everything from nuclear fusion to the theory of numbers, Asimov has illuminated for many the mysteries of science and technology. He is a skilled raconteur as well, who enlivens his writing with incidents from his own life. "In his autobiographical writings and comments," states James Gunn in Isaac Asimov: The Foundations of Science Fiction, "Asimov continually invites the reader to share his triumphs, to laugh at his blunders and lack of sophistication, and to wonder, with him, at the rise to prominence of a bright Jewish boy brought to this country from Russia at the age of three and raised in a collection of Brooklyn candy stores."

Asimov's interest in science fiction began when he first noticed several of the early science fiction magazines for sale on the newsstand of his family's candy store. Although as a boy he read and enjoyed numerous volumes of nonfiction as well as many of the literary "classics," Asimov recalls in In Memory Yet Green, his first volume of autobiography, he still longed to explore the intriguing magazines with the glossy covers. But his father refused, maintaining that fiction magazines were "junk! . . . Not fit to read. The only people who read magazines like that are bums." And bums represented "the dregs of society, apprentice gangsters."

But in August of 1929, a new magazine appeared on the scene called Science Wonder Stories. Asimov knew that as long as science fiction magazines had titles like Amazing Stories, he would have little chance of convincing his father of their worth. However, the new periodical had the word "science" in its title, and he says, "I had read enough about science to know that it was a mentally nourishing and spiritually wholesome study. What's more, I knew that my father thought so from our occasional talks about my schoolwork." When confronted with this argument, the elder Asimov consented. Soon Isaac began collecting even those periodicals that didn't have "science" in the title. He notes: "I planned to maintain with all the strength at my disposal the legal position that permission for one such magazine implied permission for all the others, regardless of title. No fight was needed, however; my harassed father conceded everything." Asimov rapidly developed into an avid fan.

Asimov first tried writing stories when he was eleven years old. He had for some time been reading stories and then retelling them to his schoolmates, and started a book like some of the popular boys' series volumes of the 1920s: "The Rover Boys," "The Bobbsey Twins," and "Pee Wee Wilson." Asimov's story was called The Greenville Chums at College, patterned after The Darewell Chums at College, and it grew to eight chapters before he abandoned it. Asimov, in In Memory Yet Green, describes the flaw in his initial literary venture: "I was trying to imitate the series books without knowing anything but what I read there. Their characters were small-town boys, so mine were, for I imagined Greenville to be a town in upstate New York. Their characters went to college, so mine did. Unfortunately, a junior-high-school youngster living in a shabby neighborhood in Brooklyn knows very little about small-town life and even less about college. Even I, myself, was forced eventually to recognize the fact that I didn't know what I was talking about.''

Despite initial discouragements, Asimov continued to write. His first published piece appeared in his high school's literary semiannual and was accepted, he says, because it was the only funny piece anyone wrote, and the editors needed something funny. In the summer of 1934, Asimov had a letter published in *Astounding Stories* in which he commented on several stories that had appeared in the magazine. His continuing activities as a fan brought him to the decision to attempt a science fiction piece of his own; in 1937, at the age of seventeen, he began a story entitled ''Cosmic Corkscrew.'' The procedure Asimov used to formulate the plot was, he says, ''typical of my science fiction. I usually thought of some scientific gimmick and built a story about that.''

By the time he finished the story on June 19, 1938, *Astounding Stories* had become *Astounding Science Fiction.* Its editor was John W. Campbell, who was to influence the work of some of the most prominent authors of modern science fiction, including Arthur C. Clarke, Robert Heinlein, Poul Anderson, L. Sprague de Camp, and Theodore Sturgeon. Since Campbell was also one of the best-known science fiction writers of the thirties and *Astounding* one of the most prestigious publications in its field at the time, Asimov was shocked by his father's suggestion that he submit ''Cosmic Corkscrew'' to the editor in person. But mailing the story would have cost twelve cents while subway fare, round trip, was only ten cents. In the interest of economy, therefore, he agreed to make the trip to the magazine's office, fully expecting to leave the manuscript with a secretary.

Campbell, however, had invited many young writers to discuss their work with him, and when Asimov arrived he was shown into the editor's office. Campbell talked for over an hour and agreed to read the story; two days later Asimov received the manuscript back in the mail. It had been rejected, but Campbell offered extensive suggestions for improvement and encouraged the young man to keep trying. This began a pattern that was to continue for several years with Campbell guiding Asimov through his formative beginnings as a science fiction writer.

Asimov's association with the field of science fiction has been a long and distinguished one. He is credited with the introduction of several innovative concepts into the genre, including the formulation of the ''Three Laws of Robotics.'' Asimov maintains that the idea for the laws was given to him by Campbell; Campbell, on the other hand, said that he had merely picked them out of Asimov's early robot stories. In any case, it was Asimov who first formally stated the three laws: ''1. A robot may not injure a human being or, through inaction, allow a human being to come to harm. 2. A robot must obey the orders given it by human beings except where such orders would conflict with the First Law. 3. A robot must protect its own existence as long as such protection does not conflict with the First or Second Laws.'' Asimov says that he used these precepts as the basis for ''over two dozen short stories and three novels . . . about robots,'' and he feels that he is ''probably more famous for

them than for anything else I have written, and they are quoted even outside the science-fiction world. The very word 'robotics' was coined by me.'' The three laws gained general acceptance among readers and among other science fiction writers; Asimov, in his autobiography, writes that they ''revolutionized'' science fiction and that ''no writer could write a *stupid* robot story if he used the Three Laws. The story might be bad on other counts, but it wouldn't be stupid.'' The laws became so popular, and seemed so logical, that many people believed real robots would eventually be designed according to Asimov's basic principles.

Also notable among Asimov's science fiction works is the ''Foundation'' series. This group of short stories, published in magazines in the forties and then collected into a trilogy in the early fifties, was inspired by Edward Gibbon's *Decline and Fall of the Roman Empire.* It was written as a ''future history,'' a story being told in a society of the distant future which relates events of that society's history. The concept was not invented by Asimov, but there can be little doubt that he became a master of the technique. *Foundation, Foundation and Empire,* and *Second Foundation* have achieved special standing among science fiction enthusiasts. In 1966, the World Science Fiction Convention honored them with a special Hugo Award as the best all-time science fiction series. Even many years after the original publication, Asimov's future history series remains popular—in the 1980s, forty years after he began the series, Asimov added a new volume, *Foundation's Edge,* and eventually linked the Foundation stories with his robot novels in *The Robots of Dawn, Robots and Empire, Foundation and Earth,* and *Prelude to Foundation.*

Asimov's first fiction written specifically for a younger audience were his ''Lucky Starr'' novels. In 1951, at the suggestion of his Doubleday editor, he began working on a series of science-fiction stories that could easily be adapted for television. ''Television was here; that was clear,'' he writes in *In Memory Yet Green.* ''Why not take advantage of it, then? Radio had its successful long-running series, 'The Lone Ranger,' so why not a 'Space Ranger' modelled very closely upon that?'' *David Starr: Space Ranger,* published under the pseudonym Paul French, introduced David 'Lucky' Starr, agent of the interplanetary law enforcement agency the Council of Science. Accompanying Lucky on his adventures is his sidekick, John Bigman Jones, a short, tough man born and raised on the great agricultural farms of Mars. Together the two of them confront and outwit space pirates, poisoners, mad scientists, and interstellar spies—humans from the Sirian star system, who have become the Earth's worst enemies.

Although the ''Lucky Starr'' series ran to six volumes, the television deal that Asimov and his editor envisioned never materialized. ''None of us dreamed that for some reason . . . television series would very rarely last more than two or three years,'' Asimov writes. ''We also didn't know that a juvenile television series to be called 'Rocky Jones: Space Ranger' was already in the works.'' Another problem the series faced was in the scientific background of the stories. ''Unfortunately,'' state Jean Fiedler and Jim Mele in

Isaac Asimov, "Asimov had the bad luck to be writing these stories on the threshold of an unprecedented exploration of our solar system's planets, an exploration which has immensely increased our astronomical knowledge. Many of his scientific premises, sound in 1952, were later found to be inaccurate." In recent editions of the books, Asimov has included forewords explaining the situation to new readers.

Asimov's first nonfiction book was a medical text entitled *Biochemistry and Human Metabolism,* begun in 1950 and written in collaboration with William Boyd and Burnham Walker, two of his colleagues at the Boston University School of Medicine. He had recognized his ability as an explainer early in life, and he enjoyed clarifying scientific principles for his family and friends. He also discovered that he was a most able and entertaining lecturer who delighted in his work as a teacher. He told *New York Times* interviewer Israel Shenker that his talent lies in the fact that he "can read a dozen dull books and make one interesting book out of them." The result was that Asimov was phenomenally successful as a writer of science books for the general public. Before his death in 1992, Asimov commented, "I'm on fire to explain, and happiest when it's something reasonably intricate which I can make clear step by step. It's the easiest way I can clarify things in my own mind."

Further Reading

Los Angeles Times, April 8, 1992.
New York Times, April 7, 1992.
Washington Post, April 7, 1992.
Asimov, Isaac, *The Bicentennial Man and Other Stories,* Doubleday, 1976.
Asimov, Isaac, *In Memory Yet Green: The Autobiography of Isaac Asimov, 1920-1954,* Doubleday, 1979.
Asimov, Isaac, *In Joy Still Felt: The Autobiography of Isaac Asimov, 1954-1979,* Doubleday, 1980.
Clareson, Thomas D., editor, *Voices for the Future: Essays on Major Science Fiction Writers,* Popular Press, 1976.
Contemporary Literary Criticism, Gale, Volume 1, 1973; Volume 3, 1975; Volume 9, 1978; Volume 19, 1981; Volume 26, 1983.
Dictionary of Literary Biography, Volume 8: *Twentieth-Century American Science Fiction Writers,* Gale, 1981. □

Asoka

Asoka (reigned ca. 273-232 B.C.), the third emperor of the Maurya dynasty, is considered ancient India's greatest ruler. He combined the piety of a saint with the practical qualities of a king, and in the history of Buddhism he ranks second only to Buddha.

By the 3d century B.C. the kingdom of Magadha under the hegemony of the Mauryas controlled almost the entire Indian subcontinent. Only the southern tip of India and Ceylon remained free of the Mauryas' political influence. However, Buddhist missionaries of Asoka extended religious influence into Ceylon, which became a stronghold of Theravada Buddhism through Asoka's efforts.

In his youth Asoka served as viceroy of Taxila and later of Ujain. He came to the throne in 273 B.C., but a disputed succession delayed his coronation until 269. In 261 he annexed Kalinga, a vast tract between the Mahanadi and Godavari rivers, killing over 100,000 people and taking 150,000 captives. This was the only aggressive war of his reign, and so shocked the King's conscience that 4 years later he publicly recorded on various edicts his profound sorrow and remorse. He devoted the rest of his life to the propagation of *dharma,* the Buddhist law of piety.

Life and Beliefs

To bring his precepts into harmony with his personal practice, Asoka gave up hunting, royal luxuries, and the use of meat in the royal kitchen. He established and endowed hospitals for men and animals, both within his own realm and in those of the neighboring powers. On the highways banyan trees were planted to provide shade, mango groves were laid to provide fruit, wells were dug, watering places constructed, and rest houses established to comfort weary men and animals.

He made pilgrimages to India's holy places, preaching the law of piety to his subjects along the way. Often he was absent from his capital for as long as 10 months. He appointed a special class of officers, *dharma mahamatras,* to propagate morality. He asked them to be teachers first, magistrates afterward. Declaring all his subjects to be his children, he considered himself to be the trustee of their welfare rather than a ruler. But Asoka, while utilizing the full force of his administration, recognized frankly that permanent improvement was to be based on genuine change of heart, not on royal measures. He exhorted his subjects to meditate; to practice nonviolence and noninjury toward fellowmen and animals; to revere parents, teachers, mendicants, and elders; to be kind to inferiors such as servants, serfs, and beasts of burden; to be truthful; and to respect the beliefs of fellowmen. He did not seek to establish a sectarian creed and lavishly gave to all religious sects.

Monuments of Faith

From the sixteenth year of his reign Asoka permanently recorded ethical doctrines by inscribing them on rocks, sandstone pillars, and cave walls in the various regional languages. There were Fourteen Rock Edicts incised at seven different places in the remoter provinces of the empire. Some of these are preserved practically complete to this day. The second great series is that of Seven Pillar Inscriptions, six of which exist in six copies each, engraved on monolithic sandstone pillars erected at various localities in the home provinces. The seventh, perhaps the most important edict, is found on one pillar only. The remaining inscriptions consist of two Kalinga Edicts in two recensions, or critical revisions, three Cave Inscriptions, two Tarai Pillar Inscriptions, and several minor pillar and rock edicts in several recensions. The number of distinct documents is perhaps 35. Some inscriptions are in Greek and Aramaic. Bilingual inscriptions have been discovered on many pillars, making possible the decipherment of Brahmi and Kharosthi scripts. Many of the pillars contain Arabic numerals, India's gift to mathematics.

Asoka is reported to have built over 8,000 temples and more than 1,000 stupas, or tombs in honor of the Buddha. The stupa at Bhilsa still survives. The surviving gray sandstone pillars of his palace at Patliputra (modern Patna) display marvelous technical execution and brilliant art detail. The huge blocks of hard stone have an exquisite polish unmatched in India since the Asokan era. Asoka's lion seal carved on the Sarnath pillar has become modern India's state seal, and Asoka's wheel is represented on the central stripe of India's flag.

Anxious to spread his message across India, Asoka sent embassies to the Near East. His edicts mention Antiochus II, Theos of Syria, Ptolemy II, Philadelphos of Egypt, Magas of Cyrene, Antigonos Gonatas of Macedonia, and Alexander of Epirus. His son Mahendra and daughter Samghamitra went to Ceylon, which has been a Buddhist country since. A mission was sent to Burma, while others went to the Himalayan region and beyond. On the Indian subcontinent he sent his views to the Cola, Cera, and Pandya rulers.

Asoka's Empire

The empire Asoka ruled comprised, in modern terminology, Afghanistan south of the Hindu Kush, Baluchistan, Sind, Kashmir, the area of the lower Himalayas, and the whole of India and Pakistan proper except the southern extremity below the latitude of Madras. The central regions were governed directly from Patliputra, the outlying domains were divided among four viceroys, who were close relatives of the imperial family. A council of ministers advised the King, but in addition there was a well-defined bureaucratic structure, and five cadres are mentioned. In spite of Asoka's personal commitment to nonviolence, a standing army was maintained, the Kalinga Edict clearly enjoined people not to rebel for the Emperor "even in his remorse" had the power to crush them, and the death penalty was retained.

Not much is known about Asoka's family life. His inscriptions speak of two queens; Buddhist legends mention several. Very little is known about his sons, and how many they were. It is also not known how, when, and where the king-turned-evangelist died. A Tibetan tradition maintains that he died at Taxila. Two grandsons, Dasratha and Samprathi, succeeded him and divided the empire. But within 50 years of Asoka's death, a Brahmanical reaction, led by Pusyamitra, brought the dynasty to an end.

Further Reading

The most authoritative study of Asoka is Romila Thapar, *Asoka and the Decline of the Mauryas* (1961), which contains complete translations of the known inscriptions. B. G. Gokhale, *Asoka Maurya* (1966), discusses the influence of Asoka's personal philosophy on his empire. Asoka is discussed at length in Gertrude Emerson Sen, *The Pageant of India's History* (1948). See also Jawaharlal Nehru, *The Discovery of India* (1946). □

Les Aspin

President Bill Clinton's first secretary of defense, Les Aspin (1938-1995) spent 20 years of service in the House of Representatives. Despite his acknowledged intellect, he was a controversial committee chair in Congress and continued in that stance in the Cabinet, being replaced in late 1993. He served as head of the President's Foreign Intelligence Advisory Board until his death in 1995.

L es Aspin was born July 21, 1938, in Milwaukee, Wisconsin, the son of a Yorkshireman, Leslie Aspin, who had moved to the United States from England via Canada, and Marie Orth. Aspin graduated *summa cum laude* from Yale University in 1960 with a degree in history. He was a Rhodes scholar at Oxford University where he earned an M.A. in economics in 1962. He then studied at the Massachusetts Institute of Technology, from which he received a Ph.D. in economics in 1965.

Even before he finished his dissertation at MIT he had landed a position as an aide to William Proxmire, senator from Wisconsin and an ardent foe of government waste and extravagance. Aspin was Proxmire's campaign manager in 1964, thus gaining an education in electoral politics.

In 1963 Aspin served as a staff assistant to Walter Heller, who was head of President John F. Kennedy's Council of Economic Advisers. Three years later, at age 28, he entered the army, but did not leave Washington, serving as an economist at the Pentagon. While there he became part of the team of Secretary of Defense Robert S. McNamara, making several trips to Vietnam and learning how to analyze the mysteries of the Pentagon budget.

Released from active duty in 1968 after fulfilling his two-year service obligation, Aspin returned to Wisconsin to manage Lyndon Johnson's presidential campaign for re-election in that state. When Johnson withdrew his name from consideration, Aspin ran for the office of state treasurer, his first bid for elective office. He failed to win the primary so he turned to teaching economics at Marquette University. In 1970 he tried politics again, this time running for the Democratic nomination for the U.S. House of Representatives from the First Congressional District. He seemed to have lost, but a recount made him the victor by a narrow margin. He campaigned in the general election on a decidedly liberal platform supporting environmental positions, opposing the Vietnam War, and promising to promote full employment. Running at a time when antiwar feeling was high, Aspin soundly defeated his Republican opponent.

Aspin's first terms in Congress showed a maverick streak. He attracted much press attention with his campaigns to expose graft, fraud, and waste in governmental operations, particularly in defense contracts. That, and his questioning of the perks of general officers, made him *persona non grata* within the military, especially since he was a vocal member of the House Armed Services Committee.

The off-year election of 1974, following the Watergate affair, brought a record crop of freshman lawmakers determined to reform the House's operations. Among the targets was the seniority system in congressional committees. Aspin led the fight to unseat F. Edward Hebert of Louisiana, a staunch friend of the military, as chair of the Armed Services Committee.

By the 1980s Aspin had seemingly become more conservative and more accepted by those supporting President Reagan's defense build-up. His record became more mixed; he was in favor of a nuclear arms freeze, but not for a moratorium on the use of nuclear weapons. He supported a 5 percent growth in defense spending and, most controversially, the MX missile. Indeed, his actions in 1983 and 1984 saved the MX missile when House liberals thought they had defeated the funding for it.

Aspin now began to be given important subcommittee assignments for the Armed Services Committee. He became chairman of the House Armed Services Subcommittee on Military Personnel and Compensation as well as serving as a member of the Subcommittee on Investigations and on the Budget Committee. By 1985 he was able to win the chairmanship of the Armed Services Committee, replacing the veteran Melvin Price.

The coalition that had supported Aspin for the chair did not hold together long. Liberals believed that he had promised them the elimination of the MX missile program, but instead he took the position of slowing down the growth of the program. These representatives felt betrayed when

Aspin again saved the system at the behest of Reagan. Aspin then became the leader of a group called Defense Democrats who supported portions of Reagan's military program although advocating less resources for them. This group wished to accelerate the midgetman program and reduce, but not eliminate, funding for research on the so-called Star Wars missile program. This only partially assuaged Aspin's foes.

Aspin again became controversial with his position on Reagan's Central American policy. Despite his anti-Vietnam War history, he supported the administration's program of aid to the El Salvadorian government in the face of that government's bad record on human rights and late in 1986 supported the Reagan effort to extend military aid to the Contra rebels in Nicaragua. This angered many congressional Democrats who had fought hard against such aid.

Military conservatives were not happy either. Aspin had continued to attack waste in the Pentagon, to demand more efficiency in the Defense Department, and to reduce what he considered to be bloated retirement pay. The result was that, although he tried to mend fences with both sides and thought that he had succeeded by mid-1986, he almost lost his chairmanship in 1987. A coalition of conservatives and some aggrieved liberals sought to replace him with arch-conservative Marvin Leath of Texas. They succeeded in ousting him in the first vote on his chairmanship; but when the vote for a new chairman was taken two weeks later he won, as his friends widely publicized Leath's record.

Aspin continued to head the Armed Services Committee through 1992. He was as controversial as ever, even as the Bush administration reduced defense growth; and when President-elect Bill Clinton selected him to be Secretary of Defense there was some opposition and grumbling in both Congress and the military.

His tenure as Secretary of Defense was quite short, lasting less than a year. Problems beset him from the start: he seemed to disagree with the president's stance on gays in the military, he refused to send tanks to Somalia when requested by the military commander, and he argued against budget director Leon Panetta's suggested cuts in his department's spending. Critics charged him with being a poor administrator and with giving discursive and unproductive testimony to Congress. Despite his short tenure, Aspin made notable contributions to the nation's military. Rather than cut weapon and troop spending at the top, he provided a detailed "bottom up" review of the Pentagon needs for the future. He also presided over the unpopular closing of many obsolete military bases and reorganized the National Guard and other reserve components into a more streamlined force. Aspin suffered health problems and had a pacemaker installed. He resigned from the cabinet on December 15, 1993. Les Aspin died in May of 1995, following a stroke. He was serving as head of the President's Foreign Intelligence Advisory Board at the time of his death.

Further Reading

Most of the information on Aspin is limited to newspapers and periodicals. See the *Bulletin of the Atomic Scientists* (April

1987); the *New Republic* (February 2, 1987; August 27, 1992); *Newsweek* (April 1, 1985); *New York Times* (April 3, 1976; January 6, 1985; December 16, 1993; December 19, 1993); *Time* (May 29, 1995; June 5, 1995); and the *Wall Street Journal* (January 5, 1985; December 16, 1993). □

Eric Gunnar Asplund

Eric Gunnar Asplund (1885-1945) was a leader of modern design whom the magazine "Architectural Review" called the "high priest of functionalism in Sweden."

Gunnar Asplund was born in Stockholm. He studied at the Technical High School and then at the Academy of Art, graduating in 1909. That year he entered an architectural competition for the Swedish Church in Paris, basing his design upon Swedish traditional architecture. He also used this approach in two competitions for schools, one at Karlshamn (1912) and the other at Hedemora (1913); the latter was not built, being considered insufficiently monumental. In 1913 he won the competition for an extension to the Town Hall in Göteborg and toured Italy and Greece.

Returning to Sweden, Asplund won, in collaboration with Sigurd Lewerentz, a competition for the South Burial Ground within a wooded area of Stockholm. Asplund's First Mortuary Chapel for the Burial Ground has the plan of an Etruscan-Roman temple, but with its steep-hipped roof covered in wood shingles it blends into the landscape.

Asplund visited the United States to investigate library design with the aim of writing a program for a Swedish competition. His investigation so impressed the Stockholm Municipal Library Committee that no competition was held, and they invited him to submit a project; this Asplund did in 1921 and the building was completed in 1928. His design utilized the severe geometric simplicity of the late-18th-century romantic-classicists (or neoclassicists), whose designs were usually based on the cube, cylinder, and sphere.

The Stockholm Exhibition buildings of 1930 not only established modern architecture in Sweden but also established Asplund as the leader of a group of young architects within the Arts and Crafts Society. Four years later Asplund was given the commission for the extension to the 17th-century Göteborg Town Hall, which he had originally won in competition in 1913. His original design had been monumental and axially designed with a symmetrical entrance from the side of the building. His design of 1934, influenced by the work of the architect Le Corbusier, used classical proportions to express the structure. Internally, a spacious hall links the courtyard of the old building with nothing more than a glass wall to prevent the free flow of space. Swedish green marble, grained plywood, and a color scheme of white and blue contribute to the feeling of a totally modern structure. Asplund's last major work was the Woodland Crematorium (1935-1940); it is monumental and yet severely simple, notably in the entrance portico.

In all, Asplund designed 68 projects, of which 32 were constructed. They include an airport, schools, housing, shops, restaurants, and mausoleums.

Further Reading

The first book-length publication on Asplund was Gustav Holmdahl, ed., *Gunnar Asplund, Architect, 1885-1940* (1943; trans. 1950); it is well illustrated with plans, sketches, and photographs. Eric de Mare published a short monograph, *Gunnar Asplund* (1955). G. E. Kidder Smith, *Sweden Builds* (1950; 2d ed. 1957), discusses modern Swedish architecture generally and places Asplund in context with other modern Swedish architects.

Additional Sources

Caldenby, Claes, *Asplund: a book,* New York: Rizzoli, 1986, 1985.

Nagy, Elemaer, *Erik Gunnar Asplund,* Budapest: Akadaemiai Kiadao, 1974. □

Herbert Henry Asquith

The English statesman Herbert Henry Asquith, Ist Earl of Oxford and Asquith (1852-1928), was prime minister of Great Britain from 1908 to 1916. His government sponsored significant social legislation, restricted the power of the House of Lords, and led Britain into World War I.

Herbert Asquith was born in Morley (near Leeds), Yorkshire, on Sept. 12, 1852, the son of a small employer in wool spinning and weaving. The death of his father when Herbert was 8 years old brought the family under the care of his mother's father, a wool stapler in Huddersfield. There Herbert and his brother, William Willans, went to day school; later they attended a Moravian boarding school in Fulneck. At the age of 11 Herbert was sent to London with his brother to live with relatives and to attend the City of London School, then under a celebrated headmaster, Dr. Edwin Abbott. Young Asquith distinguished himself as a classical scholar and, more pertinent to his ultimate career, displayed remarkable talents as a public speaker. Winner of a classical scholarship, he entered Balliol College, Oxford, in 1870. There he achieved first-class honors in humane letters, served as president of the Oxford Union, and was elected a fellow of Balliol.

The 7-year stipend from the fellowship smoothed his way as a student at Lincoln's Inn, for he chose not classical studies but the law for his career. He was admitted to the bar in 1876. The next year he married Helen Melland, daughter of a prominent Manchester physician, and settled in Hampstead on the edge of London.

Early Political Career

Asquith's law practice developed slowly, and his real ambitions, it soon became clear, were in politics. He entered the House of Commons in 1886 as Liberal member for

East Fife, a Scottish constituency which he represented for the next 32 years. His extraordinary maiden speech marked him out for future greatness. His defense (though unsuccessful) in 1888 of R. B. Cunninghame-Graham for unlawful assembly in Trafalgar Square on "Bloody Sunday" and his services (extraordinarily successful) in 1889 as junior counsel for Charles Parnell before the Commission of Enquiry (investigating Parnell's alleged approval of the Phoenix Park murders in Dublin) brought him to public notice. In 1890 he became a queen's counsel.

When William Gladstone and the Liberals returned to power in 1892, Asquith, now 40, was given Cabinet office as home secretary. In a government sharply divided over fundamental issues, he occupied himself largely with departmental details, working out a thoroughly satisfactory arrangement for public meetings in Trafalgar Square and enacting the Factory Act of 1895, which applied new standards of protection in industry. And though the Liberal government went from indifferent success under Gladstone to total failure under Lord Rosebury, Asquith emerged as a future leader of his party.

Asquith's wife had died in 1891, leaving him with five young children. Three years later he married Emma Alice Margaret (Margot) Tennant, daughter of a wealthy landed aristocrat and a woman distinguished in her own right in intellectual and social circles. Brilliant, vivacious, witty, even frivolous, she was a person altogether different from Asquith's first wife, and indeed, to all appearances, from Asquith himself. But it was an aspect of his character that, though serious in politics, for relaxation he preferred feminine company to masculine, especially if accompanied with wit and charm.

Asquith's political prospects seemed dimmed by the long Tory rule from 1895 to 1905; moreover, the Liberal party, already seriously weakened with the defection of the Unionists after 1886, was now almost hopelessly divided by the issues of the Boer War. Asquith, himself a supporter of the war, was often in conflict with Henry Campbell-Bannerman, party leader from 1898. In 1903, however, the Conservatives divided over the tariff issue, and the Liberals, the traditional party of free trade, reunited, with Asquith's oratory an instrument of revival.

Prime Minister

In the Liberal government of 1905 Asquith, as chancellor of the Exchequer, was second in command to Prime Minister Campbell-Bannerman. His extraordinary capacity in the Commons made him a leading spokesman for government policy, and when Campbell-Bannerman resigned in 1908, Asquith's succession to the premiership was a matter of course. The Asquith government represented the transition from Gladstonian liberalism with emphasis upon "Peace, Retrenchment and Reform" to the "New Liberalism" of the 20th century with objectives of social and economic reform. Under Asquith the Liberal party reached the height of its power but also suffered the first stages in its disintegration.

Asquith legislated old age pensions and national insurance against illness, disability, and unemployment. The chief obstacle was the Conservative-dominated House of Lords. Asquith forced the Lords to accept a revolutionary budget to finance pensions as well as dreadnoughts. He went on to attack the veto power of the Lords. The Lords finally gave way, and the Parliament Bill, which sharply restricted the Lords' role in legislation, became law in 1911.

However, the Asquith government was now beset with even more serious problems—the threat of prolonged turmoil in the agitation of "votes for women"; protracted and intense industrial strife, often syndicalist in spirit; and the possibility of mutiny in Ulster, supported by the Conservatives and the military in England, in opposition to imminent Irish home rule. Asquith's qualities as advocate and orator were now ineffective. They could not mask his lack of any clear philosophy of government, his failure of positive leadership, and his "wait and see" attitude.

In August 1914 the Asquith government declared Britain's entry into World War I, despite the traditional Liberal adherence to peace. Asquith's ineffectiveness as a war prime minister led to the formation of a coalition Cabinet in 1915. In December 1916 the Cabinet forced Asquith's resignation; he was replaced as prime minister by David Lloyd George. Neither the Liberal party nor Asquith ever recovered from this crisis.

Last Years

Lloyd George led the coalition until 1922 but with Liberals in Parliament divided between his adherents and those of Asquith. In the election of 1918 the Asquith Liberals were reduced to 33, and Asquith himself was not reelected.

In 1920, however, he returned to the Commons; while he was greeted by enthusiastic crowds in the streets, his reappearance in the Commons chamber brought only a "thin cheer." But it was now Lloyd George who was discredited, and the Liberals, under Asquith, made considerable recovery, although remaining less powerful than the Conservatives and Labour in the House of Commons.

In January 1924 Asquith refused overtures from the Conservatives for a new coalition, and with his support the first Labour government was formed. But later in the year the Conservatives returned to power, and Asquith again lost his seat. In 1925 he was created 1st Earl of Oxford and Asquith. Some reconciliation came within the Liberal party but very little between Asquith and Lloyd George, now the chairman of the small parliamentary party. Asquith resigned his titular party leadership in 1926. Soon after, his health failed, and he died on Feb. 15, 1928.

Further Reading

Asquith told his own story in *Memories and Reflections,* 1852-1927 (2 vols., 1928), and Margot Asquith hers in *An Autobiography* (2 vols., 1920). There are two good biographies of Asquith: J. A. Spender and Cyril Asquith, *Life of Herbert Henry Asquith, Lord Oxford and Asquith* (2 vols., 1932), is more detailed but less objective than Roy Jenkins, *Asquith* (1978, 1964). Both are based on the Asquith papers now in the Bodleian at Oxford. See also Winston Churchill, *Great Contemporaries* (1937), and for background Trevor Wilson, *The Downfall of the Liberal Party, 1914-1935* (1966).

Additional Sources

Koss, Stephen E., *Asquith,* New York: Columbia University Press, 1985, 1976; St. Martin's Press, 1976.
Levine, Naomi B., *Politics, Religion, and Love: the story of H.H. Asquith, Venetia Stanley, and Edwin Montagu, based on the life and letters of Edwin Samuel Montagu,* New York: New York University Press, 1991. □

Hafiz Assad

Hafiz Assad (al-'Asad; born 1930) took power in Syria in 1970 and became president, a position he retained longer than any other person since Syrian independence in 1946.

Hafiz Assad was born on October 6, 1930 into a large, poor peasant family that lived in a rural, mountainous village of Qurdaha, southeast of the Syrian port city of Latakia. He was one of nine children of 'Ali Assad, a farmer, who opposed the French rule that prevailed in Syria prior to independence. Assad was a member of the minority Muslim religious sect called the Alawis and of the Haddadi Clan. The Alawis sect represented roughly 12 percent of the Syrian population but was dominant in the rural areas near Syria's coastline.

Assad received his primary education in his local village. Secondary education did not exist in the poor moun-

tain regions of Syria in the 1940s so his family moved to the coast where Assad could receive the secondary education necessary to advance his career.

Assad's political views, personal attitudes, and social philosophy were molded in part by his Alawi background, the enormous poverty he witnessed in his youth, and the struggle he and his family experienced to improve their own lives. His original family name was said to be "Wahish," which means "wild beast," but the family apparently changed the name to "Asad," which means "lion." The original name reflected the lot associated with Alawis at that time. They were deprived, and many of their daughters often migrated to the rich homes in the Syrian capital of Damascus in order to seek work as servants or to take hard working, low paying jobs. Assad was determined from a young age that the next generation of Alawis would have a better life. As an adult, Assad had many colleagues who espoused his socialism, but few had the genuine humble background he did. His past resulted in both fierce determination and suspicions of his peers.

While still a teenager in the mid-1940s, Assad joined the Ba'th Party, which preached a mixture of socialism and Arab nationalism. The Ba'th Party at that time had a large following in the Alawi regions in part because the party advocated secularism in public life and a new non-sectarian national community, something always popular for many in minority groups.

His Military Career

When he was admitted to the Homs Military Academy in 1952, Assad embarked on a military career. He was attracted by the hope that a military career would offer good pay and a chance for advancement. Three years later he graduated as a lieutenant in the Syrian Air Force, one of the first Alawis to join that service. In the service, he continued his political activities but also became a proficient combat pilot and a master in aerial maneuvers. He often performed his acrobatics on parade days in the skies above Damascus.

His expertise won him a place to further study military science in Russia in 1957 at a time of intense political activity in Syria which led to the 1958 union between Syria and Egypt. In the process of that union, the careers of many known Ba'th Party members in the armed forces were sacrificed, and Assad and some of his colleagues were assigned to posts in rural Egypt, far from their political bases. While in Egypt, Captain Assad joined forces with two other exiled Alawi officers—Salah Jadid and Muhammad 'Umran—and formed a secret military committee dedicated to terminating the union with Egypt and to throwing out the old Ba'th Party civilian leadership which had promoted the union in the first place.

Although some Ba'th officers participated in the 1961 coup which ended the union with Egypt, several, including Assad, were forced to temporarily quit the air force in a political purge. Assad then worked for two years as an official of the Ministry of Sea Transportation, a period during which he concentrated on Ba'th Party activities and, with other members of the secret military committee, planned the March 8, 1963, revolution which brought the Ba'th Party to power in Syria.

Following the Ba'th Party takeover, Assad was appointed commander of the air force with the rank of major. In 1964, he was promoted to the rank of general and placed on the party's regional command, and a year later he was made commander-in-chief of the air force. In that capacity, he joined ranks with Salah Jadid in 1966 to overthrow the Ba'th government of Amin al-Hafiz. In the new government, he became minister of defense.

The year 1967 was not a happy one for Syria or for Assad. The June defeat in the Six Day War at the hands of Israel was a bitter experience. Syria had half its air force planes destroyed on the ground and the troops lost one-seventh of Syria's territory to the Israelis. As defense minister, Assad should have been a target for major blame, but he deftly passed it along to the clumsy party apparatus and leadership for having ruined the military prior to the war due to its purges and choosing party over national interests. An absolute necessity for Assad was to rebuild and strengthen the armed forces, while others in the leadership—many of them radical and doctrinaire Marxists—sought consolidation of power and the championing of Marxist economic development. Assad was able to outmaneuver many opponents in 1968 and 1969 and challenged the party leadership and Salah Jadid. He even tried in 1969 to take over the government but was thwarted by Soviet pressure. The stage, however, had been set for a showdown between Assad and Jadid.

Assad Takes the Presidency

Assad did his homework well in the party, and when the showdown came with Jadid, he prevailed and took over the reins of government in November 1970. At that time Assad became prime minister. Four months later he was elected president, a position to which he was re-elected several times. To many observers his bloodless coup in 1970 represented merely the replacement of one Alawi officer with another. But below the surface there were several changes, including a shift away from a solely Marxist-socialist socio-economic policy in internal affairs and away from the uncompromising orientations in regional and international affairs which had isolated Syria from its neighbors in the post-1967 war period.

Assad was associated with a pragmatic group which sought a more moderate path of socialism in social and economic policy. This would allow Syria's commercial sector a freer existence and a more flexible and realistic foreign policy which would permit the ability to adjust to events and changing circumstances without the constraints of any ideological straightjacket. One factor precipitating Assad's coup was a fear among some that the directions in which policies were headed under Jadid were destined to undermine the whole Ba'th revolution on one level and the new found prominence of elements of the Alawi community on another.

The political position and power of Assad and the unprecedented political continuity he provided after 1970 was the result of his three principal pillars of support: the army, the Ba'th Party, and his Alawi community. In the early 1980s, as various groups tested Assad and his leadership, and as Assad suffered a heart attack, he had to rely more on an elaborate system of security, with many key security positions occupied by Alawi officers, including his brothers, cousins and nephews.

Serious outbursts of civil unrest occurred in Syria between 1979 and 1982, and these prompted increasingly heavy-handed, often ruthless, measures by security forces of the Assad government. Discontent of Alawi rule and perceived corruption and abuse of power, along with a stagnating economy burdened by heavy military expenditures, and a developing Muslim fundamentalist challenge to Assad's rule, was fueled by resentment on the part of the Syrian Sunni Muslim majority especially in the northern Syrian towns of Aleppo and Hama. Well over 10,000 Syrians died in Hama in 1982 when security forces leveled some one-fourth of the city.

The Assad presidency of Syria was a curious combination of pragmatism and decisive action, of cool and deliberate approaches to problem solving and rash impulses, of dogged determination and live-and-let-live policies, and of impassioned rhetoric and quiet diplomacy. His opportunism, astuteness, and ability to adjust put opponents off guard time and time again.

Assad's presidency, in the eyes of many Syrians, was strengthened by his handling of foreign policy matters and his emergence as a regional figure of stature. Assad was a champion of the causes of Arab unity, Palestinian nationalism, and confrontation with Israel. He consistently said that a just and lasting solution to the Arab-Israeli conflict would only occur when the Arab world attained military parity with Israel, and he roundly attacked Egypt for breaking Arab ranks to negotiate with Israel.

A Tough Foreign Policy

His hard line toward peace negotiations and opposition to direct talks with Israel was consistent and was clearly demonstrated in his strong opposition to the Camp David Accords and the peace treaty between Israel and Egypt. He also opposed the May 17, 1983, Lebanese-Israeli withdrawal agreement, which he saw as a violation of Lebanese sovereignty and a threat to Syrian and Arab security. Syrian intentions and those of Assad in Lebanon may be unknown, but it is clear that Assad wanted a government in Lebanon he could trust and control and that he could not tolerate a Lebanon which had any separate relationship, overt or covert, with Israel.

Assad also sought to control the Palestinian national movement in order to prevent any Palestinian leadership from seeking a separate peace with Israel either directly or through Jordan. This stance would protect Syria from isolation and promote Syria as the champion of the Palestinian cause.

Assad's handling of relations with the United States and Soviet Union demonstrated the same qualities seen in his handling of other issues. While he came to rely heavily on the Soviets for military aid and political backing, he showed no intention of sacrificing Syria's independence to Soviet interference. His views of the United States were mostly negative, but he wanted to leave the door open to better ties. Assad was deeply suspicious of American policies in the region, in part because of American economic and military support for Israel, but he clearly recognized the importance of maintaining some relationship with all world powers.

Assad has carved out a unique role for himself and Syria in the Middle East peace process. He has been seen as trying to placate many sides involved in the process from the United States and the Palestinians to mending a long standing rift with Jordan. Assad was determined to remain true to his own personal agenda rather than another nation's interests and sought to act accordingly. Assad's feeble attempts at trying to come to terms with Israel and the possible return to Syria of the Golan Heights has been his in the mid 1990s. The emphasis on Syria as the one who held the key to Middle Eastern peace shifted the spotlight away from the allegations of massive domestic terrorism campaigns and rampant human rights violations Assad undertook in order to maintain power and thwart the chance for armed resistance to his policies. Wary of being viewed as the one who gave in, Assad was choosing to play his trump very carefully.

The longevity of the Assad regime in Syria resulted from Assad's ability to keep control of many diverse groups in Syria and his handling of regional issues, especially Lebanon and his confrontation with Israel. Syria's wars with Israel in 1967, 1973, and 1980 had a negative impact on the country, but Assad brought his armed forces back each time with more weapons, more men, and more sophisticated weaponry. The costs for Syria of Assad's continuous arms buildup were enormous because of the increasing share of Syria's resources needed to fuel the armed forces. President Assad was Syria's longest surviving head of state and a regional leader everyone had to reckon with, although he continued to confront and overcome serious domestic and regional challenges.

Further Reading

Assad and recent events in Syria are discussed prominently in several books written about post-independence Syria. Among the better volumes are: *Syria* by Tabitha Petran (1972); *Syria under the Ba'th, 1963-1966* by Itamar Rabinovich (1972); *Syria and the Lebanese Crisis* by Adeed Dawisha (1980); *Syria, Modern State in an Ancient Land* by John F. Devlin (1983); *The Ba'th and Syria, 1947-1982: the Evolution of Ideology, Party and State* by Robert W. Olson (1983); and *The Islamic Struggle in Syria* by Umar Ab-Allah (1984).
For further reading on Assad see also "Just Kidding," *New Republic* (January 8-15, 1996); "Holy Terror," *New Republic* (April 22, 1996); "The Shame of Lebanon," *New York Review* (April 25, 1996) and "Preparing for War," *Time* (December 9, 1996). □

Fred Astaire

Fred Astaire (1899-1987) was a preeminent dancer and choreographer who worked in vaudeville, revue, musical comedy, television, radio, and Hollywood musicals. He achieved admiring recognition not only from his peers in the entertainment world, but also from major figures in ballet and modern dance.

Fred Astaire, born Frederick Austerlitz on May 10, 1899, in Omaha, Nebraska, began performing in vaudeville with his sister, Adele, in 1905. The Astaires eventually became featured performers, and in 1917 they moved to the musical stage where they appeared in ten productions, most of them hugely successful, particularly two musical comedies with songs by George and Ira Gershwin (*Lady, Be Good* in 1924 and *Funny Face* in 1927) and a revue with songs by Arthur Schwartz and Howard Dietz (*The Band Wagon* in 1931).

When his sister retired from show business in 1932 to marry, Astaire sought to reshape his career. He settled on the featured role in *Gay Divorce*, a "musical play" with songs by Cole Porter. This show proved Astaire could flourish without his sister, and it also helped establish the pattern of most of his film musicals: it was a light, perky, unsentimental comedy, largely uncluttered by subplot, built around a love story for Astaire and his partner (Claire Luce) that was airy and amusing, but essentially serious—particularly when the pair danced together.

Astaire Goes to Hollywood

In 1933 Astaire married Phyllis Livingston Potter. Shortly after his marriage Astaire went to Hollywood. At RKO he had a featured part in the exuberant, fluttery *Flying Down to Rio* (1933). The film was a hit, and it was obvious Astaire's performance and screen appeal were a major factor in that success. *The Gay Divorcee* (1934), a film version of *Gay Divorce,* was the first of Astaire's major pictures with Ginger Rogers, and it scored even better at the box office than *Flying Down to Rio.* With this and seven more films in the 1930s (the most popular of which was *Top Hat* of 1935), they reached their full development as a team—one of the legendary partnerships in the history of dance, characterized by breathless high spirits, emotional richness, bubbling comedy, and beguiling romantic compatibility.

For these films Astaire created a rich series of romantic and playful duets for the team, as well as an array of dazzling and imaginative solos for himself. Astaire's musicality, together with the opportunity of working on such a classy, highly profitable project, made his films attractive to many of the top popular-song composers of the day: Irving Berlin, Jerome Kern, and the Gershwins.

By the end of the 1930s the revenues from the films with Rogers were beginning to decline and, after a disagreement over fees with the studio, Astaire left. The next years were nomadic but successful ones for Astaire. He made nine films at four different studios and continued to fashion splendid dances. He appeared with a variety of partners— tap virtuoso Eleanor Powell, Paulette Goddard, Rita

Hayworth, Joan Leslie, and Lucille Bremer—and he also did a pair of films with Bing Crosby. Musically, Astaire continued to attract the best: Porter, Berlin, Kern, Harold Arlen, Harry Warren, and lyricist Johnny Mercer.

Retirement and Creation of Dancing Schools

In 1946 Astaire retired from motion pictures to create a chain of dancing schools, a venture that was eventually proved to be successful. In 1947 he returned to movies to make the highly profitable *Easter Parade* at MGM, opposite Judy Garland. Nine more musicals followed. His partners in these included Ginger Rogers for one picture, as well as Vera-Ellen, Cyd Charisse, Leslie Caron, Betty Hutton, Jane Powell, and Audrey Hepburn. This period was marked by a great personal tragedy for Astaire—the agonizing death of his beloved wife from cancer in 1954 at the age of 46.

By the mid-1950s the era of the classic Hollywood musical as Astaire had experienced it—indeed, defined it— was coming to an end, and Astaire moved into other fields. On television he produced four multiple award-winning musical specials with Barrie Chase as his partner. He also tried his hand at straight acting roles with considerable success in eight films between 1959 and 1982. Over the years he played a number of characters on television— usually suave ones—in dramatic specials and series. As he entered his 80s, Astaire, a life-long horse racing enthusiast, romanced, and in 1980 married, Robyn Smith, a successful jockey in her mid-30s. He died seven years later.

Ginger Rogers, Astaire's long time dance partner, passed away in April 1995. Rogers is often quoted as having said, "I did everything Fred did, only backwards and in high heels." Their partnership lasted sixteen years, from 1933 to 1949.

Astaire's Legacy

Over the course of his long film career, Fred Astaire appeared in 212 musical numbers, of which 133 contain fully developed dance routines, a high percentage of which are of great artistic value, a contribution unrivaled in films and with few parallels in the history of dance. And, because he worked mainly in film, Astaire is that great rarity: a master choreographer the vast majority of whose works are precisely preserved.

Although the creation of many of Astaire's dances involved a degree of collaboration with others, the guiding creative hand and the final authority was Astaire himself. His choreography is notable for its inventiveness, wit, musicality, and economy. Characteristically, each dance takes two or three central ideas and carefully presents and develops them—ideas that might derive from a step, the music, the lyrics, the qualities of his partner, or the plot situation.

Astaire's dances are stylistically eclectic, an unpredictable blend of tap and ballroom with bits from other dance forms thrown in. What holds everything together is Astaire's distinctive style and sensibility: the casual sophistication, the airy wit, the transparent rhythmic intricacy, and the apparent ease of execution. Astaire also focused his attention on the problems of filming dance and settled on an approach that was to dominate Hollywood musicals for a generation: both camerawork and editing are fashioned to enhance the flow and continuity of the dances, not to undercut or overshadow it.

A perfectionist, Astaire spent weeks working out his choreography. Although his perfectionism, his propensity to worry, his shyness, and his self-doubt could make him difficult, even exasperating, to work with, he was an efficient planner and worker. His courtesy, enormous professionalism, and tireless struggle for improvement earned him the admiration of his co-workers.

Astaire's legacy continues to be revisited, sometimes with controversy. In January 1997, Astaire's image returned to television through special effects editing when Dirt Devil grafted their vacuum cleaners into dance scenes from Astaire's films for three of their commercials. The advertisements were completed and run with Robyn Astaire's blessing. The commercials, which aired during the Super Bowl, were panned by the press, the general feeling being that replacing Ginger Rogers with a vacuum cleaner was in poor taste.

Further Reading

Fred Astaire's autobiography which, shattering Hollywood tradition, he wrote himself (in longhand) is *Steps in Time* (1959). His work is discussed and analyzed in *Arlene* Croce, *The Fred Astaire & Ginger Rogers Book* (1972) and John Mueller, *Astaire Dancing: The Musical Films* (1985). Useful interviews with Astaire are included in Morton Eustis, *Players at Work* (1937) and in *Inter/View* (June 1973). Astaire can also be found on the World Wide Web. A listing of his movies can be found at http://dolphin.upenn.edu/~amatth13/fred.html. Information on Astaire can also be found at http://www.mrshowbiz.com/scoop/news/archive/1_9_97_8bogart.html. □

Francis William Aston

The British chemist and physicist Francis William Aston (1877-1945) invented the mass spectrograph and discovered the isotopic complexity of the elements.

Francis Aston was born on Sept. 1, 1877, at Harborne, Birmingham, where his father was a metal merchant and ran a small farm. He studied chemistry at Mason College (which later became the University of Birmingham). In his spare time he trained himself in the various arts of apparatus construction, especially glassblowing. When his scholarship expired, he took a post with a brewery firm. After 3 years he returned to the University of Birmingham. In 1910 an invitation arrived from J. J. Thomson to join him at the Cavendish Laboratory, Cambridge.

Separation of the Isotopes

Thomson was examining positive "rays" produced in electric-discharge tubes at low pressure. These were in fact atoms stripped of some or all of their outer electrons and thus carried an overall positive charge. Thomson had obtained parabolic tracks by submitting the rays to the simultaneous application of magnetic and electrostatic fields. With Aston's help he discovered that neon gas had a small component that gave a separate parabolic track. Since each parabola was characterized by a unique mass-charge ratio, deductions concerning particle masses could be made, and it was concluded that the atomic masses of the major and minor components of neon were 20 and 22 respectively.

Aston then attempted to separate the two components by physical means and to measure their densities on a quartz microbalance of his own devising. In 1913 he achieved a partial separation by submitting the gas to repeated diffusions through pipe clay; small, but significant, differences in gas density were found for the two samples obtained.

Mass Spectrograph

Gradually, the concept of isotopes was becoming clearer and more generally accepted, and in 1919 Aston worked out some ideas on a new instrument which could give results indicative of mass alone. Unlike Thomson's apparatus, Aston's invention employed magnetic and electrostatic fields producing opposite deflections in the same plane. By focusing the beams through fine slits, Aston ob-

tained a series of lines, each of which corresponded to a definite particle mass. The series of lines was a mass spectrum, and the original instrument was the first mass spectrograph.

With this equipment Aston began an examination of the isotopic composition of more than 50 elements. In those cases where neither the element nor any of its available compounds were volatile, he utilized a solid product containing the element as the anode of his discharge tube. In almost every case the isotopic mass was a whole number within the limits of experimental accuracy (1 in 1000). The only notable exception was hydrogen, 1.008. Thus isotopy was not a rare phenomenon, as some workers had supposed, but widespread and affecting most elements. Aston was led by these integral isotopic weights to conclude that all nuclei are composed of protons (of unit weight) and of negligibly light electrons.

The importance of precise values for the isotopic masses led Aston to design an improved mass spectrograph in 1925, with an accuracy of 1 in 10,000. A later instrument (1927) gave an accuracy improved by a factor of 10. With this refined apparatus he discovered a great many new isotopes, often present in only very small amounts in the natural element.

Assessment of His Work

Many important consequences flowed from Aston's work on the mass spectrograph. As he himself recognized, the fractional isotopic weight of hydrogen implied that if it were converted to helium substantial amounts of the mass would be converted into energy. Using Albert Einstein's relativity relationship, Aston predicted that the energy liberated in a nuclear reaction of this kind would be enormous. His opinions were justified when the first atomic bomb was exploded a few months before his death.

The more immediate importance of the mass spectrograph was its ability to give data on nuclear masses with great precision, thus laying the foundations of the atomic energy industry. More recently, the mass spectrometer has proved an indispensable tool for structural investigations in organic chemistry.

The importance of Aston's work was quickly recognized, and in 1921 he was elected a fellow of the Royal Society. The following year he received the Nobel Prize in chemistry. His authoritative book *Isotopes* first appeared in 1922 and was followed by many other editions up to 1941. His other book, *Mass Spectra and Isotopes,* appeared in 1933.

Other Interests

In addition to his work at the Cavendish Laboratory, Aston made some valuable scientific contributions to the study of astronomical eclipses. In 1925 he photographed the sun's corona from Sumatra. He made expeditions to study the solar eclipses of 1932 and 1936 in Canada and Japan respectively, though clouds prevented direct observations. However, Aston was able to study the polarization of the light in the neighborhood of the eclipsed sun.

Aston never married. He was often accompanied on his travels by his sister, Helen, to whom he was deeply devoted. He died at Trinity College, Cambridge, on Nov. 20, 1945.

Further Reading

There is no full-length biography of Aston. Edvard Farber, ed., *Great Chemists* (1961), contains a short biography, and an old but still useful source, Bernard Jaffe, *Crucibles: The Lives and Achievements of the Great Chemists* (1932), offers an adequate account of Aston's life and work. The Nobel Foundation's *Nobel Lectures, Including Presentation Speeches and Laureates' Biographies: Chemistry, 1922-1941* (1967) contains a brief biography and a résumé of the work for which Aston received the prize. F. J. Moore, *A History of Chemistry,* revision prepared by William T. Hall (1939), includes a brief sketch of Aston and places his work in historical perspective. □

John Jacob Astor

An American fur trader, merchant, and capitalist, John Jacob Astor (1763-1848) used his profits from fur trading to invest in a wide range of business enterprises. By the time of his death he was the richest man in America.

John Jacob Astor was born in Waldorf, near Heidelberg, Germany, on July 17, 1763. He was named after his father, a poor but convivial butcher. In spite of the family's poverty, Astor was sent to the local schoolmaster, who provided him with an exceptional education, considering the times. When Astor reached the age of 14, his father decided that his son should work with him. The boy assisted for 2 years before, in 1779, he struck out on his own. He joined a brother in London, where he learned English and worked to earn passage money to America. In 1783, after the peace treaty ending the American Revolution had been signed, he sailed for the United States to join another brother who had emigrated earlier. He landed at Baltimore in March 1784.

Astor soon joined his brother in New York and began to demonstrate his talent for business. He received a shipment of flutes from England, which he offered for sale. He also worked for several furriers and began buying furs on his own. In 1784 and 1785 Astor made furbuying trips to western New York for his employers, purchasing furs for himself at the same time. He acquired enough furs to make a trip to England profitable. In London he established connections with a reputable trading house, signed an agreement to act as the New York agent for a musical instrument firm, and used his profits from the furs to buy merchandise suitable for trade with the Native Americans. Not yet 22, he had already proved himself a shrewd and competent business man.

His initial success convinced Astor that a fortune could be made in the fur trade. He began to spend more time managing and expanding his business. Between 1790 and 1808 his agents collected furs from as far west as Mackinaw,

Mich. The Jay Treaty and the British evacuation of forts in the Old Northwest worked to Astor's advantage, and he expanded his operations in the Great Lakes region. Through an arrangement with the British Northwest Company, he purchased furs directly from Montreal. By about 1809 he was recognized as one of the leading fur traders in the United States.

Following the Louisiana Purchase, Astor turned his attention to the fur trade in the Pacific Northwest. Through shrewd political maneuvers he obtained a charter for the American Fur Company. His plan was to establish a main fort at the mouth of the Columbia River, with sub-forts in the interior. His fleet of ships would collect the furs and sell them in China, where goods would be purchased for sale in Europe; in Europe merchandise could be bought to sell in the United States when the ships returned.

Although the town of Astoria was established on the Columbia, the company's operations were unsuccessful. After the War of 1812 Astor renewed his efforts to gain control of the fur trade in North America. Through influence in Congress he secured legislation that prohibited foreigners from engaging in the trade except as employees and that eliminated the government's trading post serving independent traders. By the late 1820's he monopolized the fur trade in the Great Lakes region and most of the Mississippi Valley. This monopoly put him into direct competition with the Rocky Mountain Fur Company and British fur interests in the Pacific Northwest. However, by 1830 Astor's interest in the company had begun to decline.

Through his dealings in the fur trade Astor became involved in general merchandising. During the 1790s he had begun to import and sell a large variety of European goods. During this early period he showed little interest in establishing trade relations with China. Between 1800 and 1812, however, his trade with China expanded and became an integral part of his business dealings in Europe. The War of 1812 temporarily disrupted his plans, but it gave him an opportunity to purchase ships at a bargain price since declining trade had made merchants anxious to dispose of their fleets. After the war Astor had a sizable fleet of sailing vessels and again became active in the China and Pacific trade. For a time he was involved in smuggling Turkish opium into China but found the profits were not worth the risk and abandoned this venture. Between 1815 and 1820 he enjoyed a commanding position in the China trade. Thereafter his interest declined, and he turned his attention to other business activities. One explanation for Astor's success as a merchant was that he had the capital to buy superior merchandise at a low cost and a fleet of ships that could transport the goods to markets more quickly than his rivals.

Astor retired from the American Fur Company and withdrew from both domestic and foreign trade in 1834. He turned to other investments, including real estate, moneylending, insurance companies, banking, railroads and canals, public securities, and the hotel business. The most important was real estate. He had invested some capital in land early in his career. After 1800 he concentrated on real estate in New York City. He profited not only from the sale of lands and rents but from the increasing value of lands within the city. During the last decade of his life his income from rents alone exceeded $1,250,000. A reliable estimate placed his total wealth at $20-30 million (the greatest source being his land holdings on Manhattan Island) at his death in 1848, at the age of 84.

Further Reading

The most complete biography of Astor is Kenneth Wiggins Porter, *John Jacob Astor, Business Man* (2 vols., 1931). A somewhat critical work which deals extensively with Astor's interest in the fur trade is John Upton Terrell, *Furs by Astor* (1963). See also Washington Irving, *Astoria* (1836; repr. 1961); Meade Minigerode, *Certain Rich Men* (1927); and Harvey O'Connor, *The Astors* (1941). A background discussion of the fur trade that includes Astor is provided by Bernard De Voto, *Across the Wide Missouri* (1947). Social histories of New York that discuss Astor are Arthur Pound, *The Golden Earth: The Story of Manhattan's Landed Wealth* (1935); Frederick L. Collins, *Money Town* (1946); and Edward Robb Ellis, *The Epic of New York City* (1966). □

Nancy Langhorne Astor

American-born Nancy Langhorne Astor (1879-1964) became the first woman to serve as a member of the British Parliament, a position she held from 1919 to 1945.

Born in Danville, Virginia, on May 19, 1879, Nancy Langhorne grew up in the straitened circumstances of the post-Civil War South. Financial success eluded her father, Chiswell Dabney Langhorne, a former Confederate officer, until the 1890s. Then contracts with the Chesapeake and Ohio Railroad paid off, and thereafter he amassed considerable wealth. In 1892 he bought an estate, Mirador, near Charlottesville, where she spent her adolescence. She had seven brothers and sisters, one of whom, Irene, became the celebrated "Gibson girl" painted by her artist husband, Charles Dana Gibson.

Her family experience provided some of the basis for her later feminism. Her father exerted tyrannical rule, and her mother, Nancy Witcher Langhorne, accepted his authority and the conventional feminine role. Worn out by repeated unwanted pregnancies (she had 11 children, eight of whom survived) and by managing her family and household staff, she died of a heart attack at the age of 56. Astor was badly shaken by this event, but later she lamented her mother's restricted life. Women of that day, she wrote in 1951, had no "independence. It seemed to me wrong then. I think it is wrong still." Her father's refusal to send her to college was a deprivation Astor regretted throughout her life.

At the age of 18, on October 27, 1897, Nancy married Robert Gould Shaw, a proper Bostonian. They had a son, Bobbie, but the marriage did not last. The couple separated in 1902 and divorced the following year. Not long after, on an ocean voyage, she met Waldorf Astor, the heir to one of the world's greatest fortunes. An Englishman despite his American roots, Waldorf coincidentally was born on the same day as her. Apparently that was not all they had in common, for they soon announced their engagement. The marriage took place in London on April 19, 1906. They had four sons and a daughter.

In the early years of their marriage the couple became involved in reformist politics. They were largely under the influence of Lloyd George, who as chancellor of the exchequer in 1909 prepared a social welfare budget that anticipated the welfare institutions of modern England. In 1910 on his second run for office her husband was elected to Parliament from Plymouth. Astor had worked extensively and effectively in his campaign.

Elected to Parliament

In 1919 her husband had to resign his seat in order to accept a peerage (and thus a place in the House of Lords) which he inherited at his father's death. Astor decided to run as a Conservative for her husband's vacated seat in Commons. She did so successfully, advocating policies of social reform—particularly those affecting women and children. Her campaign slogan was: "Vote for Lady Astor and your children will weigh more."

On December 1, 1919, Nancy Astor became the first woman seated in the British Parliament. She considered her success a feminist triumph. Always outspoken, she believed not just in women's equality but in women's superiority. "I married beneath me," she once said. "All women do." Her commitment was, however, really to the moral transforma-

tion she believed women could effect in government. "Women," she urged, "must be as brave about peace as the men were about war" (1922).

A pacifist, she also championed temperance, women's rights, and benefits for children. In her early years in Parliament she introduced drinking-age legislation (her first speech on February 24, 1920, was on temperance) and worked on behalf of equal women's suffrage (women over 30 had received the vote in Great Britain in 1918, but not until 1928 was the age for women reduced to 21, the same as men). She also advocated equal opportunities for women in the civil service and the continuation of a women's police force. In addition, she supported the development of nursery schools for London's poor children, a project organized by Scotswoman Margaret McMillan. In the 1930s she campaigned for strict child labor laws and with her husband endorsed an extensive program of educational reform.

In international affairs, though committed to the ideals of peace, she remained a realist. On a trip to the Soviet Union in 1931 she confronted Joseph Stalin directly: "When," she asked, "are you going to stop killing people?" When George Bernard Shaw, also on the trip but more impressed with Stalin, encouraged her to become a Fabian Socialist, she was skeptical: "I would be a socialist," she said, "if I thought it would work."

"Wild Woman of God"

The Astors and their friends—collectively labeled the "Cliveden set" after the name of the Astor estate—erroneously earned a reputation in the 1930s of being pro-Nazi. In fact, both of the Astors mistrusted Hitler. She refused an opportunity to meet the German chancellor, and her husband came away from his only encounter thinking Hitler deranged. He had met with him to discuss the treatment of Christian Scientists (both of the Astors belonged to the sect) in Germany, but the conversation had turned to the treatment of the Jews, at which point Hitler had launched into a mad tirade. Both of the Astors favored, however, a policy of economic "appeasement"—that is, they believed the strict economic sanctions imposed on Germany by the Treaty of Versailles at the end of World War I should be eased. By the late 1930s, however, both had come to oppose political appeasement; throughout the period, in any event, they had both voted in favor of increased defense appropriations. She summed up her position as follows: "I am neither a Communist or a Fascist . . . I loathe all Dictatorships whether of the Russian or the German type—They are all equally cruel."

In November 1939 her husband was elected Lord Mayor of Plymouth, a position he held throughout World War II. Both were active in civic affairs during the period, she especially working to boost public morale during the extensive German bombing of the city. She was often seen visiting air raid shelters and once herself sustained a near miss. Their house in Plymouth was damaged by the bombs. She also acted as an unofficial hostess to the thousands of American troops stationed in Plymouth prior to the Normandy invasion.

She decided—under pressure from her husband—to retire from office in 1945. She continued to travel and to speak publicly on occasion, but her political career was at an end. On May 2, 1964, Astor died, 12 years after her husband's death. They are both buried at Cliveden on the Thames.

Throughout her career Astor had sustained several close friendships. The most important of these was probably with Philip Kerr, like her a Christian Scientist and an active participant in English political life. Other friends included George Bernard Shaw, T.E. Lawrence, and Eleanor and Franklin Roosevelt (the former she referred to as "Madam President"). When she met the Indian leader Mahatma Gandhi, she said, "So this is the wild man of God." He replied, "I have been warned to beware of Lady Astor— perhaps she is a wild woman of God"—a statement that seems to sum up the character of this remarkable woman.

Further Reading

Nancy herself wrote two books: *My Two Countries* (1923) and *The Astor Story* (1951, the latter her memoir). Her son Michael's *Tribal Feeling* (1963) provides further information about the family. The numerous biographies include Maurice Collis, *Nancy Astor and Her Friends* (1974), which provides many direct statements made by Astor taken from unpublished as well as published sources, some of which have been included in this article.

Additional Sources

Grigg, John, *Nancy Astor, a lady unashamed,* Boston: Little, Brown, 1980.
Grigg, John, *Nancy Astor, portrait of a pioneer,* London: Sidgwick & Jackson, 1980.
Halperin, John, *Eminent Georgians: the lives of King George V, Elizabeth Bowen, St. John Philby, and Nancy Astor,* New York: St. Martin's Press, 1995.
Harrison, Rosina., *Rose: my life in service,* New York: Viking Press, 1975.
Masters, Anthony, *Nancy Astor, a biography,* New York: McGraw-Hill, 1981.
Sykes, Christopher, *Nancy: the life of Lady Astor,* Chicago, IL: Academy Chicago, 1984, 1972. □

Miguel Angel Asturias

Miguel Angel Asturias (1899-1974) was a Guatemalan novelist and the Nobel Prize winner for literature in 1967. His profound interest in the Indian culture and a prose style inspired by surrealism give his writings a special character.

Miguel Angel Asturias was born in Guatemala City on Oct. 19, 1899, a year after the rise to power of the Guatemalan dictator Manuel Estrada Cabrera. The figure of the dictator was to exert an important influence on his life. The dictatorship forced—for political reasons—the relocation of his family to the small town of Salamá, where Asturias came into close contact with the descendants of the Maya Indians. It thus made him keenly aware of political and social issues from an early age, and it provided him with a model for the dominant presence in his most celebrated novel, *Mr. President* (1946).

The Asturias family returned to Guatemala City in 1907, but Estrada Cabrera was not removed from office until 1920. By that time the author was a militant university student who could see only oppression stemming from the military regime that had replaced the dictatorship. His family therefore found it expedient to send him to London, from where he soon departed to settle in Paris in 1923.

Maya Works and "Mr. President"

Asturias studied at the Sorbonne with Georges Raynaud, a specialist in the culture of the Mayan Quichés, and eventually finished in 1926 a translation of the *Popol Vuh,* the sacred book of the Mayas. Caught up in the legends and myths of the Indians of Guatemala, he wrote *Legends of Guatemala* (1930), a series of eight narratives and an allegorical play. The subject matter and the poetic vision of the author attracted favorable critical attention, especially in France, where the French symbolist poet Paul Valéry praised the book.

In 1933 Asturias returned to Guatemala and encountered another stifling regime—that of Jorge Ubico—which he endured until 1944, publishing only poetry, which was characterized by elegant cynicism. In 1946, with a more liberal government ruling the country, Asturias finally published the novel about an unnamed dictator in an unspecified Central American country that he had been working on as far back as 1922. It was *Mr. President,* in which the dictator is repeatedly likened to an idol of the type worshiped by the Mayas. A strikingly original novel, *Mr. President* treats a very real Spanish-American problem in a suggestive, poetic, but at the same time grotesque fashion.

From 1946 to 1954 Asturias served as ambassador to Mexico, Argentina, and El Salvador, continuing to publish throughout this time. Asturias's *Men of Corn* (1949), a novellike work of six parts, deals both realistically and imaginatively with the crisis that traditional Indian culture experiences when it is faced with modern, "progressive" technology. Here one can see the strong influence of the *Popol Vuh,* extending even to the title. (According to Maya legend, man was created from sacred corn.)

Asturias next published the three novels that make up his "Banana Cycle." Less imaginative, less artistic than his previous work, they constitute an exposé of the exploitation of the Guatemalan fruit industry by American firms. *Strong Wind* (1949), *The Green Pope* (1954), and *The Eyes of the Interred* (1960) are sincere works that are marred by an excessively aggressive tone of protest. This shortcoming is also evident in *Weekend in Guatemala* (1957), a group of stories written in anger over an invasion of Guatemala by the exiled leader Carlos Castillo Armas with, Asturias contended, the support of the U.S. government.

Works in Exile

In 1954 Asturias lost his Guatemalan citizenship and went to live in Buenos Aires, where he spent the next 8 years. When a change of government in Argentina made it advisable that he once more seek a new home, Asturias moved to Europe. He was living in Genoa when his novel *Mulata* (1963) appeared. Here again Asturias deals with Indian myths, spinning a rich and exotic narrative fabric into which he weaves ancient patterns. The moon, the sun, and the devil are all drawn into a story about an Indian peasant who sells his wife to the god of corn for wealth and a sensual concubine called Mulata. The author's poetic prose flows more freely here than in his other fiction, but at the same time it is a difficult, intensely personal book, extracted from his very private world of images.

In 1966, the same year he won the Lenin Peace Prize, Asturias was named the Guatemalan ambassador to France by the new government of President Julio Méndez Montenegro. He held the post until 1970. In 1967 Asturias won the Nobel Prize for literature. He died on June 9, 1974, while on a visit to Madrid, Spain.

Further Reading

An incisive interview with Asturias and an evaluation of his work may be found in Luis Harss and Barbara Dohmann, *Into the Mainstream: Conversations with Latin-American Writers* (1967). Asturias and his work are also discussed in Enrique Anderson-Imbert, *Spanish-American Literature: A History* (1954; trans. 1963; 2d ed., 2 vols., 1969), and Jean Franco, *The Modern Culture of Latin America: Society and the Artist* (1967).

Asturias, Miguel Angel, translated by Gerald Martin, *Men of Maize,* critical edition (University of Pittsburgh Press, 1994).

☐

Atahualpa

Atahualpa (ca. 1502-1533) was the Inca emperor of Peru whose capture and execution by Francisco Pizarro enabled the conquistadores to secure the Inca lands for the Spanish crown.

Atahualpa, whose name means "virile-sweet," was a son of the emperor Huayna Capac, last of the family of Incas to rule an undivided empire which extended from present-day southern Colombia through Ecuador, Peru, and Bolivia into northwestern Argentina and northern Chile. At Huayna Capac's death (ca. 1528) in Quito, this vast territory was divided between two of his sons: Huáscar, who won the imperial throne in the capital city of Cuzco to the south, and his half-brother Atahualpa, who gained the northern portion of the kingdom, with its center in the city of Quito.

The division led to civil war between the half-brothers, reaching a peak in 1532 with the defeat and imprisonment of Huáscar. At this point the Spaniards entered Peru. Francisco Pizarro and about 180 men reached Atahualpa's base at Cajamarca in November 1532. The confrontation between the Spanish conquistador and the Inca, who had thousands of troops camped nearby, took place in the main square of the town. The Inca rejected the call of Pizarro's emissary, the priest Valverde, to swear obedience to the king of Spain and to acknowledge Christianity as the true religion, and he threw to the ground the breviary that was proffered. Pizarro then ordered his strategically placed troops to attack the soldiers with Atahualpa; the Peruvians were routed and the Inca seized by the Spaniards.

The capture of the head of the monolithic Peruvian state was the key to the subsequent Spanish conquest of the Inca empire. Atahualpa offered to purchase his freedom by filling the large cell in which he was imprisoned with objects of gold. The Spaniards took the treasure and declared that Atahualpa had fulfilled his agreement. But they refused to release him from their "protective custody," since Pizarro feared for the safety of his vastly outnumbered and isolated troops.

Spanish accusations that Atahualpa was plotting against them and that, as was apparently the fact, he had successfully ordered, from prison, the assassination of Huáscar, gave Pizarro the excuse for placing Atahualpa on trial. The sentence that he be burned to death was changed to execution by strangulation when the Inca agreed to accept Christianity and be baptized. Atahualpa was garroted by the Spaniards on Aug. 29, 1533, leaving the leaderless empire open to complete subjugation by the European invaders.

Further Reading

The classic work by William H. Prescott, *History of the Conquest of Peru* (2 vols., 1847; many later editions), remains the best account of the conquest and the fate of Atahualpa. Philip Ainsworth Means, *Fall of the Inca Empire and the Spanish Rule in Peru: 1530-1780* (1932), relates the same events, also in a vivid prose style. J. Alden Mason, *The Ancient Civilizations of Peru* (1957; rev. ed. 1969), and Burr C. Brundage, *Empire of the Inca* (1963), describe the pre-Columbian period in Peru from an anthropological viewpoint and include brief accounts of the Spanish seizure of power. All of these works draw heavily from one of the great early Spanish narratives about the Inca empire and its conquest by the Spaniards, Garcilaso de la Vega's *Royal Commentaries of the Incas* (1609-1617; many later editions and translations).

Additional Sources

Norman, Ruth, *The last Inca, Atahualpa: an eyewitness account of the conquest of Peru in 1535,* El Cajon, CA: Unarius Academy of Science Publications, 1993. □

Ghazi Mustapha Kemal Atatürk

Ghazi Mustapha Kemal Atatürk (1881-1938) was a Turkish nationalist and political leader who was instrumental in the fall of the Ottoman sultanate and in the creation of modern Turkey.

Mustapha Kemal devoted his life to freeing Turkey from foreign domination. Under his benevolent dictatorship as president of the republic, he instituted lasting reforms that earned him the name Atatürk (the father of the Turks).

Mustapha was born in Salonika (now Greece, but then part of Turkish Macedonia), the son of a lower-middle-class Turkish customs official. He received a military education, and a teacher dubbed him Kemal (perfection) because of the youth's demand for quality performance. Kemal graduated from the military academy in Monastir in 1899 and then attended the war and staff colleges in Istanbul.

Military Career

In 1905, on the day Kemal was commissioned a lieutenant at the General Staff Academy in Istanbul, he was arrested for political agitation. Banishment to Syria failed to dampen his revolutionary ardor. He organized some officers of the 5th Army Corps in Damascus into a secret society, Vatan (fatherland). Kemal established branches during a secret visit to Salonika, where the organization became Fatherland and Liberty, then the Ottoman Society of Liberty, and subsequently part of the Committee of Union and Progress. Despite this political activity and narrow escape from a second arrest, Kemal was not active in the 1908 coup or in the Young Turk movement which toppled Abdul Hamid.

In 1911 Kemal secretly went to Libya to organize Senussi resistance against the invading Italians. A major in the Second Balkan War, he served as chief of staff to the army on Gallipoli. When World War I broke out, Col. Mustapha Kemal was serving in Bulgaria as the Ottoman military attaché. During the war he commanded armies on every one of the several Ottoman fronts. He gained national recognition during the defense of Gallipoli. Promoted to pasha and given command of the 2d Army Corps, he led his troops and 3d Army forces in the Caucasus campaigns of 1916 and then was sent to the Hejaz. Correctly predicting the reverses to be expected in the Iraq campaign, he resigned but returned to service in 1918. Kemal was in command of the 7th Army withstanding the assault on Aleppo at war's end.

Reunification of Turkey

Peace was restored by the Mudros armistice of Oct. 30, 1918. The following May, 4 days after the Greeks landed troops in Turkey, Kemal was appointed inspector general of the 3d Army in Anatolia. From here he launched an antiforeign movement that was to unify the Turkish elements in the empire against partition. At two conferences, at Erzerum on July 23 and at Sivas on September 11, he organized the Committee for the Defense of Eastern Asia Minor.

The Ferid Pasha government fell under this pressure, and new elections returned a Nationalist parliament. Its program, however, was sufficiently independent to prompt British occupation of the capital ostensibly to protect the Sultan. On March 20, 1920, the Ottoman parliament was dissolved. Some deputies fled to Ankara, where Kemal's committee convoked the first session of a new Grand National Assembly on April 23. It undertook both legislative and executive functions, with Kemal as president. Two governments were now functioning: the Sultan's in occupied Istanbul and Kemal's in Anatolia. This anomalous condition continued until the Allies forced the Sultan's assent to the Treaty of Sèvres on August 10, which established foreign control over large parts of the Turkish Empire. Thereupon the last vestige of the Sultan's power disappeared in Anatolia.

Opposition to foreign occupation was the keystone of Turkish nationalism, but dissension among the Allies was to be of major benefit to the Kemalists. Kemal's first success was peace with Russia in December. This border settlement was followed by a friendship treaty in March 1921. The Italians and the French, apparently anticipating an eventual Nationalist victory, were enticed into exchanging territorial claims for economic concessions. The result was that by mid-1921 only the Greeks and British occupied Turkish territory.

Greek troops moved through Anatolia in 1921 with considerable success to enforce the rule of the Sultan. As generalissimo of Turkish forces, Kemal had unlimited power during this campaign, and he was supplied by Russia, Italy, and France. The Greeks were stopped at Sakarya in September 1921 and driven out in a big campaign the following year. The Nationalists made Kemal a marshal and designated him Ghazi (victorious). The British concluded an armistice with the Turks at Mundanya on Oct. 11, 1922.

An international gathering at Lausanne in November 1920 set about revising the Treaty of Sèvres. The concurrent invitations issued the Nationalists and the Sultan's government precipitated the Grand National Assembly's dissolution of the sultanate of Mehmed VI on Nov. 1, 1922. On Oct. 29, 1923, Mustapha Kemal was elected president of the newly proclaimed Turkish Republic.

The interim period had been filled with the difficult task of negotiating the new treaty. The final document, signed July 24, 1923, established the compact, homogeneous entity known today as Turkey, freed of the onerous capitulations the Allies had expected to reimpose.

Turkish Republic

It had been Kemal's image as a national military hero which had assured the Nationalists a following in 1919. It was Kemal's determined leadership which assured the victory of 1923. It was to be Kemal's dictatorial guidance which subsequently defined the new Turkey.

Throughout the 1920s reform followed reform as the Turks undertook a shift from an Eastern to a Western orientation. President Kemal and his colleagues were Western-educated; the constitution of April 20, 1924, established in the republic a democratic state with elected representatives and all the typical popular guarantees. Yet Turkey remained a dictatorship throughout Kemal's time; he was a paternalistic ruler, convinced that he knew the nation's needs and how to satisfy them. Although democratic institutions were in existence, it was not the legislature which dominated but the Peoples' (in 1923 Republican Peoples') party, an outgrowth of the 1919 national group founded at Erzerum-Sivas. Kemal was party president. Policy was made in party caucus and then enacted as legislation by the Assembly. The party also selected and placed candidates, and there was no opposition slate. Kemal was reelected president of Turkey in 1927, 1931, and 1935 by the Assembly.

Kemal's Reforms

The haphazard reforms of the late 1920s were systematized by President Kemal in 1931 under six topics termed collectively "Kemalism": (1) republicanism, marked by the ending of the sultanate, the new republican constitution, and adoption of Western law codes in 1926; (2) secularism, eliminating the all-pervasive aspects of Islam from daily life, including polygamy, the Moslem calendar, and dervish religious orders; (3) populism, ending special privileges characterized formerly by religious exemptions, minority distinctions, and capitulations; the ancient Turkish peasant's democratic past was rediscovered and reemphasized, education fostered, the language purified, and the script romanized; (4) nationalism, concentrating on building Turkish pride through rewritten patriotic histories, emphasis on vernacular studies, and adoption of family names; (5) statism, introducing a form of state enterprise freed from outside manipulation and the foreign concessions of the past; it provided for the development of tariff-protected industries and increased government concern over agricultural output; (6) reformism, the continual revitalization of the movement to avoid its leadership's turning conservative and stagnating.

These Kemalist principles became the party platform in the 1935 elections and were added to the constitution in 1937. Kemal was an active president. Noted for his oratorical skill while in military school, he now utilized this asset to considerable advantage, moving readily about the country, eagerly explaining new laws. In one famous speech the President spoke over a period of 6 days.

Kemalist Turkey's foreign relations involved territorial settlements on Mosul and Alexandretta, an active role in the League of Nations after admission in 1932, and neighborly alliances in the Balkan Entente (1934) and the Saadabad Pact (1937). The most notable achievement was the Montreux Convention of 1936, by which Turkey regained control of the Straits.

Despite his posts as chief of state and party leader, Kemal was not a glory-grabber. He abhorred shallow ceremony and scorned pomp. In public life he was an incorruptible dynamo, but his riotous private life confounded many. Cirrhosis killed Atatürk on Nov. 10, 1938, his death accelerated by wild living and too much drinking.

Further Reading

Harold Armstrong, *Grey Wolf* (1932; published as *Gray Wolf: The Life of Kemal Ataturk*, 1961), and Lord Kinross, *Ataturk* (1965), are the two major works on Kemal's life. A good, thorough coverage of the period is in Donald Everett Webster, *The Turkey of Atatürk: Social Process in the Turkish Reformation* (1939). □

David Rice Atchison

David Rice Atchison (1807-1886), American lawyer and politician, was a leading Democratic senator during the 1850s. He advocated many unpopular causes, and his career reflected the rough and tumble of frontier politics.

David Atchison was born in Frogtown, near Lexington, Ky., on Aug. 11, 1807. After graduating from Transylvania College in 1825, he studied law and was admitted to the Kentucky bar in 1829. In 1830 he was admitted to the Missouri bar and established a successful law practice in the western part of the state. Between 1833 and 1838 Atchison rose from the rank of captain to major general in the Missouri militia.

During 1833 and 1834 Atchison acted as legal defense for the persecuted Mormons in Missouri and with their support was elected as a Democrat to the state legislature. Although he opposed anti-Mormon Democratic policies, his vigorous support of Andrew Jackson and his opposition to the Bank of the United States made him a leader of the state Democratic party. During the Mormon War of 1838 Atchison did much to mitigate the attacks on this religious group. He was defeated for reelection to the state legislature in 1836, won back his seat in 1838, but was defeated again in 1840.

Atchison served as judge for the Twelfth Judicial Circuit from 1841 to 1843. During this period he stood between two factions of the Missouri Democratic party, which had split over questions of representation and monetary policies. Thus when Missouri's senator died in office in 1843, Atchison was appointed to fill the vacancy and was elected for a full term in 1849.

In the Senate, Atchison served as chairman of the Committee on Indian Affairs, sponsored land grants for Missouri railroads, and served as president pro tem of the Senate some 16 times. He also supported bills to promote immigration into Oregon and advanced extensive American claims for the Oregon territory. In advocating the annexation of Texas he broke with Missouri's senior senator, the powerful Thomas Hart Benton, whose rival he became. During the debates on the Oregon and Texas questions, Atchison gradually allied himself with the Southern faction of the Democratic party; by 1850 he was an active supporter of John C. Calhoun and leader of the proslavery Democrats of Missouri, and that year he contributed importantly to Benton's defeat for reelection. Atchison supported the Southern position on the organization of the Nebraska territory and the repeal of the Missouri Compromise. Failing of reelection in 1854, he left the Senate.

After the Kansas-Nebraska Act was passed, Atchison became one of the leaders of the movement aimed at preventing Kansas from becoming a free state. He encouraged slaveholders to settle in Kansas, crossed into Kansas with large groups to vote in the state elections, and led raids by "Border Ruffians" during the Kansas civil war.

When the Civil War began, Atchison worked to bring about the secession of Missouri; he later organized a Missouri unit for Confederate military service. His lack of success caused him to leave Missouri for Texas. There he lived until 1867, when he returned to Missouri and settled permanently as a farmer, in political retirement. He died on Jan. 6, 1886.

Further Reading

The only biography of Atchison is William E. Parrish, *David Rice Atchison of Missouri, Border Politician* (1961), a judicious but highly sympathetic study of a man almost invariably maligned by scholars. Atchison's role in passing the Kansas-Nebraska Act and his senatorial race against Benton are studied in P. Orman Ray, *The Repeal of the Missouri Compromise: Its Origin and Authorship* (1909). There is a discussion of the Kansas-Nebraska Act in Allan Nevins, *Ordeal of the Union*, vol. 2: *A House Dividing, 1852-1857* (1947). □

St. Athanasius

The Christian theologian St. Athanasius (ca. 296-373) was bishop of Alexandria, in Egypt. He was the most eminent Church leader opposing Arianism on the basis of the creed adopted by the Council of Nicaea in 325.

Athanasius was probably born at Alexandria. By his early 20s he was both a deacon in the Church and secretary to Alexander, Bishop of Alexandria. In 325 he accompanied Alexander to the Council of Nicaea, a meeting of Christian bishops that has become renowned as the first ecumenical council of the Church. The council was summoned by Emperor Constantine to deal with a controversy that had first arisen between Bishop Alexander and Arius, a presbyter at Alexandria. By 325 the dispute had broadened so as to appear to pose a threat to the unity of the Church in the eastern part of the Roman Empire. The controversy concerned the compatibility of belief in the oneness and transcendence of God with belief in the full deity of Jesus Christ. Arius, influenced by certain strands of Neoplatonic philosophical thought, taught that the Son of God, incarnate in Jesus Christ, could not possibly be "God" in the full and proper sense but was rather the most exalted of all God's creatures.

At the council Athanasius, though not a bishop, appears to have distinguished himself as a disputant against the Arian position. Under pressure from the Emperor to adopt a creedal formula in the interest of peace and unity, the majority of bishops ratified a statement, the Creed of Nicaea, whose crucial anti-Arian clause asserts that the Son of God is "of one essence" with God the Father. Arius and

two bishops who would not sign the creed were sent into exile.

In 328 Athanasius succeeded Alexander as bishop of Alexandria. It soon became clear that the Council of Nicaea had only served to suppress temporarily the open expression of Arian views, and that the Emperor, susceptible to pressure from bishops close to his ear, was more interested in avoiding political problems than in supporting orthodox theological doctrine. By 330 there had occurred the first scene in a long drama of alliance between emperors and Arian leaders that was to prove so vexing for Athanasius. Constantine wrote to Athanasius, directing that he restore Arius to communion in the Church at Alexandria. Athanasius refused, and his ecclesiastical opponents then made common cause with the Melitians, a dissident Christian sect in Egypt. At a council of bishops at the city of Tyre in 335, they charged Athanasius, not completely without basis, with acts of violence committed against the Melitians and voted that he be deposed from his see. Constantine soon thereafter banished him to the German city of Trier.

Thus occurred the first of Athanasius' five exiles from Alexandria, which account for 17 of 30 years of his life from 336. It is testimony both to his determination and to his popularity in Egypt that after more than 4 decades of opposition to Arianism he lived his last 7 years as bishop of Alexandria under the vigorously Arian emperor Valens; the Emperor feared the populace would revolt if he were to take further measures against their bishop.

Athanasius' positive significance as a churchman and as an author may be suggested by three points. First, a governing theme in his anti-Arian writings is the conviction that God alone and no lesser being is the agent of man's salvation. This means that the Christian's union with Christ the Saviour is union with God, who alone can bestow immortal life. It means, too, that the traditional Christian belief in the Holy Spirit is belief in one who also is unequivocally God because he performs the activity of God in bringing man's salvation to completion. Second, Athanasius played a role as conciliatory orthodox leader. He was able to see that a large body of conservative Eastern bishops, who were uncomfortable over the Nicene formula and who preferred to say that the Son was "of like essence" to the Father, were not in fact Arians. He did important preparatory work toward a reconciliation and coalition, which he did not live to see. Third, he was a warmly enthusiastic supporter of the Christian monastic movement emanating from Egypt and wrote a widely read biography of the monastic organizer St. Anthony. Athanasius died in Alexandria in 373.

Further Reading

The best study of St. Athanasius is in French. In English see F. L. Cross, *The Study of St. Athanasius* (1945). G. L. Prestige, *Fathers and Heretics: Six Studies in Dogmatic Faith* (1940), includes a section on Athanasius. Background information is in Philip Hughes, *A History of the Church,* vol. 1: *The Church and the World in Which the Church Was Founded* (1934; rev. ed. 1949); George L. Prestige, *God in Patristic Thought* (1936; 2d ed. 1952); and H. A. Wolfson, *The Philosophy of the Church Fathers,* vol. 1: *Faith, Trinity, Incarnation* (1956; 2d ed. 1965).

Additional Sources

Barnes, Timothy David, *Athanasius and Constantius: theology and politics in the Constantinian empire,* Cambridge, Mass.: Harvard University Press, 1993.

Coray, Henry W., *Against the world: the odyssey of Athanasius,* Neerlandia, Alta., Canada; Caledonia, Mich.: Inheritance Publications, 1992. □

Farid ed-Din Attar

Farid ed-Din Attar (ca. 1140-ca. 1234) was a Persian poet and Sufi mystic. Living during a turbulent era of political uncertainty, he turned inward, exploring the realm of God and paths to Him through mystical poetry.

Little about Attar is known with certainty. His name (literally, perfume of roses) indicates that, like his father, he was a druggist and followed the calling of a medical man. Supposedly reliable Persian sources vary in the year of his death by a span of 43 years. One reason for this obscurity is that, unlike other Islamic poets, he did not write flattering panegyrics about his own life and greatness. This is to his personal credit but unfortunate for the historian. We are certain only of the fact that he was born in Nishapur in northeastern Persia; he passed 13 years of his youth in Mashad and spent much of his life collecting the poetry of other Sufi mystics.

Attar wrote over 114 books on Sufism. According to his own writings, Sufism was meant to be a spiritual search for a union with God. This search throughout history has taken many forms, but for Attar it was quite specific. Parallels may be seen with Dante. According to Attar, the spiritual pilgrimage of man brings him through seven successive "valleys." First is the valley of quest, where ascetic means are adopted; then follows the valley of love, which may be compared to Dante's earthly paradise; then follow the valleys of knowledge, detachment, unity, and amazement; and finally the valley of annihilation of the self is reached. This is the supreme state of divine union with God. Sufism was meant to be an all encompassing effort to live in a meaningful religious frame of mind.

The two best-known works of Attar are *Tadhkirat al-Awliya* (*Memoirs of Saints*), a prose work, and *Mantik al-Tayr* (*Conference of the Birds*). In *Conference* all the birds in the world are seeking God, who is called Simurgh. After a long search all but 30 birds perish. When they arrive at their destination, they realize that Simurgh (in Persian the word means 30 birds) is really themselves.

Attar died fleeing the Mongol hordes under Genghis Khan. Just before his death, Attar met a young poet, Rumi, to whom he gave some of his philosophical poems. Rumi perpetuated and added to the philosophical development of Sufism and the understanding of Attar.

Further Reading

Two of Attar's works have been translated into English. S. C. Nott translated *Conference of the Birds* (1954); and Bankey Behari (1961) and A. J. Arberry (1966) published abridged translations of *Memoirs of Saints,* both with excellent introductions. The best works about Attar are Eduard G. Browne, *A Literary History of Persia,* vol. 2 (1906), and Margaret Smith, ed., *The Persian Mystics: Attar* (1932). Attar is represented in A. J. Arberry, *Aspects of Islamic Civilization as Depicted in the Original Texts* (1964), and James Kritzeck, ed., *Anthology of Islamic Literature: From the Rise of Islam to Modern Times* (1966). For a discussion of the Sufism of Attar see A. J. Arberry, *Sufism: An Account of the Mystics of Islam* (1950), and Idries Shah, *The Sufis* (1964). □

Attila

Attila (died 453) was a chieftain who brought the Huns to their greatest strength and who posed a grave threat to the Roman Empire.

The Huns first appear in European records at the end of the 4th century A.D., when they descended from the Steppes and attacked the Germanic tribes on the northeastern edge of the Roman Empire, either subjecting them or driving them into the empire. By the 430s the scattered nomadic bands had been united into a powerful force which attacked both Germans and Romans alike.

Rua, the man responsible for much of this unity, died in 434 and left the kingdom to his nephews Attila and Bleda. For 10 years they ruled jointly and threatened the Eastern Roman Empire on several occasions. In 435 a "peace" was signed with the Romans, which among other things guaranteed the Huns an annual payment of 700 pounds of gold. In 441 the Huns attacked the provinces across the Danube. In 443 Attila so severely defeated the Roman general Aspar that the Romans had to purchase peace with an annual tribute of 6000 pounds of gold.

In 445 Attila murdered Bleda and united all the Huns under his own leadership. The Roman Priscus, an eyewitness who was an ambassador to Attila's court, describes him as short with a broad chest, flat nose, and beard sprinkled with gray. Attila ruled with absolute authority, his power based in large part on the extensive wealth from his conquests.

War with the Eastern Empire was renewed in 447, and the Romans were defeated in the bloody battle of Marcianopolis. In the peace treaty of 448 they were forced to cede extensive territory along the Danube. Attila then turned his attention to the Western Empire. Geiseric the Vandal urged Attila to attack the Goths so as to remove their pressure on the Vandals, and Attila moved to attack the Visigoths. At the same time the sister of the emperor Valentinian III, Honoria, asked Attila to rescue her from an unwelcome marriage. This gave Attila the excuse to move against Rome. Aëtius, the strongman of the Western Empire and one-time hostage of the Huns, created an alliance of Romans and Visigoths, and when the Huns invaded Gaul in 451, he defeated them on the Catalaunian Plains in Champagne.

Although defeated, the Huns escaped destruction and the next year attacked Italy. The important city of Aquileia was destroyed, but Attila did not attack Rome. An embassy from Pope Leo I was credited with dissuading him, but the growing fear of plague and famine probably determined the decision. In 453, while planning another attack on the Eastern Empire, Attila died suddenly from a hemorrhage, reportedly the result of excessive drinking at a wedding. After his death his sons divided his "empire," and the power of the Huns was soon destroyed by internal strife. Attila proved to be a major threat to Rome in his lifetime but left no permanent power to challenge the empire.

Further Reading

The major ancient source on Attila is Priscus, who visited Attila. Fragments of his work are translated in Colin D. Gordon, *The Age of Attila* (1960). A full account of Attila and the Huns is given by the 6th-century priest and historian Jordanes, *The Origin and Deeds of the Goths,* translated and edited by Charles C. Mierow (1908; rev. ed. published as *The Gothic History of Jordanes,* 1915). The best modern account is E. A. Thompson, *A History of Attila and the Huns* (1948). □

Clement Richard Attlee

Clement Richard Attlee, 1st Earl Attlee (1883-1967), was prime minister of England from 1945 to 1951. He led the labour government that established the welfare state in Great Britain.

Clement Attlee was born in Putney, near London, on Jan. 23, 1883, the son of Henry Attlee, a successful solicitor, and Ellen Watson Attlee, a cultivated and educated woman. The family was devoutly religious. Attlee attended Haileybury College and then University College, Oxford, where he read modern history and achieved second-class honors in 1904.

Heading for a legal career, Attlee joined the Inner Temple, studied and worked in chambers, was called to the bar in 1906, and set up his own office. After a visit to Haileybury House in east London, a boys' club supported by his old school, he moved to the East End. He continued practicing law, helped evenings in the club, and soon became its manager. He developed a new outlook and a new purpose. By 1908 he was a member of the Fabian Society (a socialist organization) and of the Independent Labour party, and he was a socialist in the practical sense of being committed to improving the lot of the working class.

In 1909 Attlee gave up his law practice and spent a brief period as secretary of Toynbee Hall, the best-known of the university settlements in the East End. Then he lectured at Ruskin College, Oxford, and was appointed tutor and lecturer in social science at the London School of Economics in 1913.

In 1914 he had leanings toward pacifism but concluded that the war was justified. Promptly commissioned, he served in Gallipoli and in Mesopotamia. He was discharged as a major, a title he continued to use, and returned to the London School of Economics. Still residing in the East End, he became the first labour mayor of Stepney in 1919 and a member of the executive committee of the London Labour party. In 1922 he was returned to Parliament from Limehouse, and that year he married Violet Helen Millar of Hampstead; four children were born to them.

Attlee now devoted full time to Labour politics. Ramsay MacDonald, as leader of the Opposition, appointed Attlee his parliamentary private secretary and then in 1924 in the first Labour government designated him undersecretary of state for war. Though at first excluded from the Labour Cabinet in 1929, Attlee became chancellor of the duchy of Lancaster in 1930 and a year later postmaster general. In the landslide victory for the National (coalition) government in 1931, Attlee, one of three surviving Labour members with front-bench experience, was made deputy leader of the party. Labour members of Parliament became almost hopelessly divided on armaments and diplomacy; in a tumultuous meeting in October 1935 Attlee was elected party leader, because of his demonstrated parliamentary qualities. It cannot be said that either Attlee or his party had imaginative views for dealing with Nazi Germany or Fascist Italy, but on the other hand the National government made no moves toward developing common policy. Attlee did reunite his party.

When war came and Winston Churchill formed a true coalition government in May 1940, Attlee joined the War Cabinet of five and in 1942 became deputy prime minister. He attended the San Francisco conference in April 1945, which established the United Nations. At Potsdam, the final wartime conference of the allies, in July 1945, power shifted from Churchill to Attlee after the overwhelming electoral victory of Labour at the polls. Attlee formed a strong government, and in nationalization of basic industries, the extension of social insurance, and the establishment of the National Health Service, he carried out most of his party's pledges. Under his guidance India and Pakistan became independent and England entered the North Atlantic Treaty Organization. Labour was less successful in dealing with economic problems; leadership shifted in 1951 to the Conservatives. Within the party Attlee managed to hold on, despite attacks from the left wing, until 1955, when he suffered a stroke and resigned after 20 years of leadership.

Attlee received the Order of Merit in 1951. In 1955 he was made a knight of the Garter and granted an earldom. For several years he was active in the House of Lords and devoted considerable time to writing and lecturing. He died on Oct. 8, 1967.

Further Reading

Roy Jenkins, *Mr. Attlee: An Interim Biography* (1948), is useful on Attlee's early years but continues only to 1945. Another early biography is Cyril Clemens, *The Man from Limehouse: Clement Richard Attlee* (1946). Attlee tells his own story to 1953 in *As it Happened* (1954). Francis Williams records conversations with Lord Attlee concerning the war and postwar periods in *A Prime Minister Remembers* (1961). Background studies which discuss Attlee include R. T. McKenzie, *British Political Parties* (1955; 2d ed. 1963); Henry Pelling, *A Short History of the Labour Party* (1961; 2d ed. 1965); D. N. Pritt, *The Labour Government,* 1945-51 (1963); Francis Boyd, *British Politics in Transition,* 1945-63 (1964); and Carl F. Brand, *The British Labour Party: A Short History* (1964). □

Margaret Eleanor Atwood

One of Canada's most distinguished person of letters, Margaret Eleanor Atwood (born 1939) was an internationally famous novelist, poet, critic, and politically committed cultural activist.

M argaret Eleanor Atwood was born in Ottawa, Ontario, in 1939, moving to Sault Ste. Marie in 1945 and to Toronto in 1946. Until she was 11, she spent half of each year in the northern Ontario wilderness, where her father worked as an entomologist. She studied at Victoria College, University of Toronto, where she received a B.A. in 1961, and at Radcliffe College, Cambridge, Mass. (M.A. 1962). Atwood also studied at Harvard University, Cambridge, Mass., from 1962-63 and 1965-67.

In addition to her academic accomplishments, Atwood received many honorary degrees, including: D. Litt., Trent University, 1973; LL.D., Queen's University, 1974; D. Litt., Concordia, 1980; Smith College, Northampton, Mass., 1982; University of Toronto, 1983; University of Waterloo, 1985; University of Guelph, 1985; Mount Holyoke College, 1985; Victoria College, 1987; Université de Montréal, 1991; University of Leeds, 1994; and McMaster University, 1996.

She has received more than 55 awards, including two Governor General's Awards, the first in 1966 for *The Circle Game,* her first major book of poems; the second for her 1985 novel, *The Handmaid's Tale,* which was also shortlisted for Britain's Booker Prize and made into a fairly successful wide circulation movie. Her recognition was often reflective of the diversity of her work. Among awards, honors, and prizes was a Guggenheim fellowship, the Los Angeles Times Fiction Award, 1986; Ms. Magazine's Woman of the Year, 1986; Canadian Booksellers Association Author of the Year, 1989; Government of France's Chevalier dans l'Ordre des Arts et des Lettres, 1994; the Sunday Times Award for Literary Excellence, (London, U.K.), 1994; the Humanist of the Year Award, 1987; shortlisted for the Ritz Hemingway Prize (Paris), 1987; and Arthur C. Clarke Award for best Science Fiction, 1987.

Atwood clearly—quite early—enjoyed a career of remarkable distinction and success, not only as the highly prolific author of volumes of poetry, ten novels, two books

of literary criticism, four collections of short stories, and three children's books and editor of two anthologies, as well as author of much uncollected journalism, but also as a major public figure, cultural commentator, and proponent of activist views in areas ranging from Canadian nationalism, through feminism, to such international causes as Amnesty International and PEN.

Most of her fiction has been translated into several foreign languages; a new Atwood novel becomes a Canadian, American, and international best-seller immediately (only Robertson Davies, among Canadian writers, has a comparable international public). There is a Margaret Atwood Society, a Margaret Atwood Newsletter, and an ever-increasing number of scholars studying and teachers teaching her work in women's studies courses as well as North American literature courses world wide.

Atwood is not only an acclaimed writer, serious as well as popular, in several genres, but outspoken, sardonically memorable, and distinctly quotable on moral and political private and public issues and a stalwart spokesperson for Canadian literature. Her popular and influential contribution to the never-ending quest for the Canadian identity, *Survival: A Thematic Guide to Canadian Literature* (1972), is, among other things, a manifesto for her *own* work; what began as a polemical political comment on Canadian cultural history is now a part of that very history.

She alternated prose and poetry throughout her career, often publishing a book of each in the same or consecutive years. While in a general sense the poems represent "private" myth and "personal" expression and the novels a more public and "social" expression, there is, as these dates suggest, continual interweaving and cross-connection between her prose and her poetry. The short story collections, *Dancing Girls* (1977), *Bluebeard's Egg* (1983), and especially the short stories *cum* prose poems in the remarkable, overtly metafictional collection *Murder in the Dark* (1983), bridge the gap between her poetry and her prose.

Her first six volumes of verse—*The Circle Game* (1966), *The Animals in That Country* (1968), *The Journals of Susanna Moodie* (1970), *Procedures for Underground* (1970), *Power Politics* (1971), and *You Are Happy* (1974)—are represented in *Selected Poems* (1976); the three subsequent volumes—*Two-Headed Poems* (1978), *True Stories* (1981), and *Interlunar* (1984)—in *Selected Poems II* (1986).

She wrote in an exact, vivid, witty, and often sharply discomfiting style in both prose and poetry. Her writing is often grotesque and unsparing in its gaze at pain and unfairness:

> you fit into me
> like a hook into an eye
> fish hook
> open eye
> (*Power Politics*)

"Nature" in her poems is a haunted, explicitly Canadian wilderness in which, unnervingly, man is the major predator of and terror to the "animals of that country," including himself. Her poetry works with myths, public and private; metamorphosis; process-product dualities of entrapment, like Blake's "mind-forg'd manacles"; and the vertical movement from underground to surface exemplified by such mythic figures as Persephone and Orpheus.

The Canadian critic Northrop Frye and the little-known, much underrated Canadian poet Jay Macpherson, were key influences on her early books. *The Journals of Susanna Moodie* echo the national themes of *Survival*, the individual's struggle with wilderness ending in a sort of defeat: "I planted him in that country/Like a flag," says Moodie of her drowned son. In *Power Politics* the grimmer, more mordant phases of Atwood's sex-war feminism become evident in poems with the power of a less vulnerable, more life-affirming Sylvia Plath.

Atwood's novels are social satires as well as identity quests. Her typical heroine is a modern urban woman, often a writer or artist, always with some social-professional commitment, fighting for self and survival in a society where men are the all-too-friendly enemy but women are often complicit in their own entrapment. Critics of Atwood, largely feminist in approach, see *Surfacing* (1972) as a Jungian "search for the essential female self" and *The Edible Woman* (1969) and *Lady Oracle* (1976) as comedies of female re-integration, the latter also being notable for its hilarious and skillful parodies of the female Gothic. *Life Before Man* (1979), the least comic, is slower, more somber, built on internal thought events, unified by the poetic subtexts drawn from the documentary detail of its setting in the Royal Ontario Museum.

Bodily Harm (1981) is explicitly political and feminist. Its heroine experiences violence and mutilation—bodily harm—in the double setting of the hospital where she endures her mastectomy and the tropical island from whose political violence she discovers she cannot stay aloof. She is there, it turns out, to "bear witness" to the torture inscribed on the female body of a companion, to record this mutilation in her reporter's language, and to acknowledge her own involvement through a compassion that releases the "hope" caught in "Pandora's box."

The Handmaid's Tale, a feminist rewriting (published in 1985) of the dystopia of Orwell's *1984,* is, like all dystopias, not a novel of the future but a critique of the present day in which the seeds of a destructive, misogynistic puritan revival are already planted. It is Atwood's closest approach to science fiction.

Cat's Eye (1988) is a self-portrait of the (female) artist returning to the Toronto of her childhood to recover her own past and with it a resurgence of her creativity. Her flashback recollections alternate with her satiric observations of the contemporary cultural scene in a narrative pattern found in most of Atwood's novels.

More recent books include a children's book, *For the Birds* (1990), and two volumes of short fiction, *Wilderness Tips* (1991) and *Good Bones* (1992). In 1993 Atwood published *The Robber Bride,* which was co-winner of Ontario's Trillium Book Award and won the City of Toronto Award.

Strange Things: The Malevolent North in Canadian Literature, the printed version of the four Clarendon Lectures delivered at Oxford University (England) in 1991 was published around the world in 1995. *Princess Prunella and the Purple Peanut* and *The New Oxford Book of Canadian Short Stories* were released in 1995.

Morning in the Burned House (1995) was her first book of new poetry in a decade. *Alias Grace* was first published in hardcover in the fall of 1996 and in the summer of 1997 as a paperback. It is the story of an infamous, 19th-century Canadian woman convicted as an accessory in the murder of her employer and his mistress. The lead character spends most of the novel in limbo between prison and an insane asylum, with doctors and psychologists attempting to diagnose her.

Atwood's literary works have also been recognized in other forms of artistic endeavor. In 1981, she worked on a television drama, *Snowbird* (CBC), and had her children's book *Anna's Pet* (1980) adapted for stage (1986).

One of the largest Atwood collections can be seen at The Thomas Fisher Rare Book Library, located at the University of Toronto. Manuscripts, reviews, critical responses, correspondence, and copies of both domestic and foreign editions are on display, though some areas of the collection are restricted access, requiring special permission for viewing or copying.

Atwood is known as a very accessible writer. One of her projects, the official Margaret Atwood Web site, is edited by Atwood herself and updated frequently. The Internet resource is an extensive, comprehensive guide to the literary life of the author, while also revealing a peek into

Atwood's personality with the links to her favorite charities, such as the Artists Against Racism site, or jocular blurbs she posts when the whim hits. As well, the site provides dates of lectures and appearances, updates of current writing projects, and reviews she has written. The address is: http://www.web.net/owtoad/toc.htm

She is also a talented photographer and watercolorist. Her paintings are clearly illustrative of her prose and poetry and she did, on occasion, design her own book covers. Her collages and cover for *The Journals of Susanna Moodie* bring together the visual and verbal media.

Further Reading

All Atwood's novels and her collected poems are widely and internationally available, as is considerable criticism and scholarship. Two collections, Arnold and Cathy Davidson's *The Art of Margaret Atwood: Essays in Criticism* (1981) and Kathryn VanSpanckeren and Jan Garden Castro's *Margaret Atwood: Vision and Forms* (1988), along with Sherrill Grace's book *Violent Duality: A Study of Margaret Atwood* (1980), are good places to start exploring her, but Atwood is a very accessible writer who is perhaps best approached directly. See the official Margaret Atwood Web site, edited by Atwood herself, as well as BDD Online, at http://www.bbd.com and other web sites. □

Philippe Aubert de Gaspé

Philippe Aubert de Gaspé (1786-1871) was a French-Canadian author whose historical novel, "Les Anciens Canadiens," is one of the earliest landmarks in French-Canadian literature.

Philippe Aubert de Gaspé was born on his family's seigniory at Saint-Jean-Port-Joli, on the southern shore of the St. Lawrence. The family manor had been burned down by British troops during the Seven Years War and reconstructed on a more modest scale, and this incident is transferred to the novel.

Educated and called to the bar (1813) in Quebec, Aubert de Gaspé had a career in law and public administration until 1834. His disdain for petty calculation, either in money or in friendship, led to bankruptcy and imprisonment from 1838 to 1841. He spent the next 30 years living modestly on the family estate.

Aubert de Gaspé was preceded as an author by his son, Philippe Ignace François, who has serious claims to being the first French-Canadian novelist. *L'Influence d'un livre* (1837; The Influence of a Book), subsequently published as *Le Chercheur de trésors* (The Treasure Hunter), contains a chapter sometimes attributed to the father.

His Works

Aubert de Gaspé's first signed publication, which appeared in 1862, was an extract from his novel, which was published the following year. *Les Anciens Canadiens* (The Canadians of Old) is the kind of novel in which fictitious major characters live in a world of historical minor characters. Ostensibly used by the author as a vehicle for his descriptions of traditional Canadian life, the novel and its copious notes, together with his *Mémoires* (1866), constitute a personal record of a way of life which had disappeared. The posthumously published *Divers* (1893) adds some less well known memoirs. These descriptions range from popular storytelling to the dinner conversation of the rural aristocracy, though conspicuously omitting the professional life that the author had known all too well.

Endless notes and explanations show that Aubert de Gaspé—then 75—was combining personal memories of his own time with stories handed down from his grandparents. But the novel maintains the artistic illusion of giving firsthand impressions of the period of the Conquest, then a century old. The interest of the central narrative lies in its symbolic patterns, which amount to an acceptance of British rule and a desire for reconciliation, provided that the honor and values of the French Canadians be respected, particularly among the nobility. Aubert de Gaspé's vision of a gentlemen's bond in Canada had a wide appeal, which has proved durable. Although the seigniorial system had been abolished in 1854, the author himself continued to receive the deference of his *habitants* until his death at the age of 85.

Further Reading

A biographical study of Aubert de Gaspé by James M. Tassie is in Robert L. McDougall, ed., *Our Living Tradition* (1959). □

Wystan Hugh Auden

The English-born American poet W. H. Auden (1907-1973) was one of the preeminent poets of the twentieth century. His works center on moral issues and evidence strong political, social, and psychological orientations.

In the 1930s W. H. Auden became famous when he was described by literary journalists as the leader of the so-called "Oxford Group," a circle of young English poets influenced by literary Modernism, in particular by the aesthetic principles espoused by T. S. Eliot. Rejecting the traditional poetic forms favored by their Victorian predecessors, the Modernist poets favored concrete imagery and free verse. In his work, Auden applied conceptual and scientific knowledge to traditional verse forms and metrical patterns while assimilating the industrial countryside of his youth.

Wystan Hugh Auden was born on February 21, 1907, in York, England. His father was the medical officer of the city of Birmingham and a psychologist. His mother was a devout Anglican, and the combination of religious and scientific or analytic themes are implicit throughout Auden's work. He was educated at St. Edmund's preparatory school, where he met Christopher Isherwood, who later gained a wide reputation as a novelist. At Oxford University, fellow undergraduates were Cecil Day Lewis, Louis MacNeice, and Stephen Spender, who, with Auden, formed the collective variously labeled the Oxford Group or the "Auden Generation."

At school Auden was interested in science, and at Oxford, where he studied English, his chief interest was Anglo-Saxon. He disliked the Romantic poets Shelley and Keats, whom he was inclined to refer to as "Kelly and Sheets." This break with the English post-Romantic tradition was important for his contemporaries. It is perhaps still more important that Auden was the first poet in English to use the imagery (and sometimes the terminology) of clinical psychoanalysis.

Early Travels and Publications

A small volume of his poems was privately printed by Stephen Spender in 1928, while Auden was still an undergraduate. *Poems* was published a year later by Faber and Faber (of which T. S. Eliot was a director). *The Orators* (1932), a volume consisting of odes, parodies of school speeches and sermons, and the strange, almost surreal "Journal of an Airman" provided a barrage of satire against England, "this country of ours where no one is well." It set the mood for a generation of public school boys who were in revolt against the empire of England and fox hunting.

When he had completed school, Auden traveled in Germany. In 1937 he went with MacNeice to Iceland and in 1938 with Isherwood to China. Literary results of these journeys were *Letters from Iceland* (1937) and *Journey to a*

War (1939), the first written with MacNeice and the second with Isherwood. Auden also wrote several plays in collaboration, notably 1935's *The Dog beneath the Skin* (another satire on England) and *The Ascent of F 6* (1931). More than a decade later Auden again worked in collaboration—this time with Chester Kallmann on the librettos for several operas, of which the most important was Igor Stravinsky's *The Rake's Progress* (1951).

In 1939 Auden took up residence in the United States, supporting himself by teaching at various universities. In 1946 he became a U.S. citizen, by which time his literary career had become a series of well-recognized successes. He received the Pulitzer Prize and Bollingen Award and enjoyed his standing as one of the most distinguished poets of his generation. From 1956 to 1961 he was professor of poetry at Oxford University. In his inaugural address, "Making Knowing and Judging," he explored ideas about his vocation as a poet.

Poetic Themes and Techniques

Auden's early poetry, influenced by his interest in the Anglo-Saxon language as well as in psychoanalysis, was sometimes riddle-like, sometimes jargonish and clinical. It also contained private references inaccessible to most readers. At the same time it had a clouded mysteriousness that would disappear in his later poetry. In the 1930s his poetry ceased to be mystifying; still dealing with difficult ideas, however, it could at times remain abstruse. His underlying preoccupation was a search for interpretive systems of analytic thinking and faith. Clues to the earlier poetry are to be found in the writings of Sigmund Freud and Karl Marx. In the later poems (after "New Year Letter," in which he turns to Christianity), some clues can be traced in the works of Søren Kierkegaard, Reinhold Niebuhr, and other theologians.

Among Auden's highly regarded attributes was the ability to think symbolically and rationally at the same time, so that intellectual ideas weretransformed into a uniquely personal, idiosyncratic, often witty imagistic idiom. He concretized ideas through creatures of his imagining for whom the reader could often feel affection while appreciating the austere outline of the ideas themselves. He nearly always used language that is interesting in texture as well as brilliant verbally. He employed a great variety of intricate and extremely difficult technical forms. Throughout his career he often wrote pure lyrics of grave beauty, such as "Lay Your Sleeping Head, My Love" and "Look Stranger."

Often Auden's poetry may seem a rather marginal criticism of life and society written from the sidelines. Yet sometimes it moves to the center of the time in history in which he and his contemporaries lived. In "The Shield of Achilles" he recreated the anguish of the modern world of totalitarian societies in a poem which holds one particular time in a mirror for all times. Auden was learned and intelligent, a virtuoso of form and technique. In his poetry he realized a lifelong search for a philosophical and religious position from which to analyze and comprehend the individual life in relation to society and to the human condition in general. He was able to express his scorn for authoritarian bureaucracy, his suspicion of depersonalized science, and his belief in a Christian God.

Later Works

In his final years, Auden wrote the volumes *City without Walls, and Many Other Poems,* (1969), *Epistle to a Godson, and Other Poems* (1972), and the posthumously published *Thank You, Fog: Last Poems* (1974). All three works are noted for their lexical range and humanitarian content. Auden's penchant for altering and discarding poems has prompted publication of several anthologies in the decades since his death, September 28, 1973, in Vienna, Austria. The multi-volume *Complete Works of W. H. Auden* was published in 1989.

Further Reading

Criticism and interpretation of Auden's works may be found in such studies as Stan Smith, *W. H. Auden* (1997), R. P. T. Davenport-Hines, *Auden* (1995), Anthony Hecht, *The Hidden Law: the Poetry of W. H. Auden* (1993), Allan Edwin Rodway, *A Preface to Auden* (1984), Edward Callan, *Auden: A Carnival of Intellect* (1983), Humphrey Carpenter, *W. H. Auden: A Biography* (1981), and Charles Osborne, *W. H. Auden: The Life of a Poet* (1979). In addition, Auden figures prominently in the autobiographies of some of his contemporaries. See, for example, Cyril Connolly, *Enemies of Promise* (1938; rev. ed. 1948), Christopher Isherwood, *Lions and Shadows: An Education in the Twenties* (1938), and Stephen Spender, *World within a World* (1951). The Oxford Group is examined in Michael O'Neill, *Auden, MacNeice, Spender: The Thirties Poetry* (1992). □

John James Audubon

The work of American artist and ornithologist John James Audubon (1785-1851) was the culmination of the work of natural history artists who tried to portray specimens directly from nature. He is chiefly remembered for his "Birds of America."

When John James Audubon began his work in the first decade of the 19th century, there was no distinct profession of "naturalist" in America. The men who engaged in natural history investigations came from all walks of life and generally financed their work—collecting, writing, and publication—from their own resources. The American continent, still largely unexplored, offered a fertile field, giving the amateur an unrivaled opportunity to make a genuine contribution to science—for an afternoon walk in the woods might reveal a hitherto unknown species of bird, plant, or insect to the practiced eye. Especially fortunate was the man with artistic ability, for there was an intense popular interest in the marvels of nature during this, the romantic, era; and anyone who could capture the natural beauty of wild specimens was certain to take his place among the front ranks of those recognized as "men of science." This is the context in which Audubon worked and in which he became known as

America's greatest naturalist—a title which modern scholars using other standards invariably deny him.

Audubon was born in San Domingo (now Haiti) on April 26, 1785, the illegitimate son of a French adventurer and a woman called Mademoiselle Rabin, about whom little is known except that she was a Creole of San Domingo and died soon after her son's birth. Audubon's father had made his fortune in San Domingo as a merchant, planter, and dealer in slaves. In 1789 Audubon went with his father and a half sister to France, where they joined his father's wife. The children were legalized by a regular act of adoption in 1794.

Life in France and Move to America

Audubon's education, arranged by his father, was that of a well-to-do young bourgeois; he went to a nearby school and was also tutored in mathematics, geography, drawing, music, and fencing. According to Audubon's own account, he had no interest in school, preferring instead to fish, hunt, and collect curiosities in the field. Left to the supervision of his indulgent stepmother most of the time, while his father served as a naval officer for the republic, Audubon became a spoiled, willful youth who managed to resist all efforts either to educate or discipline him. When residence at a naval base under his father's direct supervision failed to have any effect, he was sent briefly to Paris to study art, but this disciplined study also repelled him.

With the collapse of a large part of his income following the rebellion in San Domingo, the elder Audubon de-

cided to send his son to America, where he owned a farm near Philadelphia. At first the boy lived with friends of his father and they tried to teach him English and otherwise continue his education, but after a time he demanded to be allowed to live on his father's farm, which was being managed by a tenant. There Audubon continued his undisciplined ways, living the life of a country gentleman—fishing, shooting, and developing his skill at drawing birds, the only occupation to which he was ever willing to give persistent effort. He developed the new technique of inserting wires into the bodies of freshly killed birds in order to manipulate them into natural positions for his sketching. He also made the first banding experiments on the young of an American wild bird, in April 1804.

Business Career

In 1805, after a prolonged battle with his father's business agent in America, Audubon returned briefly to France, where he formed a business partnership with Ferdinand Rozier, the son of one of his father's associates. Together the two returned to America and tried to operate a lead mine on the farm. Then in August 1807 the partners decided to move to the West. There followed a series of business failures, in Louisville, Henderson, and other parts of Kentucky, caused largely by Audubon's preference for roaming the woods rather than keeping the store.

During this period he married Lucy Bakewell. After the failures with Rozier, Audubon, in association with his brother-in-law, Thomas Bakewell, and others, attempted several different enterprises, the last being a steam grist and lumber mill at Henderson. In 1819 this enterprise failed and Audubon was plunged into bankruptcy, left with only the clothes he wore, his gun, and his drawings. This disaster ended his business career.

For a time Audubon did crayon portraits at $5 a head, then he moved to Cincinnati, where he became a taxidermist in the Western Museum recently founded by Dr. Daniel Drake. In 1820 the possibility of publishing his bird drawings occurred to him; and he set out down the Ohio and Mississippi rivers, exploring the country for new birds and paying his expenses by painting portraits. For a while he supported himself in New Orleans by tutoring and painting; then his wife obtained a position as a governess and later opened a school for girls. Thereafter she was the family's main support while Audubon tried to have his drawings published.

"Birds of America"

In 1824 Audubon went to Philadelphia to seek a publisher, but he encountered the opposition of friends of Alexander Wilson, the other pioneer American ornithologist, with whom he had had a bitter rivalry dating back to a chance encounter in his store in 1810. He finally decided to raise the money for a trip to Europe, where he was assured he would find a greater interest in his subject. He arrived at Liverpool in 1826, then moved on to Edinburgh and to London, being favorably received and obtaining subscribers for his volumes in each city. Audubon finally reached an agreement with a London engraver, and in 1827 *Birds of America* began to appear in "elephant folio" size. It took 11 years in all for its serial publication and subsequent reprintings. The success of Audubon's bird drawings brought him immediate fame, and by 1831 he was acclaimed the foremost naturalist of his country. This title was bestowed upon him despite the fact that he possessed no formal scientific training and no aptitude for taxonomy (the Latin nomenclature and the scientific indentification of most of the species in *Birds of America* is largely the work of a collaborator). He had, however, succeeded in giving the world the first great collection of American birds, drawn in their natural habitats with reasonable fidelity to nature.

With his great work finally finished in 1838, and the *Ornithological Biography* (a text commentary) in publication, Audubon returned to America to prepare a "miniature" edition. Simultaneously, he began to prepare, in collaboration with John Bachman, *Viviparous Quadrupeds of North America* (2 vols., 1842-1845). Audubon himself completed only about half the drawings in this last work; his powers failed during his last few years and his son contributed the remainder.

Final Years

With old age—and success—came a more kindly attitude toward his former rivals. In 1841 he bought an estate on the Hudson River and settled down to advise and encourage young scientists. It was during this period that the romantic picture of Audubon as the "American Woodsman," the revered and adored sage and patron saint of the birds, began to emerge. (This image was kept alive by his daughter and granddaughter until 1917, when F. H. Herrick published the first critical biography of the artist-naturalist.) After several years of illness, Audubon suffered a slight stroke in January 1851, followed by partial paralysis and great pain, and died on the 27th.

Further Reading

Alice E. Ford, *John James Audubon* (1964), is a good biography by an art historian; Alexander B. Adams, *John James Audubon* (1966), gives a meticulous year-by-year chronicle of his activities. An earlier work, Francis H. Herrick, *Audubon the Naturalist* (2 vols., 1917), is still valuable for the scientific side. All of the earlier biographies, based on the account by Audubon's wife, are highly romanticized. Useful for background information on this period in American natural history is William M. and Mabel S. C. Smallwood, *Natural History and the American Mind* (1941). George H. Daniels, *American Science in the Age of Jackson* (1968), discusses the general scientific frame of reference. □

St. Augustine

The Christian philosopher and theologian St. Augustine (354-430) is best known for "The Confessions" and "The City of God." After the authors of the New Testament, he has probably been the most influential Christian writer.

The greatest of the Latin Fathers of the Church, Augustine lived during a period in which the Roman Empire was in deep decline and Christianity was taking root as the official religion. It was a time of great political stress and widespread religious anxiety. Augustine's own spiritual struggles reflect the historical transition from a dying pagan antiquity to the Christian Middle Ages. *The Confessions* reveals much about his formative years, when he strove to overcome his sensual desires, find faith, and understand religious and philosophical doctrines.

Augustine was born at Tagaste (modern Souk-Ahras, Algeria) on Nov. 13, 354. Though his father, Patricius, was to become a Christian only when he was near death, Augustine's mother, Monica, was a devout Christian. She saw to his education in this religion, but in accord with what was then the custom, his baptism into the faith of his mother was deferred. Schooled in Latin grammar and literature at Tagaste and Madaura, Augustine showed promise and was sent to Cartage in 370 to study rhetoric. In Cartage, while successfully pursuing his studies, he abandoned the Christian moral teachings of his early years. He took a mistress, with whom he was to live for 10 years, and fathered a son, Adeodatus (The God-given).

Influence of Manichaeism

At the age of 19 Augustine read Cicero's dialogue *Hortensius,* a work that was an exhortation to philosophy. According to Augustine, "Suddenly all the vanity that I had hoped in I saw as worthless, and with an incredible intensity of desire I longed after immortal wisdom" (*Confessions,* III,

4). To this end, Augustine embraced the Persian religion of Manichaeism. The Manichaeans held that in the world there were opposing forces of good and evil, called Ormuzd and Ahriman, respectively. Their struggle with one another was represented in man by the conflict between the soul, the good element, and the body, the evil one. Manichaeism made a very strong appeal to Augustine because of its materialistic outlook and account of evil.

After having taught Latin grammar and literature at Tagaste, Augustine opened a school of rhetoric in Carthage in 373. During this time his confidence in Manichaeism was eroded. In particular, he found in its doctrines neither a satisfactory reason for the conflict of the forces of good and evil nor an account of the nature of human certitude.

In 383 Augustine went to Rome to teach rhetoric. But his students had the unpleasant habit of leaving their instructors just before the payment of fees was due. So the following year he took a civic post in Milan as professor of rhetoric. In Rome, Augustine had become sympathetic to the academic skepticism of Carneades and Cicero. The skeptics thought that certitude about any topic was not attainable and that therefore all of man's beliefs should be regarded as dubious.

Influence of Platonism

In Milan, Augustine was deeply impressed by the sermons of the bishop Ambrose. Around Ambrose there was a community whose members were as much Platonists as Christians. They regarded Platonism as compatible with, and an anticipation of, Christianity. Through reading certain Platonic writings, probably those of Plotinus and Porphyry, and meetings with Christian Platonists, Augustine was brought to accept such a viewpoint. The platonists' spiritualistic metaphysics and their idea that evil was only a privation of good replaced in Augustine's mind his earlier Manichaean materialism.

Augustine's skepticism began to dissolve in the face of his newly acquired convictions. Still, this extraordinary transformation was to him only an intellectual one. What was lacking, and what he now longed for in a state of torment, was the conversion of his will to Christianity and the acceptance of Christ.

Conversion to Christianity

This event is described in the famous "garden scene" in Augustine's *Confessions* (VII, 12). Upon hearing a child's voice repeating the words "Take and read," Augustine opened his Scriptures at random and saw this passage in St. Paul's Epistle to the Romans (13:13): "Not in rioting and drunkenness, not in chambering and impurities, not in contention and envy, but put ye on the Lord Jesus Christ and make not provision for the flesh in its concupiscences." Augustine then notes, "I had no wish to read further and no need. For in that instant, with the very ending of the sentence, it was as though a light of utter confidence shone in all my heart."

From then on Augustine was a confirmed Christian, and he was baptized by Ambrose on Easter 387. In 388 Augustine returned to Tagaste and established a religious community. Ordained a priest in 391, he founded a similar community in Hippo (modern Bone, Algeria), becoming bishop there in 396. Until 430 Augustine busied himself with pastoral labors and wrote theological and philosophical works. On Aug. 28, 430, Augustine died, while Hippo was under siege by the Vandals.

Augustine's works are far too extensive to list even by title. There are commentaries on parts of the Bible and many disputatious tracts against the Manichaeans, the Donatists, and the Pelagians. His main works are *Contra academicos, De beata vita, De ordine, De immortalitate animae, Soliloquia, De libero arbitrio, De quantitate animae* (all completed between 386 and 388), *De musica* (begun between 386 and 388 and finished between 388 and 391), *De magistro* (composed between 388 and 391), *De doctrina Christiana* (composed in 396 with a fourth book added in 426), *Confessions* (400), *De Trinitate* (begun in 400 and finished in 417), *De genesi ad litteram* (begun in 401 and completed in 415), *The City of God* (begun in 413 and finished about 420), and *Retractions* (composed in 426-427).

Theory of Knowledge

One of Augustine's earliest works is *Contra academicos,* in which he attacks skepticism and lays the groundwork for the possibility of knowledge. He does so by calling attention to propositions that even the skeptic cannot doubt. First, one can be certain of exclusive disjunctive propositions. For example, it is certain that there is one world or more than one. It is also indisputable that, with respect to the world's having a beginning and an end, both are the case, or one and not the other, or neither. Second, though the senses are sometimes deceptive concerning the facts in a situation, one is certain of what appears to be the case. Error arises in man's judgments only when appearance is taken as reality. For example, one is not deceived in judging that a stick *looks* bent in water; error arises, however, when one states that the stick is *actually* bent. Third, the truth of mathematical judgments like two and two make four is immune from doubt. Lastly, in anticipation of René Descartes, Augustine points out that the experience of doubt and error presuppose the existence of oneself. A person cannot be in doubt or error unless he exists. In order to exist one has to be alive. Since both are known to be the case, one also realizes that he understands. Thus existence, life, and understanding are indubitable even to the skeptic.

Propositions of mathematics and logic have the special features of being eternally and necessarily true. Knowledge of these tends to be grouped by Augustine with the knowledge of standards that he thinks implied in comparative judgments about sensible things (for example, a standard of perfect beauty is implied in the statement, "This is more beautiful than that"). But cognitions of eternal truths and standards are acts beyond the natural capacity of man's intellect, since this faculty is mutable and temporal. Required then, says Augustine, is an illumination from a source that is itself eternal, necessary, and unchanging—namely, God.

Augustine shares the view of many Greek philosophers that the end of man is happiness or beatitude and that such a condition is a consequence of the possession of wisdom. But, by contrast, wisdom for Augustine is Christian wisdom. Philosophical conceptions are useful to faith only as preparatory and explanatory devices.

Creation from Nothing

Augustine's Christian philosophy has as one of its cornerstones the thesis that God freely created the world from nothing. Augustine thus opposed the Neoplatonic notion of a world emanating from God through necessity. "Creation from nothing" also involves the rejection of the Greek view of world formation, which is based upon the model of an artist making a finished product from materials at hand. Such a model requires preexisting and independent material for a divine craftsman to work upon. According to Augustine, either such unformed matter must be conceived so abstractly as to be the same as nothing at all, or it is something having form and made by the Creator.

At first sight, Augustine would seem to have mitigated his uncompromising position on creation by his further theory of seminal reasons (*De genesi ad litteram,* VI, 6, 12). This theory, found also in Plotinus and the Stoics, claims that things may exist in a seminal or germlike condition, having a potentiality for form that is actualized only over a period of time and if circumstance permits. Augustine's acceptance of this theory was dictated largely by considerations of scriptural interpretation. It is, however, consistent with his view of creation from nothing and affords an illustration of his use of a philosophical idea to clarify a theological issue.

According to Genesis, different forms of things appeared at different times, the successive days of creation. On the other hand, Ecclesiasticus teaches that all things were made together. The appearance of inconsistency vanishes, however, if one says, as Augustine recommends, that all things were created together from nothing but that some were created from nothing in a seminal condition, to be brought to actual formation later.

Time as Extension

The dependence of creation upon God is also stressed in Augustine's treatment of time. (His most sustained and interesting treatment is in Book XI of *The Confessions.*) The Manichaeans claimed that the doctrine of creation from nothing contains no sufficient explanation of why God should create at any given moment rather than any other and that it further poses the unanswerable question of what God was doing before he created the world. Augustine rebuts such objections by insisting that they rest upon a mistaken assimilation of time to an event in time. Creation from nothing entails that time too is a creature, which came into being with other things created. Thus the notion of events before the beginning of time becomes meaningless.

Augustine became genuinely perplexed about the existence of the past and the future. He saw that man's temporal notions require time to be measurable and that measurability requires time to have magnitude. Yet, the past is what *was* and *is not,* the future is what *will be* and *is not,* and the present is indivisible and extensionless. How then does time exist as a magnitude? His tentative answer is: "The present of things past is memory, the present of things present is sight and the present of things future is expectation. . . . It seems to me that time is nothing else than extension; but extension of what I am not sure—perhaps of the mind itself" (*Confessions,* XI, 20, 26).

Eternal Soul

Among the things that come to be in time is the soul of man. Augustine's view of the soul is thoroughly Platonic. For him it is a substance distinct from and superior to the body, which is joined to the body by a sort of vital attention. (In sensory experience the soul uses the body as an instrument, increasing its vital attention in one organ.) Augustine states that, though the soul is something that came to be, it cannot cease to be. To show this, he adapts arguments used in Plato's *Phaedo.* For example, the soul is what it is because it shares in a principle, life, which does not admit of a contrary. So, being a soul, it cannot die.

A theological problem attends the genesis of the human soul. Does God create each soul individually or did He create all souls together in making Adam's? On the former view, combined with a belief in original sin, God would create something that is evil. On the latter view, Adam would have passed on a human soul to his descendants that was made evil by his sin but was not evil when God created it. Traducianism is the name of the second position, and it was the one to which Augustine was inclined.

Philosophy of History

Augustine's interest in time also includes a view of historical time. In *The City of God* he makes a striking departure from Christian thinking about the historical significance of the Roman Empire. Before the 4th century Christians had naturally tended to look upon Rome as a satanic oppressor. When Christianity was officially recognized in 312, the empire seemed to may to have become the instrument for the fulfillment of the Gospels. Such people were stunned by the Ostrogoths' sacking of Rome in 410.

Three years later Augustine began *The City of God.* In it, Rome differs from the Church both as a reality and as an ideal. As a reality, Rome is one empire among others that have come and gone, and the fate of the Church need not be bound up with it. As an ideal, Rome is the earthly city opposed to the ideal of the heavenly city. According to Augustine, a people is a "multitude of reasonable beings united by their agreement in the things that they respect" (*City of God,* XIX, 24). The character of a society then is determined by the choices of the individuals who make it up. If the choice is of self-love rather than love of God, then one has the earthly city; if of God rather than self, then one has the heavenly city.

In contrast to Greek thinkers like Hesiod and Plato, Augustine does not talk about ideals as having existed in a remote past. Rather, he claims that the two ideals will only become historical realities at the end of time. Then the two cities will exist actually and separately. Members of the heavenly city will be with God, but members of the earthly city will suffer eternal punishment. Meanwhile, in the present, the two ideals are commingled in one historical reality. However qualified by Augustine, the implication is that Church and state can have at best an uneasy unity and that the true Christian will look elsewhere than to Rome, or any other state, for the fulfillment of his hopes.

Further Reading

One of the most commonly used translations of Augustine's works is *Basic Writings of Saint Augustine,* edited by Whitney J. Oates (2 vols., 1948). Henri I. Marrou, *Saint Augustine and His Influence through the Ages* (trans. 1957), is a fine introduction, which includes an account of Augustine's life and thought along with brief translations from his writings. Peter Brown, *Augustine of Hippo* (1967), is an outstanding biography covering both the theological and practical aspects of Augustine's career. Other works on Augustine's career and writings include Vernon J. Bourke, *Augustine's Quest for Wisdom: Life and Philosophy of the Bishop of Hippo* (1945); Jacques Chabannes, *St. Augustine* (trans. 1962); and Gerald Boner, *St. Augustine of Hippo: Life and Controversies* (1963). Written from a Thomistic perspective, but still the most thoughtful account of Augustine's philosophy, is Étienne Gilson, *The Christian Philosophy of Saint Augustine* (trans. 1960). See also Herbert A. Deane, *The Political and Social Ideas of St. Augustine* (1963). For the thought of the period consult the monumental survey, A. H. Armstrong, ed., *The Cambridge History of Later Greek and Early Medieval Philosophy* (1967). □

St. Augustine of Canterbury

The Roman monk St. Augustine of Canterbury (died ca. 606) is known as the Apostle of England. He brought Christianity to England in the 6th century and became the first archbishop of Canterbury.

G regory the Great, before he became pope, had seen in a slave market in Rome some young boys captured from the Angle tribe. He was said to have been so impressed by their light complexion and fair hair that he remarked, "These are not Angles, these are angels." When Gregory became pope, his desire to convert the Angles to Christianity led him to commission a group of monks to take the gospel message to England. To lead the mission, Gregory chose a man for whom he had gained respect when they shared a cell in the monastery of St. Andrew in Rome, a monk named Augustine.

Until this time Augustine had followed the quiet and disciplined monastic life of work, prayer, and study of Scriptures. Out of a sense of duty he responded to Pope Gregory's directive and left the peace of the monastery with a contingent of 20 monks. They landed in the southeastern corner of England in 597.

King Ethelbert of Kent received the monks with some curiosity but, suspicious that Augustine might possess magical powers, insisted on meeting them outdoors, where he would not be as vulnerable. The King was impressed by

Augustine's courage and straightforwardness. Within a year, at Christmas of 597, Ethelbert agreed to accept baptism and became a Christian himself. Ten thousand of his people followed his example, giving Augustine a base out of which to operate.

Augustine continued to receive help from Rome, and more monks came to preach under his direction. Pope Gregory sent relics, vestments, books, and answers to Augustine's questions. After being appointed bishop over all of England in 601, Augustine tried to coordinate his activities with the Christian groups among the Celts and the Britons. On the Pope's advice Augustine did not destroy pagan temples but used them as churches once the idols had been removed and the buildings purified with holy water. King Ethelbert built Augustine a monastery and encouraged the missionary to make his headquarters at Canterbury in Kent rather than London in Essex, as Pope Gregory had suggested.

Augustine met with relatively little immediate success in his relations with the other Christian groups in England, who wanted to remain independent of Kent and were not happy that the Pope had sent a Roman to supervise their activities. But the seed he planted in southeastern England was to grow throughout the entire British Isles, involving them inextricably in the course of European Christianity. Augustine died sometime between 604 and 609.

St. Augustine (seated on stage)

Further Reading

Cardinal Gasquet, *The Mission of Saint Augustine* (1924), is a thorough study of Augustine's work in England. Also a full-length study is Sir Henry H. Howorth, *Saint Augustine of Canterbury* (1913). □

Augustus

Augustus (63 B.C.-A.D. 14) was the first emperor of Rome. He established the principate, the form of government under which Rome ruled the empire for 300 years. He had an extraordinary talent for constructive statesmanship and sought to preserve the best traditions of republican Rome.

The century in which Augustus was born was a period of rapid change and, finally, civil war for Rome. Of the many factors which led to the civil wars, two are of crucial importance for understanding his career. By the middle of the 1st century B.C. Rome had conquered nearly all the lands bordering the Mediterranean, and Caesar's conquest of Gaul in 49 B.C. brought transalpine Europe into the sphere of Roman influence.

Rome and its provinces were governed throughout the republic by the Senate, composed largely of members of a small hereditary aristocracy. But the Senate was showing itself unequal to the task of governing the Mediterranean, and its authority was increasingly usurped by the generals in command of the victorious Roman legions. Because he had the support of his army and great personal popularity, Julius Caesar had become virtually a dictator in Rome following his conquest of Gaul. He was strongly opposed by the Senate and in 44 was assassinated by conspirators among them. It was at that juncture that Augustus entered the Roman political arena.

Augustus was born Gaius Octavius on Sept. 23, 63 B.C., in a house on the Palatine hill in Rome. His father, Gaius Octavius, held several political offices and had earned a fine reputation, but he died when Octavius was 4. The people who most influenced Octavius in his early years were his mother, Atia, who was Julius Caesar's niece, and Julius Caesar himself.

When Caesar's will was read, it was revealed that Caesar had adopted Octavius as his son and heir. Octavius was then at Apollonia studying oratory. Against the advice of his friends and family, Octavius—who changed his name to Gaius Julius Caesar Octavianus (English, Octavian)— immediately set out for Italy to claim his inheritance. He was only 18, rather frail physically, and although he had delivered the funeral oration for his grandmother when he was 12 and had won Caesar's admiration, he had given no previous indications of his ambitions or his genius for political maneuvering. Octavian displayed both these qualities in abundance as soon as he entered Rome in 43.

Rise to Power

Octavian's enemy in his rise to power was Mark Antony, who had assumed the command of Caesar's legions. The two men became enemies immediately when Octavian announced his intentions of taking over his inheritance. Antony had embarked on a war against the Senate to avenge Caesar's murder and to further his own ambitions, and Octavian joined the senatorial side in the battle. Antony was defeated at Mutina in 43, but the Senate refused Octavian the triumph he felt was his due. Octavian abandoned the senators and joined forces with Antony and Lepidus, another of Caesar's officers; they called themselves the Second Triumvirate. In 42 the triumvirate defeated the last republican armies, led by Brutus and Cassius, at Philippi.

The victors then divided the Mediterranean into spheres of influence; Octavian took the West; Antony, the East; and Lepidus, Africa. Lepidus became less consequential as time went on, and a clash between Antony and Octavian for sole control of the empire became increasingly inevitable. Octavian played upon Roman and Western antipathy to the Orient, and after a formidable propaganda campaign against Antony and his consort, Queen Cleopatra of Egypt, Octavian declared war against Cleopatra in 32. Octavian won a decisive naval victory, which left him master of the entire Roman world. The following year Antony and Cleopatra committed suicide, and Octavian annexed Egypt to Rome. In 29 Octavian returned to Rome in triumph.

Political Authority

Octavian's power was based on his control of the army, his financial resources, and his enormous popularity. The system of government he established, however, was designed to veil these facts by making important concessions to republican sentiment. Octavian was extremely farsighted in his political arrangements, but he continually emphasized that his rule was a return to the *mos maiorum*, the customs of the ancestors. Early in January of 27 B.C., therefore, Octavian went before the Senate and announced that he was restoring the rule of the Roman world to the Senate and the Roman people. The Senate, in gratitude, voted him special powers and on January 16 gave him the title Augustus, signifying his superior position in the state, with the added connotation of "revered." A joint government gradually evolved which in theory was a partnership; in fact, Augustus was the senior partner. Suetonius, his biographer, said that Augustus believed that "he himself would not be free from danger if he should retire" and that "it would be hazardous to trust the state to the control of the populace" so "he continued to keep it in his hands; and it is not easy to say whether his intentions or their results were the better."

The government was formalized in 23, when Augustus received two important republican titles from the Senate—Tribune of the People and Proconsul—which together gave him enormous control over the army, foreign policy, and legislation. His full nomenclature also included his adopted name, Caesar, and the title Imperator, or commander in chief of a victorious army.

Character and Achievements

Suetonius has given a description of Augustus which is confirmed by the many statues of him. "In person he was unusually handsome and exceedingly graceful at all periods of his life, though he cared nothing for personal adornment. . . . He had clear, bright eyes, in which he liked to have it thought that there was a kind of divine power, and it greatly pleased him, whenever he looked keenly at anyone, if he let his face fall as if before the radiance of the sun. . . . He was short of stature . . . but this was concealed by the fine proportion and symmetry of his figure."

Augustus concerned himself with every detail and aspect of the empire. He attended to everything with dignity, firmness, and generosity, hoping, as he said himself, that he would be "called the author of the best possible government." He stabilized the boundaries of the empire, provided for the defense of the frontiers, reorganized and reduced the size of the army, and created two fleets to form a Roman navy. His many permanent innovations included also the creation of a large civil service which attended to the general business of administering so vast an empire.

The Emperor was interested in public buildings and especially temple buildings. In 28 B.C. he undertook the repair of all the temples in Rome, 82 by his own count. He also built many new ones. In addition, he constructed a new forum, the Forum of Augustus, begun in 42 B.C. and completed 40 years later. It was with good reason that Augustus could boast that he had "found Rome built of brick and left it in marble."

Repairing the temples was only one aspect of the religious and moral revival which Augustus fostered. There seems to have been a falling away from the old gods of the state, and Augustus encouraged a return to the religious dedication and morality of the early republic. In 17 B.C. he held the Secular Games, an ancient festival which symbolized the restoration of the older religion. The poet Horace commemorated the occasion with his moving Secular Hymn.

Augustus tried to improve morals by passing laws to regulate marriage and family life and to control promiscuity. In A.D. 9, for example, he made adultery a criminal offense, and he encouraged the birthrate by granting privileges to couples with three or more children. His laws did not discourage his daughter Julia and his grand-daughter (also Julia), both of whom he banished for immoral conduct. Suetonius reports that "he bore the death of his kin with far more resignation than their misconduct."

Throughout his long reign Augustus encouraged literature, and the Augustan Age is called the Golden Age because Roman writing attained a rare perfection. It was above all an age of poets—Horace, Ovid, and most especially, Virgil. And in Virgil's great epic, the *Aeneid,* there is expressed for all time the sense of the grandeur of Rome's imperial destiny which culminated in the age of Augustus.

The Succession

Augustus suffered many illnesses, and these caused him to designate an heir early in his reign. But he had many deaths to bear and outlived his preferred choices, including his two young grandsons, and was finally forced to designate as his heir Tiberius, his third wife's son by her first marriage.

The first emperor died at Nola on Aug. 19, A.D. 14. On his deathbed, according to Suetonius, he quoted a line used by actors at the end of their performance: "Since I've played well, with joy your voices raise/ And from your stage dismiss me with your praise."

Further Reading

The main ancient source for Augustus's life is Suetonius's chapter "The Deified Augustus" in the *Lives of the Twelve Caesars.* The career of Augustus is also discussed in Tacitus's *History.* Augustus left an account of his own deeds called the *Res gestae,* or more popularly, the *Monumentum ancyranum.* John Buchan, *Augustus* (1937), is still the standard biography in English. Much that is valuable relating to Augustus's career may be found in T. Rice Holmes, *The Architect of the Roman Empire* (2 vols., 1928-1931), and in Ronald Syme, *The Roman Revolution* (1939). See also Henry Thompson Rowell, *Rome: In the Augustan Age* (1962). □

Augustus II

Augustus II (1670-1733), called Augustus the Strong, was elector of Saxony and king of Poland. Better known for his extravagance and promiscuity than for political shrewdness, he failed in his modest attempts to create a strong and independent Poland.

On May 12, 1670, Augustus was born Frederick August of Wettin, in Dresden, the second son of the Saxon elector John George III. He was trained for a military career. His powerful physique and apparently insatiable sexual appetite earned him the title "the Strong." He succeeded as elector of Saxony when his older brother, John George IV, died without heirs in 1694. The next 2 years he spent commanding the armies of the Hapsburg Empire against the Turks in Hungary. He proved an inept and unimaginative commander.

When King John III Sobieski of Poland died in June 1696, Frederick August entered the international competition for the Polish throne. He renounced his Protestant faith, to the displeasure of his Saxon subjects, and with Hapsburg support and judicious bribes he was elected king on June 27, 1697. He entered Poland a month later as Augustus II and promised to uphold that nation's aristocratic constitution. Although the union of Saxony and Poland brought real economic advantages to both states, the absolutist tendencies of Augustus gained him bitter enemies.

Allied after 1699 with Denmark and Russia, Augustus provoked a disastrous war with Sweden, whose young king, Charles XII, captured Vilna, Warsaw, and Cracow in 1701. The Polish kingdom split apart. Some of the nobles supporting Augustus prepared to fight on with Russian help, while others accepted Sweden's leadership and elected Stanislas Leszczynski king in 1704. In September 1706, after occupying Poland and invading Saxony, Charles XII forced Augustus to renounce the Polish crown and recognize Stanislas in the Treaty of Altranstädt. The displaced king went back to soldiering and spent 2 years in Flanders fighting under the English general Marlborough against France.

When Peter I of Russia defeated Charles at Poltava in July, 1709, Swedish domination of the north collapsed. Augustus was then able to return to Poland, while Stanislas fled to Sweden. Led astray by the apparent popularity of his restoration, Augustus tried briefly to rule Poland without the Diet. Even his firmest supporters, however, demanded that he adhere to the constitution. The remainder of his reign was taken up largely by his unsuccessful efforts to subdue aristocratic factions supported by foreign powers. After finally making peace with Sweden in 1719, he tried to create an alliance with Austria and England to balance increasing Russian influence, but the plan was foiled by aristocratic rebellion. He spent his last years attempting to secure the succession of his apathetic son, Frederick August, and enjoying the pleasures of wine and his large, cosmopolitan retinue of mistresses. He died on Feb. 1, 1733, leaving Poland fragmented by aristocratic factions, and a potential victim of the rapacity of its powerful neighbors.

Further Reading

The most accessible study in English on Augustus II is the chapter by Prof. W. Konopczynski in the second volume of W. F. Reddaway, ed., *Cambridge History of Poland from Augustus II* to Pilsudski (1697-1935) (1941). The most substantial biographies are in German. □

François Victor Alphonse Aulard

The French historian François Victor Alphonse Aulard (1849-1928) was a leading authority on the French Revolution.

On July 19, 1849, Alphonse Aulard was born at Montbron. His earliest interests were literary. Admitted to the École Normale in 1867, he received his doctorate in 1877. From 1871 to 1884 he taught literature, and by 1884 he had already published three volumes, *Parliamentary Eloquence during the French Revolution* (1882-1884). When, in the following year, the city of Paris founded a professorship of the history of the Revolution at the Sorbonne, he was named to fill the post.

View of the Revolution

The history of the French Revolution was at this time still the subject of violent political passions, for Frenchmen saw in the political problems of the late 19th century the continuation of conflicts and crises that had first exploded in 1789. Aulard insisted that the Revolution should be considered with the same critical detachment as all other periods of history. At the beginning of each year's lecture series, he would hand his students a list of "the historian's Ten Commandments," among them: "always use the sources; avoid unproved assertions; present facts impartially and objectively; when publishing something new do not bury interesting facts under insignificant rubbish; let your research be long and the results be short." Yet he also insisted that fervor was necessary for genuine comprehension. "He who does not sympathize with the Revolution sees only the surface. In order to understand it, it is necessary to love it."

As one who had come of age during the early years of the Third Republic, Aulard viewed the Revolution as primarily a political movement, the history of the origins of democracy and republicanism. Democracy he saw as the logical consequence of the principle of equality, and republicanism the consequence of national sovereignty. There was, however, no logic to the events themselves, which resulted from the complex interaction of men, ideas, and circumstances. His hero was Danton, whom he admired as a good republican, a patriot, an enemy of the Church, and a great compromiser.

Variety of Publications

During his lifetime Aulard wrote or edited over 60 books and pamphlets as well as hundreds of articles for *La Revolution française* (of which he was editor from 1887 until his death) and other publications. His major work on the Revolution was *Political History of the French Revolution* (1901). He believed he would be remembered mainly as the editor of *Acts of the Committee of Public Safety* (26 vols., 1889-1923). But his interests were broad, and he published extensively on the religious history of the Revolution—*The Cult of Reason and the Cult of the Supreme Being* (1892) and *The Revolution and the Congregations* (1903); economic history—*The Revolution and the Feudal Regime* (1919); and historiography—*Taine, Historian of the Revolution* (1907). He died in Paris on Oct. 23, 1928.

Further Reading

A useful work for understanding Aulard is Paul Farmer, *France Reviews Its Revolutionary Origins: Social Politics and Historical Opinion in the Third Republic* (1944). Pieter Geyl, *Napoleon: For and Against* (1946; trans. 1949), includes a chapter which compares Aulard's theories on Napoleon and the Revolution with those of other historians. Aulard's historical methodology is discussed in James L. Godfrey's chapter, "Alphonse Aulard (1849-1928)," in Bernadotte E. Schmitt, ed., *Some Historians of Modern Europe*. □

Aung San

The Burmese political leader Aung San (1915-1947) was the driving force behind the nationalist movement that won Burma (now Myanmar) its freedom from British colonial rule in 1948.

Born in the township of Natmauk on Feb. 13, 1915, Aung San was the son of fairly well-off parents. He graduated from one of the high schools set up by Burmese nationalists to demonstrate their independence of foreign-provided education, and he received his bachelor's degree from the University of Rangoon. As a university student, he was extremely active politically, serving as president of the Rangoon University Students' Union, breeding ground of nationalist leaders, and as one of the founders of the All-Burma Students' Union.

Editor of *Oway,* the Rangoon University student magazine, Aung San was expelled from the university in 1936 for printing a slashing personal attack on a college official. The attack had no connection whatsoever with mounting nationalist demands against the British colonial presence but led nonetheless to the 1936 students' strike, the major shaping event of pre-World War II Burmese nationalism.

Like various other Burmese nationalists of the period, Aung San wrote well in both Burmese and English. He was founding member of the anticolonial Red Dragon Book Club (together with U Nu, later to be independent Burma's first premier) and a member of the editorial staff of the only English-language newspaper in the prewar years, *New Burma.*

Aung San was elected general secretary of the extreme nationalist Thakin (Our Own Masters) party in 1938, and he became the leading young nationalist before World War II and one of the two or three key Burmese political figures in the country. He helped to found the All-Burma Peasants League and, together with Dr. Ba Maw, established the

Freedom Bloc to present a united front against the continuation of the British colonial presence. For such activities he was frequently interrogated and detained by the authorities.

Fight for Independence

Aung San went underground in late 1940 to escape arrest by the British and subsequently left the country surreptitiously to make contact with Japanese officials in occupied southeastern China. He traveled to Japan, then returned to Burma to lay the groundwork for subsequent Japanese-Burmese nationalist cooperation against the British.

When he returned to Japan in early 1941, he took with him 29 fellow young nationalists, none of them as prominent politically as himself. He feared that the departure of more prominent figures would arouse British suspicion. Aung San and these others were to lead the so-called Burma Independence Army into Burma from Thailand in 1942, in cooperation with the Japanese, and gain Burmese immortality as the ''Thirty Comrades.''

The Thirty Comrades were subsequently to rank as the greatest heroes of the Burmese nationalist revolution. Many were to play major political roles in postcolonial Burma, including Gen. Ne Win, who unseated elected premier U Nu in 1958 and 1962 and was Burma's head of government during most of the 1960s.

Suspicious of Japanese intentions toward Burma almost from the start, Aung San nonetheless accepted command of the Burma Defense Army, heretofore the Burma Independence Army. When Burmese ''independence'' was proclaimed in 1943, Aung San, who had been made a major general, was minister of war in the collaborationist Ba Maw government together with almost all of the other young nationalists. Despite his official position, however, he repeatedly spoke out against the sham character of Burma's alleged independence.

In August 1944 Aung San was the principal moving force behind the establishment of the Anti-Fascist Organization, the clandestine resistance force that subsequently became the Anti-Fascist People's Freedom League (AFPFL) and Burma's governing party for the first 10 years of independence after 1948. In March 1945 he led the Burma Defense Army, newly named the Patriot Burmese Forces, into open rebellion against Japan and subsequently into cooperation with the returning British military forces.

Elected president of the AFPFL in 1945 and reelected the subsequent year at a convention attended by 100,000 persons, the youthful Aung San emerged from World War II the best known and most popular of the Burmese political leaders. His demand to Britain for early independence was backed by the support of the overwhelming majority of his politically conscious countrymen. The British governor, Sir Reginald Dorman-Smith, however, regarded Aung San as a traitor and war criminal. Sir Reginald's failure to reach agreement with the Burmese leader led to his replacement by Sir Hubert Rance, with whom Aung San quickly agreed on the composition of an interim government to help rule Burma until independence and to prepare for such independence. Aung San was premier-designate of the soon-to-be independent government.

In January 1947 Aung San, now Burma's acknowledged political leader, led the Burmese delegation to London for independence talks with British premier Clement Attlee. On his return in February 1947 Aung San successfully negotiated the Panglong Agreement, which provided for the participation of various frontier-area peoples in the new Union of Burma, as the emergent Burmese federal state was to be called.

On July 19, 1947—six months before the coming of independence—Aung San, only 32, and most of the other top nationalist leaders of the country were shot to death by henchmen of an insanely jealous political rival, prewar premier U Saw. The anniversary of the assassinations, known as Martyrs Day, is Myanmar's most solemn national holiday.

Further Reading

A favorable picture of Aung San is U Maung Maung, ed., *Aung San of Burma* (1962), a compilation of sketches by persons with whom Aung San worked in the cause of Burmese nationalism. U Maung Maung, *Burma's Constitution* (1959; 2d ed. 1961), is another sympathetic work that places Aung San and his contribution to Burmese independence in an appropriate historical context. Frank N. Trager, *Burma, from Kingdom to Republic: A Historical and Political Analysis* (1966), provides an excellent historical account of the emergence of modern Myanmar, with suitable attention to Aung San's role. □

Aung San Suu Kyi

In 1988 Aung San Suu Kyi (born 1945) became the preeminent leader in Burma (now Myanmar) of the movement toward the reestablishment of democracy in that state. In 1991, while under house arrest, she was awarded the Nobel Peace Prize.

Aung San Suu Kyi was internationally recognized as a vibrant symbol of resistance to authoritarian rule. On July 20, 1989, she was placed under house arrest by the military coup leaders, called the State Law and Order Restoration Council (SLORC), who came to power in Myanmar on September 18, 1988, in the wake of a popular but crushed uprising against the previous, and also military headed socialist government. The nation's name had been changed from Burma to Myanmar in 1980.

Aung San Suu Kyi came from a distinguished Burmese family. Her father, Bogyoke (Generalissimo) Aung San, is known as the founder of independent Burma in 1948 and is widely revered in that country. He negotiated independence from the British and was able to weld the diverse ethnic groups together through the force of his personality and the trust he engendered among all groups. He was assassinated, along with most of his cabinet, by a disaffected Burmese politician, U (Mr.) Saw, on July 22, 1947, prior to independence on January 4, 1948. That day remains a national remembrance holiday in Myanmar. His loss slowed the realization of state unity.

Aung San Suu Kyi was born in Burma on June 19, 1945. She spent her early years in Burma and then joined her mother, Daw Khin Kyi (all names in Burma are individual; there are no surnames), who was appointed as Burmese ambassador to India in 1960. She was partly educated in secondary school in India and then attended St. Hugh's College, Oxford University, where she received her bachelor's and master's degrees studying politics, economics, and philosophy. For two years she worked in the United Nations Secretariat in New York. In 1972 she married Michael Vaillancourt Aris, a well-known scholar on Central Asia, Tibet, and Bhutan. They had two sons, Alexander (born in 1973 and also known by his Burmese name, Myint San Aung) and Kim (born in 1977 and also called Htein Lin).

During 1985 and 1986, Aung San Suu Kyi was a visiting scholar at the Center for Southeast Asian Studies, Kyoto University, and in 1987 she was a fellow at the Indian Institute of Advanced Studies in Simla.

Daw Khin Kyi, her mother, had a stroke in 1988, and Aung San Suu Kyi came back to Rangoon, Myanmar, to help nurse her. While there, the tumultuous events of 1988 that convulsed the country took place. The popular rising against the previous socialist regime associated with the militarily-led Burma Socialist Party regime was a mass revolt against an authoritarian and economically failed administration. This revolt started as an apolitical student brawl; it

was handled poorly by the military and spread, becoming a vehicle for expression of the pent-up political and economic frustrations dating from the earlier coup of 1962.

On August 26, 1988, Aung San Suu Kyi gained national recognition as the effective leader of the opposition National League for Democracy (NLD), later opposed to the military-led SLORC. Aung San Suu Kyi became the general secretary of the National League for Democracy and was a charismatic and effective speaker in favor of democracy throughout the country. She was placed under house arrest by the SLORC for attempting to split the army, a charge she consistently denied.

Although she was not allowed to run for election in the May 27, 1990, election, her party, the NLD, much to the astonishment and chagrin of the military, won 80 percent of the legislative seats. They were never permitted to take office. For the first years of her house arrest Aung San Suu Kyi was not allowed to have any visitors, but later her immediate family was allowed to be with her on occasional trips to Myanmar. In January of 1994 the first visitor outside of her family, U.S. Congressman Bill Richardson, a Democrat from New Mexico, was allowed to meet with her. She was recognized as a prisoner of conscience by Amnesty International. The United Nations and a large number of other national and international groups called for her unconditional release. She won many awards for democracy and human rights, including the Sakharov Prize for Freedom of Thought (European Parliament, 1991), the Nobel Peace Prize (1991), and the International Simon Bolivar Prize (UNESCO, 1992).

Aung San Suu Kyi remained under military surveillance and house arrest until July of 1995. The government continually restricted her movement throughout both the country and abroad. During Suu Kyi's first year of freedom, she was only permitted brief travel in and around her home city of Rangoon and did not travel outside of Myanmar. She continued, however, to serve as the vocal leader of the NLD and push for democracy.

Further Reading

Aung San Suu Kyi has written extensively on the life of her father, on a variety of events in Burma, on intellectual life in Burma and India under colonialism, and on literature and nationalism in Burma. These and other works and speeches, including several appreciations of her life and accomplishments, were published in English in 1991 as *Freedom From Fear and Other Writings*. See also David I. Steinberg, "The Future of Burma, Crisis and Choice in Myanmar," *Asian Agenda Report #14* (1990). More information about Aung San Suu Kyi is contained in "Stalking the Stunt Princess" *Time International* (July 8, 1996). □

Additional Sources

Parenteau, John, *Prisoner for peace: Aung San Suu Kyi and Burma's struggle for democracy*, Greensboro, N.C.: Morgan Reynolds, 1994. □

Aurangzeb (left)

Aurangzeb

Aurangzeb (1618-1707) was the sixth Mogul emperor of India and the last of the "Great Moguls." He extended the Mogul Empire to its farthest boundaries, but his reign was harsh and marked by revolts.

Mohi-ud-din Mohammed Aurangzeb was born on Oct. 24, 1618, at Dohad and was the third son of Emperor Shah Jahan. At the age of 18 Aurangzeb became viceroy of the Deccan. In 1645 he became governor of Gujarat, the empire's richest province. Two years later he led an expeditionary force against the Uzbegs in Central Asia but was unsuccessful in establishing Mogul authority over Balkh (now northern Afghanistan). An expedition against Kandahar also failed.

In 1653 he returned to the Deccan to restore law and order and extended to the south the Mogul revenue system that had been established in northern India by Emperor Akbar. During this second viceroyalty his relations with his eldest brother, Dara Shukoh, who was Emperor Shah Jahan's principal adviser, deteriorated. Aurangzeb believed in territorial expansion and Moslem orthodoxy; Dara stood for imperial consolidation and a secular empire. Thus a clash for succession became inevitable.

When Shah Jahan fell ill in September 1657, Aurangzeb challenged Dara, defeated him, imprisoned their father, and assumed imperial authority on July 21, 1658. After liquidating his three brothers, he crowned himself emperor of India, assuming the title Alamgir (Conqueror of the World) on June 5, 1659.

Committed to making India an orthodox Moslem state, Aurangzeb restricted Hindu festivals and destroyed many Hindu temples. In 1664 the practice of *sati* (immolation of widows on funeral pyres) was enjoined. Poll tax on Hindus was imposed in 1679. Censors were appointed to enforce morals, and edicts were issued against drinking, gambling, prostitution, and narcotics. When a defiant Sikh guru, Tegh Bahadur, refused to embrace Islam, he was executed. Employment of non-Moslems was restricted in the imperial bureaucracy.

Such discriminatory policies naturally led to rebellions. In 1660 the Marathas began a revolt, followed by the Jats in 1669, the Satnamis in 1672, the Sikhs in 1675, and the Rajputs in 1679. Even the English East India Company took up arms against him in 1686. One by one all these revolts were subdued, but the victories were always short-lived. Mogul imperial unity was lost, and the treasury was exhausted.

Under Aurangzeb's piety and austerity, Mogul culture also suffered. Music and arts lost royal patronage, and the position of women rapidly declined. The Emperor strove to live up to the ideals of orthodox Islam. In his spare time he copied the Koran to provide for his funeral expenses. He was a man of literary tastes, and his own letters are a model of elegant Persian prose. At the age of 90, with all his faculties, except hearing, unimpaired, he died on Feb. 20, 1707. He is buried in Daulatabad.

Further Reading

Two works by the principal authority on Aurangzeb, Jadunath Sarkarn, are *History of Aurangzib: Mainly Based on Persian Sources* (5 vols., 1912-1924; rev. ed, 1 vol., 1925) and *A Short History of Aurangzib 1618-1707* (1930; rev. ed. 1954). Chapters on Aurangzeb are in W. H. Moreland and Atul Chandra Chatterjee, *A Short History of India* (1936; 3d ed. 1953); J. C. Powell-Price, *A History of India* (1955); S. M. Ikram, *Muslim Civilization in India,* edited by Ainslie T. Embree (1964); and Bamber Gascoigne, *The Great Moghuls* (1971), which also deals with the first five Mogul emperors of India.

Additional Sources

Joshi, Rekha, *Aurangzeb, attitudes and inclinations,* New Delhi: Munshiram Manoharlal, 1979, 1978.

Lal, Muni, *Aurangzeb,* New Delhi: Vikas Pub. House, 1988.

Lane-Poole, Stanley, *Aurangzib,* Lahore: Sind Sagar Academy, 1975.

Alamgir, Delhi: Idarah-i-Adabiyat-i Delli, 1981. □

Jane Austen

The English writer Jane Austen (1775-1817) was one of the most important novelists of the 19th century.

n her intense concentration on the thoughts and feelings of a limited number of characters, Jane Austen creates as profound an understanding and as precise a vision of the potentialities of the human spirit as the art of fiction has ever achieved. Although her novels received favorable reviews, she was not celebrated as an author during her lifetime.

Jane Austen was born in 1775 at Steventon, in the south of England, where her father was rector of the parish. She was the seventh of eight children in an affectionate and high-spirited family. In 1801 she moved to Bath with her father, her mother, and her only sister, Cassandra. After the Reverend Austen's death in 1805, the three women moved to Southampton and in 1809 to the village of Chawton, where Jane Austen lived for the rest of her life. She never married, but received at least one proposal and led an active and happy life, unmarked by dramatic incident and surrounded by her sister and brothers and their families.

Austen began writing as a young girl and by the age of 14 had completed *Love and Friendship* (sic). This early work, an amusing parody of the melodramatic novels popular at that time, shows clear signs of her talent for humorous and satirical writing. Three volumes of her collected juvenilia were published more than a hundred years after her death.

Sense and Sensibility

Jane Austen's first major novel was *Sense and Sensibility,* whose main characters are Elinor Dashwood and her sister Marianne. The first draft was written in 1795 and titled

Elinor and Marianne. In 1797 Austen rewrote the novel and titled it *Sense and Sensibility.* After years of polishing, it was finally published in 1811.

As the original and final titles indicate, the novel contrasts the temperaments of the two sisters. Elinor governs her life by sense or reasonableness, while Marianne is ruled by sensibility or feeling. Elinor keeps her wits about her under the strain of an affair during which her beloved becomes entangled with another girl. After his mother disinherits him, his beloved, an avaricious schemer, jilts him and he returns to Elinor—who has the sense to take him back. A more disagreeable moral revelation is evident in Marianne Dashwood's actions. She is in love with a scoundrel, who tires of her and goes off to London. She follows him there and is bitterly disillusioned by his callous treatment. She then gives up her romantic dreams of passionate fulfillment and marries a stodgy, middle-aged suitor. Although the plot favors the value of sense over that of sensibility, the greatest emphasis is placed on the moral complexity of human affairs and on the need for enlarged and subtle thought *and* feeling in response to it.

Pride and Prejudice

In 1796, when Austen was 21 years old, she wrote the novel *First Impressions.* The work was rewritten and published under the title *Pride and Prejudice* in 1813. It is her most popular and perhaps her greatest novel. It achieves this distinction by virtue of its perfection of form, which exactly balances and expresses its human content. As in *Sense and Sensibility,* the twin abstractions of the title are closely associated with the protagonists, Elizabeth Bennet and Fitzwilliam Darcy. Elizabeth is guilty of prejudice against the aristocratic Darcy, and he manifests excessive pride in his cold and unbending attitude toward Elizabeth, her sister Jane, and other members of the Bennet family.

The form of the novel is dialectical—the opposition of ethical principles is expressed in the relations of believable characters. The resolution of the main plot with the marriage of Elizabeth and Darcy represents a reconciliation of conflicting moral extremes. The value of pride is affirmed when humanized by Elizabeth's warm personality, and the value of prejudice is affirmed when associated with Darcy's standards of traditional honor.

During 1797-1798 Austen wrote *Northanger Abbey,* which was published posthumously. It is a fine satirical novel, making sport of the popular Gothic novel of terror, but it does not rank among her major works. In the following years she wrote *The Watsons* (1803 or later), which is a fragment of a novel similar in mood to her later *Mansfield Park,* and *Lady Susan* (1804 or later), a novelette in letters.

Mansfield Park

In 1811 Jane Austen began *Mansfield Park,* which was published in 1814. It is her most severe exercise in moral analysis and presents a conservative view of ethics, politics, and religion.

The novel traces the career of Fanny Price, a Cinderella-like heroine, who is brought from a poor home to Mansfield Park, the country estate of her relative, Sir

Thomas Bertram. She is raised with some of the comforts of her cousins, the children of Sir Thomas, but her social rank is maintained at a lower level. Despite their strict upbringing, the Bertram children become involved in marital and extramarital tangles, which bring disasters and near-disasters on the family. But Fanny's upright character guides her through her own relationships with dignity—although sometimes with a chilling disdainfulness—and leads to her triumph at the close of the novel. While one may not like the rather priggish heroine, one does develop a sympathetic understanding of Fanny's thoughts and emotions and learn to value her at least as highly as the more attractive but less honest members of the Bertram family and its circle.

Emma

Shortly before *Mansfield Park* was published, Jane Austen began a new novel, *Emma,* and published it in 1816. Again the heroine, Emma Woodhouse, is difficult to love but, like Fanny Price, does engage the reader's sympathy and understanding. Emma is a girl of high intelligence and vivid imagination who is also marked by egotism and a desire to dominate the lives of others. She exercises her powers of manipulation on a number of neighbors who are not able to resist her prying into their lives. Most of Emma's attempts to control her friends, however, do not have happy effects for her or for them. But influenced by John Knightley, an old friend who is her superior in intelligence and maturity, she realizes how misguided many of her actions are. The novel ends with the decision of a warmer and less headstrong Emma to marry Mr. Knightley. The triviality of some of the characters—particularly Emma's hypochondriac father—distresses many readers, but there is much evidence to support the contention of some critics that *Emma* is Austen's most brilliant novel. The saturation of a narrow human situation with the author's satirical wit and psychological penetration is here carried to its highest point.

Persuasion

Persuasion, begun in 1815 and published posthumously (together with *Northanger Abbey*) in 1818, is Jane Austen's last complete novel and is perhaps most directly expressive of her feelings about her own life. The heroine, Anne Elliot, is a woman growing older with a sense that life has passed her by. Several years earlier she had fallen in love with Captain Wentworth but was parted from him because her class-conscious family insisted she make a more suitable match. But she still loves Wentworth, and when he again enters her life, their love deepens and ends in marriage.

Austen's satirical treatment of social pretensions and worldly motives is perhaps at its keenest in this novel, especially in her presentation of Anne's family. The predominant tone of *Persuasion,* however, is not satirical but romantic. It is, in the end, the most uncomplicated love story that Jane Austen ever wrote and to some tastes the most beautiful.

The novel *Sanditon* was unfinished at her death in 1817. She died at Winchester, where she had gone to seek medical attention, and was buried there.

Further Reading

Jane Austen's career is described in R. W. Chapman, *Jane Austen: Facts and Problems* (1949). Chapman also edited the definitive editions of her novels and letters. The best critical study of the novels is Mary Lascelles, *Jane Austen and Her Art* (1939). Marvin Mudrick presents a vigorous view of her fiction in *Jane Austen: Irony as Defense and Discovery* (1952). The context of her novels is treated in Avrom Fleishman, *A Reading of Mansfield Park: An Essay in Critical Synthesis* (1967). □

John Langshaw Austin

The English philosopher John Langshaw Austin (1911-1960) taught a generation of Oxford students a rigorous style of philosophizing based on language analysis.

John Langshaw Austin was born in Lancaster on March 26, 1911. In 1924 he entered Shrewsbury School with a scholarship in classics. His distinguished work enabled him to win a scholarship in classics to Balliol College, Oxford. To his studies in classics and linguistics Austin now added philosophy. After taking first honors, he competed successfully for a fellowship at All Souls College. In 1935 Austin gave up this research fellowship to become teaching fellow and tutor at Magdalen College.

During World War II Austin had a commission in military intelligence. He quickly displayed an extraordinary talent for analyzing and relating vast numbers of facts about the capacities of the enemy. His responsibilities steadily increased, and prior to the Normandy invasion he was the chief organizer of all the intelligence available to the Allied armies. Of his work it has been said that "he more than anybody was responsible for the life-saving accuracy of the D-Day intelligence." He retired as a lieutenant colonel, honored with the Order of the British Empire, the French Croix de Guerre, and the American Legion of Merit.

In 1945 Austin resumed teaching at Oxford, and in 1952 he was elected to the White's chair of philosophy. Austin's primary dedication was to teaching, and as a result he published very little. In his lifetime only seven short papers appeared. He once remarked to a friend: "I had to decide early on whether I was going to write books or to teach people how to do philosophy usefully."

Early in his career Austin devised a philosophical technique which grew directly out of his classical and linguistic studies. Philosophical work, he argued, could well begin with a thorough examination of the linguistic resources available. These would be the terms and usages of ordinary language rather than those of a technical vocabulary. Austin did not hold that an appeal to the usages of ordinary language should be the last word in philosophical arguments, but he did insist that "it *is* the *first* word." Any distinction which has become fixed in everyday language, surviving centuries of use and succeeding in the competition with alternative distinctions, may well be thought to point toward some real distinction in experience. Detailed investigation of such distinctions can hardly fail to get a philosophical discussion off to a productive start. As Austin put it, "we are using a sharpened awareness of words to sharpen our perception of, though not as the final arbiter of, the phenomena." With ingenuity, subtlety, and wit, Austin developed strategies to collect and classify the abundance of words, idioms, and metaphors which are ordinarily invoked in discussions having a philosophical interest.

Austin's last work, *How to Do Things with Words,* published posthumously, was based on the William James lectures which he gave at Harvard University in 1955. In it he was moving toward a more general theory of types of linguistic utterance. But his death cut short these efforts at generalization, and it is not yet clear whether, as he believed, his technique can be used by others with the same impressive results.

His death came with little warning on Feb. 8, 1960, at only 48. He was survived by his wife, Jean Courts Austin, whom he had married in 1941, and their four children.

Further Reading

K. T. Fann, ed., *Symposium on J. L. Austin* (1969), contains several interesting biographical essays and a number of distinguished critical essays, most of them by friends or former students of Austin. G. J. Warnock, *English Philosophy since 1900* (1958), includes a section on Austin.

Additional Sources

Warnock, G. J. (Geoffrey James), *J.L. Austin,* London; New York: Routledge, 1989. □

Stephen Fuller Austin

The American pioneer Stephen Fuller Austin (1793-1836) was the chief colonizer of Texas. With the exception of Utah, no other state so owes its existence to one man.

Born in Austinville, Wythe County, Va., on Nov. 3, 1793, Stephen Austin moved to Missouri in 1798, where his father, Moses Austin, engaged in lead mining and land speculation. Stephen attended Colchester Academy in Connecticut and Transylvania University in Kentucky before returning home. In Missouri he served in the state legislature from 1814 to 1820, was a director of the Bank of St. Louis and an officer in the state militia, and became active in lead mining, land speculation, and manufacturing.

When the Panic of 1819 bankrupted the family enterprises, Austin moved to Arkansas, where he was appointed a district judge. In August 1820 he moved again, seeking in Louisiana a means of making enough money to repay the family's debts. In New Orleans he read law and worked on a newspaper.

His father died in June 1821, leaving Austin a newly acquired permit to colonize 300 families in Spanish Texas. He traveled to Mexico City in 1822-1823 to secure Mexican recognition of the Spanish grant. This done, he colonized the 300 families, as well as an additional 750 families under subsequent contracts.

Small of stature, lean and wiry, with fine features, thick hair, and brown eyes, Austin was a dignified and reserved man. A bachelor given to self-analysis, he led the Texan colonists by means of his forceful personality and persuasive writings. He mapped and surveyed much of Texas, translated Mexican laws, fixed the land system, and served as civil and military liaison with the Mexican authorities. He also organized the Texan defenses against the Indians.

In 1833 he journeyed to Mexico City to represent the Texan desire for separate statehood. He was arrested on charges of sedition and imprisoned, but never tried. Released in 1835, he returned to Texas, where he joined the faction fighting the dictatorship of Antonio López de Santa Ana. At the outbreak of the fighting, he became commander in chief of the Texan military forces, but in November 1835 he was sent to the United States to seek assistance and, later, recognition of independence.

At the end of the Texas revolution, he reluctantly ran for president of the new republic against the hero of the war, Samuel Houston. Defeated, Austin accepted the position of secretary of state in the Houston administration. He died on Dec. 27, 1836, of pneumonia. His quiet, effective leadership during the years 1821-1836 is recognized in numerous

ways in Texas; the capital city, a county, and a college are named in his honor. His statue in the national capitol was placed there by grateful citizens of the Lone Star State.

Further Reading

Eugene C. Barker's standard *The Life of Stephen F. Austin* (1925) depicts in detail the career of this remarkable colonizer and places him in the context of American history. David M. Vigness, *The Revolutionary Decades, 1810-1836* (1965), traces Austin's career in the Texas revolution. Most of the known writings by Austin are contained in Eugene C. Barker, ed., *The Austin Papers* (3 vols., 1924-1928).

Additional Sources

Warren, Betsy, *Moses Austin and Stephen F. Austin: a gone to Texas dual biography*, Dallas, Tex.: Hendrick-Long Pub. Co., 1996.

Austin, Stephen F. (Stephen Fuller), *Fugitive letters, 1829-1836: Stephen F. Austin to David G. Burnet,* San Antonio, Tex.: Trinity University Press, 1981. □

Richard Avedon

The American fashion photographer Richard Avedon (born 1923) was best known for his probing portraits that go beyond recording likenesses to explore the identity of society and to reflect dreams and desires.

Richard Avedon was born in New York City on May 15, 1923. Educated in the New York City public school system, he left DeWitt Clinton High School without graduating. In 1942 he enlisted in the Merchant Marine's photographic section. Returning to civilian life in 1944, he worked as a department store photographer. A year later he was hired as a fashion photographer by Alexey Brodovitch, the art director of *Harper's Bazaar*. In 1946 he established his own studio and after that contributed photographs to *Vogue, Theatre Arts, Life, Look,* and *Graphis*.

Innovative Fashion Photography And Portraits

Traditionally, fashion photographs depicted elegant, aloof models in static poses. However, following the lead of the innovative Hungarian photographer Martin Munkasci, Avedon produced photographs blurred by the model's motion. By using a wide variety of settings and suggesting a plot through the model's expressive gestures, Avedon introduced an emotional complexity new to fashion photography. Later he took all his photographs in his studio, photographing the models in motion against the plain, white background that became his trademark. These fashion photographs, appearing in the editorial pages of *Vogue* and *Harper's Bazaar,* brought him prestige, but the lucrative part of his work was advertisements to which he seldom signed his name.

Avedon was also noted for his portraits, which first appeared in *Harper's Bazaar* but were later published in books and exhibited at museums and gallerys. Stylistically, the portraits and the fashion photographs are alike. The earliest ones, mostly of celebrities, are often blurred as the subject engages in some characteristic activity: Marian Anderson sings, Louis Armstrong plays his horn, Jimmy Durante tips his hat. Later Avedon did away with blurring and soft focus. Instead, a strobe light illuminates every pore and flaw of the subject's face, turning wrinkles into crevices. It was as if Avedon were trying to escape the elegant, youthful images of the fashion world by an intense scrutiny of old age and ugliness.

Of his portraits Avedon said, "The way someone who's being photographed presents himself to the camera, and the effect of the photographer's response on that presence, is what the making of a portrait is all about." The tension between the self image the sitter is trying to project and Avedon's response to that image is somewhat hidden in these photographs because of Avedon's technique. The sitters face forward, virtually filling the picture which is often printed with the black edges of the negative forming a funereal frame. Printed in starkly contrasted black and white, subjects are isolated against a white background. Without a context, the viewer is forced to focus on the sitters' personalities as revealed by their faces and gestures. The frontality of the pose, the empty background, and the harshly revealing light suggest that the photographer has not intervened. The viewer seems to see the bare truth, which in these portraits is seldom flattering. However, as the title of his book, *Nothing Personal,* suggests, his savage vision seems to be directed not at the subjects but at vanity and hypocrisy in general.

His portraits were virtually all of celebrities, but he did take a series of photographs of the insane, leading critics to claim that Avedon aimed his lens at the two classes of people least able to defend their privacy—the celebrated and the helpless. In any case, his later photographs are less harsh. The photographs of his father, done between October 1969 and August 1973, have been admired for their humanity as they trace his father's losing battle against incurable cancer.

Pictorial Studies of Everyday Americans

In his later work, undertaken for the Amon Carter Museum in Fort Worth, Texas, and published under the title *In the American West,* Avedon used his favorite white background and flat lighting. But the sitters were ordinary people rather than celebrities. Here he seemed to be following in the footsteps of the German photographer August Sander (1876-1964), who set about cataloguing archetypal Germans—butchers, aristocrats, Nazis. Avedon, too, labelled his sitters with their occupations: housewife, coal miner, drifter. Like Sander, Avedon believed that the human condition is essentially tragic.

Gentler but no less probing than his earlier portraits, these photographs explore the lives of marginal people, those scrabbling to fulfill the American dream. Like his earlier work, these subjects were photographed in flat light against a white background. The figures are sometimes framed off-center as if they had accidentally sidled into the camera's view, or they are cropped seemingly arbitrarily, reinforcing the notion that the viewer is seeing the people directly rather than through Avedon's eyes. The result is a sense of immediacy, of sincerity that is quite powerful.

Honors and Awards

Avedon has received many awards and honors over the years for his work. In 1958, *Popular Photography* voted him one of the ten greatest photographers in the world, and more recently, in 1989, he received an honorary doctorate from the Royal College of Art in London. He was appointed as the first and only *New Yorker* staff photographer by editor Tina Brown in 1992. In 1996, he was profiled by Helen Whitney in a television special called *Richard Avedon: Darkness and Light.*

Further Reading

Avedon's photographs appear in *Observations* (1959) with a text by Truman Capote; *Nothing Personal* (1964), with a text by James Baldwin; *Richard Avedon: Portraits* (1976), with an introduction by Harold Rosenberg; *Avedon: Photographs (1947-1977),* with text by Harold Brodkey; *In the American West* (1985); *An Autobiography* (1993); and *Evidence* (1994). Since the texts of these books are usually only loosely connected to the photographs, the best source of information on Avedon and his work is Janet Malcom's article ''Photography: Men Without Props'' in *The New Yorker,* September 22, 1975.

Avedon can be found on the Web at the A&E Biography site, http://www.biography.com, and on the *Time* site at http://www.pathfinder.com/@@EqwXNQYAtuDpY7OJ/time/magazine/domestic/1994/940328 /940328.photog. □

Averroës

The Spanish-Arabic scholar Averroës (1126-1198), also known as Ibn Rushd, was a leading philosopher of the Middle Ages. His commentaries on Aristotle became a major source for understanding the work of that thinker in the 13th and 14th centuries.

The tradition of Arabic philosophy, one of the monuments of medieval Islamic civilization, culminated in the work of Avicenna (980-1037), Avempace (died 1138), and Averroës. Avicenna expanded upon the work of such earlier Arab philosophers as al-Kindi (died 873) and al-Farabi (870-950) to form a more unified system based on Aristotelian and Neoplatonic concepts. Averroës defended that achievement against the criticism of the more conservative al-Ghazali (died 1111) and provided, through his commentaries on Aristotle's works, a view of man and the universe that conflicted with various theological dogmas of Islam and Christianity.

Averroës was a Spanish Arab. He was born in Cordova, Spain, and was educated there in mathematics, philosophy, theology, law, and medicine. He came from a family prominent in law, a profession that in Islamic society was closely associated with religion and theological concepts.

In 1153 Averroës visited Marrakesh in Morocco and caught the attention of the sultan, a noted patron of scholarship. It may have been at the sultan's suggestion that Averroës planned a commentary on all the works of Aristotle. While there Averroës observed the star Canope, which was not visible from Spain. This confirmed, for him, Aristotle's belief that the world was round.

Judge and Physician

Through the sultan's support Averroës became a judge in Seville in 1169. Later he returned to Cordova, where he became the chief judge. During this period he wrote the commentaries on Aristotle that became so important in the development of philosophy and science in Europe. These commentaries are of three types: short summations, or epitomes; long, elaborate explanations of the text; and a group intermediate in length. Their purpose was to present the true Aristotle without the accretions and misinterpretations of earlier generations.

In 1182 Averroës went to Marrakesh as physician to the sultan. He composed a medical handbook and urged other specialists to write on the subject of medicine.

In 1195, seemingly under attack by conservative theologians, Averroës retired from public life. He lived for a short time near Seville and then returned to Marrakesh, where he died in 1198.

continued to affirm personal survival, reinforced by the doctrine of the resurrection of the body. The world is eternal, for Averroës, because it depends on God, the creator, who is eternal. Averroës's God remained a personal deity who knew particular things in creation, because he knew himself and thus his creation.

Averroës's philosophical writing had a twofold purpose. First, writing after al-Ghazali, who had attacked Avicenna and all philosophy, and living in a society where conservative religious forces threatened his personal safety, Averroës defended Avicenna and Islamic philosophy. Second, within the context of philosophy itself, Averroës attempted to reconstitute a pure Aristotle, free from the corruptions of all earlier commentators and interpreters, including Avicenna.

Apart from those ideas associated with Averroës that conflicted with Christian doctrine and caused a series of theological crises during the 13th century, some aspects of Averroës's thought contributed directly to the development of Western philosophy in that period. It was largely through the work of Averroës that the Latin West became familiar with the ideas of Aristotle, ideas that had great importance for the development of medieval philosophy and science. Averroës's emphasis on logical demonstration as the major tool of scientific and philosophical inquiry was generally accepted. His emphasis on the concept of motion and the Prime Mover shaped the development of metaphysics and the conception of God in 13th-century European thought. Finally, Averroës's description of the way in which the human mind receives knowledge of the sensible world around it was generally accepted up to the 14th century. Through his association with Aristotle and the establishment of a school of Averroism, the name and thought of this Islamic philosopher were kept alive well into the 17th century.

Thought of Averroës

Only a portion of the works of Averroës were known to the Latin West in the 13th century, as many of his works were not translated until the second quarter of the 14th century. Consequently the Averroës that was known in the 13th century, on whom Latin Averroism was based, is different from the Averroës revealed through a fuller examination of his works.

On the basis of 13th-century interpretation, Averroës was held to affirm the following doctrines, which were the foundation of the school of Latin Averroism: the world was eternal rather than created; God was impersonal and, consequently, there was no divine intervention; there was one active reason, or Agent Intellect, for all mankind; there was no personal survival after death; and some truths of philosophy and theology could contradict each other and still be valid or true in their respective domains. Inasmuch as these doctrines were in direct opposition to Christian belief, Western theologians rejected them and the philosopher to whom they were attributed.

During the 14th century several other works of Averroës were translated into Latin. They indicated a more balanced, sometimes theologically conservative, thinker who seldom, if ever, denied the accepted Moslem dogma. From these works it is clear that Averroës never affirmed the possibility of double truth. Truth was one, and where philosophy contradicted religious dogma as revealed in the Koran, truth lay with the Moslem scriptures. Although there was one Agent Intellect for all men, Averroës seems to have

Further Reading

The two most important studies on the life and thought of Averroës are in French: Ernest Renan, *Averroës et l'averroisme: Essai historique* (1852; 13th ed. 1866; repr. 1949), and Léon Gauthier, *Ibn Rochd* (1948). Étienne Gilson, *History of Christian Philosophy in the Middle Ages* (1955), provides a good survey of the thought of Averroës. The distinction between the 13th-century view of Averroës and the view based on a fuller examination of his writings is described in Julius Weinberg, *A Short History of Medieval Philosophy* (1964). For an examination of the metaphysics of Averroës see Étienne Gilson, *Being and Some Philosophers* (1949; 2d ed. 1952).

Additional Sources

Leaman, Oliver., *Averroes and his philosophy*, Oxford: Clarendon Press; New York: Oxford University Press, 1988.
☐

Oswald Theodore Avery

Avery (1877?-1955) was one of the founding fathers of immunochemistry and a major contributor to the scientific evolution of microbiology.

Oswald Theodore Avery was one of the founding fathers of immunochemistry (the study of the chemical aspects of immunology) and a major contributor to the scientific evolution of microbiology. His studies of the pneumococcus virus (causing acute pneumonia) led to further classification of the virus into many distinct types and the eventual identification of the chemical differences among various pneumococci viral strains. His work on capsular polysaccharides and their role in determining immunological specificity and virulence in pneumococci led directly to the development of diagnostic tests to demonstrate circulating antibody. These studies also contributed to the development of therapeutic sera used to treat the pneumonia virus. Among his most original contributions to immunology was the identification of complex carbohydrates as playing an important role in many immunological processes. Avery's greatest impact on science, however, was his discovery that deoxyribonucleic acid (DNA)) is the molecular basis for passing on genetic information in biological self-replication. This discovery forced geneticists of that time to reevaluate their emphasis on the protein as the major means of transmitting hereditary infor-

mation. This new focus on DNA led to James Watson and Francis Crick's model of DNA in 1952 and an eventual revolution in understanding the mechanisms of heredity at the molecular level.

Avery was born on October 21, 1877 (one source says 1887), in Halifax, Nova Scotia, to Joseph Francis and Elizabeth Crowdy Avery. His father was a native of England and a clergyman in the Baptist church, with which Avery was to maintain a lifelong affiliation. In 1887 the Avery family immigrated to the United States and settled in New York City, where Avery was to spend nearly sixty-one years of his life. A private man, he guarded his personal life, even from his colleagues, and seldom spoke of his past. He believed that research should be the primary basis of evaluation for a scientific life, extending his disregard for personal matters to the point that he once refused to include details of a colleague's personal life in an obituary. Avery's argument was that knowledge of matters outside of the laboratory have no bearing on the understanding of a scientist's accomplishments. As a result, Avery, who never married, managed to keep his own personal affairs out of the public eye.

Avery graduated with a B.A. degree from Colgate University in 1900 and received his M.D. degree from Columbia University's College of Physicians and Surgeons in 1904. He then went into the clinical practice of general surgery for three years but soon turned to research and became associate director of the bacteriology division at the Hoagland Laboratory in Brooklyn. Although his time at the laboratory enabled him to study species of bacteria and their relationship to infectious diseases and was a precursor to his interest in immunology, much of his work was spent carrying out what he considered to be routine investigations. Eventually, Rufus Cole, director of the Rockefeller Institute hospital, became acquainted with Avery's research, which included work of general bacteriological interest, such as determining the optimum and limiting hydrogen-ion concentration for pneumococcus growth, developing a simple and rapid method for differentiating human and bovine streptococcus hemolyticus, and studying bacterial nutrition. Impressed with Avery's analytical capabilities, Cole asked Avery to join the institute hospital in 1913. Avery spent the remainder of his career there.

At the institute, Avery teamed up with A. Raymond Dochez in the study of the pneumococci (pneumonia) viruses, an area that was to take up a large part of his research efforts over the next several decades. Although Dochez eventually was to leave the institute, he and Avery maintained a lifelong scientific collaboration. During their early time together at the Rockefeller Institute, the two scientists further classified types of pneumococci found in patients and carriers, an effort which led to a better understanding of pneumococcus lung infection and of the causes, incidence, and distribution of lobar pneumonia. During the course of these immunological classification studies, Avery and Dochez discovered specific soluble substances of pneumococcus during growth in a cultured medium. Their subsequent identification of these substances in the blood and urine of lobar pneumonia patients showed that the substances were the result of a true metabolic process and not merely a result of disintegration during cell death.

Avery was convinced that the soluble specific substances present in pneumococci were somehow related to the immunological specificity of bacteria. In 1922, working with Michael Heidelberger and others at Rockefeller, Avery began to focus his studies on the chemical nature of these substances and eventually identified polysaccharides (complex carbohydrates) as the soluble specific substances of pneumococcus. As a result, Avery and colleagues were the first to show that carbohydrates were involved in immune reactions. His laboratory at Rockefeller went on to demonstrate that these substances, which come from the cell wall (specifically the capsular envelopes of the bacteria), can be differentiated into several different serological types by virtue of the various chemical compositions depending on the type of pneumococcus. For example, the polysaccharide in type 1 pneumococci is nitrogen-containing and partly composed of galacturonic acid. Both types 2 and 3 pneumococci contain nitrogen-free carbohydrates as their soluble substances, but the carbohydrates in type 2 are made up mainly of glucose and those of type 3 are composed of aldobionic acid units. Avery and Heidelberger went on to show that these various chemical substances account for bacterial specificity. This work opened up a new era in biochemical research, particularly in establishing the immunologic identity of the cell.

In addition to clarifying and systemizing efforts in bacteriology and immunology, Avery's work laid the foundation for modern immunological investigations in the area of antigens (parts of proteins and carbohydrates) as essential molecular markers that stimulate and, in large part, determine the success of immunological responses. Avery and his colleagues had found that specific anti-infection antibodies worked by neutralizing the bacterial capsular polysaccharide's ability to interfere with phagocytosis (the production of immune cells that recognize and attack foreign material). Eventually, Avery's discoveries led scientists to develop immunizations that worked by preventing an antigenic response from the capsular material. Avery also oversaw studies that showed similar immunological responses in *Klebsiella pneumonia* and *Hemophilus influenza*. These studies resulted in highly specific diagnostic tests and preparation of immunizing antigens and therapeutic sera. The culmination of Avery's work in this area was a paper he coauthored with Colin Munro MacLeod and Maclyn McCarty in 1944 entitled "Studies on the Chemical Nature of the Substance Inducing Transformation of Pneumococcal Types. Induction of Transformation by a Desoxyribonucleic Fraction Isolated from Pneumococcus Type III." In their article, which appeared in the *Journal of Experimental Medicine,* the scientists provided conclusive data that DNA is the molecular basis for transmitting genetic information in biological self-replication.

In 1931 Avery's focus turned to "transformation" in bacteria, building on the studies of microbiologist Frederick Griffith showing that viruses could transfer virulence. In 1928, Griffith first showed that heat-killed virulent pneumococci could make a nonvirulent strain become virulent

(produce disease). In 1932 Griffith stunned the scientific world when he announced that he had manipulated immunological specificity in pneumococci. At the time, Avery was on leave suffering from Grave's disease. He initially denounced Griffith's claim and cited inadequate experimental controls. But in 1931, after returning to work, Avery began to study transmissible hereditary changes in immunological specificity, which were confirmed by several scientists. His subsequent investigations produced one of the great milestones in biology.

In 1933 Avery's associate, James Alloway, had isolated a crude solution of the transforming agent. Immediately, the laboratory's focus turned on purifying this material. Working with type 3 capsulated pneumococcus, Avery eventually succeeded in isolating a highly purified solution of the transforming agent that could pass on the capsular polysaccharides' hereditary information to noncapsulated strains. As a result, the noncapsulated strains could now produce capsular polysaccharides, a trait continued in following generations. The substance responsible for the transfer of genetic information was DNA. These studies also were the first to alter hereditary material for treatment purposes.

Avery, however, remained cautious about the implications of the discovery, suspecting that yet another chemical component of DNA could be responsible for the phenomenon. But further work by McCarty and Moses Kunitz confirmed the findings. While some scientists, such as Peter Brian Medawar, hailed Avery's discovery as the first step out of the "dark ages" of genetics, others refused to give up the long-held notion that the protein was the basis of physical inheritance. The subsequent modeling of the DNA molecule by James Watson and Francis Crick led to an understanding of how DNA replicates, and demonstration of DNA's presence in all animals produced clear evidence of its essential role in heredity.

Avery also continued to work on other antigenic aspects of carbohydrates and the immune system. He was the first to create antibody-based treatments that were successful in protecting laboratory animals from infection, essentially by removing the protective capsular coat of the virulent cell. Collaborating with Dochez, he immunologically classified hemolytic (destructive to blood cells) streptococcus and identified many of the specific antigens at work. These efforts revealed that hemolytic streptococcus had many serological types. Eventually hemolytic streptococcus was identified as the infectious agent in scarlet and acute rheumatic fever and hemorrhagic nephritis (kidney disease). Avery's work was the foundation for the eventual discovery of effective antibiotics for hemolytic streptococcus.

Despite the fact that Avery guarded his personal life, some information is known about his interests outside of science. A musician, he played cornet with the New York Conservatory of Music Orchestra and organized his own band. He also painted water colors. An independent Republican, he was a commissioned captain in the U.S. Army Medical Corps during World War I, assigned to the Institute for Medical Research. He served on various advisory committees during World War II, including the U.S. Army Board for the Study and Control of Epidemic Disease.

A highly reserved individual, Avery preferred to be remembered by his scientific accomplishments. He was fondly remembered by many of his colleagues and former students and clearly recognized for his efforts in helping to solve the puzzle of heredity. His honors were many, including several honorary degrees, the Paul Ehrlich Gold Medal, and the Copley Medal of the Royal Society of London. He also was a member of the National Academy of Sciences and foreign member of the Royal Society of London. He continued to conduct research in laboratories at the Rockefeller Institute Hospital for several years after his retirement. Eventually, he moved to Nashville, Tennessee, in 1947. He died there on February 20, 1955.

Further Reading

Biographical Memoirs of Fellows of the Royal Society, Royal Society (London), Volume 2, 1956, pp. 34-47.

Dochez, A. R., "Oswald Theodore Avery," in *Biographical Memoirs,* Volume 32, National Academy of Sciences, 1958, pp. 31-48.

Gillispie, Charles Coulston, editor, *Dictionary of Scientific Biography,* Volume 1, Scribner's, 1970, pp. 342-343.

Magner, Lois N., *A History of the Life Sciences,* Marcel Dekker, 1979, pp. 452-454.

McGraw-Hill Modern Men of Science, McGraw-Hill, 1966, pp. 15-17. □

Avicenna

Avicenna (ca. 980-1037) was an Arabic physician and philosopher. He wove classical dicta into a rational, consistent system that dominated European medical thought from the late 12th to the 17th century.

Born in Afshana in the district of Bukhara, Avicenna, or Abu Ali al-Husain ibn Addullah ibn Sina, was the son of a government official. The family soon moved to the city of Bukhara, the capital of the province, and known throughout the Islamic world as a center of learning and culture. There Avicenna began his studies and by the age of 16 had mastered not only natural science and rudimentary metaphysics but also medical theory, having read, by his own account, all the books written on this subject. Not satisfied with merely a theoretical understanding of medicine, he began to treat the sick, obtaining empirical knowledge in this manner and also effecting remarkable cures.

The sultan of Bukhara appointed Avicenna as one of his physicians, who then had access to the sultan's vast library. By the time Avicenna was 18, he had read all the books. An early work written by Avicenna was an encyclopedia that included all branches of knowledge except mathematics; it ran to 20 volumes.

Avicenna had difficulty earning a livelihood after the sultan's death, and at the age of 22 he left Bukhara and wandered westward. At Jurjan, near the Caspian Sea, Avicenna lectured on logic and astronomy and wrote the first part of the *Canon,* his most significant medical work. He then moved to Ray (near modern Teheran), where he established a busy medical practice. There he is believed to have composed about 30 of his shorter works.

Physician to Rulers

When Ray was besieged, Avicenna fled to Hamadan, ruled by the emir Shams al-Daula. Avicenna became the emir's physician and confidant and was soon appointed to the office of vizier. Since his daylight hours were spent in attendance on the emir, Avicenna was forced to pursue his teaching and studying at night. Students would gather in his home and read the parts of his two great books, the *Shifa* and the *Canon,* already composed. He would dictate additional chapters and explain the principles underlying them to his pupils.

When Shams al-Daula died, Avicenna resigned his government office, went into hiding, and passed the time drafting a final, detailed outline of the *Shifa.* He sent a letter to the ruler of Isfahan, asking for a position in his government. When the new emir of Hamadan learned of this, he imprisoned Avicenna. While in prison Avicenna wrote several treatises. He longed to live in Isfahan, the jeweled city of central Persia, and a few months after his release from prison he, his brother, a pupil, and two slaves disguised themselves as religious ascetics and fled to Isfahan.

Avicenna spent his final years in the service of the ruler of the city, Ala al-Daula, whom he advised on scientific and literary matters and accompanied on military campaigns. An unexpected dividend of these excursions in the field was the completion of Avicenna's chapter of the *Shifa* dealing with botany and zoology.

Once, while Avicenna was ill, his slaves gave him an overdose of opium, ransacked his possessions, and escaped. Avicenna never fully recovered from this experience. In his last days he is said to have distributed alms to the poor, freed his slaves, and listened to readings from the Koran. He died during June 1037 and was buried at Hamadan.

Avicenna's Works

Although one Islamic bibliographer lists only 21 major and 24 minor works of Avicenna, other titles swell the total to at least 99 treatises dealing with philosophy, medicine, geometry, astronomy, theology, philology, and art. Young students in the Arab world still memorize his poems. The most significant of his scientific writings are the book on healing, *Kitab al Shifa,* a philosophical encyclopedia based on the Aristotelian tradition as modified by Moslem theology and Neoplatonic influences; and *Al-Qanun fi al Tibb,* or the *Canon,* which represents Avicenna's codification of Greco-Arabic medical thought.

If the *Shifa* exerted less influence in the West than did the *Canon,* this fact is explained partly by the difficulty of the subject matter and partly by the condition in which it reached Western scholars. When the *Shifa* was first translated into Latin during the 12th century, it was fragmented. The translators omitted the section on mathematics, presented only a small part of the chapters on physics and logic, and included a section on astronomy apparently written by someone else. Later translators were influenced by the efforts of their predecessors, and although parts of the *Shifa* originally overlooked or suppressed were translated subsequently, the composite nature of the work was not fully understood in the West until comparatively recently.

The *Canon,* in contrast, was rendered completely into Latin by one man, the great 12th-century translator of Arabic scientific works, Gerard of Cremona. The vast medical encyclopedia is divided into five books dealing with the theory of medicine, the simpler drugs, special pathology and therapeutics, general diseases, and pharmacopoeia.

Although much material in the second and fifth books was derived from the writings of Dioscurides, most data in the remainder of the *Canon* can be traced to three essential sources. Avicenna drew on the writings in the *Hippocratic Corpus* for fundamental doctrines. His sources for much of the anatomy and physiology were the writings of Galen. Avicenna's final authority was usually Aristotle. That Avicenna introduced the four causes of the peripatetic system into medical theory is indicative of adherence to Aristotelian principles, as is the fact that the entire *Canon* is arranged according to Aristotelian dialectic.

The synergistic quality of the *Canon* was certainly a major factor contributing to its success, and the work soon was regarded as superior even to its sources. Avicenna's

book superseded the earlier medical encyclopedias and became the most important single work on medicine in the Western world. It remained a required text in certain European medical schools until the mid-17th century, and in certain Asian countries it is influential even today.

Further Reading

Avicenna's brief autobiography, "Life of a Philosopher," completed by his student al-Juzjani, is in A. J. Arberry, *Aspects of Islamic Civilization as Depicted in the Original Texts* (1964). Soheil M. Afnan, *Avicenna: His Life and Works* (1958), covers all aspects of Avicenna's work and thought. Max Meyerhof's article, "Science and Medicine," in Sir Thomas Arnold and Alfred Guillaume, eds., *The Legacy of Islam* (1931), contains a brief biographical sketch of Avicenna. For more specialized studies see E. G. Browne, *Arabian Medicine* (1921); George Sarton, *Introduction to the History of Science,* vol. 1: *From Homer to Omar Khayyam* (1927); A. J. Arberry, *Avicenna on Theology* (1951); F. Rahman, *Avicenna's Psychology* (1952); Henry Corbin, *Avicenna and the Visionary Recital* (1960); and Seyyed Hossein Nasr, *An Introduction to Islamic Cosmological Doctrines* (1964) and *Three Muslim Sages: Avicenna, Suhrawardi, Ibn Arabi* (1964).

Additional Sources

Avicenna, 980-1037, *Avicenna on theology,* Westport, Conn.: Hyperion Press, 1979.

Afnan, Soheil Muhsin, *Avicenna, his life and works,* Westport, Conn.: Greenwood Press, 1980, 1958.

Goodman, Lenn Evan, *Avicenna,* London; New York: Routledge, 1992.

Avicenna, 980-1037, *The life of Ibn Sina; a critical edition and annotated translation,* Albany, State University of New York Press, 1974. □

Gen. Manuel Ávila Camacho

Gen. Manuel Ávila Camacho (1897-1955) was president of Mexico from 1940 to 1946. His administration is regarded as the transition from the agrarian to the industrial revolution in Mexico.

Manuel Ávila Camacho was born in Tezuitlán, in the state of Puebla. He began his military career when he entered the Constitutionalist forces as a junior officer in 1914. During the 1920s he served in various military capacities in Sonora, Michoacán, and Colima, where he directed operations against the *Cristeros* (rebels supporting the Church) as chief of the military zone. He became undersecretary of war for President Abelardo Rodriguez in 1933-1934 and secretary of defense under President Lázaro Cárdenas in 1939.

The official presidential candidate in 1940, Ávila Camacho triumphed over Gen. Juan Andreu Almazán in an election marred by violent clashes. There was little popular enthusiasm for the new president, who was not well known and heavy in appearance and speech. It was his task to consolidate the gains and heal the divisions resulting from Cárdenas's presidency, and so he called for unity, adjustment, and moderation.

Ávila Camacho slowed down agrarian reform and emphasized irrigation and increased productivity. In terms of budget there was a shift from social to economic expenditures. He reached an equitable settlement with the U.S. government for the expropriated petroleum fields. Labor leadership passed into more conservative hands, and the movement was told that the administration intended to govern for all the people and not for a special class. During Ávila Camacho's administration the Social Security Institute was established, and a dramatic national campaign ("Each One Teach One") against illiteracy was undertaken. The army was officially taken out of politics with the elimination of the military sector of the official party.

However, foreign affairs and specifically World War II dictated the course of Mexico during this period. In a radical departure from Mexico's traditional posture, Ávila Camacho aligned his nation with the United States. For Mexico it meant military and technical assistance and loans for refurbishing its transportation system and buying urgently needed machinery for industry and mining. After Pearl Harbor, Mexico severed diplomatic relations with the Axis powers and in May 1942 declared war. Despite inflation and corruption, the war significantly aided the development of the Mexican economy.

In April 1943 Ávila Camacho and President Franklin Roosevelt conferred in Monterrey on the joint war effort, beginning a pattern of visit exchanges between the executives of the two nations. At the end of his term, Ávila Camacho peacefully transferred the presidential power to his secretary of the interior, Miguel Alemán, who accelerated the industrial development of Mexico begun during his predecessor's term.

Ávila Camacho dropped out of public view after his presidency. He spent much of his time at his property La Herradura in the Federal District, where he died on Oct. 13, 1955.

Further Reading

Since there is no adequate biographical study of Ávila Camacho, one must turn to general studies of Mexico's war and postwar development: Sanford A. Mosk, *Industrial Revolution in Mexico* (1950); Frank Tannenbaum, *Mexico: The Struggle for Peace and Bread* (1950); Howard F. Cline, *Mexico: Revolution to Evolution, 1940-1960* (1962); and Frank Brandenburg, *The Making of Modern Mexico* (1964). There is a brief analysis of Ávila Camacho in Henry B. Parkes, *A History of Mexico* (1938; rev. ed. 1960), and in such standard textbooks as Hubert Herring, *A History of Latin America* (1955; 3d ed. 1968), and Helen Miller Bailey and Abraham P. Nasatir, *Latin America: The Development of Its Civilization* (1960; 2d ed. 1968). □

Lorenzo Romano Amedeo Carlo Avogadro

The Italian physicist and chemist Lorenzo Romano Amedeo Carlo Avogadro, Conte di Quaregna e di Cerreto (1776-1856), authored the hypothesis known as Avogadro's law, which ultimately clarified the foundations of molecular chemistry and physics.

B orn in Turin on Aug. 9, 1776, Amedeo Avogadro came from an ancient legal family, whose name derived from the Latin *de advocatis* (concerning the law). He took a degree in philosophy in 1789, a baccalaureate in jurisprudence in 1792, and a doctorate in ecclesiastical law a few years later.

After several years of legal experience, Avogadro found his true avocation in the study of the physical sciences. Though largely self-taught, he achieved an extensive knowledge of the then-expanding studies of matter in the gaseous state. In 1809 he was appointed professor of physics in the Royal College at Vercelli. Up to that time his only scientific paper had concerned a topic in the new field of electricity.

His Great Memoir

In July 1811 Avogadro published his memoir in the Paris *Journal de physique*. He began by drawing attention to the discovery by the French chemist Joseph Louis Gay-Lussac that when gases combine they do so in simple integral proportions by volume. Gay-Lussac supplied the experimental evidence to generalize this property of volume ratios for all gases; that is, two volumes of ammonia (NH_3) are composed of one volume of nitrogen and three volumes of hydrogen, and so forth for many similar cases of simple, integral proportions.

On the basis of this type of evidence, Avogadro drew the logical conclusion that the number of "integrant molecules" in all gases is always the same for equal volumes. He also concluded that the ratios of the masses of the molecules are the same as those of the densities of the different gases at equal temperature and pressure and that the relative number of molecules in a given compound is given at once by the ratio of volumes of the gases that form it.

In a supplementary paper sent to the *Journal de physique* in 1814, Avogadro deduced the correct formulas for $COCl_2$, H_2S, and CO_2, and from postulating an analogy between carbon and silicon he asserted the correct composition of silica, SiO_2. From available data he calculated approximately correct atomic weights for carbon, chlorine, and sulfur. He contributed massively to an understanding of the properties and reactions of the new and "changerous" element fluorine. He published these and related findings in a four-volume work entitled *Fisica de' corpi ponderabili, ossia trattato della constituzione generale de' corpi* (1837-1841). This book influenced Michael Faraday's great career of discovery.

The simplicity and clarity of Avogadro's views, though cited by leading scientists, such as André Marie Ampère, were not compelling to the majority of contemporary chemists. This lack of interest was due in part to the novelty of the atomic theories which had been presented to the world a few years before by John Dalton; furthermore, the methodological temper of the times, deeply experimentalistic and empirical, prevented careful consideration of a purely logical inference from chemical facts unsupported by masses of laboratory data.

Another confusing aspect of the Avogadro memoir was the use of the ambiguous term "molecule." Not only did this conflict with the vigorous Newtonian atomism of the English and French schools, but it implied a sequence of chemical reactions for which no decisive evidence was forthcoming. Dalton, for example, had postulated that water was formed by the simple addition of the element hydrogen to the element oxygen, or $H + O \rightarrow HO$, whereas the correct process implicit in Avogadro's hypothesis was $2H_2 + O_2$ (in the molecular form) $\rightarrow 2H_2O$.

Other Activities

When the first Italian chair in mathematical physics was established at the University of Turin in 1820, Avogadro received the professorship. Two years later, because of the turmoil gripping the country, the chair was suppressed. Avogadro returned to his position in 1834 and held it until his retirement in 1850. He married Donna Felicita Mazzi, by whom he had six sons. Two sons rose to positions of distinction: Luigi, who became general of the Italian army, and Felici, who became president of the Court of Appeal.

Avogadro also served Italy as a competent and honest civil servant. He held positions in the National Bureau of Statistics, helped to establish a national meteorological service, and in 1848 became a member of the Superior Council on Public Instruction. Modest and retiring, he was indifferent to honors and scrupulously avoided those public struggles for priority which were a characteristic of Continental scientific society in the mid-19th century.

Some indication of the fundamental nature of Avogadro's law may be seen in the fact that when modern thermodynamic theory was established at the end of the 19th century, the great German scientist and eventual Nobel laureate Walter Nernst entitled his textbook *Theoretical Chemistry from the Standpoint of Avogadro's Rule and Thermodynamics.*

Further Reading

A discussion of Avogadro's life and work appears in J. R. Partington, *A History of Chemistry*, vol. 4 (1964). See also Sir William Augustus Tilden, *Famous Chemists: The Men and Their Work* (1921); Eduard Farber, *The Evolution of Chemistry: A History of Its Ideas, Methods and Materials* (1952; 2d ed. 1969); Henry M. Leicester and Herbert S. Klickstein, eds., *A Source Book in Chemistry, 1400-1900* (1952); and Isaac Asimov, *A Short History of Chemistry: An Introduction to the Ideas and Concepts of Chemistry* (1965).

Additional Sources

Morselli, Mario, *Amedeo Avogadro, a scientific biography*, Dordrecht; Boston: D. Reidel Pub. Co.; Hingham, MA: Sold and distributed in the U.S.A. and Canada by Kluwer Academic Publishers, 1984. □

Chief Obafemi Awolowo

Chief Obafemi Awolowo (1909-1987) was a Nigerian nationalist, a political leader, and a principal participant in the struggle for Nigerian independence.

Obafemi Awolowo was born in Ikenné, Western State, Nigeria, on March 6, 1909. He received his early education in the mission schools of Ikenné, Abeokuta, and Ibadan. Often he worked at odd jobs to raise money for tuition fees, and his entrepreneurial spirit continued to express itself in the various careers which he subsequently sampled: journalist, teacher, clerk, moneylender, taxidriver, produce broker. His organizational and political inclinations became evident as he moved to high-level positions in the Nigerian Motor Transport Union, the Nigerian Produce Traders' Association, the Trades Union Congress of Nigeria, and the Nigerian Youth Movement, of which he became Western Provincial secretary.

Despite his interest in business ventures, Awolowo wanted to continue his formal education. In 1944 he completed a University of London correspondence course for the bachelor of commerce degree. His greatest ambition, however, was to study law, which he undertook in London from 1944 to 1946, when he was called to the bar. Returning to Nigeria in 1947, he developed a thriving practice as a barrister in Ibadan.

Political Career

During his residence in London, Awolowo moved to a position of prominence in the struggle for Nigerian independence. In 1945 he wrote his first book, *Path to Nigerian Freedom,* in which he was highly critical of British policies of indirect administration and called for rapid moves toward self-government and Africanization of administrative posts in Nigeria. He also expressed his belief that federalism was the form of government best suited to the diverse populations of Nigeria, a position to which he consistently adhered. Also in 1945 in London, he helped found the Egbe Omo Oduduwa (Society of the Descendants of Oduduwa, the mythical ancestor of the Yoruba-speaking peoples), an organization devoted to the study and preservation of Yoruba culture.

In 1950 Awolowo founded and organized the Action Group political party in Western Nigeria to participate in the Western Regional elections of 1951. The Action Group's platform called for immediate termination of British rule in Nigeria and for development of various public welfare programs, including universal primary education, increase of

health services in rural areas, diversification of the Western Regional economy, and democratization of local governments. The Action Group won a majority, and in 1952 Awolowo as president of the Action Group became leader of the party in power in Western Nigeria. In 1954 he became the first premier of the Western Region, on which occasion he was awarded an honorary chieftaincy. During his tenure as leader and premier, he held the regional ministerial portfolios of local government, finance, and economic planning. He was also chairman of the Regional Economic Planning Commission.

In 1959, confident of an Action Group victory in the federal elections, Awolowo resigned the premiership to stand for election to the federal House of Representatives. About that time he published his second book, *Awo: An Autobiography of Chief Obafemi Awolowo,* in which he once more endorsed federalism as the most appropriate form of government for Nigeria. He also outlined the successful history of the Action Group and was optimistic of Nigerian independence.

Power Struggle

However, the 1959 elections were to become an important turning point in Awolowo's career, for the Action Group was decisively defeated, and Awolowo found himself leader of the opposition in the Federal House of Representatives, while the deputy leader of the Action Group, Chief S. L. Akintola, remained premier of the Western Region. This situation led to a power struggle within the party which ultimately erupted in 1962 in disturbances in the Western Region House of Assembly. The federal government intervened and suspended the regional constitution. When normal government was restored, the Akintola faction had won; Akintola and his followers withdrew from the Action Group to form the Nigerian National Democratic party, which governed Western Nigeria until 1966.

In 1963 Awolowo was found guilty of conspiring to overthrow the government of Nigeria and was sentenced to ten years of imprisonment. In 1966, however, an attempted coup d'etat led to the suspension of the Nigerian federal constitution and the empowerment of a military government which promised a new constitution. That year, while in prison, Awolowo wrote *Thoughts on the Nigerian Constitution,* in which he argued for the retention of a federal form of government composed of 18 states. Later, in 1966, he was released from prison and the following year was invited to join the Federal Military Government as federal commissioner of finance and as vice chairman of the Federal Executive Council.

In 1968 Awolowo published his fourth book, *The People's Republic,* calling for federalism, democracy, and socialism as the necessary elements in a new constitution which would lead to the development of a stable and prosperous Nigeria. Although he praised the Federal Military Government for creating a 12-state federal system in 1967, he predicted further political difficulties because these states had not been based on ethnic and linguistic affinities.

Awolowo continued to serve the government as commisioner of finance and vice chairman of the Federal Executive Council throughout the years of Nigeria's civil war with Biafra (1967-1970). In his 1970 book, *The Strategy and Tactics of the People''s Republic of Nigeria,* he implied a position which he would state more firmly in subsequent years: that the government's post-war spending should be devoted to development rather than to the military. He resigned in 1971 to protest the government's continuation of military rule, and in 1975, following the overthrow of the Gowon government, issued a press release questioning the country's military spending. In 1979 and 1983 he ran for president as the candidate for the Unity Party of Nigeria, losing to Shehu Shagari. Awolowo returned to private life upon the overthrow of the Shagari government in December 1983. He died in Ikenné on May 9, 1987.

Further Reading

The most thorough treatment of Awolowo's life is his *Awo: An Autobiography of Chief Obafemi Awolowo* (1960). An excellent examination of the growth of the Action Group is in Richard L. Sklar, *Nigerian Political Parties: Power in an Emergent African Nation* (1963).

Additional Sources

Adekson, J. Bayo, *Nigeria in Search of a Stable Civil-Military System* (Westview Press, 1981).
Metz, Helen Chapin, ed., *Nigeria: A Country Study* (Federal Research Division, 1992).
New York *Times* (May 11, 1987). □

Emanuel Ax

Emanuel Ax (born 1949), American pianist, winner of the first Artur Rubinstein International Piano Competition, became a major contemporary interpreter of the traditional piano literature who was also willing to explore serious new compositions for the piano.

Emanuel Ax was born in Lwow, eastern Poland in 1949. His father, a coach at the Lwow Opera House, was the pianist's first teacher. Ax commenced his study of the piano when he was seven years old. One year later his family moved to Warsaw, and soon after, having secured exit visas, they emigrated to Winnipeg, Canada, where they had relatives. In 1961, after a year and a half in Canada, the family moved once more, this time to New York City. Emanuel Ax, then 11 years old, enrolled in the Pre-College Division at Juilliard. His only formal piano teacher at Juilliard was Mieczslaw Munz, with whom he studied for four years, eventually winning the Young Concert Artists' Michaels Award, among other honors. He majored in French at Columbia University.

Musical Career

In 1969, Ax toured Latin America. In 1970, he entered the Chopin contest in Warsaw, and came in seventh place. Continuing difficulties during this phase of his career included placing third in the Viānna da Motta competition in Lisbon in 1971 and undistinguished recognition in the Queen Elizabeth Contest in Brussels in 1972. Despite this, Ax persisted and achieved a decisive breakthrough at the first Artur Rubinstein International Piano Competition in 1974.

Rubinstein cultivated his young protegé, counseling him, occasionally soliciting his advice, and in general treating him as a fellow artist. In 1979, Ax won the prestigious Avery Fisher Prize.

Ax became one of the most sought-after concert performers of this period. He often played chamber music at summer events in Aspen, Colorado, and maintained an extremely active schedule, giving as many as 90 concerts a year. He performed with virtually every major orchestra in eastern and western Europe, the United States, Latin America, and Asia. He has compiled an extensive and essential contemporary discography. In addition to his solo recordings, he has numerous releases with cellist Yo-Yo Ma, with whom Ax claimed to have a special musical rapport over the past 20 years. He has also won Grammy Awards.

Ax's expertise was concentrated on the standard piano literature, the Romantic and Classical repertoire cultivated by such pianists as Artur Rubinstein, among others. Ax did not limit himself exclusively to this piano literature, but it was his mainstay. In 1984, he performed Hans Werner Henze's *Tristan* (1974) with the composer conducting the New York Philharmonic. Ax explored current literature to uncover little known works he could present to the listening public, but he required that they be accessible to his particular expertise and audience. More characteristically perhaps, he presented compositions from the Romantic and Classical periods, for example the *Années de Pèlerinage* of Liszt, and he had an intellectual's grasp, as well as an artist's, of the details in the standard piano repertoire.

When learning a new composition, he focused his attention not exclusively upon the score, but read the scholarly secondary source literature including music criticism, biography, and history. At the same time, he was moving away from the keyboard, thus bringing a combined technical acumen and intuitive grasp to the individual work. Ax felt his primary responsibility to be communication with his audience, providing them with a serious experience that would enliven their grasp of the music, its composer, and the tradition in which both could be found.

Further Reading

Ax is discussed briefly in *Baker's Biographical Dictionary,* 6th ed. (1978). His concerts and recordings have been reviewed in all major newspapers and music journals. The pianist himself is the subject of the following articles: "Who wants to be another Horowitz?" S. Clark, *Village Voice* 23 (March 20, 1978); "Emanuel Ax," interview with A. Kozinn, *Fugue* 4 (November 1979); "Time Off with Emanuel Ax," interview with L.P. Yost, *Clavier* 19 (1980); "Casual Conversation with a Touring Virtuoso," Paul Hertelendy, *Contemporary Keyboard* (February 1980); "An Interview with Emanuel Ax," D. Manildi, *American Record* 45 (January-February 1982); "Emanuel Ax Goes 20th Century," Allan Kozinn, *Keynote* (July 1984); "Pianist Emanuel Ax: An Adventurous Virtuoso," Karen Monson, *Ovation* (April 1985). Other articles on Ax include: "Classical Keeping Score,"*Billboard* (February 24, 1996) and "Ax & Ma: Duo Extraordinary,"*Musical America* (May 1990). □

Alfred Jules Ayer

Alfred Jules Ayer (1910-1989) was a leading philosopher of the 20th century who rigorously attacked metaphysics. His major work was *Language, Truth and Logic*.

Alfred Jules Ayer was born in 1910. He was educated at Eton and Oxford University. After his graduation from Oxford, he studied at the University of Vienna, concentrating on the philosophy of Logical Positivism. From 1933 to 1940 he was lecturer in philosophy at Christ Church (College), Oxford. During World War II he served in the Welsh Guards and was also engaged in military intelligence. In 1945, he returned to Oxford where he became a fellow and Dean of Wadham College. In the following year, he became Grote Professor of the Philosophy of Mind and Logic at University College, London. In 1959, he returned to Oxford, where he became Wykeham Professor of Logic, a position he held until his retirement in 1978. He was elected a fellow of the British Academy in 1952 and honorary fellow of Wadham College, Oxford, in 1957. Among his many awards, Ayer received an honorary doctorate from Brussels University in 1962 and was knighted in 1970. He was also an honorary member of the American Academy of Arts and Sciences and chevalier of the Legion d'Honneur.

Contributions to Philosophy

Ayer's books include: *Bertrand Russell: Philosopher of the Century* (Contribution), 1967; *British Empirical Philosophers* (editor with Raymond Winch), (1952); *The Central Questions of Philosophy* (1973); *The Concept of a Person* (1963); *The Foundations of Empirical Knowledge* (1940); *Freedom and Morality and Other Essays* (1984); *Hume* (1980); *Language, Truth and Logic* (1956); *Logical Positivism* (editor), (1960); *Metaphysics and Common Sense* (1970); *The Origins of Pragmatism: Studies in the Philosophy of Charles Sanders Peirce and William James* (1968); *Philosophical Essays* (1954); *Philosophy in the Twentieth Century* (1982); *Probability and Evidence* (1972); *The Problem of Knowledge* (1956); *The Revolution in Philosophy* (Contribution), (1956); and *Russell and Moore; The Analytical Heritage* (1971).

Language, Truth and Logic is one of Ayer's most important books and may be considered as one of the most influential philosophical works of the 20th century. In the second edition (1946), Ayer clarified some of his ideas and replied to his critics, but essentially his philosophical position remained the same. He called his philosophy "logical empiricism," a variation of logical positivism, the philosophical orientation he learned in Vienna. He was largely influenced by the thought of the 20th century philosophers Bertrand Russell and Ludwig Wittgenstein and by the earlier empiricism of George Berkeley and David Hume.

The book is a milestone in the development of philosophical thought in the 20th century. The implications of Ayer's "logical empiricism" would be felt by many branches of the discipline of philosophy, especially metaphysics, ethics, and philosophy of religion, and also logic, mathematics, and the philosophy of science. Although Ayer acknowledged the influences upon his philosophical perspective, he remained an independent thinker, accepting no position uncritically.

Ayer asserted that the criterion of meaning is found in the "verification principle": "We say that a sentence is factually significant to any given person if, and only if, he knows how to verify the proposition which it purports to express—that is, if he knows what observations would lead him, under certain conditions, to accept the proposition as being true, or reject it as being false." (*Language, Truth and Logic*). The a priori statements of logic and mathematics do not claim to provide factual content. Those statements can be said to be true only because of the conventions which govern the use of the symbols that make up the statements.

Ayer was known in the 20th century for his rigorous attack on metaphysics and as the main representative of the British empirical tradition. Genuine statements are either logical or empirical. Metaphysical statements do not purport to express either logical truths or empirical hypotheses. For that reason, metaphysical statements are pseudo-statements and do not have any meaning. The metaphysician

had been tied to the attempt to construct a deductive system of the universe from "first principles." These first principles, Ayer argued, can never be derived from experience. They are merely hypotheses. As a priori principles, they are hypotheses only, and therefore are tautologies and *not* certain empirical knowledge.

Theology, as a special branch of metaphysics which attempts to gain knowledge that transcends the limits of experience (for example, the affirmation of the existence of God) is not only false but it too has no meaning. Value statements in ethics and aesthetics are also meaningless, not genuine statements, and can be understood as emotive utterances of an imperative character.

Ayer therefore discovered for philosophy a function in the 20th century. Once the traditional tasks of philosophy have been discarded, philosophy can be seen as an intellectual discipline which endeavors to clarify the problems of science. Philosophy is, therefore, finally identical with the logic of science.

In *Language, Truth and Logic* Ayer argued that it is the task of the philosopher to give a correct definition of material things in terms of sensation. The philosopher does not deal with the properties of things in the world, but only with the way we speak of them. The propositions of philosophy are not factual, but linguistic in character: "(Propositions) ... do not describe the behavior of physical, or even mental, objects; they express definitions, or the factual consequences of definitions."

In the second edition of *Language, Truth and Logic*, Ayer provided an extended reworking of his notion of the verification principle. It was this principle which was chiefly criticized by the philosophical commentators. It would seem that the verification principle, as formulated by Ayer, is a kind of meaningless metaphysical statement that the verification principle itself was supposed to prohibit.

In his later works, Ayer proceeded boldly, and with wisdom and clarity, to deal with the major problems that have confronted and confounded other 20th century philosophers: such problems as perception, induction, knowledge, meaning, truth, value theory, other minds, the mind-body dichotomy, personal identity, and intention. Ayer was always an original and bold thinker who, in later life, espoused a more selective assessment of metaphysics due to the works of his trusted colleagues. His views on death, dying and the afterlife were slightly altered after briefly dying for four minutes and subsequently being revived. His death on June 27, 1989 marked the end of the second golden age of British philosophy.

Further Reading

Ayer provided an autobiographical volume which is filled with trenchant philosophical insights about the role of the philosopher in the 20th century; A. J. Ayer, *Part of My Life: The Memoirs of a Philosopher* (1977). Ayer was a popular broadcaster for the British Broadcasting Company (BBC). One of the most exciting broadcasts was in the form of a debate with a Jesuit Christian philosopher; see "Logical Positivism—A Debate" delivered on the BBC June 13, 1949, with A. J. Ayer and F. C. Copleston, published in P. Edwards and A. Pap (editors),

A *Modern Introduction to Philosophy* (1957). Among the many commentators of A. J. Ayer's philosophical perspective, the following are helpful: Carl G. Hempel, *Aspects of Scientific Explanation* (1965); Viktor Kraft, *The Vienna Circle: The Origin of Neo-Positivism* (1969); John Wisdom, "Note on the New Edition of Professor Ayer's *Language, Truth and Logic,*" reprinted in Wisdom's *Philosophy and Pyscho-analysis* (Oxford, 1953); H. H. Price, "Critical Notice of A. J. Ayer's *The Foundation of Empirical Knowledge,*" in *Mind* (1941); H. H. Price, "Discussion: Professor Ayer's Essays," in *Philosophical Quarterly* (1955); D. J. O'Connor, "Some Consequences of Professor A. J. Ayer's Verification Principle," in *Analysis* (1949-1950); W. V. O. Quine, "Two Dogmas of Empiricism," in *From a Logical Point of View* (1953).

Reflections on Ayer's legacy can be found in "The Logical End of an Empire,"*Economist* (July 8, 1989) and "Logic in High Gear,"*Spectator* (July 8, 1989). □

Patricio Aylwin Azócar

A leader of the Chilean Christian Democratic Party for over 40 years, Patricio Aylwin Azócar (born 1918) was elected president of Chile in 1989. Strongly committed to social and economic justice, he strove to attain those goals in an environment of freedom and economic growth.

Patricio Aylwin Azócar was born in Viña del Mar, Chile, on November 26, 1918. Eldest son of Miguel Aylwin Gajardo, an eminent lawyer who served as president of Chile's supreme court, and Laura Azócar, Patricio Aylwin was raised in a family which participated intensely in Chilean social and political life. His brother, Andrés Aylwin, became a prominent human rights advocate and congressman; Arturo, another brother, also a skilled lawyer, served in the comptroller general's office in 1990.

Tuberculosis forced Aylwin's father to move the family to the Valley of Elqui in northern Chile when Patricio was less than a year old; the family returned to Valparaiso with his father's recovery. A stint in the judiciary in Valdivia and then a move to Santiago brought the family back to the nation's capital. They settled in a pleasant San Bernardo neighborhood. Patricio attended public school, distinguished himself in studies and such extracurricular activities as student politics, and meditated the lessons of an uncle, Guillermo Azócar, a socialist senator in the Chilean congress. Aylwin credited his uncle with stimulating his concern for "social justice," a theme which would dominate his public career and his presidency.

Aylwin finished his secondary studies at the Internado Nacional Barros Arana and entered law school at the University of Chile in 1936. Classmate of a group of students who would become prominent Socialist and Radical Party politicians in the years to come—Eugenio Velasco, Clodomiro Almedya, Raul Ampuero, Felipe Herrera, Enrique Silva Cimma—Aylwin found himself also influenced by members of the Juventud de Acción Católica, under the spiritual guidance of Father Alberto Hurtado. This

influence would push Aylwin into association with Eduardo Frei, Radomiro Tomic, Bernardo Leighton, and other founders of the Falange Nacional—the origins of the Chilean Christian Democratic Party to which Aylwin would dedicate much of his life. In law school Aylwin served on student-faculty committees considering university reforms, stimulated student forums, and emerged as one of the leaders of his student generation.

In 1943 Aylwin received his law degree and in 1946 he was appointed professor of administrative law at the University of Chile. By this time he had developed his writing and rhetorical skills, publishing in student and politico-religious magazines. In 1945 he joined the Falange Nacional, a group dominated by ex-members of the Conservative Party concerned with issues of social justice and the search for a Christian alternative to capitalism and Marxism. An article published in the magazine *Política Y Espiritu* called "The Truth about the Coal," in which he defended workers against repressive measures taken by the government, drew the attention of Leonor Oyarzún Ivanovic, who met Aylwin in 1947. They were married less than a year later, in October 1948, and raised a family of five children, all of whom shared in Aylwin's political career to some degree.

Early Political Career

Aylwin is counted among the founding generation of Chilean Christian Democracy. He served as the party vice president from 1948 to 1950 and had already lost two elections by 1951—one for city council and another for congress. In 1951 Aylwin was elected president of the

Christian Democratic Party, a post he would hold repeatedly in the years to come, including the years 1965-1967 and 1987-1989, the latter during the tense transition from authoritarian to elected government in Chile.

In 1964 Christian Democrat Eduardo Frei was elected president of Chile and proclaimed his intention to carry out a "peaceful revolution." This included agrarian reform, tax reform, and encouragement of labor unionization and community organization among the urban poor. Patricio Aylwin, as senator for the provinces of Curicó, Talca, Linares, and Maule, became President Frei's staunchest ally against both the opposition from the political right and the impatience of the political left. Within the Christian Democratic Party, Aylwin also supported Frei against critics who desired a faster, more intense process of change.

Aylwin reiterated his support for Frei and the government's program frequently, coming always back to a basic theme which would reappear in the first year of his own presidency (1990): "We are carrying out an experiment, perhaps unique in this world, of pursuing at the same time social justice and economic development within the context of freedom and constrained by the fight to control inflation." Aylwin's efforts could not prevent the eventual splintering of the Christian Democratic Party nor its loss in the 1970 elections; he remained nonetheless a loyal party leader and supporter of President Frei, committed to peaceful social reform and democratic politics.

In Opposition to the Left and then the Right

When a leftist coalition, the Popular Unity Government, headed by President Salvador Allende, succeeded the Frei government, Aylwin became a vocal and effective leader of the opposition. The radical political and social reforms introduced by the Allende administration polarized Chilean politics and resulted in economic destabilization. As the political crisis came to a head, Aylwin engaged in negotiations with President Allende on behalf of the Christian Democratic Party, but was unable to arrive at a satisfactory resolution. Aylwin criticized the Allende government for not respecting the basic norms of democratic politics and noted that compromise was impossible "when official spokespersons characterize the opposition as 'enemies of the people' who must be 'crushed and destroyed.'" By July-August 1973 Aylwin emphasized that the "institutional stability of the republic was! gravely threatened."

On September 11, 1973, a military coup ended the Allende government. Aylwin initially called upon the Chilean people and his party to collaborate with the military government, believing it to be temporary, but soon became a vocal opponent of the brutal dictatorship of Augusto Pinochet that would endure almost 17 years.

Aylwin, as president of the Christian Democratic Party until 1976, gradually moved the party to open opposition against the military regime. In 1978 he formed part of the "Group for Constitutional Studies," which attempted to develop a political system to replace the dictatorship. He campaigned actively against the 1980 constitution imposed

in a plebiscite orchestrated by Pinochet, continuing this opposition until the late 1980s.

In 1984 Aylwin delivered a speech in which he declared: "The Constitution [of 1980] did not have in its origins the basic requisites for legitimacy and seeks to institutionalize an antidemocratic system." However, with the Chilean opposition unable to overthrow the Pinochet government, Aylwin would eventually be forced to abide by the rules set down by General Pinochet. In 1988, though, a plebiscite surprisingly prevented Pinochet from ruling eight more years. As a result, an election was set up in 1989 under the terms of the 1980 constitution, and Aylwin was elected president of Chile.

Aylwin had taken a key leadership role in constructing a broad coalition of parties and movements to defeat the Pinochet regime in the October 1988 plebiscite. As principal spokesperson for the "Concertation For No" he won praise and enhanced his prestige as a skilled, dedicated, sincere, and moderate politician. This made him the obvious compromise candidate of the "Concertation of Parties for Democracy" in the December 1989 elections—which he won by a 55 percent majority.

The Presidency

Aylwin took office on March 11, 1990, presiding over a coalition of 17 parties ranging from his own Christian Democrats, Socialists, and Radicals to small esoteric parties such as the Humanists. President Aylwin faced the practically impossible task of meeting the pent-up demand for social and economic improvements of the poorest of Chileans while sustaining economic growth. In addition, he inherited the legacy of human rights abuses, mass graves, and other aberrations of the military regime in a system in which the military still exercised considerable legal and physical force. Aylwin and his supporters declared that he would be "President of all Chileans," that he sought "truth and reconciliation," and that economic policy would seek gradually to improve the plight of the poor and maintain investment incentives to guarantee growth. In his first two months in the presidency Aylwin sent 28 proposed laws to the newly-opened congress, and others followed.

In 1991, the Organization of American States (OAS) held its annual meeting in Santiago in recognition of Chile's return to democracy. At that meeting, the OAS passed a resolution to defend democracy if it was threatened in any member county. Political instability and the crises in Haiti and Peru were discussed in White House meetings between the U.S. President George Bush and Aylwin. They agreed that restoring constitutional processes in Haiti and Peru was important for the democratic consolidation throughout the hemisphere.

President Aylwin was the first Chilean leader to make a state visit to the United States in 30 years. During his 1992 visit, President Bush cited Chile's transition to democracy and welcomed closer relations between the two countries. President Aylwin said, "We are not asking for help but for understanding and cooperation."

In 1993, the Chilean judicial system convicted the last two fugitives from justice in the case of Orlando Letelier, a former Chilean foreign minister who was assassinated in Washington, D.C. in 1976. Letelier and his American aide, Ronni Moffitt, were killed by a bomb planted in their car as they drove through Washington. In November of 1980, a U.S. court determined that the government of General Pinochet was responsible for the murders. When Aylwin took office, he agreed to reopen the case. Retired General Manuel Contreras and Brigadier General Pedro Espinoza were indicted for ordering the assassination. General Contreras headed the Chilean secret police during the 16 years of Pinochet's military dictatorship and Espinoza was his deputy. The man who identified them was Michael Townley, the American who confessed to planting the bomb. Townley and five other defendants were sentenced to prison for their role in the assassination.

As Aylwin approached the end of his term, many social and economic reforms had been implemented. The government had dramatically reduced unnecessary regulation of business and had opened Chile's economy, which was growing at a rate of 7.5 percent a year, to the rest of the world. Ten percent or 1.3 million Chileans had risen out of poverty, in part due to a 40 percent increase in social spending.

Aylwin was limited to a four-year term by a temporary constitutional provision. Eduardo Frei Ruiz-Tagle, son of former president Eduardo Frei Montalva, was elected to a six-year term in December of 1993, under an agreement reached on the eve of the election. Frei, also a member of the Christian Democratic Party, received the highest percentage of votes ever received by a presidential candidate. He was sworn in as president on March 11, 1994, in Chile's first transition from one democratically elected government to another in 23 years.

Further Reading

Reference material and published studies on Patricio Aylwin's career are scarce. Occasional articles and editorials in English can be found in the *Journal of Interamerican Studies & World Affairs*. With his election in 1989 a number of studies in Spanish appeared, but no serious, critical biographies. For basic information and excerpts from his speeches and writing the following may be consulted: Julio Retamal Avila, *Aylwin: La Palabra de un Demócrata* (Santiago: 1990) and *Amanecer en Chile, Patricio Aylwin Presidente* (Santiago: 1990); Patricio Aylwin, *Un Desafio Colectivo* (Santiago: 1988) and *La Alternativa Democrática* (Santiago: 1984); and Ricardo Yocelevzky, *La Demócracia Cristiana Chilena Y el Gobierno de Eduardo Frei (1964-1970)*, (Mexico:1987). □

Mohammed Ayub Khan

Mohammed Ayub Khan (1907-1974) was a president of Pakistan. Also, as commander in chief of the army and martial-law administrator, he molded the domestic and foreign policy of Pakistan.

Mohammed Ayub Khan was born on May 14, 1907, in the village of Rehanna in what is now Pakistan. His ancestors were Pathans, and his father had served as a *rissaldar*, or a noncommissioned officer, in a cavalry unit in the Indian army. Ayub attended village schools, then went to the Moslem college at Aligarh in 1922. He seems to have been an indifferent student, but his family background, ability at sports, and general intelligence led to his selection to attend Sandhurst, the officers' training school in England. He was among the first group of Indians to receive this training, and his accent, idiom, dress, and bearing always reflected his British army background.

Ayub was commissioned in 1927. He fought in Burma during World War II as second in command of his regiment. When India was partitioned in August 1947, he, like most Moslem army officers, chose to serve Pakistan. He received rapid promotion, becoming the first Pakistani army commander in chief in 1951.

Assumption of Power

Ayub's rise to power was a product of the years of economic and political instability that had followed the death of the two great leaders of Pakistan in its formative phase, M. A. Jinnah and Liaquat Ali Khan.

Ayub tells in his memoirs how, as commander in chief, he watched with growing disgust as corruption spread through every level of the nation and one ineffective government followed another. He and his fellow officers had urged the imposition of strong rule, and on Oct. 7, 1958, he

was asked by the president, Iskander Mirza, to take over the government because the civilian officials were losing control. Martial law was decreed, and shortly after taking over as chief administrator, Ayub forced Mirza to leave the country.

Although Ayub controlled the newspapers, dissolved political parties, and imprisoned those politicians he felt were disrupting the country, he did not make Pakistan into a police state. The civil service and the judiciary had a large measure of independence. Martial law had been imposed, Ayub insisted, only for "clearing up the political, social, economic mess" created by the corrupt politicians. Especially in the early years of his rule he was widely popular, and his policies brought rapid growth in agriculture and other sectors of the economy. The measure which he regarded as his greatest achievement was the creation of a new constitution. The first step had been the creation of basic democracies in 1960, giving the people the right to elect 80,000 village-level representatives, who elected Ayub president. Then in 1962 he promulgated a new constitution, under which free elections were held in 1965. Ayub ran into very strong opposition from Fatima Jinnah, who, as the sister of M.A. Jinnah, was one of the most revered figures in the nation. Ayub won with 63 percent of the votes, but the support Fatima Jinnah had received indicated the growing hostility to his regime.

Some of this hostility was related to Ayub's handling of foreign affairs, particularly relations with India. The interests of the Soviet Union, China, and the United States in the area further complicated his problems. Pakistan had entered into such American-sponsored organizations as the Central Treaty Organization (CENTO) and had received large-scale American aid. But Ayub grew disenchanted with the United States when it gave large amounts of military equipment to India during India's war with China in 1962. Pakistan's relations with India worsened, ending in the brief war in 1965, at which time the United States withdrew much of its military aid from Pakistan. Ayub then turned, with very considerable success, to building up friendly relations with Communist China and the Soviet Union. But the fact that Ayub had made peace with India rankled many Pakistanis, who believed that he should have been more aggressive.

Decline of Leadership

At the same time, charges of corruption were made against his government and his family with increasing frequency. It was alleged, apparently with considerable justification, that his sons had made vast fortunes through illegal use of their influence. Discontent was particularly strong in East Pakistan (now Bangladesh), where the people felt that they had been neglected by the officials in West Pakistan.

When Ayub became ill early in 1968, rumors spread that he had a heart attack and was paralyzed. The uncertainty about the country's future was increased when, after his recovery, an attempt was made to assassinate him in November in Peshawar. Violence became widespread in the main towns and cities, and Ayub was openly denounced. To appease his critics, Ayub announced in February 1969 that he would resign in March 1970, permitting a new president to be elected. This concession did not lessen the hostility, however, and law and order began to break down.

Ayub's Retirement

The danger to the country was increased by demands from East Pakistan leaders for virtual autonomy. Ayub considered declaring martial law once more, but the army leaders refused to give him their support, believing that he had become a liability to them. Realizing that he was without support, Ayub resigned on March 25, 1969, stating that as he had lost control of the situation, he could not preside over the destruction of his country. In a repetition of the events of 1958, martial law was decreed, and Yahya Khan, the commander in chief of the army, was appointed chief administrator. Ayub retired, apparently taking no further part in politics. Aside from the much-publicized business activities of his sons, Ayub shielded his private life from the public. Following Moslem social custom, only the most casual reference is made to his marriage in his autobiography. Ayub died at his home near Islamabad on April 19, 1974.

Further Reading

Friends, Not Masters: A Political Autobiography (1967) gives Ayub's own version of his career; he emerges as a strong-minded but modest man. Rais Ahmad Jafri, ed., *Ayub, Soldier and Statesman* (1966), is a collection of Ayub's speeches. For the general background of the period see Khalid bin Sayeed, *Pakistan: The Formative Phase, 1857-1948* (1960; 2d ed. 1968).
Newsweek (February 10, 1969; March 3, 1969; April 7, 1969). □

Manuel Azaña Diaz

The Spanish statesman and author Manuel Azaña Diaz (1880-1940) was prime minister of the republic from 1931 to 1933 and briefly in 1936. He became president in 1936, a position he held until the republic fell in March 1939 to the Nationalists.

Manuel Azaña was born on Jan. 10, 1880, in Alcalá de Henares to middle-class parents. He attended the Colegio de Maria Cristina at the Escorial. In 1898 Azaña entered the University of Madrid to study law, after which he spent several terms at the Sorbonne. The experience in Paris gave him an introduction to the kind of Europeanism that was the theme of the literary and cultural movement called the Generation of 1898 in Spain. After practicing law in Paris, Azaña returned to Spain with anticlerical views and a taste for radical politics.

During the 1920s Azaña was secretary general of the Ateneo de Madrid, the most prestigious intellectual club in Spanish society, and worked as a writer, a translator, and a journalist. Perhaps his best work is the biography of the 19th-century writer Juan Valera, an outspoken social critic. In 1930 Azaña became president of the Ateneo.

By this time he had begun to move into politics by organizing a small party called Acción Republicana. With the advent of the republic in April 1931, Azaña was named minister of war in the provisional government and immediately proceeded with a reorganization of the military, which heartened radicals who felt the services had long been too powerful. He also helped draft the republican constitution, and in October 1931, upon the resignation of Niceto Alcalá Zamora, he became premier.

Azaña remained prime minister until September 1933, a time of great importance in the history of the republic. He was particularly instrumental in solving difficult constitutional questions that threatened to divide the coalition active in republican politics. He tried hard to achieve an equitable land reform, improve education, and modernize Spanish society, but his ministry was marred in a number of ways. Azaña's anticlericalism made him reluctant to intervene in anarchist attacks on the Church, but he did pass the stringent Law for the Defense of the Republic to punish political dissenters. His harshness in January and August 1932, and again in January 1933, against his political opponents did a great deal to introduce a climate of violence into Spanish politics. Increasingly he came to rely upon Socialist support and thus fatally divided public opinion, though the division probably was inevitable. In any case, when his administration found it impossible to maintain momentum in the wake of the economic crisis of the early thirties, the right triumphed in the elections of 1933 and Azaña was succeeded by Alejandro Lerrox. Yet, despite Azaña's errors, there was no question that in just 2 years Spanish society had moved significantly forward.

The right-wing government kept a close watch on Azaña, and when, in October 1934, rioting in Asturias threatened to plunge the country into civil war, Azaña was imprisoned for some months. In 1935 he became spokesman for a renewed left coalition that in January and February 1936 won a controversial election under the banner of the Popular Front. Azaña returned to the premiership until May 10, when he replaced Alcalá Zamora once again, this time as president of the republic. When civil war broke out in July, Azaña's influence diminished after he appointed the moderate Diego Martinez Barrio as prime minister. Azaña left Madrid in the fall of 1936, never to return permanently, and he spent much of the civil war period in virtual isolation in Catalonia. After the fall of Barcelona, Azaña went into exile in France. He died in Montauban on Nov. 3, 1940.

Further Reading

A political biography of Azaña is Frank Sedwick, *The Tragedy of Manuel Azaña and the Fate of the Spanish Republic* (1963). Hugh Thomas, *The Spanish Civil War* (1961), is an authoritative history.

Additional Sources

Portrait of an unknown man: Manuel Azaña and modern Spain, Madison N.J.: Fairleigh Dickinson University Press; London; Cranbury, NJ: Associated University Presses, 1995. ☐

Félix de Azara

Félix de Azara (1746-1821) was a Spanish explorer and naturalist. His scientific work in South America showed a marked advance over that of any predecessor in the regions he visited.

Félix de Azara was a native of Barbuñales in the Spanish province of Huesca. He attended a mathematical school at Barcelona and in 1767 became an army lieutenant with an engineering specialty. In 1775 he took part in the disastrous Spanish attack on Algiers commanded by Alejandro O'Reilly and received a promotion, as well as a severe chest wound.

In 1777 Spain signed the Treaty of San Ildefonso with Portugal, followed by the Peace of El Pardo a year later, by which the two countries agreed that military commissions should survey and determine the joint boundary of their South American possessions. Azara was assigned to the Spanish delegation headed by José Varela y Ulloa. Azara reached Montevideo in 1781 and from Juan José Vértiz, viceroy of Río de la Plata, received further instructions regarding the mission; Azara became its most important member.

Azara remained 20 years in South America and for 14 of these surveyed the boundary as far north as the confluence of the Guapuré and Mamoré rivers. This involved considerable difficulties and frequent encounters with hostile Indians. It may be too much to say that he explored territory previously unvisited by white men, but certainly no such map as he skillfully prepared had ever been made. Azara, always a careful observer interested in nature, took the opportunity to collect biological specimens and make copious notes concerning the wildlife of the tributaries of the Río de la Plata and the Amazon. A Buenos Aires official, Gabriel Avilés del Fierro, confiscated Azara's map and some of the notes and tried to pass them off to the Madrid government as his own work. But Azara had companions on his travels, and too many knew the truth for the imposture to succeed. The explorer, after finishing the boundary work, undertook other missions, all involving exploration of uninviting backlands.

He returned to Spain in 1801 and visited his brother José Nicolás de Azara, the ambassador to France, and in Paris met several distinguished scientists with whom he continued to correspond throughout his life. Félix de Azara next turned to writing of his exploratory and scientific work. His most important publication appeared in France with the title *Voyage dans l'Amérique Méridionale depuis 1781 jusqu'en 1801* (1809).

When Napoleon invaded Spain in 1808, Azara offered his services to José de Palafox, the captain general of Aragon, but these were respectfully declined because of Azara's age. He nevertheless took what part he could in the Spanish resistance and sent a congratulatory message to King Ferdinand VII on his restoration in 1814. From then until his death on Oct. 20, 1821, Azara devoted himself to the agricultural and economic rehabilitation of Aargon from the devastation caused by the recent war.

Further Reading

The best summary of the Azara's life is in Spanish, Enrique Alvarez Lopez, *Félix de Azara, Siglo XVIII* (1935). The organization of the boundary commission and the division of labor are described in Ricardo Levene, *History of Argentina,* translated and edited by William Spence Robertson (1937). Brief accounts of Azara's work are found in J. N. L. Baker, *A History of Geographical Discovery and Exploration* (1931; 2d rev. ed. 1967), and in Paul Russell Cutright, *The Great Naturalists Explore South America* (1940). □

José Azcona Hoyo

José Azcona Hoyo (born 1927) was president of Honduras (1986-1990) and played an important role in the confrontation between the Contra and Sandinista forces.

José Azcona Hoyo was born in 1927. He graduated with a degree in civil engineering from the Honduran National Autonomous University and pursued additional studies in urban planning at the Technological Institute for Superior Studies in Monterrey, Mexico. Married and the father of two daughters, Azcona combined his engineering career with a growing interest in Liberal Party politics. From 1962 to 1974 he served as the director of the Liberal Action Front. In 1973 he assumed the positions of coordinator of liberal engineers in the Rodista Liberal Movement and general manager of the Honduran Federation of Housing Cooperatives. From 1975 to 1977 Azcona was a member of the Liberal Party's Central Executive Council, rising to the position of general secretary in 1982. In 1982-1983, during the presidency of Roberto Suazo Cordova, Azcona held cabinet rank as secretary of state of communications, public works, and transportation. In December of 1985 the longtime Liberal Party loyalist won the presidency of Honduras. When the new executive took office on January 27, 1986, it represented the first time in several generations that Honduras had witnessed the peaceful transfer of power from one elected civilian government to another.

The problems that President Azcona faced after his inauguration reflected a legacy of longstanding Honduran economic, social, and geo-political problems. Geography, for example, has not been kind to Honduras. Sharing frontiers with Guatemala, El Salvador, and Nicaragua meant that Honduras became, often much against her will, involved in the domestic disputes of her neighbors, disputes which frequently tended to spill across the Honduran border. Indeed, economic and political refugees from surrounding states would provide President Azcona with major challenges during his four years in office.

Furthermore, Azcona had to contend with significant economic problems. Honduras, like many other Latin American nations, had a large foreign debt. Interest on that

debt alone would drain off more than a quarter of Azcona's first budget. As one of the poorest nations in the Western Hemisphere, Honduras, with an average per capita income of less than $600 and unemployment hovering around the 25 percent mark, could not afford to allocate such a segment of national expenditures to service external obligations. The fact that interest rates and commodity prices are determined on a global scale serves to restrict Honduran options even further given the fact that most of the nation's international exchange comes from the sale of tropical commodities in the international marketplace. When these foregoing phenomena are factored into Azcona's disputed election victory, the deep divisions within his own political party, and the ever present and politically active Honduran military establishment, it was perhaps not surprising that many informed observers felt that the President would be hard pressed to serve out his constitutional term.

Azcona's controversial electoral victory in 1985 was perhaps predictive of the difficult tenure he would have as president. In terms of presidential votes cast, Azcona's opponent, Rafael Leonardo Callejas, was the clear winner. A governmental electoral commission, however, had ruled that the presidency would go to the candidate of the party that won the most votes in races for both national and municipal offices. Because Azcona's Liberal Party gained the most overall votes, it was able to claim the presidency even though Callejas had outpolled Azcona by several hundred thousand votes in their head-to-head contest. Callejas' National Party was, to say the least, bitterly disappointed with the outcome of the elections, thus providing the basis for much partisan political activity over the course of Azcona's four-year term.

Azcona's administration was also troubled by rising inflation, a weak national currency, and the repeated insistence on the part of international lending agencies that the Honduran authorities adopt stringent austerity measures to stabilize the economy. In addition to a troubled economy, President Azcona was constantly challenged during his term by internal violence that various observers attributed to such sources as the drug trade, left-wing guerrillas, military and/or right-wing death squads, and internal schisms among the Contra forces located in Honduras. Indeed, of all the problems that Azcona had to face, the Contras represented the greatest challenge of them all.

During his four year term in office, José Azcona had the difficult, if not impossible, task of attempting to reconcile the policy objectives of the United States vis-a-vis the Sandinista regime in Nicaragua with his own role as a Honduran and as a Central American. The establishment of American military bases in Honduras and the existence of Contra camps along the Honduran-Nicaraguan frontier were elements in the Central American policy of the United States that Azcona had to tolerate. Infusions of American economic and military aid represented a payment of sorts for Azcona's support, but as the Nicaraguan crisis deepened and as a series of Central American peace initiatives gained momentum, the president found himself caught between two competing forces. It is a testimony to Azcona's political and diplomatic skills, as well as more than a little bit of luck,

that he was able to lead his country through this difficult period of isthmian turmoil. Indeed, Azcona's greatest achievement might well have been his own political survival, for in January of 1990 he was able to turn executive power over to Rafael Callejas, his opponent in the 1985 election and the victor in the November 1989 presidential contest.

In 1997, the federal prosecutor's office in Tegucigalpa announced in a communique its intention to bring charges of kidnapping, torture, abuse of authority and violation of the constitution against Azcona and other officials. It was alleged that drug trafficker Juan Ramon Matta Ballesteros was "spirited" out of the country, with the help of Azcona and others, in April of 1988, and taken by U.S. agents to America. He was sentenced to life in prison for conspiracy, possession and distribution of narcotics and kidnapping-related charges. He had been linked with the kidnapping, torture and killing of U.S. Drug Enforcement Agency agent Enrique Camarena in Mexico in 1985.

Further Reading

José Azcona Hoyo is listed in the 1989 edition of *The International Year Book and Statesmen's Who's Who*. As a contemporary personality, information on Azcona can best be obtained in such periodical literature as *TIME, Current History, Newsweek, The New Republic,* and *The New York Times*. □

Sayyid Ismail al-Azhari

Sayyid Ismail al-Azhari (1898-1969) was a political leader of the Sudan and is often called the father of the Republic of the Sudan.

S ayyid Ismail al-Azhari was born in Omdurman, the son of a religious notable. He studied at Gordon College in Khartoum and the American University in Beirut. He became a teacher of mathematics and then an administrator in the Anglo-Egyptian condominium government that ruled the Sudan during the colonial period. He and other educated Sudanese demanded greater participation in the administration of the country, and to promote their objectives they formed the Graduates' General Congress in 1938. Al-Azhari's election as secretary to the congress launched him into a career in politics.

Although the congress at first had no political aspirations, in 1942 it asserted its claim to act as the spokesman for all Sudanese nationalists. When the wartime British administration rejected this claim, the congress split into two groups: the moderates, who were prepared to work with the British toward full independence, and a more extreme group, led by al-Azhari, which distrusted the British and sought unity with Egypt in the postcolonial period.

In 1943 al-Azhari and his supporters from the congress formed the Ashiqqa (Brothers') party, the first true political party in the Sudan. His main support came from the Khatmiyya brotherhood, one of the two main Moslem groups in the country. When the more moderate nationalists formed the Umma (Nation) party in 1945, its principal support came from the chief rival of the Khatmiyya, the anti-Egyptian Mahdist sect.

Between 1944 and 1953 al-Azhari, as the leading advocate for uniting the Sudan with Egypt, fought tenaciously against any act which appeared to weaken the "unity of the Nile Valley." Thus, in 1948 he boycotted the elections to establish a legislative assembly in the Sudan, and his propaganda and demonstrations led to his arrest and imprisonment for subversion in 1948-1949.

The military coup d'etat in Egypt in 1952, which ended the regime of King Farouk and brought Col. Gamal Abdel Nasser to power, dramatically changed the situation in the Sudan. Farouk's government had exerted all its influence to unite Egypt and the Sudan and block Sudanese independence. Nasser and his half-Sudanese compatriot, Col. Naquib, were more flexible and not unwilling to permit the Sudan to achieve independence.

In 1952 an agreement was reached between Egypt, the Sudanese, and their British rulers for immediate internal self-government, to be followed within 3 years by an election to determine the future relationship between Egypt and the Sudan. Although his imprisonment and the quarrels within his own party had for a time undermined al-Azhari's power and prestige, he was able to reunite his followers under the banner of the National Unionist party (NUP) in time to campaign vigorously for the combined parliament and constitutional assembly which was to rule the Sudan for

the next 2 years. Throughout the campaign al-Azhari emphasized his hostility to the British and his support for Egypt so that when the NUP won a victory in the elections of 1953, it was widely regarded as a victory for al-Azhari's efforts to link the Sudan to Egypt.

In 1954 al-Azhari became the Sudan's first prime minister. His government faced three major problems. The first was the critical constitutional question of the Sudan's relationship with Egypt. It soon became clear that the Sudanese people did not want to be tied closely to Egypt, and in his greatest act of statesmanship al-Azhari dramatically reversed the position which he had long advocated and, with the support of the principal political leaders, declared the Sudan independent on Jan. 1, 1956.

Then al-Azhari was faced with the second problem, the task of organizing a permanent government. His principal opponent, the Umma party, wanted a strong presidential system. Al-Azhari advocated a British parliamentary form of government, but he never resolved the issue during his tenure and the problem remained into the 1970s.

The third problem which confronted al-Azhari's government was the uniting of the black, non-Moslem Southern Sudanese with peoples and traditions very different if not opposed to the Arab, Moslem north. Neither by his background nor by his political convictions was al-Azhari sympathetic to the aspirations of the Southern Sudanese, and he sought to control the Southern Sudan by a combination of military and police repression on the one hand and negotiations and discussion on the other. The failure of the policy became apparent in 1955, when a mutiny in the Equatorial Corps precipitated disturbances throughout many of the districts in the south. Thereafter, relations between the Northern and the Southern Sudan remained the principal problem facing successive Sudanese governments. Their failure to meet Southern aspirations undermined their authority, just as it had drained al-Azhari's political strength.

These and other problems began to weaken al-Azhari's coalition. His reversal on unity with Egypt undermined the political strength of the NUP by depriving it of its principal ideology. The mutiny in the south damaged al-Azhari's prestige. More importantly, the fragile alliance between the Khatmiyya sect and the NUP began to disintegrate, leaving the Prime Minister without the popular support he needed to rule effectively. As a result, he reformed his coalition into a "government of all talents" in February 1956, but then his former Khatmiyya supporters deserted to form the People's Democratic party in June. In July he lost a vote of confidence in Parliament and resigned.

Al-Azhari opposed the government led by Abdullah Khalil, who replaced him, and also the succeeding military regime of Gen. Ibrahim Abboud. In 1961 al-Azhari was arrested and exiled for several months to Juba in the Southern Sudan. In 1964 the military regime resigned in the face of student-led demonstrations, and party politics reemerged in the Sudan. Al-Azhari sought to regain power, but without a strong political base even his skill as a politician was insufficient to lead a government in the Sudan. In March 1965 he became president of the Republic of the Sudan, but this was primarily an honorary position with little real power. He remained president until May 1968, when a military coup d'etat ended his political life. Known as a skilled if not crafty politician, al-Azhari was respected but not loved. His tenacity to survive the many vicissitudes of Sudanese political life was even admired. Ironically, his most statesmanlike decision—not to press for unity with Egypt—destroyed the principles upon which his political life had been constructed, leaving only manipulation to achieve political power. He died on Oct. 26, 1969.

Further Reading

There is no full-length biography of al-Azhari. P. M. Holt, *A Modern History of the Sudan* (1961), contains a great deal on the life and work of al-Azhari. In K. D. D. Henderson, *The Making of the Modern Sudan* (1952), al-Azhari figures prominently. See also Mekki Shibeika, *The Independent Sudan* (1959). □

Nnamdi Azikiwe

Nnamdi Azikiwe (1904-1996) was one of the foremost Nigerian and West African nationalists and the first president of Nigeria.

Nnamdi Azikiwe was born on Nov. 16, 1904, of Ibo parents in Zungeru, Northern Nigeria, where his father worked as a clerk in the Nigerian Regiment. His parents gave him the name Benjamin, but he later changed it to Nnamdi. He attended school in Onitsha, Lagos, and Calabar. In 1921, when he discontinued his secondary school education, he was fluent in the languages of the three major ethnic groups of Nigeria—the Hausas, the Ibos, and the Yorubas—a major asset for the future Nigerian nationalist. Between 1921 and 1924 he worked as a clerk in the Nigerian treasury in Lagos.

In 1925 Azikiwe went to the United States to study. He attended Storer College and then Howard and Lincoln universities. He received a bachelor of arts degree in political science from Lincoln in 1931 and advanced degrees from Lincoln in 1932 and the University of Pennsylvania in 1933. As a black penurious student (nicknamed Zik), Azikiwe worked at a wide range of mostly lowly jobs and was frequently a victim of racial discrimination. His American experience was certainly a source of his pan-African patriotism.

Between 1932 and 1934 Azikiwe taught political science at Lincoln University. At this time he began writing seriously, and his productions reflected his pan-African inclination. He devised a "Syllabus for African History" and wrote a book, *Liberia in World Politics* (1934), in defense of the black republic. In 1937 he published *Renascent African,* the most important single expression of his pan-African ideology.

Newspaper Career

In 1934 Azikiwe returned to Nigeria and accepted an offer to edit the *African Morning Post,* a new daily newspaper in Accra, Ghana, which he quickly made into an important organ of nationalist propaganda. In 1937 he returned to Lagos and founded the *West African Pilot,* which became "a fire-eating and aggressive nationalist paper of the highest order." In the next decade Azikiwe controlled six daily newspapers in Nigeria: two in Lagos and four strategically placed in the urban centers of Ibadan, Onitsha, Port Harcourt, and Kano. These played a crucial role in stimulating Nigerian nationalism. To support his business ventures and to express his economic nationalism, Azikiwe founded the African Continental Bank in 1944.

Political Career

Azikiwe also became directly involved in political movements. In 1937 he joined the Nigerian Youth Movement, leaving it for the Nigerian National Democratic party in 1941. In 1944, on Azikiwe's initiative, the National Council of Nigeria and the Cameroons (NCNC) was founded to "weld the heterogeneous masses of Nigeria into one solid block." Azikiwe was elected the council's general secretary and in 1946 its president. In this period his major political writings, apart from his newspaper articles, were *Political Blue Print of Nigeria* and *Economic Reconstruction in Nigeria* (both 1943).

Between 1947 and 1960 Azikiwe, as leader of the NCNC, held a number of elected public offices. He was a member of the Nigerian Legislative Council (1947- 1951), member of the Western House of Assembly (1952-1953), premier of the Eastern Region (1954-1959), and president of the Nigerian Senate (1959-1960). During these years he had continued to play the single most vigorous role in Nigeria's march toward independence. While premier, he greatly expanded educational facilities in the Eastern Region and laid the foundation of the University of Nigeria at Nsukka, formally opened in September 1960.

On Oct. 1, 1960, Nigeria became independent, and Azikiwe was appointed governor general with the primeministership going to Sir Alhaji Abubakar Tafawa Balewa, deputy governor general of the Northern People Congress, the largest single party of the federation. On Oct. 1, 1963, Nigeria became a republic, and Azikiwe was named its first president, a position he held until he was deposed by the military coup of Jan. 15, 1966.

In the Nigerian-Biafran civil war, May 1967-January 1970, Azikiwe at first reluctantly supported Biafra, but in August 1969 came out against Biafran secession and in favor of a united Nigeria.

From 1978-1983 Azikiwe led the Nigeria People's Party (NPP); he was the NPP's candidate in the presidential elections of 1979 and 1983. He retired from politics in 1986.

Azikiwe died in eastern Nigeria on May 11, 1996, following a long illness. Marking his death, the *New York Times* commented that Azikiwe "towered over the affairs of Africa's most populous nation, attaining the rare status of a truly national hero who came to be admired across the regional and ethnic lines dividing his country."

Further Reading

Two useful short biographies are Vincent Ikeotuonye, *Zik of New Africa* (1961), and K.A.B. Jones-Quartey, *A Life of Azikiwe* (1965), which is more scholarly and more readily available. Good analyses of Azikiwe's political career may be found in James Smoot Coleman, *Nigeria: Background to Nationalism* (1958), and Richard L. Sklar, *Nigerian Political Parties: Power in an Emergent African Nation* (1963).

Additional Sources

Economist (May 25, 1996).
Jet (June 3, 1996).
New York Times (May 14, 1996).
Uwazurike, P. Chudi, *The Man Called Zik of Africa: Portrait of Nigeria's Pan-African Statesman* (Triatlantic Books, 1996). □

Mariano Azuela

The Mexican novelist Mariano Azuela (1873-1952) initiated the novel of the Mexican Revolution, employing realism as a means of denouncing social injustices.

Mariano Azuela was born on Jan. 1, 1873, in Lagos de Moreno, in the state of Jalisco, where he received his primary education. Later he went to Guadalajara, the state capital, to pursue a career as a surgeon in the institute which had replaced the University of Jalisco.

Dr. Azuela's literary career began in 1896 with the publication in a Mexico City newspaper of a series of articles entitled *Impresiones de un estudiante* (A Student's Impressions). In 1907 he published his first novel, *Maria Luisa,* followed by *Los fracasados* (The Failures) in 1908 and *Mala yerba* (Weeds) in 1909. The theme of these novels was fate, continued in *Esa sangre* (That Blood), a posthumous novel published in 1956.

Having completed his medical studies, Dr. Azuela began practicing in Jalisco, where he acquired a drugstore and established his home. When Francisco I. Madero was elected president of Mexico in 1911, Dr. Azuela became mayor of Lagos and then director of education in Jalisco.

He became disillusioned with politics, however, and published *Andrés Pérez, maderista* (1911), his first novel on the theme of the Revolution; this was followed in 1912 by *Sin amor* (Without Love). With the downfall of President Madero, Azuela, persecuted by his enemies, joined the revolutionary forces of Julián Medina as a doctor and witnessed many aspects of the bloody struggle. When they were defeated, he emigrated to El Paso, Tex., and there in 1915 he wrote *Los de abajo* (*The underdogs*), his most famous novel. Its literary merit was not recognized until 1925; since then it has gone through many editions and been translated into numerous languages.

Many other novels about the Revolution followed. In 1917 Dr. Azuela moved to Mexico City, where he worked in a public dispensary, at the same time making penetrating observations of life among the lower classes, which he later used in many of his works.

In 1943 he began giving lectures in the Colegio Nacional on Mexican, French, and Spanish novelists, as well as recounting his own literary experiences. Several of his novels were dramatized, and others were made into movies. He retired after practicing medicine for 25 years.

In 1949 he won the National Prize for Literature. He died in Mexico City on March 1, 1952, and was buried there in the Panteón Civil in the Rotunda of Illustrious Men.

Further Reading

Azuela's contribution to the modern Mexican novel is assessed in Joseph Sommers, *After the Storm: Landmarks of the Modern Mexican Novel* (1968). See also John S. Brushwood, *Mexico in Its Novel: A Nation's Search for Identity* (1966).

Additional Sources

Herbst, Gerhard R., *Mexican society as seen by Mariano Azuela,* New York: Abra Ediciones, 1977. □

B

Andreas Baader and Ulrike Meinhof

Andreas Baader (1943-1977) and Ulrike Meinhof (1934-1976) were the best known founders and leading members of the West German "Red Army Faction" (RAF). Acting as Communist urban guerrillas, their names were joined by the media to make the popular designation of the "Baader-Meinhof Group," which West German police classified as a terrorist organization of violent anarchists.

Bernd Andreas Baader was born in Munich, Bavaria, on May 6, 1943. He attended several secondary schools but finally ended his formal education without graduating. In 1963 he moved to Berlin. In 1967 his girlfriend, Gudrun Ensslin, an active member of the leading organization of the extraparliamentary movement, the German Socialist Student Organization (SDS), brought him to the Berlin student protest scene, and Baader began to participate in its political activities.

On the night of April 2, 1968, Baader, together with Ensslin and two other persons, set two Frankfurt department stores on fire with fire bombs "to light a torch for Vietnam," as they put it. Baader and the others were found guilty of arson. Baader partly served his sentence and was released while his appeal was pending, but, together with Ensslin, fled the country when the appeal was rejected. On returning to Berlin he was rearrested in April 1970 and freed with guns by Ulrike Meinhof and others on May 14, 1970.

Meinhof was born in Oldenburg, Lower Saxony, on October 7, 1934. She passed her final high school examinations in 1955 and began to study education and psychology until 1960. She was strongly influenced by the political attitudes of her foster mother, Professor Renate Riemeck, a well known historian, Christian-pacifist, socialist, and protagonist of the West German extraparliamentary opposition throughout the 1950s and 1960s. Ulrike Meinhof took part in the 1958 anti-atom death campaign and joined the SDS. In 1960 she moved to Hamburg to work for the left-wing student monthly "Konkret" as chief editress. Her columns for "Konkret" helped her gain a reputation for being a serious and critically minded journalist and gave her a certain prominence within the extraparliamentary movement of the mid and late 1960s, the "Ausserparlamentarische Opposition" (APO).

Within the APO Meinhof, from an antiauthoritarian, radically socialist position, criticized the inflexible social and political structures of the West German "consumer society," calling for a fundamental change. When APO activities calmed down in the end of 1969, Meinhof belonged to those intellectuals who transformed the splitting of the APO into its most radical alternative—the "armed struggle"—thus confusing the antiauthoritarian rebellion of the students with socialist revolution. As Meinhof explained it, "to save the level of conscience of the [19]67/68 movement historically, to prevent the struggle from ceasing."

Terrorists Join Forces

With Baader—who defined politics essentially as longing for action—she shared the view that, after endless theoretical debates and verbal protests without real success, only violent political action could succeed in changing the political structures. In a "Konkret" article Meinhof had ex-

403

pressed sympathy for the Frankfurt arson, and she later revived her contacts with Baader and Ensslin. When both returned to Berlin from abroad, wanted by the police, it was Meinhof who hid and supported them, tired of seeing herself as a powerless intellectual "desk-activist."

After freeing Baader she evolved to be the theoretical head of the group, whereas Baader put his charisma to use in personal activism and organizing efforts. The first manifesto of the group was written mostly by Meinhof. It presented the concept "urban guerrilla" and constituted an uncritical adoption of South American theories of urban guerrilla warfare. Its strategic message was to provoke the state to activate its hidden repressive potential, its "latent fascism," in order to dismantle its democratic legitimacy and to revolutionize the "working masses." The RAF claimed to exert "counter-violence" in the tradition of antifascist resistance. Its practice was dominated by the primacy of military action and by the absoluteness of an all or nothing principle Baader verbalized as "victory or death."

Throughout 1970 and 1971 the group made headlines through numerous bank raids and street gun battles with police that took the first lives on both sides. In May of 1972 the RAF escalated the "people's war" by launching a massive wave of time bomb attacks against such spectacular targets as the headquarters of the Fifth U.S. Army Corps in Frankfurt and the U.S. Army Headquarters Europe (USAREUR) in Heidelberg. More than 20 people were wounded and four U.S. servicemen were killed. The RAF saw the bombing as a direct military support for the "liberation struggle of the Vietnamese people," defining itself as the ally of the liberation movements in the Third World.

Arrest and Trial

The biggest police search in the history of the Federal Republic of Germany resulted in the arrests of Baader, Meinhof, Ensslin, and other hard-core members of the group during June 1972. Baader, Meinhof, and the others were accused of murder, robbery, and the founding of a "criminal association." The Baader-Meinhof trial in a high security courthouse at Stuttgart-Stammheim began on May 21, 1975 and lasted until April 28, 1977, when all were sentenced to lifelong imprisonment.

Meinhof did not witness the outcome. Since 1972 she had been increasingly isolated within the group of RAF prisoners and, like most of them, had been held in nearly total isolation from the world outside the prison. Her relationship to Baader and Ensslin had become a rather strained one. Also, the RAF was in total political isolation within the German left. Meinhof hanged herself in her Stammheim cell the night of May 8, 1976.

The armed escalation between terrorism and the state reached its climax in the autumn of 1977, when the second generation of the RAF started another attempt to free Baader and the other prisoners by kidnapping a main representative of West German industry, Hans Martin Schleyer. As the West German government refused to exchange the RAF prisoners, the RAF, in cooperation with Palestinian terrorists, hijacked a Lufthansa jet in Mogadishu, Somalia, and took its crew and passengers hostages. A special unit of the Western German police intervened successfully, and the venture failed.

In that night of October 18, 1977, Baader shot himself with a pistol he had probably hidden in his cell. Ensslin and another leading member, Jan C. Raspe, also committed suicide in their cells at Stammheim.

Further Reading

The most detailed and biographical work on Baader and Meinhof is Jillian Becker, *Hitler's Children: The Story of the Baader-Meinhof Terrorist Gang* (1977). Careful reading is advised due to essential inaccuracies and subjective, dubious interpretations. Two solid studies of the various aspects of the theme, containing authentic documents of the RAF and an analytic precis of the group's activities are: Walter Laqueur, "Terrorism: A Study of National and International Political Violence (1977) and, by the same author, "The Terrorism Reader: A Historical Anthology" (1977). An introductory survey of the relevant literature on national and international terrorism is given by Yonah Alexander et al. (editors), "Terrorism: Theory and Practice" (1979).

Additional Sources

Becker, Jillian, *Hitler's children,* London; New York: Panther, 1978.
Horchem, Hans Josef, *West Germany's Red Army anarchists,* London: Institute for the Study of Conflict, 1974. □

Baal Shem Tov

The founder of modern Hasidism was the Polish-born Israel ben Eliezer (ca. 1700-ca. 1760), who is generally known as Baal Shem Tov (Good Master of the Name).

Israel ben Eliezer was born to aged parents in Okopy, a small town in the Ukraine. He was apprenticed to the local teacher and was later employed as an aid to the sexton of the synagogue, where he spent his nights studying the Cabala, or Jewish mystic lore.

Israel married at the traditional age of 18, but his wife died shortly afterward. He then moved to Brody in Galicia, where he met and married the rabbi's sister. They moved to a distant village in the Carpathians. There Israel worked as a laborer, but he managed to devote considerable time to prayer and contemplation in the forest. He learned the use of medicinal herbs for the treatment of disease, and he became a *Baal Shem,* a master of the occult art of manipulating the name of the Ineffable and his ministering angels as a means of exorcising demons, driving out ghosts, and avoiding other evils. He ministered to his rural neighbors, both Christians and Jews, and performed miraculous cures of both body and soul. He is said to have undergone an *Hitgalut* (self-revelation) at the age of 36, through the mediacy of a divine spirit.

About 1740 the Besht (the common abbreviation of Baal Shem Tov) settled in Miedzyboz, Podolia. His kindliness and sanctity attracted many followers, who were called Hasidim (the pious). The Besht's teachings emphasized the love of God and trust in Him. God is everywhere and there is no place free of Him. The Besht taught that devoted and fervent prayer was a channel through which divine light flows to man and leads his soul to God. Gloom and sadness were anathemas to the Besht; one of his principles was, "Serve the Lord with gladness." To aid men in their religious life, he introduced a new functionary into Judaism—the *Tzaddik* (the righteous), who has a highly developed awareness of the divine. The *Tzaddik* has become the hereditary leader of the Besht's followers.

The Besht used anecdotes and parables to illustrate his teachings. He wrote no works, but after his death compilations of his sayings and teachings were published. Hasidism had, and continues to have, a notable impact on Jewish life.

Further Reading

Rosman, Murray Jay., *Founder of Hasidism: a quest for the historical Baal Shem Tov,* Berkeley, Calif: University of California Press, 1996.
Heschel, Abraham Joshua, *A passion for truth,* Woodstock, Vt.: Jewish Lights Pub., 1995. □

Babar the Conqueror

Barbar the Conqueror (1483–1530) was a descendant of Tamerlane and Genghis Khan, who founded the Mughal (Mogul) dynasty of India and, although a devout Muslim, bequeathed a legacy of toleration for non-Muslims that characterized the Empire at its zenith.

"Strange and engrossing" was Sir Wolseley Haig's description of Babar's early life. A descendant on his father's side of the great conqueror Tamerlane and on his mother's of the Mongol overlord Genghis Khan, Babar (also known as Zahir-ud-din Muhammed Babur) inherited the legacy of division and war that had followed in these great conqueror's wakes. Tamerlane's central Asian Empire lay divided into a number of separate city-states ruled over by his Timurid descendants, who styled themselves princes and constantly fought to enlarge their domains. The cities and towns, ruled by local potentates, dominated their surrounding countryside thus giving each populated community a strategic importance which grew as they continually changed hands. Of these cities and strategic locations, Samarkand was the most important.

One such state, Farghana, was ruled by Babar's father, Umar Shaikh Mirzà. A scant 11 years after Babar's birth, his father died, leaving the child-prince the task of consolidating his hold as ruler of the kingdom in an atmosphere of intrigue and danger. His father's throne had not been particularly secure and Babar's position was threatened by older claimants to the throne and by external foes who greedily eyed their neighboring kingdom. The next 18 years were characterized by a succession of wars, battles, and treaties, as Babar sought to shore up his position. Active in spirit and mind, Babar also began a record of his life, composing poetry and prose to leave a tale that few would match in central Asian, if not world, history and literature.

Babar scored some initial successes. In 1497, after a bloody siege of some seven months, he captured Samarkand and the capital of a cousin's domain named Transoxiana, situated near present-day Iran and Afghanistan. Transoxiana and Samarkand remained Babar's obsession for the next decade. In his memoirs, his frequent and gracious references to the land of his birth provide ample illustration of his desire to secure his position in his own kingdom. He was, however, denied this wish. Driven from Samarkand in 1501 by an ally of his cousin, Babar was only granted freedom by promising his sister's hand in marriage. For the next three years, Babar was an exile in his own land, wandering homeless, accompanied by a handful of loyal followers.

Nevertheless, fate favored Babar. In 1504, his enemies were again fighting among themselves. His most powerful foe, Shaibàni Khan, chief of the Uzbegs, who had driven Babar into exile, had conquered most of Transoxiana. Khan's victories, however, propelled his former enemies' followers straight into Babar's arms, and Babar found himself at the head of an army, some 4,000 strong. But Babar did not feel sufficiently strong to attack Shaibàni Khan; instead, he turned to more profitable adventures in the

Kingdom of Kàbul, now Afghanistan. Claiming the throne of a long-deposed cousin, he led a brilliant campaign and captured the capital Kàbul and thus the city-state.

Using Kàbul as a base of power, Babar looked to the southeast and the northwest, eager to reclaim the thrones which he felt were his by divine right. He briefly ventured into the "fertile plains" of the Hindùstàn, upper India in the early months of 1506. Leading his army through the famed Khyber Pass, Babar raided throughout the upper Indian plain over a four-month period, returning to his adopted homeland to subdue a rebellion. He returned to raid again the following year. Perhaps concerned with harnessing the power of his new territory, Babar did more than just make war; he tried to bring a certain order to his kingdom, collecting taxes and centralizing some power. His passion, however, remained the recapture of Samarkand and his father's throne in Farghana.

After slowly building up his strength, Babar felt confident enough to attempt the reconquest of his homeland in earnest. In 1510, the rivalries always simmering below the surface in Transoxiana had boiled over into a full conflict. Gradually expanding his domains, Shaibàni had overreached himself and incurred the wrath of the Shàh Isma'il, the powerful leader of a rival Timurid tribe, the larger cultural group of which Babar was a member. Later that year, Isma'il's smashing of the Uzbeg armies of Shaibàni revived Babar's hopes of regaining his lost territories. Concluding a temporary alliance with Isma'il in order to confront the Uzbeg threat, Babar was able to reconquer Samarkand and Farghana. By the end of 1511, he was once again lord over an extensive central Asian territory.

Babar's success was short-lived. The alliance with Shàh Isma'il collapsed and Babar's Uzbeg enemies immediately returned to the initiative. In a series of battles over the next year and a half, they drove Babar out of Farghana and Samarkand. More importantly, they thoroughly crushed his armies. In consequence, Babar's allies turned against him, attacking his camp and pushing him back to the relative safety of his throne in Kàbul. Upon his return, finding that his subjects had revolted in his absence, Babar was forced to turn his attentions toward home, and a certain calm descended on his life as he abandoned all hopes of reclaiming his throne. Although he continued the intermittent expeditions and forays that characterized the lives of these nomadic mountain tribes—if for no other reason than to maintain his position within Kàbul—he did not mount any major expeditions aimed at reconquering his lost territories or conquering new ones until 1519. He then turned his sights on northern India, entering what was effectively the second phase of his career.

"At the dawn of the sixteenth century" writes historian Stanley Wolpert, "India was ... fragmented politically [and] divided spiritually into many relio-philosophic camps." This was perhaps an understatement. Any semblance of the old *Sultanate* (Empire) of Delhi had been shattered by Tamerlane's invasions at the end of the 14th century. In his wake, the empire had developed into a number of semi-independent governorships, the majority of these ruled by Muslim Afghani chiefs titled *Lodis*. The ex-

ception was the powerful Rànà Sàngà, chief of the Hindu Rajput confederacy, which lay to the south of the Delhi Sultanate. The elected head of this conglomerate was Ibràhim Lodi, who came to power in 1517. Ibràhim, however, was unable to secure the allegiance of all the chieftains and faced numerous threats to his hold on power. His position was so tenuous that he ignored the Portuguese trading centers and fortresses being established in the south despite their ominous implications. Ibràhim's foremost concern was the threat that was emerging from the rebellious western province of the Punjab and the capital city of Lahore.

Daulat Khàn Lodi, the governor of Lahore, was one of the key conspirators in the rebellions that plagued Ibrahim's rule. In 1523, Daulat learned that his governorship was to be rescinded and he was about to be deprived of power. Anxious to resist but lacking the forces to do so, Daulat appealed to neighboring Kàbul for aid, promising to recognize Babar as his sovereign. Babar recounts in his famous memoirs that for the past "twenty years he had never ceased to think of the conquest of Hindustan" and thus readily accepted the invitation. The truth of this statement has been questioned in light of Babar's numerous attempts to reconquer Samarkand and Farghana, and his limited incursions into northern India in the past. It is, however, of importance mainly for numbering the "invasions" of Hindùstàn by Babar and in determining whether Babar was more an opportunistic adventurer than conquering visionary. Regardless of which viewpoint one selects, Babar showed his characteristic determination as he responded to Daulat's request.

Five years of war followed, during which Babar laid the foundation of the Mughal empire, establishing a dynasty which would rule India until overcome by the Western Europeans in the 18th and 19th centuries. Employing superior military tactics and technology, Babar enjoyed successes against the Afghanis of northern India who had eluded him when he fought his own Timurid people. His first victory came in 1524 as his army defeated the Lodi army sent against Lahore by Ibràhim. Babar quickly consolidated his hold on the Punjab, unceremoniously ousting a surprised, and angry, Daulat Khàn, and formally annexed Lahore to his kingdom. Delayed for a year by concerns over another Uzbeg invasion, Babar returned to his conquest of Delhi in 1526.

Urged on by rivals to Ibràhim's throne who hoped to use Babar for their own ends, Babar cunningly played one off against the other and devoted his full attention to Delhi. In April of 1526, Babar's army met and decisively defeated the massed forces of Ibràhim at the Battle of Panipat. Facing a force, according to Babar's memoirs, of over 100,000 men and some 1,000 elephants (the ancient equivalent of the tank), Babar's army numbered only 10,000, but they included some of the finest horsemen of the day who were backed by "foreign" cannon, an innovation for the armies of central Asia. Positioning the cannon directly in front of the advancing elephants, and using the superior mobility that his mounted riders gave him to surround Ibràhim's army, Babar was able to break the back of the attacking forces. Despite the sheer weight of their numbers, the Afghans found themselves assaulted on all sides, and after battling for the better part of the morning, they began to fall. Though the battle was closely contested, the Afghans fled the field by noon, leaving behind some 15,000 dead, including Ibrāhim Lodi. It was a brilliant illustration of Babar's grasp of tactics and strategy. Delhi lay open before him.

Babar also displayed a deft touch in his dealings with the conquered Afghans, indicating that he had reflected on both the military and diplomatic lessons of his earlier failed attempts at conquest. While restraining his men from plundering and looting Delhi and the future Mughal capital of Agra as they advanced, he also protected the women and children of the upper classes from the savagery that was a common element of central Asian warfare. After securing the public treasures himself and saving those pieces with a cultural value, he liberally distributed the rest among his troops, thus ensuring their loyalty. It proved to be an astute move as the resistance to the Mughal power was not yet finished.

To the southwest, the Hindu Rajput Confederacy—under the leadership of Rānà Sàngà, "child of the sun"—was readying itself to move against the Muslim invaders. Allied with Ibrāhim's brother Mahmūd Rānà, a one-armed veteran who bore the scars of over 80 battles, Rānà Sàngà assembled a huge army of some 100,000 horsemen, representing Hindu India's united stand against the Muslim Mughal invaders. When the battle took place in 1527, Babar's smaller forces were quickly surrounded by Rānà's army. Although the morale of Babar's forces sagged, it was said that he boosted his men's spirits by vowing to never touch forbidden drink again and distributing his silver and gold wine vessels among his beleaguered troops. Whether truth or myth, Babar was able to rally his army and seize the initiative from the over-confident Rānà. Adopting the tactics that had brought him success a year earlier, Babar used his artillery to good effect, blasting a hole through Rānà's assembled force and charging with his mounted troops. Ten long hours decided the Battle of Khanua; Rānà's forces were routed and Babar was master of northern India.

Although Mahmūd Lodi made one final attempt to restore the Sultanate of Delhi, his army was crushed in May 1529. Now Babar had only internal enemies to face. His government and army was riven by disputes over whether to establish an empire in India or return to central Asia. Territory won by strength of arms had still to be organized and administered, but the internal divisions of the ruling Mughals sapped the time and energy needed to implement the sinews of empire. Babar's descendents would have the responsibility for expanding and unifying the empire, for his fate was decided before he saw his work completed. Residing in Agra to record in verse and prose his adventures, Babar died in 1530, weakened in body and spirit from his years of warfare and from concerns for his seriously ill son Humàyùn. Although Humàyùn recovered to claim the empire his father had bequeathed, he faced many rivals and the glory days of the Mughal Empire were still in the future. Babar, however, had laid the foundations and established

Muslim power in Northern India, leaving a legacy of culture and conciliation as well as power and military strength.

Further Reading

The *Memoirs of Zahir-ud-din Muhammed Babur, Emperor of Hindustan* was translated by John Leyden and William Erskine and edited by Sir Lucas King (2 vols., 1921). See also L. F. Rushbrook Williams, *An Empire Builder of the Sixteenth Century* (1918), and Harold Lamb, *Babur, the Tiger: First of the Great Moguls* (1961). There is a chapter on Babur in Bamber Gascoigne, *The Great Moghuls* (1971), a scholarly and beautifully illustrated work. Background studies include A. B. Pandey, *Later Medieval India: A History of the Mughals*, (1963); Michael Prawdin (pseudonym for Michael Charol), *The Builders of the Mogul Empire* (1963); and S. M. Ikram, *Muslim Civilization in India* (1964).

Additional Sources

Memoirs of Zehir-ed-Din Muhammed Babur, Translated by J. Leyden and W. Erskine. Revised by L. King. London: Oxford University Press, 1921.

Haig, Sir Wolseley, *The Cambridge History of India. Volume IV: the Moghul Period.* Delhi: S. Chand, 1971 [1st ed., 1957].

Streusand, Douglas E., *The Formation of the Mughal Empire.* Delhi: Oxford University Press, 1989.

Grenard, Fernand, *Babar, First of the Moguls.* Translated and adapt. by Homer White and Richard Glaenzer. London, 1930.

Habibullah, A. B. M., *The Foundation of Muslim Rule in India.* 2nd rev. ed. Allahabad, 1961.

Wolpert, Stanley A., *A New History of India.* Oxford: Oxford University Press, 1989.

The Baburnama: memoirs of Babur, prince and emperor, Washington, D.C.: Freer Gallery of Art: Arthur M. Sackler Gallery, Smithsonian Institution, 1995.

Edwardes, S. M. (Stephen Meredyth), *Babur, diarist and despot,* New York: AMS Press, 1975.

Hasan, Mohibbul, *Babur, founder of the Mughal Empire in India,* New Delhi: Manohar, 1985.

Jena, Krishnachandra, *Baburnama and Babur,* Delhi: Sundeep Prakashan, 1978.

Lal, Muni, *Babar: life and times,* New Delhi: Vikas Pub. House, 1977.

Shyam, Radhey, *Babar,* Patna: Janaki Prakashan, 1978. □

Charles Babbage

Charles Babbage (1791-1871) was an English inventor and mathematician whose mathematical machines foreshadowed the modern computer. He was a pioneer in the scientific analysis of production systems.

Charles Babbage was born on Dec. 26, 1791, in Totnes, Devonshire. Much of his early education was under private tutors. In 1810 he matriculated at Trinity College, Cambridge. Appalled by the state of mathematical instruction there, Babbage helped to organize the

Analytical Society, which played a decisive role in weakening the grip of blind Newton-worship at Cambridge and Oxford.

In 1814, the same year in which he took his degree, Babbage married Georgiana Whitmore. They had eight children, only three of whom survived to maturity. Mrs. Babbage died in 1827.

Mathematical Engines

In 1822 Babbage produced the first model of the calculating engine that would be the consuming interest of his life. The machine produced mathematical tables, and since its operation was based upon the mathematical theory of finite differences, he called it a "difference engine." The government was interested, and a vague promise of financial assistance encouraged Babbage to begin building a full-scale machine.

But he had underestimated the difficulties. Many of the precision machine tools needed to shape the wheels, gears, and cranks of the engine did not exist. Babbage and his craftsmen had to design them. The consequent delays worried the government, and the financial support was tied up in red tape.

Meanwhile the conception of a far grander engine had entered Babbage's restless brain, the "analytical engine." It would possess (in modern language) a feedback mechanism and would be able to perform any mathematical operation. Babbage asked the government for a decision on which

engine to finish. After an 8-year pause for thought, the government indicated that it wanted neither.

Between bouts with the government and work on his engines, the versatile Babbage managed to squeeze in an incredible variety of activities. He wrote on mathematics, the decline of science in England, codes and ciphers, the rationalization of manufacturing processes, religion, archeology, tool design, and submarine navigation, among other subjects. He was Lucasian professor of mathematics at Cambridge for 10 years, but he was better known for his interminable campaign against organ-grinders in the streets of London.

Always he returned to his great engines, but none of them was ever finished. He died on Oct. 18, 1871, having played a prominent part in the 19th-century revival of British science.

Further Reading

The best source on Babbage is Philip Morrison and Emily Morrison, eds., *Charles Babbage and His Calculating Engines: Selected Writings by Charles Babbage and Others* (1961). It contains an excellent short biography by the Morrisons, a selection of Babbage's works, and associated material on the engines. For more details on Babbage's life see Maboth Moseley, *Irascible Genius: A Life of Charles Babbage, Inventor* (1964). □

Bruce Edward Babbitt

Bruce Edward Babbitt (born 1938) was governor of Arizona (1978-1987), a presidential candidate (1988), and appointed secretary of the interior (1993) in the cabinet of President Bill Clinton.

Born on June 27, 1938, Bruce Babbitt was the second of six children born to Paul J. and Frances Babbitt, and grew up in Flagstaff, Arizona. His family had pioneered ranching and operated Indian trading posts in the 1880s, and they had become prosperous over time. From early childhood Babbitt enjoyed outdoor activities, including hiking and horseback riding.

A Roman Catholic, Babbitt chose to attend the University of Notre Dame, in Indiana, where he majored in geology, expecting to build a career around Arizona's array of mineral wealth. He earned a Bachelor of Science degree in 1960, graduating with honors. Two years later he completed his Master of Science degree in geophysics from the University of Newcastle in England, which he attended on a scholarship.

However, early in his career Babbitt changed his objectives. He decided, instead, on a career in political service in order to help those less fortunate than he. Babbitt entered law school to prepare for such service and received a degree from Harvard University in 1965. During his law school days he joined in civil rights marches in Selma, Alabama. After graduation he worked in the federal antipoverty pro-

programs and strategies. He also served as chairman of the Democratic Governors' Association.

Babbitt decided to seek the 1988 presidential nomination in the Democratic Party. He was the first candidate to declare for the race. His issues included increasing taxes to cut the national budget deficit, creating tax incentives for business, establishing day care programs, expanding health care coverage, reforming federal welfare programs, and promoting environmental protection laws. While he attracted interest in his policy issues, his low-keyed, quiet campaign style and personality did little to attract voters. He withdrew from the race in February 1988, after the Iowa caucuses and the New Hampshire primary.

Babbitt returned home after his short-lived campaign to renew his law practice in Phoenix. He also served as president of the nonpartisan, nonprofit League of Conservation Voters.

In 1993 President Clinton appointed Babbitt to be the nation's 47th secretary of the Department of the Interior, which manages the federal government's large land holdings and natural resources such as oil, gas, timber, and minerals. He brought his intense interest in conservation and environmental protection with him to the position. He believed in the concept of "public use," that the lands must be shared by accommodating environmental and recreational needs, along with the business needs of ranchers, miners, and loggers.

Several months later in 1993, word spread that Clinton was considering Babbitt for an appointment to the United States Supreme Court. He would have been the first nominee in decades not to have previously served as a judge. Environmental groups made a loud outcry to keep Babbitt as interior secretary. They felt that his concern for conservation and his consensus building approach to solving the issues of public land use could not be duplicated by anyone else. Whether or not this outcry affected the president's decision, Babbitt was not nominated as a justice.

As Secretary of the Interior, Bruce Babbitt often found himself in the center of debate as he dealt with many controversial issues. Upon entering office he immediately began to lobby for the establishment of a National Biological Service (NBS) to maintain baseline data concerning the country's natural resources, and to publish that information and use it to identify biological trends. His proposal drew a heavy backlash from private interest groups who did not want to see funding appropriations to the NBS. In 1993 he fought hard for a bill to impose land management controls and to increase grazing fees on public lands, but he met with intense opposition. including a filibuster by the Republican congress. During the following year Babbitt was instrumental in concluding a compromise between the environmentalist interests and sugar farmers in Florida over who would fund a massive restoration and clean-up of the Florida Everglades. In 1996 he campaigned to maintain the Environmental Species Act of 1973, which was under reassessment and scrutiny by the conservative majority. He was criticized by some because he relied heavily on moral and religious issues to argue this case. Babbitt, a master of public relations, traveled frequently to promote his agenda. As the

gram as a civil rights lawyer. Babbitt went on to be a special assistant to the director of Volunteers in Service to America (VISTA) from 1965 to 1967. Leaving government service, he returned to Arizona where he joined a law firm in Phoenix.

Babbitt was elected attorney general of Arizona in 1974. While holding that position he fought against land sale frauds, price-fixing, and insurance irregularities in his quest for consumer protection. In 1978 he became governor of Arizona. The sitting governor had resigned to become an ambassador and the first person to succeed in office passed away. As attorney general, Babbitt was next in line, becoming the youngest person to hold that office in the state's history. Shortly after assuming his new role, he had to campaign for election to a full term. He not only won that race, but sought and won reelection in 1982 for a full second term as well.

As governor, Babbitt showed a moderate ideological approach to politics. He believed that government should be streamlined and show fiscal restraint, but remain protective of civil rights and social justice. He pushed for environmental controls and water management in his first term. In his second term he supported better educational programs and child welfare programs. He also established an Office of the Child, and, having accomplished most of his major goals, chose not to run for reelection for a third full term.

While he was governor, Babbitt became active on the national level as well. He was a founding member of the Democratic Leadership Council (along with the future president, Bill Clinton), which focused on reforming the party's presidential election of 1996 drew near, he was accused by both liberals and conservatives of spending too much time "on the road." Critics argued that he was in actuality spending public moneys to fund thinly disguised campaign for Clinton. Many of these controversies were abated when the president was re-elected, and Babbitt continued in his capacity as secretary of the interior.

Known as a family man, Babbitt married Harriet Coons, a trial lawyer, with whom he had two sons, Christopher and T. J.

Further Reading

Babbitt's years in Arizona office are covered in Marie Marmo Mullaney, *Biographical Directory of the Governors of the United States, 1983-1988* (1989), and in Michael Barone, *et al., The Almanac of American Politics* (editions between 1978 and 1988). His work as secretary of the interior may be followed in *Congressional Quarterly* weekly reports, beginning with his term in 1993. Babbitt authored a book, *Color and Light: The Southwest Canvases of Louis Akin* (1973), and edited *Grand Canyon: An Anthology* (1978), which reflected his love for the southwestern region. Also see articles in *U.S. News and World Report,* May 16, 1994, and *National Parks,* September-October 1995. □

Milton Babbitt

The American composer Milton Babbitt (born 1916) is a leading figure among the most abstract and intellectual group of contemporary composers and a pioneer in the use of electronic synthesizers.

Milton Babbitt was born in Philadelphia on May 10, 1916, and grew up in Jackson, Mississippi. He attended the University of North Carolina, the University of Pennsylvania, and New York University. At school Babbitt was equally interested in mathematics and music; it was not until after World War II and study with composer Roger Sessions that he decided to devote himself to music.

Expands Schoenberg's 12-Tone Concept

Babbitt was intensely interested in Arnold Schoenberg's 12-tone music (which was little known at this time) and published several analyses that revealed new aspects of the 12-tone method of composition. Expanding Schoenberg's concept to include other elements of composition, he wrote *Three Compositions for Piano* (1947), *Composition for Four Instruments* (1948), and *Composition for Twelve Instruments* (1948), in which not only the tones but the durations, timbres, and dynamics are used in a preconceived order. This concept, called total serialization, became one of the dominant musical styles among advanced composers in the 1950s.

Calculations such as these result, of course, in a highly abstract kind of music in which the sounds simply embody the complex organization plans. Babbitt freely admitted that his music had little appeal to the general public. "I believe in cerebral music," he wrote in his 1958 essay, "Who Cares If You Listen?", "and I never choose a note unless I know why I want it there." In this essay he argues that composers should have the same intellectual freedom that abstract scientists, mathematicians, and philosophers enjoy. "Pure" thinkers such as these create for a very small audience of experts; no one but a specialist can understand their thoughts. Babbitt maintained that a composer should not worry about reaching a wide audience but must accept his isolation as a fact of modern life.

Pioneers the Use of Synthesized Sounds

In 1948 Babbitt started teaching at Princeton University and shortly thereafter became interested in the Mark I, an electronic music synthesizer; he helped design and build later models. These early synthesizers produced sounds according to specifications that were fed into the machines on punched tape; the resulting sound was then recorded. The operation was very complex, but the composer gained more control over the sound than he had in conventional electronic music of the era.

In such later compositions as *Vision and Prayer* (1961) and, his most widely acclaimed piece, *Philomel* (1963), Babbitt combined the human voice with synthesizer-produced sounds. Additional works include *Relata II* (1968), *Reflections for Piano and Synthesized Tape* (1974) and *A Solo Requiem* (1977), for soprano and two pianos. Babbitt's *Piano Quartet* (1996) was premiered at a concert held at the Kennedy Center's Terrace Theater in honor of his 80th birthday in May 1996.

In 1959 Babbitt assumed the directorship of the Columbia-Princeton Electronic Music Center. An influential teacher, his pupils formed the so-called Princeton school. He has received numerous honors and awards, including a Guggenheim Fellowship, and was elected to the National Institute of Arts and Letters in 1965. In 1982 Babbitt was awarded a special citation for electronic music by the Pulitzer Prize committee.

Further Reading

Babbitt's essay "Who Cares If You Listen?" is reprinted in Gilbert Chase, ed., *The American Composer Speaks: A Historical Anthology, 1770-1965* (1966). Eric Salzman, *Twentieth- Century Music: An Introduction* (1967), contains a discussion of Babbitt and serialism. *Sounds and Words: A Critical Celebration of Milton Babbitt at Sixty,* comprises a special issue of *Perspectives in New Music* (1976). □

Stephen Moulton Babcock

Stephen Moulton Babcock (1843-1931) was an American agricultural chemist. He perfected the Babcock test for determining the butterfat content of milk, a great stimulus to the growth of the dairy industry.

Stephen Babcock was born on Oct. 23, 1843, in Bridgewater, N.Y., of Puritan stock. After graduating from Tufts University in 1866, he attended Cornell, where he was also a chemistry instructor; he obtained his doctorate in Germany at Göttingen in 1879.

Babcock invented an early method of simple milk analysis while working at the Geneva, N.Y., agricultural experimental station in 1881. He was professor of agricultural chemistry at the University of Wisconsin from 1887 to 1913 (emeritus thereafter), where most of his discoveries were made. He helped direct the Wisconsin state experimental station from 1901 to 1913.

Babcock's central interest was the chemical analysis of milk; but in 1890 he succumbed to pressure from the dairy industry and his Wisconsin colleagues to take an interest in practical, commercial matters. After studying the previous work on butterfat testing, he favored using a chemical agent to liberate the fat globules from the casein content of milk, followed by centrifugal action to complete the milk separation; he settled on sulfuric acid as the agent. The Babcock test, which he developed in 1890, was a total success; simple and reliable, it not only tested milk quality but also made it possible to evaluate cattle, fix standards for municipal milk inspection, and set fair milk prices according to quality grading, which discouraged further watering or skimming of milk by farmers. Despite opposition the test was widely accepted by 1892. Babcock improved it over the years, refining the test as late as 1910. In view of the vast increase in milk output in the United States (ninefold growth between 1870 and 1900), Babcock's test was equaled as a technical advance in dairying only by the centrifugal cream separator. He refused a patent on the test, although it saved millions of dollars for American dairymen by providing data to improve stockbreeding and by cutting butterfat loss in cream separation. The Capper Award in 1930, worth $5,000, was the sole direct monetary gain he received for his discovery.

Babcock worked from 1896 on the biochemistry of casein and its influence on cheese making. In 1897 the enzyme galactase was isolated, to which the decomposition of protein in curd was traced. In 1900 the coordinate influence of another enzyme, pepsin, was discovered and in 1903 a cold-curing process for cheese perfected. Babcock also helped prepare the way for recognition of vitamin A by studying "hidden hunger" in animals.

A few months before his death, on July 2, 1931, the New York Legislature honored Babcock with a bill to preserve his birthplace, the farm at Babcock Hill, Bridgewater.

Further Reading

Babcock's personal papers are in the Wisconsin State Historical Society archives. The book that best describes Babcock's place in the history of the American dairy industry is Eric Lampard, *The Rise of the Dairy Industry in Wisconsin* (1963). See also T. Pirtle, *History of the Dairy Industry* (1926), and John J. Dillon, *Seven Decades of Milk* (1941). □

Isaac Emmanuelovich Babel

The Russian writer Isaac Emmanuelovich Babel (1894-1941) was a master of the short story. His compact, vivid stories of Jewish life in the Odessa of his childhood and of the Russian Revolution are written with great subtlety and intense moral passion.

Isaac Babel was born on July 1, 1894, in Odessa to middle-class orthodox Jewish parents. As a boy, he studied the Bible and the Talmud intensively at home, and at school he was an outstanding student, writing stories in French by the time he was 15. He absorbed a detailed knowledge of Jewish life and culture, which he used in many of his later stories. In 1915 he left home for St. Petersburg, where he was befriended by the writer Maxim Gorky, who as a magazine editor published two of Babel's stories in 1916. The Russian authorities, however, labeled the stories subversive and indecent, and Babel would have been prosecuted but for the outbreak of the Russian Revolution in 1917.

For the next few years Babel abandoned literature. He engaged in political, journalistic, and administrative activities for the Bolsheviks, and in 1920 he became a political commissar in a Cossack cavalry regiment fighting for the Bolsheviks in Poland. This experience was the basis of short stories he began publishing in 1923, which were collected in the volume *Red Cavalry* (1926) and established his fame. They are stories of extreme brutality, violence, and cruelty, often told with grim, ironic humor. Babel's style is ornate, with colorful imagery and startling metaphors, while his technique of moral understatement emphasizes shock and moral impact.

Babel's stories of Jewish life in Odessa, in a collection first published in 1926 but subsequently augmented, are largely based on his own, often painful boyhood and youth. "The Story of My Dovecote" recounts the terrifying experiences he and his family suffered as victims of a pogrom, or organized massacre. There are also extravagantly humorous tales of gangsters in the Odessa underworld.

Babel lived in France periodically from 1928 to 1934. He found writing increasingly difficult in the oppressive environment of Soviet literature during the 1930s. Although recognized as a major author, he was viewed with suspicion by U.S.S.R. authorities and published little during this period. He was arrested by the Soviet secret police on unspecified charges in 1939 and died in a Siberian concentration camp on March 17, 1941.

Babel's name was officially obliterated from the annals of Soviet literature for the 15 years following his arrest. In 1954 he was formally rehabilitated, and many of his works have been reprinted since then.

Further Reading

The most thorough biographical account of Babel is in his own *The Lonely Years, 1925-1939: Unpublished Stories and Private Correspondence*, edited by Nathalie Babel (trans. 1964).

There are valuable additional accounts, including reminiscences of the writer by his contemporaries, in Babel's *You Must Know Everything: Stories, 1915-1937*, edited by Nathalie Babel (trans. 1969). Both volumes contain important stories never before published. Interesting interpretations of his writing are in the introduction by Lionel Trilling to Babel's *Collected Stories* (1955), and in Edward J. Brown, *Russian Literature since the Revolution* (1963).

Additional Sources

Falen, James E., *Isaac Babel, Russian master of the short story*, Knoxville, University of Tennessee Press 1974. □

François Noel Babeuf

The French political revolutionist and writer François Noel Babeuf (1760-1797) was active during the French Revolution. He was among the first to advocate socialism as a political institution for solving the problems of society.

François Babeuf was born in Saint-Quentin on Nov. 25, 1760. Before the French Revolution he was employed as a *commissaire à terrien* at Roye, a position in which he was supposed to help the landed aristocracy assert their feudal rights over the peasants. His occupation made him unpopular among the lower classes, and he himself did not like the nobility. In 1789, on the eve of the Revolution, he wrote the section of the petition from the village of Roye which requested the king to abolish all feudal rights.

In the early years of the Revolution, Babeuf held minor government posts in Somme, in Montdidier, and finally in Paris, where he settled in 1794. He is credited with having applied the word "terrorists" to the Jacobins of 1793-1794. After the Jacobins fell on 9 Thermidor (July 27, 1794) Babeuf supported the men who had defeated them. In 1794 he began to publish the *Journal de la liberté de la presse,* later known as *Le Tribun du peuple.* In an article written shortly after the Thermidorian coup, Babeuf expressed radical democratic ideas. At this time he began to call himself Caius Gracchus Babeuf, after the Roman social reformer.

In October 1794 Babeuf was arrested for attacking the government's economic policies. After his release the following year, he became one of the Directory's most violent critics. In *Le Tribun du peuple* he put forth his socioeconomic ideas and called for the establishment of a republic of equals. His theories, which formed the basis for 19th-century socialism and communism, were offensive to the Thermidorians. But he soon attracted a following of former Jacobins, and they opened a club at the Panthéon. In February 1796 the government closed the club and planned to take actions against the group, which was becoming a political menace.

Meanwhile, Babeuf and his supporters were plotting an attack upon the government. They wanted to implement the Constitution of 1793, because they believed that it would place governmental power in the hands of the people. However, their plan was betrayed by the spy Georges Grisel, and on May 10 Babeuf and the other leaders of the movement were arrested. On April 26, 1797, Babeuf was condemned to death, and he was executed the next day.

Further Reading

The two best works on Babeuf in English are Ernest B. Bax, *The Last Episode of the French Revolution: Being a History of Gracchus Babeuf and the Conspiracy of the Equals* (1911), and Philippe M. Buonarroti, *Babeuf's Conspiracy for Equality* (1828; trans. 1836; repr. 1965). Both books are not only biographies, but histories of the "socialist" conspiracy. Also very good on the conspiracy is David Thomson, *The Babeuf Plot: The Making of a Republican Legend* (1947). □

Polly Baca-Barragán

Elected to the Colorado House of Representatives and, later, to the state senate, Polly Baca-Barragán (born 1943) was the first Hispanic woman elected to those offices. She remains active in politics working on behalf of Mexican Americans and dealing with housing issues.

Polly Baca-Barragán is a pioneer in the growing field of Hispanic woman politics. A Colorado State Senator for 12 years, Baca-Barragán was the first woman chair of the House Democratic Caucus, and in 1985 she was elected chair of the Senate Democratic Caucus. She was the first and only minority woman to be elected to the Colorado Senate and the first Hispanic Woman to serve in leadership in any State Senate in the United States. A longtime activist at the local, regional, and national levels with civic groups, she is nationally known for her leadership skills and motivational presentations.

Baca-Barragán was born in Greeley, Colorado, in 1943. She is the daughter of Spanish Americans José Manuel, a former migrant farm worker, and Leda Sierra, a strong and fiercely independent woman. From her mother Polly learned that "a woman must be her own person, independent and able to care for herself," Baca-Barragán stated in a 1988 interview contributor Gloria Bonilla-Santiago.

Encounters Racism as a Child

One of Baca-Barragán's early memories is from grade school, where she first began to notice racial discrimination. She and her family went to church and saw little girls inside in white dresses; somehow, Baca-Barragán knew she wanted to be seated with them. But the ushers came and told her family they had to sit on the side aisle because they were "Mexican Americans." The center aisles were reserved for the Anglos who went to that church. In her interview, Baca-Barragán recalled clearly the experience: "They assumed we were Mexican American from the other side of the tracks. They didn't want us there. My mother

forced my father to move into a low-income, racially mixed neighborhood, but it was not the Spanish neighborhood. We called it the Spanish American colony because we were from Colorado and from the old Spanish families. My mother was the strength in my family.''

At fourteen, Baca-Barragán's father was killed in an accident, and shortly after her mother died. She literally had to assume the role of an adult even though she had no role models. She raised her three younger brothers using common sense. She loved them and she did what she thought her mother would have done. Motivated by her neighbor, Baca-Barragán finished high school and won a scholarship to attend college. She recollected in her interview that she ''wanted to go to Colorado State University and major in Physics. My chemistry teacher told me about Madame Curie and told me I couldn't succeed in public life because I was 'Mexican American,' but I could in the scientific field because they had to judge you by what you were. So that's what I decided to be, a physics major. The principal at that high school was very bigoted. She tried to discourage me from applying to the state university.''

Although Baca-Barragán began university studies with a major in physics, she was soon drawn back to her ninth-grade desire to enter a field of power—law and politics. She plunged into campus politics, taking the vice presidency, and later the presidency, of the university Young Democrats; she was also secretary for her freshman class. Active as a volunteer for congressional campaigns, Baca-Barragán was a student volunteer of the Viva Kennedy Clubs for John

F. Kennedy and worked as an intern for the Colorado Democratic Party.

After receiving her B.A. in political science in 1962, Baca-Barragán was recruited to work as an editorial assistant for a trade union newspaper in Washington, D.C. Shortly after, she was recruited to work for President Lyndon Johnson's administration as a public information officer for a White House agency. Next she joined the national campaign staff of the late Senator Robert F. Kennedy in his bid for President of the United States in 1968. That same year she served as the director of research and information for the National Council of La Raza in Phoenix, Arizona, where she met her husband, Miguel Barragán, a Chicano activist and former priest. The marriage produced two children, Monica and Mike, before ending in divorce. A few years later, adding to a long list of ''firsts,'' Polly became an assistant to the Chairman of the Democratic National Committee. Shortly after, she opened a public relations business in Adams County after returning to Colorado, where her professional experiences blossomed into her political career.

Wins Election in Colorado

In 1974, Polly Baca-Barragán won Colorado's 34th district seat in the state's House of Representatives, and four years later she was elected to the Colorado State Legislature as the first Hispanic woman senator. In 1977, she was elected the first woman chair of the House Democratic Caucus, and in 1985, she was elected chair of the Senate Democratic caucus. She was the first minority woman to be elected to the Colorado Senate and the first Hispanic woman to serve in leadership in any State Senate in the United States.

In her interview Baca-Barragán recalled a personal note Senator Edward Kennedy sent to her with his best personal wishes during her Legislative campaign, saying, ''We need more representation of the Chicano community in public office as we need more women, and Polly's the best of both. . . . She will represent a progressive, bright, and effective addition to the state legislature, one who will speak for all the people of her district.''

As a freshman legislator in the Colorado House of Representatives, Baca-Barragán broke an old rule of the seniority system which imposed a ''watch and wait'' attitude on first termers. In the 1975 session of the Colorado Legislature, she introduced nine House bills and carried six Senate bills in the House. Two of these House bills and three of Senate bills were passed by both houses and signed into law by the governor. Throughout her term she sponsored 201 more House bills and 57 additional Senate bills. Of these, 156 passed both houses and are now law. Some of her most notable bills are Senate Bill 118, providing for the protection of deposits of public monies held by the state and national banks (1986); Senate Bill 87, providing authority to the Colorado district courts to enforce foreign subpoenas, (1985); Senate Bill 139, concerning assessment of civil money penalties by the state banking board, (1985); House Bill 1117, continuing the short-term-loan revolving fund in the division of housing, (1985); House Bill 1336, regulating the operation of non state post-secondary institutions in

Colorado by the Colorado Commission of Higher Education, and many others.

As the *Denver Post* summarized, Baca-Barragán was known in Colorado as "a democratic senator representing 63,000 Adams County resident. On the other hand, she is the Colorado politician who has the closest ties to the nation's Democratic Leadership in Washington, D.C. . . . In fact, Barragan, has better, more open links to the White House than Gov. Dick Lamm and other Democratic leaders in Colorado." Throughout her work Baca-Barragán won the respect of many leaders in the state of Colorado and nationally. By any standards, she must be judged a good policy maker.

Part of her success is attributable to her many volunteer and civic activities, which she has pursued throughout her career and which she views as a basic training ground for any politician. These activities included Chicano and minority activism, party politics, women's rights, professional and business development, and political and community organizing. Locally, she worked on the Board of Trustees of Labor's Community Agency, the Latin American Research and Service Agency, the Mile High United Way, and she has been on the Policy Advisory Council on the Division of the State Compensation Insurance Fund. On a broader scale, she served on the boards of the National Chicano Planning Council and Mexican American Legal Defense and Education Fund (MALDEF) and many others.

Baca-Barragán told the *Denver Post* that she is especially proud of her part in the founding of the National Congress of Hispanic American Citizens, better known as "El Congreso," the country's first and only full-time Latino lobby at the nation's Capitol. Her experience at the state legislative committee level reads like a Who's Who of committee assignments: Rules; Business Affairs and Labor; Finance; Local Government; Agriculture, National Resources and Energy; Transportation; School Finance; State Affairs; Health, Environment, Welfare and Institutions; Legislative Audit; and Education. Baca-Barragán's legislation, moreover, has always been people-oriented. For example, in 1986 Polly Baca-Barragán introduced innovative legislation to correct inequitable financial burdens on Colorado property tax-payers, while still providing quality education. In addition, she introduced legislation to protect public monies in state national banks. In 1980 and again in 1984, she was elected Co-Chair of the Democratic National Convention and chaired the Colorado delegation to the 1978 Democratic Mid-term Conference. Baca-Barragán also gladly shared her extensive foreign affairs experience as a participant and panelist to major international conferences in Columbia, Mexico, the USSR, Israel, Egypt, Lebanon, Canada, Belgium, and West Germany.

It was her track record of performance and success at the national level as Senator that motivated her to be a candidate for the U.S. Congress in 1986. In a personal interview for *Hispanic Women Breaking Ground and Barriers,* Baca-Barragán commented on the disappointment she felt after losing the race: "I've had two great pains in my life. The divorce was rejection by a male . . . but that's how I perceived it. The other was when I lost my race for Con-

gress. This was rejection because I was an Hispanic woman. That's the only reason I lost that race. It's a great deal of pain. I don't know of a pain that is greater and that's why people don't take risks. It's a lack of confidence that you can't succeed or the willingness to withstand the rejection if you fail."

After the long campaign, Baca-Barragán retired from public office and became President of Sierra Baca Systems, a consulting firm specializing in program development and assessment, leadership training, issue analysis and motivational presentations. In addition, Baca-Barragán has frequently appeared as a political commentator on both television and radio. She is nationally known for her leadership skills and for breaking ground in the area of politics for Latinas in the United States.

In 1988, she was honored as one of the original 14 members to be inducted into the National Hispanic Hall of Fame and being listed in the World Who's Who of Women. Though Baca-Barragán has no political aspirations at present, she continues to be active with national civic groups and serves on a bipartisan Commission on National Political Conventions. More recently, Baca-Barragán has been devoting her time to heading up the Colorado Institute for Hispanic Education and Economic Empowerment, whose mission is to "create a pool of Hispanic leaders who are sensitive to cultural differences and gender issues, and who will jump on the fast track to leadership positions," according to Mercedes Olivera in *Vista.* "If we are to have social cohesiveness as a nation," Baca-Barragán related in *Vista,* "I feel strongly that we have to value the other people, their value system, culture, history. If we honor those differences, then we can look at the human thread that unites us all as human beings." □

Carl Philipp Emanuel Bach

Carl Philipp Emanuel Bach (1714-1788), a German composer, keyboard performer, and theorist, was a prolific composer of vocal and instrumental music, especially for keyboard instruments. He contributed to the formation of the so-called Viennese classical style.

The second surviving son of Johann Sebastian Bach, Carl Philipp Emanuel Bach studied with his father and musically was the most important and influential of the sons. His career as a whole has been said, by E.F. Schmid, to mark a development "halfway between the world of his father and that of the Viennese classics." After schooling at Leipzig, he took a law degree at Frankfurt an der Oder in 1735. He moved to Berlin in 1738 and became keyboard player for the young crown prince, Frederick of Prussia, who in 1740 became King Frederick II. Bach remained in Frederick's service until 1767 as keyboard performer, composer, and accompanist to other members of the royal musical entourage, which included Frederick himself as flutist and a very distinguished circle of musicians.

Two early sets of keyboard sonatas, the "Prussian" Sonatas (1740) and the "Württemberg" Sonatas (1743), show that by the age of 30 Bach had achieved a fully mature style of composition, less rigorous in its contrapuntal organization than that of his father but with considerable power of invention and formal design and with evident stress on bringing to keyboard composition some of the intense expressivity associated mainly with vocal music; for example, the first of the 1740 Sonatas has an instrumental "recitative" as the slow movement.

The publication of his *Essay on the True Art of Playing Keyboard Instruments* (1753) made Bach the most renowned authority of the 18th century on keyboard pedagogy and composition; along with the treatises by Johann Joachim Quantz on the flute and by Leopold Mozart on the violin, it remains one of the principal monuments of 18th-century musical thought and practice. The essay also reflects Bach's preeminence as a keyboard performer, for which he was acclaimed throughout his life. When Charles Burney visited him in Hamburg in 1773, he wrote vividly of Bach's performance on his "Silbermann clavichord, his favorite instrument, upon which he played three or four of his choicest and most difficult compositions, with the delicacy, precision, and spirit for which he is so justly celebrated. . . . "

In 1767 Bach moved from the court of Berlin to a position in Hamburg as director of music at the major churches of the city, and he remained in Hamburg until his death in 1788. His duties called for extensive composition of sacred music, and his Hamburg works include two oratorios and a number of motets and cantatas. He also wrote more than 250 religious and secular songs. But by his own admission he attached the greatest importance to his instrumental music, and he continued in later years to set himself new problems in keyboard composition. The principal later works in this field are his Sonatas, Fantasias, and Rondos for Connoisseurs and Amateurs, published between 1779 and 1787.

A measure of Bach's importance to the inner development of 18th-century style may be seen in the unequivocal claim by Franz Joseph Haydn that he owed a great debt, which dated from his earliest apprentice years, to the music of C. P. E. Bach; and in Beethoven's remark in a letter of 1809 that works by C. P. E. Bach "should certainly be in the possession of every true artist, not only for the sake of real enjoyment but also for the purpose of study."

Further Reading

The best approach to the music and thought of C. P. E. Bach is through his own *Essay on the True Art of Playing Keyboard Instruments* (1753; trans. 1949). Other important early writings are his *Autobiography* (1773; trans. 1967) and Charles Burney's account of his visit with Bach in *The Present State of Music in Germany, the Netherlands, and United Provinces* (1773; 2d ed. 1775). A valuable recent study is Philip Barford, *The Keyboard Music of C. P. E. Bach Considered in Relation to His Musical Aesthetic and the Rise of the Sonata Principle* (1965).

Additional Sources

Ottenberg, Hans-Gèunter, *C.P.E. Bach,* Oxford; New York: Oxford University Press, 1987. ☐

Johann Christian Bach

The German composer Johann Christian Bach (1735-1782) was a facile and prolific writer of vocal and instrumental works in the prevailing Italianate styles of his time. He played an important role in English musical life of the period 1760-1780.

Johann Christian Bach was the youngest surviving son of Johann Sebastian Bach. On the death of his father in 1750, Johann Christian went to Berlin to continue his musical education with his brother Carl Philipp Emanuel (21 years his senior), then court keyboard performer for Frederick the Great. In 1754 Johann Christian departed for an extended period in Italy, centered in Milan. In private service with a Milanese nobleman, he continued his studies with the renowned contrapuntal teacher Padre Martini, with whom he afterward remained on good terms. Bach's conversion to Catholicism in 1760 opened the way to a secure position as organist at the Cathedral of Milan, the main significance of which, as he himself stated, was that it was not demanding and left him time to devote to composing instrumental music and, especially, Italian operas. In 1762 his opera *Alessandro nell'Indie,* on a familiar subject for *opera seria,* was performed in Naples.

Bach's active pursuit of a career as opera composer on the international circuit led to contacts with England, and in 1762 he settled there for good. He was soon appointed music master to the Queen and, together with Karl Friedrich Abel (a former pupil of his father's at Leipzig), he founded the famous Bach-Abel Concerts in London, which lasted from 1764 until 1782 and were among the most important musical events in England during this period. Bach was the leading virtuoso performer and composer of German origin in England at the time; an opera placard billed him as the "Saxon Master of Music."

In 1764 the 8-year-old Wolfgang Amadeus Mozart made his famous appearance as keyboard prodigy at the English court, beginning a close and lasting personal relationship with Bach. In 1778 Mozart wrote from Mannheim to his father that he had met Bach there and that "I love him (as you know) and respect him with all my heart.... " Mozart also wrote an aria (1778) based on the text *Non so d'onde viene,* "which has been set so beautifully by J. C. Bach; just because I know Bach's setting so well and admire it so much, and because it is always ringing in my years, I wished to try and see whether in spite of all this I could not write an aria totally unlike his.... " It is essential for an understanding of the music of Mozart and his times to realize that in the 1770s he was thoroughly familiar with the music of Johann Christian Bach and still wholly unacquainted with that of Johann Sebastian Bach.

Further Reading

The major study of the life and works of J. C. Bach is C. S. Terry, *Johann Christian Bach* (1929). His relationship to the other members of the Bach family is best approached through the source material assembled in Hans T. David and Arthur Mendel, eds., *The Bach Reader: A Life of Johann Sebastian Bach in Letters and Documents* (1945; 2d ed. 1966), and is also discussed in Karl Geiringer, *The Bach Family: Seven Generations of Creative Genius* (1954). Important too are the references to J. C. Bach in Charles Burney, *A General History of Music from the Earliest Ages to the Present Period* (4 vols., 1776-1789), and in the letters of Mozart in collections such as that edited and translated by Emily Anderson, *The Letters of Mozart and His Family* (3 vols., 1938; 2d ed., 2 vols., 1966).

Additional Sources

Gèartner, Heinz, *John Christian Bach: Mozart's friend and mentor,* Portland, Or.: Amadeus Press, 1994.
Terry, Charles Sanford, *John Christian Bach / Lando,* Westport, Conn.: Greenwood Press, 1980, 1967. ☐

Johann Sebastian Bach

The works of the German composer and organist Johann Sebastian Bach (1685-1750) are the ultimate expression of polyphony. He is probably the only composer ever able to make full use of the possibilities of art available in his time.

Johann Sebastian Bach was born on March 21, 1685, in Eisenach, the youngest child of Johann Ambrosius Bach, organist at St. George's Church, and Elizabeth Lämmerhirt Bach. He was the culmination of the family's long line of musicians, beginning with his great-grandfather, Veit Bach, who was a professional violinist in Gotha, and the name Bach was considered a synonym for musician. The Bach family was extremely loyal to the Lutheran faith. Throughout the Thirty Years War (1618-1648) the religious turmoil affected four generations of Bachs, who remained unwaveringly faithful to their Lutheran persuasion.

Bach's first music lessons were on the violin, with his father as instructor. Having a beautiful soprano voice, he also sang in the choir at St. George's Church. On May 3, 1694, his mother died; his father remarried 6 months later but died scarcely 2 months after that. The oldest brother, Johann Christoph, assumed the care of the 10-year-old Johann Sebastian. The boy moved to Ohrdruf to live with his brother, organist at St. Michael's Church. From him Johann Sebastian received his first instruction at the harpsichord and perhaps at the organ.

Lüneburg (1700-1703)

In 1700 Bach was nearing his fifteenth birthday, an age when Bachs usually began to earn their own living. When an opening developed at St. Michael's School in Lüneburg, a scholarship was awarded Bach for his fine voice and his financial need. After his voice changed, he was transferred to the orchestra and played violin. At Lüneburg, Bach met the composer Georg Böhm, organist at St. John's Church, who influenced his early organ compositions. In 1701 Bach walked 30 miles to Hamburg to hear the renowned Jan Reinken, organist at St. Catherine's Church. At neighboring Celle, Bach heard the orchestra of Georg Wilhelm, which specialized in French instrumental music. On subsequent visits to Hamburg, Bach made the acquaintance of Vincent Lübeck, organ virtuoso, and heard German opera under the baton of Reinhard Keiser, the leading operatic conductor in Germany.

The artistic weapon of the Lutheran Church was the chorale, a hymn in the vernacular sung by the people during worship. It was preceded by a chorale prelude, an organ composition based upon a chorale melody. Bach composed almost 150 chorale preludes; his earliest ones in print are from the Lüneburg period. The influence of Böhm, whose favorite form was the chorale partita or chorale variation, is evident in two Bach works: *Christ, der du bist der helle Tag* (Christ, Thou Who Art the Bright Day) and *O Gott, du frommer Gott* (O God, Thou Righteous God).

Bach graduated from St. Michael's School in 1702, and the following year he accepted the position of violinist in the chamber orchestra of Duke Johann Ernst of Weimar. As substitute organist, he had the privilege of practicing long hours on the church organ, which prepared him for future church positions.

Arnstad (1704-1707)

In the summer of 1703 Bach was invited to test and demonstrate the organ in the new church at Arnstad. He made such an impression that a month later he was formally installed as organist. Bach had much time to practice on his favorite instrument and to develop his creative talent. His dramatic flair could already be seen in his Prelude and Fugue in C Minor and Toccata and Fugue in C Major. The first of his church cantatas, No. 15, *Denn du wirst meine Seele nicht in der Hölle lassen* (For Thou Will Not Leave My Soul in Hell), was performed on Easter 1704. Evidently Bach's choir was less than adequate, because after the performance he immediately requested to be relieved of his choirmaster duties. His request was answered with a reprimand suggesting that his poor relationship with the choir was the source of the problem. A second reprimand, resulting from a street fight with his bassoonist, further deteriorated his relationships at Arnstad. He did find some comfort in his companionship with his cousin Maria Barbara Bach, who was referred to as the "stranger maiden" seen in the balcony while Bach was practicing the organ.

In 1705 Bach obtained a month's leave to hear the renowned Dietrich Buxtehude, organist at St. Mary's Church in Lübeck. Bach walked the 200 miles to Lübeck and he was so impressed by the brilliant sound of choir, organ, and 40 instrumentalists performing the annual *Abendmusiken,* or evening music, that he remained there for 4 months without sending an explanatory message to Arnstad. Bach, too, must have made an impression because he was offered Buxtehude's position on his retirement, but the offer contained the traditional stipulation that he marry one of Buxtehude's daughters. Since she was considerably older than Bach and Maria Barbara was back in Arnstad, Bach turned down the offer. when he returned to Arnstad, he imitated Buxtehude and composed long organ preludes. Soon Bach was admonished, and he countered by making the preludes extremely short. In addition, he began improvising and accompanying the hymns with what were called curious variations and irrelevant ornaments. Needless to say, the congregation felt no regret when Bach accepted a post at Mühlhausen.

Mühlhausen (1707-1708)

In 1707 Bach was appointed organist at the Church of St. Blaise in Mühlhausen. It was a free imperial city, larger and richer than Arnstad, and a rich musical tradition had been developed during the previous 50 years by Johann Rudolf Ahle and his son Johann Georg. Every year, for example, they composed a cantata for the installation of the newly elected city council. Later that year Bach married Maria Barbara.

No doubt under the influence of Buxtehude, Bach wanted to present Mühlhausen with what he called "well-ordered church music." He soon discovered that his pastor,

Johann Frohne, was an advocate of Lutheran Pietism. Frohne preferred simplicity in both the liturgy and the music, and the former organist, Johann Georg Ahle, had followed his wishes to a large extent. The very simple musical scores in the choir library reflected this approach. Bach soon became friendly with Reverend George Eilmar, an outspoken enemy of Pietism, who is thought to be the librettist of at least three cantatas which Bach wrote during the Mühlhausen tenure. The brilliant setting of Cantata No. 71, *Gott ist mein König* (God Is My King), written for the installation service of the city council on Feb. 4, 1708, certainly must have antagonized Reverend Frohne and members of the congregation who were in the audience. Bach scored the cantata for strings, woodwinds, trumpets, tympani, and the usual chorus and soloist. The council was so impressed by the performance that the music was printed and put into the city records. In spite of the council's support, the fundamental conflict between his musical ideas and those of Pietism advocated by his pastor caused Bach to look elsewhere for a new position. In his letter requesting an honorable dismissal, he states very clearly that his goal in life is "with all goodwill to conduct well-ordered church music to the honor of God."

Weimar (1708-1717)

When Bach arrived in Weimar late in the summer of 1708 as court organist to Duke Wilhelm Ernst, it marked the third time in 5 years that he had changed positions because of unfavorable circumstances. Hopefully, all would now be well, since his new position doubled his salary and he could work in an orthodox Lutheran environment. The years 1708-1710 saw an enormous output of organ music by Bach. Preludes, fugues, choral preludes, and toccatas poured from his pen. The very familiar Toccata and Fugue in D Minor dates from this early Weimar period.

Bach's primary reputation came from his organ playing, not his compositions. He was in constant demand as a recitalist and organ consultant. Typical is the reaction of Crown Prince Frederick of Sweden, who heard Bach play in Cassel in 1714. Frederick was so astonished at his virtuosity that he took a diamond ring from his finger and gave it to Bach. The musical historian Johann Mattheson, writing in 1716, refers to him as "the famous organist" of Weimar. In 1713 Bach was invited to succeed Friedrich Zachau, the teacher of George Frederick Handel, in the Liebfrauenkirche at Halle. The possibility of playing a 65-rank instrument was a great temptation to him. When he informed the duke of his leaving, the duke promptly raised his salary and promoted him to concertmeister. When the formal invitation from Halle came 2 weeks later, Bach refused it, much to the chagrin of the Halle authorities. They, in fact, accused Bach of simply using their invitation to get an increase in salary at Weimar.

For his cantata compositions Bach was blessed with two fine librettists, Erdmann Neumeister, a Lutheran pastor at St. Jacob's Church in Hamburg, who was especially interested in elaborate church music, and Salamo Franck, the custodian of the library of Duke Wilhelm Ernst. Some of the cantatas from the Weimar period are No. 142, *Uns ist ein Kind geborn* (Unto Us a Child Is Born), and No. 21, *Ich hatte viel Bekümmernis* (My Spirit Was in Heaviness). Bach also wrote a secular cantata, No. 208, *Was mir behagt* (What Pleases Me), to honor Duke Wilhelm's friend the Duke of Weissenfels. Bach did not hesitate to incorporate music from his secular cantatas into his sacred cantatas; for example, the very familiar "Sheep May Safely Graze" was taken from Cantata No. 208.

In his late Weimar years, especially beginning in 1716, Bach composed some of his grandest organ music. These compositions are not based upon a chorale but upon the architectonic nature of music itself. The brilliant preludes and fugues, with all their complexities, are miracles of tonal design. The great Passacaglia and Fugue in C Minor came from this period.

In 1716 the Kapellmeister, or court conductor, Johann Dreise died. Bach wanted this position and resented it very much when it was not offered to him. In addition, a quarrel developed between the duke and his nephew, Ernst Augustus. The duke actually forbade all his employees to have anything to do with his nephew. Bach would not tolerate such an infringement on his personal liberty and composed a birthday cantata for Ernst Augustus. At the same time Prince Leopold of Anhalt-Cöthen, a brother-in-law of Ernst Augustus, had heard of Bach through his sister's marriage. It appears that Bach investigated the musical opportunities at Cöthen and was offered a position.

If Prince Leopold had any doubts of Bach's capabilities, the proposed musical competition at Dresden between Bach and the great French organist Louis Marchand should have dispelled them. The contest was to include sight reading and improvisation. Bach welcomed the opportunity and agreed to read anything Marchand would put in front of him, provided the Frenchman would do likewise. Marchand agreed, but on the appointed day, evidently anticipating defeat, he left Dresden secretly by special coach.

When Bach requested his release to go to Cöthen, Duke Wilhelm refused on such short notice. Bach had already accepted money for the moving expenses and an advance in salary. When the duke would not release him, Bach became so angry that in punishment he was placed under arrest and confined to the country judge's place of detention from Nov. 6 to Dec. 2, 1717. Eight days later Bach began his duties at Cöthen.

Cöthen (1717-1723)

Bach's prime responsibility was to conduct the court orchestra, in which the prince himself participated. Leopold played both string instruments and the clavier. In the fall of 1719 Bach tried to meet Handel, who was visiting his family in Halle, but Handel had already left for London. An effort made 10 years later was also unsuccessful.

Tragedy struck Bach when he returned with the prince from Carlsbad in July 1720. He was informed that his wife had died and had been buried on July 4. Bach lost a great source of inspiration and encouragement in Maria Barbara. He again visited his old friend Reinken in Hamburg, from whom he had received instruction 20 years earlier. At this meeting Bach improvised on the melody *An Wasserflüssen*

Babylon (By the Waters of Babylon). Reinken paid Bach the highest compliment by saying, "I thought this art was dead; but I see that it survived in you." Since Reinken was considered the foremost extempore player of his time, this was high praise indeed.

Late in 1721 Bach married Anna Magdalena Wülken. Only 20 years old, she had to take over the momentous role of wife to a man of genius and also that of mother to his children, the oldest of whom was 12 years old. But she seems to have been equal to both tasks. In addition, during the next 20 years she presented Bach with 13 children.

Bach produced his greatest instrumental works during the Cöthen period. The Cöthen instrumental ensemble consisted of 16 skilled performers, and evidently the first-chair men were capable enough to cause Bach to write special music for them. He wrote unaccompanied violin sonatas and partitas for Josephus Spiess, violinist, and six suites for unaccompanied cello for Ferdinand Abel, principal cellist. Bach's clavier music of the Cöthen period included English and French suites, the first part of the *Well-Tempered Clavier,* inventions, and the two notebooks for Anna Magdalena Bach. Bach also wrote his principal orchestral works during this period, such as the Overtures and the six Brandenburg Concertos. Interestingly, he wrote many of his keyboard works for the instruction of his own children.

Prince Leopold married his cousin, a princess of Anhalt-Bernberg, in 1721. She had no enthusiasm for music and successfully persuaded her husband to give his time and resources to more frivolous activities. The situation became so serious that Bach, who had been quite happy in Cöthen, decided to look for another position. In addition, the education of Bach's children became more and more a concern to him, and he wanted to provide a strong orthodox Lutheran climate for his family.

In 1722 Johann Kuhnau, cantor of the Leipzig St. Thomas's Church, died. The vacant post was offered to Georg Philipp Telemann from Hamburg, who declined, and then to Christoph Graupner of Darmstadt, who, in declining, recommended Bach to the council. After Graupner's refusal a member of the council remarked that since the best musicians were unavailable an average one would have to be selected. In February 1723 Bach played a trial service and presented Cantata No. 22, *Jesu nahm zu sich die Zwölfe* (Jesus Called to Him the Twelve). At a second appearance he presented his setting of the *Passion of Our Lord according to St. John.* More than a year after the death of Kuhnau, Bach was made cantor of Leipzig.

Leipzig (1723-1750)

One can appreciate the reluctance of the Leipzig committee to appoint Bach. He did not have a university degree, and his reputation was primarily as an organist, not as a composer. The other candidates were recognized composers, and Bach's ability as an organist was not needed since the cantor was not required to play at the services. His duties, rather, were primarily to provide choral music for two large churches, St. Thomas and St. Nicholas. A cantata was performed alternately at each church every Sunday. In addition, special music was required on festive days of the church year and for other occasions such as funerals and installations.

In his arrangement with the council, Bach promised to perform not only the musical duties but also other responsibilities in connection with the St. Thomas's School, such as teaching classes in music, giving private instruction in singing, and even teaching Latin.

In Leipzig he composed the bulk of his choral music. The list includes 295 church cantatas, of which 202 have survived, 6 great motets, the 5 Masses, including the B Minor Mass, and the great Passions and oratorios.

In 1747 Bach visited his son Carl Philipp Emanuel, who was in the service of Frederick the Great at Potsdam. Frederick had expressed the desire to meet the great Bach, and for the occasion Bach improvised a six-part fugue on a theme submitted by the King. Later Bach went home and completed the work, which he called a *Musikalisches Opfer* (Musical Offering). He dedicated it to Frederick with the words, "A sovereign admired in music as in all other sciences of war and peace." Bach's last work was the *Art of the Fugue,* in which he demonstrated the complete possibilities of the fugal and canonic forms.

In his final years Bach was afflicted with gradual blindness, and he was totally blind the last year of his life. A few days before his death he dictated a setting of the hymn *Vor deinen Thron tret' ich allhier* (Before Thy Throne I Stand) to his son-in-law. The composition was prophetic. Following a stroke and a raging fever, Bach died on July 28, 1750. Four of his sons carried on the musical tradition of the Bach family: Wilhelm Friedemann and Carl Philipp Emanuel by his first marriage, and Johann Christoph and Johann Christian by his second.

For Bach, writing music was an expression of faith. His musical symbolism, his dramatic flair, even his insistence on no unnecessary notes—all served to profoundly interpret the text. Every composition, sacred and secular, was "in the name of Jesus" and "to the glory of God alone." His influence on music is well stated in the words of Johannes Brahms: "Study Bach: there you will find everything."

Further Reading

The principal source for the life and works of Bach is Philipp Spitta, *Johann Sebastian Bach: His Work and Influence on the Music of Germany, 1685-1750* (2 vols., 1873-1880; trans., 3 vols., 1951). Albert Schweitzer, *J. S. Bach* (1905; trans., 2 vols., 1911), enumerates the principal sources of Bach's tonal language and his chief uses of it. Excellent short biographies of Bach are Wilibald Gurlitt, *Johann Sebastian Bach: The Master and His Work* (1936; trans. 1957), and Russell Hancock Miles, *Johann Sebastian Bach: An Introduction to His Life and Works* (1962). Hans T. David and Arthur Mendel, eds., *The Bach Reader: A Life of Johann Sebastian Bach in Letters and Documents* (1945), treats Bach from the human-interest viewpoint. See also Karl Geiringer, *Johann Sebastian Bach: The Culmination of an Era* (1966). Bach's work in the context of the times is discussed in Manfred F. Bukofzer, *Music in the Baroque Era: From Monteverdi to Bach* (1947), and in Paul Henry Lang, *Music in Western Civilization* (1941). □

Alexander Dallas Bache

American educator and scientist Alexander Dallas Bache (1806-1867) was the first president of the National Academy of Sciences.

lexander Bache, the great-grandson of Benjamin Franklin, was born in Philadelphia on July 19, 1806. He entered West Point at the age of 15. The youngest in his class, he graduated with highest achievement on July 1, 1825, and stayed on for a year as an assistant in engineering. During the following 2 years he worked as an Army construction engineer, assigned to Newport, R.I. There he met Nancy Clarke Fowler, whom he married in 1828. That year he resigned from the Army and accepted a professorship in chemistry at the University of Pennsylvania. As a member of the Franklin Institute for the Promotion of Mechanic Arts and of the American Philosophical Society in Philadelphia, he conducted notable scientific studies in general mechanics, terrestrial magnetism, and weights and measures.

Bache's interest in the broader problems of education became a full-time occupation in 1836, when he accepted the presidency of a new college for the education of "poor male white orphan children." The college bore the name of its benefactor, Stephen Girard, a wealthy Philadelphia merchant who had died in 1831. Bache's first duty was to travel to Europe to find out how such a school could be organized according to Girard's innovative desires. After 26 months of intense investigation into 278 schools, he published the lengthy, exacting *Report on Education in Europe* (1839). This study of comparative education, covering "the systems of general education" as well as the education of orphans, was very influential.

Ironically, the knowledge that Bache acquired in order to set up Girard College was used more for the advancement of public education in Philadelphia. When the opening of the college was delayed by financial and political problems, he offered to help organize the city's newly established Central High School and became its first principal in 1839. Adapting ideas derived from his observations of the Prussian educational system, he planned the curriculum with emphasis on science (*Report to the Controllers of the Public Schools on the Reorganization of Central High School,* 1839).

During his years of involvement with public education, Bache continued to engage in scientific study. In 1843 President Tyler appointed Bache superintendent of the U.S. Coast Survey, a position he held until his death. Bache directed the expansion of the office's scientific activity. He was influential in establishing the National Academy of Sciences and was its first president (1863-1867). He died after a long, debilitating illness at Newport on Feb. 17, 1867.

Further Reading

Merle M. Odgers, *Alexander Dallas Bache: Scientist and Educator* (1947), is a substantial biography. A useful work is Benjamin Apthorp Gould, *An Address in Commemoration of*

Alexander Dallas Bache (1868), which contains a bibliography of Bache's writings. A good background study is Adolph E. Meyer, *An Educational History of the American People* (1957; 2d ed. 1967). □

Isaac Backus

Isaac Backus (1724-1806), an American Baptist leader, was a major figure in New England church history and was instrumental in the eventual securing of the separation of church and state for the new United States.

saac Backus was born of Puritan parents on Jan. 9, 1724, and belonged to the first family to settle Norwich, Conn. His father died when Isaac was 16, leaving an estate which included an iron foundry that became, later, an indispensable source of munitions for the American Revolution. Backus grew up during the Great Awakening; his experience of the mystery of "rebirth" at the age of 17 induced him to leave Congregationalism for the New Light Separatists. In 1746 he preached his first sermon and acknowledged his special calling for the ministry. In early 1748 he became pastor of the First Baptist Church of Middleboro, Mass., a post he held until his death. His career revealed his shrewd organizational gifts and natural intelligence.

Backus's contributions to church history fall into three categories: his efforts for church growth, his theological undertakings, and his political action to separate church and state. In pursuit of the first, Backus traveled extensively on evangelistic missions throughout New England and even into the south. Moreover, he overcame initial misgivings about dangers to congregational autonomy and supported the Warren Association, a powerful vehicle of communication and counsel for New England's Baptist churches. He also served as a trustee of Rhode Island College (later Brown University) and helped soothe Baptist suspicions of higher learning. Backus's *History of New England Baptists,* in three volumes, chronicled the remarkable expansion of the Baptists.

Theologically Backus developed a modified Calvinism suited to the demands of the burgeoning, democratic society in which he lived. Though he was committed to the doctrine of human inability, his writings stressed a gospel of love, millennial hope, and evolving divine revelation through intuitional, not churchly, means. In 1756 he began to advocate adult immersion and closed communion to protect the faithful from the cold intellectualism of Congregationalist orthodoxy.

Finally, Backus labored tirelessly to free the Baptists from the encumbrances of state taxation for the Congregationalist establishment. Basing his arguments upon the Bible, John Locke, and Revolutionary experience, Backus formulated a clear justification for the separation of church and state. After 1769 he led the Grievance Committee of the Warren Association in handling Baptist tax delinquency suits and in petitioning the General Assembly, the British Crown, and, in 1774, the First Continental Congress for redress against civil coercion. Though a Revolutionary patriot, Backus vigorously but vainly protested the church establishment clauses of the Massachusetts constitutions of 1779 and 1780. He was also a delegate to the ratification convention in Boston, 1789, where he praised the national constitution for prohibiting a national church establishment.

Backus's most significant works on religious liberty were *A Seasonable Plea for Liberty of Conscience* (1770) and *Appeal to the Public* (1773). By the time of his death, on Nov.20, 1806, he had provided his successors with the instruments needed to convince Americans that church voluntarism, not church establishment, conformed to divine wishes and American ideals of freedom.

Further Reading

For Backus's writings see William G. McLoughlin, ed., *Isaac Backus on Church, State, and Calvinism: Pamphlets, 1754-1789* (1968), which includes a bibliography. Two studies of Backus are William G. McLoughlin, *Isaac Backus and the American Pietistic Tradition* (1967), and Alvah Hovey, *A Memoir of the Life and Times of the Rev. Isaac Backus, A.M.* (1858).

Additional Sources

Grenz, Stanley, *Isaac Backus—Puritan and Baptist: his place in history, his thought, and their implications for modern Baptist theology,* Macon, Ga.: Mercer University Press, 1983. □

Francis Bacon

The English artist Francis Bacon (1909-1992) was one of the most powerful and original figure painters in contemporary art, particularly noted for the obsessive intensity of his work.

Francis Bacon (a collateral descendant of the great Elizabethan statesman and essayist of the same name) was born in Dublin on October 28, 1909, to English parents. He left home at the age of 16, and after spending two years in Berlin and Paris he settled in London with the intention of establishing himself as an interior decorator and furniture designer. However, he soon gave up interior decorating for painting, in which he was self-taught. The few early paintings that survive (he destroyed most of them) show that he began as a late cubist and then turned by 1932 to an agonized form of surrealism based partly on Pablo Picasso's works of about 1925 to 1928.

Gains Prominence after World War II

Bacon exhibited very rarely until 1945, and it was only after World War II that his paintings became known outside his immediate circle of friends. At this time he also began to paint the human figure, subjecting it at first to weird distortions and combining it with bizarre and disturbing imagery. The pictures that made his reputation are of such subjects as a vaporizing head in front of a curtain and a screaming figure crouching under an umbrella. These startlingly original works are impressive not only as a powerful expression of anguish but also for the grandeur of their presentation and painterly quality.

By the early 1950s Bacon had developed a more direct treatment of the human figure, working almost always from photographs rather than from life. Images taken from newspaper clippings or from the photographs of humans and animals in movement by the 19th-century photographer Eadweard Muybridge were sometimes combined with borrowings from the well-recognized paintings of the old masters. For instance, a series of paintings inspired by the portrait of Pope Innocent X by the Spanish painter Diego Velázquez also incorporate a screaming face and pince-nez derived from a close-up of a wounded nurse in Sergei Eisenstein's film *The Battleship Potemkin*. Such a combination of motifs drawn from completely unrelated sources is very characteristic of Bacon's work. At the same time contemporary imagery is given a grandeur presentation akin to that of 16th- and 17th- century painting.

Major Themes and Subjects

From the 1950s through the end of Bacon's painting career and life in the early 1990s, the recurrent theme of his work was the isolation and anguish of the individual, with a single figure (usually male) seated or standing in a claustrophobic, windowless interior as if confined in a private hell. His subjects were artists, friends, lovers, and even himself. Working without preliminary studies and relying to a great extent on improvisation, Bacon used expressive deformations to extract every nuance of feeling and tension. His painting technique consisted of using rags, his hands and whorls of dust along with paint and brush.

Although Bacon had consistently denied the illustrational nature of his paintings, the facts of his life have tempted art critics and historians to draw links between his personal life and the subject matter of his paintings. One of the great tragedies of his life was the death, an apparent suicide, of his long time lover George Dyer. Dyer's death, the result of ingesting large quantities of drugs and alcohol, occurred just before the opening of Bacon's major retrospective in Paris, France, in 1971. Bacon's famous and moving *Triptych—May-June 1973,* was a three-paneled work of his dying friend hunched fetus-like on a toilet, shadowed in a door frame and vomiting into a sink. While admitting this to be his most personal work, Bacon was still loath to allow its narrative nature, insisting that the panels be framed individually to avoid the impact of storytelling.

In a period dominated by abstract art, Bacon stood out as one of the few great exponents of the figure-painting tradition. During the last decade of his life major retrospective exhibitions were mounted at such sites as the Marlborough Gallery in New York in 1984, Moscow in 1989, and the museum of Modern Art in New York in 1990. Bacon died of heart failure brought on by asthma in Madrid, Spain, on April 28, 1992.

Further Reading

Biographical and critical examinations of Bacon and his works include: Daniel Farson, *The Gilded Gutter Life of Francis Bacon* (1993); Michael Peppiatt, *Francis Bacon: Anatomy of an Enigma* (1997); Wieland Schmied, *Francis Bacon: Commitment and Conflict* (1996); John Russell, *Francis Bacon* (1993); and Hugh Marlais Davies, *Francis Bacon* (1986). □

Sir Francis Bacon

The English philosopher, statesman, and author Sir Francis Bacon (1561-1626) was the chief figure of the English Renaissance. His advocacy of "active science" influenced the culture of the English-speaking world.

Francis Bacon was born in London on Jan. 22, 1561, the younger son of Sir Nicholas Bacon and his second wife, Lady Anne Bacon. Through the families of both parents he had important connections with the political and cultural life of Tudor England. His father was lord keeper of the great seal under Elizabeth I, and his maternal grandfather had been tutor to Edward VI.

Bacon entered Trinity College, Cambridge, in April 1573 and completed his studies there in December 1575. He began to study law at Gray's Inn, but his studies were interrupted for 2 1/2 years while he served with Sir Amyas Paulet, the English ambassador to France. Upon his father's death Bacon returned to England, reentered Gray's Inn, and became a barrister in June 1592.

Bacon's literary work was accomplished, for the most part, during a life taken up with affairs of state. His public career began with his first election to Parliament in 1584. He early sought a position at court and Elizabeth I did make him Queen's counsel, but his ambitions for higher positions, supported by the Earl of Essex, were frustrated.

In 1592, on the anniversary of the Queen's coronation, Essex presented an entertainment composed by Bacon. In the speech in praise of knowledge he states his lifelong theme: "the sovereignty of man lieth hid in knowledge . . . now we govern nature in opinions, but are thrall to her in necessities; but if we would be led by her in invention, we should command her in action." Bacon tied himself closely to Essex and received many favors from him but later helped prosecute him for treason. While his part in the fate of Essex has been criticized as an ungrateful betrayal, it has also been defended as a duty painfully performed.

His Publications

Bacon's first publication, in 1597, was a collection of 10 essays mainly devoted to aphorisms on political behavior. These were expanded and 29 new essays published with them in 1612. A still further enlarged edition, including 58 essays, appeared in 1625.

Bacon was knighted 4 months after the accession of James I in 1603, and in 1607 he was appointed solicitor general. In the meantime he had published *The Advancement of Learning* (1605), hoping to move James to support science. *De sapientia veterum* (*On the Wisdom of the Ancients*), an interpretation of ancient myths, was published in 1609. In the next dozen years Bacon's fortunes soared. In 1613 he was appointed attorney general; in 1616 to the Privy Council; in 1617 lord keeper; and in 1618 lord chancellor and Baron Verulam.

In 1620 *Novum organum* (*New Method*), was published as Part II of *The Great Instauration*. The entire project was never completed, and this part is not complete itself, but Bacon's reputation as a philosopher of science rests mainly upon it. The plan for the renewal of the sciences had six parts: a survey of existing knowledge, Bacon's inductive logic, an encyclopedia of all natural phenomena, examples of the New Method's application, Bacon's discoveries, and an exposition of the New Philosophy that would finally emerge.

Last Years

In 1621, on his sixtieth birthday, Bacon was at the height of his career. He celebrated the occasion with a party at York House on the Strand, his birthplace. Among the guests was Ben Jonson. Five days later Bacon was created Viscount St. Albans. Disaster struck soon after. He was convicted by the High Court of Parliament for accepting bribes, sentenced to a fine and imprisonment, and banned from public office and Parliament. Here again, the degree of

Bacon's guilt, which he admitted, and its moral evaluation have raised controversy.

The last 4 years of his life he devoted to writing *History of Henry VII, De augmentis scientiarum* (1623), *The New Atlantis* (1624), *Sylva sylvarum* (1627), and a number of other pieces.

He died on April 9, 1626, appropriately, however unfortunately, as the combined result of a scientific experiment and a political gesture. Leaving London, he decided to try the effect of cold in inhibiting putrefaction, and he stuffed with snow a hen he purchased from a woman along the way. He caught a chill and went to the nearby house of Lord Arundel, where the servants, in deference to his importance, made available the best bed. It, disastrously, was in a room that had not been adequately warmed or aired out, and Bacon contracted the bronchitis that brought about his death a week later.

Bacon's Philosophy

Bacon developed a dislike for Aristotelian philosophy at Trinity College, and he also opposed Platonism. He felt that Aristotle's system was more suited to disputation than to discovery of new truth and that Plato's doctrine of innate knowledge turned the mind inward upon itself, "away from observation and away from things." Bacon's new method emphasized "the commerce of the mind with things." Science was to be experimental, to take note of how human activity produces changes in things and not merely to record what happens independently of what men do. This is part of what Bacon means by "active science." Still more fundamental is an ethical component. Science should be a practical instrument for human betterment. Bacon's attitude is best summed up in a passage from "Plan of the Work" in *The Great Instauration*, describing the sixth part, on "The New Philosophy or Active Science." "Man is the helper and interpreter of Nature. He can only act and understand insofar as by working upon her he has come to perceive her order. Beyond this he has neither knowledge nor power. For there is no strength that can break the causal chain. Accordingly these twin goals, human science and human power, come in the end to one. To be ignorant of causes is to be frustrated in action."

In the aphorism which concludes Book I of *Novum organum,* two rules of scientific procedure are emphasized: "to drop all preconceived notions and make a fresh start; and . . . to refrain for a while from trying to rise to the most general conclusions or even near to them." The fresh start requires the mind to overcome the influence of four "Idols," tendencies that inhibit the search for truth. The Idols of the Tribe are common to mankind generally. The Idols of the Cave are the tendencies of each man to see truth in relation to his own particular interests and disposition. The Idols of the Theater are the traditional philosophical systems. The Idols of the Market Place are errors that arise from language.

Science should start with what Bacon called Tables of Investigation. The Table of Presence lists instances in which the phenomenon being studied occurs. The Table of Absence in Proximity includes the important negative instances; these are the ones most like the positive instances.

The Table of Comparison compares the degrees of the phenomenon.

Interpretation begins with a brief survey which will suggest the correct explanation of the phenomenon. Although this "anticipation" resembles a hypothesis, there is in Bacon's discussions no clear indication that he recognized the central scientific importance of devising and testing hypotheses. He goes on to consider "prerogative instances," those most likely to facilitate interpretation, of which he classifies 27 different types. By following the method outlined, scientific investigation is supposed to produce, almost mechanically, a gradually increasing generality of understanding, a "ladder of axioms" upon which the mind can climb up or down.

Bacon's program was too ambitious and in its particulars it has been of little influence. His approach did serve, however, to encourage detailed, concrete observation and experimentation and a system of scientific theory tied to them. His identification as the Moses of modern science or the Columbus of the mind is therefore not entirely inapt.

Further Reading

The definitive edition of Bacon is James Spedding, Robert L. Ellis, and Douglas D. Heath, eds., *The Works of Francis Bacon* (14 vols., 1857-1874). The last seven volumes, edited by Spedding, were also printed separately as *The Letters and Life of Francis Bacon Including All His Occasional Works*. Among the most helpful works on Bacon are C. D. Broad, *The Philosophy of Francis Bacon* (1926); Fulton H. Anderson, *The Philosophy of Francis Bacon* (1948) and *Francis Bacon: His Career and Thought* (1962); Benjamin Farrington, *Francis Bacon, Philosopher of Industrial Science* (1949); Karl R. Wallace, *Francis Bacon on the Nature of Man* (1967); Paolo Rossi, *Francis Bacon: From Magic to Science* (trans. 1968); and Brian Vickers, ed., *Essential Articles for the Study of Francis Bacon* (1968), which includes selected articles and useful bibliographical references. □

Nathaniel Bacon

Nathaniel Bacon (1647-1676) was an American colonial leader in Virginia and the leader of Bacon's Rebellion in 1676.

The period of American colonial history which followed the restoration of the Stuart monarchy in England (1660) was an era of political and economic instability. Typical of the way converging problems could lead to civil conflict was Bacon's Rebellion. The youthful Nathaniel Bacon took charge of discontented frontiersmen and, during the course of an Indian war, virtually assumed control of the colony of Virginia. The results of Bacon's Rebellion were not lasting; most of the legislative reforms were repealed at its end, and 23 of its leaders met their death by hanging.

Nathaniel Bacon was born on Jan. 2, 1647, at Friston Hall, Suffolk, England. He was the only son of Thomas Bacon, a wealthy landowner. A contemporary remembered him as being tall and slender, "blackhair'd and of an ominous, pensive melancholy Aspect . . . not much given to talk, . . . of a most imperious and dangerous Pride of heart, despising the wiser of his neighbours for their Ignorance, and very ambitious and arrogant." These traits of character were evident in Bacon's withdrawal from Cambridge without completing a degree. Upon his marriage to Elizabeth Duke, the bride's father rejected the match and disinherited his daughter. Shortly thereafter, the impetuous Bacon became involved in a scheme to defraud an acquaintance. Disturbed by his errant son's behavior, Thomas Bacon helped Nathaniel and his wife leave England to settle in Virginia.

Arrival in Virginia

Nathaniel Bacon arrived in Virginia in 1674 with both money and influence to aid him. His father and brother-in-law had sent him off with £1,800 and with forewarning to influential relatives in Virginia. Hearing of Bacon's wish to settle on the frontier, Governor William Berkeley helped arrange the purchase of two estates; the governor also assisted Bacon by granting his application to engage in Indian trade. The governor later paid the new planter the honor of a seat on the Council. "Gentlemen of your quality come very rarely into this country," he explained, "and therefore when they do come are used by me with all respect."

Bacon's Rebellion

A variety of causes contributed to Bacon's Rebellion. The immediate cause was the resumption of violent clashes with frontier Indians, including the killing of Bacon's overseer. Vigilante groups sprang up to protect the colonial settlements, and Bacon accepted command of the hastily organized forces. The underlying factors giving rise to the rebellion are variously described by contemporaries. Doubtless, the depressed price of tobacco exports (Virginia's main crop) and unhappiness with English mercantile laws laid bases for discontent. Other causes for dissatisfaction were the vast land grants in northern Virginia made arbitrarily by Charles II to his courtiers. Complaints also arose about the arbitrary governing system of Virginia, especially at the local level, and the inequities of heavy tax assessments. There can be little question, however, that the Indian troubles and Governor Berkeley's failure to react vigorously to demands for action by frontier settlers gave cohesion to Bacon's movement.

Bacon wrote to Governor Berkeley seeking permission to attack the Indians and then, without waiting for a reply, moved his vigilantes against the tribes. But instead of supporting this effort, the governor was furious, believing Bacon's actions would further antagonize the Indians. Hoping to marshal popular support, Berkeley proclaimed Bacon a rebel and dissolved the General Assembly, which had sat for 16 years, calling for new elections. Meanwhile, Bacon had returned a hero from an apparently successful foray against the Indians and was elected to the House of Burgesses.

When the General Assembly met in June 1676, Governor Berkeley decided to try to patch up his quarrel with Bacon. An elaborate public reconciliation was arranged, and Bacon was restored to a seat on the Council. But shortly afterward, the struggle was renewed. Probably, Bacon had expected to receive a formal commission from the governor and to return to his Indian campaign without delay. When this appointment was not forthcoming, he fled Jamestown, regrouped his men, and captured the city. Under duress, Berkeley issued the commission and also signed into law the series of legislative acts known as "Bacon's Laws." It is doubtful that Bacon had much influence over this legislation, but the new laws did indicate some of the issues which had contributed to the controversies of the past months. The most important bill established universal manhood suffrage, while other acts provided for the popular election of church vestries, eliminated tax privileges for councilors, abolished plural office holding, and instituted rules to make the local county government more responsive. This action completed, Berkeley again tried to raise troops to reassert his authority. Failing in an open confrontation with Bacon's superior forces, Berkeley fled Jamestown and a civil war ensued.

Then Bacon's Rebellion collapsed. The immediate cause was Bacon's death, from disease and exposure, on Oct. 26, 1676. Important too was the English government's continuing support of Governor Berkeley: desperate reports of the "uproars" in Virginia had induced Charles II to send 1,130 troops to support the constituted government. Yet even before the troops landed, the rebellion had collapsed, and Governor Berkeley, gathering strength as the rebel forces disintegrated, was able to disperse the remaining rebels and execute their leaders. Berkeley's vindictiveness, however, led to conflicts with the King's representatives and his eventual recall to England in disgrace.

Further Reading

Two opposing views of Bacon are Thomas Jefferson Wertenbaker, *Torchbearer of the Revolution: The Story of Bacon's Rebellion and Its Leader* (1940), and Wilcomb E. Washburn, *The Governor and the Rebel: A History of Bacon's Rebellion in Virginia* (1957). An excellent short appraisal is in Wesley Frank Craven, *The Colonies in Transition: 1660-1713* (1967). A good general account of the Southern colonies during this period is Craven's *The Southern Colonies in the Seventeenth Century: 1607-1689* (1949). For a penetrating comparison of Bacon's Rebellion with other colonial conflicts see Clarence L. Ver Steeg, *The Formative Years: 1607-1763* (1964). □

Roger Bacon

The medieval English philosopher Roger Bacon (ca. 1214-1294) insisted on the importance of a so-called science of experience, or "scientia experimentalis." In this respect he is often regarded as a forerunner of modern science.

Little is known about the details of Roger Bacon's life or about the chronology and motivation of his major works, the *Opus majus,* the *Opus minus,* and the *Opus tertium.* It appears that he was born in Ilchester, Somerset. At 13 he entered Oxford University, where he spent 8 years. Contrasting himself to other scholastics who received only a baccalaureate in the arts and then moved on to theology, Bacon took delight in having the advanced arts degree.

In the 1240s, perhaps in the early years of the decade, Bacon lectured at the University of Paris on the works of Aristotle. During this period he also wrote three works on logic. Within relatively few years there were three important events in Bacon's life: his return to England from France, the awakening of his scientific interests, and his entry into the Franciscan order.

A Universal Science

Early in his empirical pursuits Bacon envisioned a universal science which would promote the spread of Christianity, prolong life, aid health, and form a synthesis between theology and the science of experience. Theology for Bacon was more or less biblical theology, not the scholastic theology based on the *Sentences* of Peter Lombard, which Bacon may have known only superficially. He praised science as being "most beautiful and most useful." Bacon had other reasons for urging Christians to take up a science of experience. In many respects his age had an

apocalyptic character, and there was considerable belief that a struggle with the antichrist was imminent. Bacon saw a science of experience as a Christian weapon for the fray.

It is quite likely that Bacon became a Franciscan in 1252. By Bacon's time, as even more so during the following century, the work begun by St. Francis had posed problems for his followers. Franciscans were required to take a vow of poverty, but their work had swelled to such size and importance that it was impossible to continue it unless the order owned or at least administered property and other possessions. However, the acquisition of property by the Franciscan order was seriously questioned by a group of friars who claimed a literal allegiance to St. Francis. Bacon joined this group.

Moreover, during this very period of struggle over the vow of poverty, the new orders, Dominican as well as Franciscan, were being attacked by the secular clergy, whose power was being diminished as the religious clergy grew in numbers and influence.

Period of Confinement

About 1257 Bacon was taken from England to France and, for unknown reasons, underwent some kind of confinement, perhaps even an imprisonment, in a French monastery. One theory is that his scientific interests made him suspect, but it is more likely that his views on Franciscan life proved unpopular with the friars in England. Actually, there are no grounds for thinking that this confinement had any-

thing to do with an alleged conflict between science and religion.

During his period of confinement Bacon wrote his greatest works: the *Opus majus,* the *Opus minus,* and the *Opus tertium.* Differences among scholars concerning the order and purposes of these works underscore once again the many unknowns concerning Bacon's life. It seems that he intended to write a treatise on the sciences but soon realized the magnitude of such a task. Instead, he composed what is now known as the *Opus majus,* in which he made use of materials already written, added new material, and climaxed the work with a section on moral theory. With respect to the sciences, the overall tone of the *Opus majus* is a rhetorical plea, attempting to persuade the pope about the importance of experimental knowledge. There is no evidence that Bacon made any important contribution to science and much evidence that he was, instead, a reader, writer, and rhetorician in behalf of science. Concerning the *Opus minus,* a convincing theory is that it was written while the *Opus majus* was still in the hands of copyists and Bacon was reflecting on his omissions from the earlier manuscript. The *Opus minus* is thus a supplement to the *Opus majus.* The *Opus tertium* may well have been an expansion of what began as a preface to the earlier two works.

Observations and Writings

In many ways Bacon was ahead of his time. His works mention flying machines, self-driven boats, and an "instrument small in size, which can raise and lower things of almost infinite weight." He studied the heavens. He seems to have studied the refraction of light under experimental conditions, but in his so-called science of experience he did not make any known advances into what is today called physics; and he did not make any known practical inventions.

After the three works previously mentioned, Bacon wrote a great part of *Communium naturalium,* one of his finest works. He also wrote a Greek grammar and a Hebrew grammar, and in 1272 he published *Compendium of the Study of Philosophy,* in which the old, angry, polemical Bacon reemerges. It is possible that an imprisonment in the final years of his life stems from the *Compendium,* in which he claimed to see in the then-warring factions of Christendom the presence of the antichrist and in which he took in general the extreme view of Franciscan life identified with Joachim of Fiore.

The length of his imprisonment and the causes of his release are again matters of educated guesswork. He was free enough late in life to write *Compendium of Theology.* He was not imprisoned at the time of his death, which occurred in 1294 (according to one account, on June 11).

Further Reading

The best work on Bacon is Stewart C. Easton, *Roger Bacon and His Search for a Universal Science* (1952). See also John Henry Bridges, *The Life and Work of Roger Bacon* (1914); Theodore Crowley, *Roger Bacon* (1950); and E. Westacott, *Roger Bacon in Life and Legend* (1953). Appreciative discussions of Bacon are in A. G. Little, ed., *Roger Bacon: Essays*

Contributed by Various Writers on the Occasion of the Commemoration of the Seventh Centenary of His Birth (1914). See also Lynn Thorndike, *A History of Magic and Experimental Science* (2 vols., 1923), and a chapter by Robert Steele, ''Roger Bacon and the State of Science in the Thirteenth Century,'' in Charles Singer, ed., *Studies in the History and Method of Science,* vol. 2 (1921).

Additional Sources

Bridges, John Henry, *The life & work of Roger Bacon: an introduction to the Opus majus,* Merrick, N.Y.: Richwood Pub. Co., 1976.

Westacott, Evalyn, *Roger Bacon in life and legend,* Norwood, PA: Norwood Editions, c1953, 1978. □

Amos Bad Heart Bull

Amos Bad Heart Bull (1869-1913) was an Oglala Lakota Sioux tribal historian and artist known for his pictographs.

Amos Bad Heart Bull (bottom)

Amos Bad Heart Bull was called ''the Herodotus of his people'' by Helen Blish, who rescued his 400 pictographs by having had them photographed before their interment. Through her intervention *A Pictographic History of the Oglala Sioux* was published to relate the transition of these proud Plains warriors into reservation Indians. The illustrations from this book have been featured in every television documentary about the Ghost Dance, the Battle of the Little Big Horn, and the deaths of Sitting Bull and Crazy Horse. The artist's pictures of Crazy Horse, his cousin, are the only surviving likenesses of him since Crazy Horse never allowed himself to be photographed. Fortunately, Blish was able to interview two of the artist's uncles, He Dog (Sunka Bloka) and Short Bull (Tatanka Ptecela), on the Pine Ridge Reservation in South Dakota, to learn a little about his life. Short Bull and He Dog told her that Amos Bad Heart Bull the Elder had been a band historian, a keeper of the winter count, and had created a hide chronicle on which the outstanding single event of each year was recorded. Since he died young, the task of bringing up his son fell to them, and to their brothers, Little Shield and Only Man. They told him stories of the battles they had fought in, and observed his interest in collecting treaties and documents about Indian-white encounters.

Self-Taught Artistry

Without any formal instruction, Bad Heart Bull began creating annotated drawings. Although he had been given no education, he taught himself to write using a system devised by the missionaries for the transcription of Lakota. He also learned English from the soldiers at Fort Robinson, where he had enlisted as a scout for the United States Army in 1890. From a clothing dealer in Crawford, Nebraska, he bought a used ledger in which he began his 415 drawings using black pen, indelible pencil, and blue, yellow, green, and brown crayons, and red ink. In some instances he painted with a brush so fine that the strokes can be seen only under magnification. In addition, some of the pictures are touched with a gray or brown wash in places. He worked at this project for about two decades recording the civic, religious, social, economic, and military life of the Oglala.

His technical innovations permitted multiple perspectives of an event. He portrayed masses of people engaged in dramatic actions by assuming a panoramic view. Depicting hundreds of men and horses in battle, or in religious ceremonies, or in processionals to a buffalo hunt from above, he captured tribal activities in long-shots or topographic views. Then, he would render close-ups of some aspect on the same page, framed and set-off to one side, so that one could study the psychological impact of the sweeping event upon an individual participant by means of a near-view insert. He experimented with other than stylized profile renditions, using full-face depictions, rear-views, rendering wounded horses from below, or showing dancers in three-quarter view. Another innovation was his use of foreshortening. These techniques added drama and realism to his pictures.

Each set of drawings tells part of a heroic epic. The first group shows tribal events before 1856. The councilmen (wakicunza) and their marshals (akicita) are shown deliberating in the camp council, a buffalo hunt, a sun dance, and the eight warrior societies in their regalia are shown. The next set of pictures tells the story of the conflicts with the Crow, their hereditary enemies on the Plains in sporadic skirmishes from 1856 to 1875. The third set narrates the defeat of U.S. General George A. Custer on the Little Big Horn River in Montana. The next group of pictures shows the reorganization of Oglala society as it was forced to accept reservation existence. It opens with the ceremonies: the Sacred Bow, the Victory Dance, the Dance of the Black Tailed Deer, the Horse Dance, and the Vision Quest. These are followed by eight depictions of courting scenes, and ten of games. This section closes with the transition to agriculture. The next to last set depicts the Ghost Dance and the Battle of Wounded Knee. And the final set shows the fourth of July being celebrated in 1898 and in 1903 on the Pine Ridge Reservation. By grouping his pictures in these narrative sequences, the artist has conveyed the history of his band over 60 years. Because he preserved the most minute details of daily life, this constitutes an unparalleled historical record.

Rescued for Posterity

In 1926, Helen Blish was a graduate student at the University of Nebraska searching for examples of Plains art. From W. O. Roberts of the Pine Ridge Agency, she learned about Bad Heart Bull's drawings, which had been given, after the artist's death in 1913, to his sister, Dolly Pretty Cloud. Speaking through an interpreter, Blish spent her summer vacations from teaching in a Detroit high school, studying the art of Pretty Cloud's brother, kept in a trunk on the dirt floor of the one-room cabin on the reservation. It was only after much persuasion that she was permitted to rent it for a modest annual fee and to analyze the renderings for her master's thesis under the noted art historian Hartley Burr Alexander.

Following Lakota custom, the prized ledger book was buried with Pretty Cloud upon her death in 1947. Fortunately, though, Blish's work had been given to the American Museum of Natural History in New York City before her death in 1941. In 1959, the University of Nebraska Press decided to publish Bad Heart Bull's pictorial history and attempted to get permission to disinter the ledger, to no avail. However, it was found that Alexander had photographed the priceless document page-by-page in 1927; therefore, these illustrations were collated with Blish's manuscript and published in book form. Mari Sandoz, the biographer of Bad Heart Bull's cousin, Crazy Horse, encouraged the project from its inception, and wrote its introduction in the last year of her life. She said, ''Without doubt, the Amos Bad Heart Bull picture history is the most comprehensive, the finest statement as art and as report of the North American Indian so far discovered anywhere.''

Further Reading

Blish, Helen H., *A Pictographic History of the Oglala Sioux*, Lincoln, University of Nebraska Press, 1967.
Dockstader, Frederick J., *Great North American Indians*, New York, Van Nostrand Reinhold, 1977.
The Indians' Book, edited by Natalie Cirtis Burlin, New York, Harper, 1923.
Sandoz, Mari, *Crazy Horse: The Strange Man of the Oglalas*, Lincoln, University of Nebraska Press, 1942. □

Pietro Badoglio

The Italian general and statesman Pietro Badoglio (1871-1956) played a large part in the Italian victories in World War I and in Ethiopia in 1936. He shared the responsibility for the Italian disaster in World War II.

Pietro Badoglio was born in Grazzano Monferrato. He graduated from military academy in 1890, served his first campaign in Africa from 1895 to 1898, and was attached to the general staff in Rome as a captain in 1906. An intelligent, though tough and taciturn, officer, he gained battlefield promotion to major in the Libyan campaign in 1911-1912. With the outbreak of World War I, he became a lieutenant colonel of the general staff. Defying the stationary warfare that ensued, Badoglio brilliantly broke through the Austrian lines in 1916, conquered Mount Sabotino (Gorizia), and brought a much-needed victory to Italy. Battle promotions to the top military hierarchy followed. As major general and assistant chief of general staff, he distinguished himself further, both in Italy's recovery from disaster in 1917 and in the crushing of Austria in 1918. Badoglio then headed the armistice commission and negotiated the Austrian surrender.

A senator and chief of army staff in 1919, Badoglio was appointed successively ambassador to Brazil in 1924, chief of general staff in 1925, field marshal in 1926, and governor of Libya in 1928. In 1929 he was ennobled as the Marchese of Sabotino and was awarded the highest Italian honor, the Collar of the Annunziata.

When the Fascist government bungled the early Ethiopian campaign in 1935, Mussolini hastily appointed Badoglio supreme commissar, and he achieved a rapid, total victory in 1936. Although promptly named viceroy of Ethiopia and titled the Duke of Addis Ababa, Badoglio preferred to return to Rome, the center of activity, rather than remain isolated in Africa. A Royalist rather than a Fascist soldier, a suspicious, calculating politician as much as a military professional, he remained aloof from Benito Mussolini and reserved his loyalties for King Victor Emmanuel III.

In 1936 Badoglio resumed the position of chief of staff, but his star had already begun to decline. When World War II broke out, he was aware of, as well as inherently responsible for, Italy's military unpreparedness, and he opposed Italian entry timidly and without conviction. He was forced to resign in 1940 after the first military defeats.

When the King deposed Mussolini in 1943, he appointed the 72-year-old Badoglio prime minister with a mandate to end the war. But Badoglio, no longer resolute or capable, brought Italy to the worst possible armistice in 1943: German occupation, Allied invasion, and civil war. He disgraced himself further by abandoning Rome to the Nazis and fleeing south with his government. He held power precariously and only through Allied support, which ceased with Rome's liberation in 1944. Futilely defending

his record in his last years, he died in Grazzano Monferrato in 1956.

Further Reading

There is a good summary of Badoglio's life in Italian, A. Mosti, *Pietro Badoglio* (1956). Studies in English concentrate on Badoglio's war government. The best military narrative is C. R. S. Harris, *Allied Military Administration of Italy, 1943-45* (1957); the best general account is F. W. Deakin, *The Brutal Friendship: Mussolini, Hitler, and the Fall of Italian Fascism* (1962).

Additional Sources

Bertoldi, Silvio, *Badoglio,* Milano: Rizzoli, 1982. □

Leo Baeck

Leo Baeck (1873-1956)—rabbi, teacher, hero of the concentration camps, and Jewish leader—represented in his life and writings the drama, tragedy, and hopefulness of modern Judaism.

L eo Baeck was born May 23, 1873, in Lissa, a city in the Prussian province of Posen where his father was an Orthodox rabbi. There he received both a traditional Jewish education and secular training in the Lissa Gymnasium. He continued this dual interest in Judaism and

secular thought through his studies at the Orthodox seminary Judische-Theologisches Seminar, the University of Breslau, the Berlin Hochschule fuer die Wissenschaft des Judentums (a liberal Jewish seminary), and the Friedrich Wilhelm University. In 1897 he received a rabbinical degree from the Hochschule and a doctorate from the University of Berlin.

Baeck's rabbinical experience included that of a traditional synagogue in the town of Oppeln, Silesia, and of the larger synagogue in Dusseldorf. Finally he was elected senior rabbi of the autonomous Jewish community of Berlin, a post which he held from 1912 until 1943 when he was deported by the Nazis to the concentration camp at Theresienstadt. He was a noted teacher, rabbi, and preacher, respected by Jew and non-Jew alike.

His reputation was built not only upon his scholarship but also upon his concern for the entire Jewish community. He was active in civic organizations like B'nai Brith and also in the Zionist movement, which was unusual for a German rabbi of his time. He was also known and respected by Christian leaders after the publication of his first book, *The Essence of Judaism* (1905), which responded to a critique of Judaism offered in Adolf von Harnack's book *What is Christianity.*

The Nazi Years and Their Aftermath

Baeck's reputation was sorely tried during the Nazi years. He served as leader of the council of German Jews established by Hitler in 1933 and later in Theresienstadt

served as head of the *Aeltestenrat,* a council of elders which was more a facade of Jewish autonomy than an actually independent body. Baeck has been criticized for his cooperation with the Nazis in their attempts to mask their atrocities with the appearance of justice. Nevertheless Baeck was able to utilize these positions to promote prayers of protest and to mobilize Jewish learning as a means of resistance to the Nazi effort to dehumanize the Jews.

After World War II Baeck went to London, and in 1953 he became a British citizen. While continuing his educational activities in England he also served on the faculty of the Reform Seminary, the Hebrew Union College, in Cincinnati, Ohio. He thus became associated with the Liberal Movement in Judaism, and the Liberal Jewish seminary in London is named after him. During this time he also travelled to Israel, lecturing at the Hebrew University.

His Thought

Baeck's thought had three central concerns: Jewish ethics, Judaism and Christianity, and the Jewish people. These are represented by three major works. His first book, *The Essence of Judaism,* began as an exposition on the continuity of Jewish thinking from the Bible through the great rabbinic teachers. By the time it was revised and expanded in 1922 Baeck had developed a three-fold understanding of Judaism. Jewish religion, he contended, is made up of, first, prophetic universalism, proclaiming God's unity to humanity; second, an optimistic and dynamic faith in God, in oneself, in others, and in humanity as a whole; and third, the historical task of the Jewish people as God's emissary to the world.

In each section of his book Baeck weaves quotations from the Bible and later Jewish writings into a compressed compendium of Jewish thinking. The first section gives primacy to the religious experience, the second to ethics, and the third to history. The book comprises a sketch of Judaism richly studded with authentic Jewish texts.

Baeck's various essays on Christianity explore the differences among the rabbis, Jesus, Paul, and the later church (his earliest writings on Christianity date from 1922; see in English *Judaism and Christianity,* 1958). Judaism, he contended, is a classical religion, by which he meant a religious tradition seeking a positive, active social life, while Christianity is a romantic religion, a tradition that is inward looking. This contention stimulated considerable controversy among German biblical scholars (see Krister Stendal's introduction to Baeck's *The Pharisees and Other Essays,* 1947).

Baeck continually emphasized the Jewish people as a cultural and historical group. His final work, *This People Israel* (1955, and in English translation 1964), captures the sweep and majesty of Jewish history while revealing his commitment to the Jewish people. The book, which began as an exposition of the greatness of biblical Judaism, was written in 1938 and destroyed by the Nazis. The rest of the book was composed while in the Theresienstadt concentration camp. The first half covers biblical history, giving insightful summaries of such perplexing problems as the levitical laws. The second half follows Jewish culture in its various incarnations in Europe, whether under Muslim or Christian domination, and into the modern world, including mention of all the major trends in Jewish thought and social development. The book concludes with an affirmation of the Jewish task.

Further Reading

A short introduction to Baeck's life and thought by a colleague and disciple can be found in Fritz Bamberger, *Leo Baeck: The Man and the Idea* (1958). An interesting, if laudatory, biography by one of Baeck's American students after World War II is Albert H. Friedlander, *Leo Baeck: Teacher of Theresienstadt* (1959). Leonard Baker's *Days of Pain and Sorrow: Leo Baeck and the Berlin Jews* (1978) presents a well researched, critical, and scholarly analysis of Baeck's life in its German context. Useful information is also included in the introductions to the English translations of Baeck's writings. Walter Kaufmann's remarks in Leo Baeck, *Judaism and Christianity,* translated with an introduction by Walter Kaufmann (1958), are particularly illuminating.

Additional Sources

Baker, Leonard, *Days of sorrow and pain: Leo Baeck and the Berlin Jews,* New York: Macmillan, 1978. □

Leo Hendrik Baekeland

An American chemist, inventor, and manufacturer, Leo Hendrik Baekeland (1863-1944) invented Bakelite, the first plastic to be used widely in industry.

Leo Ernst Baekeland was born in 1863 in Ghent, Belgium. He took a bachelor of science degree from the University of Ghent in 1882 and began to teach there as an assistant professor; he received his doctorate in natural science in 1884 and continued to teach for another 5 years. In 1889 he went to the United States on a traveling scholarship, liked the country, received a job offer from a photographic firm, and decided to make America his home.

These were the years when science was first coming to the attention of American industry. In some European countries, notably Germany, industrial research was already helping to improve old products and processes and to develop new ones. This wedding of science and technology was just beginning in the United States, first in those industries that had been close to science from their beginnings, such as the chemical and electrical industries. The manufacture of photographic equipment and materials was one such industry. Baekeland began work to improve photographic film, and in 1893 he established the Nepera Chemical Company to manufacture Velox paper, a film of his invention which could be handled in the light. In 1899 he sold out to the leading firm in the field, Eastman Kodak, and used the money to set up his own private industrial research laboratory in a converted barn behind his home in Yonkers, N.Y.

At this laboratory Baekeland began a large number of experiments covering a range of subjects. One of these was an attempt to produce a synthetic shellac by mixing formaldehyde and phenolic bodies. Other experimenters had worked with these two substances, and it was known that the interaction was greatly influenced by the proportions used and the conditions under which they were brought together. Baekeland failed to synthesize shellac but instead discovered Bakelite, the first successful plastic.

Earlier plastics had only limited usefulness because of their tendency to soften when heated, harden when cooled, and interact readily with many chemical substances. Baekeland's new material did not suffer from any of these defects. Using temperatures much higher than previously thought possible, he developed a process for placing the material in a hot mold and adding both pressure and more heat so that a chemical change would take place, transforming the material in composition as well as shape.

He patented this process in 1909 and formed the Bakelite Corporation the following year to market the material. Bakelite soon became very successful and was widely used in industry as a substitute for hard rubber and amber, particularly in electrical devices. He retired from the company in 1939, honored for his success as a manufacturer and for his effectiveness as a spokesman for the whole concept of scientific research in the aid of industry.

Further Reading

There is no available biography of Baekeland. A sketch of his activities is in John Jewkes, David Sawers, and Richard Stillerman, *The Sources of Invention* (1958). An exhaustive study of the American Chemical industry is Williams Haynes, *American Chemical Industry* (6 vols., 1945-1954). The best study of plastics is Morris Kaufman, *The First Century of Plastics: Celluloid and its Sequel* (1963). □

Karl Ernst von Baer

The Estonian anatomist and embryologist Karl Ernst von Baer (1792-1876) was the first to describe the mammalian ovum. He also developed the germ-layer theory, which became the basis for modern embryology.

Karl Ernst von Baer was born in Piep on Feb. 29, 1792. He began his medical studies at the University of Dorpat in Estonia in 1810, and after graduating in 1814 he continued his studies at Vienna. After realizing his limitations as a practitioner, he studied comparative anatomy at the University of Würzburg, where he was taught by the influential anatomist Johann Döllinger. On completion of his studies, Baer accepted a position as prosector in anatomy at the University of Königsberg, and in 1819 he was appointed associate professor of zoology there. In 1822 he achieved the rank of professor.

At Königsberg he undertook his famous studies in embryology in collaboration with C. H. Pander. He worked first on the embryology of the chick but later investigated the problem of identifying the structure of the ovum of the dog and found it to be a small yellow spot floating in the follicular fluid. As a result of this work, he published in 1827 the first description of a mammalian egg, *Epistola de ovi mammalium et hominis genesi* (On the Origin of the Mammalian and Human Ovum). His reputation was further increased by the publication of his most famous work, *Entwicklungsgeschichte der Tiere* (1828-1837; Developmental History in Animals). In this work he developed the germ-layer theory, in which he held that in vertebrate eggs four "layers" of cells are formed and that each layer always gives rise to certain tissues in the adult organism. (The two middle layers were later regarded as one.) In this same work he outlined his discovery of the notochord in the chick embryo. He described it as a rod of cells which runs the length of the vertebrate embryo and around which the future backbone is laid down.

Laws of Development

Baer's work on the embryological development of animals led him to frame four laws. In these laws he was concerned with the question of how closely the development of an embryo of one species resembles that of other species and how closely its various embryonic stages resemble the adult stages of other species. His laws state that the embryo of a given species never resembles the adult of another species and that the embryos of even the most

similar species do not pass through the same states but, rather, become progressively different from each other. These "laws of development," though much misunderstood by other biologists and in some cases used by them to support opposite views, were fruitful in later interpretations of embryology and evolution. Herbert Spencer used Baer's law (later known as the biogenetic law) to support his theory that the world is becoming increasingly differentiated and complicated.

In 1834 Baer left Germany to take up the position of librarian of the Academy of Science at St. Petersburg. In this position he advised the Russian government on a number of scientific matters. In 1837 he led a scientific expedition into Arctic regions, and from 1851 until 1856 he studied Russian fisheries and suggested many improvements. He retired to his native Estonia and died on Nov. 28, 1876, in Dorpat.

Further Reading

There is a very good account of Baer's biological work and influence in Edward Stuart Russell, *Form and Function: A Contribution to the History of Animal Morphology* (1916). Information is also in Joseph Needham, *A History of Embryology* (1934; 2d ed. 1959); Arthur William Meyer, *The Rise of Embryology* (1939); and Jane M. Oppenheimer, *Essays in the History of Embryology and Biology* (1967).

Additional Sources

Baer, Karl Ernst von, *Autobiography of Dr. Karl Ernst von Baer,* Canton, MA: Science History Publications U.S.A., 1986. □

Johann Friedrich Adolf von Baeyer

The German chemist Johann Friedrich Adolf von Baeyer (1835-1917) experimented in the organic field, notably achieving the synthesis of indigo. He received the Nobel Prize in chemistry in 1905.

Adolf von Baeyer was born in Berlin on Oct. 31, 1835. From an early age Adolf was devoted to the study of nature; for example, he planted date seeds in a series of pots which were nourished successively by milk, wine, and ink. The 8-year-old who conducted such endeavors was destined to become a superb experimentalist during 60 years of leadership and to garner many scientific honors.

Analysis of Organic Molecules

After comprehensive studies in physics and mathematics at the Friedrich Wilhelm Gymnasium in Berlin, Baeyer went to the University of Berlin, where he pursued the same course. One year later, convinced that chemistry was to be his life, Baeyer moved to Heidelberg to study. His doctoral research on arsenical organic compounds was completed in 1858 and indicated his future scientific focus—the analysis and synthesis of organic molecules.

At the new laboratories established in the Gewerbe institute in Berlin, Baeyer assembled a brilliant circle of chemists that rivaled the group gathered by A. W. von Hofmann at the University of Berlin. To this period belong Baeyer's studies of uric acid, which contributed to the clarification of the biochemical differences in the metabolic processes of mammals and reptiles.

The years from 1865 to 1885 were devoted to the painstaking investigation of the organic dyes, particularly indigo, alizarin, and isatin. This work contributed immensely to the German dye industry's phenomenal growth but brought no material rewards to Baeyer, who generously shared his insights and techniques with his students.

Other Investigations

Baeyer and his pupils also pioneered in the study of polyacetylenes, oxonium salts, and the internal architecture of aromatic compounds and other ring structures. Generally an experimentalist, he used the structure theory of his friend August Kekulé as the theoretical base on which to build his life's work. Baeyer proposed a "centric" formula for benzene, and a "strain" theory, correlating the stability of cyclic compounds with the ring angles, to account for the submolecular properties of complex compounds. His studies in the condensation reactions of ketones and aldehydes, plus his abiding interest in plant physiology, led him to propose a photosynthetic theory which stimulated much research on this important topic.

Baeyer was married and the father of four children. He was active in the German Chemical Society and occupied some of the most prestigious chairs in the German academic world. He lived for his science, his students, and his collaborators. These included Emil and Otto Fischer, Edward Hepp, and Richard Willstäter, all of whom achieved the highest ranking in the international chemical world. Baeyer's 300 important papers are one of the great monuments of German intellectual life.

Further Reading

Baeyer's autobiography, which covers only the first half of his life, is not available in English. The best short account of Baeyer is the essay by Richard Willstäter in Eduard Farber, ed., *Great Chemists* (1961). His technical achievements are treated in Eduard Farber, *The Evolution of Chemistry: A History of Its Ideas, Methods, and Materials* (1952; 2d ed. 1969), and in J. R. Partington, *A History of Chemistry,* vol. 4 (1964). □

Buenaventura Baez

Buenaventura Baez (1812-1884) was five times president of the Dominican Republic and dominated his country's history for 3 decades.

Born of wealthy mulatto parents in Azua de Compostela, Buenaventura Baez was educated in Europe and returned to his homeland as one of the best-educated Dominicans of his day. He opposed continuation of Haitian rule over the eastern part of Hispaniola. By 1843, and after the ouster of the Haitian ruler Jean Pierre Boyer, this rule existed in name only. When the Dominican Republic declared independence, Baez became a member of the Dominican constitutional assembly and speaker of the first congress.

Baez was a compromise choice for president in 1849. At the end of his term in 1853, he handed over power to his legally chosen successor, Pedro Santana—one of the rare times in Dominican history when this happened. Thereafter, Santana and Baez became implacable enemies, and Baez was soon exiled and did not return until 1856. In the personalistic manner of Dominican politics, this feud dominated the country's political life as the two leaders' followers struggled for control.

By 1855 Santana's harsh rule had caused a revolt, and he resigned. Baez returned and maneuvered himself into the presidency. Naturally, his first move was to exile Santana.

A revolt by tobacco growers in the Cibao Valley sent Baez into exile in Curaçao in June 1858, and Santana replaced him as president as the Dominican Republic entered the era of Spanish rule known as the Third Spanish Colony. The Dominican War of the Restoration against Spain began in 1863. After much fighting, the last Spanish troops departed in July 1865. A constitutional assembly elected Baez president, and he entered his third term on Nov. 14, 1865. However, by early May 1866 the country was again in revolt, and Baez returned to Curaçao.

Before Baez claimed the presidency for the fourth time, in May 1868, the Dominican government had made serious efforts to lease the Bay of Samaná area, one of the world's great natural harbors, to the U.S. government. Baez went even further, attempting to have his country annexed by the United States. On Nov. 29, 1869, representatives of both governments signed two treaties in Santo Domingo, one leasing the Bay of Samaná and the other annexing the Dominican Republic. In spite of a questionable Dominican plebiscite in favor of the annexation and U.S. President Ulysses S. Grant's firm support, U.S. Senate opposition killed the treaty. The lease treaty lapsed, and finally in December 1872 Baez rented the Samaná peninsula to an American corporation for $150,000 a year. The contract was rescinded a few months later, and by the end of 1873 Baez was toppled by yet another revolution.

The next few years were very confused; 1876 saw four presidents, the last being Baez as he started his fifth and final term in December. By February 1878 he was again in exile, this time in Mayagüez, Puerto Rico, where he died on March 21, 1884.

Further Reading

An excellent account of Baez's career is in Selden Rodman, *Quisqueya: A History of the Dominican Republic* (1964). Probably the classic work on the Dominican Republic is Sumner Welles, *Naboth's Vinyard: The Dominican Republic, 1844-1924* (2 vols., 1928). This work explains and interprets the history, culture, and society of the nation. Another useful work is Otto Schoenrich, *Santo Domingo: A Country with a Future* (1918). □

Joan Baez

American folk singer Joan Baez (born 1941) was recognized for her non-violent, anti-establishment, and anti-war positions. She used her singing and speaking talents to denounce violations of human rights in a number of countries.

By the age of 22, Joan Baez was already known as the "queen of folk singers." Her rich and varied early experiences contributed significantly to her later "anti-establishment" attitudes. Her father, Albert V. Baez, was a physicist who came to the United States from Mexico at a very early age, and her mother was of West-European descent. Joan inherited her father's dark complexion, and the occasional racial prejudice she suffered as a child probably led to her later involvement in the civil rights movement. Although as an adult she claimed not to share her parents' Quaker faith, it undoubtedly contributed to what some called her keen "social conscience."

One of three sisters, Baez was born on January 9, 1941, in Staten Island, New York. She was exposed to an intellectual atmosphere with classical music during her childhood, but rejected piano lessons in favor of the guitar and rock and roll.

Her father's research and teaching positions took the family to various American and foreign cities. She attended high school in Palo Alto, California, where she excelled in music more than in academic subjects. Shortly after her high school graduation in 1958, her family moved to Boston where Baez's interest in folk music surfaced after visiting a coffeeshop where amateur folk singers performed.

From Boston Coffee Houses to Newport

She briefly attended Boston University where she made friends with several semi-professional folk singers from whom she learned much about the art. In addition to simple folk songs, she began to sing Anglo-American ballads, blues, spirituals, and songs from various countries. As she worked to develop her technique and repertoire, Baez began to perform professionally in Boston coffeehouses and quickly became a favorite of Harvard students. She was also noticed by other folk singers, including Harry Belafonte, who offered her a job with his singing group.

In the summer of 1959 she was invited to sing at the Newport (Rhode Island) Folk Festival. That performance made her a soaring phenomenon—especially to young people—and led to friendships with other important folk singers such as the Seeger family and Odetta. Although that

performance brought her offers to make recordings and concert tours, she decided to resume her Boston coffeeshop appearances.

After her second Newport appearance in 1960, Baez made her first album for Vanguard Records, simply labelled *Joan Baez,* which was an immediate success. She was then such a "hot item" that she could tell CBS what songs she would sing and what props she would use in her appearance. In the following years Baez sang to capacity crowds on American college campuses and concert halls and on several foreign tours. Her eight gold album and one gold single awards attested to her popularity as a singer.

Her soprano voice has been described as "so clear and so luminously sensual that it reminded everyone of their first loves." She had no need to take lessons to enhance her voice, which ranged over three octaves, but she needed practice in order to achieve command of the guitar.

Politics a Source of Controversy

While many critics agreed that her untrained singing voice was unusually haunting, beautiful, and very soothing, they saw her spoken words, lifestyle, and actions as discordant and sometimes anti-American. In the turbulent 1960s, Baez became a center of controversy when she used her singing and speaking talents to urge non-payment of taxes used for war purposes and to urge men to resist the draft during the Vietnam War. She helped block induction centers and was twice arrested for such violations of the law. She had already studied, understood, and adopted non-violent strategies as a way to effect changes where she perceived injustices to exist.

She was married to David Harris, a draft resister, in March 1968. She was pregnant with their son, Gabriel, in April 1969 and three months later saw her husband arrested for refusing induction into the military forces. (He spent the next 20 months in a federal prison in Texas.)

Baez Creates A Stir Among American Left

In the early 1970s, Baez began to speak with less stridence and by the end of the decade had offended dozens of her former peace-activist allies, such as Jane Fonda and attorney William Kunstler, when she publicly denounced the atrocities in Vietnam's Communist "re-education" centers. As she had done in the case of Chile and Argentina (without public outcries from former associates), Baez called for human rights to be extended to those centers in post-war Vietnam. Although her position seemed similar to that of Western intellectuals, it nevertheless created a stir among the American left (some of whom called for her own re-education). When some asked what right any American had to criticize the Communist government for anything it was doing after what the United States had done to the Vietnamese, she responded: "The same right we have to help anyone anywhere who is a prisoner of conscience."

Baez' Career Through the 1980s and '90s

In later years Baez' singing career faltered despite various attempts to revive it. Her 1985 effort featured a more conventional hairstyle and attire. Her supporters believed

she would regain her prominence in the entertainment industry because her voice, although deeper, retained the
same qualities which earlier made her so successful. Meanwhile, she was quite busy throughout the world as the head
of the Humanitas International Human Rights Committee,
which concentrated on distracting (in any possible nonviolent way) those whom it believed exercised illegitimate
power.

Baez has continued to make music and to influence
younger performers. In 1987, Baez released *Recently,* her
first studio solo album in eight years. She was nominated for
a 1988 Best Contemporary Folk Recording Grammy Award
for the song "Asimbonanga" from the album. Also in 1988,
Baez recorded *Diamonds and Rust in the Bullring* in Bilbao,
Spain. The album was released the following April. In 1990,
Baez toured with the Indigo Girls and the threesome were
recorded for a PBS video presentation, *Joan Baez In Concert.* In 1991, she released a compilation album, *Brothers In
Arms,* featuring two new tracks. In 1993, two more Baez
recordings were released: *Play Me Backwards,* consisting of
new material; and *Rare, Live & Classic,* a retrospective of
her career from 1958 to 1989, featuring 22 previously unreleased tracks. Another compilation CD, *Live At Newport,*
containing previously unreleased performances from the
1963,1964 and 1965 Newport Folk Festivals was released
by Vanguard records in 1996. Baez released another solo
album, *Gone from Danger,* in early 1997.

The singer's interest in politics and human rights has
continued as well. In 1993, she was invited by Refugees
International to travel to Bosnia-Herzegovina in order to
help bring attention to the suffering there. In September of
that same year, Baez became the first major artist to perform
in a professional concert on Alcatraz Island (the former
Federal Penitentiary) in San Francisco to benefit her sister
Mimi Farina's organization, Bread & Roses. She returned to
the island for a second benefit in 1996 along with the Indigo
Girls and Dar Williams. She has also supported the gay and
lesbian cause, joining Janis Ian in a performance at the
National Gay and Lesbian Task Force's *Fight the Right* fundraising event in San Francisco in 1995.

Further Reading

Bits of biographical data about Joan Baez may be found in her
    book *Daybreak* (1968) and in *Coming Out* (1971), which she
    co-authored with husband, David Harris. The latter chron-
    icles a brief period after Harris's release from prison for draft
    evasion. The best sources for additional information about her
    anti-war activities are news and popular periodicals from
    1968 to 1977.
Baez's 1987 autobiography, *And A Voice To Sing With*, is an
    excellent source of information as well. Other current sources
    include the January 17, 1997 issue of *Goldmine* in which she
    is profiled in an extensive 14-page cover story by Bill Carpen-
    ter.
Baez can be found on the web at http://baez.woz.org and on the
    A&E Biography site at http://www.biography.com/find/
    find.html. □

William Baffin

**The English navigator and explorer William Baffin
(ca. 1584-1622) discovered Baffin Bay and was active in the early exploration of the Arctic.**

Williaam Baffin's background and his activities
prior to 1612 are either unknown or based on
conjecture. He was probably born in London
and appears to have been of humble birth. Self-educated
but remarkably skilled in his profession, he wrote several
accounts of voyages which demonstrate some exposure to
classical literature. Little is known of his personal life,
though Baffin's elderly widow appears in official documents
as a somewhat quarrelsome petitioner of the East India
Company. There is no evidence of any children surviving
Baffin's death.

Baffin first appears in history in 1612, when he served
as chief pilot aboard a vessel off the western coast of Green-
land. In 1613 and 1614 he was with the Muscovy Company's whaling fleets off Svalbard (Spitsbergen), and in 1615
he explored the Hudson Strait. In 1616 the Northwest Passage Company employed Baffin as pilot aboard the ship
Discovery under the command of Robert Bylot. This company, which had previously dispatched several other expeditions under such men as Henry Hudson and Sir Thomas
Button, sought to discover a westward route to Asia.

The *Discovery* left England in March 1616. It passed
beyond the farthest point reached by earlier expeditions,
and Baffin explored the coast and inlets of the large bay
subsequently named in his honor. Though Baffin failed to
realize that Lancaster Sound, which he named in honor of
one of the sponsors of the expedition, constituted an opening into the strait for which he was searching, he did chart
and name the main features of Baffin Bay. The *Discovery*
returned safely to England in August 1616.

Baffin, apparently convinced that the Northwest Passage could not be discovered from the western approaches,
sought employment with the East India Company. His last
two voyages (1617-1619 and 1620-1622) were to the East.
In 1622 the fleet with which his ship sailed engaged in
hostilities with a rival Portuguese fleet and besieged a Portuguese fortress in the Strait of Ormuz. During this siege Baffin
"received a shot from the castle into his belly, wherewith he
gave three leaps, and died immediately."

While chiefly known as the discoverer of Baffin Bay,
Baffin made a significant contribution to early geography as
a scientific navigator as well. He may have been the first
seaman to determine longitude by use of the angular distance of the moon from some other celestial body. He was
required to keep accurate logs, and in addition to astronomical observations he also recorded tidal movements and
other phenomena. Some of the most important data collected by Baffin concerned magnetic variation in the Far
North. His records of compass variations are permanently
important in tracing the changes in the magnetic pole.
Baffin was also an accomplished map maker.

Further Reading

An old but complete and interesting study of Baffin is Sir Clements R. Markham, *The Voyages of William Baffin, 1612-1622* (1881). This work includes an excellent historical introduction and numerous accounts of Baffin's voyages written either by himself or by others who accompanied him. Augustine Courtauld, *From the Ends of the Earth: An Anthology of Polar Writings* (1958), also includes excerpts from Baffin's writings. A brief account is in Jeanette Mirsky, *To the North! The Story of the Arctic Exploration from Earliest Times to the Present* (1934; rev. ed. entitled *To the Arctic! The Story of Northern Exploration from Earliest Times to the Present,* 1948). Other books of interest are Sir Clements R. Markham, *The Lands of Silence: A History of Arctic and Antarctic Exploration* (1921); Nellis M. Crouse, *The Search for the Northwest Passage* (1934); and Paul Emile Victor, *Man and the Conquest of the Poles* (trans. 1963). □

Walter Bagehot

The English economist, social theorist, and literary critic Walter Bagehot (1826-1877) was virtually the founder in England of political psychology and political sociology.

Walter Bagehot, born on Feb. 23, 1826, at Langport, Somerset, came of well-to-do, middle-class banking stock with literary leanings. At Bristol College (1839-1842) he was deeply influenced by studying anthropology with J. C. Prichard. He then spent 4 years at University College, London, where he and some friends formed a debating society. They also wandered about London in search of the great free-trade and Chartist orators. Even more crucial was his year of reading for a master's degree, especially in moral philosophy and political economy and in the early-19th-century English poets. Out of this reading came his first published essays, literary and economic, in a Unitarian journal, the *Prospective Review.* Yet he fumbled in finding his vocation, spending several wretched years reading for the bar at Lincoln's Inn before he decided against law as a career.

Bagehot sent letters back from a holiday trip in Paris which were published in seven installments as "Letters on the French Coup d'Etat of 1851." He was absorbed with the problem of national character and saw the convergence between culture, social structure, and personality structure.

Victorian England was neither the time nor the place for a free-wheeling writer's career, except perhaps in fiction. Bagehot was too closely in touch with the reality principle to forsake a day-to-day base for a career as a man of letters. He decided upon a life as a banker.

In 1857, his life changed. He met James Wilson, founder and editor of the *Economist,* a political, literary, and financial weekly. Bagehot married Wilson's daughter, and when Wilson died suddenly, Bagehot became managing director and then editor, a post he held until his death. Every week he wrote several leaders, or editorials, on the money market and political trends.

Three Great Books

The new direction of his writings bore fruit in the three great books of his career. The first, *The English Constitution* (1867), is the one for which he is best known. It described and analyzed not how the Constitution was supposed to work but how it did actually work, especially in its fusion of powers rather than formal separation of powers, with stress on the Cabinet as "a hyphen which joins, a buckle which fastens" the legislative and executive parts of the state.

His second book, *Physics and Politics* (1872), made less of a splash but dug deeper. From his reading in the evolutionists and anthropologists Bagehot asked what the new sciences could show about the source of political societies and their development from primitive human life. He used as an evolutionary frame a scheme of three stages: the preliminary age, when the problem was to get any sort of government started; the fighting age, when cohesion was sought through enlarging loyalties and through custom and law; and the age of discussion, when innovation broke the "cake of custom" and offered freer choices to the members of society.

His third book, *Lombard Street* (1873), a classic in financial writing, was an exposition of how the money market actually works. In the last decade of his life Bagehot became immersed not only in the normal functioning of the money market but also in its neuroses, pathology, and therapy, so that his suggestions for getting greater liquidity by enlarging the central gold reserves and his invention of the treasury bill as a means of government borrowing were taken seriously.

Bagehot died at Langport on March 24, 1877. The only unfulfilled part of his life lay in the frustration of his ambition to be a member of Parliament. A man of ironic detachment and biting wit, he lacked any warmth of relation to an audience and the needed "common touch."

His pamphlet "Parliamentary Reform" clearly shows that, while he was formally a liberal, his deeper instincts were those of a Burkean conservative; that he had little enchantment with the liberal and radical cult of the common man; and that membership in the polity was for him not a "leaves-of-grass" abstraction but an operational fact which depended on political education and intelligence. His viability rests with his profound understanding of political psychology.

Further Reading

Norman St. John-Stevas, ed., *The Collected Works of Walter Bagehot* (4 vols., 1965-1968), supersedes the editions by R. H. Hutton (1889) and by Mrs. Russell Barrington (1915). Bagehot's *The English Constitution* has been reprinted many times; see the editions by Lord Balfour (1933) and R. H. S. Crossman (1963). Good editions of Bagehot's *Physics and Politics* are by Jacques Barzun (1948) and Hans Kohn (1956). Hartley Withers's edition of Bagehot's *Lombard Street* (1915) is also recommended. A selection of Bagehot's political and historical essays, including "Letters on the French Coup d'Etat of 1851," is in Norman St. John-Stevas, ed., *Bagehot's Histori-cal Essays* (1965).

The best biography of Bagehot is Alastair Buchan, *The Spare Chancellor: The Life of Walter Bagehot* (1959). The best bibli-ography is in Norman St. John-Stevas, *Walter Bagehot: A Study of His Life and Thought* (1959). See also Leslie Stephen, *Studies of a Biographer,* vol, 3 (1902; published in one vol-ume, 1907); C. H. Driver, "Walter Bagehot and the Social Psychologists," in Fossey John Cobb Hearnshaw, ed., *The Social and Political Ideas of Some Representative Thinkers of the Victorian Age* (1933); Herbert Read, *Collected Essays in Literary Criticism* (1938; 2d ed. 1951); Max Lerner, "Walter Bagehot: A Credible Victorian," in his *Ideas Are Weapons* (1939); George Malcolm Young, *Today and Yesterday* (1948); Asa Briggs, *Victorian People* (1954); and Walter Edwards Houghton, *The Victorian Frame of Mind, 1830-1870* (1957).
☐

William Chandler Bagley

William Chandler Bagley (1874-1946) was an educa-tor and theorist of educational "essentialism."

William Chandler Bagley was born March 15, 1874, in Detroit, Michigan, to William Chase and Ruth (Walker) Bagley. The family came originally from Massachusetts but moved west for his fa-ther's employment as a hospital superintendent in Detroit. Bagley attended high school in Detroit and in 1891 enrolled in the Michigan Agricultural College (now Michigan State University) to study scientific agriculture. He received his bachelor's degree in 1895, but finding no immediate em-ployment in his field, he took a position as a teacher in a one-room school in the town of Garth, a lumber community in the Upper Peninsula of Michigan.

His interest in teaching awakened with this experience, and in the summer of 1896 he began studies at the Univer-sity of Chicago in the field of education and learning theory. Then, after a second year teaching at Garth, he enrolled as a full-time student, on borrowed money, at the University of Wisconsin, completing his master's degree in 1898. He then began work toward a doctorate in education and psychol-ogy at Cornell University, studying with Edward Bradford Titchener, a leading laboratory psychologist at that time. He completed the Ph.D. degree in 1900 with a dissertation entitled "The Apperception of the Spoken Sentence." In the following year he was appointed to an elementary school principalship in St. Louis, and there he met and married Florence MacLean Winger. They had four children, two sons and two daughters.

Bagley's first faculty appointment was in 1902 at the Montana State Normal College at Dillon as professor of psychology and pedagogy and director of teacher training. He also served as superintendent of the local Dillon public schools, where he promoted such innovations as the use of college student teachers in the schools.

After several years there and in a similar faculty ap-pointment at the State Normal School in Oswego, New York, in 1909 Bagley was appointed professor and director of the School of Education at the University of Illinois. During this period of expansion of American schools and of teacher education institutions, Bagley worked to create a strong faculty and to build an influential program in educa-tion at the University of Illinois. In 1917 he left Illinois to accept a professorship at Teachers College, Columbia Uni-versity, in New York City. There he organized a department for the study of normal schools and teacher education. He continued in this position at Teachers College until his re-tirement in 1939.

Bagley's central professional goal was to determine the scientific theoretical basis for the professionalization of teacher education. His writings, books, and journal articles were widely influential at a formative time in American education. Most notable was his textbook *Classroom Man-agement* (1907), which was a guide for beginning teachers to help them master the necessary skills and techniques for effectively controlling the classroom. Over 100,000 copies of the book were sold, and it remained in print until 1946. Management of the classroom was perceived as a strict "chain of command" model. The building principal, he wrote, was like the captain of the ship who issued orders (i.e., the course of study) to the teachers, who in turn saw that each student executed the assigned tasks (skills and knowledge). An efficient school system in Bagley's view required the "unquestioned obedience" of teachers and of students to the authority of principal and superintendent, though, he wrote, there might be some latitude, some choice and initiative on the part of individuals in the actual day-to-day execution of the orders. The ultimate aim of education in Bagley's view was indeed efficiency—that is, social efficiency, or the "development of the socially efficient individual."

Other books by Bagley that were used extensively in teacher education classes were *The Educative Process* (1905) and *Educational Values* (1911), works that explored the limitations of the then current "transfer of training" theories and outlined his ideas on the need for a scientific basis for educational practice. For effective teaching, he stated, it is necessary that "an adequate conception of principles based on the best data that science can offer . . . be added to a mastery of technique." Science, he concluded, rather than narrow psychological studies, must be the foundation of good teaching.

Bagley was also active in other publications' efforts to advance the professionalization of teaching. As early as 1905 he organized the *Inter-Mountain Educator,* the first journal of education studies in the northern Rocky Mountain region. He joined with several colleagues to found and edit the *Journal of Educational Psychology* (1910). He was editor of *School and Home Education* (1912 to 1914) and of the *Journal of the National Education Association* (1920 to 1925), and he worked with the Carnegie Foundation to create the Society for the Advancement of Education and to edit its journal, *School and Society,* in his retirement years. He collaborated on several grade school textbook projects, the most notable of which was the *History of the American People* which was written in cooperation with historian Charles A. Beard.

As an educational theorist Bagley was best known for his statement of an "essentialist" position in education, a view that emphasized the firm facts of the physical and social sciences as the "essential" basis of subject matter that all students must acquire. The view stressed the conservative function of education: schools must pass on the accepted values of the society as well as the realities of scientific fact and should not concern themselves with the satisfaction of individual interests and desires. In a widely influential address in 1938, "An Essentialist's Platform for the Advancement of American Education," Bagley stated his socially conservative position in contrast with the "soft" pedagogy of the then current progressive education theory, which in his view overemphasized individual interests and freedom. It was time, he declared, to reassert the values of discipline, authority, tradition, and scientific truth. Language and mathematics skills were the essentials upon which any curriculum must be built, and these basics must underlie the socially useful curriculum and effective education for citizenship. The term "essentialist" passed from fashion by the 1950s, but the ideas contained in it remained a persistent force in American educational thinking over the years.

William Bagley remained active through continuing work with Teachers College students and colleagues in his retirement years. He died in 1946, at age 72, in New York City.

Further Reading

The following publications contain information on Bagley and his work: Erwin V. Johanningmeier, "William Chandler Bagley's Changing Views on the Relationship Between Psychology and Education," *History of Education Quarterly* (Spring 1969); Henry C. Johnson, Jr., and Erwin V. Johanningmeier, *Teachers for the Prairie: The University of Illinois and the Schools, 1868-1945* (1972); and I. L. Kandel, *William Chandler Bagley: Stalwart Educator* (1961). □

Egon Bahr

The West German politician Egon Bahr (born 1922) made significant contributions to the lessening of tensions between the German Democratic Republic and the Federal Republic of Germany, which eventually led to the crumbling of the Berlin Wall in 1989 and reunification a year later.

E gon Bahr is a typical representative of the generation of Social Democratic leaders who rose to prominence in West Germany in the years immediately following World War II. Like Willy Brandt, his long-time mentor and associate, Bahr was too young to have been active in the politics of the Weimar Republic.

Bahr was born on March 18, 1922, in the small Thuringian town of Treffurt. After obtaining his high school diploma (*Abitur*), he was immediately drafted first into the compulsory labor service in Nazi Germany and later into the *Wehrmacht.* He served in the German army from 1942 to 1944, when he was dismissed because of his Jewish heritage. (Under the scheme of "racial" classifications introduced by the Nazis' Nuremberg Laws, Bahr counted as "partially Jewish.")

After the war Bahr turned to journalism. Although he had no formal training in this field, he was a natural talent. His first job was with the *Neue Zeitung,* the German-language newspaper founded by the American occupation forces. (The *Neue Zeitung* was a major nurturing ground for postwar German literary and journalistic talent. Its writers included, in addition to the brilliant editor Hans Habe, such later luminaries as the East German dissident novelist Stefan Heym). After the *Neue Zeitung* ceased publication, Bahr moved to West Berlin where he worked first for the newspaper *Tagesspiegel* and later became the Bonn correspondent for the West Berlin radio station RIAS (Radio in the American Sector).

Launching a Political Career

It was in Berlin that Bahr met Willy Brandt, whose "idealistic alter ego" he was to become. Brandt, too, started out as a journalist, although by the early 1950s he was already a rising star in the Social Democratic Party (SPD). When Brandt was elected mayor of West Berlin in 1960, he appointed Bahr his press secretary, a position that Egon Bahr was to keep until Brandt became the West German foreign

1969, Bahr became his chief of staff in the chancellor's office. It was in the foreign ministry and later the chancellor's office that Bahr elaborated the ideas and diplomatic tactics that were to result in the series of treaties between West Germany, the Soviet Union, the East European countries, and the German Democratic Republic (GDR) that collectively became known as the *Ostpolitik.*

Bahr had aired the ideas that underlay the *Ostpolitik* concept some years before he and Brandt moved to Bonn. In retrospect, a famous speech which he delivered in July 1963 represented a turning point in the conceptualization of West Germany's foreign policy. Bahr summed up his ideas with the catchy slogan *"Wandel durch Annäherung"* (change through contact). Rejecting the earlier policies of confrontation with the East as counterproductive, Bahr argued that only by recognizing both the GDR's existence and acknowledging the Soviet Union's key role in the evolution of the relationship between East and West Germany could West Germany hope to overcome the division of the country. Put in the terms of old-fashioned diplomatic history, the road to East Berlin lay through Moscow.

In retrospect, of course, later changes in Germany and Eastern Europe proved Bahr right, but at the time his ideas aroused a great deal of controversy. The Christian Democrats accused him of deserting the united anti-Communist front of all West German political groups and of giving in to Moscow's demands for control of Eastern Europe and East Germany.

Bridging the Two Germanys

After 1969 Brandt, now chancellor, and Bahr had a chance to put their willingness to "recognize the realities of 1945" into practice. The *Ostpolitik* was a complicated process, but it was Bahr who played a crucial role in bringing about the most important of the so-called Eastern treaties, the pact between West Germany and the Soviet Union. Beginning in January 1970 Bahr was in charge of handling negotiations with the Soviet foreign minister, Andrei Gromyko. The talks with Gromyko resulted in the so-called Bahr-Gromyko paper, the basic outline of an agreement that became the basis for the formal treaty signed by West Germany and the Soviet Union in August 1970. Once that treaty had been achieved, the subsequent pacts with Poland, Czechoslovakia, and Hungary proved less difficult.

Bahr had in the meantime turned his attention to the East Germans. In 1972 he was appointed a member of the cabinet as minister for special affairs, and it was in this capacity that Bahr and his East German counterpart, Michael Kohl, sought to put relations between the Federal Republic of Germany and the German Democratic Republic on a new footing. The result was a package of agreements that ranged from treaties on transport between East and West Germany and between West Germany and the isolated West Berlin to the so-called Basic Treaty, which specified the terms of mutual recognition between the two countries.

These pacts laid the groundwork for the special relationship (for example, the West Germans insisted that the two states exchange "permanent representatives" rather

minister in 1966. As Willy Brandt's close personal friend, Bahr managed Brandt's public relations and more. Along with a group of other young Social Democrats in Berlin, which included Klaus Schütz and Heinrich Albertz, Bahr was a member of Willy Brandt's "brain trust," a group of informal advisers which the mayor used as both a sounding board for his own ideas and as a source for generating new initiatives.

It was from the specific vantage point of politics in the former German capital after the building of the Berlin Wall that Bahr made his contributions to the theory and practice of East-West relations, the field in which he was to achieve his greatest triumphs. The building of the Berlin Wall demonstrated the futility of hoping for the success of "rolling-back" Communism in East Germany. At the same time, as leaders of West Berlin, Willy Brandt and his associates were acutely aware of the human consequences which the wall brought for the average citizen of the now completely divided city. It was to alleviate these human tragedies without yielding on matters of principle that Brandt and his "brain trust" developed the policy of dealing with, rather than attempting to ignore, the East German authorities. The aim was not to challenge the wall, but to make it more porous. The most important outcomes of that policy were the agreements at Christmas 1962 and Easter 1963 which allowed more than one million West Berliners to visit close relatives in East Berlin during these two holidays.

When Brandt became West German foreign minister in 1966 he appointed Bahr chief of the planning staff in the foreign office. After Brandt was elected federal chancellor in than ambassadors) between East and West Germany that was to prevail until the Communist regime in East Germany was toppled in the fall of 1989. Under the terms of the agreements West Germany recognized the existence and boundaries of East Germany, although the West Germans did not yield their claim that there should be a united Germany at some point in the future. In return, East Germany gave up its attempt to interfere in the relations between West Germany and West Berlin and permitted greater freedom of travel by West Germans in the GDR.

Willy Brandt was forced to resign as chancellor in 1974 after one of his personal assistants was unmasked as an East German spy. Egon Bahr stayed on in the cabinet of Helmut Schmidt as minister for economic cooperation, but he and Schmidt did not get along particularly well and after only two years Bahr resigned from the cabinet.

When Willy Brandt left the government he retained his position as chairman of the SPD, and Bahr's next major appointment, general secretary of the Social Democratic Party, once again brought him into close contact with Brandt. Unfortunately, Egon Bahr proved a far less successful party administrator than diplomat and international relations theorist. In the 1983 federal election the SPD suffered its worst defeat since 1961, and Bahr resigned as general secretary. He remained active in politics, however. In 1990 he was a member of the West German Bundestag and an alternate member of the European Parliament. In addition, he continued his writings on the problems of future European security arrangements.

Bahr's most important legacy was undoubtedly the *Ostpolitik.* Commenting in 1982 upon the treaties that he had helped to negotiate ten years earlier, Bahr took pride in the fact that the *Ostpolitik* had begun the process of reducing tensions between East and West and that this process, in turn, had made possible increased contacts and travel between East and West Germans. By 1990 he could go a major step further and point out that the *Ostpolitik* also began the process which undermined the viability of the East German regime. The developments that had made the Berlin Wall porous also inaugurated the process that would eventually make it crumble.

Further Reading

There is no full-scale English-language biography of *Egon Bahr,* but there are two good German-language introductions to his life and work. One is Karsten Schröder, *Egon Bahr* (Rastatt: 1988); the other is the chapter on *Egon Bahr* in Otto Borst, editor, *Persönlichkeit und Politik in der Bundesrepublik Deutschland* (Göttingen: 1982). Two English-language analyses of Bahr's role in the *Ostpolitik* are Lawrence L. Whetten, *The Ostpolitik* (1983); and Timothy Garton Ash, *In Europe's Name: Germany and the Divided Continent* (1993). □

William Balfour Baikie

The Scottish explorer William Balfour Baikie (1825-1864) proved in an expedition up the Niger and Benue rivers that Europeans could penetrate the interior of tropical Africa and survive.

William Baikie was born on Aug. 27, 1825, at Kirkwall, in the Orkneys, the son of John Baikie, a Royal Navy captain. Young Baikie attended medical school in Edinburgh and in 1848 entered the Royal Navy as an assistant surgeon. During 1850-1851 he saw service with the fleet in the Mediterranean. He was a man of wide interests, which included literature, natural history, and foreign languages.

The third McGregor Laird trading expedition to the Niger River was formed in 1854. Its purpose was to explore the Benue River to the limit of navigation, open up trade with peoples on the banks of the river, collect objects of natural history, and inquire about the slave trade. Laird built a special vessel, the *Pleiad,* for this effort and put it under the command of Capt. John Beecroft. Baikie was appointed surgeon and naturalist, but when Beecroft died at Fernando Po before the expedtion left, the command fell to Baikie.

The venture proved highly successful. It was established that steamships could be taken up the Niger and Benue rivers, which was instrumental in opening up the interior to foreign commerce. Missionary stations were established, and over 250 miles of previously unexplored river (Benue) were explored and charted. No lives were lost to malaria due to the pioneering prophylactic use of quinine. Baikie's 118-day stay on the rivers proved that Europeans from temperate zones could penetrate the interior and survive there. Baikie described his 1854 expedition in his *Narrative of an Exploring Voyage up the Rivers Kwora and Binue.*

In 1857 he again set out for Africa on the fourth Niger expedition. This and another attempt in 1859 met the same fate: the steamer was wrecked shortly after starting up the river. Undaunted, Baikie decided not to return to England but established himself near the confluence of the Niger and Benue at Lokoja as an unofficial British consul and agent. He remained there until 1864, studying the country and its peoples. Most of his work from that 5-year period remains unpublished.

In 1864 Baikie finally left Lokoja to return home but died en route in Sierra Leone. In an age which called for daring and courage from explorers in Africa, Baikie was a match for other British explorers, but he differed from many in that he was an educated, scientific observer of the African scene, an intellectual rather than a daredevil.

Further Reading

Baikie's own account of the famous expedition of 1854 is *Narrative of an Exploring Voyage up the Rivers Kwora and Binue* (1856; repr. 1966). The Nigerian bishop Samuel Crowther was a member of the expedition and wrote his impressions in *Journal of an Expedition up the Niger and Tshadda Rivers* (1855). □

F. Lee Bailey

Francis Lee Bailey (born 1933) is a high-profile superstar attorney and best-selling author.

"The legal profession is a business with a tremendous collection of egos," proclaimed F. Lee Bailey to *U.S. News & World Report.* "Few people who are not strong egotistically gravitate to it." Not many would deny that Bailey is well-suited to his vocation; he has generated significant controversy throughout his career, often due to his capacity for self-promotion. He became the preeminent superstar lawyer, appearing on television and publishing books at a time when such activities were often criticized as grandstanding. Furthermore, noted Edward Felsenthal of the *Wall Street Journal,* the often flamboyant attorney "didn't get to be rich and famous by being cautious or carefully following rules. His career is pockmarked with run-ins with judicial authorities and others." Bailey has been involved in a number of high-profile cases, notably the trials of Patty Hearst, the Boston Strangler, and O.J. Simpson.

Bailey was born June 10, 1933, in Waltham, Massachusetts; his mother was a teacher and nursery school director. An outstanding student, he nonetheless dropped out of Harvard to serve as a fighter pilot in the U.S. Marine Corps; flying would become one of his few passions rivaling litigation. Bailey then moved on to law school at Boston University—achieving the highest grade point average in the school's history—and was admitted to the Massachusetts bar shortly after graduating in 1960. He married Florence Gott the same year; the two divorced in 1961.

Bailey attended Keeler Polygraph Institute in Chicago, where he became an expert in lie detector tests. It was in this capacity that he was enlisted by the defense in the case of George Elderly, a physician charged with murdering his wife. When Elderly's attorney was incapacitated by a heart attack, Bailey took over the defense. The doctor—whose story served as the basis for the television series and film *The Fugitive*—was acquitted. Soon thereafter, Bailey won a reversal of the conviction of another doctor, Samuel H. Sheppard, who was also accused of murdering his wife. Felsenthal cited a *New York Times* article from the period that labeled the dynamic young lawyer "the shiniest new star in the criminal law field."

This new standout did not shy away from the spotlight. Indeed, Bailey drew criticism for appearing on television talk shows and discussing various cases and was censured by the Massachusetts bar in 1970. While the idea of the "celebrity lawyer" sounding off to the press about the cases he pursues may sound ordinary, it was highly unconventional at the time. Bailey's contemptuous words regarding a New Jersey ruling so outraged the Supreme Court of that state that he was forbidden to practice there for a year. Meanwhile, he was profiled in magazines much the way a film star might be, with his second wife, Froma—formerly his secretary—standing by. He divorced her in 1972, marrying Lynda Hart that same year.

Around the same time, Bailey defended Ernest L. Medina in a court-martial over the Vietnam War's notorious My Lai massacre, an incident of extreme violence against Vietnamese civilians that gave impetus to the anti-war movement in the United States. Bailey won Medina's acquittal after calling a vast number of witnesses—including Medina himself. This victory was one of his greatest courtroom triumphs. As Felsenthal observed, Bailey "already was gaining renown for his eloquent oratory, his nearly photographic memory and his mastery at cross-examining witnesses."

Again, Bailey used this renown to further his career, writing *The Defense Never Rests* and *For the Defense,* books on the lawyer's craft for a popular audience, in addition to writing legal textbooks. He also became publisher of *Gallery* magazine in 1972. Though Bailey lost his defense of Albert DeSalvo, a mental patient who admitted to being the Boston Strangler—a serial killer who had murdered 13 women—the case did not damage his reputation. The same could not be said, however, for his defense of Patty Hearst. The daughter of a publishing tycoon, Hearst was allegedly kidnapped by a terrorist organization called the Symbionese Liberation Army (SLA) and forced to participate in a series of bank robberies. Despite her claim that she was coerced, the heiress was tried for the holdups.

Defends Hearst

Bailey conducted a spirited defense, placing Hearst on the stand along with 71 witnesses. It was his intention to show that his client went along with the SLA to save her life.

The jury felt otherwise, apparently, and convicted her; she served 22 months in prison and eventually hired another attorney, hoping to overturn her conviction on the grounds that Bailey had not represented her adequately. His insufficient attention to her legal needs, she asserted, was due in part to his focus on the book he planned to write about the case. President Jimmy Carter eventually commuted her sentence, and she abandoned her claim against the attorney. Even so, a San Francisco appeals court suggested that Hearst's argument had some merit. Bailey's loss marked a turning point in the public's perception of his courtroom prowess.

Bailey divorced Hart in 1980, waiting a full five years before getting married again, this time to flight attendant Patricia Shiers. He continued to publish books, including a book about flying and a novel, *Secrets;* he also lent his name to ads for a variety of office machinery, collected $10,000 per speaking engagement, and stumped regularly for one of his pet causes, the necessity of reducing lawsuits. "Americans are the most litigious people in the world," he remarked in an interview with *U.S. News & World Report,* asserting that a variety of reforms—fewer jury trials, restructuring of legal fees to discourage the padding of hours, laws forbidding the possession of large sums of cash, and other changes—would help accomplish this goal. In *USA Today* magazine, Bailey claimed that he had "never seen a major trial which lacked significant perjury, and I have yet to see that perjury punished." The government, he insisted, often overlooked such mendacity when it came from its own witnesses.

In 1982 Bailey was arrested for drunk driving in California; he was acquitted, thanks in large part to the defense conducted by Robert Shapiro, who would summon Bailey to the O.J. Simpson defense team some 12 years later. The drunk driving trial so enraged Bailey that he wrote a book, *How to Protect Yourself against Cops in California and Other Strange Places,* which alleged serious abuses by police and argued that driving under the influence of alcohol had become "a number, not a condition." He furthermore asserted that political pressure had motivated police to go after celebrities in particular. While *Los Angeles* magazine called it "a small (96 pages) gem of a book," *Newsweek* writer Mark Starr found Bailey's mini-opus less than compelling, calling much of its advice "impractical," "sophomoric," or "just plain obvious."

Another strike to Bailey's credibility came when he took on the case of aggrieved families of passengers on Korean Airlines flight 007, which was shot down over the Soviet Union in 1983. Though he made several public statements attesting to his commitment to the case, his firm put in a much smaller number of hours on the case than did the two other law firms working on it. Bailey aggravated other clients by traveling to Libya to discuss defending two men who were charged with blowing up Pan American flight 103 over Lockerbie, Scotland, even after undertaking the cause of relatives of that bombing's victims. To the latter, the expedition to Tripoli was a clear conflict of interest; Bailey denied that he intended to defend the Libyans, though a letter he had written to the U.S. government suggested otherwise.

Joins O.J. Defense Team

When Robert Shapiro enlisted Bailey to join the defense team of O.J. Simpson, opinion among the throngs of professional observers was divided. The football star turned actor was accused (and later acquitted) of murdering his ex-wife Nicole and her friend Ronald Goldman in Los Angeles. In the words of *Los Angeles Times* reporter Bill Boyarsky, "a lot of lawyers and reporters wondered why the 'dream team' had hired a has-been." Although Boyarsky found these commentators "off the mark," he found that at times during his early Simpson trial appearances Bailey didn't follow the advice of his own books. After a grueling nine-month trial the jury on October 3, 1995, announced the verdict of "not guilty" on two counts of homicide, making it seem clear that Bailey and the rest of the team knew their jobs well.

Bailey's questioning of Los Angeles police detective Mark Fuhrman—alleged by the defense team to be a racist who hoped to frame Simpson, who is black—was one of the most anticipated moments of the exhaustively chronicled trial. The attorney, perhaps not surprisingly, gave himself high marks. "I'm not [stalwart television lawyer] Perry Mason," he stated in *Time,* adding, "nobody is. Other lawyers whom I respect told me that given what I had to work with, it was good. [Celebrated author] Norman Mailer called me and said it was flawless. So I feel good." Whether it was, in *Los Angeles Times* commentator Boyarsky's phrase, "Bailey's test, his chance to exhibit the skills he showed when he freed Sam Sheppard, to reclaim the reputation that was diminished after Patty Hearst, to prove that this is one lawyer who's not ready for retirement," remained to be seen.

Bailey and the rest of the Simpson team insisted that they had a witness who could attest to Fuhrman's racism, and Bailey himself claimed to have spoken "marine to marine" with the witness in question, Maximo Cordoba. Yet Cordoba's testimony was so inconsistent that in the minds of many observers it compromised the defense's Fuhrman strategy. Elizabeth Gleick of *Time* quoted prosecutor Marcia Clark's exclamation: "This is the kind of nonsense that gives lawyers a bad name."

Gleick felt that "the defining face-off of the trial was not exactly what most observers expected," adding that Bailey, "once America's most famous trial lawyer, was, by turns, sputtering, enraged and embarrassed. Instead of regaining his former glory after nearly two decades out of the limelight, he may in the end have scarred his reputation." Felsenthal of the *Wall Street Journal* similarly asserted that "Americans who recently named F. Lee Bailey the most admired lawyer in the country might feel differently now that they have actually watched him in action in the O.J. Simpson case."

Perhaps most off-putting to many observers was an apparent spat between Bailey and Shapiro. Though the two lawyers had been so close that Bailey had served as the godfather for Shapiro's child, reported Felsenthal, "Bailey was accused of getting involved in a whispering campaign to the media" against his colleague. Central to this controversy was an article in the *New York Daily News* that was strongly critical of Shapiro while reporting his demotion from the position of lead counsel in the Simpson case; Bailey was alleged by some to have been the article's primary source.

If the celebrated attorney had indeed leaked damaging information about Shapiro to the media, said a legal-ethics expert quoted in the *Wall Street Journal* piece, he "was putting his own interest ahead of those of his client." Bailey himself denied having said anything negative about Shapiro. In an analysis of the defense team—which also included Alan Dershowitz, a celebrity lawyer of a different sort—*Newsweek'*s David Kaplan wondered how Shapiro and Bailey might "share courtroom time" and concluded that "there's no way both of them can play center stage." After the trial was over, Shapiro stated he would never talk to Bailey again, and *People* quoted Bailey openly assaulting Shapiro's courtroom skills. "All Shapiro knew how to do was plead [guilty]," stated Bailey. "He was not a trial lawyer." Shapiro denied considering a plea bargain for Simpson.

In a television appearance, Bailey argued—as he long had—that a person "in the business of defending criminal cases is going to live in controversy all of his or her life." Whether or not this is universally true, he has certainly been exemplary in this respect. At the same time, he has demonstrated unquestionable skills as a "trial maven," as *Newsweek'*s Kaplan called him, and has been a trailblazer for the superstar attorneys that have followed in his wake. And after all, as Bailey noted to *U.S. News,* "each lawyer makes somebody unhappy either by beating him, embarrassing him or tying him in knots."

In 1996 Bailey's reputation again came under questioning. He was jailed after being slapped with contempt of court for failing to hand over illegally obtained shares of stock and money from a former drug-dealer client. The legendary defense lawyer was released from federal prison on his 44th day behind bars on April 16, 1996 after surrendering $16 million in disputed stock and his yacht.

Further Reading

Los Angeles, November 1982, p. 325.
Los Angeles Times, February 16, 1995, p. A14; April 20, 1996, p. A4.
Newsweek, November 22, 1982, p. 91; July 11, 1994, pp. 26-27.
New York Times, October 4, 1995, p. A18.
People, November 16, 1995, pp. 55-58.
Time, March 27, 1995, pp. 65-66.
USA Today, July 1988, Magazine, pp. 30-32.
U.S. News & World Report, September 14, 1981, pp. 72-73.
Wall Street Journal, March 20, 1995, pp. A1, A8. □

Florence Merriam Bailey

Florence Merriam Bailey (1863-1948) wrote numerous works for a wide range of people interested in birding.

A prominent ornithologist, Florence Merriam Bailey wrote numerous works for a wide range of people interested in birding. In addition to publishing technical guides for specialists in the field, Bailey was able to pique the interest of young people and novices through her informative and entertaining books.

The last of four children, Florence Augusta Merriam was born to Clinton Levi Merriam and Caroline Hart Merriam on August 8, 1863, in Locust Grove, a New York village in Lewis County. Merriam's mother was the daughter of County Judge Levi Hart. Her father, a merchant banker, retired about the time Merriam was born.

Merriam's love of nature was inspired by the natural setting of her family's home in the foothills of the Adirondack Mountains. It was also nurtured by her father and by her brother, Clinton, a physician and a naturalist, who eventually became the chief of the U.S. Biological Survey.

Because she planned to be a writer, Merriam attended the newly-opened Smith College in Northampton, Massachusetts, for four years as a special student. Although she left in 1886 without a degree, Smith awarded her one in 1921. While at Smith, Merriam led nature groups into the countryside, founded one of the nation's first Audubon societies, and wrote articles on birds for *Audubon Magazine.*

The Audubon articles became the core of her first book, *Birds through an Opera Glass* (1889), which was part of a series for young people. The first book's entertaining style, enhanced by close observation and enthusiasm for the subjects, became Merriam's hallmark.

In addition to her love of nature, Merriam was also interested in people. During the summer of 1891 she worked a month at a Chicago school for working girls, and that same winter she worked in a working girl's club in New York City. Her social service was curtailed when she contracted tuberculosis, an illness that prompted Merriam to travel west in 1893 in search of a better climate in which to recover.

Life in a small Utah town led to Merriam's *My Summer in a Mormon Village* (1894), a description of everyday Mormon life. From Utah, Merriam traveled to Palo Alto, California, where she attended Stanford University for six months. In the spring of 1894, she visited Twin Oaks, an area of California, to take notes on birds, and then moved on to observe in the mountains of Arizona.

Her trip west had a profound influence on her career. *A Birding on a Bronco* (1896), her first big western bird book, written for beginners in ornithology, became one of the first popular American bird guides. Merriam's *Handbook of the Birds of the Western United States* (1902) complemented Frank Chapman's *Handbook of Birds of Eastern North America* (1895). The handbook became a standard reference book—informative, succinct, technical, and filled with illustrations of the area's hundreds of species.

Birds of New Mexico (1928), originally intended for inclusion in a Biological Survey report, became in Merriam's hands a comprehensive book for general use. It won her the Brewster Medal of the American Ornithologist's

Union in 1931—she was the first woman to be thus honored. Two years later she received an honorary LL.D. from the University of New Mexico.

Both the handbook and the New Mexico volumes contain substantial contributions by biologist Vernon Bailey, who later became the chief naturalist of the U.S. Biological Survey. Merriam met Vernon at her brother's home in Washington, D.C., and married him on December 16, 1899. Shortly after their marriage, Vernon began a series of biological field trips to New Mexico, often accompanied by Florence. Over the years, each contributed to the other's books. Her New Mexico book and his *Mammals of New Mexico* (1931) are considered classics on western natural history.

Although Florence looked delicate, her arduous travels testified to her stamina and unflagging spirit. From one end of the country to the other, the Baileys journeyed by railroad, wagon, pack train, or on foot. Although the couple remained childless, Florence aimed to transmit her love of birds to young people. The subtitle of her fourth book, *Birds of Village and Field: A Bird Book for Beginners,* suggests that she had youngsters in mind.

When the Baileys were not away on a field trip, their home in Washington, D.C., was a gathering place for amateur and professional naturalists, young and old. Florence tirelessly promoted the Audubon Society of Washington, D.C., which she helped to found in 1887. She also directed and taught the society's program for teachers of nature studies.

The last major work of Florence Merriam Bailey, *Among the Birds in the Grand Canyon National Park* (1939), was published by the National Park Service just four years before her husband's death and nearly ten years before her own death on September 22, 1948, of myocardial degeneration. She is buried on the grounds of her childhood home in Locust Grove, New York.

In addition to Bailey's books, a tribute to her work in the West lives on in a resident of the higher mountains of southern California. A form of a chickadee, *Parus gambeli baileyae,* was named for her in 1908.

Further Reading

Oehser, Paul H., "Bailey, Florence Augusta Merriam," in *Notable American Women: A Biographical Dictionary,* edited by Edward James, Belknap Press, 1971.
Welker, Robert H., "Bailey, Florence Augusta Merriam," in *Dictionary of American Biography,* Supplement Four, 1946-1950, edited by John Garraty and Edward James, Scribner, 1974. □

Gamaliel Bailey

An American antislavery editor and a founder of the Republican party, Gamaliel Bailey (1807-1859) helped make the antislavery movement a major force in national politics in the mid-19th century.

Gamaliel Bailey was born on Dec. 3, 1807, in Mount Holly, N.J., the son of a Methodist minister. He was raised in Philadelphia, Pa., and graduated in 1827 from Jefferson Medical College. Restless and ill, Bailey shipped out on a trading vessel, which took him to China. He returned home expecting to practice medicine, but instead became the editor of *Mutual Rights and Methodist Baptist* in Baltimore, Md. When the paper failed, he joined an expedition to Oregon but was stranded in St. Louis, Mo. He walked east to Cincinnati, Ohio, where he settled.

In 1834 the great debate over slavery that took place at Lane Seminary in Cincinnati persuaded Bailey of the virtues of abolitionism. He became secretary of the Ohio Anti-Slavery society and joined James G. Birney in editing Birney's weekly, the *Philanthropist.* With Birney away lecturing and engaging in organizational activities much of the time, Bailey became the active and competent editor of this conservative abolitionist journal. He soon fully succeeded Birney and made the paper a strong western voice of gradualist abolition.

Bailey's appeal to reason did not save him from mob assaults, which he bore with fortitude, and from which he gained increasing respect. The 1840 schism in antislavery ranks separated radicals from moderates, and Bailey supported the new, moderate American and Foreign Anti-Slavery Society. Bailey's vision, however, went beyond the Liberty party of 1840 and 1844; he desired a broad-based party which could attract all shades of antislavery opinion. In 1847 he founded the *National Era* in Washington, D.C. Although William Lloyd Garrison derogated it as "tainted with the spirit of compromise," it had an immediate effect on national politics.

Bailey drew together varied contributors, including the poet-reformer John Greenleaf Whittier. He mixed articles of general interest with those of sharp antislavery opinion. In July 1851 he began to serialize Harriet Beecher Stowe's epoch-making *Uncle Tom's Cabin.* By 1853 the *National Era* had 25,000 subscribers. Bailey also developed an antislavery "salon," which brought together congressmen and others concerned with antislavery measures.

In 1855 Bailey met with antislavery Democrats to organize opposition to the Federal government's plans to make Kansas a proslavery territory. In 1856, at great sacrifice, he issued a daily edition of the *National Era* on behalf of the Republican presidential candidate John C. Frémont. Bailey interested himself in the Dred Scott case of 1857, which engaged hitherto-neutral northerners in the struggle against slavery extension.

Bailey did not live to witness the Republican triumph in 1860, and, indeed, he was superseded by practical Republicans, to whom antislavery was more a political issue than a moral crusade. His health, always delicate, required a trip to Europe in 1853. In 1859 he set out for Europe again; he died aboard ship on June 5. He was buried in Washington.

Further Reading

Histories of the Republican party pay Bailey scant attention. Theodore Clarke Smith, *The Liberty and Free Soil Parties in the*

Northwest (1897; repr. 1967), recognizes his importance. Louis Filler, *The Crusade against Slavery, 1830-1860* (1960), places him in the antislavery movement.

Additional Sources

Harrold, Stanley, *Gamaliel Bailey and antislavery union*, Kent, Ohio: Kent State University Press, 1986. □

D. (Donald) M. (Macpherson) Baillie

The younger of the famous "Baillie Brothers," D. (Donald) M. (Macpherson) Baillie (1887-1954) was a central figure in the theological debates attempting to reconcile Christian faith and the modern mind in Scotland before, during, and after World War II.

D. M. Baillie, D.D., professor of systematic theology at the University of St. Andrews from 1934 to 1954 and brother of Professor John Baillie of New College, Edinburgh, was born November 5, 1887, in Gairloch, West Ross-shire, Scotland. His father, the Rev. John Baillie, died when Donald was three, and the following year his mother moved her three sons to the Highland capital of Inverness to begin their formal education at the Royal Academy. The family moved to Edinburgh in 1905 to continue the boys' education at the university. Donald began in literary studies, but like his older brother he soon changed to philosophy, winning first class medals in both metaphysics and moral philosophy as well as the George Saintsbury Prize for English Verse. He matriculated at New College, Edinburgh in 1909, where he concentrated on theological and biblical studies with H. R. MacKintosh, H. A. A. Kennedy, and Alexander Martin. He also spent two semesters at the German universities in Marburg under Wilhelm Herrmann and Adolf Julicher and in Heidelberg under Ernst Troeltsch and Johannes Weiss. Baillie completed his ministerial training at New College in March 1913.

The outbreak of World War I coincided with the tragic death by drowning of Baillie's younger brother, Peter, who was just beginning work as a medical missionary in India. Baillie began his own pastoral work as an assistant in North Morningside Church, Edinburgh and in 1917 volunteered to serve with the Young Men's Christian Association (Y.M.C.A.) in France. He had to be relieved of his duties there due to a chronic asthmatic condition which plagued him all his life. He then filled an interim position at St. Boswell's Church in Edinburgh before accepting his first regular call to the United Free Church at Inverbie (1918-1923). He later served St. John's Church in Cupar, Fife (1923-1930) and St. Columbia's, Kilmacolm, near Glasgow (1930-1934), from which he was called by the recently reunited Church of Scotland to St. Mary's College, St. Andrews.

A devout and ecumenical spirit, though not without moments of severe depression and spiritual distress, much of Baillie's acute intellect and intense will were exerted in the preparation and delivery of more than 650 sermons, several of which have been gathered in two posthumous volumes, *To Whom Shall We Go?* (1955) and *Out of Nazareth* (1958). His earliest theological publication, done at the request of Professor MacKintosh, was a summary translation from the German of F. D. E. Schleiermacher's *The Christian Faith in Outline* (1922), followed by the exceptional Kerr Lectures delivered in Glasgow in 1926 and later published as *Faith in God and Its Christian Consummation* (1927, 1964). Without question, however, Donald Baillie's best known work was his widely acclaimed essay on incarnation and atonement, *God Was in Christ* (1948), which went through five printings including a separate German edition.

Baillie's ecumenical interests and contributions were highlighted by his participation as a steward in the World Missionary Conference in Edinburgh in 1910, as a Church of Scotland delegate to the Second World Conference on Faith and Order in Edinburgh in 1937, and as chairman of the Theological Commission of the Third World Conference on Faith and Order in Lund, Sweden, in 1952. In preparation for the latter he co-edited (with John Marsh) an inspiring challenge to Christian unity titled *Intercommunion* (1952).

As an elder in Martyrs Church, St. Andrews, during World War II Baillie chaired the local refugee committee, was the Scottish secretary of the Student Christian Movement, and was a leading sponsor of the experimental Iona Community. Although not doctrinaire politically, he believed strongly in the need not only for increasing religious but also social, political, and economic freedom tempered by a prophetic critique of any unjustifiable inequities in these areas. In his last years Baillie served as convener of the Church of Scotland's Committee on Inter-Church Relations, which was exploring closer ties with the Church of England. Several themes of these discussions were expressed in *The Theology of the Sacraments* (1957, 1964), edited by his brother John and published after his death.

A rare combination of pastor, preacher, scholar, and teacher, Baillie died of emphysema in Maryfield Hospital, Dundee, on October 31, 1954, at the age of 67 years. Perhaps his life is best summed up in the biographical tribute of an American student who, like so many others, had travelled thousands of miles to study with him. "The death of Professor D. M. Baillie is more than the passing of a great Scottish theologian, more than the passing of a great world-Church leader, it is the passing of a saint among men." □

John Baillie

The Scottish theologian and ecumenical churchman John Baillie (1886-1960) was a major influence mediating the conflicting currents of British, American, and European religious and philosophical thought during the middle years of the 20th century.

John Baillie, D.Litt., D.D., S.T.D., professor of divinity at Edinburgh University from 1934 to 1956 and brother of Professor D. M. Baillie of St. Mary's College, St. Andrews, was born March 6, 1886, in Gairloch, West Ross-shire, Scotland. John was the eldest of three sons born to the Free Church minister Rev. John Baillie and Annie Macpherson. His father died when John was four, and the following year his mother moved the three boys to the Highland capital of Inverness where they began their formal education at the Royal Academy. After finishing first in his class, he moved to Edinburgh in 1904 to attend the university, and the rest of the family joined him the following year. With the aid of several generous scholarships he was able to explore a wide variety of subjects, particularly English literature, though he confessed he gave up the art of poetry when his younger brother bested him for the Saintsbury Prize. During Baillie's undergraduate days all other academic interests were soon subordinated to his new-found passion for philosophy. He won first class medals in virtually every philosophical subject and was especially influenced by the brothers James and Andrew Seth (Pringle-Pattison).

Upon graduation in 1908 Baillie proceeded to New College, Edinburgh, to take up the four-year course preparatory to the United Free Church ministry. During this period he spent summers at the German Universities of Marburg and Jena, attending the lectures of philosophers Rudolf Eucken, Herrmann Cohen, and Paul Natorp as well as theologians Wilhelm Herrmann and Adolf Julicher. After finishing New College in 1912, he divided his energies between an assistantship in moral philosophy at Edinburgh under Pringle-Pattison and a pastoral position assisting James Black at Broughton Place Church.

The first severe shock to Baillie's youthful outlook came in May 1914 with the tragic news that his youngest brother, Peter, had drowned accidentally while preparing himself for work as a medical missionary in India. Coupled with the outbreak of World War I later that August and the death in battle of two close friends, Baillie soon volunteered for service under the Young Men's Christian Association (Y.M.C.A.) with the British armies in France. There he met Jewel Fowler, whom he married in April 1919, shortly before being released from service.

After the war Baillie took up the chair of Christian theology in Auburn Theological Seminary, New York, where he remained for seven years (1920-1927) prior to moving to Emmanuel College, Toronto, for another three years (1927-1930). In 1930 he was called to succeed William Adams Brown as Roosevelt Professor of Systematic Theology in Union Seminary, New York City. After four stimulating years on that distinguished faculty, Baillie was invited to return to New College at the same time that his brother had been appointed to the new chair in systematic theology at nearby St. Andrews. For the next 20 years the "Baillie Brothers" exercised an extraordinary influence upon each other, their students, and the major theological debates of their time.

Widely regarded as one of the great "mediating" theologians of the 20th century, Baillie's theological development can be briefly but accurately traced through several representative samples from his prolific writings. His sermons and addresses have been collected in three posthumous volumes: *Christian Devotion* (1962), *Baptism and Regeneration* (1963), and *A Reasoned Faith* (1963). His more strictly theological writings range from the massive and somewhat "liberal" *Interpretation of Religion* (1928), *The Place of Jesus Christ in Modern Christianity* (1929), and *And the Life Everlasting* (1933) through a more conservative phase represented by *Our Knowledge of God* (1939, regarded by many as his best book), *Invitation to Pilgrimage* (1942), and *What is Christian Civilization?* (1945) to the relatively moderate view exemplified by his insightful critique of *The Belief in Progress* (1950); the masterful British Association Lecture, *Natural Science and the Spiritual Life* (1952); the Bampton Lectures published as *The Idea of Revelation in Recent Thought* (1956); and finally his posthumously published Gifford Lectures, *The Sense of the Presence of God* (1962). However, no account of John Baillie's theological contribution would be complete without reference to his enormously influential *Diary of Private Prayer* (1937), which went through numerous editions and more than 20 translations, and its companion volume, *A Diary of Readings* (1955), which contains selections from Baillie's own devotional readings.

Like his brother, Baillie embodied a rare combination of theological reflection and religious practice. Beginning as a student steward at the epochal World Missionary Conference in Edinburgh in 1910, he went on to become an active worker in the Faith and Order Movement from the early 1930s and a member of the British Council of Churches almost from its inception. In 1943, the centennial of the Great Disruption, this son of a Free Church minister was elected moderator of the recently reunited Church of Scotland and convenor of its very influential Committee for the Interpretation of God's Will in the Present Crisis, whose report was later published as *God's Will for Church and Nation* (1946). He was also a member of the central committee of the first assembly of the World Council of Churches in Amsterdam (1948) and was elected one of its six presidents at the second assembly in Evanston, Illinois in 1954.

Perhaps the crowning achievement of Baillie's career was bestowed upon him in 1957 after his retirement as professor of divinity and principal (1950-1956) of New College when he was named a Companion of Honour to Queen Elizabeth II. After a brief tour of the southern United States and South America, Baillie returned to Edinburgh to work on his Gifford Lectures. The last year of his life was a tireless struggle against illness and pain, and upon completion of his lectures John Baillie died September 29, 1960, at the age of 74 years.

Further Reading

The life and thought of John Baillie is available in *The Theology of the Sacraments* by D. M. Baillie (London, 1957), which includes a biographical essay by John Baillie. John Baillie's works include *The Interpretation of Religion* (1928); "Confessions of a Transplanted Scot," in *Contemporary American Theology,* edited by Vergilius Ferm (1933); *A Diary of Private Prayer* (1937); *Our Knowledge of God* (1939);

Invitation to Pilgrimage (1942); *The Belief in Progress* (London, 1950); *The Idea of Revelation in Recent Thought* (1956); *Christian Devotion* (1962), which includes a biographical memoir by Baillie's cousin, Isobel M. Forrester; and *The Sense of the Presence of God* (1962). Additional material about Baillie can also be found in Donald S. Klinefelter, "The Theology of John Baillie: A Biographical Introduction," in *Scottish Journal of Theology* (December 1969) and in John A. MacKay, "John Baillie, A Lyrical Tribute and Appraisal," in *Scottish Journal of Theology* (Summer 1956). □

James Addison Baker III

A Republican Party campaign leader, James Addison Baker, III (born 1930) helped elect as president both Ronald Reagan and George Bush. He also served as Chief of Staff and Secretary of the Treasury for Reagan and as Secretary of State for Bush.

James Addison Baker, III, was born April 28, 1930, into a wealthy Houston, Texas, family. His great-grandfather had opened a law office in Houston that was to become one of the largest law firms in the country. His grandfather helped the firm grow and founded a bank. His father continued the legal tradition and had a great influence over Baker's formative years. His mother was the former Bonner Means.

Baker attended a college prep school in Pennsylvania. He studied classics at Princeton University and earned his Bachelor of Arts degree in 1952. After two years of active duty as a lieutenant in the United States Marine Corps, he entered the University of Texas School of Law at Austin. He received his law degree, with honors, in 1957. He later joined the American, Texas, and Houston Bar associations. As a corporate attorney, Baker practiced with the Houston firm of Andrews and Kurth from 1957 to 1975.

Baker had a long-term personal and political friendship with George Bush, who was a U.S. representative from Texas. Bush asked Baker to help manage his campaign for the U.S. Senate in 1970. Although Bush lost that race, Baker's political activities thrived. He switched political parties, becoming a Republican that year. Two years later he was working in the campaign for President Richard Nixon's reelection. In 1972 he became a state party official in Texas.

President Gerald R. Ford, with Bush's recommendation, appointed Baker as the Under Secretary of Commerce in August 1975. Baker joined Ford's campaign for reelection to the presidency in May 1976 as Deputy Chairman for Delegate Operations, and in August became National Chairman of the President Ford Committee.

Deciding to seek public office for himself, Baker entered the race for Attorney General of Texas in 1978, but lost the election. Afterward, he went back to campaigning for others.

Baker's friend and tennis partner George Bush decided to seek the presidency, and from January 1979 to May 1980,

he headed Bush's campaign team for the Republican nomination. Bush faltered in his effort and became, instead, Ronald Reagan's teammate as the vice presidential candidate. Baker moved with Bush and became a senior adviser to the Reagan-Bush ticket.

Reagan was impressed with Baker's organizational skills and political strategies during the 1980 campaign. After the election, President Reagan appointed Baker White House Chief of Staff, beginning January 1981. He became a trusted adviser, reporting directly to the president. Because of his political contacts and experience, he also became an important link between the White House and Congress. Baker worked hard to win congressional acceptance of Reagan's tax reduction proposals.

In January 1985, at the start of Reagan's second term, Baker switched positions with Secretary of the Treasury Donald T. Regan.

Baker served as the 67th Secretary of the Treasury from February 1985 to August 1988. While in this office, he was active in trying to solve such problems as Third World debts and stabilizing the international monetary system, while continuing to support Reagan's tax reforms.

Baker resigned his cabinet position to direct the successful presidential campaign of George Bush. Within hours of his election, Bush nominated Baker to be Secretary of State. Baker was sworn in as the 61st Secretary of State on January 25, 1989 and served in this role till 1992, during which time he traveled to 90 foreign countries. He presided over American foreign affairs at the time of historic changes in American-Soviet relations, with the tearing down of the Berlin Wall, the emerging democratic participation in Eastern European countries, arms control, and American troop withdrawal in Europe.

When Iraq invaded Kuwait on August 2, 1990, Baker played a key role in lining up wide support in the community of nations against the Iraqi dictator Saddam Hussein. In mid-January, 1991, U.S.-led coalition forces launched massive air strikes on Iraqi military targets in Iraq and Kuwait (Desert Storm). Thirty-seven countries shared the financial or military burdens of the effort to liberate Kuwait. The allies took great care to keep civilian casualties to a minimum. But Iraq directed most of its military attacks against civilians, firing numerous Scud missiles at cities in Saudi Arabia and Israel, a noncombatant. In late February, the allies launched a ground attack, and a few days later, Kuwait was liberated and the Gulf War was over.

Baker was honored in 1993 with a National Association of Arab Americans Peace Award, marking the second anniversary of the Madrid Conference, where he had played a key role. The historic handshake on the South Lawn of the White House "was not just old enemies stepping across an important diplomatic threshold," but "a decisive commitment to peace," said Baker. "Palestinian autonomy and Israeli security have become inextricably linked."

In 1997, Baker was asked by United Nations Secretary General Kofi Annan to be his personal envoy to the Western Sahara. He was asked to help get the faltering efforts to settle the differences between the Government of Morocco and the Frente POLISARIO over governing the former Spanish territory in the Sahara back on track.

In a 1995 interview with David Gergen, editor-at-large of *U.S. News & World Report,* Baker spoke of his book *The Politics of Diplomacy: Revolution, War & Peace, 1989-1992.* Baker told Gergen that to include his entire 12 years of service in government would have resulted in a book of unreasonable length. "I wrote the book about my time as Secretary of State because the world changed during that 43 months. The world, as I had known it for my entire adult life, changed. There were so many historic things that happened with the collapse of Communism, the fall of the Wall, the implosion of the Soviet Union, the reunification of Germany, NATO, a Mideast peace, the Persian Gulf War, a war in Panama."

Baker received the Presidential Medal of Freedom in 1991, and has been the recipient of many other awards for distinguished public service, including Princeton University's Woodrow Wilson Award, The American Institute for Public Service's Jefferson Award, Harvard University's John F. Kennedy School of Government Award, The Hans J. Morgenthau Award, The George F. Kennan Award, the Department of the Treasury's Alexander Hamilton Award, the Department of State's Distinguished Service Award and numerous honorary academic degrees.

Baker was a senior partner in the law firm of Baker & Botts and Senior Counselor to The Carlyle Group, a merchant banking firm in Washington, DC. He served on the boards of Rice University, Princeton University, the Woodrow Wilson International Center for Scholars in the Smithsonian, and the Howard Hughes Medical Institute.

Baker was Honorary Chairman of the James A. Baker, III Institute for Public Policy at Rice University in Houston. The institute was established in 1993 and named in his honor. Baker had early and strong ties with the university, and his grandfather has served as first chairman of the board of trustees.

Baker was described as an outstanding administrator. He was labeled a pragmatist, with a belief in negotiation rather than confrontation when dealing with Congress and foreign governments.

Baker married Mary McHenry in 1953, and they had four sons. She died of cancer in 1970. Three years later, he married Susan Garrett Winston, a mother of two sons and a daughter. Together they had another daughter, who was born in 1977.

Further Reading

Baker's *The Politics of Diplomacy: Revolution, War & Peace, 1989-1992* (1995) is also available in audio format. There is no book-length biography of Baker, but aspects of his activities have been discussed by people with whom he worked. Some campaign-related events are recorded in George Bush's autobiography, *Looking Forward* (1987), and in Jack W. Germond and Jules Witcover, *Whose Broad Stripes and Bright Stars?* (1989). Insight into his role as Chief of Staff and in his cabinet positions can be found in Donald T. Regan, *For the Record* (1988); Michael K. Deaver, *Behind the Scenes* (1987); and Larry Speakes, *Speaking Out* (1988). Biographical material is found in Ronald Brownstein and Nina Easton, *Reagan's Ruling Class* (1982). Articles on various issues authored by Baker can be found in *The Los Angeles Times* articles "Will Netanyahu have the will to fight for peace?" (June 9, 1996), "NAFTA fight offers competing visions of U.S. international role" (October 17, 1993), and "China plays its China card: N. Korea or human rights?" (April 10, 1994); and *The New York Times* article "Our best defense" (February 16, 1997). □

Josephine Baker

Josephine Baker (1906-1975) was a Parisian dancer and singer, the most famous American expatriate in France.

Josephine Baker was born in a poor, Black slum in East St. Louis, Illinois, on June 3, 1906, to 21-year-old Carrie MacDonald. Her mother hoped to be a music hall dancer; meanwhile, she was forced to take in laundry. She was of mixed ethnic background: Indian/Negro (as they would say in 1906) or Native American/African American (as we would say today). She descended from Apalachee Indians and Black slaves in South Carolina. Olive-skinned Eddie Carson, her father, was a vaudeville drummer and was not seen much by his daughter.

At the age of eight Josephine was hired out to a white woman as a maid; she was forced to sleep in the coal cellar with a pet dog and was scalded on the hands when she used too much soap in the laundry. At the age of ten she returned, thankfully, to school. "There is no Santa Claus," she said. "I'm Santa Claus." Josephine witnessed the cruel East St. Louis race riot of 1917. She moved from the St. Louis area at the age of 13 and emigrated out of the United States at 19. "That such a childhood produced an expatriate is not surprising," Phyllis Rose, one of her biographers, commented.

"Because I was born in a cold city, because I felt cold throughout my childhood . . . I always wanted to dance on the stage," Josephine offered as explanation of why she was determined to be a dancer (in the first of her five autobiographies). From watching the dancers in a local vaudeville house she "graduated" to dancing in a touring show based in Philadelphia (where her grandmother lived) at age 16. She had already been married twice: to Willie Wells (for a few weeks in 1919) and to Will Baker (for a short time in 1921). She took her second husband's name as her own—Josephine Baker.

It is hard to discover true biographical facts, especially when it comes to show people. We know that Josephine joined the chorus line of the touring show of *Shuffle Along* in Boston in August 1922. The comedy was produced in Manhattan by a renowned African American songwriting team, Noble Sissle and Eubie Blake; it was the first all-Black Broadway musical. Subsequently, Josephine was in New York for the *Chocolate Dandies* (at the Cotton Club) and the floor show at the Plantation Club in Harlem (with Ethel Waters). She drew the attention of the audience (at the end of the chorus line) by clowning, mugging, and improvising.

With her long legs, slim figure, and comic interludes, her special style as an entertainer evolved.

Baker Goes to Paris

African American performers were established in France already in the 1920s. "Bricktop" (Ada Smith, with her signature red hair) had moved from Harlem to Paris, where she owned a locally famous nightclub on the rue Pigalle. Bricktop claimed to have taught Josephine personal grooming, clothes-sense, and even writing—everything—from the moment the younger woman's arrived in Paris in October 1925. This is an exaggeration. Josephine went to Paris for a top salary ($250 a week; more than twice what she was paid in New York) to gyrate at the Théâtre des Champs Elysées as a variety dancer in *La Revue Nègre*. With other African Americans, including jazz star Sidney Bechet, she introduced *le jazz hot* and went on to international fame on the wave of French intoxication for American jazz and exotic nudity.

The Parisian cultural scene was ready for things African in the 1920s. African American music had penetrated to such European classical composers as Debussy, Ravel, and Stravinsky since at least 1908. But Parisians became aware of jazz only in the 1920s (the first jazz band in Paris played in 1917). African art and sculpture was one of the influences on the Cubist movement and Art Deco. Josephine's oval head, resembling a temple sculpture, and lithe body, her "geometry" (according to *Dance Magazine*) was perfect for anything Cubist or in the Art Deco style.

She was the favorite of artists and left-intellectuals such as Picasso, Pirandello, Georges Roualt, Le Corbusier, e.e. cummings, Jean Cocteau, Aleksander Wat, and Ernest Hemingway (who thought she was "the most beautiful woman there is, there ever was, or ever will be," in hyperbole). But Josephine had not been to Africa and she knew nothing of the culture there, at that time. She had a relatively small repertoire of dance steps ("Charleston knock-knees for eight counts, camel-walk eight counts") and a small vocal repertoire, too (her keynote song, "J'ai deux amours," was repeated over and over again in various contexts); but the core materials were absolutely perfect with her body style and fitted to the era.

Josephine endured a breach-of-contract lawsuit about her abandoning *Le Revue Nègre* for a star billing at the *Folies-Bergère* in 1926. (The legal case was one of many in her life.) She was 20 when she was a sensation in the "jungle" banana dance: naked but for a string of rubber bananas around her waist. Soon banana-clad Josephine dolls were selling like hot cakes! Feet stomping, elbows flapping, knees bent, she would bump and grind a Charleston, puffing out her cheeks and crossing her eyes and always having a perpetual grin on her face (as stated by *American Heritage*). She was likened to a snake, a giraffe, and a hummingbird. Also, in 1926, she recorded her throaty voice for the first time. Magazine covers and posters added to her fame.

In December 1926 she opened her own nightclub in Pigalle called Chez Joséphine (later moved to rue Francois I, a more fashionable spot). She became a chic, affluent woman with expensive idiosyncracies, like parading her pet leopard down the elegant Champs Elysées. She went on a world tour for two years in 1928-1930, and received thousands of love letters. But back in France she said: "I don't want to live without Paris. . . . It's my country. . . . I want to be worthy of Paris." In addition she met, in the fall of 1926, Pepito Abatino, a Sicilian "count" who became her lover and manager (until about 1935, when they split up in anger, Abatino still loving her). In 1934 she took a title part in an operetta, a revival of Offenbach's *La Créole* at the Théâtre Marigny, opening in December for a six-month run. Josephine was in America with the *Ziegfeld Follies* in 1936 when Abatino died. While he was alive, Abatino helped Josephine evolve from a mere eccentric dancer to integrating her songs and speech and dance in performances; from being "the highest-paid chorus girl in vaudeville" to being "one of the high-paid stars in the world," in part by controlling her scripts and the first two volumes of her memoirs. Returning to the *Follies* in the 1930s, her photographs, 20 feet high, flanked the theater entrance. In France she was called simply "Joséphine" or "La Baker." In 1937 Josephine officially became a French citizen.

A Heroine in World War II

She married Jean Lion, a French industrialist. She had a miscarriage in 1938, and Lion divorced her in 1940, during the early months of World War II. When Germany occupied Belgium, Josephine became a Red Cross nurse, watching over refugees. When Germany finally occupied France itself, she worked for the French Resistance as an underground courier, transmitting information "pinned inside her underwear" to Captain Jacques Abtey. In October 1940 she began complicated journeys from London to Pau in southwestern France, through Spain and Portugal, and to Rio de Janeiro, Brazil (where she had theatrical bookings), back to Marseilles. In December 1940 she had the leading role in the Marseilles municipal opera production of *La Créole,* but she was sued for breach of contract after leaving Algiers, Algeria in 1941. A mysterious near-fatal illness with peritonitis kept her in a Casablanca clinic from June 1941 to December 1942. It left Josephine weak, but not too weak to entertain troops in North Africa and the Middle East as a sublieutenant in the women's auxiliary of the Free French forces. She was awarded the Croix de Guerre and the Légion d'Honneur by General Charles de Gaulle and the Rosette of the Résistance.

After the war Josephine returned to her beloved Paris, regularly appearing in the *Follies.* In June 1947 she married Jo Bouillon, a jazz bandleader; after several miscarriages they separated in 1957. In 1950 at her 300-acre estate in the Dordogne (with a medieval chateau), Les Milandes, she began adopting orphaned babies of all races and religions. She retired to look after the estate and family in 1956, but soon debts amounting to $400,000 were accrued, and she was forced back into show business in 1959, in a musical autobiography called *Paris mes Amours,* which opened at the Olympia Theatre in Paris in May.

Josephine more than once looked back to her childhood in America disconsolately. She was in a bind which many find themselves in: bound to one country but in love with another. She could never forgive the United States for its racism. But her song (written by Vincent Scotto), *J'ai deux amours,* was a constant reminder: "I have two loves: my country and Paris." She visited America in the 1930s and 1940s and was disappointed. In 1951 her trip to New York was sullied by a racial incident at the Stork Club, where she was at first refused service. Walter Winchell, a columnist, linked her to communism (the "Communist conspiracy" was in the news, led by Senator J. McCarthy). In 1952 she told a reporter in Buenos Aires, Argentina: "The U.S. is not a free country. . . . They treat Negroes as though they were dogs." As late as 1955, on her return to the United States, she was questioned by immigration officials about her alleged anti-American sentiments.

President John F. Kennedy made a difference to America. Josephine returned in August 1963 to attend the civil rights march in Washington, D.C. In October of that year she made a trip to Manhattan to sing, dance, and "fight bias" (as *The New York Times* said). She flaunted her age: she said she was 60 (she was only 57), but she seemed ageless to reporters.

Problems in Her "True" Home

In France there were also problems: she was evicted from her chateau with her adopted family in 1969. Princess Grace Kelly of Monte Carlo (who was also an American expatriate) and her husband, Prince Rainier, offered the Baker family a villa in Monaco. The Rainiers helped to put on the spectacle *Joséphine* in 1975, in which Josephine, aged 69, had a dozen costume changes and, with tears streaming down from sequined eyelids, "stole the show" once again.

Describing herself, Josephine Baker said "I have never really been a great artist. I have been a human being that has loved art, which is not the same thing. But I have loved and believed in art and the idea of universal brotherhood so much, that I have put everything I have into them, and I have been blessed." (*Ebony* report of interview in 1975.) More than that, Josephine Baker pulled herself out of poverty and the trauma of humiliation and made herself an international star, principally due to her love of dancing.

She died in her sleep of a stroke on April 12, 1975, after 14 successful performances of *Joséphine.* The Roman Catholic funeral service was held at the Church of the Madeleine in Paris, which was, after all, her true home.

Further Reading

There are five autobiographies of Josephine Baker: *Les Mémoires de Josephine Baker,* Vol. I (Paris, 1927); *Voyages et Aventures de Joséphine Baker* (with Marcel Sauvage), Vol. II (Paris, 1931); *Une Vie de Toutes Couleurs* (memories presented by André Rivollet), Vol. III (Grenoble, 1935); *Les Memoires de Josephine Baker* (collected and adapted by Marcel Sauvage), Vol. IV (Paris, 1949); and *Joséphine* (with Jo Bouillon and Jacqueline Cartier), Vol. V (Paris, 1976). Books about Baker include *Bricktop* (1983) by her friend Bricktop (with Jim Haskins), *Josephine Baker* (1988) by Bryan Hammond (personal collection) and Patrick O'Connor (theatrical biography), *Jazz Cleopatra* (1988) by Phyllis Rose, and *Josephine:*

The *Hungry Heart* (1993) by Jean-Claude Baker (who called Josephine "Mother" although he was never legally adopted) and Chris Chase. Among the best articles are *Ebony* (June 1991), *Dance Magazine* (July 1989), *American Heritage* (November 1989), and *New Republic* (6 November 1989). ☐

Newton Diehl Baker

Newton Diehl Baker (1871-1937) was an American lawyer, mayor of Cleveland, and secretary of war from 1916 to 1921. He made his most indelible mark as a municipal reformer in Cleveland.

Newton D. Baker was born in Martinsburg, W.Va., of a family with deep southern roots. In 1892, after graduating from Johns Hopkins University, he took a law degree at Washington and Lee University. A disciple of Edmund Burke, he also admired Thomas Jefferson.

After practicing law briefly in Martinsburg, Baker went first to Washington, D.C., where he served as secretary to Postmaster General William L. Wilson, and then to Cleveland to resume practice. There his astuteness and speaking ability soon won the attention of Thomas L. Johnson, who began an extraordinarily constructive career as a reform mayor in 1901. The youngest man in Johnson's administration, Baker was also one of the most influential. As city solicitor from 1902 through 1912, he brilliantly handled most of the 55 suits brought by the traction interests to prevent reductions in streetcar fares. He also did much to publicize the inequitable tax structure.

Baker early supported Woodrow Wilson for the presidential nomination in 1912, and his success in breaking the unit rule at the convention helped assure Wilson's nomination. Baker had been elected mayor of Cleveland in 1911 and in 1913 was reelected. Furthering Johnson's ideal of a utopia of civic righteousness, he constructed a municipally owned power plant, organized a symphony orchestra supported by civic funds, improved hospital facilities, and in general raised the quality of Cleveland life.

Appointed secretary of war in March 1916, Baker served to the end of Wilson's second term. He was slow to revitalize the Army and Navy, partly because of Wilson's indecisiveness and partly because of his own pacifist leanings. He approved the decision to go to war, however, and despite much Republican criticism of his administration of the War Department, he proved a creditable, though not truly distinguished, secretary.

In 1921 Baker returned to Cleveland and the law. As successful at the bar as he had been as a municipal reformer, he was called the outstanding lawyer of the 1920s by Justice Oliver Wendell Holmes. Baker's practice was largely corporate. He became more conservative as he grew older and spent much of his time in the service of the utility interests he had once opposed. He was an ardent proponent of the League of Nations, and in 1928 he was appointed to

the World Court. Though critical of the New Deal, he did not break with his party. Baker died on Christmas Day, 1937, and was survived by his wife, two daughters, and a son.

A gracious and learned man, Baker had an unusually open mind. Though small and slightly built, he was a powerful orator. He was widely regarded as one of the most kindly and charming public men of his time.

Further Reading

Clarence H. Cramer, *Newton D. Baker* (1961), is the standard biography. Though appreciative in tone, it is quite objective. It should be supplemented by Frederick Palmer, *Newton D. Baker: America at War* (2 vols., 1931).

Additional Sources

Cramer, C. H. (Clarence Henley), *Newton D. Baker, a biography*, New York: Garland Pub., 1979, 1961. ☐

Ray Stannard Baker

The American author Ray Stannard Baker (1870-1946) was a noted muckraking journalist before he became the official biographer of Woodrow Wilson.

Ray Stannard Baker was born in Lansing, Mich., on April 17, 1870. An 1889 graduate of Michigan Agricultural College (now Michigan State University), he later studied law and literature at the University of Michigan.

In 1892 Baker went to work for the *Chicago Record,* remaining for 6 years as reporter and editor. This introduced him to the misery of Chicago's poor, soup kitchens, charity wards, and thousands of homeless, starving men in the streets. "My attitude was that of the frontier where I had grown up. Bums, tramps! Why didn't they get out and hustle? Why didn't they quit Chicago?" he said. But his attitude began to change after he tried fruitlessly to help a youth find a job. He was haunted for the rest of his life by this "Potato-Car Boy," whom he wanted to make the central figure in a novel.

Baker's experiences as a reporter in Chicago reversed, or at least challenged, his early attitudes. In 1894 he was assigned to go with Coxey's Army on their march on Washington to demand relief from unemployment. When Coxey's "petition in boots" left Massilon, Ohio, Baker thought it was a "dishonest way for freemen to redress wrongs." But 12 days later he wrote sympathetically that the army was a "manifestation of unrest in the laboring classes" and should be looked upon as "more than a huge joke." He returned to Illinois in time to cover the Pullman strike that began in May 1894 and broke into violence in July. Baker gave a full, sympathetic account of the strikers' complaints and of the violence on the company's part. He was critical of George Pullman's "model city," with its high rents, and he handled the *Chicago Record* relief fund for the strikers.

In 1896 Baker married Jessie Beal, and they had two children. Baker went east in 1898 to work for *McClure's Magazine.* Other staff members were muckrakers (exposé journalists) Ida Tarbell, Lincoln Steffens, and Frank Norris. Baker wrote about conditions in industry and moved politically toward independent "progressivism." But in *Native American* (1941) he said he had never belonged to a political party and had "never been a Socialist, nor a Communist, nor a Single Taxer"; and he looked back on his actions in the *McClure's* days as "sheer bumptiousness."

By 1906 he and the other muckrakers had become disenchanted. They broke away from *McClure's* and gained control of *American Magazine.* Although *American Magazine* was also a muckraking publication, Baker was about to enter a new phase of life. He had long wanted to write the "great American novel," but instead he shifted to two new areas—writing essays under the pen name of David Grayson and producing the official biography of President Wilson. Baker wrote *Adventures in Contentment* and eight other books on the same theme under the Grayson name for 35 years. Baker spent 14 years on the Wilson project, going through 5 tons of the President's personal papers and becoming his intimate. The last two books of Baker's eight-volume *Woodrow Wilson: Life and Letters* won the Pulitzer Prize for biography in 1940. Baker died of a heart attack in Amherst, Mass., on July 12, 1946.

Further Reading

Baker's own writings include *Native American: The Book of My Youth* (1941) and *American Chronicle: The Autobiography of Ray Stannard Baker (David Grayson)* (1945). The best study of Baker is Robert C. Bannister, Jr., *Ray Stannard Baker: The Mind and Thought of a Progressive* (1966).

For background, works sympathetic to Baker are C. C. Regier, *Era of the Muckrakers* (1932), and Louis Filler, *Crusaders for American Liberalism* (1939; new ed. 1961). Studies critical of him are John Chamberlain, *Farewell to Reform: The Rise, Life and Decay of the Progressive Mind in America* (1932; 2d ed. 1933), and Granville Hicks, *The Great Tradition: An Interpretation of American Literature since the Civil War* (1933; rev. ed. 1935). See also Arthur S. Link, *Woodrow Wilson and the Progressive Era, 1910-1917* (1954), and David Noble, *The Paradox of Progressive Thought* (1958).

Additional Sources

Bannister, Robert C., *Ray Stannard Baker: the mind and thought of a progressive,* New York: Garland Pub., 1979, 1966. □

Russell Baker

Russell Baker (born 1925) was one of the most distinguished practitioners of the personal-political essay in the English language.

Russell Baker was born in rural Morrisonville, Virginia on August 14, 1925. His early upbringing was not conducive to the development of the elegant, urbane literary style and trenchant criticism of contemporary city life he was to indulge in later. One of his earliest memories was of being nosed in his crib by an inquisitive cow. There were some pleasant memories of growing up close to nature: "summer days drenched in sunlight, fields yellow with buttercups." However, it was not a very progressive community; Baker's father, a stonemason, died of untreated diabetes when the boy was five, even though insulin had been discovered nearly a decade earlier.

Baker's mother, trained as a schoolteacher, had studied for a year in college and encouraged her son's aptitude for language. During these earliest years there was much contention over child-rearing tactics between mother and mother-in-law, both of whom were strong-willed women. When Baker's father died in 1930, the younger woman took the occasion to leave her husband's large family—and Virginia—for good. Her destitution at the time was attested by the fact that she gave her youngest child, who was still a baby, up for adoption. Baker's mother moved to Newark, New Jersey, with Baker and his younger sister, boarding with her brother, who continued to have a steady job during this Depression era. What started out in 1931 as a temporary arrangement—until his mother should find work—lasted for six years, including a move by the combined families to nearby suburban Belleville. The best Baker's mother could manage was work as a laundress.

During this second phase of his life, Baker exchanged maternal for paternal uncles, resulting in an early exposure to heated political debate in the home, often centering on the relative merits of Herbert Hoover and Franklin Roosevelt. In the Belleville elementary school which he attended at this time, came the first taste of literary success: faced with a writing assignment on produce, the youngster came up with an essay on wheat. An ecstatic teacher read this production to her class, although they appeared to be unmoved

In 1937, on the advice of another brother, Baker's mother took her two children to live in Baltimore, home of a great essayist of that period, H. L. Mencken. The family struggled financially. Baker was able to contribute a bit with a part-time job as newspaper deliverer, but the nightmare of having to go on relief, of having to accept government-surplus food, smuggled surreptitiously into the home under flimsy camouflage, became a reality for these proud people.

By the end of the 1930s, however, the situation had eased. Baker, without any definite prospects of attending college, nevertheless completed secondary school in Baltimore's fine "City College"—a college preparatory school with a rigorous traditional curriculum, including requirements in German, French, and Latin. When Baker was 16, his mother remarried and the family was able to move into a home of its own. At this time Baker remembers that he had only one strong professional ambition—to become a writer—although this did not seem likely to provide a viable livelihood. "It gave me a way of thinking about myself which satisfied my need to have an identity." He was persuaded by a high school classmate to take the entrance examination for Johns Hopkins University, passed, and was admitted on scholarship in the summer of 1942—six months after America's entrance into World War II. Baker was able to complete only one year of college; he enlisted in the navy in 1943, spending the rest of the war in flight training in Florida, Georgia, and South Carolina.

After the war, Baker returned to Johns Hopkins. Visions of becoming another Hemingway obsessed him. After graduation in 1947, with the help of his creative writing teacher, he got a job on the *Baltimore Sun*. The idea was that this experience would be good training for a fledgling novelist (it had been so for Hemingway). But for two years Baker did not have an opportunity to write a single published sentence. Phoning in stories, he worked as a night police reporter "prowling the slums of Baltimore, studying the psychology of cops, watching people's homes burn, deciphering semiliterate police reports of dented fenders and suicides."

Baker was married in 1950. Four years later his big break came—but for the professional journalist rather than for the novelist. He landed a job with the Washington Bureau of the *New York Times* covering the White House, Congress, and national politics in general. For more than two decades, starting in 1962, he continuously wrote the "Observer" column for the *New York Times,* the medium through which he became known to millions of readers. Writing at the rate of two or three columns a week, Baker managed to maintain a level of excellence sustained over comparable time by few others. The hallmarks of his style were irony and understatement, applied to a variety of subjects, political and personal. For example, topics on which he wrote included: stopping smoking, trimming a Christmas tree, the merchandising of presidential images, and the common cold as alibi.

Perhaps over the years there was a shift from the political to the more purely personal, but Baker continued to represent both broad streams of the English essay—the greater formality of 18th century Addison-Steele and the comparative subjectivity of Romantic Charles Lamb. In America, his predecessors were Ralph Waldo Emerson and Mencken. Baker was less acerbic than Mencken and more subtle than his only contemporary rival in quality and longevity, Art Buchwald. A unifying theme in all of Baker's writing was the glory of language and the need to safeguard it against depredation of both political jargon and commercial advertising.

In 1979, Baker won the George Polk award for commentary and a Pulitzer Prize for distinguished commentary. In 1983 he was awarded a second Pulitzer, in autobiography, for *Growing Up*. Baker embarked on a new facet of his career—college hall lecturer and wit—in the 1980s. Yet another career change was in the works for him in the early 1990s: PBS asked him to replace Alistair Cooke as host of the program "Masterpiece Theater."

Further Reading

An American in Washington (1961) and *No Cause for Panic* (1964) are volumes which represent the earlier, more formal Baker. *Poor Baker's Almanac* (1972) and *So This is Depravity* (1980) are "Observer" collections of essays which typify his later personal style. Baker can also be heard speaking about humor on a tape available through CBS.

Additional information can be found in "Beyond Words," in *Entertainment Weekly* (December 31, 1993) and "Master Observer," *Time* (March 8, 1993). □

Sir Samuel White Baker

Sir Samuel White Baker (1821-1893) was an English explorer, author, and administrator who explored the Upper Nile and discovered Lake Albert. He also sought to suppress the slave trade in the southern Sudan.

Samuel Baker was born in London on June 8, 1821. He was a large man with prodigious energy and great bravery and determination. A firm believer in the economic potential of the tropics, he went to manage his family's plantations in Mauritius in 1844 and later established his own estates in Ceylon. The plantations in Ceylon prospered, and he returned to England with his family. After his first wife, Henrietta, died in 1855, Baker traveled in the Crimea, Asia Minor, and the Balkans. In 1860 he married Florence Ninian von Sass, a young and beautiful Hungarian, and the following year he arrived in Cairo determined to seek the source of the River Nile.

Traveling up the Nile to Berber, Baker spent a year wandering along the Atbara River and the Blue Nile, hunting and learning Arabic before returning to Khartoum, from which he and his wife launched an expedition up the White Nile in December 1862. Arriving at Gondokoro, the Bakers met the British explorers John Hanning Speke and James Augustus Grant, who had reached Lake Victoria and the Nile from the East African coast. In 1863-1864 Baker and his wife discovered and explored the eastern shore of Lake Albert, visited Kamrasi, the ruler of Bunyoro, and after many delays returned to London, where Baker wrote an extremely popular book about his explorations and the horrors of the Sudanese slave trade.

In the spring of 1869 Baker was approached by Ismail, the khedive of Egypt, to lead an Egyptian expedition to the Upper Nile to extend Egyptian control to Lake Victoria, to claim the territory for Egypt, and to end the slave trade. Baker was consequently appointed governor general of Equatoria Province and sailed up the Nile with a large expedition of 1200 troops, the most expensive expedition to penetrate Africa.

Baker had agreed to serve for 4 years. Unfortunately, the first year was wasted breaking through the great swamps of the Nile, whose sudd formations provide an almost impenetrable barrier to navigation. Baker reached Gondokoro

in 1870 and spent the second year organizing his men and establishing stations in Equatoria.

Frustrated at every turn, he began to employ increasing force to pacify the people and acquire supplies for his troops and followers. Although these raids alienated important tribes, Baker continued to push south into Bunyoro in 1872, where he was again forced to fight, this time against Kabarega, who had succeeded Kamrasi as ruler. Like most African leaders who had to deal with Baker and his forces, Kabarega refused to trust the intruders, and Baker possessed neither the tact nor the tolerance to allay his fears.

Nevertheless, when Baker retired to England and fame and fortune in 1873, he had struck the first blow against the Nilotic slave trade and had laid the foundations for colonial rule in the southern Sudan. He died in Devonshire on Dec. 30, 1893.

Further Reading

Dorothy Middleton, *Baker of the Nile* (1949), is a full-length biography. Also useful for information on Baker are Emile Ludwig, *The Nile: The Life-Story of a River* (1935; trans. 1937), and Alan Moorehead, *The White Nile* (1961). □

Sara Josephine Baker

Sara Josephine Baker (1873–1945) was a physician working toward improving the public health care and reducing infant mortality rates substantially in New York City.

Sara Josephine Baker was a pioneer in the field of public health and an activist in the women's movement. She was the first woman to receive a doctorate in public health. As the head of the Department of Health's newly created division of child hygiene, she reduced New York City's infant mortality rate to the lowest of all major cities worldwide. From 1922 to 1924 she represented the United States on the health committee of the League of Nations.

Born on November 15, 1873, in Poughkeepsie, New York, Baker was the daughter of affluent parents. Her Quaker father, Orlando Daniel Mosser Baker, was a lawyer and her mother was one of the first women to attend Vassar College. Baker's Quaker Aunt Abby stimulated her intellectually and instilled in her the courage to be a nonconformist. This background influenced her decision to enter medicine and establish innovative programs in preventive health, particularly in obstetrics (childbirth) and pediatrics (treatment of children).

Becomes a doctor

When Baker was 16 years old both her father and brother died in a typhoid epidemic. Devastated, she abandoned plans for attending Vassar and decided to go directly to New York Women's Medical College. She was determined to become a doctor in order to help support her mother and sister. In 1898, after four years of intensive study, Baker graduated second in a class of 18. She interned, or gained practical experience in medicine, at the New England Hospital for Women and Children, an outpatient clinic serving residents in one of the worst slums in Boston, Massachusetts. Later she moved to New York City with her roommate and fellow intern, where they set up a practice near Central Park West. Unable to make ends meet, Baker took a job as a medical inspector for the New York City Department of Health. She examined sick children in schools and worked toward controlling the spread of contagious disease.

Becomes first woman health official

In 1902 Baker was given the job of searching for sick infants in Hell's Kitchen. Located near the docks of Manhattan's West Side, Hell's Kitchen was a slum area where 1,500 children were dying each week of dysentery (a disease that causes severe diarrhea and dehydration). In 1908 the Department of Health established a division of child hygiene, with Baker as its director. She was the first woman in the United States to hold an executive position in a health department. There she shaped policies for innovative health reform and made preventive medicine and health education the responsibility of government. As Baker's program saved the lives of countless infants, she revolutionized pediatric health care in the United States and in other nations as well.

Starts innovative projects

One of Baker's projects was establishing "milk stations" throughout the city, where nurses examined babies, dispensed low-cost, high-quality milk, and scheduled checkups. In 1911 alone 15 milk stations prevented more than 1,000 deaths, and the next year 40 more stations were opened. Another of Baker's programs was the training and licensing of midwives, or persons who assist women in childbirth. Since many immigrant women were used to midwifery, they were reluctant to allow their babies to be delivered by male doctors in hospitals. Midwives were often unqualified, however, and infant death rates were high. Baker instituted a mandatory licensing program with results so successful that she was able to demonstrate that rates of infection for home deliveries were lower than those for hospitals.

Baker also started a program called the Little Mothers League to train young girls in the care of babies, since many girls were put in charge of their younger siblings while their mothers worked. Through this program nurses instructed schoolgirls in the feeding, exercising, dressing, and general care of infants. An even more significant method of reducing infant mortality was a foster care system Baker founded to give orphaned babies a better environment than that available in institutions. Her efforts helped reduce death rates from one-half to one-third of infants born in a year. She also introduced the concept of prenatal care to prevent infant mortality during and following childbirth.

Contributes to nation's public health system

Among Baker's other accomplishments were a school inspection system and the organization and streamlining of record-keeping procedures for health departments, which was adopted nationwide. She opened specialized clinics and instituted parent training by public health nurses. In 1912 she established the Federal Children's Bureau and made plans for creating a division of child hygiene in every state. Besides being a leader in the medical field, Baker was in the forefront of the fledgling women's movement. In 1915 she was invited by officials at the New York University (NYU) Medical School to lecture on child hygiene for a new course leading to a degree of doctor of public health. Since she did not have an actual degree in the field of public health herself, she offered to teach in return for the opportunity to earn the diploma. When Dean William Park turned down her request on the grounds that the medical school did not admit women, Baker refused the appointment.

Park searched in vain for a year for another instructor, finally giving up and admitting Baker and other women to the program. Baker's reception by some of the male students was hostile, but she continued teaching at NYU for 15 years. Along with five other women Baker founded the College Equal Suffrage League, an organization that campaigned for women's voting rights, and she marched in the first annual Fifth Avenue suffrage parade.

Appointed League of Nations representative

During her term as U.S. representative on the health committee of the League of Nations from 1922 to 1924, Baker was appointed consulting director in maternity and child hygiene of the U.S. Children's Bureau. After retirement she participated in more than 25 committees devoted to improving children's health care. She also served a term as president of the American Medical Women's Association. Baker died of cancer on February 22, 1945, in New York City. Her work laid the foundation for preventive health procedures that saved the lives of hundreds of thousands of babies, resulting in an improvement in mortality rates from one in six in 1907 to one in 20 by 1943.

Further Reading

Peavy, Linda, and Ursula Smith, *Women Who Changed Things,* Charles Scribner's Sons, 1983, p. 122.
Morantz-Sanchez, Regina Markell, *Sympathy and Science: Women Physicians in American Medicine,* Oxford University Press, 1985.
Morantz, Regina Markell, Cynthia Stodola Pomerleau, and Carol Fenichel, eds., *In Her Own Words: Oral Histories of Women Physicians,* Yale University Press, 1982, p. 30. □

Mikhail Mikhailovich Bakhtin

Russian philosopher and literary critic Mikhail Mikhailovich Bakhtin (1895-1975) was the central figure of an intellectual circle that focused on the social nature of language, literature, and meaning in the years between World War I and World War II. Though his major works were not widely read until after the 1960s, his ideas were later adopted by many academic spheres and have contributed to new directions in philosophy, linguistics, and literary theory.

Although relatively unknown outside Soviet intellectual circles during his lifetime, the writings of Mikhail Mikhailovich Bakhtin have a had a significant influence in the fields of literary theory, linguistics, and philosophy. In works such as *Problems of Dostoevsky's Poetics* (1929, 1963), *Rabelais and His World* (1965), and *The Dialogic Imagination* (1975), Bakhtin outlined theories on the social nature of language, literature, and meaning. With the spread of his ideas in the Western academic world, Bakhtin has become one of the major figures of twentieth-century literary theory.

Bakhtin was born on November 16, 1895, in the city of Orel in the southern part of Russia. He was the third of five children in a family that had been part of the nobility since the Middle Ages, but no longer held land or title. His father was a state bank official, as his grandfather had been. Although the family relocated at various times throughout Bakhtin's childhood, he was provided with a thorough education. At home, he and his older brother, Nikolai, received lessons in Greek poetry from a German governess. After the family moved to Vilnius, Lithuania, when he was nine, he attended schools in the Russian-ruled city. At the age of 15, Bakhtin traveled with his family to Odessa in the Ukraine, where he graduated from the First Gymnasium and then studied philology (the study of literature and language) at the University of Odessa for a year.

Attracted by Philosophical Ideas

In his early adolescent years, Bakhtin began to develop an interest in radical philosophical ideas. He immersed himself in a wide range of books, including the works of German philosophers Friedrich Nietzsche and Georg Wilhelm Friedrich Hegel. He was encouraged in his pursuits and exposed to a developing spirit of revolutionary change by his brother and a circle of friends, with whom he would hold discussions and debates about new concepts. This early habit of questioning established ideas would become a lifelong practice for Bakhtin. Another important theme of his life first appeared during these years. At the age of 16, he was stricken with osteomyelitis, a disease that causes inflammation and destruction of bone tissue. This chronic condition and other bouts of poor health affected his work and activities for the rest of his life.

Bakhtin entered the University of St. Petersburg in Russia in 1914. There he studied philosophy and literature with a number of professors while sharing living quarters with his older brother. When the political turmoil of the Russian Revolution broke out in 1917, Nikolai joined the White Army, the military group supporting Russian royal rule against the Bolshevik revolutionary forces. With the defeat of the royal forces, Nikolai left for England. Bakhtin, however, stayed in school throughout this time and graduated in 1918.

Bakhtin Circle Established

Over the next ten years, Bakhtin began to develop the ideas that would lead to his major writings. Having moved with his family to the Belorussian town of Nevel in 1918, Bakhtin began meeting with a group of intellectuals that would become known as the "Bakhtin Circle." The members of the group discussed such topics as the effects of the Russian Revolution on the social and cultural lives of Soviet citizens and the role of social reality in the meaning of artistic works and language. Bakhtin published his first paper the following year in a local journal. The two-page article was titled, "Art and Responsibility." He would not publish again for another decade.

In 1920, he moved to the town of Vitebsk, where he held a number of jobs, including a teaching position at the Vitebsk Higher Institute of Education. His intellectual work from this time included a number of unpublished writings, including the notebooks he kept. At Vitebsk, Bakhtin was joined by his friends from his circle in Nevel, including Lev Vasilyevich Pumpiansky and Valentin Nikolayevich Voloshinov. In addition, new people such as Ivan Ivanovich Sollertinsky and Pavel Nikolayevich Medvedev joined the group. In 1921, Bakhtin formed another important relationship. Suffering from his continued battle with osteomyelitis, his health declined even further when he contracted typhoid. A woman who nursed him through this period of illness, Elena Aleksandrova Okolovich, became his wife later in the same year.

From 1924 to 1929, Bakhtin lived in Leningrad (the name given to St. Petersburg after the Revolution). Prevented from working because of his poor health, his only income was a small medical pension. He did, however, continue to meet with the members of the Bakhtin Circle in their homes, where he would occasionally give lectures. Papers published by his associates during this time reflect many of Bakhtin's ideas; whether the critic was the sole author, co-author, or simply the philosophical inspiration for these writings is a matter of debate. Some of the works in question include the book *The Formal Method in Literary Scholarship,* published in 1928 by Medvedev and the 1929 work *Marxism and the Philosophy of Language* by Voloshinov. These works reflect the basic idea of the Bakhtin Circle that language is fundamentally a sociological force. Just as society, or popular culture, is continually changing and growing with the exchange of experiences and ideas, so does the meaning of language take on new

dimensions with every act of reading, listening, or responding. In this way, Bakhtin and his colleagues established the concept of the "dialogic," or social nature of language, which was also extended to all artistic acts and utterances. These works by Medvedev and Voloshinov were couched in the language and themes of Marxism, making them acceptable for publication in the young communist state.

First Book Focuses on Dostoevsky

In 1929, Bakhtin published his first major work, a study of Russian novelist Fyodor Dostoevsky titled *Problems of Dostoevsky's Poetics.* Continuing the themes raised by Medvedev and Voloshinov, Bakhtin argued that in Dostoevsky's novels, the author does not use a single authoritative narrator to dictate the motives and meanings of actions and characters to the reader. Rather, characters are allowed to take on meaning through their interactions with others, gradually revealing their own world view, or ideology. This interaction of all the voices in the novel, including that of the narrator, is called a "polyphonic dialogue" by Bakhtin. He goes on to demonstrate this type of dynamic in other interactions of language, including the literary forms of parody and satire.

In 1929, Bakhtin and several members of his circle were arrested. The official reasons for Bakhtin's arrest included his religious practices—he had retained his Christian practices and beliefs even after all expressions of religion had been banned in the Soviet Union. He was sentenced, without a trial, to ten years of exile in the northern Soviet region of Siberia. With his health problems, such a severe sentence was a serious threat to Bakhtin's life. Several prominent political and cultural figures sympathized with the author's plight and lobbied for a reduced sentence. Due perhaps in large part to a favorable review of his Dostoevsky book by the Commissar of Enlightenment, Bakhtin's sentence was eventually reduced to six years in Kazakhstan. In 1930 he received permission to travel to the city of Kustani and find work himself, rather than being assigned a job by the government. He secured a position as an accountant in a local government office; he also helped train workers in the area in clerical skills. Although his exile officially ended in 1934, Bakhtin opted to remain in Kustani for another two years.

He returned to Russia in 1936, settling in Saransk and taking a teaching job at the Mordovian Pedagogical Institute. In 1937, he moved to the town of Savelovo; being only a hundred kilometers outside Moscow, he was able to once again appear in intellectual and academic gatherings. But the coming years were filled with a number of frustrations and disappointments. His physical health suffered another blow in 1938 when his right leg was amputated. Professionally, he seemed assured of success when a number of his papers were accepted for publication. But with the start of World War II, these works were not printed.

Carnival Theory Applied to Literature

This adversity seemed to spark a period of great productivity in Bakhtin. He gave lectures on the novel at Moscow's Gorky Institute and completed a dissertation on sixteenth-century French satirist Francois Rabelais for the institute in 1940. This work, which was expanded and published in 1965 as *Rabelais and His World,* stands alongside *Problems of Dostoevsky's Poetics* as one of Bakhtin's most important writings. In this work, Bakhtin examines the cultural and political hierarchies that existed in European society in the Middle Ages and the early Renaissance period. He postulated that popular culture embraced an earlier way of life that stressed communal living and working that directly clashed with the increasing power of central governments and noble classes. The tension between the "official" world of power, government, and religion and the unacknowledged world of popular culture was only free to be expressed, according to Bakhtin, in the environment of the carnival—a holiday atmosphere in which all things held sacred and mighty were free to be subjected to laughter and satire, a time when all boundaries were temporarily dissolved. Bakhtin finds this kind of carnivalesque subversion in the novels of Rabelais, whom he credits with heralding the modern era and a new philosophy of history.

Although he began working as a German instructor in the schools of Savelovo in 1941, Bakhtin continued to concentrate on his writing, turning out articles on the novel that were later collected in *The Dialogic Imagination,* published in 1975. Bakhtin worked in Savelovo from 1942 to 1945 as an instructor in Russian. He returned to the Mordovian Pedagogical Institute in Saransk in 1945, where he attained the rank of department chair. After submitting and defending his dissertation in the late 1940s, he was finally awarded a degree of candidate in 1951. When the institute became a university six years later, Bakhtin's scholarship and reputation as a teacher earned him the position of head of the department of Russian and foreign literatures.

Reputation Increased in Later Years

Despite these advancements, Bakhtin's ideas were little known outside his academic and intellectual circles of friends. Beginning in the mid-1950s, his work began to earn a limited amount of recognition elsewhere. His book on Dostoevsky was mentioned in articles by American Vladimir Sedeno in 1955, Soviet critic Viktor Shklovsky in 1956, and literary critic Roman Jakobson in 1959. This increased interest by younger intellectuals resulted in a demand for publication of other works by Bakhtin, bringing about a revised version of the Dostoevsky book in 1963 and the first printing of his dissertation on Rabelais in 1965.

At this time of rising acclaim, Bakhtin continued to publish, but once again ill health limited his activities. He and his wife—who was also unwell—moved to Moscow in 1967 and then to Grevno in 1970 for medical care. After his wife's death in 1971 from a heart condition, Bakhtin settled in an apartment in Moscow. He spent his last years fighting both emphysema and his osteomyelitis, but he did not abandon his writing. He died in Moscow on March 7, 1975. After his death, more of his works were published and his influence gradually spread throughout the world, due in great part to the interest of Western academics. In this way, his own work took on a life of ongoing growth and interpretation—the kind of existence that Bakhtin had claimed for all

acts of language. Long after the moment of writing and years after the death of the author, the works of Bakhtin have been the subject of numerous readings and responses that have added new dimensions to fields concerned with language and the nature of meaning, including linguistics, philosophy, and literary criticism.

Further Reading

For more information see Brandist, Craig, "The Bakhtin Circle," *The Internet Encyclopedia of Philosophy,* 1997; Clark, Katerina, and Holquist, Michael, *Mikhail Bakhtin,* The Belknap Press of Harvard University Press, 1984; Morson, Gary Saul, editor, *Bakhtin Essays and Dialogues on His Work,* University of Chicago Press, 1986; Morson, Gary Saul, and Caryl Emerson, editors, *Rethinking Bakhtin: Extensions and Challenges,* Northwestern University Press, 1989; and Patterson, David, *Essays on Bakhtin and His Contemporaries,* University of Kentucky Press, 1988. □

Mikhail Aleksandrovich Bakunin

Russian revolutionary agitator Mikhail Aleksandrovich Bakunin (1814-1876) was the leading spirit of 19th-century anarchism. He viewed revolution as the necessary means of destroying the political domination of individuals by the state.

M ikhail Bakunin was born on May 18, 1814, in Premukhino in the Tver Province to a retired diplomat and landowner. After finishing his studies at the artillery school, he received a commission as an officer in the Guards. It is said that his father was angry with him and asked that Mikhail be transferred to the regular army. Stranded in a desolate village of White Russia with his battery, Bakunin became depressed and unsociable. He neglected his duties and would lie for days wrapped in a sheepskin. The battery commander felt sorry for him; he had no alternative, however, but to remind Bakunin that he must either perform his duties or be discharged. Bakunin chose to take the latter course and asked to be relieved of his commission.

Bakunin went to Moscow in 1836, and from that date life began in earnest for him. He had studied nothing before, he had read nothing, and his knowledge of German was very poor. But he was blessed with a gift for dialectics and for constant, persistent thinking. He mastered German to study the philosophies of Immanuel Kant, Johann Fichte, and G. W. F. Hegel. In 1842, while living in Berlin, Bakunin published an impassioned essay declaring Hegelianism a revolutionary tool and ending with the dictum that was to become the motto of international anarchism: "The passion for destruction is also a creative passion." Bakunin participated in the Paris Revolution of 1848, made a fruitless attempt to organize a secret revolutionary international campaign for a Czech revolt, and participated in the Dres-

den rebellion of 1849. He was imprisoned in Russia until 1857 and then exiled to Siberia. In 1861 he escaped from Siberia to Japan, and on his way to Europe he stopped off in the United States. He declared his intention of becoming an American citizen. The poet Henry Wadsworth Longfellow portrayed the Russian in his diary as "a giant of a man with a most ardent, seething temperament."

Mission in Life

In 1862 Bakunin joined the revolutionary leaders Aleksandr Herzen and Nicholas Ogarev in London. Bakunin's intention was to devote all his energies to fighting for the freedom of the Russians and all the Slavs. He had not yet devised his anarchist doctrines, and he found himself advocating some of Herzen's views. Temperamentally the two men were so incompatible that they could not be comrades-in-arms, though they remained good friends. Bakunin's instincts were all against moderation, and conspiratorial intrigue was his goal. He embraced the cause of land and liberty and plunged into plotting with immense zest. He had plans for agitating in the army and among the peasantry, and he played with the idea of a vast revolutionary organization ringing Russia with a network of agents at strategic points on the border. Siberia was to be served by a branch located on the western coast of the United States.

Concept of Revolution

Bakunin reached the conclusion that revolution is necessary, regardless of the point of the critique of society from which it starts. He frequently attempted to give a philosoph-

ical foundation to revolution. The whole history of mankind appeared to him as "the revolutionary negation of the past. . . . Man has liberated himself (by breaking the divine commandment not to eat of the tree of knowledge); he has divided himself from animal and made himself man; he began his history and his human development with his act of disobedience and knowledge, that is, with rebellion and thought."

Bakunin held that there are principles which are the moving force of both the individual and the historical process. These are human animality, thought, and revolt. Social and private economy correspond to the first, science to the second, and freedom to the third. Man has an innate instinct for revolt. therefore, man's perpetual rebellion, which may lead to self-sacrifice and self-destruction, does not depend on either right or obligation but is immediately bestowed along with his humanity. Revolution can be looked upon as a theoretically perpetual situation or as an almost-infinite process. In theory, revolution may at some time cease and be replaced by a new order; in practice, it lasts so long that it must claim the attention of at least a whole generation. According to Bakunin, the goal of his generation was to destroy; the reconstruction would be done by others who would be better, fresher, and wiser. Bakunin never abandoned this view.

Exponent of Anarchism

The failure of the Polish insurrection in 1863 was a big disappointment to Bakunin, who henceforth became absorbed in a campaign of universal anarchy. Anarchism called for the replacement of the state with a loose confederation of autonomous units that would both end the injustices of private property and assure individual freedom. The millennium was to be achieved through an international rebellion set off by small groups of anarchist conspirators. Bakunin's anarchism, in theory, meant not disorder but lack of domination, a system without political power. Bakunin was also a militant atheist and thought religion was as great an enemy of freedom as the state was. At the end he appears to have lost his confidence in spontaneous popular uprising as the only sure method of destroying state governments.

Bakunin died in Bern, Switzerland, on July 1, 1876. His lifelong friend Herzen once remarked about Bakunin: "This man was born not under an ordinary star, but under a comet."

Further Reading

An early biography of Bakunin is Edward H. Carr, *Michael Bakunin* (1937). Grigorii P. Maximoff, *The Political Philosophy of Bakunin: Scientific Anarchism* (1953), studies source material. Eugene Pyziur, *The Doctrine of Anarchism of Michael A. Bakunin* (1955), gives a fine analysis. Recommended for general historical background is Thomas G. Masaryk, *The Spirit of Russia: Studies in History, Literature, and Philosophy* (1913; trans., 2 vols., 1919; 2d ed. 1955); the author, a scholar and the first president of Czechoslovakia, makes a comprehensive survey of Russian culture and values. Franco Venturi, *Roots of Revolution: A History of the Populist and Socialist Movements in Nineteenth Century Russia* (1952;

trans. 1960), is the fullest treatment since Masaryk's of the development of 19th-century Russian radical thought.

Additional Sources

Bienek, Horst, *Bakunin, an invention,* London: Gollancz, 1977.

Carr, Edward Hallett, *Michael Bakunin,* New York: Octagon Books, 1975.

Kelly, Aileen, *Mikhail Bakunin: a study in the psychology and politics of Utopianism,* New Haven: Yale University Press, 1987.

Mendel, Arthur P., *Michael Bakunin: roots of apocalypse,* New York, N.Y.: Praeger, 1981. □

Joaquin Balaguer y Ricardo

An author and politician, Joaquin Balaguer (born 1907) served seven nonconsecutive terms as president of the Dominican Republic between 1960 and 1996.

Joaquin Balaguer y Ricardo was born on September 1, 1907. He received most of his education in the Dominican Republic, graduating with a law degree from the national university in Santo Domingo. He also did advanced studies in France.

Gains Prominence during Trujillo Regime

During the dictatorship of Rafael Trujillo Molina, Balaguer gained recognition both as a scholar and as a government official. His particular fields of scholarly research were history and international affairs, and he wrote a number of books on these topics.

Soon after completing his education, Balaguer went to work in 1932 for the Dominican government, rising through the ranks. By the 1940s he was in the diplomatic service and served as ambassador, first to Colombia and then to Mexico. Following these appointments he became secretary to the president.

When Trujillo arranged to have his brother Hector re-elected to the presidency in 1957, he chose Balaguer as vice-president. Three years later, when pressure from the Organization of American States convinced the dictator that it was inappropriate to have a member of his family as president, Trujillo forced his brother to resign, and Balaguer succeeded to the post.

The position of Balaguer in the Trujillo regime was unusual. Mild of manner, soft-spoken, and short of stature, he had a reputation for being honest, which was rare among high officials of the dictatorship. It was also well known within the administration that he had used his limited influence to save a number of individuals from the vengeance of the dictator. Balaguer himself described his situation as president during the last months of the Trujillo dictatorship as that of being "the most important prisoner in the republic." He was kept under strictest surveillance by Trujillo's various police forces and was given little opportunity to

wield effectively the theoretical power of the office he occupied.

Political Turmoil and Exile in the Early 1960s

With the assassination of Rafael Trujillo in May 1961, Balaguer's role changed dramatically. During the remainder of the year he devoted himself to dismantling the dictatorship which he had inherited. He used the influence of Trujillo's son Rafael, Jr., to disarm private armies of the dictator's brothers but subsequently cooperated in exiling Rafael and his uncles. At the end of January 1962 the air force chief Rodriguez Echeverria ousted Balaguer and established a short-lived dictatorship.

Balaguer went into exile, and during most of the next three years lived in New York City. After the outbreak of civil war in April 1965 and intervention by U.S. troops, Balaguer returned home. With the establishment of a provisional government under President Hector Garcia Godoy and the calling of elections, Balaguer and former president Juan Bosch became the principal opponents for the presidency. Balaguer defeated Bosch by a substantial majority.

Elected to Presidency Six Times

The second Balaguer regime was turbulent. He sought to pacify the enmities surviving from the Trujillo regime and from the 1965 civil war, but political murders were frequent during his administration. He succeeded in partially rehabilitating the government's finances, which were in a chaotic state, and pushed through a modest program of economic development. Attempting to rehabilitate his reputation, Balaguer sought to maintain a democratic regime, but he was impeded by remnants of the Trujillo government, by left-wing extremists, and even by elements of the Partido Revolucionario Dominicano of Juan Bosch, who had lost all faith in democratic procedures in the Dominican Republic. Balaguer won re-election in 1970 and 1974, but he was defeated by Antonio Guzman in 1978 amid national economic strife and allegations of corruption within his administration.

Although in his mid-seventies, Balaguer continued his engagement in political life with an unsuccessful bid to regain the presidency in 1982. The candidate of the Social Christian Reform Party, he was returned to office in the election of 1986 and held the presidency through subsequent elections in 1990 and 1994. Labor unrest, violent anti-government protests, and calls for Balaguer's resignation followed his 1990 victory, when food and fuel shortages plagued the country, and Balaguer initiated a program of tight economic controls in an effort to limit inflation and reduce the government deficit. Ultimately, charges of election fraud led to the shortening of his seventh term to two rather than four years. In a special election held June 30, 1996, Lionel Fernandez Reyna emerged as Balaguer's successor with an international delegation that included former U.S. President Jimmy Carter monitoring the ballot procedures.

In November of that same year, Balaguer was named in a suit charging the misappropriation of more than $700 million in government funds during his time in office. Two additional suits named Balaguer as a conspirator in the murders of opposition journalists in 1975 and 1994. Balaguer's *History of Dominican Literature* (1955) was issued in English translation in 1978. His memoirs of the Trujillo era were published in 1996.

Further Reading

Because his career in public life extended over several decades, information on Balaguer may be found in such surveys as Frank Moya Pons, *The Dominican Republic: A National History* (1995), Emelio Betances, *State and Society in the Dominican Republic* (1995), Jan Knippers Black, *The Dominican Republic: Politics and Development in an Unsovereign State* (1986), and G. Pope Atkins, *Arms and Politics in the Dominican Republic* (1981). ☐

George Balanchine

The Russian-born American choreographer George Balanchine (1904-1983) formed and established the classical style of contemporary ballet in America. His choreography emphasized form rather than content, technique rather than interpretation.

George Balanchine, born Georgi Melitonovitch Balanchivadze in St. Petersburg, Russia, on January 22, 1904, was the son of a famous Russian composer. At the age of 10, he entered the Imperial Ballet School, where he learned the technically precise and athletic Russian dancing style. After the Russian Revolution of 1917, Balanchine continued his training in a new government theater. In 1921 he entered the St. Petersburg Conservatory of Music to study piano while continuing work in ballet at the State Academy of Opera and Ballet. He used a group of dancers from the school to present his earliest choreographed works. One of the students was Tamara Gevergeyeva, later known as Tamara Geva, whom Balanchine married in 1922. She was the first of his four wives, who were all dancers. In 1924, when the group was invited to tour Europe as the Soviet State Dancers, Balanchine defected.

He was discovered in 1925 in Paris by the ballet impresario Sergei Diaghilev. When Diaghilev's most famous choreographer, Nijinska, left his ballet company, Balanchine took her place; at the age of 21 he was the ballet master and principal choreographer of the most famous ballet corps in the world. It was Diaghilev who changed the Russian's name to Balanchine. Balanchine did 10 ballets for him. When Diaghilev died and the company disbanded in 1929, Balanchine moved from one company to another until in 1933 he formed his own company, Les Ballets. That year he met Lincoln Kirstein, a young, rich American, who invited him to head the new School of American Ballet in New York City.

With the School of American Ballet and later with the New York City Ballet, Balanchine established himself as one of the world's leading contemporary classical choreographers. Almost single-handedly he brought academic excellence and quality performance to the American ballet, which had been merely a weak copy of the great European companies.

In 1934 the American Ballet Company became the resident company at the Metropolitan Opera in New York. Audiences were treated to three new Balanchine ballets: *Apollo, The Card Party,* and *The Fairy's Kiss*—works that revolutionized American classical ballet style. But Balanchine's daring ballet style and the Metropolitan's conservative artistic policy caused a breach that ultimately terminated the alliance in 1938. His work in the next several years included choreography for Broadway shows and films and two ballets created in 1941 for the American Ballet Caravan, a touring group: *Ballet Imperial* and *Concerto Barocco.*

In 1946, following Kirstein's return from service in World War II, he and Balanchine established a new company, the Ballet Society. Initially financed by and limited to subscribers, in 1948 it was opened to the public. The performance of Balanchine's *Orpheus* was so successful that his company was invited to establish permanent residence at the New York City Center. It did so and was renamed the New York City Ballet. Finally, Balanchine had a school, a company, and a permanent theater. He developed the New York City Ballet into the foremost classical company in America, and to some critics, in the world. Here he created some of his most enduring works, including his *Nutcracker* and *Agon.* After the New York City Ballet moved to Lincoln Center's New York State Theatre in 1964, Balanchine added such wide-ranging works as *Don Quixote* and *Union Jack.*

Balanchine's choreography was not tied to the virtuosity of the ballerina, the plot, or the decor but to pure dance. The drama was in the dance, and movement was solely related to the music—a perfect dance equivalent to music. For Balanchine, the movement of the body alone created artistic excitement and evoked images of fantasy or reality. He emphasized balance, control, precision, and ease of movement. He rejected the traditional sweet style of romantic ballet, as well as the more acrobatic style of theatrical ballet, in favor of a neoclassic style stripped to its essentials—motion, movement, and music. His dancers became precision instruments of the choreographer, whose ideas and designs came from the music itself.

Balanchine died in New York City on April 30, 1983. Summing up his career in the *New York Times,* Anna Kisselgoff said, "More than anyone else, he elevated choreography in ballet to an independent art. . . . In an age when ballet had been dependent on a synthesis of spectacle, storytelling, décor, mime, acting and music, and only partly on dancing, George Balanchine insisted that the dance element come first."

Further Reading

Bernard Taper, *Balanchine* (1963), is a popular biography. Balanchine is given extensive coverage in George Amberg, *Ballet in America: The Emergence of an American Art* (1949); Olga Maynard, *The American Ballet* (1959); Joan Lawson, *A History of Ballet and Its Makers* (1964); and Ferdinando Reyna, *A Concise History of Ballet* (trans. 1965).

Additional Sources

Buckle, Richard, and John Taras, *George Balanchine: Ballet Master* (Random House, 1988).
Mason, Francis, *I Remember Balanchine: Recollections of the Ballet Master by Those Who Knew Him* (Doubleday, 1991).
New York Times (May 1, 1983). □

Vasco Núñez de Balboa

The Spanish conquistador Vasco Núñez de Balboa (ca. 1475-1519) explored Central America and discovered the Pacific Ocean. He was the first Spanish explorer to gain a permanent foothold on the American mainland.

Vasco Núñez de Balboa was born at Jerez de los Caballeros in the province of Estremadura. He was descended from an old and noble Galician family. To improve his meager fortune, Balboa went to the new Spanish colonies in America. In 1500 he sailed with Rodrigo de Bastidas on a preliminary reconnaissance of the Colombian and northern Panamanian coasts. He then settled in Hispaniola (present-day Haiti and the Dominican Republic) and tried farming but failed and fell heavily into debt.

Meanwhile, two would-be conquistadores, Alonso de Ojeda and Diego de Nicuesa, received crown licenses to settle the regions explored by Bastidas. Ojeda headed for the northern Colombian coast late in 1509 with 300 men, while Nicuesa sailed toward the Panamanian Isthmus with a force numbering over 700. Within a few months hostile Native Americans, disease, and starvation had reduced their combined forces to less than 100. Ojeda returned to Hispaniola, leaving his remnant under Francisco Pizarro to wait for the relief expedition of Martin Fernández de Enciso.

One of Enciso's provision casks contained an unusual cargo: Balboa had stowed away to escape his creditors in Hispaniola. At 35 the intelligent and willful Balboa was at the height of his physical powers. With these qualities and his knowledge of the area he soon became the group's leader. He convinced the men to leave the inhospitable site of Ojeda's camp at San Sebastián and to cross the Gulf of Urabá (now the Gulf of Darién) to a new location on the Isthmus (Santa Maria la Antigua, commonly called Darién).

There Balboa dispensed with the nominal authority of Enciso, sending him back to Spain. Nicuesa, another potential rival, was picked up with survivors and brought to Darién. They were soon returned to the mercies of the sea in a leaky, meagerly supplied ship.

By the end of 1510 Balboa's authority was certified by King Ferdinand, who commissioned him captain general

and interim governor of Darién. Balboa extended his conquest westward along the Central American coast and into the interior, subjugating the Native Americans or allying with them by a combination of terror and diplomacy. Strengthened by reinforcements form Spain and Hispanola, the group accumulated hoards of gold ornaments; they also learned about a sea to the south, bordered (so the Native Americans said) by fabulously gold-rich kingdoms.

While Balboa foraged the countryside, Encisco was undermining him at the court in Spain. Eventually, he persuaded the King to replace Balboa with the elderly Pedrarias (Pedro Arias de Ávila), who was sent off with a company of 1,500 men. Getting wind of this development, Balboa hastened to redeem himself by discovering the "South Sea." With a small band of Spaniards and a larger number of Native American allies, he journeyed to the narrowest part of the Isthmus, fought his way across the hilly, swampy country, and on Sept. 25, 1513, ascended the summit of Darién. From that point he saw the vast expanse of the Pacific to the south. Balboa then marched down to the coast of the Gulf of San Miguel, waded into the water, and claimed the "South Sea" and all its adjacent territories for Spain. A nearby pearl fishery provided more material rewards.

King Ferdinand did not rescind his appointment of Pedrarias but made Balboa governor of the South Sea province and two bordering ones. The king was greatly pleased by the pearls and gold Balboa had sent him, and for the next 5 years a jealous Pedrarias was forced to share his authority with the conquistador. During that time Balboa sent back

complaints about his rival's mistreatment of friendly Native Americans, while Pedrarias attempted to win over Balboa by offering his daughter in marriage.

At last Balboa decided to strike out once more on his own. On the southern Panamanian coast he constructed four brigantines and was about to sail off on another voyage of conquest when he was summoned to confer with Pedrarias. On his way to the meeting Pizarro arrested him. Balboa was accused of plotting treason and condemned, and in January 1519 he was beheaded.

Further Reading

Balboa's career is explored in detail in Kathleen Romoli, *Balboa of Darién* (1953). Charles L.G. Anderson *Life and Letters of Vasco Núñez de Balboa* (1941), may also be consulted. There is a short account of Balboa in F. A. Kirkpatrick, *The Spanish Conquistadores* (1946). See also C. H. Haring, *The Spanish Empire in America* (1947), and J. H. Parry, *The Age of Reconnaissance* (1963). □

Emily Greene Balch

Pacifist, political activist, college professor, and social reformer, Emily Greene Balch (1867-1961) dedicated her life to humanitarian causes. In 1946 she shared the Nobel Peace Prize with John R. Mott.

Emily Greene Balch was born in Jamaica Plain, Massachusetts, on January 8, 1867. Her father and mother, Ellen Noyes and Francis V. Balch, were educated Unitarians who raised their six children to cherish high moral and religious standards.

When selecting a college after attending Miss Catherine Ireland's School in Boston, Balch chose Bryn Mawr. Entering in 1886, she studied economics and graduated with an A.B. degree in 1889. The initial recipient of the European Fellowship at Bryn Mawr, she went first to New York City to work under social reformer Jacob Riis, then used her award to attend the Sorbonne. From 1890 to 1891 she applied herself to "the social question," and upon her return to the United States she worked in Boston with Charles W. Birtwell at the Children's Aid Society.

Now in her element, Balch became acquainted in 1892 with three other reform-minded women: Jane Addams, Katherine Coman, and Vida Scudder. That same year she helped found the Boston settlement Denison House, acting as its director for a brief time.

Following her social work experience, Balch turned to college teaching as a way to further advance the cause of reform. She prepared for this by studying at the University of Chicago, at Harvard University, and at the University of Berlin. In 1896 Balch joined Coman at Wellesley College as an assistant, teaching economics courses. She illustrated her lectures with her social work experiences and was highly regarded as an imaginative and dedicated teacher.

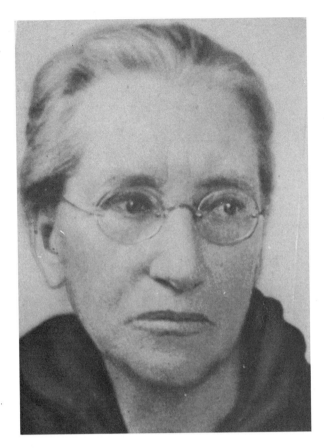

of Nations, helping to ensure that the interests of smaller nations and of women and children were upheld.

By 1922, due to poor health, Balch resigned as secretary-treasurer of the WILPF, although she continued to work for the group on a voluntary basis. She travelled to Haiti with a commission established by Herbert Hoover in 1930 to investigate conditions in that occupied nation. Hoover subsequently removed U.S. troops from Haiti on the basis of the commission's report.

In 1935 Wellesley College invited Balch to speak at an Armistice Day program, ending its public disapproval of the former faculty member.

Balch worked tirelessly on behalf of world peace and in 1939 published *Refugees as Assets,* urging the United States to admit refugees from Nazis out of respect for humanitarian principles. After Pearl Harbor in 1941, Balch advocated support for Japanese-Americans held in U.S. detention camps.

Balch won the Nobel Peace Prize in 1946, an award she shared with John R. Mott, international Young Men's Christian Association (YMCA) official. Among those supporting Balch's nomination for the prize was Wellesley president Mildred McAfee Horton. Balch donated her $17,000 share of the prize money to the WILPF.

In poor health and living on a limited income during her later years, Balch nevertheless continued her activism. She was honorary chairwoman of the Women's International League, and in 1959 served on a commission that organized a 100th anniversary celebration in honor of Jane Addam's birth held the following year.

Balch entered Mr. Vernon Nursing Home in Cambridge, Massachusetts, in 1956 and died there of pneumonia at age 94 on January 10, 1961.

Further Reading

Both John Herman Randall, Jr.'s *Emily Greene Balch of New England, Citizen of the World* (1946) and *Improper Bostonian: Emily Greene Balch* (1964) by Mercedes M. Randall, are biographies of note. Further insight into Balch's activism can be found in *Beyond Nationalism: The Social Thought of Emily Greene Balch* (1972) by Mercedes M. Randall. □

In 1902 Balch became president of the Women's Trade Union League of Boston, which she co-founded, and sat on a state commission organized to investigate minimum wages for women. In 1906 she announced her affinity for socialism and worked closely with others to advance its principles. These radical activities cost her the chance to move up quickly in the academic hierarchy at Wellesley.

Balch's research led to the publication of *Our Slavic Fellow Citizens* in 1910. She was appointed chairwoman of the economics and sociology department at Wellesley College in 1913. Two years later, in April 1915, she travelled to The Hague, where she was an American delegate to the International Congress of Women. The 42-member delegation included such notables as Addams, Alice Hamilton, and Louis Lochner.

Balch was on leave from Wellesley between 1916 and 1918. During that period she became active in pacifism and was connected with such groups as the American Union Against Militarism and the Women's Peace Party. Because of her outspoken views and radical behavior, renewal of Balch's contract at Wellesley was denied in 1919. That same year she accompanied another delegation to the International Congress of Women. While there, she was elected secretary-treasurer of the newly-formed Women's International League for Peace and Freedom (WILPF), which had Addams as its president.

Balch relied heavily on her spiritual convictions during these years and in 1921 joined the London Society of Friends. She dedicated herself to the success of the League

Baldwin I

Baldwin I (ca. 1058-1118), a Norman known earlier as Baldwin of Boulogne and a chief lay leader of the First Crusade, reigned as king of Jerusalem from 1100 to 1118.

S on of the Norman Count of Boulogne, Baldwin joined the First Crusade with his brothers, Eustace and Godfrey of Bouillon. Baldwin soon left the main army to establish himself in Edessa (modern Urfa, Turkey), a Byzantine town beyond the Euphrates River, at the invitation of the Armenian prince Thoros. Upon the latter's death in 1098 Baldwin became head of the first crusading state in the

East. His wife, Godvere of Tosni, died shortly before this successful venture, and Baldwin soon authenticated his position by marrying Arda, an Armenian princess.

When Godfrey of Bouillon died in 1100, a group of knights in Jerusalem asked Baldwin to succeed him. This succession was opposed by the patriarch Daimbert, who wished to maintain his ecclesiastical control of the city, and by the crusader Tancred, who was suspicious of the use to which Baldwin might put his new power. It is indicative of Baldwin's strength that not only did he force Daimbert to crown him king (albeit in Bethlehem, not in Jerusalem), but he also kept Tancred at a distance until the latter departed the following year to assume the lordship of Antioch. In 1102 Baldwin deposed Daimbert, and his successors were all royal appointees.

Baldwin then set about to make his military position more secure. He had little effective power until he was able to control the coastal towns, which were vital for communications and supplies. He depended heavily on the loyalty of the vassals of the great fiefs, such as Tiberias, Haifa, and Caesarea, and to a lesser extent on mercenary troops and ships from the Italian cities. Once assured of the oaths of his knights, Baldwin commenced a systematic reduction of the ports so that by 1113 he controlled all the important ones in the vicinity of Jerusalem except Ascalon and Tyre. Although he still opposed Tancred, Baldwin was not above joining him on at least two occasions, in 1109 and in 1112, when preservation of the kingdom made cooperation advisable.

In 1113 Baldwin gave up Queen Arda for Adelaide of Salona, Countess of Sicily and mother of Count Roger II. The historian is obliged to see this as a political marriage which brought a dowry and possibly an heir to the kingdom, since Roger II was named as successor. Baldwin had never been divorced from his former wife, however, and 3 years later he approved the annulment of his union with Adelaide at the price of the enmity of the Sicilian court. Baldwin died near Ascalon on a raiding expedition in Egypt in April 1118. His successor in Jerusalem was his cousin, Baldwin II.

Baldwin I was an impressive figure. By his personal authority, with limited resources, and in the face of constant and powerful opposition from Cairo, Damascus, and his own associates, he established and maintained the kingdom of Jerusalem for 18 years.

Further Reading

There is no biography of Baldwin I in English. Useful sources are John L. La Monte, *Feudal Monarchy in the Latin Kingdom of Jerusalem, 1100-1291* (1932); Sir Steven Runciman, *A History of the Crusades,* (3 vols., 1951-1954); and *A History of the Crusades,* vol. 1: *The First Hundred Years,* edited by Marshall W. Baldwin (1955; 2d ed. 1969). □

James Arthur Baldwin

The author James Arthur Baldwin (1924-1987) achieved international recognition for his bold ex-pressions of African American life in the United States.

James Baldwin was born in Harlem, New York City, on August 2, 1924, the oldest of nine children. His father was a lay preacher in the Holiness-Pentecostal sect, and at the age of 14 Baldwin was also ordained a preacher. At 18 he graduated from DeWitt Clinton High School, and in 1944 he met Richard Wright, who helped secure a fellowship that allowed Baldwin the financial freedom to devote himself solely to literature. By 1948 Baldwin had concluded that the social tenor of the United States was stifling his creativity, and he went to Europe with the financial assistance of a Rosenwald fellowship. In Europe, Baldwin completed *Go Tell It on the Mountain* (1953), *Notes of a Native Son* (1955), and *Giovanni's Room* (1956).

Spokesperson for Civil Rights Movement

Returning to the United States after nine years abroad, Baldwin became known as the most eloquent literary spokesperson for the civil rights of African Americans. A popular speaker on the lecture circuit, Baldwin quickly discovered that social conditions for African Americans had become even more bleak while he was abroad. As the 1960s began—and violence in the South escalated—he became increasingly outraged. Baldwin responded with three powerful books of essays: *Nobody Knows My Name* (1961), *The Fire Next Time* (1963), in which he all but predicts the outbursts of black anger to come, and *More*

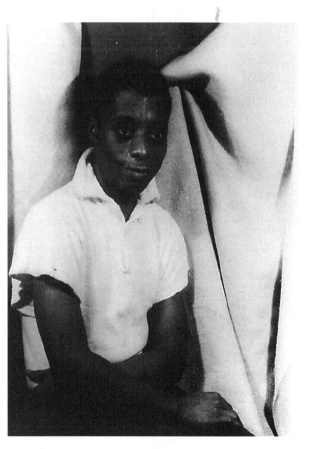

Notes of a Native Son. These highly inflammatory works were accompanied by *Another Country* (1962), his third novel. *Going to Meet the Man* (1965) is a group of cogent short stories of the same period. During this time Baldwin's commentary to Richard Avedon's photography was published under the title *Nothing Personal* (1964), and four years later came another novel, *Tell Me How Long the Train's Been Gone.*

In addition, the mid-1960s saw Baldwin's two published plays produced on Broadway. *The Amen Corner,* first staged in Washington, D.C., in 1955, was mounted at New York City's Ethel Barrymore Theatre in April 1965. Similar in tone to *Go Tell It on the Mountain,* it communicates the religious emotion of the Holiness-Pentecostal sect. *Blues for Mr. Charlie,* which premiered at Broadway's ANTA Theatre in April 1964, is based on the Emmett Till murder case.

The assassinations of three of Baldwin's friends—civil rights marcher Medgar Evers, the Reverend Martin Luther King, Jr., and the black Muslim leader Malcolm X— shattered any hopes Baldwin maintained for racial reconciliation in the United States, and he returned to France in the early 1970s. His subsequent works of fiction include *If Beale Street Could Talk* (1974) and *Just Above My Head* (1979). Nonfiction writings of this period include *No Name in the Street* (1972), *The Devil Finds Work* (1976), an examination of African Americans in the motion picture industry, and *The Evidence of Things Not Seen* (1985), a consideration of racial issues surrounding the Atlanta child murders of 1979 and 1980. A volume of poetry, *Jimmy's Blues* was issued in 1985.

Literary Achievement

Baldwin's greatest achievement as a writer was his ability to address American race relations from a psychological perspective. In his essays and fiction he explored the implications of racism for both the oppressed and the oppressor, suggesting repeatedly that all people suffer in a racist climate. Baldwin's fiction and plays also explore the burdens a callous society can impose on a sensitive individual. Two of his best-known works, the novel *Go Tell It on the Mountain* and the play *The Amen Corner* were inspired by his years with the Pentecostal church in Harlem. In *Go Tell It on the Mountain,* for instance, a teenaged boy struggles with a repressive stepfather and experiences a charismatic spiritual awakening. Later Baldwin novels deal frankly with homosexuality and interracial love affairs— love in both its sexual and spiritual forms became an essential component of the quest for self-realization for both Baldwin and his characters.

Themes and Techniques

Baldwin's prose is characterized by a style of beauty and telling power. His language seems deliberately chosen to shock and disturb, arouse, repel, and finally shake the reader out of complacency into a concerned state of action. His major themes are repeated: the terrible pull of love and hate between black and white Americans; the constant war in one possessed by inverted sexuality between guilt or shame and ecstatic abandon; and such moral, spiritual, and ethical values as purity of motive and inner wholeness, the gift of sharing and extending love, the charm of goodness versus evil. He tunes an inner ear to the disturbing social upheaval of contemporary life and to the rewarding ecstasy of artistic achievement. All such positive values are set in continual warfare against racism, industrialism, materialism, and a global power struggle. Everything demeaning to the human spirit is attacked with vigor and righteous indignation.

Final Works

Baldwin remained abroad much of the last 15 years of his life, but he never gave up his American citizenship. The citizens of France nevertheless embraced Baldwin as one of their own, and in 1986 he was accorded one of the country's highest accolades when he was named Commander of the Legion of Honor. He died of stomach cancer, November 30, 1987, in Saint-Paul-de-Vance, France, and was buried in Harlem. One of his last works to see publication during his lifetime was a well-regarded anthology of essays *The Price of the Ticket: Collected Nonfiction, 1948-1985.*

Further Reading

Biographical studies include David Adams Leeming, *James Baldwin: A Biography* (1994) and William J. Weatherby, *James Baldwin: Artist on Fire* (1989). Aspects of Baldwin's writings are examined in such studies as Bryan R. Washington, *The Politics of Exile: Ideology in Henry James, F. Scott Fitzgerald, and James Baldwin* (1995), R. Jothiprakash, *Commitment as a Theme in African American Literature: A Study of James Baldwin and Ralph Ellison* (1994), Jean-Francois Gounard, *The Racial Problem in the Works of Richard Wright and James Baldwin* (1992), and Horace A. Porter, *Stealing the Fire: The Art and Protest of James Baldwin* (1989). □

Robert Baldwin

The Canadian politician Robert Baldwin (1804-1858) played a decisive role in articulating and applying the concept of "responsible government" that underlies the constitutional development of the Commonwealth.

Robert Baldwin was born on May 12, 1804, in York, Upper Canada, the son of a well-to-do physician. He studied law and was called to the bar in 1825. In 1829 he was elected to the House of Assembly of Upper Canada but was defeated in another election in the following year.

Responsible Government

For most of his political career Baldwin was a man of a single idea—responsible government. This principle alone, he felt, could cure the evils of the existing system of government in the British North American colonies. The root of the trouble lay in an irresponsible executive. The British-appointed governor was surrounded by a group of advisers and hangers-on who filled most of the offices in the colonial administration and controlled all aspects of policy. Their privileged position allowed them to acquire large holdings of public lands and to obtain valuable bank and transportation charters for themselves. As a power elite, they were arbitrary and self-perpetuating, accountable only to the governor and, through him, to the British government in London.

Against this system, which was creating dangerous tensions in the colony, Baldwin proposed the simple principle of responsible government. By this he meant the British cabinet system, whereby a ministry or cabinet holds office only so long as it commands the support of the majority of elected members in the legislature. The ministers are thus responsible to the people's representatives and must leave office if their policies lose popular favor. Baldwin felt that the adoption of this form of government in the Canadas would ensure the loyalty of the majority of people to the British connection and at the same time would allow the colonies to develop along lines of local autonomy.

Political Struggle

Baldwin asserted the principle of responsible government unsuccessfully in 1836, when, after a difference of opinion on the workings of the principle, he resigned a position in the Executive Council, to which he had been appointed by the governor, Sir Francis Bond Head. The same year Baldwin submitted a memorandum on the subject to the Colonial Office in London which, if it did not impress the colonial secretary, was read and digested by

Lord Durham, soon to be sent to the Canadas as a special commissioner to look into the breakdown of government after the rebellions of 1837.

Baldwin had no sympathy with the resort to arms undertaken in Upper and Lower Canada in a desperate effort to remedy grievances. At Bond Head's request he negotiated with the leader of the rebels at York, William Lyon Mackenzie, but took no part in the unpleasant aftermath of the uprisings. Baldwin was cheered when Lord Durham recommended the establishment of responsible government as an essential political reform in his famous *Report on the Affairs of British North America* (1839).

A member of the new parliament for the united Province of Canada that came into existence in 1841, Baldwin became solicitor general for the western part of the province. When the new governor general, Lord Sydenham, refused to include French-Canadian reformers in the ministry, Baldwin again resigned and went into opposition. He introduced resolutions in favor of responsible government into the Assembly in 1841 and gained a thorough debate on the issue. A year later Sydenham's successor, Sir Charles Bagot, asked Baldwin to take office again, this time in association with French-speaking reformers from Canada East led by Louis-Hippolyte Lafontaine. The attempt to establish responsible government was frustrated once more when another governor, Sir Charles Metcalfe, refused to accept his ministers' advice on political appointments; 9 of the 10 ministers resigned in 1843, and for the next 5 years Baldwin and Lafontaine acted in opposition to the governor and his measures.

Achievement of the Principle

Finally, in 1847, a new governor, Lord Elgin, was sent to Canada with instructions to apply the principle of responsible government in its full implications. With a majority of members of the legislature behind them, Baldwin and Lafontaine were invited in 1848 to from a second ministry, the so-called Great Ministry. The test came the following year when, in spite of hesitations, Elgin endorsed a controversial measure which had been recommended by his ministers and passed in the legislature, indemnifying those who had suffered property losses in the recent rebellion. The Rebellion Losses Act created an intense storm in which the parliament buildings in Montreal were burned to the ground by a furious mob. But the principle of cabinet government was now established in Canadian constitutional practice.

The ministry headed by Baldwin and Lafontaine went on to further reforms: the provision of new municipal institutions to Canada West, a new system of financial guarantees to aid in the building of railroads, and a scheme to secularize the Anglican King's College as the University of Toronto. In 1851, feeling out of temper with the impatient mood of younger reformers, the conservative-minded Baldwin resigned office. He left public life after an electoral defeat later in the year. Subsequently he gave his blessing to an alliance between his followers and another group led by Francis Hincks, a political merger which produced a liberal-conservative party and eventually the Conservative party.

Baldwin died in Toronto on Dec. 9, 1858. He was a man of serious purpose and outstanding integrity. During his lifetime he did not receive due recognition for his determined struggle to establish in Canada a great constructive principle for the management of public affairs.

Further Reading

The best biography of Baldwin is George E. Wilson, *The Life of Robert Baldwin* (1933). An earlier study, which treats the three reformers of the period, is Stephen Leacock, *Baldwin, Lafontaine, Hincks: Responsible Government* (1907; revised and enlarged as *Mackenzie, Baldwin, Lafontaine, Hincks*, 1926). The achievement of "responsible government" in British North America is fully described in Chester Martin, *Empire and Commonwealth* (1929). □

Stanley Baldwin

Stanley Baldwin, 1st Earl Baldwin of Bewdley (1867-1947), was three times prime minister of Great Britain. He was involved in the settlement of the general strike of 1926 and in the abdication of Edward VIII in 1936.

Stanley Baldwin was born on Aug. 3, 1867, at Lower Park, Bewdley, Worcestershire. An only child, he was the son of Alfred Baldwin, an ironmaster, and Louisa Macdonald, the daughter of a Wesleyan minister. Baldwin attended Harrow and then Trinity College, Cambridge, where his record was undistinguished. He entered his father's business and, characteristically, came to know every workman in the foundry. He became a magistrate and a member of local councils. In 1892 he married Lucy Ridsdale of Rottingdean; to them seven children were born.

In 1908 Baldwin entered Parliament as a Conservative from the Bewdley division of Worcestershire, succeeding his father. Baldwin spoke infrequently and attracted little attention. When the new War Cabinet was formed in 1916, Bonar Law, a friend of his father and chancellor of the Exchequer, asked Baldwin to be his parliamentary private secretary. He soon became joint financial secretary to the Treasury. In 1921 he entered the Lloyd George Cabinet as president of the Board of Trade.

Baldwin came to national attention in 1922 at the Carlton Club Conference, at which the Conservatives in the House of Commons, after a stormy meeting, voted to end the coalition under David Lloyd George. Baldwin's passionate attack on Lloyd George materially influenced the result and brought Baldwin the chancellorship of the Exchequer. He successfully negotiated the settlement of the American war debt and, because of Bonar Law's illness, was, in effect, leader of the House of Commons. In a series of speeches Baldwin's appeal became clear—a plain earnestness of manner, an unashamed morality and patriotism, an absence of showmanship, and a certain provincialism. His plea for "tranquility" and a return to normalcy reached the average voter. In 1923, on Bonar Law's retirement, the King, on the advice of elder statesmen, selected Baldwin as prime minister, passing over Lord Curzon because he was in the House of Lords.

In an effort to reunite the Conservatives, Baldwin proposed a protective tariff and plunged the country into a general election in 1923, which brought Conservative defeat and the first Labour government. Before the end of the following year another election returned the Conservatives to power with Baldwin as prime minister. In the coal crisis and the general strike of 1926 Baldwin acted firmly but with conciliation. But just when his influence was at its height, he failed to deal with the basic issues in the coal industry. His administration proved a disappointment even to some members of his government, for he produced no policy to deal with unemployment, gave no lead to education, and made no important contribution in foreign or colonial affairs. Social legislation was enacted only on the initiative of Neville Chamberlain, the minister of health. Baldwin himself was content to rest on the slogans "Safety First" and "Trust Baldwin" in the election of 1929, which brought defeat to the Conservatives.

In the financial and political crisis of 1931 Baldwin readily acquiesced in the formation of a national government under the Labour leader, Ramsay MacDonald, with Baldwin himself taking the post of lord president of the council. For 4 years he was content to remain in the background, where in fact he was the real power. But in the crucial area of foreign affairs his role was unimaginative, and, like most of his countrymen, he was slow to see the necessity for rearmament in the face of Nazi and Fascist power.

In 1935 Baldwin replaced MacDonald. In this, Baldwin's third, administration he was at once confronted with the Abyssinian crisis, which was settled in Italy's favor and sharply lowered his prestige. His reputation was not revived in 1936 by the policy of nonintervention in the Spanish Civil War—a fiction so far as Continental powers were concerned. But 1936 was also the year of his greatest triumph— his masterful handling of the constitutional crisis over the proposed marriage of Edward VIII, the new king, to Mrs. Wallis Simpson. In his opposition Baldwin had the country behind him, as he knew he would.

Baldwin resigned in 1937. He was created an earl. He largely withdrew from public affairs, spending his declining years at Astley Hall in Worcestershire, where he died on Dec. 14, 1947.

Further Reading

Keith Middlemas and John Barnes, *Baldwin: A Biography* (1969), is the authoritative work. G. M. Young's brilliant but unsympathetic *Stanley Baldwin* (1952) was answered by D. C. Somervell, *Stanley Baldwin: An Examination of Some Features of Mr. G.M. Young's Biography* (1953), and by Arthur W. Baldwin, *My Father: The True Story* (1955). Background information is in Charles L. Mowat, *Britain between the Wars 1918-1940* (1955).

Additional Sources

Jenkins, Roy, *Baldwin,* London: Papermac, 1995. □

Arthur James Balfour

The British statesman and philosopher Arthur James Balfour, 1st Earl of Balfour (1848-1930), was prime minister of Great Britain. He later was chiefly responsible for the Balfour Declaration, favoring the establishment of Palestine as the national Jewish home.

Arthur James Balfour was born on July 25, 1848, at Whittinghame House, East Lothian, Scotland, the son of James Maitland Balfour, a country gentleman, and Lady Blanche Balfour, daughter of the 2d Marquess of Salisbury. Well educated, strong-minded, and evangelical in outlook, Lady Blanche dominated the early years of her children. Balfour was educated at Eton and at Trinity College, Cambridge.

Balfour pursued two careers, philosophy and politics, often simultaneously. As a metaphysician, his main concern was to find bases for modern religious belief. The doctrine of naturalism repelled him; he believed that one should be no more skeptical about religion than about science. His writings include *A Defense of Philosophical Doubt* (1879), *Foundations of Belief* (1896), and most important, his Gifford Lectures at the University of Glasgow, published as

Theism and Humanism (1915) and *Theism and Thought* (1923). His scholarly honors were legion, including the presidency of the British Association for the Advancement of Science (1904) and of the British Academy (1921). In 1891 he was named chancellor of Edinburgh University and in 1919 chancellor of Cambridge. His cultivation of mind, social graces, and gift for conversation brought him a prestige in English life for which, it is said, one must go back to the 18th century British statesman Charles James Fox for an equal. He never married.

At the suggestion of his uncle, Lord Salisbury, Balfour entered politics and won a Conservative seat in the House of Commons in 1874. As parliamentary private secretary he accompanied Salisbury, now foreign secretary, to the Congress of Berlin in 1878. Balfour's own parliamentary gifts were not fully revealed until the Salisbury administration (1886-1892). Balfour served successively as secretary for Scotland, as chief secretary for Ireland (he restored order and enacted salutary land reforms), and finally in 1891 as first lord of the Treasury and leader of the House of Commons. When Salisbury retired in 1902 during his second administration, the succession as prime minister fell naturally to Balfour.

During his own government (1902-1905) Balfour proved more successful as a statesman than as a politician. His leadership brought proposals for military reform and legislation of monumental significance: the Education Act of 1902, unifying elementary education, and the Irish Land Act of 1903, greatly simulating outright ownership of land by Irish peasants. Also there came an end to diplomatic

isolation, with the Entente Cordiale with France (1904) and the Anglo-Japanese Alliance (1905). But when Joseph Chamberlain challenged the sacred doctrine of free trade, splitting the party asunder, Balfour proved incapable either of restoring unity or indeed of developing a policy; the Conservatives, including Balfour, suffered total defeat in the election of 1906. A safe seat from the City of London was soon found for Balfour, who directed Conservative efforts to block the Liberal government's legislation program of fiscal and social reform. With the Parliament Act of 1911, which limited the role of the Lords, it was clear that Balfour had failed and he resigned the party leadership.

Balfour's political career was by no means at an end, however. In 1915 he joined the coalition War Cabinet as first lord of the Admiralty and was foreign secretary in the Lloyd George Cabinet. Balfour was largely responsible for the declaration (1917) which bears his name, authorized by the War Cabinet and affirming British support for a Jewish national home in Palestine. At the peace conference after World War I Balfour was active in the Council of Ten. In 1919 he shifted to the office of lord president of the Council and rendered distinguished service at the Washington Arms Conference (1922). He was created an earl in 1922. He presented the Balfour Report at the Imperial Conference of 1926, enunciating the doctrine of "equality of status" of the Dominions with Great Britain, which was formalized in the Statute of Westminster in 1931. Lord Balfour left office in 1929. He died on March 19, 1930.

Further Reading

Kenneth Young, *Arthur James Balfour* (1963), is the standard biography. An older, more personal treatment is Blanche E. C. Dugdale, *Arthur James Balfour, First Earl of Balfour* (2 vols., 1936). For special topics consult Denis Judd, *Balfour and the British Empire* (1968), and Alfred Gollin, *Balfour's Burden* (1965), a study of the tariff issue during 1903-1905.

Additional Sources

Harris, Paul, *Life in a Scottish country house: the story of A.J. Balfour and Whittingehame House,* Whittingehame, Haddington: Whittingehame House Pub., 1989. □

George Ball

George Ball (1909-1994) was a classic Atlanticist who promoted both strong ties between the United States and Western Europe and the development of an economically united Europe. He served as undersecretary of state during the Kennedy and Johnson administrations and wrote extensively on foreign affairs.

George W(ildman) Ball was born in Des Moines, Iowa, on December 21, 1909. He received both bachelor of arts and doctor of jurisprudence degrees from Northwestern University. Graduating from law

school in 1933, Ball went to Washington, D.C., where he worked for Henry Morgenthau, first at the Farm Credit Administration and then at the Department of Treasury. In 1935 he returned to Chicago to practice law. In the late 1930s he became greatly interested in world affairs. When war began in Europe, Ball followed his friend and colleague, Adlai Stevenson, into the Committee to Defend America by Aiding the Allies, an interventionist organization usually known as the White Committee.

When the United States entered World War II, Ball reentered government service, developing a specialty in international economic affairs. From 1942 to 1944 he served in the Office of Lend-Lease Administration and the Foreign Economic Administration. In 1944 he was appointed director of the U.S. Strategic Bombing Survey in London. He returned to Washington in 1945 to work for Jean Monnet as general counsel for the French Supply Council, a post he held until his return to private practice in 1946.

Monnet's Influence on Ball

Monnet was probably the greatest single influence on Ball's subsequent thought and career. Out of the shambles left by the war, the brilliant French visionary sought to create a united Europe with an integrated economy. His dream captured Ball, who worked with him toward creation of the European Coal and Steel Community and the European Common Market. Ball also represented a number of Common Market agencies in the United States in the years that followed.

Ball became a classic Atlanticist, profoundly committed to the idea that Western Europe was central to America's future, as it had been to America's past, and that the well-being of the North Atlantic Treaty Organization (NATO) and the vitality of the European Common Market were the essential interests of the United States. He believed that events in the Afro-Asian world were relatively less important and should never be allowed to corrode the links between the United States and Great Britain and France.

Economic Affairs and Trade Matters

In the 1950s Ball aided Henry Wallace in his defense against McCarthyism and, most importantly, helped orchestrate the "drafting" of Stevenson as Democratic presidential candidate. He remained with Stevenson through the 1960 campaign, managing the candidate's affairs at the Los Angeles convention. Nonetheless, the victorious John F. Kennedy was induced to appoint him undersecretary of state for economic affairs in January 1961.

Secretary of State Dean Rusk had little taste for economic affairs and left Ball a clear field. For most of 1961 Ball concentrated on trade matters, working to eliminate trade barriers by reducing American tariffs and giving the president broad powers to retaliate against nations that restricted imports. He helped draft the Trade Expansion Act of 1962, which embodied his ideas.

In November 1961, Ball replaced Chester Bowles as undersecretary of state, the second-ranking position in the department. Rusk delegated power easily, giving Ball full authority whenever the secretary travelled or was otherwise preoccupied. Rusk was also unusually tolerant of dissent and allowed Ball free rein to express his views to the president.

The Congo Crisis

Spared complicity in the Bay of Pigs debacle and the Laotian situation Kennedy inherited, Ball was less fortunate in the Congo crisis. In the Congo, a government which had won independence from Belgium in 1960 was threatened by internal strife from which the former Soviet Union, Belgian industrialists, other western investors, and various Congolese politicians sought to benefit. Moise Tshombe, who became the darling of American conservatives, led a secessionist movement in the mineral-rich province of Katanga. Ball was probably more sympathetic to the Belgians than Rusk, but no less aware that colonialism in any form was doomed. Both men were obsessed with fear that the Soviet Union might gain a foothold in the Congo, which Ball purported to believe was the key to the destiny of Africa in the Cold War struggle. Neither man was as committed to the United Nation's policy of suppressing the Katanga secession by force as were Bowles, Stevenson, and Assistant Secretary for African Affairs G. Mennen "Soapy" Williams. Indeed, Ball and Stevenson argued bitterly on the issue. Taking charge of the problem, Ball successfully negotiated the political minefields, contained the Left, pacified the Right, satisfied advocates of the United Nations, and minimized the irritation of NATO allies.

Antagonized By de Gaulle

Ball's arch-antagonist in Europe was Charles de Gaulle, whose intensive nationalism could not abide the Monnet-Ball images of France's place in a united Europe. Ball led the "theologians" who sought the further integration of Europe. He was the force behind the American effort to drive Britain into the Common Market and to solve the nuclear weapons control issue with the Multilateral Force (MLF). Always de Gaulle thwarted him, and neither Kennedy nor Lyndon Johnson would allow him to undertake a broader challenge to the French leader.

Questioned American Involvement in Vietnam

Ball's most memorable role was not widely known until publication of The Pentagon Papers in 1971. Alone among senior foreign policy advisors of Presidents Kennedy and Johnson, he consistently questioned American involvement in Vietnam and argued that intervention would not succeed. In part his views were based on understanding of the futility of the earlier French effort. They were also based on an Atlanticist's conviction that Southeast Asia, like the rest of the Afro-Asian world, mattered little. If the United States could protect the sources of industrial power in Europe, the Middle East, and Japan, it would prevail in the struggle against Communism.

Life After Politics

In September 1966, weary of the struggle, Ball resigned—in a quiet, establishment-approved way that preserved future opportunities to serve. He returned to government briefly as ambassador to the United Nations in 1968. He resigned that post to help Hubert Humphrey's presidential campaign.

In private life, Ball built his fortune as an investment banker with Lehman Brothers and wrote regularly on foreign affairs. His criticism of the policies of the administrations of the 1970s and 1980s appeared in frequent articles and books. An articulate and forceful writer, he never lacked a forum for his views. Ball passed away in 1994, but his legacy as a friend of Europe lives on.

Further Reading

The most useful sources of information are Ball's own memoir, *The Past Has Another Pattern* (1982), *George Ball: Behind the Scenes In U.S. Foreign Policy* by James A. Bill, Yale University Press (1997), and Warren I. Cohen, *Dean Rusk*, volume 19 in Samuel F. Bemis and Robert H. Ferrell, editors, *The American Secretaries of State and Their Diplomacy* (1980). See also David Halberstam, *The Best and the Brightest* (1972); Lyndon B. Johnson, *The Vantage Point* (1971); *The Pentagon Papers* (1971); and *Jean Monnet: The First Statesman of Independence* by François Duché, with a foreword by George W. Ball (1995). ☐

Lucille Ball

The face of comedienne Lucille Ball (Lucille Desiree Hunt; 1911-1989), immortalized as Lucy Ricardo on *I Love Lucy*, is said to have been seen by more people worldwide than any other. "Lucy" to generations of television viewers who delighted at her rubber-faced antics and zany impersonations (among them Charlie Chaplin's Little Tramp), she was a shrewd businesswoman, serious actress, and Broadway star as well.

Born Lucille Desiree Hunt on August 6, 1911, she and her mother, DeDe, made their home with her grandparents in Celoron, outside Jamestown, New York, after her father's death in 1915.

Lucy's mother encouraged her daughter's penchant for the theater. The two were close, and DeDe Ball's laugh can be heard on almost every *I Love Lucy* sound track. But from Lucy's first unsuccessful foray to New York, where she won—and lost—a chorus part in the Shubert musical *Stepping Stones*, through her days in Hollywood as "Queen of the B's" (grade B movies), the road to *I Love Lucy* was not an easy one.

In 1926 she enrolled at the John Murray Anderson/Robert Milton School of Theater and Dance in New York. Her participation there, unlike that of star student Bette

Davis, was a dismal failure. The proprietor even wrote to tell Lucy's mother that she was wasting her money. It was back to Celoron for the future star.

After a brief respite, the indomitable Lucy returned to New York with the stage name Diane Belmont. She was chosen to appear in Earl Carroll's *Vanities,* for the third road company of Ziegfeld's *Rio Rita,* and for *Step Lively,* but none of these performances materialized. She found employment at a Rexall drugstore on Broadway; then she worked in Hattie Carnegie's elegant dress salon, moonlighting as a model. Lucille Ball's striking beauty always differentiated her from other comediennes.

At the age of 17, Lucy was stricken with rheumatoid arthritis and returned to Celoron yet again, where her mother nursed her through an almost three-year bout with the illness.

Determined, she found more success in New York the next time when she became the Chesterfield Cigarette Girl. In 1933 she was cast as a last-minute replacement for one of the twelve Goldwyn girls in the Eddie Canter movie *Roman Scandals,* directed by Busby Berkeley. (Ball's first on-screen appearance was actually a walk-on in the 1933 *Broadway Thru a Keyhole.*) During the filming, when Lucy volunteered to take a pie in the face, the legendary Berkeley is said to have commented, "Get that girl's name. That's the one who will make it."

Favorable press from her first speaking role in 1935 and the second lead in *That Girl from Paris* (1936) helped win her a major part in the Broadway musical *Hey Diddle Diddle,* but the project was aborted by the premature death of the male lead. It would take roughly another 15 years for Lucy to attain stardom.

She worked with many comic "greats," including the Three Stooges, the Marx Brothers, Laurel and Hardy, and Buster Keaton, with whom she honed her extraordinary skill in the handling of props. She gave a creditable performance as an aspiring actress in *Stage Door* (1937) and earned praise from critic James Agee for her portrayal of a bitter, handicapped nightclub singer in *The Big Street* (1942).

Lucy first acquired her flaming red hair in 1943 when, after *The Big Street,* MGM officials signed her to appear opposite Red Skelton in Cole Porter's *DuBarry Was a Lady.* (Throughout the years, rumors flew as to the color's origin, including one that Lucy decided upon the dye job in an effort to somehow rival Betty Grable.)

It was on the set of an innocuous film, *Dance, Girl, Dance,* that Lucille Ball first met her future husband, Cuban bandleader Desi Arnaz. Married in 1940, they were separated by Desi's travels for much of the first decade of their marriage. The union, plagued by Arnaz's alcoholism, workaholism, and philandering, dissolved in 1960.

The decade prior to Lucy's television debut was filled with intermittent parts in films and the more satisfying role of Liz Cooper, the scatterbrained wife on the radio program *My Favorite Husband* (July 1947 to March 1951).

Determined to work together and to save their marriage, the couple conceived a television pilot. Studio executives were dubious. The duo was forced to take their "act" on the road to prove its viability and to borrow $5,000 to found Desilu Productions. (After buying out Arnaz's share and changing the corporation's name, Lucy eventually sold it to Gulf Western for $18 million.) They persevered, and *I Love Lucy* premiered on October 15, 1951.

Within six months the show as rated number one. It ran six seasons in its original format and then evolved into hour-long specials, accumulating over 20 awards, among them five Emmys. *I Love Lucy* is one of television's four "all-time hits."

. The characters Lucy and Ricky Ricardo became household words, with William Frawley and Vivian Vance superbly cast as long-suffering neighbors Fred and Ethel Mertz. More viewers tuned in for the television birth of "Little Ricky" Ricardo than for President Eisenhower's inauguration. The show was the first in television history to claim viewing in more than ten million homes. It was filmed before a studio audience, in sequence, and helped to revolutionize television production by utilizing three cameras.

I Love Lucy begat *Lucy in Connecticut* (1960); in turn, *The Lucy-Desi Comedy Hour* (1962-1967); then *The Lucy Show* (1962, with Vivian Vance, later called *The Lucille Ball Show,* running until 1974); and, finally, in 1986, the ill-fated *Life with Lucy,* with Gale Gordon.

The Lucy Ricardo character may be viewed as a downtrodden housewife, but compared to other situation comedy wives of television's "golden years' she was liberated. The show's premise was her desire to share the show-biz limelight with her performer husband and to leave the pots and pans behind. Later series featured Lucy as a single mother and as a working woman "up against" her boss.

Following her initial retirement from prime time in 1974 Lucy continued to make guest appearances on television, too numerous to mention. Broadway saw her starring in *Mame* (1974), a role with which she identified. (Her other Broadway appearance after her career had "taken off" was in *Wildcat* in 1960.) Her last serious role was that of a bag lady in the 1983 made-for-television movie *Stone Pillow.*

Lucy was married to comic Gary Morton from 1961 until the time of her death on April 26, 1989, eight days after open-heart surgery. She was survived by her husband, her two children by Arnaz, Luci and Desi Junior, and millions of fans who continue to watch her in re-runs of *I Love Lucy,* which is now also available on video cassette.

Further Reading

Chapters devoted to Lucille Ball can be found in *Women in Comedy* (1986) by Linda Martin and Kerry Segrave and in *Funny Women* (1987) by Mary Unterbrink. Biographies include *The Lucille Ball Story* (1974) by James Gregory, *Lucy* (1986) by Charles Higham, and *Forever Lucy* (1986) by Joe Morella and Edward Z. Epstein. Desi Arnaz's 1976 autobiography, *A Book,* chronicles their years together from his perspective, and Bart Andrews' *Lucy and Ricky and Fred and Ethel: The Story of "I Love Lucy"* (1976) features a complete plot summary for each of the show's episodes. *People* magazine paid special tribute to Lucy in its August 14, 1989, issue.

☐

Giacomo Balla

The Italian painter Giacomo Balla (1871-1958) was one of the founders of futurism, an Italian art movement.

Giacomo Balla was born on July 24, 1871, in Turin. He was already appreciated as an academic painter when he first encountered impressionist and divisionist painting during a visit to Paris at the turn of the century. The problems of light and color intrigued him. On his return to Rome he enthusiastically imparted his new-found postimpressionist theories to the painters Gino Severini and Umberto Boccioni. The poet F. T. Marinetti converted Balla to futurism.

Futurism was a movement with a program of belligerent modernism, both in an ethical and esthetic sense. A determined acceptance of the age of the machine and an admiration of speed were its main points. As a style, futurism evolved from the revolutionary tenets of analytical cubism. It brought to modern art an emphasis on the visualization of the kinetic principle and a contempt for all traditional modes of esthetic expression. Thus Marinetti declared: "We have already put behind us the grotesque burial of passéist Beauty. . . . We shall sing the love of danger, the habit of energy and boldness. . . . We declare that the world's splendor has been enriched by a new beauty, the beauty of speed. A speeding motor car . . . is more beautiful than the Victory of Samothrace."

Although Balla was one of five painters who signed the Futurist Manifesto of 1910, he did not take part (despite the fact that his name figured in the catalog) in the important exhibition of futurist painting in Paris in 1912. It was Balla, however, who that year painted the first, most original, and somewhat witty visual depiction of movement in the novel futurist manner; it depicted the legs of a lady and a dog on a leash in successive phases of the action of walking. Another painting in a similar style was *Rhythm of the Violinist.*

A more complex interpretation of the kinetic principle occurred to Balla after reading Severini's *Expansion sphérique dans l'espace* (Spherical Expansion in Space). In 1913/1914 Balla showed a marked preference for massive scrolls, with the help of which he re-created the illusion of depth. Also dating from this period are his cosmogonic themes (such as *Mercury Passing in front of the Sun*), which are among the most abstract pictures produced by the futurists.

During the 1920s Balla remained faithful to the futurist movement. Later on he painted figurative compositions and abstract studies. What he aimed at as a mature artist was a synthesis of physical movement and emotional and mental attitudes. Balla lived most of his life in Rome, where he died on March 6, 1958.

Further Reading

Information on Balla is in Alfred H. Barr, Jr., *Cubism and Abstract Art* (1936); James Thrall Soby and Alfred H. Barr, Jr., *Twenti-*

eth-Century Italian Art (1949); and Raffaele Carrieri, *Avant-Grade Painting and Sculpture* (*1890-1955*) *in Italy* (1955) and *Futurism* (1961; trans. 1963). ☐

Edouard Balladur

Edouard Balladur (born 1929) took the leadership of the French Government in March 1993, after a long career in civil service and, beginning in 1986, in politics. After an unsuccessful bid for the presidency in 1995, Balladur retired from the public spotlight.

Edouard Balladur became premier (prime minister) of the French Government in March 1993. After his election he distinguished himself perhaps more for his highly unusual popularity in the midst of deep economic crisis than for the solutions he attempted for France's economic woes.

Balladur became premier after conservative parties, including his own Gaullist Rally for the Republic (RPR), inflicted a resounding election defeat on the incumbent Socialists. As a result, Socialist President François Mitterrand found himself compelled, for the second time in his presidential career, to appoint a head of government from an adversary party. However, due to Balladur's conciliatory posture and personality, this second episode in *cohabitation* proved far less controversial than the previous one in 1986-1988 (with Jacques Chirac).

Balladur was described as a somewhat distant and haughty man of great poise, always elegant in manner, speech, and dress, yet endowed with a wry sense of humor. His personality apparently aided his relationship with the French president, but it cannot alone explain such success. Balladur's own political moderation was at the core of the relationship between president and premier. When the conservatives swept the elections, many commentators and pundits in Europe feared a sharp right-wing political turn in France. Yet, Balladur proved them wrong time and again.

While a staunch advocate of free-market economics, Balladur raised taxes in order to reduce a staggering budget deficit and promised to curtail the 10 to 11 percent unemployment rate. Even before his election he pointed out that the French economy was at its worst since the end of World War II and that the French public should not expect miraculous solutions to the crisis. Progress would come slowly and painfully. Balladur also pledged to do the following: keep the French franc as strong as his Socialist predecessors had; strengthen the process of European economic and political integration as much as possible; and privatize a number of state-owned enterprises. With the first two proposals Balladur was sure to appease Mitterrand, and with the latter his own conservative supporters and party allies.

Balladur's political and managerial abilities developed over a long period of time during which he stood out of the limelight. Born in 1929 in Smyrna, Turkey, into a French family, he was brought up in Marseilles in southern France.

He attended the two top series of courses for future civil servants, the Faculty of Political Sciences and the National School of Administration (ENA) in Paris. After graduation, in the 1960s and 1970s he worked for Gaullist premier and president Georges Pompidou. At first he was the premier's adviser, and later he became Pompidou's deputy chief and then chief of staff at the Presidential (Elysée) Palace. After the death of Pompidou and a brief spell as a businessman, Balladur became a sort of "gray eminence" for Jacques Chirac, who had become the Gaullists' leader.

Balladur officially entered politics only in 1986, when he became minister of finance in Chirac's *cohabitation* cabinet. In that capacity between 1986 and 1988 Balladur embarked upon a major program of privatization of state-owned industries. While he left that task unfinished after a Socialist electoral victory in 1988, he reprised it immediately upon becoming premier.

While Balladur maintained a considerable degree of popularity in the few months after his appointment, he faced a number of serious and diverse crises. First of all, he was compelled to retreat to some extent from his pledge to keep a strong French franc. Tied to an intra-European monetary system, the franc had difficulty in maintaining its value *vis-à-vis* the German mark. The German central bank (Bundesbank) in turn kept interest rates high to defeat possible inflation within Germany. In order to keep a strong franc the French had to keep interest rates high as well, or capital would fly to Germany. High interest rates in turn helped deepen the recession. After Balladur's appointment, speculation against the franc began, in the expectation that interest rates would be lowered and/or the French currency devalued. Balladur then opted for a massive currency-rescue operation by the Bank of France, coupled with a small devaluation *vis-à-vis* the mark. While this was a risky course, it did help stop the speculators, at least for a time.

Another thorny issue for Balladur was the General Agreements on Tariffs and Trade (GATT). While the United States (and most European countries) preferred lower agricultural tariffs, France insisted on protection of French farmers from foreign competition. Militant French farmers periodically engaged in violent protests in order to keep the government on its protectionist course. At the same time, several French motion picture industry personalities campaigned to limit the number of American films shown in French theaters. After months of difficult negotiations, in December 1993 the Balladur government managed to settle for a compromise with the United States that left many French farmers and cinema personalities unhappy.

One more difficult episode involved the attempt to streamline the administration of state-owned Air France. When 4,000 job cuts at the airline were announced, Air France personnel went on strike. Since the French public, worried about unemployment, sided solidly with the Air France employees, the Balladur government chose to retreat. Balladur feared the strikes might spread to other sectors, and his problems worsened throughout 1994. French leftists protested Balladur's policy to increase government funding to private schools. Rioting fishermen demanded government price guarantees. Students took to the streets in contempt of expansion of the welfare state.

Despite these problems Balladur remained surprisingly popular, and he sought the French presidency in the election of 1995. Near the end of 1994, shortly before the first round of voting was scheduled (in April of 1995), Balladur and his administration were plagued by a series of scandals. The prime minister's popularity plunged desperately amid charges of illegal wiretapping, kickbacks to magistrates, and financial scandals involving various cabinet ministers. Jacques Chirac, an old friend and colleague of Balladur, ultimately won the presidency, but the friendship between the two was dissolved in the contest, and Balladur disappeared from from the public spotlight.

Further Reading

The only sources on Edouard Balladur in English are books on the Mitterrand presidency and/or national newspapers and magazines. For Balladur's role in the first *cohabitation* cabinet see Julius W. Friend, *Seven Years in France: François Mitterrand and the Unintended Revolution, 1981-1988* (1989); for the experience of that Gaullist cabinet in general see Wayne Northcutt, *Mitterrand: A Political Biography* (1992).

Additional Sources

The Economist, March 12, 1994; September 17, 1994; October 22, 1994; February 25, 1995; March 11, 1995.
National Review,, March 21, 1994.
Insight on the News, May 9, 1994.
The Nation, February 7, 1994. □

José Ballivián

José Ballivián (1805-1852) was a Bolivian patriot officer in the movement for independence from Spain, defended his country from invasion from Peru, and was president of Bolivia from 1841 to 1847.

José Ballivián was born to an aristocratic Spanish family in La Paz on Nov. 30, 1805. After a routine, local education, he entered the military as a cadet in the Spanish army stationed in Bolivia (Alto Peru) during the South American revolutions for independence. By 1820 he had changed sides, and he spent the next 5 years fighting for the patriot cause under Simón Bolivar and other great war heroes. At war's end in 1825, Ballivián was a young but respected colonel.

Little is known of Ballivián after independence until he helped lead a rebellion against the confederation of Peru and Bolivia under a single executive. The revolt failed, but the confederation was dissolved during war with Chile in 1839.

In 1839 Ballivián became a presidential aspirant; when he lost, he again led an unsuccessful revolt and was forced to flee to Peru and exile. In 1841, however, when Bolivia was invaded by the Peruvian general Agustin Gamarra, who dreamed of a union of the two nations, Ballivián was back in

Bolivia heading its army as a general. He defeated the superior army of Gamarra at Ingavi in November 1841.

As Bolivia's second Great Liberator, Ballivián encountered little opposition when he claimed the presidency and began his firm rule. Ballivián was one of Bolivia's best 19th-century rulers. A cultured man, he began to work toward his dream of a modern Bolivia. He had the vast, unknown eastern section of the country surveyed, mapped, and made into the new and separate department (state) of El Beni, integrating the primitive section into the nation. He surrounded himself with competent men and worked toward a broader educational system, better river transportation, an adequate seaport on the Pacific coast, and creation of a free press.

In 1843 a grateful Congress formally elected Ballivián president and ratified the constitution he had prepared. He was reelected in 1846, but unrest was growing and revolutions were breaking out all over the country. For more than a year he repressed all serious opposition, but his growing harshness prompted even more unrest until Gen. Isidro Belzu and a large part of the army revolted in mid-1847. In December, convinced of the futility of resistance, Ballivián resigned the presidency and in January fled to Peru. After several unsuccessful attempts at a comeback, Ballivián left Peru and traveled to Brazil, where he died in Rio de Janeiro on Oct. 16, 1852.

The ghastly procession of dictators who followed Ballivián seriously retarded the development of Bolivia and made the Ballivián years appear a "golden age" of progress.

Further Reading

There is no adequate biography of Ballivián in any language. The best treatment of the man and his rule may be found in Alcides Arguedas, *Historia general de Bolivia . . . 1809-1921,* in Spanish (1922). Ballivián's career is recounted in Robert Barton, *A Short History of the Republic of Bolivia* (La Paz, 2d ed. 1968). Also of value are Enrique Finot, *Nueva historia de Bolivia: Ensayo de interpretación sociológia,* in Spanish (1946; 3d ed. 1964), and Harold Osborne, *Bolivia: A Land Divided* (1954; 3d ed. 1965). □

José Manuel Balmaceda Fernández

José Manuel Balmaceda Fernández (1840-1891) was the last of the strong 19th-century presidents of Chile. His personality and policies provoked a constitutional crisis between Congress and the presidency and led to a civil war.

José Balmaceda was born in Santiago, Chile. He was destined for the Church but entered politics instead as a liberal reformer. In 1878, after gaining a reputation as an orator and a forceful politician, he was sent as Chilean envoy to Buenos Aires, where his diplomatic skill helped to keep Argentina from joining Peru and Bolivia against Chile in the War of the Pacific. He then was made minister of foreign affairs and of the interior, and in 1886 he became president of Chile.

Balmaceda's presidency was one of the stormiest in Chilean history. Despite the instability of his cabinets and the turbulence of opposing congressional factions, Balmaceda carried through an energetic program of public works. Though the country suffered setbacks from the 1886-1887 cholera epidemic and from incipient labor troubles, its flourishing nitrate industry brought growing prosperity. Balmaceda held that the state should have the major voice in controlling the economic expansion, and he thereby came into conflict with the business circles who believed in a laissez-faire policy.

In 1890 Balmaceda's policies and increasingly autocratic conduct of affairs precipitated a major constitutional crisis. The opposition made use of its majority in Congress to withhold funds and impose the appointment of a cabinet acceptable to itself. Balmaceda then replaced this cabinet by one of his own choice, dissolved Congress, and began to assume openly dictatorial powers. Congress attempted to depose him and civil war broke out. The navy supported Congress, and most of the army, the president. Congressional leaders established a junta at Iquique and set about raising an army in northern Chile, which they financed from the nitrate revenues. Balmaceda summoned a fresh Congress and began energetically to organize his forces. These forces, however, suffered defeat in the battles of Concón and Placilla, and the President was forced to abdicate and seek asylum in the Argentine embassy. There he committed suicide on Sept. 18, 1891.

Balmaceda—the handsome, gifted, and wealthy liberal reformer whose evolution into the most authoritarian of presidents ended in civil war and personal tragedy—remains one of the most striking and controversial figures in Chilean history. His defeat, vindicating the ultimate supremacy of Congress over the presidency, was regarded by his opponents as the triumph of democracy over dictatorship. His admirers claimed that it represented only the triumph of an oligarchy of wealthy families, backed by foreign nitrate interests, who felt threatened by the President's nationalist policies and his concern for social justice.

Further Reading

Balmaceda is the subject of a large and mainly polemical literature in Spanish. In English there is an essay by Lewis W. Bealer in A. Curtis Wilgus, ed., *South American Dictators during the First Century of Independence* (1937). Background studies that include a discussion of Balmaceda are Isaac J. Cox's chapter in A. Curtis Wilgus, ed., *Argentina, Brazil and Chile since Independence* (1934), and Luis Galdames, *A History of Chile* (1925; trans. 1941). Fredrick B. Pike, *Chile and the United States, 1880-1962* (1963), has exhaustive Chilean material and extensive footnotes and bibliography, but it has been criticized for the author's politically leftist outlook. □

Balthus

Balthus (born 1908) was a European painter and stage designer who worked within the Western tradition of figure painting. He is best known for his paintings of everyday life invested with a sense of mystery, symbolism, and eroticism.

Balthus was born Balthasar Klossowski in Paris, France, on February 29, 1908, to a Prussian family that had left Silesia five years before. His parents were both painters, as was his brother, and they lived in Switzerland and Berlin during the turbulent years before, during, and after World War I. Balthus did not study at the Academy of Fine Arts or in the studio of another painter. Instead, he taught himself by copying masterpieces at the Louvre Museum, as had many painters in the 19th century. He did attend sketching classes at the Grand Chaumiere, an informal art school, where he received criticism from Maurice Vlaminck and Pierre Bonnard, two prominent painters associated with the Ecole de Paris.

Balthus copied works by the French Neo-Classic painter Nicolas Poussin and the Italian Renaissance painter Piero della Francesca. The German poet Rainer Maria Rilke, a close friend of his mother, urged him to use his childhood nickname, Balthus, as his artistic name. Married twice with three children, Balthus lived most of his life in Paris but moved in 1977 to near Beatenburg, Switzerland.

Painting Style and Subject Matter

Balthus' work was always figurative, despite the strong tendency toward abstraction in the 20th century. Throughout his career the subject matter of his work was fairly constant, depicting street scenes, landscapes, portraits, and interior domestic scenes. He is best known for his paintings of adolescents, especially young girls who are often nude or partially clothed in intimate, indoor settings where the painter—and by extension the viewer—appear to be peeking. His manner of painting is often considered classical: the figures and objects are weighty geometric forms that appear frozen in time. Balthus' composition, derived from Renaissance models, used the inter-relationship of figures, objects, and setting to create a sense of space. The atmospheric stillness in Balthus' painting infuses the everyday activities he depicted with a psychological sense of mystery and intrigue.

Balthus worked outside the main artistic currents that developed in Paris, but during the 1930s he was in contact with the Surrealist group and he became friendly with the Swiss sculptor Alberto Giacometti. The Surrealists, who were interested in the psychology of the unconscious, were drawn to the dream-like quality of Balthus' paintings, their sexual ambiguity, and his confessed desire to shock. Balthus himself disavowed the erotic content in his work.

Later, he built up thick layers of oil paint on his canvases, called an impasto, and painted with bright, warm colors which made the paintings look like frescos executed in plaster. The sense of bright light in them is almost Mediterranean, and it appears to dissolve distinctions between things, a pronounced difference from the sharp focus of his earlier work. Besides this further reference to Renaissance art he also executed work based on Japanese prints.

Designed Stage Sets for Artaud

Balthus did not paint continuously throughout his life. He also designed stage sets and costumes for the theater, most notably for his close friend Antonin Artaud, the dramatist, actor, and poet. Balthus did the set for Artaud's *Les Cencis* in 1935, a violent and scandalous story, and for productions of Shakespeare and Mozart's *Cosi fan Tutti*. Balthus fought in World War II in Alsace and was the director of the French Academy in Rome between 1961 and 1977.

Career Flourished First in U.S.A.

Earlier in his life Balthus was better known as a painter in the United States than in Europe where he had only two one-person shows between 1934 and 1946. The artist owes much of his fame to two American businessmen who took note of him in the 1930s. Connecticut millionaire James Thrall Soby, purchased Balthus' *The Street* in 1937 and then donated the painting, revised by the artist himself to censor an image of a boy grabbing a girl's crotch, to The Museum of Modern Art in 1956. Pierre Matisse, an art dealer, gallery owner, and son of Henri Matisse, began selling Balthus' work in New York in the 1930s. Matisse gave Balthus seven one-man shows in his gallery over the years as well. He was shown more in New York during the 1930s and 1940s and was the subject of an exhibition at the Museum of Modern Art in 1956 and at the Metropolitan Museum of Art in 1984.

Work Difficult to Categorize

Balthus' work is difficult to place within the history of 20th century art as he never embraced any of this century's major art trends and he was never associated with any group of artists. He remained a kind of solitary figure. His insistence on working figuratively ran counter to much of the mainstream art of this century, although he was held in esteem by many abstract painters for his purely formal strengths. Picasso owned at least one of Balthus' major paintings. What identifies his work as modern is the presence of a highly personal psychology in his painting and the challenging nature of his subject matter. Balthus' art is not an art of experimentation or innovation, but one of reinvestigation of traditional painting attitudes and techniques and of an attempt to reinvest Western painting conventions with new meaning. A renewed interest in Balthus can be explained by recent attempts by art historians to revise the orthodox history of modernism to explain the work of ideosyncratic artists such as Balthus and to acknowledge the continuing presence of figurative art throughout the 20th century.

Further Reading

For a thorough account of Balthus' life and a good number of color illustrations of work from all periods see Sabine Re-

wald's *Balthus* (1984), a catalog for his retrospective at the Metropolitan Museum of Art in New York in 1984. Another monograph with a text by Jean Leymarie, *Balthus* (1979), was published earlier. There are various catalogs on specific aspects of Balthus' work, such as *Balthus, Drawings and Watercolors* by Giovanni Carandente, but there is no real examination of the psycho-sexual content in his work. See also *Balthus Receives A Visitor* by Ted Morgan in the *New York Times Magazine,* January 9, 1994; and *Solitary In the City of Art* by Jed Perl in *The New Republic,* March 13, 1995. Balthus can be found on the Web at *A&E Biography,* http://www.biography.com/find/find.html. □

David Baltimore

The American virologist David Baltimore (born 1938) received the Nobel Prize in Physiology and Medicine for his work on retrovirus biochemistry and its significance for cancer research.

David Baltimore was born on March 7, 1938, in New York City, the son of Richard I. and Gertrude (Lipschitz) Baltimore. While still a high school student, he spent a summer at the Jackson Memorial Laboratory in Bar Harbor, Maine, experiencing biology under actual research conditions. This so affected him that upon entering Swarthmore College in 1956 he declared himself a biology major. Later he switched to chemistry to complete a research thesis and graduated in 1960 with a B.A. and high honors. Between his sophomore and junior years at Swarthmore, he spent a summer at the Cold Spring Harbor Laboratories, where the influence of George Streisinger led him to molecular biology.

Baltimore spent two years of graduate work at Massachusetts Institute of Technology (MIT) in biophysics, then left for a summer with Philip Marcus at the Albert Einstein Medical College and to take the animal virus course at Cold Spring Harbor under Richard Franklin and Edward Simon. He then joined Franklin at the Rockefeller Institute, completing his thesis by 1964 and staying on as a postdoctoral fellow in animal virology with James Darnell.

In 1965 he became a research associate at the Salk Institute of Biological Studies, working in association with Renato Dulbecco. Here he first met Alice S. Huang, with whom he also conducted research. He and Huang were married on October 5, 1968, and that same year they returned to MIT, where he held the position of associate professor of microbiology until 1971. In 1972 he rose to full professorship, and in 1974 he joined the staff of the MIT Center for Cancer Research under Salvador Luria.

Received Recognition For Cancer and Immunology Research

Baltimore received many awards for his work. In 1971 he was the recipient of the Gustav Stern award in virology, the Warren Triennial Prize, and the Eli Lilly and Co. award in microbiology and immunology. A year after being promoted to full professorship at MIT, he was rewarded a lifetime research professorship by the American Cancer Society. In 1974 he was presented with the U.S. Steel Foundation award in molecular biology and the Gairdner Foundation Annual Award. His most prestigious award came in 1975 when he shared the Nobel Prize in Physiology and Medicine with Howard M. Temin and Renato Dulbecco for research on retro-viruses and cancer. Much of this work concentrated upon protein and nucleic acid synthesis of RNA (ribonucleic acid) animal viruses, especially poliovirus and the RNA tumor virus. His research demonstrated that the flow of genetic information in such viruses did not have to go from DNA (deoxyribonucleic acid) to RNA but could flow from RNA to DNA, a finding which undermined the central dogma of molecular biology—i.e., unilinear information flow from DNA to proteins. This process came to be called, facetiously, "reverse transcriptase."

Baltimore's interests later took him further into the study of how viruses reproduce themselves and into work on the immune systems of animals and humans, where he concentrated upon the process by which antibodies may develop. Central to much of this work was DNA technology, in which he maintained an active interest.

Baltimore proved himself an effective educator, conducting seminars with graduate students and younger colleagues. He also became successful at directing research rather than doing it himself, again working closely with students.

Research Debacle

In 1989 Thereza Imanishi-Kari, a collegue with whom he co-authored a 1986 paper on immunology for *Cell*, was charged with falsifying data. Imanishi-Kari, a Massachussets Institute of Technology Assistant Professor, was absolved when a top government ethics panel declared they found no wrongdoing in 1996. Although Baltimore was never implicated in any wrongdoing, the incident caused him to withdraw the paper. He was also pressured by colleagues to resign from his presidency at New York's Rockefeller University, which he did in 1991.

Baltimore Chairs AIDS Vaccine Research Panel

In December 1996, Baltimore became the head of a new AIDS vaccine research panel for the Office of AIDS Research at the National Institute of Health. The panel was formed to step up the search for an AIDS vaccine. He also became the President of the California Institute of Technology in 1997.

Further Reading

Short biographies of David Baltimore can be found in the 39th edition of *Who's Who in America* (1976-1977) and in the 14th edition of *American Men and Women of Science: Physical and Biological Sciences* (1979). He provided an autobiographical sketch in the *Nobel Lectures* (1977), and a *New York Times* interview (August 26, 1980) gives additional information.

For further reading, see: *Appeals Panel Reverses Fraud Finding* by K. Fackelmann in *Science News*, July 6, 1996; *Baltimore to Head New Vaccine Panel* by Jon Cohen in *Science*, December 20, 1996; and *A Shot In the Arm* by Mark Schoofs, *The Village Voice*, December 24, 1996. □

Honoré de Balzac

The French novelist Honoré de Balzac (1799-1850) was the first writer to use fiction to convey the total social scene prevailing within one country at a particular period in its history. Commonly regarded as the founder of social realism, he also had affinities with the romantics.

Born at Tours on May 20, 1799, Honoré de Balzac was sent as a boarder, at the age of 8, to the Oratorian College of Vendôme, an old-fashioned school where the discipline was harsh and conditions primitive. The semiautobiographical work *Louis Lambert* (1832) gives a fairly faithful account of this period of Balzac's life. The boy sought refuge from his surroundings in books, but excessive reading eventually brought on some kind of nervous malady, and he was brought home in 1813. The following year his family moved to Paris, where he completed his secondary education and in 1819 took a degree in law. The not inconsiderable legal knowledge Balzac acquired at this time, both in the lecture hall and in the office of the solicitor for whom he worked, was put to good use in a number of the novels and stories of his maturity that turn on disputed legacies (*Le Cousin Pons*, 1846-1847), marriage settlements (*Le Contrat de mariage*, 1835), petitions in lunacy (*L'Interdiction*, 1836), and bankruptcy proceedings (*César Birotteau*, 1837; *Illusions perdues*, 1837-1843).

Early Life

To his parents' disappointment, Balzac refused to enter the legal profession and instead declared his intention to devote himself to a literary career. His father gave him a small allowance on the understanding that at the end of 2 years he should produce a masterpiece or else abandon his ambitions. Although the expected great work did not materialize, Balzac persisted, and between 1820 and 1825 he wrote a number of sensational or humorous novels, some of them in collaboration with friends and none signed with his own name. These books were devoid of literary merit, but he earned his living by them and learned some useful lessons in the art of fiction.

Casting about for ways of making his fortune more rapidly, Balzac next set himself up as a publisher. In 1825, he launched one-volume editions of the works of the French authors Molière and La Fontaine, but they did not sell well. Undaunted, he acquired a printing business on borrowed capital and later a type foundry. These commercial ventures were also failures, and Balzac's brief business career ended in 1828, when his affairs were liquidated, leaving him with very large debts.

day, keeping himself awake by frequent cups of strong coffee.

Whenever Balzac earned a respite from his herculean toil, he would plunge into bouts of social dissipation which were only a little less exhausting. Though of sober disposition—he never drank to excess and considered the use of tobacco to be enfeebling—he enjoyed good food and was capable of devouring gargantuan meals. In appearance he was unprepossessing, a thick-set man with massive neck and fleshy chin, his enormous head crowned by a mop of greasy black hair. But his magnetic gaze unfailingly compelled attention. He did his best to offset the inelegance of his person by dressing splendidly and wearing ostentatious jewels. In spite of this strain of vulgarity, the liveliness of his conversation and the reputation his books had given him of being an expert on feminine psychology made him a welcome guest in a number of fashionable salons.

The Human Comedy

Balzac's lifework, apart from the early novels already mentioned and a few plays toward the end of his career, consists of a massive series of some 90 novels and short stories collected under the title *La Comédie humaine* (*The Human Comedy*). It was not until 1841 that this title, probably suggested to him by Dante's *Divine Comedy*, made its appearance. *The Human Comedy* was subdivided into smaller cycles of novels: "Scenes of Private Life," "Scenes of Political Life," Scenes of "Parisian," "Provincial," "Country" Life, and so on. There was a separate group of "Philosophical Studies," in which Balzac gave freer rein to his love of the fantastic and the macabre and to his interest in metapsychical phenomena such as thought transference and mesmerism. The "Philosophical Studies" often have historical settings, whereas the rest of *The Human Comedy* consists of stories that are set in Balzac's own time and describe various aspects of French society during the period of the Bourbon restoration (1814-1830) and of the July Monarchy, which followed.

Apart from the unifying element provided by a common historical background, Balzac also devised an original method of linking the novels by causing characters that he had introduced into one novel to reappear in subsequent stories. This practice, extended more and more as *The Human Comedy* took shape, enhanced the realistic illusion and also permitted Balzac to develop the psychology of individual characters more fully than would have been feasible within the limits of a single novel.

Thereafter he returned to literature and in 1829 published the first novel that he signed with his own name. This was *Le Dernier Chouan* (the title was changed in later editions to *Les Chouans*), a historical novel based on the Breton rebellion against the republican government in 1799. Balzac had undertaken careful research on the background, traveling to Britanny in order to ensure that his descriptions of the countryside and its inhabitants would be authentic. Since there was a vogue for historical novels, the book was well received. But real fame came to him 2 years later, when he published *La Peau de chagrin,* a semifantastic story in which the talismanic shagreen skin of the title is discovered to have the magical property of granting whatever wish the owner utters. Every time the skin is used in this way, however, it shrinks, and the young man who has acquired it knows that his own life-span contracts correspondingly. The tale thus becomes an allegory of the conflict between the will to enjoy and the will to survive, two principles which, according to Balzac, are utterly irreconcilable.

Author and Socialite

Throughout the 1830s Balzac engaged in furious activity, working hard and enjoying himself hugely, in reckless disregard of the moral he had enunciated in *La Peau de chagrin,* The constant struggle to earn enough to keep his creditors at bay drove him to impose on himself a timetable of work that eventually ruined even his robust constitution. And as the pressure of his commitments to publishers mounted, he increased his hours from 10 to 14 or even 18 a

Social and Ethical Assumptions

In the important preface to his collected works that Balzac wrote in 1842, he defined his function as that of "secretary of French society." Accordingly, every class of people, from the cultivated aristocrat down to the brutish peasant, has a place in *The Human Comedy*. In the novel *Le Père Goriot,* lodging-house keepers, usurers, duchesses, students, retired clerks, and gangsters rub shoulders in a manner strangely convincing in spite of the inherent improbability of the situations.

Balzac often ascribed the basest motivations to his characters. He once wrote that the lust for gold and the search for pleasure were the sole principles that ruled humanity. Although capable of dramatizing cases of magnificent self-sacrifice or touching expiation (as he does in *Le Lys dans la vallée,* 1836, and *Le Curé de village,* 1838-1839), in the vast majority of instances Balzac presents naked self-seeking served by feverish energy and unflagging willpower. This is where the realism of his work shades off into something else. It was the French poet Baudelaire who first pointed out that Balzac was primarily a visionary, and it was he too who said that Balzac's characters were all replicas of their creator since they were all possessed of "genius." In the sense that single-minded determination to achieve one's aim is part of genius, the remark has considerable validity. The monomaniac-the man obsessed by some transcendent purpose or passion or perhaps by some vice, to the point of sacrificing his own comfort and the welfare of his dependents—is constantly encountered in Balzac's more impressive novels, among them *Eugénie Grandet* (1833), *Le Père Goriot* (1834), *La Recherche de l'absolu* (1834), and *La Cousine Bette* (1846).

It is true that Balzac was writing in an age characterized more by individual endeavor than by collective effort. This was a period when the struggle for existence among the poor or for social advancement among the less fortunate was at its fiercest. The rigidly hierarchical framework of society which had existed before the French Revolution had disappeared, and no solidly stratified social organization had yet replaced it. Balzac himself deplored the anarchic individualism that he observed around him, and in the comments strewn through his novels he argues desperately in favor of restoring the authority of central government under an absolute monarch as a means of extinguishing the jungle warfare of conflicting interests. Human nature, in his view, was fundamentally depraved; any machinery, legal, political, or religious, whereby the inherent wickedness of men could be held in check ought to be repaired and strengthened. But this teaching went against the tendencies of the age; toward the end of his career, in the mid-1840s, Balzac could see France heading for a new popular revolution which would finally sweep away the domination of "throne and altar." This gloomy prospect partly accounts for the deeper pessimism of his last works.

Marriage and Death

During his last years Balzac suffered increasingly from poor health, and his morale had been weakened by the constant frustrations and disappointments he endured in the one great love affair of his life. In 1832 he had received his first letter from Madame Hanska, the wife of a Polish nobleman who owned extensive estates in the Russian Empire. Balzac was flattered and excited, and he met her in Switzerland the following year. Thereafter they kept up an ardent correspondence, interrupted by occasional vacations spent together in different parts of Europe. In 1841 her husband died, but Madame Hanska obstinately refused to marry Balzac despite his earnest pleas. Only when he fell gravely ill, during a last visit to her mansion in the Ukraine, did she consent. The wedding took place at her home on March 14,

1850. The long journey back to France took a serious toll on Balzac's health, and he died in Paris on Aug. 18, 1850, only a few weeks after his return.

Further Reading

Herbert J. Hunt, *Honoré de Balzac* (1957) is a concise biography. More detailed is André Maurois, *Prometheus: The Life of Balzac* (1965; trans. 1965). Stefan Zweig, *Balzac* (1946; trans. 1947), still repays study. The fullest account of Balzac's literary output is Herbert J. Hunt, *Balzac's Comédie Humaine* (1959), in which the novels and other writings are studied in chronological order. In F.W.J. Hemmings, *Balzac: An Interpretation of "La Comédie Humaine"* (1967), an attempt has been made to trace certain thematic patterns in the work as a whole. A thorough study of *The Comédie humaine* is Félicien Marceau, *Balzac and His World* (1955; trans. 1967). Other useful general studies are Samuel Rogers, *Balzac and the Novel* (1953), and E.J. Oliver, *Honoré de Balzac* (1964). □

Ba Maw

Ba Maw (1893-1977) was the first premier of independent Burma (now Myanmar) and the leader of the wartime government that ruled in cooperation with the occupying Japanese from 1942 to 1945.

B a Maw was born in Maubin on February 8, 1893. His father was U Kye, who had been an official of the courts of former Burmese kings Mindon and Thibaw and who had actively opposed the establishment of British colonial rule. By far the most learned of the first generation of active nationalist agitators against the British imperial presence, Ba Maw was educated at Rangoon College and at Calcutta University in India. Like many other Burmese nationalists, Ba Maw turned first to teaching as a profession, becoming the first Burmese to be appointed to the faculty of British-run Rangoon College in 1917. He later studied at Cambridge University in England, qualified as a barrister-at-law at Gray's Inn, London, in 1924, and received a doctorate in philosophy from Bordeaux University in France. Upon his return to Burma in 1924, he entered the practice of law.

Nationalist Political Activities of the 1930s

Opposed to the detachment of Burma from British India because it might delay Burmese independence from Britain, Ba Maw was a leader of the faction of the divided General Council of Burmese Associations (GCBA, the country's first avowedly nationalist political organization) that became the Anti-Separation League. This wing of the GCBA won a majority in the 1932 elections. Two years later, Ba Maw became minister of education and public health in the government.

Ba Maw's advance in political prominence was partly the result of his defense of the nationalist Saya San, whose minor rebellion from 1930 to 1932 captured the popular imagination, though it did not inspire widespread participation. Ba Maw—highly Europeanized, Christian (in a Buddhist country), and partly Mon (a minority among the racially proud Burman majority)—courageously, if opportunistically, defended Saya San against a charge of seditious treason. Saya San was convicted and, after various appeals by Ba Maw, executed in 1937.

Ba Maw exploited the Saya San revolt and trial to augment his image as a nationalist and patriot. His defense of the rebel, whose unarmed followers had used "magic" and amulets to protect themselves against British bullets, was probably the main factor in his rise to the premiership.

In 1936, building on the popularity derived from his defense of Saya San, Ba Maw founded the Sinyetha Wunthanu (Poor Man's) party, the first Burmese political organization to appeal directly to the economic interests of the masses. Only 16 Sinyetha candidates were elected to the 132-seat legislature, but in 1937 Ba Maw nonetheless managed to emerge as the first Burmese premier after independence from India. He seemed to suffer a steady decline in popularity during his two-year premiership, which was far less radical in practice than it had been in electoral promises.

Allying himself with such younger and more radical Thakin (Our Masters) nationalists as Aung San and U Nu, Ba Maw was the chief founder in 1939 of the Freedom Bloc, which sought to establish contacts with the expanding Japanese to assist in ousting the colonial British from Burma. Jailed by the British in August 1940, he escaped from Mogok jail in April 1942, when the Japanese advanced into the country.

Heads Provisional Government under Japanese Occupation

The same year Ba Maw was appointed head of the Provisional Administrative Committee by the Japanese, and in 1943 he assumed leadership of the Independence Preparatory Commission. When "independence" was granted by Japan on August 1, 1943, Ba Maw was named *adipati* (pseudo-royalist head of state) as well as premier.

Publicly Ba Maw seemed to revel in his new high status despite the restrictions inherent in the Japanese presence. Vanity had been one of his hallmarks, and he clearly enjoyed the privileges of his role as a pseudo-monarch. However, he was too wise and patriotic to be taken in by the Japanese or to feel no compassion for the material and psychological hardships of his countrymen, who had swapped a benevolent colonial ruler for a comparatively harsh one. Accordingly, he played a major role in mitigating the effects of the Japanese presence on his countrymen from 1942 to 1945.

Jailed by the Allies in Sugamo Prison, Japan, after the war, Ba Maw returned to Burma in 1946 but never again played a major political role. As a highly articulate critic, however, he persisted in challenging his country's younger rulers. He was jailed by military dictator Gen. Ne Win in 1966 for contact with proclaimed rebels against the regime. Following his release with other political detainees in 1968,

Ba Maw returned to the private practice of law. He died on May 28, 1977.

Further Reading

Ba Maw's own perceptive account of the important years 1939-1946 can be read in his *Breakthrough in Burma: Memoirs of a Revolution* (1968). The same period is also treated by U Nu in *Burma under the Japanese: Pictures and Portraits* (1945; trans. 1954). A broader perspective is provided in, John F. Cady, *A History of Modern Burma* (1958). Also recommended is Frank N. Trager, *Burma: From Kingdom to Republic: A Historical and Political Analysis* (1966). A brief obituary appears in the *New York Times* (May 31, 1977). □

Amadou Bamba

The Senegalese religious leader Amadou Bamba (1850-1927) was the founder of the Mourides, the strongest and most influential African Islamic brotherhood in black Africa.

Amadou Bamba was born in M'Backe, Senegal, into a Wolof family of Toucouleur origins, the son of a minor Islamic holy man and teacher. A charismatic personality, Bamba aided in the mass conversion of the Wolof peoples from tribal paganism to Islam at the end of the 19th century, becoming the founder and marabout of the Mouride sect of Islam. Many Senegalese looked to the Mouride brotherhood for leadership and organization in the fight against the colonial invaders. Fearing a holy war against the Europeans under Bamba's inspired leadership, the French exiled him to Gabon from 1895 until November 1902, and again to Mauritania from June 1903 to 1907.

After 1911, however, fear of a popular uprising in Senegal declined, and the French began to regard Bamba in a new light. Upon his urging, thousands of his followers volunteered for the French army and worked to increase agricultural production during World War I. In 1919 Bamba was named a chevalier in the Legion of Honor. Until he died in 1927, however, he was never again allowed to return permanently to the holy village where he had become convinced of his calling, and he remained always under a cloud of suspicion. In Senegal, nationalists reassessed his historical role and now praise Bamba for his early resistance to the colonial regime.

Bamba was a legend in his own time because of his reputed mystical powers and saintly behavior. Two aspects of his credo powerfully affected the strength and devotion of his following. One was the belief that every Mouride who had worked for his marabout and had given him his tithe would go to heaven because of the marabout's personal intervention; there would be no need for the person to do anything more for his own salvation, even if he had sinned. The other aspect was the doctrine that work was like prayer and sanctified the individual. This belief resulted in a Calvinistic zeal for hard labor that made the Mouride brotherhood into a tremendous ally of the most powerful economic forces in West Africa.

Further Reading

A work in French, E. Marty, *Études sur l'Islam en Senegal* (1917), provides the earliest and most comprehensive account of Bamba and the Mourides. The French administration used the study as the basis of their policy. In English see John Spencer Trimingham, *Islam in West Africa* (1959); Martin A. Klein, *Islam and Imperialism in Senegal: Sine-Saloum, 1847-1914* (1968); and Donald B. Cruse O'Brien, *The Mourides of Senegal* (1971). □

Toni Cade Bambara

Toni Cade Bambara (1939-1995), who initially gained recognition as a short story writer, has branched out into other genres and media in the course of her career, yet she continues to focus on issues of racial awareness and feminism in her work.

Born Toni Cade on March 25, 1939, in New York City, she later acquired the name "Bambara" after discovering it as part of a signature on a sketchbook in her great-grandmother's trunk. Bambara was generally silent about her childhood, but she revealed a few details from her youth. In an interview with Beverly Guy-Sheftall in *Sturdy Black Bridges: Visions of Black Women in Literature,* Bambara discussed some women who influenced her work: "For example, in every neighborhood I lived in there were always two types of women that somehow pulled me and sort of got their wagons in a circle around me. I call them Miss Naomi and Miss Gladys, although I'm sure they came under various names. The Miss Naomi types . . . would give me advice like, 'When you meet a man, have a birthday, demand a present that's hockable, and be careful.' . . . The Miss Gladyses were usually the type that hung out the window in Apartment 1-A leaning on the pillow giving single-action advice on numbers or giving you advice about how to get your homework done or telling you to stay away from those cruising cars that moved through the neighborhood patrolling little girls." After attending Queens College in New York City and several European institutions, Bambara worked as a free-lance writer and lecturer, social investigator for the New York State Department of Welfare, and director of recreation in the psychiatry department at Metropolitan Hospital in New York City. As she told Guy-Sheftall, writing at that time seemed to her "rather frivolous . . . something you did because you didn't feel like doing any work. But . . . I've come to appreciate that it is a perfectly legitimate way to participate in a struggle."

Bambara's interest in black liberation and women's movements led her to edit and publish an anthology entitled *The Black Woman* in 1970. The work is a collection of poetry, short stories, and essays by such celebrated writers as Nikki Giovanni, Audre Lorde, Alice Walker, and Paule Marshall. *The Black Woman* also contains short stories by Bambara, who was at that time still writing under the name of Cade. According to Deck, Bambara saw the work as "a response to all the male 'experts' both black and white who had been publishing articles and conducting sociological studies on black women." Another anthology, *Tales and Stories for Black Folks,* followed in 1971. Bambara explained in the introduction to this short story collection that the work's aim is to instruct young blacks about "Our Great Kitchen Tradition," Bambara's term for the black tradition of storytelling. In the first part of *Tales and Stories,* Bambara included works by writers like Langston Hughes, Alice Walker, and Ernest Gaines—stories she wished she had read while growing up. The second part of the collection contains stories by students in a first year composition class Bambara was teaching at Livingston College, Rutgers University. Deck wrote that Bambara's inclusion of professional writers and students in a single work "shows her desire to give young writers a chance to make their talents known to a large audience." Additionally, such a mixture "would have helped her inspire young adults to read, to think critically, and to write."

Most of Bambara's early writings—short stories written between 1959 and 1970 under the name Toni Cade—were collected in her next work, *Gorilla, My Love* (1972). Bambara told Claudia Tate in an interview published in *Black Women Writers at Work* that when her agent suggested she assemble some old stories for a book, she thought, "Aha, I'll get the old kid stuff out and see if I can't clear some space to get into something else." Nevertheless, *Gorilla, My Love* remains her most widely read collection.

Deck noted that after the publication of her first collection, "major events took place in Toni Cade Bambara's life which were to have an effect on her writing." Bambara traveled to Cuba in 1973 and Vietnam in 1975, meeting with both the Federation of Cuban Women and the Women's Union in Vietnam. She was impressed with both groups, particularly with the ability of the Cuban women to surpass class and color conflicts and with the Vietnamese women's resistance to their traditional place in society. Furthermore, upon returning to the United States, Bambara moved to the South, where she became a founding member of the Southern Collective of African-American Writers. Her travels and her involvement with community groups like the collective influenced the themes and settings of *The Sea Birds Are Still Alive* (1977), her second collection of short stories. These stories take place in diverse geographical areas, and they center chiefly around communities instead of individuals. With both collections, critics noted Bambara's skill in the genre, and many praised the musical nature of language and dialogue in her stories, which she herself likens to "riffs" and "be-bop."

Although Bambara admittedly favored the short story genre, her next work, *The Salt Eaters* (1980), is a novel. She explained in *Black Women Writers:* "Of all the writing forms, I've always been partial to the short story. . . . But the major publishing industry, the academic establishment, reviewers, and critics favor the novel . . . Murder for the gene-deep loyalist who readily admits in interviews that the move to the novel was not occasioned by a recognition of having reached the limits of the genre or the practitioner's disillusion with it, but rather Career. Economics. Critical Attention. A major motive behind the production of *Salt*." The novel, which focuses on the recovery of community organizer Velma Henry from an attempted suicide, consists of a "fugue-like interweaving of voices," Bambara's speciality. *The Salt Eaters* succeeded in gaining more critical attention for Bambara, but many reviewers found the work to be confusing, particularly because of breaks in the story line and the use of various alternating narrators. Others appreciated her "complex vision," however, and further praised her ability to write dialogue.

Since the publication of *The Salt Eaters* in 1980, Bambara devoted herself to another medium, film. She told Tate in *Black Women Writers at Work:* "Quite frankly, I've always considered myself a film person. . . . There's not too much more I want to experiment with in terms of writing. It gives me pleasure, insight, keeps me centered, sane. But, oh, to get my hands on some movie equipment." Bambara nevertheless remained committed to working within black communities, continuing to address issues of black awareness and feminism in her art.

On December 9, 1995, Bambara died of colon cancer in Philadelphia.

Further Reading

Beizer, Janet L., *Black Women Writers (1950-1980): A Critical Evaluation,* edited by Mari Evans, Anchor Books, 1979.
Contemporary Literary Criticism, Volume 19, Gale, 1984.
Dictionary of Literary Biography, Volume 38: Afro-American Writers after 1955: Dramatists and Prose Writers, Gale, 1985.
Parker, Bell and Beverly Guy-Sheftall, *Sturdy Black Bridges: Visions of Black Women in Literature,* Doubleday, 1979.
Pearlman, Mickey, editor, *American Women Writing Fiction: Memory, Identity, Family, Space,* Universty Press of Kentucky, 1989.
Prenshaw, Peggy Whitman, editor, *Women Writers of the Contemporary South,* University Press of Mississippi, 1984.
Tate, Claudia, editor, *Black Women Writers at Work,* Continuum, 1983. □

George Bancroft

George Bancroft (1800-1891) was an eminent American historian and a diplomat and politician. He also founded the U.S. Naval Academy.

George Bancroft was born in Worcester, Mass., on Oct. 3, 1800. His father was a Unitarian minister. At 17 George went from Harvard to the University of Göttingen, Germany, where he received his doctorate in 1820. Returning in 1822 to America, he briefly joined the Harvard faculty, teaching Greek.

Unable to reform Harvard's teaching methods, Bancroft left to found (with J. G. Cogswell) a progressive school at Northampton, Mass. For 11 years the Round Hill School was a model of advanced pedagogy, attracting wide attention. For much of his life Bancroft was important in acquainting Americans with German culture.

Bancroft had left the school in 1831, having been drawn to politics and history. To the dismay of fellow intellectuals he ardently supported Andrew Jackson and Martin Van Buren. In 1837 he was named collector of the Port of Boston. Now high in the councils of the Democratic party, he was appointed secretary of the Navy by President James Polk. Bancroft instituted reforms in the service and founded the Naval Academy at Annapolis, Md.

From 1846 to 1849 Bancroft was minister to England, where he gathered additional materials to continue the history he had been working on for many years. The first volume of Bancroft's *History of the United States from the Discovery of the Continent* appeared in 1834. In the next 40 years nine more volumes were published, carrying the narrative to the close of the American Revolution.

In his first volume Bancroft stated his main theme, which, with variations, echoed throughout the history: "The spirit of the colonies demanded freedom from the beginning." Like his fellow romantic historians John Lothrop Motley and William Prescott, Bancroft believed that liberty and progress had found their highest fulfillment in the United States.

Bancroft's writing was at its best in detailing the events during the 2 years leading up to July 4, 1776. In these pages he evoked with great skill the spirit of the Revolution. From 1849 to 1867 Bancroft remained busy at his history. In 1867 President Andrew Johnson, indebted to Bancroft as ghost

writer, named him minister to Berlin, where he remained until 1874, delighting in the company of Bismarck and distinguished German historians.

After Bancroft's diplomatic career ended, he published the two-volume *History of the Formation of the Constitution of the United States of America* (1882). Now past 80 he continued to write in the spirit of his youth. It was his "loud and uncritical Americanism" which repelled some of his contemporaries as well as later critics. His scholarship was not impeccable, his prose too lush. Yet he performed a remarkable pioneer service in organizing the materials of American history, giving it coherence and a foundation on which later scholars built. One of them said that they could see farther because they stood on his shoulders.

Fame and wealth from his histories came to the vigorous little man who stood tall in his country's esteem. His many admirers joined in mourning his death, in Washington, D.C., on Jan. 17, 1891.

Further Reading

The best biography of Bancroft is Russel B. Nye, *George Bancroft: Brahmin Rebel* (1944). Chapters on Bancroft appear in Michael Kraus, *The Writing of American History* (1953), and in William T. Hutchinson, ed., *The Marcus W. Jernegan Essays in American Historiography*, selection by Watt Stewart (1958). John S. Bassett, *The Middle Group of American Historians* (1917), and John F. Jameson, *The History of Historical Writing in America* (1891), are critical of Bancroft's work. An excellent analysis of Bancroft's writing is in David Levin,

History as Romantic Art: Bancroft, Prescott, Motley and Parkman (1959).

Additional Sources

Handlin, Lilian, *George Bancroft, the intellectual as Democrat,* New York: Harper & Row, 1984. □

Hubert Howe Bancroft

The historian Hubert Howe Bancroft (1832-1918) was the first major collector of American documentary materials and the first historian of the Far West.

Hubert Howe Bancroft was born in Granville, Ohio, on May 5, 1832. He attended a local academy, was tutored by his mother, and planned to go to college. When he realized that the costs were too high for his parents, he left home at the age of 16 to work in his brother-in-law's bookstore in Buffalo, N.Y.

In 1852 Bancroft accompanied a consignment of his brother-in-law's books to California, where his father and brother had already gone. While there, Bancroft learned of his brother-in-law's death. After disposing of the books, he worked at odd jobs and then established a bookstore in Crescent City, Calif.

At the request of his sister, Bancroft returned to New York State. Unhappy there, he soon returned to California with another stock of books. He set up as a printer, publisher, and bookseller in San Francisco in 1858 and became an immediate business success.

In 1859 Bancroft married Emily Ketchum and began collecting books, originally to publish a *Hand-Book Almanac for 1860* on the Pacific Coast. The collecting fever had infected him. Spending the summer of 1862 and the year of 1866 in Europe, Bancroft looked for books about the Pacific Coast as well as for representatives to send books to him. By 1867 Bancroft was rich enough to consider retiring. Instead, he cast about for a use for his books and in 1869, the year of his wife's death, decided to write a history of the entire western half of the North American continent.

Bancroft began the writing of the history in 1871, utilizing a staff of assistants ranging in number from 6 to 50 to do research, condensing, and writing for him. The *History of the Pacific States* began with the 5-volume *Native Races of the Pacific States* (1874-1876). These anthropological accounts were criticized by professional scholars, so Bancroft traveled to the East Coast to solicit support but was not very successful.

Undaunted, Bancroft pushed ahead with his project, which was to include political and cultural, as well as natural, history. He put together another 28 volumes, including a 6-volume *History of Mexico* and a 7-volume *History of California*. A comprehensive edition, *The Works of Hubert Howe Bancroft* (1882-1890), which included books on the Indians, was sold throughout the West by

skillful promotion—some 6,000 sets worth over a million dollars.

Bancroft failed to achieve the literary fame he desired. Critics attacked him for his use of assistants, emphasis on local history, and pro-British and pro-vigilante positions. His reputation became better later, largely because of a change of emphasis in historical research in the United States and because of his historical collection. Bancroft tried for 20 years to sell his library to the University of California; not until 1905 were his efforts successful. The library was named after him, as was a professorship of history.

Bancroft continued to write on the history of the West as well as on other topics of the day. His election as president of the Pacific Coast branch of the American Historical Association in 1911 signaled increased respect for his work. He died in California, his adopted state, on March 2, 1918.

Further Reading

Bancroft's *Retrospection, Political and Personal* (1912; 3d ed. 1915) contains his view of his life, while his *Literary Industries* (1890) describes his "factory" methods. John Walton Caughey, *Hubert Howe Bancroft: Historian of the West* (1946), portrays Bancroft as an entrepreneur-historian and discusses his weaknesses. Michael Kraus, *The Writing of American History* (1953), and David D. Van Tassel, *Recording America's Past: An Interpretation of the Development of Historical Studies in America, 1607-1884* (1960), give short evaluations of Bancroft that are kinder to him than his contemporaries were. □

Hastings Kamuzu Banda

Hastings Kamuzu Banda (born 1905) was a leader in Malawi's struggle for independence, and he became the country's first president. An acknowledged nationalist, he nevertheless frankly advocated trade and diplomatic relations with white-dominated African countries.

Hastings Banda was born to poor parents of the Chewa tribe in the Kasungu District of Nyasaland, a British protectorate, which achieved independence as Malawi in 1964. Banda's early education at the Church of Scotland's Livingstonia Mission school in Kasungu fired his ambition for learning. About age 13 he set out to walk to South Africa to continue his education. He stopped to work in an African hospital near Salisbury, Southern Rhodesia (now Zimbabwe). An uncle helped him to reach Johannesburg, where he worked as a clerk in a gold mine.

Studies and Medical Career

Banda traveled to the United States in 1923 and earned a high school diploma from Wilberforce Academy in 1928. He worked as a Bantu language adviser at the University of Chicago until he earned a doctorate in 1931. He then entered Meharry Medical College in Nashville, Tennessee, and in 1937 received a doctorate of medicine. To qualify for practice in Great Britain, he went to Scotland and earned medical diplomas at the universities of Glasgow and Edinburgh in 1941. He also became an elder in the Church of Scotland. Banda first practiced at the Tyneside Mission for Colored Seamen (1944) and then in a London suburb from 1945 to 1953. His home was a gathering place for Nyasas and for early African nationalist leaders. In 1951 he published a paper criticizing racial policies in Southern Rhodesia, which was then pressing for a federation of Rhodesia and Nyasaland. When the federation was imposed in August 1953, Banda went to Ghana as a physician to the poor Zongo people and to campaign for the independence of his homeland.

Political Career

Banda agreed in 1958 to return home to lead Nyasaland out of the federation. However, he first headed a delegation to London to petition for a new constitution. He returned to Nyasaland on July 6, 1958. On August 1, 1958, he was elected president of the Congress party. Mounting anti-federation riots led to a state of emergency on March 3, 1959, and Banda was imprisoned in Southern Rhodesia for 13 months. Upon his release he assumed leadership of the Malawi Congress Party. In June 1960 he accepted a new constitution from Britain which gave Africans a majority in the Legislative Council. On February 1, 1963, he became his country's first prime minister. Independence came on July 6, 1964, and on July 6, 1966—when Malawi became a

republic within the Commonwealth—Banda became Malawi's first president.

After independence and the creation of a one-party state, Banda had to reconcile the left-wing younger leadership with his own more conservative policies. His firm control—some called him dictatorial—was challenged by dissident ministers in an unsuccessful coup d'etat that lasted from 1964 to 1965. However, Banda's wide-based support among the people of Malawi was shown in 1967, when villagers directed police to conspirators plotting to kill him. Opposition was based partly on Banda's retention of British civil servants as department heads and partly on his frank recognition of landlocked Malawi's economic dependence on nearby white-ruled South African countries. Banda deplored segregation, but he believed the country could secure badly needed development loans from Rhodesia and South Africa. He maintained reasonable rapport with black African states while initiating trade, loan, and diplomatic relations with white African states.

Elected president for life in 1971, Banda maintained his leadership until economic issues associated with the loss of Western aid in 1992 and a serious illness in 1993 led to his defeat in Malawi's first multiparty elections, held in May 1994. He was succeeded in office by Bakili Muluzi of the United Democratic Front (UDF).

Legal Difficulties in the Mid-1990s

In 1995 Banda and two others were charged with conspiracy to commit murder in connection with the 1983 deaths of four political adversaries. Although the three were later acquitted, the scandal still raged in 1997 as the prosecution appealed a ruling made by the presiding judge in the case that blocked key evidence from the trial. In addition, the UDF government began a thorough inquiry into Banda's financial affairs, especially concerning the personal wealth he amassed from business ventures believed to have been bankrolled by public funds.

In 1995 Banda was dispossessed of the Press Trust, a successful conglomerate, and charged with fraud in the misappropriation of funds intended for the construction of a school in his home district. Banda was later pardoned in the fraud case due to his extreme age and ill health. In May 1997 the UDF Minister of Lands and Valuation directed the reallocation of 2,000 acres that Banda had illegally seized in 1978 and on which he had established a cattle ranch. Despite Banda's myriad legal woes, advanced age, and failing health, he remained a dominant force within the Malawi Congress Party, which in July 1997 was poised to merge with another opposition party, the Alliance for Democracy.

Further Reading

A full-length examination of Banda's career may be found in John Lloyd Lwanda, *Kamuzu Banda of Malawi: A Study in Promise, Power, and Paralysis* (1993). An earlier consideration is Philip Short, *Banda* (1974). His regime is discussed in relation to recent Malawi history in T. David Williams, *Malawi: The Politics of Despair* (1978). □

Sirimavo Bandaranaike

Sirimavo Bandaranaike (born 1916) became the first woman prime minister in the world when she was chosen to head the Sri Lankan Freedom Party government in 1960, following the assassination of her husband. She pursued policies of nonalignment abroad and democratic socialism at home.

Sirimavo (also Sirima) Ratwatte Dias Bandaranaike was born on April 17, 1916, to an aristocratic Kandyan family and was educated in a Roman Catholic convent in Colombo. Married to Solomon West Ridgeway Dias (SWRD) Bandaranaike in 1940 when he was a minister in the government of Ceylon, then a British crown colony, Bandaranaike's life was politically uneventful. She had the preoccupations of a housewife married to an eminent national leader who became the prime minister of Ceylon in 1956, eight years after its independence. In 1959, however, SWRD Bandaranaike was assassinated by a Buddhist monk, and such was SWRD's charisma that his party, the Sri Lankan Freedom Party (SLFP), chose Sirimavo Bandaranaike to be its leader.

First Woman Prime Minister

SWRD's assassination resulted in a brief period of political instability. The minority government of the United National Party (UNP) was unable to sustain itself in power after the elections in March 1960. Consequently, the country went to the polls again in July 1960. In this election Bandaranaike succeeded in mobilizing a parliamentary majority for her party and became the first woman prime minister in the world. When Bandaranaike became the prime minister she was not a member of the House of Representatives but of the Senate—the upper house—that her party was to abolish in 1971.

In office, Bandaranaike sought to carry forward her husband's policies, which had been tempered with socialist principles of a government-directed and controlled economy in contrast to the free economy advocated by the main opposition UNP party.

In foreign affairs, Bandaranaike staunchly believed in pursuing a policy of nonalignment (with neither East nor West), as her husband had done. She actively participated in the nonaligned conferences and also mediated the India-China border conflict during 1962.

Bandaranaik is credited with successfully negotiating with Indian Prime Minister Lal Bahadur Shastri an agreement pertaining to the political status of the plantation workers of Indian origin in Ceylon, most of whom had been disenfranchised soon after Ceylon became independent. The agreement, known as the Sirimavo-Shastri Pact, was signed in October 1964 at New Delhi. It specified the

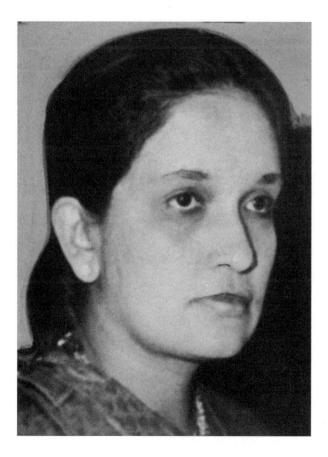

modalities of granting Ceylonese or Indian citizenship to the workers of Indian origin on a proportionate basis. In the domestic sphere, during her premiership, the American and British oil companies operating in Ceylon were nationalized and a state controlled commercial banking system was established.

Fall of Bandaranaike's Government

As the Parliament was nearing the end of its five year term, differences began to surface in the SLFP. A group of 14 members of Parliament revolted against Bandaranaike and crossed over to the opposition in protest against the enactment of the Press Bill, which enabled the government to take over the well-established independent media. Consequently, Bandaranaike's government fell.

Bandaranaike Returns As Prime Minister

In the elections that ensued in 1965, the SLFP was defeated by the UNP, although Bandaranaike herself retained her seat and became the leader of the opposition. She utilized the opportunity to consolidate the "opposition party," concluding an agreement with the left parties that they would not contest each other in the event of a general election. This agreement paid off in the 1970 elections, and Bandaranaike was back as the prime minister and the SLFP and its allies secured a massive majority.

Soon, however, Bandaranaike found herself confronted with an insurrectionary situation of considerable magnitude. With unemployment among the Sinhalese educated youth swelling, a group of radicals calling itself the Jatika Vimukti Perumana (JVP)—National Liberation Front— launched an insurrection. With military assistance from the United States, the United Kingdom, the Soviet Union, Yugoslavia, India, and Pakistan, Bandaranaike finally overcame the insurrection and restored normalcy in the island.

Thereafter, Bandaranaike set about implementing her electoral promises, a major one of which was that the SLFP would convene a constituent assembly and give the country a republican constitution. This was duly done in 1972, and the island reacquired its ancient name, Sri Lanka.

Apart from this, major socialist measures taken by the government included the abolition of agency houses as well as the nationalization of tea estates and the imposition of land ownership ceilings. Credit also goes to her for having successfully negotiated an agreement with India over the disputed status of an uninhabited island, Kachchathivu, in the Palk Straits. Finally, Sri Lanka hosted the fifth summit of the nonaligned movement in Colombo and Bandaranaike became its chairperson in 1976.

Disastrous Defeat

Despite implementing its electoral pledge, the SLFP suffered a disastrous defeat in the parliamentary elections of 1977, and the party won just eight seats while the UNP won 140 of the 168 seats.

Yet Bandaranaike's worst days in her political life were to follow. The UNP government set up a presidential commission of inquiry to investigate charges that Bandaranaike misused her office as prime minister for personal and family benefit. She refused to participate in the proceedings of the commission on the ground that she considered it to be a political vendetta against her. The commission sustained the charges against her and deprived her of civic rights for a period of seven years. Consequently, in October 1980 she was expelled from the Parliament. Intraparty factionalism also weakened her support basis. Her daughter Chandrika, along with her actor husband, formed one of the several splinter parties formed in this period. Stripped of her political rights, Bandaranaike took a place offstage. Early in 1986, however, she received a pardon from her successor, President Junius Jayewardene.

An Unprecedented Comeback

Bandaranaike turned heads by making an unprecedented comeback after 17 years out of office. She and her Sri Lanka Freedom Party, along with the People's Alliance coalition, emerged victorious in a March 24, 1994 provincial council election in the southern province of the country. Later that same year, Bandaranaike again became Prime Minister. Her daughter, Chandrika Kumaratunge, also briefly Prime Minister in 1994, became the President.

Further Reading

Two biographical studies are available. K. P. Mukerji's *Madame Prime Minister Sirimavo Bandaranaike* (Colombo, 1960) provides a survey of her life and activities before Mrs. Bandaranaike became the prime minister. The other, written by a journalist, Maureen Seneviratne, is entitled *Sirimavo Bandaranaike: The World's First Woman Prime Minister* (Colombo, 1975). For a brief biographical sketch, readers are advised to look up Ceylon Daily News, *Parliament of Sri Lanka, 1977* (Colombo, 1980). For more current information, see: *Sri Lanka: Southern Surprise* in *Far Eastern Economic Review 1994,* April 7, p.25; and on the World Wide Web on the Women Political Leaders page at http://www.info.london.on.ca/~barnes/women/priminist.htm. □

Surendranath Banerjee

Surendranath Banerjee (1848-1925) was a major figure in early Indian nationalism. A believer in moderate means, he was deeply committed to achieving constitutional objectives by constitutional methods.

Surendranath Banerjee was born in Calcutta on Nov. 10, 1848, into a Brahmin family. His father was a distinguished physician. Banerjee received his early education at Doveton College in Calcutta. Upon taking a degree in English literature from Calcutta University, he went to London and in 1869 became the second Indian to succeed in the Indian civil service competitive examination, after an official effort to exclude him had failed.

Banerjee was appointed to a post in Sylhet in his homeland; however, in 1874 he was dismissed for a minor and apparently inadvertent procedural error. His efforts at reinstatement failed, and as a dismissed civil servant he was also refused admission to the bar. Banerjee felt he had been discriminated against because he was Indian. He embarked on a political career to organize Indian public opinion, to redress wrongs and protect rights, and to give Indians a serious role in the administration of their country and a voice in the counsels of their government.

On returning to Calcutta in 1875, he took a chair in English literature at the Metropolitan Institution (now Vidyasagar College) and subsequently founded and taught at the Ripon College (now Surendranath College). Banerjee was active in teaching for 37 years and considered it his chief vocation, though inseparable from his political work. In 1878 he became proprietor of the *Bengalee,* an English-language newspaper, through which he espoused liberal causes for nearly half a century. Banerjee was instrumental in founding the Indian Association in 1876, and he played a prominent role in the Indian National Congress from the time of its founding in 1885. He was president of the Congress in 1895 and 1902.

Banerjee was a believer in moderate means of political agitation, meetings, petitions, and legislative action. His grasp of the English language and his skills as an orator and debater made him an outstanding public speaker and a master parliamentarian. He reached the peak of his political career in opposing the partition of Bengal in 1905, an official action which was modified in 1911. During these years he was often called "the uncrowned king of Bengal."

But nationalist politics in India meant opposition, and increasingly there were others whose opposition was more vigorous and who came to center stage. Banerjee could accept neither the extremist view of political action nor the noncooperation of Gandhi, then emerging as a major factor in the nationalist movement. Banerjee saw the Montagu-Chelmsford reforms of 1919 as substantially fulfilling Congress's demands, a position which further isolated him. He was elected to the reformed Legislative Council of Bengal in 1921, knighted in the same year, and held office as minister for local self-government from 1921 to 1924. He was defeated at the polls in 1923. He died at Barrackpore on Aug. 6, 1925.

Further Reading

The basic source on Banerjee is his autobiography, *A Nation in Making: Being the Reminiscences of Fifty Years of Public Life* (1925), a classic account of the early nationalist movement. Recent studies of the period with interesting assessments of Banerjee's role are Daniel Argov, *Moderates and Extremists in the Indian National Movement, 1883-1920: With Special Reference to Surendranath Banerjea and Lajpat Raj* (1967), and J.H. Broomfield, *Elite Conflict in a Plural Society: Twentieth-Century Bengal* (1968). □

Dennis J. Banks

As one of the founders of the American Indian Movement (AIM), Dennis Banks (born 1932) has spent much of his life protecting the traditional ways of

Indian people and engaging in legal cases protecting treaty rights of Native Americans. He travels the globe lecturing, teaching Native American customs, and sharing his experiences.

Dennis Banks, Native American leader, teacher, lecturer, activist, and author, was born in 1932 on the Leech Lake Indian Reservation in northern Minnesota. In 1968, he helped found the American Indian Movement (AIM), which was established to protect the traditional ways of Indian people and to engage in legal cases protecting treaty rights of Native Americans, such as treaty and aboriginal rights to hunting and fishing, trapping, and gathering wild rice.

AIM has been quite successful in bringing Native American issues to the public. Among other activities, AIM members participated in the occupation of Alcatraz Island, where demands were made that all federal surplus property be returned to Indian control. In 1972, AIM organized and led the Trail of Broken Treaties Caravan across the United States to Washington, D.C., calling attention to the plight of Native Americans. The refusal of congressional leaders to meet with the Trail of Broken Treaties delegation led to the 1972 takeover of the Bureau of Indian Affairs offices in Washington, D.C.

Under the leadership of Banks, AIM led a protest in Custer, South Dakota, in 1973 against the judicial process that found a non-Indian innocent of murdering an Indian. As

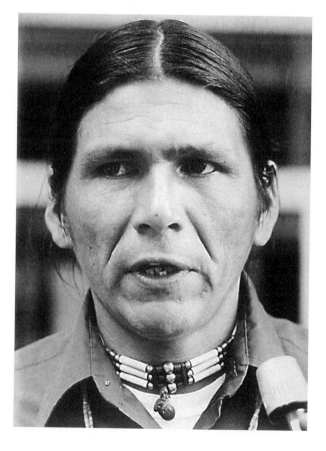

a result of his involvement in the 71-day occupation of Wounded Knee, South Dakota, in 1973, and his activities at Custer, Banks and 300 others were arrested. Banks was acquitted of charges stemming from his participation in the Wounded Knee takeover, but was convicted of riot and assault stemming from the confrontation at Custer. Refusing to serve time in prison, Banks went underground but later received amnesty from Governor Jerry Brown of California.

Between 1976 and 1983, Banks earned an associate of arts degree at the University of California, Davis, and taught at Deganawidah-Quetzecoatl (DQ) University (an all-Indian controlled institution), where he became the first American Indian university chancellor. In the spring of 1979, he taught at Stanford University in Palo Alto, California.

After Governor Brown left office, Banks received sanctuary on the Onondaga Reservation in upstate New York in 1984. While living there, Banks organized the Great Jim Thorpe Run from New York City to Los Angeles, California. A spiritual run, this event ended in Los Angeles, where the Jim Thorpe Memorial Games were held and where the gold medals that Thorpe had previously won in the 1912 Olympic games were restored to the Thorpe family.

In 1985, Banks left the Onondaga Reservation to surrender to law enforcement officials in South Dakota, and served 18 months in prison. When released, he worked as a drug and alcohol counselor on the Pine Ridge Reservation in South Dakota.

In 1987, Banks was active in convincing the states of Kentucky and Indiana to pass laws against desecration of Indian graves and human remains. He organized reburial ceremonies for over 1,200 Indian grave sites that were disturbed by graverobbers in Uniontown, Kentucky.

In 1988, Banks organized and led a spiritual run called the Sacred Run from New York to San Francisco, and then across Japan from Hiroshima to Hakkaido. Also in 1988, his autobiography *Sacred Soul* was published in Japan, and won the 1988 Non-fiction Book of the Year Award.

In addition to leading and organizing sacred runs (1988, 1990, 1991), Banks stays involved in American Indian issues, including AIM, and travels the globe lecturing, teaching Native American traditions, and sharing his experiences. He had key roles in the films *War Party, The Last of the Mohicans* (1992), and *Thunderheart* (1992). Banks is writing a book on Native American philosophy which will be published in Japan. He is a single parent and lives with his children in Kentucky. □

Sir Joseph Banks

Sir Joseph Banks (1743-1820) was an English traveler and animal and plant breeder, but most of all a scientific promoter. His whole adult life was directed toward the advancement of science.

Joseph Banks, born on Feb. 13, 1743, in London, was the son of William Banks of Revesby Abbey, Lincolnshire. At age 9 Joseph entered Harrow; 4 years later he transferred to Eton, where at age 15 he started a lifelong interest in natural history. He entered Christ Church, Oxford, in 1761, but he found botanical studies so stagnant that he had to go to Cambridge for tutoring.

In 1764 Banks began his travels. He collected plants in Newfoundland, toured western England and observed its natural and human history, and then in 1768 embarked on the *Endeavour* on Capt. James Cook's first voyage of exploration in the Pacific. Although most of the results of Banks's expeditions were never published, these findings did seep into the general body of knowledge through his key positions in science and his personal generosity in allowing people to use his materials.

After 1772 Banks became increasingly involved in administering scientific undertakings in England; his personal botanical collections, which were to become the finest private ones in England, consumed some time, however. By the mid-1770s Banks was supervising the collection and propagation of plants from all over the world at the Royal Botanical Gardens at Kew. In 1778 he became president of the Royal Society. For the next 42 years he presided over the scientific academy, developed an acquaintance with most branches of science, and became one of the most distinguished members of the scientific community. He encouraged and administered George III's introduction of Merino sheep into England between 1788 and 1820.

Banks used his considerable power and influence beneficently. During the dark years between 1789 and 1815, when the English government was almost exclusively concerned about surviving the French Revolution and Napoleonic Wars, Banks helped plan and looked after the interests of New South Wales, Australia, in London. On several occasions he also intervened with his own government and Napoleon's to protect scientists and their property against seizure.

Further Reading

Banks's personal papers were widely scattered in the 1880s but are slowly coming into print. See, for example, Warren R. Dawson, ed., *The Banks Letters: A Calendar of the Manuscript Correspondence of Sir Joseph Banks . . . in Great Britain* (1958). A major collection of material on Banks is in the Sutro Library of the California State Library, San Francisco Branch, which issued some material in *New Source Material on Sir Joseph Banks and Iceland* (1941). J.C. Beaglehole, ed., *The Endeavour Journal of Joseph Banks, 1768-1771* (2 vols., 1962), is a model for other editors to follow.

A recent biography of Banks is Hector C. Cameron, *Sir Joseph Banks, The Autocrat of the Philosophers* (1952). Older, but also of value, is Edward Smith, *The Life of Sir Joseph Banks* (1911). □

Benjamin Banneker

Benjamin Banneker (1731-1806), an African American mathematician and amateur astronomer, calculated ephemerides for almanacs for the years 1792 through 1797 that were widely distributed.

On Nov. 9, 1731, Benjamin Banneker was born in Baltimore County, Md. He was the son of an African slave named Robert, who had bought his own freedom, and of Mary Banneky, who was the daughter of an Englishwoman and a free African slave. Benjamin lived on his father's farm and attended a nearby Quaker country school for several seasons. He received no further formal education but enjoyed reading and taught himself literature, history, and mathematics. He worked as a tobacco planter for most of his life.

In 1761, at the age of 30, Banneker constructed a striking wooden clock without having seen a clock before that time, although he had examined a pocket watch. The clock operated successfully until the time of his death.

At the age of 58 Banneker became interested in astronomy through the influence of a neighbor, George Ellicott, who lent him several books on astronomy as well as a telescope and drafting instruments. Without further guidance or assistance, Banneker taught himself the science of astronomy; he made projections for solar and lunar eclipses and computed ephemerides (tables of the locations of celestial bodies) for an almanac.

In February 1791 Maj. Andrew Ellicott was appointed to survey the 10-mile square of the Federal Territory for a

new national capital, and Banneker worked in the field as his scientific assistant for several months. After the base lines and boundaries had been established and Banneker had returned home, he prepared an ephemeris for the following year, which was published in Baltimore in *Benjamin Banneker's Pennsylvania, Delaware, Maryland and Virginia Almanack and Ephemeris, for the Year of Our Lord, 1792; Being Bissextile, or Leap-Year, and the Sixteenth Year of American Independence, which commenced July 4, 1776.*

Banneker forwarded a manuscript copy of his calculations to Thomas Jefferson, then secretary of state, with a letter rebuking Jefferson for his proslavery views and urging the abolishment of slavery of the African American, which he compared to the enslavement of the American colonies by the British crown. Jefferson acknowledged Banneker's letter and forwarded the manuscript to the Marquis de Condorcet, the secretary of the Académie des Sciences in Paris. The exchange of letters between Banneker and Jefferson was published as a separate pamphlet and given wide publicity at the time the first almanac was published. The two letters were reprinted in Banneker's almanac for 1793, which also included "A Plan for an Office of Peace," which was the work of Dr. Benjamin Rush. The abolition societies of Maryland and Pennsylvania were largely instrumental in the publication of Banneker's almanacs, which were widely distributed as an example of the work of an African American that demonstrated the equal mental abilities of the races.

The last known issue of Banneker's almanacs appeared for the year 1797, because of diminishing interest in the antislavery movement; nevertheless, he prepared ephemerides for each year until 1804. He also published a treatise on bees and computed the cycle of the 17-year locust.

Banneker never married. He died on Oct. 9, 1806, and was buried in the family burial ground near his house. Among the memorabilia preserved was his commonplace book and the manuscript journal in which he had entered astronomical calculations and personal notations.

Banneker's memory was kept alive by writers who described his achievements as the first African American scientist. Recent studies have verified Banneker's status as an extremely competent mathematician and amateur astronomer.

Further Reading

Two good biographical studies of Banneker are Martha E. Tyson, *A Sketch of the Life of Benjamin Banneker* (1854), and her *Banneker: The Afric-American Astronomer,* edited by Anne T. Kirk (1884). All the available source material has been brought together in Silvio A. Bedini, *The Life of Benjamin Banneker* (1972). Other treatments include a brief account in John Hope Franklin, *From Slavery to Freedom: A History of American Negroes* (1947; 3d ed. 1967); Shirley Graham's fictionalized biography, *Your Most Humble Servant* (1949); Wilhemena S. Robinson's sketch in *Historical Negro Biographies* (1968); and a chapter in William J. Simmons, *Men of Mark: Eminent, Progressive and Rising* (1968). Banneker's famous letter to Thomas Jefferson is in vol. 1 of Milton Meltzer, ed., *In Their Own Words: A History of the American Negro, 1619-1865* (3 vols., 1964-1967). For general background see E. Franklin Frazier, *The Negro in The United States* (1949; rev. ed. 1963), and Winthrop D. Jordan's monumental *White over Black: American Attitudes toward the Negro, 1550-1812* (1968). □

Edward Mitchell Bannister

African American artist Edward Bannister (1828-1901), though never afforded the opportunity of studying in a formal academic setting, earned praise and many honors for his New England landscape paintings.

E dward Bannister was a prominent New England landscape painter of the nineteenth century and enjoyed a career notable for the lack of prejudice with which it was judged. The African-American artist, though regretting to his death that he was not given a chance to study his art in a formal academic setting, nevertheless succeeded admirably and won great acclaim in his day. Sadly, most of his works did not survive the ages, but an essay on his work in *A History of African-American Artists, from 1790 to the Present,* described him as "a professional artist who lived by his painting. . . . Bannister painted primarily what he knew intimately—the somber blue-gray skies with breezy white cumulus clouds in the late afternoon and the hilly sweep of the Rhode Island landscape and its Narragansett dunes and shores."

Heritage Brought Good Fortune

Bannister was born in November of 1828 in Canada, a British colony that soon made the practice of indentured servitude illegal. His mother was of Scottish descent, his father a native of Barbados. The family lived in St. Andrews, a coastal village in New Brunswick, close to the border of Maine. Economic hardship came when Bannister reached the age of six and his father died; his mother later passed away when Edward was a teenager. After the death of his mother, he became a live-in servant for one of St. Andrews's more affluent citizens and his wife. When he left there, he joined the crew of a boat as a cook.

The sailing life suited Bannister well; he could supplement the adequate education he had received in St. Andrews with visits to museums and libraries in ports of call like Boston and New York. He eventually settled in Boston and took up the barber trade. With the introduction of the daguerreotype in the 1840s, a new market opened up in portraiture, and those with artistic skills were needed to tint these works, which were forerunners of the photograph. Bannister obtained a job doing so, but also continued to work as a barber. Through his profession he met his wife, Christiana Babcock Carteaux, an accomplished hairdresser and proprietor of two tony establishments in Providence and Boston. The couple married in 1857. His rendering of his wife is Bannister's only surviving portrait.

Won Acclaim with Earliest Artistic Endeavors

The new Mrs. Bannister encouraged her husband's artistic pursuits. Within a few years he had given up both barbering and tinting photographs and kept studio hours. He produced a number of paintings that were soon exhibited and sold around Boston. His efforts were also selected for group exhibitions at the Boston Art Club and Museum. Much of Bannister's artistic subject matter from this period was lifted from biblical themes, although he did execute portraits, landscapes, and scenes from history. He also received encouragement from other prominent African-Americans—and African-American artists—of the day. Yet Bannister felt his lack of formal training in the arts hindered him. In 1856 he attended lectures given by D. William Rimmer, a sculptor noted for his accuracy and verve in rendering the human figure. Soon Bannister and other artists began using the principles they had acquired from the lecture in drawing live figure models.

That same year, famed Boston artist William Morris Hunt returned from France. He brought with him a new style of landscape painting known as the Barbizon school, which Bannister soon adopted. "It was a style that permitted Bannister to express both his observation of and reverence for nature," noted *A History of African-American Artists*. This love of nature had been a preoccupation with the artist since his childhood in the fishing village of St. Andrews, and as an adult he came to consider nature itself as a holy entity. Such an attitude mirrored philosophical trends then gaining currency in New England, especially in the writings of Ralph Waldo Emerson and Henry David Thoreau.

Bannister was also fortunate to reside in a city that was extremely tolerant. Boston was home to many African-Americans who were either born free or had escaped from slavery in the South. The city was the center of the abolitionist movement, where many of the most prominent opponents of slavery resided. Bannister's achievements as an artist were honored when he was still in his thirties. He was one of two artists included in the 1863 book *The Black Man: His Antecedents, His Genius, and His Achievements*. The Bannisters also became politically active during this Civil War period, enjoying particular success with a fundraising drive to address pay iniquities between black and white soldiers in the Union army. Christiana Bannister herself took part in the ceremonies sending off Massachusetts's first black regiment.

Achieved American Art's Highest Honor

In 1870 the Bannisters moved to Providence, Rhode Island, in part because of Christiana Bannister's connections there. The move allowed Bannister to more easily partake of the woods and natural landscapes just outside the town. He joined other prominent creative individuals in Providence in a building that housed numerous artists' studios. This period also marked an evolution in his subject matter, away from his usual biblical themes and toward more depictions of landscapes and shorelines. Around 1874 he visited a nearby farm to do some sketching, and from this he executed a painting he called *Under the Oaks*. He entered the work in the 1876 U.S. Centennial Exposition in Philadelphia, the country's first national art exhibition. The art of American masters from both the past and present—such as John Singleton Copley and Frederick E. Church—were part of the famed exhibition as well. Bannister's work took the bronze medal, the highest honor awarded to oil paintings by the Centennial jury.

When Bannister heard a report that his work had taken the prize, he rushed to the Exposition and asked about it at the information desk, where he was treated rudely. "I was not an artist to them, simply an inquisitive colored man," he said in a conversation with a friend of his quoted in *A History of African-American Artists*. "Controlling myself, I said deliberately, 'I am interested in the report that *Under the Oaks* has received a prize. I painted the picture.' An explosion could not have made a more marked impression. Without hesitation he apologized to me, and soon everyone in the room was bowing and scraping to me." After the Exposition, *Under the Oaks* was sold by an art dealer for $1,500, a large sum at the time. Unfortunately, its whereabouts (as well as that of the bronze medal) are unknown.

Integral Member of Local Arts Community

Bannister's success brought great civic pride to Providence and inspired its artistic community. A small group of prominent arts supporters soon founded the Rhode Island Museum of Art and School of Design in the city. A century later, the school remains one of the most prestigious art schools in the nation. In 1880 Bannister and a group of other artists chartered the Providence Art Club. It included both artists and supporters of the arts, and its first exhibition in the spring of that year hosted the work of 64 artists. Bannister's silhouette can still be seen in the building's portrait gallery of its founders. He participated in discussion groups and readings of academic papers at the club's regular meetings and was honored with the title "Artist Laureate." One colleague, according to *A History of African-American Artists,* described him as "a person of gentlemanly bearing who could enter and leave a room with ease and grace. He conversed with more than ordinary intelligence on the principal topics of the day and all deemed it a privilege to be in his company."

Bannister's hobbies included reading music, and sailing. His landscapes reflected the tranquillity of his personality. As his career matured, he accumulated other honors, including several from the Massachusetts Charitable Mechanics Association, which put on an important Boston juried show every year. Meanwhile, his wife established a nursing home for elderly black women that was still in operation in 1993. Yet Bannister's—and the Barbizon—style of painting eventually passed out of favor and what became known as the Hudson School rose to prominence in American art. In addition to suffering financially later in life, Bannister was plagued by memory loss, which restricted his activities. He died of a heart attack at a prayer meeting among his congregation at the Elmwood Avenue Free Baptist Church on January 8, 1901. Later that year, his friends among Providence's artistic community erected a memorial boulder at his grave site containing a bronze palette, a replica of his favorite pipe, and a poetic inscription. *Free Within Ourselves: African-American Artists in the Collection of the National Museum of American Art* praised Bannister as "the only major African American artist of the late nineteenth century who developed his talents without the benefit of European exposure."

Further Reading

Bearden, Romare, and Harry Henderson, *A History of African-American Artists, from 1790 to the Present,* Pantheon, 1993.
Perry, Regenia, *Free Within Ourselves: African-American Artists in the Collection of the National Museum of American Art,* Pomegranate, 1992, p. 23. □

Frederick Grant Banting

The Canadian medical scientist Frederick Grant Banting (1891-1941) was codiscoverer of insulin and a leader in other fields of medical research, including suprarenal cortex, cancer, silicosis, and aviation medicine.

Frederick Banting was born in Alliston, Ontario, on Nov. 14, 1891, to William Thompson Banting, a well-established farmer, and Margaret Grant Banting. He enrolled at the University of Toronto in 1911 in an arts course leading to theology. However, he decided that he wanted to be a doctor, and in 1912 he registered as a medical student.

With World War I under way, Banting left college in 1915 to join the medical corps as a private. Doctors were urgently needed, however, and he was sent back to finish his studies, graduating in 1916. He was commissioned in the Royal Canadian Army Medical Corps and proceeded to England, where he received exceptional surgical experience in several army hospitals.

On returning to Toronto in 1919, Banting was appointed to a residency in surgery at the Hospital for Sick Children, but in 1920 he set up practice for himself. He moved to London, Ontario, and opened an office. One evening, he read an article dealing with the relation of the islands of Langerhans to diabetes. Banting had been interested in diabetes since his school days when a classmate had died in coma. This event impressed him deeply, and now his mind eagerly seized upon possibilities which might be worthy of investigation.

Initiation of the Insulin Work

In 1920 Banting went to Toronto for an interview with the professor of physiology Dr. J.J.R. Macleod, a world authority in the field of carbohydrate metabolism. Banting described his ideas and his desire to search for the internal secretion of the pancreas; he begged for an opportunity to try out his theories in the physiology laboratory, but Macleod refused for he knew that Banting had no training in

research. Banting returned to Toronto several times to try to persuade Macleod. Finally, impressed by his enthusiasm and determination, Macleod promised Banting the use of the laboratory for 8 weeks during the summer. Macleod knew that if Banting was to have any success whatever, someone who knew the latest chemical techniques must work with him. Charles Best, completing the final year in the physiology and biochemistry course, had been working on a problem related to diabetes in Macleod's department. Banting and Best met and talked things over. Although no stipends were available, both were determined and decided that work would begin on May 17, 1921, the day following Best's final examination.

Discovery of Insulin

The first attempts to produce a diabetic condition upon which to study the effect of a pancreatic extract were not successful. Every effort was made to show that a neutral or preferably an acid aqueous or alcoholic extract of degenerated or intact dog pancreas and of fetal or adult beef pancreas always produced a potent antidiabetic material. The observations were repeated time and again until there was convincing evidence that the extract did produce the dramatic effect which was being sought in depancreatized animals.

As the material was extracted from the microscopic islands of Langerhans (cells of the pancreas, different from the majority, which are grouped together as islets of tissue named after Paul Langerhans, the German physician who first observed them), it was called "isletin"; later the named was changed to "insulin," meaning island. Again and again the same successful results were obtained, and when Macleod returned to Toronto, he was finally convinced that the elusive hormone had indeed been captured. On Nov. 14, 1921, Banting and Best presented their findings before the Physiological Journal Club of the University of Toronto, and later that month a paper entitled "The Internal Secretion of the Pancreas" was submitted for publication in the *Journal of Laboratory and Clinical Medicine*.

News of the discovery brought scientists from many parts of the world, as well as diabetics and their families, to Toronto. To accelerate production of the precious extract, Macleod suggested turning over further purification and development to Dr. J.B. Collip, a trained biochemist. Banting was then free to devote himself to clinical aspects of insulin.

Banting subsequently made a vigorous and sustained attack on the physiological problems associated with the suprarenal gland, facilitated studies on silicosis, made significant advances in knowledge of the etiology of cancer, and was mainly responsible for the initiation of aviation medical research in Canada even before the outbreak of war.

Nobel Prize and Other Honors

In 1923 Banting received the Nobel Prize in medicine jointly with Macleod. With characteristic generosity he divided his share with Best; Macleod did the same with Collip. That year the Banting and Best Department of Medical Research was established by the university with a special grant from the Ontario Legislature. In 1934 Banting was

created a knight commander of the British Empire and the following year was elected a fellow of the Royal Society of London. He was killed in a plane crash on the coast of Newfoundland, Feb. 21, 1941, while on a war mission to England.

Further Reading

Two studies of Banting are Seale Harris, *Banting's Miracle: The Story of the Discoverer of Insulin* (1946), and Lloyd Stevenson, *Sir Frederick Banting* (1946; rev. ed. 1947). See also G.A. Wrenshall, G. Hetenyi, and W.R. Feasby, *The Story of Insulin: Forty Years of Success against Diabetes* (1962). □

Hugo Banzer Suárez

Hugo Banzer Suárez (born 1926), Bolivian president from 1971 to 1979, presided over the nation's largest economic boom. He remained politically active as head of the ADN party, and succeeded in winning the presidential election to reclaim power in 1997.

Hugo Banzer Suárez was born July 10, 1926, in Bolivia's (then) sparsely-populated Eastern Lowlands at Santa Cruz. He came from a family of pure Spanish blood in this ranching region noted for its fierce independence and its difference from the highlands, where the majority of Bolivians lived.

He was educated at La Paz and entered the military academy there, graduating as a cavalry lieutenant. After routine postings he was selected to receive training at the U.S. Army School of the Americas in Panama, beginning a long contact with the United States. In 1960 he was sent to train at the Fort Hood, Texas, Armored Cavalry School, and, after several years' command of the key 4th Cavalry Regiment in Bolivia, was sent as Bolivian military attaché to Washington, a post of great prestige. There, he expanded his already wide circle of American friends (chiefly military) and perfected his English. In this period he also served for one year under President Rene Barrientos Ortuño as minister of education.

In 1969 he returned home to the prized position of director of the military academy, a post he held until his dismissal by the left-leaning president Gen. Juan José Torres in January 1971. Torres reassigned Banzer to a "safe" frontier garrison, but the conservative, anti-Communist Banzer instead rallied other officers and seized the La Paz military headquarters. The coup, however, was abortive, and he was soon in exile in Argentina.

With unflagging energy, Banzer plotted and built up an anti-Torres organization from Argentina, often sneaking into Bolivia covertly. Within a few months he had gained support of the powerful MNR (National Revolutionary Movement) of ex-president Victor Paz Estenssoro, the ultra-conservative Falange, and much of the military.

Sparks Revolution

Arrested in August 1971 during one of his secret visits to his native Santa Cruz, Banzer became the sparkplug of a revolution which broke out the next day, spearheaded by the elite Ranger regiment trained by American Green Berets—and, it is said, by a handful of American military advisors in that city. Most of the nation accepted the Banzer revolution (Bolivia's 187th), but there was considerable fighting for several days in La Paz.

Forms New Government

Nine days later, recognized by the United States, Banzer formed his government with a judicious mix of MNR and Falange leaders on the cabinet. In short order he dissolved the Soviet-style People's Assembly formed by Torres, invited back the Peace Corps, expanded the size of the Army, announced a campaign to attract foreign investment (he soon passed a very liberal law to facilitate this), and put a team to work on a five-year plan for social and economic development.

Early in 1972, to Washington's pleasure, Banzer expelled almost all Soviet diplomatic personnel for spying, and soon (under pressure from the International Monetary Fund) announced a devaluation of the peso from 12 to 20 per dollar. While a sound economic move, this angered many and put crowds in the streets, which in turn resulted in imposition of martial law.

Early in 1973 Banzer unveiled Bolivia's first five-year plan—a series of economic reforms together with a school-building program and social security benefits for the Indian majority. By and large, the plan was successful, albeit due to events beyond Banzer's control. The years 1973 through 1976 saw a major economic boom, as OPEC's price increases greatly boosted Bolivia's oil sales earnings; as tin prices rose dramatically; as natural gas exports began and grew phenomenally; as for the first time in history Bolivia exported agricultural products (mainly sugar and cotton from the Santa Cruz area).

To these gains were added substantial foreign loans, which, while adding a debt burden, *did* stimulate a great building boom. In short, through a combination of choice and chance Banzer found himself champion of the middle classes rather than of all Bolivians, and, since most benefits accrued to that sector, the poor again took to the streets. Banzer, incidentally, would survive a record 13 coup attempts.

Innovative Responses To Unrest

The innovative president responded in a very unique way; in late 1974 he informed Bolivians that he had just performed an "autogolpe," or coup from above. This legerdemain permitted him to disband all political parties and rule by decree. In essence, he was following the post-1964 "Brazilian Model" of authoritarian rule hinged upon economic development. In fact, he reoriented Bolivia away from its traditional symbiotic relationship with Argentina to a heavy dependency upon Brazil both diplomatically and economically. So many long term economic packages were negotiated with Brazil that some Bolivians felt he "sold out" the nation's natural resources to that giant neighbor.

More than most Bolivian presidents, Banzer was willing to use force to suppress his critics. He literally invaded (and had the Air Force strafe) San Andrés University in La Paz, enacted censorship in the media, frequently used troops against striking miners, and often jailed or exiled dissidents. In the process, Bolivia was turning in the largest trade surpluses in its history and the middle classes—including importers, manufacturers, Santa Cruz agribusinessmen, and others—raked in the profits.

Turmoil In the Late 1970s

This situation could not last in faction-ridden Bolivia. The external debt multiplied, corruption flourished, inflation soared, and negotiations with Chile for access to the Pacific collapsed. With pressures building, Banzer suspended his autogolpe decrees in 1977 and agreed to an election in 1978 without his candidacy. The elections, patently fraudulent, were disallowed, and Banzer promptly resigned. Genuine elections held in 1979 were invalidated when no candidate received a majority, and in 1980, in new elections, Banzer himself ran at the head of a new party, the ADN (National Democratic Action), coming in second. He was hardly through with politics, however, and built the ADN into a major force for the July 1985 elections. Running against Victor Paz and the MNR (and a host of minor candidates), the supposedly unpopular Banzer took 32 percent of the vote to Paz's 27 percent, but Congress, charged with deciding the issue, favored Paz.

Not one to sulk in Santa Cruz, Banzer let himself be wooed by the increasingly conservative Paz—who needed ADN votes in Congress—and in October 1985 he signed the ADN/MNR ''Pact for Democracy,'' which assured Paz control of Congress and Banzer a probable 1990 presidency.

Changed Leader Announces Comeback

Controversial Banzer, who held continuous power in Bolivia longer than anyone else in the 20th century, was denounced for his harsh rule yet praised for continuing and accelerating distribution of land to the peasants. He was criticized for ''militarizing'' politics, yet he stepped aside voluntarily in 1978 rather than risk violence. He was castigated for becoming a ''tool'' of imperialism, yet he diversified Bolivia's economy and trading partners. He was, in short, a paradox unresolved. In August 1997, Banzer was elected president, after working hard to convince Bolivians that he is not the same repressive, dictatorial figure he was in the 1970s.

Further Reading

There is no adequate biography of Banzer in print. However, a great deal of information about him and the Bolivia of his era can be found in the following books: Christopher Mitchell, *The Legacy of Populism in Bolivia, from the MNR to Military Rule* (1977); Jorge Gallardo Lozado, *De Torres a Banzer* (Buenos Aires, 1972); Jonathan Kelly and Herbert S. Klein, *Revolution and the Rebirth of Inequality* (1981); J. Lademan, *Bolivia Since 1964* (1985); William J. McEwen, *Changing Rural Society. A Study of Communities in Bolivia* (1975); *To Get Votes, Bolivian General Changes Tune* in *The Christian Science Monitor,* November 19, 1996, by Jack Epstein; and *The General Tries Again* in *Economist,* May 31, 1997, pp. 34-36. □

Bao Dai

Bao Dai (1913–1997) was the last emperor of Vietnam. Opportunism, absence of a nationalist outlook, and lack of concern for social reform contributed to his political eclipse as a result of the 1955 referendum.

The son of Khai Dinah, who became emperor in 1916, Bao Dai was born in the protectorate of Annam, part of French-governed Indochina, on Oct. 22, 1913. At the age of 9 he was sent to school in France, where he later continued his primary education at the École des Sciences Politiques in Paris.

Named thirteenth emperor of Annam in 1926 upon his father's death, Bao Dai did not then ascend the throne because of his age and instead went back to Paris to continue his studies. He returned from France in September 1932 to be enthroned at the age of 19.

Bao Dai was subservient to the French during the pre-World War II years, developing in the same period a deserved reputation as a playboy. In 1933 he appointed Ngo Dinh Diem, later to be South Vietnam's first premier and president, the minister of interior in his government, but encouraged by the French, failed to cooperate when Diem proposed various reforms. Bao Dai's unsympathetic attitude and his subsequent canceling of various of Diem's awards and decorations encouraged a strong personal enmity between the two men.

Continuing on the throne during the wartime Japanese occupation, Bao Dai abdicated as emperor in 1945 under Communist pressure in favor of Ho Chi Minh's Democratic Republic of Vietnam. He was named supreme councilor by Ho but fled to luxurious retirement in Hong Kong in 1946. During the next 3 years he divided his time between Hong Kong and the French Riviera, adding to his already considerable reputation for self-indulgence.

In an attempt to undercut the appeal of Ho by exploiting the traditional office of emperor while retaining real power, France in 1949 encouraged Bao Dai to quit his comfortable retirement and to become head of state of the less than fully independent nation of Vietnam. The Bao Dai regime was quickly recognized by the United States, Britain, and various other Western states—primarily as a means of checkmating the Communists. Their actions, however, merely moved the Soviet Union and China to recognize Ho's Democratic Republic.

Much against Bao Dai's wishes, the French, encouraged by the United States, asked Diem to become premier after the 1954 fall of Dien Bien Phu. When a separate South

Vietnam came into being in July 1954 as part of the Geneva settlement, Diem was its political leader with Bao Dai its figurehead ceremonial chief. In a referendum in 1955, in which Bao Dai did not take part, Diem won endorsement for his plan to make South Vietnam a republic with himself as president (and Bao Dai once again a private citizen).

During the campaigning Bao Dai stayed in southern France, where he subsequently remained. In 1980 he published an historical memoir in French under the title *Le Dragon d'Annam* (The Dragon of Vietnam). A Vietnamese version of the book, *Con Rong Viet Nam,* was published in California in 1990. "The dragon" here is a Vietnamese idiom referring to the emperor, Bao Dai.

Meanwhile in Vietnam, the government initiated a project to rebuild the old capitol city of Hue and to restore the imperial palace of the Nguyen Dynasty to its original splendor. Bao Dai died in Paris, at the age of 83, on July 31, 1997.

Further Reading

Ellen J. Hammer, *The Struggle for Indochina* (1954; rev. ed. 1966), is a contemporary and scholarly account of the early 1950s and offers one of the best views of French policy, and Bao Dai's role in it, during these years. Robert Shaplen, *The Lost Revolution* (1955; rev. ed. 1966), also offers an excellent treatment of the Bao Dai-French relationship and the subsequent clash between the former emperor and Ngo Dinh Diem. A background book of outstanding quality is Bernard Fall, *The Two Viet-Nams: A Political and Military Analysis* (1963; 2d ed. 1967). □

the 1969-1970 War of Attrition with Egypt along the Suez Canal he was in charge of an armored company; and during the 1973 Yom Kippur War he directed an armored battalion.

Meanwhile, Barak's secret exploits included leading a squad disguised as airport maintenance men that successfully stormed a Sabena airliner hijacked to Tel-Aviv in May 1972, safely rescuing 97 hostages. A month later, his special operations team reportedly captured five Syrian officers who were on an inspection tour in southern Lebanon. In spring 1973 Barak participated in the daring IDF raid into central Beirut that eliminated three Palestinian extremist leaders masterminding Palestine Liberation Organization (PLO) terrorist activities against Israeli, Jewish, and European targets. In 1976 Barak took part in the celebrated Entebbe rescue, and he is believed to have planned the April 1988 assassination in Tunis of Abu Jihad, the PLO's operations chief.

In 1974 Barak was appointed head of the IDF's Tank Commanders Course, and in the next six years he rotated from command of a regular armored battalion, a regular armored brigade, a reserve division and, finally, a regular division. Moving from field posts, in 1980 he directed the IDF Battalion Commander Course and then served in various staff positions, including both the General Headquarters' Intelligence Branch and the Operations Department.

In grooming him for top command as a professional soldier, the army sponsored Barak's higher education. He earned a Bachelor of Science degree from the Hebrew

Ehud Barak

On April 1, 1991, Ehud Barak (born 1942) was elevated to the rank of lieutenant general, becoming Israel's 14th chief of staff, and, at the age of 49, also the youngest in the history of the Israel Defense Forces (I.D.F.). In 1995, following the assassination of Yitzhak Rabin, Ehud Barak was named Israel's Foreign Minister. He became the leader of Israel's Labor Party in 1997.

A list of Barak's numerous military postings and career promotions after joining the army in 1959 traces his steady rise to the top of the Israel Defense Forces (IDF) chain of command. His immense contributions to Israeli national security were signified by the awarding of an *itur limofet,* the army's medal for distinguished combat service, plus four other citations for valor in secret operations, the details of which remain classified.

Ehud Barak was born in kibbutz Mishmar HaSharon in 1942. Soon after his IDF induction, when nearly 18, Ehud Barak was selected for the *sayeret matkal* elite special operations unit, going from platoon and company leader to its deputy commander and commander. During the 1967 Six Day War he commanded a mobile reconnaissance unit; in

University in Jerusalem in 1968, majoring in both physics and mathematics, and in 1978 he received an advanced Master of Science degree from Stanford University in systems analysis. Known for his sharp intellect and analytical skill, Barak was also an accomplished classical pianist and weekend gardener at his home in Kochav Yair, north of Tel-Aviv, where he lived with his wife and three daughters.

Barak's career took another leap on January 1, 1982, when he was promoted to the rank of major general and appointed director of the General Headquarters Planning Branch. During the 1982 "Peace for Galilee" War he returned to a field command and was deputy leader of a formation that operated in the Beka'a Valley in eastern Lebanon. From there he went on to become chief of IDF military intelligence on April 15, 1983, a position he filled until January 19, 1986, and his appointment as commander of the Central Command. After a year in that position Barak, on May 7, 1987, was chosen deputy chief of staff under General Dan Shomron, succeeding him as chief of staff four years later.

Ehud Barak pledged himself to restructuring the IDF, sensing that under the combined impact of the 1973 Yom Kippur trauma, the prolonged Lebanese intervention, and the added burden of coping with the *intifada* uprising in the annexed West Bank territories and Gaza Strip, the Israeli military had become a less-effective fighting machine. Convinced the army had become simply too large, too cumbersome, and too costly, he set about to fashion a smaller, more disciplined, and more mobile IDF, yet one equipped with and trained in the use of sophisticated state-of-the-art weaponry and capable of conducting multiple missions.

This agenda involved Barak in a number of far-reaching issues and decisions. First was the need to formulate a longer range defense doctrine. Second, he needed to find ways of maximizing a shrinking defense budget. Next, in conjunction with the budget, he needed to adopt a weapons procurement policy that assured a supply of modern equipment on a cost-benefit basis while sustaining Israel's own indigenous military industries and weapons development program. In the fourth place he needed to strengthen a strategic relationship with the United States. Fifth and finally, it was necessary to help define the societal role of the IDF, which was traditionally regarded as the social equalizer in Israel, and whose changing manpower needs no longer could cope with the increasing numbers of 18-year-old young adults registering for military service. In the midst of preparing the Israeli army for possible war threats beyond the year 2000, General Barak was unexpectedly summoned to cope with the more immediate security implications of the September 1993 Israeli-Palestinian act of mutual recognition. According to the joint declaration of principles and timetable, Barak's IDF were called upon to effect a phased withdrawal from Gaza and Jericho, redeploying forces while continuing to assure the safety of Israeli settlers in the disputed territories as well as of Israel as a whole.

Even before his scheduled retirement from the military, Ehud Barak was already touted as a natural contender for high political office as a prospective defense minister, and possibly even future prime minister. He made the transition to civilian life in 1994 at age 52 after 35 years of military service. The young chief of staff was taken into confidence by the late Yitzhak Rabin, then Prime Minister, who became a mentor to Barak. When Yitzhak Rabin was assassinated In 1995, Barak was appointed to the post of Foreign Minister by Shimon Peres, Rabin's successor. In 1996 Peres failed at his bid for election to the post, losing to Binyamin Netanyahu. Barak was then chosen on June 3, 1997 to replace Peres as leader of Israel's Labour Party. Barak favors a separatist compromise in the disputed territories of Israel and Palestine. He maintains an optimistic stance that a lasting peace can be realized without the sacrifice of Palestinian independence, but insists that Israel must retain an amount of the territory sufficient to insure perpetual security. He is a formidable contender to become the next Prime Minister of Israel in the elections that are scheduled for the year 2000.

Further Reading

There is little information published in English about Barak, although he is listed in *The International Who's Who, 1993-1994* (1993). Also see *U.S. News & World Report,* December 26, 1994; December 25, 1995; June 16, 1997, and *The Economist,* June 7, 1997. □

Imamu Amiri Baraka

The African American author Imamu Amiri Baraka (born 1934 as Everett LeRoi Jones) became influential during the 1960s as a spokesperson for radical black literature and theater.

B orn as Everett LeRoi Jones in Newark, New Jersey, on October 30, 1934, Baraka studied at Rutgers, Columbia, and Howard universities and at the New School for Social Research. After taking a bachelor of arts degree at Howard in 1953, he spent two years in the U.S. Air Force in Puerto Rico.

Baraka's life may be divided into two major periods. As a resident of New York City's Greenwich Village, LeRoi Jones led the life of a typical white American. He married a caucasian woman, Hettie Cohen, and they had two children. He and his wife published *Yugen,* a poetry magazine, and he coedited a literary newsletter, *Floating Bear.* Jones's political commitment began when he visited Cuba in 1960.

In 1965 Jones moved to Harlem and began the second period of his life. Here he lived a totally African American and separatist life. As founder and director of the Black Arts Repertory Theatre School, he made every aspect of his life "black" and opposite to the "white" life he had previously known.

Religious Conversion and Political Activism

Converted to the Kewaida sect of the Muslim faith, he took the name Imamu Amiri Baraka and moved to Newark,

New Jersey. "Imamu" is the Swahili word for spiritual leader; "Amiri Baraka" is the Arabic name Jones adopted. In Newark he directed Spirit House, a religious, cultural, and educational black community. He lived with his second wife, their son, and his wife's three daughters by a previous marriage.

During the 1967 racial rebellions in Newark, Baraka was severely beaten and then arrested and charged with carrying a concealed weapon. The judge fined him $25,000 and read one of Baraka's poems, which he regarded as obscene, as justification for the exorbitant fine. National indignation was aroused by this injustice, and the fine was paid by the contributions of Baraka's supporters. He later appealed the case and won. The 1970 election of the African American Kenneth Gibson as mayor of Newark was due partly to Baraka's leadership of a fervent voter registration campaign among African Americans of the city.

As a black nationalist political leader, Baraka was a key figure in the organization of the Congress of African Peoples in 1970 and the National Black Political Assembly in 1972. Political writings during this period cover such topics as the development of a black value system and black political institutions and include the essay collection *Raise, Race, Rays, Raze: Essays since 1965* (1971). However, by 1974 Baraka had undergone yet another reassessment of his cultural and political orientation. In a dramatic turnabout he rejected black nationalism and proclaimed himself a Marxist-Leninist-Maoist. After 1974 Baraka produced a great deal of socialist poetry and essays espousing revolutionary politics.

Literary Achievement

The most startling feature of Baraka's literary work is his arresting vocabulary, which communicates shocking states of emotion as well as ideas that indicate new intellectual dimensions and frontiers of the mind. He was a brilliant myth-maker, breaking icons and clichés and destroying the stereotypes and shibboleths of the old racist myth—the myth of race and sex in America. As poet, essayist, and playwright, he pressed for new cultural understanding in the turbulent society of modern America.

Baraka's writing reveals the influence of black music on his sensibilities. Jazz especially influenced the rhythms of his poetry, although the imagery and style of his early poetry reflect wide reading in classical poetry of all countries and especially the influence of contemporary "beat" poetry. However, his subject matter was from the start almost entirely the plight of African Americans.

During the 1960s Baraka wrote three volumes of poetry: *Preface to a Twenty Volume Suicide Note* (1961), *The Dead Lecturer* (1964), and *Black Magic Poetry* (1969). His many plays of the period include *Dutchman* (1964), which won the Obie Award and marked the beginning of black revolutionary theater, *The Slave, Slave Ship, Arm Yrself or Harm Yrself or Harm Yrself, Jello,* and *The Toilet. Experimental Death Unit #1, A Black Mass, Great Goodness of Life,* and *Madheart* were published as *Four Black Revolutionary Plays* (1969). He authored three collections of nonfiction, *Blues People* (1963), *Home,* a group of social essays

(1966), and *Black Music* (1967); a novel, *The System of Dante's Hell* (1965); and a group of short stories entitled *Tales* (1967). During this period he also edited *The Moderns: An Anthology of New Writing in America* (1963) and coedited an anthology of new African American writing, *Black Fire* (1968).

Later Works

While Baraka produced numerous political writings during the 1970s—some of which were later collected in 1984's *Daggers and Javelins: Essays, 1974-1979*—his literary efforts of the decade include the drama collection *The Motion of History, and Other Plays* (1978), as well as *The Sidnee Poet Heroical, in Twenty-Nine Scenes* (1979). A first *Selected Poetry* was issued in 1979 in addition to such later verse collections as *Reggae or Not! Poems* (1981) and *Transbluesency: The Selected Poems of Amiri Baraka/LeRoi Jones (1961-1995)* (1995). *Funk Lore* (1996) features poems written from 1984 to 1995. Both 1995's *Wise, Why's, Y's* and 1996's *Eulogies* offer his insight into notable African American figures of the 20th century. Baraka's autobiography was published in 1984.

Further Reading

Examinations of Baraka's literary achievement may be found in William J. Harris *The Poetry and Poetics of Amiri Baraka: The Jazz Aesthetic* (1985), Henry C. Lacey, *To Raise, Destroy, and Create: The Poetry, Drama, and Fiction of Imamu Amiri Baraka* (1981), Lloyd Wellesley Brown, *Amiri Baraka* (1980), Werner Sollors, *Amiri Baraka/LeRoi Jones: The Quest for a "Populist Modernism"* (1978), Kimberly W. Benston, *Baraka: The Renegade and the Mask* (1978), Theodore R. Hudson, *From LeRoi Jones to Amiri Baraka: The Literary Works* (1973), and Robert Elliot Fox, *Conscientious Sorcerers: The Black Postmodernist Fiction of LeRoi Jones /Amiri Baraka, Ishmael Reed, and Samuel R. Delany* (1987). □

Aleksandr Andreievich Baranov

The Russian merchant and explorer Aleksandr Andreievich Baranov (1747-1819) was the manager of the Russian American Company and governor of Russian America from 1799 to 1818.

Aleksandr Baranov was born in Kargopol, a small town near the Finnish border, on April 16, 1747, where he received a rudimentary education. He worked for a German merchant in Moscow as a youth and then returned to his home to marry and become a merchant. In 1780 he left his wife and emigrated to Siberia, where he became manager of a glass factory at Irkutsk and a fur trader.

Many fur-trading companies were operating in the Aleutian Islands, and in 1790 Baranov accepted the position of general manager of the American interests of the Shelekhov-Golikov Company on Kodiak Island, at Three

Saints Bay. For the next 28 years the development of Russian America was furthered by his aggressive administration. At first Baranov engaged in ruthless competition with the other fur-trading companies, establishing his reputation and making dividends for his company. In 1793 he launched the first ship built of native timber in Russian America, a crude vessel of about 100 tons.

In 1799 Czar Paul I and his Board of Commerce decided to establish a single powerful company in the Russian American colonies to better protect the natives and resist foreign penetration. An imperial charter was granted to the newly formed Russian American Company, giving it a trade monopoly on the American coast from latitude 55° to the Bering Strait, including the Aleutian, Kuril, and other islands in the northern seas. Its task was to discover new territories, occupy them as Russian possessions, and serve as the agent for the Russian government in America. A board of directors supervised affairs from St. Petersburg, but because of the long distances involved and Russian involvement in the Napoleonic Wars, Baranov, as manager of the company and governor of Russian America, exercised a great deal of independent authority.

Baranov overcame tremendous obstacles to become successful in the Alaskan frontier. He transferred company headquarters in 1808 from Kodiak Island to Sitka, where he built a fortified post and named it New Archangel. He was faced with the problems of hostile Native Americans, who were able to purchase firearms from traders, and shipping— bringing in food and supplies and sending furs out of Alaska. The colony, criminals from Siberia and natives who were

little more than slaves, was short on manpower and food and racked with disease. Baranov began to rely more and more on American traders, including John Jacob Astor, who sent in food and items to trade with the Native Americans and took out cargoes of fur.

After 19 years in Alaska, Baranov requested a replacement, and after 9 more years one appeared. In November 1818 he finally left Alaska on a ship bound for European Russia, but he became ill when the ship stopped at Batavia. Baranov died on April 28, 1819, a few days after leaving port, and was buried at sea.

Further Reading

The best biography of Baranov is Hector Chevigny, *Lord of Alaska: Baranov and the Russian Adventure* (1942); his *Russian America: The Great Alaskan Venture, 1741-1867* (1965) devotes several chapters to the Baranov period. The American view of the Russian American Company is presented in Hubert Howe Bancroft, *History of Alaska, 1730-1885* (1886; many later editions), and Clarence Charles Hulley, *Alaska, 1741-1953* (1953). For a Russian view see S.B. Okun, *The Russian American Company* (trans. 1951). □

Samuel Barber

Samuel Barber (1910-1981) was among the leading figures in 20th-century American music and is perhaps best known for his *Adagio for Strings*, which has become one of the most recognized pieces in contemporary orchestral music.

S amuel Barber was born on March 9, 1910, in West Chester, Pennsylvania, into a middle-class professional family. His maternal aunt was the well-known singer Louise Homer. Barber's mother was an accomplished pianist, and his own musical studies started early. He began composing at the age of seven. In 1924 he entered the Curtis Institute of Music in Philadelphia, where he remained for nine years, studying composition and piano. He also studied voice, which undoubtedly influenced the cultivation of a strong lyrical style in his musical composition. It was at Curtis that Barber began a lifelong friendship with Gian Carlo Menotti, a newly arrived student from Italy. Although Barber made frequent trips to Europe (as a recipient of the Prix de Rome he spent several years at the American Academy in Rome), he was among the first American composers trained in his own country. The roots of European tradition nevertheless had been assimilated. Except for a brief period of teaching at the Curtis Institute, he maintained his independence, primarily through grants, commissions, and royalties.

Early Works

Barber's music covers a wide range. Vocal works include choral compositions and solo settings with piano, chamber ensemble, and orchestra. Barber set to music the texts of such literary figures as Matthew Arnold, James

remain outside experimental trends of the period. His structure is tonal, yet the earlier works are more simple and direct. Later works, such as *Symphony No. 2,* the *Piano Sonata,* and the *Piano Concerto,* another Pulitzer Prize winner, are more chromatic and dissonant. Twelve-tone serial technique is used in the *Piano Sonata.* Barber's instrumental works reveal traditional attitudes toward musical articulation and form. His themes are carefully molded and highly motivic. His contrapuntal texture is strong, and he used canonic, fugal, and ostinato procedures. His various settings for solo voice are very sensitive and expressive, especially in the evocation of youth. A beautiful example is *Knoxville: Summer of 1915,* derived from Agee's *A Death in the Family.* Because of his direct expressivity and warm lyricism he is generally regarded as a "neoromantic," but this is a classification of attitude rather than of style.

After a period of artistic inactivity in the 1970s, Barber returned to composing with his *Third Essay for Orchestra,* which was performed by the New York Philharmonic orchestra in 1980. The premier of a second new work, an oboe concerto, was planned at the time of his death, January 23, 1981, following a long illness.

Further Reading

A sympathetic biography and analysis of Barber's music is Nathan Broder, *Samuel Barber* (1954; revised, 1985). A penetrating interpretation of Barber is given by Wilfrid Mellers in *Music in a New Found Land* (1965). A consideration of Barber's life and career may also be found in Barbara B. Heyman, *Samuel Barber: The Composer and His Music* (1992; reprinted, 1994). For additional information, see Don A. Hennessee, *Samuel Barber: A Bio-Bibliography* (1985). □

Joyce, William Butler Yeats, James Agee, Rainer Maria Rilke, and the philosopher Søren Kierkegaard. Among his orchestral works are three *Essays for Orchestra* and two symphonies. The performance in 1938 of his first *Essay* and of his best-known work, *Adagio for Strings,* with Arturo Toscanini conducting the NBC Symphony Orchestra, won Barber immediate national recognition. *Symphony No. 2* was commissioned by the Army Air Forces while Barber served as a corporal during World War II. Three concertos for violin, violoncello, and piano reveal his grasp of instrumental idiomatic virtuosity. He also wrote ballet music for Martha Graham (*Medea*) and the Ballet Society (*Souvenirs*).

Operas

It was inevitable that Barber would turn to opera. The Pulitzer Prize-winning *Vanessa,* with a libretto by Menotti (1958), was commissioned by the Metropolitan Opera, New York City. Limited to a few roles, it is a lyrical work of passionate intensity. Following the success of *Vanessa,* Barber was honored by another commission, *Antony and Cleopatra,* adapted from Shakespeare by Franco Zeffirelli, for the opening of the Metropolitan Opera House at Lincoln Center, New York City, in September 1966. This opera is more complex musically and more grandiose in scope and theatricality.

Major Themes and Techniques

It is difficult to classify Barber's style. His early works represent a conservative, traditional style based on European prototypes, and his later, more complex compositions

Klaus Barbie

Klaus Barbie (1913-1991) was a Nazi SS leader who was head of anti-Resistance operations in France during its occupation by Germany in World War II. After the war, Barbie worked covertly for U.S. Army intelligence in Germany prior to his escape to Bolivia. There he lived for over 30 years as Klaus Altmann before his arrest and return to France for trial as a war criminal.

Klaus Barbie was born October 25, 1913, in the town of Bad Godesberg, a few miles down the Rhine River from Bonn. The son of a school teacher, he spent an uneventful childhood as a good but not brilliant student with a gift for languages.

Barbie Joins Nazi SS

In 1935, three years after Hitler became chancellor of Germany, the 22-year-old Barbie joined the SS (*Shutzstaffel*), the Nazi party's cadre that swore loyalty not to Germany but to Hitler. He served in the SD (*Sicherheitsdienst*), the intelligence and security branch of the SS, headed by Reinhold Heydrich.

The young Barbie was assigned to a number of posts in Europe in the next six years as the German war machine swept westward. He won a reputation as a shrewd, dedicated SS officer, earning promotions and commendations from admiring superiors.

Head of Anti-Resistance Operations in France

After Germany invaded France in 1941, Barbie became head of anti-Resistance operations there. He is widely believed to have been responsible for the torture and death of Jean Moulin, the clandestine head of France's anti-Nazi coalition. As head of the Gestapo at Lyon, Barbie also appears to have been responsible for a number of "actions" against innocent French Jews, including a raid on an orphanage in the town of Izieu which sent over 50 boys and girls to the gas chambers at the death camp of Auschwitz.

Recruited by U.S. Counter Intelligence Corps

When the war in Europe ended in the spring of 1945 with the Nazis' defeat, Barbie hid from the Allies until April 1947, when he was recruited by the Counter Intelligence Corps (CIC) of the U.S. Army in occupied Germany. Although the Army had a warrant for Barbie's arrest as a suspected subversive, the regional commander decided that his skills as an interrogator made him more valuable as a spy

than as a prisoner, and over the next four years Barbie took on increasing responsibility for the Army, at one time running a "net" or spy network that included scores of informants in East and West Germany and France. By all accounts a crafty and skilled interrogator, Barbie soon became one of the Army's most trusted spies. In 1949, however, his presence became known to French war crimes investigators, who demanded that the "Butcher of Lyon" be turned over to them to stand trial for his crimes.

Army Hides Barbie

The Army took a fateful step. It decided not to surrender Barbie to the French, fearing that it would be embarrassed by his service and apprehensive that he might disclose wide-ranging U.S. intelligence efforts to the French. With the aid of Krunoslav Dragonovich, a shadowy Croatian priest, it placed Barbie in a so-called "rat line" that had previously been used to help Soviet and Eastern bloc citizens who had spied on behalf of the United States.

Aided by false papers that Dragonovich obtained from the International Red Cross under the name of "Klaus Altmann," the Army delivered Barbie to Genoa, Italy. Here he and his wife and two young children boarded an Italian liner to Buenos Aires, Argentina. The "Altmann" family quickly moved to the mountainous city of La Paz, Bolivia, where Barbie supported himself as an auto mechanic.

Barbie Spies For Bolivia

His skills as a spy did not go unnoticed in the military government of Bolivia, and before long Barbie became a confidant of high-ranking generals. It is likely that he served as an adviser to that country's secret police; it is known that he became the director of Transmaritima Boliviana, a company organized to charter ships to bring supplies to landlocked Bolivia. He lived openly as any prosperous businessman might and was often seen in La Paz' cafes and restaurants.

True Identity Discovered

The past began to catch up with Barbie in 1971, when Beate Klarsfeld, a German-born homemaker married to French lawyer Serge Klarsfeld, discovered from a German prosecutor's files that Barbie was living in Bolivia under the name of Altmann. In a dramatic move, she went to La Paz and chained herself to a fence, demanding that "Altmann" be tried for his crimes.

Although her initial effort was unsuccessful—she was hustled to the airport by indignant Bolivian police—the spotlight of publicity was on Barbie to stay. For over a decade, "Altmann" denied that he was Barbie, but his identity was no secret to Bolivian military regimes. Finally, in 1982, a civilian government came to power, and in February 1983 it arrested Barbie and turned him over to French officials.

Barbie's return to France created tremendous publicity and soul-searching in that country, which had never fully come to terms with its mixed record of collaboration with, and resistance to, the Nazis. Shortly after his return, the prosecutor in Lyon announced that Barbie would stand trial on several charges of "crimes against humanity"—including the deaths of the French children from Izieu.

Barbie's expulsion to France had ramifications in America as well. The U.S. Department of Justice, following a five-month investigation, revealed Barbie's post-war role for U.S. intelligence and issued a formal apology to France for "delaying justice in Lyon" for nearly 33 years.

Like nearly all others who committed horrifying atrocities under the Nazi regimes, Barbie showed little remorse for his crimes. "There are no war crimes," he said. "There are only acts of war." When he was expelled from Bolivia, he seemed indifferent: "I did my duty. I have forgotten. If they (the French) have not forgotten, that is their business."

The French had not forgotten, but three years after his return, Barbie languished in a jail cell in Lyon, with no date set for his trial. A further postponement came in 1986 when the French Court of Indictments ruled that he could be tried for crimes against resistance fighters as well as for "crimes against humanity." Barbie was imprisoned for life in 1987 for crimes including the murders of at least four Jews and Resistance Workers and 15,000 deportations to death camps. He was the last German war criminal of rank to be tried. Barbie died of cancer in a prison hospital in Lyons, France on September 25, 1991.

Further Reading

A recent biography of Barbie, which devotes considerable attention to the impact of his return on France, is *Unhealed Wounds: France and the Klaus Barbie Affair,* by Erna Paris (Methuen, 1985). Serge Klarsfeld's *The Children of Izieu* (1985) contains the full story of that tragic crime. A chapter on Barbie's affiliation with the United States is found in *Quiet Neighbors: Prosecuting Nazi War Criminals in America,* by Allan A. Ryan, Jr. (1984). The complete Justice Department report was published in 1983 by the Government Printing Office under the title *Klaus Barbie and the United States Government.* See also, *Voices From the Barbie Trial* by Ted Morgan in the August 2, 1987 edition of the *New York Times Magazine* and *Gestapo Chief Dies In Prison* by Paul Webster in the September 26, 1991 issue of *The Guardian.* □

Ruy Barbosa

Ruy Barbosa (1849-1923) was a Brazilian lawyer, journalist, and politician. He was probably the most intellectually gifted Latin American political figure of his time.

Ruy Barbosa was born on Nov. 5, 1849, in São Salvador, Bahia, into a long-established family of Portuguese descent. From 1866 to 1870 he studied in the law schools of Recife and São Paulo, where he enthusiastically joined the abolitionist movement. His liberal ideas were equally well articulated in his own abolitionist paper, *O Radical Paulistano,* and in his stirring speeches before organizations and student groups in São Paulo. Returning to Bahia after graduation, he joined the Liberal party and became the editor of the *Diário da Bahia* to continue his antislavery campaign.

Barbosa's first major publication appeared in 1877 with his translation of *The Pope and the Council,* a German work published about a decade earlier which attacked the doctrine of papal infallibility. The preface to this work is an outstanding example of his excellent prose style.

In 1878 he was elected to the national Chamber of Deputies, where he staunchly supported educational reform and abolition. In recognition of his detailed report on the national educational system, he was granted the title of Counselor of the Empire in 1881. His position on abolition, however, doomed his bid for reelection.

Long an admirer of British parliamentary monarchy, Barbosa favored decentralization of the empire rather than a republic. When abolition was decreed in May 1888, Barbosa immediately accelerated his demand for federalization of the empire in another of his papers, the *Diário de Noticias.* After the military coup which deposed Pedro II, Barbosa was selected as Manoel Deodoro da Fonseca's vice chief of the provisional government and was given the portfolios of the ministries of finance and justice, as well as being charged with writing the constitution.

As minister of finance, Barbosa inherited the failing imperial economy. His continuance of the *encilhmento* (a period of frenzied financial speculation on the Brazilian stock market) and authorization of the issuance of paper money only exacerbated the financial crisis. He resigned his position, along with the rest of Deodoro's Cabinet, during the ministerial crisis in January 1891, and later attacked Deodoro's successor, Floriano Peixoto, for his disregard of the constitution.

Accused of being one of the conspirators in the September 1893 naval revolt, Barbosa fled to Buenos Aires and later to London. While in London he wrote a series of letters giving his impressions and observations of the European scene. This series, later published as his excellent *Cartas da Inglaterra* (Letters from England), began in January 1895 with an eloquent plea for justice in the Dreyfus case.

Returning to Brazil after the election of Prudente de Morais in late 1895, he won a seat in the Senate and urged a general amnesty for all those implicated in the revolts of 1893-1894. He led the Brazilian delegation to the Second Hague Conference in 1907 and won international acclaim as "The Eagle of The Hague" for his stout defense of the legal equality of nations, his mastery of international law, and his splendid oratory in several languages. The next year he became a member of the Permanent Court of Arbitration at The Hague.

In 1909 Barbosa resigned his position as vice president of the Senate to oppose the military candidate Hermes da Fonseca for the Brazilian presidency. Although his anti-militarist campaign was the greatest popular electoral drive that Brazil had ever seen, political manipulation deprived him of victory.

During World War I Barbosa advised Brazilian neutrality and later refused, for personal and political reasons, to head the Brazilian delegation to the Versailles Peace Conference. He died in Rio de Janeiro on March 1, 1923.

In addition to his political renown, Barbosa is also considered one of Brazil's greatest scholars and perhaps the outstanding prose writer of the Portuguese language. He was a preeminent linguist who spoke fluent English, French, Spanish, and Italian and possessed a commanding knowledge of the classical languages. His 40,000-volume multilanguage library was purported to be the largest private collection in Latin America.

Further Reading

The best book in English on Ruy Barbosa is Charles W. Turner's laudatory *Ruy Barbosa: Brazilian Crusader for the Essential Freedoms* (1945). By no means a complete biography, it does present an interpretation of the man and his thought based on extensive study of his writings and public activities. Harold E. Davis, *Latin American Leaders* (1949), includes an excellent biographical sketch of Barbosa. □